Collins

Collins
Spanish
Dictionary

HarperCollins Publishers
Westerhill Road
Bishopbriggs
Glasgow
G64 2QT

This Edition 2013

Reprint 10 9 8 7 6 5 4 3 2

© HarperCollins Publishers 2006, 2013

ISBN 978-0-00-793353-2

Collins® is a registered trademark of
HarperCollins Publishers Limited

www.collinslanguage.com

A catalogue record for this book is
available from the British Library

Typeset by Wordcraft, Glasgow

Printed in Great Britain by Clays,
St Ives plc

Acknowledgements
We would like to thank those
authors and publishers who kindly
gave permission for copyright
material to be used in the Collins
Corpus. We would also like to thank
Times Newspapers Ltd for providing
valuable data.

MANAGING EDITOR
Michela Clari

CONTRIBUTORS
José Martín Galera
Wendy Lee
José María Ruiz Vaca
Cordelia Lilly

EDITORIAL COORDINATION
Maree Airlie
Joyce Littlejohn
Marianne Noble

SERIES EDITOR
Lorna Knight

William Collins' dream of knowledge for all began with the publication of his first book in 1819. A self-educated mill worker, he not only enriched millions of lives, but also founded a flourising publishing house. Today, staying true to this spirit, Collins books are packed with inspiration, innovation, and practical expertise. They place you at the centre of a world of possibility and give you exactly what you need to explore it.

Language is the key to this exploration, and at the heart of Collins Dictionaries is language as it is really used. New words, phrases, and meanings spring up every day, and all of them are captured and analysed by the Collins Word Web. Constantly updated, and with over 2.5 billion entries, this living language resource is unique to our dictionaries.

Words are tools for life. And a Collins Dictionary makes them work for you.

Collins. Do more.

ÍNDICE

CONTENTS

INTRODUCCIÓN

Estamos muy satisfechos de que hayas decidido comprar
este diccionario y esperamos que lo disfrutes y que te sirva
de gran ayuda ya sea en el colegio, en el trabajo, en tus
vacaciones o en casa.

Esta introducción pretende darte algunas indicaciones
para ayurdarte a sacar el mayor provecho de este diccionario;
no sólo de su extenso vocabulario, sino de toda la información
que te proporciona cada entrada. Esta te ayudará a leer y
comprender – y también a comunicarte y a expresarte –
en inglés moderno. Este diccionario comienza con una lista
de abreviaturas utilizadas en el texto y con una ilustración
de los sonidos representados por los símbolos fonéticos.

EL MANEJO DE TU DICCIONARIO

La amplia información que te ofrece este diccionario
aparece presentada en distintas tipografías, con caracteres
de diversos tamaños y con distintos símbolos, abreviaturas
y paréntesis. Los apartados siguientes explican las reglas y
símbolos utilizados.

ENTRADAS

Las palabras que consultas en el diccionario – las entradas
– aparecen ordenades alfabéticamente en negrita y en un
nuevo párrafo para una identificación más rápida. La palabra
que aparece en la parte superior de cada página es la primera
entrada (si aparece en la página izquierda) y la última entrada
(si aparece en la página derecha) de la página en cuestión.
La información sobre el uso o la forma de determinadas
entradas aparece entre paréntesis, detrás de la transcripción
fonética, y generalmente en forma abreviada y en cursiva

(p. ej.: (*fam*), (*Com*)). En algunos casos se ha considerado oportuno agrupar palabras de una misma familia (**nación, nacionalismo; accept, acceptance**) bajo una misma entrada que aparece en negrita.

Las expresiones de uso corriente en las que aparece una entrada se dan en negrita (p. ej.: **hurry:** [...] **to be in a ~**).

SÍMBOLOS FONÉTICOS

La transcripción fonética de cada entrada inglesa (que indica su pronunciación) aparece entre corchetes, inmediatamente después de la entrada (p. ej. **knife** [naif]). En las páginas xv-xviii encontrarás una lista de los símbolos fonéticos utilizados en este diccionario.

TRADUCCIONES

Las traducciones de las entradas aparecen en caracteres normales, y en los casos en los que existen significados o usos diferentes, éstos aparecen separados mediante un punto y coma. A menudo encontrarás también otras palabras en cursiva y entre paréntesis antes de las traducciones. Estas sugieren contextos en los que la entrada podría aparecer (p. ej.: **alto** (*persona*) o (*sonido*)) o proporcionan sinónimos (p. ej.: **mismo** (*semejante*)).

PALABRAS CLAVE

Particular relevancia reciben ciertas palabras inglesas y españolas que han sido consideradas palabras 'clave' en cada lengua. Estas pueden, por ejemplo, ser de utilización muy corriente o tener distintos usos (**de, haber; get, that**). La combinación de triángulos y números te permitirá distinguir las diferentes categorías gramaticales y los diferentes significados. Las indicaciones en cursiva y entre paréntesis proporcionan además importante información adicional.

FALSOS AMIGOS

Las palabras que se prestan a confusión al traducir han sido identificadas. En tales entradas existen unas notas que te ayudaran a evitar errores.

INFORMACIÓN GRAMATICAL

Las categorías gramaticales aparecen en forma abreviada y en cursiva después de la transcripción fonética de cada entrada (*vt, adv, conj*). También se indican la forma femenina y los plurales irregulares de los sustantivos del inglés (**child, -ren**).

INTRODUCTION

We are delighted that you have decided to buy this Spanish dictionary and hope you will enjoy and benefit from using it at school, at home, on holiday or at work.

This introduction gives you a few tips on how to get the most out of your dictionary – not simply from its comprehensive wordlist but also from the information provided in each entry. This will help you to read and understand modern Spanish, as well as communicate and express yourself in the language. This dictionary begins by listing the abbreviations used in the text and illustrating the sounds shown by the phonetic symbols.

USING YOUR DICTIONARY

A wealth of information is presented in the dictionary, using various typefaces, sizes of type, symbols, abbreviations and brackets. The various conventions and symbols used are explained in the following sections.

HEADWORDS

The words you look up in a dictionary – 'headwords' – are listed alphabetically. They are printed in **bold** and on a new line for rapid identification. The headwords appearing at the top of each page indicate the first (if it appears on a left-hand page and last word (if it appears on a right-hand page) dealt with on the page in question.

Information about the usage or form of certain headwords is given in brackets after the phonetic spelling. This usually appears in abbreviated form and in italics (e.g. (*fam*), (*Com*)).

Where appropriate, words related to headwords are grouped in the same entry (**nación, nacionalismo; accept, acceptance**) and are also in bold. Common expressions in which the headword appears are shown in a different bold roman type (e.g. **cola:** [...] **hacer ~**).

PHONETIC SPELLINGS
The phonetic spelling of each headword (indicating its pronunciation) is given in square brackets immediately after the headword (e.g. **cohete** [ko'ete]). A list of these symbols is given on pages xv-xviii.

TRANSLATIONS
Headword translations are given in ordinary type and, where more than one meaning or usage exists, these are separated by a semi-colon. You will often find other words in italics in brackets before the translations. These offer suggested contexts in which the headword might appear (e.g. **fare** (*on trains, buses*)) or provide synonyms (e.g. **litter** (*rubbish*) o (*young animals*)). The gender of the Spanish translation also appears in italics immediately following the key element of the translation, except where this is a regular masculine singular noun ending in 'o', or a regular feminine noun ending in 'a'.

KEY WORDS
Special status is given to certain Spanish and English words which are considered as 'key' words in each language. They may, for example, occur very frequently or have several types of usage (e.g. **de, haber; get, that**). A combination of triangles and numbers helps you to distinguish different

parts of speech and different meanings. Further helpful information is provided in brackets and italics.

FALSE FRIENDS
Words which can be easily confused have been identified in the dictionary. Notes at such entries will help you to avoid these common translation pitfalls.

GRAMMATICAL INFORMATION
Parts of speech are given in abbreviated form in italics after the phonetic spellings of headwords (e.g. *vt, adv, conj*). Genders of Spanish nouns are indicated as follows: *nm* for a masculine and *nf* for a feminine noun. Feminine and irregular plural forms of nouns are also shown (**irlandés, esa; luz** (*pl* **luces**)).

ABREVIATURAS

ABBREVIATIONS

abreviatura	*ab(b)r*	abbreviation
adjetivo, locución adjetiva	*adj*	adjective, adjectival phrase
administración	*Admin*	administration
adverbio, locución adverbial	*adv*	adverb, adverbial phrase
agricultura	*Agr*	agriculture
anatomía	*Anat*	anatomy
Argentina	*Arg*	Argentina
arquitectura	*Arq, Arch*	architecture
el automóvil	*Aut(o)*	the motor car and motoring
aviación, viajes aéreos	*Aviac, Aviat*	flying, air travel
biología	*Bio(l)*	biology
botánica, flores	*Bot*	botany
inglés británico	BRIT	British English
Centroamérica	CAM	Central America
química	*Chem*	chemistry
comercio, finanzas, banca	*Com(m)*	commerce, finance, banking
informática	*Comput*	computing
conjunción	*conj*	conjunction
construcción	*Constr*	building
compuesto	*cpd*	compound element
Cono Sur	CS	Southern Cone
cocina	*Culin*	cookery
economía	*Econ*	economics
eletricidad, electrónica	*Elec*	electricity, electronics
enseñanza, sistema escolar y universitario	*Escol*	schooling, schools and universities
España	ESP	Spain
especialmente	*esp*	especially
exclamación, interjección	*excl*	exclamation, interjection
femenino	f	feminine
lengua familiar (! vulgar)	*fam(!)*	colloquial usage (! particularly offensive)
ferrocarril	*Ferro*	railways
uso figurado	*fig*	figurative use
fotografía	*Foto*	photography
(verbo inglés) del cual la partícula es inseparable	*fus*	(phrasal verb) where the particle is inseparable
generalmente	*gen*	generally
geografía, geología	*Geo*	geography, geology
geometría	*Geom*	geometry

ABREVIATURAS

historia	*Hist*	history
uso familiar	*inf(!)*	colloquial usage
(! vulgar)		(! particularly offensive)
infinitivo	*infin*	infinitive
informática	*Inform*	computing
invariable	*inv*	invariable
irregular	*irreg*	irregular
lo jurídico	*Jur*	law
América Latina	LAM	Latin America
gramática, lingüística	*Ling*	grammar, linguistics
masculino	*m*	masculine
matemáticas	*Mat(h)*	mathematics
masculino/femenino	*m/f*	masculine/feminine
medicina	*Med*	medicine
México	MÉX, MEX	Mexico
lo militar, ejército	*Mil*	military matters
música	*Mús, Mus*	music
substantivo, nombre	*n*	noun
navegación, náutica	*Náut, Naut*	sailing, navigation
sustantivo numérico	*num*	numeral noun
complemento	*obj*	(grammatical) object
	o.s.	oneself
peyorativo	*pey, pej*	derogatory, pejorative
fotografía	*Phot*	photography
fisiología	*Physiol*	physiology
plural	*pl*	plural
política	*Pol*	politics
participio de pasado	*pp*	past participle
preposición	*prep*	preposition
pronombre	*pron*	pronoun
psicología, psiquiatría	*Psico, Psych*	psychology, psychiatry
tiempo pasado	*pt*	past tense
química	*Quím*	chemistry
ferrocarril	*Rail*	railways
religión	*Rel*	religion
Río de la Plata	RPL	River Plate
	sb	somebody
Cono Sur	SC	Southern Cone
enseñanza, sistema escolar	*Scol*	schooling, schools
y universitario		and universities
singular	*sg*	singular
España	SP	Spain
	sth	something

ABREVIATURAS

sujeto	*su(b)j*	(grammatical) subject
subjuntivo	*subjun*	subjunctive
tauromaquia	*Taur*	bullfighting
también	*tb*	also
técnica, tecnología	*Tec(h)*	technical term, technology
telecomunicaciones	*Telec, Tel*	telecommunications
imprenta, tipografía	*Tip, Typ*	typography, printing
televisión	*TV*	television
universidad	*Univ*	university
inglés norteamericano	*US*	American English
verbo	*vb*	verb
verbo intransitivo	*vi*	intransitive verb
verbo pronominal	*vr*	reflexive verb
verbo transitivo	*vt*	transitive verb
zoología	*Zool*	zoology
marca registrada	®	registered trademark
indica un equivalente cultural	≈	introduces a cultural equivalent

SPANISH PRONUNCIATION

VOWELS

a	[a]	pata	not as long as *a* in *far*. When followed by a consonant in the same syllable (i.e. in a closed syllable), as in *a*mante, the *a* is short, as in b*a*t
e	[e]	me	like *e* in th*ey*. In a closed syllable, as in g*e*nte, the *e* is short as in p*e*t
i	[i]	pino	as in m*ea*n or mach*i*ne
o	[o]	lo	as in l*o*cal. In a closed syllable, as in c*o*ntrol, the *o* is short as in c*o*t
u	[u]	lunes	as in r*u*le. It is silent after q, and in *gue*, *gui*, unless marked *güe*, *güi* e.g. antig*ü*edad, when it is pronounced like *w* in *w*olf

SEMIVOWELS

i, y	[j]	bien	pronounced like *y* in *y*es
		hielo	
		yunta	
u	[w]	huevo	unstressed *u* between consonant and vowel is pronounced like *w* in *w*ell.
		fuento	See notes on *u* above.
		antigüedad	

DIPHTHONGS

ai, ay	[ai]	baile	as *i* in r*i*de
au	[au]	auto	as *ou* in sh*ou*t
ei, ey	[ei]	buey	as *ey* in gr*ey*
eu	[eu]	deuda	both elements pronounced independently [e] + [u]
oi, oy	[oi]	hoy	as *oy* in t*oy*

CONSONANTS

b	[b, β]	boda	see notes on *v* below
		bomba	
		labor	
c	[k]	caja	*c* before *a*, *o*, *u* is pronounced as in *c*at
ce, ci	[θe, θi]	cero	*c* before *e* or *i* is pronounced as in *th*in
		cielo	
ch	[tʃ]	chiste	*ch* is pronounced as *ch* in *ch*air
d	[d, ð]	danés	at the beginning of a phrase or after *l* or *n*, *d* is pronounced as in English. In any other position it is pronounced like *th* in *th*e
		ciudad	

g	[g, ɣ]	**g**afas	*g* before *a*, *o* or *u* is pronounced as in
		pa**g**a	*g*ap, if at the beginning of a phrase
			or after *n*. In other positions the sound
			is softened
ge, gi	[xe, xi]	**g**ente	*g* before *e* or *i* is pronounced similar
		girar	to *ch* in Scottish lo*ch*
h		**h**aber	*h* is always silent in Spanish
j	[x]	**j**ugar	*j* is pronounced similar to *ch* in
			Scottish lo*ch*
ll	[ʎ]	ta**ll**e	*ll* is pronounced like the *y* in *y*et or the
			lli in mi*lli*on
ñ	[ʃ]	ni**ñ**o	*ñ* is pronounced like the *ni* in o*ni*on
q	[k]	**q**ue	*q* is pronounced as *k* in *k*ing
r, rr	[r, rr]	quita**r**	*r* is always pronounced in Spanish,
		ga**rr**a	unlike the silent *r* in dance*r*. *rr* is trilled,
			like a Scottish *r*
s	[s]	quizá**s**	*s* is usually pronounced as in pa*ss*,
		i**s**la	but before *b*, *d*, *g*, *l*, *m* or *n* it is
			pronounced as in ro*s*e
v	[b, β]	**v**ía	*v* is pronounced something like *b*.
			At the beginning of a phrase or after
			m or *n* it is pronounced as *b* in *b*oy.
			In any other position the sound is
			softened
z	[θ]	tena**z**	*z* is pronounced as *th* in *th*in

f, k, l, m, n, p, t and x are pronounced as in English.

STRESS

The rules of stress in Spanish are as follows:

(a) when a word ends in a vowel or in *n* or *s*, the second last syllable is stressed:
   pa*ta*ta, pa*ta*tas; *co*me, *co*men

(b) when a word ends in a consonant other than *n* or *s*, the stress falls on the last syllable:
   pa*red*, ha*blar*

(c) when the rules set out in (a) and (b) are not applied, an acute accent appears over the stressed vowel:
   co*mún*, geogra*fía*, in*glés*

In the phonetic transcription, the symbol [¹] precedes the syllable on which the stress falls.

LA PRONUNCIACIÓN INGLESA

VOCALES

	Ejemplo inglés	Explicación
[ɑː]	father	Entre *a* de p*a*dre y *o* de n*o*che
[ʌ]	but, come	*a* muy breve
[æ]	man, cat	Con los labios en la posición de *e* en p*e*na y luego se pronuncia el sonido *a* parecido a la *a* de c*a*rro
[ə]	father, ago	Vocal neutra parecida a una *e* u *o* casi muda
[əː]	bird, heard	Entre *e* abierta y *o* cerrada, sonido alargado
[ε]	get, bed	Como en p*e*rro
[ɪ]	it, big	Más breve que en s*i*
[iː]	tea, see	Como en f*i*no
[ɔ]	hot, wash	Como en t*o*rre
[ɔː]	saw, all	Como en p*o*r
[u]	put, book	Sonido breve, más cerrado que b*u*rro
[uː]	too, you	Sonido largo, como en *u*no

DIPTONGOS

	Ejemplo inglés	Explicación
[aɪ]	fly, high	Como en fr*ai*le
[au]	how, house	Como en p*au*sa
[εə]	there, bear	Casi como en v*ea*, pero el sonido *a* se mezcla con el indistinto [ə]
[eɪ]	day, obey	*e* cerrada seguida por una *i* débil
[ɪə]	here, hear	Como en man*ía*, mezclándose el sonido *a* con el indistinto [ə]
[əu]	go, note	[ə] seguido por una breve *u*
[ɔɪ]	boy, oil	Como en v*oy*
[uə]	poor, sure	*u* bastante larga más el sonido indistinto [ə]

CONSONANTES

	Ejemplo inglés	Explicación
[b]	big, lobby	Como en tumban
[d]	mended	Como en conde, andar
[g]	go, get, big	Como en grande, gol
[dʒ]	gin, judge	Como en la ll andaluza y en Generalitat (catalán)
[ŋ]	sing	Como en vínculo
[h]	house, he	Como la jota hispanoamericana
[j]	young, yes	Como en ya
[k]	come, mock	Como en caña, Escocia
[r]	red, tread	Se pronuncia con la punta de la lengua hacia atrás y sin hacerla vibrar
[s]	sand, yes	Como en casa, sesión
[z]	rose, zebra	Como en desde, mismo
[ʃ]	she, machine	Como en chambre (francés), roxo (portugués)
[tʃ]	chin, rich	Como en chocolate
[v]	valley	Como f, pero se retiran los dientes superiores vibrándolos contra el labio inferior
[w]	water, which	Como la u de huevo, puede
[ʒ]	vision	Como en journal (francés)
[θ]	think, myth	Como en receta, zapato
[ð]	this, the	Como en hablado, verdad

f, l, m, n, p, t y x iguales que en español.

El signo [*] indica que la r final escrita apenas se pronuncia en inglés británico cuando la palabra siguiente empieza con vocal. El signo [¹] indica la sílaba acentuada.

LOS NÚMEROS

NUMBERS

un, uno(a)	1	one
dos	2	two
tres	3	three
cuatro	4	four
cinco	5	five
seis	6	six
siete	7	seven
ocho	8	eight
nueve	9	nine
diez	10	ten
once	11	eleven
doce	12	twelve
trece	13	thirteen
catorce	14	fourteen
quince	15	fifteen
dieciséis	16	sixteen
diecisiete	17	seventeen
dieciocho	18	eighteen
diecinueve	19	nineteen
veinte	20	twenty
veintiuno	21	twenty-one
veintidós	22	twenty-two
treinta	30	thirty
cuarenta	40	forty
cincuenta	50	fifty
sesenta	60	sixty
setenta	70	seventy
ochenta	80	eighty
noventa	90	ninety
cien, ciento	100	a hundred, one hundred
ciento uno(a)	101	a hundred and one
doscientos(as)	200	two hundred
trescientos(as)	300	three hundred
cuatrocientos(as)	400	four hundred
quiniento(as)	500	five hundred
seiscientos(as)	600	six hundred
setecientos(as)	700	seven hundred
ochocientos(as)	800	eight hundred
novecientos(as)	900	nine hundred
mil	1000	a thousand
cinco mil	5000	five thousand
un millón	1000000	a million

LOS NÚMEROS	NUMBERS
primer, primero(a), 1º, 1ᵉʳ, (1ª, 1ᵉʳᵃ)	first, 1st
segundo(a), 2º (2ª)	second, 2nd
tercer, tercero(a), 3º (3ª)	third, 3rd
cuarto(a), 4º (4ª)	fourth, 4th
quinto(a), 5º (5ª)	fifth, 5th
sexto(a), 6º (6ª)	sixth, 6th
séptimo(a)	seventh
octavo(a)	eighth
noveno(a)	ninth
décimo(a)	tenth
undécimo(a)	eleventh
duodécimo(a)	twelfth
decimotercio(a)	thirteenth
decimocuarto(a)	fourteenth
decimoquinto(a)	fifteenth
decimosexto(a)	sixteenth
decimoséptimo(a)	seventeenth
decimoctavo(a)	eighteenth
decimonoveno(a)	nineteenth
vigésimo(a)	twentieth
trigésimo(a)	thirtieth
centésimo(a)	hundredth
milésimo(a)	thousandth

NÚMEROS QUEBRADOS ETC	FRACTIONS ETC
un medio	a half
un tercio	a third
un cuarto	a quarter
un quinto	a fifth
cero coma cinco, 0,5	(nought) point five, 0.5
tres coma cuatro, 3,4	three point four, 3.4
diez por cien(to)	ten per cent
cien por cien	a hundred per cent

EJEMPLOS	EXAMPLES
va a llegar el 7 (de mayo)	he's arriving on the 7th (of May)
vive en el número 7	he lives at number 7
el capítulo/la página 7	chapter/page 7
llegó séptimo	he came in 7th

N.B. In Spanish the ordinal numbers from 1 to 10 are commonly used; from 11 to 20 rather less; above 21 they are rarely written and almost never heard in speech.

LA HORA

¿qué hora es?

es/son

medianoche, las doce (de la noche)
la una (de la madrugada)

la una y cinco
la una y diez
la una y cuarto *or* quince

la una y veinticinco

la una y media *or* treinta
las dos menos veinticinco, la una
    treinta y cinco
las dos menos veinte, la una cuarenta
las dos menos cuarto, la una cuarenta
    y cinco
las dos menos diez, la una cincuenta
mediodía, las doce (de la tarde)

la una (de la tarde)

las siete (de la tarde)

¿a qué hora?

a medianoche
a las siete

en veinte minutos
hace quince minutos

THE TIME

what time is it?

it's o it is

midnight, twelve p.m.
one o'clock (in the
    morning), one (a.m.)
five past one
ten past one
a quarter past one,
    one fifteen
twenty-five past one,
    one twenty-five
half-past one, one thirty
twenty-five to two,
    one thirty-five
twenty to two, one forty
a quarter to two,
    one forty-five
ten to two, one fifty
twelve o'clock, midday,
    noon
one o'clock (in the
    afternoon), one (p.m.)
seven o'clock (in the
    evening), seven (p.m.)

(at) what time?

at midnight
at seven o'clock

in twenty minutes
fifteen minutes ago

VERBOS IRREGULARES EN INGLÉS

PRESENTE	PASADO	PARTICIPIO	PRESENTE	PASADO	PARTICIPIO
arise	arose	arisen	dream	dreamed,	dreamed,
awake	awoke	awoken		dreamt	dreamt
be (am, is,	was, were	been	drink	drank	drunk
are; being)			drive	drove	driven
bear	bore	born(e)	dwell	dwelt	dwelt
beat	beat	beaten	eat	ate	eaten
become	became	become	fall	fell	fallen
begin	began	begun	feed	fed	fed
bend	bent	bent	feel	felt	felt
bet	bet,	bet,	fight	fought	fought
	betted	betted	find	found	found
bid (at auction,	bid	bid	flee	fled	fled
cards)			fling	flung	flung
bid (say)	bade	bidden	fly	flew	flown
bind	bound	bound	forbid	forbad(e)	forbidden
bite	bit	bitten	forecast	forecast	forecast
bleed	bled	bled	forget	forgot	forgotten
blow	blew	blown	forgive	forgave	forgiven
break	broke	broken	forsake	forsook	forsaken
breed	bred	bred	freeze	froze	frozen
bring	brought	brought	get	got	got,
build	built	built			(us) gotten
burn	burnt,	burnt,	give	gave	given
	burned	burned	go (goes)	went	gone
burst	burst	burst	grind	ground	ground
buy	bought	bought	grow	grew	grown
can	could	(been able)	hang	hung	hung
cast	cast	cast	hang (suspend)	hanged	hanged
catch	caught	caught	(execute)		
choose	chose	chosen	have	had	had
cling	clung	clung	hear	heard	heard
come	came	come	hide	hid	hidden
cost (be	cost	cost	hit	hit	hit
valued at)			hold	held	held
cost (work	costed	costed	hurt	hurt	hurt
out price of)			keep	kept	kept
creep	crept	crept	kneel	knelt,	knelt,
cut	cut	cut		kneeled	kneeled
deal	dealt	dealt	know	knew	known
dig	dug	dug	lay	laid	laid
do (does)	did	done	lead	led	led
draw	drew	drawn	lean	leant,	leant,

PRESENTE	PASADO	PARTICIPIO	PRESENTE	PASADO	PARTICIPIO
	leaned	leaned	shine	shone	shone
leap	leapt,	leapt,	shoot	shot	shot
	leaped	leaped	show	showed	shown
learn	learnt,	learnt,	shrink	shrank	shrunk
	learned	learned	shut	shut	shut
leave	left	left	sing	sang	sung
lend	lent	lent	sink	sank	sunk
let	let	let	sit	sat	sat
lie (lying)	lay	lain	slay	slew	slain
light	lit,	lit,	sleep	slept	slept
	lighted	lighted	slide	slid	slid
lose	lost	lost	sling	slung	slung
make	made	made	slit	slit	slit
may	might	–	smell	smelt,	smelt,
mean	meant	meant		smelled	smelled
meet	met	met	sow	sowed	sown,
mistake	mistook	mistaken			sowed
mow	mowed	mown,	speak	spoke	spoken
		mowed	speed	sped,	sped,
must	(had to)	(had to)		speeded	speeded
pay	paid	paid	spell	spelt,	spelt,
put	put	put		spelled	spelled
quit	quit,	quit,	spend	spent	spent
	quitted	quitted	spill	spilt,	spilt,
read	read	read		spilled	spilled
rid	rid	rid	spin	spun	spun
ride	rode	ridden	spit	spat	spat
ring	rang	rung	spoil	spoiled,	spoiled,
rise	rose	risen		spoilt	spoilt
run	ran	run	spread	spread	spread
saw	sawed	sawed,	spring	sprang	sprung
		sawn	stand	stood	stood
say	said	said	steal	stole	stolen
see	saw	seen	stick	stuck	stuck
seek	sought	sought	sting	stung	stung
sell	sold	sold	stink	stank	stunk
send	sent	sent	stride	strode	stridden
set	set	set	strike	struck	struck
sew	sewed	sewn	strive	strove	striven
shake	shook	shaken	swear	swore	sworn
shear	sheared	shorn,	sweep	swept	swept
		sheared	swell	swelled	swollen,
shed	shed	shed			swelled

PRESENTE	PASADO	PARTICIPIO	PRESENTE	PASADO	PARTICIPIO
swim	swam	swum	**wear**	wore	worn
swing	swung	swung	**weave** (*on*	wove	woven
take	took	taken	*loom*)		
teach	taught	taught	**weave** (*wind*)	weaved	weaved
tear	tore	torn	**wed**	wedded,	wedded,
tell	told	told		wed	wed
think	thought	thought	**weep**	wept	wept
throw	threw	thrown	**win**	won	won
thrust	thrust	thrust	**wind**	wound	wound
tread	trod	trodden	**wring**	wrung	wrung
wake	woke,	woken,	**write**	wrote	written
	waked	waked			

a

7 (*razón*): **a 30 céntimos el kilo** at 30 cents a kilo; **a más de 50 km/h** at more than 50 kms per hour
8 (*dativo*): **se lo di a él** I gave it to him; **vi al policía** I saw the policeman; **se lo compré a él** I bought it from him
9 (*tras ciertos verbos*): **voy a verle** I'm going to see him; **empezó a trabajar** he started working *o* to work
10 (+ *infin*): **al verlo, lo reconocí inmediatamente** when I saw him I recognized him at once; **el camino a recorrer** the distance we *etc* have to travel; **¡a callar!** keep quiet!; **¡a comer!** let's eat!

abad, esa [a'βað, 'ðesa] *nm/f* abbot/abbess; **abadía** *nf* abbey

abajo [a'βaxo] *adv* (*situación*) (down) below, underneath; (*en edificio*) downstairs; (*dirección*) down, downwards; **el piso de ~** the downstairs flat; **la parte de ~** the lower part; **¡~ el gobierno!** down with the government!; **cuesta/río ~** downhill/downstream; **de arriba ~** from top to bottom; **el ~ firmante** the undersigned; **más ~** lower *o* further down

abalanzarse [aβalan'θarse] *vr*: **~ sobre** *o* **contra** to throw o.s. at

abanderado, -a [aβande'raðo] *nm/f* (*portaestandarte*) standard bearer; (*de un movimiento*) champion, leader; (*MÉX: linier*) linesman, assistant referee

abandonado, -a [aβando'naðo, a] *adj* derelict; (*desatendido*) abandoned; (*desierto*) deserted; (*descuidado*) neglected

abandonar [aβando'nar] *vt* to leave; (*persona*) to abandon, desert; (*cosa*) to abandon, leave behind; (*descuidar*) to neglect; (*renunciar a*) to give up; (*Inform*) to quit; **abandonarse** *vr*: **~se a** to abandon o.s. to; **abandono** *nm* (*acto*) desertion, abandonment; (*estado*) abandon, neglect; (*renuncia*) withdrawal, retirement; **ganar por**

a [a] (*a* + *el* = *al*) *prep* **1** (*dirección*) to; **fueron a Madrid/Grecia** they went to Madrid/Greece; **me voy a casa** I'm going home
2 (*distancia*): **está a 15 km de aquí** it's 15 kms from here
3 (*posición*): **estar a la mesa** to be at table; **al lado de** next to, beside; V *tb* **puerta**
4 (*tiempo*): **a las 10/a medianoche** at 10/midnight; **a la mañana siguiente** the following morning; **a los pocos días** after a few days; **estamos a 9 de julio** it's the ninth of July; **a los 24 años** at the age of 24; **al año/a la semana** a year/week later
5 (*manera*): **a la francesa** the French way; **a caballo** on horseback; **a oscuras** in the dark
6 (*medio, instrumento*): **a lápiz** in pencil; **a mano** by hand; **cocina a gas** gas stove

abandono to win by default

abanico [aβa'niko] *nm* fan; (*Náut*) derrick

abarcar [aβar'kar] *vt* to include, embrace; (*LAM: acaparar*) to monopolize

abarrotado, -a [aβarro'taðo, a] *adj* packed

abarrotar [aβarro'tar] *vt* (*local, estadio, teatro*) to fill, pack

abarrotero, -a [aβarro'tero, a] (*MÉX*) *nm/f* grocer; **abarrotes** (*MÉX*) *nmpl* groceries; **tienda de abarrotes** (*MÉX, CAM*) grocery store

abastecer [aβaste'θer] *vt*: **~ (de)** to supply (with); **abastecimiento** *nm* supply

abasto [a'βasto] *nm* supply; **no dar ~ a** to be unable to cope with

abatible [aβa'tiβle] *adj*: **asiento ~** tip-up seat; (*Auto*) reclining seat

abatido, -a [aβa'tiðo, a] *adj* dejected, downcast

abatir [aβa'tir] *vt* (*muro*) to demolish; (*pájaro*) to shoot *o* bring down; (*fig*) to depress

abdicar [aβði'kar] *vi* to abdicate

abdomen [aβ'ðomen] *nm* abdomen; **abdominales** *nmpl* (*tb:* **ejercicios abdominales**) sit-ups

abecedario [aβeθe'ðarjo] *nm* alphabet

abedul [aβe'ðul] *nm* birch

abeja [a'βexa] *nf* bee

abejorro [aβe'xorro] *nm* bumblebee

abertura [aβer'tura] *nf* = **apertura**

abeto [a'βeto] *nm* fir

abierto, -a [a'βjerto, a] *pp de* **abrir** ▷ *adj* open

abismal [aβis'mal] *adj* (*fig*) vast, enormous

abismo [a'βismo] *nm* abyss

ablandar [aβlan'dar] *vt* to soften; **ablandarse** *vr* to get softer

abocado, -a [aβo'kaðo, a] *adj* (*vino*) smooth, pleasant

abochornar [aβot∫or'nar] *vt* to embarrass

abofetear [aβofete'ar] *vt* to slap

(in the face)

abogado, -a [aβo'xaðo, a] *nm/f* lawyer; (*notario*) solicitor; (*en tribunal*) barrister (*BRIT*), attorney (*US*); **abogado defensor** defence lawyer *o* (*US*) attorney

abogar [aβo'xar] *vi*: **~ por** to plead for; (*fig*) to advocate

abolir [aβo'lir] *vt* to abolish; (*cancelar*) to cancel

abolladura [aβoλa'ðura] *nf* dent

abollar [aβo'λar] *vt* to dent

abombarse [aβom'barse] (*LAM*) *vr* to go bad

abominable [aβomi'naβle] *adj* abominable

abonado, -a [aβo'naðo, a] *adj* (*deuda*) paid(-up) ▷ *nm/f* subscriber

abonar [aβo'nar] *vt* (*deuda*) to settle; (*terreno*) to fertilize; (*idea*) to endorse; **abonarse** *vr* to subscribe; **abono** *nm* payment; fertilizer; subscription

abordar [aβor'ðar] *vt* (*barco*) to board; (*asunto*) to broach

aborigen [aβo'rixen] *nmf* aborigine

aborrecer [aβorre'θer] *vt* to hate, loathe

abortar [aβor'tar] *vi* (*malparir*) to have a miscarriage; (*deliberadamente*) to have an abortion; **aborto** *nm* miscarriage; abortion

abovedado, -a [aβoβe'ðaðo, a] *adj* vaulted, domed

abrasar [aβra'sar] *vt* to burn (up); (*Agr*) to dry up, parch

abrazar [aβra'θar] *vt* to embrace, hug

abrazo [a'βraθo] *nm* embrace, hug; **un ~** (*en carta*) with best wishes

abrebotellas [aβreβo'teλas] *nm inv* bottle opener

abrecartas [aβre'kartas] *nm inv* letter opener

abrelatas [aβre'latas] *nm inv* tin (*BRIT*) *o* can opener

abreviatura [aβreβja'tura] *nf* abbreviation

abridor [aβri'ðor] *nm* bottle opener;

(*de latas*) tin (BRIT) o can opener

abrigador, a [aβriɣa'ðor, a] (MÉX) *adj* warm

abrigar [aβri'ɣar] *vt* (*proteger*) to shelter; (*ropa*) to keep warm; (*fig*) to cherish

abrigo [a'βriɣo] *nm* (*prenda*) coat, overcoat; (*lugar protegido*) shelter

abril [a'βril] *nm* April

abrillantador [aβriʎanta'ðor] *nm* polish

abrillantar [aβriʎan'tar] *vt* to polish

abrir [a'βrir] *vt* to open (up) ▷ *vi* to open; **abrirse** *vr* to open (up); (*extenderse*) to open out; (*cielo*) to clear; **~se paso** to find o force a way through

abrochar [aβro'tʃar] *vt* (*con botones*) to button (up); (*zapato, con broche*) to do up

abrupto, -a [a'βrupto, a] *adj* abrupt; (*empinado*) steep

absoluto, -a [aβso'luto, a] *adj* absolute; **en ~** *adv* not at all

absolver [aβsol'βer] *vt* to absolve; (*Jur*) to pardon; (: *acusado*) to acquit

absorbente [aβsor'βente] *adj* absorbent; (*interesante*) absorbing

absorber [aβsor'βer] *vt* to absorb; (*embeber*) to soak up

absorción [aβsor'θjon] *nf* absorption; (*Com*) takeover

abstemio, -a [aβs'temjo, a] *adj* teetotal

abstención [aβsten'θjon] *nf* abstention

abstenerse [aβste'nerse] *vr*: **~ (de)** to abstain o refrain (from)

abstinencia [aβsti'nenθja] *nf* abstinence; (*ayuno*) fasting

abstracto, -a [aβs'trakto, a] *adj* abstract

abstraer [aβstra'er] *vt* to abstract; **abstraerse** *vr* to be o become absorbed

abstraído, -a [aβstra'iðo, a] *adj* absent-minded

absuelto [aβ'swelto] *pp de* **absolver**

absurdo, -a [aβ'surðo, a] *adj* absurd

abuchear [aβutʃe'ar] *vt* to boo

abuelo, -a [a'βwelo, a] *nm/f* grandfather(-mother); **abuelos** *nmpl* grandparents

abultado, -a [aβul'taðo, a] *adj* bulky

abultar [aβul'tar] *vi* to be bulky

abundancia [aβun'danθja] *nf*: **una ~ de** plenty of; **abundante** *adj* abundant, plentiful

abundar [aβun'dar] *vi* to abound, be plentiful

aburrido, -a [aβu'rriðo, a] *adj* (*hastiado*) bored; (*que aburre*) boring; **aburrimiento** *nm* boredom, tedium

aburrir [aβu'rrir] *vt* to bore; **aburrirse** *vr* to be bored, get bored

abusado, -a [aβu'saðo, a] (MÉX: *fam*) *adj* (*astuto*) sharp, cunning ▷ *excl*: **¡~!** (*inv*) look out!, careful!

abusar [aβu'sar] *vi* to go too far; **~ de** to abuse

abusivo, -a [aβu'siβo, a] *adj* (*precio*) exorbitant

abuso [a'βuso] *nm* abuse

acá [a'ka] *adv* (*lugar*) here

acabado, -a [aka'βaðo, a] *adj* finished, complete; (*perfecto*) perfect; (*agotado*) worn out; (*fig*) masterly ▷ *nm* finish

acabar [aka'βar] *vt* (*llevar a su fin*) to finish, complete; (*consumir*) to use up; (*rematar*) to finish off ▷ *vi* to finish, end; **acabarse** *vr* to finish, stop; (*terminarse*) to be over; (*agotarse*) to run out; **~ con** to put an end to; **~ de llegar** to have just arrived; **~ por hacer** to end (up) by doing; **¡se acabó!** it's all over!; (*¡basta!*) that's enough!

acábose [aka'βose] *nm*: **esto es el ~** this is the last straw

academia [aka'ðemja] *nf* academy; **academia de idiomas** language school; **académico, -a** *adj* academic

acalorado, -a [akalo'raðo, a] *adj* (*discusión*) heated

acampar [akam'par] *vi* to camp

acantilado [akanti'laðo] *nm* cliff

acaparar [akapa'rar] *vt* to

monopolize; (*acumular*) to hoard

acariciar [akari'θjar] *vt* to caress; (*esperanza*) to cherish

acarrear [akarre'ar] *vt* to transport; (*fig*) to cause, result in

acaso [a'kaso] *adv* perhaps, maybe; **(por) si ~** (just) in case

acatar [aka'tar] *vt* to respect; (*ley*) obey

acatarrarse [akata'rrarse] *vr* to catch a cold

acceder [akθe'ðer] *vi*: **~ a** (*petición etc*) to agree to; (*tener acceso a*) to have access to; (*Inform*) to access

accesible [akθe'siβle] *adj* accessible

acceso [ak'θeso] *nm* access, entry; (*camino*) access, approach; (*Med*) attack, fit

accesorio, -a [akθe'sorjo, a] *adj*, *nm* accessory

accidentado, -a [akθiðen'taðo, a] *adj* uneven; (*montañoso*) hilly; (*azaroso*) eventful ▷ *nm/f* accident victim

accidental [akθiðen'tal] *adj* accidental

accidente [akθi'ðente] *nm* accident; **accidentes** *nmpl* (*de terreno*) unevenness *sg*; **accidente laboral** *o* **de trabajo/de tráfico** industrial/road *o* traffic accident

acción [ak'θjon] *nf* action; (*acto*) action, act; (*Com*) share; (*Jur*) action, lawsuit; **accionar** *vt* to work, operate; (*Inform*) to drive

accionista [akθjo'nista] *nmf* shareholder, stockholder

acebo [a'θeβo] *nm* holly; (*árbol*) holly tree

acechar [aθe'tʃar] *vt* to spy on; (*aguardar*) to lie in wait for; **acecho** *nm*: **estar al acecho (de)** to lie in wait (for)

aceite [a'θeite] *nm* oil; **aceite de girasol/oliva** olive/sunflower oil; **aceitera** *nf* oilcan; **aceitoso, -a** *adj* oily

aceituna [aθei'tuna] *nf* olive; **aceituna rellena** stuffed olive

acelerador [aθelera'ðor] *nm* accelerator

acelerar [aθele'rar] *vt* to accelerate

acelga [a'θelɣa] *nf* chard, beet

acento [a'θento] *nm* accent; (*acentuación*) stress

acentuar [aθen'twar] *vt* to accent; to stress; (*fig*) to accentuate

acepción [aθep'θjon] *nf* meaning

aceptable [aθep'taβle] *adj* acceptable

aceptación [aθepta'θjon] *nf* acceptance; (*aprobación*) approval

aceptar [aθep'tar] *vt* to accept; (*aprobar*) to approve; **~ hacer algo** to agree to do sth

acequia [a'θekja] *nf* irrigation ditch

acera [a'θera] *nf* pavement (BRIT), sidewalk (US)

acerca [a'θerka]: **~ de** *prep* about, concerning

acercar [aθer'kar] *vt* to bring *o* move nearer; **acercarse** *vr* to approach, come near

acero [a'θero] *nm* steel

acérrimo, -a [a'θerrimo, a] *adj* (*partidario*) staunch; (*enemigo*) bitter

acertado, -a [aθer'taðo, a] *adj* correct; (*apropiado*) apt; (*sensato*) sensible

acertar [aθer'tar] *vt* (*blanco*) to hit; (*solución*) to get right; (*adivinar*) to guess ▷ *vi* to get it right, be right; **~ a** to manage to; **~ con** to happen *o* hit on

acertijo [aθer'tixo] *nm* riddle, puzzle

achacar [atʃa'kar] *vt* to attribute

achacoso, -a [atʃa'koso, a] *adj* sickly

achicar [atʃi'kar] *vt* to reduce; (*Náut*) to bale out

achicharrar [atʃitʃa'rrar] *vt* to scorch, burn

achichincle [atʃi'tʃinkle] (*MÉX: fam*) *nmf* minion

achicoria [atʃi'korja] *nf* chicory

achuras [a'tʃuras] (*RPL*) *nfpl* offal *sg*

acicate [aθi'kate] *nm* spur

acidez [aθi'ðeθ] nf acidity
ácido, -a ['aθiðo, a] adj sour, acid
▷ nm acid
acierto etc [a'θjerto] vb V **acertar**
▷ nm success; (buen paso) wise move;
(solución) solution; (habilidad) skill,
ability
acitronar [aθitro'nar] (MÉX: fam) vt
to brown
aclamar [akla'mar] vt to acclaim;
(aplaudir) to applaud
aclaración [aklara'θjon] nf
clarification, explanation
aclarar [akla'rar] vt to clarify,
explain; (ropa) to rinse ▷ vi to clear
up; **aclararse** vr (explicarse) to
understand; **~se la garganta** to clear
one's throat
aclimatación [aklimata'θjon] nf
acclimatization
aclimatar [aklima'tar] vt to
acclimatize; **aclimatarse** vr to
become acclimatized
acné [ak'ne] nm acne
acobardar [akoβar'ðar] vt to
intimidate
acogedor, a [akoxe'ðor, a] adj
welcoming; (hospitalario) hospitable
acoger [ako'xer] vt to welcome;
(abrigar) to shelter
acogida [ako'xiða] nf reception;
refuge
acomedido, -a [akome'ðiðo, a]
(MÉX) adj helpful, obliging
acometer [akome'ter] vt to attack;
(emprender) to undertake; **acometida**
nf attack, assault
acomodado, -a [akomo'ðaðo, a] adj
(persona) well-to-do
acomodador, a [akomoða'ðor, a]
nm/f usher(ette)
acomodar [akomo'ðar] vt to adjust;
(alojar) to accommodate; **acomodarse**
vr to conform; (instalarse) to install o.s.;
(adaptarse): **~se (a)** to adapt (to)
acompañar [akompa'ɲar] vt to
accompany; (documentos) to enclose
acondicionar [akondiθjo'nar] vt to

arrange, prepare; (pelo) to condition
aconsejar [akonse'xar] vt to advise,
counsel; **~ a algn hacer** o **que haga
algo** to advise sb to do sth
acontecer [akonte'θer] vi to happen,
occur; **acontecimiento** nm event
acopio [a'kopjo] nm store, stock
acoplar [ako'plar] vt to fit; (Elec) to
connect; (vagones) to couple
acorazado, -a [akora'θaðo, a]
adj armour-plated, armoured ▷ nm
battleship
acordar [akor'ðar] vt (resolver) to
agree, resolve; (recordar) to remind;
acordarse vr to agree; **~ hacer algo**
to agree to do sth; **~se (de algo)** to
remember (sth); **acorde** adj (Mús)
harmonious; **acorde con** (medidas etc)
in keeping with ▷ nm chord
acordeón [akorðe'on] nm accordion
acordonado, -a [akorðo'naðo, a]
adj (calle) cordoned-off
acorralar [akorra'lar] vt to round
up, corral
acortar [akor'tar] vt to shorten;
(duración) to cut short; (cantidad) to
reduce; **acortarse** vr to become
shorter
acosar [ako'sar] vt to pursue
relentlessly; (fig) to hound, pester;
acoso nm harassment; **acoso sexual**
sexual harassment
acostar [akos'tar] vt (en cama) to
put to bed; (en suelo) to lay down;
acostarse vr to go to bed; to lie down;
~se con algn to sleep with sb
acostumbrado, -a [akostum'braðo,
a] adj usual; **~ a** used to
acostumbrar [akostum'brar] vt: **~
a algn a algo** to get sb used to sth
▷ vi: **~ (a) hacer** to be in the habit of
doing; **acostumbrarse** vr: **~se a** to
get used to
acotación [akota'θjon] nf marginal
note; (Geo) elevation mark; (de
límite) boundary mark; (Teatro) stage
direction
acotamiento [akota'mjento] (MÉX)

nm hard shoulder (BRIT), berm (US)

acre ['akre] *adj* (*olor*) acrid; (*fig*) biting ▷ *nm* acre

acreditar [akreði'tar] *vt* (*garantizar*) to vouch for, guarantee; (*autorizar*) to authorize; (*dar prueba de*) to prove; (*Com: abonar*) to credit; (*embajador*) to accredit

acreedor, a [akree'ðor, a] *nm/f* creditor

acribillar [akriβi'ʎar] *vt*: ~ **a balazos** to riddle with bullets

acróbata [a'kroβata] *nmf* acrobat

acta ['akta] *nf* certificate; (*de comisión*) minutes *pl*, record; **acta de matrimonio/nacimiento** (MÉX) marriage/birth certificate; **acta notarial** affidavit

actitud [akti'tuð] *nf* attitude; (*postura*) posture

activar [akti'βar] *vt* to activate; (*acelerar*) to speed up

actividad [aktiβi'ðað] *nf* activity

activo, -a [ak'tiβo, a] *adj* active; (*vivo*) lively ▷ *nm* (*Com*) assets *pl*

acto ['akto] *nm* act, action; (*ceremonia*) ceremony; (*Teatro*) act; **en el ~** immediately

actor [ak'tor] *nm* actor; (*Jur*) plaintiff ▷ *adj*: **parte ~a** prosecution

actriz [ak'triθ] *nf* actress

actuación [aktwa'θjon] *nf* action; (*comportamiento*) conduct, behaviour; (*Jur*) proceedings *pl*; (*desempeño*) performance

actual [ak'twal] *adj* present(-day), current

> No confundir **actual** con la palabra inglesa *actual*.

actualidad *nf* present; **actualidades** *nfpl* (*noticias*) news *sg*; **en la actualidad** at present; (*hoy día*) nowadays; **actualizar** [aktwali'θar] *vt* to update, modernize; **actualmente** [aktwal'mente] *adv* at present; (*hoy día*) nowadays

> No confundir **actualmente** con la palabra inglesa *actually*.

actuar [ak'twar] *vi* (*obrar*) to work, operate; (*actor*) to act, perform ▷ *vt* to work, operate; ~ **de** to act as

acuarela [akwa'rela] *nf* watercolour

acuario [a'kwarjo] *nm* aquarium; (*Astrología*): **A~** Aquarius

acuático, -a [a'kwatiko, a] *adj* aquatic

acudir [aku'ðir] *vi* (*asistir*) to attend; (*ir*) to go; ~ **a** (*fig*) to turn to; ~ **a una cita** to keep an appointment; ~ **en ayuda de** to go to the aid of

acuerdo *etc* [a'kwerðo] *vb* V **acordar** ▷ *nm* agreement; **¡de ~!** agreed!; **de ~ con** (*persona*) in agreement with; (*acción, documento*) in accordance with; **estar de ~** to be agreed, agree

acumular [akumu'lar] *vt* to accumulate, collect

acuñar [aku'ɲar] *vt* (*moneda*) to mint; (*frase*) to coin

acupuntura [akupun'tura] *nf* acupuncture

acurrucarse [akurru'karse] *vr* to crouch; (*ovillarse*) to curl up

acusación [akusa'θjon] *nf* accusation

acusar [aku'sar] *vt* to accuse; (*revelar*) to reveal; (*denunciar*) to denounce

acuse [a'kuse] *nm*: ~ **de recibo** acknowledgement of receipt

acústica [a'kustika] *nf* acoustics *pl*

acústico, -a [a'kustiko, a] *adj* acoustic

adaptación [aðapta'θjon] *nf* adaptation

adaptador [aðapta'ðor] *nm* (*Elec*) adapter, adaptor; **adaptador universal** universal adapter *o* adaptor

adaptar [aðap'tar] *vt* to adapt; (*acomodar*) to fit

adecuado, -a [aðe'kwaðo, a] *adj* (*apto*) suitable; (*oportuno*) appropriate

a. de J.C. *abr* (= *antes de Jesucristo*) B.C.

adelantado, -a [aðelan'taðo, a] *adj* advanced; (*reloj*) fast; **pagar por ~** to pay in advance

adelantamiento [aðelanta'mjento]

nm (*Auto*) overtaking

adelantar [aðelan'tar] *vt* to move forward; (*avanzar*) to advance; (*acelerar*) to speed up; (*Auto*) to overtake ▷ *vi* to go forward, advance; **adelantarse** *vr* to go forward, advance

adelante [aðe'lante] *adv* forward(s), ahead ▷ *excl* come in!; **de hoy en ~** from now on; **más ~** later on; (*más allá*) further on

adelanto [aðe'lanto] *nm* advance; (*mejora*) improvement; (*progreso*) progress

adelgazar [aðelɣa'θar] *vt* to thin (down) ▷ *vi* to get thin; (*con régimen*) to slim down, lose weight

ademán [aðe'man] *nm* gesture; **ademanes** *nmpl* manners

además [aðe'mas] *adv* besides; (*por otra parte*) moreover; (*también*) also; **~ de** besides, in addition to

adentrarse [aðen'trarse] *vr*: **~ en** to go into, get inside; (*penetrar*) to penetrate (into)

adentro [a'ðentro] *adv* inside, in; **mar ~** out at sea; **tierra ~** inland

adepto, -a [a'ðepto, a] *nm/f* supporter

aderezar [aðere'θar] *vt* (*ensalada*) to dress; (*comida*) to season; **aderezo** *nm* dressing; seasoning

adeudar [aðeu'ðar] *vt* to owe

adherirse [aðe'rirse] *vr*: **~ a** to adhere to; (*partido*) to join

adhesión [aðe'sjon] *nf* adhesion; (*fig*) adherence

adicción [aðik'θjon] *nf* addiction

adición [aði'θjon] *nf* addition

adicto, -a [a'ðikto, a] *adj*: **~ a** addicted to; (*dedicado*) devoted to ▷ *nm/f* supporter, follower; (*toxicómano*) addict

adiestrar [aðjes'trar] *vt* to train, teach; (*conducir*) to guide, lead

adinerado, -a [aðine'raðo, a] *adj* wealthy

adiós [a'ðjos] *excl* (*para despedirse*) goodbye!, cheerio!; (*al pasar*) hello!

aditivo [aði'tiβo] *nm* additive

adivinanza [aðiβi'nanθa] *nf* riddle

adivinar [aðiβi'nar] *vt* to prophesy; (*conjeturar*) to guess; **adivino, -a** *nm/f* fortune-teller

adj *abr* (= *adjunto*) encl

adjetivo [aðxe'tiβo] *nm* adjective

adjudicar [aðxuði'kar] *vt* to award; **adjudicarse** *vr*: **~se algo** to appropriate sth

adjuntar [aðxun'tar] *vt* to attach, enclose; **adjunto, -a** *adj* attached, enclosed ▷ *nm/f* assistant

administración [aðministra'θjon] *nf* administration; (*dirección*) management; **administrador, a** *nm/f* administrator, manager(ess)

administrar [aðminis'trar] *vt* to administer; **administrativo, -a** *adj* administrative

admirable [aðmi'raβle] *adj* admirable

admiración [aðmira'θjon] *nf* admiration; (*asombro*) wonder; (*Ling*) exclamation mark

admirar [aðmi'rar] *vt* to admire; (*extrañar*) to surprise

admisible [aðmi'siβle] *adj* admissible

admisión [aðmi'sjon] *nf* admission; (*reconocimiento*) acceptance

admitir [aðmi'tir] *vt* to admit; (*aceptar*) to accept

adobar [aðo'βar] *vt* (*Culin*) to season

adobe [a'ðoβe] *nm* adobe, sun-dried brick

adolecer [aðole'er] *vi*: **~ de** to suffer from

adolescente [aðoles'θente] *nmf* adolescent, teenager

adonde [a'ðonðe] *conj* (to) where

adónde [a'ðonðe] *adv* = **dónde**

adopción [aðop'θjon] *nf* adoption

adoptar [aðop'tar] *vt* to adopt

adoptivo, -a [aðop'tiβo, a] *adj* (*padres*) adoptive; (*hijo*) adopted

adoquín [aðo'kin] *nm* paving stone

adorar [aðo'rar] *vt* to adore

adornar [aðor'nar] *vt* to adorn

adorno [a'ðorno] *nm* ornament; (*decoración*) decoration

adosado, -a [aðo'saðo, a] *adj*: **casa adosada** semi-detached house

adosar [aðo'sar] (*MÉX*) *vt* (*adjuntar*) to attach, enclose (*with a letter*)

adquiero *etc vb* V **adquirir**

adquirir [aðki'rir] *vt* to acquire, obtain

adquisición [aðkisi'θjon] *nf* acquisition

adrede [a'ðreðe] *adv* on purpose

ADSL *nm abr* broadband

aduana [a'ðwana] *nf* customs *pl*

aduanero, -a [aðwa'nero, a] *adj* customs *cpd* ▷ *nm/f* customs officer

adueñarse [aðwe'ɲarse] *vr*: **~ de** to take possession of

adular [aðu'lar] *vt* to flatter

adulterar [aðulte'rar] *vt* to adulterate

adulterio [aðul'terjo] *nm* adultery

adúltero, -a [a'ðultero, a] *adj* adulterous ▷ *nm/f* adulterer/ adulteress

adulto, -a [a'ðulto, a] *adj, nm/f* adult

adverbio [að'βerβjo] *nm* adverb

adversario, -a [aðβer'sarjo, a] *nm/f* adversary

adversidad [aðβersi'ðað] *nf* adversity; (*contratiempo*) setback

adverso, -a [að'βerso, a] *adj* adverse

advertencia [aðβer'tenθja] *nf* warning; (*prefacio*) preface, foreword

advertir [aðβer'tir] *vt* to notice; (*avisar*): **~ a algn de** to warn sb about *o* of

Adviento [að'βjento] *nm* Advent

advierto *etc vb* V **advertir**

aéreo, -a [a'ereo, a] *adj* aerial

aerobic [ae'roβik] *nm* aerobics *sg*; **aerobics** (*MÉX*) *nmpl* aerobics *sg*

aeromozo, -a [aero'moθo, a] (*LAM*) *nm/f* air steward(ess)

aeronáutica [aero'nautika] *nf* aeronautics *sg*

aeronave [aero'naβe] *nm* spaceship

aeroplano [aero'plano] *nm* aeroplane

aeropuerto [aero'pwerto] *nm* airport

aerosol [aero'sol] *nm* aerosol

afamado, -a [afa'maðo, a] *adj* famous

afán [a'fan] *nm* hard work; (*deseo*) desire

afanador, a [afana'ðor, a] (*MÉX*) *nm/f* (*de limpieza*) cleaner

afanar [afa'nar] *vt* to harass; (*fam*) to pinch

afear [afe'ar] *vt* to disfigure

afección [afek'θjon] *nf* (*Med*) disease

afectado, -a [afek'taðo, a] *adj* affected

afectar [afek'tar] *vt* to affect

afectísimo, -a [afek'tisimo, a] *adj* affectionate; **suyo ~** yours truly

afectivo, -a [afek'tiβo, a] *adj* (*problema etc*) emotional

afecto [a'fekto] *nm* affection; **tenerle ~ a algn** to be fond of sb

afectuoso, -a [afek'twoso, a] *adj* affectionate

afeitar [afei'tar] *vt* to shave; **afeitarse** *vr* to shave

afeminado, -a [afemi'naðo, a] *adj* effeminate

Afganistán [afɣanis'tan] *nm* Afghanistan

afianzar [afjan'θar] *vt* to strengthen; to secure; **afianzarse** *vr* to become established

afiche [a'fitʃe] (*RPL*) *nm* poster

afición [afi'θjon] *nf* fondness, liking; **la ~** the fans *pl*; **pinto por ~** I paint as a hobby; **aficionado, -a** *adj* keen, enthusiastic; (*no profesional*) amateur ▷ *nm/f* enthusiast, fan; amateur; **ser aficionado a algo** to be very keen on *o* fond of sth

aficionar [afiθjo'nar] *vt*: **~ a algn a algo** to make sb like sth; **aficionarse** *vr*: **~se a algo** to grow fond of sth

afilado, -a [afi'laðo, a] *adj* sharp

afilar [afi'lar] *vt* to sharpen

afiliarse [afi'ljarse] vr to affiliate

afín [a'fin] adj (parecido) similar; (conexo) related

afinar [afi'nar] vt (Tec) to refine; (Mús) to tune ▷ vi (tocar) to play in tune; (cantar) to sing in tune

afincarse [afin'karse] vr to settle

afinidad [afini'ðað] nf affinity; (parentesco) relationship; **por ~** by marriage

afirmación [afirma'θjon] nf affirmation

afirmar [afir'mar] vt to affirm, state; **afirmativo, -a** adj affirmative

afligir [afli'xir] vt to afflict; (apenar) to distress

aflojar [aflo'xar] vt to slacken; (desatar) to loosen, undo; (relajar) to relax ▷ vi (drop); (bajar) to go down; **aflojarse** vr to relax

afluente [aflu'ente] adj flowing ▷ nm tributary

afmo, -a abr (= afectísimo(a) suyo(a)) Yours

afónico, -a [a'foniko, a] adj: **estar ~** to have a sore throat; to have lost one's voice

aforo [a'foro] nm (de teatro etc) capacity

afortunado, -a [afortu'naðo, a] adj fortunate, lucky

África ['afrika] nf Africa; **África del Sur** South Africa; **africano, -a** adj, nm/f African

afrontar [afron'tar] vt to confront; (poner cara a cara) to bring face to face

afrutado, -a [afru'taðo, a] adj fruity

after ['after] (pl **~s**) nm after-hours club; **afterhours** [after'aurs] nm inv =**after**

afuera [a'fwera] adv out, outside; **afueras** nfpl outskirts

agachar [aɣa'tʃar] vt to bend, bow; **agacharse** vr to stoop, bend

agalla [a'ɣaʎa] nf (Zool) gill; **tener ~s** (fam) to have guts

agarradera [aɣarra'ðera] (MÉX) nf handle

agarrado, -a [aɣa'rraðo, a] adj mean, stingy

agarrar [aɣa'rrar] vt to grasp, grab; (LAM: tomar) to take, catch; (recoger) to pick up ▷ vi (planta) to take root; **agarrarse** vr to hold on (tightly)

agencia [a'xenθja] nf agency; **agencia de viajes** travel agency; **agencia inmobiliaria** estate (BRIT) o real estate (US) agent's (office)

agenciarse [axen'θjarse] vr to obtain, procure

agenda [a'xenda] nf diary; **~ electronica** PDA

▍No confundir **agenda** con la palabra inglesa agenda.

agente [a'xente] nmf agent; (tb: **~ de policía**) policeman/policewoman; **agente de seguros** insurance agent; **agente de tránsito** (MÉX) traffic cop; **agente inmobiliario** estate agent (BRIT), realtor (US)

ágil ['axil] adj agile, nimble; **agilidad** nf agility, nimbleness

agilizar [axili'θar] vt (trámites) to speed up

agiotista [axjo'tista] (MÉX) nmf (usurero) usurer

agitación [axita'θjon] nf (de mano etc) shaking, waving; (de líquido etc) stirring; (fig) agitation

agitado, -a [axi'aðo, a] adj hectic; (viaje) bumpy

agitar [axi'tar] vt to wave, shake; (líquido) to stir; (fig) to stir up, excite; **agitarse** vr to get excited; (inquietarse) to get worried o upset

aglomeración [aɣlomera'θjon] nf agglomeration; **aglomeración de gente/tráfico** mass of people/traffic jam

agnóstico, -a [aɣ'nostiko, a] adj, nm/f agnostic

agobiar [aɣo'βjar] vt to weigh down; (oprimir) to oppress; (cargar) to burden

agolparse [aɣol'parse] vr to crowd together

agonía [aɣo'nia] nf death throes pl;

(*fig*) agony, anguish
agonizante [aɣoni'θante] *adj* dying
agonizar [aɣoni'θar] *vi* to be dying
agosto [a'ɣosto] *nm* August
agotado, -a [aɣo'taðo, a] *adj*
(*persona*) exhausted; (*libros*) out of
print; (*acabado*) finished; (*Com*) sold
out; **agotador, a** [aɣota'ðor, a] *adj*
exhausting
agotamiento [aɣota'mjento] *nm*
exhaustion
agotar [aɣo'tar] *vt* to exhaust;
(*consumir*) to drain; (*recursos*) to use up,
deplete; **agotarse** *vr* to be exhausted;
(*acabarse*) to run out; (*libro*) to go out
of print
agraciado, -a [aɣra'θjaðo, a] *adj*
(*atractivo*) attractive; (*en sorteo etc*)
lucky
agradable [aɣra'ðaβle] *adj* pleasant,
nice
agradar [aɣra'ðar] *vt*: **él me agrada**
I like him
agradecer [aɣraðe'θer] *vt* to
thank; (*favor etc*) to be grateful
for; **agradecido, -a** *adj* grateful;
¡muy agradecido! thanks a lot!;
agradecimiento *nm* thanks *pl*;
gratitude
agradezco *etc vb* V **agradecer**
agrado [a'ɣraðo] *nm*: **ser de tu** *etc* **~** to
be to your *etc* liking
agrandar [aɣran'dar] *vt* to enlarge;
(*fig*) to exaggerate; **agrandarse** *vr* to
get bigger
agrario, -a [a'ɣrarjo, a] *adj* agrarian,
land *cpd*; (*política*) agricultural, farming
agravante [aɣra'βante] *adj*
aggravating ▷ *nm*: **con el ~ de que ...**
with the further difficulty that ...
agravar [aɣra'βar] *vt* (*pesar sobre*)
to make heavier; (*irritar*) to aggravate;
agravarse *vr* to worsen, get worse
agraviar [aɣra'βjar] *vt* to offend; (*ser
injusto con*) to wrong
agredir [aɣre'ðir] *vt* to attack
agregado, -a [aɣre'ɣaðo, a] *nm/f*: **A~**
= teacher (*who is not head of department*)

▷ *nm* aggregate; (*persona*) attaché
agregar [aɣre'ɣar] *vt* to gather;
(*añadir*) to add; (*persona*) to appoint
agresión [aɣre'sjon] *nf* aggression
agresivo, -a [aɣre'siβo, a] *adj*
aggressive
agriar [a'ɣrjar] *vt* to (turn) sour
agrícola [a'ɣrikola] *adj* farming *cpd*,
agricultural
agricultor, a [aɣrikul'tor, a] *nm/f*
farmer
agricultura [aɣrikul'tura] *nf*
agriculture, farming
agridulce [aɣri'ðulθe] *adj*
bittersweet; (*Culin*) sweet and sour
agrietarse [aɣrje'tarse] *vr* to crack;
(*piel*) to chap
agrio, -a ['aɣrjo, a] *adj* bitter
agrupación [aɣrupa'θjon] *nf* group;
(*acto*) grouping
agrupar [aɣru'par] *vt* to group
agua ['aɣwa] *nf* water; (*Náut*) wake;
(*Arq*) slope of a roof; **aguas** *nfpl* (*de
piedra*) water *sg*, sparkle *sg*; (*Med*)
water *sg*, urine *sg*; (*Náut*) waters;
agua bendita/destilada/potable
holy/distilled/drinking water; **agua
caliente** hot water; **agua corriente**
running water; **agua de colonia** eau
de cologne; **agua mineral (con/sin
gas)** (sparkling/still) mineral water;
agua oxigenada hydrogen peroxide;
aguas abajo/arriba downstream/
upstream; **aguas jurisdiccionales**
territorial waters
aguacate [aɣwa'kate] *nm* avocado
(pear)
aguacero [aɣwa'θero] *nm* (heavy)
shower, downpour
aguado, -a [a'ɣwaðo, a] *adj* watery,
watered down
aguafiestas [aɣwa'fjestas] *nmf inv*
spoilsport, killjoy
aguamiel [aɣwa'mjel] (*MÉX*) *nf*
fermented maguey *o* agave juice
aguanieve [aɣwa'njeβe] *nf* sleet
aguantar [aɣwan'tar] *vt* to bear, put
up with; (*sostener*) to hold up ▷ *vi* to

last; **aguantarse** vr to restrain o.s.;
aguante nm (paciencia) patience;
(resistencia) endurance

aguar [a'ɣwar] vt to water down

aguardar [aɣwar'ðar] vt to wait for

aguardiente [aɣwar'ðjente] nm
brandy, liquor

aguarrás [aɣwa'rras] nm turpentine

aguaviva [aɣwa'biβa] (RPL) nf
jellyfish

agudeza [aɣu'ðeθa] nf sharpness;
(ingenio) wit

agudo, -a [a'ɣuðo, a] adj sharp;
(voz) high-pitched, piercing; (dolor,
enfermedad) acute

agüero [a'ɣwero] nm: **buen/mal ~**
good/bad omen

aguijón [aɣi'xon] nm sting; (fig) spur

águila ['aɣila] nf eagle; (fig) genius

aguileño, -a [aɣi'leɲo, a] adj (nariz)
aquiline; (rostro) sharp-featured

aguinaldo [aɣi'naldo] nm Christmas
box

aguja [a'ɣuxa] nf needle; (de reloj)
hand; (Arq) spire; (Tec) firing-pin;
agujas nfpl (Zool) ribs; (Ferro) points

agujerear [aɣuxere'ar] vt to make
holes in

agujero [aɣu'xero] nm hole

agujetas [aɣu'xetas] nfpl stitch sg;
(rigidez) stiffness sg

ahí [a'i] adv there; **de ~ que** so that,
with the result that; **~ llega** here he
comes; **por ~** that way; (allá) over
there; **zoo o por ~** 200 or so

ahijado, -a [ai'xaðo, a] nm/f
godson/daughter

ahogar [ao'ɣar] vt to drown; (asfixiar)
to suffocate, smother; (fuego) to put
out; **ahogarse** vr (en el agua) to drown;
(por asfixia) to suffocate

ahogo [a'oɣo] nm breathlessness;
(fig) financial difficulty

ahondar [aon'dar] vt to deepen,
make deeper; (fig) to study thoroughly
▷ vi to study thoroughly

ahora [a'ora] adv now; (hace poco)
a moment ago, just now; (dentro de
poco) in a moment; **~ voy** I'm coming;
~ mismo right now; **~ bien** now then;
por ~ for the present

ahorcar [aor'kar] vt to hang

ahorita [ao'rita] (fam) adv (LAM: en
este momento) right now; (MÉX: hace
poco) just now; (: dentro de poco) in a
minute

ahorrar [ao'rrar] vt (dinero) to save;
(esfuerzos) to save, avoid; **ahorro** nm
(acto) saving; **ahorros** nmpl (dinero)
savings

ahuecar [awe'kar] vt to hollow (out);
(voz) to deepen; **ahuecarse** vr to give
o.s. airs

ahumar [au'mar] vt to smoke, cure;
(llenar de humo) to fill with smoke ▷ vi
to smoke; **ahumarse** vr to fill with
smoke

ahuyentar [aujen'tar] vt to drive off,
frighten off; (fig) to dispel

aire ['aire] nm air; (viento) wind;
(corriente) draught; (Mús) tune;
al ~ libre in the open air; **aire
acondicionado** air conditioning;
airear vt to air; **airearse** vr (persona)
to go out for a breath of fresh air;
airoso, -a adj windy; draughty; (fig)
graceful

aislado, -a [ais'laðo, a] adj isolated;
(incomunicado) cut-off; (Elec) insulated

aislar [ais'lar] vt to isolate; (Elec) to
insulate

ajardinado, -a [axarði'naðo, a] adj
landscaped

ajedrez [axe'ðreθ] nm chess

ajeno, -a [a'xeno, a] adj (que
pertenece a otro) somebody else's; **~ a**
foreign to

ajetreado, -a [axetre'aðo, a] adj
busy

ajetreo [axe'treo] nm bustle

ají [a'xi] (cs) nm chil(l)i, red pepper;
(salsa) chil(l)i sauce

ajillo [a'xiʎo] nm: **gambas al ~** garlic
prawns

ajo ['axo] nm garlic

ajuar [a'xwar] nm household

furnishings pl; (de novia) trousseau; (de niño) layette

ajustado, -a [axus'taðo, a] adj (tornillo) tight; (cálculo) right; (ropa) tight(-fitting); (resultado) close

ajustar [axus'tar] vt (adaptar) to adjust; (encajar) to fit; (Tec) to engage; (Imprenta) to make up; (apretar) to tighten; (concertar) to agree (on); (reconciliar) to reconcile; (cuentas, deudas) to settle ▷ vi to fit; **ajustarse** vr: **~se a** (precio etc) to be in keeping with, fit in with; **~ las cuentas a algn** to get even with sb

ajuste [a'xuste] nm adjustment; (Costura) fitting; (acuerdo) compromise; (de cuenta) settlement

al [al] = **a + el**; V **a**

ala ['ala] nf wing; (de sombrero) brim; winger; **ala delta** nf hang-glider

alabanza [ala'βanθa] nf praise

alabar [ala'βar] vt to praise

alacena [ala'θena] nf kitchen cupboard (BRIT) o closet (US)

alacrán [ala'kran] nm scorpion

alambrada [alam'braða] nf wire fence; (red) wire netting

alambre [a'lambre] nm wire; **alambre de púas** barbed wire

alameda [ala'meða] nf (plantío) poplar grove; (lugar de paseo) avenue, boulevard

álamo ['alamo] nm poplar

alarde [a'larðe] nm show, display; **hacer ~ de** to boast of

alargador [alarxa'ðor] nm (Elec) extension lead

alargar [alar'xar] vt to lengthen, extend; (paso) to hasten; (brazo) to stretch out; (cuerda) to pay out; (conversación) to spin out; **alargarse** vr to get longer

alarma [a'larma] nf alarm; **alarma de incendios** fire alarm; **alarmar** vt to alarm; **alarmarse** to get alarmed; **alarmante** [alar'mante] adj alarming

alba ['alβa] nf dawn

albahaca [al'βaka] nf basil

Albania [al'βanja] nf Albania

albañil [alβa'ɲil] nm bricklayer; (cantero) mason

albarán [alβa'ran] nm (Com) delivery note, invoice

albaricoque [alβari'koke] nm apricot

albedrío [alβe'ðrio] nm: **libre ~** free will

alberca [al'βerka] nf reservoir; (MÉX: piscina) swimming pool

albergar [alβer'xar] vt to shelter

albergue etc [al'βerxe] vb V **albergar** ▷ nm shelter, refuge; **albergue juvenil** youth hostel

albóndiga [al'βondixa] nf meatball

albornoz [alβor'noθ] nm (de los árabes) burnous; (para el baño) bathrobe

alborotar [alβoro'tar] vi to make a row ▷ vt to agitate, stir up; **alborotarse** vr to get excited; (mar) to get rough; **alboroto** nm row, uproar

álbum ['alβum] (pl **~s, ~es**) nm album; **álbum de recortes** scrapbook

albur [al'βur] (MÉX) nm (juego de palabras) pun; (doble sentido) double entendre

alcachofa [alka'tʃofa] nf artichoke

alcalde, -esa [al'kalde, esa] nm/f mayor(ess)

alcaldía [alkal'dia] nf mayoralty; (lugar) mayor's office

alcance etc [al'kanθe] vb V **alcanzar** ▷ nm reach; (Com) adverse balance; **al ~ de algn** available to sb

alcancía [alkan'θia] (LAM) nf (para ahorrar) money box; (para colectas) collection box

alcantarilla [alkanta'riʎa] nf (de aguas cloacales) sewer; (en la calle) gutter

alcanzar [alkan'θar] vt (algo: con la mano, el pie) to reach; (alguien: en el camino etc) to catch up (with); (autobús) to catch; (bala) to hit, strike ▷ vi (ser suficiente) to be enough; **~ a hacer** to manage to do

alcaparra [alka'parra] nf caper
alcayata [alka'jata] nf hook
alcázar [al'kaθar] nm fortress; (Náut) quarter-deck
alcoba [al'koβa] nf bedroom
alcohol [al'kol] nm alcohol; **alcohol metílico** methylated spirits pl (BRIT), wood alcohol (US); **alcohólico, -a** adj, nm/f alcoholic; **alcoholímetro** [alko'limetro] nm Breathalyser® (BRIT), drunkometer (US); **alcoholismo** [alko'lismo] nm alcoholism
alcornoque [alkor'noke] nm cork tree; (fam) idiot
aldea [al'dea] nf village; **aldeano, -a** adj village cpd ▷ nm/f villager
aleación [alea'θjon] nf alloy
aleatorio, -a [alea'torjo, a] adj random
aleccionar [alekθjo'nar] vt to instruct; (adiestrar) to train
alegar [ale'ɣar] vt to claim; (Jur) to plead ▷ vi (LAM: discutir) to argue
alegoría [aleɣo'ria] nf allegory
alegrar [ale'ɣrar] vt (causar alegría) to cheer (up); (fuego) to poke; (fiesta) to liven up; **alegrarse** vr (fam) to get merry o tight; **~se de** to be glad about
alegre [a'leɣre] adj happy, cheerful; (fam) merry, tight; (chiste) risqué, blue; **alegría** nf happiness; merriment
alejar [ale'xar] vt to remove; (fig) to estrange; **alejarse** vr to move away
alemán, -ana [ale'man, ana] adj, nm/f German ▷ nm (Ling) German
Alemania [ale'manja] nf Germany
alentador, a [alenta'ðor, a] adj encouraging
alentar [alen'tar] vt to encourage
alergia [a'lerxja] nf allergy
alero [a'lero] nm (de tejado) eaves pl; (guardabarros) mudguard
alerta [a'lerta] adj, nm alert
aleta [a'leta] nf (de pez) fin; (ala) wing; (de foca, Deporte) flipper; (Auto) mudguard
aletear [alete'ar] vi to flutter
alevín [ale'βin] nm fry, young fish

alevosía [aleβo'sia] nf treachery
alfabeto [alfa'βeto] nm alphabet
alfalfa [al'falfa] nf alfalfa, lucerne
alfarería [alfare'ria] nf pottery; (tienda) pottery shop; **alfarero, -a** nm/f potter
alféizar [al'feiθar] nm window-sill
alférez [al'fereθ] nm (Mil) second lieutenant; (Náut) ensign
alfil [al'fil] nm (Ajedrez) bishop
alfiler [alfi'ler] nm pin; (broche) clip
alfombra [al'fombra] nf carpet; (más pequeña) rug; **alfombrilla** nf rug, mat; (Inform) mouse mat o pad
alforja [al'forxa] nf saddlebag
algas ['alɣas] nfpl seaweed
álgebra ['alxeβra] nf algebra
algo ['alɣo] pron something; anything ▷ adv somewhat, rather; **¿~ más?** anything else?; (en tienda) is that all?; **por ~ será** there must be some reason for it
algodón [alɣo'ðon] nm cotton; (planta) cotton plant; **algodón de azúcar** candy floss (BRIT), cotton candy (US); **algodón hidrófilo** cotton wool (BRIT), absorbent cotton (US)
alguien ['alɣjen] pron someone, somebody; (en frases interrogativas) anyone, anybody
alguno, -a [al'ɣuno, a] adj (delante de nm): **algún** some; (después de n): **no tiene talento ~** he has no talent, he doesn't have any talent ▷ pron (alguien) someone, somebody; **algún que otro libro** some book or other; **algún día iré** I'll go one o some day; **sin interés ~** without the slightest interest; **~ que otro** an occasional one; **~s piensan** some (people) think
alhaja [a'laxa] nf jewel; (tesoro) precious object, treasure
alhelí [ale'li] nm wallflower, stock
aliado, -a [a'ljaðo, a] adj allied
alianza [a'ljanθa] nf alliance; (anillo) wedding ring
aliar [a'ljar] vt to ally; **aliarse** vr to form an alliance

alias ['aljas] *adv* alias
alicatado [alika'taðo] (*ESP*) *nm*
tiling
alicates [ali'kates] *nmpl* pliers
aliciente [ali'θjente] *nm* incentive;
(*atracción*) attraction
alienación [aljena'θjon] *nf*
alienation
aliento [a'ljento] *nm* breath;
(*respiración*) breathing; **sin ~** breathless
aligerar [alixe'rar] *vt* to lighten;
(*reducir*) to shorten; (*aliviar*) to alleviate;
(*mitigar*) to ease; (*paso*) to quicken
alijo [a'lixo] *nm* consignment
alimaña [ali'maɲa] *nf* pest
alimentación [alimenta'θjon] *nf*
(*comida*) food; (*acción*) feeding; (*tienda*)
grocer's (shop)
alimentar [alimen'tar] *vt* to feed;
(*nutrir*) to nourish; **alimentarse** *vr*
to feed
alimenticio, -a [alimen'tiθjo, a]
adj food *cpd*; (*nutritivo*) nourishing,
nutritious
alimento [ali'mento] *nm* food;
(*nutrición*) nourishment
alineación [alinea'θjon] *nf*
alignment; (*Deporte*) line-up
alinear [aline'ar] *vt* to align; (*Deporte*)
to select, pick
aliñar [ali'ɲar] *vt* (*Culin*) to season;
aliño *nm* (*Culin*) dressing
alioli [ali'oli] *nm* garlic mayonnaise
alisar [ali'sar] *vt* to smooth
alistarse [alis'tarse] *vr* to enlist;
(*inscribirse*) to enrol
aliviar [ali'βjar] *vt* (*carga*) to lighten;
(*persona*) to relieve; (*dolor*) to relieve,
alleviate
alivio [a'liβjo] *nm* alleviation, relief
aljibe [al'xiβe] *nm* cistern
allá [a'ʎa] *adv* (*lugar*) there; (*por ahí*)
over there; (*tiempo*) then; **~ abajo** down
there; **más ~** further on; **más ~ de**
beyond; **¡~ tú!** that's your problem!; **¡~
voy!** I'm coming!
allanamiento [aʎana'mjento] *nm*
(*LAM: de policía*) raid; **allanamiento de**

morada burglary
allanar [aʎa'nar] *vt* to flatten, level
(out); (*igualar*) to smooth (out); (*fig*) to
subdue; (*Jur*) to burgle, break into
allegado, -a [aʎe'ɣaðo, a] *adj* near,
close ▷ *nm/f* relation
allí [a'ʎi] *adv* there; **~ mismo** right
there; **por ~** over there; (*por ese camino*)
that way
alma ['alma] *nf* soul; (*persona*) person
almacén [alma'θen] *nm* (*depósito*)
warehouse, store; (*Mil*) magazine;
(*cs: de comestibles*) grocer's (shop);
grandes almacenes department store
sg; **almacenaje** *nm* storage
almacenar [almaθe'nar] *vt* to store,
put in storage; (*proveerse*) to stock
up with
almanaque [alma'nake] *nm*
almanac
almeja [al'mexa] *nf* clam
almendra [al'mendra] *nf* almond;
almendro *nm* almond tree
almíbar [al'miβar] *nm* syrup
almidón [almi'ðon] *nm* starch
almirante [almi'rante] *nm* admiral
almohada [almo'aða] *nf* pillow;
(*funda*) pillowcase; **almohadilla** *nf*
cushion; (*para alfileres*) pincushion;
(*Tec*) pad
almohadón [almoa'ðon] *nm* large
pillow; bolster
almorranas [almo'rranas] *nfpl*
piles, haemorrhoids
almorzar [almor'θar] *vt*: **~ una
tortilla** to have an omelette for lunch
▷ *vi* to (have) lunch
almuerzo *etc* [al'mwerθo] *vb* V
almorzar ▷ *nm* lunch
alocado, -a [alo'kaðo, a] *adj* crazy
alojamiento [aloxa'mjento] *nm*
lodging(s) *pl*; (*viviendas*) housing
alojar [alo'xar] *vt* to lodge; **alojarse**
vr to lodge, stay
alondra [a'londra] *nf* lark, skylark
alpargata [alpar'ɣata] *nf* rope-soled
sandal, espadrille
Alpes ['alpes] *nmpl*: **los ~** the Alps

alpinismo [alpi'nismo] *nm*
mountaineering, climbing; **alpinista**
nmf mountaineer, climber
alpiste [al'piste] *nm* birdseed
alquilar [alki'lar] *vt*
(*propietario*: *inmuebles*) to let, rent
(out); (: *coche*) to hire out; (: *TV*) to rent
(out); (*alquilador*: *inmuebles*, *TV*) to rent;
(: *coche*) to hire; **"se alquila casa"**
"house to let (BRIT) *o* for rent (US)"
alquiler [alki'ler] *nm* renting; letting;
hiring; (*arriendo*) rent; hire charge; **de**
~ for hire; **alquiler de automóviles** *o*
coches car hire
alquimia [al'kimja] *nf* alchemy
alquitrán [alki'tran] *nm* tar
alrededor [alreðe'ðor] *adv* around,
about; **~ de** around, about; **mirar**
a su ~ to look (round) about one;
alrededores *nmpl* surroundings
alta ['alta] *nf* (certificate of)
discharge
altar [al'tar] *nm* altar
altavoz [alta'βoθ] *nm* loudspeaker;
(*amplificador*) amplifier
alteración [altera'θjon] *nf*
alteration; (*alboroto*) disturbance
alterar [alte'rar] *vt* to alter; to
disturb; **alterarse** *vr* (*persona*) to
get upset
altercado [alter'kaðo] *nm* argument
alternar [alter'nar] *vt* to alternate
▷ *vi* to alternate; (*turnar*) to take turns;
alternarse *vr* to alternate; to take
turns; **~ con** to mix with; **alternativa**
nf alternative; (*elección*) choice;
alternativo, -a *adj* alternative;
(*alterno*) alternating; **alterno, -a** *adj*
alternate; (*Elec*) alternating
Alteza [al'teθa] *nf* (*tratamiento*)
Highness
altibajos [alti'βaxos] *nmpl* ups and
downs
altiplano [alti'plano] *nm* =
altiplanicie
altisonante [altiso'nante] *adj* high-
flown, high-sounding
altitud [alti'tuð] *nf* height; (*Aviac*,

Geo) altitude
altivo, -a [al'tiβo, a] *adj* haughty,
arrogant
alto, -a ['alto, a] *adj* high; (*persona*)
tall; (*sonido*) high, sharp; (*noble*) high,
lofty ▷ *nm* halt; (*Mús*) alto; (*Geo*) hill
▷ *adv* (*de sitio*) high; (*de sonido*) loud,
loudly ▷ *excl* halt!; **la pared tiene**
2 metros de ~ the wall is 2 metres
high; **en alta mar** on the high seas;
en voz alta in a loud voice; **las altas**
horas de la noche the small *o* wee
hours; **en lo ~ de** at the top of; **pasar**
por ~ to overlook; **altoparlante**
[altopar'lante] (LAM) *nm* loudspeaker
altura [al'tura] *nf* height; (*Náut*)
depth; (*Geo*) latitude; **la pared tiene**
1.80 de ~ the wall is 1 metre 80cm high;
a estas ~s at this stage; **a estas ~s del**
año at this time of the year
alubia [a'luβja] *nf* bean
alucinación [aluθina'θjon] *nf*
hallucination
alucinar [aluθi'nar] *vi* to hallucinate
▷ *vt* to deceive; (*fascinar*) to fascinate
alud [a'luð] *nm* avalanche; (*fig*) flood
aludir [alu'ðir] *vi*: **~ a** to allude to;
darse por aludido to take the hint
alumbrado [alum'braðo] *nm*
lighting
alumbrar [alum'brar] *vt* to light (up)
▷ *vi* (*Med*) to give birth
aluminio [alu'minjo] *nm* aluminium
(BRIT), aluminum (US)
alumno, -a [a'lumno, a] *nm/f* pupil,
student
alusión [alu'sjon] *nf* allusion
alusivo, -a [alu'siβo, a] *adj* allusive
aluvión [alu'βjon] *nm* alluvium;
(*fig*) flood
alverja [al'βerxa] (LAM) *nf* pea
alza ['alθa] *nf* rise; (*Mil*) sight
alzamiento [alθa'mjento] *nm*
(*rebelión*) rising
alzar [al'θar] *vt* to lift (up); (*precio*,
muro) to raise; (*cuello de abrigo*) to
turn up; (*Agr*) to gather in; (*Imprenta*)
to gather; **alzarse** *vr* to get up,

rise; (*rebelarse*) to revolt; (*Com*) to go
fraudulently bankrupt; (*Jur*) to appeal

ama ['ama] *nf* lady of the house;
(*dueña*) owner; (*institutriz*) governess;
(*madre adoptiva*) foster mother; **ama
de casa** housewife; **ama de llaves**
housekeeper

amabilidad [amaβili'ðað] *nf*
kindness; (*simpatía*) niceness; **amable**
adj kind; nice; **es usted muy amable**
that's very kind of you

amaestrado, -a [amaes'traðo, a]
adj (*animal: en circo etc*) performing

amaestrar [amaes'trar] *vt* to train

amago [a'maɣo] *nm* threat; (*gesto*)
threatening gesture; (*Med*) symptom

amainar [amai'nar] *vi* (*viento*) to
die down

amamantar [amaman'tar] *vt* to
suckle, nurse

amanecer [amane'θer] *vi* to dawn
▷ *nm* dawn; **~ afiebrado** to wake up
with a fever

amanerado, -a [amane'raðo, a]
adj affected

amante [a'mante] *adj*: **~ de** fond of
▷ *nmf* lover

amapola [ama'pola] *nf* poppy

amar [a'mar] *vt* to love

amargado, -a [amar'ɣaðo, a] *adj*
bitter

amargar [amar'ɣar] *vt* to make
bitter; (*fig*) to embitter; **amargarse** *vr*
to become embittered

amargo, -a [a'marɣo, a] *adj* bitter

amarillento, -a [amari'ʎento, a]
adj yellowish; (*tez*) sallow; **amarillo, -a**
adj, nm yellow

amarrado, -a [ama'rraðo, a]
(*MÉX: fam*) *adj* mean, stingy

amarrar [ama'rrar] *vt* to moor;
(*sujetar*) to tie up

amarras [a'marras] *nfpl*: **soltar ~**
to set sail

amasar [ama'sar] *vt* (*masa*) to knead;
(*mezclar*) to mix, prepare; (*confeccionar*)
to concoct

amateur [ama'ter] *nmf* amateur

amazona [ama'θona] *nf*
horsewoman; **Amazonas** *nm*: **el
Amazonas** the Amazon

ámbar ['ambar] *nm* amber

ambición [ambi'θjon] *nf* ambition;
ambicionar *vt* to aspire to;
ambicioso, -a *adj* ambitious

ambidextro, -a [ambi'ðekstro, a]
adj ambidextrous

ambientación [ambjenta'θjon] *nf*
(*Cine, Teatro etc*) setting; (*Radio*) sound
effects

ambiente [am'bjente] *nm*
atmosphere; (*medio*) environment

ambigüedad [ambiɣwe'ðað]
nf ambiguity; **ambiguo, -a** *adj*
ambiguous

ámbito ['ambito] *nm* (*campo*) field;
(*fig*) scope

ambos, -as ['ambos, as] *adj pl, pron
pl* both

ambulancia [ambu'lanθja] *nf*
ambulance

ambulante [ambu'lante] *adj*
travelling *cpd*, itinerant

ambulatorio [ambula'torio] *nm*
state health-service clinic

amén [a'men] *excl* amen; **~ de**
besides

amenaza [ame'naθa] *nf* threat;
amenazar [amena'θar] *vt* to
threaten ▷ *vi*: **amenazar con hacer** to
threaten to do

ameno, -a [a'meno, a] *adj* pleasant

América [a'merika] *nf* America;
América Central/Latina Central/
Latin America; **América del Norte/del
Sur** North/South America; **americana**
nf coat, jacket; V *tb* **americano**;
americano, -a *adj, nm/f* American

ametralladora [ametraʎa'ðora] *nf*
machine gun

amigable [ami'ɣaβle] *adj* friendly

amígdala [a'miɣðala] *nf* tonsil;
amigdalitis *nf* tonsillitis

amigo, -a [a'miɣo, a] *adj* friendly
▷ *nm/f* friend; (*amante*) lover; **ser ~ de
algo** to be fond of sth; **ser muy ~s** to be

close friends

aminorar [amino'rar] vt to diminish; (reducir) to reduce; ~ **la marcha** to slow down

amistad [amis'tað] nf friendship; **amistades** nfpl (amigos) friends; **amistoso, -a** adj friendly

amnesia [am'nesja] nf amnesia

amnistía [amnis'tia] nf amnesty

amo ['amo] nm owner; (jefe) boss

amolar [amo'lar] (MÉX: fam) vt to ruin, damage

amoldar [amol'dar] vt to mould; (adaptar) to adapt

amonestación [amonesta'θjon] nf warning; **amonestaciones** nfpl (Rel) marriage banns

amonestar [amones'tar] vt to warn; (Rel) to publish the banns of

amontonar [amonto'nar] vt to collect, pile up; **amontonarse** vr to crowd together; (acumularse) to pile up

amor [a'mor] nm love; (amante) lover; **hacer el ~** to make love; **amor propio** self-respect

amoratado, -a [amora'taðo, a] adj purple

amordazar [amorða'θar] vt to muzzle; (fig) to gag

amorfo, -a [a'morfo, a] adj amorphous, shapeless

amoroso, -a [amo'roso, a] adj affectionate, loving

amortiguador [amortigwa'ðor] nm shock absorber; (parachoques) bumper; **amortiguadores** nmpl (Auto) suspension sg

amortiguar [amorti'xwar] vt to deaden; (ruido) to muffle; (color) to soften

amotinar [amoti'nar] vt to stir up, incite (to riot); **amotinarse** vr to mutiny

amparar [ampa'rar] vt to protect; **ampararse** vr to seek protection; (de la lluvia etc) to shelter; **amparo** nm help, protection; **al amparo de** under the protection of

amperio [am'perjo] nm ampère, amp

ampliación [amplja'θjon] nf enlargement; (extensión) extension

ampliar [am'pljar] vt to enlarge; to extend

amplificador [amplifika'ðor] nm amplifier

amplificar [amplifi'kar] vt to amplify

amplio, -a ['ampljo, a] adj spacious; (de falda etc) full; (extenso) extensive; (ancho) wide; **amplitud** nf spaciousness; extent; (fig) amplitude

ampolla [am'poʎa] nf blister; (Med) ampoule

amputar [ampu'tar] vt to cut off, amputate

amueblar [amwe'βlar] vt to furnish

anales [a'nales] nmpl annals

analfabetismo [analfaβe'tismo] nm illiteracy; **analfabeto, -a** adj, nm/f illiterate

analgésico [anal'xesiko] nm painkiller, analgesic

análisis [a'nalisis] nm inv analysis

analista [ana'lista] nmf (gen) analyst

analizar [anali'θar] vt to analyse

analógico, -a [ana'loxiko, a] adj (Inform) analog; (reloj) analogue (BRIT), analog (US)

análogo, -a [a'naloxo, a] adj analogous, similar

ananá [ana'na] (RPL) nm pineapple

anarquía [anar'kia] nf anarchy; **anarquista** nmf anarchist

anatomía [anato'mia] nf anatomy

anca ['anka] nf rump, haunch; **ancas** nfpl (fam) behind sg

ancho, -a ['antʃo, a] adj wide; (falda) full; (fig) liberal ▷ nm width; (Ferro) gauge; **ponerse ~** to get conceited; **estar a sus anchas** to be at one's ease

anchoa [an'tʃoa] nf anchovy

anchura [an'tʃura] nf width; (extensión) wideness

anciano, -a [an'θjano, a] adj old, aged ▷ nm/f old man/woman; elder

ancla ['ankla] nf anchor

Andalucía [andalu'θia] nf
Andalusia; **andaluz, -a** adj, nm/f
Andalusian

andamio [an'damjo] nm
scaffold(ing)

andar [an'dar] vt to go, cover, travel
▷ vi to go, walk, travel; (funcionar) to
go, work; (estar) to be ▷ nm walk,
gait, pace; **andarse** vr to go away;
~ a pie/a caballo/en bicicleta to go
on foot/on horseback/by bicycle; **~
haciendo algo** to be doing sth; **¡anda!**
(sorpresa) go on!; **anda por** o **en los 40**
he's about 40

andén [an'den] nm (Ferro) platform;
(Náut) quayside; (CAM: de la calle)
pavement (BRIT), sidewalk (US)

Andes ['andes] nmpl: **los ~** the Andes

andinismo [andi'nismo] (LAM) nm
mountaineering, climbing

Andorra [an'dorra] nf Andorra

andrajoso, -a [andra'xoso, a] adj
ragged

anduve etc vb V **andar**

anécdota [a'nekðota] nf anecdote,
story

anegar [ane'xar] vt to flood; (ahogar)
to drown

anemia [a'nemja] nf anaemia

anestesia [anes'tesja] nf (sustancia)
anaesthetic; (proceso) anaesthesia;
anestesia general/local general/
local anaesthetic

anexar [anek'sar] vt to annex;
(documento) to attach; **anexión** nf
annexation; **anexo, -a** adj attached
▷ nm annexe

anfibio, -a [an'fiβjo, a] adj
amphibious ▷ nm amphibian

anfiteatro [anfite'atro] nm
amphitheatre; (Teatro) dress circle

anfitrión, -ona [anfi'trjon, ona]
nm/f host(ess)

ánfora ['anfora] nf (cántaro)
amphora; (MÉx Pol) ballot box

ángel ['anxel] nm angel; **ángel de la
guarda** guardian angel

angina [an'xina] nf (Med)

inflammation of the throat; **tener ~s**
to have tonsillitis; **angina de pecho**
angina

anglicano, -a [angli'kano, a] adj,
nm/f Anglican

anglosajón, -ona [anglosa'xon,
ona] adj Anglo-Saxon

anguila [an'gila] nf eel

angula [an'gula] nf elver, baby eel

ángulo ['angulo] nm angle; (esquina)
corner; (curva) bend

angustia [an'gustja] nf anguish

anhelar [ane'lar] vt to be eager for;
(desear) to long for, desire ▷ vi to pant,
gasp; **anhelo** nm eagerness; desire

anidar [ani'ðar] vi to nest

anillo [a'niʎo] nm ring; **anillo de
boda/compromiso** wedding/
engagement ring

animación [anima'θjon] nf
liveliness; (vitalidad) life; (actividad)
activity; bustle

animado, -a [ani'maðo, a] adj
lively; (vivaz) animated; **animador, a**
nm/f (TV) host(ess), compère; (Deporte)
cheerleader

animal [ani'mal] adj animal; (fig)
stupid ▷ nm animal; (fig) fool; (bestia)
brute

animar [ani'mar] vt (Bio) to animate,
give life to; (fig) to liven up, brighten
up, cheer up; (estimular) to stimulate;
animarse vr to cheer up; to feel
encouraged; (decidirse) to make up
one's mind

ánimo ['animo] nm (alma) soul;
(mente) mind; (valentía) courage ▷ excl
cheer up!

animoso, -a [ani'moso, a] adj brave;
(vivo) lively

aniquilar [aniki'lar] vt to annihilate,
destroy

anís [a'nis] nm aniseed; (licor)
anisette

aniversario [aniβer'sarjo] nm
anniversary

anoche [a'notʃe] adv last night;
antes de ~ the night before last

anochecer [anotʃe'θer] *vi* to get dark
▷ *nm* nightfall, dark; **al ~** at nightfall
anodino, -a [ano'ðino, a] *adj* dull,
anodyne
anomalía [anoma'lia] *nf* anomaly
anonadado, -a [anona'ðaðo,
a] *adj*: **estar ~** to be overwhelmed *o*
amazed
anonimato [anoni'mato] *nm*
anonymity
anónimo, -a [a'nonimo, a] *adj*
anonymous; (*Com*) limited ▷ *nm* (*carta
anónima*) anonymous letter; (: *maliciosa*)
poison-pen letter
anormal [anor'mal] *adj* abnormal
anotación [anota'θjon] *nf* note;
annotation
anotar [ano'tar] *vt* to note down;
(*comentar*) to annotate
ansia ['ansja] *nf* anxiety; (*añoranza*)
yearning; **ansiar** *vt* to long for
ansiedad [ansje'ðað] *nf* anxiety
ansioso, -a [an'sjoso, a] *adj* anxious;
(*anhelante*) eager; **~ de** *o* **por algo**
greedy for sth
antaño [an'taɲo] *adv* long ago,
formerly
Antártico [an'tartiko] *nm*: **el ~** the
Antarctic
ante ['ante] *prep* before, in the
presence of; (*problema etc*) faced with
▷ *nm* (*piel*) suede; **~ todo** above all
anteanoche [antea'notʃe] *adv* the
night before last
anteayer [antea'jer] *adv* the day
before yesterday
antebrazo [ante'βraθo] *nm* forearm
antecedente [anteθe'ðente]
adj previous ▷ *nm* antecedent;
antecedentes *nmpl* (*historial*) record
sg; **antecedentes penales** criminal
record
anteceder [anteθe'ðer] *vt* to
precede, go before
antecesor, a [anteθe'sor, a] *nm/f*
predecessor
antelación [antela'θjon] *nf*: **con ~**
in advance

antemano [ante'mano]: **de ~** *adv*
beforehand, in advance
antena [an'tena] *nf* antenna; (*de
televisión etc*) aerial; **antena parabólica**
satellite dish
antenoche [ante'notʃe] (*LAM*) *adv*
the night before last
anteojo [ante'oxo] *nm* eyeglass;
anteojos *nmpl* (*LAM*: *gafas*) glasses,
spectacles
antepasados [antepa'saðos] *nmpl*
ancestors
anteponer [antepo'ner] *vt* to place
in front; (*fig*) to prefer
anterior [ante'rjor] *adj* preceding,
previous; **anterioridad** *nf*: **con
anterioridad a** prior to, before
antes ['antes] *adv* (*con prioridad*)
before ▷ *prep*: **~ de** before ▷ *conj*: **~
de ir/de que te vayas** before going/
before you go; **~ bien** (but) rather; **dos
días ~** two days before *o* previously;
no quiso venir ~ she didn't want to
come any earlier; **tomo el avión ~ que
el barco** I take the plane rather than
the boat; **~ de** *o* **que nada** (*en el tiempo*)
first of all; (*indicando preferencia*) above
all; **~ que yo** before me; **lo ~ posible** as
soon as possible; **cuanto ~ mejor** the
sooner the better
antibalas [anti'βalas] *adj inv*:
chaleco ~ bullet-proof jacket
antibiótico [anti'βjotiko] *nm*
antibiotic
anticaspa [anti'kaspa] *adj inv* anti-
dandruff *cpd*
anticipación [antiθipa'θjon] *nf*
anticipation; **con 10 minutos de ~** 10
minutes early
anticipado, -a [antiθi'paðo, a] *adj*
(*pago*) advance; **por ~** in advance
anticipar [antiθi'par] *vt* to
anticipate; (*adelantar*) to bring
forward; (*Com*) to advance; **anticiparse**
vr: **~se a su época** to be ahead of
one's time
anticipo [anti'θipo] *nm* (*Com*)
advance

anticonceptivo, -a
[antikonθep'tiβo, a] *adj, nm*
contraceptive

anticongelante [antikonxe'lante]
nm antifreeze

anticuado, -a [anti'kwaðo, a] *adj*
out-of-date, old-fashioned; (*desusado*)
obsolete

anticuario [anti'kwarjo] *nm*
antique dealer

anticuerpo [anti'kwerpo] *nm* (*Med*)
antibody

antidepresivo [antiðepre'siβo] *nm*
antidepressant

antidóping [anti'dopin] *adj*
inv: **control ~** drugs test

antídoto [an'tiðoto] *nm* antidote

antiestético, -a [anties'tetiko, a]
adj unsightly

antifaz [anti'faθ] *nm* mask; (*velo*) veil

antiglobalización
[antigloβaliθa'θjon] *nf* anti-
globalization; **antiglobalizador, a** *adj*
anti-globalization *cpd*

antiguamente [antiɣwa'mente]
adv formerly; (*hace mucho tiempo*)
long ago

antigüedad [antiɣwe'ðað] *nf*
antiquity; (*artículo*) antique; (*rango*)
seniority

antiguo, -a [an'tiɣwo, a] *adj* old,
ancient; (*que fue*) former

Antillas [an'tiʎas] *nfpl*: **las ~** the
West Indies

antílope [an'tilope] *nm* antelope

antinatural [antinatu'ral] *adj*
unnatural

antipatía [antipa'tia] *nf* antipathy,
dislike; **antipático, -a** *adj*
disagreeable, unpleasant

antirrobo [anti'rroβo] *adj inv* (*alarma
etc*) anti-theft

antisemita [antise'mita] *adj* anti-
Semitic ▷ *nmf* anti-Semite

antiséptico, -a [anti'septiko, a] *adj*
antiseptic ▷ *nm* antiseptic

antivirus [anti'birus] *nm inv*
(*Comput*) antivirus program

antojarse [anto'xarse] *vr* (*desear*): **se
me antoja comprarlo** I have a mind to
buy it; (*pensar*): **se me antoja que ...** I
have a feeling that ...

antojitos [anto'xitos] (*MÉX*) *nmpl*
snacks, nibbles

antojo [an'toxo] *nm* caprice, whim;
(*rosa*) birthmark; (*lunar*) mole

antología [antolo'xia] *nf* anthology

antorcha [an'tortʃa] *nf* torch

antro ['antro] *nm* cavern

antropología [antropolo'xia] *nf*
anthropology

anual [a'nwal] *adj* annual

anuario [a'nwarjo] *nm* yearbook

anulación [anula'θjon] *nf*
annulment; (*cancelación*) cancellation

anular [anu'lar] *vt* (*contrato*) to
annul, cancel; (*ley*) to revoke, repeal;
(*suscripción*) to cancel ▷ *nm* ring finger

anunciar [anun'θjar] *vt* to
announce; (*proclamar*) to proclaim;
(*Com*) to advertise

anuncio [a'nunθjo] *nm*
announcement; (*señal*) sign; (*Com*)
advertisement; (*cartel*) poster

anzuelo [an'θwelo] *nm* hook; (*para
pescar*) fish hook

añadidura [aɲaði'ðura] *nf* addition,
extra; **por ~** besides, in addition

añadir [aɲa'ðir] *vt* to add

añejo, -a [a'ɲexo, a] *adj* old; (*vino*)
mellow

añicos [a'ɲikos] *nmpl*: **hacer ~** to
smash, shatter

año ['aɲo] *nm* year; **¡Feliz A~ Nuevo!**
Happy New Year!; **tener 15 ~s** to be 15
(years old); **los ~s 90** the nineties; **el
~ que viene** next year; **año bisiesto/
escolar/fiscal/sabático** leap/school/
tax/sabbatical year

añoranza [aɲo'ranθa] *nf* nostalgia;
(*anhelo*) longing

apa ['apa] (*MÉX*) *excl* goodness me!,
good gracious!

apabullar [apaβu'ʎar] *vt* to crush,
squash

apacible [apa'θiβle] *adj* gentle, mild

apaciguar [apaθiˈɣwar] vt to pacify, calm (down)

apadrinar [apaðriˈnar] vt to sponsor, support; (Rel) to be godfather to

apagado, -a [apaˈɣaðo, a] adj (volcán) extinct; (color) dull; (voz) quiet; (sonido) muted, muffled; (persona: apático) listless; **estar ~** (fuego, luz) to be out; (Radio, TV etc) to be off

apagar [apaˈɣar] vt to put out; (Elec, Radio, TV) to turn off; (sonido) to silence, muffle; (sed) to quench

apagón [apaˈɣon] nm blackout; power cut

apalabrar [apalaˈβrar] vt to agree to; (contratar) to engage

apalear [apaleˈar] vt to beat, thrash

apantallar [apantaˈʎar] (MÉX) vt to impress

apañar [apaˈɲar] vt to pick up; (asir) to take hold of, grasp; (reparar) to mend, patch up; **apañarse** vr to manage, get along

apapachar [apapaˈtʃar] (MÉX: fam) vt to cuddle, hug

aparador [aparaˈðor] nm sideboard; (MÉX: escaparate) shop window

aparato [apaˈrato] nm apparatus; (máquina) machine; (doméstico) appliance; (boato) ostentation; **aparato digestivo** (Anat) digestive system; **aparatoso, -a** adj showy, ostentatious

aparcamiento [aparkaˈmjento] nm car park (BRIT), parking lot (US)

aparcar [aparˈkar] vt, vi to park

aparear [apareˈar] vt (objetos) to pair, match; (animales) to mate; **aparearse** vr to make a pair; to mate

aparecer [apareˈθer] vi to appear; **aparecerse** vr to appear

aparejador, a [aparexaˈðor, a] nm/f (Arq) master builder

aparejo [apaˈrexo] nm harness; rigging; (de poleas) block and tackle

aparentar [aparenˈtar] vt (edad) to look; (fingir) **~ tristeza** to pretend to be sad

aparente [apaˈrente] adj apparent; (adecuado) suitable

aparezco etc vb V **aparecer**

aparición [apariˈθjon] nf appearance; (de libro) publication; (espectro) apparition

apariencia [apaˈrjenθja] nf (outward) appearance; **en ~** outwardly, seemingly

apartado, -a [aparˈtaðo, a] adj separate; (lejano) remote ⊳ nm (tipográfico) paragraph; **apartado de correos** (ESP) post office box; **apartado postal** (LAM) post office box

apartamento [apartaˈmento] nm apartment, flat (BRIT)

apartar [aparˈtar] vt to separate; (quitar) to remove; **apartarse** vr to separate, part; (irse) to move away; to keep away

aparte [aˈparte] adv (separadamente) separately; (además) besides ⊳ nm aside; (tipográfico) new paragraph

aparthotel [apartoˈtel] nm serviced apartments

apasionado, -a [apasjoˈnaðo, a] adj passionate

apasionar [apasjoˈnar] vt to excite; **le apasiona el fútbol** she's crazy about football; **apasionarse** vr to get excited

apatía [apaˈtia] nf apathy

apático, -a [aˈpatiko, a] adj apathetic

Apdo abr (= Apartado (de Correos)) PO Box

apeadero [apeaˈðero] nm halt, stop, stopping place

apearse [apeˈarse] vr (jinete) to dismount; (bajarse) to get down o out; (Auto, Ferro) to get off o out

apechugar [apetʃuˈɣar] vr: **~ con algo** to face up to sth

apegarse [apeˈɣarse] vr: **~ a** to become attached to; **apego** nm attachment, devotion

apelar [apeˈlar] vi to appeal; **~ a** (fig) to resort to

apellidar [apeʎi'ðar] *vt* to call, name;
apellidarse *vr*: **se apellida Pérez** her
(sur)name's Pérez

apellido [ape'ʎiðo] *nm* surname

apenar [ape'nar] *vt* to grieve,
trouble; (*LAM*: *avergonzar*) to
embarrass; **apenarse** *vr* to grieve;
(*LAM*: *avergonzarse*) to be embarrassed

apenas [a'penas] *adv* scarcely, hardly
▷ *conj* as soon as, no sooner

apéndice [a'pendiθe] *nm* appendix;
apendicitis *nf* appendicitis

aperitivo [aperi'tiβo] *nm* (*bebida*)
aperitif; (*comida*) appetizer

apertura [aper'tura] *nf* opening;
(*Pol*) liberalization

apestar [apes'tar] *vt* to infect ▷ *vi*: ~
(**a**) to stink (of)

apetecer [apete'θer] *vt*: **¿te apetece
un café?** do you fancy a (cup of) coffee?;
apetecible *adj* desirable; (*comida*)
appetizing

apetito [ape'tito] *nm* appetite;
apetitoso, -a *adj* appetizing; (*fig*)
tempting

apiadarse [apja'ðarse] *vr*: ~ **de** to
take pity on

ápice ['apiθe] *nm* whit, iota

apilar [api'lar] *vt* to pile o heap up

apiñarse [api'narse] *vr* to crowd o
press together

apio ['apjo] *nm* celery

apisonadora [apisona'ðora] *nf*
steamroller

aplacar [apla'kar] *vt* to placate

aplastante [aplas'tante] *adj*
overwhelming; (*lógica*) compelling

aplastar [aplas'tar] *vt* to squash
(flat); (*fig*) to crush

aplaudir [aplau'ðir] *vt* to applaud

aplauso [a'plauso] *nm* applause; (*fig*)
approval, acclaim

aplazamiento [aplaθa'mjento] *nm*
postponement

aplazar [apla'θar] *vt* to postpone,
defer

aplicación [aplika'θjon] *nf*
application; (*esfuerzo*) effort

aplicado, -a [apli'kaðo, a] *adj*
diligent, hard-working

aplicar [apli'kar] *vt* (*ejecutar*) to
apply; **aplicarse** *vr* to apply o.s.

aplique *etc* [a'plike] *vb* V **aplicar**
▷ *nm* wall light

aplomo [a'plomo] *nm* aplomb,
self-assurance

apodar [apo'ðar] *vt* to nickname

apoderado [apoðe'raðo] *nm* agent,
representative

apoderarse [apoðe'rarse] *vr*: ~ **de** to
take possession of

apodo [a'poðo] *nm* nickname

apogeo [apo'xeo] *nm* peak, summit

apoquinar [apoki'nar] (*fam*) *vt* to
fork out, cough up

aporrear [aporre'ar] *vt* to beat (up)

aportar [apor'tar] *vt* to contribute
▷ *vi* to reach port; **aportarse** *vr*
(*LAM*: *llegar*) to arrive, come

aposta [a'posta] *adv* deliberately,
on purpose

apostar [apos'tar] *vt* to bet, stake;
(*tropas etc*) to station, post ▷ *vi* to bet

apóstol [a'postol] *nm* apostle

apóstrofo [a'postrofo] *nm*
apostrophe

apoyar [apo'jar] *vt* to lean, rest; (*fig*)
to support, back; **apoyarse** *vr*: ~**se en**
to lean on; **apoyo** *nm* (*gen*) support;
backing, help

apreciable [apre'θjaβle] *adj*
considerable; (*fig*) esteemed

apreciar [apre'θjar] *vt* to evaluate,
assess; (*Com*) to appreciate, value;
(*persona*) to respect; (*tamaño*) to gauge,
assess; (*detalles*) to notice

aprecio [a'preθjo] *nm* valuation,
estimate; (*fig*) appreciation

aprehender [apreen'der] *vt* to
apprehend, detain

apremio [a'premjo] *nm* urgency

aprender [apren'der] *vt, vi* to learn;
~ **algo de memoria** to learn sth (off)
by heart

aprendiz, a [apren'diθ, a] *nm/f*
apprentice; (*principiante*) learner;

aprendizaje *nm* apprenticeship

aprensión [apren'sjon] *nm* apprehension, fear; **aprensivo, -a** *adj* apprehensive

apresar [apre'sar] *vt* to seize; (*capturar*) to capture

apresurado, -a [apresu'raðo, a] *adj* hurried, hasty

apresurar [apresu'rar] *vt* to hurry, accelerate; **apresurarse** *vr* to hurry, make haste

apretado, -a [apre'taðo, a] *adj* tight; (*escritura*) cramped

apretar [apre'tar] *vt* to squeeze; (*Tec*) to tighten; (*presionar*) to press together, pack ▷ *vi* to be too tight

apretón [apre'ton] *nm* squeeze; **apretón de manos** handshake

aprieto [a'prjeto] *nm* squeeze; (*dificultad*) difficulty; **estar en un ~** to be in a fix

aprisa [a'prisa] *adv* quickly, hurriedly

aprisionar [aprisjo'nar] *vt* to imprison

aprobación [aproβa'θjon] *nf* approval

aprobar [apro'βar] *vt* to approve (of); (*examen, materia*) to pass ▷ *vi* to pass

apropiado, -a [apro'pjaðo, a] *adj* suitable

apropiarse [apro'pjarse] *vr*: **~ de** to appropriate

aprovechado, -a [aproβe'tʃaðo, a] *adj* industrious, hard-working; (*económico*) thrifty; (*pey*) unscrupulous

aprovechar [aproβe'tʃar] *vt* to use; (*explotar*) to exploit; (*experiencia*) to profit from; (*oferta, oportunidad*) to take advantage of ▷ *vi* to progress, improve; **aprovecharse** *vr*: **~se de** to make use of; to take advantage of; **¡que aproveche!** enjoy your meal!

aproximación [aproksima'θjon] *nf* approximation; (*de lotería*) consolation prize

aproximar [aproksi'mar] *vt* to bring nearer; **aproximarse** *vr* to come near, approach

apruebo *etc vb* V **aprobar**

aptitud [apti'tuð] *nf* aptitude

apto, -a ['apto, a] *adj* suitable

apuesta [a'pwesta] *nf* bet, wager

apuesto, -a [a'pwesto, a] *adj* neat, elegant

apuntar [apun'tar] *vt* (*con arma*) to aim at; (*con dedo*) to point at o to; (*anotar*) to note (down); (*Teatro*) to prompt; **apuntarse** *vr* (*Deporte: tanto, victoria*) to score; (*Escol*) to enrol

> No confundir **apuntar** con la palabra inglesa *appoint*.

apunte [a'punte] *nm* note

apuñalar [apuɲa'lar] *vt* to stab

apurado, -a [apu'raðo, a] *adj* needy; (*difícil*) difficult; (*peligroso*) dangerous; (*LAM: con prisa*) hurried, rushed

apurar [apu'rar] *vt* (*agotar*) to drain; (*recursos*) to use up; (*molestar*) to annoy; **apurarse** *vr* (*preocuparse*) to worry; (*LAM: darse prisa*) to hurry

apuro [a'puro] *nm* (*aprieto*) fix, jam; (*escasez*) want, hardship; (*vergüenza*) embarrassment; (*LAM: prisa*) haste, urgency

aquejado, -a [ake'xaðo, a] *adj*: **~ de** (*Med*) afflicted by

aquel, aquella [a'kel, a'keʎa] *adj* that; **~los(as)** those

aquél, aquélla [a'kel, a'keʎa] *pron* that (one); **~los(as)** those (ones)

aquello [a'keʎo] *pron* that, that business

aquí [a'ki] *adv* (*lugar*) here; (*tiempo*) now; **~ arriba** up here; **~ mismo** right here; **~ yace** here lies; **de ~ a siete días** a week from now

ara ['ara] *nf*: **en ~s de** for the sake of

árabe ['araβe] *adj, nmf* Arab ▷ *nm* (*Ling*) Arabic

Arabia [a'raβja] *nf* Arabia; **Arabia Saudí** o **Saudita** Saudi Arabia

arado [a'raðo] *nm* plough

Aragón [ara'ɣon] *nm* Aragon; **aragonés, -esa** *adj, nm/f* Aragonese

arancel [aran'θel] *nm* tariff, duty

arandela [aran'dela] *nf* (*Tec*) washer

araña [a'raɲa] nf (Zool) spider; (lámpara) chandelier

arañar [ara'ɲar] vt to scratch

arañazo [ara'ɲaθo] nm scratch

arbitrar [arβi'trar] vt to arbitrate in; (Deporte) to referee ▷ vi to arbitrate

arbitrario, -a [arβi'trarjo, a] adj arbitrary

árbitro ['arβitro] nm arbitrator; (Deporte) referee; (Tenis) umpire

árbol ['arβol] nm (Bot) tree; (Náut) mast; (Tec) axle, shaft; **árbol de Navidad** Christmas tree

arboleda [arβo'leða] nf grove, plantation

arbusto [ar'βusto] nm bush, shrub

arca ['arka] nf chest, box

arcada [ar'kaða] nf arcade; (de puente) arch, span; **arcadas** nfpl (náuseas) retching sg

arcaico, -a [ar'kaiko, a] adj archaic

arce [ar'θe] nm maple tree

arcén [ar'θen] nm (de autopista) hard shoulder; (de carretera) verge

archipiélago [artʃi'pjelaɣo] nm archipelago

archivador [artʃiβa'ðor] nm filing cabinet

archivar [artʃi'βar] vt to file (away); **archivo** nm file, archive(s) pl; **archivo adjunto** (Inform) attachment; **archivo de seguridad** (Inform) backup file

arcilla [ar'θiʎa] nf clay

arco ['arko] nm arch; (Mat) arc; (Mil, Mús) bow; **arco iris** rainbow

arder [ar'ðer] vi to burn; **estar que arde** (persona) to fume

ardid [ar'ðið] nm ploy, trick

ardiente [ar'ðjente] adj burning, ardent

ardilla [ar'ðiʎa] nf squirrel

ardor [ar'ðor] nm (calor) heat; (fig) ardour; **ardor de estómago** heartburn

arduo, -a ['arðwo, a] adj arduous

área ['area] nf area; (Deporte) penalty area

arena [a'rena] nf sand; (de una lucha) arena; **arenas movedizas** quicksand

sg; **arenal** [are'nal] nm (terreno arenoso) sandy spot

arenisca [are'niska] nf sandstone; (cascajo) grit

arenoso, -a [are'noso, a] adj sandy

arenque [a'renke] nm herring

arete [a'rete] (MÉX) nm earring

Argel [ar'xel] n Algiers; **Argelia** nf Algeria; **argelino, -a** adj, nm/f Algerian

Argentina [arxen'tina] nf (tb: la ~) Argentina

argentino, -a [arxen'tino, a] adj Argentinian; (de plata) silvery ▷ nm/f Argentinian

argolla [ar'ɣoʎa] nf (large) ring

argot [ar'ɣo] (pl ~s) nm slang

argucia [ar'ɣuθja] nf subtlety, sophistry

argumentar [arɣumen'tar] vt, vi to argue

argumento [arɣu'mento] nm argument; (razonamiento) reasoning; (de novela etc) plot; (Cine, TV) storyline

aria ['arja] nf aria

aridez [ari'ðeθ] nf aridity, dryness

árido, -a ['ariðo, a] adj arid, dry

Aries ['arjes] nm Aries

arisco, -a [a'risko, a] adj surly; (insociable) unsociable

aristócrata [aris'tokrata] nmf aristocrat

arma ['arma] nf arm; **armas** nfpl arms; **arma blanca** blade, knife; **arma de doble filo** double-edged sword; **arma de fuego** firearm; **armas de destrucción masiva** weapons of mass destruction

armada [ar'maða] nf armada; (flota) fleet

armadillo [arma'ðiʎo] nm armadillo

armado, -a [ar'maðo, a] adj armed; (Tec) reinforced

armadura [arma'ðura] nf (Mil) armour; (Tec) framework; (Zool) skeleton; (Física) armature

armamento [arma'mento] nm armament; (Náut) fitting-out

armar [ar'mar] vt (soldado) to arm;
(máquina) to assemble; (navío) to fit
out; **~la, ~ un lío** to start a row, kick
up a fuss

armario [ar'marjo] nm wardrobe;
(de cocina, baño) cupboard; **armario
empotrado** built-in cupboard

armatoste [arma'toste] nm (mueble)
monstrosity; (máquina) contraption

armazón [arma'θon] nf o m body,
chassis; (de mueble etc) frame; (Arq)
skeleton

armiño [ar'mijno] nm stoat; (piel)
ermine

armisticio [armis'tiθjo] nm
armistice

armonía [armo'nia] nf harmony

armónica [ar'monika] nf harmonica

armonizar [armoni'θar] vt to
harmonize; (diferencias) to reconcile

aro ['aro] nm ring; (tejo) quoit;
(cs: pendiente) earring

aroma [a'roma] nm aroma, scent;
aromaterapia n aromatherapy;
aromático, -a [aro'matiko, a] adj
aromatic

arpa ['arpa] nf harp

arpía [ar'pia] nf shrew

arpón [ar'pon] nm harpoon

arqueología [arkeolo'xia] nf
archaeology; **arqueólogo, -a** nm/f
archaeologist

arquetipo [arke'tipo] nm archetype

arquitecto [arki'tekto] nm
architect; **arquitectura** nf
architecture

arrabal [arra'βal] nm poor suburb,
slum; **arrabales** nmpl (afueras)
outskirts

arraigar [arrai'xar] vt to establish
▷ vi to take root

arrancar [arran'kar] vt (sacar) to
extract, pull out; (arrebatar) to snatch
(away); (Inform) to boot; (fig) to extract
▷ vi (Auto, máquina) to start; (ponerse en
marcha) to get going; **~ de** to stem from

arranque etc ['arranke] vb V
arrancar ▷ nm sudden start; (Auto)

start; (fig) fit, outburst

arrasar [arra'sar] vt (aplanar) to level,
flatten; (destruir) to demolish

arrastrar [arras'trar] vt to drag
(along); (fig) to drag down, degrade;
(agua, viento) to carry away ▷ vi to
drag, trail on the ground; **arrastrarse**
vr to crawl; (fig) to grovel; **llevar algo
arrastrado** to drag sth along

arrear [arre'ar] vt to drive on, urge on
▷ vi to hurry along

arrebatar [arreβa'tar] vt to snatch
(away), seize; (fig) to captivate

arrebato [arre'βato] nm fit of rage,
fury; (éxtasis) rapture

arrecife [arre'θife] nm reef

arreglado, -a [arre'xlaðo, a] adj
(ordenado) neat, orderly; (moderado)
moderate, reasonable

arreglar [arre'xlar] vt (poner orden)
to tidy up; (algo roto) to fix, repair;
(problema) to solve; **arreglarse** vr to
reach an understanding; **arreglárselas**
(fam) to get by, manage

arreglo [a'rrexlo] nm settlement;
(orden) order; (acuerdo) agreement;
(Mús) arrangement, setting

arremangar [arreman'gar] vt to roll
up, turn up; **arremangarse** vr to roll
up one's sleeves

arremeter [arreme'ter] vi: **~ contra**
to attack, rush at

arrendamiento [arrenda'mjento]
nm letting; (alquilar) hiring; (contrato)
lease; (alquiler) rent; **arrendar** vt to
let, lease; to rent; **arrendatario, -a**
nm/f tenant

arreos [a'rreos] nmpl (de caballo)
harness sg, trappings

arrepentimiento
[arrepenti'mjento] nm regret,
repentance

arrepentirse [arrepen'tirse] vr to
repent; **~ de** to regret

arresto [a'rresto] nm arrest; (Mil)
detention; (audacia) boldness, daring;
arresto domiciliario house arrest

arriar [a'rrjar] vt (velas) to haul down;

(*bandera*) to lower, strike; (*cable*) to pay out

○ **PALABRA CLAVE**

arriba [a'rriβa] *adv* **1** (*posición*) above; **desde arriba** from above; **arriba de todo** at the very top, right on top; **Juan está arriba** Juan is upstairs; **lo arriba mencionado** the aforementioned **2** (*dirección*): **calle arriba** up the street **3** **de arriba abajo** from top to bottom; **mirar a algn de arriba abajo** to look sb up and down
4 **para arriba: de 5000 euros para arriba** from 5000 euros up(wards)
▷ *adj*: **de arriba: el piso de arriba** the upstairs (*BRIT*) flat *o* apartment; **la parte de arriba** the top *o* upper part
▷ *prep*: **arriba de** (*LAM: por encima de*) above; **arriba de 200 dólares** more than 200 dollars
▷ *excl*: **¡arriba!** up!; **¡manos arriba!** hands up!; **¡arriba España!** long live Spain!

arribar [arri'βar] *vi* to put into port; (*llegar*) to arrive
arriendo *etc* [a'rrjendo] *vb* V **arrendar** ▷ *nm* = **arrendamiento**
arriesgado, -a [arrjes'ɣaðo, a] *adj* (*peligroso*) risky; (*audaz*) bold, daring
arriesgar [arrjes'ɣar] *vt* to risk; (*poner en peligro*) to endanger; **arriesgarse** *vr* to take a risk
arrimar [arri'mar] *vt* (*acercar*) to bring close; (*poner de lado*) to set aside; **arrimarse** *vr* to come close *o* closer; **~se a** to lean on
arrinconar [arrinko'nar] *vt* (*colocar*) to put in a corner; (*enemigo*) to corner; (*fig*) to put on one side; (*abandonar*) to push aside
arroba [a'rroβa] *nf* (*Internet*) at (sign)
arrodillarse [arroði'ʎarse] *vr* to kneel (down)
arrogante [arro'ɣante] *adj* arrogant

arrojar [arro'xar] *vt* to throw, hurl; (*humo*) to emit, give out; (*Com*) to yield, produce; **arrojarse** *vr* to throw *o* hurl o.s.
arrojo [a'rroxo] *nm* daring
arrollador, a [arroʎa'ðor, a] *adj* overwhelming
arrollar [arro'ʎar] *vt* (*Auto etc*) to run over, knock down; (*Deporte*) to crush
arropar [arro'par] *vt* to cover, wrap up; **arroparse** *vr* to wrap o.s. up
arroyo [a'rrojo] *nm* stream; (*de la calle*) gutter
arroz [a'rroθ] *nm* rice; **arroz con leche** rice pudding
arruga [a'rruɣa] *nf* (*de cara*) wrinkle; (*de vestido*) crease; **arrugar** [arru'ɣar] *vt* to wrinkle; to crease; **arrugarse** *vr* to get creased
arruinar [arrwi'nar] *vt* to ruin, wreck; **arruinarse** *vr* to be ruined, go bankrupt
arsenal [arse'nal] *nm* naval dockyard; (*Mil*) arsenal
arte ['arte] (*gen m en sg y siempre f en pl*) *nm* art; (*maña*) skill, guile; **artes** *nfpl* (*bellas artes*) arts
artefacto [arte'fakto] *nm* appliance
arteria [ar'terja] *nf* artery
artesanía [artesa'nia] *nf* craftsmanship; (*artículos*) handicrafts *pl*; **artesano, -a** *nm/f* artisan, craftsman(-woman)
ártico, -a ['artiko, a] *adj* Arctic ▷ *nm*: **el Á~** the Arctic
articulación [artikula'θjon] *nf* articulation; (*Med, Tec*) joint
artículo [ar'tikulo] *nm* article; (*cosa*) thing, article; **artículos** *nmpl* (*Com*) goods; **artículos de escritorio** stationery
artífice [ar'tifiθe] *nmf* (*fig*) architect
artificial [artifi'θjal] *adj* artificial
artillería [artiʎe'ria] *nf* artillery
artilugio [arti'luxjo] *nm* gadget
artimaña [arti'maɲa] *nf* trap, snare; (*astucia*) cunning
artista [ar'tista] *nmf* (*pintor*) artist,

painter; (*Teatro*) artist, artiste; **artista de cine** film actor/actress; **artístico, -a** *adj* artistic

artritis [ar'tritis] *nf* arthritis

arveja [ar'βexa] (*LAM*) *nf* pea

arzobispo [arθo'βispo] *nm* archbishop

as [as] *nm* ace

asa ['asa] *nf* handle; (*fig*) lever

asado [a'saðo] *nm* roast (meat); (*LAM: barbacoa*) barbecue

⬤ **ASADO**
⬤
⬤
⬤ Traditional Latin American
⬤ barbecues, especially in the River
⬤ Plate area, are celebrated in
⬤ the open air around a large grill
⬤ which is used to grill mainly beef
⬤ and various kinds of spicy pork
⬤ sausage. They are usually very
⬤ common during the summer and
⬤ can go on for several days. The
⬤ head cook is nearly always a man.

asador [asa'ðor] *nm* spit

asadura [asa'ðura] *nf* entrails *pl*, offal

asalariado, -a [asala'rjaðo, a] *adj* paid, salaried ▷ *nm/f* wage earner

asaltar [asal'tar] *vt* to attack, assault; (*fig*) to assail; **asalto** *nm* attack, assault; (*Deporte*) round

asamblea [asam'blea] *nf* assembly; (*reunión*) meeting

asar [a'sar] *vt* to roast

ascendencia [asθen'denθja] *nf* ancestry; (*LAM: influencia*) ascendancy; **de ~ francesa** of French origin

ascender [asθen'der] *vi* (*subir*) to ascend, rise; (*ser promovido*) to gain promotion ▷ *vt* to promote; **~ a** to amount to; **ascendiente** *nm* influence ▷ *nmf* ancestor

ascensión [asθen'sjon] *nf* ascent; (*Rel*): **la A~** the Ascension

ascenso [as'θenso] *nm* ascent; (*promoción*) promotion

ascensor [asθen'sor] *nm* lift (*BRIT*), elevator (*US*)

asco ['asko] *nm*: **¡qué ~!** how revolting o disgusting; **el ajo me da ~** I hate o loathe garlic; **estar hecho un ~** to be filthy

ascua ['askwa] *nf* ember

aseado, -a [ase'aðo, a] *adj* clean; (*arreglado*) tidy; (*pulcro*) smart

asear [ase'ar] *vt* to clean, wash; to tidy (up)

asediar [ase'ðjar] *vt* (*Mil*) to besiege, lay siege to; (*fig*) to chase, pester; **asedio** *nm* siege; (*Com*) run

asegurado, -a [aseɣu'raðo, a] *adj* insured

asegurador, a [aseɣura'ðor, a] *nm/f* insurer

asegurar [aseɣu'rar] *vt* (*consolidar*) to secure, fasten; (*dar garantía de*) to guarantee; (*preservar*) to safeguard; (*afirmar, dar por cierto*) to assure, affirm; (*tranquilizar*) to reassure; (*tomar un seguro*) to insure; **asegurarse** *vr* to assure o.s., make sure

asemejarse [aseme'xarse] *vr* to be alike; **~ a** to be like, resemble

asentado, -a [asen'taðo, a] *adj* established, settled

asentar [asen'tar] *vt* (*sentar*) to seat, sit down; (*poner*) to place, establish; (*alisar*) to level, smooth down o out; (*anotar*) to note down ▷ *vi* to be suitable, suit

asentir [asen'tir] *vi* to assent, agree; **~ con la cabeza** to nod (one's head)

aseo [a'seo] *nm* cleanliness; **aseos** *nmpl* (*servicios*) toilet *sg* (*BRIT*), cloakroom *sg* (*BRIT*), restroom *sg* (*US*)

aséptico, -a [a'septiko, a] *adj* germ-free, free from infection

asequible [ase'kiβle] *adj* (*precio*) reasonable; (*meta*) attainable; (*persona*) approachable

asesinar [asesi'nar] *vt* to murder; (*Pol*) to assassinate; **asesinato** *nm* murder; assassination

asesino, -a [ase'sino, a] *nm/f*

murderer, killer; (*Pol*) assassin

asesor, a [ase'sor, a] *nm/f* adviser,
consultant; **asesorar** [aseso'rar]
vt (*Jur*) to advise, give legal advice
to; (*Com*) to act as consultant to;
asesorarse *vr*: **asesorarse con** *o* **de**
to take advice from, consult; **asesoría**
nf (*cargo*) consultancy; (*oficina*)
consultant's office

asestar [ases'tar] *vt* (*golpe*) to deal,
strike

asfalto [as'falto] *nm* asphalt

asfixia [as'fiksja] *nf* asphyxia,
suffocation; **asfixiar** [asfik'sjar] *vt* to
asphyxiate, suffocate; **asfixiarse** *vr* to
be asphyxiated, suffocate

así [a'si] *adv* (*de esta manera*) in this
way, like this, thus; (*aunque*) although;
(*tan pronto como*) as soon as; ~ **que** so;
~ **como** as well as; ~ **y todo** even so;
¿no es ~? isn't it?, didn't you? *etc*; ~ **de
grande** this big

Asia ['asja] *nf* Asia; **asiático, -a** *adj*,
nm/f Asian, Asiatic

asiduo, -a [a'siðwo, a] *adj*
assiduous; (*frecuente*) frequent ▷ *nm/f*
regular (customer)

asiento [a'sjento] *nm* (*mueble*) seat,
chair; (*de coche, en tribunal etc*) seat;
(*localidad*) seat, place; (*fundamento*)
site; **asiento delantero/trasero**
front/back seat

asignación [asiɣna'θjon] *nf*
(*atribución*) assignment; (*reparto*)
allocation; (*sueldo*) salary; **asignación
(semanal)** pocket money

asignar [asiɣ'nar] *vt* to assign,
allocate

asignatura [asiɣna'tura] *nf* subject;
course

asilo [a'silo] *nm* (*refugio*) asylum,
refuge; (*establecimiento*) home,
institution; **asilo político** political
asylum

asimilar [asimi'lar] *vt* to assimilate

asimismo [asi'mismo] *adv* in the
same way, likewise

asistencia [asis'tenθja] *nf* audience;

(*Med*) attendance; (*ayuda*) assistance;
asistencia en carretera roadside
assistance; **asistente** *nmf* assistant;
los asistentes those present;
asistente social social worker

asistido, -a [asis'tiðo, a] *adj*: ~ **por
ordenador** computer-assisted

asistir [asis'tir] *vt* to assist, help
▷ *vi*: ~ **a** to attend, be present at

asma ['asma] *nf* asthma

asno ['asno] *nm* donkey; (*fig*) ass

asociación [asoθja'θjon] *nf*
association; (*Com*) partnership;
asociado, -a *adj* associate ▷ *nm/f*
associate; (*Com*) partner

asociar [aso'θjar] *vt* to associate

asomar [aso'mar] *vt* to show, stick
out ▷ *vi* to appear; **asomarse** *vr* to
appear, show up; ~ **la cabeza por la
ventana** to put one's head out of the
window

asombrar [asom'brar] *vt* to
amaze, astonish; **asombrarse**
vr (*sorprenderse*) to be amazed;
(*asustarse*) to get a fright; **asombro**
nm amazement, astonishment;
(*susto*) fright; **asombroso, -a** *adj*
astonishing, amazing

asomo [a'somo] *nm* hint, sign

aspa ['aspa] *nf* (*cruz*) cross; (*de molino*)
sail; **en ~** X-shaped

aspaviento [aspa'βjento] *nm*
exaggerated display of feeling; (*fam*)
fuss

aspecto [as'pekto] *nm* (*apariencia*)
look, appearance; (*fig*) aspect

áspero, -a ['aspero, a] *adj* rough;
bitter; sour; harsh

aspersión [asper'sjon] *nf* sprinkling

aspiración [aspira'θjon] *nf* breath,
inhalation; (*Mús*) short pause;
aspiraciones *nfpl* (*ambiciones*)
aspirations

aspirador [aspira'ðor] *nm* =
aspiradora

aspiradora [aspira'ðora] *nf* vacuum
cleaner, Hoover®

aspirante [aspi'rante] *nmf*

(*candidato*) candidate; (*Deporte*) contender

aspirar [aspi'rar] *vt* to breathe in ▷ *vi*: **~ a** to aspire to

aspirina [aspi'rina] *nf* aspirin

asqueroso, -a [aske'roso, a] *adj* disgusting, sickening

asta ['asta] *nf* lance; (*arpón*) spear; (*mango*) shaft, handle; (*Zool*) horn; **a media ~** at half mast

asterisco [aste'risko] *nm* asterisk

astilla [as'tiʎa] *nf* splinter; (*pedacito*) chip; **astillas** *nfpl* (*leña*) firewood *sg*

astillero [asti'ʎero] *nm* shipyard

astro ['astro] *nm* star

astrología [astrolo'xia] *nf* astrology; **astrólogo, -a** *nm/f* astrologer

astronauta [astro'nauta] *nmf* astronaut

astronomía [astrono'mia] *nf* astronomy

astucia [as'tuθja] *nf* astuteness; (*ardid*) clever trick

asturiano, -a [astu'rjano, a] *adj, nm/f* Asturian

astuto, -a [as'tuto, a] *adj* astute; (*taimado*) cunning

asumir [asu'mir] *vt* to assume

asunción [asun'θjon] *nf* assumption; (*Rel*): **A~** Assumption

asunto [a'sunto] *nm* (*tema*) matter, subject; (*negocio*) business

asustar [asus'tar] *vt* to frighten; **asustarse** *vr* to be (*o* become) frightened

atacar [ata'kar] *vt* to attack

atadura [ata'ðura] *nf* bond, tie

atajar [ata'xar] *vt* (*enfermedad, mal*) to stop ▷ *vi* (*persona*) to take a short cut

atajo [a'taxo] *nm* short cut

atañer [ata'ɲer] *vi*: **~ a** to concern

ataque *etc* [a'take] *vb* V **atacar** ▷ *nm* attack; **ataque cardíaco** heart attack

atar [a'tar] *vt* to tie, tie up

atarantado, -a [ataran'taðo, a] (*MÉX*) *adj* (*aturdido*) dazed

atardecer [atarðe'θer] *vi* to get dark ▷ *nm* evening; (*crepúsculo*) dusk

atareado, -a [atare'aðo, a] *adj* busy

atascar [atas'kar] *vt* to clog up; (*obstruir*) to jam; (*fig*) to hinder; **atascarse** *vr* to stall; (*cañería*) to get blocked up; **atasco** *nm* obstruction; (*Auto*) traffic jam

ataúd [ata'uð] *nm* coffin

ataviar [ata'βjar] *vt* to deck, array

atemorizar [atemori'θar] *vt* to frighten, scare

Atenas [a'tenas] *n* Athens

atención [aten'θjon] *nf* attention; (*bondad*) kindness ▷ *excl* (be) careful!, look out!

atender [aten'der] *vt* to attend to, look after; (*Tel*) to answer ▷ *vi* to pay attention

atenerse [ate'nerse] *vr*: **~ a** to abide by, adhere to

atentado [aten'taðo] *nm* crime, illegal act; (*asalto*) assault; (*tb*: **~ terrorista**) terrorist attack; **~ contra la vida de algn** attempt on sb's life; **atentado suicida** suicide bombing

atentamente [atenta'mente] *adv*: **Le saluda ~** Yours faithfully

atentar [aten'tar] *vi*: **~ a** *o* **contra** to commit an outrage against

atento, -a [a'tento, a] *adj* attentive, observant; (*cortés*) polite, thoughtful; **estar ~ a** (*explicación*) to pay attention to

atenuar [ate'nwar] *vt* (*disminuir*) to lessen, minimize

ateo, -a [a'teo, a] *adj* atheistic ▷ *nm/f* atheist

aterrador, a [aterra'ðor, a] *adj* frightening

aterrizaje [aterri'θaxe] *nm* landing; **aterrizaje forzoso** emergency *o* forced landing

aterrizar [aterri'θar] *vi* to land

aterrorizar [aterrori'θar] *vt* to terrify

atesorar [ateso'rar] *vt* to hoard

atestar [ates'tar] *vt* to pack, stuff; (*Jur*) to attest, testify to

atestiguar [atesti'ɣwar] *vt* to testify

to, bear witness to

atiborrar [atiβo'rrar] vt to fill, stuff;
atiborrarse vr to stuff o.s.

ático ['atiko] nm (*desván*) attic;
(*apartamento*) penthouse

atinado, -a [ati'naðo, a] adj
(*sensato*) wise; (*correcto*) right, correct

atinar [ati'nar] vi (*al disparar*): ~ **al
blanco** to hit the target; (*fig*) to be right

atizar [ati'θar] vt to poke; (*horno etc*)
to stoke; (*fig*) to stir up, rouse

atlántico, -a [at'lantiko, a] adj
Atlantic ▷ nm: **el (océano) A~** the
Atlantic (Ocean)

atlas ['atlas] nm inv atlas

atleta [at'leta] nm athlete; **atlético,
-a** adj athletic; **atletismo** nm
athletics sg

atmósfera [at'mosfera] nf
atmosphere

atolladero [atoʎa'ðero] nm (*fig*)
jam, fix

atómico, -a [a'tomiko, a] adj
atomic

átomo ['atomo] nm atom

atónito, -a [a'tonito, a] adj
astonished, amazed

atontado, -a [aton'taðo, a] adj
stunned; (*bobo*) silly, daft

atormentar [atormen'tar] vt to
torture; (*molestar*) to torment; (*acosar*)
to plague, harass

atornillar [atorni'ʎar] vt to screw
on o down

atosigar [atosi'ɣar] vt to harass,
pester

atracador, a [atraka'ðor, a] nm/f
robber

atracar [atra'kar] vt (*Náut*) to moor;
(*robar*) to hold up, rob ▷ vi to moor;
atracarse vr: ~**se (de)** to stuff o.s.
(with)

atracción [atrak'θjon] nf attraction

atraco [a'trako] nm holdup, robbery

atracón [atra'kon] nm: **darse** o
pegarse un ~ (de) (*fam*) to stuff o.s.
(with)

atractivo, -a [atrak'tiβo, a] adj

attractive ▷ nm appeal

atraer [atra'er] vt to attract

atragantarse [atraɣan'tarse]
vr: ~ **(con)** to choke (on); **se me ha
atragantado el chico** I can't stand
the boy

atrancar [atran'kar] vt (*puerta*) to
bar, bolt

atrapar [atra'par] vt to trap; (*resfriado
etc*) to catch

atrás [a'tras] adv (*movimiento*)
back(-wards); (*lugar*) behind;
(*tiempo*) previously; **ir hacia ~** to go
back(wards), to go to the rear; **estar ~**
to be behind o at the back

atrasado, -a [atra'saðo, a] adj slow;
(*pago*) overdue, late; (*país*) backward

atrasar [atra'sar] vi to be slow;
atrasarse vr to remain behind; (*tren*)
to be o run late; **atraso** nm slowness;
lateness, delay; (*de país*) backwardness;
atrasos nmpl (*Com*) arrears

atravesar [atraβe'sar] vt (*cruzar*) to
cross (over); (*traspasar*) to pierce; to go
through; (*poner al través*) to lay o put
across; **atravesarse** vr to come in
between; (*intervenir*) to interfere

atravieso etc vb V **atravesar**

atreverse [atre'βerse] vr to dare;
(*insolentarse*) to be insolent; **atrevido,
-a** adj daring; insolent; **atrevimiento**
nm daring; insolence

atribución [atriβu'θjon] nf
attribution; **atribuciones** nfpl (*Pol*)
powers; (*Admin*) responsibilities

atribuir [atriβu'ir] vt to attribute;
(*funciones*) to confer

atributo [atri'βuto] nm attribute

atril [a'tril] nm (*para libro*) lectern;
(*Mús*) music stand

atropellar [atrope'ʎar] vt (*derribar*)
to knock over o down; (*empujar*) to
push (aside); (*Auto*) to run over, run
down; (*agraviar*) to insult; **atropello**
nm (*Auto*) accident; (*empujón*) push;
(*agravio*) wrong; (*atrocidad*) outrage

atroz [a'troθ] adj atrocious, awful

ATS nmf abr (= *Ayudante Técnico*

Sanitario) nurse

atuendo [a'twendo] *nm* attire

atún [a'tun] *nm* tuna

aturdir [atur'ðir] *vt* to stun; (*de ruido*) to deafen; (*fig*) to dumbfound, bewilder

audacia [au'ðaθja] *nf* boldness, audacity; **audaz** *adj* bold, audacious

audición [auði'θjon] *nf* hearing; (*Teatro*) audition

audiencia [au'ðjenθja] *nf* audience; (*Jur: tribunal*) court

audífono [au'ðifono] *nm* (*para sordos*) hearing aid

auditor [auði'tor] *nm* (*Jur*) judge advocate; (*Com*) auditor

auditorio [auði'torjo] *nm* audience; (*sala*) auditorium

auge ['auxe] *nm* boom; (*clímax*) climax

augurar [auɣu'rar] *vt* to predict; (*presagiar*) to portend

augurio [au'ɣurjo] *nm* omen

aula ['aula] *nf* classroom; (*en universidad etc*) lecture room

aullar [au'ʎar] *vi* to howl, yell

aullido [au'ʎiðo] *nm* howl, yell

aumentar [aumen'tar] *vt* to increase; (*precios*) to put up; (*producción*) to step up; (*con microscopio, anteojos*) to magnify ▷ *vi* to increase, be on the increase; **aumentarse** *vr* to increase, be on the increase; **aumento** *nm* increase; rise

aun [a'un] *adv* even; ~ **así** even so; ~ **más** even o yet more

aún [a'un] *adv*: ~ **está aquí** he's still here; ~ **no lo sabemos** we don't know yet; **¿no ha venido ~?** hasn't she come yet?

aunque [a'unke] *conj* though, although, even though

aúpa [a'upa] *excl* come on!

auricular [auriku'lar] *nm* (*Tel*) receiver; **auriculares** *nmpl* (*cascos*) headphones

aurora [au'rora] *nf* dawn

ausencia [au'senθja] *nf* absence

ausentarse [ausen'tarse] *vr* to go away; (*por poco tiempo*) to go out

ausente [au'sente] *adj* absent

austero, -a [aus'tero, a] *adj* austere

austral [aus'tral] *adj* southern ▷ *nm* monetary unit of Argentina

Australia [aus'tralja] *nf* Australia; **australiano, -a** *adj, nm/f* Australian

Austria ['austrja] *nf* Austria; **austríaco, -a** *adj, nm/f* Austrian

auténtico, -a [au'tentiko, a] *adj* authentic

auto ['auto] *nm* (*Jur*) edict, decree; (: *orden*) writ; (*Auto*) car; **autos** *nmpl* (*Jur*) proceedings; (: *acta*) court record *sg*

autoadhesivo [autoaðe'siβo] *adj* self-adhesive; (*sobre*) self-sealing

autobiografía [autoβjoɣra'fia] *nf* autobiography

autobomba [auto'bomba] (*RPL*) *nm* fire engine

autobronceador [autoβronθea'ðor] *adj* self-tanning

autobús [auto'βus] *nm* bus; **autobús de línea** long-distance coach

autocar [auto'kar] *nm* coach (*BRIT*), (passenger) bus (*US*)

autóctono, -a [au'toktono, a] *adj* native, indigenous

autodefensa [autoðe'fensa] *nf* self-defence

autodidacta [autoði'ðakta] *adj* self-taught

autoescuela [autoes'kwela] (*ESP*) *nf* driving school

autógrafo [au'toɣrafo] *nm* autograph

autómata [au'tomata] *nm* automaton

automático, -a [auto'matiko, a] *adj* automatic ▷ *nm* press stud

automóvil [auto'moβil] *nm* (motor) car (*BRIT*), automobile (*US*); **automovilismo** *nm* (*actividad*) motoring; (*Deporte*) motor racing; **automovilista** *nmf* motorist, driver

autonomía [auto'nomia] *nf* autonomy; **autónomo, -a** (*ESP*), **autonómico, -a** (*ESP*) *adj* (*Pol*) autonomous

autopista [auto'pista] *nf* motorway (BRIT), freeway (US); **autopista de cuota** (ESP) *o* **peaje** (MÉX) toll (BRIT) *o* turnpike (US) road

autopsia [au'topsja] *nf* autopsy, postmortem

autor, a [au'tor, a] *nm/f* author

autoridad [autori'ðað] *nf* authority; **autoritario, -a** *adj* authoritarian

autorización [autoriθa'θjon] *nf* authorization; **autorizado, -a** *adj* authorized; (*aprobado*) approved

autorizar [autori'θar] *vt* to authorize; (*aprobar*) to approve

autoservicio [autoser'βiβjo] *nm* (*tienda*) self-service shop (BRIT) *o* store (US); (*restaurante*) self-service restaurant

autostop [auto'stop] *nm* hitch-hiking; **hacer ~** to hitch-hike; **autostopista** *nmf* hitch-hiker

autovía [auto'βia] *nf* ≈ A-road (BRIT), dual carriageway (BRIT), ≈ state highway (US)

auxiliar [auksi'ljar] *vt* to help ▷ *nmf* assistant; **auxilio** *nm* assistance, help; **primeros auxilios** first aid *sg*

Av *abr* (= *Avenida*) Av(e)

aval [a'βal] *nm* guarantee; (*persona*) guarantor

avalancha [aβa'lantʃa] *nf* avalanche

avance [a'βanθe] *nm* advance; (*pago*) advance payment; (*Cine*) trailer

avanzar [aβan'θar] *vt, vi* to advance

avaricia [aβa'riθja] *nf* avarice, greed; **avaricioso, -a** *adj* avaricious, greedy

avaro, -a [a'βaro, a] *adj* miserly, mean ▷ *nm/f* miser

Avda *abr* (= *Avenida*) Av(e)

AVE ['aβe] *nm abr* (= *Alta Velocidad Española*) ≈ bullet train

ave ['aβe] *nf* bird; **ave de rapiña** bird of prey

avecinarse [aβeθi'narse] *vr* (*tormenta*: *fig*) to be on the way

avellana [aβe'ʎana] *nf* hazelnut; **avellano** *nm* hazel tree

avemaría [aβema'ria] *nm* Hail Mary, Ave Maria

avena [a'βena] *nf* oats *pl*

avenida [aβe'niða] *nf* (*calle*) avenue

aventajar [aβenta'xar] *vt* (*sobrepasar*) to surpass, outstrip

aventón [aβen'ton] (MÉX: *fam*) *nm* ride; **dar ~ a algn** to give sb a ride

aventura [aβen'tura] *nf* adventure; **aventurero, -a** *adj* adventurous

avergonzar [aβerɣon'θar] *vt* to shame; (*desconcertar*) to embarrass; **avergonzarse** *vr* to be ashamed; to be embarrassed

avería [aβe'ria] *nf* (*Tec*) breakdown, fault

averiado, -a [aβe'rjaðo, a] *adj* broken down; **"~"** "out of order"

averiguar [aβeri'ɣwar] *vt* to investigate; (*descubrir*) to find out, ascertain

avestruz [aβes'truθ] *nm* ostrich

aviación [aβja'θjon] *nf* aviation; (*fuerzas aéreas*) air force

aviador, a [aβja'ðor, a] *nm/f* aviator, airman(-woman)

ávido, -a ['aβiðo, a] *adj* avid, eager

avinagrado, -a [aβina'xraðo, a] *adj* sour, acid

avión [a'βjon] *nm* aeroplane; (*ave*) martin; **avión de reacción** jet (plane)

avioneta [aβjo'neta] *nf* light aircraft

avisar [aβi'sar] *vt* (*advertir*) to warn, notify; (*informar*) to tell; (*aconsejar*) to advise, counsel; **aviso** *nm* warning; (*noticia*) notice

avispa [a'βispa] *nf* wasp

avispado, -a [aβis'paðo, a] *adj* sharp, clever

avivar [aβi'βar] *vt* to strengthen, intensify

axila [ak'sila] *nf* armpit

ay [ai] *excl* (*dolor*) ow!, ouch!; (*aflicción*) oh!, oh dear!; **¡~ de mi!** poor me!

ayer [a'jer] *adv, nm* yesterday; **antes de ~** the day before yesterday; **~ mismo** only yesterday

ayote [a'jote] (CAM) *nm* pumpkin

ayuda [a'juða] nf help, assistance
▷ nm page; **ayudante** nmf assistant,
helper; (*Escol*) assistant; (*Mil*) adjutant
ayudar [aju'ðar] vt to help, assist
ayunar [aju'nar] vi to fast; **ayunas**
nfpl: **estar en ayunas** to be fasting;
ayuno nm fast; fasting
ayuntamiento [ajunta'mjento] nm
(*consejo*) town (o city) council; (*edificio*)
town (o city) hall
azafata [aθa'fata] nf air stewardess
azafrán [aθa'fran] nm saffron
azahar [aθa'ar] nm orange/lemon
blossom
azar [a'θar] nm (*casualidad*) chance,
fate; (*desgracia*) misfortune, accident;
por ~ by chance; **al ~** at random
Azores [a'θores] nfpl: **las ~** the Azores
azotar [aθo'tar] vt to whip, beat;
(*pegar*) to spank; **azote** nm (*látigo*)
whip; (*latigazo*) lash, stroke; (*en las
nalgas*) spank; (*calamidad*) calamity
azotea [aθo'tea] nf (flat) roof
azteca [aθ'teka] adj, nmf Aztec
azúcar [a'θukar] nm sugar;
azucarado, -a adj sugary, sweet
azucarero, -a [aθuka'rero, a] adj
sugar cpd ▷ nm sugar bowl
azucena [aθu'θena] nf white lily
azufre [a'θufre] nm sulphur
azul [a'θul] adj, nm blue; **azul
celeste/marino** sky/navy blue
azulejo [aθu'lexo] nm tile
azuzar [aθu'θar] vt to incite, egg on

baba ['baβa] nf spittle, saliva; **babear**
vi to drool, slaver
babero [ba'βero] nm bib
babor [ba'βor] nm port (side)
babosada [baβo'saða] (*MÉX, CAM*:
fam) nf drivel; **baboso, -a** [ba'βoso, a]
(*LAM: fam*) adj silly
baca ['baka] nf (*Auto*) luggage o
roof rack
bacalao [baka'lao] nm cod (fish)
bache ['batʃe] nm pothole, rut; (*fig*)
bad patch
bachillerato [batʃiʎe'rato] nm *higher
secondary school course*
bacinica [baθi'nika] (*LAM*) nf potty
bacteria [bak'terja] nf bacterium,
germ
Bahama [ba'ama]: **las (Islas) ~** nfpl
the Bahamas
bahía [ba'ia] nf bay
bailar [bai'lar] vt, vi to dance;
bailarín, -ina nm/f (ballet) dancer;
baile nm dance; (*formal*) ball
baja ['baxa] nf drop, fall; (*Mil*)

casualty; **dar de ~** (*soldado*) to
discharge; (*empleado*) to dismiss
bajada [ba'xaða] *nf* descent; (*camino*)
slope; (*de aguas*) ebb
bajar [ba'xar] *vi* to go down, come
down; (*temperatura, precios*) to drop,
fall ▷ *vt* (*cabeza*) to bow; (*escalera*)
to go down, come down; (*precio, voz*)
to lower; (*llevar abajo*) to take down;
bajarse *vr* (*de coche*) to get out; (*de
autobús, tren*) to get off; **~ de** (*coche*) to
get out of; (*autobús, tren*) to get off; **~se
algo de Internet** to download sth from
the Internet
bajío [ba'xio] (*LAM*) *nm* lowlands *pl*
bajo, -a ['baxo] *adj* (*mueble, número,
precio*) low; (*piso*) ground; (*de estatura*)
small, short; (*color*) pale; (*sonido*) faint,
soft, low; (*voz: en tono*) deep; (*metal*)
base; (*humilde*) low, humble ▷ *adv*
(*hablar*) softly, quietly; (*volar*) low ▷ *prep*
under, below, underneath ▷ *nm* (*Mús*)
bass; **~ la lluvia** in the rain
bajón [ba'xon] *nm* fall, drop
bakalao [baka'lao] (*ESP: fam*) *nm*
rave (music)
bala ['bala] *nf* bullet
balacear [balaθe'ar] (*MÉX, CAM*) *vt*
to shoot
balance [ba'lanθe] *nm* (*Com*) balance;
(: *libro*) balance sheet; (: *cuenta general*)
stocktaking
balancear [balanθe'ar] *vt* to balance
▷ *vi* to swing (to and fro); (*vacilar*) to
hesitate; **balancearse** *vr* to swing (to
and fro), to hesitate
balanza [ba'lanθa] *nf* scales *pl*,
balance; **balanza comercial** balance
of trade; **balanza de pagos** balance
of payments
balaustrada [balaus'traða] *nf*
balustrade; (*pasamanos*) banisters *pl*
balazo [ba'laθo] *nm* (*golpe*) shot;
(*herida*) bullet wound
balbucear [balβuθe'ar] *vi, vt* to
stammer, stutter
balcón [bal'kon] *nm* balcony
balde ['balde] *nm* bucket, pail; **de ~**

(for) free, for nothing; **en ~** in vain
baldosa [bal'dosa] *nf* (*azulejo*) floor
tile; (*grande*) flagstone; **baldosín** *nm*
(small) tile
Baleares [bale'ares] *nfpl*: **las (Islas) ~**
the Balearic Islands
balero [ba'lero] (*LAM*) *nm* (*juguete*)
cup-and-ball toy
baliza [ba'liθa] *nf* (*Aviac*) beacon;
(*Náut*) buoy
ballena [ba'ʎena] *nf* whale
ballet [ba'le] (*pl* **~s**) *nm* ballet
balneario [balne'arjo] *nm* spa; (*CS: en
la costa*) seaside resort
balón [ba'lon] *nm* ball
baloncesto [balon'θesto] *nm*
basketball
balonmano [balon'mano] *nm*
handball
balsa ['balsa] *nf* raft; (*Bot*) balsa wood
bálsamo ['balsamo] *nm* balsam,
balm
baluarte [ba'lwarte] *nm* bastion,
bulwark
bambú [bam'bu] *nm* bamboo
banana [ba'nana] (*LAM*) *nf* banana;
banano *nm* (*LAM: árbol*) banana tree;
(*CAM: fruta*) banana
banca ['banka] *nf* (*Com*) banking
bancario, -a [ban'karjo, a] *adj*
banking *cpd*, bank *cpd*
bancarrota [banka'rrota] *nf*
bankruptcy; **hacer ~** to go bankrupt
banco ['banko] *nm* bench; (*Escol*)
desk; (*Com*) bank; (*Geo*) stratum; **banco
de arena** sandbank; **banco de crédito**
credit bank; **banco de datos** databank
banda ['banda] *nf* band; (*pandilla*)
gang; (*Náut*) side, edge; **banda ancha**
broadband; **banda sonora** soundtrack
bandada [ban'daða] *nf* (*de pájaros*)
flock; (*de peces*) shoal
bandazo [ban'daθo] *nm*: **dar ~s** to
sway from side to side
bandeja [ban'dexa] *nf* tray
bandera [ban'dera] *nf* flag
banderilla [bande'riʎa] *nf* banderilla
bandido [ban'diðo] *nm* bandit

bando ['bando] nm (edicto) edict,
proclamation; (facción) faction;
bandos nmpl (Rel) banns

bandolera [bando'lera] nf: **llevar en
~** to wear across one's chest

banquero [ban'kero] nm banker

banqueta [ban'keta] nf stool;
(MÉX: en calle) pavement (BRIT),
sidewalk (US)

banquete [ban'kete] nm banquet;
(para convidados) formal dinner;
banquete de boda(s) wedding
reception

banquillo [ban'kiʎo] nm (Jur) dock,
prisoner's bench; (banco) bench; (para
los pies) footstool

banquina [ban'kina] (RPL) nf hard
shoulder (BRIT), berm (US)

bañadera [baɲa'ðera] (RPL) nf
bathtub

bañador [baɲa'ðor] (ESP) nm
swimming costume (BRIT), bathing
suit (US)

bañar [ba'ɲar] vt to bath, bathe;
(objeto) to dip; (de barniz) to coat;
bañarse vr (en el mar) to bathe, swim;
(en la bañera) to have a bath

bañera [ba'ɲera] (ESP) nf bath(tub)

bañero, -a [ba'ɲero, a] (CS) nm/f
lifeguard

bañista [ba'ɲista] nmf bather

baño ['baɲo] nm (en bañera) bath;
(en río) dip, swim; (cuarto) bathroom;
(bañera) bath(tub); (capa) coating;
darse o tomar un ~ (en bañera) to have
o take a bath; (en mar, piscina) to have a
swim; **baño María** bain-marie

bar [bar] nm bar

barahúnda [bara'unda] nf uproar,
hubbub

baraja [ba'raxa] nf pack (of cards);
barajar vt (naipes) to shuffle; (fig) to
jumble up

baranda [ba'randa] nf = **barandilla**

barandilla [baran'diʎa] nf rail,
railing

barata [ba'rata] (MÉX) nf (bargain)
sale

baratillo [bara'tiʎo] nm (tienda)
junkshop; (subasta) bargain sale;
(conjunto de cosas) secondhand goods pl

barato, -a [ba'rato, a] adj cheap
▷ adv cheap, cheaply

barba ['barβa] nf (mentón) chin;
(pelo) beard

barbacoa [barβa'koa] nf (parrilla)
barbecue; (carne) barbecued meat

barbaridad [barβari'ðað] nf
barbarity; (acto) barbarism; (atrocidad)
outrage; **una ~** (fam) loads; **¡qué ~!**
(fam) how awful!

barbarie [bar'βarje] nf barbarism,
savagery; (crueldad) barbarity

bárbaro, -a ['barβaro, a] adj
barbarous, cruel; (grosero) rough,
uncouth ▷ nm/f barbarian ▷ adv: **lo
pasamos ~** (fam) we had a great time;
¡qué ~! (fam) how marvellous!; **un
éxito ~** (fam) a terrific success; **es un
tipo ~** (fam) he's a great bloke

barbero [bar'βero] nm barber,
hairdresser

barbilla [bar'βiʎa] nf chin, tip of
the chin

barbudo, -a [bar'βuðo, a] adj
bearded

barca ['barka] nf (small) boat;
barcaza nf barge

Barcelona [barθe'lona] n Barcelona

barco ['barko] nm boat; (grande) ship;
barco de carga/pesca cargo/fishing
boat; **barco de vela** sailing ship

barda ['barða] (MÉX) nf (de madera)
fence

baremo [ba'remo] nm (Mat: fig) scale

barítono [ba'ritono] nm baritone

barman ['barman] nm barman

barniz [bar'niθ] nm varnish; (en loza)
glaze; (fig) veneer; **barnizar** vt to
varnish; (loza) to glaze

barómetro [ba'rometro] nm
barometer

barquillo [bar'kiʎo] nm cone, cornet

barra ['barra] nf bar, rod; (de un bar,
café) bar; (de pan) French stick; (palanca)
lever; **barra de labios** lipstick; **barra**

libre free bar

barraca [ba'rraka] nf hut, cabin

barranco [ba'rranko] nm ravine; (fig) difficulty

barrena [ba'rrena] nf drill

barrer [ba'rrer] vt to sweep; (quitar) to sweep away

barrera [ba'rrera] nf barrier

barriada [ba'rrjaða] nf quarter, district

barricada [barri'kaða] nf barricade

barrida [ba'rriða] nf sweep, sweeping

barriga [ba'rriɣa] nf belly; (panza) paunch; **barrigón, -ona** adj potbellied; **barrigudo, -a** adj potbellied

barril [ba'rril] nm barrel, cask

barrio ['barrjo] nm (vecindad) area, neighborhood (US); (en afueras) suburb; **barrio chino** (ESP) red-light district

barro ['barro] nm (lodo) mud; (objetos) earthenware; (Med) pimple

barroco, -a [ba'rroko, a] adj, nm baroque

barrote [ba'rrote] nm (de ventana) bar

bartola [bar'tola] nf: **tirarse** o **tumbarse a la ~** to take it easy, be lazy

bártulos ['bartulos] nmpl things, belongings

barullo [ba'ruʎo] nm row, uproar

basar [ba'sar] vt to base; **basarse** vr: **~se en** to be based on

báscula ['baskula] nf (platform) scales

base ['base] nf base; **a ~ de** on the basis of; (mediante) by means of; **base de datos** (Inform) database

básico, -a ['basiko, a] adj basic

basílica [ba'silika] nf basilica

básquetbol ['basketbol] (LAM) nm basketball

bastante [bas'tante] adj **1** (suficiente) enough; **bastante dinero** enough o sufficient money; **bastantes libros**
enough books

2 (valor intensivo): **bastante gente** quite a lot of people; **tener bastante calor** to be rather hot

▷ adv: **bastante bueno/malo** quite good/rather bad; **bastante rico** pretty rich; **(lo) bastante inteligente (como) para hacer algo** clever enough o sufficiently clever to do sth

bastar [bas'tar] vi to be enough o sufficient; **bastarse** vr to be self-sufficient; **~ para** to be enough to; **¡basta!** (that's) enough!

bastardo, -a [bas'tarðo, a] adj, nm/f bastard

bastidor [basti'ðor] nm frame; (de coche) chassis; (Teatro) wing; **entre ~es** (fig) behind the scenes

basto, -a ['basto, a] adj coarse, rough; **bastos** nmpl (Naipes) ≈ clubs

bastón [bas'ton] nm stick, staff; (para pasear) walking stick

bastoncillo [baston'θiʎo] nm cotton bud

basura [ba'sura] nf rubbish (BRIT), garbage (US) ▷ adj: **comida/televisión ~** junk food/TV

basurero [basu'rero] nm (hombre) dustman (BRIT), garbage man (US); (lugar) dump; (cubo) (rubbish) bin (BRIT), trash can (US)

bata ['bata] nf (gen) dressing gown; (cubretodo) smock, overall; (Med, Tec etc) lab(oratory) coat

batalla [ba'taʎa] nf battle; **de ~** (fig) for everyday use; **batalla campal** pitched battle

batallón [bata'ʎon] nm battalion

batata [ba'tata] nf sweet potato

batería [bate'ria] nf battery; (Mús) drums; **batería de cocina** kitchen utensils

batido, -a [ba'tiðo, a] adj (camino) beaten, well-trodden ▷ nm (Culin: de leche) milk shake

batidora [bati'ðora] nf beater, mixer; **batidora eléctrica** food mixer, blender

batir [ba'tir] vt to beat, strike; (vencer) to beat, defeat; (revolver) to beat, mix; **batirse** vr to fight; **~ palmas** to applaud

batuta [ba'tuta] nf baton; **llevar la ~** (fig) to be the boss, be in charge

baúl [ba'ul] nm trunk; (Auto) boot (BRIT), trunk (US)

bautismo [bau'tismo] nm baptism, christening

bautizar [bauti'θar] vt to baptize, christen; (fam: diluir) to water down; **bautizo** nm baptism, christening

bayeta [ba'jeta] nf floorcloth

baza ['baθa] nf trick; **meter ~** to butt in

bazar [ba'θar] nm bazaar

bazofia [ba'θofja] nf trash

be [be] nf name of the letter B; **be chica/grande** (MÉX) V/B; **be larga** (LAM) B

beato, -a [be'ato, a] adj blessed; (piadoso) pious

bebé [be'βe] (pl **~s**) nm baby

bebedero [beβe'ðero, a] (MÉX, CS) nm drinking fountain

bebedor, a [beβe'ðor, a] adj hard-drinking

beber [be'βer] vt, vi to drink

bebida [be'βiða] nf drink; **bebido, -a** adj drunk

beca ['beka] nf grant, scholarship; **becario, -a** [be'karjo, a] nm/f scholarship holder, grant holder

bedel [be'ðel] nm (Escol) janitor; (Univ) porter

béisbol ['beisβol] nm baseball

Belén [be'len] nm Bethlehem; **belén** nm (de Navidad) nativity scene, crib

belga ['belxa] adj, nmf Belgian

Bélgica ['belxika] nf Belgium

bélico, -a ['beliko, a] adj (actitud) warlike

belleza [be'ʎeθa] nf beauty

bello, -a ['beʎo, a] adj beautiful, lovely; **Bellas Artes** Fine Art

bellota [be'ʎota] nf acorn

bemol [be'mol] nm (Mús) flat; **esto tiene ~es** (fam) this is a tough one

bencina [ben'θina] nf (Quím) benzine

bendecir [bende'θir] vt to bless

bendición [bendi'θjon] nf blessing

bendito, -a [ben'dito, a] pp de **bendecir** ▷ adj holy; (afortunado) lucky; (feliz) happy; (sencillo) simple ▷ nm/f simple soul

beneficencia [benefi'θenθja] nf charity

beneficiario, -a [benefi'θjarjo, a] nm/f beneficiary

beneficio [bene'fiθjo] nm (bien) benefit, advantage; (ganancia) profit, gain; **a ~ de algn** in aid of sb; **beneficioso, -a** adj beneficial

benéfico, -a [be'nefiko, a] adj charitable

beneplácito [bene'plaθito] nm approval, consent

benévolo, -a [be'neβolo, a] adj benevolent, kind

benigno, -a [be'nixno, a] adj kind; (suave) mild; (Med: tumor) benign, non-malignant

berberecho [berβe'retʃo] nm (Zool, Culin) cockle

berenjena [beren'xena] nf aubergine (BRIT), eggplant (US)

Berlín [ber'lin] n Berlin

berlinesa [berli'nesa] (RPL) nf doughnut, donut (US)

bermudas [ber'muðas] nfpl Bermuda shorts

berrido [be'rriðo] nm bellow(ing)

berrinche [be'rrintʃe] (fam) nm temper, tantrum

berro ['berro] nm watercress

berza ['berθa] nf cabbage

besamel [besa'mel] nf (Culin) white sauce, bechamel sauce

besar [be'sar] vt to kiss; (fig: tocar) to graze; **besarse** vr to kiss (one another); **beso** nm kiss

bestia ['bestja] nf beast, animal; (fig) idiot; **bestia de carga** beast of burden; **bestial** [bes'tjal] adj bestial; (fam) terrific; **bestialidad** nf bestiality; (fam) stupidity

besugo [be'suɣo] *nm* sea bream;
(*fam*) idiot
besuquear [besuke'ar] *vt* to cover
with kisses; **besuquearse** *vr* to kiss
and cuddle
betabel [beta'bel] (*MÉX*) *nm* beetroot
(*BRIT*), beet (*US*)
betún [be'tun] *nm* shoe polish;
(*Quím*) bitumen
biberón [biβe'ron] *nm* feeding bottle
Biblia ['biβlja] *nf* Bible
bibliografía [biβljoɣra'fia] *nf*
bibliography
biblioteca [biβljo'teka] *nf* library;
(*mueble*) bookshelves; **biblioteca
de consulta** reference library;
bibliotecario, -a *nm/f* librarian
bicarbonato [bikarβo'nato] *nm*
bicarbonate
bicho ['bitʃo] *nm* (*animal*) small
animal; (*sabandija*) bug, insect;
(*Taur*) bull
bici ['biθi] (*fam*) *nf* bike
bicicleta [biθi'kleta] *nf* bicycle, cycle;
ir en ~ to cycle
bidé [bi'ðe] (*pl* ~**s**) *nm* bidet
bidón [bi'ðon] *nm* (*de aceite*) drum; (*de
gasolina*) can

○ **PALABRA CLAVE**

bien [bjen] *nm* **1** (*bienestar*) good; **te
lo digo por tu bien** I'm telling you for
your own good; **el bien y el mal** good
and evil
2 (*posesión*): **bienes** goods; **bienes de
consumo** consumer goods; **bienes
inmuebles** *o* **raíces/bienes muebles**
real estate *sg*/personal property *sg*
▷ *adv* **1** (*de manera satisfactoria, correcta
etc*) well; **trabaja/come bien** she
works/eats well; **contestó bien** he
answered correctly; **me siento bien**
I feel fine; **no me siento bien** I don't
feel very well; **se está bien aquí** it's
nice here
2 (*frases*): **hiciste bien en llamarme**
you were right to call me

3 (*valor intensivo*) very; **un cuarto bien
caliente** a nice warm room; **bien se ve
que ...** it's quite clear that ...
4 estar bien: estoy muy bien aquí
I feel very happy here; **está bien que
vengan** it's all right for them to come;
¡está bien! lo haré oh all right, I'll do it
5 (*de buena gana*): **yo bien que
iría pero ...** I'd gladly go but ...
▷ *excl*: **¡bien!** (*aprobación*) O.K.!; **¡muy
bien!** well done! ▷ *adj inv* (*matiz
despectivo*): **gente bien** posh people
▷ *conj* **1 bien ... bien: bien en coche
bien en tren** either by car or by train
2 (*LAM*): **no bien: no bien llegue te
llamaré** as soon as I arrive I'll call you
3 si bien even though; *V tb* **más**

bienal [bje'nal] *adj* biennial
bienestar [bjenes'tar] *nm* well-
being, welfare
bienvenida [bjembe'niða] *nf*
welcome; **dar la ~ a algn** to welcome
sb
bienvenido [bjembe'niðo] *excl*
welcome!
bife ['bife] (*cs*) *nm* steak
bifurcación [bifurka'θjon] *nf* fork
bígamo, -a ['biɣamo, a] *adj*
bigamous ▷ *nm/f* bigamist
bigote [bi'ɣote] *nm* moustache;
bigotudo, -a *adj* with a big
moustache
bikini [bi'kini] *nm* bikini; (*Culin*)
toasted ham and cheese sandwich
bilingüe [bi'lingwe] *adj* bilingual
billar [bi'ʎar] *nm* billiards *sg*; **billares**
nmpl (*lugar*) billiard hall; (*sala de juegos*)
amusement arcade; **billar americano**
pool
billete [bi'ʎete] *nm* ticket; (*de banco*)
(bank)note; (*carta*) note;
~ de 20 libras £20 note; **billete de ida
y vuelta** return (*BRIT*) *o* round-trip (*US*)
ticket; **billete sencillo** *o* **de ida** single
(*BRIT*) *o* one-way (*US*) ticket; **billete
electrónico** e-ticket
billetera [biʎe'tera] *nf* wallet

billón [bi'ʎon] *nm* billion

bimensual [bimen'swal] *adj* twice monthly

bingo ['bingo] *nm* bingo

biodegradable [bioðeɣra'ðaβle] *adj* biodegradable

biografía [bjoɣra'fia] *nf* biography

biología [bjolo'xia] *nf* biology; **biológico, -a** *adj* biological; (*cultivo, producto*) organic; **biólogo, -a** *nm/f* biologist

biombo ['bjombo] *nm* (folding) screen

bioterrorismo [bjoterro'rismo] *nm* bioterrorism

biquini [bi'kini] *nm o* (*RPL*) *f* bikini

birlar [bir'lar] (*fam*) *vt* to pinch

Birmania [bir'manja] *nf* Burma

birome [bi'rome] (*RPL*) *nf* ballpoint (pen)

birria ['birrja] *nf*: **ser una ~** (*película, libro*) to be rubbish

bis [bis] *excl* encore!

bisabuelo, -a [bisa'βwelo, a] *nm/f* great-grandfather(-mother)

bisagra [bi'saɣra] *nf* hinge

bisiesto [bi'sjesto] *adj*: **año ~** leap year

bisnieto, -a [bis'njeto, a] *nm/f* great-grandson/daughter

bisonte [bi'sonte] *nm* bison

bisté [bis'te] *nm* = **bistec**

bistec [bis'tek] *nm* steak

bisturí [bistu'ri] *nm* scalpel

bisutería [bisute'ria] *nf* imitation *o* costume jewellery

bit [bit] *nm* (*Inform*) bit

bizco, -a ['biθko, a] *adj* cross-eyed

bizcocho [biθ'kotʃo] *nm* (*Culin*) sponge cake

blanca ['blanka] *nf* (*Mús*) minim; **estar sin ~** (*ESP: fam*) to be broke; *V tb* **blanco**

blanco, -a ['blanko, a] *adj* white ▷ *nm/f* white man/woman, white ▷ *nm* (*color*) white; (*en texto*) blank; (*Mil, fig*) target; **en ~** blank; **noche en ~** sleepless night

blandir [blan'dir] *vt* to brandish

blando, -a ['blando, a] *adj* soft; (*tierno*) tender, gentle; (*carácter*) mild; (*fam*) cowardly

blanqueador [blankea'ðor] (*MÉX*) *nm* bleach

blanquear [blanke'ar] *vt* to whiten; (*fachada*) to whitewash; (*paño*) to bleach ▷ *vi* to turn white

blanquillo [blan'kiʎo] (*MÉX, CAM*) *nm* egg

blasfemar [blasfe'mar] *vi* to blaspheme, curse

bledo ['bleðo] *nm*: **me importa un ~** I couldn't care less

blindado, -a [blin'daðo, a] *adj* (*Mil*) armour-plated; (*antibala*) bullet-proof; **coche** (*ESP*) *o* **carro** (*LAM*) **~** armoured car

bloc [blok] (*pl* **~s**) *nm* writing pad

blof [blof] (*MÉX*) *nm* bluff; **blofear** (*MÉX*) *vi* to bluff

blog [bloɣ] (*pl* **~s**) *nm* blog

bloque ['bloke] *nm* block; (*Pol*) bloc

bloquear [bloke'ar] *vt* to blockade; **bloqueo** *nm* blockade; (*Com*) freezing, blocking; **bloqueo mental** mental block

blusa ['blusa] *nf* blouse

bobada [bo'βaða] *nf* foolish action; foolish statement; **decir ~s** to talk nonsense

bobina [bo'βina] *nf* (*Tec*) bobbin; (*Foto*) spool; (*Elec*) coil

bobo, -a ['boβo, a] *adj* (*tonto*) daft, silly; (*cándido*) naïve ▷ *nm/f* fool, idiot ▷ *nm* (*Teatro*) clown, funny man

boca ['boka] *nf* mouth; (*de crustáceo*) pincer; (*de cañón*) muzzle; (*entrada*) mouth, entrance; **bocas** *nfpl* (*de río*) mouth *sg*; **~ abajo/arriba** face down/up; **se me hace la ~ agua** my mouth is watering; **boca de incendios** hydrant; **boca del estómago** pit of the stomach; **boca de metro** underground (*BRIT*) *o* subway (*US*) entrance

bocacalle [boka'kaʎe] *nf* (entrance to a) street; **la primera ~** the first turning o street

bocadíllo [boka'ðiʎo] *nm* sandwich

bocado [bo'kaðo] *nm* mouthful, bite; (*de caballo*) bridle

bocajarro [boka'xarro]: **a ~** *adv* (*disparar*) point-blank

bocanada [boka'naða] *nf* (*de vino*) mouthful, swallow; (*de aire*) gust, puff

bocata [bo'kata] (*fam*) *nm* sandwich

bocazas [bo'kaθas] (*fam*) *nm inv* bigmouth

boceto [bo'θeto] *nm* sketch, outline

bochorno [bo'tʃorno] *nm* (*vergüenza*) embarrassment; (*calor*): **hace ~** it's very muggy

bocina [bo'θina] *nf* (*Mús*) trumpet; (*Auto*) horn; (*para hablar*) megaphone

boda [bo'ða] *nf* (*tb*: **~s**) wedding, marriage; (*fiesta*) wedding reception; **bodas de oro/plata** golden/silver wedding *sg*

bodega [bo'ðexa] *nf* (*de vino*) (wine) cellar; (*depósito*) storeroom; (*de barco*) hold

bodegón [boðe'xon] *nm* (*Arte*) still life

bofetada [bofe'taða] *nf* slap (in the face)

boga ['boxa] *nf*: **en ~** (*fig*) in vogue

Bogotá [boxo'ta] *n* Bogotá

bohemio, -a [bo'emjo, a] *adj*, *nm/f* Bohemian

bohío [bo'io] (*CAM*) *nm* shack, hut

boicot [boi'kot] (*pl* **~s**) *nm* boycott; **boicotear** *vt* to boycott

bóiler ['boiler] (*MÉX*) *nm* boiler

boina ['boina] *nf* beret

bola ['bola] *nf* ball; (*canica*) marble; (*Naipes*) (grand) slam; (*betún*) shoe polish; (*mentira*) tale, story; **bolas** *nfpl* (*LAM*: *caza*) bolas *sg*; **bola de billar** billiard ball; **bola de nieve** snowball

boleadoras [bolea'ðoras] *nfpl* bolas *sg*

bolear [bole'ar] (*MÉX*) *vt* (*zapatos*) to polish, shine

bolera [bo'lera] *nf* skittle o bowling alley

bolero, -a (*MÉX*) [bo'lero] *nm/f* (*limpiabotas*) shoeshine boy/girl

boleta [bo'leta] (*LAM*) *nf* (*de rifa*) ticket; (*cs*: *recibo*) receipt; **boleta de calificaciones** (*MÉX*) report card

boletería [bolete'ria] (*LAM*) *nf* ticket office

boletín [bole'tin] *nm* bulletin; (*periódico*) journal, review; **boletín de noticias** news bulletin

boleto [bo'leto] *nm* (*LAM*) ticket; **boleto de ida y vuelta** (*LAM*) round trip ticket; **boleto electrónico** (*LAM*) e-ticket; **boleto redondo** (*MÉX*) round trip ticket

boli ['boli] (*fam*) *nm* Biro®

bolígrafo [bo'lixrafo] *nm* ball-point pen, Biro®

bolilla [bo'liʎa] (*RPL*) *nf* topic

bolillo [bo'liʎo] (*MÉX*) *nm* (bread) roll

bolita [bo'lita] (*cs*) *nf* marble

bolívar [bo'liβar] *nm* monetary unit of Venezuela

Bolivia [bo'liβja] *nf* Bolivia; **boliviano, -a** *adj*, *nm/f* Bolivian

bollería [boʎe'ria] *nf* cakes *pl* and pastries *pl*

bollo ['boʎo] *nm* (*pan*) roll; (*bulto*) bump, lump; (*abolladura*) dent

bolo ['bolo] *nm* skittle; (*píldora*) (large) pill; **(juego de) bolos** *nmpl* skittles *sg*

bolsa ['bolsa] *nf* (*para llevar algo*) bag; (*MÉX*, *CAM*: *bolsillo*) pocket; (*MÉX*: *de mujer*) handbag; (*Anat*) cavity, sac; (*Com*) stock exchange; (*Minería*) pocket; **de ~** pocket *cpd*; **bolsa de agua caliente** hot water bottle; **bolsa de aire** air pocket; **bolsa de dormir** (*MÉX*, *RPL*) sleeping bag; **bolsa de la compra** shopping bag; **bolsa de papel/plástico** paper/plastic bag

bolsear [bolse'ar] (*MÉX*, *CAM*) *vt*: **~ a algn** to pick sb's pocket

bolsillo [bol'siʎo] *nm* pocket; (*cartera*) purse; **de ~** pocket(-size)

bolso ['bolso] *nm* (*bolsa*) bag; (*de mujer*) handbag

bomba ['bomba] *nf* (*Mil*) bomb; (*Tec*)

pump ▷ *adj* (*fam*): **noticia ~** bombshell ▷ *adv* (*fam*): **pasarlo ~** to have a great time; **bomba atómica/de efecto retardado/de humo** atomic/time/smoke bomb

bombacha [bom'batʃa] (*RPL*) *nf* panties *pl*

bombardear [bombarðe'ar] *vt* to bombard; (*Mil*) to bomb; **bombardeo** *nm* bombardment; bombing

bombazo [bom'baθo] (*MÉX*) *nm* (*explosión*) explosion; (*fam: notición*) bombshell; (: *éxito*) smash hit

bombear [bombe'ar] *vt* (*agua*) to pump (out *o* up)

bombero [bom'bero] *nm* fireman

bombilla [bom'biʎa] (*ESP*) *nf* (light) bulb

bombita [bom'bita] (*RPL*) *nf* (light) bulb

bombo ['bombo] *nm* (*Mús*) bass drum; (*Tec*) drum

bombón [bom'bon] *nm* chocolate; (*MÉX: de caramelo*) marshmallow

bombona [bom'bona] (*ESP*) *nf* (*de butano, oxígeno*) cylinder

bonachón, -ona [bona'tʃon, ona] *adj* good-natured, easy-going

bonanza [bo'nanθa] *nf* (*Náut*) fair weather; (*fig*) bonanza; (*Minería*) rich pocket *o* vein

bondad [bon'dað] *nf* goodness, kindness; **tenga la ~ de** (please) be good enough to

bonito, -a [bo'nito, a] *adj* pretty; (*agradable*) nice ▷ *nm* (*atún*) tuna (fish)

bono ['bono] *nm* voucher; (*Finanzas*) bond

bonobús [bono'βus] (*ESP*) *nm* bus pass

bonoloto [bono'loto] *nf* state-run weekly lottery

boquerón [boke'ron] *nm* (*pez*) (kind of) anchovy; (*agujero*) large hole

boquete [bo'kete] *nm* gap, hole

boquiabierto, -a [bokia'βjerto, a] *adj*: **quedarse ~** to be amazed *o* flabbergasted

boquilla [bo'kiʎa] *nf* (*para riego*) nozzle; (*para cigarro*) cigarette holder; (*Mús*) mouthpiece

borbotón [borβo'ton] *nm*: **salir a borbotones** to gush out

borda ['borða] *nf* (*Náut*) (ship's) rail; **tirar algo/caerse por la ~** to throw sth/fall overboard

bordado [bor'ðaðo] *nm* embroidery

bordar [bor'ðar] *vt* to embroider

borde ['borðe] *nm* edge, border; (*de camino etc*) side; (*en la costura*) hem; **al ~ de** (*fig*) on the verge *o* brink of; **ser ~** (*ESP: fam*) to be rude; **bordear** *vt* to border

bordillo [bor'ðiʎo] *nm* kerb (*BRIT*), curb (*US*)

bordo ['borðo] *nm* (*Náut*) side; **a ~** on board

borlote [bor'lote] (*MÉX*) *nm* row, uproar

borrachera [borra'tʃera] *nf* (*ebriedad*) drunkenness; (*orgía*) spree, binge

borracho, -a [bo'rratʃo, a] *adj* drunk ▷ *nm/f* (*habitual*) drunkard, drunk; (*temporal*) drunk, drunk man/woman

borrador [borra'ðor] *nm* (*escritura*) first draft, rough sketch; (*goma*) rubber (*BRIT*), eraser

borrar [bo'rrar] *vt* to erase, rub out

borrasca [bo'rraska] *nf* storm

borrego, -a [bo'rreɣo, a] *nm/f* (*Zool: joven*) (yearling) lamb; (*adulto*) sheep ▷ *nm* (*MÉX: fam*) false rumour

borrico, -a [bo'rriko, a] *nm/f* donkey/she-donkey; (*fig*) stupid man/woman

borrón [bo'rron] *nm* (*mancha*) stain

borroso, -a [bo'rroso, a] *adj* vague, unclear; (*escritura*) illegible

bosque ['boske] *nm* wood; (*grande*) forest

bostezar [boste'θar] *vi* to yawn; **bostezo** *nm* yawn

bota ['bota] *nf* (*calzado*) boot; (*para vino*) leather wine bottle; **botas de agua** *o* **goma** Wellingtons

botana [bo'tana] (*MÉX*) *nf* snack,

appetizer

botánica [bo'tanika] nf (ciencia)
botany; V tb **botánico**

botánico, -a [bo'taniko, a] adj
botanical ▷ nm/f botanist

botar [bo'tar] vt to throw, hurl; (Náut)
to launch; (LAM: echar) to throw out ▷ vi
(ESP: saltar) to bounce

bote ['bote] nm (salto) bounce;
(golpe) thrust; (ESP: envase) tin,
can; (embarcación) boat; (MÉX,
CAM: pey: cárcel) jail; **de ~ en ~** packed,
jammed full; **bote de la basura** (MÉX)
dustbin (BRIT), trashcan (US); **bote
salvavidas** lifeboat

botella [bo'teʎa] nf bottle; **botellín**
nm small bottle; **botellón** nm
(ESP: fam) outdoor drinking session

botijo [bo'tixo] nm (earthenware) jug

botín [bo'tin] nm (calzado) half boot;
(polaina) spat; (Mil) booty

botiquín [boti'kin] nm (armario)
medicine cabinet; (portátil) first-aid kit

botón [bo'ton] nm button; (Bot) bud

botones [bo'tones] nm inv bellboy
(BRIT), bellhop (US)

bóveda ['boβeða] nf (Arq) vault

boxeador [boksea'ðor] nm boxer

boxeo [bok'seo] nm boxing

boya ['boja] nf (Náut) buoy; (de
caña) float

boyante [bo'jante] adj prosperous

bozal [bo'θal] nm (para caballos)
halter; (de perro) muzzle

bragas ['braɣas] nfpl (de mujer)
panties, knickers (BRIT)

bragueta [bra'ɣeta] nf fly, flies pl

braille [breil] nm braille

brasa ['brasa] nf live o hot coal

brasero [bra'sero] nm brazier

brasier [bra'sjer] (MÉX) nm bra

Brasil [bra'sil] nm (tb: **el ~**) Brazil;
brasileño, -a adj, nm/f Brazilian

brassier [bra'sjer] (MÉX) nm V
brasier

bravo, -a ['braβo, a] adj (valiente)
brave; (feroz) ferocious; (salvaje) wild;
(mar etc) rough, stormy ▷ excl bravo!;

bravura nf bravery; ferocity

braza ['braθa] nf fathom; **nadar a ~**
to swim breast-stroke

brazalete [braθa'lete] nm (pulsera)
bracelet; (banda) armband

brazo ['braθo] nm arm; (Zool) foreleg;
(Bot) limb, branch; **luchar a ~ partido**
to fight hand-to-hand; **ir cogidos del ~**
to walk arm in arm

brebaje [bre'βaxe] nm potion

brecha ['bretʃa] nf (hoyo, vacío) gap,
opening; (Mil, fig) breach

brega ['breɣa] nf (lucha) struggle;
(trabajo) hard work

breva ['breβa] nf early fig

breve ['breβe] adj short, brief ▷ nf
(Mús) breve; **en ~** (pronto) shortly,
before long; **brevedad** nf brevity,
shortness

bribón, -ona [bri'βon, ona] adj idle,
lazy ▷ nm/f (pícaro) rascal, rogue

bricolaje [briko'laxe] nm do-it-
yourself, DIY

brida ['briða] nf bridle, rein; (Tec)
clamp

bridge [britʃ] nm bridge

brigada [bri'ɣaða] nf (unidad)
brigade; (de trabajadores) squad, gang
▷ nm ≈ staff-sergeant, sergeant-major

brillante [bri'ʎante] adj brilliant
▷ nm diamond

brillar [bri'ʎar] vi to shine; (joyas)
to sparkle

brillo ['briʎo] nm shine; (brillantez)
brilliance; (fig) splendour; **sacar ~ a**
to polish

brincar [brin'kar] vi to skip about,
hop about, jump about

brinco ['brinko] nm jump, leap

brindar [brin'dar] vi: **~ a o por** to
drink (a toast) to ▷ vt to offer, present

brindis ['brindis] nm inv toast

brío ['brio] nm spirit, dash

brisa ['brisa] nf breeze

británico, -a [bri'taniko, a] adj
British ▷ nm/f Briton, British person

brizna ['briθna] nf (de hierba, paja)
blade; (de tabaco) leaf

broca ['broka] *nf* (*Tec*) drill, bit

brocha ['brotʃa] *nf* (*large*) paintbrush; **brocha de afeitar** shaving brush

broche ['brotʃe] *nm* brooch

broma ['broma] *nf* joke; **de** *o* **en ~** in fun, as a joke; **broma pesada** practical joke; **bromear** *vi* to joke

bromista [bro'mista] *adj* fond of joking ▷ *nmf* joker, wag

bronca ['bronka] *nf* row; **echar una ~ a algn** to tick sb off

bronce ['bronθe] *nm* bronze; **bronceado, -a** *adj* bronze; (*por el sol*) tanned ▷ *nm* (sun)tan; (*Tec*) bronzing

bronceador [bronθea'ðor] *nm* suntan lotion

broncearse [bronθe'arse] *vr* to get a suntan

bronquio ['bronkjo] *nm* (*Anat*) bronchial tube

bronquitis [bron'kitis] *nf inv* bronchitis

brotar [bro'tar] *vi* (*Bot*) to sprout; (*aguas*) to gush (forth); (*Med*) to break out

brote ['brote] *nm* (*Bot*) shoot; (*Med*, *fig*) outbreak

bruces ['bruθes]: **de bruces** *adv*: **caer** *o* **dar de ~** to fall headlong, fall flat

bruja ['bruxa] *nf* witch; **brujería** *nf* witchcraft

brujo ['bruxo] *nm* wizard, magician

brújula ['bruxula] *nf* compass

bruma ['bruma] *nf* mist

brusco, -a ['brusko, a] *adj* (*súbito*) sudden; (*áspero*) brusque

Bruselas [bru'selas] *n* Brussels

brutal [bru'tal] *adj* brutal; **brutalidad** [brutali'ðað] *nf* brutality

bruto, -a ['bruto, a] *adj* (*idiota*) stupid; (*bestial*) brutish; (*peso*) gross; **en ~** raw, unworked

Bs.As. *abr* (= *Buenos Aires*) B.A.

bucal [bu'kal] *adj* oral; **por vía ~** orally

bucear [buθe'ar] *vi* to dive ▷ *vt* to explore; **buceo** *nm* diving

bucle ['bukle] *nm* curl

budismo [bu'ðismo] *nm* Buddhism

buen [bwen] *adj m* V **bueno**

buenamente [bwena'mente] *adv* (*fácilmente*) easily; (*voluntariamente*) willingly

buenaventura [bwenaßen'tura] *nf* (*suerte*) good luck; (*adivinación*) fortune

buenmozo [bwen'moθo] (*MÉX*) *adj* handsome

○ **PALABRA CLAVE**

bueno, -a ['bweno, a] (*antes de nmsg*: **buen**) *adj* **1** (*excelente etc*) good; **es un libro bueno, es un buen libro** it's a good book; **hace bueno, hace buen tiempo** the weather is fine, it is fine; **el bueno de Paco** good old Paco; **fue muy bueno conmigo** he was very nice *o* kind to me

2 (*apropiado*): **ser bueno para** to be good for; **creo que vamos por buen camino** I think we're on the right track

3 (*irónico*): **le di un buen rapapolvo** I gave him a good *o* real ticking off; **¡buen conductor estás hecho!** some *o* a fine driver you are!; **¡estaría bueno que ...!** a fine thing it would be if ...!

4 (*atractivo, sabroso*): **está bueno este bizcocho** this sponge is delicious; **Carmen está muy buena** Carmen is gorgeous

5 (*saludos*): **¡buen día!, ¡buenos días!** (good) morning!; **¡buenas (tardes)!** (good) afternoon!; (*más tarde*) (good) evening!; **¡buenas noches!** good night!

6 (*otras locuciones*): **estar de buenas** to be in a good mood; **por las buenas** *o* **por las malas** by hook or by crook; **de buenas a primeras** all of a sudden ▷ *excl*: **¡bueno!** all right!; **bueno, ¿y qué?** well, so what?

Buenos Aires [bweno'saires] *nm* Buenos Aires

buey [bwei] *nm* ox

búfalo ['bufalo] *nm* buffalo

bufanda [bu'fanda] *nf* scarf

bufete [bu'fete] *nm* (*despacho de abogado*) lawyer's office

bufón [bu'fon] *nm* clown

buhardilla [buar'ðiʎa] *nf* attic

búho ['buo] *nm* owl; (*fig*) hermit, recluse

buitre ['bwitre] *nm* vulture

bujía [bu'xia] *nf* (*vela*) candle; (*Elec*) candle (power); (*Auto*) spark plug

bula ['bula] *nf* (*papal*) bull

bulbo ['bulβo] *nm* bulb

bulevar [bule'βar] *nm* boulevard

Bulgaria [bul'ɣarja] *nf* Bulgaria; **búlgaro, -a** *adj*, *nm/f* Bulgarian

bulla ['buʎa] *nf* (*ruido*) uproar; (*de gente*) crowd

bullicio [bu'ʎiθjo] *nm* (*ruido*) uproar; (*movimiento*) bustle

bulto ['bulto] *nm* (*paquete*) package; (*fardo*) bundle; (*tamaño*) size, bulkiness; (*Med*) swelling, lump; (*silueta*) vague shape

buñuelo [bu'ɲwelo] *nm* ≈ doughnut (*BRIT*), ≈ donut (*US*); (*fruta de sartén*) fritter

buque ['buke] *nm* ship, vessel; **buque de guerra** warship

burbuja [bur'βuxa] *nf* bubble

burdel [bur'ðel] *nm* brothel

burgués, -esa [bur'xes, esa] *adj* middle-class, bourgeois; **burguesía** *nf* middle class, bourgeoisie

burla ['burla] *nf* (*mofa*) gibe; (*broma*) joke; (*engaño*) trick; **burlar** [bur'lar] *vt* (*engañar*) to deceive ▷ *vi* to joke; **burlarse** *vr* to joke; **burlarse de** to make fun of

burlón, -ona [bur'lon, ona] *adj* mocking

buró [bu'ro] (*MÉX*) *nm* bedside table

burocracia [buro'kraθja] *nf* civil service

burrada [bu'rraða] *nf*: **decir** o **soltar ~s** to talk nonsense; **hacer ~s** to act stupid; **una ~** (*ESP*: *mucho*) a (hell of a) lot

burro, -a ['burro, a] *nm/f* donkey/

she-donkey; (*fig*) ass, idiot

bursátil [bur'satil] *adj* stock-exchange *cpd*

bus [bus] *nm* bus

busca ['buska] *nf* search, hunt ▷ *nm* (*Tel*) bleeper; **en ~ de** in search of

buscador [buska'ðor] *nm* (*Internet*) search engine

buscar [bus'kar] *vt* to look for, search for, seek ▷ *vi* to look, search, seek; **se busca secretaria** secretary wanted

busque *etc vb* V **buscar**

búsqueda ['buskeða] *nf* = **busca**

busto ['busto] *nm* (*Anat, Arte*) bust

butaca [bu'taka] *nf* armchair; (*de cine, teatro*) stall, seat

butano [bu'tano] *nm* butane (gas)

buzo ['buθo] *nm* diver

buzón [bu'θon] *nm* (*en puerta*) letter box; (*en calle*) pillar box

C

C. *abr* (= *centígrado*) C; (*compañía*) Co.

C/ *abr* (= *calle*) St

cabal [ka'βal] *adj* (*exacto*) exact; (*correcto*) right, proper; (*acabado*) finished, complete; **cabales** *nmpl*: **no está en sus cabales** she isn't in her right mind

cábalas ['kaβalas] *nfpl*: **hacer ~** to guess

cabalgar [kaβal'ɣar] *vt, vi* to ride

cabalgata [kaβal'ɣata] *nf* procession

caballa [ka'βaʎa] *nf* mackerel

caballería [kaβaʎe'ria] *nf* mount; (*Mil*) cavalry

caballero [kaβa'ʎero] *nm* gentleman; (*de la orden de caballería*) knight; (*trato directo*) sir

caballete [kaβa'ʎete] *nm* (*Arte*) easel; (*Tec*) trestle

caballito [kaβa'ʎito] *nm* (*caballo pequeño*) small horse, pony; **caballitos** *nmpl* (*en verbena*) roundabout, merry-go-round

caballo [ka'βaʎo] *nm* horse; (*Ajedrez*) knight; (*Naipes*) queen; **ir en ~** to ride; **caballo de carreras** racehorse; **caballo de fuerza** *o* **vapor** horsepower

cabaña [ka'βaɲa] *nf* (*casita*) hut, cabin

cabecear [kaβeθe'ar] *vt, vi* to nod

cabecera [kaβe'θera] *nf* head; (*Imprenta*) headline

cabecilla [kaβe'θiʎa] *nm* ringleader

cabellera [kaβe'ʎera] *nf* (head of) hair; (*de cometa*) tail

cabello [ka'βeʎo] *nm* (*tb*: **~s**) hair; **cabello de ángel** confectionery and pastry filling made of pumpkin and syrup

caber [ka'βer] *vi* (*entrar*) to fit, go; **caben 3 más** there's room for 3 more

cabestrillo [kaβes'triʎo] *nm* sling

cabeza [ka'βeθa] *nf* head; (*Pol*) chief, leader; **cabeza de ajo** bulb of garlic; **cabeza de familia** head of the household; **cabeza rapada** skinhead; **cabezada** *nf* (*golpe*) butt; **dar cabezadas** to nod off; **cabezón, -ona** *adj* (*vino*) heady; (*fam: persona*) pig-headed

cabida [ka'βiða] *nf* space

cabina [ka'βina] *nf* cabin; (*de avión*) cockpit; (*de camión*) cab; **cabina telefónica** telephone (*BRIT*) box *o* booth

cabizbajo, -a [kaβiθ'βaxo, a] *adj* crestfallen, dejected

cable ['kaβle] *nm* cable

cabo ['kaβo] *nm* (*de objeto*) end, extremity; (*Mil*) corporal; (*Náut*) rope, cable; (*Geo*) cape; **al ~ de 3 días** after 3 days; **llevar a ~** to carry out

cabra ['kaβra] *nf* goat

cabré *etc vb* V **caber**

cabrear [kaβre'ar] (*fam*) *vt* to bug; **cabrearse** *vr* (*enfadarse*) to fly off the handle

cabrito [ka'βrito] *nm* kid

cabrón [ka'βron] *nm* cuckold; (*fam!*) bastard (!)

caca ['kaka] (*fam*) *nf* pooh

cacahuete [kaka'wete] (*ESP*) *nm* peanut

cacao [ka'kao] nm cocoa; (Bot) cacao

cacarear [kakare'ar] vi (persona) to boast; (gallina) to crow

cacería [kaθe'ria] nf hunt

cacarizo, -a [kaka'riθo, a] (MÉX) adj pockmarked

cacerola [kaθe'rola] nf pan, saucepan

cachalote [katʃa'lote] nm (Zool) sperm whale

cacharro [ka'tʃarro] nm earthenware pot; **cacharros** nmpl pots and pans

cachear [katʃe'ar] vt to search, frisk

cachemir [katʃe'mir] nm cashmere

cachetada [katʃe'taða] (LAM: fam) nf (bofetada) slap

cachete [ka'tʃete] nm (Anat) cheek; (ESP: bofetada) slap (in the face)

cachivache [katʃi'βatʃe] nm (trasto) piece of junk; **cachivaches** nmpl junk sg

cacho ['katʃo] nm (small) bit; (LAM: cuerno) horn

cachondeo [katʃon'deo] (ESP: fam) nm farce, joke

cachondo, -a [ka'tʃondo, a] adj (Zool) on heat; (fam: sexualmente) randy; (: gracioso) funny

cachorro, -a [ka'tʃorro, a] nm/f (perro) pup, puppy; (león) cub

cachucha [ka'tʃuka] (MÉX: fam) nf cap

cacique [ka'θike] nm chief, local ruler; (Pol) local party boss

cactus ['kaktus] nm inv cactus

cada ['kaða] adj inv each; (antes de número) every; **~ día** each day, every day; **~ dos días** every other day; **~ uno/a** each one, every one; **~ vez más/menos** more and more/less and less; **~ vez que ...** whenever, every time (that) ...; **uno de ~ diez** one out of every ten

cadáver [ka'ðaβer] nm (dead) body, corpse

cadena [ka'ðena] nf chain; (TV) channel; **trabajo en ~** assembly line work; **cadena montañosa** mountain range; **cadena perpetua** (Jur) life imprisonment

cadera [ka'ðera] nf hip

cadete [ka'ðete] nm cadet

caducar [kaðu'kar] vi to expire; **caduco, -a** adj expired; (persona) very old

caer [ka'er] vi to fall (down); **caerse** vr to fall (down); **me cae bien/mal** I get on well with him/I can't stand him; **~ en la cuenta** to realize; **dejar ~** to drop; **su cumpleaños cae en viernes** her birthday falls on a Friday

café [ka'fe] (pl **~s**) nm (bebida, planta) coffee; (lugar) café ▷ adj (MÉX: color) brown, tan; **café con leche** white coffee; **café negro** (LAM) black coffee; **café solo** (ESP) black coffee

cafetera [kafe'tera] nf coffee pot

cafetería [kafete'ria] nf (gen) café

cafetero, -a [kafe'tero, a] adj coffee cpd; **ser muy ~** to be a coffee addict

cafishio [ka'fiʃjo] (CS) nm pimp

cagar [ka'ɣar] (fam!) vt to bungle, mess up ▷ vi to have a shit (!)

caída [ka'iða] nf fall; (declive) slope; (disminución) fall, drop

caído, -a [ka'iðo, a] adj drooping

caiga etc vb V **caer**

caimán [kai'man] nm alligator

caja ['kaxa] nf box; (para reloj) case; (de ascensor) shaft; (Com) cashbox; (donde se hacen los pagos) cashdesk; (: en supermercado) checkout, till; **caja de ahorros** savings bank; **caja de cambios** gearbox; **caja de fusibles** fuse box; **caja fuerte** o **de caudales** safe, strongbox

cajero, -a [ka'xero, a] nm/f cashier; **cajero automático** cash dispenser

cajetilla [kaxe'tiʎa] nf (de cigarrillos) packet

cajón [ka'xon] nm big box; (de mueble) drawer

cajuela (MÉX) nf (Auto) boot (BRIT), trunk (US)

cal [kal] nf lime

cala ['kala] nf (Geo) cove, inlet; (de barco) hold

calabacín [kalaβa'θin] nm (Bot) baby marrow; (: más pequeño) courgette (BRIT), zucchini (US)

calabacita [kalaβa'θita] (MÉX) nf courgette (BRIT), zucchini (US)

calabaza [kala'βaθa] nf (Bot) pumpkin

calabozo [kala'βoθo] nm (cárcel) prison; (celda) cell

calada [ka'laða] (ESP) nf (de cigarrillo) puff

calado, -a [ka'laðo, a] adj (prenda) lace cpd ▷ nm (Náut) draught

calamar [kala'mar] nm squid no pl

calambre [ka'lambre] nm (Elec) shock

calar [ka'lar] vt to soak, drench; (penetrar) to pierce, penetrate; (comprender) to see through; (vela) to lower; **calarse** vr (Auto) to stall; **~se las gafas** to stick one's glasses on

calavera [kala'βera] nf skull

calcar [kal'kar] vt (reproducir) to trace; (imitar) to copy

calcetín [kalθe'tin] nm sock

calcio ['kalθjo] nm calcium

calcomanía [kalkoma'nia] nf transfer

calculador, a [kalkula'ðor, a] adj (persona) calculating; **calculadora** [kalkula'ðora] nf calculator

calcular [kalku'lar] vt (Mat) to calculate, compute; **~ que ...** to reckon that ...

caldera [kal'dera] nf boiler

calderilla [kalde'riʎa] nf (moneda) small change

caldo ['kaldo] nm stock; (consomé) consommé

calefacción [kalefak'θjon] nf heating; **calefacción central** central heating

calefón [kale'fon] (RPL) nm boiler

calendario [kalen'darjo] nm calendar

calentador [kalenta'ðor] nm heater

calentamiento [kalenta'mjento] nm (Deporte) warm-up;

calentamiento global global warming

calentar [kalen'tar] vt to heat (up); **calentarse** vr to heat up, warm up; (fig: discusión etc) to get heated

calentón [kalen'ton] (RPL: fam) adj (sexualmente) horny, randy (BRIT)

calentura [kalen'tura] nf (Med) fever, (high) temperature

calesita [kale'sita] (RPL) nf merry-go-round, carousel

calibre [ka'liβre] nm (de cañón) calibre, bore; (diámetro) diameter; (fig) calibre

calidad [kali'ðað] nf quality; **de ~** quality cpd; **en ~ de** in the capacity of, as

cálido, -a ['kaliðo, a] adj hot; (fig) warm

caliente etc [ka'ljente] vb V **calentar** ▷ adj hot; (fig) fiery; (disputa) heated; (fam: cachondo) randy

calificación [kalifika'θjon] nf qualification; (de alumno) grade, mark

calificado, -a [kalifi'kaðo, a] (LAM) adj (competente) qualified; (obrero) skilled

calificar [kalifi'kar] vt to qualify; (alumno) to grade, mark; **~ de** to describe as

calima [ka'lima] nf (cerca del mar) mist

cáliz ['kaliθ] nm chalice

caliza [ka'liθa] nf limestone

callado, -a [ka'ʎaðo, a] adj quiet

callar [ka'ʎar] vt (asunto delicado) to keep quiet about, say nothing about; (persona, opinión) to silence ▷ vi to keep quiet, be silent; **callarse** vr to keep quiet, be silent; **¡cállate!** be quiet!, shut up!

calle ['kaʎe] nf street; (Deporte) lane; **~ arriba/abajo** up/down the street; **calle de sentido único** one-way street; **calle mayor** (ESP) high (BRIT) o main (US) street; **calle peatonal** pedestrianized o pedestrian street; **calle principal** (LAM) high (BRIT) o main

(US) street; **callejear** vi to wander (about) the streets; **callejero, -a** adj street cpd ▷ nm street map; **callejón** nm alley, passage; **callejón sin salida** cul-de-sac; **callejuela** nf side-street, alley

callista [ka'ʎista] nmf chiropodist

callo ['kaʎo] nm callus; (en el pie) corn; **callos** nmpl (Culin) tripe sg

calma ['kalma] nf calm

calmante [kal'mante] nm sedative, tranquillizer

calmar [kal'mar] vt to calm, calm down ▷ vi (tempestad) to abate; (mente etc) to become calm

calor [ka'lor] nm heat; (agradable) warmth; **hace ~** it's hot; **tener ~** to be hot

caloría [kalo'ria] nf calorie

calumnia [ka'lumnja] nf calumny, slander

caluroso, -a [kalu'roso, a] adj hot; (sin exceso) warm; (fig) enthusiastic

calva ['kalβa] nf bald patch; (en bosque) clearing

calvario [kal'βarjo] nm stations pl of the cross

calvicie [kal'βiθje] nf baldness

calvo, -a ['kalβo, a] adj bald; (terreno) bare, barren; (tejido) threadbare

calza ['kalθa] nf wedge, chock

calzada [kal'θaða] nf roadway, highway

calzado, -a [kal'θaðo, a] adj shod ▷ nm footwear

calzador [kalθa'ðor] nm shoehorn

calzar [kal'θar] vt (zapatos etc) to wear; (mueble) to put a wedge under; **calzarse** vr: **~se los zapatos** to put on one's shoes; **¿qué (número) calza?** what size do you take?

calzón [kal'θon] nm (ESP: pantalón corto) shorts; (LAM: ropa interior: de hombre) underpants, pants (BRIT), shorts (US); (: de mujer) panties, knickers (BRIT)

calzoncillos [kalθon'θiʎos] nmpl underpants

cama ['kama] nf bed; **hacer la ~** to make the bed; **cama individual/de matrimonio** single/double bed

camaleón [kamale'on] nm chameleon

cámara ['kamara] nf chamber; (habitación) room; (sala) hall; (Cine) cine camera; (fotográfica) camera; **cámara de aire** (ESP) inner tube; **cámara de comercio** chamber of commerce; **cámara de gas** gas chamber; **cámara digital** digital camera; **cámara frigorífica** cold-storage room

camarada [kama'raða] nmf comrade, companion

camarera [kama'rera] nf (en restaurante) waitress; (en casa, hotel) maid

camarero [kama'rero] nm waiter

camarógrafo, -a [kama'rografo, a] (LAM) nm/f cameraman/camerawoman

camarón [kama'ron] nm shrimp

camarote [kama'rote] nm cabin

cambiable [kam'bjaβle] adj (variable) changeable, variable; (intercambiable) interchangeable

cambiante [kam'bjante] adj variable

cambiar [kam'bjar] vt to change; (dinero) to exchange ▷ vi to change; **cambiarse** vr (mudarse) to move; (de ropa) to change; **~ de idea** u **opinión** to change one's mind; **~se de ropa** to change (one's clothes)

cambio ['kambjo] nm change; (trueque) exchange; (Com) rate of exchange; (oficina) bureau de change; (dinero menudo) small change; **a ~ de** in return o exchange for; **en ~** on the other hand; (en lugar de) instead; **cambio climático** climate change; **cambio de divisas** foreign exchange; **cambio de marchas** o **velocidades** gear lever

camelar [kame'lar] vt to sweet-talk

camello [ka'meʎo] nm camel; (fam: traficante) pusher

camerino [kame'rino] nm dressing

room

camilla [ka'miʎa] nf (Med) stretcher

caminar [kami'nar] vi (marchar) to walk, go ▷ vt (recorrer) to cover, travel

caminata [kami'nata] nf long walk; (por el campo) hike

camino [ka'mino] nm way, road; (sendero) track; **a medio ~** halfway (there); **en el ~** on the way, en route; **~ de** on the way to; **Camino de Santiago** Way of St James; **camino particular** private road

- **CAMINO DE SANTIAGO**
-
- The **Camino de Santiago** is a
- medieval pilgrim route stretching
- from the Pyrenees to Santiago de
- Compostela in north-west Spain,
- where tradition has it the body
- of the Apostle James is buried.
- Nowadays it is a popular tourist
- route as well as a religious one.

camión [ka'mjon] nm lorry (BRIT), truck (US); (MÉX: autobús) bus; **camión cisterna** tanker; **camión de la basura** dustcart, refuse lorry; **camión de mudanzas** removal (BRIT) o moving (US) van; **camionero, -a** nm/f lorry o truck driver

camioneta [kamjo'neta] nf van, light truck

camisa [ka'misa] nf shirt; (Bot) skin; **camisa de fuerza** straitjacket

camiseta [kami'seta] nf (prenda) tee-shirt; (ropa interior) vest; (de deportista) top

camisón [kami'son] nm nightdress, nightgown

camorra [ka'morra] nf: **buscar ~** to look for trouble

camote [ka'mote] nm (MÉX, CS: batata) sweet potato, yam; (MÉX: bulbo) tuber, bulb; (CS: fam: enamoramiento) crush

campamento [kampa'mento] nm camp

campana [kam'pana] nf bell; **campanada** nf peal; **campanario** nm belfry

campanilla [kampa'niʎa] nf small bell

campaña [kam'paɲa] nf (Mil, Pol) campaign; **campaña electoral** election campaign

campechano, -a [kampe'tʃano, a] adj (franco) open

campeón, -ona [kampe'on, ona] nm/f champion; **campeonato** nm championship

cámper ['kamper] (LAM) nm o f caravan (BRIT), trailer (US)

campera [kam'pera] (RPL) nf anorak

campesino, -a [kampe'sino, a] adj country cpd, rural; (gente) peasant cpd ▷ nm/f countryman/woman; (agricultor) farmer

campestre [kam'pestre] adj country cpd, rural

camping ['kampin] (pl **~s**) nm camping; (lugar) campsite; **ir** o **estar de ~** to go camping

campo ['kampo] nm (fuera de la ciudad) country, countryside; (Agr, Elec) field; (de fútbol) pitch; (de golf) course; (Mil) camp; **campo de batalla** battlefield; **campo de concentración** concentration camp; **campo de deportes** sports ground, playing field; **campo visual** field of vision, visual field

camuflaje [kamu'flaxe] nm camouflage

cana ['kana] nf white o grey hair; **tener ~s** to be going grey

Canadá [kana'ða] nm Canada; **canadiense** adj, nmf Canadian ▷ nf fur-lined jacket

canal [ka'nal] nm canal; (Geo) channel, strait; (de televisión) channel; (de tejado) gutter; **canal de Panamá** Panama Canal

canaleta [kana'leta] (LAM) nf (de tejado) gutter

canalizar [kanali'θar] vt to channel

canalla [ka'naʎa] *nf* rabble, mob
▷ *nm* swine

canapé [kana'pe] (*pl* **~s**) *nm* sofa,
settee; (*Culin*) canapé

Canarias [ka'narjas] *nfpl* (*tb*: **las
Islas ~**) the Canary Islands, the
Canaries

canario, -a [ka'narjo, a] *adj, nm/f*
(native) of the Canary Isles ▷ *nm* (*Zool*)
canary

canasta [ka'nasta] *nf* (round) basket

canasto [ka'nasto] *nm* large basket

cancela [kan'θela] *nf* gate

cancelación [kanθela'θjon] *nf*
cancellation

cancelar [kanθe'lar] *vt* to cancel;
(*una deuda*) to write off

cáncer ['kanθer] *nm* (*Med*) cancer; **C~**
(*Astrología*) Cancer

cancha ['kantʃa] *nf* (*de baloncesto*)
court; (*LAM: campo*) pitch; **cancha de
tenis** (*LAM*) tennis court

canciller [kanθi'ʎer] *nm* chancellor

canción [kan'θjon] *nf* song; **canción
de cuna** lullaby

candado [kan'daðo] *nm* padlock

candente [kan'dente] *adj* red-hot;
(*fig: tema*) burning

candidato, -a [kandi'ðato, a] *nm/f*
candidate

cándido, -a ['kandiðo, a] *adj* simple;
naive

No confundir **cándido** con la
palabra inglesa *candid*.

candil [kan'dil] *nm* oil lamp;
candilejas *nfpl* (*Teatro*) footlights

canela [ka'nela] *nf* cinnamon

canelones [kane'lones] *nmpl*
cannelloni

cangrejo [kan'grexo] *nm* crab

canguro [kan'guro] *nm* kangaroo;
hacer de ~ to babysit

caníbal [ka'niβal] *adj, nmf* cannibal

canica [ka'nika] *nf* marble

canijo, -a [ka'nixo, a] *adj* frail, sickly

canilla [ka'niʎa] (*RPL*) *nf* tap (*BRIT*),
faucet (*US*)

canjear [kanxe'ar] *vt* to exchange

canoa [ka'noa] *nf* canoe

canon ['kanon] *nm* canon; (*pensión*)
rent; (*Com*) tax

canonizar [kanoni'θar] *vt* to
canonize

canoso, -a [ka'noso, a] *adj* grey-
haired

cansado, -a [kan'saðo, a] *adj* tired,
weary; (*tedioso*) tedious, boring

cansancio [kan'sanθjo] *nm*
tiredness, fatigue

cansar [kan'sar] *vt* (*fatigar*) to tire,
tire out; (*aburrir*) to bore; (*fastidiar*) to
bother; **cansarse** *vr* to tire, get tired;
(*aburrirse*) to get bored

cantábrico, -a [kan'taβriko, a] *adj*
Cantabrian

cantante [kan'tante] *adj* singing
▷ *nmf* singer

cantar [kan'tar] *vt* to sing ▷ *vi* to
sing; (*insecto*) to chirp ▷ *nm* (*acción*)
singing; (*canción*) song; (*poema*) poem

cántaro ['kantaro] *nm* pitcher, jug;
llover a ~s to rain cats and dogs

cante ['kante] *nm* (*Mús*) Andalusian
folk song; **cante jondo** flamenco
singing

cantera [kan'tera] *nf* quarry

cantero [kan'tero] (*RPL*) *nm* (*arriate*)
border

cantidad [kanti'ðað] *nf* quantity,
amount; **~ de** lots of

cantimplora [kantim'plora] *nf*
(*frasco*) water bottle, canteen

cantina [kan'tina] *nf* canteen; (*de
estación*) buffet; (*LAM: bar*) bar

cantinero, -a [kanti'nero, a] (*MÉX*)
nm/f barman/barmaid, bartender (*US*)

canto ['kanto] *nm* singing; (*canción*)
song; (*borde*) edge, rim; (*de cuchillo*)
back; **canto rodado** boulder

cantor, a [kan'tor, a] *nm/f* singer

canturrear [kanturre'ar] *vi* to
sing softly

canuto [ka'nuto] *nm* (*tubo*) small
tube; (*fam: droga*) joint

caña ['kaɲa] *nf* (*Bot: tallo*) stem, stalk;
(*carrizo*) reed; (*vaso*) tumbler; (*de cerveza*)

glass of beer; (*Anat*) shinbone; **caña de azúcar** sugar cane; **caña de pescar** fishing rod

cañada [ka'ɲaða] *nf* (*entre dos montañas*) gully, ravine; (*camino*) cattle track

cáñamo ['kaɲamo] *nm* hemp

cañería [kaɲe'ria] *nf* (*tubo*) pipe

caño ['kaɲo] *nm* (*tubo*) tube, pipe; (*de albañal*) sewer; (*Mús*) pipe; (*de fuente*) jet

cañón [ka'ɲon] *nm* (*Mil*) cannon; (*de fusil*) barrel; (*Geo*) canyon, gorge

caoba [ka'oβa] *nf* mahogany

caos ['kaos] *nm* chaos

capa ['kapa] *nf* cloak, cape; (*Geo*) layer, stratum; **capa de ozono** ozone layer

capacidad [kapaθi'ðað] *nf* (*medida*) capacity; (*aptitud*) capacity, ability

caparazón [kapara'θon] *nm* shell

capataz [kapa'taθ] *nm* foreman

capaz [ka'paθ] *adj* able, capable; (*amplio*) capacious, roomy

capellán [kape'ʎan] *nm* chaplain; (*sacerdote*) priest

capicúa [kapi'kua] *adj inv* (*número, fecha*) reversible

capilla [ka'piʎa] *nf* chapel

capital [kapi'tal] *adj* capital ▷ *nm* (*Com*) capital ▷ *nf* (*ciudad*) capital; **capital social** share *o* authorized capital

capitalismo [kapita'lismo] *nm* capitalism; **capitalista** *adj, nmf* capitalist

capitán [kapi'tan] *nm* captain

capítulo [ka'pitulo] *nm* chapter

capó [ka'po] *nm* (*Auto*) bonnet

capón [ka'pon] *nm* (*gallo*) capon

capota [ka'pota] *nf* (*de mujer*) bonnet; (*Auto*) hood (BRIT), top (US)

capote [ka'pote] *nm* (*abrigo: de militar*) greatcoat; (*de torero*) cloak

capricho [ka'pritʃo] *nm* whim, caprice; **caprichoso, -a** *adj* capricious

Capricornio [kapri'kornjo] *nm* Capricorn

cápsula ['kapsula] *nf* capsule

captar [kap'tar] *vt* (*comprender*) to understand; (*Radio*) to pick up; (*atención, apoyo*) to attract

captura [kap'tura] *nf* capture; (*Jur*) arrest; **capturar** *vt* to capture; to arrest

capucha [ka'putʃa] *nf* hood, cowl

capuchón [kapu'tʃon] (ESP) *nm* (*de bolígrafo*) cap

capullo [ka'puʎo] *nm* (*Bot*) bud; (*Zool*) cocoon; (*fam*) idiot

caqui ['kaki] *nm* khaki

cara ['kara] *nf* (*Anat: de moneda*) face; (*de disco*) side; (*descaro*) boldness; ~ **a** facing; **de** ~ opposite, facing; **dar la** ~ to face the consequences; **¿~ o cruz?** heads or tails?; **¡qué ~ (más dura)!** what a nerve!

Caracas [ka'rakas] *n* Caracas

caracol [kara'kol] *nm* (*Zool*) snail; (*concha*) (sea) shell

carácter [ka'rakter] (*pl* **caracteres**) *nm* character; **tener buen/mal** ~ to be good natured/bad tempered

característica [karakte'ristika] *nf* characteristic

característico, -a [karakte'ristiko, a] *adj* characteristic

caracterizar [karakteri'θar] *vt* to characterize, typify

caradura [kara'ðura] *nmf*: **es un** ~ he's got a nerve

carajillo [kara'xiʎo] *nm* *coffee with a dash of brandy*

carajo [ka'raxo] (*fam!*) *nm*: **¡~!** shit! (!)

caramba [ka'ramba] *excl* good gracious!

caramelo [kara'melo] *nm* (*dulce*) sweet; (*azúcar fundida*) caramel

caravana [kara'βana] *nf* caravan; (*fig*) group; (*Auto*) tailback

carbón [kar'βon] *nm* coal; **papel** ~ carbon paper

carbono [kar'βono] *nm* carbon

carburador [karβura'ðor] *nm* carburettor

carburante [karβu'rante] *nm* (*para motor*) fuel

carcajada [karka'xaða] *nf* (loud)

laugh, guffaw

cárcel ['karθel] *nf* prison, jail; (*Tec*) clamp

carcoma [kar'koma] *nf* woodworm

cardar [kar'ðar] *vt* (*pelo*) to backcomb

cardenal [karðe'nal] *nm* (*Rel*) cardinal; (*Med*) bruise

cardíaco, -a [kar'ðiako, a] *adj* cardiac, heart *cpd*

cardinal [karði'nal] *adj* cardinal

cardo ['karðo] *nm* thistle

carecer [kare'θer] *vi*: ~ **de** to lack, be in need of

carencia [ka'renθja] *nf* lack; (*escasez*) shortage; (*Med*) deficiency

careta [ka'reta] *nf* mask

carga ['karɣa] *nf* (*peso, Elec*) load; (*de barco*) cargo, freight; (*Mil*) charge; (*responsabilidad*) duty, obligation

cargado, -a [kar'ɣaðo, a] *adj* loaded; (*Elec*) live; (*café, té*) strong; (*cielo*) overcast

cargamento [karɣa'mento] *nm* (*acción*) loading; (*mercancías*) load, cargo

cargar [kar'ɣar] *vt* (*barco, arma*) to load; (*Elec*) to charge; (*Com: algo en cuenta*) to charge; (*Inform*) to load ▷ *vi* (*Mil*) to charge; (*Auto*) to load (up); ~ **con** to pick up, carry away; (*peso: fig*) to shoulder, bear; **cargarse** *vr* (*fam: estropear*) to break; (: *matar*) to bump off

cargo ['karɣo] *nm* (*puesto*) post, office; (*responsabilidad*) duty, obligation; (*Jur*) charge; **hacerse ~ de** to take charge of *o* responsibility for

carguero [kar'ɣero] *nm* freighter, cargo boat; (*avión*) freight plane

Caribe [ka'riβe] *nm*: **el ~** the Caribbean; **del ~** Caribbean; **caribeño, -a** [kari'βeɲo, a] *adj* Caribbean

caricatura [karika'tura] *nf* caricature

caricia [ka'riθja] *nf* caress

caridad [kari'ðað] *nf* charity

caries ['karjes] *nf inv* tooth decay

cariño [ka'riɲo] *nm* affection, love;

(*caricia*) caress; (*en carta*) love ...; **tener ~ a** to be fond of; **cariñoso, -a** *adj* affectionate

carisma [ka'risma] *nm* charisma

caritativo, -a [karita'tiβo, a] *adj* charitable

cariz [ka'riθ] *nm*: **tener** *o* **tomar buen/mal ~** to look good/bad

carmín [kar'min] *nm* lipstick

carnal [kar'nal] *adj* carnal; **primo ~** first cousin

carnaval [karna'βal] *nm* carnival

carne ['karne] *nf* flesh; (*Culin*) meat; **se me pone la ~ de gallina sólo verlo** I get the creeps just seeing it; **carne de cerdo/cordero/ternera/vaca** pork/lamb/veal/beef; **carne de gallina** (*fig*) gooseflesh; **carne molida** (*LAM*) mince (*BRIT*), ground meat (*US*); **carne picada** (*ESP, RPL*) mince (*BRIT*), ground meat (*US*)

carné [kar'ne] (*ESP*) (*pl* ~**s**) *nm*: ~ **de conducir** driving licence (*BRIT*), driver's license (*US*); ~ **de identidad** identity card; ~ **de socio** membership card

carnero [kar'nero] *nm* sheep, ram; (*carne*) mutton

carnet [kar'ne] (*ESP*) (*pl* ~**s**) *nm* = **carné**

carnicería [karniθe'ria] *nf* butcher's (shop); (*fig: matanza*) carnage, slaughter

carnicero, -a [karni'θero, a] *adj* carnivorous ▷ *nm/f* butcher; (*carnívoro*) carnivore

carnívoro, -a [kar'niβoro, a] *adj* carnivorous

caro, -a ['karo, a] *adj* dear; (*Com*) dear, expensive ▷ *adv* dear, dearly

carpa ['karpa] *nf* (*pez*) carp; (*de circo*) big top; (*LAM: tienda de campaña*) tent

carpeta [kar'peta] *nf* folder, file; **carpeta de anillas** ring binder

carpintería [karpinte'ria] *nf* carpentry, joinery; **carpintero** *nm* carpenter

carraspear [karraspe'ar] *vi* to clear one's throat

carraspera [karras'pera] *nf* hoarseness

carrera [ka'rrera] *nf* (*acción*) run(ning); (*espacio recorrido*) run; (*competición*) race; (*trayecto*) course; (*profesión*) career; (*licenciatura*) degree; **a la ~** at (full) speed; **carrera de obstáculos** (*Deporte*) steeplechase

carrete [ka'rrete] *nm* reel, spool; (*Tec*) coil

carretera [karre'tera] *nf* (main) road, highway; **carretera de circunvalación** ring road; **carretera nacional** ≈ A road (*BRIT*), ≈ state highway (*US*)

carretilla [karre'tiʎa] *nf* trolley; (*Agr*) (wheel)barrow

carril [ka'rril] *nm* furrow; (*de autopista*) lane; (*Ferro*) rail; **carril-bici** cycle lane

carrito [ka'rrito] *nm* trolley

carro ['karro] *nm* cart, wagon; (*Mil*) tank; (*LAM: coche*) car; **carro patrulla** (*LAM*) patrol o panda (*BRIT*) car

carrocería [karroθe'ria] *nf* bodywork, coachwork

carroña [ka'rroɲa] *nf* carrion *no pl*

carroza [ka'rroθa] *nf* (*carruaje*) coach

carrusel [karru'sel] *nm* merry-go-round, roundabout

carta ['karta] *nf* letter; (*Culin*)

menu; (*naipe*) card; (*mapa*) map; (*Jur*) document; **carta certificada/urgente** registered/special-delivery letter

cartabón [karta'βon] *nm* set square

cartel [kar'tel] *nm* (*anuncio*) poster, placard; (*Escol*) wall chart; (*Com*) cartel; **cartelera** *nf* hoarding, billboard; (*en periódico etc*) entertainments guide; **"en cartelera"** "showing"

cartera [kar'tera] *nf* (*de bolsillo*) wallet; (*de colegial, cobrador*) satchel; (*de señora*) handbag; (*para documentos*) briefcase; (*Com*) portfolio; **ocupa la ~ de Agricultura** she is Minister of Agriculture

carterista [karte'rista] *nmf* pickpocket

cartero [kar'tero] *nm* postman

cartilla [kar'tiʎa] *nf* primer, first reading book; **cartilla de ahorros** savings book

cartón [kar'ton] *nm* cardboard; **cartón piedra** papier-mâché

cartucho [kar'tutʃo] *nm* (*Mil*) cartridge

cartulina [kartu'lina] *nf* card

casa ['kasa] *nf* house; (*hogar*) home; (*Com*) firm, company; **en ~** at home; **casa consistorial** town hall; **casa de campo** country house; **casa de huéspedes** boarding house; **casa de socorro** first aid post; **casa rodante** (*CS*) caravan (*BRIT*), trailer (*US*)

casado, -a [ka'saðo, a] *adj* married ▷ *nm/f* married man/woman

casar [ka'sar] *vt* to marry; (*Jur*) to quash, annul; **casarse** *vr* to marry, get married

cascabel [kaska'βel] *nm* (small) bell

cascada [kas'kaða] *nf* waterfall

cascanueces [kaska'nweθes] *nm inv* nutcrackers *pl*

cascar [kas'kar] *vt* to crack, split, break (open); **cascarse** *vr* to crack, split, break (open)

cáscara ['kaskara] *nf* (*de huevo, fruta seca*) shell; (*de fruta*) skin; (*de limón*) peel

casco ['kasko] *nm* (*de bombero,*

soldado) helmet; (*Náut: de barco*) hull; (*Zool: de caballo*) hoof; (*botella*) empty bottle; (*de ciudad*): **el ~ antiguo** the old part; **el ~ urbano** the town centre; **los ~s azules** the UN peace-keeping force, the blue berets

cascote [kas'kote] *nm* rubble

caserío [kase'rio] (*ESP*) *nm* farmhouse; (*casa*) country mansion

casero, -a [ka'sero, a] *adj* (*pan etc*) home-made ▷ *nm/f* (*propietario*) landlord/lady; **ser muy ~** to be home-loving; **"comida casera"** "home cooking"

caseta [ka'seta] *nf* hut; (*para bañista*) cubicle; (*de feria*) stall

casete [ka'sete] *nm o f* cassette

casi ['kasi] *adv* almost, nearly; **~ nada** hardly anything; **~ nunca** hardly ever, almost never; **~ te caes** you almost fell

casilla [ka'siʎa] *nf* (*casita*) hut, cabin; (*Ajedrez*) square; (*para cartas*) pigeonhole; **casilla de correo** (*cs*) P.O. Box; **casillero** *nm* (*para cartas*) pigeonholes *pl*

casino [ka'sino] *nm* club; (*de juego*) casino

caso ['kaso] *nm* case; **en ~ de** in case of; **en ~ de que ...** in case ...; **el ~ es que ...** the fact is that ...; **en ese/todo ~** in that/any case; **hacer ~ a** to pay attention to; **venir al ~** to be relevant

caspa ['kaspa] *nf* dandruff

cassette [ka'sete] *nm o f* = **casete**

castaña [kas'taɲa] *nf* chestnut

castaño, -a [kas'taɲo, a] *adj* chestnut(-coloured), brown ▷ *nm* chestnut tree

castañuelas [kasta'ɲwelas] *nfpl* castanets

castellano, -a [kaste'ʎano, a] *adj, nm/f* Castilian ▷ *nm* (*Ling*) Castilian, Spanish

castigar [kasti'ɣar] *vt* to punish; (*Deporte*) to penalize; **castigo** *nm* punishment; (*Deporte*) penalty

Castilla [kas'tiʎa] *nf* Castille

castillo [kas'tiʎo] *nm* castle

castizo, -a [kas'tiθo, a] *adj* (*Ling*) pure

casto, -a ['kasto, a] *adj* chaste, pure

castor [kas'tor] *nm* beaver

castrar [kas'trar] *vt* to castrate

casual [ka'swal] *adj* chance, accidental

▎ No confundir **casual** con la palabra inglesa *casual*.

casualidad *nf* chance, accident; (*combinación de circunstancias*) coincidence; **da la casualidad de que ...** it (just) so happens that ...; **¡qué casualidad!** what a coincidence!

cataclismo [kata'klismo] *nm* cataclysm

catador, a [kata'ðor, a] *nm/f* wine taster

catalán, -ana [kata'lan, ana] *adj, nm/f* Catalan ▷ *nm* (*Ling*) Catalan

catalizador [kataliθa'ðor] *nm* catalyst; (*Auto*) catalytic convertor

catalogar [katalo'ɣar] *vt* to catalogue; **~ a algn (de)** (*fig*) to categorize sb (as)

catálogo [ka'taloxo] *nm* catalogue

Cataluña [kata'luɲa] *nf* Catalonia

catar [ka'tar] *vt* to taste, sample

catarata [kata'rata] *nf* (*Geo*) waterfall; (*Med*) cataract

catarro [ka'tarro] *nm* catarrh; (*constipado*) cold

catástrofe [ka'tastrofe] *nf* catastrophe

catear [kate'ar] (*fam*) *vt* (*examen, alumno*) to fail

cátedra ['kateðra] *nf* (*Univ*) chair, professorship

catedral [kate'ðral] *nf* cathedral

catedrático, -a [kate'ðratiko, a] *nm/f* professor

categoría [katexo'ria] *nf* category; (*rango*) rank, standing; (*calidad*) quality; **de ~** (*hotel*) top-class

cateto, -a ['kateto, a] (*ESP: pey*) *nm/f* peasant

catolicismo [katoli'θismo] *nm* Catholicism

católico, -a [ka'toliko, a] *adj, nm/f* Catholic

catorce [ka'torθe] *num* fourteen

cauce ['kauθe] *nm* (*de río*) riverbed; (*fig*) channel

caucho ['kautʃo] (ESP) *nm* rubber

caudal [kau'ðal] *nm* (*de río*) volume, flow; (*fortuna*) wealth; (*abundancia*) abundance

caudillo [kau'ðiʎo] *nm* leader, chief

causa ['kausa] *nf* cause; (*razón*) reason; (*Jur*) lawsuit, case; **a ~ de** because of; **causar** [kau'sar] *vt* to cause

cautela [kau'tela] *nf* caution, cautiousness; **cauteloso, -a** *adj* cautious, wary

cautivar [kauti'βar] *vt* to capture; (*atraer*) to captivate

cautiverio [kauti'βerjo] *nm* captivity

cautividad [kautiβi'ðað] *nf* = **cautiverio**

cautivo, -a [kau'tiβo, a] *adj, nm/f* captive

cauto, -a ['kauto, a] *adj* cautious, careful

cava ['kaβa] *nm* champagne-type wine

cavar [ka'βar] *vt* to dig

caverna [ka'βerna] *nf* cave, cavern

cavidad [kaβi'ðað] *nf* cavity

cavilar [kaβi'lar] *vt* to ponder

cayendo *etc vb* V **caer**

caza ['kaθa] *nf* (*acción: gen*) hunting; (*: con fusil*) shooting; (*una caza*) hunt, chase; (*de animales*) game ▷ *nm* (*Aviac*) fighter; **ir de ~** to go hunting; **caza mayor** game hunting; **cazador, a** [kaθa'ðor, a] *nm/f* hunter; **cazadora** *nf* jacket; **cazar** [ka'θar] *vt* to hunt; (*perseguir*) to chase; (*prender*) to catch

cazo ['kaθo] *nm* saucepan

cazuela [ka'θwela] *nf* (*vasija*) pan; (*guisado*) casserole

CD *nm abr* (= *compact disc*) CD

CD-ROM [θeðe'rom] *nm abr* CD-ROM

CE *nf abr* (= *Comunidad Europea*) EC

cebada [θe'βaða] *nf* barley

cebar [θe'βar] *vt* (*animal*) to fatten (up); (*anzuelo*) to bait; (*Mil, Tec*) to prime

cebo ['θeβo] *nm* (*para animales*) feed, food; (*para peces, fig*) bait; (*de arma*) charge

cebolla [θe'βoʎa] *nf* onion; **cebolleta** *nf* spring onion

cebra ['θeβra] *nf* zebra

cecear [θeθe'ar] *vi* to lisp

ceder [θe'ðer] *vt* to hand over, give up, part with ▷ *vi* (*renunciar*) to give in, yield; (*disminuir*) to diminish, decline; (*romperse*) to give way

cedro ['θeðro] *nm* cedar

cédula ['θeðula] *nf* certificate, document; **cédula de identidad** (LAM) identity card; **cédula electoral** (LAM) ballot

cegar [θe'ɣar] *vt* to blind; (*tubería etc*) to block up, stop up ▷ *vi* to go blind; **cegarse** *vr*: **~se (de)** to be blinded (by)

ceguera [θe'ɣera] *nf* blindness

ceja ['θexa] *nf* eyebrow

cejar [θe'xar] *vi* (*fig*) to back down

celador, a [θela'ðor, a] *nm/f* (*de edificio*) watchman; (*de museo etc*) attendant

celda ['θelda] *nf* cell

celebración [θeleβra'θjon] *nf* celebration

celebrar [θele'βrar] *vt* to celebrate; (*alabar*) to praise ▷ *vi* to be glad; **celebrarse** *vr* to occur, take place

célebre ['θeleβre] *adj* famous

celebridad [θeleβri'ðað] *nf* fame; (*persona*) celebrity

celeste [θe'leste] *adj* (*azul*) sky-blue

celestial [θeles'tjal] *adj* celestial, heavenly

celo¹ ['θelo] *nm* zeal; (*Rel*) fervour; (*Zool*): **en ~** on heat; **celos** *nmpl* jealousy *sg*; **dar ~s a algn** to make sb jealous; **tener ~s** to be jealous

celo²® ['θelo] *nm* Sellotape®

celofán [θelo'fan] *nm* cellophane

celoso, -a [θe'loso, a] *adj* jealous; (*trabajador*) zealous

celta ['θelta] *adj* Celtic ▷ *nmf* Celt

célula ['θelula] nf cell
celulitis [θelu'litis] nf cellulite
cementerio [θemen'terjo] nm cemetery, graveyard
cemento [θe'mento] nm cement; (hormigón) concrete; (LAM: cola) glue
cena ['θena] nf evening meal, dinner; **cenar** [θe'nar] vt to have for dinner ▷ vi to have dinner
cenicero [θeni'θero] nm ashtray
ceniza [θe'niθa] nf ash, ashes pl
censo ['θenso] nm census; **censo electoral** electoral roll
censura [θen'sura] nf (Pol) censorship; **censurar** [θensu'rar] vt (idea) to censure; (cortar: película) to censor
centella [θen'teʎa] nf spark
centenar [θente'nar] nm hundred
centenario, -a [θente'narjo, a] adj centenary; hundred-year-old ▷ nm centenary
centeno [θen'teno] nm (Bot) rye
centésimo, -a [θen'tesimo, a] adj hundredth
centígrado [θen'tiɣraðo] adj centigrade
centímetro [θen'timetro] nm centimetre (BRIT), centimeter (US)
céntimo ['θentimo] nm cent
centinela [θenti'nela] nm sentry, guard
centollo [θen'toʎo] nm spider crab
central [θen'tral] adj central ▷ nf head office; (Tec) plant; (Tel) exchange; **central eléctrica** power station; **central nuclear** nuclear power station; **central telefónica** telephone exchange
centralita [θentra'lita] nf switchboard
centralizar [θentrali'θar] vt to centralize
centrar [θen'trar] vt to centre
céntrico, -a ['θentriko, a] adj central
centrifugar [θentrifu'xar] vt to spin-dry

centro ['θentro] nm centre; **centro comercial** shopping centre; **centro de atención al cliente** call centre; **centro de salud** health centre; **centro escolar** school; **centro juvenil** youth club; **centro turístico** (lugar muy visitado) tourist centre; **centro urbano** urban area, city
centroamericano, -a [θentroameri'kano, a] adj, nm/f Central American
ceñido, -a [θe'ɲiðo, a] adj (chaqueta, pantalón) tight(-fitting)
ceñir [θe'ɲir] vt (rodear) to encircle, surround; (ajustar) to fit (tightly)
ceño ['θeɲo] nm frown, scowl; **fruncir el ~** to frown, knit one's brow
cepillar [θepi'ʎar] vt to brush; (madera) to plane (down)
cepillo [θe'piʎo] nm brush; (para madera) plane; **cepillo de dientes** toothbrush
cera ['θera] nf wax
cerámica [θe'ramika] nf pottery; (arte) ceramics
cerca ['θerka] nf fence ▷ adv near, nearby, close; **~ de** near, close to
cercanías [θerka'nias] nfpl (afueras) outskirts, suburbs
cercano, -a [θer'kano, a] adj close, near
cercar [θer'kar] vt to fence in; (rodear) to surround
cerco ['θerko] nm (Agr) enclosure; (LAM: valla) fence; (Mil) siege
cerdo, -a ['θerðo, a] nm/f pig/sow
cereal [θere'al] nm cereal; **cereales** nmpl cereals, grain sg
cerebro [θe'reβro] nm brain; (fig) brains pl
ceremonia [θere'monja] nf ceremony; **ceremonioso, -a** adj ceremonious
cereza [θe'reθa] nf cherry
cerilla [θe'riʎa] nf (fósforo) match
cerillo [θe'riʎo] (MÉX) nm match
cero ['θero] nm nothing, zero
cerquillo [θer'kiʎo] (CAM, RPL) nm

fringe (BRIT), bangs pl (US)

cerrado, -a [θe'rraðo, a] adj closed, shut; (con llave) locked; (tiempo) cloudy, overcast; (curva) sharp; (acento) thick, broad

cerradura [θerra'ðura] nf (acción) closing; (mecanismo) lock

cerrajero [θerra'xero] nm locksmith

cerrar [θe'rrar] vt to close, shut; (paso, carretera) to close; (grifo) to turn off; (cuenta, negocio) to close ▷ vi to close, shut; (noche) to come down; **cerrarse** vr to close, shut; **~ con llave** to lock; **~ un trato** to strike a bargain

cerro ['θerro] nm hill

cerrojo [θe'rroxo] nm (herramienta) bolt; (de puerta) latch

certamen [θer'tamen] nm competition, contest

certero, -a [θer'tero, a] adj (gen) accurate

certeza [θer'teθa] nf certainty

certidumbre [θerti'ðumbre] nf = **certeza**

certificado, -a [θertifi'kaðo, a] adj (carta, paquete) registered; (aprobado) certified ▷ nm certificate; **certificado médico** medical certificate

certificar [θertifi'kar] vt (asegurar, atestar) to certify

cervatillo [θerβa'tiʎo] nm fawn

cervecería [θerβeθe'ria] nf (fábrica) brewery; (bar) public house, pub

cerveza [θer'βeθa] nf beer

cesar [θe'sar] vi to cease, stop ▷ vt (funcionario) to remove from office

cesárea [θe'sarea] nf (Med) Caesarean operation o section

cese ['θese] nm (de trabajo) dismissal; (de pago) suspension

césped ['θespeð] nm grass, lawn

cesta ['θesta] nf basket

cesto ['θesto] nm (large) basket, hamper

cfr abr (= confróntese) cf.

chabacano, -a [tʃaβa'kano, a] adj vulgar, coarse

chabola [tʃa'βola] (ESP) nf shack;

barrio de chabolas shanty town

chacal [tʃa'kal] nm jackal

chacha ['tʃatʃa] (fam) nf maid

cháchara ['tʃatʃara] nf chatter; **estar de ~** to chatter away

chacra ['tʃakra] (cs) nf smallholding

chafa ['tʃafa] (MÉX: fam) adj useless, dud

chafar [tʃa'far] vt (aplastar) to crush; (plan etc) to ruin

chal [tʃal] nm shawl

chalado, -a [tʃa'lado, a] (fam) adj crazy

chalé [tʃa'le] (pl ~s) nm villa, ≈ detached house

chaleco [tʃa'leko] nm waistcoat, vest (US); **chaleco de seguridad** (Aut) reflective safety vest; **chaleco salvavidas** life jacket

chalet [tʃa'le] (pl ~s) nm = **chalé**

chamaco, -a (MÉX) [tʃa'mako, a] nm/f (niño) kid

chambear [tʃambe'ar] (MÉX: fam) vi to earn one's living

champán [tʃam'pan] nm champagne

champiñón [tʃampi'ɲon] nm mushroom

champú [tʃam'pu] (pl ~es, ~s) nm shampoo

chamuscar [tʃamus'kar] vt to scorch, sear, singe

chance ['tʃanθe] (LAM) nm chance

chancho, -a ['tʃantʃo, a] (LAM) nm/f pig

chanchullo [tʃan'tʃuʎo] (fam) nm fiddle

chandal [tʃan'dal] nm tracksuit

chantaje [tʃan'taxe] nm blackmail

chapa ['tʃapa] nf (de metal) plate, sheet; (de madera) board, panel; (RPL Auto) number plate o license (US) plate; **chapado, -a** adj: **chapado en oro** gold-plated

chaparrón [tʃapa'rron] nm downpour, cloudburst

chaperón [tʃape'ron] (MÉX) nm: **hacer de ~** to play gooseberry;

chaperona (*LAM*) *nf*: **hacer de chaperona** to play gooseberry
chapopote [tʃapoˈpote] (*MÉX*) *nm* tar
chapulín [tʃapuˈlin] (*MÉX, CAM*) *nm* grasshopper
chapurrear [tʃapurreˈar] *vt* (*idioma*) to speak badly
chapuza [tʃaˈpuθa] *nf* botched job
chapuzón [tʃapuˈθon] *nm*: **darse un ~** to go for a dip
chaqueta [tʃaˈketa] *nf* jacket
chaquetón [tʃakeˈton] *nm* long jacket
charca [ˈtʃarka] *nf* pond, pool
charco [ˈtʃarko] *nm* pool, puddle
charcutería [tʃarkuteˈria] *nf* (*tienda*) shop selling chiefly pork meat products; (*productos*) cooked pork meats *pl*
charla [ˈtʃarla] *nf* talk, chat; (*conferencia*) lecture; **charlar** [tʃarˈlar] *vi* to talk, chat; **charlatán, -ana** [tʃarlaˈtan, ana] *nm/f* (*hablador*) chatterbox; (*estafador*) trickster
charol [tʃaˈrol] *nm* varnish; (*cuero*) patent leather
charola [tʃaˈrola] (*MÉX*) *nf* tray
charro [ˈtʃarro, a] (*MÉX*) *nm* typical Mexican
chasco [ˈtʃasko] *nm* (*desengaño*) disappointment
chasis [ˈtʃasis] *nm inv* chassis
chasquido [tʃasˈkiðo] *nm* crack; click
chat [tʃat] *nm* (*Internet*) chat room
chatarra [tʃaˈtarra] *nf* scrap (metal)
chatear [tʃateˈar] *vi* (*Internet*) to chat
chato, -a [ˈtʃato, a] *adj* flat; (*nariz*) snub
chaucha [ˈtʃautʃa] (*RPL*) *nf* runner (*BRIT*) o pole (*US*) bean
chaval, a [tʃaˈβal, a] (*ESP*) *nm/f* kid, lad/lass
chavo, -a [ˈtʃaβo] (*MÉX: fam*) *nm/f* guy/girl
checar [tʃeˈkar] (*MÉX*) *vt*: **~ tarjeta** (*al entrar*) to clock in o on; (: *al salir*) to clock off o out
checo, -a [ˈtʃeko, a] *adj, nm/f* Czech

▷ *nm* (*Ling*) Czech
checoslovaco, -a [tʃekosloˈβako, a] *adj, nm/f* Czech, Czechoslovak
Checoslovaquia [tʃekosloˈβakja] *nf* (*Hist*) Czechoslovakia
cheque [ˈtʃeke] *nm* cheque (*BRIT*), check (*US*); **cobrar un ~** to cash a cheque; **cheque al portador** cheque payable to bearer; **cheque de viaje** traveller's cheque (*BRIT*), traveler's check (*US*); **cheque en blanco** blank cheque
chequeo [tʃeˈkeo] *nm* (*Med*) check-up; (*Auto*) service
chequera [tʃeˈkera] (*LAM*) *nf* chequebook (*BRIT*), checkbook (*US*)
chévere [ˈtʃeβere] (*LAM: fam*) *adj* great
chícharo [ˈtʃitʃaro] (*MÉX, CAM*) *nm* pea
chichón [tʃiˈtʃon] *nm* bump, lump
chicle [ˈtʃikle] *nm* chewing gum
chico, -a [ˈtʃiko, a] *adj* small, little ▷ *nm/f* (*niño*) child; (*muchacho*) boy/girl
chiflado, -a [tʃiˈflaðo, a] *adj* crazy
chiflar [tʃiˈflar] *vt* to hiss, boo
chilango, -a [tʃiˈlango, a] (*MÉX*) *adj* of o from Mexico City
Chile [ˈtʃile] *nm* Chile; **chileno, -a** *adj, nm/f* Chilean
chile [ˈtʃile] *nm* chilli pepper
chillar [tʃiˈʎar] *vi* (*persona*) to yell, scream; (*animal salvaje*) to howl; (*cerdo*) to squeal
chillido [tʃiˈʎiðo] *nm* (*de persona*) yell, scream; (*de animal*) howl
chimenea [tʃimeˈnea] *nf* chimney; (*hogar*) fireplace
China [ˈtʃina] *nf* (*tb*: **la ~**) China
chinche [ˈtʃintʃe] *nf* (*insecto*) (bed)bug; (*Tec*) drawing pin (*BRIT*), thumbtack (*US*) ▷ *nmf* nuisance, pest
chincheta [tʃinˈtʃeta] *nf* drawing pin (*BRIT*), thumbtack (*US*)
chingada [tʃinˈgaða] (*MÉX: fam!*) *nf*: **hijo de la ~** bastard
chino, -a [ˈtʃino, a] *adj, nm/f* Chinese ▷ *nm* (*Ling*) Chinese
chipirón [tʃipiˈron] *nm* (*Zool, Culin*)

squid

Chipre ['tʃipre] nf Cyprus; **chipriota** adj, nmf Cypriot

chiquillo, -a [tʃi'kiʎo, a] nm/f (fam) kid

chirimoya [tʃiri'moja] nf custard apple

chiringuito [tʃirin'ɣito] nm small open-air bar

chiripa [tʃi'ripa] nf fluke

chirriar [tʃi'rrjar] vi to creak, squeak

chirrido [tʃi'rriðo] nm creak(ing), squeak(ing)

chisme ['tʃisme] nm (habladurías) piece of gossip; (fam: objeto) thingummyjig

chismoso, -a [tʃis'moso, a] adj gossiping ▷ nm/f gossip

chispa ['tʃispa] nf spark; (fig) sparkle; (ingenio) wit; (fam) drunkenness

chispear [tʃispe'ar] vi (lloviznar) to drizzle

chiste ['tʃiste] nm joke, funny story

chistoso, -a [tʃis'toso, a] adj funny, amusing

chivo, -a ['tʃiβo, a] nm/f (billy-/nanny-)goat; **chivo expiatorio** scapegoat

chocante [tʃo'kante] adj startling; (extraño) odd; (ofensivo) shocking

chocar [tʃo'kar] vi (coches etc) to collide, crash ▷ vt to shock; (sorprender) to startle; **~ con** to collide with; (fig) to run into, run up against; **¡chócala!** (fam) put it there!

chochear [tʃotʃe'ar] vi to be senile

chocho, -a ['tʃotʃo, a] adj doddering, senile; (fig) soft, doting

choclo ['tʃoklo] (cs) nm (grano) sweet corn; (mazorca) corn on the cob

chocolate [tʃoko'late] adj, nm chocolate; **chocolatina** nf chocolate

chofer [tʃo'fer] nm = **chófer**

chófer ['tʃofer] nm driver

chollo ['tʃoʎo] (ESP: fam) nm bargain, snip

choque etc ['tʃoke] vb V **chocar** ▷ nm (impacto) impact; (golpe) jolt; (Auto)

crash; (fig) conflict; **choque frontal** head-on collision

chorizo [tʃo'riθo] nm hard pork sausage, (type of) salami

chorrada [tʃo'rraða] (ESP: fam) nf: **¡es una ~!** that's crap! (!); **decir ~s** to talk crap (!)

chorrear [tʃorre'ar] vi to gush (out), spout (out); (gotear) to drip, trickle

chorro ['tʃorro] nm jet; (fig) stream

choza ['tʃoθa] nf hut, shack

chubasco [tʃu'βasko] nm squall

chubasquero [tʃuβas'kero] nm lightweight raincoat

chuchería [tʃutʃe'ria] nf trinket

chuleta [tʃu'leta] nf chop, cutlet

chulo ['tʃulo] nm (de prostituta) pimp

chupaleta [tʃupa'leta] (MÉX) nf lollipop

chupar [tʃu'par] vt to suck; (absorber) to absorb; **chuparse** vr to grow thin

chupete [tʃu'pete] (ESP, cs) nm dummy (BRIT), pacifier (US)

chupetín [tʃupe'tin] (RPL) nf lollipop

chupito [tʃu'pito] (fam) nm shot

chupón [tʃu'pon] nm (piruleta) lollipop; (LAM: chupete) dummy (BRIT), pacifier (US)

churro ['tʃurro] nm (type of) fritter

chusma ['tʃusma] nf rabble, mob

chutar [tʃu'tar] vi to shoot (at goal)

Cía abr (= compañía) Co.

cianuro [θja'nuro] nm cyanide

cibercafé [θiβerka'fe] nm cybercafé

cibernauta [θiβer'nauta] nmf web surfer, Internet user

ciberterrorista [θiβerterro'rista] nmf cyberterrorist

cicatriz [θika'triθ] nf scar; **cicatrizarse** vr to heal (up), form a scar

ciclismo [θi'klismo] nm cycling

ciclista [θi'klista] adj cycle cpd ▷ nmf cyclist

ciclo ['θiklo] nm cycle; **cicloturismo** nm touring by bicycle

ciclón [θi'klon] nm cyclone

ciego, -a ['θjeɣo, a] adj blind ▷ nm/f

blind man/woman

cielo ['θjelo] nm sky; (Rel) heaven; **¡~s!** good heavens!

ciempiés [θjem'pjes] nm inv centipede

cien [θjen] num V **ciento**

ciencia ['θjenθja] nf science; **ciencias** nfpl (Escol) science sg; **ciencia-ficción** nf science fiction

científico, -a [θjen'tifiko, a] adj scientific ▷ nm/f scientist

ciento ['θjento] num hundred; **pagar al 10 por ~** to pay at 10 per cent; V tb **cien**

cierre etc ['θjerre] vb V **cerrar** ▷ nm closing, shutting; (con llave) locking; (LAM: cremallera) zip (fastener)

cierro etc vb V **cerrar**

cierto, -a ['θjerto, a] adj sure, certain; (un tal) a certain; (correcto) right, correct; **por ~** by the way; **~ hombre** a certain man; **ciertas personas** certain o some people; **sí, es ~** yes, that's correct

ciervo ['θjerβo] nm deer; (macho) stag

cifra ['θifra] nf number; (secreta) code; **cifrar** [θi'frar] vt to code, write in code

cigala [θi'xala] nf Norway lobster

cigarra [θi'xarra] nf cicada

cigarrillo [θixa'rriʎo] nm cigarette

cigarro [θi'xarro] nm cigarette; (puro) cigar

cigüeña [θi'xweɲa] nf stork

cilíndrico, -a [θi'lindriko, a] adj cylindrical

cilindro [θi'lindro] nm cylinder

cima ['θima] nf (de montaña) top, peak; (de árbol) top; (fig) height

cimentar [θimen'tar] vt to lay the foundations of; (fig: fundar) to found

cimiento [θi'mjento] nm foundation

cincel [θin'θel] nm chisel

cinco ['θinko] num five

cincuenta [θin'kwenta] num fifty

cine ['θine] nm cinema; **cinematográfico, -a** [θinemato'xrafiko, a] adj cine-,

film cpd

cínico, -a ['θiniko, a] adj cynical ▷ nm/f cynic

cinismo [θi'nismo] nm cynicism

cinta ['θinta] nf band, strip; (de tela) ribbon; (película) reel; (de máquina de escribir) ribbon; **cinta adhesiva/aislante** sticky/insulating tape; **cinta de vídeo** videotape; **cinta magnetofónica** tape; **cinta métrica** tape measure

cintura [θin'tura] nf waist

cinturón [θintu'ron] nm belt; **cinturón de seguridad** safety belt

ciprés [θi'pres] nm cypress (tree)

circo ['θirko] nm circus

circuito [θir'kwito] nm circuit

circulación [θirkula'θjon] nf circulation; (Auto) traffic

circular [θirku'lar] adj, nf circular ▷ vi, vt to circulate ▷ vi (Auto) to drive; **"circule por la derecha"** "keep (to the) right"

círculo ['θirkulo] nm circle; **círculo vicioso** vicious circle

circunferencia [θirkunfe'renθja] nf circumference

circunstancia [θirkuns'tanθja] nf circumstance

cirio ['θirjo] nm (wax) candle

ciruela [θi'rwela] nf plum; **ciruela pasa** prune

cirugía [θiru'xia] nf surgery; **cirugía estética** o **plástica** plastic surgery

cirujano [θiru'xano] nm surgeon

cisne ['θisne] nm swan

cisterna [θis'terna] nf cistern, tank

cita ['θita] nf appointment, meeting; (de novios) date; (referencia) quotation

citación [θita'θjon] nf (Jur) summons sg

citar [θi'tar] vt (gen) to make an appointment with; (Jur) to summons; (un autor, texto) to quote; **citarse** vr: **se ~on en el cine** they arranged to meet at the cinema

cítricos ['θitrikos] nmpl citrus fruit(s

ciudad [θju'ðað] nf town; (más

grande) city; **ciudadano, -a** *nm/f* citizen

cívico, -a ['θiβiko, a] *adj* civic

civil [θi'βil] *adj* civil ▷ *nm* (*guardia*) policeman; **civilización** [θiβiliθa'θjon] *nf* civilization; **civilizar** [θiβili'θar] *vt* to civilize

cizaña [θi'θaɲa] *nf* (*fig*) discord

cl. *abr* (= *centilitro*) cl.

clamor [kla'mor] *nm* clamour, protest

clandestino, -a [klandes'tino, a] *adj* clandestine; (*Pol*) underground

clara ['klara] *nf* (*de huevo*) egg white

claraboya [klara'βoja] *nf* skylight

clarear [klare'ar] *vi* (*el día*) to dawn; (*el cielo*) to clear up, brighten up; **clarearse** *vr* to be transparent

claridad [klari'ðað] *nf* (*de día*) brightness; (*de estilo*) clarity

clarificar [klarifi'kar] *vt* to clarify

clarinete [klari'nete] *nm* clarinet

claro, -a ['klaro, a] *adj* clear; (*luminoso*) bright; (*color*) light; (*evidente*) clear, evident; (*poco espeso*) thin ▷ *nm* (*en bosque*) clearing ▷ *adv* clearly ▷ *excl*: **¡~ que sí!** of course!; **¡~ que no!** of course not!

clase ['klase] *nf* class; **dar ~(s)** to teach; **clase alta/media/obrera** upper/middle/working class; **clases particulares** private lessons *o* tuition *sg*

clásico, -a ['klasiko, a] *adj* classical

clasificación [klasifika'θjon] *nf* classification; (*Deporte*) league (table)

clasificar [klasifi'kar] *vt* to classify

claustro ['klaustro] *nm* cloister

cláusula ['klausula] *nf* clause

clausura [klau'sura] *nf* closing, closure

clavar [kla'βar] *vt* (*clavo*) to hammer in; (*cuchillo*) to stick, thrust

clave ['klaβe] *nf* key; (*Mús*) clef; **clave de acceso** password; **clave lada** (*MÉX*) dialling (*BRIT*) *o* area (*US*) code

clavel [kla'βel] *nm* carnation

clavícula [kla'βikula] *nf* collar bone

clavija [kla'βixa] *nf* peg, dowel, pin; (*Elec*) plug

clavo ['klaβo] *nm* (*de metal*) nail; (*Bot*) clove

claxon ['klakson] (*pl* **~s**) *nm* horn

clérigo ['klerixo] *nm* priest

clero ['klero] *nm* clergy

clicar [kli'kar] *vi* (*Internet*) to click; **~ en el icono** to click on an icon; **~ dos veces** to double-click

cliché [kli'tʃe] *nm* cliché; (*Foto*) negative

cliente, -a ['kljente, a] *nm/f* client, customer; **clientela** [kljen'tela] *nf* clientele, customers *pl*

clima ['klima] *nm* climate; **climatizado, -a** [klimati'θaðo, a] *adj* air-conditioned

clímax ['klimaks] *nm inv* climax

clínica ['klinika] *nf* clinic; (*particular*) private hospital

clip [klip] (*pl* **~s**) *nm* paper clip

clítoris ['klitoris] *nm inv* (*Anat*) clitoris

cloaca [klo'aka] *nf* sewer

clonar [klo'nar] *vt* to clone

cloro ['kloro] *nm* chlorine

clóset ['kloset] (*MÉX*) *nm* cupboard

club [klub] (*pl* **~s** *o* **~es**) *nm* club; **club nocturno** night club

cm *abr* (= *centímetro, centímetros*) cm

coágulo [ko'axulo] *nm* clot

coalición [koali'θjon] *nf* coalition

coartada [koar'taða] *nf* alibi

coartar [koar'tar] *vt* to limit, restrict

coba ['koβa] *nf*: **dar ~ a algn** (*adular*) to suck up to sb

cobarde [ko'βarðe] *adj* cowardly ▷ *nm* coward; **cobardía** *nf* cowardice

cobaya [ko'βaja] *nf* guinea pig

cobertizo [koβer'tiθo] *nm* shelter

cobertura [koβer'tura] *nf* cover; **aquí no hay ~** (*Tel*) I can't get a signal

cobija [ko'βixa] (*LAM*) *nf* blanket; **cobijar** [koβi'xar] *vt* (*cubrir*) to cover; (*proteger*) to shelter; **cobijo** *nm* shelter

cobra ['koβra] *nf* cobra

cobrador, a [koβra'ðor, a] *nm/f* (*de*

autobús) conductor/conductress; (*de impuestos, gas*) collector

cobrar [ko'βɾaɾ] *vt* (*cheque*) to cash; (*sueldo*) to collect, draw; (*objeto*) to recover; (*precio*) to charge; (*deuda*) to collect ▷ *vi* to be paid; **cóbrese al entregar** cash on delivery; **¿me cobra, por favor?** how much do I owe you?, can I have the bill, please?

cobre ['koβɾe] *nm* copper; **cobres** *nmpl* (*Mús*) brass instruments

cobro ['koβɾo] *nm* (*de cheque*) cashing; **presentar al ~** to cash

cocaína [koka'ina] *nf* cocaine

cocción [kok'θjon] *nf* (*Culin*) cooking; (*en agua*) boiling

cocer [ko'θeɾ] *vt, vi* to cook; (*en agua*) to boil; (*en horno*) to bake

coche ['kotʃe] *nm* (*Auto*) car (BRIT), automobile (US); (*de tren, de caballos*) coach, carriage; (*para niños*) pram (BRIT), baby carriage (US); **ir en ~** to drive; **coche celular** police van; **coche de bomberos** fire engine; **coche de carreras** racing car; **coche fúnebre** hearse; **coche-cama** (*pl* **coches-cama**) *nm* (*Ferro*) sleeping car, sleeper

cochera [ko'tʃeɾa] *nf* garage; (*de autobuses, trenes*) depot

coche restaurante (*pl* **coches restaurante**) *nm* (*Ferro*) dining car, diner

cochinillo [kotʃi'niʎo] *nm* (*Culin*) suckling pig, sucking pig

cochino, -a [ko'tʃino, a] *adj* filthy, dirty ▷ *nm/f* pig

cocido [ko'θiðo] *nm* stew

cocina [ko'θina] *nf* kitchen; (*aparato*) cooker, stove; (*acto*) cookery; **cocina eléctrica/de gas** electric/gas cooker; **cocina francesa** French cuisine; **cocinar** *vt, vi* to cook

cocinero, -a [koθi'neɾo, a] *nm/f* cook

coco ['koko] *nm* coconut

cocodrilo [koko'ðɾilo] *nm* crocodile

cocotero [koko'teɾo] *nm* coconut palm

cóctel ['koktel] *nm* cocktail; **cóctel molotov** petrol bomb, Molotov cocktail

codazo [ko'ðaθo] *nm*: **dar un ~ a algn** to nudge sb

codicia [ko'ðiθja] *nf* greed; **codiciar** *vt* to covet

código ['koðiχo] *nm* code; **código civil** common law; **código de barras** bar code; **código de circulación** highway code; **código de la zona** (LAM) dialling (BRIT) o area (US) code; **código postal** postcode

codillo [ko'ðiʎo] *nm* (*Zool*) knee; (*Tec*) elbow (joint)

codo ['koðo] *nm* (*Anat, de tubo*) elbow; (*Zool*) knee

codorniz [koðoɾ'niθ] *nf* quail

coexistir [koe(k)sis'tiɾ] *vi* to coexist

cofradía [kofɾa'ðia] *nf* brotherhood, fraternity

cofre ['kofɾe] *nm* (*de joyas*) case; (*de dinero*) chest

coger [ko'xeɾ] (ESP) *vt* to take (hold of); (*objeto caído*) to pick up; (*frutas*) to pick, harvest; (*resfriado, ladrón, pelota*) to catch ▷ *vi*: **~ por el buen camino** to take the right road; **cogerse** *vr* (*el dedo*) to catch; **~se a algo** to get hold of sth

cogollo [ko'ɣoʎo] *nm* (*de lechuga*) heart

cogote [ko'ɣote] *nm* back o nape of the neck

cohabitar [koaβi'taɾ] *vi* to live together, cohabit

coherente [koe'ɾente] *adj* coherent

cohesión [koe'sjon] *nm* cohesion

cohete [ko'ete] *nm* rocket

cohibido, -a [koi'βiðo, a] *adj* (*Psico*) inhibited; (*tímido*) shy

coincidencia [koinθi'ðenθja] *nf* coincidence

coincidir [koinθi'ðiɾ] *vi* (*en idea*) to coincide, agree; (*en lugar*) to coincid◄

coito [ko'ito] *nm* intercourse, coitus

coja *etc vb* V **coger**

cojear [koxe'aɾ] *vi* (*persona*) to limp,

hobble; (*mueble*) to wobble, rock
cojera [ko'xera] *nf* limp
cojín [ko'xin] *nm* cushion
cojo, -a etc ['koxo, a] *vb* V **coger**
▷ *adj* (*que no puede andar*) lame,
crippled; (*mueble*) wobbly ▷ *nm/f* lame
person, cripple
cojón [ko'xon] (*fam!*) *nm*: ¡**cojones!**
shit! (*!*); **cojonudo, -a** (*fam*) *adj* great,
fantastic
col [kol] *nf* cabbage; **coles de
Bruselas** Brussels sprouts
cola ['kola] *nf* tail; (*de gente*) queue;
(*lugar*) end, last place; (*para pegar*) glue,
gum; **hacer ~** to queue (up)
colaborador, a [kolaβora'ðor, a]
nm/f collaborator
colaborar [kolaβo'rar] *vi* to
collaborate
colada [ko'laða] (*ESP*) *nf*: **hacer la ~** to
do the washing
colador [kola'ðor] *nm* (*para líquidos*)
strainer; (*para verduras etc*) colander
colapso [ko'lapso] *nm* collapse
colar [ko'lar] *vt* (*líquido*) to strain
off; (*metal*) to cast ▷ *vi* to ooze, seep
(through); **colarse** *vr* to jump the
queue; **~se en** to get into without
paying; (*fiesta*) to gatecrash
colcha ['koltʃa] *nf* bedspread
colchón [kol'tʃon] *nm* mattress;
colchón inflable air bed *o* mattress
colchoneta [koltʃo'neta] *nf* (*en
gimnasio*) mat; (*de playa*) air bed
colección [kolek'θjon] *nf*
collection; **coleccionar** *vt* to collect;
coleccionista *nmf* collector
colecta [ko'lekta] *nf* collection
colectivo, -a [kolek'tiβo, a] *adj*
collective, joint ▷ *nm* (*ARG: autobús*)
(small) bus
colega [ko'leɣa] *nmf* colleague; (*fam*)
(*ESP: amigo*) mate
colegial, a [kole'xjal, a] *nm/f*
schoolboy(-girl)
colegio [ko'lexjo] *nm* college;
(*escuela*) school; (*de abogados etc*)
association; **colegio electoral** polling

station; **colegio mayor** (*ESP*) hall of
residence

- **COLEGIO**
-
- A **colegio** is normally a private
- primary or secondary school.
- In the state system it means a
- primary school although there
- are also called **escuelas**. State
- secondary schools are called
- **institutos**.

cólera ['kolera] *nf* (*ira*) anger; (*Med*)
cholera
colesterol [koleste'rol] *nm*
cholesterol
coleta [ko'leta] *nf* pigtail
colgante [kol'ɣante] *adj* hanging
▷ *nm* (*joya*) pendant
colgar [kol'ɣar] *vt* to hang (up);
(*ropa*) to hang out ▷ *vi* to hang; (*Tel*)
to hang up
cólico ['koliko] *nm* colic
coliflor [koli'flor] *nf* cauliflower
colilla [ko'liʎa] *nf* cigarette end, butt
colina [ko'lina] *nf* hill
colisión [koli'sjon] *nf* collision,
colisión frontal head-on crash
collar [ko'ʎar] *nm* necklace; (*de
perro*) collar
colmar [kol'mar] *vt* to fill to the brim;
(*fig*) to fulfil, realize
colmena [kol'mena] *nf* beehive
colmillo [kol'miʎo] *nm* (*diente*) eye
tooth; (*de elefante*) tusk; (*de perro*) fang
colmo ['kolmo] *nm*: ¡**es el ~!** it's
the limit!
colocación [koloka'θjon] *nf* (*acto*)
placing; (*empleo*) job, position
colocar [kolo'kar] *vt* to place, put,
position; (*dinero*) to invest; (*poner en
empleo*) to find a job for; **colocarse** *vr*
to get a job
Colombia [ko'lombja] *nf* Colombia;
colombiano, -a *adj*, *nm/f* Colombian
colonia [ko'lonja] *nf* colony; (*agua
de colonia*) cologne; (*MÉX: de casas*)

residential area; **colonia proletaria** (MÉX) shantytown

colonización [koloniθa'θjon] nf colonization; **colonizador, a** [koloniθa'ðor, a] adj colonizing ▷ nm/f colonist, settler

colonizar [koloni'θar] vt to colonize

coloquio [ko'lokjo] nm conversation; (congreso) conference

color [ko'lor] nm colour

colorado, -a [kolo'raðo, a] adj (rojo) red; (MÉX: chiste) smutty, rude

colorante [kolo'rante] nm colouring

colorear [kolore'ar] vt to colour

colorete [kolo'rete] nm blusher

colorido [kolo'riðo] nm colouring

columna [ko'lumna] nf column; (pilar) pillar; (apoyo) support; (tb: ~ **vertebral**) spine, spinal column; (fig) backbone

columpiar [kolum'pjar] vt to swing; **columpiarse** vr to swing; **columpio** nm swing

coma ['koma] nf comma ▷ nm (Med) coma

comadre [ko'maðre] nf (madrina) godmother; (chismosa) gossip; **comadrona** nf midwife

comal [ko'mal] (MÉX, CAM) nm griddle

comandante [koman'dante] nm commandant

comarca [ko'marka] nf region

comba ['komba] nf (cuerda) skipping rope; **saltar a la ~** to skip

combate [kom'bate] nm fight

combatir [komba'tir] vt to fight, combat

combinación [kombina'θjon] nf combination; (Quím) compound; (prenda) slip

combinar [kombi'nar] vt to combine

combustible [kombus'tiβle] nm fuel

comedia [ko'meðja] nf comedy; (Teatro) play, drama; **comediante** [kome'ðjante] nmf (comic) actor/actress

comedido, -a [kome'ðiðo, a] adj moderate

comedor, a [kome'ðor, a] nm (habitación) dining room; (cantina) canteen

comensal [komen'sal] nmf fellow guest (o diner)

comentar [komen'tar] vt to comment on; **comentario** [komen'tarjo] nm comment, remark; (literario) commentary; **comentarios** nmpl (chismes) gossip sg; **comentarista** [komenta'rista] nmf commentator

comenzar [komen'θar] vt, vi to begin, start; **~ a hacer algo** to begin o start doing sth

comer [ko'mer] vt to eat; (Damas, Ajedrez) to take, capture ▷ vi to eat; (ESP, MÉX: almorzar) to have lunch; **comerse** vr to eat up

comercial [komer'θjal] adj commercial; (relativo al negocio) business cpd; **comercializar** vt (producto) to market; (pey) to commercialize

comerciante [komer'θjante] nmf trader, merchant

comerciar [komer'θjar] vi to trade, do business

comercio [ko'merθjo] nm commerce, trade; (tienda) shop, store; (negocio) business; (fig) dealings pl; **comercio electrónico** e-commerce; **comercio exterior/interior** foreign/domestic trade

comestible [komes'tiβle] adj eatable, edible; **comestibles** nmpl food sg, foodstuffs

cometa [ko'meta] nm comet ▷ nf kite

cometer [kome'ter] vt to commit

cometido [kome'tiðo] nm task, assignment

cómic ['komik] nm comic

comicios [ko'miθjos] nmpl elections

cómico, -a ['komiko, a] adj comic(al) ▷ nm/f comedian

comida [ko'miða] nf (*alimento*) food; (*almuerzo, cena*) meal; (*de mediodía*) lunch; **comida basura** junk food; **comida chatarra** (MÉX) junk food

comidilla [komi'ðiʎa] nf: **ser la ~ del barrio** o **pueblo** to be the talk of the town

comienzo *etc* [ko'mjenθo] *vb* V **comenzar** ▷ *nm* beginning, start

comillas [komi'miʎas] nfpl quotation marks

comilona [komi'lona] (*fam*) nf blow-out

comino [ko'mino] nm: **(no) me importa un ~** I don't give a damn

comisaría [komisa'ria] nf (*de policía*) police station; (*Mil*) commissariat

comisario [komi'sarjo] nm (*Mil etc*) commissary; (*Pol*) commissar

comisión [komi'sjon] nf commission; **Comisiones Obreras** (ESP) Communist trade union

comité [komi'te] (*pl* ~**s**) nm committee

comitiva [komi'tiβa] nf retinue

como ['komo] *adv* as; (*tal* ~) like; (*aproximadamente*) about, approximately ▷ *conj* (*ya que, puesto que*) as, since; **¡~ no!** of course!; **~ no lo haga hoy** unless he does it today; **~ si** as if; **es tan alto ~ ancho** it is as high as it is wide

cómo ['komo] *adv* how?, why? ▷ *excl* what?, I beg your pardon? ▷ *nm*: **el ~ y el porqué** the whys and wherefores

cómoda ['komoða] nf chest of drawers

comodidad [komoði'ðað] nf comfort

comodín [komo'ðin] nm joker

cómodo, -a ['komoðo, a] *adj* comfortable; (*práctico, de fácil uso*) convenient

compact [kom'pakt] (*pl* ~**s**) nm (*tb*: ~ **disc**) compact disk player

compacto, -a [kom'pakto, a] *adj* compact

compadecer [kompaðe'θer] *vt* to

pity, be sorry for; **compadecerse** *vr*: **~se de** to pity, be o feel sorry for

compadre [kom'paðre] nm (*padrino*) godfather; (*amigo*) friend, pal

compañero, -a [kompa'ɲero, a] nm/f companion; (*novio*) boy/girlfriend; **compañero de clase** classmate

compañía [kompa'ɲia] nf company; **hacer ~ a algn** to keep sb company

comparación [kompara'θjon] nf comparison; **en ~ con** in comparison with

comparar [kompa'rar] *vt* to compare

comparecer [kompare'θer] *vi* to appear (in court)

comparsa [kom'parsa] nmf (*Teatro*) extra

compartimiento [komparti'mjento] nm (*Ferro*) compartment

compartir [kompar'tir] *vt* to share; (*dinero, comida etc*) to divide (up), share (out)

compás [kom'pas] nm (*Mús*) beat, rhythm; (*Mat*) compasses pl; (*Náut etc*) compass

compasión [kompa'sjon] nf compassion, pity

compasivo, -a [kompa'siβo, a] *adj* compassionate

compatible [kompa'tiβle] *adj* compatible

compatriota [kompa'trjota] nmf compatriot, fellow countryman/woman

compenetrarse [kompene'trarse] *vr* to be in tune

compensación [kompensa'θjon] nf compensation

compensar [kompen'sar] *vt* to compensate

competencia [kompe'tenθja] nf (*incumbencia*) domain, field; (*Jur, habilidad*) competence; (*rivalidad*) competition

competente [kompe'tente] *adj*

competent

competición [kompeti'θjon] nf
competition

competir [kompe'tir] vi to compete

compinche [kom'pintʃe] (LAM) nmf
mate, buddy (US)

complacer [kompla'θer] vt to
please; **complacerse** vr to be pleased

complaciente [kompla'θjente] adj
kind, obliging, helpful

complejo, -a [kom'plexo, a] adj,
nm complex

complementario, -a
[komplemen'tarjo, a] adj
complementary

completar [komple'tar] vt to
complete

completo, -a [kom'pleto, a] adj
complete; (perfecto) perfect; (lleno) full
▷ nm full complement

complicado, -a [kompli'kaðo,
a] adj complicated; **estar ~ en** to be
mixed up in

cómplice ['kompliθe] nmf
accomplice

complot [kom'plo(t)] (pl ~s) nm plot

componer [kompo'ner] vt (Mús,
Literatura, Imprenta) to compose; (algo
roto) to mend, repair; (arreglar) to
arrange; **componerse** vr: **~se de** to
consist of

comportamiento
[komporta'mjento] nm behaviour,
conduct

comportarse [kompor'tarse] vr
to behave

composición [komposi'θjon] nf
composition

compositor, a [komposi'tor, a]
nm/f composer

compostura [kompos'tura] nf
(actitud) composure

compra ['kompra] nf purchase;
hacer la ~ to do the shopping; **ir de ~s**
to go shopping; **comprador, a** nm/f
buyer, purchaser; **comprar** [kom'prar]
vt to buy, purchase

comprender [kompren'der] vt to

understand; (incluir) to comprise,
include

comprensión [kompren'sjon] nf
understanding; **comprensivo, -a** adj
(actitud) understanding

compresa [kom'presa] nf (para
mujer) sanitary towel (BRIT) o napkin
(US)

comprimido, -a [kompri'miðo, a]
adj compressed ▷ nm (Med) pill, tablet

comprimir [kompri'mir] vt to
compress; (Internet) to zip

comprobante [kompro'βante] nm
proof; (Com) voucher; **comprobante de
compra** proof of purchase

comprobar [kompro'βar] vt to
check; (probar) to prove; (Tec) to
check, test

comprometer [komprome'ter]
vt to compromise; (poner en peligro)
to endanger; **comprometerse** vr
(involucrarse) to get involved

compromiso [kompro'miso] nm
(obligación) obligation; (cometido)
commitment; (convenio) agreement;
(apuro) awkward situation

compuesto, -a [kom'pwesto, a]
adj: **~ de** composed of, made up of ▷ nm
compound

computadora [komputa'ðora]
(LAM) nf computer; **computadora
central** mainframe (computer);
computadora personal personal
computer

cómputo ['komputo] nm calculation

comulgar [komul'ɣar] vi to receive
communion

común [ko'mun] adj common
▷ nm: **el ~** the community

comunicación [komunika'θjon] nf
communication; (informe) report

comunicado [komuni'kaðo] nm
announcement; **comunicado de
prensa** press release

comunicar [komuni'kar] vt, vi to
communicate; **comunicarse** vr to
communicate; **está comunicando**
(Tel) the line's engaged (BRIT) o

busy (US); **comunicativo, -a** adj
communicative

comunidad [komuni'ðað] nf
community; **comunidad autónoma**
(ESP) autonomous region; **Comunidad
(Económica) Europea** European
(Economic) Community; **comunidad
de vecinos** residents' association

comunión [komu'njon] nf
communion

comunismo [komu'nismo] nm
communism; **comunista** adj, nmf
communist

○ **PALABRA CLAVE**

con [kon] prep **1**(medio, compañía)
with; **comer con cuchara** to eat with
a spoon; **pasear con algn** to go for a
walk with sb
2 (a pesar de): **con todo, merece
nuestros respetos** all the same, he
deserves our respect
3 (para con): **es muy bueno para con
los niños** he's very good with (the)
children
4 (+ infin): **con llegar a las seis estará
bien** if you come by six it will be fine
▷ conj: **con que: será suficiente con
que le escribas** it will be sufficient if
you write to her

concebir [konθe'βir] vt, vi to
conceive

conceder [konθe'ðer] vt to concede

concejal, a [konθe'xal, a] nm/f
town councillor

concentración [konθentra'θjon] nf
concentration

concentrar [konθen'trar] vt to
concentrate; **concentrarse** vr to
concentrate

concepto [kon'θepto] nm concept

concernir [konθer'nir] vi to concern;
en lo que concierne a ... as far as ... is
concerned; **en lo que a mí concierne**
as far as I'm concerned

concertar [konθer'tar] vt (Mús)

to harmonize; (acordar: precio) to
agree; (: tratado) to conclude; (trato)
to arrange, fix up; (combinar: esfuerzos)
to coordinate ▷ vi to harmonize,
be in tune

concesión [konθe'sjon] nf
concession

concesionario [konθesjo'narjo] nm
(licensed) dealer, agent

concha ['kontʃa] nf shell

conciencia [kon'θjenθja] nf
conscience; **tomar ~ de** to become
aware of; **tener la ~ tranquila** to have
a clear conscience

concienciar [konθjen'θjar] vt to
make aware; **concienciarse** vr to
become aware

concienzudo, -a [konθjen'θuðo, a]
adj conscientious

concierto etc [kon'θjerto] vb V
concertar ▷ nm concert; (obra)
concerto

conciliar [konθi'ljar] vt to reconcile;
~ el sueño to get to sleep

concilio [kon'θiljo] nm council

conciso, -a [kon'θiso, a] adj concise

concluir [konklu'ir] vt, vi to
conclude; **concluirse** vr to conclude

conclusión [konklu'sjon] nf
conclusion

concordar [konkor'ðar] vt to
reconcile ▷ vi to agree, tally

concordia [kon'korðja] nf harmony

concretar [konkre'tar] vt to
make concrete, make more specific;
concretarse vr to become more
definite

concreto, -a [kon'kreto, a] adj,
nm (LAM: hormigón) concrete; **en ~** (en
resumen) to sum up; (específicamente)
specifically; **no hay nada en ~** there's
nothing definite

concurrido, -a [konku'rriðo, a] adj
(calle) busy; (local, reunión) crowded

concursante [konkur'sante] nmf
competitor

concurso [kon'kurso] nm (de público)
crowd; (Escol, Deporte, competencia)

competition; (*ayuda*) help, cooperation

condal [kon'dal] *adj*: **la Ciudad C~** Barcelona

conde ['konde] *nm* count

condecoración [kondekora'θjon] *nf* (*Mil*) medal

condena [kon'dena] *nf* sentence; **condenación** [kondena'θjon] *nf* condemnation; (*Rel*) damnation; **condenar** [konde'nar] *vt* to condemn; (*Jur*) to convict; **condenarse** *vr* (*Rel*) to be damned

condesa [kon'desa] *nf* countess

condición [kondi'θjon] *nf* condition; **a ~ de que ...** on condition that ...; **condicional** *adj* conditional

condimento [kondi'mento] *nm* seasoning

condominio [kondo'minjo] (*LAM*) *nm* condominium

condón [kon'don] *nm* condom

conducir [kondu'θir] *vt* to take, convey; (*Auto*) to drive ▷ *vi* to drive; (*fig*) to lead; **conducirse** *vr* to behave

conducta [kon'dukta] *nf* conduct, behaviour

conducto [kon'dukto] *nm* pipe, tube; (*fig*) channel

conductor, a [konduk'tor, a] *adj* leading, guiding ▷ *nm* (*Física*) conductor; (*de vehículo*) driver

conduje *etc vb* V **conducir**

conduzco *etc vb* V **conducir**

conectado, -a [konek'taðo, a] *adj* (*Inform*) on-line

conectar [konek'tar] *vt* to connect (up); (*enchufar*) plug in

conejillo [kone'xiʎo] *nm*: **~ de Indias** guinea pig

conejo [ko'nexo] *nm* rabbit

conexión [konek'sjon] *nf* connection

confección [confe(k)'θjon] *nf* preparation; (*industria*) clothing industry

confeccionar [konfekθjo'nar] *vt* to make (up)

conferencia [konfe'renθja] *nf* conference; (*lección*) lecture; (*ESP Tel*) call; **conferencia de prensa** press conference

conferir [konfe'rir] *vt* to award

confesar [konfe'sar] *vt* to confess, admit

confesión [konfe'sjon] *nf* confession

confesionario [konfesjo'narjo] *nm* confessional

confeti [kon'feti] *nm* confetti

confiado, -a [kon'fjaðo, a] *adj* (*crédulo*) trusting; (*seguro*) confident

confianza [kon'fjanθa] *nf* trust; (*seguridad*) confidence; (*familiaridad*) intimacy, familiarity

confiar [kon'fjar] *vt* to entrust ▷ *vi* to trust; **~ en algn** to trust sb; **~ en que ...** to hope that ...

confidencial [konfiðen'θjal] *adj* confidential

confidente [konfi'ðente] *nmf* confidant/e; (*policial*) informer

configurar [konfiɣu'rar] *vt* to shape, form

confín [kon'fin] *nm* limit; **confines** *nmpl* confines, limits

confirmar [konfir'mar] *vt* to confirm

confiscar [konfis'kar] *vt* to confiscate

confite [kon'fite] *nm* sweet (*BRIT*), candy (*US*); **confitería** [konfite'ria] *nf* (*tienda*) confectioner's (shop)

confitura [konfi'tura] *nf* jam

conflictivo, -a [konflik'tiβo, a] *adj* (*asunto, propuesta*) controversial; (*país, situación*) troubled

conflicto [kon'flikto] *nm* conflict; (*fig*) clash

confluir [kon'flwir] *vi* (*ríos*) to meet; (*gente*) to gather

conformar [konfor'mar] *vt* to shape, fashion ▷ *vi* to agree; **conformarse** *vr* to conform; (*resignarse*) to resign o.s.; **~se con algo** to be happy with sth

conforme [kon'forme] *adj*

(correspondiente): **~ con** in line with; *(de acuerdo):* **estar ~s (con algo)** to be in agreement (with sth) ▷ *adv* as ▷ *excl* agreed! ▷ *prep:* **~ a** in accordance with; **quedarse ~ (con algo)** to be satisfied (with sth)

confortable [konfor'taβle] *adj* comfortable

confortar [konfor'tar] *vt* to comfort

confrontar [konfron'tar] *vt* to confront; *(dos personas)* to bring face to face; *(cotejar)* to compare

confundir [konfun'dir] *vt (equivocar)* to mistake, confuse; *(turbar)* to confuse; **confundirse** *vr (turbarse)* to get confused; *(equivocarse)* to make a mistake; *(mezclarse)* to mix

confusión [konfu'sjon] *nf* confusion

confuso, -a [kon'fuso, a] *adj* confused

congelado, -a [konxe'laðo, a] *adj* frozen; **congelados** *nmpl* frozen food(s); **congelador** *nm (aparato)* freezer, deep freeze

congelar [konxe'lar] *vt* to freeze; **congelarse** *vr (sangre, grasa)* to congeal

congeniar [konxe'njar] *vi* to get on *(BRIT) o* along *(US)* well

congestión [konxes'tjon] *nf* congestion

congestionar [konxestjo'nar] *vt* to congest

congraciarse [kongra'θjarse] *vr* to ingratiate o.s.

congratular [kongratu'lar] *vt* to congratulate

congregar [kongre'ɣar] *vt* to gather together; **congregarse** *vr* to gather together

congresista [kongre'sista] *nmf* delegate, congressman/woman

congreso [kon'greso] *nm* congress

conjetura [konxe'tura] *nf* guess; **conjeturar** *vt* to guess

conjugar [konxu'ɣar] *vt* to combine, fit together; *(Ling)* to conjugate

conjunción [konxun'θjon] *nf* conjunction

conjunto, -a [kon'xunto, a] *adj* joint, united ▷ *nm* whole; *(Mús)* band; **en ~** as a whole

conmemoración [konmemora'θjon] *nf* commemoration

conmemorar [konmemo'rar] *vt* to commemorate

conmigo [kon'miɣo] *pron* with me

conmoción [konmo'θjon] *nf* shock; *(fig)* upheaval; **conmoción cerebral** *(Med)* concussion

conmovedor, a [konmoβe'ðor, a] *adj* touching, moving; *(emocionante)* exciting

conmover [konmo'βer] *vt* to shake, disturb; *(fig)* to move

conmutador [konmuta'ðor] *nm* switch; *(LAM: centralita)* switchboard; *(: central)* telephone exchange

cono ['kono] *nm* cone; **Cono Sur** Southern Cone

conocedor, a [konoθe'ðor, a] *adj* expert, knowledgeable ▷ *nm/f* expert

conocer [kono'θer] *vt* to know; *(por primera vez)* to meet, get to know; *(entender)* to know about; *(reconocer)* to recognize; **conocerse** *vr (una persona)* to know o.s.; *(dos personas)* to (get to) know each other; **~ a algn de vista** to know sb by sight

conocido, -a [kono'θiðo, a] *adj* (well-)known ▷ *nm/f* acquaintance

conocimiento [konoθi'mjento] *nm* knowledge; *(Med)* consciousness; **conocimientos** *nmpl (saber)* knowledge *sg*

conozco *etc vb* V **conocer**

conque ['konke] *conj* and so, so then

conquista [kon'kista] *nf* conquest; **conquistador, a** *adj* conquering ▷ *nm* conqueror; **conquistar** [konkis'tar] *vt* to conquer

consagrar [konsa'ɣrar] *vt (Rel)* to consecrate; *(fig)* to devote

consciente [kons'θjente] *adj* conscious

consecución [konseku'θjon] *nf*
acquisition; (*de fin*) attainment

consecuencia [konse'kwenθja] *nf*
consequence, outcome; (*coherencia*)
consistency

consecuente [konse'kwente] *adj*
consistent

consecutivo, -a [konseku'tiβo, a]
adj consecutive

conseguir [konse'ɣir] *vt* to get,
obtain; (*objetivo*) to attain

consejero, -a [konse'xero, a] *nm/f*
adviser, consultant; (*Pol*) councillor

consejo [kon'sexo] *nm* advice; (*Pol*)
council; **consejo de administración**
(*Com*) board of directors; **consejo de
guerra** court martial; **consejo de
ministros** cabinet meeting

consenso [kon'senso] *nm* consensus

consentimiento [konsenti'mjento]
nm consent

consentir [konsen'tir] *vt* (*permitir,
tolerar*) to consent to; (*mimar*) to
pamper, spoil; (*aguantar*) to put up with
▷ *vi* to agree, consent; **~ que algn
haga algo** to allow sb to do sth

conserje [kon'serxe] *nm* caretaker;
(*portero*) porter

conservación [konserβa'θjon]
nf conservation; (*de alimentos, vida*)
preservation

conservador, a [konserβa'ðor,
a] *adj* (*Pol*) conservative ▷ *nm/f*
conservative

conservante [konser'βante] *nm*
preservative

conservar [konser'βar] *vt* to
conserve, keep; (*alimentos, vida*) to
preserve; **conservarse** *vr* to survive

conservas [kon'serβas] *nfpl* canned
food(s) *pl*

conservatorio [konserβa'torjo] *nm*
(*Mús*) conservatoire, conservatory

considerable [konsiðe'raβle] *adj*
considerable

consideración [konsiðera'θjon] *nf*
consideration; (*estimación*) respect

considerado, -a [konsiðe'raðo, a]
adj (*atento*) considerate; (*respetado*)
respected

considerar [konsiðe'rar] *vt* to
consider

consigna [kon'siɣna] *nf* (*orden*)
order, instruction; (*para equipajes*) left-
luggage office

consigo *etc* [kon'siɣo] *vb* V
conseguir ▷ *pron* (*m*) with him; (*f*)
with her; (*Vd*) with you; (*reflexivo*)
with o.s.

consiguiendo *etc vb* V **conseguir**

consiguiente [konsi'ɣjente] *adj*
consequent; **por ~** and so, therefore,
consequently

consistente [konsis'tente] *adj*
consistent; (*sólido*) solid, firm; (*válido*)
sound

consistir [konsis'tir] *vi*: **~ en**
(*componerse de*) to consist of

consola [kon'sola] *nf* (*mueble*)
console table; (*de videojuegos*)
console

consolación [konsola'θjon] *nf*
consolation

consolar [konso'lar] *vt* to console

consolidar [konsoli'ðar] *vt* to
consolidate

consomé [konso'me] (*pl* **~s**) *nm*
consommé, clear soup

consonante [konso'nante]
adj consonant, harmonious ▷ *nf*
consonant

consorcio [kon'sorθjo] *nm*
consortium

conspiración [konspira'θjon] *nf*
conspiracy

conspirar [konspi'rar] *vi* to conspire

constancia [kon'stanθja] *nf*
constancy; **dejar ~ de** to put on record

constante [kons'tante] *adj, nf*
constant

constar [kons'tar] *vi* (*evidenciarse*) to
be clear o evident; **~ de** to consist of

constipado, -a [konsti'paðo, a]
adj: **estar ~** to have a cold ▷ *nm* cold
No confundir **constipado** con la
palabra inglesa *constipated*.

constitución [konstitu'θjon] *nf*
constitution

constituir [konstitu'ir] *vt (formar,*
componer) to constitute, make up;
(fundar, erigir, ordenar) to constitute,
establish

construcción [konstruk'θjon] *nf*
construction, building

constructor, a [konstruk'tor, a]
nm/f builder

construir [konstru'ir] *vt* to build,
construct

construyendo *etc vb* V **construir**

consuelo [kon'swelo] *nm*
consolation, solace

cónsul ['konsul] *nm* consul;
consulado *nm* consulate

consulta [kon'sulta] *nf*
consultation; *(Med)*: **horas de ~**
surgery hours; **consultar** [konsul'tar]
vt to consult; **consultar algo con**
algn to discuss sth with sb;
consultorio [konsul'torjo] *nm (Med)*
surgery

consumición [konsumi'θjon] *nf*
consumption; *(bebida)* drink; *(comida)*
food; **consumición mínima** cover
charge

consumidor, a [konsumi'ðor, a]
nm/f consumer

consumir [konsu'mir] *vt* to
consume; **consumirse** *vr* to be
consumed; *(persona)* to waste away

consumismo [konsu'mismo] *nm*
consumerism

consumo [kon'sumo] *nm*
consumption

contabilidad [kontaβili'ðað]
nf accounting, book-keeping;
(profesión) accountancy; **contable** *nmf*
accountant

contacto [kon'takto] *nm* contact;
(Auto) ignition; **estar/ponerse en ~**
con algn to be/to get in touch with sb

contado, -a [kon'taðo, a] *adj*: **~s**
(escasos) numbered, scarce, few
▷ *nm*: **pagar al ~** to pay (in) cash

contador [konta'ðor] *nm*

(ESP: aparato) meter ▷ *nmf (LAM Com)*
accountant

contagiar [konta'xjar] *vt*
(enfermedad) to pass on, transmit;
(persona) to infect; **contagiarse** *vr* to
become infected

contagio [kon'taxjo] *nm* infection;
contagioso, -a *adj* infectious; *(fig)*
catching

contaminación [kontamina'θjon]
nf contamination; *(polución)* pollution

contaminar [kontami'nar] *vt* to
contaminate; *(aire, agua)* to pollute

contante [kon'tante] *adj*: **dinero ~ (y**
sonante) cash

contar [kon'tar] *vt (páginas, dinero)* to
count; *(anécdota, chiste etc)* to tell ▷ *vi*
to count; **~ con** to rely on, count on

contemplar [kontem'plar] *vt* to
contemplate; *(mirar)* to look at

contemporáneo, -a
[kontempo'raneo, a] *adj, nm/f*
contemporary

contenedor [kontene'ðor] *nm*
container

contener [konte'ner] *vt* to contain,
hold; *(retener)* to hold back, contain;
contenerse *vr* to control *o* restrain
o.s.

contenido, -a [konte'niðo, a]
adj (moderado) restrained; *(risa etc)*
suppressed ▷ *nm* contents *pl*, content

contentar [konten'tar] *vt (satisfacer)*
to satisfy; *(complacer)* to please;
contentarse *vr* to be satisfied

contento, -a [kon'tento, a] *adj*
(alegre) pleased; *(feliz)* happy

contestación [kontesta'θjon] *nf*
answer, reply

contestador [kontesta'ðor] *nm*
(tb: ~ automático) answering
machine

contestar [kontes'tar] *vt* to answer,
reply; *(Jur)* to corroborate, confirm

 No confundir **contestar** con la
palabra inglesa *contest*.

contexto [kon'te(k)sto] *nm* context

contigo [kon'tixo] *pron* with you

contiguo, -a [kon'tiɣwo, a] adj
adjacent, adjoining

continente [konti'nente] adj, nm
continent

continuación [kontinwa'θjon] nf
continuation; **a ~** then, next

continuar [konti'nwar] vt to
continue, go on with ▷ vi to continue,
go on; **~ hablando** to continue talking
o to talk

continuidad [kontinwi'ðað] nf
continuity

continuo, -a [kon'tinwo, a] adj
(sin interrupción) continuous; (acción
perseverante) continual

contorno [kon'torno] nm outline;
(Geo) contour; **contornos** nmpl
neighbourhood sg, surrounding area sg

contra ['kontra] prep, adv against
▷ nm inv con ▷ nf: **la C~** (de Nicaragua)
the Contras pl

contraataque [kontraa'take] nm
counter-attack

contrabajo [kontra'βaxo] nm
double bass

contrabandista [kontraβan'dista]
nmf smuggler

contrabando [kontra'βando]
nm (acción) smuggling; (mercancías)
contraband

contracción [kontrak'θjon] nf
contraction

contracorriente [kontrako'rrjente]
nf cross-current

contradecir [kontraðe'θir] vt to
contradict

contradicción [kontraðik'θjon] nf
contradiction

contradictorio, -a
[kontraðik'torjo, a] adj contradictory

contraer [kontra'er] vt to contract;
(limitar) to restrict; **contraerse** vr to
contract; (limitarse) to limit o.s.

contraluz [kontra'luθ] nm view
against the light

contrapartida [kontrapar'tiða]
nf: **como ~ (de)** in return (for)

contrapelo [kontra'pelo]: **a ~** adv the
wrong way

contrapeso [kontra'peso] nm
counterweight

contraportada [kontrapor'taða] nf
(de revista) back cover

contraproducente
[kontraproðu'θente] adj
counterproductive

contrario, -a [kon'trarjo, a] adj
contrary; (persona) opposed; (sentido,
lado) opposite ▷ nm/f enemy,
adversary; (Deporte) opponent; **al o por
el ~** on the contrary; **de lo ~** otherwise

contrarreloj [kontrarre'lo] nf
(tb: **prueba ~**) time trial

contrarrestar [kontrarres'tar] vt to
counteract

contrasentido [kontrasen'tiðo] nm
(contradicción) contradiction

contraseña [kontra'seɲa] nf (Inform)
password

contrastar [kontras'tar] vt, vi to
contrast

contraste [kon'traste] nm contrast

contratar [kontra'tar] vt firmar un
acuerdo para, to contract for; (empleados,
obreros) to hire, engage

contratiempo [kontra'tjempo]
nm setback

contratista [kontra'tista] nmf
contractor

contrato [kon'trato] nm contract

contraventana [kontraβen'tana]
nf shutter

contribución [kontriβu'θjon] nf
(municipal etc) tax; (ayuda) contribution

contribuir [kontriβu'ir] vt, vi to
contribute; (Com) to pay (in taxes)

contribuyente [kontriβu'jente] nmf
(Com) taxpayer; (que ayuda) contributor

contrincante [kontrin'kante] nmf
opponent

control [kon'trol] nm control;
(inspección) inspection, check; **control
de pasaportes** passport inspection;
controlador, a nm/f controller;
controlador aéreo air-traffic
controller; **controlar** [kontro'lar] vt

to control; (*inspeccionar*) to inspect, check

contundente [kontun'dente] *adj* (*instrumento*) blunt; (*argumento, derrota*) overwhelming

contusión [kontu'sjon] *nf* bruise

convalecencia [kombale'θenθja] *nf* convalescence

convalecer [kombale'θer] *vi* to convalesce, get better

convalidar [kombali'ðar] *vt* (*título*) to recognize

convencer [komben'θer] *vt* to convince; **~ a algn (de** o **para hacer algo)** to persuade sb (to do sth)

convención [komben'θjon] *nf* convention

conveniente [kombe'njente] *adj* suitable; (*útil*) useful

convenio [kom'benjo] *nm* agreement, treaty

convenir [kombe'nir] *vi* (*estar de acuerdo*) to agree; (*venir bien*) to suit, be suitable

> No confundir **convenir** con la palabra inglesa *convene*.

convento [kom'bento] *nm* convent

convenza *etc vb* V **convencer**

convergir [komber'xir] *vi* = **converger**

conversación [kombersa'θjon] *nf* conversation

conversar [komber'sar] *vi* to talk, converse

conversión [komber'sjon] *nf* conversion

convertir [komber'tir] *vt* to convert

convidar [kombi'ðar] *vt* to invite; **~ a algn a una cerveza** to buy sb a beer

convincente [kombin'θente] *adj* convincing

convite [kom'bite] *nm* invitation; (*banquete*) banquet

convivencia [kombi'βenθja] *nf* coexistence, living together

convivir [kombi'βir] *vi* to live together

convocar [kombo'kar] *vt* to summon, call (together)

convocatoria [komboka'torja] *nf* (*de oposiciones, elecciones*) notice; (*de huelga*) call

cónyuge ['konjuxe] *nmf* spouse

coñac [ko'ɲa(k)] (*pl* ~**s**) *nm* cognac, brandy

coño ['koɲo] (*fam!*) *excl* (*enfado*) shit! (*!*); (*sorpresa*) bloody hell! (*!*)

cool [kul] *adj* (*fam*) cool

cooperación [koopera'θjon] *nf* cooperation

cooperar [koope'rar] *vi* to cooperate

cooperativa [koopera'tiβa] *nf* cooperative

coordinadora [koorðina'ðora] *nf* (*comité*) coordinating committee

coordinar [koorði'nar] *vt* to coordinate

copa ['kopa] *nf* cup; (*vaso*) glass; (*bebida*): **tomar una ~** (to have a) drink; (*de árbol*) top; (*de sombrero*) crown; **copas** *nfpl* (*Naipes*) ≈ hearts

copia ['kopja] *nf* copy; **copia de respaldo** o **seguridad** (*Inform*) back-up copy; **copiar** *vt* to copy

copla ['kopla] *nf* verse; (*canción*) (popular) song

copo ['kopo] *nm*: **~ de nieve** snowflake; **~s de maíz** cornflakes

coqueta [ko'keta] *adj* flirtatious, coquettish; **coquetear** *vi* to flirt

coraje [ko'raxe] *nm* courage; (*ánimo*) spirit; (*ira*) anger

coral [ko'ral] *adj* choral ▷ *nf* (*Mús*) choir ▷ *nm* (*Zool*) coral

coraza [ko'raθa] *nf* (*armadura*) armour; (*blindaje*) armour-plating

corazón [kora'θon] *nm* heart

corazonada [koraθo'naða] *nf* impulse; (*presentimiento*) hunch

corbata [kor'βata] *nf* tie

corchete [kor'tʃete] *nm* catch, clasp

corcho ['kortʃo] *nm* cork; (*Pesca*) float

cordel [kor'ðel] *nm* cord, line

cordero [kor'ðero] *nm* lamb

cordial [kor'ðjal] *adj* cordial

cordillera [korði'ʎera] nf range (of mountains)

Córdoba ['korðoβa] n Cordova

cordón [kor'ðon] nm (cuerda) cord, string; (de zapatos) lace; (Mil etc) cordon; **cordón umbilical** umbilical cord

cordura [kor'ðura] nf: **con ~** (obrar, hablar) sensibly

corneta [kor'neta] nf bugle

cornisa [kor'nisa] nf (Arq) cornice

coro ['koro] nm chorus; (conjunto de cantores) choir

corona [ko'rona] nf crown; (de flores) garland

coronel [koro'nel] nm colonel

coronilla [koro'niʎa] nf (Anat) crown (of the head)

corporal [korpo'ral] adj corporal, bodily

corpulento, -a [korpu'lento, a] adj (persona) heavily-built

corral [ko'rral] nm farmyard

correa [ko'rrea] nf strap; (cinturón) belt; (de perro) lead, leash; **correa del ventilador** (Auto) fan belt

corrección [korrek'θjon] nf correction; (reprensión) rebuke; **correccional** nm reformatory

correcto, -a [ko'rrekto, a] adj correct; (persona) well-mannered

corredizo, -a [korre'ðiθo, a] adj (puerta etc) sliding

corredor, a [korre'ðor, a] nm (pasillo) corridor; (balcón corrido) gallery; (Com) agent, broker ▷ nm/f (Deporte) runner

corregir [korre'xir] vt (error) to correct; **corregirse** vr to reform

correo [ko'rreo] nm post, mail; (persona) courier; **Correos** nmpl (ESP) Post Office sg; **correo aéreo** airmail; **correo basura** (Inform) spam; **correo electrónico** e-mail, electronic mail; **correo web** webmail

correr [ko'rrer] vt to run; (cortinas) to draw; (cerrojo) to shoot ▷ vi to run; (líquido) to run, flow; **correrse** vr to slide, move; (colores) to run

correspondencia

[korrespon'denθja] nf correspondence; (Ferro) connection

corresponder [korrespon'der] vi to correspond; (convenir) to be suitable; (pertenecer) to belong; (concernir) to concern; **corresponderse** vr (por escrito) to correspond; (amarse) to love one another

correspondiente [korrespon'djente] adj corresponding

corresponsal [korrespon'sal] nmf correspondent

corrida [ko'rriða] nf (de toros) bullfight

corrido, -a [ko'rriðo, a] adj (avergonzado) abashed; **un kilo ~** a good kilo

corriente [ko'rrjente] adj (agua) running; (dinero etc) current; (común) ordinary, normal ▷ nf current ▷ nm current month; **estar al ~ de** to be informed about; **corriente eléctrica** electric current

corrija etc vb V **corregir**

corro ['korro] nm ring, circle (of people)

corromper [korrom'per] vt (madera) to rot; (fig) to corrupt

corrosivo, -a [korro'siβo, a] adj corrosive

corrupción [korrup'θjon] nf rot, decay; (fig) corruption

corsé [kor'se] nm corset

cortacésped [korta'θespeð] nm lawn mower

cortado, -a [kor'taðo, a] adj (gen) cut; (leche) sour; (tímido) shy; (avergonzado) embarrassed ▷ nm coffee (with a little milk)

cortafuegos [korta'fweɣos] nm inv (en el bosque) firebreak, fire lane (us); (Internet) firewall

cortar [kor'tar] vt to cut; (suministro) to cut off; (un pasaje) to cut out ▷ vi to cut; **cortarse** vr (avergonzarse) to become embarrassed; (leche) to turn, curdle; **~se el pelo** to have one's hair cut

cortauñas [korta'uɲas] nm inv nail clippers pl

corte ['korte] nm cut, cutting; (de tela) piece, length ▷ nf: **las C~s** the Spanish Parliament; **corte de luz** power cut; **corte y confección** dressmaking

cortejo [kor'texo] nm entourage; **cortejo fúnebre** funeral procession

cortés [kor'tes] adj courteous, polite

cortesía [korte'sia] nf courtesy

corteza [kor'teθa] nf (de árbol) bark; (de pan) crust

cortijo [kor'tixo] (ESP) nm farm, farmhouse

cortina [kor'tina] nf curtain

corto, -a ['korto, a] adj (breve) short; (tímido) bashful; **~ de luces** not very bright; **~ de vista** short-sighted; **estar ~ de fondos** to be short of funds; **cortocircuito** nm short circuit; **cortometraje** nm (Cine) short

cosa ['kosa] nf thing; **~ de** about; **eso es ~ mía** that's my business

coscorrón [kosko'rron] nm bump on the head

cosecha [ko'setʃa] nf (Agr) harvest; (de vino) vintage; **cosechar** [kose'tʃar] vt to harvest, gather (in)

coser [ko'ser] vt to sew

cosmético, -a [kos'metiko, a] adj, nm cosmetic

cosquillas [kos'kiʎas] nfpl: **hacer ~** to tickle; **tener ~** to be ticklish

costa ['kosta] nf (Geo) coast; **a toda ~** at all costs; **Costa Brava** Costa Brava; **Costa Cantábrica** Cantabrian Coast; **Costa del Sol** Costa del Sol

costado [kos'taðo] nm side

costanera [kosta'nera] (CS) nf promenade, sea front

costar [kos'tar] vt (valer) to cost; **me cuesta hablarle** I find it hard to talk to him

Costa Rica [kosta'rika] nf Costa Rica; **costarricense** adj, nmf Costa Rican; **costarriqueño, -a** adj, nm/f Costa Rican

coste ['koste] nm = **costo**

costear [koste'ar] vt to pay for

costero, -a [kos'tero, a] adj (pueblecito, camino) coastal

costilla [kos'tiʎa] nf rib; (Culin) cutlet

costo ['kosto] nm cost, price; **costo de (la) vida** cost of living; **costoso, -a** adj costly, expensive

costra ['kostra] nf (corteza) crust; (Med) scab

costumbre [kos'tumbre] nf custom, habit

costura [kos'tura] nf sewing, needlework; (zurcido) seam

costurera [kostu'rera] nf dressmaker

costurero [kostu'rero] nm sewing box o case

cotidiano, -a [koti'ðjano, a] adj daily, day to day

cotilla [ko'tiʎa] (ESP: fam) nmf gossip; **cotillear** (ESP) vi to gossip; **cotilleo** (ESP) nm gossip(ing)

cotizar [koti'θar] vt (Com) to quote, price; **cotizarse** vr: **~se a** to sell at, fetch; (Bolsa) to stand at, be quoted at

coto ['koto] nm (terreno cercado) enclosure; (de caza) reserve

cotorra [ko'torra] nf parrot

coyote [ko'jote] nm coyote, prairie wolf

coz [koθ] nf kick

crack [krak] nm (droga) crack

cráneo ['kraneo] nm skull, cranium

cráter ['krater] nm crater

crayón [kra'jon] (MÉX, RPL) nm crayon, chalk

creación [krea'θjon] nf creation

creador, a [krea'ðor, a] adj creative ▷ nm/f creator

crear [kre'ar] vt to create, make

crecer [kre'θer] vi to grow; (precio) to rise

creces ['kreθes]: **con ~** adv amply, fully

crecido, -a [kre'θiðo, a] adj (persona, planta) full-grown; (cantidad) large

crecimiento [kreθi'mjento] nm growth; (aumento) increase

credencial [kreðen'θjal] nf

(LAM: tarjeta) card; **credenciales** nfpl credentials; **credencial de socio** (LAM) membership card

crédito ['kreðito] nm credit

credo ['kreðo] nm creed

creencia [kre'enθja] nf belief

creer [kre'er] vt, vi to think, believe; **creerse** vr to believe o.s. (to be); **~ en** to believe in; **creo que sí/no** I think/don't think so; **¡ya lo creo!** I should think so!

creído, -a [kre'iðo, a] adj (engreído) conceited

crema ['krema] nf cream; **crema batida** (LAM) whipped cream; **crema pastelera** (confectioner's) custard

cremallera [krema'ʎera] nf zip (fastener)

crepe ['krepe] (ESP) nf pancake

cresta ['kresta] nf (Geo, Zool) crest

creyendo etc vb V **creer**

creyente [kre'jente] nmf believer

creyó etc vb V **creer**

crezco etc vb V **crecer**

cría etc ['kria] vb V **criar** ▷ nf (de animales) rearing, breeding; (animal) young; V tb **crío**

criadero [kria'ðero] nm (Zool) breeding place

criado, -a [kri'aðo, a] nm servant ▷ nf servant, maid

criador [kria'ðor] nm breeder

crianza [kri'anθa] nf rearing, breeding; (fig) breeding

criar [kri'ar] vt (educar) to bring up; (producir) to grow, produce; (animales) to breed

criatura [kria'tura] nf creature; (niño) baby, (small) child

cribar [kri'βar] vt to sieve

crimen ['krimen] nm crime

criminal [krimi'nal] adj, nmf criminal

crines ['krines] nfpl mane

crío, -a ['krio, a] (fam) nm/f (niño) kid

crisis ['krisis] nf inv crisis; **crisis nerviosa** nervous breakdown

crismas ['krismas] (ESP) nm inv Christmas card

cristal [kris'tal] nm crystal; (de ventana) glass, pane; (lente) lens; **cristalino, -a** adj crystalline; (fig) clear ▷ nm lens (of the eye)

cristianismo [kristja'nismo] nm Christianity

cristiano, -a [kris'tjano, a] adj, nm/f Christian

Cristo ['kristo] nm Christ; (crucifijo) crucifix

criterio [kri'terjo] nm criterion; (juicio) judgement

crítica ['kritika] nf criticism; V tb **crítico**

criticar [kriti'kar] vt to criticize

crítico, -a ['kritiko, a] adj critical ▷ nm/f critic

Croacia [kro'aθja] nf Croatia

cromo ['kromo] nm chrome

crónica ['kronika] nf chronicle, account

crónico, -a ['kroniko, a] adj chronic

cronómetro [kro'nometro] nm stopwatch

croqueta [kro'keta] nf croquette

cruce etc ['kruθe] vb V **cruzar** ▷ nm (para peatones) crossing; (de carreteras) crossroads

crucero [kru'θero] nm (viaje) cruise

crucificar [kruθifi'kar] vt to crucify

crucifijo [kruθi'fixo] nm crucifix

crucigrama [kruθi'ɣrama] nm crossword (puzzle)

cruda ['kruða] (MÉX, CAM: fam) nf hangover

crudo, -a ['kruðo, a] adj raw; (no maduro) unripe; (petróleo) crude; (rudo, cruel) cruel ▷ nm crude (oil)

cruel [krwel] adj cruel; **crueldad** nf cruelty

crujiente [kru'xjente] adj (galleta etc) crunchy

crujir [kru'xir] vi (madera etc) to creak; (dedos) to crack; (dientes) to grind; (nieve, arena) to crunch

cruz [kruθ] nf cross; (de moneda) tails sg; **cruz gamada** swastika

cruzada [kru'θaða] nf crusade

cruzado, -a [kru'θaðo, a] *adj*
crossed ▷ *nm* crusader

cruzar [kru'θar] *vt* to cross; **cruzarse**
vr (*líneas etc*) to cross; (*personas*) to pass
each other

Cruz Roja *nf* Red Cross

cuaderno [kwa'ðerno] *nm*
notebook; (*de escuela*) exercise book;
(*Náut*) logbook

cuadra ['kwaðra] *nf* (*caballeriza*)
stable; (*LAM: entre calles*) block

cuadrado, -a [kwa'ðraðo, a] *adj*
square ▷ *nm* (*Mat*) square

cuadrar [kwa'ðrar] *vt* to square
▷ *vi*: **~ con** to square with, tally with;
cuadrarse *vr* (*soldado*) to stand to
attention

cuadrilátero [kwaðri'latero]
nm (*Deporte*) boxing ring; (*Geom*)
quadrilateral

cuadrilla [kwa'ðriʎa] *nf* party, group

cuadro ['kwaðro] *nm* square; (*Arte*)
painting; (*Teatro*) scene; (*diagrama*)
chart; (*Deporte, Med*) team; **tela a**
~s checked (*BRIT*) o chequered (*US*)
material

cuajar [kwa'xar] *vt* (*leche*) to curdle;
(*sangre*) to congeal; (*Culin*) to set;
cuajarse *vr* to curdle; to congeal; to
set; (*llenarse*) to fill up

cuajo ['kwaxo] *nm*: **de ~** (*arrancar*) by
the roots; (*cortar*) completely

cual [kwal] *adv* like, as ▷ *pron*: **el** *etc*
~ which; (*persona sujeto*) who; (*: objeto*)
whom ▷ *adj* such as; **cada ~** each one;
déjalo tal ~ leave it just as it is

cuál [kwal] *pron interr* which (one)

cualesquier, a [kwales'kjer(a)] *pl de*
cualquier(a)

cualidad [kwali'ðað] *nf* quality

cualquier [kwal'kjer] *adj V*
cualquiera

cualquiera [kwal'kjera] (*pl*
cualesquiera) *adj* (*delante de nm y f*
cualquier) any ▷ *pron* anybody; **un**
coche ~ servirá any car will do; **no es**
un hombre ~ he isn't just anybody;
cualquier día/libro any day/book; **eso**

~ lo sabe hacer anybody can do that;
es un ~ he's a nobody

cuando ['kwando] *adv* when; (*aún*
si) if, even if ▷ *conj* (*puesto que*) since
▷ *prep*: **yo, ~ niño ...** when I was a child
...; **~ no sea así** even if it is not so; **~**
más at (the) most; **~ menos** at least;
~ no if not, otherwise; **de ~ en ~** from
time to time

cuándo ['kwando] *adv* when; **¿desde**
~? since when?

cuantía [kwan'tia] *nf* extent

○ **PALABRA CLAVE**

cuanto, -a ['kwanto, a] *adj* **1** (*todo*):
tiene todo cuanto desea he's got
everything he wants; **le daremos**
cuantos ejemplares necesite we'll
give him as many copies as o all the
copies he needs; **cuantos hombres la**
ven all the men who see her
2 unos cuantos: había unos
cuantos periodistas there were a few
journalists
3 (+ *más*): **cuanto más vino bebes peor**
te sentirás the more wine you drink
the worse you'll feel
▷ *pron*: **tiene cuanto desea** he has
everything he wants; **tome cuanto/**
cuantos quiera take as much/many
as you want
▷ *adv*: **en cuanto: en cuanto profesor**
as a teacher; **en cuanto a mí** as for me;
V tb **antes**
▷ *conj* **1 cuanto más gana menos**
gasta the more he earns the less
he spends; **cuanto más joven más**
confiado the younger you are the more
trusting you are
2 en cuanto: en cuanto llegue/
llegué as soon as I arrive/arrived

cuánto, -a ['kwanto, a] *adj*
(*exclamación*) what a lot of; (*interr: sg*)
how much?; (*: pl*) how many? ▷ *pron,*
adv how; (*: interr: sg*) how much?; (*: pl*)
how many?; **¡cuánta gente!** what a

lot of people!; **¿~ cuesta?** how much does it cost?; **¿a ~s estamos?** what's the date?

cuarenta [kwa'renta] *num* forty

cuarentena [kwaren'tena] *nf* quarantine

cuaresma [kwa'resma] *nf* Lent

cuarta ['kwarta] *nf* (*Mat*) quarter, fourth; (*palmo*) span

cuartel [kwar'tel] *nm* (*Mil*) barracks *pl*; **cuartel de bomberos** (*RPL*) fire station; **cuartel general** headquarters *pl*

cuarteto [kwar'teto] *nm* quartet

cuarto, -a ['kwarto, a] *adj* fourth ▷ *nm* (*Mat*) quarter, fourth; (*habitación*) room; **cuarto de baño** bathroom; **cuarto de estar** living room; **cuarto de hora** quarter (of an) hour; **cuarto de kilo** quarter kilo; **cuartos de final** quarter finals

cuatro ['kwatro] *num* four

Cuba ['kuβa] *nf* Cuba

cuba ['kuβa] *nf* cask, barrel

cubano, -a [ku'βano, a] *adj, nm/f* Cuban

cubata [ku'βata] *nm* (*fam*) large drink (*of rum and coke etc*)

cubeta [ku'βeta] (*ESP, MÉX*) *nf* (*balde*) bucket, tub

cúbico, -a ['kuβiko, a] *adj* cubic

cubierta [ku'βjerta] *nf* cover, covering; (*neumático*) tyre; (*Náut*) deck

cubierto, -a [ku'βjerto, a] *pp de* **cubrir** ▷ *adj* covered ▷ *nm* cover; (*lugar en la mesa*) place; **cubiertos** *nmpl* cutlery *sg*; **a ~** under cover

cubilete [kuβi'lete] *nm* (*en juegos*) cup

cubito [ku'βito] *nm* (*tb*: **~ de hielo**) ice-cube

cubo ['kuβo] *nm* (*Mat*) cube; (*ESP: balde*) bucket, tub; (*Tec*) drum; **cubo de (la) basura** dustbin (*BRIT*), trash can (*US*)

cubrir [ku'βrir] *vt* to cover; **cubrirse** *vr* (*cielo*) to become overcast

cucaracha [kuka'ratʃa] *nf* cockroach

cuchara [ku'tʃara] *nf* spoon; (*Tec*) scoop; **cucharada** *nf* spoonful; **cucharadita** *nf* teaspoonful

cucharilla [kutʃa'riʎa] *nf* teaspoon

cucharón [kutʃa'ron] *nm* ladle

cuchilla [ku'tʃiʎa] *nf* (*large*) knife; (*de arma blanca*) blade; **cuchilla de afeitar** razor blade

cuchillo [ku'tʃiʎo] *nm* knife

cuchitril [kutʃi'tril] *nm* hovel

cuclillas [ku'kliʎas] *nfpl*: **en ~** squatting

cuco, -a ['kuko, a] *adj* pretty; (*astuto*) sharp ▷ *nm* cuckoo

cucurucho [kuku'rutʃo] *nm* cornet

cueca ['kweka] *nf* Chilean national dance

cuello ['kweʎo] *nm* (*Anat*) neck; (*de vestido, camisa*) collar

cuenca ['kwenka] *nf* (*Anat*) eye socket; (*Geo*) bowl, deep valley

cuenco ['kwenko] *nm* bowl

cuenta *etc* ['kwenta] *vb* V **contar** ▷ *nf* (*cálculo*) count, counting; (*en café, restaurante*) bill (*BRIT*), check (*US*); (*Com*) account; (*de collar*) bead; **a fin de ~s** in the end; **caer en la ~** to catch on; **darse ~ de** to realize; **tener en ~** to bear in mind; **echar ~s** to take stock; **cuenta atrás** countdown; **cuenta corriente/de ahorros** current/savings account; **cuenta de correo (electrónica)** (*Inform*) email account; **cuentakilómetros** *nm inv* ≈ milometer; (*de velocidad*) speedometer

cuento *etc* ['kwento] *vb* V **contar** ▷ *nm* story; **cuento chino** tall story; **cuento de hadas** a fairy tale

cuerda ['kwerða] *nf* rope; (*fina*) string; (*de reloj*) spring; **dar ~ a un reloj** to wind up a clock; **cuerda floja** tightrope; **cuerdas vocales** vocal cords

cuerdo, -a ['kwerðo, a] *adj* sane; (*prudente*) wise, sensible

cuerno ['kwerno] *nm* horn

cuero ['kwero] *nm* leather; **en ~s** stark naked; **cuero cabelludo** scalp

cuerpo ['kwerpo] *nm* body

cuervo ['kwerβo] nm crow

cuesta etc ['kwesta] vb V **costar**
▷ nf slope; (en camino etc) hill; **~ arriba/abajo** uphill/downhill; **a ~s** on one's back

cueste etc vb V **costar**

cuestión [kwes'tjon] nf matter, question, issue

cuete ['kwete] adj (MÉX: fam) drunk
▷ nm (LAM: cohete) rocket; (MÉX, RPL: fam: embriaguez) drunkenness; (MÉX: Culin) steak

cueva ['kweβa] nf cave

cuidado [kwi'ðaðo] nm care, carefulness; (preocupación) care, worry
▷ excl careful!, look out!; **eso me tiene sin ~** I'm not worried about that

cuidadoso, -a [kwiða'ðoso, a] adj careful; (preocupado) anxious

cuidar [kwi'ðar] vt (Med) to care for; (ocuparse de) to take care of, look after
▷ vi: **~ de** to take care of, look after; **cuidarse** vr to look after o.s.; **~se de hacer algo** to take care to do sth

culata [ku'lata] nf (de fusil) butt

culebra [ku'leβra] nf snake

culebrón [kule'βron] (fam) nm (TV) soap(-opera)

culo ['kulo] nm bottom, backside; (de vaso, botella) bottom

culpa ['kulpa] nf fault; (Jur) guilt; **por ~ de** because of; **echar la ~ a algn** to blame sb for sth; **tener la ~ (de)** to be to blame (for); **culpable** adj guilty
▷ nmf culprit; **culpar** [kul'par] vt to blame; (acusar) to accuse

cultivar [kulti'βar] vt to cultivate

cultivo [kul'tiβo] nm (acto) cultivation; (plantas) crop

culto, -a ['kulto, a] adj (que tiene cultura) cultured, educated ▷ nm (homenaje) worship; (religión) cult

cultura [kul'tura] nf culture

culturismo [kultu'rismo] nm body-building

cumbia ['kumbja] nf popular Colombian dance

cumbre ['kumbre] nf summit, top

cumpleaños [kumple'aɲos] nm inv birthday

cumplido, -a [kum'pliðo, a] adj (abundante) plentiful; (cortés) courteous
▷ nm compliment; **visita de ~** courtesy call

cumplidor, a [kumpli'ðor, a] adj reliable

cumplimiento [kumpli'mjento] nm (de un deber) fulfilment; (acabamiento) completion

cumplir [kum'plir] vt (orden) to carry out, obey; (promesa) to carry out, fulfil; (condena) to serve ▷ vi: **~ con** (deber) to carry out, fulfil; **cumplirse** vr (plazo) to expire; **hoy cumple dieciocho años** he is eighteen today

cuna ['kuna] nf cradle, cot

cundir [kun'dir] vi (noticia, rumor, pánico) to spread; (rendir) to go a long way

cuneta [ku'neta] nf ditch

cuña ['kuɲa] nf wedge

cuñado, -a [ku'ɲaðo, a] nm/f brother-/sister-in-law

cuota ['kwota] nf (parte proporcional) share; (cotización) fee, dues pl

cupe etc vb V **caber**

cupiera etc vb V **caber**

cupo ['kupo] vb V **caber** ▷ nm quota

cupón [ku'pon] nm coupon

cúpula ['kupula] nf dome

cura ['kura] nf (curación) cure; (método curativo) treatment ▷ nm priest

curación [kura'θjon] nf cure; (acción) curing

curandero, -a [kuran'dero, a] nm/f quack

curar [ku'rar] vt (Med: herida) to treat, dress; (: enfermo) to cure; (Culin) to cure, salt; (cuero) to tan; **curarse** vr to get well, recover

curiosear [kurjose'ar] vt to glance at, look over ▷ vi to look round, wander round; (explorar) to poke about

curiosidad [kurjosi'ðað] nf curiosity

curioso, -a [ku'rjoso, a] adj curious
▷ nm/f bystander, onlooker

curita [ku'rita] (*LAM*) *nf* (sticking) plaster (*BRIT*), Bandaid® (*US*)

currante [ku'rrante] (*ESP: fam*) *nmf* worker

currar [ku'rrar] (*ESP: fam*) *vi* to work

currículo [ku'rrikulo] = **curriculum**

curriculum [ku'rrikulum] *nm* curriculum vitae

cursi ['kursi] (*fam*) *adj* affected

cursillo [kur'siʎo] *nm* short course

cursiva [kur'siβa] *nf* italics *pl*

curso ['kurso] *nm* course; **en ~** (*año*) current; (*proceso*) going on, under way

cursor [kur'sor] *nm* (*Inform*) cursor

curul [ku'rul] (*MÉX*) *nm* (*escaño*) seat

curva ['kurβa] *nf* curve, bend

custodia [kus'toðja] *nf* safekeeping; custody

cutis ['kutis] *nm inv* skin, complexion

cutre ['kutre] (*ESP: fam*) *adj* (*lugar*) grotty

cuyo, -a ['kujo, a] *pron* (*de quien*) whose; (*de que*) whose, of which; **en ~ caso** in which case

C.V. *abr* (= *caballos de vapor*) H.P.

D. *abr* (= *Don*) Esq

dado, -a ['daðo, a] *pp de* **dar** ▷ *nm* die; **dados** *nmpl* dice; **~ que** given that

daltónico, -a [dal'toniko, a] *adj* colour-blind

dama ['dama] *nf* (*gen*) lady; (*Ajedrez*) queen; **damas** *nfpl* (*juego*) draughts *sg*; **dama de honor** bridesmaid

damasco [da'masko] (*RPL*) *nm* apricot

danés, -esa [da'nes, esa] *adj* Danish ▷ *nm/f* Dane

dañar [da'ɲar] *vt* (*objeto*) to damage; (*persona*) to hurt; **dañarse** *vr* (*objeto*) to get damaged

dañino, -a [da'ɲino, a] *adj* harmful

daño ['daɲo] *nm* (*objeto*) damage; (*persona*) harm, injury; **~s y perjuicios** (*Jur*) damages; **hacer ~ a** to damage; (*persona*) to hurt, injure; **hacerse ~** to hurt o.s.

○ **PALABRA CLAVE**

dar [dar] *vt* **1** (*gen*) to give; (*obra de*

teatro) to put on; (*film*) to show; (*fiesta*) to hold; **dar algo a algn** to give sb sth *o* sth to sb; **dar de beber a algn** to give sb a drink

2 (*producir: intereses*) to yield; (*fruta*) to produce

3 (*locuciones + n*): **da gusto escucharle** it's a pleasure to listen to him; *V tb* **paseo**

4 (*+ n: = perífrasis de verbo*): **me da asco** it sickens me

5 (*considerar*): **dar algo por descontado/entendido** to take sth for granted/as read; **dar algo por concluido** to consider sth finished

6 (*hora*): **el reloj dio las 6** the clock struck 6 (o'clock)

7: **me da lo mismo** it's all the same to me; *V tb* **igual, más**

▷*vi* **1** **dar con: dimos con él dos horas más tarde** we came across him two hours later; **al final di con la solución** I eventually came up with the answer

2: **dar en** (*blanco, suelo*) to hit; **el sol me da en la cara** the sun is shining (right) on my face

3: **dar de sí** (*zapatos etc*) to stretch, give

darse *vr* **1**: **darse por vencido** to give up

2 (*ocurrir*): **se han dado muchos casos** there have been a lot of cases

3: **darse a: se ha dado a la bebida** he's taken to drinking

4: **se me dan bien/mal las ciencias** I'm good/bad at science

5: **dárselas de: se las da de experto** he fancies himself *o* poses as an expert

dardo ['darðo] *nm* dart

dátil ['datil] *nm* date

dato ['dato] *nm* fact, piece of information; **datos personales** personal details

dcha. *abr* (= *derecha*) r.h.

d. de C. *abr* (= *después de Cristo*) A.D.

○ **PALABRA CLAVE**

de [de] (*de + el = del*) *prep* **1** (*posesión*) of; **la casa de Isabel/mis padres** Isabel's/my parents' house; **es de ellos** it's theirs

2 (*origen, distancia, con números*) from; **soy de Gijón** I'm from Gijón; **de 8 a 20** from 8 to 20; **salir del cine** to go out of *o* leave the cinema; **de 2 en 2** 2 by 2, 2 at a time

3 (*valor descriptivo*): **una copa de vino** a glass of wine; **la mesa de la cocina** the kitchen table; **un billete de 10 euros** a 10 euro note; **un niño de tres años** a three-year-old (child); **una máquina de coser** a sewing machine; **ir vestido de gris** to be dressed in grey; **la niña del vestido azul** the girl in the blue dress; **trabaja de profesora** she works as a teacher; **de lado** sideways; **de atrás/delante** rear/front

4 (*hora, tiempo*): **a las 8 de la mañana** at 8 o'clock in the morning; **de día/noche** by day/night; **de hoy en ocho días** a week from now; **de niño era gordo** as a child he was fat

5 (*comparaciones*): **más/menos de cien personas** more/less than a hundred people; **el más caro de la tienda** the most expensive in the shop; **menos/más de lo pensado** less/more than expected

6 (*causa*): **del calor** from the heat

7 (*tema*) about; **clases de inglés** English classes; **¿sabes algo de él?** do you know anything about him?; **un libro de física** a physics book

8 (*adj + de + infin*): **fácil de entender** easy to understand

9 (*oraciones pasivas*): **fue respetado de todos** he was loved by all

10 (*condicional + infin*) if; **de ser posible** if possible; **de no terminarlo hoy** if I *etc* don't finish it today

dé [de] vb V **dar**

debajo [de'βaxo] adv underneath; **~ de** below, under; **por ~ de** beneath

debate [de'βate] nm debate; **debatir** vt to debate

deber [de'βer] nm duty ⊳ vt to owe ⊳ vi: **debe (de)** it must, it should; **deberes** nmpl (Escol) homework; **deberse** vr: **~se a** to be owing o due to; **debo hacerlo** I must do it; **debe de ir** he should go

debido, -a [de'βiðo, a] adj proper, just; **~ a** to, because of

débil ['deβil] adj (persona, carácter) weak; (luz) dim; **debilidad** nf weakness; dimness

debilitar [deβili'tar] vt to weaken; **debilitarse** vr to grow weak

débito ['deβito] nm debit; **débito bancario** (LAM) direct debit (BRIT) o billing (US)

debutar [deβu'tar] vi to make one's debut

década ['dekaða] nf decade

decadencia [deka'ðenθja] nf (estado) decadence; (proceso) decline, decay

decaído, -a [deka'iðo, a] adj: **estar ~** (abatido) to be down

decano, -a [de'kano, a] nm/f (de universidad etc) dean

decena [de'θena] nf: **una ~** ten (or so)

decente [de'θente] adj decent

decepción [deθep'θjon] nf disappointment

> No confundir **decepción** con la palabra inglesa deception.

decepcionar [deθepθjo'nar] vt to disappoint

decidir [deθi'ðir] vt, vi to decide; **decidirse** vr: **~se a** to make up one's mind to

décimo, -a ['deθimo, a] adj tenth ⊳ nm tenth

decir [de'θir] vt to say; (contar) to tell; (hablar) to speak ⊳ nm saying; **decirse** vr: **se dice que** it is said that; **es ~** that is (to say); **~ para sí** to say to o.s.;

querer ~ to mean; **¡dígame!** (Tel) hello!; (en tienda) can I help you?

decisión [deθi'sjon] nf (resolución) decision; (firmeza) decisiveness

decisivo, -a [deθi'siβo, a] adj decisive

declaración [deklara'θjon] nf (manifestación) statement; (de amor) declaration; **declaración fiscal** o **de la renta** income-tax return

declarar [dekla'rar] vt to declare ⊳ vi to declare; (Jur) to testify; **declararse** vr to propose

decoración [dekora'θjon] nf decoration

decorado [deko'raðo] nm (Cine, Teatro) scenery, set

decorar [deko'rar] vt to decorate; **decorativo, -a** adj ornamental, decorative

decreto [de'kreto] nm decree

dedal [de'ðal] nm thimble

dedicación [deðika'θjon] nf dedication

dedicar [deði'kar] vt (libro) to dedicate; (tiempo, dinero) to devote; (palabras: decir, consagrar) to dedicate, devote; **dedicatoria** nf (de libro) dedication

dedo ['deðo] nm finger; **hacer ~** (fam) to hitch (a lift); **dedo anular** ring finger; **dedo corazón** middle finger; **dedo (del pie)** toe; **dedo gordo** (de la mano) thumb; (del pie) big toe; **dedo índice** index finger; **dedo meñique** little finger; **dedo pulgar** thumb

deducción [deðuk'θjon] nf deduction

deducir [deðu'θir] vt (concluir) to deduce, infer; (Com) to deduct

defecto [de'fekto] nm defect, flaw; **defectuoso, -a** adj defective, faulty

defender [defen'der] vt to defend; **defenderse** vr (desenvolverse) to get by

defensa [de'fensa] nf defence ⊳ nm (Deporte) defender, back; **defensivo, -a** adj defensive; **a la defensiva** on the defensive

defensor, a [defen'sor, a] *adj*
defending ▷ *nm/f* (*abogado defensor*)
defending counsel; (*protector*) protector

deficiencia [defi'θjenθja] *nf*
deficiency

deficiente [defi'θjente] *adj*
(*defectuoso*) defective; **~ en** lacking o
deficient in; **ser un ~ mental** to be
mentally handicapped

déficit ['defiθit] (*pl* **~s**) *nm* deficit

definición [defini'θjon] *nf* definition

definir [defi'nir] *vt* (*determinar*) to
determine, establish; (*decidir*) to define;
(*aclarar*) to clarify; **definitivo, -a** *adj*
definitive; **en definitiva** definitively;
(*en resumen*) in short

deformación [deforma'θjon] *nf*
(*alteración*) deformation; (*Radio etc*)
distortion

deformar [defor'mar] *vt* (*gen*) to
deform; **deformarse** *vr* to become
deformed; **deforme** *adj* (*informe*)
deformed; (*feo*) ugly; (*malhecho*)
misshapen

defraudar [defrau'ðar] *vt*
(*decepcionar*) to disappoint; (*estafar*)
to defraud

defunción [defun'θjon] *nf* death,
demise

degenerar [dexene'rar] *vi* to
degenerate

degradar [dexra'ðar] *vt* to debase,
degrade; **degradarse** *vr* to demean
o.s.

degustación [dexusta'θjon] *nf*
sampling, tasting

dejar [de'xar] *vt* to leave; (*permitir*)
to allow, let; (*abandonar*) to abandon,
forsake; (*beneficios*) to produce, yield
▷ *vi*: **~ de** (*parar*) to stop; (*no hacer*) to
fail to; **~ a un lado** to leave o set aside;
~ entrar/salir to let in/out; **~ pasar** to
let through

del [del] (=**de** + **el**) *V* **de**

delantal [delan'tal] *nm* apron

delante [de'lante] *adv* in front;
(*enfrente*) opposite; (*adelante*) ahead; **~**
de in front of, before

delantera [delan'tera] *nf* (*de vestido,
casa etc*) front part; (*Deporte*) forward
line; **llevar la ~ (a algn)** to be ahead
(of sb)

delantero, -a [delan'tero, a] *adj*
front ▷ *nm* (*Deporte*) forward,
striker

delatar [dela'tar] *vt* to inform on
o against, betray; **delator, a** *nm/f*
informer

delegación [delexa'θjon] *nf* (*acción,
delegados*) delegation; (*Com: oficina*)
office, branch; **delegación de policía**
(*MÉX*) police station

delegado, -a [dele'xaðo, a] *nm/f*
delegate; (*Com*) agent

delegar [dele'xar] *vt* to delegate

deletrear [deletre'ar] *vt* to spell (out)

delfín [del'fin] *nm* dolphin

delgado, -a [del'xaðo, a] *adj* thin;
(*persona*) slim, thin; (*tela etc*) light,
delicate

deliberar [deliβe'rar] *vt* to debate,
discuss

delicadeza [delika'ðeθa] *nf* (*gen*)
delicacy; (*refinamiento, sutileza*)
refinement

delicado, -a [deli'kaðo, a] *adj*
(*gen*) delicate; (*sensible*) sensitive;
(*quisquilloso*) touchy

delicia [de'liθja] *nf* delight

delicioso, -a [deli'θjoso, a] *adj*
(*gracioso*) delightful; (*exquisito*)
delicious

delimitar [delimi'tar] *vt* (*función,
responsabilidades*) to define

delincuencia [delin'kwenθja]
nf delinquency; **delincuente** *nmf*
delinquency; (*criminal*) criminal

delineante [deline'ante] *nmf*
draughtsman/woman

delirante [deli'rante] *adj* delirious

delirar [deli'rar] *vi* to be delirious,
rave

delirio [de'lirjo] *nm* (*Med*)
delirium; (*palabras insensatas*)
ravings *pl*

delito [de'lito] *nm* (*gen*) crime;

(*infracción*) offence

delta ['delta] *nm* delta

demacrado, -a [dema'krado, a] *adj*: **estar ~** to look pale and drawn, be wasted away

demanda [de'manda] *nf* (*pedido, Com*) demand; (*petición*) request; (*Jur*) action, lawsuit; **demandar** [deman'dar] *vt* (*gen*) to demand; (*Jur*) to sue, file a lawsuit against

demás [de'mas] *adj*: **los ~ niños** the other *o* remaining children ▷ *pron*: **los/las ~** the others, the rest (of them); **lo ~** the rest (of it)

demasía [dema'sia] *nf* (*exceso*) excess, surplus; **comer en ~** to eat to excess

demasiado, -a [dema'sjaðo, a] *adj*: **~ vino** too much wine ▷ *adv* (*antes de adj, adv*) too; **~s libros** too many books; **¡esto es ~!** that's the limit!; **hace ~ calor** it's too hot; **~ despacio** too slowly; **~s** too many

demencia [de'menθja] *nf* (*locura*) madness

democracia [demo'kraθja] *nf* democracy

demócrata [de'mokrata] *nmf* democrat; **democrático, -a** *adj* democratic

demoler [demo'ler] *vt* to demolish; **demolición** *nf* demolition

demonio [de'monjo] *nm* devil, demon; **¡~s!** hell!, damn!; **¿cómo ~s?** how the hell?

demora [de'mora] *nf* delay

demos ['demos] *vb* V **dar**

demostración [demostra'θjon] *nf* (*Mat*) proof; (*de afecto*) show, display

demostrar [demos'trar] *vt* (*probar*) to prove; (*mostrar*) to show; (*manifestar*) to demonstrate

den [den] *vb* V **dar**

denegar [dene'xar] *vt* (*rechazar*) to refuse; (*Jur*) to reject

denominación [denomina'θjon] *nf* (*acto*) naming; **Denominación de**

Origen *see note*

densidad [densi'ðað] *nf* density; (*fig*) thickness

denso, -a ['denso, a] *adj* dense; (*espeso, pastoso*) thick; (*fig*) heavy

dentadura [denta'ðura] *nf* (set of) teeth *pl*; **dentadura postiza** false teeth *pl*

dentera [den'tera] *nf* (*grima*): **dar ~ a algn** to set sb's teeth on edge

dentífrico, -a [den'tifriko, a] *adj* dental ▷ *nm* toothpaste

dentista [den'tista] *nmf* dentist

dentro ['dentro] *adv* inside ▷ *prep*: **~ de** in, inside, within; **por ~** (on the) inside; **mirar por ~** to look inside; **~ de tres meses** within three months

denuncia [de'nunθja] *nf* (*delación*) denunciation; (*acusación*) accusation; (*de accidente*) report; **denunciar** *vt* to report; (*delatar*) to inform on *o* against

departamento [departa'mento] *nm sección administrativa*, department, section; (*LAM: apartamento*) flat (*BRIT*), apartment

depender [depen'der] *vi*: **~ de** to depend on; **depende** it (all) depends

dependienta [depen'djenta] *nf* saleswoman, shop assistant

dependiente [depen'djente] *adj* dependent ▷ *nm* salesman, shop assistant

depilar [depi'lar] *vt* (*con cera*) to wax; (*cejas*) to pluck

deportar [depor'tar] *vt* to deport

deporte [de'porte] nm sport; **hacer ~** to play sports; **deportista** adj sports cpd ▷ nmf sportsman/woman; **deportivo, -a** adj (club, periódico) sports cpd ▷ nm sports car

depositar [deposi'tar] vt (dinero) to deposit; (mercancías) to put away, store; **depositarse** vr to settle

depósito [de'posito] nm (gen) deposit; (almacén) warehouse, store; (de agua, gasolina etc) tank; **depósito de cadáveres** mortuary

depredador, a [depreða'ðor, a] adj predatory ▷ nm predator

depresión [depre'sjon] nf depression; **depresión nerviosa** nervous breakdown

deprimido, -a [depri'miðo, a] adj depressed

deprimir [depri'mir] vt to depress; **deprimirse** vr (persona) to become depressed

deprisa [de'prisa] adv quickly, hurriedly

depurar [depu'rar] vt to purify; (purgar) to purge

derecha [de'retʃa] nf right(-hand) side; (Pol) right; **a la ~** (estar) on the right; (torcer etc) (to the) right

derecho, -a [de'retʃo, a] adj right, right-hand ▷ nm (privilegio) right; (lado) right(-hand) side; (leyes) law ▷ adv straight, directly; **derechos** nmpl (de aduana) duty sg; (de autor) royalties; **tener ~ a** to have a right to; **derechos de autor** royalties

deriva [de'riβa] nf: **ir** o **estar a la ~** to drift, be adrift

derivado [deri'βaðo] nm (Com) by-product

derivar [deri'βar] vt to derive; (desviar) to direct ▷ vi to be derived; (Náut) to drift; **derivarse** vr to derive, be derived; to drift

derramamiento [derrama'mjento] nm (dispersión) spilling; **derramamiento de sangre** bloodshed

derramar [derra'mar] vt to spill; (verter) to pour out; (esparcir) to scatter; **derramarse** vr to pour out

derrame [de'rrame] nm (de líquido) spilling; (de sangre) shedding; (de tubo etc) overflow; (pérdida) leakage; **derrame cerebral** brain haemorrhage

derredor [derre'ðor] adv: **al** o **en ~ de** around, about

derretir [derre'tir] vt (gen) to melt; (nieve) to thaw; **derretirse** vr to melt

derribar [derri'βar] vt to knock down; (construcción) to demolish; (persona, gobierno, político) to bring down

derrocar [derro'kar] vt (gobierno) to bring down, overthrow

derrochar [derro'tʃar] vt to squander; **derroche** nm (despilfarro) waste, squandering

derrota [de'rrota] nf (Náut) course; (Mil, Deporte etc) defeat, rout; **derrotar** vt (gen) to defeat; **derrotero** nm (rumbo) course

derrumbar [derrum'bar] vt (edificio) to knock down; **derrumbarse** vr to collapse

des etc vb V **dar**

desabrochar [desaβro'tʃar] vt (botones, broches) to undo, unfasten; **desabrocharse** vr (ropa etc) to come undone

desacato [desa'kato] nm (falta de respeto) disrespect; (Jur) contempt

desacertado, -a [desaθer'taðo, a] adj (equivocado) mistaken; (inoportuno) unwise

desacierto [desa'θjerto] nm mistake, error

desaconsejar [desakonse'xar] vt to advise against

desacreditar [desakreði'tar] vt (desprestigiar) to discredit, bring into disrepute; (denigrar) to run down

desacuerdo [desa'kwerðo] nm disagreement, discord

desafiar [desa'fjar] vt (retar) to challenge; (enfrentarse a) to defy

desafilado, -a [desafi'laðo, a]

adj blunt

desafinado, -a [desafi'naðo, a] *adj*: **estar ~** to be out of tune

desafinar [desafi'nar] *vi* (*al cantar*) to be *o* go out of tune

desafío *etc* [desa'fio] *vb* V **desafiar** ▷ *nm* (*reto*) challenge; (*combate*) duel; (*resistencia*) defiance

desafortunado, -a [desafortu'naðo, a] *adj* (*desgraciado*) unfortunate, unlucky

desagradable [desaɣra'ðaβle] *adj* (*fastidioso, enojoso*) unpleasant; (*irritante*) disagreeable

desagradar [desaɣra'ðar] *vi* (*disgustar*) to displease; (*molestar*) to bother

desagradecido, -a [desaɣraðe'θiðo, a] *adj* ungrateful

desagrado [desa'ɣraðo] *nm* (*disgusto*) displeasure; (*contrariedad*) dissatisfaction

desagüe [des'aɣwe] *nm* (*de un líquido*) drainage; (*cañería*) drainpipe; (*salida*) outlet, drain

desahogar [desao'ɣar] *vt* (*aliviar*) to ease, relieve; (*ira*) to vent; **desahogarse** *vr* (*relajarse*) to relax; (*desfogarse*) to let off steam

desahogo [desa'oxo] *nm* (*alivio*) relief; (*comodidad*) comfort, ease

desahuciar [desau'θjar] *vt* (*enfermo*) to give up hope for; (*inquilino*) to evict

desairar [desai'rar] *vt* (*menospreciar*) to slight, snub

desalentador, a [desalenta'ðor, a] *adj* discouraging

desaliño [desa'liɲo] *nm* slovenliness

desalmado, -a [desal'maðo, a] *adj* (*cruel*) cruel, heartless

desalojar [desalo'xar] *vt* (*expulsar, echar*) to eject; (*abandonar*) to move out of ▷ *vi* to move out

desamor [desa'mor] *nm* (*frialdad*) indifference; (*odio*) dislike

desamparado, -a [desampa'raðo, a] *adj* (*persona*) helpless; (*lugar: expuesto*) exposed; (*desierto*)

deserted

desangrar [desan'grar] *vt* to bleed; (*fig: persona*) to bleed dry; **desangrarse** *vr* to lose a lot of blood

desanimado, -a [desani'maðo, a] *adj* (*persona*) downhearted; (*espectáculo, fiesta*) dull

desanimar [desani'mar] *vt* (*desalentar*) to discourage; (*deprimir*) to depress; **desanimarse** *vr* to lose heart

desapacible [desapa'θiβle] *adj* (*gen*) unpleasant

desaparecer [desapare'θer] *vi* (*gen*) to disappear; (*el sol, la luz*) to vanish; **desaparecido, -a** *adj* missing; **desaparición** *nf* disappearance

desapercibido, -a [desaperθi'βiðo, a] *adj* (*desprevenido*) unprepared; **pasar ~** to go unnoticed

desaprensivo, -a [desapren'siβo, a] *adj* unscrupulous

desaprobar [desapro'βar] *vt* (*reprobar*) to disapprove of; (*condenar*) to condemn; (*no consentir*) to reject

desaprovechado, -a [desaproβe'tʃaðo, a] *adj* (*oportunidad, tiempo*) wasted; (*estudiante*) slack

desaprovechar [desaproβe'tʃar] *vt* to waste

desarmador [desarma'ðor] (MÉX) *nm* screwdriver

desarmar [desar'mar] *vt* (*Mil, fig*) to disarm; (*Tec*) to take apart, dismantle; **desarme** *nm* disarmament

desarraigar [desarrai'ɣar] *vt* to uproot; **desarraigo** *nm* uprooting

desarreglar [desarre'ɣlar] *vt* (*desordenar*) to disarrange; (*trastocar*) to upset, disturb

desarrollar [desarro'ʎar] *vt* (*gen*) to develop; **desarrollarse** *vr* to develop; (*ocurrir*) to take place; (*Foto*) to develop; **desarrollo** *nm* development

desarticular [desartiku'lar] *vt* (*hueso*) to dislocate; (*objeto*) to take apart; (*fig*) to break up

desasosegar [desasose'ɣar] *vt* (*inquietar*) to disturb, make uneasy

desasosiego etc [desaso'sjeɣo] vb
V **desasosegar** ▷ nm (intranquilidad)
uneasiness, restlessness; (ansiedad)
anxiety

desastre [de'sastre] nm disaster;
desastroso, -a adj disastrous

desatar [desa'tar] vt (nudo) to untie;
(paquete) to undo; (separar) to detach;
desatarse vr (zapatos) to come
untied; (tormenta) to break

desatascar [desatas'kar] vt (cañería)
to unblock, clear

desatender [desaten'der] vt no
prestar atención a, to disregard;
(abandonar) to neglect

desatino [desa'tino] nm (idiotez)
foolishness, folly; (error) blunder

desatornillar [desatorni'ʎar] vt to
unscrew

desatrancar [desatran'kar] vt
(puerta) to unbolt; (cañería) to clear,
unblock

desautorizado, -a [desautori'θaðo,
a] adj unauthorized

desautorizar [desautori'θar]
vt (oficial) to deprive of authority;
(informe) to deny

desayunar [desaju'nar] vi to have
breakfast ▷ vt to have for breakfast;
desayuno nm breakfast

desazón [desa'θon] nf anxiety

desbarajuste [desβara'xuste] nm
confusion, disorder

desbaratar [desβara'tar] vt
(deshacer, destruir) to ruin

desbloquear [desβloke'ar] vt
(negociaciónes, tráfico) to get going
again; (Com: cuenta) to unfreeze

desbordar [desβor'ðar] vt
(sobrepasar) to go beyond; (exceder)
to exceed; **desbordarse** vr (río) to
overflow; (entusiasmo) to erupt

descabellado, -a [deskaβe'ʎaðo, a]
adj (disparatado) wild, crazy

descafeinado, -a [deskafei'naðo, a]
adj decaffeinated ▷ nm decaffeinated
coffee

descalabro [deska'laβro] nm blow;

(desgracia) misfortune

descalificar [deskalifi'kar] vt to
disqualify; (desacreditar) to discredit

descalzar [deskal'θar] vt (zapato) to
take off; **descalzo, -a** adj barefoot(ed)

descambiar [deskam'bjar] vt to
exchange

descaminado, -a [deskami'naðo,
a] adj (equivocado) on the wrong road;
(fig) misguided

descampado [deskam'paðo] nm
open space

descansado, -a [deskan'saðo, a] adj
(gen) rested; (que tranquiliza) restful

descansar [deskan'sar] vt (gen) to
rest ▷ vi to rest, have a rest; (echarse)
to lie down

descansillo [deskan'siʎo] nm (de
escalera) landing

descanso [des'kanso] nm (reposo)
rest; (alivio) relief; (pausa) break;
(Deporte) interval, half time

descapotable [deskapo'taβle] nm
(tb: **coche ~**) convertible

descarado, -a [deska'raðo, a] adj
shameless; (insolente) cheeky

descarga [des'karɣa] nf (Arq, Elec,
Mil) discharge; (Náut) unloading;
descargar [deskar'ɣar] vt to unload;
(golpe) to let fly; **descargarse** vr to
unburden o.s.; **descargarse algo de
Internet** to download sth from the
Internet

descaro [des'karo] nm nerve

descarriar [deska'rrjar] vt
(descaminar) to misdirect; (fig) to lead
astray; **descarriarse** vr (perderse) to
lose one's way; (separarse) to stray;
(pervertirse) to err, go astray

descarrilamiento
[deskarrila'mjento] nm (de tren)
derailment

descarrilar [deskarri'lar] vi to be
derailed

descartar [deskar'tar] vt (rechazar)
to reject; (eliminar) to rule out;
descartarse vr (Naipes) to discard;
~se de to shirk

descendencia [desθen'denθja] nf
(origen) origin, descent; (hijos) offspring

descender [desθen'der] vt
(bajar: escalera) to go down ▷ vi to
descend; (temperatura, nivel) to fall,
drop; **~ de** to be descended from

descendiente [desθen'djente] nmf
descendant

descenso [des'θenso] nm descent;
(de temperatura) drop

descifrar [desθi'frar] vt to decipher;
(mensaje) to decode

descolgar [deskol'ɣar] vt (bajar)
to take down; (teléfono) to pick up;
descolgarse vr to let o.s. down

descolorido, -a [deskolo'riðo, a] adj
faded; (pálido) pale

descompasado, -a
[deskompa'saðo, a] adj (sin
proporción) out of all proportion;
(excesivo) excessive

descomponer [deskompo'ner] vt
(desordenar) to disarrange, disturb; (Tec)
to put out of order; (dividir) to break
down (into parts); (fig) to provoke;
descomponerse vr (corromperse) to
rot, decompose; (LAM Tec) to break
down

descomposición [deskomposi'θjon]
nf (de un objeto) breakdown; (de fruta
etc) decomposition; **descomposición
de vientre** (ESP) stomach upset,
diarrhoea

descompostura [deskompos'tura]
nf (MÉX: avería) breakdown, fault;
(LAM: diarrea) diarrhoea

descomprimir [deskompri'mir]
(Internet) to unzip

descompuesto, -a
[deskom'pwesto, a] adj (corrompido)
decomposed; (roto) broken

desconcertado, -a
[deskonθer'taðo, a] adj disconcerted,
bewildered

desconcertar [deskonθer'tar] vt
(confundir) to baffle; (incomodar) to
upset, put out; **desconcertarse** vr
(turbarse) to be upset

desconchado, -a [deskon'tʃaðo, a]
adj (pintura) peeling

desconcierto etc [deskon'θjerto] vb
V **desconcertar** ▷ nm (gen) disorder;
(desorientación) uncertainty; (inquietud)
uneasiness

desconectar [deskonek'tar] vt to
disconnect

desconfianza [deskon'fjanθa] nf
distrust

desconfiar [deskon'fjar] vi to be
distrustful; **~ de** to distrust, suspect

descongelar [deskonxe'lar] vt to
defrost; (Com, Pol) to unfreeze

descongestionar
[deskonxestjo'nar] vt (cabeza, tráfico)
to clear

desconocer [deskono'θer] vt
(ignorar) not to know, be ignorant of

desconocido, -a [deskono'θiðo, a]
adj unknown ▷ nm/f stranger

desconocimiento
[deskonoθi'mjento] nm falta de
conocimientos, ignorance

desconsiderado, -a
[deskonsiðe'raðo, a] adj
inconsiderate; (insensible) thoughtless

desconsuelo etc [deskon'swelo] vb
V **desconsolar** ▷ nm (tristeza) distress;
(desesperación) despair

descontado, -a [deskon'taðo, a]
adj: **dar por ~ (que)** to take (it) for
granted (that)

descontar [deskon'tar] vt (deducir)
to take away, deduct; (rebajar) to
discount

descontento, -a [deskon'tento, a]
adj dissatisfied ▷ nm dissatisfaction,
discontent

descorchar [deskor'tʃar] vt to
uncork

descorrer [desko'rrer] vt (cortinas,
cerrojo) to draw back

descortés [deskor'tes] adj (mal
educado) discourteous; (grosero) rude

descoser [desko'ser] vt to unstitch;
descoserse vr to come apart (at the
seams)

descosido, -a [desko'siðo, a] *adj*
(*Costura*) unstitched

descreído, -a [deskre'iðo, a] *adj*
(*incrédulo*) incredulous; (*falto de fe*)
unbelieving

descremado, -a [deskre'maðo, a]
adj skimmed

describir [deskri'βir] *vt* to describe;
descripción [deskrip'θjon] *nf*
description

descrito [des'krito] *pp de* **describir**

descuartizar [deskwarti'θar] *vt*
(*animal*) to cut up

descubierto, -a [desku'βjerto, a] *pp*
de **descubrir** ▷ *adj* uncovered, bare;
(*persona*) bareheaded ▷ *nm* (*bancario*)
overdraft; **al ~** in the open

descubrimiento [deskuβri'mjento]
nm (*hallazgo*) discovery; (*revelación*)
revelation

descubrir [desku'βrir] *vt* to discover,
find; (*inaugurar*) to unveil; (*vislumbrar*)
to detect; (*revelar*) to reveal, show;
(*destapar*) to uncover; **descubrirse** *vr*
to reveal o.s.; (*quitarse sombrero*) to take
off one's hat; (*confesar*) to confess

descuento *etc* [des'kwento] *vb* V
descontar ▷ *nm* discount

descuidado, -a [deskwi'ðaðo, a]
adj (*sin cuidado*) careless; (*desordenado*)
untidy; (*olvidadizo*) forgetful;
(*dejado*) neglected; (*desprevenido*)
unprepared

descuidar [deskwi'ðar] *vt* (*dejar*)
to neglect; (*olvidar*) to overlook;
descuidarse *vr* (*distraerse*) to be
careless; (*abandonarse*) to let o.s. go;
(*desprevenirse*) to drop one's guard;
¡descuida! don't worry!; **descuido**
nm (*dejadez*) carelessness; (*olvido*)
negligence

○ **PALABRA CLAVE**

desde ['desðe] *prep* **1** (*lugar*) from;
**desde Burgos hasta mi casa hay 30
km** it's 30 km from Burgos to my house
2 (*posición*): **hablaba desde el balcón**

she was speaking from the balcony
3 (*tiempo*: + *adv*, *n*): **desde ahora** from
now on; **desde la boda** since the
wedding; **desde niño** since I *etc* was
a child; **desde 3 años atrás** since 3
years ago
4 (*tiempo*: + *vb*, *fecha*) since; for; **nos
conocemos desde 1992/desde hace
20 años** we've known each other since
1992/for 20 years; **no le veo desde
1997/desde hace 5 años** I haven't seen
him since 1997/for 5 years
5 (*gama*): **desde los más lujosos hasta
los más económicos** from the most
luxurious to the most reasonably
priced
6: **desde luego (que no)** of course
(not)
▷ *conj*: **desde que**: **desde que
recuerdo** for as long as I can
remember; **desde que llegó no ha
salido** he hasn't been out since he
arrived

desdén [des'ðen] *nm* scorn

desdeñar [desðe'ɲar] *vt* (*despreciar*)
to scorn

desdicha [des'ðitʃa] *nf* (*desgracia*)
misfortune; (*infelicidad*) unhappiness;
desdichado, -a *adj* (*sin suerte*)
unlucky; (*infeliz*) unhappy

desear [dese'ar] *vt* to want, desire,
wish for

desechar [dese'tʃar] *vt* (*basura*) to
throw out *o* away; (*ideas*) to reject,
discard; **desechos** *nmpl* rubbish *sg*,
waste *sg*

desembalar [desemba'lar] *vt* to
unpack

desembarazar [desembara'θar] *vt*
(*desocupar*) to clear; (*desenredar*) to free;
desembarazarse *vr*: **~se de** to free o.s.
of, get rid of

desembarcar [desembar'kar] *vt*
(*mercancías etc*) to unload ▷ *vi* to
disembark

desembocadura [desemboka'ðura]
nf (*de río*) mouth; (*de calle*) opening

desembocar [desembo'kar] vi (río) to flow into; (fig) to result in

desembolso [desem'bolso] nm payment

desembrollar [desembro'ʎar] vt (madeja) to unravel; (asunto, malentendido) to sort out

desemejanza [deseme'xanθa] nf dissimilarity

desempaquetar [desempake'tar] vt (regalo) to unwrap; (mercancía) to unpack

desempate [desem'pate] nm (Fútbol) replay, play-off; (Tenis) tie-break(er)

desempeñar [desempe'ɲar] vt (cargo) to hold; (papel) to perform; (lo empeñado) to redeem; **~ un papel** (fig) to play (a role)

desempleado, -a [desemple'aðo, a] nm/f unemployed person; **desempleo** nm unemployment

desencadenar [desenkaðe'nar] vt to unchain; (ira) to unleash; **desencadenarse** vr to break loose; (tormenta) to burst; (guerra) to break out

desencajar [desenka'xar] vt (hueso) to dislocate; (mecanismo, pieza) to disconnect, disengage

desencanto [desen'kanto] nm disillusionment

desenchufar [desentʃu'far] vt to unplug

desenfadado, -a [desenfa'ðaðo, a] adj (desenvuelto) uninhibited; (descarado) forward; **desenfado** nm (libertad) freedom; (comportamiento) free and easy manner; (descaro) forwardness

desenfocado, -a [desenfo'kaðo, a] adj (Foto) out of focus

desenfreno [desen'freno] nm wildness; (de las pasiones) lack of self-control

desenganchar [desengan'tʃar] vt (gen) to unhook; (Ferro) to uncouple

desengañar [desenga'ɲar] vt to disillusion; **desengañarse** vr to become disillusioned; **desengaño** nm disillusionment; (decepción) disappointment

desenlace [desen'laθe] nm outcome

desenmascarar [desenmaska'rar] vt to unmask

desenredar [desenre'ðar] vt (pelo) to untangle; (problema) to sort out

desenroscar [desenros'kar] vt to unscrew

desentenderse [desenten'derse] vr: **~ de** to pretend not to know about; (apartarse) to have nothing to do with

desenterrar [desente'rrar] vt to exhume; (tesoro, fig) to unearth, dig up

desentonar [desento'nar] vi (Mús) to sing (o play) out of tune; (color) to clash

desentrañar [desentra'ɲar] vt (misterio) to unravel

desenvoltura [desenβol'tura] nf ease

desenvolver [desenβol'βer] vt (paquete) to unwrap; (fig) to develop; **desenvolverse** vr (desarrollarse) to unfold, develop; (arreglárselas) to cope

deseo [de'seo] nm desire, wish; **deseoso, -a** adj: **estar deseoso de** to be anxious to

desequilibrado, -a [desekili'βraðo, a] adj unbalanced

desertar [deser'tar] vi to desert

desértico, -a [de'sertiko, a] adj desert cpd

desesperación [desespera'θjon] nf (impaciencia) desperation, despair; (irritación) fury

desesperar [desespe'rar] vt to drive to despair; (exasperar) to drive to distraction ▷ vi: **~ de** to despair of; **desesperarse** vr to despair, lose hope

desestabilizar [desestaβili'θar] vt to destabilize

desestimar [desesti'mar] vt (menospreciar) to have a low opinion of; (rechazar) to reject

desfachatez [desfatʃa'teθ] nf (insolencia) impudence; (descaro) rudeness

desfalco [des'falko] *nm* embezzlement

desfallecer [desfaʎe'θer] *vi* (*perder las fuerzas*) to become weak; (*desvanecerse*) to faint

desfasado, -a [desfa'saðo, a] *adj* (*anticuado*) old-fashioned; **desfase** *nm* (*diferencia*) gap

desfavorable [desfaβo'raβle] *adj* unfavourable

desfigurar [desfixu'rar] *vt* (*cara*) to disfigure; (*cuerpo*) to deform

desfiladero [desfila'ðero] *nm* gorge

desfilar [desfi'lar] *vi* to parade; **desfile** *nm* procession; **desfile de modelos** fashion show

desgana [des'ɣana] *nf* (*falta de apetito*) loss of appetite; (*apatía*) unwillingness; **desganado, -a** *adj*: **estar desganado** (*sin apetito*) to have no appetite; (*sin entusiasmo*) to have lost interest

desgarrar [desɣa'rrar] *vt* to tear (up); (*fig*) to shatter; **desgarro** *nm* (*en tela*) tear; (*aflicción*) grief

desgastar [desɣas'tar] *vt* (*deteriorar*) to wear away o down; (*estropear*) to spoil; **desgastarse** *vr* to get worn out; **desgaste** *nm* wear (and tear)

desglosar [desɣlo'sar] *vt* (*factura*) to break down

desgracia [des'ɣraθja] *nf* misfortune; (*accidente*) accident; (*vergüenza*) disgrace; (*contratiempo*) setback; **por ~** unfortunately; **desgraciado, -a** [desɣra'θjaðo, a] *adj* (*sin suerte*) unlucky, unfortunate; (*miserable*) wretched; (*infeliz*) miserable

desgravar [desɣra'βar] *vt* (*impuestos*) to reduce the tax o duty on

desguace [des'ɣwaθe] (*ESP*) *nm* junkyard

deshabitado, -a [desaβi'taðo, a] *adj* uninhabited

deshacer [desa'θer] *vt* (*casa*) to break up; (*Tec*) to take apart; (*enemigo*) to defeat; (*diluir*) to melt; (*contrato*) to break; (*intriga*) to solve; **deshacerse**

vr (*disolverse*) to melt; (*despedazarse*) to come apart o undone; **~se de** to get rid of; **~se en lágrimas** to burst into tears

deshecho, -a [des'etʃo, a] *adj* undone; (*roto*) smashed; (*persona*) **estar ~** to be shattered

desheredar [desere'ðar] *vt* to disinherit

deshidratar [desiðra'tar] *vt* to dehydrate

deshielo [des'jelo] *nm* thaw

deshonesto, -a [deso'nesto, a] *adj* indecent

deshonra [des'onra] *nf* (*deshonor*) dishonour; (*vergüenza*) shame

deshora [des'ora]: **a ~** *adv* at the wrong time

deshuesadero [deswesa'ðero] (*MÉX*) *nm* junkyard

deshuesar [deswe'sar] *vt* (*carne*) to bone; (*fruta*) to stone

desierto, -a [de'sjerto, a] *adj* (*casa, calle, negocio*) deserted ▷ *nm* desert

designar [desix'nar] *vt* (*nombrar*) to designate; (*indicar*) to fix

desigual [desi'ɣwal] *adj* (*terreno*) uneven; (*lucha etc*) unequal

desilusión [desilu'sjon] *nf* disillusionment; (*decepción*) disappointment; **desilusionar** *vt* to disillusion; to disappoint; **desilusionarse** *vr* to become disillusioned

desinfectar [desinfek'tar] *vt* to disinfect

desinflar [desin'flar] *vt* to deflate

desintegración [desinteɣra'θjon] *nf* disintegration

desinterés [desinte'res] *nm* (*desgana*) lack of interest; (*altruismo*) unselfishness

desintoxicarse [desintoksi'karse] *vr* (*drogadicto*) to undergo detoxification

desistir [desis'tir] *vi* (*renunciar*) to stop, desist

desleal [desle'al] *adj* (*infiel*) disloyal; (*Com: competencia*) unfair; **deslealtad**

nf disloyalty

desligar [desli'xar] *vt* (*desatar*) to untie, undo; (*separar*) to separate; **desligarse** *vr* (*de un compromiso*) to extricate o.s.

desliz [des'liθ] *nm* (*fig*) lapse; **deslizar** *vt* to slip, slide

deslumbrar [deslum'brar] *vt* to dazzle

desmadrarse [desma'ðrarse] (*fam*) *vr* (*descontrolarse*) to run wild; (*divertirse*) to let one's hair down; **desmadre** (*fam*) *nm* (*desorganización*) chaos; (*jaleo*) commotion

desmán [des'man] *nm* (*exceso*) outrage; (*abuso de poder*) abuse

desmantelar [desmante'lar] *vt* (*deshacer*) to dismantle; (*casa*) to strip

desmaquillador [desmakiʎa'ðor] *nm* make-up remover

desmayar [desma'jar] *vi* to lose heart; **desmayarse** *vr* (*Med*) to faint; **desmayo** *nm* (*Med: acto*) faint; (*: estado*) unconsciousness

desmemoriado, -a [desmemo'rjaðo, a] *adj* forgetful

desmentir [desmen'tir] *vt* (*contradecir*) to contradict; (*refutar*) to deny

desmenuzar [desmenu'θar] *vt* (*deshacer*) to crumble; (*carne*) to chop; (*examinar*) to examine closely

desmesurado, -a [desmesu'raðo, a] *adj* disproportionate

desmontable [desmon'taβle] *adj* (*que se quita: pieza*) detachable; (*plegable*) collapsible, folding

desmontar [desmon'tar] *vt* (*deshacer*) to dismantle; (*tierra*) to level ▷ *vi* to dismount

desmoralizar [desmorali'θar] *vt* to demoralize

desmoronar [desmoro'nar] *vt* to wear away, erode; **desmoronarse** *vr* (*edificio, dique*) to collapse; (*economía*) to decline

desnatado, -a [desna'taðo, a] *adj* skimmed

desnivel [desni'βel] *nm* (*de terreno*) unevenness

desnudar [desnu'ðar] *vt* (*desvestir*) to undress; (*despojar*) to strip; **desnudarse** *vr* (*desvestirse*) to get undressed; **desnudo, -a** *adj* naked ▷ *nm/f* nude; **desnudo de** devoid o bereft of

desnutrición [desnutri'θjon] *nf* malnutrition; **desnutrido, -a** *adj* undernourished

desobedecer [desoβeðe'θer] *vt*, *vi* to disobey; **desobediencia** *nf* disobedience

desocupado, -a [desoku'paðo, a] *adj* at leisure; (*desempleado*) unemployed; (*deshabitado*) empty, vacant

desodorante [desoðo'rante] *nm* deodorant

desolación [desola'θjon] *nf* (*de lugar*) desolation; (*fig*) grief

desolar [deso'lar] *vt* to ruin, lay waste

desorbitado, -a [desorβi'taðo, a] *adj* (*excesivo: ambición*) boundless; (*deseos*) excessive; (*: precio*) exorbitant

desorden [des'orðen] *nm* confusion; (*político*) disorder, unrest

desorganización [desorxaniθa'θjon] *nf* (*de persona*) disorganization; (*en empresa, oficina*) disorder, chaos

desorientar [desorjen'tar] *vt* (*extraviar*) to mislead; (*confundir, desconcertar*) to confuse; **desorientarse** *vr* (*perderse*) to lose one's way

despabilado, -a [despaβi'laðo, a] *adj* (*despierto*) wide-awake; (*fig*) alert, sharp

despachar [despa'tʃar] *vt* (*negocio*) to do, complete; (*enviar*) to send, dispatch; (*vender*) to sell, deal in; (*billete*) to issue; (*mandar ir*) to send away

despacho [des'patʃo] *nm* (*oficina*) office; (*de paquetes*) dispatch; (*venta*) sale; (*comunicación*) message

despacio [des'paθjo] *adv* slowly

desparpajo [despar'paxo] *nm* self-confidence; (*pey*) nerve

desparramar [desparra'mar] *vt*
(*esparcir*) to scatter; (*líquido*) to spill

despecho [des'petʃo] *nm* spite

despectivo, -a [despek'tiβo, a]
adj (*despreciativo*) derogatory; (*Ling*)
pejorative

despedida [despe'ðiða] *nf* (*adiós*)
farewell; (*de obrero*) sacking

despedir [despe'ðir] *vt* (*visita*) to see
off, show out; (*empleado*) to dismiss;
(*inquilino*) to evict; (*objeto*) to hurl; (*olor
etc*) to give out o off; **despedirse** *vr*: **~se
de** to say goodbye to

despegar [despe'ɣar] *vt* to unstick
▷ *vi* (*avión*) to take off; **despegarse** *vr*
to come loose, come unstuck; **despego**
nm detachment

despegue *etc* [des'peɣe] *vb* V
despegar ▷ *nm* takeoff

despeinado, -a [despei'naðo, a] *adj*
dishevelled, unkempt

despejado, -a [despe'xaðo, a] *adj*
(*lugar*) clear, free; (*cielo*) clear; (*persona*)
wide-awake, bright

despejar [despe'xar] *vt* (*gen*) to clear;
(*misterio*) to clear up ▷ *vi* (*el tiempo*) to
clear; **despejarse** *vr* (*tiempo, cielo*) to
clear (up); (*misterio*) to become clearer;
(*cabeza*) to clear

despensa [des'pensa] *nf* larder

despeñarse [despe'ɲarse] *vr* to hurl
o.s. down; (*coche*) to tumble over

desperdicio [desper'ðiθjo] *nm*
(*despilfarro*) squandering; **desperdicios**
nmpl (*basura*) rubbish *sg* (BRIT), garbage
sg (US); (*residuos*) waste *sg*

desperezarse [despere'θarse] *vr*
to stretch

desperfecto [desper'fekto] *nm*
(*deterioro*) slight damage; (*defecto*) flaw,
imperfection

despertador [desperta'ðor] *nm*
alarm clock

despertar [desper'tar] *nm*
awakening ▷ *vt* (*persona*) to wake
up; (*recuerdos*) to revive; (*sentimiento*)
to arouse ▷ *vi* to awaken, wake up;

despertarse *vr* to awaken, wake up

despido *etc* [des'piðo] *vb* V **despedir**
▷ *nm* dismissal, sacking

despierto, -a etc [des'pjerto, a]
vb V **despertar** ▷ *adj* awake; (*fig*)
sharp, alert

despilfarro [despil'farro] *nm*
(*derroche*) squandering; (*lujo desmedido*)
extravagance

despistar [despis'tar] *vt* to throw off
the track o scent; (*confundir*) to mislead,
confuse; **despistarse** *vr* to take the
wrong road; (*confundirse*) to become
confused

despiste [des'piste] *nm* absent-
mindedness; **un ~** a mistake o slip

desplazamiento [desplaθa'mjento]
nm displacement

desplazar [despla'θar] *vt* to move;
(*Náut*) to displace; (*Inform*) to scroll;
(*fig*) to oust; **desplazarse** *vr* (*persona*)
to travel

desplegar [desple'ɣar] *vt* (*tela, papel*)
to unfold, open out; (*bandera*) to unfurl;
despliegue *etc* [des'pleɣe] *vb* V
desplegar ▷ *nm* display

desplomarse [desplo'marse] *vr*
(*edificio, gobierno, persona*) to collapse

desplumar [desplu'mar] *vt* (*ave*) to
pluck; (*fam: estafar*) to fleece

despoblado, -a [despo'βlaðo, a] *adj*
(*sin habitantes*) uninhabited

despojar [despo'xar] *vt* (*alguien: de
sus bienes*) to divest of, deprive of; (*casa*)
to strip, leave bare; (*alguien: de su cargo*)
to strip of

despojo [des'poxo] *nm* (*acto*)
plundering; (*objetos*) plunder, loot;
despojos *nmpl* (*de ave, res*) offal *sg*

desposado, -a [despo'saðo, a] *adj,
nm/f* newly-wed

despreciar [despre'θjar] *vt* (*desdeñar*)
to despise, scorn; (*afrentar*) to slight;
desprecio *nm* scorn, contempt; slight

desprender [despren'der] *vt*
(*broche*) to unfasten; (*olor*) to give off;
desprenderse *vr* (*botón: caerse*) to fall
off; (*broche*) to come unfastened; (*olor,*

perfume) to be given off; **~se de algo que ...** to draw from sth that ...

desprendimiento
[desprendi'mjento] *nm* (*gen*) loosening; (*generosidad*) disinterestedness; (*de tierra, rocas*) landslide; **desprendimiento de retina** detachment of the retina

despreocupado, -a
[despreoku'paðo, a] *adj* (*sin preocupación*) unworried, nonchalant; (*negligente*) careless

despreocuparse [despreoku'parse] *vr* not to worry; **~ de** to have no interest in

desprestigiar [despresti'xjar] *vt* (*criticar*) to run down; (*desacreditar*) to discredit

desprevenido, -a [despreβe'niðo, a] *adj* (*no preparado*) unprepared, unready

desproporcionado, -a [despropor θjo'naðo, a] *adj* disproportionate, out of proportion

desprovisto, -a [despro'βisto, a] *adj*: **~ de** devoid of

después [des'pwes] *adv* afterwards, later; (*próximo paso*) next; **~ de comer** after lunch; **un año ~** a year later; **~ se debatió el tema** next the matter was discussed; **~ de corregido el texto** after the text had been corrected; **~ de todo** after all

desquiciado, -a [deski'θjaðo, a] *adj* deranged

destacar [desta'kar] *vt* to emphasize, point up; (*Mil*) to detach, detail ⊳ *vi* (*resaltarse*) to stand out; (*persona*) to be outstanding *o* exceptional; **destacarse** *vr* to stand out; to be outstanding *o* exceptional

destajo [des'taxo] *nm*: **trabajar a ~** to do piecework

destapar [desta'par] *vt* (*botella*) to open; (*cacerola*) to take the lid off; (*descubrir*) to uncover; **destaparse** *vr* (*revelarse*) to reveal one's true character

destartalado, -a [destarta'laðo,

a] *adj* (*desordenado*) untidy; (*ruinoso*) tumbledown

destello [des'teʎo] *nm* (*de estrella*) twinkle; (*de faro*) signal light

destemplado, -a [destem'plaðo, a] *adj* (*Mús*) out of tune; (*voz*) harsh; (*Med*) out of sorts; (*tiempo*) unpleasant, nasty

desteñir [deste'ɲir] *vt* to fade ⊳ *vi* to fade; **desteñirse** *vr* to fade; **esta tela no destiñe** this fabric will not run

desternillarse [desterni'ʎarse] *vr*: **~ de risa** to split one's sides laughing

desterrar [deste'rrar] *vt* (*exiliar*) to exile; (*fig*) to banish, dismiss

destiempo [des'tjempo] **a ~** *adv* out of turn

destierro *etc* [des'tjerro] *vb* V **desterrar** ⊳ *nm* exile

destilar [desti'lar] *vt* to distil; **destilería** *nf* distillery

destinar [desti'nar] *vt* (*funcionario*) to appoint, assign; (*fondos*) **~ (a)** to set aside (for)

destinatario, -a [destina'tarjo, a] *nm/f* addressee

destino [des'tino] *nm* (*suerte*) destiny; (*de avión, viajero*) destination; **con ~ a Londres** (*barco*) (bound) for London; (*avión, carta*) to London

destituir [destitu'ir] *vt* to dismiss

destornillador [destorniʎa'ðor] *nm* screwdriver

destornillar [destorni'ʎar] *vt* (*tornillo*) to unscrew; **destornillarse** *vr* to unscrew

destreza [des'treθa] *nf* (*habilidad*) skill; (*maña*) dexterity

destrozar [destro'θar] *vt* (*romper*) to smash, break (up); (*estropear*) to ruin; (*nervios*) to shatter

destrozo [des'troθo] *nm* (*acción*) destruction; (*desastre*) smashing; **destrozos** *nmpl* (*pedazos*) pieces; (*daños*) havoc *sg*

destrucción [destruk'θjon] *nf* destruction

destruir [destru'ir] *vt* to destroy

desuso [des'uso] *nm* disuse; **caer en**

~ to become obsolete

desvalijar [desβali'xar] vt (persona) to rob; (casa, tienda) to burgle; (coche) to break into

desván [des'βan] nm attic

desvanecer [desβane'θer] vt (disipar) to dispel; (borrar) to blur; **desvanecerse** vr (humo etc) to vanish, disappear; (color) to fade; (recuerdo, sonido) to fade away; (Med) to pass out; (duda) to be dispelled

desvariar [desβa'rjar] vi (enfermo) to be delirious

desvelar [desβe'lar] vt to keep awake; **desvelarse** vr (no poder dormir) to stay awake; (preocuparse) to be vigilant o watchful

desventaja [desβen'taxa] nf disadvantage

desvergonzado, -a [desβerɣon'θaðo, a] adj shameless

desvestir [desβes'tir] vt to undress; **desvestirse** vr to undress

desviación [desβja'θjon] nf deviation; (Auto) diversion, detour

desviar [des'βjar] vt to turn aside; (río) to alter the course of; (navío) to divert, re-route; (conversación) to sidetrack; **desviarse** vr (apartarse del camino) to turn aside; (: barco) to go off course

desvío etc [des'βio] vb V **desviar** ▷ nm (desviación) detour, diversion; (fig) indifference

desvivirse [desβi'βirse] vr: ~ por (anhelar) to long for, crave for; (hacer lo posible por) to do one's utmost for

detallar [deta'ʎar] vt to detail

detalle [de'taʎe] nm detail; (gesto) gesture, token; **al** ~ in detail; (Com) retail

detallista [deta'ʎista] nmf (Com) retailer

detective [detek'tiβe] nmf detective; **detective privado** private detective

detener [dete'ner] vt (gen) to stop; (Jur) to arrest; (objeto) to keep; **detenerse** vr to stop; (demorarse): ~se

en to delay over, linger over

detenidamente [deteniða'mente] adv (minuciosamente) carefully; (extensamente) at great length

detenido, -a [dete'niðo, a] adj (arrestado) under arrest ▷ nm/f person under arrest, prisoner

detenimiento [deteni'mjento] nm: **con** ~ thoroughly; (observar, considerar) carefully

detergente [deter'xente] nm detergent

deteriorar [deterjo'rar] vt to spoil, damage; **deteriorarse** vr to deteriorate; **deterioro** nm deterioration

determinación [determina'θjon] nf (empeño) determination; (decisión) decision; **determinado, -a** adj specific

determinar [determi'nar] vt (plazo) to fix; (precio) to settle; **determinarse** vr to decide

detestar [detes'tar] vt to detest

detractor, a [detrak'tor, a] nm/f slanderer, libeller

detrás [de'tras] adv (tb: **por** ~) behind; (atrás) at the back; ~ **de** behind

detrimento [detri'mento] nm: **en** ~ **de** to the detriment of

deuda ['deuða] nf debt; **deuda exterior/pública** foreign/national debt

devaluación [deβalwa'θjon] nf devaluation

devastar [deβas'tar] vt (destruir) to devastate

deveras [de'βeras] (MÉX) nf inv: **un amigo de (a)** ~ a true o real friend

devoción [deβo'θjon] nf devotion

devolución [deβolu'θjon] nf (reenvío) return, sending back; (reembolso) repayment; (Jur) devolution

devolver [deβol'βer] vt to return; (lo extraviado, lo prestado) to give back; (carta al correo) to send back; (Com) to repay, refund ▷ vi (vomitar) to be sick

devorar [deβo'rar] vt to devour

devoto, -a [de'βoto, a] *adj* devout
▷ *nm/f* admirer

devuelto *pp de* **devolver**

devuelva *etc vb* ∨ **devolver**

di *etc vb* ∨ **dar; decir**

día ['dia] *nm* day; **¿qué ~ es?** what's
the date?; **estar/poner al ~** to be/keep
up to date; **el ~ de hoy/de mañana**
today/tomorrow; **al ~ siguiente** (on)
the following day; **vivir al ~** to live from
hand to mouth; **de ~** by day, in daylight;
en pleno ~ in full daylight; **Día de la
Independencia** Independence Day;
Día de los Muertos (*MÉX*) All Souls'
Day; **Día de Reyes** Epiphany; **día
feriado** (*LAM*) holiday; **día festivo** (*ESP*)
holiday; **día lectivo** teaching day; **día
libre** day off

diabetes [dja'βetes] *nf* diabetes

diablo ['djaβlo] *nm* devil; **diablura**
nf prank

diadema [dja'ðema] *nf* tiara

diafragma [dja'fraxma] *nm*
diaphragm

diagnóstico [diax'nostiko] *nm* =
diagnosis

diagonal [djaxo'nal] *adj* diagonal

diagrama [dja'xrama] *nm* diagram

dial [djal] *nm* dial

dialecto [dja'lekto] *nm* dialect

dialogar [djalo'xar] *vi*: **~ con** (*Pol*) to
hold talks with

diálogo ['djaloxo] *nm* dialogue

diamante [dja'mante] *nm* diamond

diana ['djana] *nf* (*Mil*) reveille; (*de
blanco*) centre, bull's-eye

diapositiva [djaposi'tiβa] *nf* (*Foto*)
slide, transparency

diario, -a ['djarjo, a] *adj* daily ▷ *nm*
newspaper; **a ~** daily; **de ~** everyday

diarrea [dja'rrea] *nf* diarrhoea

dibujar [diβu'xar] *vt* to draw,
sketch; **dibujo** *nm* drawing; **dibujos
animados** cartoons

diccionario [dikθjo'narjo] *nm*
dictionary

dice *etc vb* ∨ **decir**

dicho, -a ['ditʃo, a] *pp de*

decir ▷ *adj*: **en ~s países** in the
aforementioned countries ▷ *nm*
saying

dichoso, -a [di'tʃoso, a] *adj* happy

diciembre [di'θjembre] *nm*
December

dictado [dik'taðo] *nm* dictation

dictador [dikta'ðor] *nm* dictator;
dictadura *nf* dictatorship

dictar [dik'tar] *vt* (*carta*) to dictate;
(*Jur: sentencia*) to pronounce; (*decreto*) to
issue; (*LAM: clase*) to give

didáctico, -a [di'ðaktiko, a] *adj*
educational

diecinueve [djeθi'nweβe] *num*
nineteen

dieciocho [djeθi'otʃo] *num* eighteen

dieciséis [djeθi'seis] *num* sixteen

diecisiete [djeθi'sjete] *num*
seventeen

diente ['djente] *nm* (*Anat, Tec*) tooth;
(*Zool*) fang; (: *de elefante*) tusk; (*de
ajo*) clove

diera *etc vb* ∨ **dar**

diesel ['disel] *adj*: **motor ~** diesel
engine

diestro, -a ['djestro, a] *adj* (*derecho*)
right; (*hábil*) skilful

dieta ['djeta] *nf* diet; **estar a ~** to be
on a diet

diez [djeθ] *num* ten

diferencia [dife'renθja] *nf*
difference; **a ~ de** unlike; **diferenciar**
vt to differentiate between ▷ *vi* to
differ; **diferenciarse** *vr* to differ, be
different; (*distinguirse*) to distinguish
o.s.

diferente [dife'rente] *adj* different

diferido [dife'riðo] *nm*: **en ~** (*TV etc*)
recorded

difícil [di'fiθil] *adj* difficult

dificultad [difikul'tað] *nf* difficulty;
(*problema*) trouble

dificultar [difikul'tar] *vt* (*complicar*)
to complicate, make difficult; (*estorbar*)
to obstruct

difundir [difun'dir] *vt* (*calor, luz*)
to diffuse; (*Radio, TV*) to broadcast; **~**

una noticia to spread a piece of news;
difundirse vr to spread (out)
difunto, -a [di'funto, a] adj dead,
deceased ▷ nm/f deceased (person)
difusión [difu'sjon] nf (Radio, TV)
broadcasting
diga etc vb V **decir**
digerir [dixe'rir] vt to digest; (fig)
to absorb; **digestión** nf digestion;
digestivo, -a adj digestive
digital [dixi'tal] adj digital
dignarse [dix'narse] vr to deign to
dignidad [dixni'ðað] nf dignity
digno, -a ['dixno, a] adj worthy
digo etc vb V **decir**
dije etc vb V **decir**
dilatar [dila'tar] vt (cuerpo) to dilate;
(prolongar) to prolong
dilema [di'lema] nm dilemma
diluir [dilu'ir] vt to dilute
diluvio [di'luβjo] nm deluge, flood
dimensión [dimen'sjon] nf
dimension
diminuto, -a [dimi'nuto, a] adj tiny,
diminutive
dimitir [dimi'tir] vi to resign
dimos vb V **dar**
Dinamarca [dina'marka] nf
Denmark
dinámico, -a [di'namiko, a] adj
dynamic
dinamita [dina'mita] nf dynamite
dínamo ['dinamo] nf dynamo
dineral [dine'ral] nm large sum of
money, fortune
dinero [di'nero] nm money; **dinero
en efectivo** o **metálico** cash; **dinero
suelto** (loose) change
dio vb V **dar**
dios [djos] nm god; **¡D~ mío!** (oh,) my
God!; **¡por D~!** for heaven's sake!; **diosa**
['djosa] nf goddess
diploma [di'ploma] nm diploma
diplomacia [diplo'maθja] nf
diplomacy; (fig) tact
diplomado, -a [diplo'maðo, a] adj
qualified
diplomático, -a [diplo'matiko, a]

adj diplomatic ▷ nm/f diplomat
diputación [diputa'θjon] nf (tb: **~
provincial**) ≈ county council
diputado, -a [dipu'taðo, a] nm/f
delegate; (Pol) ≈ member of parliament
(BRIT) ≈ representative (US)
dique ['dike] nm dyke
diré etc vb V **decir**
dirección [direk'θjon] nf direction;
(señas) address; (Auto) steering;
(gerencia) management; (Pol)
leadership; **dirección única/
prohibida** one-way street/no entry
direccional [direkθjo'nal] (MÉX) nf
(Auto) indicator
directa [di'rekta] nf (Auto) top gear
directiva [direk'tiβa] nf (tb: **junta ~**)
board of directors
directo, -a [di'rekto, a] adj direct;
(Radio, TV) live; **transmitir en ~** to
broadcast live
director, a [direk'tor, a] adj leading
▷ nm/f director; (Escol) head (teacher)
(BRIT), principal (US); (gerente)
manager/ess; (Prensa) editor; **director
de cine** film director; **director general**
managing director
directorio [direk'torjo] (MÉX) nm
(telefónico) phone book
dirigente [diri'xente] nmf (Pol)
leader
dirigir [diri'xir] vt to direct; (carta) to
address; (obra de teatro, film) to direct;
(Mús) to conduct; (negocio) to manage;
dirigirse vr: **~se a** to go towards,
make one's way towards; (hablar con)
to speak to
dirija etc vb V **dirigir**
disciplina [disθi'plina] nf discipline
discípulo, -a [dis'θipulo, a] nm/f
disciple
Discman® ['diskman] nm
Discman®
disco ['disko] nm disc; (Deporte)
discus; (Tel) dial; (Auto: semáforo) light;
(Mús) record; **disco compacto/de
larga duración** compact disc/long-
playing record; **disco de freno** brake

disc; **disco flexible/duro** o **rígido** (*Inform*) floppy/hard disk

disconforme [diskon'forme] *adj* differing; **estar ~ (con)** to be in disagreement (with)

discordia [dis'korðja] *nf* discord

discoteca [disko'teka] *nf* disco(theque)

discreción [diskre'θjon] *nf* discretion; (*reserva*) prudence; **comer a ~** to eat as much as one wishes

discreto, -a [dis'kreto, a] *adj* discreet

discriminación [diskrimina'θjon] *nf* discrimination

disculpa [dis'kulpa] *nf* excuse; (*pedir perdón*) apology; **pedir ~s a/por** to apologize to/for; **disculpar** *vt* to excuse, pardon; **disculparse** *vr* to excuse o.s.; to apologize

discurso [dis'kurso] *nm* speech

discusión [disku'sjon] *nf* (*diálogo*) discussion; (*riña*) argument

discutir [disku'tir] *vt* (*debatir*) to discuss; (*pelear*) to argue about; (*contradecir*) to argue against ▷ *vi* (*debatir*) to discuss; (*pelearse*) to argue

disecar [dise'kar] *vt* (*conservar*: *animal*) to stuff; (: *planta*) to dry

diseñar [dise'ɲar] *vt, vi* to design

diseño [di'seɲo] *nm* design

disfraz [dis'fraθ] *nm* (*máscara*) disguise; (*excusa*) pretext; **disfrazar** *vt* to disguise; **disfrazarse** *vr*: **disfrazarse de** to disguise o.s. as

disfrutar [disfru'tar] *vt* to enjoy ▷ *vi* to enjoy o.s.; **~ de** to enjoy, possess

disgustar [disɣus'tar] *vt* (*no gustar*) to displease; (*contrariar, enojar*) to annoy, upset; **disgustarse** *vr* (*enfadarse*) to get upset; (*dos personas*) to fall out

> No confundir **disgustar** con la palabra inglesa *disgust*.

disgusto [dis'ɣusto] *nm* (*contrariedad*) annoyance; (*tristeza*) grief; (*riña*) quarrel

disimular [disimu'lar] *vt* (*ocultar*) to hide, conceal ▷ *vi* to dissemble

dislocarse [dislo'karse] *vr* (*articulación*) to sprain, dislocate

disminución [disminu'θjon] *nf* decrease, reduction

disminuido, -a [disminu'iðo, a] *nm/f*: **~ mental/físico** mentally/physically handicapped person

disminuir [disminu'ir] *vt* to decrease, diminish

disolver [disol'βer] *vt* (*gen*) to dissolve; **disolverse** *vr* to dissolve; (*Com*) to go into liquidation

dispar [dis'par] *adj* different

disparar [dispa'rar] *vt, vi* to shoot, fire

disparate [dispa'rate] *nm* (*tontería*) foolish remark; (*error*) blunder; **decir ~s** to talk nonsense

disparo [dis'paro] *nm* shot

dispersar [disper'sar] *vt* to disperse; **dispersarse** *vr* to scatter

disponer [dispo'ner] *vt* (*arreglar*) to arrange; (*ordenar*) to put in order; (*preparar*) to prepare, get ready ▷ *vi*: **~ de** to have, own; **disponerse** *vr*: **~se a** o **para hacer** to prepare to do

disponible [dispo'niβle] *adj* available

disposición [disposi'θjon] *nf* arrangement, disposition; (*voluntad*) willingness; (*Inform*) layout; **a su ~** at your service

dispositivo [disposi'tiβo] *nm* device, mechanism

dispuesto, -a [dis'pwesto, a] *pp de* **disponer** ▷ *adj* (*arreglado*) arranged; (*preparado*) disposed

disputar [dispu'tar] *vt* (*carrera*) to compete in

disquete [dis'kete] *nm* floppy disk, diskette

distancia [dis'tanθja] *nf* distance; **distanciar** [distan'θjar] *vt* to space out; **distanciarse** *vr* to become estranged; **distante** [dis'tante] *adj* distant

diste *vb* V **dar**

disteis *vb* V **dar**

distinción [distin'θjon] *nf*
distinction; (*elegancia*) elegance;
(*honor*) honour

distinguido, -a [distin'giðo, a] *adj*
distinguished

distinguir [distin'gir] *vt* to
distinguish; (*escoger*) to single out;
distinguirse *vr* to be distinguished

distintivo [distin'tiβo] *nm* badge;
(*fig*) characteristic

distinto, -a [dis'tinto, a] *adj*
different; (*claro*) clear

distracción [distrak'θjon] *nf*
distraction; (*pasatiempo*) hobby,
pastime; (*olvido*) absent-mindedness,
distraction

distraer [distra'er] *vt* (*atención*) to
distract; (*divertir*) to amuse; (*fondos*) to
embezzle; **distraerse** *vr* (*entretenerse*)
to amuse o.s.; (*perder la concentración*) to
allow one's attention to wander

distraído, -a [distra'iðo, a] *adj* (*gen*)
absent-minded; (*entretenido*) amusing

distribuidor, a [distriβui'ðor, a]
nm/f distributor; **distribuidora** *nf*
(*Com*) dealer, agent; (*Cine*) distributor

distribuir [distriβu'ir] *vt* to
distribute

distrito [dis'trito] *nm* (*sector,
territorio*) region; (*barrio*) district;
Distrito Federal (*MÉX*) Federal District;
distrito postal postal district

disturbio [dis'turβjo] *nm*
disturbance; (*desorden*) riot

disuadir [diswa'ðir] *vt* to dissuade

disuelto [di'swelto] *pp de* **disolver**

DIU *nm abr* (= *dispositivo intrauterino*)
IUD

diurno, -a ['djurno, a] *adj* day *cpd*

divagar [diβa'xar] *vi* (*desviarse*) to
digress

diván [di'βan] *nm* divan

diversidad [diβersi'ðað] *nf* diversity,
variety

diversión [diβer'sjon] *nf* (*gen*)
entertainment; (*actividad*) hobby,
pastime

diverso, -a [di'βerso, a] *adj* diverse;

~s libros several books; **diversos** *nmpl*
sundries

divertido, -a [diβer'tiðo, a] *adj*
(*chiste*) amusing; (*fiesta etc*) enjoyable

divertir [diβer'tir] *vt* (*entretener,
recrear*) to amuse; **divertirse** *vr*
(*pasarlo bien*) to have a good time;
(*distraerse*) to amuse o.s.

dividendos [diβi'ðendos] *nmpl*
(*Com*) dividends

dividir [diβi'ðir] *vt* (*gen*) to divide;
(*distribuir*) to distribute, share out

divierta *etc vb* V **divertir**

divino, -a [di'βino, a] *adj* divine

divirtiendo *etc vb* V **divertir**

divisa [di'βisa] *nf* (*emblema*)
emblem, badge; **divisas** *nfpl* foreign
exchange *sg*

divisar [diβi'sar] *vt* to make out,
distinguish

división [diβi'sjon] *nf* (*gen*) division;
(*de partido*) split; (*de país*) partition

divorciar [diβor'θjar] *vt* to divorce;
divorciarse *vr* to get divorced;
divorcio *nm* divorce

divulgar [diβul'xar] *vt* (*ideas*) to
spread; (*secreto*) to divulge

DNI (*ESP*) *nm abr* (= *Documento Nacional
de Identidad*) *national identity card*

> ● **DNI**
> ●
> ● The **Documento Nacional de**
> ● **Identidad** is a Spanish ID card
> ● which must be carried at all times
> ● and produced on request for the
> ● police. It contains the holder's
> ● photo, fingerprints and personal
> ● details. It is also known as the **DNI**
> ● or "carnet de identidad".

Dña. *abr* (= *doña*) Mrs

do [do] *nm* (*Mús*) do, C

dobladillo [doβla'ðiʎo] *nm* (*de
vestido*) hem; (*de pantalón: vuelta*) turn-
up (*BRIT*), cuff (*US*)

doblar [do'βlar] *vt* to double; (*papel*)
to fold; (*caño*) to bend; (*la esquina*) to

turn, go round; (*film*) to dub ▷ *vi* to turn; (*campana*) to toll; **doblarse** *vr* (*plegarse*) to fold (up), crease; (*encorvarse*) to bend; **~ a la derecha/izquierda** to turn right/left

doble ['doβle] *adj* double; (*de dos aspectos*) dual; (*fig*) two-faced ▷ *nm* double ▷ *nmf* (*Teatro*) double, stand-in; **dobles** *nmpl* (*Deporte*) doubles *sg*; **con ~ sentido** with a double meaning

doce ['doθe] *num* twelve; **docena** *nf* dozen

docente [do'θente] *adj*: **centro/personal ~** teaching establishment/staff

dócil ['doθil] *adj* (*pasivo*) docile; (*obediente*) obedient

doctor, a [dok'tor, a] *nm/f* doctor

doctorado [dokto'raðo] *nm* doctorate

doctrina [dok'trina] *nf* doctrine, teaching

documentación [dokumenta'θjon] *nf* documentation, papers *pl*

documental [dokumen'tal] *adj, nm* documentary

documento [doku'mento] *nm* (*certificado*) document; **documento adjunto** (*Inform*) attachment; **documento nacional de identidad** identity card

dólar ['dolar] *nm* dollar

doler [do'ler] *vt, vi* to hurt; (*fig*) to grieve; **dolerse** *vr* (*de su situación*) to grieve, feel sorry; (*de las desgracias ajenas*) to sympathize; **me duele el brazo** my arm hurts

dolor [do'lor] *nm* pain; (*fig*) grief, sorrow; **dolor de cabeza/estómago/muelas** headache/stomachache/toothache

domar [do'mar] *vt* to tame

domesticar [domesti'kar] *vt* = **domar**

doméstico, -a [do'mestiko, a] *adj* (*vida, servicio*) home; (*tareas*) household; (*animal*) tame, pet

domicilio [domi'θiljo] *nm* home;

servicio a **~** home delivery service; **sin ~ fijo** of no fixed abode; **domicilio particular** private residence

dominante [domi'nante] *adj* dominant; (*persona*) domineering

dominar [domi'nar] *vt* (*gen*) to dominate; (*idiomas*) to be fluent in ▷ *vi* to dominate, prevail

domingo [do'mingo] *nm* Sunday; **Domingo de Ramos/Resurrección** Palm/Easter Sunday

dominio [do'minjo] *nm* (*tierras*) domain; (*autoridad*) power, authority; (*de las pasiones*) grip, hold; (*de idiomas*) command

don [don] *nm* (*talento*) gift; **~ Juan Gómez** Mr Juan Gómez, Juan Gómez Esq (*BRIT*)

- **DON/DOÑA**
-
- The term **don/doña** often
- abbreviated to **D./Dña** is placed
- before the first name as a mark
- of respect to an older or more
- senior person – eg Don Diego,
- Doña Inés. Although becoming
- rarer in Spain it is still used
- with names and surnames on
- official documents and formal
- correspondence – eg "Sr. D. Pedro
- Rodríguez Hernández", "Sra. Dña.
- Inés Rodríguez Hernández".

dona ['dona] (*MÉX*) *nf* doughnut, donut (*US*)

donar [do'nar] *vt* to donate

donativo [dona'tiβo] *nm* donation

donde ['donde] *adv* where ▷ *prep*: **el coche está allí ~ el farol** the car is over there by the lamppost *o* where the lamppost is; **en ~** where, in which

dónde ['donde] *adv* where?; **¿a ~ vas?** where are you going (to)?; **¿de ~ vienes?** where have you been?; **¿por ~?** where?, whereabouts?

dondequiera [donde'kjera] *adv* anywhere; **por ~** everywhere, all over the place ▷ *conj*: **~ que** wherever

donut® [do'nut] (*ESP*) *nm* doughnut, donut (*US*)

doña ['doɲa] *nf*: **~ Alicia** Alicia; **~ Victoria Benito** Mrs Victoria Benito

dorado, -a [do'raðo, a] *adj* (*color*) golden; (*Tec*) gilt

dormir [dor'mir] *vt*: **~ la siesta** to have an afternoon nap ▷ *vi* to sleep; **dormirse** *vr* to fall asleep

dormitorio [dormi'torjo] *nm* bedroom

dorsal [dor'sal] *nm* (*Deporte*) number

dorso ['dorso] *nm* (*de mano*) back; (*de hoja*) other side

dos [dos] *num* two

dosis ['dosis] *nf inv* dose, dosage

dotado, -a [do'taðo, a] *adj* gifted; **~ de** endowed with

dotar [do'tar] *vt* to endow; **dote** *nf* dowry; **dotes** *nfpl* (*talentos*) gifts

doy [doj] *vb* V **dar**

drama ['drama] *nm* drama; **dramaturgo** [drama'turxo] *nm* dramatist, playwright

drástico, -a [a ['drastiko, a] *adj* drastic

drenaje [dre'naxe] *nm* drainage

droga ['droxa] *nf* drug; **drogadicto, -a** [droxa'ðikto, a] *nm/f* drug addict

droguería [droxe'ria] *nf* hardware shop (*BRIT*) o store (*US*)

ducha ['dutʃa] *nf* (*baño*) shower; (*Med*) douche; **ducharse** *vr* to take a shower

duda ['duða] *nf* doubt; **no cabe ~** there is no doubt about it; **dudar** *vt, vi* to doubt; **dudoso, -a** [du'ðoso, a] *adj* (*incierto*) hesitant; (*sospechoso*) doubtful

duela *etc vb* V **doler**

duelo ['dwelo] *vb* V **doler** ▷ *nm* (*combate*) duel; (*luto*) mourning

duende ['dwende] *nm* imp, goblin

dueño, -a ['dweɲo, a] *nm/f* (*propietario*) owner; (*de pensión, taberna*) landlord/lady; (*empresario*) employer

duermo *etc vb* V **dormir**

dulce ['dulθe] *adj* sweet ▷ *adv* gently, softly ▷ *nm* sweet

dulcería [dulθe'ria] (*LAM*) *nf* confectioner's (shop)

dulzura [dul'θura] *nf* sweetness; (*ternura*) gentleness

dúo ['duo] *nm* duet

duplicar [dupli'kar] *vt* (*hacer el doble de*) to duplicate

duque ['duke] *nm* duke; **duquesa** *nf* duchess

duración [dura'θjon] *nf* (*de película, disco etc*) length; (*de pila etc*) life; (*curso: de acontecimientos etc*) duration

duradero, -a [dura'ðero, a] *adj* (*tela etc*) hard-wearing; (*fe, paz*) lasting

durante [du'rante] *prep* during

durar [du'rar] *vi* to last; (*recuerdo*) to remain

durazno [du'raθno] (*LAM*) *nm* (*fruta*) peach; (*árbol*) peach tree

durex ['dureks] (*MÉX, ARG*) *nm* (*tira adhesiva*) Sellotape® (*BRIT*), Scotch tape® (*US*)

dureza [du'reθa] *nf* (*calidad*) hardness

duro, -a ['duro, a] *adj* hard; (*carácter*) tough ▷ *adv* hard ▷ *nm* (*moneda*) five-peseta coin o piece

DVD *nm abr* (= *disco de vídeo digital*) DVD

environmentalist

economía [ekono'mia] *nf* (*sistema*) economy; (*carrera*) economics

económico, -a [eko'nomiko, a] *adj* (*barato*) cheap, economical; (*ahorrativo*) thrifty; (*Com: año etc*) financial; (: *situación*) economic

economista [ekono'mista] *nmf* economist

Ecuador [ekwa'ðor] *nm* Ecuador; **ecuador** *nm* (*Geo*) equator

ecuatoriano, -a [ekwato'rjano, a] *adj, nm/f* Ecuadorian

ecuestre [e'kwestre] *adj* equestrian

edad [e'ðað] *nf* age; **¿qué ~ tienes?** how old are you?; **tiene ocho años de ~** he's eight (years old); **de ~ mediana/ avanzada** middle-aged/advanced in years; **la E~ Media** the Middle Ages

edición [eði'θjon] *nf* (*acto*) publication; (*ejemplar*) edition

edificar [edifi'kar] *vt, vi* to build

edificio [eði'fiθjo] *nm* building; (*fig*) edifice, structure

Edimburgo [eðim'burxo] *nm* Edinburgh

editar [eði'tar] *vt* (*publicar*) to publish; (*preparar textos*) to edit

editor, a [eði'tor, a] *nm/f* (*que publica*) publisher; (*redactor*) editor ▷ *adj* publishing *cpd*; **editorial** *adj* editorial ▷ *nm* leading article, editorial; **casa editorial** publisher

edredón [eðre'ðon] *nm* duvet

educación [eðuka'θjon] *nf* education; (*crianza*) upbringing; (*modales*) (good) manners *pl*

educado, -a [eðu'kaðo, a] *adj*: **bien/ mal ~** well/badly behaved

educar [eðu'kar] *vt* to educate; (*criar*) to bring up; (*voz*) to train

EE. UU. *nmpl abr* (= *Estados Unidos*) US(A)

efectivamente [efecti'βa'mente] *adv* (*como respuesta*) exactly, precisely; (*verdaderamente*) really; (*de hecho*) in fact

efectivo, -a [efek'tiβo, a] *adj* effective; (*real*) actual, real ▷ *nm*: **pagar**

E *abr* (= *este*) E

e [e] *conj* and

ébano ['eβano] *nm* ebony

ebrio, -a ['eβrjo, a] *adj* drunk

ebullición [eβuʎi'θjon] *nf* boiling

echar [e'tʃar] *vt* to throw; (*agua, vino*) to pour (out); (*empleado: despedir*) to fire, sack; (*hojas*) to sprout; (*cartas*) to post; (*humo*) to emit, give out ▷ *vi*: **~ a correr** to run off; **echarse** *vr* to lie down; **~ llave a** to lock (up); **~ abajo** (*gobierno*) to overthrow; (*edificio*) to demolish; **~ mano a** to lay hands on; **~ una mano a algn** (*ayudar*) to give sb a hand; **~ de menos** to miss; **~se atrás** (*fig*) to back out

eclesiástico, -a [ekle'sjastiko, a] *adj* ecclesiastical

eco ['eko] *nm* echo; **tener ~** to catch on

ecología [ekolo'xia] *nf* ecology; **ecológico, -a** *adj* (*producto, método*) environmentally-friendly; (*agricultura*) organic; **ecologista** *adj* ecological, environmental ▷ *nmf*

en ~ to pay (in) cash; **hacer ~ un cheque** to cash a cheque
efecto [e'fekto] nm effect, result; **efectos** nmpl (efectos personales) effects; (bienes) goods; (Com) assets; **en ~** in fact; (respuesta) exactly, indeed; **efecto invernadero** greenhouse effect; **efectos especiales/secundarios/sonoros** special/side/sound effects
efectuar [efek'twar] vt to carry out; (viaje) to make
eficacia [efi'kaθja] nf (de persona) efficiency; (de medicamento etc) effectiveness
eficaz [efi'kaθ] adj (persona) efficient; (acción) effective
eficiente [efi'θjente] adj efficient
egipcio, -a [e'xipθjo, a] adj, nm/f Egyptian
Egipto [e'xipto] nm Egypt
egoísmo [exo'ismo] nm egoism
egoísta [exo'ista] adj egoistical, selfish ▷ nmf egoist
Eire ['eire] nm Eire
ej. abr (= ejemplo) eg
eje ['exe] nm (Geo, Mat) axis; (de rueda) axle; (de máquina) shaft, spindle
ejecución [exeku'θjon] nf execution; (cumplimiento) fulfilment; (Mús) performance; (Jur: embargo de deudor) attachment
ejecutar [exeku'tar] vt to execute, carry out; (matar) to execute; (cumplir) to fulfil; (Mús) to perform; (Jur: embargar) to attach, distrain (on)
ejecutivo, -a [exeku'tiβo, a] adj executive; **el (poder) ~** the executive (power)
ejemplar [exem'plar] adj exemplary ▷ nm example; (Zool) specimen; (de libro) copy; (de periódico) number, issue
ejemplo [e'xemplo] nm example; **por ~** for example
ejercer [exer'θer] vt to exercise; (influencia) to exert; (un oficio) to practise ▷ vi (practicar): **~ (de)** to practise (as)

ejercicio [exer'θiθjo] nm exercise; (período) tenure; **hacer ~** to take exercise; **ejercicio comercial** financial year
ejército [e'xerθito] nm army; **entrar en el ~** to join the army, join up; **ejército del aire/de tierra** Air Force/Army
ejote [e'xote] (MÉX) nm green bean

○ **PALABRA CLAVE**

el [el] (f **la**, pl **los, las**, neutro **lo**) art def **1** the; **el libro/la mesa/los estudiantes** the book/table/students
2 (con n abstracto: no se traduce): **el amor/la juventud** love/youth
3 (posesión: se traduce a menudo por adj posesivo): **romperse el brazo** to break one's arm; **levantó la mano** he put his hand up; **se puso el sombrero** she put her hat on
4 (valor descriptivo): **tener la boca grande/los ojos azules** to have a big mouth/blue eyes
5 (con días) on; **me iré el viernes** I'll leave on Friday; **los domingos suelo ir a nadar** on Sundays I generally go swimming
6 (lo +adj): **lo difícil/caro** what is difficult/expensive; (cuán): **no se da cuenta de lo pesado que es** he doesn't realise how boring he is
▷ pron demos **1**: **mi libro y el de usted** my book and yours; **las de Pepe son mejores** Pepe's are better; **no la(s) blanca(s) sino la(s) gris(es)** not the white one(s) but the grey one(s)
2: **lo de: lo de ayer** what happened yesterday; **lo de las facturas** that business about the invoices
▷ pron relativo **1** (indef): **el que: el (los) que quiera(n) que se vaya(n)** anyone who wants to can leave; **llévese el que más le guste** take the one you like best
2 (def): **el que: el que compré ayer** the one I bought yesterday; **los que se van** those who leave

3: **lo que: lo que pienso yo/más me gusta** what I think/like most
▷ *conj*: **el que: el que lo diga** the fact that he says so; **el que sea tan vago me molesta** his being so lazy bothers me
▷ *excl*: **¡el susto que me diste!** what a fright you gave me!
▷ *pron personal* **1** (*persona: m*) him; (: *f*) her; (: *pl*) them; **lo/las veo** I can see him/them
2 (*animal, cosa: sg*) it; (: *pl*) them; **lo** (*o* **la**) **veo** I can see it; **los** (*o* **las**) **veo** I can see them
3 (*como sustituto de frase*): **lo: no lo sabía** I didn't know; **ya lo entiendo** I understand now

él [el] *pron* (*persona*) he; (*cosa*) it; (*después de prep: persona*) him; (: *cosa*) it; **de ~** his

elaborar [elaβo'rar] *vt* (*producto*) to make, manufacture; (*preparar*) to prepare; (*madera, metal etc*) to work; (*proyecto etc*) to work on o out

elástico, -a [e'lastiko, a] *adj* elastic; (*flexible*) flexible ▷ *nm* elastic; (*un elástico*) elastic band

elección [elek'θjon] *nf* election; (*selección*) choice, selection; **elecciones generales** general election *sg*

electorado [elekto'raðo] *nm* electorate, voters *pl*

electricidad [elektriθi'ðað] *nf* electricity

electricista [elektri'θista] *nmf* electrician

eléctrico, -a [e'lektriko, a] *adj* electric

electro... [elektro] *prefijo* electro...; **electrocardiograma** *nm* electrocardiogram; **electrocutar** *vt* to electrocute; **electrodo** *nm* electrode; **electrodomésticos** *nmpl* (electrical) household appliances

electrónica [elek'tronika] *nf* electronics *sg*

electrónico, -a [elek'troniko, a] *adj* electronic

elefante [ele'fante] *nm* elephant

elegancia [ele'ɣanθja] *nf* elegance, grace; (*estilo*) stylishness

elegante [ele'ɣante] *adj* elegant, graceful; (*estiloso*) stylish, fashionable

elegir [ele'xir] *vt* (*escoger*) to choose, select; (*optar*) to opt for; (*presidente*) to elect

elemental [elemen'tal] *adj* (*claro, obvio*) elementary; (*fundamental*) elemental, fundamental

elemento [ele'mento] *nm* element; (*fig*) ingredient; **elementos** *nmpl* elements, rudiments

elevación [eleβa'θjon] *nf* elevation; (*acto*) raising, lifting; (*de precios*) rise; (*Geo etc*) height, altitude

elevar [ele'βar] *vt* to raise, lift (up); (*precio*) to put up; **elevarse** *vr* (*edificio*) to rise; (*precios*) to go up

eligiendo *etc vb V* **elegir**

elija *etc vb V* **elegir**

eliminar [elimi'nar] *vt* to eliminate, remove

eliminatoria [elimina'torja] *nf* heat, preliminary (round)

élite ['elite] *nf* elite

ella ['eʎa] *pron* (*persona*) she; (*cosa*) it; (*después de prep: persona*) her; (: *cosa*) it; **de ~** hers

ellas ['eʎas] *pron* (*personas y cosas*) they; (*después de prep*) them; **de ~** theirs

ello ['eʎo] *pron* it

ellos ['eʎos] *pron* they; (*después de prep*) them; **de ~** theirs

elogiar [elo'xjar] *vt* to praise; **elogio** *nm* praise

elote [e'lote] (*MÉX*) *nm* corn on the cob

eludir [elu'ðir] *vt* to avoid

email [i'mel] *nm* email; (*dirección*) email address; **mandar un ~ a algn** to email sb, send sb an email

embajada [emba'xaða] *nf* embassy

embajador, a [embaxa'ðor, a] *nm/f* ambassador/ambassadress

embalar [emba'lar] *vt* to parcel, wrap (up); **embalarse** *vr* to go fast

embalse [em'balse] nm (presa) dam; (lago) reservoir

embarazada [embara'θaða] adj pregnant ▷ nf pregnant woman
No confundir **embarazada** con la palabra inglesa embarrassed.

embarazo [emba'raθo] nm (de mujer) pregnancy; (impedimento) obstacle, obstruction; (timidez) embarrassment; **embarazoso, -a** adj awkward, embarrassing

embarcación [embarka'θjon] nf (barco) boat, craft; (acto) embarkation, boarding

embarcadero [embarka'ðero] nm pier, landing stage

embarcar [embar'kar] vt (cargamento) to ship, stow; (persona) to embark, put on board; **embarcarse** vr to embark, go on board

embargar [embar'xar] vt (Jur) to seize, impound

embargo [em'barxo] nm (Jur) seizure; (Com, Pol) embargo

embargue etc vb V **embargar**

embarque etc [em'barke] vb V **embarcar** ▷ nm shipment, loading

embellecer [embeʎe'θer] vt to embellish, beautify

embestida [embes'tiða] nf attack, onslaught; (carga) charge

embestir [embes'tir] vt to attack, assault; to charge, attack ▷ vi to attack

emblema [em'blema] nm emblem

embobado, -a [embo'βaðo, a] adj (atontado) stunned, bewildered

embolia [em'bolja] nf (Med) clot

émbolo ['embolo] nm (Auto) piston

emborrachar [emborra'tʃar] vt to make drunk, intoxicate; **emborracharse** vr to get drunk

emboscada [embos'kaða] nf ambush

embotar [embo'tar] vt to blunt, dull

embotellamiento [emboteʎa'mjento] nm (Auto) traffic jam

embotellar [embote'ʎar] vt to bottle

embrague [em'braxe] nm (tb: **pedal de ~**) clutch

embrión [em'brjon] nm embryo

embrollo [em'broʎo] nm (enredo) muddle, confusion; (aprieto) fix, jam

embrujado, -a [embru'xaðo, a] adj bewitched; **casa embrujada** haunted house

embrutecer [embrute'θer] vt (atontar) to stupefy

embudo [em'buðo] nm funnel

embuste [em'buste] nm (mentira) lie; **embustero, -a** adj lying, deceitful ▷ nm/f (mentiroso) liar

embutido [embu'tiðo] nm (Culin) sausage; (Tec) inlay

emergencia [emer'xenθja] nf emergency; (surgimiento) emergence

emerger [emer'xer] vi to emerge, appear

emigración [emixra'θjon] nf emigration; (de pájaros) migration

emigrar [emi'xrar] vi (personas) to emigrate; (pájaros) to migrate

eminente [emi'nente] adj eminent, distinguished; (elevado) high

emisión [emi'sjon] nf (acto) emission; (Com etc) issue; (Radio, TV: acto) broadcasting; (: programa) broadcast, programme (BRIT), program (US)

emisora [emi'sora] nf radio o broadcasting station

emitir [emi'tir] vt (olor etc) to emit, give off; (moneda etc) to issue; (opinión) to express; (Radio) to broadcast

emoción [emo'θjon] nf emotion; (excitación) excitement; (sentimiento) feeling

emocionante [emoθjo'nante] adj (excitante) exciting, thrilling

emocionar [emoθjo'nar] vt (excitar) to excite, thrill; (conmover) to move, touch; (impresionar) to impress

emoticón [emoti'kon], **emoticono** [emoti'kono] nm smiley

emotivo, -a [emo'tiβo, a] adj emotional

empacho [em'patʃo] nm (Med)
indigestion; (fig) embarrassment

empalagoso, -a [empala'ɣoso, a]
adj cloying; (fig) tiresome

empalmar [empal'mar] vt to join,
connect ▷ vi (dos caminos) to meet,
join; **empalme** nm joint, connection;
junction; (de trenes) connection

empanada [empa'naða] nf pie,
pasty

empañarse [empa'ɲarse] vr
(cristales etc) to steam up

empapar [empa'par] vt (mojar)
to soak, saturate; (absorber) to soak
up, absorb; **empaparse** vr: **~se de**
to soak up

empapelar [empape'lar] vt (paredes)
to paper

empaquetar [empake'tar] vt to
pack, parcel up

empastar [empas'tar] vt
(embadurnar) to paste; (diente) to fill

empaste [em'paste] nm (de diente)
filling

empatar [empa'tar] vi to draw, tie;
~on a dos they drew two-all; **empate**
nm draw, tie

empecé etc vb V **empezar**

empedernido, -a [empeðer'niðo,
a] adj hard, heartless; (fumador)
inveterate

empeine [em'peine] nm (de pie,
zapato) instep

empeñado, -a [empe'ɲaðo, a] adj
(persona) determined; (objeto) pawned

empeñar [empe'ɲar] vt (objeto) to
pawn, pledge; (persona) to compel;
empeñarse vr (endeudarse) to get
into debt; **~se en** to be set on, be
determined to

empeño [em'peɲo] nm
(determinación, insistencia)
determination, insistence; **casa de ~s**
pawnshop

empeorar [empeo'rar] vt to make
worse, worsen ▷ vi to get worse,
deteriorate

empezar [empe'θar] vt, vi to begin,
start

empiece etc vb V **empezar**

empiezo etc vb V **empezar**

emplasto [em'plasto] nm (Med)
plaster

emplazar [empla'θar] vt (ubicar) to
site, place, locate; (Jur) to summons;
(convocar) to summon

empleado, -a [emple'aðo, a] nm/f
(gen) employee; (de banco etc) clerk

emplear [emple'ar] vt (usar) to use,
employ; (dar trabajo a) to employ;
emplearse vr (conseguir trabajo) to be
employed; (ocuparse) to occupy o.s.

empleo [em'pleo] nm (puesto) job;
(puestos: colectivamente) employment;
(uso) use, employment

empollar [empo'ʎar] (ESP: fam) vt, vi
to swot (up); **empollón, -ona** (ESP: fam)
nm/f swot

emporio [em'porjo] (LAM) nm (gran
almacén) department store

empotrado, -a [empo'traðo, a] adj
(armario etc) built-in

emprender [empren'der] vt
(empezar) to begin, embark on;
(acometer) to tackle, take on

empresa [em'presa] nf (de espíritu
etc) enterprise; (Com) company,
firm; **empresariales** nfpl business
studies; **empresario, -a** nm/f (Com)
businessman(-woman)

empujar [empu'xar] vt to push,
shove

empujón [empu'xon] nm push,
shove

empuñar [empu'ɲar] vt (asir) to
grasp, take (firm) hold of

○ **PALABRA CLAVE**

en [en] prep **1** (posición) in; (: sobre)
on; **está en el cajón** it's in the drawer; **en
Argentina/La Paz** in Argentina/La
Paz; **en la oficina/el colegio** at the
office/school; **está en el suelo/quinto
piso** it's on the floor/the fifth floor
2 (dirección) into; **entró en el aula** she

went into the classroom; **meter algo en el bolso** to put sth into one's bag

3 (*tiempo*) in; on; **en 1605/3 semanas/ invierno** in 1605/3 weeks/winter; **en (el mes de) enero** in (the month of) January; **en aquella ocasión/época** on that occasion/at that time

4 (*precio*) for; **lo vendió en 20 dólares** he sold it for 20 dollars

5 (*diferencia*) by; **reducir/aumentar en una tercera parte/un 20 por ciento** to reduce/increase by a third/20 per cent

6 (*manera*): **en avión/autobús** by plane/bus; **escrito en inglés** written in English

7 (*después de vb que indica gastar etc*) on; **han cobrado demasiado en dietas** they've charged too much to expenses; **se le va la mitad del sueldo en comida** he spends half his salary on food

8 (*tema, ocupación*): **experto en la materia** expert on the subject; **trabaja en la construcción** he works in the building industry

9 (*adj + en + infin*): **lento en reaccionar** slow to react

enaguas [e'naɣwas] *nfpl* petticoat *sg*, underskirt *sg*

enajenación [enaxena'θjon] *nf* (*Psico: tb*: **~ mental**) mental derangement

enamorado, -a [enamo'raðo, a] *adj* in love ▷ *nm/f* lover; **estar ~ (de)** to be in love (with)

enamorar [enamo'rar] *vt* to win the love of; **enamorarse** *vr*: **~se de algn** to fall in love with sb

enano, -a [e'nano, a] *adj* tiny ▷ *nm/f* dwarf

encabezamiento [enkaβeθa'mjento] *nm* (*de carta*) heading; (*de periódico*) headline

encabezar [enkaβe'θar] *vt* (*movimiento, revolución*) to lead, head; (*lista*) to head, be at the top of; (*carta*) to put a heading to

encadenar [enkaðe'nar] *vt* to chain (together); (*poner grilletes a*) to shackle

encajar [enka'xar] *vt* (*ajustar*): **~ (en)** to fit (into); (*fam: golpe*) to take ▷ *vi* to fit (well); (*fig: corresponder a*) to match

encaje [en'kaxe] *nm* (*labor*) lace

encallar [enka'ʎar] *vi* (*Náut*) to run aground

encaminar [enkami'nar] *vt* to direct, send

encantado, -a [enkan'taðo, a] *adj* (*hechizado*) bewitched; (*muy contento*) delighted; **¡~!** how do you do, pleased to meet you

encantador, a [enkanta'ðor, a] *adj* charming, lovely ▷ *nm/f* magician, enchanter/enchantress

encantar [enkan'tar] *vt* (*agradar*) to charm, delight; (*hechizar*) to bewitch, cast a spell on; **me encanta eso** I love that; **encanto** *nm* (*hechizo*) spell, charm; (*fig*) charm, delight

encarcelar [enkarθe'lar] *vt* to imprison, jail

encarecer [enkare'θer] *vt* to put up the price of; **encarecerse** *vr* to get dearer

encargado, -a [enkar'ɣaðo, a] *adj* in charge ▷ *nm/f* agent, representative; (*responsable*) person in charge

encargar [enkar'ɣar] *vt* to entrust; (*recomendar*) to urge, recommend; **encargarse** *vr*: **~se de** to look after, take charge of; **~ algo a algn** to put sb in charge of sth; **~ a algn que haga algo** to ask sb to do sth

encargo [en'karɣo] *nm* (*tarea*) assignment, job; (*responsabilidad*) responsibility; (*Com*) order

encariñarse [enkari'ɲarse] *vr*: **~ con** to grow fond of, get attached to

encarnación [enkarna'θjon] *nf* incarnation, embodiment

encarrilar [enkarri'lar] *vt* (*tren*) to put back on the rails; (*fig*) to correct, put on the right track

encasillar [enkasiˈʎar] vt (fig) to pigeonhole; (actor) to typecast

encendedor [enθendeˈðor] nm lighter

encender [enθenˈder] vt (con fuego) to light; (luz, radio) to put on, switch on; (avivar: pasión) to inflame; **encenderse** vr to catch fire; (excitarse) to get excited; (de cólera) to flare up; (el rostro) to blush

encendido [enθenˈdiðo] nm (Auto) ignition

encerado [enθeˈraðo] nm (Escol) blackboard

encerrar [enθeˈrrar] vt (confinar) to shut in, shut up; (comprender, incluir) to include, contain

encharcado, -a [entʃarˈkaðo, a] adj (terreno) flooded

encharcarse [entʃarˈkarse] vr to get flooded

enchufado, -a [entʃuˈfaðo, a] (fam) nm/f well-connected person

enchufar [entʃuˈfar] vt (Elec) to plug in; (Tec) to connect, fit together; **enchufe** nm (Elec: clavija) plug; (: toma) socket; (do dos tubos) joint, connection; (fam: influencia) contact, connection; (: puesto) cushy job

encía [enˈθia] nf gum

encienda etc vb V **encender**

encierro etc [enˈθjerro] vb V **encerrar** ▷ nm shutting in, shutting up; (calabozo) prison

encima [enˈθima] adv (sobre) above, over; (además) besides; **~ de** (en) on, on top of; (sobre) above, over; (además de) besides, on top of; **por ~ de** over; **¿llevas dinero ~?** have you (got) any money on you?; **se me vino ~** it took me by surprise

encina [enˈθina] nf holm oak

encinta [enˈθinta] adj pregnant

enclenque [enˈklenke] adj weak, sickly

encoger [enkoˈxer] vt to shrink, contract; **encogerse** vr to shrink, contract; (fig) to cringe; **~se de**

hombros to shrug one's shoulders

encomendar [enkomenˈdar] vt to entrust, commend; **encomendarse** vr: **~se a** to put one's trust in

encomienda etc [enkoˈmjenda] vb V **encomendar** ▷ nf (encargo) charge, commission; (elogio) tribute; **encomienda postal** (LAM) package

encontrar [enkonˈtrar] vt (hallar) to find; (inesperadamente) to meet, run into; **encontrarse** vr to meet (each other); (situarse) to be (situated); **~se con** to meet; **~se bien (de salud)** to feel well

encrucijada [enkruθiˈxaða] nf crossroads sg

encuadernación [enkwaðernaˈθjon] nf binding

encuadrar [enkwaˈðrar] vt (retrato) to frame; (ajustar) to fit, insert; (contener) to contain

encubrir [enkuˈβrir] vt (ocultar) to hide, conceal; (criminal) to harbour, shelter

encuentro etc [enˈkwentro] vb V **encontrar** ▷ nm (de personas) meeting; (Auto etc) collision, crash; (Deporte) match, game; (Mil) encounter

encuerado, -a (MÉX) [enkweˈraðo, a] adj nude, naked

encuesta [enˈkwesta] nf inquiry, investigation; (sondeo) (public) opinion poll

encumbrar [enkumˈbrar] vt (persona) to exalt

endeble [enˈdeβle] adj (persona) weak; (argumento, excusa, persona) weak

endemoniado, -a [endemoˈnjaðo, a] adj possessed (of the devil); (travieso) devilish

enderezar [endereˈθar] vt (poner derecho) to straighten (out); (: verticalmente) to set upright; (situación) to straighten o sort out; (dirigir) to direct; **enderezarse** vr (persona sentada) to straighten up

endeudarse [endeuˈðarse] vr to get into debt

endiablado, -a [endja'βlaðo, a] *adj* devilish, diabolical; (*travieso*) mischievous

endilgar [endil'xar] (*fam*) *vt*: **~le algo a algn** to lumber sb with sth

endiñar [endi'ɲar] (*ESP: fam*) *vt* (*bofetón*) to land, belt

endosar [endo'sar] *vt* (*cheque etc*) to endorse

endulzar [endul'θar] *vt* to sweeten; (*suavizar*) to soften

endurecer [endure'θer] *vt* to harden; **endurecerse** *vr* to harden, grow hard

enema [e'nema] *nm* (*Med*) enema

enemigo, -a [ene'mixo, a] *adj* enemy, hostile ▷ *nm/f* enemy

enemistad [enemis'taθ] *nf* enmity

enemistar [enemis'tar] *vt* to make enemies of, cause a rift between; **enemistarse** *vr* to become enemies; (*amigos*) to fall out

energía [ener'xia] *nf* (*vigor*) energy, drive; (*empuje*) push; (*Tec, Elec*) energy, power; **energía eólica** wind power; **energía solar** solar energy *o* power

enérgico, -a [e'nerxiko, a] *adj* (*gen*) energetic; (*voz, modales*) forceful

energúmeno, -a [ener'xumeno, a] (*fam*) *nm/f* (*fig*) madman(-woman)

enero [e'nero] *nm* January

enfadado, -a [enfa'ðaðo, a] *adj* angry, annoyed

enfadar [enfa'ðar] *vt* to anger, annoy; **enfadarse** *vr* to get angry *o* annoyed

enfado [en'faðo] *nm* (*enojo*) anger, annoyance; (*disgusto*) trouble, bother

énfasis ['enfasis] *nm* emphasis, stress

enfático, -a [en'fatiko, a] *adj* emphatic

enfermar [enfer'mar] *vt* to make ill ▷ *vi* to fall ill, be taken ill

enfermedad [enferme'ðaθ] *nf* illness; **enfermedad venérea** venereal disease

enfermera [enfer'mera] *nf* nurse

enfermería [enferme'ria] *nf* infirmary; (*de colegio etc*) sick bay

enfermero [enfer'mero] *nm* (male) nurse

enfermizo, -a [enfer'miθo, a] *adj* (*persona*) sickly, unhealthy; (*fig*) unhealthy

enfermo, -a [en'fermo, a] *adj* ill, sick ▷ *nm/f* invalid, sick person; (*en hospital*) patient; **caer** *o* **ponerse ~** to fall ill

enfocar [enfo'kar] *vt* (*foto etc*) to focus; (*problema etc*) to approach

enfoque *etc* [en'foke] *vb* V **enfocar** ▷ *nm* focus

enfrentar [enfren'tar] *vt* (*peligro*) to face (up to), confront; (*oponer*) to bring face to face; **enfrentarse** *vr* (*dos personas*) to face *o* confront each other; (*Deporte: dos equipos*) to meet; **~se a** *o* **con** to face up to, confront

enfrente [en'frente] *adv* opposite; **la casa de ~** the house opposite, the house across the street; **~ de** opposite, facing

enfriamiento [enfria'mjento] *nm* chilling, refrigeration; (*Med*) cold, chill

enfriar [enfri'ar] *vt* (*alimentos*) to cool, chill; (*algo caliente*) to cool down; **enfriarse** *vr* to cool down; (*Med*) to catch a chill; (*amistad*) to cool

enfurecer [enfure'θer] *vt* to enrage, madden; **enfurecerse** *vr* to become furious, fly into a rage; (*mar*) to get rough

enganchar [engan'tʃar] *vt* to hook; (*dos vagones*) to hitch up; (*Tec*) to couple, connect; (*Mil*) to recruit; **engancharse** *vr* (*Mil*) to enlist, join up

enganche [en'gantʃe] *nm* hook; (*ESP Tec*) coupling, connection; (*acto*) hooking (up); (*Mil*) recruitment, enlistment; (*MÉX: depósito*) deposit

engañar [enga'ɲar] *vt* to deceive; (*estafar*) to cheat, swindle; **engañarse** *vr* (*equivocarse*) to be wrong; (*disimular la verdad*) to deceive o.s.

engaño [en'gaɲo] *nm* deceit;

(*estafa*) trick, swindle; (*error*) mistake, misunderstanding; (*ilusión*) delusion; **engañoso, -a** *adj* (*tramposo*) crooked; (*mentiroso*) dishonest, deceitful; (*aspecto*) deceptive; (*consejo*) misleading

engatusar [engatu'sar] (*fam*) *vt* to coax

engendro [en'xendro] *nm* (*Bio*) foetus; (*fig*) monstrosity

englobar [englo'βar] *vt* to include, comprise

engordar [engor'ðar] *vt* to fatten ▷ *vi* to get fat, put on weight

engorroso, -a [engo'rroso, a] *adj* bothersome, trying

engranaje [engra'naxe] *nm* (*Auto*) gear

engrasar [engra'sar] *vt* (*Tec: poner grasa*) to grease; (: *lubricar*) to lubricate, oil; (*manchar*) to make greasy

engreído, -a [engre'iðo, a] *adj* vain, conceited

enhebrar [ene'βrar] *vt* to thread

enhorabuena [enora'βwena] *excl* ¡~! congratulations! ▷ *nf*: **dar la ~ a** to congratulate

enigma [e'niɣma] *nm* enigma; (*problema*) puzzle; (*misterio*) mystery

enjambre [en'xambre] *nm* swarm

enjaular [enxau'lar] *vt* to (put in a) cage; (*fam*) to jail, lock up

enjuagar [enxwa'ɣar] *vt* (*ropa*) to rinse (out)

enjuague *etc* [en'xwaxe] *vb* V **enjuagar** ▷ *nm* (*Med*) mouthwash; (*de ropa*) rinse, rinsing

enlace [en'laθe] *nm* link, connection; (*relación*) relationship; (*tb*: **~ matrimonial**) marriage; (*de carretera, trenes*) connection; **enlace sindical** shop steward

enlatado, -a [enla'taðo, a] *adj* (*alimentos, productos*) tinned, canned

enlazar [enla'θar] *vt* (*unir con lazos*) to bind together; (*atar*) to tie; (*conectar*) to link, connect; (*LAM: caballo*) to lasso

enloquecer [enloke'θer] *vt* to drive

mad ▷ *vi* to go mad

enmarañar [enmara'ɲar] *vt* (*enredar*) to tangle (up), entangle; (*complicar*) to complicate; (*confundir*) to confuse

enmarcar [enmar'kar] *vt* (*cuadro*) to frame

enmascarar [enmaska'rar] *vt* to mask; **enmascararse** *vr* to put on a mask

enmendar [enmen'dar] *vt* to emend, correct; (*constitución etc*) to amend; (*comportamiento*) to reform; **enmendarse** *vr* to reform, mend one's ways; **enmienda** *nf* correction; amendment; reform

enmudecer [enmuðe'θer] *vi* (*perder el habla*) to fall silent; (*guardar silencio*) to remain silent

ennoblecer [ennoβle'θer] *vt* to ennoble

enojado, -a [eno'xaðo, a] (*LAM*) *adj* angry

enojar [eno'xar] *vt* (*encolerizar*) to anger; (*disgustar*) to annoy, upset; **enojarse** *vr* to get angry; to get annoyed

enojo [e'noxo] *nm* (*cólera*) anger; (*irritación*) annoyance

enorme [e'norme] *adj* enormous, huge; (*fig*) monstrous

enredadera [enreða'ðera] *nf* (*Bot*) creeper, climbing plant

enredar [enre'ðar] *vt* (*cables, hilos etc*) to tangle (up), entangle; (*situación*) to complicate, confuse; (*meter cizaña*) to sow discord among o between; (*implicar*) to embroil, implicate; **enredarse** *vr* to get entangled, get tangled (up); (*situación*) to get complicated; (*persona*) to get embroiled; (*LAM: fam*) to meddle

enredo [en'reðo] *nm* (*maraña*) tangle; (*confusión*) mix-up, confusion; (*intriga*) intrigue

enriquecer [enrike'θer] *vt* to make rich, enrich; **enriquecerse** *vr* to get rich

enrojecer [enroxe'θer] vt to redden
▷ vi (persona) to blush; **enrojecerse**
vr to blush

enrollar [enro'ʎar] vt to roll (up),
wind (up)

ensalada [ensa'laða] nf salad;
ensaladilla (rusa) nf Russian salad

ensanchar [ensan'tʃar] vt (hacer
más ancho) to widen; (agrandar) to
enlarge, expand; (Costura) to let out;
ensancharse vr to get wider, expand

ensayar [ensa'jar] vt to test, try
(out); (Teatro) to rehearse

ensayo [en'sajo] nm test, trial;
(Quím) experiment; (Teatro) rehearsal;
(Deporte) try; (Escol, Literatura) essay

enseguida [ense'ɣiða] adv at once,
right away

ensenada [ense'naða] nf inlet, cove

enseñanza [ense'nanθa] nf
(educación) education; (acción)
teaching; (doctrina) teaching, doctrine;
enseñanza (de) primaria/secundaria
elementary/secondary education

enseñar [ense'nar] vt (educar) to
teach; (mostrar, señalar) to show

enseres [en'seres] nmpl belongings

ensuciar [ensu'θjar] vt (manchar) to
dirty, soil; (fig) to defile; **ensuciarse** vr
to get dirty; (bebé) to dirty one's nappy

entablar [enta'βlar] vt (recubrir) to
board (up); (Ajedrez, Damas) to set up;
(conversación) to strike up; (Jur) to file
▷ vi to draw

ente ['ente] nm (organización) body,
organization; (fam: persona) odd
character

entender [enten'der] vt (comprender)
to understand; (darse cuenta) to realize
▷ vi to understand; (creer) to think,
believe; **entenderse** vr (comprenderse)
to be understood; (ponerse de acuerdo)
to agree, reach an agreement; **~ de**
to know all about; **~ algo de** to know
a little about; **~ en** to deal with, have
to do with; **~ mal** to misunderstand;
~se con algn (llevarse bien) to get on o
along with sb; **~se mal** (dos personas) to
get on badly

entendido, -a [enten'diðo, a] adj
(comprendido) understood; (hábil)
skilled; (inteligente) knowledgeable
▷ nm/f (experto) expert ▷ excl agreed!;
entendimiento nm (comprensión)
understanding; (inteligencia) mind,
intellect; (juicio) judgement

enterado, -a [ente'raðo, a] adj well-
informed; **estar ~ de** to know about,
be aware of

enteramente [entera'mente] adv
entirely, completely

enterar [ente'rar] vt (informar) to
inform, tell; **enterarse** vr to find out,
get to know

enterito [ente'rito] (RPL) nm boiler
suit (BRIT), overalls (US)

entero, -a [en'tero, a] adj (total)
whole, entire; (fig: honesto) honest;
(: firme) firm, resolute ▷ nm
(Com: punto) point

enterrar [ente'rrar] vt to bury

entidad [enti'ðað] nf (empresa) firm,
company; (organismo) body; (sociedad)
society; (Filosofía) entity

entiendo etc vb V **entender**

entierro [en'tjerro] nm (acción)
burial; (funeral) funeral

entonación [entona'θjon] nf (Ling)
intonation

entonar [ento'nar] vt (canción) to
intone; (colores) to tone; (Med) to tone
up ▷ vi to be in tune

entonces [en'tonθes] adv then,
at that time; **desde ~** since then; **en
aquel ~** at that time; **(pues) ~** and so

entornar [entor'nar] vt (puerta,
ventana) to half-close, leave ajar; (los
ojos) to screw up

entorpecer [entorpe'θer] vt
(entendimiento) to dull; (impedir) to
obstruct, hinder; (: tránsito) to slow
down, delay

entrada [en'traða] nf (acción) entry,
access; (sitio) entrance, way in; (Inform)
input; (Com) receipts pl, takings pl;
(Culin) starter; (Deporte) innings sg;

(*Teatro*) house, audience; (*billete*) ticket; **~s y salidas** (*Com*) income and expenditure; **de ~** from the outset; **entrada de aire** (*Tec*) air intake o inlet

entrado, -a [en'traðo, a] *adj*: **~ en años** elderly; **una vez ~ el verano** in the summer(time), when summer comes

entramparse [entram'parse] *vr* to get into debt

entrante [en'trante] *adj* next, coming; **mes/año ~** next month/year; **entrantes** *nmpl* starters

entraña [en'traɲa] *nf* (*fig: centro*) heart, core; (*raíz*) root; **entrañas** *nfpl* (*Anat*) entrails; (*fig*) heart *sg*; **entrañable** *adj* close, intimate; **entrañar** *vt* to entail

entrar [en'trar] *vt* (*introducir*) to bring in; (*Inform*) to input ▷ *vi* (*meterse*) to go in, come in, enter; (*comenzar*): **~ diciendo** to begin by saying; **hacer ~** to show in; **me entró sed/sueño** I started to feel thirsty/sleepy; **no me entra** I can't get the hang of it

entre ['entre] *prep* (*dos*) between; (*más de dos*) among(st)

entreabrir [entrea'βrir] *vt* to half-open, open halfway

entrecejo [entre'θexo] *nm*: **fruncir el ~** to frown

entredicho [entre'ðitʃo] *nm* (*Jur*) injunction; **poner en ~** to cast doubt on; **estar en ~** to be in doubt

entrega [en'treɣa] *nf* (*de mercancías*) delivery; (*de novela etc*) instalment; **entregar** [entre'ɣar] *vt* (*dar*) to hand (over), deliver; **entregarse** *vr* (*rendirse*) to surrender, give in, submit; (*dedicarse*) to devote o.s.

entremeses [entre'meses] *nmpl* hors d'œuvres

entremeter [entreme'ter] *vt* to insert, put in; **entremeterse** *vr* to meddle, interfere; **entremetido, -a** *adj* meddling, interfering

entremezclar [entremeθ'klar] *vt* to intermingle; **entremezclarse** *vr* to intermingle

entrenador, a [entrena'ðor, a] *nm/f* trainer, coach

entrenarse [entre'narse] *vr* to train

entrepierna [entre'pjerna] *nf* crotch

entresuelo [entre'swelo] *nm* mezzanine

entretanto [entre'tanto] *adv* meanwhile, meantime

entretecho [entre'tetʃo] (*cs*) *nm* attic

entretejer [entrete'xer] *vt* to interweave

entretener [entrete'ner] *vt* (*divertir*) to entertain, amuse; (*detener*) to hold up, delay; **entretenerse** *vr* (*divertirse*) to amuse o.s.; (*retrasarse*) to delay, linger; **entretenido, -a** *adj* entertaining, amusing; **entretenimiento** *nm* entertainment, amusement

entrever [entre'βer] *vt* to glimpse, catch a glimpse of

entrevista [entre'βista] *nf* interview; **entrevistar** *vt* to interview; **entrevistarse** *vr* to have an interview

entristecer [entriste'θer] *vt* to sadden, grieve; **entristecerse** *vr* to grow sad

entrometerse [entrome'terse] *vr*: **~ (en)** to interfere (in o with)

entumecer [entume'θer] *vt* to numb, benumb; **entumecerse** *vr* (*por el frío*) to go o become numb

enturbiar [entur'βjar] *vt* (*el agua*) to make cloudy; (*fig*) to confuse; **enturbiarse** *vr* (*oscurecerse*) to become cloudy; (*fig*) to get confused, become obscure

entusiasmar [entusjas'mar] *vt* to excite, fill with enthusiasm; (*gustar mucho*) to delight; **entusiasmarse** *vr*: **~se con** o **por** to get enthusiastic o excited about

entusiasmo [entu'sjasmo] *nm* enthusiasm; (*excitación*) excitement

entusiasta [entu'sjasta] *adj*
enthusiastic ▷ *nmf* enthusiast
enumerar [enume'rar] *vt* to
enumerate
envainar [embai'nar] *vt* to sheathe
envalentonar [embalento'nar] *vt*
to give courage to; **envalentonarse** *vr*
(*pey: jactarse*) to boast, brag
envasar [emba'sar] *vt* (*empaquetar*)
to pack, wrap; (*enfrascar*) to bottle;
(*enlatar*) to can; (*embolsar*) to pocket
envase [em'base] *nm* (*en paquete*)
packing, wrapping; (*en botella*)
bottling; (*en lata*) canning; (*recipiente*)
container; (*paquete*) package; (*botella*)
bottle; (*lata*) tin (BRIT), can
envejecer [embexe'θer] *vt* to make
old, age ▷ *vi* (*volverse viejo*) to grow old;
(*parecer viejo*) to age
envenenar [embene'nar] *vt* to
poison; (*fig*) to embitter
envergadura [emberxa'ðura] *nf*
(*fig*) scope, compass
enviar [em'bjar] *vt* to send; **~ un**
mensaje a algn (*por movil*) to text sb, to
send sb a text message
enviciarse [embi'θjarse] *vr*: **~ (con)**
to get addicted (to)
envidia [em'biðja] *nf* envy; **tener**
~ a to envy, be jealous of; **envidiar**
vt to envy
envío [em'bio] *nm* (*acción*) sending;
(*de mercancías*) consignment; (*de dinero*)
remittance
enviudar [embju'ðar] *vi* to be
widowed
envoltura [embol'tura] *nf* (*cobertura*)
cover; (*embalaje*) wrapper, wrapping;
envoltorio *nm* package
envolver [embol'βer] *vt* to wrap (up);
(*cubrir*) to cover; (*enemigo*) to surround;
(*implicar*) to involve, implicate
envuelto [em'bwelto] *pp de*
envolver
enyesar [enje'sar] *vt* (*pared*) to
plaster; (*Med*) to put in plaster
enzarzarse [enθar'θarse] *vr*: **~ en**
(*pelea*) to get mixed up in; (*disputa*) to

get involved in
épica ['epika] *nf* epic
epidemia [epi'ðemja] *nf* epidemic
epilepsia [epi'lepsja] *nf* epilepsy
episodio [epi'soðjo] *nm* episode
época ['epoka] *nf* period, time; (*Hist*)
age, epoch; **hacer ~** to be epoch-
making
equilibrar [ekili'βrar] *vt* to balance;
equilibrio *nm* balance, equilibrium;
mantener/perder el equilibrio to
keep/lose one's balance; **equilibrista**
nmf (*funámbulo*) tightrope walker;
(*acróbata*) acrobat
equipaje [eki'paxe] *nm* luggage;
(*avíos*): **hacer el ~** to pack; **equipaje de**
mano hand luggage
equipar [eki'par] *vt* (*proveer*) to equip
equipararse [ekipa'rarse] *vr*: **~ con**
to be on a level with
equipo [e'kipo] *nm* (*conjunto de*
cosas) equipment; (*Deporte*) team; (*de*
obreros) shift
equis ['ekis] *nf inv* (the letter) X
equitación [ekita'θjon] *nf* horse
riding
equivalente [ekiβa'lente] *adj, nm*
equivalent
equivaler [ekiβa'ler] *vi* to be
equivalent o equal
equivocación [ekiβoka'θjon] *nf*
mistake, error
equivocado, -a [ekiβo'kaðo, a] *adj*
wrong, mistaken
equivocarse [ekiβo'karse] *vr* to be
wrong, make a mistake; **~ de camino**
to take the wrong road
era ['era] *vb V* **ser** ▷ *nf* era, age
erais *vb V* **ser**
éramos *vb V* **ser**
eran *vb V* **ser**
eras *vb V* **ser**
erección [erek'θjon] *nf* erection
eres *vb V* **ser**
erigir [eri'xir] *vt* to erect, build;
erigirse *vr*: **~se en** to set o.s. up as
erizo [e'riθo] *nm* (*Zool*) hedgehog;
erizo de mar sea-urchin

ermita [er'mita] *nf* hermitage;
ermitaño, -a [ermi'taɲo, a] *nm/f*
hermit

erosión [ero'sjon] *nf* erosion

erosionar [erosjo'nar] *vt* to erode

erótico, -a [e'rotiko, a] *adj* erotic;
erotismo *nm* eroticism

errante [e'rrante] *adj* wandering,
errant

erróneo, -a [e'rroneo, a] *adj*
(*equivocado*) wrong, mistaken

error [e'rror] *nm* error, mistake;
(*Inform*) bug; **error de imprenta**
misprint

eructar [eruk'tar] *vt* to belch, burp

erudito, -a [eru'ðito, a] *adj* erudite,
learned

erupción [erup'θjon] *nf* eruption;
(*Med*) rash

es *vb* V **ser**

esa ['esa] (*pl* ~**s**) *adj demos* V **ese**

ésa ['esa] (*pl* ~**s**) *pron* V **ése**

esbelto, -a [es'βelto, a] *adj* slim,
slender

esbozo [es'βoθo] *nm* sketch, outline

escabeche [eska'βetʃe] *nm* brine; (*de
aceitunas etc*) pickle; **en ~** pickled

escabullirse [eskaβu'ʎirse] *vr* to slip
away, to clear out

escafandra [eska'fandra] *nf* (*buzo*)
diving suit; (*escafandra espacial*)
space suit

escala [es'kala] *nf* (*proporción, Mús*)
scale; (*de mano*) ladder; (*Aviac*) stopover;
hacer ~ en to stop o call in at

escalafón [eskala'fon] *nm* (*escala de
salarios*) salary scale, wage scale

escalar [eska'lar] *vt* to climb, scale

escalera [eska'lera] *nf* stairs *pl*,
staircase; (*escala*) ladder; (*Naipes*) run;
escalera de caracol spiral staircase;
escalera de incendios fire escape;
escalera mecánica escalator

escalfar [eskal'far] *vt* (*huevos*) to
poach

escalinata [eskali'nata] *nf* staircase

escalofriante [eskalo'frjante] *adj*
chilling

escalofrío [eskalo'frio] *nm* (*Med*)
chill; **escalofríos** *nmpl* (*fig*) shivers

escalón [eska'lon] *nm* step, stair; (*de
escalera*) rung

escalope [eska'lope] *nm* (*Culin*)
escalope

escama [es'kama] *nf* (*de pez,
serpiente*) scale; (*de jabón*) flake; (*fig*)
resentment

escampar [eskam'par] *vb impers* to
stop raining

escandalizar [eskandali'θar] *vt* to
scandalize, shock; **escandalizarse**
vr to be shocked; (*ofenderse*) to be
offended

escándalo [es'kandalo] *nm* scandal;
(*alboroto, tumulto*) row, uproar;
escandaloso, -a *adj* scandalous,
shocking

escandinavo, -a [eskandi'naβo, a]
adj, nm/f Scandinavian

escanear [eskane'ar] *vt* to scan

escaño [es'kaɲo] *nm* bench; (*Pol*) seat

escapar [eska'par] *vi* (*gen*) to escape,
run away; (*Deporte*) to break away;
escaparse *vr* to escape, get away;
(*agua, gas*) to leak (out)

escaparate [eskapa'rate] *nm* shop
window

escape [es'kape] *nm* (*de agua, gas*)
leak; (*de motor*) exhaust

escarabajo [eskara'βaxo] *nm* beetle

escaramuza [eskara'muθa] *nf*
skirmish

escarbar [eskar'βar] *vt* (*tierra*) to
scratch

escarceos [eskar'θeos] *nmpl*: **en mis
~ con la política ...** in my dealings
with politics ...; **escarceos amorosos**
love affairs

escarcha [es'kartʃa] *nf* frost;
escarchado, -a [eskar'tʃaðo, a] *adj*
(*Culin: fruta*) crystallized

escarlatina [eskarla'tina] *nf* scarlet
fever

escarmentar [eskarmen'tar] *vt* to
punish severely ▷ *vi* to learn one's
lesson

escarmiento etc [eskar'mjento] vb
V **escarmentar** ▷ nm (ejemplo) lesson;
(castigo) punishment
escarola [eska'rola] nf endive
escarpado, -a [eskar'paðo, a] adj
(pendiente) sheer, steep; (rocas) craggy
escasear [eskase'ar] vi to be scarce
escasez [eska'seθ] nf (falta) shortage,
scarcity; (pobreza) poverty
escaso, -a [es'kaso, a] adj (poco)
scarce; (raro) rare; (ralo) thin, sparse;
(limitado) limited
escatimar [eskati'mar] vt to skimp
(on), be sparing with
escayola [eska'jola] nf plaster
escena [es'θena] nf scene; **escenario**
[esθe'narjo] nm (Teatro) stage; (Cine)
set; (fig) scene

▌No confundir **escenario** con la
palabra inglesa *scenery*.

escenografía nf set design
escéptico, -a [es'θeptiko, a] adj
sceptical ▷ nm/f sceptic
esclarecer [esklare'θer] vt (misterio,
problema) to shed light on
esclavitud [esklaβi'tuð] nf slavery
esclavizar [esklaβi'θar] vt to enslave
esclavo, -a [es'klaβo, a] nm/f slave
escoba [es'koβa] nf broom; **escobilla**
nf brush
escocer [esko'θer] vi to burn, sting;
escocerse vr to chafe, get chafed
escocés, -esa [esko'θes, esa] adj
Scottish ▷ nm/f Scotsman(-woman),
Scot
Escocia [es'koθja] nf Scotland
escoger [esko'xer] vt to choose,
pick, select; **escogido, -a** adj chosen,
selected
escolar [esko'lar] adj school cpd
▷ nmf schoolboy(-girl), pupil
escollo [es'koʎo] nm (obstáculo) pitfall
escolta [es'kolta] nf escort; **escoltar**
vt to escort
escombros [es'kombros] nmpl
(basura) rubbish sg; (restos) debris sg
esconder [eskon'der] vt to hide,
conceal; **esconderse** vr to hide;

escondidas (LAM) nfpl: **a escondidas**
secretly; **escondite** nm hiding place;
(ESP: juego) hide-and-seek; **escondrijo**
nm hiding place, hideout
escopeta [esko'peta] nf shotgun
escoria [es'korja] nf (de alto horno)
slag; (fig) scum, dregs pl
Escorpio [es'korpjo] nm Scorpio
escorpión [eskor'pjon] nm scorpion
escotado, -a [esko'taðo, a] adj
low-cut
escote [es'kote] nm (de vestido) low
neck; **pagar a ~** to share the expenses
escotilla [esko'tiʎa] nf (Náut)
hatch(way)
escozor [esko'θor] nm (dolor)
sting(ing)
escribible [eskri'βiβle] adj writable
escribir [eskri'βir] vt, vi to write; **~ a
máquina** to type; **¿cómo se escribe?**
how do you spell it?
escrito, -a [es'krito, a] pp de
escribir ▷ nm (documento) document;
(manuscrito) text, manuscript; **por ~**
in writing
escritor, a [eskri'tor, a] nm/f writer
escritorio [eskri'torjo] nm desk
escritura [eskri'tura] nf (acción)
writing; (caligrafía) (hand)writing;
(Jur: documento) deed
escrúpulo [es'krupulo] nm scruple;
(minuciosidad) scrupulousness;
escrupuloso, -a adj scrupulous
escrutinio [eskru'tinjo] nm (examen
atento) scrutiny; (Pol: recuento de votos)
count(ing)
escuadra [es'kwaðra] nf (Mil etc)
squad; (Náut) squadron; (flota: de coches
etc) fleet; **escuadrilla** nf (de aviones)
squadron; (LAM: de obreros) gang
escuadrón [eskwa'ðron] nm
squadron
escuálido, -a [es'kwaliðo, a] adj
skinny, scraggy; (sucio) squalid
escuchar [esku'tʃar] vt to listen to
▷ vi to listen
escudo [es'kuðo] nm shield
escuela [es'kwela] nf school; **escuela**

de artes y oficios (*ESP*) ≈ technical
college; **escuela de choferes** (*LAM*),
driving school; **escuela de manejo**
(*MÉX*) driving school

escueto, -a [es'kweto, a] *adj* plain;
(*estilo*) simple

escuincle, -a [es'kwinkle, a]
(*MÉX: fam*) *nm/f* kid

esculpir [eskul'pir] *vt* to sculpt;
(*grabar*) to engrave; (*tallar*) to carve;
escultor, a *nm/f* sculptor(-tress);
escultura *nf* sculpture

escupidera [eskupi'ðera] *nf*
spittoon

escupir [esku'pir] *vt, vi* to spit (out)

escurreplatos [eskurre'platos]
(*ESP*) *nm inv* draining board (*BRIT*),
drainboard (*US*)

escurridero [eskurri'ðero] (*LAM*) *nm*
draining board (*BRIT*), drainboard (*US*)

escurridizo, -a [eskurri'ðiθo, a]
adj slippery

escurridor [eskurri'ðor] *nm*
colander

escurrir [esku'rrir] *vt* (*ropa*) to wring
out; (*verduras, platos*) to drain ▷ *vi*
(*líquidos*) to drip; **escurrirse** *vr* (*secarse*)
to drain; (*resbalarse*) to slip, slide;
(*escaparse*) to slip away

ese ['ese] (*f* **esa**, *pl* **esos, esas**) *adj*
demos (*sg*) that; (*pl*) those

ése ['ese] (*f* **ésa**, *pl* **ésos, ésas**) *pron*
(*sg*) that (one); (*pl*) those (ones); **~ ...
éste ...** the former ... the latter ...; **no
me vengas con ésas** don't give me any
more of that nonsense

esencia [e'senθja] *nf* essence;
esencial *adj* essential

esfera [es'fera] *nf* sphere; (*de reloj*)
face; **esférico, -a** *adj* spherical

esforzarse [esfor'θarse] *vr* to exert
o.s., make an effort

esfuerzo *etc* [es'fwerθo] *vb* V
esforzarse ▷ *nm* effort

esfumarse [esfu'marse] *vr* (*apoyo,
esperanzas*) to fade away

esgrima [es'ɣrima] *nf* fencing

esguince [es'ɣinθe] *nm* (*Med*) sprain

eslabón [esla'βon] *nm* link

eslip [ez'lip] *nm* pants *pl* (*BRIT*),
briefs *pl*

eslovaco, -a [eslo'βako, a] *adj, nm/f*
Slovak, Slovakian ▷ *nm* (*Ling*) Slovak,
Slovakian

Eslovaquia [eslo'βakja] *nf* Slovakia

esmalte [es'malte] *nm* enamel;
esmalte de uñas nail varnish *o* polish

esmeralda [esme'ralda] *nf* emerald

esmerarse [esme'rarse] *vr* (*aplicarse*)
to take great pains, exercise great care;
(*afanarse*) to work hard

esmero [es'mero] *nm* (great) care

esnob [es'nob] (*pl* **~s**) *adj* (*persona*)
snobbish ▷ *nmf* snob

eso ['eso] *pron* that, that thing *o*
matter; **~ de su coche** that business
about his car; **~ de ir al cine** all that
about going to the cinema; **a ~ de
las cinco** at about five o'clock; **en ~**
thereupon, at that point; **~ es** that's
it; **¡~ sí que es vida!** now that is really
living!; **por ~ te lo dije** that's why I told
you; **y ~ que llovía** in spite of the fact
it was raining

esos *adj demos* V **ese**

ésos *pron* V **ése**

espabilar *etc* [espaβi'lar] = **despabilar**
etc

espacial [espa'θjal] *adj* (*del espacio*)
space *cpd*

espaciar [espa'θjar] *vt* to space (out)

espacio [es'paθjo] *nm* space; (*Mús*)
interval; (*Radio, TV*) programme (*BRIT*),
program (*US*); **el ~** space; **espacio
aéreo/exterior** air/outer space;
espacioso, -a *adj* spacious, roomy

espada [es'paða] *nf* sword; **espadas**
nfpl (*Naipes*) spades

espaguetis [espa'ɣetis] *nmpl*
spaghetti *sg*

espalda [es'palda] *nf* (*gen*) back;
espaldas *nfpl* (*hombros*) shoulders; **a
~s de algn** behind sb's back; **estar de
~s** to have one's back turned; **tenderse
de ~s** to lie (down) on one's back;
volver la ~ a algn to cold-shoulder sb

espantajo [espan'taxo] *nm* =
espantapájaros

espantapájaros [espanta'paxaros]
nm inv scarecrow

espantar [espan'tar] *vt* (*asustar*) to
frighten, scare; (*ahuyentar*) to frighten
off; (*asombrar*) to horrify, appal;
espantarse *vr* to get frightened *o*
scared; to be appalled

espanto [es'panto] *nm* (*susto*) fright;
(*terror*) terror; (*asombro*) astonishment;
espantoso, -a *adj* frightening;
terrifying; astonishing

España [es'paɲa] *nf* Spain; **español,
a** *adj* Spanish ▷ *nm/f* Spaniard ▷ *nm*
(*Ling*) Spanish

esparadrapo [espara'ðrapo] *nm*
(sticking) plaster (*BRIT*), adhesive
tape (*US*)

esparcir [espar'θir] *vt* to spread;
(*diseminar*) to scatter; **esparcirse** *vr*
to spread (out), to scatter; (*divertirse*)
to enjoy o.s.

espárrago [es'parraxo] *nm*
asparagus

esparto [es'parto] *nm* esparto (grass)

espasmo [es'pasmo] *nm* spasm

espátula [es'patula] *nf* spatula

especia [es'peθja] *nf* spice

especial [espe'θjal] *adj* special;
especialidad *nf* speciality (*BRIT*),
specialty (*US*)

especie [es'peθje] *nf* (*Bio*) species;
(*clase*) kind, sort; **en ~** in kind

especificar [espeθifi'kar] *vt* to
specify; **específico, -a** *adj* specific

espécimen [es'peθimen] (*pl*
especímenes) *nm* specimen

espectáculo [espek'takulo] *nm* (*gen*)
spectacle; (*Teatro etc*) show

espectador, a [espekta'ðor, a] *nm/f*
spectator

especular [espeku'lar] *vt, vi* to
speculate

espejismo [espe'xismo] *nm* mirage

espejo [es'pexo] *nm* mirror; (**espejo**)
retrovisor rear-view mirror

espeluznante [espeluθ'nante] *adj*

horrifying, hair-raising

espera [es'pera] *nf* (*pausa, intervalo*)
wait; (*Jur: plazo*) respite; **en ~ de**
waiting for; (*con expectativa*) expecting

esperanza [espe'ranθa] *nf*
(*confianza*) hope; (*expectativa*)
expectation; **hay pocas ~s de que
venga** there is little prospect of his
coming; **esperanza de vida** life
expectancy

esperar [espe'rar] *vt* (*aguardar*) to
wait for; (*tener expectativa de*) to expect;
(*desear*) to hope for ▷ *vi* to wait; to
expect; to hope; **hacer ~ a algn** to keep
sb waiting; **~ un bebé** to be expecting
(a baby)

esperma [es'perma] *nf* sperm

espeso, -a [es'peso, a] *adj* thick;
espesor *nm* thickness

espía [es'pia] *nmf* spy; **espiar** *vt*
(*observar*) to spy on

espiga [es'pixa] *nf* (*Bot: de trigo
etc*) ear

espigón [espi'xon] *nm* (*Bot*) ear;
(*Náut*) breakwater

espina [es'pina] *nf* thorn; (*de pez*)
bone; **espina dorsal** (*Anat*) spine

espinaca [espi'naka] *nf* spinach

espinazo [espi'naθo] *nm* spine,
backbone

espinilla [espi'niʎa] *nf* (*Anat: tibia*)
shin(bone); (*grano*) blackhead

espinoso, -a [espi'noso, a] *adj*
(*planta*) thorny, prickly; (*asunto*)
difficult

espionaje [espjo'naxe] *nm* spying,
espionage

espiral [espi'ral] *adj, nf* spiral

espirar [espi'rar] *vt* to breathe out,
exhale

espiritista [espiri'tista] *adj, nmf*
spiritualist

espíritu [es'piritu] *nm* spirit;
Espíritu Santo Holy Ghost *o* Spirit;
espiritual *adj* spiritual

espléndido, -a [es'plendiðo, a] *adj*
(*magnífico*) magnificent, splendid;
(*generoso*) generous

esplendor [esplen'dor] *nm* splendour

espolvorear [espolβore'ar] *vt* to dust, sprinkle

esponja [es'ponxa] *nf* sponge; (*fig*) sponger; **esponjoso, -a** *adj* spongy

espontaneidad [espontanei'ðað] *nf* spontaneity; **espontáneo, -a** *adj* spontaneous

esposa [es'posa] *nf* wife; **esposas** *nfpl* handcuffs; **esposar** *vt* to handcuff

esposo [es'poso] *nm* husband

espray [es'prai] *nm* spray

espuela [es'pwela] *nf* spur

espuma [es'puma] *nf* foam; (*de cerveza*) froth, head; (*de jabón*) lather; **espuma de afeitar** shaving foam; **espumadera** *nf* (*utensilio*) skimmer; **espumoso, -a** *adj* frothy, foamy; (*vino*) sparkling

esqueleto [eske'leto] *nm* skeleton

esquema [es'kema] *nm* (*diagrama*) diagram; (*dibujo*) plan; (*Filosofía*) schema

esquí [es'ki] (*pl* **~s**) *nm* (*objeto*) ski; (*Deporte*) skiing; **esquí acuático** water-skiing; **esquiar** *vi* to ski

esquilar [eski'lar] *vt* to shear

esquimal [eski'mal] *adj, nmf* Eskimo

esquina [es'kina] *nf* corner; **esquinazo** [eski'naθo] *nm*: **dar esquinazo a algn** to give sb the slip

esquirol [eski'rol] (*ESP*) *nm* strikebreaker, scab

esquivar [eski'βar] *vt* to avoid

esta ['esta] *adj demos* V **este²**

está *vb* V **estar**

ésta *pron* V **éste**

estabilidad [estaβili'ðað] *nf* stability; **estable** *adj* stable

establecer [estaβle'θer] *vt* to establish; **establecerse** *vr* to establish o.s.; (*echar raíces*) to settle (down); **establecimiento** *nm* establishment

establo [es'taβlo] *nm* (*Agr*) stable

estaca [es'taka] *nf* stake, post; (*de tienda de campaña*) peg

estacada [esta'kaða] *nf* (*cerca*) fence, fencing; (*palenque*) stockade

estación [esta'θjon] *nf* station; (*del año*) season; **estación balnearia** seaside resort; **estación de autobuses** bus station; **estación de servicio** service station

estacionamiento [estaθjona'mjento] *nm* (*Auto*) parking; (*Mil*) stationing

estacionar [estaθjo'nar] *vt* (*Auto*) to park; (*Mil*) to station

estadía [esta'ðia] (*LAM*) *nf* stay

estadio [es'taðjo] *nm* (*fase*) stage, phase; (*Deporte*) stadium

estadista [esta'ðista] *nm* (*Pol*) statesman; (*Mat*) statistician

estadística [esta'ðistika] *nf* figure, statistic; (*ciencia*) statistics *sg*

estado [es'taðo] *nm* (*Pol: condición*) state; **estar en ~** to be pregnant; **estado civil** marital status; **estado de ánimo** state of mind; **estado de cuenta** bank statement; **estado de sitio** state of siege; **estado mayor** staff; **Estados Unidos** United States (of America)

estadounidense [estaðouni'ðense] *adj* United States *cpd*, American ▷ *nmf* American

estafa [es'tafa] *nf* swindle, trick; **estafar** *vt* to swindle, defraud

estáis *vb* V **estar**

estallar [esta'ʎar] *vi* to burst; (*bomba*) to explode, go off; (*epidemia, guerra, rebelión*) to break out; **~ en llanto** to burst into tears; **estallido** *nm* explosion; (*fig*) outbreak

estampa [es'tampa] *nf* print, engraving; **estampado, -a** [estam'paðo, a] *adj* printed ▷ *nm* (*impresión: acción*) printing; (: *efecto*) print; (*marca*) stamping

estampar [estam'par] *vt* (*imprimir*) to print; (*marcar*) to stamp; (*metal*) to engrave; (*poner sello en*) to stamp; (*fig*) to stamp, imprint

estampida [estam'piða] *nf* stampede

estampido [estam'piðo] *nm* bang, report

estampilla [estam'piʎa] (*LAM*) *nf* (postage) stamp

están *vb* V **estar**

estancado, -a [estan'kaðo, a] *adj* stagnant

estancar [estan'kar] *vt* (*aguas*) to hold up, hold back; (*Com*) to monopolize; (*fig*) to block, hold up; **estancarse** *vr* to stagnate

estancia [es'tanθja] *nf* (*ESP*, *MÉX: permanencia*) stay; (*sala*) room; (*RPL: de ganado*) farm, ranch; **estanciero** (*RPL*) *nm* farmer, rancher

estanco, -a [es'tanko, a] *adj* watertight ▷ *nm* tobacconist's (shop), cigar store (*US*)

- **ESTANCO**
-
- Cigarettes, tobacco, postage
- stamps and official forms are all
- sold under state monopoly in
- shops called **estancos**. Although
- tobacco products can also be
- bought in bars and quioscos they
- are generally more expensive.

estándar [es'tandar] *adj, nm* standard

estandarte [estan'darte] *nm* banner, standard

estanque [es'tanke] *nm* (*lago*) pool, pond; (*Agr*) reservoir

estanquero, -a [estan'kero, a] *nm/f* tobacconist

estante [es'tante] *nm* (*armario*) rack, stand; (*biblioteca*) bookcase; (*anaquel*) shelf; **estantería** *nf* shelving, shelves *pl*

○ **PALABRA CLAVE**

estar [es'tar] *vi* **1** (*posición*) to be; **está en la plaza** it's in the square; **¿está**

Juan? is Juan in?; **estamos a 30 km de Junín** we're 30 kms from Junín

2 (*+ adj: estado*) to be; **estar enfermo** to be ill; **está muy elegante** he's looking very smart; **¿cómo estás?** how are you keeping?

3 (*+ gerundio*) to be; **estoy leyendo** I'm reading

4 (*uso pasivo*): **está condenado a muerte** he's been condemned to death; **está envasado en ...** it's packed in ...

5 (*con fechas*): **¿a cuántos estamos?** what's the date today?; **estamos a 5 de mayo** it's the 5th of May

6 (*locuciones*): **¿estamos?** (*¿de acuerdo?*) okay?; (*¿listo?*) ready?

7: **estar de: estar de vacaciones/ viaje** to be on holiday/away o on a trip; **está de camarero** he's working as a waiter

8: **estar para: está para salir** he's about to leave; **no estoy para bromas** I'm not in the mood for jokes

9: **estar por** (*propuesta etc*) to be in favour of; (*persona etc*) to support, side with; **está por limpiar** it still has to be cleaned

10: **estar sin: estar sin dinero** to have no money; **está sin terminar** it isn't finished yet

estarse *vr*: **se estuvo en la cama toda la tarde** he stayed in bed all afternoon

estas ['estas] *adj demos* V **este²**

éstas *pron* V **éste**

estatal [esta'tal] *adj* state *cpd*

estático, -a [es'tatiko, a] *adj* static

estatua [es'tatwa] *nf* statue

estatura [esta'tura] *nf* stature, height

este¹ ['este] *nm* east

este² ['este] (*f* **esta**, *pl* **estos, estas**) *adj demos* (*sg*) this; (*pl*) these

esté *etc vb* V **estar**

éste ['este] (*f* **ésta**, *pl* **éstos, éstas**) *pron* (*sg*) this (one); (*pl*) these (ones);

ése ... ~ ... the former ... the latter ...

estén etc vb V **estar**

estepa [es'tepa] nf (Geo) steppe

estera [es'tera] nf mat(ting)

estéreo [es'tereo] adj inv, nm stereo;
  estereotipo nm stereotype

estéril [es'teril] adj sterile, barren;
  (fig) vain, futile; **esterilizar** vt to
  sterilize

esterlina [ester'lina] adj: **libra ~**
  pound sterling

estés etc vb V **estar**

estética [es'tetika] nf aesthetics sg

estético, -a [es'tetiko, a] adj
  aesthetic

estiércol [es'tjerkol] nm dung, manure

estigma [es'tixma] nm stigma

estilo [es'tilo] nm style; (Tec) stylus;
  (Natación) stroke; **algo por el ~**
  something along those lines

estima [es'tima] nf esteem,
  respect; **estimación** [estima'θjon]
  nf (evaluación) estimation; (aprecio,
  afecto) esteem, regard; **estimado, a** adj
  esteemed; **E~ señor** Dear Sir

estimar [esti'mar] vt (evaluar) to
  estimate; (valorar) to value; (apreciar) to
  esteem, respect; (pensar, considerar) to
  think, reckon

estimulante [estimu'lante] adj
  stimulating ▷ nm stimulant

estimular [estimu'lar] vt to
  stimulate; (excitar) to excite

estímulo [es'timulo] nm stimulus;
  (ánimo) encouragement

estirar [esti'rar] vt to stretch; (dinero,
  suma etc) to stretch out; **estirarse** vr
  to stretch

estirón [esti'ron] nm pull, tug;
  (crecimiento) spurt, sudden growth; **dar
  o pegar un ~** (fam: niño) to shoot up (inf)

estirpe [es'tirpe] nf stock, lineage

estival [esti'βal] adj summer cpd

esto ['esto] pron this, this thing o
  matter; **~ de la boda** this business
  about the wedding

Estocolmo [esto'kolmo] nm
  Stockholm

estofado [esto'faðo] nm stew

estómago [es'tomaxo] nm stomach;
  tener ~ to be thick-skinned

estorbar [estor'βar] vt to hinder,
  obstruct; (molestar) to bother, disturb
  ▷ vi to be in the way; **estorbo** nm
  (molestia) bother, nuisance; (obstáculo)
  hindrance, obstacle

estornudar [estornu'ðar] vi to
  sneeze

estos ['estos] adj demos V **este²**

éstos pron V **éste**

estoy vb V **estar**

estrado [es'traðo] nm platform

estrafalario, -a [estrafa'larjo, a] adj
  odd, eccentric

estrago [es'traxo] nm ruin,
  destruction; **hacer ~s en** to wreak
  havoc among

estragón [estra'xon] nm tarragon

estrambótico, -a [estram'botiko,
  a] adj (persona) eccentric; (peinado,
  ropa) outlandish

estrangular [estrangu'lar] vt
  (persona) to strangle; (Med) to
  strangulate

estratagema [estrata'xema] nf
  (Mil) stratagem; (astucia) cunning

estrategia [estra'texja] nf strategy;
  estratégico, -a adj strategic

estrato [es'trato] nm stratum, layer

estrechar [estre'tʃar] vt (reducir) to
  narrow; (Costura) to take in; (abrazar)
  to hug, embrace; **estrecharse** vr
  (reducirse) to narrow, grow narrow;
  (abrazarse) to embrace; **~ la mano** to
  shake hands

estrechez [estre'tʃeθ] nf narrowness;
  (de ropa) tightness; **estrecheces** nfpl
  (dificultades económicas) financial
  difficulties

estrecho, -a [es'tretʃo, a] adj
  narrow; (apretado) tight; (íntimo) close,
  intimate; (miserable) mean ▷ nm strait;
  ~ de miras narrow-minded

estrella [es'treʎa] nf star; **estrella
  de mar** (Zool) starfish; **estrella fugaz**
  shooting star

estrellar [estre'ʎar] vt (hacer añicos) to smash (to pieces); (huevos) to fry; **estrellarse** vr to smash; (chocarse) to crash; (fracasar) to fail

estremecer [estreme'θer] vt to shake; **estremecerse** vr to shake, tremble

estrenar [estre'nar] vt (vestido) to wear for the first time; (casa) to move into; (película, obra de teatro) to première; **estrenarse** vr (persona) to make one's début; **estreno** nm (Cine etc) première

estreñido, -a [estre'ɲiðo, a] adj constipated

estreñimiento [estreɲi'mjento] nm constipation

estrepitoso, -a [estrepi'toso, a] adj noisy; (fiesta) rowdy

estría [es'tria] nf groove

estribar [estri'βar] vi: ~ **en** to lie on

estribillo [estri'βiʎo] nm (Literatura) refrain; (Mús) chorus

estribo [es'triβo] nm (de jinete) stirrup; (de coche, tren) step; (de puente) support; (Geo) spur; **perder los ~s** to fly off the handle

estribor [estri'βor] nm (Náut) starboard

estricto, -a [es'trikto, a] adj (riguroso) strict; (severo) severe

estridente [estri'ðente] adj (color) loud; (voz) raucous

estropajo [estro'paxo] nm scourer

estropear [estrope'ar] vt to spoil; (dañar) to damage; **estropearse** vr (objeto) to get damaged; (persona, piel) to be ruined

estructura [estruk'tura] nf structure

estrujar [estru'xar] vt (apretar) to squeeze; (aplastar) to crush; (fig) to drain, bleed

estuario [es'twarjo] nm estuary

estuche [es'tutʃe] nm box, case

estudiante [estu'ðjante] nmf student; **estudiantil** adj student cpd

estudiar [estu'ðjar] vt to study

estudio [es'tuðjo] nm study; (Cine, Arte, Radio) studio; **estudios** nmpl studies; (erudición) learning sg; **estudioso, -a** adj studious

estufa [es'tufa] nf heater, fire

estupefaciente [estupefa'θjente] nm drug, narcotic

estupefacto, -a [estupe'fakto, a] adj speechless, thunderstruck

estupendo, -a [estu'pendo, a] adj wonderful, terrific; (fam) great; ¡~! that's great!, fantastic!

estupidez [estupi'ðeθ] nf (torpeza) stupidity; (acto) stupid thing (to do)

estúpido, -a [es'tupiðo, a] adj stupid, silly

estuve etc vb V **estar**

ETA ['eta] (ESP) nf abr (= Euskadi ta Askatasuna) ETA

etapa [e'tapa] nf (de viaje) stage; (Deporte) leg; (parada) stopping place; (fase) stage, phase

etarra [e'tarra] nmf member of ETA

etc. abr (= etcétera) etc

etcétera [et'θetera] adv etcetera

eternidad [eterni'ðað] nf eternity; **eterno, -a** adj eternal, everlasting

ética ['etika] nf ethics pl

ético, -a ['etiko, a] adj ethical

etiqueta [eti'keta] nf (modales) etiquette; (rótulo) label, tag

Eucaristía [eukaris'tia] nf Eucharist

euforia [eu'forja] nf euphoria

euro ['euro] nm (moneda) euro

eurodiputado, -a [eurodipu'taðo, a] nm/f Euro MP, MEP

Europa [eu'ropa] nf Europe; **europeo, -a** adj, nm/f European

Euskadi [eus'kaði] nm the Basque Country o Provinces pl

euskera [eus'kera] nm (Ling) Basque

evacuación [eβakwa'θjon] nf evacuation

evacuar [eβa'kwar] vt to evacuate

evadir [eβa'ðir] vt to evade, avoid; **evadirse** vr to escape

evaluar [eβa'lwar] vt to evaluate

evangelio [eβan'xeljo] nm gospel

evaporar [eβapo'rar] *vt* to evaporate; **evaporarse** *vr* to vanish

evasión [eβa'sjon] *nf* escape, flight; (*fig*) evasion; **evasión de capitales** flight of capital

evasiva [eβa'siβa] *nf* (*pretexto*) excuse

evento [e'βento] *nm* event

eventual [eβen'twal] *adj* possible, conditional (upon circumstances); (*trabajador*) casual, temporary

⬛ No confundir **eventual** con la palabra inglesa *eventual*.

evidencia [eβi'ðenθja] *nf* evidence, proof

evidente [eβi'ðente] *adj* obvious, clear, evident

evitar [eβi'tar] *vt* (*evadir*) to avoid; (*impedir*) to prevent; **~ hacer algo** to avoid doing sth

evocar [eβo'kar] *vt* to evoke, call forth

evolución [eβolu'θjon] *nf* (*desarrollo*) evolution, development; (*cambio*) change; (*Mil*) manoeuvre; **evolucionar** *vi* to evolve; to manoeuvre

ex [eks] *adj* ex-; **el ~ ministro** the former minister, the ex-minister

exactitud [eksakti'tuð] *nf* exactness; (*precisión*) accuracy; (*puntualidad*) punctuality; **exacto, -a** *adj* exact; accurate; punctual; **¡exacto!** exactly!

exageración [eksaxera'θjon] *nf* exaggeration

exagerar [eksaxe'rar] *vt, vi* to exaggerate

exaltar [eksal'tar] *vt* to exalt, glorify; **exaltarse** *vr* (*excitarse*) to get excited *o* worked up

examen [ek'samen] *nm* examination; **examen de conducir** driving test; **examen de ingreso** entrance examination

examinar [eksami'nar] *vt* to examine; **examinarse** *vr* to be examined, take an examination

excavadora [ekskaβa'ðora] *nf* excavator

excavar [ekska'βar] *vt* to excavate

excedencia [eksθe'ðenθja] *nf*: **estar en ~** to be on leave; **pedir** *o* **solicitar la ~** to ask for leave

excedente [eksθe'ðente] *adj, nm* excess, surplus

exceder [eksθe'ðer] *vt* to exceed, surpass; **excederse** *vr* (*extralimitarse*) to go too far

excelencia [eksθe'lenθja] *nf* excellence; **su E~** his Excellency; **excelente** *adj* excellent

excéntrico, -a [eks'θentriko, a] *adj, nm/f* eccentric

excepción [eksθep'θjon] *nf* exception; **a ~ de** with the exception of, except for; **excepcional** *adj* exceptional

excepto [eks'θepto] *adv* excepting, except (for)

exceptuar [eksθep'twar] *vt* to except, exclude

excesivo, -a [eksθe'siβo, a] *adj* excessive

exceso [eks'θeso] *nm* (*gen*) excess; (*Com*) surplus; **exceso de equipaje/peso** excess luggage/weight; **exceso de velocidad** speeding

excitado, -a [eksθi'taðo, a] *adj* excited; (*emociónes*) aroused

excitar [eksθi'tar] *vt* to excite; (*incitar*) to urge; **excitarse** *vr* to get excited

exclamación [eksklama'θjon] *nf* exclamation

exclamar [ekskla'mar] *vi* to exclaim

excluir [eksklu'ir] *vt* to exclude; (*dejar fuera*) to shut out; (*descartar*) to reject

exclusiva [eksklu'siβa] *nf* (*Prensa*) exclusive, scoop; (*Com*) sole right

exclusivo, -a [eksklu'siβo, a] *adj* exclusive; **derecho ~** sole *o* exclusive right

Excmo. *abr* = **excelentísmo**

excomulgar [ekskomul'ɣar] *vt* (*Rel*) to excommunicate

excomunión [ekskomu'njon] *nf* excommunication

excursión [ekskur'sjon] *nf*
excursion, outing; **excursionista** *nmf*
(*turista*) sightseer

excusa [eks'kusa] *nf* excuse;
(*disculpa*) apology; **excusar**
[eksku'sar] *vt* to excuse

exhaustivo, -a [eksaus'tiβo, a] *adj*
(*análisis*) thorough; (*estudio*) exhaustive

exhausto, -a [ek'sausto, a] *adj*
exhausted

exhibición [eksiβi'θjon] *nf*
exhibition, display, show

exhibir [eksi'βir] *vt* to exhibit,
display, show

exigencia [eksi'xenθja] *nf*
demand, requirement; **exigente** *adj*
demanding

exigir [eksi'xir] *vt* (*gen*) to demand,
require; ~ **el pago** to demand payment

exiliado, -a [eksi'ljaðo, a] *adj* exiled
▷ *nm/f* exile

exilio [ek'siljo] *nm* exile

eximir [eksi'mir] *vt* to exempt

existencia [eksis'tenθja] *nf*
existence; **existencias** *nfpl* stock(s) *pl*

existir [eksis'tir] *vi* to exist, be

éxito ['eksito] *nm* (*triunfo*) success;
(*Mús etc*) hit; **tener ~** to be successful
No confundir **éxito** con la palabra
inglesa *exit*.

exorbitante [eksorβi'tante] *adj*
(*precio*) exorbitant; (*cantidad*) excessive

exótico, -a [ek'sotiko, a] *adj* exotic

expandir [ekspan'dir] *vt* to expand

expansión [ekspan'sjon] *nf*
expansion

expansivo, -a [ekspan'siβo, a]
adj: **onda expansiva** shock wave

expatriarse [ekspa'trjarse] *vr* to
emigrate; (*Pol*) to go into exile

expectativa [ekspekta'tiβa] *nf*
(*espera*) expectation; (*perspectiva*)
prospect

expedición [ekspeði'θjon] *nf*
(*excursión*) expedition

expediente [ekspe'ðjente] *nm*
expedient; (*Jur: procedimento*) action,
proceedings *pl*; (: *papeles*) dossier,

file, record

expedir [ekspe'ðir] *vt* (*despachar*) to
send, forward; (*pasaporte*) to issue

expensas [eks'pensas] *nfpl*: **a ~ de** at
the expense of

experiencia [ekspe'rjenθja] *nf*
experience

experimentado, -a
[eksperimen'taðo, a] *adj* experienced

experimentar [eksperimen'tar] *vt*
(*en laboratorio*) to experiment with;
(*probar*) to test, try out; (*notar, observar*)
to experience; (*deterioro, pérdida*) to
suffer; **experimento** *nm* experiment

experto, -a [eks'perto, a] *adj* expert,
skilled ▷ *nm/f* expert

expirar [ekspi'rar] *vi* to expire

explanada [eskpla'naða] *nf* (*llano*)
plain

explayarse [ekspla'jarse] *vr* (*en
discurso*) to speak at length; ~ **con algn**
to confide in sb

explicación [eksplika'θjon] *nf*
explanation

explicar [ekspli'kar] *vt* to explain;
explicarse *vr* to explain (o.s.)

explícito, -a [eks'pliθito, a] *adj*
explicit

explique *etc vb* ∨ **explicar**

explorador, a [eksplora'ðor, a] *nm/f*
(*pionero*) explorer; (*Mil*) scout ▷ *nm*
(*Med*) probe; (*Tec*) (*radar*) scanner

explorar [eksplo'rar] *vt* to explore;
(*Med*) to probe; (*radar*) to scan

explosión [eksplo'sjon] *nf*
explosion; **explosivo, -a** *adj* explosive

explotación [eksplota'θjon] *nf*
exploitation; (*de planta etc*) running

explotar [eksplo'tar] *vt* to exploit to
run, operate ▷ *vi* to explode

exponer [ekspo'ner] *vt* to expose;
(*cuadro*) to display; (*vida*) to risk;
(*idea*) to explain; **exponerse** *vr*: ~**se
a (hacer) algo** to run the risk of
(doing) sth

exportación [eksporta'θjon] *nf*
(*acción*) export; (*mercancías*) exports *pl*

exportar [ekspor'tar] *vt* to export

exposición [eksposi'θjon] nf (gen) exposure; (de arte) show, exhibition; (explicación) explanation; (declaración) account, statement

expresamente [ekspresa'mente] adv (decir) clearly; (a propósito) expressly

expresar [ekspre'sar] vt to express; **expresión** nf expression

expresivo, -a [ekspre'siβo, a] adj (persona, gesto, palabras) expressive; (cariñoso) affectionate

expreso, -a [eks'preso, a] pp de **expresar** ▷ adj (explícito) express; (claro) specific, clear; (tren) fast ▷ adv: **enviar ~** to send by express (delivery)

express [eks'pres] (LAM) adv: **enviar algo ~** to send sth special delivery

exprimidor [eksprimi'ðor] nm squeezer

exprimir [ekspri'mir] vt (fruta) to squeeze; (zumo) to squeeze out

expuesto, -a [eks'pwesto, a] pp de **exponer** ▷ adj exposed; (cuadro etc) on show, on display

expulsar [ekspul'sar] vt (echar) to eject, throw out; (alumno) to expel; (despedir) to sack, fire; (Deporte) to send off; **expulsión** nf expulsion; sending-off

exquisito, -a [ekski'sito, a] adj exquisite; (comida) delicious

éxtasis ['ekstasis] nm ecstasy

extender [eksten'der] vt to extend; (los brazos) to stretch out, hold out; (mapa, tela) to spread (out), open (out); (mantequilla) to spread; (certificado) to issue; (cheque, recibo) to make out; (documento) to draw up; **extenderse** vr (gen) to extend; (persona: en el suelo) to stretch out; (epidemia) to spread; **extendido, -a** adj (abierto) spread out, open; (brazos) outstretched; (costumbre) widespread

extensión [eksten'sjon] nf (de terreno, mar) expanse, stretch; (de tiempo) length, duration; (Tel) extension; **en toda la ~ de la palabra** in every sense of the word

extenso, -a [eks'tenso, a] adj extensive

exterior [ekste'rjor] adj (de fuera) external; (afuera) outside, exterior; (apariencia) outward; (deuda, relaciónes) foreign ▷ nm (gen) exterior, outside; (aspecto) outward appearance; (Deporte) wing(er); (países extranjeros) abroad; **en el ~** abroad; **al ~** outwardly, on the surface

exterminar [ekstermi'nar] vt to exterminate

externo, -a [eks'terno, a] adj (exterior) external, outside; (superficial) outward ▷ nm/f day pupil

extinguir [ekstin'gir] vt (fuego) to extinguish, put out; (raza, población) to wipe out; **extinguirse** vr (fuego) to go out; (Bio) to die out, become extinct

extintor [ekstin'tor] nm (fire) extinguisher

extirpar [ekstir'par] vt (Med) to remove (surgically)

extra ['ekstra] adj inv (tiempo) extra; (chocolate, vino) good-quality ▷ nmf extra ▷ nm extra; (bono) bonus

extracción [ekstrak'θjon] nf extraction; (en lotería) draw

extracto [eks'trakto] nm extract

extradición [ekstraði'θjon] nf extradition

extraer [ekstra'er] vt to extract, take out

extraescolar [ekstraesko'lar] adj: **actividad ~** extracurricular activity

extranjero, -a [ekstran'xero, a] adj foreign ▷ nm/f foreigner ▷ nm foreign countries pl; **en el ~** abroad

▌No confundir **extranjero** con la palabra inglesa stranger.

extrañar [ekstra'ɲar] vt (sorprender) to find strange o odd; (echar de menos) to miss; **extrañarse** vr (sorprenderse) to be amazed, be surprised; **me extraña** I'm surprised

extraño, -a [eks'traɲo, a] adj (extranjero) foreign; (raro, sorprendente) strange, odd

extraordinario, -a
[ekstraorði'narjo, a] *adj*
extraordinary; (*edición, número*) special
▷ *nm* (*de periódico*) special edition;
horas extraordinarias overtime *sg*

extrarradio [ekstra'rraðjo] *nm*
suburbs

extravagante [ekstraβa'ɣante]
adj (*excéntrico*) eccentric; (*estrafalario*)
outlandish

extraviado, -a [ekstra'βjaðo, a] *adj*
lost, missing

extraviar [ekstra'βjar] *vt*
(*persona: desorientar*) to mislead,
misdirect; (*perder*) to lose, misplace;
extraviarse *vr* to lose one's way,
get lost

extremar [ekstre'mar] *vt* to carry
to extremes

extremaunción [ekstremaun'θjon]
nf extreme unction

extremidad [ekstremi'ðað] *nf*
(*punta*) extremity; **extremidades** *nfpl*
(*Anat*) extremities

extremo, -a [eks'tremo, a] *adj*
extreme; (*último*) last ▷ *nm* end; (*límite,
grado sumo*) extreme; **en último ~** as
a last resort

extrovertido, -a [ekstroβer'tiðo, a]
adj, nm/f extrovert

exuberante [eksuβe'rante] *adj*
exuberant; (*fig*) luxuriant, lush

eyacular [ejaku'lar] *vt, vi* to
ejaculate

adj, nm/f extrovert
exuberante [eksuβe'rante] *adj*
exuberant; (*fig*) luxuriant, lush
eyacular [ejaku'lar] *vt, vi* to
ejaculate

o lose one's way, get lost

extremar [ekstre'mar] *vt* to carry
to extremes

extremaunción [ekstremaun'θjon]
nf extreme unction

extremidad [ekstremi'ðað] *nf*
(*punta*) extremity; **extremidades** *nfpl*
(*Anat*) extremities

extremo, -a [eks'tremo, a] *adj*
extreme; (*último*) last ▷ *nm* end; (*límite,
grado sumo*) extreme; **en último ~** as
a last resort

extrovertido, -a [ekstroβer'tiðo, a]

f

fa [fa] *nm* (*Mús*) fa, F

fabada [fa'βaða] *nf* bean and sausage stew

fábrica ['faβrika] *nf* factory; **marca de ~** trademark; **precio de ~** factory price

> No confundir **fábrica** con la palabra inglesa *fabric*.

fabricación [faβrika'θjon] *nf* (*manufactura*) manufacture; (*producción*) production; **de ~ casera** home-made; **fabricación en serie** mass production

fabricante [faβri'kante] *nmf* manufacturer

fabricar [faβri'kar] *vt* (*manufacturar*) to manufacture, make; (*construir*) to build; (*cuento*) to fabricate, devise

fábula ['faβula] *nf* (*cuento*) fable; (*chisme*) rumour; (*mentira*) fib

fabuloso, -a [faβu'loso, a] *adj* (*oportunidad, tiempo*) fabulous, great

facción [fak'θjon] *nf* (*Pol*) faction; **facciones** *nfpl* (*de rostro*) features

faceta [fa'θeta] *nf* facet

facha ['fatʃa] (*fam*) *nf* (*aspecto*) look; (*cara*) face

fachada [fa'tʃaða] *nf* (*Arq*) façade, front

fácil ['faθil] *adj* (*simple*) easy; (*probable*) likely

facilidad [faθili'ðað] *nf* (*capacidad*) ease; (*sencillez*) simplicity; (*de palabra*) fluency; **facilidades** *nfpl* facilities; **facilidades de pago** credit facilities

facilitar [faθili'tar] *vt* (*hacer fácil*) to make easy; (*proporcionar*) to provide

factor [fak'tor] *nm* factor

factura [fak'tura] *nf* (*cuenta*) bill; **facturación** *nf* (*de equipaje*) check-in; **facturar** *vt* (*Com*) to invoice, charge for; (*equipaje*) to check in

facultad [fakul'tað] *nf* (*aptitud, Escol etc*) faculty; (*poder*) power

faena [fa'ena] *nf* (*trabajo*) work; (*quehacer*) task, job

faisán [fai'san] *nm* pheasant

faja ['faxa] *nf* (*para la cintura*) sash; (*de mujer*) corset; (*de tierra*) strip

fajo ['faxo] *nm* (*de papeles*) bundle; (*de billetes*) wad

falda ['falda] *nf* (*prenda de vestir*) skirt; **falda pantalón** culottes *pl*, split skirt

falla ['faʎa] *nf* (*defecto*) fault, flaw; **falla humana** (*LAM*) human error

fallar [fa'ʎar] *vt* (*Jur*) to pronounce sentence on ▷ *vi* (*memoria*) to fail; (*motor*) to miss

Fallas ['faʎas] *nfpl Valencian celebration of the feast of St Joseph*

- **FALLAS**
-
- In the week of 19 March (the feast
- of San José), Valencia honours its
- patron saint with a spectacular
- fiesta called **Las Fallas**. The **Fallas**
- are huge papier-mâché, cardboard
- and wooden sculptures which
- are built by competing teams
- throughout the year. They depict
- politicians and well-known public
- figures and are thrown onto

bonfires and set alight once a jury
has judged them – only the best
sculpture escapes the flames.

fallecer [faʎe'θer] *vi* to pass away,
die; **fallecimiento** *nm* decease,
demise

fallido, -a [fa'ʎiðo, a] *adj* (*gen*)
frustrated, unsuccessful

fallo ['faʎo] *nm* (*Jur*) verdict, ruling;
(*fracaso*) failure; **fallo cardíaco** heart
failure; **fallo humano** (*ESP*) human
error

falsificar [falsifi'kar] *vt* (*firma etc*) to
forge; (*moneda*) to counterfeit

falso, -a ['falso, a] *adj* false;
(*documento, moneda etc*) fake; **en ~**
falsely

falta ['falta] *nf* (*defecto*) fault, flaw;
(*privación*) lack, want; (*ausencia*)
absence; (*carencia*) shortage;
(*equivocación*) mistake; (*Deporte*) foul;
echar en ~ to miss; **hacer ~ hacer algo**
to be necessary to do sth; **me hace
~ una pluma** I need a pen; **falta de
educación** bad manners *pl*; **falta de
ortografía** spelling mistake

faltar [fal'tar] *vi* (*escasear*) to be
lacking, be wanting; (*ausentarse*) to
be absent, be missing; **faltan 2 horas
para llegar** there are 2 hours to go
till arrival; **~ al respeto a algn** to be
disrespectful to sb; **¡no faltaba más!**
(*no hay de qué*) don't mention it

fama ['fama] *nf* (*renombre*) fame;
(*reputación*) reputation

familia [fa'milja] *nf* family; **familia
numerosa** large family; **familia
política** in-laws *pl*

familiar [fami'ljar] *adj* (*relativo a la
familia*) family *cpd*; (*conocido, informal*)
familiar ▷ *nm* relative, relation

famoso, -a [fa'moso, a] *adj*
(*renombrado*) famous

fan [fan] (*pl* **~s**) *nmf* fan

fanático, -a [fa'natiko, a] *adj*
fanatical ▷ *nm/f* fanatic; (*Cine,
Deporte*) fan

fanfarrón, -ona [fanfa'rron, ona]
adj boastful

fango ['fango] *nm* mud

fantasía [fanta'sia] *nf* fantasy,
imagination; **joyas de ~** imitation
jewellery *sg*

fantasma [fan'tasma] *nm* (*espectro*)
ghost, apparition; (*fanfarrón*) show-off

fantástico, -a [fan'tastiko, a] *adj*
fantastic

farmacéutico, -a [farma'θeutiko,
a] *adj* pharmaceutical ▷ *nm/f*
chemist (*BRIT*), pharmacist

farmacia [far'maθja] *nf* chemist's
(shop) (*BRIT*), pharmacy; **farmacia de
guardia** all-night chemist

fármaco ['farmako] *nm* drug

faro ['faro] *nm* (*Náut*: *torre*)
lighthouse; (*Auto*) headlamp;
faros antiniebla fog lamps; **faros
delanteros/traseros** headlights/rear
lights

farol [fa'rol] *nm* lantern, lamp

farola [fa'rola] *nf* street lamp (*BRIT*)
o light (*US*)

farra ['farra] (*LAM*: *fam*) *nf* party; **ir de
~** to go on a binge

farsa ['farsa] *nf* (*gen*) farce

farsante [far'sante] *nmf* fraud, fake

fascículo [fas'θikulo] *nm* (*de revista*)
part, instalment

fascinar [fasθi'nar] *vt* (*gen*) to
fascinate

fascismo [fas'θismo] *nm* fascism;
fascista *adj, nmf* fascist

fase ['fase] *nf* phase

fashion ['faʃon] *adj* (*fam*) trendy

fastidiar [fasti'ðjar] *vt* (*molestar*)
to annoy, bother; (*estropear*) to spoil;
fastidiarse *vr*: **¡que se fastidie!** (*fam*)
he'll just have to put up with it!

fastidio [fas'tiðjo] *nm* (*molestia*)
annoyance; **fastidioso, -a** *adj*
(*molesto*) annoying

fatal [fa'tal] *adj* (*gen*) fatal;
(*desgraciado*) ill-fated; (*fam*: *malo,
pésimo*) awful; **fatalidad** *nf* (*destino*)
fate; (*mala suerte*) misfortune

fatiga [fa'tiɣa] nf (cansancio) fatigue, weariness

fatigar [fati'ɣar] vt to tire, weary

fatigoso, -a [fati'ɣoso, a] adj (cansador) tiring

fauna ['fauna] nf fauna

favor [fa'βor] nm favour; **estar a ~ de** to be in favour of; **haga el ~ de ...** would you be so good as to ..., kindly ...; **por ~** please; **favorable** adj favourable

favorecer [faβore'θer] vt to favour; (vestido etc) to become, flatter; **este peinado le favorece** this hairstyle suits him

favorito, -a [faβo'rito, a] adj, nm/f favourite

fax [faks] nm inv fax; **mandar por ~** to fax

fe [fe] nf (Rel) faith; (documento) certificate; **actuar con buena/mala ~** to act in good/bad faith

febrero [fe'βrero] nm February

fecha ['fetʃa] nf date; **con ~ adelantada** postdated; **en ~ próxima** soon; **hasta la ~** to date, so far; **poner ~** to date; **fecha de caducidad** (de producto alimenticio) sell-by date; (de contrato etc) expiry date; **fecha de nacimiento** date of birth; **fecha límite** o **tope** deadline

fecundo, -a [fe'kundo, a] adj (fértil) fertile; (fig) prolific; (productivo) productive

federación [feðera'θjon] nf federation

felicidad [feliθi'ðað] nf happiness; **¡~es!** (deseos) best wishes, congratulations!; (en cumpleaños) happy birthday!

felicitación [feliθita'θjon] nf (tarjeta) greeting(s) card

felicitar [feliθi'tar] vt to congratulate

feliz [fe'liθ] adj happy

felpudo [fel'puðo] nm doormat

femenino, -a [feme'nino, a] adj, nm feminine

feminista [femi'nista] adj, nmf feminist

fenómeno [fe'nomeno] nm phenomenon; (fig) freak, accident ▷ adj great ▷ excl great!, marvellous!; **fenomenal** adj =**fenómeno**

feo, -a ['feo, a] adj (gen) ugly; (desagradable) bad, nasty

féretro ['feretro] nm (ataúd) coffin; (sarcófago) bier

feria ['ferja] nf (gen) fair; (descanso) holiday, rest day; (MÉx: cambio) small o loose change; (CS: mercado) village market

feriado [fe'rjaðo] (LAM) nm holiday

fermentar [fermen'tar] vi to ferment

feroz [fe'roθ] adj (cruel) cruel; (salvaje) fierce

férreo, -a ['ferreo, a] adj iron

ferretería [ferrete'ria] nf (tienda) ironmonger's (shop) (BRIT), hardware store (US)

ferrocarril [ferroka'rril] nm railway

ferroviario, -a [ferro'βjarjo, a] adj rail cpd

ferry ['ferri] (pl **~s** o **ferries**) nm ferry

fértil ['fertil] adj (productivo) fertile; (rico) rich; **fertilidad** nf (gen) fertility; (productividad) fruitfulness

fervor [fer'βor] nm fervour

festejar [feste'xar] vt (celebrar) to celebrate

festejo [fes'texo] nm celebration; **festejos** nmpl (fiestas) festivals

festín [fes'tin] nm feast, banquet

festival [festi'βal] nm festival

festividad [festiβi'ðað] nf festivity

festivo, -a [fes'tiβo, a] adj (de fiesta) festive; (Cine, Literatura) humorous; **día ~** holiday

feto ['feto] nm foetus

fiable ['fjaβle] adj (persona) trustworthy; (máquina) reliable

fiambre ['fjambre] nm cold meat

fiambrera [fjam'brera] nf (para almuerzo) lunch box

fianza ['fjanθa] nf surety; (Jur): **libertad bajo ~** release on bail

fiar [fi'ar] vt (salir garante de) to guarantee; (vender a crédito) to sell on credit ▷ vi to trust; **fiarse** vr to trust (in), rely on; **~ a** (secreto) to confide (to); **~se de algn** to rely on sb

fibra ['fiβra] nf fibre; **fibra óptica** optical fibre

ficción [fik'θjon] nf fiction

ficha ['fitʃa] nf (Tel) token; (en juegos) counter, marker; (tarjeta) (index) card; **fichaje** nm (Deporte) signing; **fichar** vt (archivar) to file, index; (Deporte) to sign; **estar fichado** to have a record; **fichero** nm box file; (Inform) file

ficticio, -a [fik'tiθjo, a] adj (imaginario) fictitious; (falso) fabricated

fidelidad [fiðeli'ðað] nf (lealtad) fidelity, loyalty; **alta ~** high fidelity, hi-fi

fideos [fi'ðeos] nmpl noodles

fiebre ['fjeβre] nf (Med) fever; (fig) fever, excitement; **tener ~** to have a temperature; **fiebre aftosa** foot-and-mouth disease

fiel [fjel] adj (leal) faithful, loyal; (fiable) reliable; (exacto) accurate, faithful ▷ nm: **los ~es** the faithful

fieltro ['fjeltro] nm felt

fiera ['fjera] nf (animal feroz) wild animal o beast; (fig) dragon; V tb **fiero**

fiero, -a ['fjero, a] adj (cruel) cruel; (feroz) fierce; (duro) harsh

fierro ['fjerro] (LAM) nm (hierro) iron

fiesta ['fjesta] nf party; (de pueblo) festival; (vacaciones: tb: **~s**) holiday sg; **fiesta mayor** annual festival; **fiesta patria** (LAM) independence day

- **FIESTAS**
-
- **Fiestas** can be official public
- holidays or holidays set by each
- autonomous region, many of
- which coincide with religious
- festivals. There are also many
- **fiestas** all over Spain for a local
- patron saint or the Virgin Mary.
- These often last several days and

- can include religious processions,
- carnival parades, bullfights and
- dancing.

figura [fi'ɣura] nf (gen) figure; (forma, imagen) shape, form; (Naipes) face card

figurar [fiɣu'rar] vt (representar) to represent; (fingir) to figure ▷ vi to figure; **figurarse** vr (imaginarse) to imagine; (suponer) to suppose

fijador [fixa'ðor] nm (Foto etc) fixative; (de pelo) gel

fijar [fi'xar] vt (gen) to fix; (estampilla) to affix, stick (on); **fijarse** vr: **~se en** to notice

fijo, -a ['fixo, a] adj (gen) fixed; (firme) firm; (permanente) permanent ▷ adv: **mirar ~** to stare

fila ['fila] nf row; (Mil) rank; **ponerse en ~** to line up, get into line; **fila india** single file

filatelia [fila'telja] nf philately, stamp collecting

filete [fi'lete] nm (de carne) fillet steak; (de pescado) fillet

filiación [filja'θjon] nf (Pol) affiliation

filial [fi'ljal] adj filial ▷ nf subsidiary

Filipinas [fili'pinas] nfpl: **las (Islas) ~** the Philippines; **filipino, -a** adj, nm/f Philippine

filmar [fil'mar] vt to film, shoot

filo ['filo] nm (gen) edge; **sacar ~ a** to sharpen; **al ~ del mediodía** at about midday; **de doble ~** double-edged

filología [filolo'ɣia] nf philology; **filología inglesa** (Univ) English Studies

filón [fi'lon] nm (Minería) vein, lode; (fig) goldmine

filosofía [filoso'fia] nf philosophy; **filósofo, -a** nm/f philosopher

filtrar [fil'trar] vt, vi to filter, strain; **filtrarse** vr to filter; **filtro** nm (Tec, utensilio) filter

fin [fin] nm end; (objetivo) aim, purpose; **al ~ y al cabo** when all's said and done; **a ~ de** in order to; **por ~** finally; **en ~** in short; **fin de semana**

weekend

final [fi'nal] *adj* final ▷ *nm* end,
conclusion ▷ *nf* final; **al ~** in the
end; **a ~es de** at the end of; **finalidad**
nf (*propósito*) purpose, intention;
finalista *nmf* finalist; **finalizar** *vt* to
end, finish; (*Inform*) to log out *o* off ▷ *vi*
to end, come to an end

financiar [finan'θjar] *vt* to finance;
financiero, -a *adj* financial ▷ *nm/f*
financier

finca ['finka] *nf* (*casa de campo*)
country house; (*ESP: bien inmueble*)
property, land; (*LAM: granja*) farm

finde ['finde] *nm abr* (*fam: fin de
semana*) weekend

fingir [fin'xir] *vt* (*simular*) to simulate,
feign ▷ *vi* (*aparentar*) to pretend

finlandés, -esa [finlan'des, esa]
adj Finnish ▷ *nm/f* Finn ▷ *nm* (*Ling*)
Finnish

Finlandia [fin'landja] *nf* Finland

fino, -a ['fino, a] *adj* fine; (*delgado*)
slender; (*de buenas maneras*) polite,
refined; (*jerez*) fino, dry

firma ['firma] *nf* signature; (*Com*)
firm, company

firmamento [firma'mento] *nm*
firmament

firmar [fir'mar] *vt* to sign

firme ['firme] *adj* firm; (*estable*)
stable; (*sólido*) solid; (*constante*) steady;
(*decidido*) resolute ▷ *nm* road (surface);
firmeza *nf* firmness; (*constancia*)
steadiness; (*solidez*) solidity

fiscal [fis'kal] *adj* fiscal ▷ *nmf* public
prosecutor; **año ~** tax *o* fiscal year

fisgonear [fisxone'ar] *vt* to poke
one's nose into ▷ *vi* to pry, spy

física ['fisika] *nf* physics *sg*; V *tb* **físico**

físico, -a ['fisiko, a] *adj* physical
▷ *nm* physique ▷ *nm/f* physicist

fisura [fi'sura] *nf* crack; (*Med*) fracture

flác(c)ido, -a ['fla(k)θiðo, a] *adj*
flabby

flaco, -a ['flako, a] *adj* (*muy delgado*)
skinny, thin; (*débil*) weak, feeble

flagrante [fla'xrante] *adj* flagrant

flama ['flama] (*MÉX*) *nf* flame;
flamable (*MÉX*) *adj* flammable

flamante [fla'mante] (*fam*) *adj*
brilliant; (*nuevo*) brand-new

flamenco, -a [fla'menko, a] *adj*
(*de Flandes*) Flemish; (*baile, música*)
flamenco ▷ *nm* (*baile, música*)
flamenco; (*Zool*) flamingo

flamingo [fla'mingo] (*MÉX*) *nm*
flamingo

flan [flan] *nm* creme caramel

No confundir **flan** con la palabra
inglesa *flan*.

flash [flaʃ] (*pl ~ o ~es*) *nm* (*Foto*) flash

flauta ['flauta] *nf* (*Mús*) flute

flecha ['fletʃa] *nf* arrow

flechazo [fle'tʃaθo] *nm* love at
first sight

fleco ['fleko] *nm* fringe

flema ['flema] *nm* phlegm

flequillo [fle'kiʎo] *nm* (*pelo*) fringe

flexible [flek'siβle] *adj* flexible

flexión [flek'sjon] *nf* press-up

flexo ['flekso] *nm* adjustable
table-lamp

flirtear [flirte'ar] *vi* to flirt

flojera [flo'xera] (*LAM: fam*) *nf*: **me da
~** I can't be bothered

flojo, -a ['floxo, a] *adj* (*gen*) loose; (*sin
fuerzas*) limp; (*débil*) weak

flor [flor] *nf* flower; **a ~ de** on the
surface of; **flora** *nf* flora; **florecer**
vi (*Bot*) to flower, bloom; (*fig*) to
flourish; **florería** (*LAM*) *nf* florist's
(shop); **florero** *nm* vase; **floristería** *nf*
florist's (shop)

flota ['flota] *nf* fleet

flotador [flota'ðor] *nm* (*gen*) float;
(*para nadar*) rubber ring

flotar [flo'tar] *vi* (*gen*) to float; **flote**
nm: **a flote** afloat; **salir a flote** (*fig*) to
get back on one's feet

fluidez [flui'ðeθ] *nf* fluidity; (*fig*)
fluency

fluido, -a ['fluiðo, a] *adj, nm* fluid

fluir [flu'ir] *vi* to flow

flujo ['fluxo] *nm* flow; **flujo y reflujo**
ebb and flow

flúor ['fluor] nm fluoride

fluorescente [flwores'θente] adj fluorescent ▷ nm fluorescent light

fluvial [flu'βi'al] adj (navegación, cuenca) fluvial, river cpd

fobia ['fobja] nf phobia; **fobia a las alturas** fear of heights

foca ['foka] nf seal

foco ['foko] nm focus; (Elec) floodlight; (MÉX: bombilla) (light) bulb

fofo, -a ['fofo, a] adj soft, spongy; (carnes) flabby

fogata [fo'ɣata] nf bonfire

fogón [fo'ɣon] nm (de cocina) ring, burner

folio ['foljo] nm folio, page

follaje [fo'ʎaxe] nm foliage

folleto [fo'ʎeto] nm (Pol) pamphlet

follón [fo'ʎon] (ESP: fam) nm (lío) mess; (conmoción) fuss; **armar un ~** to kick up a row

fomentar [fomen'tar] vt (Med) to foment

fonda ['fonda] nf inn

fondo ['fondo] nm (de mar) bottom; (de coche, sala) back; (Arte etc) background; (reserva) fund; **fondos** nmpl (Com) funds, resources; **una investigación a ~** a thorough investigation; **en el ~** at bottom, deep down

fonobuzón [fonoβu'θon] nm voice mail

fontanería [fontane'ria] nf plumbing; **fontanero, -a** nm/f plumber

footing ['futin] nm jogging; **hacer ~** to jog, go jogging

forastero, -a [foras'tero, a] nm/f stranger

forcejear [forθexe'ar] vi (luchar) to struggle

forense [fo'rense] nmf pathologist

forma ['forma] nf (figura) form, shape; (Med) fitness; (método) way, means; **las ~s** the conventions; **estar en ~** to be fit; **de ~ que ...** so that ...; **de todas ~s** in any case

formación [forma'θjon] nf (gen) formation; (educación) education; **formación profesional** vocational training

formal [for'mal] adj (gen) formal; (fig: serio) serious; (: de fiar) reliable; **formalidad** nf formality; seriousness; **formalizar** vt (Jur) to formalize; (situación) to put in order, regularize; **formalizarse** vr (situación) to be put in order, be regularized

formar [for'mar] vt (componer) to form, shape; (constituir) to make up, constitute; (Escol) to train, educate; **formarse** vr (Escol) to be trained, educated; (cobrar forma) to form, take form; (desarrollarse) to develop

formatear [formate'ar] vt to format

formato [for'mato] nm format

formidable [formi'ðaβle] adj (temible) formidable; (estupendo) tremendous

fórmula ['formula] nf formula

formulario [formu'larjo] nm form

fornido, -a [for'niðo, a] adj well-built

foro ['foro] nm (Pol, Inform etc) forum

forrar [fo'rrar] vt (abrigo) to line; (libro) to cover; **forro** nm (de cuaderno) cover; (Costura) lining; (de sillón) upholstery; **forro polar** fleece

fortalecer [fortale'θer] vt to strengthen

fortaleza [forta'leθa] nf (Mil) fortress, stronghold; (fuerza) strength; (determinación) resolution

fortuito, -a [for'twito, a] adj accidental

fortuna [for'tuna] nf (suerte) fortune, (good) luck; (riqueza) fortune, wealth

forzar [for'θar] vt (puerta) to force (open); (compeler) to compel

forzoso, -a [for'θoso, a] adj necessary

fosa ['fosa] nf (sepultura) grave; (en tierra) pit; **fosas nasales** nostrils

fósforo ['fosforo] nm (Quím) phosphorus; (cerilla) match

fósil ['fosil] nm fossil

foso ['foso] nm ditch; (Teatro) pit; (Auto) inspection pit

foto ['foto] nf photo, snap(shot); **sacar una ~** to take a photo o picture; **foto (de) carné** passport(-size) photo

fotocopia [foto'kopja] nf photocopy; **fotocopiadora** nf photocopier; **fotocopiar** vt to photocopy

fotografía [fotoɣra'fia] nf (Arte) photography; (una fotografía) photograph; **fotografiar** vt to photograph

fotógrafo, -a [fo'toɣrafo, a] nm/f photographer

fotomatón [fotoma'ton] nm photo booth

FP (ESP) nf abr (= Formación Profesional) vocational courses for 14- to 18-year-olds

fracasar [fraka'sar] vi (gen) to fail

fracaso [fra'kaso] nm failure

fracción [frak'θjon] nf fraction

fractura [frak'tura] nf fracture, break

fragancia [fra'ɣanθja] nf (olor) fragrance, perfume

frágil ['fraxil] adj (débil) fragile; (Com) breakable

fragmento [fraɣ'mento] nm (pedazo) fragment

fraile ['fraile] nm (Rel) friar; (: monje) monk

frambuesa [fram'bwesa] nf raspberry

francés, -esa [fran'θes, esa] adj French ▷ nm/f Frenchman(-woman) ▷ nm (Ling) French

Francia ['franθja] nf France

franco, -a ['franko, a] adj (cándido) frank, open; (Com: exento) free ▷ nm (moneda) franc

francotirador, a [frankotira'ðor, a] nm/f sniper

franela [fra'nela] nf flannel

franja ['franxa] nf fringe

franquear [franke'ar] vt (camino) to clear; (carta, paquete postal) to frank, stamp; (obstáculo) to overcome

franqueo [fran'keo] nm postage

franqueza [fran'keθa] nf (candor) frankness

frasco ['frasko] nm bottle, flask

frase ['frase] nf sentence; **frase hecha** set phrase; (pey) stock phrase

fraterno, -a [fra'terno, a] adj brotherly, fraternal

fraude ['frauðe] nm (cualidad) dishonesty; (acto) fraud

frazada [fra'saða] (LAM) nf blanket

frecuencia [fre'kwenθja] nf frequency; **con ~** frequently, often

frecuentar [frekwen'tar] vt to frequent

frecuente [fre'kwente] adj (gen) frequent

fregadero [freɣa'ðero] nm (kitchen) sink

fregar [fre'ɣar] vt (frotar) to scrub; (platos) to wash (up); (LAM: fam: fastidiar) to annoy; (: malograr) to screw up

fregona [fre'ɣona] nf mop

freír [fre'ir] vt to fry

frenar [fre'nar] vt to brake; (fig) to check

frenazo [fre'naθo] nm: **dar un ~** to brake sharply

frenesí [frene'si] nm frenzy

freno ['freno] nm (Tec, Auto) brake; (de cabalgadura) bit; (fig) check; **freno de mano** handbrake

frente ['frente] nm (Arq, Pol) front; (de objeto) front part ▷ nf forehead, brow; **~ a** in front of; (en situación opuesta de) opposite; **al ~ de** (fig) at the head of; **chocar de ~** to crash head-on; **hacer ~ a** to face up to

fresa ['fresa] (ESP) nf strawberry

fresco, -a ['fresko, a] adj (nuevo) fresh; (frío) cool; (descarado) cheeky ▷ nm (aire) fresh air; (Arte) fresco; (LAM: jugo) fruit drink ▷ nm/f (fam): **ser un ~** to have a nerve; **tomar el ~** to get some fresh air; **frescura** nf freshness; (descaro) cheek, nerve

frialdad [frial'dað] nf (gen) coldness; (indiferencia) indifference

frigidez [frixi'ðeθ] nf frigidity

frigorífico [friʝo'rifiko] nm refrigerator

frijol [fri'xol] nm kidney bean

frío, -a etc ['frio, a] vb V **freír** ▷ adj cold; (indiferente) indifferent ▷ nm cold; indifference; **hace ~** it's cold; **tener ~** to be cold

frito, -a ['frito, a] adj fried; **me trae ~ ese hombre** I'm sick and tired of that man; **fritos** nmpl fried food

frívolo, -a ['friβolo, a] adj frivolous

frontal [fron'tal] adj frontal; **choque ~** head-on collision

frontera [fron'tera] nf frontier; **fronterizo, -a** adj frontier cpd; (contiguo) bordering

frontón [fron'ton] nm (Deporte: cancha) pelota court; (: juego) pelota

frotar [fro'tar] vt to rub; **frotarse** vr: **~se las manos** to rub one's hands

fructífero, -a [fruk'tifero, a] adj fruitful

fruncir [frun'θir] vt to pucker; (Costura) to pleat; **~ el ceño** to knit one's brow

frustrar [frus'trar] vt to frustrate

fruta ['fruta] nf fruit; **frutería** nf fruit shop; **frutero, -a** adj fruit cpd ▷ nm/f fruiterer ▷ nm fruit bowl

frutilla [fru'tiʎa] (cs) nf strawberry

fruto ['fruto] nm fruit; (fig: resultado) result; (: beneficio) benefit; **frutos secos** nuts and dried fruit pl

fucsia ['fuksja] nf fuchsia

fue [fwe] vb V **ser**; **ir**

fuego ['fweɣo] nm (gen) fire; **a ~ lento** on a low heat; **¿tienes ~?** have you (got) a light?; **fuego amigo** friendly fire; **fuegos artificiales** fireworks

fuente ['fwente] nf fountain; (manantial: fig) spring; (origen) source; (plato) large dish

fuera etc ['fwera] vb V **ser**; **ir** ▷ adv out(side); (en otra parte) away; (excepto, salvo) except, save ▷ prep: **~ de** outside; (fig) besides; **~ de sí** beside o.s.; **por ~** (on the) outside

fuera-borda [fwera'βorða] nm speedboat

fuerte ['fwerte] adj strong; (golpe) hard; (ruido) loud; (comida) rich; (lluvia) heavy; (dolor) intense ▷ adv strongly; hard; loud(ly)

fuerza etc ['fwerθa] vb V **forzar** ▷ nf (fortaleza) strength; (Tec, Elec) power; (coacción) force; (Mil, Pol) force; **a ~ de** by dint of; **cobrar ~s** to recover one's strength; **tener ~s para** to have the strength to; **a la ~** forcibly, by force; **por ~** of necessity; **fuerza de voluntad** willpower; **fuerzas aéreas** air force sg; **fuerzas armadas** armed forces

fuga ['fuɣa] nf (huida) flight, escape; (de gas etc) leak

fugarse [fu'ɣarse] vr to flee, escape

fugaz [fu'ɣaθ] adj fleeting

fugitivo, a [fuxi'tiβo, a] adj, nm/f fugitive

fui [fwi] vb V **ser**; **ir**

fulano, -a [fu'lano, a] nm/f so-and-so, what's-his-name/what's-her-name

fulminante [fulmi'nante] adj (fig: mirada) fierce; (Med: enfermedad, ataque) sudden; (fam: éxito, golpe) sudden

fumador, a [fuma'ðor, a] nm/f smoker

fumar [fu'mar] vt, vi to smoke; **~ en pipa** to smoke a pipe

función [fun'θjon] nf function; (en trabajo) duties pl; (espectáculo) show; **entrar en funciones** to take up one's duties

funcionar [funθjo'nar] vi (gen) to function; (máquina) to work; **"no funciona"** "out of order"

funcionario, -a [funθjo'narjo, a] nm/f civil servant

funda ['funda] nf (gen) cover; (de almohada) pillowcase

fundación [funda'θjon] nf foundation

fundamental [fundamen'tal] adj fundamental, basic

fundamento [funda'mento] nm

(*base*) foundation

fundar [fun'dar] *vt* to found;
fundarse *vr*: **~se en** to be founded on

fundición [fundi'θjon] *nf* fusing;
(*fábrica*) foundry

fundir [fun'dir] *vt* (*gen*) to fuse;
(*metal*) to smelt, melt down; (*nieve etc*) to melt; (*Com*) to merge; (*estatua*)
to cast; **fundirse** *vr* (*colores etc*) to
merge, blend; (*unirse*) to fuse together;
(*Elec: fusible, lámpara etc*) to fuse, blow;
(*nieve etc*) to melt

fúnebre ['funeβre] *adj* funeral *cpd*,
funereal

funeral [fune'ral] *nm* funeral;
funeraria *nf* undertaker's

funicular [funiku'lar] *nm* (*tren*)
funicular; (*teleférico*) cable car

furgón [fur'xon] *nm* wagon;
furgoneta *nf* (*Auto, Com*) (transit) van
(*BRIT*), pick-up (truck) (*US*)

furia ['furja] *nf* (*ira*) fury; (*violencia*)
violence; **furioso, -a** *adj* (*iracundo*)
furious; (*violento*) violent

furtivo, -a [fur'tiβo, a] *adj* furtive
▷ *nm* poacher

fusible [fu'siβle] *nm* fuse

fusil [fu'sil] *nm* rifle; **fusilar** *vt* to
shoot

fusión [fu'sjon] *nf* (*gen*) melting;
(*unión*) fusion; (*Com*) merger

fútbol ['futβol] *nm* football (*BRIT*),
soccer (*US*); **fútbol americano**
American football (*BRIT*), football
(*US*); **fútbol sala** indoor football (*BRIT*)
o soccer (*US*); **futbolín** *nm* table
football; **futbolista** *nmf* footballer

futuro, -a [fu'turo, a] *adj, nm* future

g

gabardina [gaβar'ðina] *nf* raincoat,
gabardine

gabinete [gaβi'nete] *nm* (*Pol*)
cabinet; (*estudio*) study; (*de abogados etc*) office

gachas ['gatʃas] *nfpl* porridge *sg*

gafas ['gafas] *nfpl* glasses; **gafas de
sol** sunglasses

gafe ['gafe] (*ESP*) *nmf* jinx

gaita ['gaita] *nf* bagpipes *pl*

gajes ['gaxes] *nmpl*: **~ del oficio**
occupational hazards

gajo ['gaxo] *nm* (*de naranja*) segment

gala ['gala] *nf* (*traje de etiqueta*) full
dress; **galas** *nfpl* (*ropa*) finery *sg*; **estar
de ~** to be in one's best clothes; **hacer
~ de** to display

galápago [ga'lapaxo] *nm* (*Zool*)
turtle

galardón [galar'ðon] *nm* award,
prize

galaxia [ga'laksja] *nf* galaxy

galera [ga'lera] *nf* (*nave*) galley; (*carro*)
wagon; (*Imprenta*) galley

galería [gale'ria] *nf* (*gen*) gallery;

(*balcón*) veranda(h); (*pasillo*) corridor; **galería comercial** shopping mall

Gales ['gales] *nm* (*tb:* **País de ~**) Wales; **galés, -esa** *adj* Welsh ▷ *nm/f* Welshman(-woman) ▷ *nm* (*Ling*) Welsh

galgo, -a ['galɣo, a] *nm/f* greyhound

gallego, -a [ga'ʎeɣo, a] *adj, nm/f* Galician

galleta [ga'ʎeta] *nf* biscuit (*BRIT*), cookie (*US*)

gallina [ga'ʎina] *nf* hen ▷ *nmf* (*fam: cobarde*) chicken; **gallinero** *nm* henhouse; (*Teatro*) top gallery

gallo ['gaʎo] *nm* cock, rooster

galopar [galo'par] *vi* to gallop

gama ['gama] *nf* (*fig*) range

gamba ['gamba] *nf* prawn (*BRIT*), shrimp (*US*)

gamberro, -a [gam'berro, a] (*ESP*) *nm/f* hooligan, lout

gamuza [ga'muθa] *nf* chamois

gana ['gana] *nf* (*deseo*) desire, wish; (*apetito*) appetite; (*voluntad*) will; (*añoranza*) longing; **de buena ~** willingly; **de mala ~** reluctantly; **me da ~s de** I feel like, I want to; **no me da la ~** I don't feel like it; **tener ~s de** to feel like

ganadería [ganaðe'ria] *nf* (*ganado*) livestock; (*ganado vacuno*) cattle *pl*; (*cría, comercio*) cattle raising

ganadero, -a [gana'ðero, a] (*ESP*) *nm/f* (*hacendado*) rancher

ganado [ga'naðo] *nm* livestock; **ganado porcino** pigs *pl*

ganador, a [gana'ðor, a] *adj* winning ▷ *nm/f* winner

ganancia [ga'nanθja] *nf* (*lo ganado*) gain; (*aumento*) increase; (*beneficio*) profit; **ganancias** *nfpl* (*ingresos*) earnings; (*beneficios*) profit *sg*, winnings

ganar [ga'nar] *vt* (*obtener*) to get, obtain; (*sacar ventaja*) to gain; (*salario etc*) to earn; (*Deporte, premio*) to win; (*derrotar a*) to beat; (*alcanzar*) to reach ▷ *vi* (*Deporte*) to win; **ganarse** *vr*: **~se**

la vida to earn one's living

ganchillo [gan'tʃiʎo] *nm* crochet

gancho ['gantʃo] *nm* (*gen*) hook; (*colgador*) hanger

gandul, a [gan'dul, a] *adj, nm/f* good-for-nothing, layabout

ganga ['ganga] *nf* bargain

gangrena [gan'grena] *nf* gangrene

ganso, -a ['ganso, a] *nm/f* (*Zool*) goose; (*fam*) idiot

ganzúa [gan'θua] *nf* skeleton key

garabato [gara'βato] *nm* (*escritura*) scrawl, scribble

garaje [ga'raxe] *nm* garage

garantía [garan'tia] *nf* guarantee

garantizar [garanti'θar] *vt* to guarantee

garbanzo [gar'βanθo] *nm* chickpea (*BRIT*), garbanzo (*US*)

garfio ['garfjo] *nm* grappling iron

garganta [gar'ɣanta] *nf* (*Anat*) throat; (*de botella*) neck; **gargantilla** *nf* necklace

gárgaras ['garɣaras] *nfpl*: **hacer ~** to gargle

gargarear [garɣare'ar] (*LAM*) *vi* to gargle

garita [ga'rita] *nf* cabin, hut; (*Mil*) sentry box

garra ['garra] *nf* (*de gato, Tec*) claw; (*de ave*) talon; (*fam: mano*) hand, paw

garrafa [ga'rrafa] *nf* carafe, decanter

garrapata [garra'pata] *nf* tick

gas [gas] *nm* gas; **gases lacrimógenos** tear gas *sg*

gasa ['gasa] *nf* gauze

gaseosa [gase'osa] *nf* lemonade

gaseoso, -a [gase'oso, a] *adj* gassy, fizzy

gasoil [ga'soil] *nm* diesel (oil)

gasóleo [ga'soleo] *nm* = **gasoil**

gasolina [gaso'lina] *nf* petrol (*BRIT*), gas(oline) (*US*); **gasolinera** *nf* petrol (*BRIT*) o gas (*US*) station

gastado, -a [gas'taðo, a] *adj* (*dinero*) spent; (*ropa*) worn out; (*usado: frase etc*) trite

gastar [gas'tar] *vt* (*dinero, tiempo*) to

spend; (*fuerzas*) to use up; (*desperdiciar*)
to waste; (*llevar*) to wear; **gastarse** *vr*
to wear out; (*estropearse*) to waste; **~ en**
to spend on; **~ bromas** to crack jokes;
¿qué número gastas? what size (shoe)
do you take?

gasto ['gasto] *nm* (*desembolso*)
expenditure, spending; (*consumo,
uso*) use; **gastos** *nmpl* (*desembolsos*)
expenses; (*cargos*) charges, costs

gastronomía [gastrono'mia] *nf*
gastronomy

gatear [gate'ar] *vi* (*andar a gatas*) to
go on all fours

gatillo [ga'tiʎo] *nm* (*de arma de fuego*)
trigger; (*de dentista*) forceps

gato, -a ['gato, a] *nm/f* cat ▷ *nm*
(*Tec*) jack; **andar a gatas** to go on
all fours

gaucho ['gautʃo] *nm* gaucho

- GAUCHO

  Gauchos are the herdsmen or
  riders of the Southern Cone plains.
  Although popularly associated
  with Argentine folklore, **gauchos**
  belong equally to the cattle-
  raising areas of Southern Brazil
  and Uruguay. **Gauchos'** traditions
  and clothing reflect their mixed
  ancestry and cultural roots. Their
  baggy trousers are Arabic in
  origin, while the horse and guitar
  are inherited from the Spanish
  conquistadors; the poncho, maté
  and **boleadoras** (strips of leather
  weighted at either end with
  stones) form part of the Indian
  tradition.

gaviota [ga'βjota] *nf* seagull
gay [ge] *adj inv*, *nm* gay, homosexual
gazpacho [gaθ'patʃo] *nm* gazpacho
gel [xel] *nm*: **~ de baño/ducha**
bath/shower gel
gelatina [xela'tina] *nf* jelly; (*polvos
etc*) gelatine

gema ['xema] *nf* gem
gemelo, -a [xe'melo, a] *adj*,
nm/f twin; **gemelos** *nmpl* (*de camisa*)
cufflinks; (*prismáticos*) field glasses,
binoculars

gemido [xe'miðo] *nm* (*quejido*) moan,
groan; (*aullido*) howl

Géminis ['xeminis] *nm* Gemini

gemir [xe'mir] *vi* (*quejarse*) to moan,
groan; (*aullar*) to howl

generación [xenera'θjon] *nf*
generation

general [xene'ral] *adj* general ▷ *nm*
general; **por lo** *o* **en ~** in general;
Generalitat *nf* Catalan parliament;
generalizar *vt* to generalize;
generalizarse *vr* to become
generalized, spread

generar [xene'rar] *vt* to generate

género ['xenero] *nm* (*clase*) kind, sort;
(*tipo*) type; (*Bio*) genus; (*Ling*) gender;
(*Com*) material; **género humano**
human race

generosidad [xenerosi'ðað]
nf generosity; **generoso, -a** *adj*
generous

genial [xe'njal] *adj* inspired; (*idea*)
brilliant; (*estupendo*) wonderful

genio ['xenjo] *nm* (*carácter*) nature,
disposition; (*humor*) temper; (*facultad
creadora*) genius; **de mal ~** bad-
tempered

genital [xeni'tal] *adj* genital;
genitales *nmpl* genitals

genoma [xe'noma] *nm* genome

gente ['xente] *nf* (*personas*) people *pl*;
(*parientes*) relatives *pl*

gentil [xen'til] *adj* (*elegante*) graceful;
(*encantador*) charming

⎸ No confundir **gentil** con la palabra
inglesa *gentle*.

genuino, -a [xe'nwino, a] *adj*
genuine

geografía [xeoɣra'fia] *nf* geography
geología [xeolo'xia] *nf* geology
geometría [xeome'tria] *nf* geometry
gerente [xe'rente] *nmf* (*supervisor*)
manager; (*jefe*) director

geriatría [xeria'tria] nf (Med) geriatrics sg

germen ['xermen] nm germ

gesticular [xestiku'lar] vi to gesticulate; (hacer muecas) to grimace; **gesticulación** nf gesticulation; (mueca) grimace

gestión [xes'tjon] nf management; (diligencia, acción) negotiation

gesto ['xesto] nm (mueca) grimace; (ademán) gesture

Gibraltar [xiβral'tar] nm Gibraltar; **gibraltareño, -a** adj, nm/f Gibraltarian

gigante [xi'ɣante] adj, nmf giant; **gigantesco, -a** adj gigantic

gilipollas [xili'poʎas] (fam) adj inv daft ▷ nmf inv wally

gimnasia [xim'nasja] nf gymnastics pl; **gimnasio** nm gymnasium; **gimnasta** nmf gymnast

ginebra [xi'neβra] nf gin

ginecólogo, -a [xine'koloɣo, a] nm/f gynaecologist

gira ['xira] nf tour, trip

girar [xi'rar] vt (dar la vuelta) to turn (around); (: rápidamente) to spin; (Com: giro postal) to draw; (: letra de cambio) to issue ▷ vi to turn (round); (rápido) to spin

girasol [xira'sol] nm sunflower

giratorio, -a [xira'torjo, a] adj revolving

giro ['xiro] nm (movimiento) turn, revolution; (Ling) expression; (Com) draft; **giro bancario/postal** bank draft/money order

gis [xis] (MÉX) nm chalk

gitano, -a [xi'tano, a] adj, nm/f gypsy

glacial [gla'θjal] adj icy, freezing

glaciar [gla'θjar] nm glacier

glándula ['glandula] nf gland

global [glo'βal] adj global; **globalización** nf globalization

globo ['gloβo] nm (esfera) globe, sphere; (aerostato, juguete) balloon

glóbulo ['gloβulo] nm globule; (Anat) corpuscle

gloria ['glorja] nf glory

glorieta [glo'rjeta] nf (de jardín) bower, arbour; (plazoleta) roundabout (BRIT), traffic circle (US)

glorioso, -a [glo'rjoso, a] adj glorious

glotón, -ona [glo'ton, ona] adj gluttonous, greedy ▷ nm/f glutton

glucosa [glu'kosa] nf glucose

gobernador, a [goβerna'ðor, a] adj governing ▷ nm/f governor; **gobernante** adj governing

gobernar [goβer'nar] vt (dirigir) to guide, direct; (Pol) to rule, govern ▷ vi to govern; (Náut) to steer

gobierno etc [go'βjerno] vb V **gobernar** ▷ nm (Pol) government; (dirección) guidance, direction; (Náut) steering

goce etc ['goθe] vb V **gozar** ▷ nm enjoyment

gol [gol] nm goal

golf [golf] nm golf

golfa ['golfa] (fam!) nf (mujer) slut, whore

golfo, -a ['golfo, a] nm (Geo) gulf ▷ nm/f (fam: niño) urchin; (gamberro) lout

golondrina [golon'drina] nf swallow

golosina [golo'sina] nf (dulce) sweet; **goloso, -a** adj sweet-toothed

golpe ['golpe] nm blow; (de puño) punch; (de mano) smack; (de remo) stroke; (fig: choque) clash; **no dar ~** to be bone idle; **de un ~** with one blow; **de ~** suddenly; **golpe (de estado)** coup (d'état); **golpear** vt, vi to strike, knock; (asestar) to beat; (de puño) to punch; (golpetear) to tap

goma ['goma] nf (caucho) rubber; (elástico) elastic; (una goma) elastic band; **goma de borrar** eraser, rubber (BRIT); **goma espuma** foam rubber

gomina [go'mina] nf hair gel

gomita [go'mita] (RPL) nf rubber band

gordo, -a ['gorðo, a] *adj* (*gen*) fat;
(*fam*) enormous; **el (premio) ~** (*en
lotería*) first prize

gorila [go'rila] *nm* gorilla

gorra ['gorra] *nf* cap; (*de bebé*) bonnet;
(*militar*) bearskin; **entrar de ~** (*fam*) to
gatecrash; **ir de ~** to sponge

gorrión [go'rrjon] *nm* sparrow

gorro ['gorro] *nm* (*gen*) cap; (*de bebé,
mujer*) bonnet

gorrón, -ona [go'rron, ona]
nm/f scrounger; **gorronear** (*fam*) *vi*
to scrounge

gota ['gota] *nf* (*gen*) drop; (*de sudor*)
bead; (*Med*) gout; **gotear** *vi* to drip;
(*lloviznar*) to drizzle; **gotera** *nf* leak

gozar [go'θar] *vi* to enjoy o.s.; **~ de**
(*disfrutar*) to enjoy; (*poseer*) to possess

gr. *abr* (= *gramo, gramos*) g

grabación [graβa'θjon] *nf* recording

grabado [gra'βaðo] *nm* print,
engraving

grabadora [graβa'ðora] *nf* tape-
recorder; **grabadora de CD/DVD**
CD/DVD writer

grabar [gra'βar] *vt* to engrave; (*discos,
cintas*) to record

gracia ['graθja] *nf* (*encanto*) grace,
gracefulness; (*humor*) humour, wit;
¡(muchas) ~s! thanks (very much)!;
~s a thanks to; **dar las ~s a algn por
algo** to thank sb for sth; **tener ~** (*chiste
etc*) to be funny; **no me hace ~** I am
not keen; **gracioso, -a** *adj* (*divertido*)
funny, amusing; (*cómico*) comical
▷ *nm/f* (*Teatro*) comic character

grada ['graða] *nf* (*de escalera*) step;
(*de anfiteatro*) tier, row; **gradas** *nfpl*
(*Deporte: de estadio*) terraces

grado ['graðo] *nm* degree; (*de aceite,
vino*) grade; (*grada*) step; (*Mil*) rank; **de
buen ~** willingly; **grado centígrado/
Fahrenheit** degree centigrade/
Fahrenheit

graduación [graðwa'θjon] *nf*
(*del alcohol*) proof, strength; (*Escol*)
graduation; (*Mil*) rank

gradual [gra'ðwal] *adj* gradual

graduar [gra'ðwar] *vt* (*gen*) to
graduate; (*Mil*) to commission;
graduarse *vr* to graduate; **~se la
vista** to have one's eyes tested

gráfica ['grafika] *nf* graph

gráfico, -a ['grafiko, a] *adj* graphic
▷ *nm* diagram; **gráficos** *nmpl* (*Inform*)
graphics

grajo ['graxo] *nm* rook

gramática [gra'matika] *nf* grammar

gramo ['gramo] *nm* gramme (*BRIT*),
gram (*US*)

gran [gran] *adj* V **grande**

grana ['grana] *nf* (*color, tela*) scarlet

granada [gra'naða] *nf* pomegranate;
(*Mil*) grenade

granate [gra'nate] *adj* deep red

Gran Bretaña [-bre'taɲa] *nf* Great
Britain

grande ['grande] (*antes de nmsg* **gran**)
adj (*de tamaño*) big, large; (*alto*) tall;
(*distinguido*) great; (*impresionante*) grand
▷ *nm* grandee

granel [gra'nel]: **a ~** *adv* (*Com*) in bulk

granero [gra'nero] *nm* granary, barn

granito [gra'nito] *nm* (*Agr*) small
grain; (*roca*) granite

granizado [grani'θaðo] *nm* iced
drink

granizar [grani'θar] *vi* to hail;
granizo *nm* hail

granja ['granxa] *nf* (*gen*) farm;
granjero, -a *nm/f* farmer

grano ['grano] *nm* grain; (*semilla*)
seed; (*de café*) bean; (*Med*) pimple, spot

granuja [gra'nuxa] *nmf* rogue;
(*golfillo*) urchin

grapa ['grapa] *nf* staple; (*Tec*) clamp;
grapadora *nf* stapler

grasa ['grasa] *nf* (*gen*) grease; (*de
cocinar*) fat, lard; (*sebo*) suet; (*mugre*)
filth; **grasiento, -a** *adj* greasy; (*de
aceite*) oily; **graso, -a** *adj* (*leche, queso,
carne*) fatty; (*pelo, piel*) greasy

gratinar [grati'nar] *vt* to cook au
gratin

gratis ['gratis] *adv* free

grato, -a ['grato, a] *adj* (*agradable*)

pleasant, agreeable

gratuito, -a [gra'twito, a] *adj* (*gratis*) free; (*sin razón*) gratuitous

grave ['graβe] *adj* heavy; (*serio*) grave, serious; **gravedad** *nf* gravity

Grecia ['greθja] *nf* Greece

gremio ['gremjo] *nm* trade, industry

griego, -a ['grjexo, a] *adj, nm/f* Greek

grieta ['grjeta] *nf* crack

grifo ['grifo] (*ESP*) *nm* tap (*BRIT*), faucet (*US*)

grillo ['griʎo] *nm* (*Zool*) cricket

gripa ['gripa] (*MÉX*) *nf* flu, influenza

gripe ['gripe] *nf* flu, influenza; **gripe aviar** bird flu

gris [gris] *adj* (*color*) grey

gritar [gri'tar] *vt, vi* to shout, yell; **grito** *nm* shout, yell; (*de horror*) scream

grosella [gro'seʎa] *nf* (red)currant

grosero, -a [gro'sero, a] *adj* (*poco cortés*) rude, bad-mannered; (*ordinario*) vulgar, crude

grosor [gro'sor] *nm* thickness

grúa ['grua] *nf* (*Tec*) crane; (*de petróleo*) derrick

grueso, -a ['grweso, a] *adj* thick; (*persona*) stout ▷ *nm* bulk; **el ~ de** the bulk of

grulla ['gruʎa] *nf* crane

grumo ['grumo] *nm* clot, lump

gruñido [gru'ɲiðo] *nm* grunt; (*de persona*) grumble

gruñir [gru'ɲir] *vi* (*animal*) to growl; (*persona*) to grumble

grupo ['grupo] *nm* group; (*Tec*) unit, set; **grupo de presión** pressure group; **grupo sanguíneo** blood group

gruta ['gruta] *nf* grotto

guacho, -a ['gwatʃo, a] (*CS*) *nm/f* homeless child

guajolote [gwaxo'lote] (*MÉX*) *nm* turkey

guante ['gwante] *nm* glove; **guantes de goma** rubber gloves; **guantera** *nf* glove compartment

guapo, -a ['gwapo, a] *adj* good-looking, attractive; (*elegante*) smart

guarda ['gwarða] *nmf* (*persona*)

guard, keeper ▷ *nf* (*acto*) guarding; (*custodia*) custody; **guarda jurado** (armed) security guard; **guardabarros** *nm inv* mudguard (*BRIT*), fender (*US*); **guardabosques** *nm inv* gamekeeper; **guardacostas** *nm inv* coastguard vessel ▷ *nmf* guardian, protector; **guardaespaldas** *nmf inv* bodyguard; **guardameta** *nmf* goalkeeper; **guardar** *vt* (*gen*) to keep; (*vigilar*) to guard, watch over; (*dinero: ahorrar*) to save; **guardarse** *vr* (*preservarse*) to protect o.s.; (*evitar*) to avoid; **guardar cama** to stay in bed; **guardarropa** *nm* (*armario*) wardrobe; (*en establecimiento público*) cloakroom

guardería [gwarðe'ria] *nf* nursery

guardia ['gwarðja] *nf* (*Mil*) guard; (*cuidado*) care, custody ▷ *nmf* guard; (*policía*) policeman(-woman); **estar de ~** to be on guard; **montar ~** to mount guard; **Guardia Civil** Civil Guard

guardián, -ana [gwar'ðjan, ana] *nm/f* (*gen*) guardian, keeper

guarida [gwa'riða] *nf* (*de animal*) den, lair; (*refugio*) refuge

guarnición [gwarni'θjon] *nf* (*de vestimenta*) trimming; (*de piedra*) mount; (*Culin*) garnish; (*arneses*) harness; (*Mil*) garrison

guarro, -a ['gwarro, a] *nm/f* pig

guasa ['gwasa] *nf* joke; **guasón, -ona** *adj* (*bromista*) joking ▷ *nm/f* wit; joker

Guatemala [gwate'mala] *nf* Guatemala

guay [gwai] (*fam*) *adj* super, great

güero, -a ['gwero, a] (*MÉX*) *adj* blond(e)

guerra ['gerra] *nf* war; **dar ~** to annoy; **guerra civil** civil war; **guerra fría** cold war; **guerrero, -a** *adj* fighting; (*carácter*) warlike ▷ *nm/f* warrior

guerrilla [ge'rriʎa] *nf* guerrilla warfare; (*tropas*) guerrilla band o group

guía *etc* ['gia] *vb* V **guiar** ▷ *nmf* (*persona*) guide; (*nf: libro*) guidebook; **guía telefónica** telephone directory;

guía turística tourist guide

guiar [gi'ar] *vt* to guide, direct; (*Auto*) to steer; **guiarse** *vr*: **~se por** to be guided by

guinda ['ginda] *nf* morello cherry

guindilla [gin'diʎa] *nf* chilli pepper

guiñar [gi'ɲar] *vt* to wink

guión [gi'on] *nm* (*Ling*) hyphen, dash; (*Cine*) script; **guionista** *nmf* scriptwriter

guiri ['giri] (*ESP: fam, pey*) *nmf* foreigner

guirnalda [gir'nalda] *nf* garland

guisado [gi'saðo] *nm* stew

guisante [gi'sante] *nm* pea

guisar [gi'sar] *vt, vi* to cook; **guiso** *nm* cooked dish

guitarra [gi'tarra] *nf* guitar

gula ['gula] *nf* gluttony, greed

gusano [gu'sano] *nm* worm; (*lombriz*) earthworm

gustar [gus'tar] *vt* to taste, sample ▷ *vi* to please, be pleasing; **~ de algo** to like *o* enjoy sth; **me gustan las uvas** I like grapes; **le gusta nadar** she likes *o* enjoys swimming

gusto ['gusto] *nm* (*sentido, sabor*) taste; (*placer*) pleasure; **tiene ~ a menta** it tastes of mint; **tener buen ~** to have good taste; **coger el *o* tomar ~ a algo** to take a liking to sth; **sentirse a ~** to feel at ease; **mucho ~ (en conocerle)** pleased to meet you; **el ~ es mío** the pleasure is mine; **con ~** willingly, gladly

ha *vb V* **haber**

haba ['aβa] *nf* bean

Habana [a'βana] *nf*: **la ~** Havana

habano [a'βano] *nm* Havana cigar

habéis *vb V* **haber**

○ **PALABRA CLAVE**

haber [a'βer] *vb aux* **1** (*tiempos compuestos*) to have; **había comido** I had eaten; **antes/después de haberlo visto** before seeing/after seeing *o* having seen it

2: **¡haberlo dicho antes!** you should have said so before!

3: **haber de: he de hacerlo** I have to do it; **ha de llegar mañana** it should arrive tomorrow

▷ *vb impers* **1** (*existencia: sg*) there is; (: *pl*) there are; **hay un hermano/dos hermanos** there is one brother/there are two brothers; **¿cuánto hay de aquí a Sucre?** how far is it from here to Sucre?

2 (*obligación*): **hay que hacer algo**

something must be done; **hay que apuntarlo para acordarse** you have to write it down to remember
3: **¡hay que ver!** well I never!
4: **¡no hay de o por** (LAM) **qué!** don't mention it!, not at all!
5: **¿qué hay?** (¿qué pasa?) what's up?, what's the matter?; (¿qué tal?) how's it going?
▷ vt: **he aquí unas sugerencias** here are some suggestions; **no hay cintas blancas pero sí las hay rojas** there aren't any white ribbons but there are some red ones
▷ nm (en cuenta) credit side; **haberes** nmpl assets; **¿cuánto tengo en el haber?** how much do I have in my account?; **tiene varias novelas en su haber** he has several novels to his credit
haberse vr: **habérselas con algn** to have it out with sb

habichuela [aβi'tʃwela] nf kidney bean
hábil ['aβil] adj (listo) clever, smart; (capaz) fit, capable; (experto) expert; **día ~** working day; **habilidad** nf skill, ability
habitación [aβita'θjon] nf (cuarto) room; (Bio: morada) habitat; **habitación doble o de matrimonio** double room; **habitación individual o sencilla** single room
habitante [aβi'tante] nmf inhabitant
habitar [aβi'tar] vt (residir en) to inhabit; (ocupar) to occupy ▷ vi to live
hábito ['aβito] nm habit
habitual [aβi'twal] adj usual
habituar [aβi'twar] vt to accustom; **habituarse** vr: **~se a** to get used to
habla ['aβla] nf (capacidad de hablar) speech; (idioma) language; (dialecto) dialect; **perder el ~** to become speechless; **de ~ francesa** French-speaking; **estar al ~** to be in contact; (Tel) to be on the line; **¡González al ~!** (Tel) González speaking!
hablador, a [aβla'ðor, a] adj

talkative ▷ nm/f chatterbox
habladuría [aβlaðu'ria] nf rumour; **habladurías** nfpl gossip sg
hablante [a'βlante] adj speaking ▷ nmf speaker
hablar [a'βlar] vt to speak, talk ▷ vi to speak; **hablarse** vr to speak to each other; **~ con** to speak to; **~ de** to speak of o about; **¡ni ~!** it's out of the question!; **"se habla inglés"** "English spoken here"
habré etc [a'βre] vb V **haber**
hacendado [aθen'daðo] (LAM) nm rancher, farmer
hacendoso, -a [aθen'doso, a] adj industrious

○ **PALABRA CLAVE**

hacer [a'θer] vt **1** (fabricar, producir) to make; (construir) to build; **hacer una película/un ruido** to make a film/noise; **el guisado lo hice yo** I made o cooked the stew
2 (ejecutar: trabajo etc) to do; **hacer la colada** to do the washing; **hacer la comida** to do the cooking; **¿qué haces?** what are you doing?; **hacer el malo o el papel del malo** (Teatro) to play the villain
3 (estudios, algunos deportes) to do; **hacer español/económicas** to do o study Spanish/economics; **hacer yoga/gimnasia** to do yoga/go to gym
4 (transformar, incidir en): **esto lo hará más difícil** this will make it more difficult; **salir te hará sentir mejor** going out will make you feel better
5 (cálculo): **2 y 2 hacen 4** 2 and 2 make 4; **éste hace 100** this one makes 100
6 (+ sub): **esto hará que ganemos** this will make us win; **harás que no quiera venir** you'll stop him wanting to come
7 (como sustituto de vb) to do; **él bebió y yo hice lo mismo** he drank and I did likewise
8 no hace más que criticar all he does is criticize

▷ vb semi-aux (directo): **hacer** +infin: **les hice venir** I made o had them come; **hacer trabajar a los demás** to get others to work
▷ vi **1** **haz como que no lo sabes** act as if you don't know
2 (ser apropiado): **si os hace** if it's alright with you
3 **hacer de: hacer de Otelo** to play Othello
▷ vb impers **1** **hace calor/frío** it's hot/cold; V tb **bueno, sol, tiempo**
2 (tiempo): **hace 3 años** 3 years ago; **hace un mes que voy/no voy** I've been going/I haven't been for a month
3 **¿cómo has hecho para llegar tan rápido?** how did you manage to get here so quickly?
hacerse vr **1** (volverse) to become; **se hicieron amigos** they became friends
2 (acostumbrarse): **hacerse a** to get used to
3 **se hace con huevos y leche** it's made out of eggs and milk; **eso no se hace** that's not done
4 (obtener): **hacerse de** o **con algo** to get hold of sth
5 (fingirse): **hacerse el sueco** to turn a deaf ear

hacha ['atʃa] nf axe; (antorcha) torch
hachís [a'tʃis] nm hashish
hacia ['aθja] prep (en dirección de) towards; (cerca de) near; (actitud) towards; **~ adelante/atrás** forwards/backwards; **~ arriba/abajo** up(wards)/down(wards); **~ mediodía/las cinco** about noon/five
hacienda [a'θjenda] nf (propiedad) property; (finca) farm; (LAM: rancho) ranch; **(Ministerio de) H~** Exchequer (BRIT), Treasury Department (US); **hacienda pública** public finance
hada ['aða] nf fairy
hago etc vb V **hacer**
Haití [ai'ti] nm Haiti
halagar [ala'ɣar] vt to flatter
halago [a'laɣo] nm flattery

halcón [al'kon] nm falcon, hawk
hallar [a'ʎar] vt (gen) to find; (descubrir) to discover; (toparse con) to run into; **hallarse** vr to be (situated)
halterofilia [alteɾo'filja] nf weightlifting
hamaca [a'maka] nf hammock
hambre ['ambre] nf hunger; (plaga) famine; (deseo) longing; **tener ~** to be hungry; **¡me muero de ~!** I'm starving!; **hambriento, -a** adj hungry, starving
hamburguesa [ambur'ɣesa] nf hamburger; **hamburguesería** nf burger bar
han vb V **haber**
harapos [a'rapos] nmpl rags
haré vb V **hacer**
harina [a'rina] nf flour; **harina de maíz** cornflour (BRIT), cornstarch (US); **harina de trigo** wheat flour
hartar [ar'tar] vt to satiate, glut; (fig) to tire, sicken; **hartarse** vr (de comida) to fill o.s., gorge o.s.; (cansarse): **~se (de)** to get fed up (with); **harto, -a** adj (lleno) full; (cansado) fed up ▷ adv (bastante) enough; (muy) very; **estar harto de hacer algo/de algn** to be fed up of doing sth/with sb
has vb V **haber**
hasta ['asta] adv even ▷ prep (alcanzando a) as far as; up to; down to; (de tiempo: a tal hora) till, until; (antes de) before ▷ conj: **~ que ...** until; **~ luego/el sábado** see you soon/on Saturday; **~ ahora** (al despedirse) see you in a minute; **~ pronto** see you soon
hay vb V **haber**
Haya ['aja] nf: **la ~** The Hague
haya etc ['aja] vb V **haber** ▷ nf beech tree
haz [aθ] vb V **hacer** ▷ nm (de luz) beam
hazaña [a'θaɲa] nf feat, exploit
hazmerreír [aθmerre'ir] nm inv laughing stock
he vb V **haber**
hebilla [e'βiʎa] nf buckle, clasp
hebra ['eβra] nf thread; (Bot: fibra)

fibre, grain

hebreo, -a [e'βreo, a] *adj, nm/f*
Hebrew ▷ *nm* (*Ling*) Hebrew

hechizar [etʃi'θar] *vt* to cast a spell
on, bewitch

hechizo [e'tʃiθo] *nm* witchcraft,
magic; (*acto de magía*) spell, charm

hecho, -a ['etʃo, a] *pp de* **hacer** ▷ *adj*
(*carne*) done; (*Costura*) ready-to-wear
▷ *nm* deed, act; (*dato*) fact; (*cuestión*)
matter; (*suceso*) event ▷ *excl* agreed!,
done!; **de ~** in fact, as a matter of fact;
el ~ es que ... the fact is that ...; **¡bien
~!** well done!

hechura [e'tʃura] *nf* (*forma*) form,
shape; (*de persona*) build

hectárea [ek'tarea] *nf* hectare

helada [e'laða] *nf* frost

heladera [ela'ðera] (*LAM*) *nf*
(*refrigerador*) refrigerator

helado, -a [e'laðo, a] *adj* frozen;
(*glacial*) icy; (*fig*) chilly, cold ▷ *nm* ice
cream

helar [e'lar] *vt* to freeze, ice (up);
(*dejar atónito*) to amaze; (*desalentar*)
to discourage ▷ *vi* to freeze; **helarse**
vr to freeze

helecho [e'letʃo] *nm* fern

hélice ['eliθe] *nf* (*Tec*) propeller

helicóptero [eli'koptero] *nm*
helicopter

hembra ['embra] *nf* (*Bot, Zool*)
female; (*mujer*) woman; (*Tec*) nut

hemorragia [emo'rraxja] *nf*
haemorrhage

hemorroides [emo'rroiðes] *nfpl*
haemorrhoids, piles

hemos *vb* V **haber**

heno ['eno] *nm* hay

heredar [ere'ðar] *vt* to inherit;
heredero, -a *nm/f* heir(ess)

hereje [e'rexe] *nmf* heretic

herencia [e'renθja] *nf* inheritance

herida [e'riða] *nf* wound, injury; V
tb **herido**

herido, -a [e'riðo, a] *adj* injured,
wounded ▷ *nm/f* casualty

herir [e'rir] *vt* to wound, injure; (*fig*)

to offend

hermanastro, -a [erma'nastro, a]
nm/f stepbrother/sister

hermandad [erman'daθ] *nf*
brotherhood

hermano, -a [er'mano, a]
nm/f brother/sister; **hermano**(-a)
gemelo(-a), twin brother/sister;
hermano(-a) político(-a), brother-in-
law/sister-in-law

hermético, -a [er'metiko, a] *adj*
hermetic; (*fig*) watertight

hermoso, -a [er'moso, a] *adj*
beautiful, lovely; (*estupendo*) splendid;
(*guapo*) handsome; **hermosura** *nf*
beauty

hernia ['ernja] *nf* hernia; **hernia
discal** slipped disc

héroe ['eroe] *nm* hero

heroína [ero'ina] *nf* (*mujer*) heroine;
(*droga*) heroin

herradura [erra'ðura] *nf* horseshoe

herramienta [erra'mjenta] *nf* tool

herrero [e'rrero] *nm* blacksmith

hervidero [erβi'ðero] *nm* (*fig*)
swarm; (*Pol etc*) hotbed

hervir [er'βir] *vi* to boil; (*burbujear*)
to bubble; **~ a fuego lento** to simmer;
hervor *nm* boiling; (*fig*) ardour,
fervour

heterosexual [eterosek'swal] *adj*
heterosexual

hice *etc vb* V **hacer**

hidratante [iðra'tante] *adj*: **crema
~** moisturizing cream, moisturizer;
hidratar *vt* (*piel*) to moisturize;
hidrato *nm* hydrate; **hidratos de
carbono** carbohydrates

hidráulico, -a [i'ðrauliko, a] *adj*
hydraulic

hidro... [iðro] *prefijo* hydro...,
water-...; **hidroeléctrico, -a** *adj*
hydroelectric; **hidrógeno** *nm*
hydrogen

hiedra ['jeðra] *nf* ivy

hiel [jel] *nf* gall, bile; (*fig*) bitterness

hiela *etc vb* V **helar**

hielo ['jelo] *nm* (*gen*) ice; (*escarcha*)

frost; (fig) coldness, reserve
hiena ['jena] nf hyena
hierba ['jerβa] nf (pasto) grass; (Culin,
Med: planta) herb; **mala ~** weed; (fig)
evil influence; **hierbabuena** nf mint
hierro ['jerro] nm (metal) iron; (objeto)
iron object
hígado ['iɣaðo] nm liver
higiene [i'xjene] nf hygiene;
higiénico, -a adj hygienic
higo ['iɣo] nm fig; **higo seco** dried fig;
higuera nf fig tree
hijastro, -a [i'xastro, a] nm/f
stepson/daughter
hijo, -a ['ixo, a] nm/f son/daughter,
child; **hijos** nmpl children, sons and
daughters; **hijo adoptivo** adopted
child; **hijo de papá/mamá** daddy's/
mummy's boy; **hijo de puta** (fam!)
bastard (!), son of a bitch (!); **hijo/a
político/a** son-/daughter-in-law
hilera [i'lera] nf row, file
hilo ['ilo] nm thread; (Bot) fibre; (metal)
wire; (de agua) trickle, thin stream
hilvanar [ilβa'nar] vt (Costura)
to tack (BRIT), baste (US); (fig) to do
hurriedly
himno ['imno] nm hymn; **himno
nacional** national anthem
hincapié [inka'pje] nm: **hacer ~ en**
to emphasize
hincar [in'kar] vt to drive (in),
thrust (in)
hincha ['intʃa] (fam) nmf fan
hinchado, -a [in'tʃaðo, a] adj (gen)
swollen; (persona) pompous
hinchar [in'tʃar] vt (gen) to swell;
(inflar) to blow up, inflate; (fig) to
exaggerate; **hincharse** vr (inflarse) to
swell up; (fam: de comer) to stuff o.s.;
hinchazón nf (Med) swelling; (altivez)
arrogance
hinojo [i'noxo] nm fennel
hipermercado [ipermer'kaðo] nm
hypermarket, superstore
hípico, -a ['ipiko, a] adj horse cpd
hipnotismo [ipno'tismo] nm
hypnotism; **hipnotizar** vt to

hypnotize
hipo ['ipo] nm hiccups pl
hipocresía [ipokre'sia] nf hypocrisy;
hipócrita adj hypocritical ▷ nmf
hypocrite
hipódromo [i'poðromo] nm
racetrack
hipopótamo [ipo'potamo] nm
hippopotamus
hipoteca [ipo'teka] nf mortgage
hipótesis [i'potesis] nf inv
hypothesis
hispánico, -a [is'paniko, a] adj
Hispanic
hispano, -a [is'pano, a] adj
Hispanic, Spanish, Hispano- ▷ nm/f
Spaniard; **Hispanoamérica** nf Latin
America; **hispanoamericano, -a** adj,
nm/f Latin American
histeria [is'terja] nf hysteria
historia [is'torja] nf history; (cuento)
story, tale; **historias** nfpl (chismes)
gossip sg; **dejarse de ~s** to come to
the point; **pasar a la ~** to go down
in history; **historiador, a** nm/f
historian; **historial** nm (profesional)
curriculum vitae, C.V.; (Med) case
history; **histórico, -a** adj historical;
(memorable) historic
historieta [isto'rjeta] nf tale,
anecdote; (dibujos) comic strip
hito ['ito] nm (fig) landmark
hizo vb V **hacer**
hocico [o'θiko] nm snout
hockey ['xokei] nm hockey; **hockey
sobre hielo/patines** ice/roller hockey
hogar [o'ɣar] nm fireplace, hearth;
(casa) home; (vida familiar) home life;
hogareño, -a adj home cpd; (persona)
home-loving
hoguera [o'ɣera] nf (gen) bonfire
hoja ['oxa] nf (gen) leaf; (de flor) petal;
(de papel) sheet; (página) page; **hoja
de afeitar** (LAM) razor blade; **hoja
electrónica o de cálculo** spreadsheet;
hoja informativa leaflet, handout
hojalata [oxa'lata] nf tin(plate)
hojaldre [o'xaldre] nm (Culin) puff

pastry
hojear [oxe'ar] *vt* to leaf through,
turn the pages of
hojuela [o'xwela] (*MÉX*) *nf* flake
hola ['ola] *excl* hello!
holá [o'la] (*RPL*) *excl* hello!
Holanda [o'landa] *nf* Holland;
holandés, -esa *adj* Dutch ▷ *nm/f*
Dutchman(-woman) ▷ *nm* (*Ling*)
Dutch
holgado, -a [ol'xaðo, a] *adj* (*ropa*)
loose, baggy; (*rico*) comfortable
holgar [ol'xar] *vi* (*descansar*) to rest;
(*sobrar*) to be superfluous
holgazán, -ana [olxa'θan, ana] *adj*
idle, lazy ▷ *nm/f* loafer
hollín [o'ʎin] *nm* soot
hombre ['ombre] *nm* (*gen*) man; (*raza
humana*): **el ~** man(kind) ▷ *excl*: **¡sí
~!** (*claro*) of course!; (*para énfasis*)
man, old boy; **hombre de negocios**
businessman; **hombre de pro** honest
man; **hombre-rana** frogman
hombrera [om'brera] *nf* shoulder
strap
hombro ['ombro] *nm* shoulder
homenaje [ome'naxe] *nm* (*gen*)
homage; (*tributo*) tribute
homicida [omi'θiða] *adj* homicidal
▷ *nmf* murderer; **homicidio** *nm*
murder, homicide
homologar [omolo'ðar] *vt*
(*Com: productos, tamaños*) to
standardize
homólogo, -a [o'moloxo, a] *nm/f*: **su**
etc **~** his *etc* counterpart *o* opposite
number
homosexual [omosek'swal] *adj, nmf*
homosexual
honda ['onda] (*CS*) *nf* catapult
hondo, -a ['ondo, a] *adj* deep;
lo ~ the depth(s) *pl*, the bottom;
hondonada *nf* hollow, depression;
(*cañón*) ravine
Honduras [on'duras] *nf* Honduras
hondureño, -a [ondu'reɲo, a] *adj,
nm/f* Honduran
honestidad [onesti'ðað] *nf* purity,

chastity; (*decencia*) decency; **honesto,
-a** *adj* chaste; decent; honest; (*justo*)
just
hongo ['ongo] *nm* (*Bot: gen*) fungus;
(*: comestible*) mushroom; (*: venenoso*)
toadstool
honor [o'nor] *nm* (*gen*) honour; **en ~
a la verdad** to be fair; **honorable** *adj*
honourable
honorario, -a [ono'rarjo, a] *adj*
honorary; **honorarios** *nmpl* fees
honra ['onra] *nf* (*gen*) honour;
(*renombre*) good name; **honradez**
nf honesty; (*de persona*) integrity;
honrado, -a *adj* honest, upright;
honrar [on'rar] *vt* to honour
hora ['ora] *nf* (*una hora*) hour; (*tiempo*)
time; **¿qué ~ es?** what time is it?; **¿a
qué ~?** at what time?; **media ~** half an
hour; **a la ~ de recreo** at playtime; **a
primera ~** first thing (in the morning);
a última ~ at the last moment; **a
altas ~s** in the small hours; **¡a buena
~!** about time too!; **pedir ~** to make
an appointment; **dar la ~** to strike
the hour; **horas de oficina/trabajo**
office/working hours; **horas de
visita** visiting times; **horas extras** *o*
extraordinarias overtime *sg*; **horas
pico** (*LAM*) rush *o* peak hours; **horas
punta** (*ESP*) rush hours
horario, -a [o'rarjo, a] *adj* hourly,
hour *cpd* ▷ *nm* timetable; **horario
comercial** business hours *pl*
horca ['orka] *nf* gallows *sg*
horcajadas [orka'xaðas]: **a ~** *adv*
astride
horchata [or'tʃata] *nf* cold drink made
from tiger nuts and water, tiger nut milk
horizontal [oriθon'tal] *adj*
horizontal
horizonte [ori'θonte] *nm* horizon
horma ['orma] *nf* mould
hormiga [or'mixa] *nf* ant; **hormigas**
nfpl (*Med*) pins and needles
hormigón [ormi'xon] *nm* concrete;
hormigón armado/pretensado
reinforced/prestressed concrete;

hormigonera nf cement mixer

hormigueo [ormiˈɣeo] nm (comezón) itch

hormona [orˈmona] nf hormone

hornillo [orˈniʎo] nm (cocina) portable stove; **hornillo de gas** gas ring

horno [ˈorno] nm (Culin) oven; (Tec) furnace; **alto ~** blast furnace

horóscopo [oˈroskopo] nm horoscope

horquilla [orˈkiʎa] nf hairpin; (Agr) pitchfork

horrendo, -a [oˈrrendo, a] adj horrendous, frightful

horrible [oˈrriβle] adj horrible, dreadful

horripilante [orripiˈlante] adj hair-raising, horrifying

horror [oˈrror] nm horror, dread; (atrocidad) atrocity; ¡qué ~! (fam) how awful!; **horrorizar** vt to horrify, frighten; **horrorizarse** vr to be horrified; **horroroso, -a** adj horrifying, ghastly

hortaliza [ortaˈliθa] nf vegetable

hortelano, -a [orteˈlano, a] nm/f (market) gardener

hortera [orˈtera] (fam) adj tacky

hospedar [ospeˈðar] vt to put up; **hospedarse** vr to stay, lodge

hospital [ospiˈtal] nm hospital

hospitalario, -a [ospitaˈlarjo, a] adj (acogedor) hospitable; **hospitalidad** nf hospitality

hostal [osˈtal] nm small hotel

hostelería [osteleˈria] nf hotel business o trade

hostia [ˈostja] nf (Rel) host, consecrated wafer; (fam!: golpe) whack, punch ▷ excl (fam!): ¡~(s)! damn!

hostil [osˈtil] adj hostile

hotdog [otˈdog] (LAM) nm hot dog

hotel [oˈtel] nm hotel; **hotelero, -a** adj hotel cpd ▷ nm/f hotelier

● **HOTEL**
●
● In Spain you can choose from
● the following categories of
● accommodation, in descending
● order of quality and price: **hotel**
● (from 5 stars to 1), **hostal**, **pensión**,
● **casa de huéspedes**, **fonda**. The
● State also runs luxury hotels called
● **paradores**, which are usually sited
● in places of particular historical
● interest and are often historic
● buildings themselves.

hoy [oi] adv (este día) today; (la actualidad) now(adays) ▷ nm present time; **~ (en) día** now(adays)

hoyo [ˈojo] nm hole, pit

hoz [oθ] nf sickle

hube etc vb V **haber**

hucha [ˈutʃa] nf money box

hueco, -a [ˈweko, a] adj (vacío) hollow, empty; (resonante) booming ▷ nm hollow, cavity

huelga etc [ˈwelɣa] vb V **holgar** ▷ nf strike; **declararse en ~** to go on strike, come out on strike; **huelga de hambre** hunger strike; **huelga general** general strike

huelguista [welˈɣista] nmf striker

huella [ˈweʎa] nf (pisada) tread; (marca del paso) footprint, footstep; (: de animal, máquina) track; **huella dactilar** fingerprint

huelo etc vb V **oler**

huérfano, -a [ˈwerfano, a] adj orphan(ed) ▷ nm/f orphan

huerta [ˈwerta] nf market garden; (en Murcia y Valencia) irrigated region

huerto [ˈwerto] nm kitchen garden; (de árboles frutales) orchard

hueso [ˈweso] nm (Anat) bone; (de fruta) stone

huésped [ˈwespeð] nmf guest

hueva [ˈweβa] nf roe

huevera [weˈβera] nf eggcup

huevo [ˈweβo] nm egg; **huevo a la copa** (CS) soft-boiled egg; **huevo duro/escalfado** hard-boiled/poached egg; **huevo estrellado** (LAM) fried egg; **huevo frito** (ESP) fried egg; **huevo**

pasado por agua soft-boiled egg;
huevos revueltos scrambled eggs;
huevo tibio (MÉX) soft-boiled egg
huida [u'iða] nf escape, flight
huir [u'ir] vi (escapar) to flee, escape;
(evitar) to avoid
hule ['ule] nm oilskin; (MÉX: goma)
rubber
hulera [u'lera] (MÉX) nf catapult
humanidad [umani'ðað] nf
(género humano) man(kind); (cualidad)
humanity
humanitario, -a [umani'tarjo, a]
adj humanitarian
humano, -a [u'mano, a] adj (gen)
human; (humanitario) humane ▷ nm
human; **ser ~** human being
humareda [uma'reða] nf cloud
of smoke
humedad [ume'ðað] nf (de clima)
humidity; (de pared etc) dampness; **a
prueba de ~** damp-proof; **humedecer**
vt to moisten, wet; **humedecerse** vr
to get wet
húmedo, -a ['umeðo, a] adj (mojado)
damp, wet; (tiempo etc) humid
humilde [u'milde] adj humble,
modest
humillación [umiʎa'θjon] nf
humiliation; **humillante** adj
humiliating
humillar [umi'ʎar] vt to humiliate
humo ['umo] nm (de fuego) smoke;
(gas nocivo) fumes pl; (vapor) steam,
vapour; **humos** nmpl (fig) conceit sg
humor [u'mor] nm (disposición)
mood, temper; (lo que divierte) humour;
de buen/mal ~ in a good/bad mood;
humorista nmf comic; **humorístico,
-a** adj funny, humorous
hundimiento [undi'mjento] nm
(gen) sinking; (colapso) collapse
hundir [un'dir] vt to sink; (edificio,
plan) to ruin, destroy; **hundirse** vr to
sink, collapse
húngaro, -a ['ungaro, a] adj, nm/f
Hungarian
Hungría [un'gria] nf Hungary

huracán [ura'kan] nm hurricane
huraño, -a [u'raɲo, a] adj (antisocial)
unsociable
hurgar [ur'ɣar] vt to poke, jab;
(remover) to stir (up); **hurgarse** vr: **~se
(las narices)** to pick one's nose
hurón, -ona [u'ron, ona] nm (Zool)
ferret
hurtadillas [urta'ðiʎas]: **a ~** adv
stealthily, on the sly
hurtar [ur'tar] vt to steal; **hurto** nm
theft, stealing
husmear [usme'ar] vt (oler) to sniff
out, scent; (fam) to pry into
huyo etc vb V **huir**

iba etc vb V **ir**

ibérico, -a [i'βeriko, a] adj Iberian

iberoamericano, -a [iβeroameri'kano, a] adj, nm/f Latin American

Ibiza [i'βiθa] nf Ibiza

iceberg [iθe'βer] nm iceberg

icono [i'kono] nm ikon, icon

ida ['iða] nf going, departure; **~ y vuelta** round trip, return

idea [i'ðea] nf idea; **no tengo la menor ~** I haven't a clue

ideal [iðe'al] adj, nm ideal; **idealista** nmf idealist; **idealizar** vt to idealize

ídem ['iðem] pron ditto

idéntico, -a [i'ðentiko, a] adj identical

identidad [iðenti'ðað] nf identity

identificación [iðentifika'θjon] nf identification

identificar [iðentifi'kar] vt to identify; **identificarse** vr: **~se con** to identify with

ideología [iðeolo'xia] nf ideology

idilio [i'ðiljo] nm love-affair

idioma [i'ðjoma] nm (gen) language

No confundir **idioma** con la palabra inglesa *idiom*.

idiota [i'ðjota] adj idiotic ▷ nmf idiot

ídolo [i'ðolo] nm (tb fig) idol

idóneo, -a [i'ðoneo, a] adj suitable

iglesia [i'ɣlesja] nf church

ignorante [iɣno'rante] adj ignorant, uninformed ▷ nmf ignoramus

ignorar [iɣno'rar] vt not to know, be ignorant of; (no hacer caso a) to ignore

igual [i'ɣwal] adj (gen) equal; (similar) like, similar; (mismo) (the) same; (constante) constant; (temperatura) even ▷ nmf equal; **~ que** like, the same as; **me da** o **es ~** I don't care; **son ~es** they're the same; **al ~ que** (prep, conj) like, just like

igualar [iɣwa'lar] vt (gen) to equalize, make equal; (allanar, nivelar) to level (off), even (out); **igualarse** vr (platos de balanza) to balance out

igualdad [iɣwal'dað] nf equality; (similaridad) sameness; (uniformidad) uniformity

igualmente [iɣwal'mente] adv equally; (también) also, likewise ▷ excl the same to you!

ilegal [ile'ɣal] adj illegal

ilegítimo, -a [ile'xitimo, a] adj illegitimate

ileso, -a [i'leso, a] adj unhurt

ilimitado, -a [ilimi'taðo, a] adj unlimited

iluminación [ilumina'θjon] nf illumination; (alumbrado) lighting

iluminar [ilumi'nar] vt to illuminate, light (up); (fig) to enlighten

ilusión [ilu'sjon] nf illusion; (quimera) delusion; (esperanza) hope; **hacerse ilusiones** to build up one's hopes; **ilusionado, -a** adj excited; **ilusionar** vi: **le ilusiona ir de vacaciones** he's looking forward to going on holiday; **ilusionarse** vr: **ilusionarse (con)** to get excited (about)

iluso, -a [i'luso, a] adj easily deceived ▷ nm/f dreamer

ilustración [ilustra'θjon] *nf*
illustration; *(saber)* learning, erudition;
la I~ the Enlightenment; **ilustrado, -a**
adj illustrated; learned

ilustrar [ilus'trar] *vt* to illustrate;
(instruir) to instruct; *(explicar)* to
explain, make clear

ilustre [i'lustre] *adj* famous,
illustrious

imagen [i'maxen] *nf (gen)* image;
(dibujo) picture

imaginación [imaxina'θjon] *nf*
imagination

imaginar [imaxi'nar] *vt (gen)* to
imagine; *(idear)* to think up; *(suponer)* to
suppose; **imaginarse** *vr* to imagine;
imaginario, -a *adj* imaginary;
imaginativo, -a *adj* imaginative

imán [i'man] *nm* magnet

imbécil [im'beθil] *nmf* imbecile, idiot

imitación [imita'θjon] *nf* imitation;
de ~ imitation *cpd*

imitar [imi'tar] *vt* to imitate;
(parodiar, remedar) to mimic, ape

impaciente [impa'θjente] *adj*
impatient; *(nervioso)* anxious

impacto [im'pakto] *nm* impact

impar [im'par] *adj* odd

imparcial [impar'θjal] *adj* impartial,
fair

impecable [impe'kaβle] *adj*
impeccable

impedimento [impeði'mento] *nm*
impediment, obstacle

impedir [impe'ðir] *vt (obstruir)* to
impede, obstruct; *(estorbar)* to prevent;
~ a algn hacer *o* **que algn haga algo**
to prevent sb (from) doing sth, stop
sb doing sth

imperativo, -a [impera'tiβo, a] *adj*
(urgente, Ling) imperative

imperdible [imper'ðiβle] *nm*
safety pin

imperdonable [imperðo'naβle] *adj*
unforgivable, inexcusable

imperfecto, -a [imper'fekto, a] *adj*
imperfect

imperio [im'perjo] *nm* empire;

(autoridad) rule, authority; *(fig)* pride,
haughtiness

impermeable [imperme'aβle] *adj*
waterproof ▷ *nm* raincoat, mac (BRIT)

impersonal [imperso'nal] *adj*
impersonal

impertinente [imperti'nente] *adj*
impertinent

ímpetu ['impetu] *nm (impulso)*
impetus, impulse; *(impetuosidad)*
impetuosity; *(violencia)* violence

implantar [implan'tar] *vt* to
introduce

implemento [imple'mento] (LAM)
nm tool, implement

implicar [impli'kar] *vt* to involve;
(entrañar) to imply

implícito, -a [im'pliθito, a] *adj*
(tácito) implicit; *(sobreentendido)*
implied

imponente [impo'nente] *adj*
(impresionante) impressive, imposing;
(solemne) grand

imponer [impo'ner] *vt (gen)* to
impose; *(exigir)* to exact; **imponerse**
vr to assert o.s.; *(prevalecer)* to prevail;
imponible *adj (Com)* taxable

impopular [impopu'lar] *adj*
unpopular

importación [importa'θjon]
nf (acto) importing; *(mercancías)*
imports *pl*

importancia [impor'tanθja] *nf*
importance; *(valor)* value, significance;
(extensión) size, magnitude; **no
tiene ~** it's nothing; **importante** *adj*
important; valuable, significant

importar [impor'tar] *vt (del
extranjero)* to import; *(costar)* to amount
to ▷ *vi* to be important, matter; **me
importa un rábano** I couldn't care
less; **no importa** it doesn't matter;
¿le importa que fume? do you mind
if I smoke?

importe [im'porte] *nm (total)*
amount; *(valor)* value

imposible [impo'siβle] *adj (gen)*
impossible; *(insoportable)* unbearable,

intolerable

imposición [imposi'θjon] *nf*
imposition; (*Com: impuesto*) tax;
(: *inversión*) deposit

impostor, a [impos'tor, a] *nm/f*
impostor

impotencia [impo'tenθja] *nf*
impotence; **impotente** *adj* impotent

impreciso, -a [impre'θiso, a] *adj*
imprecise, vague

impregnar [impreɣ'nar] *vt* to
impregnate; **impregnarse** *vr* to
become impregnated

imprenta [im'prenta] *nf* (*acto*)
printing; (*aparato*) press; (*casa*)
printer's; (*letra*) print

imprescindible [impresθin'diβle]
adj essential, vital

impresión [impre'sjon] *nf* (*gen*)
impression; (*Imprenta*) printing;
(*edición*) edition; (*Foto*) print; (*marca*)
imprint; **impresión digital** fingerprint

impresionante [impresjo'nante]
adj impressive; (*tremendo*) tremendous;
(*maravilloso*) great, marvellous

impresionar [impresjo'nar] *vt*
(*conmover*) to move; (*afectar*) to impress,
strike; (*película fotográfica*) to expose;
impresionarse *vr* to be impressed;
(*conmoverse*) to be moved

impreso, -a [im'preso, a] *pp de*
imprimir ▷ *adj* printed; **impresos**
nmpl printed matter; **impresora** *nf*
printer

imprevisto, -a [impre'βisto, a]
adj (*gen*) unforeseen; (*inesperado*)
unexpected

imprimir [impri'mir] *vt* to imprint,
impress, stamp; (*textos*) to print;
(*Inform*) to output, print out

improbable [impro'βaβle] *adj*
improbable; (*inverosímil*) unlikely

impropio, -a [im'propjo, a] *adj*
improper

improvisado, -a [improβi'saðo, a]
adj improvised

improvisar [improβi'sar] *vt* to
improvise

improviso, -a [impro'βiso, a] *adj*: **de**
~ unexpectedly, suddenly

imprudencia [impru'ðenθja] *nf*
imprudence; (*indiscreción*) indiscretion;
(*descuido*) carelessness; **imprudente**
adj unwise, imprudent; (*indiscreto*)
indiscreet

impuesto, -a [im'pwesto, a] *adj*
imposed ▷ *nm* tax; **impuesto al valor**
agregado o **añadido** (*LAM*) value added
tax (*BRIT*) ≈ sales tax (*US*); **impuesto**
sobre el valor añadido (*ESP*) value
added tax (*BRIT*) ≈ sales tax (*US*)

impulsar [impul'sar] *vt* to drive;
(*promover*) to promote, stimulate

impulsivo, -a [impul'siβo, a] *adj*
impulsive; **impulso** *nm* impulse;
(*fuerza, empuje*) thrust, drive;
(*fig: sentimiento*) urge, impulse

impureza [impu'reθa] *nf* impurity;
impuro, -a *adj* impure

inaccesible [inakθe'siβle] *adj*
inaccessible

inaceptable [inaθep'taβle] *adj*
unacceptable

inactivo, -a [inak'tiβo, a] *adj*
inactive

inadecuado, -a [inaðe'kwaðo, a]
adj (*insuficiente*) inadequate; (*inapto*)
unsuitable

inadvertido, -a [inaðβer'tiðo, a] *adj*
(*no visto*) unnoticed

inaguantable [inaɣwan'taβle] *adj*
unbearable

inanimado, -a [inani'maðo, a] *adj*
inanimate

inaudito, -a [inau'ðito, a] *adj*
unheard-of

inauguración [inauɣura'θjon] *nf*
inauguration; opening

inaugurar [inauɣu'rar] *vt* to
inaugurate; (*exposición*) to open

inca ['inka] *nmf* Inca

incalculable [inkalku'laβle] *adj*
incalculable

incandescente [inkandes'θente]
adj incandescent

incansable [inkan'saβle] *adj*

tireless, untiring

incapacidad [inkapaθi'ðað]
nf incapacity; (*incompetencia*)
incompetence; **incapacidad física/
mental** physical/mental disability

incapacitar [inkapaθi'tar] *vt*
(*inhabilitar*) to incapacitate, render
unfit; (*descalificar*) to disqualify

incapaz [inka'paθ] *adj* incapable

incautarse [inkau'tarse] *vr*: **~ de** to
seize, confiscate

incauto, -a [in'kauto, a] *adj*
(*imprudente*) incautious, unwary

incendiar [inθen'djar] *vt* to set
fire to; (*fig*) to inflame; **incendiarse**
vr to catch fire; **incendiario, -a** *adj*
incendiary

incendio [in'θendjo] *nm* fire

incentivo [inθen'tiβo] *nm* incentive

incertidumbre [inθerti'ðumbre] *nf*
(*inseguridad*) uncertainty; (*duda*) doubt

incesante [inθe'sante] *adj* incessant

incesto [in'θesto] *nm* incest

incidencia [inθi'ðenθja] *nf* (*Mat*)
incidence

incidente [inθi'ðente] *nm* incident

incidir [inθi'ðir] *vi* (*influir*) to
influence; (*afectar*) to affect

incienso [in'θjenso] *nm* incense

incierto, -a [in'θjerto, a] *adj*
uncertain

incineración [inθinera'θjon] *nf*
incineration; (*de cadáveres*) cremation

incinerar [inθine'rar] *vt* to burn;
(*cadáveres*) to cremate

incisión [inθi'sjon] *nf* incision

incisivo, -a [inθi'siβo, a] *adj* sharp,
cutting; (*fig*) incisive

incitar [inθi'tar] *vt* to incite, rouse

inclemencia [inkle'menθja] *nf*
(*severidad*) harshness, severity; (*del
tiempo*) inclemency

inclinación [inklina'θjon] *nf* (*gen*)
inclination; (*de tierras*) slope, incline;
(*de cabeza*) nod, bow; (*fig*) leaning, bent

inclinar [inkli'nar] *vt* to incline;
(*cabeza*) to nod, bow ▷ *vi* to lean, slope;
inclinarse *vr* to bow; (*encorvarse*) to

stoop; **~se a** (*parecerse a*) to take after,
resemble; **~se ante** to bow down
to; **me inclino a pensar que ...** I'm
inclined to think that ...

incluir [inklu'ir] *vt* to include;
(*incorporar*) to incorporate; (*meter*) to
enclose

inclusive [inklu'siβe] *adv* inclusive
▷ *prep* including

incluso [in'kluso] *adv* even

incógnita [in'koɣnita] *nf* (*Mat*)
unknown quantity

incógnito [in'koɣnito] *nm*: **de ~**
incognito

incoherente [inkoe'rente] *adj*
incoherent

incoloro, -a [inko'loro, a] *adj*
colourless

incomodar [inkomo'ðar] *vt* to
inconvenience; (*molestar*) to bother,
trouble; (*fastidiar*) to annoy

incomodidad [inkomoði'ðað]
nf inconvenience; (*fastidio, enojo*)
annoyance; (*de vivienda*) discomfort

incómodo, -a [in'komoðo, a] *adj*
(*inconfortable*) uncomfortable; (*molesto*)
annoying; (*inconveniente*) inconvenient

incomparable [inkompa'raβle] *adj*
incomparable

incompatible [inkompa'tiβle] *adj*
incompatible

incompetente [inkompe'tente] *adj*
incompetent

incompleto, -a [inkom'pleto, a] *adj*
incomplete, unfinished

incomprensible [inkompren'siβle]
adj incomprehensible

incomunicado, -a [inkomuni'kaðo,
a] *adj* (*aislado*) cut off, isolated;
(*confinado*) in solitary confinement

incondicional [inkondiθjo'nal] *adj*
unconditional; (*apoyo*) wholehearted;
(*partidario*) staunch

inconfundible [inkonfun'diβle] *adj*
unmistakable

incongruente [inkon'grwente] *adj*
incongruous

inconsciente [inkons'θjente] *adj*

unconscious; thoughtless

inconsecuente [inkonse'kwente]
adj inconsistent

inconstante [inkons'tante] *adj*
inconstant

incontable [inkon'taβle] *adj*
countless, innumerable

inconveniencia [inkombe'njenθja]
nf unsuitability, inappropriateness;
(*descortesía*) impoliteness;
inconveniente *adj* unsuitable;
impolite ▷ *nm* obstacle; (*desventaja*)
disadvantage; **el inconveniente es
que ...** the trouble is that ...

incordiar [inkor'ðjar] (*fam*) *vt* to
bug, annoy

incorporar [inkorpo'rar] *vt* to
incorporate; **incorporarse** *vr* to sit
up; **~se a** to join

incorrecto, -a [inko'rrekto,
a] *adj* (*gen*) incorrect, wrong;
(*comportamiento*) bad-mannered

incorregible [inkorre'xiβle] *adj*
incorrigible

incrédulo, -a [in'kreðulo, a] *adj*
incredulous, unbelieving; sceptical

increíble [inkre'iβle] *adj* incredible

incremento [inkre'mento] *nm*
increment; (*aumento*) rise, increase

increpar [inkre'par] *vt* to reprimand

incruento, -a [in'krwento, a] *adj*
bloodless

incrustar [inkrus'tar] *vt* to incrust;
(*piedras: en joya*) to inlay

incubar [inku'βar] *vt* to incubate

inculcar [inkul'kar] *vt* to inculcate

inculto, -a [in'kulto, a] *adj* (*persona*)
uneducated; (*grosero*) uncouth ▷ *nm/f*
ignoramus

incumplimiento
[inkumpli'mjento] *nm* non-
fulfilment; **incumplimiento de
contrato** breach of contract

incurrir [inku'rrir] *vi*: **~ en** to incur;
(*crimen*) to commit

indagar [inda'xar] *vt* to investigate;
to search; (*averiguar*) to ascertain

indecente [inde'θente] *adj* indecent,

improper; (*lascivo*) obscene

indeciso, -a [inde'θiso, a] *adj* (*por
decidir*) undecided; (*vacilante*) hesitant

indefenso, -a [inde'fenso, a] *adj*
defenceless

indefinido, -a [indefi'niðo, a] *adj*
indefinite; (*vago*) vague, undefined

indemne [in'demne] *adj* (*objeto*)
undamaged; (*persona*) unharmed,
unhurt

indemnizar [indemni'θar] *vt* to
indemnify; (*compensar*) to compensate

independencia [indepen'denθja] *nf*
independence

independiente [indepen'djente]
adj (*libre*) independent; (*autónomo*)
self-sufficient

indeterminado, -a
[indetermi'naðo, a] *adj* indefinite;
(*desconocido*) indeterminate

India ['indja] *nf*: **la ~** India

indicación [indika'θjon] *nf*
indication; (*señal*) sign; (*sugerencia*)
suggestion, hint

indicado, -a [indi'kaðo, a] *adj*
(*momento, método*) right; (*tratamiento*)
appropriate; (*solución*) likely

indicador [indika'ðor] *nm* indicator;
(*Tec*) gauge, meter

indicar [indi'kar] *vt* (*mostrar*) to
indicate, show; (*termómetro etc*) to
read, register; (*señalar*) to point to

índice ['indiθe] *nm* index; (*catálogo*)
catalogue; (*Anat*) index finger,
forefinger; **índice de materias** table
of contents

indicio [in'diθjo] *nm* indication, sign;
(*en pesquisa etc*) clue

indiferencia [indife'renθja]
nf indifference; (*apatía*) apathy;
indiferente *adj* indifferent

indígena [in'dixena] *adj* indigenous,
native ▷ *nmf* native

indigestión [indixes'tjon] *nf*
indigestion

indigesto, -a [indi'xesto, a] *adj*
(*alimento*) indigestible; (*fig*) turgid

indignación [indixna'θjon] *nf*

indignation

indignar [indix'nar] *vt* to anger, make indignant; **indignarse** *vr*: **~se por** to get indignant about

indigno, -a [in'dixno, a] *adj* (*despreciable*) low, contemptible; (*inmerecido*) unworthy

indio, -a ['indjo, a] *adj, nm/f* Indian

indirecta [indi'rekta] *nf* insinuation, innuendo; (*sugerencia*) hint

indirecto, -a [indi'rekto, a] *adj* indirect

indiscreción [indiskre'θjon] *nf* (*imprudencia*) indiscretion; (*irreflexión*) tactlessness; (*acto*) gaffe, faux pas

indiscreto, -a [indis'kreto, a] *adj* indiscreet

indiscutible [indisku'tiβle] *adj* indisputable, unquestionable

indispensable [indispen'saβle] *adj* indispensable, essential

indispuesto, -a [indis'pwesto, a] *adj* (*enfermo*) unwell, indisposed

indistinto, -a [indis'tinto, a] *adj* indistinct; (*vago*) vague

individual [indiβi'ðwal] *adj* individual; (*habitación*) single ▷ *nm* (*Deporte*) singles *sg*

individuo, -a [indi'βiðwo, a] *adj, nm* individual

índole ['indole] *nf* (*naturaleza*) nature; (*clase*) sort, kind

inducir [indu'θir] *vt* to induce; (*inferir*) to infer; (*persuadir*) to persuade

indudable [indu'ðaβle] *adj* undoubted; (*incuestionable*) unquestionable

indultar [indul'tar] *vt* (*perdonar*) to pardon, reprieve; (*librar de pago*) to exempt; **indulto** *nm* pardon; exemption

industria [in'dustrja] *nf* industry; (*habilidad*) skill; **industrial** *adj* industrial ▷ *nm* industrialist

inédito, -a [in'eðito, a] *adj* (*texto*) unpublished; (*nuevo*) new

ineficaz [inefi'kaθ] *adj* (*inútil*) ineffective; (*ineficiente*) inefficient

ineludible [inelu'ðiβle] *adj* inescapable, unavoidable

ineptitud [inepti'tuð] *nf* ineptitude, incompetence; **inepto, -a** *adj* inept, incompetent

inequívoco, -a [ine'kiβoko, a] *adj* unequivocal; (*inconfundible*) unmistakable

inercia [in'erθja] *nf* inertia; (*pasividad*) passivity

inerte [in'erte] *adj* inert; (*inmóvil*) motionless

inesperado, -a [inespe'raðo, a] *adj* unexpected, unforeseen

inestable [ines'taβle] *adj* unstable

inevitable [ineβi'taβle] *adj* inevitable

inexacto, -a [inek'sakto, a] *adj* inaccurate; (*falso*) untrue

inexperto, -a [inek'sperto, a] *adj* (*novato*) inexperienced

infalible [infa'liβle] *adj* infallible; (*plan*) foolproof

infame [in'fame] *adj* infamous; (*horrible*) dreadful; **infamia** *nf* infamy; (*deshonra*) disgrace

infancia [in'fanθja] *nf* infancy, childhood

infantería [infante'ria] *nf* infantry

infantil [infan'til] *adj* (*pueril, aniñado*) infantile; (*cándido*) childlike; (*literatura, ropa etc*) children's

infarto [in'farto] *nm* (*tb:* **~ de miocardio**) heart attack

infatigable [infati'xaβle] *adj* tireless, untiring

infección [infek'θjon] *nf* infection; **infeccioso, -a** *adj* infectious

infectar [infek'tar] *vt* to infect; **infectarse** *vr* to become infected

infeliz [infe'liθ] *adj* unhappy, wretched ▷ *nmf* wretch

inferior [infe'rjor] *adj* inferior; (*situación*) lower ▷ *nmf* inferior, subordinate

inferir [infe'rir] *vt* (*deducir*) to infer, deduce; (*causar*) to cause

infidelidad [infiðeli'ðað] *nf* (*gen*)

infidelity, unfaithfulness

infiel [inˈfjel] *adj* unfaithful, disloyal; (*erróneo*) inaccurate ▷ *nmf* infidel, unbeliever

infierno [inˈfjerno] *nm* hell

infiltrarse [infilˈtrarse] *vr*: ~ **en** to infiltrate in(to); (*persona*) to work one's way in(to)

ínfimo, -a [ˈinfimo, a] *adj* (*más bajo*) lowest; (*despreciable*) vile, mean

infinidad [infiniˈðað] *nf* infinity; (*abundancia*) great quantity

infinito, -a [infiˈnito, a] *adj, nm* infinite

inflación [inflaˈθjon] *nf* (*hinchazón*) swelling; (*monetaria*) inflation; (*fig*) conceit

inflamable [inflˈmaβle] *adj* flammable

inflamar [inflaˈmar] *vt* (*Med: fig*) to inflame; **inflamarse** *vr* to catch fire; to become inflamed

inflar [inˈflar] *vt* (*hinchar*) to inflate, blow up; (*fig*) to exaggerate; **inflarse** *vr* to swell (up); (*fig*) to get conceited

inflexible [inflekˈsiβle] *adj* inflexible; (*fig*) unbending

influencia [influˈenθja] *nf* influence

influir [influˈir] *vt* to influence

influjo [inˈfluxo] *nm* influence

influya *etc vb* V **influir**

influyente [influˈjente] *adj* influential

información [informaˈθjon] *nf* information; (*noticias*) news *sg*; (*Jur*) inquiry; **I~** (*oficina*) Information Office; (*mostrador*) Information Desk; (*Tel*) Directory Enquiries

informal [inforˈmal] *adj* (*gen*) informal

informar [inforˈmar] *vt* (*gen*) to inform; (*revelar*) to reveal, make known ▷ *vi* (*Jur*) to plead; (*denunciar*) to inform; (*dar cuenta de*) to report on; **informarse** *vr* to find out; ~**se de** to inquire into

informática [inforˈmatika] *nf* computer science, information technology

informe [inˈforme] *adj* shapeless ▷ *nm* report

infracción [infrakˈθjon] *nf* infraction, infringement

infravalorar [infrabaloˈrar] *vt* to undervalue, underestimate

infringir [infrinˈxir] *vt* to infringe, contravene

infundado, -a [infunˈdaðo, a] *adj* groundless, unfounded

infundir [infunˈdir] *vt* to infuse, instil

infusión [infuˈsjon] *nf* infusion; **infusión de manzanilla** camomile tea

ingeniería [inxenjeˈria] *nf* engineering; **ingeniería genética** genetic engineering; **ingeniero, -a** *nm/f* engineer; **ingeniero civil** *o* **de caminos** civil engineer

ingenio [inˈxenjo] *nm* (*talento*) talent; (*agudeza*) wit; (*habilidad*) ingenuity, inventiveness; **ingenio azucarero** (*LAM*) sugar refinery; **ingenioso, -a** [inxeˈnjoso, a] *adj* ingenious, clever; (*divertido*) witty; **ingenuo, -a** *adj* ingenuous

ingerir [inxeˈrir] *vt* to ingest; (*tragar*) to swallow; (*consumir*) to consume

Inglaterra [inglaˈterra] *nf* England

ingle [ˈingle] *nf* groin

inglés, -esa [inˈgles, esa] *adj* English ▷ *nm/f* Englishman(-woman) ▷ *nm* (*Ling*) English

ingrato, -a [inˈgrato, a] *adj* (*gen*) ungrateful

ingrediente [ingreˈðjente] *nm* ingredient

ingresar [ingreˈsar] *vt* (*dinero*) to deposit ▷ *vi* to come in; ~ **en el hospital** to go into hospital

ingreso [inˈgreso] *nm* (*entrada*) entry; (*en hospital etc*) admission; **ingresos** *nmpl* (*dinero*) income *sg*; (*Com*) takings *pl*

inhabitable [inaβiˈtaβle] *adj* uninhabitable

inhalar [inaˈlar] *vt* to inhale

inhibir [iniˈβir] *vt* to inhibit

inhóspito, -a [i'nospito, a] *adj*
(*región, paisaje*) inhospitable

inhumano, -a [inu'mano, a] *adj*
inhuman

inicial [ini'θjal] *adj, nf* initial

iniciar [ini'θjar] *vt* (*persona*) to
initiate; (*empezar*) to begin, commence;
(*conversación*) to start up

iniciativa [iniθja'tiβa] *nf* initiative;
iniciativa privada private enterprise

ininterrumpido, -a
[ininterrum'piðo, a] *adj*
uninterrupted

injertar [inxer'tar] *vt* to graft;
injerto *nm* graft

injuria [in'xurja] *nf* (*agravio, ofensa*)
offence; (*insulto*) insult
▌No confundir **injuria** con la palabra
inglesa *injury*.

injusticia [inxus'tiθja] *nf* injustice

injusto, -a [in'xusto, a] *adj* unjust,
unfair

inmadurez [inmaðu'reθ] *nf*
immaturity

inmediaciones [inmeðja'θjones]
nfpl neighbourhood *sg*, environs

inmediato, -a [inme'ðjato,
a] *adj* immediate; (*contiguo*)
adjoining; (*rápido*) prompt; (*próximo*)
neighbouring, next; **de ~** immediately

inmejorable [inmexo'raβle] *adj*
unsurpassable; (*precio*) unbeatable

inmenso, -a [in'menso, a] *adj*
immense, huge

inmigración [inmixra'θjon] *nf*
immigration

inmobiliaria [inmoβi'ljarja] *nf*
estate agency

inmolar [inmo'lar] *vt* to immolate,
sacrifice

inmoral [inmo'ral] *adj* immoral

inmortal [inmor'tal] *adj* immortal;
inmortalizar *vt* to immortalize

inmóvil [in'moβil] *adj* immobile

inmueble [in'mweβle] *adj*: **bienes
~s** real estate, landed property ▷ *nm*
property

inmundo, -a [in'mundo, a] *adj*
filthy

inmune [in'mune] *adj*: **~ (a)** (*Med*)
immune (to)

inmunidad [inmuni'ðað] *nf*
immunity

inmutarse [inmu'tarse] *vr* to turn
pale; **no se inmutó** he didn't turn a hair

innato, -a [in'nato, a] *adj* innate

innecesario, -a [inneθe'sarjo, a] *adj*
unnecessary

innovación [innoβa'θjon] *nf*
innovation

innovar [inno'βar] *vt* to introduce

inocencia [ino'θenθja] *nf* innocence

inocentada [inoθen'taða] *nf*
practical joke

inocente [ino'θente] *adj* (*ingenuo*)
naive, innocent; (*inculpable*) innocent;
(*sin malicia*) harmless ▷ *nmf* simpleton;
el día de los (Santos) l~s ≈ April
Fools' Day

⬤ **DÍA DE LOS (SANTOS)**
⬤ **INOCENTES**
⬤
⬤ The 28th December, el **día de los**
⬤ **(Santos) Inocentes**, is when
⬤ the Church commemorates the
⬤ story of Herod's slaughter of the
⬤ innocent children of Judaea.
⬤ On this day Spaniards play
⬤ **inocentadas** (practical jokes) on
⬤ each other, much like our April
⬤ Fool's Day pranks.

inodoro [ino'ðoro] *nm* toilet,
lavatory (*BRIT*)

inofensivo, -a [inofen'siβo, a] *adj*
inoffensive, harmless

inolvidable [inolβi'ðaβle] *adj*
unforgettable

inoportuno, -a [inopor'tuno, a] *adj*
untimely; (*molesto*) inconvenient

inoxidable [inoksi'ðaβle] *adj*: **acero
~** stainless steel

inquietar [inkje'tar] *vt* to worry,
trouble; **inquietarse** *vr* to worry,
get upset; **inquieto, -a** *adj* anxious,

worried; **inquietud** *nf* anxiety, worry

inquilino, -a [inki'lino, a] *nm/f*
tenant

insaciable [insa'θjaβle] *adj*
insatiable

inscribir [inskri'βir] *vt* to inscribe; ~
a algn en (*lista*) to put sb on; (*censo*) to
register sb on

inscripción [inskrip'θjon] *nf*
inscription; (*Escol etc*) enrolment; (*en
censo*) registration

insecticida [insekti'θiða] *nm*
insecticide

insecto [in'sekto] *nm* insect

inseguridad [inseɣuri'ðað] *nf*
insecurity; **inseguridad ciudadana**
lack of safety in the streets

inseguro, -a [inse'ɣuro, a] *adj*
insecure; (*inconstante*) unsteady;
(*incierto*) uncertain

insensato, -a [insen'sato, a] *adj*
foolish, stupid

insensible [insen'siβle] *adj*
(*gen*) insensitive; (*movimiento*)
imperceptible; (*sin sentido*) numb

insertar [inser'tar] *vt* to insert

inservible [inser'βiβle] *adj* useless

insignia [in'siɣnja] *nf* (*señal
distintiva*) badge; (*estandarte*) flag

insignificante [insiɣnifi'kante] *adj*
insignificant

insinuar [insi'nwar] *vt* to insinuate,
imply

insípido, -a [in'sipiðo, a] *adj* insipid

insistir [insis'tir] *vi* to insist; ~ **en
algo** to insist on sth; (*enfatizar*) to
stress sth

insolación [insola'θjon] *nf* (*Med*)
sunstroke

insolente [inso'lente] *adj* insolent

insólito, -a [in'solito, a] *adj* unusual

insoluble [inso'luβle] *adj* insoluble

insomnio [in'somnjo] *nm* insomnia

insonorizado, -a [insonori'θaðo, a]
adj (*cuarto etc*) soundproof

insoportable [insopor'taβle] *adj*
unbearable

inspección [inspek'θjon] *nf*

inspection, check; **inspeccionar**
vt (*examinar*) to inspect, examine;
(*controlar*) to check

inspector, a [inspek'tor, a] *nm/f*
inspector

inspiración [inspira'θjon] *nf*
inspiration

inspirar [inspi'rar] *vt* to inspire;
(*Med*) to inhale; **inspirarse** *vr*: ~**se en**
to be inspired by

instalación [instala'θjon] *nf* (*equipo*)
fittings *pl*, equipment; **instalación
eléctrica** wiring

instalar [insta'lar] *vt* (*establecer*)
to instal; (*erguir*) to set up, erect;
instalarse *vr* to establish o.s.; (*en una
vivienda*) to move into

instancia [ins'tanθja] *nf* (*Jur*)
petition; (*ruego*) request; **en última** ~
as a last resort

instantáneo, -a [instan'taneo,
a] *adj* instantaneous; **café** ~ instant
coffee

instante [ins'tante] *nm* instant,
moment; **al** ~ right now

instar [ins'tar] *vt* to press, urge

instaurar [instau'rar] *vt* (*costumbre*)
to establish; (*normas, sistema*) to bring
in, introduce; (*gobierno*) to instal

instigar [insti'ɣar] *vt* to instigate

instinto [ins'tinto] *nm* instinct; **por**
~ instinctively

institución [institu'θjon] *nf*
institution, establishment

instituir [institu'ir] *vt* to establish;
(*fundar*) to found; **instituto** *nm* (*gen*)
institute; (*ESP Escol*) ≈ comprehensive
(*BRIT*) o high (*US*) school

institutriz [institu'triθ] *nf*
governess

instrucción [instruk'θjon] *nf*
instruction

instruir [instru'ir] *vt* (*gen*) to
instruct; (*enseñar*) to teach, educate

instrumento [instru'mento] *nm*
(*gen*) instrument; (*herramienta*) tool,
implement

insubordinarse [insuβorði'narse]

vr to rebel

insuficiente [insufi'θjente] *adj*
(*gen*) insufficient; (*Escol: calificación*)
unsatisfactory

insular [insu'lar] *adj* insular

insultar [insul'tar] *vt* to insult;
insulto *nm* insult

insuperable [insupe'raβle] *adj*
(*excelente*) unsurpassable; (*problema etc*)
insurmountable

insurrección [insurrek'θjon] *nf*
insurrection, rebellion

intachable [inta'tʃaβle] *adj*
irreproachable

intacto, -a [in'takto, a] *adj* intact

integral [inte'xral] *adj* integral;
(*completo*) complete; **pan ~** wholemeal
(*BRIT*) *o* wholewheat (*US*) bread

integrar [inte'xrar] *vt* to make up,
compose; (*Mat: fig*) to integrate

integridad [intexri'ðað] *nf*
wholeness; (*carácter*) integrity;
íntegro, -a *adj* whole, entire;
(*honrado*) honest

intelectual [intelek'twal] *adj, nmf*
intellectual

inteligencia [inteli'xenθja]
nf intelligence; (*ingenio*) ability;
inteligente *adj* intelligent

intemperie [intem'perje] *nf*: **a
la ~** out in the open, exposed to the
elements

intención [inten'θjon] *nf* (*gen*)
intention, purpose; **con segundas
intenciones** maliciously; **con ~**
deliberately

intencionado, -a [intenθjo'naðo,
a] *adj* deliberate; **mal ~** ill-disposed,
hostile

intensidad [intensi'ðað] *nf* (*gen*)
intensity; (*Elec, Tec*) strength; **llover
con ~** to rain hard

intenso, -a [in'tenso, a] *adj* intense;
(*sentimiento*) profound, deep

intentar [inten'tar] *vt* (*tratar*) to try,
attempt; **intento** *nm* attempt

interactivo, -a [interak'tiβo, a] *adj*
(*Inform*) interactive

intercalar [interka'lar] *vt* to insert

intercambio [inter'kambjo] *nm*
exchange, swap

interceder [interθe'ðer] *vi* to
intercede

interceptar [interθep'tar] *vt* to
intercept

interés [inte'res] *nm* (*gen*) interest;
(*parte*) share, part; (*pey*) self-interest;
intereses creados vested interests

interesado, -a [intere'saðo, a] *adj*
interested; (*prejuiciado*) prejudiced;
(*pey*) mercenary, self-seeking

interesante [intere'sante] *adj*
interesting

interesar [intere'sar] *vt, vi* to
interest, be of interest to; **interesarse**
vr: **~se en** *o* **por** to take an interest in

interferir [interfe'rir] *vt* to interfere
with; (*Tel*) to jam ▷ *vi* to interfere

interfón [inter'fon] (*MÉX*) *nm* entry
phone

interino, -a [inte'rino, a] *adj*
temporary ▷ *nm/f* temporary holder
of a post; (*Med*) locum; (*Escol*) supply
teacher

interior [inte'rjor] *adj* inner,
inside; (*Com*) domestic, internal
▷ *nm* interior, inside; (*fig*) soul, mind;
Ministerio del I~ ≈ Home Office
(*BRIT*) ≈ Department of the Interior
(*US*); **interiorista** (*ESP*) *nmf* interior
designer

interjección [interxek'θjon] *nf*
interjection

interlocutor, a [interloku'tor, a]
nm/f speaker

intermedio, -a [inter'meðjo, a] *adj*
intermediate ▷ *nm* interval

interminable [intermi'naβle] *adj*
endless

intermitente [intermi'tente] *adj*
intermittent ▷ *nm* (*Auto*) indicator

internacional [internaθjo'nal] *adj*
international

internado [inter'naðo] *nm* boarding
school

internar [inter'nar] *vt* to intern; (*en*

un manicomio) to commit; **internarse** *vr (penetrar)* to penetrate

internauta [inter'nauta] *nmf* web surfer, Internet user

Internet, internet [inter'net] *nm* o f Internet

interno, -a [in'terno, a] *adj* internal, interior; *(Pol etc)* domestic ▷ *nm/f (alumno)* boarder

interponer [interpo'ner] *vt* to interpose, put in; **interponerse** *vr* to intervene

interpretación [interpreta'θjon] *nf* interpretation

interpretar [interpre'tar] *vt* to interpret; *(Teatro, Mús)* to perform, play; **intérprete** *nmf (Ling)* interpreter, translator; *(Mús, Teatro)* performer, artist(e)

interrogación [interroɣa'θjon] *nf* interrogation; *(Ling: tb: signo de ~)* question mark

interrogar [interro'ɣar] *vt* to interrogate, question

interrumpir [interrum'pir] *vt* to interrupt

interrupción [interrup'θjon] *nf* interruption

interruptor [interrup'tor] *nm (Elec)* switch

intersección [intersek'θjon] *nf* intersection

interurbano, -a [interur'βano, a] *adj*: **llamada interurbana** long-distance call

intervalo [inter'βalo] *nm* interval; *(descanso)* break

intervenir [interβe'nir] *vt (controlar)* to control, supervise; *(Med)* to operate on ▷ *vi (participar)* to take part, participate; *(mediar)* to intervene

interventor, a [interβen'tor, a] *nm/f* inspector; *(Com)* auditor

intestino [intes'tino] *nm (Med)* intestine

intimar [inti'mar] *vi* to become friendly

intimidad [intimi'ðað] *nf* intimacy;

(familiaridad) familiarity; *(vida privada)* private life; *(Jur)* privacy

íntimo, -a ['intimo, a] *adj* intimate

intolerable [intole'raβle] *adj* intolerable, unbearable

intoxicación [intoksika'θjon] *nf* poisoning; **intoxicación alimenticia** food poisoning

intranet [intra'net] *nf* intranet

intranquilo, -a [intran'kilo, a] *adj* worried

intransitable [intransi'taβle] *adj* impassable

intrépido, -a [in'trepiðo, a] *adj* intrepid

intriga [in'triɣa] *nf* intrigue; *(plan)* plot; **intrigar** *vt, vi* to intrigue

intrínseco, -a [in'trinseko, a] *adj* intrinsic

introducción [introðuk'θjon] *nf* introduction

introducir [introðu'θir] *vt (gen)* to introduce; *(moneda etc)* to insert; *(Inform)* to input, enter

intromisión [intromi'sjon] *nf* interference, meddling

introvertido, -a [introβer'tiðo, a] *adj, nm/f* introvert

intruso, -a [in'truso, a] *adj* intrusive ▷ *nm/f* intruder

intuición [intwi'θjon] *nf* intuition

inundación [inunda'θjon] *nf* flood(ing); **inundar** *vt* to flood; *(fig)* to swamp, inundate

inusitado, -a [inusi'taðo, a] *adj* unusual, rare

inútil [in'util] *adj* useless; *(esfuerzo)* vain, fruitless

inutilizar [inutili'θar] *vt* to make o render useless

invadir [imba'ðir] *vt* to invade

inválido, -a [im'baliðo, a] *adj* invalid ▷ *nm/f* invalid

invasión [imba'sjon] *nf* invasion

invasor, a [imba'sor, a] *adj* invadin ▷ *nm/f* invader

invención [imben'θjon] *nf* inventio

inventar [imben'tar] *vt* to invent

inventario [imben'tarjo] *nm*
inventory
invento [im'bento] *nm* invention
inventor, a [imben'tor, a] *nm/f*
inventor
invernadero [imberna'ðero] *nm*
greenhouse
inverosímil [imbero'simil] *adj*
implausible
inversión [imber'sjon] *nf* (Com)
investment
inverso, -a [im'berso, a] *adj* inverse,
opposite; **en el orden ~** in reverse
order; **a la inversa** inversely, the other
way round
inversor, a [imber'sor, a] *nm/f*
(Com) investor
invertir [imber'tir] *vt* (Com) to invest;
(volcar) to turn upside down; (tiempo
etc) to spend
investigación [imbestiɣa'θjon]
nf investigation; (Escol) research;
investigación y desarrollo research
and development
investigar [imbesti'ɣar] *vt* to
investigate; (Escol) to do research
into
invierno [im'bjerno] *nm* winter
invisible [imbi'siβle] *adj* invisible
invitado, -a [imbi'taðo, a] *nm/f*
guest
invitar [imbi'tar] *vt* to invite; (incitar)
to entice; (pagar) to buy, pay for
invocar [imbo'kar] *vt* to invoke,
call on
involucrar [imbolu'krar] *vt*: **~
en** to involve in; **involucrarse** *vr*
(persona); **~se en** to get mixed up in
involuntario, -a [imbolun'tarjo,
a] *adj* (movimiento, gesto) involuntary;
(error) unintentional
inyección [injek'θjon] *nf* injection
inyectar [injek'tar] *vt* to inject
iPod® ['ipoð] (pl **~s**) *nm* iPod®

○ **PALABRA CLAVE**

r [ir] *vi* **1** to go; (a pie) to walk; (viajar)

to travel; **ir caminando** to walk; **fui
en tren** I went o travelled by train;
¡(ahora) voy! (I'm just) coming!
2: **ir (a) por**: **ir (a) por el médico** to
fetch the doctor
3 (progresar: persona, cosa) to go; **el
trabajo va muy bien** work is going
very well; **¿cómo te va?** how are things
going?; **me va muy bien** I'm getting on
very well; **le fue fatal** it went awfully
badly for him
4 (funcionar): **el coche no va muy bien**
the car isn't running very well
5: **te va estupendamente ese color**
that colour suits you fantastically well
6 (locuciones): **¿vino? – ¡que va!** did
he come? – of course not!; **vamos, no
llores** come on, don't cry; **¡vaya coche!**
what a car!, that's some car!
7: **no vaya a ser: tienes que correr,
no vaya a ser que pierdas el tren**
you'll have to run so as not to miss
the train
8 (+ pp): **iba vestido muy bien** he was
very well dressed
9: **ni me** etc **va ni me** etc **viene** I etc
don't care
▷ *vb aux* **1** **ir a**: **voy/iba a hacerlo hoy**
I am/was going to do it today
2 (+ gerundio): **iba anocheciendo** it
was getting dark; **todo se me iba
aclarando** everything was gradually
becoming clearer to me
3 (+ pp: = pasivo): **van vendidos 300
ejemplares** 300 copies have been
sold so far
irse *vr* **1**: **¿por dónde se va al
zoológico?** which is the way to the
zoo?
2 (marcharse) to leave; **ya se habrán ido**
they must already have left o gone

ira ['ira] *nf* anger, rage
Irak [i'rak] *nm* = **Iraq**
Irán [i'ran] *nm* Iran; **iraní** *adj, nmf*
Iranian
Iraq [i'rak] *nm* Iraq; **iraquí** *adj,
nmf* Iraqi

iris ['iris] *nm inv* (*tb*: **arco ~**) rainbow;
(*Anat*) iris
Irlanda [ir'landa] *nf* Ireland;
irlandés, -esa *adj* Irish ▷ *nm/f*
Irishman(-woman); **los irlandeses**
the Irish
ironía [iro'nia] *nf* irony; **irónico, -a**
adj ironic(al)
IRPF *nm abr* (= *Impuesto sobre la Renta
de las Personas Físicas*) (personal)
income tax
irreal [irre'al] *adj* unreal
irregular [irreɣu'lar] *adj* (*gen*)
irregular; (*situación*) abnormal
irremediable [irreme'ðjaβle] *adj*
irremediable; (*vicio*) incurable
irreparable [irrepa'raβle] *adj* (*daños*)
irreparable; (*pérdida*) irrecoverable
irrespetuoso, -a [irrespe'twoso, a]
adj disrespectful
irresponsable [irrespon'saβle] *adj*
irresponsible
irreversible [irreβer'sible] *adj*
irreversible
irrigar [irri'ɣar] *vt* to irrigate
irrisorio, -a [irri'sorjo, a] *adj*
derisory, ridiculous
irritar [irri'tar] *vt* to irritate, annoy
irrupción [irrup'θjon] *nf* irruption;
(*invasión*) invasion
isla ['isla] *nf* island
Islam [is'lam] *nm* Islam; **las
enseñanzas del ~** the teachings of
Islam; **islámico, -a** *adj* Islamic
islandés, -esa [islan'des, esa] *adj*
Icelandic ▷ *nm/f* Icelander
Islandia [is'landja] *nf* Iceland
isleño, -a [is'leɲo, a] *adj* island *cpd*
▷ *nm/f* islander
Israel [isra'el] *nm* Israel; **israelí** *adj*,
nmf Israeli
istmo ['istmo] *nm* isthmus
Italia [i'talja] *nf* Italy; **italiano, -a** *adj*,
nm/f Italian
itinerario [itine'rarjo] *nm* itinerary,
route
ITV (*ESP*) *nf abr* (= *inspección técnica
de vehículos*) roadworthiness test, ≈

MOT (*BRIT*)
IVA ['iβa] *nm abr* (= *impuesto sobre el
valor añadido*) VAT
izar [i'θar] *vt* to hoist
izdo, -a *abr* (= *izquierdo, a*) l
izquierda [iθ'kjerda] *nf* left; (*Pol*) left
(wing); **a la ~** (*estar*) on the left; (*torcer
etc*) (to the) left
izquierdo, -a [iθ'kjerðo, a] *adj* left

J

jabalí [xaβa'li] *nm* wild boar

jabalina [xaβa'lina] *nf* javelin

jabón [xa'βon] *nm* soap

jaca ['xaka] *nf* pony

jacal [xa'kal] (*MÉX*) *nm* shack

jacinto [xa'θinto] *nm* hyacinth

jactarse [xak'tarse] *vr* to boast, brag

jadear [xaðe'ar] *vi* to pant, gasp
  for breath

jaguar [xa'ɣwar] *nm* jaguar

jaiba ['xaiβa] (*LAM*) *nf* crab

jalar [xa'lar] (*LAM*) *vt* to pull

jalea [xa'lea] *nf* jelly

jaleo [xa'leo] *nm* racket, uproar;
  armar un ~ to kick up a racket

jalón [xa'lon] (*LAM*) *nm* tug

jamás [xa'mas] *adv* never

jamón [xa'mon] *nm* ham; **jamón
  dulce** o **de York** cooked ham; **jamón
  serrano** cured ham

Japón [xa'pon] *nm* Japan; **japonés,
  -esa** *adj, nm/f* Japanese ▷ *nm* (*Ling*)
  Japanese

jaque ['xake] *nm* (*Ajedrez*) check;
  jaque mate checkmate

jaqueca [xa'keka] *nf* (very bad)
  headache, migraine

jarabe [xa'raβe] *nm* syrup

jardín [xar'ðin] *nm* garden; **jardín
  infantil** o **de infancia** nursery (school);
  jardinería *nf* gardening; **jardinero, -a**
  nm/f gardener

jarra ['xarra] *nf* jar; (*jarro*) jug

jarro ['xarro] *nm* jug

jarrón [xa'rron] *nm* vase

jaula ['xaula] *nf* cage

jauría [xau'ria] *nf* pack of hounds

jazmín [xaθ'min] *nm* jasmine

J.C. *abr* (= *Jesucristo*) J.C.

jeans [jins, dʒins] (*LAM*) *nmpl* jeans,
  denims; **unos ~** a pair of jeans

jefatura [xefa'tura] *nf* (*tb*: **~ de
  policía**) police headquarters *sg*

jefe, -a ['xefe, a] *nm/f* (*gen*) chief,
  head; (*patrón*) boss; **jefe de cocina**
  chef; **jefe de estación** stationmaster;
  jefe de Estado head of state; **jefe de
  estudios** (*Escol*) director of studies;
  jefe de gobierno head of government

jengibre [xen'xiβre] *nm* ginger

jeque ['xeke] *nm* sheik

jerárquico, -a [xe'rarkiko, a] *adj*
  hierarchic(al)

jerez [xe'reθ] *nm* sherry

jerga ['xerɣa] *nf* jargon

jeringa [xe'ringa] *nf* syringe;
  (*LAM: molestia*) annoyance, bother;
  jeringuilla *nf* syringe

jeroglífico [xero'ɣlifiko] *nm*
  hieroglyphic

jersey [xer'sei] (*pl* **~s**) *nm* jersey,
  pullover, jumper

Jerusalén [xerusa'len] *n* Jerusalem

Jesucristo [xesu'kristo] *nm* Jesus
  Christ

jesuita [xe'swita] *adj, nm* Jesuit

Jesús [xe'sus] *nm* Jesus; **¡~!** good
  heavens!; (*al estornudar*) bless you!

jinete [xi'nete] *nmf*
  horseman(-woman), rider

jipijapa [xipi'xapa] (*LAM*) *nm* straw
  hat

jirafa [xi'rafa] *nf* giraffe

jirón [xi'ron] nm rag, shred

jitomate [xito'mate] (MÉX) nm tomato

joder [xo'ðer] (fam!) vt, vi to fuck (!)

jogging ['joɣin] (RPL) nm tracksuit (BRIT), sweat suit (US)

jornada [xor'naða] nf (viaje de un día) day's journey; (camino o viaje entero) journey; (día de trabajo) working day

jornal [xor'nal] nm (day's) wage; **jornalero** nm (day) labourer

joroba [xo'roβa] nf hump, hunched back; **jorobado, -a** adj hunchbacked ▷ nm/f hunchback

jota ['xota] nf (the letter) J; (danza) Aragonese dance; **no saber ni ~** to have no idea

joven ['xoβen] (pl **jóvenes**) adj young ▷ nm young man, youth ▷ nf young woman, girl

joya ['xoja] nf jewel, gem; (fig: persona) gem; **joyas de fantasía** costume o imitation jewellery; **joyería** nf (joyas) jewellery; (tienda) jeweller's (shop); **joyero** nm (persona) jeweller; (caja) jewel case

juanete [xwa'nete] nm (del pie) bunion

jubilación [xuβila'θjon] nf (retiro) retirement

jubilado, -a [xuβi'laðo, a] adj retired ▷ nm/f pensioner (BRIT), senior citizen

jubilar [xuβi'lar] vt to pension off, retire; (fam) to discard; **jubilarse** vr to retire

júbilo ['xuβilo] nm joy, rejoicing; **jubiloso, -a** adj jubilant

judía [xu'ðia] nf (ESP) (Culin) bean; **judía blanca/verde** haricot/French bean; V tb **judío**

judicial [xuði'θjal] adj judicial

judío, -a [xu'ðio, a] adj Jewish ▷ nm/f Jew(ess)

judo ['juðo] nm judo

juego etc ['xweɣo] vb V **jugar** ▷ nm (gen) play; (pasatiempo, partido) game; (en casino) gambling; (conjunto) set; **fuera de ~** (Deporte: persona) offside;

(: pelota) out of play; **juego de palabras** pun, play on words; **Juegos Olímpicos** Olympic Games

juerga ['xwerɣa] (ESP: fam) nf binge; (fiesta) party; **ir de ~** to go out on a binge

jueves ['xweβes] nm inv Thursday

juez [xweθ] nmf judge; **juez de instrucción** examining magistrate; **juez de línea** linesman; **juez de salida** starter

jugada [xu'ɣaða] nf play; **buena ~** good move o shot o stroke etc

jugador, a [xuɣa'ðor, a] nm/f player; (en casino) gambler

jugar [xu'ɣar] vt, vi to play; (en casino) to gamble; (apostar) to bet; **~ al fútbol** to play football

juglar [xu'ɣlar] nm minstrel

jugo ['xuɣo] nm (Bot) juice; (fig) essence, substance; **jugo de naranja** (LAM) orange juice; **jugoso, -a** adj juicy; (fig) substantial, important

juguete [xu'ɣete] nm toy; **juguetear** vi to play; **juguetería** nf toyshop

juguetón, -ona [xuɣe'ton, ona] adj playful

juicio ['xwiθjo] nm judgement; (razón) sanity, reason; (opinión) opinion

julio ['xuljo] nm July

jumper ['dʒumper] (LAM) nm pinafore dress (BRIT), jumper (US)

junco ['xunko] nm rush, reed

jungla ['xungla] nf jungle

junio ['xunjo] nm June

junta ['xunta] nf (asamblea) meeting, assembly; (comité, consejo) council, committee; (Com, Finanzas) board; (Tec) joint; **junta directiva** board of directors

juntar [xun'tar] vt to join, unite; (maquinaria) to assemble, put together; (dinero) to collect; **juntarse** vr to join, meet; (reunirse: personas) to meet, assemble; (arrimarse) to approach, draw closer; **~se con algn** to join sb

junto, -a ['xunto, a] adj joined; (unido) united; (anexo) near, close;

(*contiguo, próximo*) next, adjacent
▷ *adv*: **todo ~** all at once; **~s** together;
~ a near (to), next to; **~ con** (together)
with

jurado [xu'raðo] *nm* (*Jur: individuo*)
juror; (: *grupo*) jury; (*de concurso*: *grupo*)
panel (of judges); (: *individuo*) member
of a panel

juramento [xura'mento] *nm* oath;
(*maldición*) oath, curse; **prestar ~** to
take the oath; **tomar ~ a** to swear in,
administer the oath to

jurar [xu'rar] *vt, vi* to swear; **~ en
falso** to commit perjury; **tenérsela
jurada a algn** to have it in for sb

jurídico, -a [xu'riðiko, a] *adj* legal

jurisdicción [xurisðik'θjon]
nf (*poder, autoridad*) jurisdiction;
(*territorio*) district

justamente [xusta'mente] *adv*
justly, fairly; (*precisamente*) just, exactly

justicia [xus'tiθja] *nf* justice;
(*equidad*) fairness, justice

justificación [xustifika'θjon] *nf*
justification; **justificar** *vt* to justify

justo, -a ['xusto, a] *adj* (*equitativo*)
just, fair, right; (*preciso*) exact, correct;
(*ajustado*) tight ▷ *adv* (*precisamente*)
exactly, precisely; (*LAM: apenas a tiempo*)
just in time

juvenil [xuβe'nil] *adj* youthful

juventud [xuβen'tuð] *nf*
(*adolescencia*) youth; (*jóvenes*) young
people *pl*

juzgado [xuθ'ɣaðo] *nm* tribunal;
(*Jur*) court

juzgar [xuθ'ɣar] *vt* to judge; **a ~ por
...** to judge by ..., judging by ...

kárate ['karate] *nm* karate

kg *abr* (= *kilogramo*) kg

kilo ['kilo] *nm* kilo; **kilogramo**
nm kilogramme; **kilometraje** *nm*
distance in kilometres ≈ mileage;
kilómetro *nm* kilometre; **kilovatio**
nm kilowatt

kiosco ['kjosko] *nm* = **quiosco**

kleenex® [kli'neks] *nm* paper
handkerchief, tissue

Kosovo [ko'soβo] *nm* Kosovo

km *abr* (= *kilómetro*) km

kv *abr* (= *kilovatio*) kw

l abr (= litro) l

la [la] art def the ▷ pron her; (Ud.) you; (cosa) it ▷ nm (Mús) la; **~ del sombrero rojo** the girl in the red hat; V tb **el**

laberinto [laβe'rinto] nm labyrinth

labio ['laβjo] nm lip

labor [la'βor] nf labour; (Agr) farm work; (tarea) job, task; (Costura) needlework; **labores domésticas** o **del hogar** household chores; **laborable** adj (Agr) workable; **día laborable** working day; **laboral** adj (accidente) at work; (jornada) working

laboratorio [laβora'torjo] nm laboratory

laborista [laβo'rista] adj: **Partido L~** Labour Party

labrador, a [laβra'ðor, a] adj farming cpd ▷ nm/f farmer

labranza [la'βranθa] nf (Agr) cultivation

labrar [la'βrar] vt (gen) to work; (madera etc) to carve; (fig) to cause, bring about

laca ['laka] nf lacquer

lacio, -a ['laθjo, a] adj (pelo) straight

lacón [la'kon] nm shoulder of pork

lactancia [lak'tanθja] nf lactation

lácteo, -a ['lakteo, a] adj: **productos ~s** dairy products

ladear [laðe'ar] vt to tip, tilt ▷ vi to tilt; **ladearse** vr to lean

ladera [la'ðera] nf slope

lado ['laðo] nm (gen) side; (fig) protection; (Mil) flank; **al ~ de** beside; **poner de ~** to put on its side; **poner a un ~** to put aside; **por todos ~s** on all sides, all round (BRIT)

ladrar [la'ðrar] vi to bark; **ladrido** nm bark, barking

ladrillo [la'ðriʎo] nm (gen) brick; (azulejo) tile

ladrón, -ona [la'ðron, ona] nm/f thief

lagartija [laɣar'tixa] nf (Zool) (small) lizard

lagarto [la'ɣarto] nm (Zool) lizard

lago ['laɣo] nm lake

lágrima ['laɣrima] nf tear

laguna [la'ɣuna] nf (lago) lagoon; (hueco) gap

lamentable [lamen'taβle] adj lamentable, regrettable; (miserable) pitiful

lamentar [lamen'tar] vt (sentir) to regret; (deplorar) to lament; **lamentarse** vr to lament; **lo lamento mucho** I'm very sorry

lamer [la'mer] vt to lick

lámina ['lamina] nf (plancha delgada) sheet; (para estampar, estampa) plate

lámpara ['lampara] nf lamp; **lámpara de alcohol/gas** spirit/gas lamp; **lámpara de pie** standard lamp

lana ['lana] nf wool

lancha ['lantʃa] nf launch; **lancha motora** motorboat, speedboat

langosta [lan'gosta] nf (crustáceo) lobster; (: de río) crayfish; **langostino** nm Dublin Bay prawn

lanza ['lanθa] nf (arma) lance, spear

lanzamiento [lanθa'mjento] nm (gen) throwing; (Náut, Com) launch, launching; **lanzamiento de peso** putting the shot

lanzar [lan'θar] *vt* (*gen*) to throw; (*Deporte: pelota*) to bowl; (*Náut, Com*) to launch; (*Jur*) to evict; **lanzarse** *vr* to throw o.s.

lapa ['lapa] *nf* limpet

lapicero [lapi'θero] (*CAM*) *nm* (*bolígrafo*) ballpoint pen, Biro®

lápida ['lapiða] *nf* stone; **lápida mortuoria** headstone

lápiz ['lapiθ] *nm* pencil; **lápiz de color** coloured pencil; **lápiz de labios** lipstick; **lápiz de ojos** eyebrow pencil

largar [lar'xar] *vt* (*soltar*) to release; (*aflojar*) to loosen; (*lanzar*) to launch; (*fam*) to let fly; (*velas*) to unfurl; (*LAM: lanzar*) to throw; **largarse** *vr* (*fam*) to beat it; **~se a** (*CS: empezar*) to start to

largo, -a ['larxo, a] *adj* (*longitud*) long; (*tiempo*) lengthy; (*fig*) generous ▷ *nm* length; (*Mús*) largo; **dos años ~s** two long years; **tiene 9 metros de ~** it is 9 metres long; **a la larga** in the long run; **a lo ~ de** along; (*tiempo*) all through, throughout

> No confundir **largo** con la palabra inglesa *large*.

largometraje *nm* feature film

laringe [la'rinxe] *nf* larynx; **laringitis** *nf* laryngitis

las [las] *art def* the ▷ *pron* them; **~ que cantan** the ones *o* women *o* girls who sing; *V tb* **el**

lasaña [la'saɲa] *nf* lasagne, lasagna

láser ['laser] *nm* laser

lástima ['lastima] *nf* (*pena*) pity; **dar ~** to be pitiful; **es una ~ que ...** it's a pity that ...; **¡qué ~!** what a pity!; **está hecha una ~** she looks pitiful

lastimar [lasti'mar] *vt* (*herir*) to wound; (*ofender*) to offend; **lastimarse** *vr* to hurt o.s.

lata ['lata] *nf* (*metal*) tin; (*caja*) tin (*BRIT*), can; (*fam*) nuisance; **en ~** tinned (*BRIT*), canned; **dar la ~** to be a nuisance

latente [la'tente] *adj* latent

lateral [late'ral] *adj* side *cpd*, lateral ▷ *nm* (*Teatro*) wings

latido [la'tiðo] *nm* (*de corazón*) beat

latifundio [lati'fundjo] *nm* large estate

latigazo [lati'xaθo] *nm* (*golpe*) lash; (*sonido*) crack

látigo [la'tixo] *nm* whip

latín [la'tin] *nm* Latin

latino, -a [la'tino, a] *adj* Latin; **latinoamericano, -a** *adj*, *nm/f* Latin-American

latir [la'tir] *vi* (*corazón, pulso*) to beat

latitud [lati'tuð] *nf* (*Geo*) latitude

latón [la'ton] *nm* brass

laurel [lau'rel] *nm* (*Bot*) laurel; (*Culin*) bay

lava ['laβa] *nf* lava

lavabo [la'βaβo] *nm* (*pila*) washbasin; (*tb:* **~s**) toilet

lavado [la'βaðo] *nm* washing; (*de ropa*) laundry; (*Arte*) wash; **lavado de cerebro** brainwashing; **lavado en seco** dry-cleaning

lavadora [laβa'ðora] *nf* washing machine

lavanda [la'βanda] *nf* lavender

lavandería [laβande'ria] *nf* laundry; (*automática*) launderette

lavaplatos [laβa'platos] *nm inv* dishwasher

lavar [la'βar] *vt* to wash; (*borrar*) to wipe away; **lavarse** *vr* to wash o.s.; **~se las manos** to wash one's hands; **~se los dientes** to brush one's teeth; **~ y marcar** (*pelo*) to shampoo and set; **~ en seco** to dry-clean; **~ los platos** to wash the dishes

lavarropas [laβa'rropas] (*RPL*) *nm inv* washing machine

lavavajillas [laβaβa'xiʎas] *nm inv* dishwasher

laxante [lak'sante] *nm* laxative

lazarillo [laθa'riʎo] *nm* (*tb:* **perro ~**) guide dog

lazo ['laθo] *nm* knot; (*lazada*) bow; (*para animales*) lasso; (*trampa*) snare;

(vínculo) tie

le [le] pron (directo) him (o her); (: usted) you; (indirecto) to him (o her o it); (: usted) to you

leal [le'al] adj loyal; **lealtad** nf loyalty

lección [lek'θjon] nf lesson

leche ['letʃe] nf milk; **tiene mala ~** (fam!) he's a swine (!); **leche condensada** condensed milk; **leche desnatada** skimmed milk

lecho ['letʃo] nm (cama: de río) bed; (Geo) layer

lechón [le'tʃon] nm sucking (BRIT) o suckling (US) pig

lechoso, -a [le'tʃoso, a] adj milky

lechuga [le'tʃuɣa] nf lettuce

lechuza [le'tʃuθa] nf owl

lector, a [lek'tor, a] nm/f reader ▷ nm: **~ de discos compactos** CD player

lectura [lek'tura] nf reading

leer [le'er] vt to read

legado [le'ɣaðo] nm (don) bequest; (herencia) legacy; (enviado) legate

legajo [le'ɣaxo] nm file

legal [le'ɣal] adj (gen) legal; (persona) trustworthy; **legalizar** [leɣali'θar] vt to legalize; (documento) to authenticate

legaña [le'ɣaɲa] nf sleep (in eyes)

legión [le'xjon] nf legion; **legionario, -a** adj legionary ▷ nm legionnaire

legislación [lexisla'θjon] nf legislation

legislar [lexis'lar] vi to legislate

legislatura [lexisla'tura] nf (Pol) period of office

legítimo, -a [le'xitimo, a] adj (genuino) authentic; (legal) legitimate

legua ['leɣwa] nf league

legumbres [le'ɣumbres] nfpl pulses

leído, -a [le'iðo, a] adj well-read

lejanía [lexa'nia] nf distance; **lejano, -a** adj far-off; (en el tiempo) distant; (fig) remote

lejía [le'xia] nf bleach

lejos ['lexos] adv far, far away; **a lo ~** in the distance; **de** o **desde ~** from afar; **~ de** far from

lema ['lema] nm motto; (Pol) slogan

lencería [lenθe'ria] nf linen, drapery

lengua ['lengwa] nf tongue; (Ling) language; **morderse la ~** to hold one's tongue

lenguado [len'gwaðo] nm sole

lenguaje [len'gwaxe] nm language; **lenguaje de programación** program(m)ing language

lengüeta [len'gweta] nf (Anat) epiglottis; (zapatos) tongue; (Mús) reed

lente ['lente] nf lens; (lupa) magnifying glass; **lentes** nfpl lenses ▷ nmpl (LAM: gafas) glasses; **lentes bifocales/de sol** (LAM) bifocals/sunglasses; **lentes de contacto** contact lenses

lenteja [len'texa] nf lentil; **lentejuela** nf sequin

lentilla [len'tiʎa] nf contact lens

lentitud [lenti'tuð] nf slowness; **con ~** slowly

lento, -a ['lento, a] adj slow

leña ['leɲa] nf firewood; **leñador, a** nm/f woodcutter

leño ['leɲo] nm (trozo de árbol) log; (madero) timber; (fig) blockhead

Leo ['leo] nm Leo

león [le'on] nm lion; **león marino** sea lion

leopardo [leo'parðo] nm leopard

leotardos [leo'tarðos] nmpl tights

lepra ['lepra] nf leprosy; **leproso, -a** nm/f leper

les [les] pron (directo) them; (: ustedes) you; (indirecto) to them; (: ustedes) to you

lesbiana [les'βjana] adj, nf lesbian

lesión [le'sjon] nf wound, lesion; (Deporte) injury; **lesionado, -a** adj injured ▷ nm/f injured person

letal [le'tal] adj lethal

letanía [leta'nia] nf litany

letra ['letra] nf letter; (escritura) handwriting; (Mús) lyrics pl; **letra de cambio** bill of exchange; **letra de imprenta** print; **letrado, -a** adj learned ▷ nm/f lawyer; **letrero** nm (*cartel*) sign; (*etiqueta*) label

letrina [le'trina] *nf* latrine

leucemia [leu'θemja] *nf* leukaemia

levadura [leβa'ðura] *nf* (*para el pan*) yeast; (*de cerveza*) brewer's yeast

levantar [leβan'tar] *vt* (*gen*) to raise; (*del suelo*) to pick up; (*hacia arriba*) to lift (up); (*plan*) to make, draw up; (*mesa*) to clear; (*campamento*) to strike; (*fig*) to cheer up, hearten; **levantarse** *vr* to get up; (*enderezarse*) to straighten up; (*rebelarse*) to rebel; **~ el ánimo** to cheer up

levante [le'βante] *nm* east coast; **el L~** *region of Spain extending from Castellón to Murcia*

levar [le'βar] *vt* to weigh

leve ['leβe] *adj* light; (*fig*) trivial

levita [le'βita] *nf* frock coat

léxico ['leksiko] *nm* (*vocabulario*) vocabulary

ley [lei] *nf* (*gen*) law; (*metal*) standard

leyenda [le'jenda] *nf* legend

leyó *etc vb* V **leer**

liar [li'ar] *vt* to tie (up); (*unir*) to bind; (*envolver*) to wrap (up); (*enredar*) to confuse; (*cigarrillo*) to roll; **liarse** *vr* (*fam*) to get involved; **~se a palos** to get involved in a fight

Líbano ['liβano] *nm*: **el ~** the Lebanon

libélula [li'βelula] *nf* dragonfly

liberación [liβera'θjon] *nf* liberation; (*de la cárcel*) release

liberal [liβe'ral] *adj, nmf* liberal

liberar [liβe'rar] *vt* to liberate

libertad [liβer'tað] *nf* liberty, freedom; **libertad bajo fianza** bail; **libertad bajo palabra** parole; **libertad condicional** probation; **libertad de culto/de prensa/de comercio** freedom of worship/of the press/of trade

libertar [liβer'tar] *vt* (*preso*) to set free; (*de una obligación*) to release; (*eximir*) to exempt

libertino, -a [liβer'tino, a] *adj* permissive ▷ *nm/f* permissive person

libra ['liβra] *nf* pound; **L~** (*Astrología*) Libra; **libra esterlina** pound sterling

libramiento [liβra'mjento] (*MÉX*) *nm* ring road (*BRIT*), beltway (*US*)

librar [li'βrar] *vt* (*de peligro*) to save; (*batalla*) to wage, fight; (*de impuestos*) to exempt; (*cheque*) to make out; (*Jur*) to exempt; **librarse** *vr*: **~se de** to escape from, free o.s. from

libre ['liβre] *adj* free; (*lugar*) unoccupied; (*asiento*) vacant; (*de deudas*) free of debts; **~ de impuestos** free of tax; **tiro ~** free kick; **los 100 metros ~s** the 100 metres free-style (*race*); **al aire ~** in the open air

librería [liβre'ria] *nf* (*tienda*) bookshop

▌ No confundir **librería** con la palabra inglesa **library**.

librero, -a *nm/f* bookseller

libreta [li'βreta] *nf* notebook

libro ['liβro] *nm* book; **libro de bolsillo** paperback; **libro de texto** textbook; **libro electrónico** e-book

Lic. *abr* = **licenciado, a**

licencia [li'θenθja] *nf* (*gen*) licence; (*permiso*) permission; **licencia de caza** game licence; **licencia por enfermedad** (*MÉX, RPL*) sick leave; **licenciado, -a** *adj* licensed ▷ *nm/f* graduate; **licenciar** *vt* (*empleado*) to dismiss; (*permitir*) to permit, allow; (*soldado*) to discharge; (*estudiante*) to confer a degree upon; **licenciarse** *vr*: **licenciarse en Derecho** to graduate in law

lícito, -a ['liθito, a] *adj* (*legal*) lawful; (*justo*) fair, just; (*permisible*) permissible

licor [li'kor] *nm* spirits *pl* (*BRIT*), liquor (*US*); (*de frutas etc*) liqueur

licuadora [likwa'ðora] *nf* blender

líder ['liðer] *nmf* leader; **liderato** *nm* leadership; **liderazgo** *nm* leadership

lidia ['liðja] *nf* bullfighting; (*una lidia*) bullfight; **toros de ~** fighting bulls; **lidiar** *vt, vi* to fight

liebre ['ljeβre] *nf* hare

lienzo ['ljenθo] *nm* linen; (*Arte*) canvas; (*Arq*) wall

liga ['liɣa] nf (de medias) garter, suspender; (LAM: goma) rubber band; (confederación) league

ligadura [liɣa'ðura] nf bond, tie; (Med, Mús) ligature

ligamento [liɣa'mento] nm ligament

ligar [li'ɣar] vt (atar) to tie; (unir) to join; (Med) to bind up; (Mús) to slur ▷ vi to mix, blend; (fam): (él) **liga mucho** he pulls a lot of women; **ligarse** vr to commit o.s.

ligero, -a [li'ɣero, a] adj (de peso) light; (tela) thin; (rápido) swift, quick; (ágil) agile, nimble; (de importancia) slight; (de carácter) flippant, superficial ▷ adv: **a la ligera** superficially

liguero [li'ɣero] nm suspender (BRIT) o garter (US) belt

lija ['lixa] nf (Zool) dogfish; (tb: **papel de** ~) sandpaper

lila ['lila] nf lilac

lima ['lima] nf file; (Bot) lime; **lima de uñas** nailfile; **limar** vt to file

limitación [limita'θjon] nf limitation, limit

limitar [limi'tar] vt to limit; (reducir) to reduce, cut down ▷ vi: ~ **con** to border on; **limitarse** vr: ~**se a** to limit o.s. to

límite ['limite] nm (gen) limit; (fin) end; (frontera) border; **límite de velocidad** speed limit

limítrofe [li'mitrofe] adj neighbouring

limón [li'mon] nm lemon ▷ adj: **amarillo** ~ lemon-yellow; **limonada** nf lemonade

limosna [li'mosna] nf alms pl; **vivir de** ~ to live on charity

limpiador [limpja'ðor] (MÉX) nm = **limpiaparabrisas**

limpiaparabrisas [limpjapara'βrisas] nm inv windscreen (BRIT) o windshield (US) wiper

limpiar [lim'pjar] vt to clean; (con trapo) to wipe; (quitar) to wipe away;

(zapatos) to shine, polish; (fig) to clean up

limpieza [lim'pjeθa] nf (estado) cleanliness; (acto) cleaning; (: de las calles) cleansing; (: de zapatos) polishing; (habilidad) skill; (fig: Policía) clean-up; (pureza) purity; (Mil): **operación de** ~ mopping-up operation; **limpieza en seco** dry cleaning

limpio, -a ['limpjo, a] adj clean; (moralmente) pure; (Com) clear, net; (fam) honest ▷ adv: **jugar** ~ to play fair; **pasar a** (ESP) o **en** (LAM) ~ to make a clean copy of

lince ['linθe] nm lynx

linchar [lin'tʃar] vt to lynch

lindar [lin'dar] vi to adjoin; ~ **con** to border on

lindo, -a ['lindo, a] adj pretty, lovely ▷ adv: **nos divertimos de lo** ~ we had a marvellous time; **canta muy** ~ (LAM) he sings beautifully

línea ['linea] nf (gen) line; **en** ~ (Inform) on line; **línea aérea** airline; **línea de meta** goal line; (en carrera) finishing line; **línea discontinua** (Auto) broken line; **línea recta** straight line

lingote [lin'gote] nm ingot

lingüista [lin'gwista] nmf linguist; **lingüística** nf linguistics sg

lino ['lino] nm linen; (Bot) flax

linterna [lin'terna] nf torch (BRIT), flashlight (US)

lío ['lio] nm bundle; (fam) fuss; (desorden) muddle, mess; **armar un** ~ to make a fuss

liquen ['liken] nm lichen

liquidación [likiða'θjon] nf liquidation; **venta de** ~ clearance sale

liquidar [liki'ðar] vt (mercancías) to liquidate; (deudas) to pay off; (empresa) to wind up

líquido, -a ['likiðo, a] adj liquid; (ganancia) net ▷ nm liquid; **líquido imponible** net taxable income

lira ['lira] nf (Mús) lyre; (moneda) lira

lírico, -a ['liriko, a] adj lyrical

lirio ['lirjo] nm (Bot) iris
lirón [li'ron] nm (Zool) dormouse; (fig)
sleepyhead
Lisboa [lis'βoa] n Lisbon
lisiar [li'sjar] vt to maim
liso, -a ['liso, a] adj (terreno) flat;
(cabello) straight; (superficie) even;
(tela) plain
lista ['lista] nf list; (de alumnos) school
register; (de libros) catalogue; (de platos)
menu; (de precios) price list; **pasar ~** to
call the roll; **tela de ~s** striped material;
lista de espera waiting list; **lista de
precios** price list; **listín** nm (tb: **listín
telefónico** o **de teléfonos**) telephone
directory
listo, -a ['listo, a] adj (perspicaz)
smart, clever; (preparado) ready
listón [lis'ton] nm (de madera, metal)
strip
litera [li'tera] nf (en barco, tren) berth;
(en dormitorio) bunk, bunk bed
literal [lite'ral] adj literal
literario, -a [lite'rarjo, a] adj literary
literato, -a [lite'rato, a] adj literary
▷ nm/f writer
literatura [litera'tura] nf literature
litigio [li'tixjo] nm (Jur) lawsuit;
(fig): **en ~ con** in dispute with
litografía [litoɣra'fia] nf
lithography; (una litografía) lithograph
litoral [lito'ral] adj coastal ▷ nm
coast, seaboard
litro ['litro] nm litre
lívido, -a ['liβiðo, a] adj livid
llaga ['ʎaɣa] nf wound
llama ['ʎama] nf flame; (Zool) llama
llamada [ʎa'maða] nf call; **llamada a
cobro revertido** reverse-charge (BRIT)
o collect (US) call; **llamada al orden**
call to order; **llamada de atención**
warning; **llamada local** (LAM) local call;
llamada metropolitana (ESP) local
call; **llamada por cobrar** (MÉX) reverse-
charge (BRIT) o collect (US) call
llamamiento [ʎama'mjento]
nm call
llamar [ʎa'mar] vt to call; (atención) to

attract ▷ vi (por teléfono) to telephone;
(a la puerta) to knock (o ring); (por señas)
to beckon; (Mil) to call up; **llamarse**
vr to be called, be named; **¿cómo se
llama (usted)?** what's your name?
llamativo, -a [ʎama'tiβo, a] adj
showy; (color) loud
llano, -a ['ʎano, a] adj (superficie) flat;
(persona) straightforward; (estilo) clear
▷ nm plain, flat ground
llanta ['ʎanta] nf (ESP) (wheel) rim;
llanta (de goma) (LAM: neumático)
tyre; (: cámara) inner (tube); **llanta de
repuesto** (LAM) spare tyre
llanto ['ʎanto] nm weeping
llanura [ʎa'nura] nf plain
llave ['ʎaβe] nf key; (del agua) tap;
(Mecánica) spanner; (de la luz) switch;
(Mús) key; **echar la ~ a** to lock up;
llave de contacto (ESP Auto) ignition
key; **llave de encendido** (LAM Auto)
ignition key; **llave de paso** stopcock;
llave inglesa monkey wrench; **llave
maestra** master key; **llavero** nm
keyring
llegada [ʎe'ɣaða] nf arrival
llegar [ʎe'ɣar] vi to arrive; (alcanzar) to
reach; (bastar) to be enough; **llegarse
vr: ~se a** to approach; **~ a** to manage
to, succeed in; **~ a saber** to find out; **~
a ser** to become; **~ a las manos de** to
come into the hands of
llenar [ʎe'nar] vt to fill; (espacio) to
cover; (formulario) to fill in o up; (fig)
to heap
lleno, -a ['ʎeno, a] adj full, filled;
(repleto) full up ▷ nm (Teatro) full house;
dar de ~ contra un muro to hit a wall
head-on
llevadero, -a [ʎeβa'ðero, a] adj
bearable, tolerable
llevar [ʎe'βar] vt to take; (ropa) to
wear; (cargar) to carry; (quitar) to take
away; (en coche) to drive; (transportar)
to transport; (traer: dinero) to carry;
(conducir) to lead; (Mat) to carry ▷ vi
(suj: camino etc): **~ a** to lead to; **llevarse
vr** to carry off, take away; **llevamos**

dos días aquí we have been here for two days; **él me lleva 2 años** he's 2 years older than me; **~ los libros** (Com) to keep the books; **~se bien** to get on well (together)

llorar [ʎo'rar] vt, vi to cry, weep; **~ de risa** to cry with laughter

llorón, -ona [ʎo'ron, ona] adj tearful ▷ nm/f cry-baby

lloroso, -a [ʎo'roso, a] adj (gen) weeping, tearful; (triste) sad, sorrowful

llover [ʎo'βer] vi to rain

llovizna [ʎo'βiθna] nf drizzle; **lloviznar** vi to drizzle

llueve etc vb V **llover**

lluvia ['ʎuβja] nf rain; **lluvia radioactiva** (radioactive) fallout; **lluvioso, -a** adj rainy

lo [lo] art def: **~ bel-** the beautiful, what is beautiful, that which is beautiful ▷ pron (persona) him; (cosa) it; **~ que sea** whatever; V tb **el**

loable [lo'aβle] adj praiseworthy

lobo ['loβo] nm wolf; **lobo de mar** (fig) sea dog

lóbulo ['loβulo] nm lobe

local [lo'kal] adj local ▷ nm place, site; (oficinas) premises pl; **localidad** nf (barrio) locality; (lugar) location; (Teatro) seat, ticket; **localizar** vt (ubicar) to locate, find; (restringir) to localize; (situar) to place

loción [lo'θjon] nf lotion

loco, -a ['loko, a] adj mad ▷ nm/f lunatic, mad person; **estar ~ con** o **por algo/por algn** to be mad about sth/sb

locomotora [lokomo'tora] nf engine, locomotive

locuaz [lo'kwaθ] adj loquacious

locución [loku'θjon] nf expression

locura [lo'kura] nf madness; (acto) crazy act

locutor, a [loku'tor, a] nm/f (Radio) announcer; (comentarista) commentator; (TV) newsreader

locutorio [loku'torjo] nm (en telefónica) telephone booth

lodo ['loðo] nm mud

lógica ['loxika] nf logic

lógico, -a ['loxiko, a] adj logical

login ['loxin] nm login

logística [lo'xistika] nf logistics sg

logotipo [loðo'tipo] nm logo

logrado, -a [lo'ðraðo, a] adj (interpretación, reproducción) polished, excellent

lograr [lo'ɣrar] vt to achieve; (obtener) to get, obtain; **~ hacer** to manage to do; **~ que algn venga** to manage to get sb to come

logro ['loɣro] nm achievement, success

lóker ['loker] (LAM) nm locker

loma ['loma] nf hillock (BRIT), small hill

lombriz [lom'briθ] nf worm

lomo ['lomo] nm (de animal) back; (Culin: de cerdo) pork loin; (: de vaca) rib steak; (de libro) spine

lona ['lona] nf canvas

loncha ['lontʃa] nf = **lonja**

lonchería [lontʃe'ria] (LAM) nf snack bar, diner (US)

Londres ['londres] n London

longaniza [longa'niθa] nf pork sausage

longitud [lonxi'tuð] nf length; (Geo) longitude; **tener 3 metros de ~** to be 3 metres long; **longitud de onda** wavelength

lonja ['lonxa] nf slice; (de tocino) rasher; **lonja de pescado** fish market

loro ['loro] nm parrot

los [los] art def the ▷ pron them; (ustedes) you; **mis libros y ~ tuyos** my books and yours; V tb **el**

losa ['losa] nf stone

lote ['lote] nm portion; (Com) lot

lotería [lote'ria] nf lottery; (juego) lotto

● **LOTERÍA**
●
● Millions of pounds are spent
● on lotteries each year in Spain,
● two of which are state-run: the

- **Lotería Primitiva** and the **Lotería**
- **Nacional**, with money raised
- going directly to the government.
- One of the most famous lotteries is
- run by the wealthy and influential
- society for the blind, "la ONCE".

loza ['loθa] nf crockery

lubina [lu'βina] nf sea bass

lubricante [luβri'kante] nm lubricant

lubricar [luβri'kar] vt to lubricate

lucha ['lutʃa] nf fight, struggle; **lucha de clases** class struggle; **lucha libre** wrestling; **luchar** vi to fight

lúcido, -a [lu'θiðo, a] adj (persona) lucid; (mente) logical; (idea) crystal-clear

luciérnaga [lu'θjernaxa] nf glow-worm

lucir [lu'θir] vt to illuminate, light (up); (ostentar) to show off ▷ vi (brillar) to shine; **lucirse** vr (irónico) to make a fool of o.s.

lucro ['lukro] nm profit, gain

lúdico, -a ['ludiko, a] adj (aspecto, actividad) play cpd

luego ['lweɣo] adv (después) next; (más tarde) later, afterwards

lugar [lu'ɣar] nm place; (sitio) spot; **en primer ~** in the first place, firstly; **en ~ de** instead of; **hacer ~** to make room; **fuera de ~** out of place; **sin ~ a dudas** without doubt, undoubtedly; **dar ~ a** to give rise to; **tener ~** to take place; **yo en su ~** if I were him; **lugar común** commonplace

lúgubre ['luɣuβre] adj mournful

lujo ['luxo] nm luxury; (fig) profusion, abundance; **de ~** luxury cpd, de luxe; **lujoso, -a** adj luxurious

lujuria [lu'xurja] nf lust

lumbre ['lumbre] nf fire; (para cigarrillo) light

luminoso, -a [lumi'noso, a] adj luminous, shining

luna ['luna] nf moon; (de un espejo) glass; (de gafas) lens; (fig) crescent; **estar en la ~** to have one's head in the clouds; **luna de miel** honeymoon; **luna llena/nueva** full/new moon

lunar [lu'nar] adj lunar ▷ nm (Anat) mole; **tela de ~es** spotted material

lunes ['lunes] nm inv Monday

lupa ['lupa] nf magnifying glass

lustre ['lustre] nm polish; (fig) lustre; **dar ~ a** to polish

luto ['luto] nm mourning; **llevar el o vestirse de ~** to be in mourning

Luxemburgo [luksem'burɣo] nm Luxembourg

luz [luθ] (pl **luces**) nf light; **dar a ~ un niño** to give birth to a child; **sacar a la ~** to bring to light; **dar o encender** (ESP) o **prender** (LAM)**/apagar la ~** to switch the light on/off; **tener pocas luces** to be dim o stupid; **traje de luces** bullfighter's costume; **luces de tráfico** traffic lights; **luz de freno** brake light; **luz roja/verde** red/green light

m

m *abr* (= *metro*) m; (= *minuto*) m

macana [ma'kana] (*MÉX*) *nf*
truncheon (*BRIT*), billy club (*US*)

macarrones [maka'rrones] *nmpl*
macaroni *sg*

macedonia [maθe'ðonja] *nf* (*tb*: **~ de
frutas**) fruit salad

maceta [ma'θeta] *nf* (*de flores*) pot of
flowers; (*para plantas*) flowerpot

machacar [matʃa'kar] *vt* to crush,
pound ▷ *vi* (*insistir*) to go on, keep on

machete [ma'tʃete] *nm* machete,
(large) knife

machetear [matʃete'ar] (*MÉX*) *vt* to
swot (*BRIT*), grind away (*US*)

machismo [ma'tʃismo] *nm* male
chauvinism; **machista** *adj, nm* sexist

macho ['matʃo] *adj* male; (*fig*) virile
▷ *nm* male; (*fig*) he-man

macizo, -a [ma'θiθo, a] *adj* (*grande*)
massive; (*fuerte, sólido*) solid ▷ *nm*
mass, chunk

madeja [ma'ðexa] *nf* (*de lana*) skein,
hank; (*de pelo*) mass, mop

madera [ma'ðera] *nf* wood; (*fig*)
nature, character; **una ~** a piece of
wood

madrastra [ma'ðrastra] *nf*
stepmother

madre ['maðre] *adj* mother *cpd* ▷ *nf*
mother; (*de vino etc*) dregs *pl*; **madre
política/soltera** mother-in-law/
unmarried mother

Madrid [ma'ðrið] *n* Madrid

madriguera [maðri'ɣera] *nf* burrow

madrileño, -a [maðri'leɲo, a] *adj* of
o from Madrid ▷ *nm/f* native of Madrid

madrina [ma'ðrina] *nf* godmother;
(*Arq*) prop, shore; (*Tec*) brace; (*de boda*)
bridesmaid

madrugada [maðru'ɣaða] *nf* early
morning; (*alba*) dawn, daybreak

madrugador, a [maðruxa'ðor, a]
adj early-rising

madrugar [maðru'ɣar] *vi* to get up
early; (*fig*) to get ahead

madurar [maðu'rar] *vt, vi* (*fruta*)
to ripen; (*fig*) to mature; **madurez** *nf*
ripeness; maturity; **maduro, -a** *adj*
ripe; mature

maestra *nf* V **maestro**

maestría [maes'tria] *nf* mastery;
(*habilidad*) skill, expertise

maestro, -a [ma'estro, a] *adj*
masterly; (*principal*) main ▷ *nm/f*
master/mistress; (*profesor*) teacher
▷ *nm* (*autoridad*) authority; (*Mús*)
maestro; (*experto*) master; **maestro
albañil** master mason

magdalena [maɣða'lena] *nf* fairy
cake

magia ['maxja] *nf* magic; **mágico, -a**
adj magic(al) ▷ *nm/f* magician

magisterio [maxis'terjo] *nm*
(*enseñanza*) teaching; (*profesión*)
teaching profession; (*maestros*)
teachers *pl*

magistrado [maxis'traðo] *nm*
magistrate

magistral [maxis'tral] *adj*
magisterial; (*fig*) masterly

magnate [maɣ'nate] *nm* magnate,
tycoon

magnético, -a [max'netiko, a] *adj*
magnetic

magnetofón [maxneto'fon] *nm*
tape recorder

magnetófono [maxne'tofono] *nm* =
magnetofón

magnífico, -a [max'nifiko, a] *adj*
splendid, magnificent

magnitud [maxni'tuð] *nf*
magnitude

mago, -a ['maxo, a] *nm/f* magician;
los Reyes M~s the Three Wise Men

magro, -a ['maxro, a] *adj* (*carne*) lean

mahonesa [mao'nesa] *nf*
mayonnaise

maître ['metre] *nm* head waiter

maíz [ma'iθ] *nm* maize (BRIT), corn
(US); sweet corn

majestad [maxes'tað] *nf* majesty

majo, -a ['maxo, a] *adj* nice; (*guapo*)
attractive, good-looking; (*elegante*)
smart

mal [mal] *adv* badly; (*equivocadamente*)
wrongly ▷ *adj* = **malo** ▷ *nm* evil;
(*desgracia*) misfortune; (*daño*) harm,
damage; (*Med*) illness; **~ que**
rightly or wrongly; **ir de ~ en peor** to
get worse and worse

malabarista [malaβa'rista] *nmf*
juggler

malaria [ma'larja] *nf* malaria

malcriado, -a [mal'krjaðo, a] *adj*
spoiled

maldad [mal'dað] *nf* evil,
wickedness

maldecir [malde'θir] *vt* to curse

maldición [maldi'θjon] *nf* curse

maldito, -a [mal'dito, a] *adj*
(*condenado*) damned; (*perverso*) wicked;
¡~ sea! damn it!

malecón [male'kon] (LAM) *nm* sea
front, promenade

maleducado, -a [maleðu'kaðo, a]
adj bad-mannered, rude

malentendido [malenten'diðo] *nm*
misunderstanding

malestar [males'tar] *nm* (*gen*)
discomfort; (*fig: inquietud*) uneasiness;

(*Pol*) unrest

maleta [ma'leta] *nf* case, suitcase;
(*Auto*) boot (BRIT), trunk (US); **hacer las
~s** to pack; **maletero** *nm* (*Auto*) boot
(BRIT), trunk (US); **maletín** *nm* small
case, bag

maleza [ma'leθa] *nf* (*malas hierbas*)
weeds *pl*; (*arbustos*) thicket

malgastar [malxas'tar] *vt* (*tiempo,
dinero*) to waste; (*salud*) to ruin

malhechor, a [male'tʃor, a] *nm/f*
delinquent

malhumorado, -a [malumo'raðo,
a] *adj* bad-tempered

malicia [ma'liθja] *nf* (*maldad*)
wickedness; (*astucia*) slyness, guile;
(*mala intención*) malice, spite; (*carácter
travieso*) mischievousness

maligno, -a [ma'lixno, a] *adj* evil;
(*malévolo*) malicious; (*Med*) malignant

malla ['maʎa] *nf* mesh; (*de baño*)
swimsuit; (*de ballet, gimnasia*) leotard;
mallas *nfpl* tights; **malla de alambre**
wire mesh

Mallorca [ma'ʎorka] *nf* Majorca

malo, -a ['malo, a] *adj* bad, false
▷ *nm/f* villain; **estar ~** to be ill

malograr [malo'xrar] *vt* to spoil;
(*plan*) to upset; (*ocasión*) to waste

malparado, -a [malpa'raðo, a]
adj: **salir ~** to come off badly

malpensado, -a [malpen'saðo, a]
adj nasty

malteada [malte'aða] (LAM) *nf*
milkshake

maltratar [maltra'tar] *vt* to ill-treat,
mistreat

malvado, -a [mal'βaðo, a] *adj* evil,
villainous

Malvinas [mal'βinas] *nfpl* (*tb*: **Islas
~**) Falklands, Falkland Islands

mama ['mama] *nf* (*de animal*) teat; (*de
mujer*) breast

mamá [ma'ma] (*pl* **~s**) (*fam*) *nf* mum,
mummy

mamar [ma'mar] *vt, vi* to suck

mamarracho [mama'rratʃo] *nm*
sight, mess

mameluco [mame'luko] (RPL) nm
dungarees pl (BRIT), overalls pl (US)

mamífero [ma'mifero] nm mammal

mampara [mam'para] nf (entre
habitaciones) partition; (biombo) screen

mampostería [mamposte'ria] nf
masonry

manada [ma'naða] nf (Zool) herd;
(: de leones) pride; (: de lobos) pack

manantial [manan'tjal] nm spring

mancha ['mantʃa] nf stain, mark;
(Zool) patch; **manchar** vt (gen) to
stain, mark; (ensuciar) to soil, dirty

manchego, -a [man'tʃexo, a] adj of
o from La Mancha

manco, -a ['manko, a] adj (de un
brazo) one-armed; (de una mano) one-
handed; (fig) defective, faulty

mancuernas [man'kwernas] (MÉX)
nfpl cufflinks

mandado [man'daðo] (LAM) nm
errand

mandamiento [manda'mjento]
nm (orden) order, command; (Rel)
commandment

mandar [man'dar] vt (ordenar) to
order; (dirigir) to lead, command;
(enviar) to send; (pedir) to order, ask for
▷ vi to be in charge; (pey) to be bossy;
¿mande? (MÉX: ¿cómo dice?) pardon?,
excuse me?; **~ hacer un traje** to have
a suit made

mandarina [manda'rina] (ESP) nf
tangerine, mandarin (orange)

mandato [man'dato] nm (orden)
order; (Pol: período) term of office;
(: territorio) mandate

mandíbula [man'diβula] nf jaw

mandil [man'dil] nm apron

mando ['mando] nm (Mil) command;
(de país) rule; (el primer lugar) lead; (Pol)
term of office; (Tec) control; **~ a la
izquierda** left-hand drive; **mando a
distancia** remote control

mandón, -ona [man'don, ona] adj
bossy, domineering

manejar [mane'xar] vt to manage;
(máquina) to work, operate; (caballo
etc) to handle; (casa) to run, manage;
(LAM: coche) to drive; **manejarse**
vr (comportarse) to act, behave;
(arreglárselas) to manage; **manejo**
nm (de bicicleta) handling; (de negocio)
management, running; (LAM Auto)
driving; (facilidad de trato) ease,
confidence; **manejos** nmpl (intrigas)
intrigues

manera [ma'nera] nf way, manner,
fashion; **maneras** nfpl (modales)
manners; **su ~ de ser** the way he
is; (aire) his manner; **de ninguna
~** no way, by no means; **de otra ~**
otherwise; **de todas ~s** at any rate; **no
hay ~ de persuadirle** there's no way of
convincing him

manga ['manga] nf (de camisa) sleeve;
(de riego) hose

mango ['mango] nm handle; (Bot)
mango

manguera [man'gera] nf hose

maní [ma'ni] (LAM) nm peanut

manía [ma'nia] nf (Med) mania;
(fig: moda) rage, craze; (disgusto) dislike;
(malicia) spite; **coger ~ a algn** to take a
dislike to sb; **tener ~ a algn** to dislike
sb; **maníaco, -a** adj maniac(al) ▷ nm/f
maniac

maniático, -a [ma'njatiko, a] adj
maniac(al) ▷ nm/f maniac

manicomio [mani'komjo] nm
mental hospital (BRIT), insane asylum
(US)

manifestación [manifesta'θjon] nf
(declaración) statement, declaration;
(de emoción) show, display; (Pol: desfile)
demonstration; (: concentración) mass
meeting

manifestar [manifes'tar] vt to
show, manifest; (declarar) to state,
declare; **manifiesto, -a** adj clear,
manifest ▷ nm manifesto

manillar [mani'ʎar] nm handlebars pl

maniobra [ma'njoβra] nf
manoeuvre; **maniobras** nfpl (Mil)
manoeuvres; **maniobrar** vt to
manoeuvre

manipulación [manipula'θjon] *nf* manipulation

manipular [manipu'lar] *vt* to manipulate; (*manejar*) to handle

maniquí [mani'ki] *nm* dummy ▷ *nmf* model

manivela [mani'βela] *nf* crank

manjar [man'xar] *nm* (tasty) dish

mano ['mano] *nf* hand; (*Zool*) foot, paw; (*de pintura*) coat; (*serie*) lot, series; **a ~** by hand; **a ~ derecha/izquierda** on the right(-hand side)/left(-hand side); **de ~** (at) first hand; **de segunda ~** (at) second hand; **robo a ~ armada** armed robbery; **estrechar la ~ a algn** to shake sb's hand; **mano de obra** labour, manpower; **manos libres** *adj inv* (*teléfono, dispositivo*) hands-free ▷ *nm inv* hands-free kit

manojo [ma'noxo] *nm* handful, bunch; (*de llaves*) bunch

manopla [ma'nopla] *nf* mitten

manosear [manose'ar] *vt* (*tocar*) to handle, touch; (*desordenar*) to mess up, rumple; (*insistir en*) to overwork; (*LAM: acariciar*) to caress, fondle

manotazo [mano'taθo] *nm* slap, smack

mansalva [man'salβa]: **a ~** *adv* indiscriminately

mansión [man'sjon] *nf* mansion

manso, -a ['manso, a] *adj* gentle, mild; (*animal*) tame

manta ['manta] (*ESP*) *nf* blanket

manteca [man'teka] *nf* fat; (*cs: mantequilla*) butter; **manteca de cerdo** lard

mantecado [mante'kaðo] (*ESP*) *nm* Christmas sweet made from flour, almonds and lard

mantel [man'tel] *nm* tablecloth

mantendré *etc vb* V **mantener**

mantener [mante'ner] *vt* to support, maintain; (*alimentar*) to sustain; (*conservar*) to keep; (*Tec*) to maintain, service; **mantenerse** *vr* (*seguir de pie*) to be still standing; (*no ceder*) to hold one's ground;

(*subsistir*) to sustain o.s., keep going; **mantenimiento** *nm* maintenance; sustenance; (*sustento*) support

mantequilla [mante'kiʎa] *nf* butter

mantilla [man'tiʎa] *nf* mantilla; **mantillas** *nfpl* (*de bebé*) baby clothes

manto ['manto] *nm* (*capa*) cloak; (*de ceremonia*) robe, gown

mantuve *etc vb* V **mantener**

manual [ma'nwal] *adj* manual ▷ *nm* manual, handbook

manuscrito, -a [manus'krito, a] *adj* handwritten ▷ *nm* manuscript

manutención [manuten'θjon] *nf* maintenance; (*sustento*) support

manzana [man'θana] *nf* apple; (*Arq*) block (of houses)

manzanilla [manθa'niʎa] *nf* (*planta*) camomile; (*infusión*) camomile tea

manzano [man'θano] *nm* apple tree

maña ['maɲa] *nf* (*gen*) skill, dexterity; (*pey*) guile; (*destreza*) trick, knack

mañana [ma'ɲana] *adv* tomorrow ▷ *nm* future ▷ *nf* morning; **de** *o* **por la ~** in the morning; **¡hasta ~!** see you tomorrow!; **~ por la ~** tomorrow morning

mapa ['mapa] *nm* map

maple ['maple] (*LAM*) *nm* maple

maqueta [ma'keta] *nf* (scale) model

maquiladora [makila'ðora] (*MÉX*) *nf* (*Com*) bonded assembly plant

maquillaje [maki'ʎaxe] *nm* make-up; (*acto*) making up

maquillar [maki'ʎar] *vt* to make up; **maquillarse** *vr* to put on (some) make-up

máquina ['makina] *nf* machine; (*de tren*) locomotive, engine; (*Foto*) camera; (*fig*) machinery; **escrito a ~** typewritten; **máquina de coser** sewing machine; **máquina de escribir** typewriter; **máquina fotográfica** camera

maquinaria [maki'narja] *nf* (*máquinas*) machinery; (*mecanismo*) mechanism, works *pl*

maquinilla [maki'niʎa] (*ESP*) *nf*

(*tb*: **~ de afeitar**) razor

maquinista [maki'nista] *nmf* (*de tren*) engine driver; (*Tec*) operator; (*Náut*) engineer

mar [mar] *nm o f* sea; **~ adentro** out at sea; **en alta ~** on the high seas; **la ~ de** (*fam*) lots of; **el Mar Negro/Báltico** the Black/Baltic Sea

maraña [ma'raɲa] *nf* (*maleza*) thicket; (*confusión*) tangle

maravilla [mara'βiʎa] *nf* marvel, wonder; (*Bot*) marigold; **maravillar** *vt* to astonish, amaze; **maravillarse** *vr* to be astonished, be amazed; **maravilloso, -a** *adj* wonderful, marvellous

marca ['marka] *nf* (*gen*) mark; (*sello*) stamp; (*Com*) make, brand; **de ~** excellent, outstanding; **marca de fábrica** trademark; **marca registrada** registered trademark

marcado, -a [mar'kaðo, a] *adj* marked, strong

marcador [marka'ðor] *nm* (*Deporte*) scoreboard; (: *persona*) scorer

marcapasos [marka'pasos] *nm inv* pacemaker

marcar [mar'kar] *vt* (*gen*) to mark; (*número de teléfono*) to dial; (*gol*) to score; (*números*) to record, keep a tally of; (*pelo*) to set ▷ *vi* (*Deporte*) to score; (*Tel*) to dial

marcha ['martʃa] *nf* march; (*Tec*) running, working; (*Auto*) gear; (*velocidad*) speed; (*fig*) progress; (*dirección*) course; **poner en ~** to put into gear; (*fig*) to set in motion, get going; **dar ~ atrás** to reverse, put into reverse; **estar en ~** to be under way, be in motion

marchar [mar'tʃar] *vi* (*ir*) to go; (*funcionar*) to work, go; **marcharse** *vr* to go (away), leave

marchitar [martʃi'tar] *vt* to wither, dry up; **marchitarse** *vr* (*Bot*) to wither; (*fig*) to fade away; **marchito, -a** *adj* withered, faded; (*fig*) in decline

marciano, -a [mar'θjano, a] *adj,* *nm/f* Martian

marco ['marko] *nm* frame; (*moneda*) mark; (*fig*) framework

marea [ma'rea] *nf* tide; **marea negra** oil slick

marear [mare'ar] *vt* (*fig*) to annoy, upset; (*Med*): **~ a algn** to make sb feel sick; **marearse** *vr* (*tener náuseas*) to feel sick; (*desvanecerse*) to feel faint; (*aturdirse*) to feel dizzy; (*fam: emborracharse*) to get tipsy

maremoto [mare'moto] *nm* tidal wave

mareo [ma'reo] *nm* (*náusea*) sick feeling; (*en viaje*) travel sickness; (*aturdimiento*) dizziness; (*fam: lata*) nuisance

marfil [mar'fil] *nm* ivory

margarina [marɣa'rina] *nf* margarine

margarita [marɣa'rita] *nf* (*Bot*) daisy; (*Tip*) daisywheel

margen ['marxen] *nm* (*borde*) edge, border; (*fig*) margin, space ▷ *nf* (*de río etc*) bank; **dar ~ para** to give an opportunity for; **mantenerse al ~** to keep out (of things)

marginar [marxi'nar] *vt* (*socialmente*) to marginalize, ostracize

mariachi [ma'rjatʃi] *nm* (*persona*) mariachi musician; (*grupo*) mariachi band

MARIACHI

Mariachi music is the musical style most characteristic of Mexico. From the state of Jalisco in the 19th century, this music spread rapidly throughout the country, until each region had its own particular style of the Mariachi "sound". A Mariachi band can be made up of several singers, up to eight violins, two trumpets, guitars, a "vihuela" (an old form of guitar), and a harp. The dance associated with this music is called the "zapateado".

marica [ma'rika] (*fam*) *nm*
sissy

maricón [mari'kon] (*fam*) *nm*
queer

marido [ma'riðo] *nm* husband

marihuana [mari'wana] *nf*
marijuana, cannabis

marina [ma'rina] *nf* navy; **marina
mercante** merchant navy

marinero, -a [mari'nero, a] *adj* sea
cpd ▷ *nm* sailor, seaman

marino, -a [ma'rino, a] *adj* sea *cpd*,
marine ▷ *nm* sailor

marioneta [marjo'neta] *nf*
puppet

mariposa [mari'posa] *nf*
butterfly

mariquita [mari'kita] *nf* ladybird
(*BRIT*), ladybug (*US*)

marisco [ma'risko] (*ESP*) *nm* shellfish
inv, seafood; **mariscos** (*LAM*) *nmpl* =
marisco

marítimo, -a [ma'ritimo, a] *adj* sea
cpd, maritime

mármol ['marmol] *nm* marble

marqués, -esa [mar'kes, esa] *nm/f*
marquis/marchioness

marrón [ma'rron] *adj* brown

marroquí [marro'ki] *adj*, *nmf*
Moroccan ▷ *nm* Morocco (leather)

Marruecos [ma'rrwekos] *nm*
Morocco

martes ['martes] *nm inv* Tuesday; **~ y
trece** ≈ Friday 13th

martillo [mar'tiʎo] *nm* hammer

mártir ['martir] *nmf* martyr;
martirio *nm* martyrdom; (*fig*) torture,
torment

marxismo [mark'sismo] *nm*
Marxism

marzo ['marθo] *nm* March

○ **PALABRA CLAVE**

más [mas] *adj*, *adv* **1**: **más (que** *o* **de)**
(*compar*) more (than), ...+ er (than); **más
grande/inteligente** bigger/
more intelligent; **trabaja más (que
yo)** he works more (than me); *V tb* **cada**
2 (*superl*): **el más** the most, ...+ est; **el
más grande/inteligente (de)** the
biggest/most intelligent (in)
3 (*negativo*): **no tengo más dinero** I
haven't got any more money; **no viene
más por aquí** he doesn't come round
here any more
4 (*adicional*): **no le veo más solución
que ...** I see no other solution than to
...; **¿quién más?** anybody else?
5 (+ *adj*: *valor intensivo*): **¡qué perro
más sucio!** what a filthy dog!; **¡es más
tonto!** he's so stupid!
6 (*locuciones*): **más o menos** more or
less; **los más** most people; **es más**
furthermore; **más bien** rather;
¡qué más da! what does it matter!;
V tb **no**
7: **por más: por más que te esfuerces**
no matter how hard you try; **por más
que quisiera ...** much as I should
like to ...
8: **de más: veo que aquí estoy de más**
I can see I'm not needed here; **tenemos
uno de más** we've got one extra
▷ *prep*: **2 más 2 son 4** 2 and o plus 2 are 4
▷ *nm inv*: **este trabajo tiene sus más
y sus menos** this job's got its good
points and its bad points

mas [mas] *conj* but

masa ['masa] *nf* (*mezcla*) dough;
(*volumen*) volume, mass; (*Física*) mass;
en ~ en masse; **las ~s** (*Pol*) the masses

masacre [ma'sakre] *nf* massacre

masaje [ma'saxe] *nm* massage

máscara ['maskara] *nf* mask;
máscara antigás/de oxígeno
gas/oxygen mask; **mascarilla** *nf* (*de*

belleza, Med) mask

masculino, -a [masku'lino, a] *adj* masculine; (*Bio*) male

masía [ma'sia] *nf* farmhouse

masivo, -a [ma'siβo, a] *adj* mass *cpd*

masoquista [maso'kista] *nmf* masochist

máster ['master] (*ESP*) *nm* master

masticar [masti'kar] *vt* to chew

mástil ['mastil] *nm* (*de navío*) mast; (*de guitarra*) neck

mastín [mas'tin] *nm* mastiff

masturbarse [mastur'βarse] *vr* to masturbate

mata ['mata] *nf* (*arbusto*) bush, shrub; (*de hierba*) tuft

matadero [mata'ðero] *nm* slaughterhouse, abattoir

matamoscas [mata'moskas] *nm inv* (*pala*) fly swat

matanza [ma'tanθa] *nf* slaughter

matar [ma'tar] *vt, vi* to kill; **matarse** *vr* (*suicidarse*) to kill o.s., commit suicide; (*morir*) to be o get killed; **~ el hambre** to stave off hunger

matasellos [mata'seλos] *nm inv* postmark

mate ['mate] *adj* matt ▷ *nm* (*en ajedrez*) (check)mate; (*LAM: hierba*) maté; (: *vasija*) gourd

matemáticas [mate'matikas] *nfpl* mathematics; **matemático, -a** *adj* mathematical ▷ *nm/f* mathematician

materia [ma'terja] *nf* (*gen*) matter; (*Tec*) material; (*Escol*) subject; **en ~ de** on the subject of; **materia prima** raw material; **material** *adj* material ▷ *nm* material; (*Tec*) equipment; **materialista** *adj* materialist(ic); **materialmente** *adv* materially; (*fig*) absolutely

maternal [mater'nal] *adj* motherly, maternal

maternidad [materni'ðað] *nf* motherhood, maternity; **materno, -a** *adj* maternal; (*lengua*) mother *cpd*

matinal [mati'nal] *adj* morning *cpd*

matiz [ma'tiθ] *nm* shade; **matizar** *vt*

(*variar*) to vary; (*Arte*) to blend; **matizar de** to tinge with

matón [ma'ton] *nm* bully

matorral [mato'rral] *nm* thicket

matrícula [ma'trikula] *nf* (*registro*) register; (*Auto*) registration number; (: *placa*) number plate; **matrícula de honor** (*Univ*) top marks in a subject at university with the right to free registration the following year; **matricular** *vt* to register, enrol

matrimonio [matri'monjo] *nm* (*pareja*) (married) couple; (*unión*) marriage

matriz [ma'triθ] *nf* (*Anat*) womb; (*Tec*) mould

matrona [ma'trona] *nf* (*persona de edad*) matron; (*comadrona*) midwife

matufia [ma'tufja] (*RPL: fam*) *nf* put-up job

maullar [mau'λar] *vi* to mew, miaow

maxilar [maksi'lar] *nm* jaw(bone)

máxima ['maksima] *nf* maxim

máximo, -a ['maksimo, a] *adj* maximum; (*más alto*) highest; (*más grande*) greatest ▷ *nm* maximum; **como ~** at most

mayo ['majo] *nm* May

mayonesa [majo'nesa] *nf* mayonnaise

mayor [ma'jor] *adj* main, chief; (*adulto*) adult; (*de edad avanzada*) elderly; (*Mús*) major; (*compar: de tamaño*) bigger; (: *de edad*) older; (*superl: de tamaño*) biggest; (: *de edad*) oldest ▷ *nm* (*adulto*) adult; **mayores** *nmpl* (*antepasados*) ancestors; **al por ~** wholesale; **mayor de edad** adult

mayoral [majo'ral] *nm* foreman

mayordomo [major'ðomo] *nm* butler

mayoría [majo'ria] *nf* majority, greater part

mayorista [majo'rista] *nmf* wholesaler

mayoritario, -a [majori'tarjo, a] *adj* majority *cpd*

mayúscula [ma'juskula] *nf* capital

letter

mazapán [maθa'pan] *nm* marzipan

mazo ['maθo] *nm* (*martillo*) mallet; (*de flores*) bunch; (*Deporte*) bat

me [me] *pron* (*directo*) me; (*indirecto*) (to) me; (*reflexivo*) (to) myself; **¡dá~lo!** give it to me!

mear [me'ar] (*fam*) *vi* to pee, piss (!)

mecánica [me'kanika] *nf* (*Escol*) mechanics *sg*; (*mecanismo*) mechanism; *V tb* **mecánico**

mecánico, -a [me'kaniko, a] *adj* mechanical ▷ *nm/f* mechanic

mecanismo [meka'nismo] *nm* mechanism; (*marcha*) gear

mecanografía [mekanoɣra'fia] *nf* typewriting; **mecanógrafo, -a** *nm/f* typist

mecate [me'kate] (*MÉX, CAM*) *nm* rope

mecedora [meθe'ðora] *nf* rocking chair

mecer [me'θer] *vt* (*cuna*) to rock; **mecerse** *vr* to rock; (*rama*) to sway

mecha ['metʃa] *nf* (*de vela*) wick; (*de bomba*) fuse

mechero [me'tʃero] *nm* (cigarette) lighter

mechón [me'tʃon] *nm* (*gen*) tuft; (*de pelo*) lock

medalla [me'ðaʎa] *nf* medal

media ['meðja] *nf* stocking; (*LAM: calcetín*) sock; (*promedio*) average

mediado, -a [me'ðjaðo, a] *adj* half-full; (*trabajo*) half-completed; **a ~s de** in the middle of, halfway through

mediano, -a [me'ðjano, a] *adj* (*regular*) medium, average; (*mediocre*) mediocre

medianoche [meðja'notʃe] *nf* midnight

mediante [me'ðjante] *adv* by (means of), through

mediar [me'ðjar] *vi* (*interceder*) to mediate, intervene

medicamento [meðika'mento] *nm* medicine, drug

medicina [meði'θina] *nf* medicine

médico, -a ['meðiko, a] *adj* medical

▷ *nm/f* doctor

medida [me'ðiða] *nf* measure; (*medición*) measurement; (*prudencia*) moderation, prudence; **en cierta/ gran ~** up to a point/to a great extent; **un traje a la ~** a made-to-measure suit; **~ de cuello** collar size; **a ~ de** in proportion to; (*de acuerdo con*) in keeping with; **a ~ que** (*conforme*) as; **medidor** (*LAM*) *nm* meter

medio, -a ['meðjo, a] *adj* half (a); (*punto*) mid, middle; (*promedio*) average ▷ *adv* half ▷ *nm* (*centro*) middle, centre; (*promedio*) average; (*método*) means, way; (*ambiente*) environment; **medios** *nmpl* means, resources; **~ litro** half a litre; **las tres y media** half past three; **a ~ terminar** half finished; **pagar a medias** to share the cost; **medio ambiente** environment; **medio de transporte** means of transport; **Medio Oriente** Middle East; **medios de comunicación** media; **medioambiental** *adj* (*política, efectos*) environmental

mediocre [me'ðjokre] *adj* mediocre

mediodía [meðjo'ðia] *nm* midday, noon

medir [me'ðir] *vt, vi* (*gen*) to measure

meditar [meði'tar] *vt* to ponder, think over, meditate on; (*planear*) to think out

mediterráneo, -a [meðite'rraneo, a] *adj* Mediterranean ▷ *nm*: **el M~** the Mediterranean

médula ['meðula] *nf* (*Anat*) marrow; **médula espinal** spinal cord

medusa [me'ðusa] (*ESP*) *nf* jellyfish

megáfono [me'ɣafono] *nm* megaphone

megapíxel [meɣa'piksel] (*pl* **megapixels** *or* **~es**) *nm* megapixel

mejilla [me'xiʎa] *nf* cheek

mejillón [mexi'ʎon] *nm* mussel

mejor [me'xor] *adj, adv* (*compar*) better; (*superl*) best; **a lo ~** probably; (*quizá*) maybe; **~ dicho** rather; **tanto ~**

so much the better

mejora [me'xora] *nf* improvement;
mejorar *vt* to improve, make better
▷ *vi* to improve, get better; **mejorarse**
vr to improve, get better

melancólico, -a [melan'koliko, a]
adj (*triste*) sad, melancholy; (*soñador*)
dreamy

melena [me'lena] *nf* (*de persona*) long
hair; (*Zool*) mane

mellizo, -a [me'ʎiθo, a] *adj*, *nm/f*
twin

melocotón [meloko'ton] (*ESP*) *nm*
peach

melodía [melo'ðia] *nf* melody, tune

melodrama [melo'ðrama] *nm*
melodrama; **melodramático, -a** *adj*
melodramatic

melón [me'lon] *nm* melon

membrete [mem'brete] *nm*
letterhead

membrillo [mem'briʎo] *nm* quince;
(carne de) ~ quince jelly

memoria [me'morja] *nf* (*gen*)
memory; **memorias** *nfpl* (*de autor*)
memoirs; **memorizar** *vt* to memorize

menaje [me'naxe] *nm* (*tb*: **artículos
de ~**) household items

mencionar [menθjo'nar] *vt* to
mention

mendigo, -a [men'diɣo, a] *nm/f*
beggar

menear [mene'ar] *vt* to move;
menearse *vr* to shake; (*balancearse*)
to sway; (*moverse*) to move; (*fig*) to get
a move on

menestra [me'nestra] *nf* (*tb*: **~ de
verduras**) vegetable stew

menopausia [meno'pausja] *nf*
menopause

menor [me'nor] *adj* (*más
pequeño*: *compar*) smaller; (: *superl*)
smallest; (*más joven*: *compar*) younger;
(: *superl*) youngest; (*Mús*) minor ▷ *nmf*
(*joven*) young person, juvenile; **no
tengo la ~ idea** I haven't the faintest
idea; **al por ~** retail; **menor de edad**
person under age

Menorca [me'norka] *nf* Minorca

○ **PALABRA CLAVE**

menos [menos] *adj* **1**: **menos
(que** *o* **de)** (*compar*: *cantidad*) less
(than); (: *número*) fewer (than);
con menos entusiasmo with less
enthusiasm; **menos gente** fewer
people; V *tb* **cada**
2 (*superl*): **es el que menos culpa tiene**
he is the least to blame
▷ *adv* **1** (*compar*): **menos (que** *o* **de)** less
(than); **me gusta menos que el otro** I
like it less than the other one
2 (*superl*): **es el menos listo (de su
clase)** he's the least bright in his class;
**de todas ellas es la que menos me
agrada** out of all of them she's the one
I like least
3 (*locuciones*): **no quiero verle y menos
visitarle** I don't want to see him, let
alone visit him; **tenemos siete de
menos** we're seven short; **(por) lo
menos** at (the very) least; **¡menos mal!**
thank goodness!
▷ *prep* except; (*cifras*) minus; **todos
menos él** everyone except (for) him;
5 menos 2 5 minus 2
▷ *conj*: **a menos que: a menos que
venga mañana** unless he comes
tomorrow

menospreciar [menospre'θjar] *vt*
to underrate, undervalue; (*despreciar*)
to scorn, despise

mensaje [men'saxe] *nm* message;
enviar un ~ a algn (*por móvil*) to text
sb, send sb a text message; **mensaje
de texto** text message; **mensajero, -a**
nm/f messenger

menso, -a ['menso, a] (*MÉX*: *fam*)
adj stupid

menstruación [menstrua'θjon] *nf*
menstruation

mensual [men'swal] *adj* monthly;
100 euros ~es 100 euros a month;
mensualidad *nf* (*salario*) monthly

salary; (*Com*) monthly payment,
monthly instalment
menta ['menta] *nf* mint
mental [men'tal] *adj* mental;
mentalidad *nf* mentality; **mentalizar**
vt (*sensibilizar*) to make aware;
(*convencer*) to convince; (*padres*) to
prepare (mentally); **mentalizarse**
vr (*concienciarse*) to become aware;
mentalizarse (de) to get used to the
idea (of); **mentalizarse de que ...**
(*convencerse*) to get it into one's head
that ...
mente ['mente] *nf* mind
mentir [men'tir] *vi* to lie
mentira [men'tira] *nf* (*una mentira*)
lie; (*acto*) lying; (*invención*) fiction;
parece mentira que ... it seems
incredible that ..., I can't believe that
...; **mentiroso, -a** [menti'roso, a] *adj*
lying ▷ *nm/f* liar
menú [me'nu] (*pl* **~s**) *nm* menu;
menú del día set menu; **menú
turístico** tourist menu
menudencias [menu'ðenθjas] (*LAM*)
nfpl giblets
menudo, -a [me'nuðo, a] *adj*
(*pequeño*) small, tiny; (*sin importancia*)
petty, insignificant; **¡~ negocio!** (*fam*)
some deal!; **a ~** often, frequently
meñique [me'ɲike] *nm* little finger
mercadillo [merka'ðiʎo] (*ESP*) *nm*
flea market
mercado [mer'kaðo] *nm* market;
mercado de pulgas (*LAM*) flea market
mercancía [merkan'θia] *nf*
commodity; **mercancías** *nfpl* goods,
merchandise *sg*
mercenario, -a [merθe'narjo, a]
adj, *nm* mercenary
mercería [merθe'ria] *nf*
haberdashery (*BRIT*), notions *pl* (*US*);
(*tienda*) haberdasher's (*BRIT*), notions
store (*US*)
mercurio [mer'kurjo] *nm* mercury
merecer [mere'θer] *vt* to deserve,
merit ▷ *vi* to be deserving, be worthy;
merece la pena it's worthwhile;

merecido, -a *adj* (well) deserved;
llevar su merecido to get one's deserts
merendar [meren'dar] *vt* to have
for tea ▷ *vi* to have tea; (*en el campo*)
to have a picnic; **merendero** *nm*
open-air cafe
merengue [me'renge] *nm* meringue
meridiano [meri'ðjano] *nm* (*Geo*)
meridian
merienda [me'rjenda] *nf* (light) tea,
afternoon snack; (*de campo*) picnic
mérito ['merito] *nm* merit; (*valor*)
worth, value
merluza [mer'luθa] *nf* hake
mermelada [merme'laða] *nf* jam
mero, -a ['mero, a] *adj* mere; (*MÉX,
CAM*: *fam*) very
merodear [meroðe'ar] *vi*: **~ por** to
prowl about
mes [mes] *nm* month
mesa ['mesa] *nf* table; (*de trabajo*)
desk; (*Geo*) plateau; **poner/quitar la ~**
to lay/clear the table; **mesa electoral**
officials in charge of a polling station;
mesa redonda (*reunión*) round table;
mesero, -a (*LAM*) *nm/f* waiter/
waitress
meseta [me'seta] *nf* (*Geo*) plateau,
tableland
mesilla [me'siʎa] *nf* (*tb*: **~ de noche**)
bedside table
mesón [me'son] *nm* inn
mestizo, -a [mes'tiθo, a] *adj* half-
caste, of mixed race ▷ *nm/f* half-caste
meta ['meta] *nf* goal; (*de carrera*)
finish
metabolismo [metaβo'lismo] *nm*
metabolism
metáfora [me'tafora] *nf* metaphor
metal [me'tal] *nm* (*materia*) metal;
(*Mús*) brass; **metálico, -a** *adj* metallic;
(*de metal*) metal ▷ *nm* (*dinero contante*)
cash
meteorología [meteorolo'xia] *nf*
meteorology
meter [me'ter] *vt* (*colocar*) to put,
place; (*introducir*) to put in, insert;
(*involucrar*) to involve; (*causar*) to make,

cause; **meterse** *vr*: **~se en** to go into, enter; (*fig*) to interfere in, meddle in; **~se a** to start; **~se a escritor** to become a writer; **~se con uno** to provoke sb, pick a quarrel with sb

meticuloso, -a [metiku'loso, a] *adj* meticulous, thorough

metódico, -a [me'toðiko, a] *adj* methodical

método ['metoðo] *nm* method

metralleta [metra'ʎeta] *nf* sub-machine-gun

métrico, -a ['metriko, a] *adj* metric

metro ['metro] *nm* metre; (*tren*) underground (BRIT), subway (US)

metrosexual [metrosek'swal] *adj*, *nm* metrosexual

mexicano, -a [mexi'kano, a] *adj*, *nm/f* Mexican

México ['mexiko] *nm* Mexico; **Ciudad de ~** Mexico City

mezcla ['meθkla] *nf* mixture; **mezcladora** (*MÉX*) *nf* (*tb*: **mezcladora de cemento**) cement mixer; **mezclar** *vt* to mix (up); **mezclarse** *vr* to mix, mingle; **mezclarse en** to get mixed up in, get involved in

mezquino, -a [meθ'kino, a] *adj* mean

mezquita [meθ'kita] *nf* mosque

mg. *abr* (= *miligramo*) mg

mi [mi] *adj pos* my ▷ *nm* (*Mús*) E

mí [mi] *pron* me; myself

mía *pron* V **mío**

michelín [mitʃe'lin] (*fam*) *nm* (*de grasa*) spare tyre

microbio [mi'kroβjo] *nm* microbe

micrófono [mi'krofono] *nm* microphone

microondas [mikro'ondas] *nm inv* (*tb*: **horno ~**) microwave (oven)

microscopio [mikro'skopjo] *nm* microscope

miedo ['mjeðo] *nm* fear; (*nerviosismo*) apprehension, nervousness; **tener ~** to be afraid; **de ~** wonderful, marvellous; **hace un frío de ~** (*fam*) it's terribly cold; **miedoso, -a** *adj* fearful, timid

miel [mjel] *nf* honey

miembro ['mjembro] *nm* limb; (*socio*) member; **miembro viril** penis

mientras ['mjentras] *conj* while; (*duración*) as long as ▷ *adv* meanwhile; **~ tanto** meanwhile

miércoles ['mjerkoles] *nm inv* Wednesday

mierda ['mjerða] (*fam!*) *nf* shit (!)

miga ['mixa] *nf* crumb; (*fig: meollo*) essence; **hacer buenas ~s** (*fam*) to get on well

mil [mil] *num* thousand; **dos ~ libras** two thousand pounds

milagro [mi'laxro] *nm* miracle; **milagroso, -a** *adj* miraculous

milésima [mi'lesima] *nf* (*de segundo*) thousandth

mili ['mili] (*ESP: fam*) *nf*: **hacer la ~** to do one's military service

milímetro [mi'limetro] *nm* millimetre

militante [mili'tante] *adj* militant

militar [mili'tar] *adj* military ▷ *nmf* soldier ▷ *vi* (*Mil*) to serve; (*en un partido*) to be a member

milla ['miʎa] *nf* mile

millar [mi'ʎar] *nm* thousand

millón [mi'ʎon] *num* million; **millonario, -a** *nm/f* millionaire

milusos [mi'lusos] (*MÉX*) *nm inv* odd-job man

mimar [mi'mar] *vt* to spoil, pamper

mimbre ['mimbre] *nm* wicker

mímica ['mimika] *nf* (*para comunicarse*) sign language; (*imitación*) mimicry

mimo ['mimo] *nm* (*caricia*) caress; (*de niño*) spoiling; (*Teatro*) mime; (: *actor*) mime artist

mina ['mina] *nf* mine

mineral [mine'ral] *adj* mineral ▷ *nm* (*Geo*) mineral; (*mena*) ore

minero, -a [mi'nero, a] *adj* mining *cpd* ▷ *nm/f* miner

miniatura [minja'tura] *adj inv*, *nf* miniature

minidisco [mini'disko] *nm*

MiniDisc®

minifalda [mini'falda] nf miniskirt

mínimo, -a ['minimo, a] adj, nm minimum

minino, -a [mi'nino, a] (fam) nm/f puss, pussy

ministerio [minis'terjo] nm Ministry; **Ministerio de Hacienda/de Asuntos Exteriores** Treasury (BRIT), Treasury Department (US)/Foreign Office (BRIT), State Department (US)

ministro, -a [mi'nistro, a] nm/f minister

minoría [mino'ria] nf minority

minúscula [mi'nuskula] nf small letter

minúsculo, -a [mi'nuskulo, a] adj tiny, minute

minusválido, -a [minus'βaliðo, a] adj (physically) handicapped ▷ nm/f (physically) handicapped person

minuta [mi'nuta] nf (de comida) menu

minutero [minu'tero] nm minute hand

minuto [mi'nuto] nm minute

mío, -a ['mio, a] pron: **el ~/la mía** mine; **un amigo ~** a friend of mine; **lo ~** what is mine

miope [mi'ope] adj short-sighted

mira ['mira] nf (de arma) sight(s) (pl); (fig) aim, intention

mirada [mi'raða] nf look, glance; (expresión) look, expression; **clavar la ~ en** to stare at; **echar una ~ a** to glance at

mirado, -a [mi'raðo, a] adj (sensato) sensible; (considerado) considerate; **bien/mal ~** (estimado) well/not well thought of; **bien ~ ...** all things considered ...

mirador [mira'ðor] nm viewpoint, vantage point

mirar [mi'rar] vt to look at; (observar) to watch; (considerar) to consider, think over; (vigilar, cuidar) to watch, look after ▷ vi to look; (Arq) to face; **mirarse** vr (dos personas) to look at each other; **~**

bien/mal to think highly of/have a poor opinion of; **~se al espejo** to look at o.s. in the mirror

mirilla [mi'riʎa] nf spyhole, peephole

mirlo ['mirlo] nm blackbird

misa ['misa] nf mass

miserable [mise'raβle] adj (avaro) mean, stingy; (nimio) miserable, paltry; (lugar) squalid; (fam) vile, despicable ▷ nmf (malvado) rogue

miseria [mi'serja] nf (pobreza) poverty; (tacañería) meanness, stinginess; (condiciones) squalor; **una ~** a pittance

misericordia [miseri'korðja] nf (compasión) compassion, pity; (piedad) mercy

misil [mi'sil] nm missile

misión [mi'sjon] nf mission; **misionero, -a** nm/f missionary

mismo, -a ['mismo, a] adj (semejante) same; (después de pron) -self; (para énfasis) very ▷ adv: **aquí/hoy ~** right here/this very day; **ahora ~** right now ▷ conj: **lo ~ que** just like o as; **el ~ traje** the same suit; **en ese ~ momento** at that very moment; **vino el ~ ministro** the minister himself came; **yo ~ lo vi** I saw it myself; **lo ~** the same (thing); **da lo ~** it's all the same; **quedamos en las mismas** we're no further forward; **por lo ~** for the same reason

misterio [mis'terjo] nm mystery; **misterioso, -a** adj mysterious

mitad [mi'tað] nf (medio) half; (centro) middle; **a ~ de precio** (at) half-price; **en o a ~ del camino** halfway along the road; **cortar por la ~** to cut through the middle

mitin ['mitin] (pl **mítines**) nm meeting

mito ['mito] nm myth

mixto, -a ['miksto, a] adj mixed

ml. abr (= mililitro) ml

mm. abr (= milímetro) mm

mobiliario [moβi'ljarjo] nm furniture

mochila [mo'tʃila] nf rucksack (BRIT), back-pack

moco ['moko] nm mucus; **mocos** nmpl (fam) snot; **limpiarse los ~s de la nariz** (fam) to wipe one's nose

moda ['moða] nf fashion; (estilo) style; **a la o de ~** in fashion, fashionable; **pasado de ~** out of fashion

modales [mo'ðales] nmpl manners

modelar [moðe'lar] vt to model

modelo [mo'ðelo] adj inv, nmf model

módem ['moðem] nm (Inform) modem

moderado, -a [moðe'raðo, a] adj moderate

moderar [moðe'rar] vt to moderate; (violencia) to restrain, control; (velocidad) to reduce; **moderarse** vr to restrain o.s., control o.s.

modernizar [moðerni'θar] vt to modernize

moderno, -a [mo'ðerno, a] adj modern; (actual) present-day

modestia [mo'ðestja] nf modesty; **modesto, -a** adj modest

modificar [moðifi'kar] vt to modify

modisto, -a [mo'ðisto, a] nm/f (diseñador) couturier, designer; (que confecciona) dressmaker

modo ['moðo] nm way, manner; (Mús) mode; **modos** nmpl manners; **de ningún ~** in no way; **de todos ~s** at any rate; **modo de empleo** directions pl (for use)

mofarse [mo'farse] vr: **~ de** to mock, scoff at

mofle ['mofle] (MÉX, CAM) nm silencer (BRIT), muffler (US)

mogollón [moɣo'ʎon] (ESP: fam) adv a hell of a lot

moho ['moo] nm mould, mildew; (en metal) rust

mojar [mo'xar] vt to wet; (humedecer) to damp(en), moisten; (calar) to soak; **mojarse** vr to get wet

molcajete [molka'xete] (MÉX) nm mortar

molde ['molde] nm mould; (Costura)

pattern; (fig) model; **moldeado** nm soft perm; **moldear** vt to mould

mole ['mole] nf mass, bulk; (edificio) pile

moler [mo'ler] vt to grind, crush

molestar [moles'tar] vt to bother; (fastidiar) to annoy; (incomodar) to inconvenience, put out ▷ vi to be a nuisance; **molestarse** vr to bother; (incomodarse) to go to trouble; (ofenderse) to take offence; **¿(no) te molesta si ...?** do you mind if ...?

▌ No confundir **molestar** con la palabra inglesa molest.

molestia [mo'lestja] nf bother, trouble; (incomodidad) inconvenience; (Med) discomfort; **es una ~** it's a nuisance; **molesto, -a** adj (que fastidia) annoying; (incómodo) inconvenient; (inquieto) uncomfortable, ill at ease; (enfadado) annoyed

molido, -a [mo'liðo, a] adj: **estar ~** (fig) to be exhausted o dead beat

molinillo [moli'niʎo] nm hand mill; **molinillo de café** coffee grinder

molino [mo'lino] nm (edificio) mill; (máquina) grinder

momentáneo, -a [momen'taneo, a] adj momentary

momento [mo'mento] nm moment; **de ~** at o for the moment

momia ['momja] nf mummy

monarca [mo'narka] nmf monarch, ruler; **monarquía** nf monarchy

monasterio [monas'terjo] nm monastery

mondar [mon'dar] vt to peel; **mondarse** vr (ESP): **~se de risa** (fam) to split one's sides laughing

mondongo [mon'dongo] (LAM) nm tripe

moneda [mo'neða] nf (tipo de dinero) currency, money; (pieza) coin; **una ~ de 2 euros** a 2 euro piece; **monedero** nm purse

monitor, a [moni'tor, a] nm/f instructor, coach ▷ nm (TV) set; (Inform) monitor

monja ['monxa] nf nun

monje ['monxe] nm monk

mono, -a ['mono, a] adj (bonito) lovely, pretty; (gracioso) nice, charming ▷ nm/f monkey, ape ▷ nm dungarees pl; (overoles) overalls pl

monopatín [monopa'tin] nm skateboard

monopolio [mono'poljo] nm monopoly; **monopolizar** vt to monopolize

monótono, -a [mo'notono, a] adj monotonous

monstruo ['monstrwo] nm monster ▷ adj inv fantastic; **monstruoso, -a** adj monstrous

montaje [mon'taxe] nm assembly; (Teatro) décor; (Cine) montage

montaña [mon'taɲa] nf (monte) mountain; (sierra) mountains pl, mountainous area; **montaña rusa** roller coaster; **montañero, -a** nm/f mountaineer; **montañismo** nm mountaineering

montar [mon'tar] vt (subir a) to mount, get on; (Tec) to assemble, put together; (negocio) to set up; (arma) to cock; (colocar) to lift on to; (Culin) to beat ▷ vi to mount, get on; (sobresalir) to overlap; **~ en bicicleta** to ride a bicycle; **~ en cólera** to get angry; **~ a caballo** to ride, go horseriding

monte ['monte] nm (montaña) mountain; (bosque) woodland; (área sin cultivar) wild area, wild country; **monte de piedad** pawnshop

montón [mon'ton] nm heap, pile; (fig) **un ~ de** heaps o lots of

monumento [monu'mento] nm monument

moño ['moɲo] nm bun

moqueta [mo'keta] nf fitted carpet

mora ['mora] nf blackberry; V tb **moro**

morado, -a [mo'raðo, a] adj purple, violet ▷ nm bruise

moral [mo'ral] adj moral ▷ nf (ética) ethics pl; (moralidad) morals pl,

morality; (ánimo) morale

moraleja [mora'lexa] nf moral

morboso, -a [mor'βoso, a] adj morbid

morcilla [mor'θiʎa] nf blood sausage ≈ black pudding (BRIT)

mordaza [mor'ðaθa] nf (para la boca) gag; (Tec) clamp

morder [mor'ðer] vt to bite; (fig: consumir) to eat away, eat into; **mordisco** nm bite

moreno, -a [mo'reno, a] adj (color) (dark) brown; (de tez) dark; (de pelo moreno) dark-haired; (negro) black

morfina [mor'fina] nf morphine

moribundo, -a [mori'βundo, a] adj dying

morir [mo'rir] vi to die; (fuego) to die down; (luz) to go out; **morirse** vr to die; (fig) to be dying; **murió en un accidente** he was killed in an accident; **~se por algo** to be dying for sth

moro, -a ['moro, a] adj Moorish ▷ nm/f Moor

moroso, -a [mo'roso, a] nm/f bad debtor, defaulter

morraña [mo'rraɲa] (MÉX) nf (cambio) small o loose change

morro ['morro] nm (Zool) snout, nose; (Auto, Aviac) nose

morsa ['morsa] nf walrus

mortadela [morta'ðela] nf mortadella

mortal [mor'tal] adj mortal; (golpe) deadly; **mortalidad** nf mortality

mortero [mor'tero] nm mortar

mosca ['moska] nf fly

Moscú [mos'ku] n Moscow

mosquearse [moske'arse] (fam) vr (enojarse) to get cross; (ofenderse) to take offence

mosquitero [moski'tero] nm mosquito net

mosquito [mos'kito] nm mosquito

mostaza [mos'taθa] nf mustard

mosto ['mosto] nm (unfermented)

grape juice

mostrador [mostra'ðor] *nm* (*de tienda*) counter; (*de café*) bar

mostrar [mos'trar] *vt* to show; (*exhibir*) to display, exhibit; (*explicar*) to explain; **mostrarse** *vr*: **~se amable** to be kind; to prove to be kind; **no se muestra muy inteligente** he doesn't seem (to be) very intelligent

mota ['mota] *nf* speck, tiny piece; (*en diseño*) dot

mote ['mote] *nm* nickname

motín [mo'tin] *nm* (*del pueblo*) revolt, rising; (*del ejército*) mutiny

motivar [moti'βar] *vt* (*causar*) to cause, motivate; (*explicar*) to explain, justify; **motivo** *nm* motive, reason

moto ['moto] (*fam*) *nf* = **motocicleta**

motocicleta [motoθi'kleta] *nf* motorbike (BRIT), motorcycle

motoneta [moto'neta] (CS) *nf* scooter

motor [mo'tor] *nm* motor, engine; **motor a chorro** *o* **de reacción/de explosión** jet engine/internal combustion engine

motora [mo'tora] *nf* motorboat

movedizo, -a *adj* V **arena**

mover [mo'βer] *vt* to move; (*cabeza*) to shake; (*accionar*) to drive; (*fig*) to cause, provoke; **moverse** *vr* to move; (*fig*) to get a move on

móvil ['moβil] *adj* mobile; (*pieza de máquina*) moving; (*mueble*) movable ▷ *nm* (*motivo*) motive; (*teléfono*) mobile

movimiento [moβi'mjento] *nm* movement; (*Tec*) motion; (*actividad*) activity

mozo, -a ['moθo, a] *adj* (*joven*) young ▷ *nm/f* (*joven*) youth, young man/girl; (CS: *mesero*) waiter/waitress

MP3 *nm* MP3; **reproductor (de) ~** MP3 player

mucama [mu'kama] (RPL) *nf* maid

muchacho, -a [mu'tʃatʃo, a] *nm/f* (*niño*) boy/girl; (*criado*) servant; (*criada*)

maid

muchedumbre [mutʃe'ðumbre] *nf* crowd

○ **PALABRA CLAVE**

mucho, -a ['mutʃo, a] *adj* **1** (*cantidad*) a lot of, much; (*número*) lots of, a lot of, many; **mucho dinero** a lot of money; **hace mucho calor** it's very hot; **muchas amigas** lots *o* a lot of friends **2** (*sg: grande*): **ésta es mucha casa para él** this house is much too big for him

▷ *pron*: **tengo mucho que hacer** I've got a lot to do; **muchos dicen que ...** a lot of people say that ...; V *tb* **tener**

▷ *adv* **1** **me gusta mucho** I like it a lot; **lo siento mucho** I'm very sorry; **come mucho** he eats a lot; **¿te vas a quedar mucho?** are you going to be staying long?

2 (*respuesta*) very; **¿estás cansado? – ¡mucho!** are you tired? – very!

3 (*locuciones*): **como mucho** at (the) most; **con mucho: el mejor con mucho** by far the best; **ni mucho menos: no es rico ni mucho menos** he's far from being rich

4: **por mucho que: por mucho que le creas** no matter how *o* however much you believe her

muda ['muða] *nf* change of clothes

mudanza [mu'ðanθa] *nf* (*de casa*) move

mudar [mu'ðar] *vt* to change; (*Zool*) to shed ▷ *vi* to change; **mudarse** *vr* (*ropa*) to change; **~se de casa** to move house

mudo, -a ['muðo, a] *adj* dumb; (*callado, Cine*) silent

mueble ['mweβle] *nm* piece of furniture; **muebles** *nmpl* furniture *sg*

mueca ['mweka] *nf* face, grimace; **hacer ~s a** to make faces at

muela ['mwela] *nf* back tooth; **muela del juicio** wisdom tooth

muelle ['mweʎe] *nm* spring; (*Náut*)
wharf; (*malecón*) pier

muero *etc vb* V **morir**

muerte ['mwerte] *nf* death;
(*homicidio*) murder; **dar ~ a** to kill

muerto, -a ['mwerto, a] *pp de* **morir**
▷ *adj* dead ▷ *nm/f* dead man/woman;
(*difunto*) deceased; (*cadáver*) corpse;
estar ~ de cansancio to be dead tired;
Día de los Muertos (*MÉX*) All Souls' Day

> **DÍA DE LOS MUERTOS**
>
> All Souls' Day (or "Day of the Dead")
> in Mexico coincides with All
> Saints' Day, which is celebrated
> in the Catholic countries of Latin
> America on November 1st and
> 2nd. All Souls' Day is actually
> a celebration which begins
> in the evening of October 31st
> and continues until November
> 2nd. It is a combination of the
> Catholic tradition of honouring
> the Christian saints and martyrs,
> and the ancient Mexican or Aztec
> traditions, in which death was not
> something sinister. For this reason
> all the dead are honoured by
> bringing offerings of food, flowers
> and candles to the cemetery.

muestra ['mwestra] *nf* (*señal*)
indication, sign; (*demostración*)
demonstration; (*prueba*) proof;
(*estadística*) sample; (*modelo*) model,
pattern; (*testimonio*) token

muestro *etc vb* V **mostrar**

muevo *etc vb* V **mover**

mugir [mu'xir] *vi* (*vaca*) to moo

mugre ['muxre] *nf* dirt, filth

mujer [mu'xer] *nf* woman; (*esposa*)
wife; **mujeriego** *nm* womanizer

mula ['mula] *nf* mule

muleta [mu'leta] *nf* (*para andar*)
crutch; (*Taur*) stick with red cape attached

multa ['multa] *nf* fine; **poner una ~ a**
to fine; **multar** *vt* to fine

multicines [multi'θines] *nmpl*
multiscreen cinema *sg*

multinacional [multinaθjo'nal] *nf*
multinational

múltiple ['multiple] *adj* multiple; (*pl*)
many, numerous

multiplicar [multipli'kar] *vt*
(*Mat*) to multiply; (*fig*) to increase;
multiplicarse *vr* (*Bio*) to multiply; (*fig*)
to be everywhere at once

multitud [multi'tuð] *nf*
(*muchedumbre*) crowd; **~ de** lots of

mundial [mun'djal] *adj* world-wide,
universal; (*guerra, récord*) world *cpd*

mundo ['mundo] *nm* world; **todo el ~**
everybody; **tener ~** to be experienced,
know one's way around

munición [muni'θjon] *nf*
ammunition

municipal [muniθi'pal] *adj*
municipal, local

municipio [muni'θipjo] *nm*
(*ayuntamiento*) town council,
corporation; (*territorio administrativo*)
town, municipality

muñeca [mu'ɲeka] *nf* (*Anat*) wrist;
(*juguete*) doll

muñeco [mu'ɲeko] *nm* (*figura*)
figure; (*marioneta*) puppet; (*fig*) puppet,
pawn

mural [mu'ral] *adj* mural, wall *cpd*
▷ *nm* mural

muralla [mu'raʎa] *nf* (city) wall(s)
(*pl*)

murciélago [mur'θjelaxo] *nm* bat

murmullo [mur'muʎo] *nm*
murmur(ing); (*cuchicheo*) whispering

murmurar [murmu'rar] *vi* to
murmur, whisper; (*cotillear*) to gossip

muro ['muro] *nm* wall

muscular [musku'lar] *adj* muscular

músculo ['muskulo] *nm* muscle

museo [mu'seo] *nm* museum; **museo
de arte** art gallery

musgo ['musxo] *nm* moss

música ['musika] *nf* music; V *tb*
músico

músico, -a ['musiko, a] *adj* musical

▷ *nm/f* musician

muslo ['muslo] *nm* thigh

musulmán, -ana [musul'man, ana] *nm/f* Moslem

mutación [muta'θjon] *nf* (*Bio*) mutation; (*cambio*) (sudden) change

mutilar [muti'lar] *vt* to mutilate; (*a una persona*) to maim

mutuo, -a ['mutwo, a] *adj* mutual

muy [mwi] *adv* very; (*demasiado*) too; **M~ Señor mío** Dear Sir; **~ de noche** very late at night; **eso es ~ de él** that's just like him

N *abr* (= *norte*) N

nabo ['naβo] *nm* turnip

nacer [na'θer] *vi* to be born; (*de huevo*) to hatch; (*vegetal*) to sprout; (*río*) to rise; **nací en Barcelona** I was born in Barcelona; **nacido, -a** *adj* born; **recién nacido** newborn; **nacimiento** *nm* birth; (*de Navidad*) Nativity; (*de río*) source

nación [na'θjon] *nf* nation; **nacional** *adj* national; **nacionalismo** *nm* nationalism

nada ['naða] *pron* nothing ▷ *adv* not at all, in no way; **no decir ~** to say nothing, not to say anything; **~ más** nothing else; **de ~** don't mention it

nadador, a [naða'ðor, a] *nm/f* swimmer

nadar [na'ðar] *vi* to swim

nadie ['naðje] *pron* nobody, no-one; **~ habló** nobody spoke; **no había ~** there was nobody there, there wasn't anybody there

nado ['naðo] **a nado**: *adv*: **pasar a ~** to swim across

nafta ['nafta] (RPL) nf petrol (BRIT),
gas (US)

naipe ['naipe] nm (playing) card;
naipes nmpl cards

nalgas ['nalɣas] nfpl buttocks

nalguear [nalɣe'ar] (MÉX, CAM) vt
to spank

nana ['nana] (ESP) nf lullaby

naranja [na'ranxa] adj inv, nf orange;
media ~ (fam) better half; **naranjada**
nf orangeade; **naranjo** nm orange
tree

narciso [nar'θiso] nm narcissus

narcótico, -a [nar'kotiko, a] adj,
nm narcotic; **narcotizar** vt to drug;
narcotráfico nm drug trafficking
o running

nariz [na'riθ] nf nose; **nariz chata/
respingona** snub/turned-up nose

narración [narra'θjon] nf narration

narrar [na'rrar] vt to narrate,
recount; **narrativa** nf narrative

nata ['nata] nf cream; **nata montada**
whipped cream

natación [nata'θjon] nf swimming

natal [na'tal] adj: **ciudad ~** home
town; **natalidad** nf birth rate

natillas [na'tiʎas] nfpl custard sg

nativo, -a [na'tiβo, a] adj, nm/f
native

natural [natu'ral] adj natural;
(fruta etc) fresh ▷ nmf native ▷ nm
(disposición) nature

naturaleza [natura'leθa] nf nature;
(género) nature, kind; **naturaleza
muerta** still life

naturalmente [natural'mente] adv
(de modo natural) in a natural way; **¡~!**
of course!

naufragar [naufra'ɣar] vi to sink;
naufragio nm shipwreck

nauseabundo, -a [nausea'βundo,
a] adj nauseating, sickening

náuseas ['nauseas] nfpl nausea sg;
me da ~ it makes me feel sick

náutico, -a ['nautiko, a] adj
nautical

navaja [na'βaxa] nf knife; (de barbero,

peluquero) razor

naval [na'βal] adj naval

Navarra [na'βarra] n Navarre

nave ['naβe] nf (barco) ship, vessel;
(Arq) nave; **nave espacial** spaceship;
nave industrial factory premises pl

navegador [naβeɣa'ðor] nm (Inform)
browser

navegante [naβe'ɣante] nmf
navigator

navegar [naβe'ɣar] vi (barco) to
sail; (avión) to fly; **~ por Internet** to
surf the Net

Navidad [naβi'ðað] nf Christmas;
Navidades nfpl Christmas time;
¡Feliz ~! Merry Christmas!; **navideño,
-a** adj Christmas cpd

nazca etc vb V nacer

nazi ['naθi] adj, nmf Nazi

NE abr (= nor(d)este) NE

neblina [ne'βlina] nf mist

necesario, -a [neθe'sarjo, a] adj
necessary

neceser [neθe'ser] nm toilet bag;
(bolsa grande) holdall

necesidad [neθesi'ðað] nf need;
(lo inevitable) necessity; (miseria)
poverty; **en caso de ~** in case of
need o emergency; **hacer sus ~es** to
relieve o.s.

necesitado, -a [neθesi'taðo, a] adj
needy, poor; **~ de** in need of

necesitar [neθesi'tar] vt to need,
require

necio, -a ['neθjo, a] adj foolish

nectarina [nekta'rina] nf nectarine

nefasto, -a [ne'fasto, a] adj ill-fated,
unlucky

negación [neɣa'θjon] nf negation;
(rechazo) refusal, denial

negar [ne'ɣar] vt (renegar, rechazar)
to refuse; (prohibir) to refuse, deny;
(desmentir) to deny; **negarse** vr: **~se a**
to refuse to

negativa [neɣa'tiβa] nf negative;
(rechazo) refusal, denial

negativo, -a [neɣa'tiβo, a] adj, nm
negative

negociante [neɣo'θjante] *nmf*
businessman/woman

negociar [neɣo'θjar] *vt, vi* to
negotiate; **~ en** to deal *o* trade in

negocio [ne'ɣoθjo] *nm* (*Com*)
business; (*asunto*) affair, business;
(*operación comercial*) deal, transaction;
(*lugar*) place of business; **los ~s**
business *sg*; **hacer ~** to do business

negra [neɣra] *nf* (*Mús*) crotchet; V
tb **negro**

negro, -a ['neɣro, a] *adj* black;
(*suerte*) awful ▷ *nm* black ▷ *nm/f* black
man/woman

nene, -a ['nene, a] *nm/f* baby,
small child

neón [ne'on] *nm*: **luces/lámpara de ~**
neon lights/lamp

neoyorquino, -a [neojor'kino, a]
adj (of) New York

nervio ['nerβjo] *nm* nerve;
nerviosismo *nm* nervousness, nerves
pl; **nervioso, -a** *adj* nervous

neto, -a ['neto, a] *adj* net

neumático, -a [neu'matiko, a] *adj*
pneumatic ▷ *nm* (*Esp*) tyre (*Brit*),
tire (*Us*); **neumático de recambio**
spare tyre

neurólogo, -a [neu'roloɣo, a] *nm/f*
neurologist

neurona [neu'rona] *nf* nerve cell

neutral [neu'tral] *adj* neutral;
neutralizar *vt* to neutralize;
(*contrarrestar*) to counteract

neutro, -a ['neutro, a] *adj* (*Bio*,
Ling) neuter

neutrón [neu'tron] *nm* neutron

nevada [ne'βaða] *nf* snowstorm;
(*caída de nieve*) snowfall

nevar [ne'βar] *vi* to snow

nevera [ne'βera] (*Esp*) *nf* refrigerator
(*Brit*), icebox (*Us*)

nevería [neβe'ria] (*Méx*) *nf* ice-cream
parlour

nexo ['nekso] *nm* link, connection

ni [ni] *conj* nor, neither; (*tb*: **~ siquiera**)
not ... even; **~ aunque que** not even
if; **~ blanco ~ negro** neither white

nor black

Nicaragua [nika'raɣwa] *nf*
Nicaragua; **nicaragüense** *adj, nmf*
Nicaraguan

nicho ['nitʃo] *nm* niche

nicotina [niko'tina] *nf* nicotine

nido ['niðo] *nm* nest

niebla ['njeβla] *nf* fog; (*neblina*) mist

niego *etc vb* V **negar**

nieto, -a ['njeto, a] *nm/f* grandson/
daughter; **nietos** *nmpl* grandchildren

nieve *etc* ['njeβe] *vb* V **nevar** ▷ *nf*
snow; (*Méx: helado*) ice cream

NIF *nm abr* (= *Número de Identificación*
Fiscal) *personal identification number used*
for financial and tax purposes

ninfa ['ninfa] *nf* nymph

ningún *adj* V **ninguno**

ninguno, -a [nin'guno, a] (*adj*
ningún) no *pron* (*nadie*) nobody; (*ni*
uno) none, not one; (*ni uno ni otro*)
neither; **de ninguna manera** by no
means, not at all

niña ['nina] *nf* (*Anat*) pupil; V *tb* **niño**

niñera [ni'nera] *nf* nursemaid, nanny

niñez [ni'neθ] *nf* childhood; (*infancia*)
infancy

niño, -a ['nino, a] *adj* (*joven*) young;
(*inmaduro*) immature ▷ *nm/f* child,
boy/girl

nipón, -ona [ni'pon, ona] *adj, nm/f*
Japanese

níquel ['nikel] *nm* nickel

níspero ['nispero] *nm* medlar

nítido, -a ['nitiðo, a] *adj* clear; sharp

nitrato [ni'trato] *nm* nitrate

nitrógeno [ni'troxeno] *nm* nitrogen

nivel [ni'βel] *nm* (*Geo*) level; (*norma*)
level, standard; (*altura*) height; **nivel**
de aceite oil level; **nivel de aire** spirit
level; **nivel de vida** standard of living;
nivelar *vt* to level out; (*fig*) to even up;
(*Com*) to balance

no [no] *adv* no; not; (*con verbo*) not
▷ *excl* no!; **~ tengo nada** I don't have
anything, I have nothing; **~ es el mío**
it's not mine; **ahora ~** not now; **¿~ lo**
sabes? don't you know?; **~ mucho** not

much; **~ bien termine, lo entregaré** as soon as I finish, I'll hand it over; **~ más: ayer ~ más** just yesterday; **¡pase ~ más!** come in!; **¡a que ~ lo sabes!** I bet you don't know!; **¡cómo ~!** of course!; **la ~ intervención** non-intervention

noble ['noβle] *adj, nmf* noble; **nobleza** *nf* nobility

noche ['notʃe] *nf* night, night-time; (*la tarde*) evening; **de ~, por la ~** at night; **es de ~** it's dark; **Noche de San Juan** *see note*

nochebuena [notʃe'βwena] *nf* Christmas Eve

nochevieja [notʃe'βjexa] *nf* New Year's Eve

nocivo, -a [no'θiβo, a] *adj* harmful

noctámbulo, -a [nok'tambulo, a]

nm/f sleepwalker

nocturno, -a [nok'turno, a] *adj* (*de la noche*) nocturnal, night *cpd*; (*de la tarde*) evening *cpd* ▷ *nm* nocturne

nogal [no'ɣal] *nm* walnut tree

nómada ['nomaða] *adj* nomadic ▷ *nmf* nomad

nombrar [nom'brar] *vt* (*designar*) to name; (*mencionar*) to mention; (*dar puesto a*) to appoint

nombre ['nombre] *nm* name; (*sustantivo*) noun; **~ y apellidos** name in full; **poner ~ a** to call, name; **nombre común/propio** common/proper noun; **nombre de pila/de soltera** Christian/maiden name

nómina ['nomina] *nf* (*lista*) payroll; (*hoja*) payslip

nominal [nomi'nal] *adj* nominal

nominar [nomi'nar] *vt* to nominate

nominativo, -a [nomina'tiβo, a] *adj* (*Com*): **cheque ~ a X** cheque made out to X

nordeste [nor'ðeste] *adj* north-east, north-eastern, north-easterly ▷ *nm* north-east

nórdico, -a ['norðiko, a] *adj* Nordic

noreste [no'reste] *adj, nm* = **nordeste**

noria ['norja] *nf* (*Agr*) waterwheel; (*de carnaval*) big (BRIT) o Ferris (US) wheel

norma ['norma] *nf* rule (of thumb)

normal [nor'mal] *adj* (*corriente*) normal; (*habitual*) usual, natural; **normalizarse** *vr* to return to normal; **normalmente** *adv* normally

normativa [norma'tiβa] *nf* (set of) rules *pl*, regulations *pl*

noroeste [noro'este] *adj* north-west, north-western, north-westerly ▷ *nm* north-west

norte ['norte] *adj* north, northern, northerly ▷ *nm* north; (*fig*) guide

norteamericano, -a [norteameri'kano, a] *adj, nm/f* (North) American

Noruega [no'rweɣa] *nf* Norway

noruego, -a [no'rweɣo, a] *adj, nm/f* Norwegian

nos [nos] *pron* (*directo*) us; (*indirecto*) us; to us; for us; from us; (*reflexivo*) (to) ourselves; (*recíproco*) (to) each other; **~ levantamos a las 7** we get up at 7

nosotros, -as [no'sotros, as] *pron* (*sujeto*) we; (*después de prep*) us

nostalgia [nos'talxja] *nf* nostalgia

nota ['nota] *nf* note; (*Escol*) mark

notable [no'taβle] *adj* notable; (*Escol*) outstanding

notar [no'tar] *vt* to notice, note; **notarse** *vr* to be obvious; **se nota que** ... one observes that ...

notario [no'tarjo] *nm* notary

noticia [no'tiθja] *nf* (*información*) piece of news; **las ~s** the news *sg*; **tener ~s de algn** to hear from sb

▌ No confundir **noticia** con la palabra inglesa *notice*.

noticiero [noti'θjero] (*LAM*) *nm* news bulletin

notificar [notifi'kar] *vt* to notify, inform

notorio, -a [no'torjo, a] *adj* (*público*) well-known; (*evidente*) obvious

novato, -a [no'βato, a] *adj* inexperienced ▷ *nm/f* beginner, novice

novecientos, -as [noβe'θjentos, as] *num* nine hundred

novedad [noβe'ðað] *nf* (*calidad de nuevo*) newness; (*noticia*) piece of news; (*cambio*) change, (new) development

novel [no'βel] *adj* new; (*inexperto*) inexperienced ▷ *nmf* beginner

novela [no'βela] *nf* novel

noveno, -a [no'βeno, a] *adj* ninth

noventa [no'βenta] *num* ninety

novia *nf* V **novio**

novicio, -a [no'βiθjo, a] *nm/f* novice

noviembre [no'βjembre] *nm* November

novillada [noβi'ʎaða] *nf* (*Taur*) bullfight with young bulls; **novillero** *nm* novice bullfighter; **novillo** *nm* young bull, bullock; **hacer novillos** (*fam*) to play truant

novio, -a ['noβjo, a] *nm/f* boyfriend/ girlfriend; (*prometido*) fiancé/fiancée; (*recién casado*) bridegroom/bride; **los ~s** the newly-weds

nube ['nuβe] *nf* cloud

nublado, -a [nu'βlaðo, a] *adj* cloudy; **nublarse** *vr* to grow dark

nubosidad [nuβosi'ðað] *nf* cloudiness; **había mucha ~** it was very cloudy

nuca ['nuka] *nf* nape of the neck

nuclear [nukle'ar] *adj* nuclear

núcleo ['nukleo] *nm* (*centro*) core; (*Física*) nucleus; **núcleo urbano** city centre

nudillo [nu'ðiʎo] *nm* knuckle

nudista [nu'ðista] *adj* nudist

nudo ['nuðo] *nm* knot; (*de carreteras*) junction

nuera ['nwera] *nf* daughter-in-law

nuestro, -a ['nwestro, a] *adj pos* our ▷ *pron* ours; **~ padre** our father; **un amigo ~** a friend of ours; **es el ~** it's ours

Nueva York [-jork] *n* New York

Nueva Zelanda [-θe'landa] *nf* New Zealand

nueve ['nweβe] *num* nine

nuevo, -a ['nweβo, a] *adj* (*gen*) new; **de ~** again

nuez [nweθ] *nf* walnut; (*Anat*) Adam's apple; **nuez moscada** nutmeg

nulo, -a ['nulo, a] *adj* (*inepto, torpe*) useless; (*inválido*) (null and) void; (*Deporte*) drawn, tied

núm. *abr* (= *número*) no.

numerar [nume'rar] *vt* to number

número ['numero] *nm* (*gen*) number; (*tamaño: de zapato*) size; (*ejemplar: de diario*) number, issue; **sin ~** numberless, unnumbered; **número atrasado** back number; **número de matrícula/ teléfono** registration/telephone number; **número impar/par** odd/even number; **número romano** Roman numeral

numeroso, -a [nume'roso, a] *adj* numerous

nunca ['nunka] *adv* (*jamás*) never; **~**

lo pensé I never thought it; **no viene ~** he never comes; **~ más** never again; **más que ~** more than ever

nupcias ['nupθjas] *nfpl* wedding *sg*, nuptials

nutria ['nutrja] *nf* otter

nutrición [nutri'θjon] *nf* nutrition

nutrir [nu'trir] *vt* (*alimentar*) to nourish; (*dar de comer*) to feed; (*fig*) to strengthen; **nutritivo, -a** *adj* nourishing, nutritious

nylon [ni'lon] *nm* nylon

ñango, -a ['ɲango, a] (*MÉX*) *adj* puny

ñapa ['ɲapa] (*LAM*) *nf* extra

ñata ['ɲata] (*LAM: fam*) *nf* nose; V *tb* **ñato**

ñato, -a ['ɲato, a] (*LAM*) *adj* snub-nosed

ñoñería [ɲoɲe'ria] *nf* insipidness

ñoño, -a ['ɲoɲo, a] *adj* (*fam: tonto*) silly, stupid; (*soso*) insipid; (*persona*) spineless; (*ESP: película, novela*) sentimental

O

O *abr* (= *oeste*) W

o [o] *conj* or

oasis [o'asis] *nm inv* oasis

obcecarse [oβθe'karse] *vr* to get o become stubborn

obedecer [oβeðe'θer] *vt* to obey; **obediente** *adj* obedient

obertura [oβer'tura] *nf* overture

obeso, -a [o'βeso, a] *adj* obese

obispo [o'βispo] *nm* bishop

obituario [oβɪ'twarjo] (*LAM*) *nm* obituary

objetar [oβxe'tar] *vt, vi* to object

objetivo, -a [oβxe'tiβo, a] *adj, nm* objective

objeto [oβ'xeto] *nm* (*cosa*) object; (*fin*) aim

objetor, a [oβxe'tor, a] *nm/f* objector

obligación [oβlixa'θjon] *nf* obligation; (*Com*) bond

obligar [oβli'xar] *vt* to force; **obligarse** *vr* to bind o.s.; **obligatorio, -a** *adj* compulsory, obligatory

oboe [o'βoe] *nm* oboe

obra ['oβra] *nf* work; (*Arq*) construction, building; (*Teatro*) play; **por ~ de** thanks to (the efforts of); **obra maestra** masterpiece; **obras públicas** public works; **obrar** *vt* to work; (*tener efecto*) to have an effect on ▷ *vi* to act, behave; (*tener efecto*) to have an effect; **la carta obra en su poder** the letter is in his/her possession

obrero, -a [o'βrero, a] *adj* (*clase*) working; (*movimiento*) labour *cpd* ▷ *nm/f* (*gen*) worker; (*sin oficio*) labourer

obsceno, -a [oβs'θeno, a] *adj* obscene

obscu... = **oscu...**

obsequiar [oβse'kjar] *vt* (*ofrecer*) to present with; (*agasajar*) to make a fuss of, lavish attention on; **obsequio** *nm* (*regalo*) gift; (*cortesía*) courtesy, attention

observación [oβserβa'θjon] *nf* observation; (*reflexión*) remark

observador, a [oβserβa'ðor, a] *nm/f* observer

observar [oβser'βar] *vt* to observe; (*anotar*) to notice; **observarse** *vr* to keep to, observe

obsesión [oβse'sjon] *nf* obsession; **obsesivo, -a** *adj* obsessive

obstáculo [oβs'takulo] *nm* obstacle; (*impedimento*) hindrance, drawback

obstante [oβs'tante]: **no ~** *adv* nevertheless

obstinado, -a [oβsti'naðo, a] *adj* obstinate, stubborn

obstinarse [oβsti'narse] *vr* to be obstinate; **~ en** to persist in

obstruir [oβstru'ir] *vt* to obstruct

obtener [oβte'ner] *vt* (*gen*) to obtain; (*premio*) to win

obturador [oβtura'ðor] *nm* (*Foto*) shutter

obvio, -a ['oββjo, a] *adj* obvious

oca ['oka] *nf* (*animal*) goose; (*juego*) ≈ snakes and ladders

ocasión [oka'sjon] *nf* (*oportunidad*) opportunity, chance; (*momento*) occasion, time; (*causa*) cause; **de ~**

secondhand; **ocasionar** *vt* to cause

ocaso [o'kaso] *nm* (*fig*) decline

occidente [okθi'ðente] *nm* west

OCDE *nf abr* (= *Organización de Cooperación y Desarrollo Económico*) OECD

océano [o'θeano] *nm* ocean; **Océano Índico** Indian Ocean

ochenta [o'tʃenta] *num* eighty

ocho ['otʃo] *num* eight; **dentro de ~ días** within a week

ocio ['oθjo] *nm* (*tiempo*) leisure; (*pey*) idleness

octavilla [okta'viʎa] *nf* leaflet, pamphlet

octavo, -a [ok'taβo, a] *adj* eighth

octubre [ok'tuβre] *nm* October

oculista [oku'lista] *nmf* oculist

ocultar [okul'tar] *vt* (*esconder*) to hide; (*callar*) to conceal; **oculto, -a** *adj* hidden; (*fig*) secret

ocupación [okupa'θjon] *nf* occupation

ocupado, -a [oku'paðo, a] *adj* (*persona*) busy; (*plaza*) occupied, taken; (*teléfono*) engaged; **ocupar** *vt* (*gen*) to occupy; **ocuparse** *vr*: **ocuparse de** *o* **en** (*gen*) to concern o.s. with; (*cuidar*) to look after

ocurrencia [oku'rrenθja] *nf* (*idea*) bright idea

ocurrir [oku'rrir] *vi* to happen; **ocurrirse** *vr*: **se me ocurrió que ...** it occurred to me that ...

odiar [o'ðjar] *vt* to hate; **odio** *nm* hate, hatred; **odioso, -a** *adj* (*gen*) hateful; (*malo*) nasty

odontólogo, -a [oðon'toloxo, a] *nm/f* dentist, dental surgeon

oeste [o'este] *nm* west; **una película del ~** a western

ofender [ofen'der] *vt* (*agraviar*) to offend; (*insultar*) to insult; **ofenderse** *vr* to take offence; **ofensa** *nf* offence; **ofensiva** *nf* offensive; **ofensivo, -a** *adj* offensive

oferta [o'ferta] *nf* offer; (*propuesta*) proposal; **la ~ y la demanda** supply

and demand; **artículos en ~** goods on offer

oficial [ofi'θjal] *adj* official ▷ *nm* (*Mil*) officer

oficina [ofi'θina] *nf* office; **oficina de correos** post office; **oficina de información** information bureau; **oficina de turismo** tourist office; **oficinista** *nmf* clerk

oficio [o'fiθjo] *nm* (*profesión*) profession; (*puesto*) post; (*Rel*) service; **ser del ~** to be an old hand; **tener mucho ~** to have a lot of experience; **oficio de difuntos** funeral service

ofimática [ofi'matika] *nf* office automation

ofrecer [ofre'θer] *vt* (*dar*) to offer; (*proponer*) to propose; **ofrecerse** *vr* (*persona*) to offer o.s., volunteer; (*situación*) to present itself; **¿qué se le ofrece?, ¿se le ofrece algo?** what can I do for you?, can I get you anything?

ofrecimiento [ofreθi'mjento] *nm* offer

oftalmólogo, -a [oftal'moloxo, a] *nm/f* ophthalmologist

oída [o'iða] *nf*: **de ~s** by hearsay

oído [o'iðo] *nm* (*Anat*) ear; (*sentido*) hearing

oigo *etc vb V* **oír**

oír [o'ir] *vt* (*gen*) to hear; (*atender a*) to listen to; **¡oiga!** listen!; **~ misa** to attend mass

OIT *nf abr* (= *Organización Internacional del Trabajo*) ILO

ojal [o'xal] *nm* buttonhole

ojalá [oxa'la] *excl* if only (it were so)!, some hope! ▷ *conj* if only ...!, would that ...!; **~ (que) venga hoy** I hope he comes today

ojeada [oxe'aða] *nf* glance

ojera [o'xera] *nf*: **tener ~s** to have bags under one's eyes

ojo ['oxo] *nm* eye; (*de puente*) span; (*de cerradura*) keyhole ▷ *excl* careful!; **tener ~ para** to have an eye for; **ojo de buey** porthole

okey ['okei] (*LAM*) *excl* O.K.

okupa [o'kupa] (ESP: fam) nmf
squatter

ola ['ola] nf wave

olé [o'le] excl bravo!, olé!

oleada [ole'aða] nf big wave, swell;
(fig) wave

oleaje [ole'axe] nm swell

óleo ['oleo] nm oil; **oleoducto** nm
(oil) pipeline

oler [o'ler] vt (gen) to smell; (inquirir)
pry into; (fig: sospechar) to sniff out ▷ vi
to smell; **~ a** to smell of

olfatear [olfate'ar] vt to smell;
(inquirir) to pry into; **olfato** nm sense
of smell

olimpiada [olim'piaða] nf: **las
O~s** the Olympics; **olímpico, -a**
[o'limpiko, a] adj Olympic

oliva [o'liβa] nf (aceituna) olive; **aceite
de ~** olive oil; **olivo** nm olive tree

olla ['oʎa] nf pan; (comida) stew; **olla
exprés** o **a presión** (ESP) pressure
cooker; **olla podrida** type of Spanish
stew

olmo ['olmo] nm elm (tree)

olor [o'lor] nm smell; **oloroso, -a** adj
scented

olvidar [olβi'ðar] vt to forget; (omitir)
to omit; **olvidarse** vr (fig) to forget
o.s.; **se me olvidó** I forgot

olvido [ol'βiðo] nm oblivion; (despiste)
forgetfulness

ombligo [om'blixo] nm navel

omelette [ome'lete] (LAM) nf
omelet(te)

omisión [omi'sjon] nf (abstención)
omission; (descuido) neglect

omiso, -a [o'miso, a] adj: **hacer caso
~ de** to ignore, pass over

omitir [omi'tir] vt to omit

omnipotente [omnipo'tente] adj
omnipotent

omóplato [o'moplato] nm shoulder
blade

OMS nf abr (= Organización Mundial de
la Salud) WHO

once ['onθe] num eleven; **onces** (cs)
nfpl tea break sg

onda ['onda] nf wave; **onda corta/
larga/media** short/long/medium
wave; **ondear** vt, vi to wave; (tener
ondas) to be wavy; (agua) to ripple

ondulación [ondula'θjon] nf
undulation; **ondulado, -a** adj wavy

ONG nf abr (= organización no
gubernamental) NGO

ONU ['onu] nf abr (= Organización de las
Naciones Unidas) UNO

opaco, -a [o'pako, a] adj opaque

opción [op'θjon] nf (gen) option;
(derecho) right, option

OPEP ['opep] nf abr (= Organización de
Países Exportadores de Petróleo) OPEC

ópera ['opera] nf opera; **ópera bufa** o
cómica comic opera

operación [opera'θjon] nf (gen)
operation; (Com) transaction, deal

operador, a [opera'ðor, a]
nm/f operator; (Cine: de proyección)
projectionist; (: de rodaje) cameraman

operar [ope'rar] vt (producir) to
produce, bring about; (Med) to operate
on ▷ vi (Com) to operate, deal;
operarse vr to occur; (Med) to have
an operation

opereta [ope'reta] nf operetta

opinar [opi'nar] vt to think ▷ vi
to give one's opinion; **opinión** nf
(creencia) belief; (criterio) opinion

opio ['opjo] nm opium

oponer [opo'ner] vt (resistencia) to
put up, offer; **oponerse** vr (objetar)
to object; (estar frente a frente) to be
opposed; (dos personas) to oppose each
other; **~ A a B** to set A against B; **me
opongo a pensar que ...** I refuse to
believe o think that ...

oportunidad [oportuni'ðað] nf
(ocasión) opportunity; (posibilidad)
chance

oportuno, -a [opor'tuno, a] adj
(en su tiempo) opportune, timely;
(respuesta) suitable; **en el momento ~**
at the right moment

oposición [oposi'θjon] nf
opposition; **oposiciones** nfpl (Escol)

public examinations

opositor, a [oposi'tor, a] *nm/f* (*adversario*) opponent; (*candidato*): **~ (a)** candidate (for)

opresión [opre'sjon] *nf* oppression; **opresor, a** *nm/f* oppressor

oprimir [opri'mir] *vt* to squeeze; (*fig*) to oppress

optar [op'tar] *vi* (*elegir*) to choose; **~ por** to opt for; **optativo, -a** *adj* optional

óptico, -a ['optiko, a] *adj* optic(al) ▷ *nm/f* optician; **óptica** *nf* optician's (shop); **desde esta óptica** from this point of view

optimismo [opti'mismo] *nm* optimism; **optimista** *nmf* optimist

opuesto, -a [o'pwesto, a] *adj* (*contrario*) opposite; (*antagónico*) opposing

oración [ora'θjon] *nf* (*Rel*) prayer; (*Ling*) sentence

orador, a [ora'ðor, a] *nm/f* (*conferenciante*) speaker, orator

oral [o'ral] *adj* oral

orangután [orangu'tan] *nm* orangutan

orar [o'rar] *vi* to pray

oratoria [ora'torja] *nf* oratory

órbita [or'βita] *nf* orbit

orden ['orðen] *nm* (*gen*) order ▷ *nf* (*gen*) order; (*Inform*) command; **en ~ de prioridad** in order of priority; **orden del día** agenda

ordenado, -a [orðe'naðo, a] *adj* (*metódico*) methodical; (*arreglado*) orderly

ordenador [orðena'ðor] *nm* computer; **ordenador central** mainframe computer

ordenar [orðe'nar] *vt* (*mandar*) to order; (*poner orden*) to put in order, arrange; **ordenarse** *vr* (*Rel*) to be ordained

ordeñar [orðe'nar] *vt* to milk

ordinario, -a [orði'narjo, a] *adj* (*común*) ordinary, usual; (*vulgar*) vulgar, common

orégano [o'reɣano] *nm* oregano

oreja [o'rexa] *nf* ear; (*Mecánica*) lug, flange

orfanato [orfa'nato] *nm* orphanage

orfebrería [orfeβre'ria] *nf* gold/silver work

orgánico, -a [or'ɣaniko, a] *adj* organic

organismo [orɣa'nismo] *nm* (*Bio*) organism; (*Pol*) organization

organización [orɣaniθa'θjon] *nf* organization; **organizar** *vt* to organize

órgano ['orɣano] *nm* organ

orgasmo [or'ɣasmo] *nm* orgasm

orgía [or'xia] *nf* orgy

orgullo [or'ɣuʎo] *nm* pride; **orgulloso, -a** *adj* (*gen*) proud; (*altanero*) haughty

orientación [orjenta'θjon] *nf* (*posición*) position; (*dirección*) direction

oriental [orjen'tal] *adj* eastern; (*del Extremo Oriente*) oriental

orientar [orjen'tar] *vt* (*situar*) to orientate; (*señalar*) to point; (*dirigir*) to direct; (*guiar*) to guide; **orientarse** *vr* to get one's bearings

oriente [o'rjente] *nm* east; **el O~ Medio** the Middle East; **el Próximo/ Extremo O~** the Near/Far East

origen [o'rixen] *nm* origin

original [orixi'nal] *adj* (*nuevo*) original; (*extraño*) odd, strange; **originalidad** *nf* originality

originar [orixi'nar] *vt* to start, cause; **originarse** *vr* to originate; **originario, -a** *adj* original; **originario de** native of

orilla [o'riʎa] *nf* (*borde*) border; (*de río*) bank; (*de bosque, tela*) edge; (*de mar*) shore

orina [o'rina] *nf* urine; **orinal** *nm* (chamber) pot; **orinar** *vi* to urinate; **orinarse** *vr* to wet o.s.

oro ['oro] *nm* gold; **oros** *nmpl* (*Naipes*) hearts

orquesta [or'kesta] *nf* orchestra; **orquesta sinfónica** symphony orchestra

orquídea [or'kiðea] nf orchid
ortiga [or'tiɣa] nf nettle
ortodoxo, -a [orto'ðokso, a] adj orthodox
ortografía [ortoɣra'fia] nf spelling
ortopedia [orto'peðja] nf orthopaedics sg; **ortopédico, -a** adj orthopaedic
oruga [o'ruɣa] nf caterpillar
orzuelo [or'θwelo] nm stye
os [os] pron (gen) you; (a vosotros) to you
osa ['osa] nf (she-)bear; **Osa Mayor/ Menor** Great/Little Bear
osadía [osa'ðia] nf daring
osar [o'sar] vi to dare
oscilación [osθila'θjon] nf (movimiento) oscillation; (fluctuación) fluctuation
oscilar [osθi'lar] vi to oscillate; to fluctuate
oscurecer [oskure'θer] vt to darken ▷ vi to grow dark; **oscurecerse** vr to grow o get dark
oscuridad [oskuri'ðað] nf obscurity; (tinieblas) darkness
oscuro, -a [os'kuro, a] adj dark; (fig) obscure; **a oscuras** in the dark
óseo, -a ['oseo, a] adj bone cpd
oso ['oso] nm bear; **oso de peluche** teddy bear; **oso hormiguero** anteater
ostentar [osten'tar] vt (gen) to show; (pey) to flaunt, show off; (poseer) to have, possess
ostión [os'tjon] (MÉX) nm = **ostra**
ostra ['ostra] nf oyster
OTAN ['otan] nf abr (= Organización del Tratado del Atlántico Norte) NATO
otitis [o'titis] nf earache
otoñal [oto'ɲal] adj autumnal
otoño [o'toɲo] nm autumn
otorgar [otor'ɣar] vt (conceder) to concede; (dar) to grant
otorrino, -a [oto'rrino, a], **otorrinolaringólogo, -a** [otorrinolarin'goloɣo, a] nm/f ear,

nose and throat specialist

O PALABRA CLAVE

otro, -a ['otro, a] adj 1 (distinto: sg) another; (: pl) other; **con otros amigos** with other o different friends
2 (adicional): **tráigame otro café (más), por favor** can I have another coffee please; **otros diez días más** another ten days
▷ pron 1 **el otro** the other one; **(los) otros** (the) others; **de otro** somebody else's; **que lo haga otro** let somebody else do it
2 (recíproco): **se odian (la) una a (la) otra** they hate one another o each other
3: **otro tanto: comer otro tanto** to eat the same o as much again; **recibió una decena de telegramas y otras tantas llamadas** he got about ten telegrams and as many calls

ovación [oβa'θjon] nf ovation
oval [o'βal] adj oval; **ovalado, -a** adj oval; **óvalo** nm oval
ovario [o'βario] nm ovary
oveja [o'βexa] nf sheep
overol [oβe'rol] (LAM) nm overalls pl
ovillo [o'βiʎo] nm (de lana) ball of wool
OVNI ['oβni] nm abr (= objeto volante no identificado) UFO
ovulación [oβula'θjon] nf ovulation; **óvulo** nm ovum
oxidación [oksiða'θjon] nf rusting
oxidar [oksi'ðar] vt to rust; **oxidarse** vr to go rusty
óxido ['oksiðo] nm oxide
oxigenado, -a [oksixe'naðo, a] adj (Quím) oxygenated; (pelo) bleached
oxígeno [ok'sixeno] nm oxygen
oyente [o'jente] nmf listener
oyes etc vb V **oír**
ozono [o'θono] nm ozone

P

pabellón [paβe'ʎon] *nm* bell tent; (*Arq*) pavilion; (*de hospital etc*) block, section; (*bandera*) flag

pacer [pa'θer] *vi* to graze

paciencia [pa'θjenθja] *nf* patience

paciente [pa'θjente] *adj, nmf* patient

pacificación [paθifika'θjon] *nf* pacification

pacífico, -a [pa'θifiko, a] *adj* (*persona*) peaceable; (*existencia*) peaceful; **el (Océano) P~** the Pacific (Ocean)

pacifista [paθi'fista] *nmf* pacifist

pacotilla [pako'tiʎa] *nf*: **de ~** (*actor, escritor*) third-rate

pactar [pak'tar] *vt* to agree to o on ▷ *vi* to come to an agreement

pacto ['pakto] *nm* (*tratado*) pact; (*acuerdo*) agreement

padecer [paðe'θer] *vt* (*sufrir*) to suffer; (*soportar*) to endure, put up with; **padecimiento** *nm* suffering

padrastro [pa'ðrastro] *nm* stepfather

padre ['paðre] *nm* father ▷ *adj* (*fam*): **un éxito ~** a tremendous success; **padres** *nmpl* parents; **padre político** father-in-law

padrino [pa'ðrino] *nm* (*Rel*) godfather; (*tb*: **~ de boda**) best man; (*fig*) sponsor, patron; **padrinos** *nmpl* godparents

padrón [pa'ðron] *nm* (*censo*) census, roll

padrote [pa'ðrote] (*MÉX: fam*) *nm* pimp

paella [pa'eʎa] *nf* paella, *dish of rice with meat, shellfish etc*

paga ['paɣa] *nf* (*pago*) payment; (*sueldo*) pay, wages *pl*

pagano, -a [pa'ɣano, a] *adj, nm/f* pagan, heathen

pagar [pa'ɣar] *vt* to pay; (*las compras, crimen*) to pay for; (*fig: favor*) to repay ▷ *vi* to pay; **~ al contado/a plazos** to pay (in) cash/in instalments

pagaré [paɣa're] *nm* I.O.U.

página ['paxina] *nf* page; **página de inicio** (*Inform*) home page; **página web** (*Inform*) web page

pago ['paɣo] *nm* (*dinero*) payment; **en ~ de** in return for; **pago anticipado/a cuenta/contra reembolso/en especie** advance payment/payment on account/cash on delivery/payment in kind

pág(s). *abr* (= *página(s)*) p(p).

pague *etc vb V* **pagar**

país [pa'is] *nm* (*gen*) country; (*región*) land; **los P~es Bajos** the Low Countries; **el P~ Vasco** the Basque Country

paisaje [pai'saxe] *nm* landscape, scenery

paisano, -a [pai'sano, a] *adj* of the same country ▷ *nm/f* (*compatriota*) fellow countryman/woman; **vestir de ~** (*soldado*) to be in civvies; (*guardia*) to be in plain clothes

paja ['paxa] *nf* straw; (*fig*) rubbish (*BRIT*), trash (*US*)

pajarita [paxa'rita] *nf* (*corbata*) bow tie

pájaro ['paxaro] *nm* bird; **pájaro carpintero** woodpecker

pajita [pa'xita] *nf* (drinking) straw

pala ['pala] *nf* spade, shovel; (*raqueta etc*) bat; (: *de tenis*) racquet; (*Culin*) slice; **pala mecánica** power shovel

palabra [pa'laβra] *nf* word; (*facultad*) (power of) speech; (*derecho de hablar*) right to speak; **tomar la ~** (*en mitin*) to take the floor

palabrota [pala'brota] *nf* swearword

palacio [pa'laθjo] *nm* palace; (*mansión*) mansion, large house; **palacio de justicia** courthouse; **palacio municipal** town *o* city hall

paladar [pala'ðar] *nm* palate; **paladear** *vt* to taste

palanca [pa'lanka] *nf* lever; (*fig*) pull, influence

palangana [palan'gana] *nf* washbasin

palco ['palko] *nm* box

Palestina [pales'tina] *nf* Palestine; **palestino, -a** *nm/f* Palestinian

paleta [pa'leta] *nf* (*de pintor*) palette; (*de albañil*) trowel; (*de ping-pong*) bat; (*MÉX, CAM: helado*) ice lolly (*BRIT*), Popsicle® (*US*)

palidecer [paliðe'θer] *vi* to turn pale; **palidez** *nf* paleness; **pálido, -a** *adj* pale

palillo [pa'liʎo] *nm* (*mondadientes*) toothpick; (*para comer*) chopstick

palito [pa'lito] (*RPL*) *nm* (*helado*) ice lolly (*BRIT*), Popsicle® (*US*)

paliza [pa'liθa] *nf* beating, thrashing

palma ['palma] *nf* (*Anat*) palm; (*árbol*) palm tree; **batir** *o* **dar ~s** to clap, applaud; **palmada** *nf* slap; **palmadas** *nfpl* clapping *sg*, applause *sg*

palmar [pal'mar] (*fam*) *vi* (*tb*: **~la**) to die, kick the bucket

palmear [palme'ar] *vi* to clap

palmera [pal'mera] *nf* (*Bot*) palm tree

palmo ['palmo] *nm* (*medida*) span; (*fig*) small amount; **~ a ~** inch by inch

palo ['palo] *nm* stick; (*poste*) post; (*de tienda de campaña*) pole; (*mango*) handle, shaft; (*golpe*) blow, hit; (*de golf*) club; (*de béisbol*) bat; (*Náut*) mast; (*Naipes*) suit

paloma [pa'loma] *nf* dove, pigeon

palomitas [palo'mitas] *nfpl* popcorn *sg*

palpar [pal'par] *vt* to touch, feel

palpitar [palpi'tar] *vi* to palpitate; (*latir*) to beat

palta ['palta] (*CS*) *nf* avocado

paludismo [palu'ðismo] *nm* malaria

pamela [pa'mela] *nf* picture hat, sun hat

pampa ['pampa] *nf* pampas, prairie

pan [pan] *nm* bread; (*una barra*) loaf; **pan integral** wholemeal (*BRIT*) *o* wholewheat (*US*) bread; **pan rallado** breadcrumbs *pl*; **pan tostado** (*MÉX: tostada*) toast

pana ['pana] *nf* corduroy

panadería [panaðe'ria] *nf* baker's (shop); **panadero, -a** *nm/f* baker

Panamá [pana'ma] *nm* Panama; **panameño, -a** *adj* Panamanian

pancarta [pan'karta] *nf* placard, banner

panceta [pan'θeta] (*ESP, RPL*) *nf* bacon

pancho ['pantʃo] (*RPL*) *nm* hot dog

pancito [pan'θito] *nm* (*bread*) roll

panda ['panda] *nm* (*Zool*) panda

pandereta [pande'reta] *nf* tambourine

pandilla [pan'diʎa] *nf* set, group; (*de criminales*) gang; (*pey: camarilla*) clique

panecillo [pane'θiʎo] (*ESP*) *nm* (*bread*) roll

panel [pa'nel] *nm* panel; **panel solar** solar panel

panfleto [pan'fleto] *nm* pamphlet

pánico [paniko] *nm* panic

panorama [pano'rama] *nm* panorama; (*vista*) view

panqueque [pan'keke] (*LAM*) *nm* pancake

pantalla [pan'taʎa] *nf* (*de cine*) screen; (*de lámpara*) lampshade

pantalón [panta'lon] nm trousers;
  pantalones nmpl trousers;
  pantalones cortes shorts
pantano [pan'tano] nm (ciénaga)
  marsh, swamp; (depósito: de agua)
  reservoir; (fig) jam, difficulty
panteón [pante'on] nm (monumento)
  pantheon
pantera [pan'tera] nf panther
pantimedias [panti'meðjas] (MÉX)
  nfpl = **pantis**
pantis ['pantis] nmpl tights (BRIT),
  pantyhose (US)
pantomima [panto'mima] nf
  pantomime
pantorrilla [panto'rriʎa] nf calf
  (of the leg)
pants [pants] (MÉX) nmpl tracksuit
  (BRIT), sweat suit (US)
pantufla [pan'tufla] nf slipper
panty(s) ['panti(s)] nm(pl) tights
  (BRIT), pantyhose (US)
panza ['panθa] nf belly, paunch
pañal [pa'ɲal] nm nappy (BRIT),
  diaper (US); **pañales** nmpl (fig) early
  stages, infancy sg
paño ['paɲo] nm (tela) cloth; (pedazo de
  tela) (piece of) cloth; (trapo) duster, rag;
  paños menores underclothes
pañuelo [pa'ɲwelo] nm
  handkerchief, hanky; (fam: para la
  cabeza) (head)scarf
papa ['papa] nm: **el P~** the Pope ▷ nf
  (LAM: patata) potato; **papas fritas** (LAM)
  French fries, chips (BRIT); (de bolsa)
  crisps (BRIT), potato chips (US)
papá [pa'pa] (fam) nm dad(dy), pa (US)
papada [pa'paða] nf double chin
papagayo [papa'ɣajo] nm parrot
papalote [papa'lote] (MÉX, CAM)
  nm kite
papanatas [papa'natas] (fam) nm
  inv simpleton
papaya [pa'paja] nf papaya
papear [pape'ar] (fam) vt, vi to scoff
papel [pa'pel] nm paper; (hoja de
  papel) sheet of paper; (Teatro: fig) role;
  papel de aluminio aluminium (BRIT)

o aluminum (US) foil; **papel de arroz/
envolver/fumar** rice/wrapping/
cigarette paper; **papel de estaño** o
plata tinfoil; **papel de lija** sandpaper;
papel higiénico toilet paper; **papel
moneda** paper money; **papel secante**
blotting paper
papeleo [pape'leo] nm red tape
papelera [pape'lera] nf wastepaper
basket; (en la calle) litter bin; **papelera
(de reciclaje)** (Inform) wastebasket
papelería [papele'ria] nf stationer's
(shop)
papeleta [pape'leta] (ESP) nf (Pol)
ballot paper
paperas [pa'peras] nfpl mumps sg
papilla [pa'piʎa] nf (de bebé) baby
food
paquete [pa'kete] nm (de cigarrillos
etc) packet; (Correos etc) parcel
par [par] adj (igual) like, equal; (Mat)
even ▷ nm equal; (de guantes) pair; (de
veces) couple; (Pol) peer; (Golf, Com) par;
abrir de ~ en ~ to open wide
para ['para] prep for; **no es ~ comer**
it's not for eating; **decir ~ sí** to say to
o.s.; **¿~ qué lo quieres?** what do you
want it for?; **se casaron ~ separarse
otra vez** they married only to separate
again; **lo tendré ~ mañana** I'll have
it (for) tomorrow; **ir ~ casa** to go
home, head for home; **~ profesor es
muy estúpido** he's very stupid for a
teacher; **¿quién es usted ~ gritar así?**
who are you to shout like that?; **tengo
bastante ~ vivir** I have enough to live
on; V tb **con**
parabién [para'βjen] nm
congratulations pl
parábola [pa'raβola] nf parable;
(Mat) parabola; **parabólica** nf
(tb: **antena parabólica**) satellite dish
parabrisas [para'βrisas] nm inv
windscreen (BRIT), windshield (US)
paracaídas [paraka'iðas] nm
inv parachute; **paracaidista** nmf
parachutist; (Mil) paratrooper
parachoques [para'tʃokes] nm inv

(*Auto*) bumper; (*Mecánica etc*) shock absorber

parada [pa'raða] *nf* stop; (*acto*) stopping; (*de industria*) shutdown, stoppage; (*lugar*) stopping place; **parada de autobús** bus stop; **parada de taxis** taxi stand *o* rank (BRIT)

paradero [para'ðero] *nm* stopping-place; (*situación*) whereabouts

parado, -a [pa'raðo, a] *adj* (*persona*) motionless, standing still; (*fábrica*) closed, at a standstill; (*coche*) stopped; (LAM: *de pie*) standing (up); (ESP: *sin empleo*) unemployed, idle

paradoja [para'ðoxa] *nf* paradox

parador [para'ðor] *nm* parador, state-run hotel

paragolpes [para'golpes] (RPL) *nm inv* (*Auto*) bumper, fender (US)

paraguas [pa'raxwas] *nm inv* umbrella

Paraguay [para'xwai] *nm* Paraguay; **paraguayo, -a** *adj, nm/f* Paraguayan

paraíso [para'iso] *nm* paradise, heaven

paraje [pa'raxe] *nm* place, spot

paralelo, -a [para'lelo, a] *adj* parallel

parálisis [pa'ralisis] *nf inv* paralysis; **paralítico, -a** *adj, nm/f* paralytic

paralizar [parali'θar] *vt* to paralyse; **paralizarse** *vr* to become paralysed; (*fig*) to come to a standstill

páramo ['paramo] *nm* bleak plateau

paranoico, -a [para'noiko, a] *nm/f* paranoiac

parapente [para'pente] *nm* (*deporte*) paragliding; (*aparato*) paraglider

parapléjico, -a [para'plexiko, a] *adj, nm/f* paraplegic

parar [pa'rar] *vt* to stop; (*golpe*) to ward off ▷ *vi* to stop; **pararse** *vr* to stop; (LAM: *ponerse de pie*) to stand up; **ha parado de llover** it has stopped raining; **van a ir a ~ a comisaría** they're going to end up in the police station; **~se en** to pay attention to

pararrayos [para'rrajos] *nm inv*

lightning conductor

parásito, -a [pa'rasito, a] *nm/f* parasite

parcela [par'θela] *nf* plot, piece of ground

parche ['partʃe] *nm* (*gen*) patch

parchís [par'tʃis] *nm* ludo

parcial [par'θjal] *adj* (*pago*) part-; (*eclipse*) partial; (*Jur*) prejudiced, biased; (*Pol*) partisan

parecer [pare'θer] *nm* (*opinión*) opinion, view; (*aspecto*) looks *pl* ▷ *vi* (*tener apariencia*) to seem, look; (*asemejarse*) to look *o* seem like; (*aparecer, llegar*) to appear; **parecerse** *vr* to look alike, resemble each other; **al ~** apparently; **según parece** evidently, apparently; **~se a** to look like, resemble; **me parece que** I think (that), it seems to me that

parecido, -a [pare'θiðo, a] *adj* similar ▷ *nm* similarity, likeness, resemblance; **bien ~** good-looking, nice-looking

pared [pa'reð] *nf* wall

pareja [pa'rexa] *nf* (*par*) pair; (*dos personas*) couple; (*otro: de un par*) other one (of a pair); (*persona*) partner

parentesco [paren'tesko] *nm* relationship

paréntesis [pa'rentesis] *nm inv* parenthesis; (*en escrito*) bracket

parezco *etc vb* V **parecer**

pariente [pa'rjente] *nmf* relative, relation

> No confundir **pariente** con la palabra inglesa *parent*.

parir [pa'rir] *vt* to give birth to ▷ *vi* (*mujer*) to give birth, have a baby

París [pa'ris] *n* Paris

parka ['parka] (LAM) *nf* anorak

parking ['parkin] *nm* car park (BRIT), parking lot (US)

parlamentar [parlamen'tar] *vi* to parley

parlamentario, -a [parlamen'tarjo, a] *adj* parliamentary ▷ *nm/f* member of parliament

parlamento [parla'mento] *nm*
parliament

parlanchín, -ina [parlan'tʃin, ina]
adj indiscreet ▷ *nm/f* chatterbox

parlar [par'lar] *vi* to chatter (away)

paro ['paro] *nm* (*huelga*) stoppage
(of work), strike; (*ESP: desempleo*)
unemployment; (: *subsidio*)
unemployment benefit; **estar en ~**
(*ESP*) to be unemployed; **paro cardíaco**
cardiac arrest

parodia [pa'roðja] *nf* parody;
parodiar *vt* to parody

parpadear [parpaðe'ar] *vi* (*ojos*) to
blink; (*luz*) to flicker

párpado ['parpaðo] *nm* eyelid

parque ['parke] *nm* (*lugar verde*)
park; (*MÉX: munición*) ammunition;
parque de atracciones fairground;
parque de bomberos (*ESP*) fire station;
parque infantil/temático/zoológico
playground/theme park/zoo

parqué [par'ke] *nm* parquet
(flooring)

parquímetro [par'kimetro] *nm*
parking meter

parra ['parra] *nf* (grape)vine

párrafo ['parrafo] *nm* paragraph;
echar un ~ (*fam*) to have a chat

parranda [pa'rranda] (*fam*) *nf* spree,
binge

parrilla [pa'rriʎa] *nf* (*Culin*) grill; (*de
coche*) grille; **(carne a la) ~** barbecue;
parrillada *nf* barbecue

párroco ['parroko] *nm* parish priest

parroquia [pa'rrokja] *nf* parish;
(*iglesia*) parish church; (*Com*) clientele,
customers *pl*; **parroquiano, -a** *nm/f*
parishioner; (*Com*) client, customer

parte ['parte] *nm* message; (*informe*)
report ▷ *nf* part; (*lado, cara*) side; (*de
reparto*) share; (*Jur*) party; **en alguna
~ de Europa** somewhere in Europe;
en *o* **por todas ~s** everywhere; **en
gran ~** to a large extent; **la mayor ~
de los españoles** most Spaniards;
de un tiempo a esta ~ for some time
past; **de ~ de algn** on sb's behalf; **¿de**

~ de quién? (*Tel*) who is speaking?;
por ~ de on the part of; **yo por mi ~** I
for my part; **por otra ~** on the other
hand; **dar ~** to inform; **tomar ~** to take
part; **parte meteorológico** weather
forecast *o* report

participación [partiθipa'θjon] *nf*
(*acto*) participation, taking part; (*parte,
Com*) share; (*de lotería*) shared prize;
(*aviso*) notice, notification

participante [partiθi'pante] *nmf*
participant

participar [partiθi'par] *vt* to notify,
inform ▷ *vi* to take part, participate

partícipe [par'tiθipe] *nmf*
participant

particular [partiku'lar] *adj* (*especial*)
particular, special; (*individual, personal*)
private, personal ▷ *nm* (*punto, asunto*)
particular, point; (*individuo*) individual;
tiene coche ~ he has a car of his own

partida [par'tiða] *nf* (*salida*)
departure; (*Com*) entry, item; (*juego*)
game; (*grupo de personas*) band,
group; **mala ~** dirty trick; **partida de
nacimiento/matrimonio/defunción**
(*ESP*) birth/marriage/death certificate

partidario, -a [parti'ðarjo, a] *adj*
partisan ▷ *nm/f* supporter, follower

partido [par'tiðo] *nm* (*Pol*) party;
(*Deporte*) game, match; **sacar ~ de**
to profit *o* benefit from; **tomar ~** to
take sides

partir [par'tir] *vt* (*dividir*) to split,
divide; (*compartir, distribuir*) to share
(out), distribute; (*romper*) to break
open, split open; (*rebanada*) to cut (off)
▷ *vi* (*ponerse en camino*) to set off *o* out;
(*comenzar*) to start (off *o* out); **partirse**
vr to crack *o* split *o* break (in two *etc*); **a
~ de** (starting) from

partitura [parti'tura] *nf* (*Mús*) score

parto ['parto] *nm* birth; (*fig*) product,
creation; **estar de ~** to be in labour

parvulario [parβu'larjo] (*ESP*) *nm*
nursery school, kindergarten

pasa ['pasa] *nf* raisin; **pasa de
Corinto** currant

pasacintas [pasa'θintas] (*LAM*) *nm* cassette player

pasada [pa'saða] *nf* passing, passage; **de ~** in passing, incidentally; **una mala ~** a dirty trick

pasadizo [pasa'ðiθo] *nm* (*pasillo*) passage, corridor; (*callejuela*) alley

pasado, -a [pa'saðo, a] *adj* past; (*malo: comida, fruta*) bad; (*muy cocido*) overdone; (*anticuado*) out of date ▷ *nm* past; **~ mañana** the day after tomorrow; **el mes ~** last month

pasador [pasa'ðor] *nm* (*cerrojo*) bolt; (*de pelo*) hair slide; (*horquilla*) grip

pasaje [pa'saxe] *nm* passage; (*pago de viaje*) fare; (*los pasajeros*) passengers *pl*; (*pasillo*) passageway

pasajero, -a [pasa'xero, a] *adj* passing; (*situación, estado*) temporary; (*amor, enfermedad*) brief ▷ *nm/f* passenger

pasamontañas [pasamon'tañas] *nm inv* balaclava helmet

pasaporte [pasa'porte] *nm* passport

pasar [pa'sar] *vt* to pass; (*tiempo*) to spend; (*desgracias*) to suffer, endure; (*noticia*) to give, pass on; (*río*) to cross; (*barrera*) to pass through; (*falta*) to overlook, tolerate; (*contrincante*) to surpass, do better than; (*coche*) to overtake; (*Cine*) to show; (*enfermedad*) to give, infect with ▷ *vi* (*gen*) to pass; (*terminarse*) to be over; (*ocurrir*) to happen; **pasarse** *vr* (*flores*) to fade; (*comida*) to go bad o off; (*fig*) to overdo it, go too far; **~ de** to go beyond, exceed; **~ por** (*LAM*) to fetch; **~lo bien/mal** to have a good/bad time; **¡pase!** come in!; **hacer ~** to show in; **lo que pasa es que ...** the thing is ...; **~se al enemigo** to go over to the enemy; **se me pasó** I forgot; **no se le pasa nada** he misses nothing; **pase lo que pase** come what may; **¿qué pasa?** what's going on?, what's up?; **¿qué te pasa?** what's wrong?

pasarela [pasa'rela] *nf* footbridge; (*en barco*) gangway

pasatiempo [pasa'tjempo] *nm* pastime, hobby

Pascua ['paskwa] *nf* (*en Semana Santa*) Easter; **Pascuas** *nfpl* Christmas (time); **¡felices ~s!** Merry Christmas!

pase ['pase] *nm* pass; (*Cine*) performance, showing

pasear [pase'ar] *vt* to take for a walk; (*exhibir*) to parade, show off ▷ *vi* to walk, go for a walk; **pasearse** *vr* to walk, go for a walk; **~ en coche** to go for a drive; **paseo** *nm* (*avenida*) avenue; (*distancia corta*) walk, stroll; **dar un** o **ir de paseo** to go for a walk; **paseo marítimo** (*ESP*) promenade

pasillo [pa'siλo] *nm* passage, corridor

pasión [pa'sjon] *nf* passion

pasivo, -a [pa'siβo, a] *adj* passive; (*inactivo*) inactive ▷ *nm* (*Com*) liabilities *pl*, debts *pl*

pasmoso, -a [pas'moso, a] *adj* amazing, astonishing

paso, -a ['paso, a] *adj* dried ▷ *nm* step; (*modo de andar*) walk; (*huella*) footprint; (*rapidez*) speed, pace, rate; (*camino accesible*) way through, passage; (*cruce*) crossing; (*pasaje*) passing, passage; (*Geo*) pass; (*estrecho*) strait; **a ese ~** (*fig*) at that rate; **salir al ~ de** o **a** to waylay; **estar de ~** to be passing through; **prohibido el ~** no entry; **ceda el ~** give way; **paso a nivel** (*Ferro*) level-crossing; **paso (de) cebra** (*ESP*) zebra crossing; **paso de peatones** pedestrian crossing; **paso elevado** flyover

pasota [pa'sota] (*ESP: fam*) *adj, nmf* ≈ dropout; **ser un ~** to be a bit of a dropout; (*ser indiferente*) not to care about anything

pasta ['pasta] *nf* paste; (*Culin: masa*) dough; (: *de bizcochos etc*) pastry; (*fam*) dough; **pastas** *nfpl* (*bizcochos*) pastries, small cakes; (*fideos, espaguetis etc*) pasta; **pasta dentífrica** o **de dientes** toothpaste

pastar [pas'tar] *vt, vi* to graze

pastel [pas'tel] *nm* (*dulce*) cake; (*Arte*)

pastel; **pastel de carne** meat pie;
pastelería nf cake shop
pastilla [pas'tiʎa] nf (de jabón,
chocolate) bar; (píldora) tablet, pill
pasto ['pasto] nm (hierba) grass;
(lugar) pasture, field; **pastor, a**
[pas'tor, a] nm/f shepherd/ess
▷ nm (Rel) clergyman, pastor; **pastor
alemán** Alsatian
pata ['pata] nf (pierna) leg; (pie) foot;
(de muebles) leg; **~s arriba** upside down;
metedura de ~ (fam) gaffe; **meter la
~** (fam) to put one's foot in it; **tener
buena/mala ~** to be lucky/unlucky;
pata de cabra (Tec) crowbar; **patada**
nf kick; (en el suelo) stamp
patata [pa'tata] nf potato; **patatas
fritas** chips, French fries; (de bolsa)
crisps
paté [pa'te] nm pâté
patente [pa'tente] adj obvious,
evident; (Com) patent ▷ nf patent
paternal [pater'nal] adj fatherly,
paternal; **paterno, -a** adj paternal
patético, -a [pa'tetiko, a] adj
pathetic, moving
patilla [pa'tiʎa] nf (de gafas)
side(piece); **patillas** nfpl sideburns
patín [pa'tin] nm skate; (de trineo)
runner; **patín de ruedas** roller skate;
patinaje nm skating; **patinar** vi to
skate; (resbalarse) to skid, slip; (fam) to
slip up, blunder
patineta [pati'neta] nf (MÉX: patinete)
scooter; (cs: monopatín) skateboard
patinete [pati'nete] nm scooter
patio ['patjo] nm (de casa) patio,
courtyard; **patio de recreo** playground
pato ['pato] nm duck; **pagar el ~** (fam)
to take the blame, carry the can
patoso, -a [pa'toso, a] (fam) adj
clumsy
patotero [pato'tero] (cs) nm
hooligan, lout
patraña [pa'traɲa] nf story, fib
patria ['patrja] nf native land,
mother country
patrimonio [patri'monjo] nm

inheritance; (fig) heritage
patriota [pa'trjota] nmf patriot
patrocinar [patroθi'nar] vt to
sponsor
patrón, -ona [pa'tron, ona] nm/f
(jefe) boss, chief, master(mistress);
(propietario) landlord/lady; (Rel) patron
saint ▷ nm (Tec, Costura) pattern
patronato [patro'nato] nm
sponsorship; (acto) patronage;
(fundación benéfica) trust, foundation
patrulla [pa'truʎa] nf patrol
pausa ['pausa] nf pause, break
pauta ['pauta] nf line, guide line
pava ['paβa] (RPL) nf kettle
pavimento [paβi'mento] nm (de
losa) pavement, paving
pavo ['paβo] nm turkey; **pavo real**
peacock
payaso, -a [pa'jaso, a] nm/f clown
payo, -a ['pajo, a] nm/f non-gipsy
paz [paθ] nf peace; (tranquilidad)
peacefulness, tranquillity; **hacer las
paces** to make peace; (fig) to make up;
¡déjame en ~! leave me alone!
PC nm PC, personal computer
P.D. abr (= posdata) P.S., p.s.
peaje [pe'axe] nm toll
peatón [pea'ton] nm pedestrian;
peatonal adj pedestrian
peca ['peka] nf freckle
pecado [pe'kaðo] nm sin; **pecador, a**
adj sinful ▷ nm/f sinner
pecaminoso, -a [pekami'noso, a]
adj sinful
pecar [pe'kar] vi (Rel) to sin; **peca de
generoso** he is generous to a fault
pecera [pe'θera] nf fish tank;
(redonda) goldfish bowl
pecho ['petʃo] nm (Anat) chest; (de
mujer) breast; **dar el ~ a** to breast-feed;
tomar algo a ~ to take sth to heart
pechuga [pe'tʃuxa] nf breast
peculiar [peku'ljar] adj special,
peculiar; (característico) typical,
characteristic
pedal [pe'ðal] nm pedal; **pedalear**
vi to pedal

pedante [pe'ðante] *adj* pedantic
 ▷ *nmf* pedant

pedazo [pe'ðaθo] *nm* piece, bit;
 hacerse ~s to smash, shatter

pediatra [pe'ðjatra] *nmf*
 paediatrician

pedido [pe'ðiðo] *nm* (*Com*) order;
 (*petición*) request

pedir [pe'ðir] *vt* to ask for, request;
 (*comida, Com: mandar*) to order;
 (*necesitar*) to need, demand, require
 ▷ *vi* to ask; **me pidió que cerrara la
 puerta** he asked me to shut the door;
 ¿cuánto piden por el coche? how
 much are they asking for the car?

pedo ['peðo] (*fam!*) *nm* fart

pega ['peɣa] *nf* snag; **poner ~s (a)** to
 complain (about)

pegadizo, -a [peɣa'ðiθo, a] *adj*
 (*Mús*) catchy

pegajoso, -a [peɣa'xoso, a] *adj*
 sticky, adhesive

pegamento [peɣa'mento] *nm*
 gum, glue

pegar [pe'ɣar] *vt* (*papel, sellos*) to
 stick (on); (*cartel*) to stick up; (*coser*)
 to sew (on); (*unir: partes*) to join, fix
 together; (*Comput*) to paste; (*Med*) to
 give, infect with; (*dar: golpe*) to give,
 deal ▷ *vi* (*adherirse*) to stick, adhere; (*ir
 juntos: colores*) to match, go together;
 (*golpear*) to hit; (*quemar: el sol*) to strike
 hot, burn; **pegarse** *vr* (*gen*) to stick;
 (*dos personas*) to hit each other, fight;
 (*fam*): **~ un grito** to let out a yell; **~ un
 salto** to jump (with fright); **~ en** to
 touch; **~se un tiro** to shoot o.s.

pegatina [peɣa'tina] *nf* sticker

pegote [pe'ɣote] (*fam*) *nm* eyesore,
 sight

peinado [pei'naðo] *nm* hairstyle

peinar [pei'nar] *vt* to comb; (*hacer
 estilo*) to style; **peinarse** *vr* to comb
 one's hair

peine ['peine] *nm* comb; **peineta** *nf*
 ornamental comb

p.ej. *abr* (= *por ejemplo*) e.g.

Pekín [pe'kin] *n* Pekin(g)

pelado, -a [pe'laðo, a] *adj* (*fruta,
 patata etc*) peeled; (*cabeza*) shorn;
 (*campo, fig*) bare; (*fam: sin dinero*) broke

pelar [pe'lar] *vt* (*fruta, patatas etc*) to
 peel; (*cortar el pelo a*) to cut the hair of;
 (*quitar la piel: animal*) to skin; **pelarse** *vr*
 (*la piel*) to peel off; **voy a ~me** I'm going
 to get my hair cut

peldaño [pel'daɲo] *nm* step

pelea [pe'lea] *nf* (*lucha*) fight;
 (*discusión*) quarrel, row; **peleado, -a**
 [pele'aðo, a] *adj*: **estar peleado (con
 algn)** to have fallen out (with sb);
 pelear [pele'ar] *vi* to fight; **pelearse**
 vr to fight; (*reñirse*) to fall out, quarrel

pelela [pe'lela] (*cs*) *nf* potty

peletería [pelete'ria] *nf* furrier's,
 fur shop

pelícano [pe'likano] *nm* pelican

película [pe'likula] *nf* film; (*cobertura
 ligera*) thin covering; (*Foto: rollo*) roll
 o reel of film; **película de dibujos
 (animados)/del oeste** cartoon/
 western

peligro [pe'liɣro] *nm* danger; (*riesgo*)
 risk; **correr ~ de** to run the risk of;
 peligroso, -a *adj* dangerous; risky

pelirrojo, -a [peli'rroxo, a] *adj* red-
 haired, red-headed ▷ *nm/f* redhead

pellejo [pe'ʎexo] *nm* (*de animal*)
 skin, hide

pellizcar [peʎiθ'kar] *vt* to pinch, nip

pelma ['pelma] (*ESP: fam*) *nmf* pain
 (in the neck)

pelmazo [pel'maθo] (*fam*) *nm* =
 pelma

pelo ['pelo] *nm* (*cabellos*) hair;
 (*de barba, bigote*) whisker; (*de
 animal: pellejo*) hair, fur, coat; **venir al
 ~** to be exactly what one needs; **un
 hombre de ~ en pecho** a brave man;
 por los ~s by the skin of one's teeth; **no
 tener ~s en la lengua** to be outspoken
 not to mince one's words; **con ~s y
 señales** in minute detail; **tomar el ~ a
 algn** to pull sb's leg

pelota [pe'lota] *nf* ball; **en ~** stark
 naked; **hacer la ~ (a algn)** (*ESP: fam*) to

creep (to sb); **pelota vasca** pelota

pelotón [pelo'ton] nm (Mil) squad, detachment

peluca [pe'luka] nf wig

peluche [pe'lutʃe] nm: **oso/muñeco de ~** teddy bear/soft toy

peludo, -a [pe'luðo, a] adj hairy, shaggy

peluquería [peluke'ria] nf hairdresser's; **peluquero, -a** nm/f hairdresser

pelusa [pe'lusa] nf (Bot) down; (en tela) fluff

pena ['pena] nf (congoja) grief, sadness; (remordimiento) regret; (dificultad) trouble; (dolor) pain; (Jur) sentence; **merecer** o **valer la ~** to be worthwhile; **a duras ~s** with great difficulty; **¡qué ~!** what a shame!; **pena capital** capital punishment; **pena de muerte** death penalty

penal [pe'nal] adj penal ▷ nm (cárcel) prison

penalidad [penali'ðað] nf (problema, dificultad) trouble, hardship; (Jur) penalty, punishment; **penalidades** nfpl trouble sg, hardship sg

penalti [pe'nalti] nm = **penalty**

penalty [pe'nalti] (pl **~s** o **penalties**) nm penalty (kick)

pendiente [pen'djente] adj pending, unsettled ▷ nm earring ▷ nf hill, slope

pene ['pene] nm penis

penetrante [pene'trante] adj (herida) deep; (persona, arma) sharp; (sonido) penetrating, piercing; (mirada) searching; (viento, ironía) biting

penetrar [pene'trar] vt to penetrate, pierce; (entender) to grasp ▷ vi to penetrate, go in; (entrar) to enter, go in; (líquido) to soak in; (fig) to pierce

penicilina [peniθi'lina] nf penicillin

península [pe'ninsula] nf peninsula; **peninsular** adj peninsular

penique [pe'nike] nm penny

penitencia [peni'tenθja] nf penance

penoso, -a [pe'noso, a] adj (lamentable) distressing; (difícil)

arduous, difficult

pensador, a [pensa'ðor, a] nm/f thinker

pensamiento [pensa'mjento] nm thought; (mente) mind; (idea) idea

pensar [pen'sar] vt to think; (considerar) to think over, think out; (proponerse) to intend, plan; (imaginarse) to think up, invent ▷ vi to think; **~ en** to aim at, aspire to; **pensativo, -a** adj thoughtful, pensive

pensión [pen'sjon] nf (casa) boarding o guest house; (dinero) pension; (cama y comida) board and lodging; **media ~** half-board; **pensión completa** full board; **pensionista** nmf (jubilado) (old-age) pensioner; (huésped) lodger

penúltimo, -a [pe'nultimo, a] adj penultimate, last but one

penumbra [pe'numbra] nf half-light

peña ['pena] nf (roca) rock; (cuesta) cliff, crag; (grupo) group, circle; (LAM: club) folk club

peñasco [pe'nasko] nm large rock, boulder

peñón [pe'non] nm wall of rock; **el P~** the Rock (of Gibraltar)

peón [pe'on] nm labourer; (LAM Agr) farm labourer, farmhand; (Ajedrez) pawn

peonza [pe'onθa] nf spinning top

peor [pe'or] adj (comparativo) worse; (superlativo) worst ▷ adv worse; worst; **de mal en ~** from bad to worse

pepinillo [pepi'niʎo] nm gherkin

pepino [pe'pino] nm cucumber; **(no) me importa un ~** I don't care one bit

pepita [pe'pita] nf (Bot) pip; (Minería) nugget

pepito [pe'pito] (ESP) nm (tb: **~ de ternera**) steak sandwich

pequeño, -a [pe'keno, a] adj small, little

pera ['pera] nf pear; **peral** nm pear tree

percance [per'kanθe] nm setback, misfortune

percatarse [perka'tarse] vr: **~ de** to

notice, take note of

percebe [per'θeβe] *nm* barnacle

percepción [perθep'θjon] *nf* (*vista*) perception; (*idea*) notion, idea

percha ['pertʃa] *nf* (coat)hanger; (*ganchos*) coat hooks *pl*; (*de ave*) perch

percibir [perθi'βir] *vt* to perceive, notice; (*Com*) to earn, get

percusión [perku'sjon] *nf* percussion

perdedor, a [perðe'ðor, a] *adj* losing ▷ *nm/f* loser

perder [per'ðer] *vt* to lose; (*tiempo, palabras*) to waste; (*oportunidad*) to lose, miss; (*tren*) to miss ▷ *vi* to lose; **perderse** *vr* (*extraviarse*) to get lost; (*desaparecer*) to disappear, be lost to view; (*arruinarse*) to be ruined; **echar a ~** (*comida*) to spoil, ruin; (*oportunidad*) to waste

pérdida ['perðiða] *nf* loss; (*de tiempo*) waste; **pérdidas** *nfpl* (*Com*) losses

perdido, -a [per'ðiðo, a] *adj* lost

perdiz [per'ðiθ] *nf* partridge

perdón [per'ðon] *nm* (*disculpa*) pardon, forgiveness; (*clemencia*) mercy; **¡~!** sorry!, I beg your pardon!; **perdonar** *vt* to pardon, forgive; (*la vida*) to spare; (*excusar*) to exempt, excuse; **¡perdone (usted)!** sorry!, I beg your pardon!

perecedero, -a [pereθe'ðero, a] *adj* perishable

perecer [pere'θer] *vi* to perish, die

peregrinación [pereɣrina'θjon] *nf* (*Rel*) pilgrimage

peregrino, -a [pere'ɣrino, a] *adj* (*idea*) strange, absurd ▷ *nm/f* pilgrim

perejil [pere'xil] *nm* parsley

perenne [pe'renne] *adj* everlasting, perennial

pereza [pe'reθa] *nf* laziness, idleness; **perezoso, -a** *adj* lazy, idle

perfección [perfek'θjon] *nf* perfection; **perfeccionar** *vt* to perfect; (*mejorar*) to improve; (*acabar*) to complete, finish

perfecto, -a [per'fekto, a] *adj* perfect; (*total*) complete

perfil [per'fil] *nm* profile; (*contorno*) silhouette, outline; (*Arq*) (cross) section; **perfiles** *nmpl* features

perforación [perfora'θjon] *nf* perforation; (*con taladro*) drilling; **perforadora** *nf* punch

perforar [perfo'rar] *vt* to perforate; (*agujero*) to drill, bore; (*papel*) to punch a hole in ▷ *vi* to drill, bore

perfume [per'fume] *nm* perfume, scent

periferia [peri'ferja] *nf* periphery; (*de ciudad*) outskirts *pl*

periférico [peri'feriko] (*LAM*) *nm* ring road (*BRIT*), beltway (*US*)

perilla [pe'riʎa] *nf* (*barba*) goatee; (*LAM: de puerta*) doorknob, door handle

perímetro [pe'rimetro] *nm* perimeter

periódico, -a [pe'rjoðiko, a] *adj* periodic(al) ▷ *nm* newspaper

periodismo [perjo'ðismo] *nm* journalism; **periodista** *nmf* journalist

periodo [pe'rjoðo] *nm* period

período [pe'rioðo] *nm* = **periodo**

periquito [peri'kito] *nm* budgerigar, budgie

perito, -a [pe'rito, a] *adj* (*experto*) expert; (*diestro*) skilled, skilful ▷ *nm/f* expert; skilled worker; (*técnico*) technician

perjudicar [perxuði'kar] *vt* (*gen*) to damage, harm; **perjudicial** *adj* damaging, harmful; (*en detrimento*) detrimental; **perjuicio** *nm* damage, harm

perjurar [perxu'rar] *vi* to commit perjury

perla ['perla] *nf* pearl; **me viene de ~s** it suits me fine

permanecer [permane'θer] *vi* (*quedarse*) to stay, remain; (*seguir*) to continue to be

permanente [perma'nente] *adj* permanent, constant ▷ *nf* perm

permiso [per'miso] *nm* permission; (*licencia*) permit, licence; **con ~** excuse me; **estar de ~** (*Mil*) to be on leave;

permiso de conducir driving licence (BRIT), driver's license (US); **permiso por enfermedad** (LAM) sick leave

permitir [permi'tir] vt to permit, allow

pernera [per'nera] nf trouser leg

pero ['pero] conj but; (aún) yet ▷ nm (defecto) flaw, defect; (reparo) objection

perpendicular [perpendiku'lar] adj perpendicular

perpetuo, -a [per'petwo, a] adj perpetual

perplejo, -a [per'plexo, a] adj perplexed, bewildered

perra ['perra] nf (Zool) bitch; **estar sin una ~** (ESP: fam) to be flat broke

perrera [pe'rrera] nf kennel

perrito [pe'rrito] nm (tb: **~ caliente**) hot dog

perro ['perro] nm dog

persa ['persa] adj, nmf Persian

persecución [perseku'θjon] nf pursuit, chase; (Rel, Pol) persecution

perseguir [perse'xir] vt to pursue, hunt; (cortejar) to chase after; (molestar) to pester, annoy; (Rel, Pol) to persecute

persiana [per'sjana] nf (Venetian) blind

persistente [persis'tente] adj persistent

persistir [persis'tir] vi to persist

persona [per'sona] nf person; **persona mayor** elderly person

personaje [perso'naxe] nm important person, celebrity; (Teatro etc) character

personal [perso'nal] adj (particular) personal; (para una persona) single, for one person ▷ nm personnel, staff; **personalidad** nf personality

personarse [perso'narse] vr to appear in person

personificar [personifi'kar] vt to personify

perspectiva [perspek'tiβa] nf perspective; (vista, panorama) view, panorama; (posibilidad futura) outlook, prospect

persuadir [perswa'ðir] vt (gen) to persuade; (convencer) to convince; **persuadirse** vr to become convinced; **persuasión** nf persuasion

pertenecer [pertene'θer] vi to belong; (fig) to concern; **perteneciente** adj: **perteneciente a** belonging to; **pertenencia** nf ownership; **pertenencias** nfpl (bienes) possessions, property sg

pertenezca etc vb V **pertenecer**

pértiga ['pertixa] nf: **salto de ~** pole vault

pertinente [perti'nente] adj relevant, pertinent; (apropiado) appropriate; **~ a** concerning, relevant to

perturbación [perturβa'θjon] nf (Pol) disturbance; (Med) upset, disturbance

Perú [pe'ru] nm Peru; **peruano, -a** adj, nm/f Peruvian

perversión [perβer'sjon] nf perversion; **perverso, -a** adj perverse; (depravado) depraved

pervertido, -a [perβer'tiðo, a] adj perverted ▷ nm/f pervert

pervertir [perβer'tir] vt to pervert, corrupt

pesa ['pesa] nf weight; (Deporte) shot

pesadez [pesa'ðeθ] nf (peso) heaviness; (lentitud) slowness; (aburrimiento) tediousness

pesadilla [pesa'ðiʎa] nf nightmare, bad dream

pesado, -a [pe'saðo, a] adj heavy; (lento) slow; (difícil, duro) tough, hard; (aburrido) boring, tedious; (tiempo) sultry

pésame ['pesame] nm expression of condolence, message of sympathy; **dar el ~** to express one's condolences

pesar [pe'sar] vt to weigh ▷ vi to weigh; (ser pesado) to weigh a lot, be heavy; (fig: opinión) to carry weight; **no pesa mucho** it's not very heavy ▷ nm (arrepentimiento) regret; (pena) grief, sorrow; **a ~ de** o **pese a (que)** in spite of, despite

pesca ['peska] nf (acto) fishing; (lo pescado) catch; **ir de ~** to go fishing

pescadería [peskaðe'ria] nf fish shop, fishmonger's (BRIT)

pescadilla [peska'ðiʎa] nf whiting

pescado [pes'kaðo] nm fish

pescador, a [peska'ðor, a] nm/f fisherman/woman

pescar [pes'kar] vt (tomar) to catch; (intentar tomar) to fish for; (conseguir: trabajo) to manage to get ▷ vi to fish, go fishing

pesebre [pe'seβre] nm manger

peseta [pe'seta] nf (Hist) peseta

pesimista [pesi'mista] adj pessimistic ▷ nmf pessimist

pésimo, -a ['pesimo, a] adj awful, dreadful

peso ['peso] nm weight; (balanza) scales pl; (moneda) peso; **vender al ~** to sell by weight; **peso bruto/neto** gross/net weight; **peso pesado/pluma** heavyweight/featherweight

pesquero, -a [pes'kero, a] adj fishing cpd

pestaña [pes'taɲa] nf (Anat) eyelash; (borde) rim

peste ['peste] nf plague; (mal olor) stink, stench

pesticida [pesti'θiða] nm pesticide

pestillo [pes'tiʎo] nm (cerrojo) bolt; (picaporte) door handle

petaca [pe'taka] nf (de cigarros) cigarette case; (de pipa) tobacco pouch; (MÉX: maleta) suitcase

pétalo ['petalo] nm petal

petardo [pe'tarðo] nm firework, firecracker

petición [peti'θjon] nf (pedido) request, plea; (memorial) petition; (Jur) plea

peto ['peto] (ESP) nm dungarees pl, overalls pl (US)

petróleo [pe'troleo] nm oil, petroleum; **petrolero, -a** adj petroleum cpd ▷ nm (oil) tanker

peyorativo, -a [pejora'tiβo, a] adj pejorative

pez [peθ] nm fish; **pez espada** swordfish

pezón [pe'θon] nm teat, nipple

pezuña [pe'θuɲa] nf hoof

pianista [pja'nista] nmf pianist

piano ['pjano] nm piano

piar [pjar] vi to cheep

pibe, -a ['piβe, a] (RPL) nm/f boy/girl

picadero [pika'ðero] nm riding school

picadillo [pika'ðiʎo] nm mince, minced meat

picado, -a [pi'kaðo, a] adj pricked, punctured; (Culin) minced, chopped; (mar) choppy; (diente) bad; (tabaco) cut; (enfadado) cross

picador [pika'ðor] nm (Taur) picador; (minero) faceworker

picadura [pika'ðura] nf (pinchazo) puncture; (de abeja) sting; (de mosquito) bite; (tabaco picado) cut tobacco

picante [pi'kante] adj hot; (comentario) racy, spicy

picaporte [pika'porte] nm (manija) doorhandle; (pestillo) latch

picar [pi'kar] vt (agujerear, perforar) to prick, puncture; (abeja) to sting; (mosquito, serpiente) to bite; (Culin) to mince, chop; (incitar) to incite, goad; (dañar, irritar) to annoy, bother; (quemar: lengua) to burn, sting ▷ vi (pez) to bite, take the bait; (sol) to burn, scorch; (abeja, Med) to sting; (mosquito) to bite; **picarse** vr (agriarse) to turn sour, go off; (ofenderse) to take offence

picardía [pikar'ðia] nf villainy; (astucia) slyness, craftiness; (una picardía) dirty trick; (palabra) rude/bad word o expression

pícaro, -a ['pikaro, a] adj (malicioso) villainous; (travieso) mischievous ▷ nm (astuto) crafty sort; (sinvergüenza) rascal, scoundrel

pichi ['pitʃi] (ESP) nm pinafore dress (BRIT), jumper (US)

pichón [pi'tʃon] nm young pigeon

pico ['piko] nm (de ave) beak; (punta)

sharp point; (*Tec*) pick, pickaxe; (*Geo*) peak, summit; **y ~** and a bit; **las seis y ~** six and a bit

picor [pi'kor] *nm* itch

picoso, -a [pi'koso, a] (*MÉX*) *adj* (*comida*) hot

picudo, -a [pi'kuðo, a] *adj* pointed, with a point

pidió *etc vb* V **pedir**

pido *etc vb* V **pedir**

pie [pje] (*pl* **~s**) *nm* foot; (*fig: motivo*) motive, basis; (: *fundamento*) foothold; **ir a ~** to go on foot, walk; **estar de ~** to be standing (up); **ponerse de ~** to stand up; **de ~s a cabeza** from top to bottom; **al ~ de la letra** (*citar*) literally, verbatim; (*copiar*) exactly, word for word; **en ~ de guerra** on a war footing; **dar ~ a** to give cause for; **hacer ~** (*en el agua*) to touch (the) bottom

piedad [pje'ðað] *nf* (*lástima*) pity, compassion; (*clemencia*) mercy; (*devoción*) piety, devotion

piedra ['pjeðra] *nf* stone; (*roca*) rock; (*de mechero*) flint; (*Meteorología*) hailstone; **piedra preciosa** precious stone

piel [pjel] *nf* (*Anat*) skin; (*Zool*) skin, hide, fur; (*cuero*) leather; (*Bot*) skin, peel

pienso *etc vb* V **pensar**

pierdo *etc vb* V **perder**

pierna ['pjerna] *nf* leg

pieza ['pjeθa] *nf* piece; (*habitación*) room; **pieza de recambio** o **repuesto** spare (part)

pigmeo, -a [pix'meo, a] *adj, nm/f* pigmy

pijama [pi'xama] *nm* pyjamas *pl* (*BRIT*), pajamas *pl* (*US*)

pila ['pila] *nf* (*Elec*) battery; (*montón*) heap, pile; (*lavabo*) sink

píldora ['pildora] *nf* pill; **la ~ (anticonceptiva)** the (contraceptive) pill

pileta [pi'leta] (*RPL*) *nf* (*fregadero*) (kitchen) sink; (*piscina*) swimming pool

pillar [pi'ʎar] *vt* (*saquear*) to pillage, plunder; (*fam: coger*) to catch; (: *agarrar*)

to grasp, seize; (: *entender*) to grasp, catch on to; **pillarse** *vr*: **~se un dedo con la puerta** to catch one's finger in the door

pillo, -a ['piʎo, a] *adj* villainous; (*astuto*) sly, crafty ▷ *nm/f* rascal, rogue, scoundrel

piloto [pi'loto] *nm* pilot; (*de aparato*) (pilot) light; (*Auto: luz*) tail o rear light; (: *conductor*) driver; **piloto automático** automatic pilot

pimentón [pimen'ton] *nm* paprika

pimienta [pi'mjenta] *nf* pepper

pimiento [pi'mjento] *nm* pepper, pimiento

pin [pin] (*pl* **~s**) *nm* badge

pinacoteca [pinako'teka] *nf* art gallery

pinar [pi'nar] *nm* pine forest (*BRIT*), pine grove (*US*)

pincel [pin'θel] *nm* paintbrush

pinchadiscos [pintʃa'ðiskos] (*ESP*) *nmf inv* disc-jockey, DJ

pinchar [pin'tʃar] *vt* (*perforar*) to prick, pierce; (*neumático*) to puncture; (*fig*) to prod; (*Inform*) to click

pinchazo [pin'tʃaθo] *nm* (*perforación*) prick; (*de neumático*) puncture; (*fig*) prod

pincho ['pintʃo] *nm* savoury (snack); **pincho de tortilla** small slice of omelette; **pincho moruno** shish kebab

ping-pong ['pin'pon] *nm* table tennis

pingüino [pin'gwino] *nm* penguin

pino ['pino] *nm* pine (tree)

pinta ['pinta] *nf* spot; (*de líquidos*) spot, drop; (*aspecto*) appearance, look(s) (*pl*); **pintado, -a** *adj* spotted; (*de colores*) colourful; **pintadas** *nfpl* graffiti *sg*

pintalabios [pinta'laβjos] (*ESP*) *nm inv* lipstick

pintar [pin'tar] *vt* to paint ▷ *vi* to paint; (*fam*) to count, be important; **pintarse** *vr* to put on make-up

pintor, a [pin'tor, a] *nm/f* painter

pintoresco, -a [pinto'resko, a] *adj* picturesque

pintura [pin'tura] *nf* painting;
pintura al óleo oil painting
pinza ['pinθa] *nf* (Zool) claw; (para
colgar ropa) clothes peg; (Tec) pincers
pl; **pinzas** *nfpl* (para depilar etc)
tweezers *pl*
piña ['piɲa] *nf* (de pino) pine cone;
(fruta) pineapple; (fig) group
piñata [pi'ɲata] *nf* container hung up
at parties to be beaten with sticks until
sweets or presents fall out

● **PIÑATA**
●
● **Piñata** is a very popular party
● game in Mexico. The **piñata** itself
● is a hollow figure made of papier
● maché, or, traditionally, from
● adobe, in the shape of an object,
● a star, a person or an animal. It is
● filled with either sweets and toys,
● or fruit and yam beans. The game
● consists of hanging the **piñata**
● from the ceiling, and beating it
● with a stick, blindfolded, until it
● breaks and the presents fall out.

piñón [pi'ɲon] *nm* (fruto) pine nut;
(Tec) pinion
pío, -a ['pio, a] *adj* (devoto) pious,
devout; (misericordioso) merciful
piojo ['pjoxo] *nm* louse
pipa ['pipa] *nf* pipe; **pipas** *nfpl* (Bot)
(edible) sunflower seeds
pipí [pi'pi] (fam) *nm*: **hacer ~** to have
a wee(-wee) (BRIT), have to go (wee-
wee) (US)
pique ['pike] *nm* (resentimiento)
pique, resentment; (rivalidad)
rivalry, competition; **irse a ~** to sink;
(esperanza, familia) to be ruined
piqueta [pi'keta] *nf* pick(axe)
piquete [pi'kete] *nm* (Mil) squad,
party; (de obreros) picket; (MÉX: de
insecto) bite; **piquetear** (LAM) *vt* to
picket
pirado, -a [pi'raðo, a] (fam) *adj*
round the bend ▷ *nm/f* nutter

piragua [pi'raxwa] *nf* canoe;
piragüismo *nm* canoeing
pirámide [pi'ramiðe] *nf* pyramid
pirata [pi'rata] *adj*, *nmf* pirate; **pirata
informático** hacker
Pirineo(s) [piri'neo(s)] *nm(pl)*
Pyrenees *pl*
pirómano, -a [pi'romano, a] *nm/f*
(Med, Jur) arsonist
piropo [pi'ropo] *nm* compliment,
(piece of) flattery
pirueta [pi'rweta] *nf* pirouette
piruleta [piru'leta] (ESP) *nf* lollipop
pis [pis] (fam) *nm* pee, piss; **hacer ~** to
have a pee; (para niños) to wee-wee
pisada [pi'saða] *nf* (paso) footstep;
(huella) footprint
pisar [pi'sar] *vt* (caminar sobre) to walk
on, tread on; (apretar con el pie) to press;
(fig) to trample on, walk all over ▷ *vi* to
tread, step, walk
piscina [pis'θina] *nf* swimming pool
Piscis ['pisθis] *nm* Pisces
piso ['piso] *nm* (suelo, planta)
floor; (ESP: apartamento) flat (BRIT),
apartment; **primer ~** (ESP) first floor;
(LAM: planta baja) ground floor
pisotear [pisote'ar] *vt* to trample (on
o underfoot)
pista ['pista] *nf* track, trail; (indicio)
clue; **pista de aterrizaje** runway; **pista
de baile** dance floor; **pista de hielo** ice
rink; **pista de tenis** (ESP) tennis court
pistola [pis'tola] *nf* pistol; (Tec)
spray-gun
pistón [pis'ton] *nm* (Tec) piston;
(Mús) key
pitar [pi'tar] *vt* (silbato) to blow;
(rechiflar) to whistle at, boo ▷ *vi* to
whistle; (Auto) to sound o toot one's
horn; (LAM: fumar) to smoke
pitillo [pi'tiʎo] *nm* cigarette
pito ['pito] *nm* whistle; (de coche) horn
pitón [pi'ton] *nm* (Zool) python
pitonisa [pito'nisa] *nf* fortune-teller
pitorreo [pito'rreo] *nm* joke; **estar
de ~** to be joking
píxel ['piksel] (*pl* **pixels** or **~es**) *nm*

pixel

piyama [pi'jama] (*LAM*) *nm* pyjamas *pl* (*BRIT*), pajamas *pl* (*US*)

pizarra [pi'θarra] *nf* (*piedra*) slate; (*ESP: encerado*) blackboard; **pizarra blanca** whiteboard; **pizarra interactiva** interactive whiteboard

pizarrón [piθa'rron] (*LAM*) *nm* blackboard

pizca ['piθka] *nf* pinch, spot; (*fig*) spot, speck; **ni ~** not a bit

placa ['plaka] *nf* plate; (*distintivo*) badge, insignia; **placa de matrícula** (*LAM*) number plate

placard [pla'kar] (*RPL*) *nm* cupboard

placer [pla'θer] *nm* pleasure ▷ *vt* to please

plaga ['plaɣa] *nf* pest; (*Med*) plague; (*abundancia*) abundance

plagio ['plaxjo] *nm* plagiarism

plan [plan] *nm* (*esquema, proyecto*) plan; (*idea, intento*) idea, intention; **tener ~** (*fam*) to have a date; **tener un ~** (*fam*) to have an affair; **en ~ económico** (*fam*) on the cheap; **vamos en ~ de turismo** we're going as tourists; **si te pones en ese ~ ...** if that's your attitude ...

plana ['plana] *nf* sheet (of paper), page; (*Tec*) trowel; **en primera ~** on the front page

plancha ['plantʃa] *nf* (*para planchar*) iron; (*rótulo*) plate, sheet; (*Náut*) gangway; **a la ~** (*Culin*) grilled; **planchar** *vt* to iron ▷ *vi* to do the ironing

planear [plane'ar] *vt* to plan ▷ *vi* to glide

planeta [pla'neta] *nm* planet

plano, -a ['plano, a] *adj* flat, level, even ▷ *nm* (*Mat, Tec*) plane; (*Foto*) shot; (*Arq*) plan; (*Geo*) map; (*de ciudad*) map, street plan; **primer ~** close-up

planta ['planta] *nf* (*Bot, Tec*) plant; (*Anat*) sole of the foot, foot; (*piso*) floor; (*LAM: personal*) staff; **planta baja** ground floor

plantar [plan'tar] *vt* (*Bot*) to plant;

(*levantar*) to erect, set up; **plantarse** *vr* to stand firm; **~ a algn en la calle** to throw sb out; **dejar plantado a algn** (*fam*) to stand sb up

plantear [plante'ar] *vt* (*problema*) to pose; (*dificultad*) to raise

plantilla [plan'tiʎa] *nf* (*de zapato*) insole; (*ESP: personal*) personnel; **ser de ~** (*ESP*) to be on the staff

plantón [plan'ton] *nm* (*Mil*) guard, sentry; (*fam*) long wait; **dar (un) ~ a algn** to stand sb up

plasta ['plasta] (*ESP: fam*) *adj inv* boring ▷ *nmf* bore

plástico, -a ['plastiko, a] *adj* plastic ▷ *nm* plastic

Plastilina® [plasti'lina] *nf* Plasticine®

plata ['plata] *nf* (*metal*) silver; (*cosas hechas de plata*) silverware; (*cs: dinero*) cash, dough

plataforma [plata'forma] *nf* platform; **plataforma de lanzamiento/perforación** launch(ing) pad/drilling rig

plátano ['platano] *nm* (*fruta*) banana; (*árbol*) plane tree; banana tree

platea [pla'tea] *nf* (*Teatro*) pit

plática ['platika] *nf* talk, chat; **platicar** *vi* to talk, chat

platillo [pla'tiʎo] *nm* saucer; **platillos** *nmpl* (*Mús*) cymbals; **platillo volante** flying saucer

platino [pla'tino] *nm* platinum; **platinos** *nmpl* (*Auto*) contact points

plato ['plato] *nm* plate, dish; (*parte de comida*) course; (*comida*) dish; **primer ~** first course; **plato combinado** set main course (*served on one plate*); **plato fuerte** main course

playa ['plaja] *nf* beach; (*costa*) seaside; **playa de estacionamiento** (*cs*) car park (*BRIT*), parking lot (*US*)

playera [pla'jera] *nf* (*MÉX: camiseta*) T-shirt; **playeras** *nfpl* (*zapatos*) canvas shoes

plaza ['plaθa] *nf* square; (*mercado*) market(place); (*sitio*) room, space; (*de* *vehículo*) seat, place; (*colocación*) post, job; **plaza de toros** bullring

plazo ['plaθo] *nm* (*lapso de tiempo*) time, period; (*fecha de vencimiento*) expiry date; (*pago parcial*) instalment; **a corto/largo~** short-/long-term; **comprar algo a ~s** to buy sth on hire purchase (*BRIT*) o on time (*US*)

plazoleta [plaθo'leta] *nf* small square

plebeyo, -a [ple'βejo, a] *adj* plebeian; (*pey*) coarse, common

plegable [ple'ɣaβle] *adj* collapsible; (*silla*) folding

pleito ['pleito] *nm* (*Jur*) lawsuit, case; (*fig*) dispute, feud

plenitud [pleni'tuð] *nf* plenitude, fullness; (*abundancia*) abundance

pleno, -a ['pleno, a] *adj* full; (*completo*) complete ▷ *nm* plenum; **en ~ día** in broad daylight; **en ~ verano** at the height of summer; **en plena cara** full in the face

pliego *etc* ['pljeɣo] *vb* V **plegar** ▷ *nm* (*hoja*) sheet (of paper); (*carta*) sealed letter/document; **pliego de condiciones** details *pl*, specifications *pl*

pliegue *etc* ['pljeɣe] *vb* V **plegar** ▷ *nm* fold, crease; (*de vestido*) pleat

plomería [plome'ria] (*LAM*) *nf* plumbing; **plomero** (*LAM*) *nm* plumber

plomo ['plomo] *nm* (*metal*) lead; (*Elec*) fuse; **sin ~** unleaded

pluma ['pluma] *nf* feather; (*para escribir*): **~ (estilográfica)** ink pen; **~ fuente** (*LAM*) fountain pen

plumero [plu'mero] *nm* (*para el polvo*) feather duster

plumón [plu'mon] *nm* (*de ave*) down

plural [plu'ral] *adj* plural

pluriempleo [pluriem'pleo] *nm* having more than one job

plus [plus] *nm* bonus

población [poβla'θjon] *nf* population; (*pueblo, ciudad*) town, city

poblado, -a [po'βlaðo, a] *adj* inhabited ▷ *nm* (*aldea*) village; (*pueblo*)

(*small*) town; **densamente ~** densely populated

poblador, a [poβla'ðor, a] *nm/f* settler, colonist

pobre ['poβre] *adj* poor ▷ *nmf* poor person; **pobreza** *nf* poverty

pocilga [po'θilɣa] *nf* pigsty

○ **PALABRA CLAVE**

poco, -a ['poko, a] *adj* **1** (*sg*) little, not much; **poco tiempo** little o not much time; **de poco interés** of little interest, not very interesting; **poca cosa** not much
2 (*pl*) few, not many; **unos pocos** a few, some; **pocos niños comen lo que les conviene** few children eat what they should
▷ *adv* **1** little, not much; **cuesta poco** it doesn't cost much
2 (*+ adj: negativo, antónimo*): **poco amable/inteligente** not very nice/intelligent
3: **por poco me caigo** I almost fell
4: **a poco: a poco de haberse casado** shortly after getting married
5: **poco a poco** little by little
▷ *nm* a little, a bit; **un poco triste/de dinero** a little sad/money

podar [po'ðar] *vt* to prune

○ **PALABRA CLAVE**

poder [po'ðer] *vi* **1** (*tener capacidad*) can, be able to; **no puedo hacerlo** I can't do it, I'm unable to do it
2 (*tener permiso*) can, may, be allowed to; **¿se puede?** may I (o we)?; **puedes irte ahora** you may go now; **no se puede fumar en este hospital** smoking is not allowed in this hospital
3 (*tener posibilidad*) may, might, could; **puede llegar mañana** he may o might arrive tomorrow; **pudiste haberte hecho daño** you might o could have

hurt yourself; **¡podías habérmelo dicho antes!** you might have told me before!

4: **puede ser** perhaps; **puede ser que lo sepa Tomás** Tomás may o might know

5: **¡no puedo más!** I've had enough!; **es tonto a más no poder** he's as stupid as they come

6: **poder con: no puedo con este crío** this kid's too much for me
▷ *nm* power; **detentar** o **ocupar** o **estar en el poder** to be in power; **poder adquisitivo/ejecutivo/ legislativo** purchasing/executive/ legislative power; **poder judicial** judiciary

poderoso, -a [poðe'roso, a] *adj* (*político, país*) powerful
podio ['poðjo] *nm* (*Deporte*) podium
podium ['poðjum] = **podio**
podrido, -a [po'ðriðo, a] *adj* rotten, bad; (*fig*) rotten, corrupt
podrir [po'ðrir] = **pudrir**
poema [po'ema] *nm* poem
poesía [poe'sia] *nf* poetry
poeta [po'eta] *nmf* poet; **poético, -a** *adj* poetic(al)
poetisa [poe'tisa] *nf* (woman) poet
póker ['poker] *nm* poker
polaco, -a [po'lako, a] *adj* Polish
▷ *nm/f* Pole
polar [po'lar] *adj* polar
polea [po'lea] *nf* pulley
polémica [po'lemika] *nf* polemics *sg*; (*una polémica*) controversy, polemic
polen ['polen] *nm* pollen
policía [poli'θia] *nmf* policeman/ woman ▷ *nf* police; **policíaco, -a** *adj* police *cpd*; **novela policíaca** detective story; **policial** *adj* police *cpd*
polideportivo [poliðepor'tiβo] *nm* sports centre o complex
polígono [po'liɣono] *nm* (*Mat*) polygon; **polígono industrial** (*ESP*) industrial estate

polilla [po'liʎa] *nf* moth
polio ['poljo] *nf* polio
política [po'litika] *nf* politics *sg*; (*económica, agraria etc*) policy; *V tb* **político**
político, -a [po'litiko, a] *adj* political; (*discreto*) tactful; (*de familia*) ...-in-law ▷ *nm/f* politician; **padre ~** father-in-law
póliza ['poliθa] *nf* certificate, voucher; (*impuesto*) tax stamp; **póliza de seguro(s)** insurance policy
polizón [poli'θon] *nm* stowaway
pollera [po'ʎera] (*cs*) *nf* skirt
pollo ['poʎo] *nm* chicken
polo ['polo] *nm* (*Geo, Elec*) pole; (*helado*) ice lolly (*BRIT*), Popsicle® (*US*); (*Deporte*) polo-neck; **polo Norte/Sur** North/South Pole
Polonia [po'lonja] *nf* Poland
poltrona [pol'trona] *nf* easy chair
polución [polu'θjon] *nf* pollution
polvera [pol'βera] *nf* powder compact
polvo ['polβo] *nm* dust; (*Quím, Culin, Med*) powder; **polvos** *nmpl* (*maquillaje*) powder *sg*; **en ~** powdered; **quitar el ~** to dust; **estar hecho ~** (*fam*) to be worn out o exhausted; **polvos de talco** talcum powder *sg*
pólvora ['polβora] *nf* gunpowder
polvoriento, -a [polβo'rjento, a] *adj* (*superficie*) dusty; (*sustancia*) powdery
pomada [po'maða] *nf* cream, ointment
pomelo [po'melo] *nm* grapefruit
pómez ['pomeθ] *nf*: **piedra ~** pumice stone
pomo ['pomo] *nm* doorknob
pompa ['pompa] *nf* (*burbuja*) bubble; (*bomba*) pump; (*esplendor*) pomp, splendour
pómulo ['pomulo] *nm* cheekbone
pon [pon] *vb* V **poner**
ponchadura [pontʃa'dura] (*MÉX*) *nf* puncture (*BRIT*), flat (*US*); **ponchar** (*MÉX*) *vt* (*llanta*) to puncture

ponche ['pontʃe] *nm* punch
poncho ['pontʃo] *nm* poncho
pondré *etc vb* V **poner**

○ **PALABRA CLAVE**

poner [po'ner] *vt* **1** (*colocar*) to put;
(*telegrama*) to send; (*obra de teatro*)
to put on; (*película*) to show; **ponlo
más fuerte** turn it up; **¿qué ponen
en el Excelsior?** what's on at the
Excelsior?
2 (*tienda*) to open; (*instalar: gas etc*) to
put in; (*radio, TV*) to switch *o* turn on
3 (*suponer*): **pongamos que ...** let's
suppose that ...
4 (*contribuir*): **el gobierno ha puesto
otro millón** the government has
contributed another million
5 (*Tel*): **póngame con el Sr. López** can
you put me through to Mr. López?
6: **poner de: le han puesto de
director general** they've appointed
him general manager
7 (+ *adj*) to make; **me estás poniendo
nerviosa** you're making me nervous
8 (*dar nombre*): **al hijo le pusieron
Diego** they called their son Diego
▷ *vi* (*gallina*) to lay
ponerse *vr* **1** (*colocarse*): **se puso a mi
lado** he came and stood beside me;
tú ponte en esa silla you go and sit
on that chair
2 (*vestido, cosméticos*) to put on; **¿por
qué no te pones el vestido nuevo?**
why don't you put on *o* wear your
new dress?
3 (+ *adj*) to turn; to get, become; **se
puso muy serio** he got very serious;
**después de lavarla la tela se puso
azul** after washing it the material
turned blue
4: **ponerse a: se puso a llorar** he
started to cry; **tienes que ponerte
a estudiar** you must get down to
studying

pongo *etc vb* V **poner**

poniente [po'njente] *nm* (*occidente*)
west; (*viento*) west wind
pontífice [pon'tifiθe] *nm* pope,
pontiff
popa ['popa] *nf* stern
popote [po'pote] (*MÉX*) *nm* straw
popular [popu'lar] *adj* popular;
(*cultura*) of the people, folk *cpd*;
popularidad *nf* popularity

○ **PALABRA CLAVE**

por [por] *prep* **1** (*objetivo*) for; **luchar
por la patria** to fight for one's
country
2 (+ *infin*): **por no llegar tarde** so as not
to arrive late; **por citar unos ejemplos**
to give a few examples
3 (*causa*) out of, because of; **por
escasez de fondos** through *o* for lack
of funds
4 (*tiempo*): **por la mañana/noche** in
the morning/at night; **se queda por
una semana** she's staying (for) a week
5 (*lugar*): **pasar por Madrid** to pass
through Madrid; **ir a Guayaquil por
Quito** to go to Guayaquil via Quito;
caminar por la calle to walk along the
street; V *tb* **todo**
6 (*cambio, precio*): **te doy uno nuevo
por el que tienes** I'll give you a new
one (in return) for the one you've got
7 (*valor distributivo*): **6 euros por
hora/cabeza** 6 euros an *o* per hour/a
o per head
8 (*modo, medio*) by; **por correo/avión**
by post/air; **entrar por la entrada
principal** to go in through the main
entrance
9: **10 por 10 son 100** 10 times 10 is 100
10 (*en lugar de*): **vino él por su jefe** he
came instead of his boss
11: **por mí que revienten** as far as I'm
concerned they can drop dead
12: **¿por qué?** why?; **¿por qué no?**
why not?

porcelana [porθe'lana] *nf* porcelain;

(*china*) china

porcentaje [porθen'taxe] *nm* percentage

porción [por'θjon] *nf* (*parte*) portion, share; (*cantidad*) quantity, amount

porfiar [por'fjar] *vi* to persist, insist; (*disputar*) to argue stubbornly

pormenor [porme'nor] *nm* detail, particular

pornografía [pornoxra'fia] *nf* pornography

poro ['poro] *nm* pore

pororó [poro'ro] (*RPL*) *nm* popcorn

poroso, -a [po'roso, a] *adj* porous

poroto [po'roto] (*CS*) *nm* bean

porque ['porke] *conj* (*a causa de*) because; (*ya que*) since; (*con el fin de*) so that, in order that

porqué [por'ke] *nm* reason, cause

porquería [porke'ria] *nf* (*suciedad*) filth, dirt; (*acción*) dirty trick; (*objeto*) small thing, trifle; (*fig*) rubbish

porra ['porra] (*ESP*) *nf* (*arma*) stick, club

porrazo [po'rraθo] *nm* blow, bump

porro ['porro] (*fam*) *nm* (*droga*) joint (*fam*)

porrón [po'rron] *nm* glass wine jar with a long spout

portaaviones [porta'(a)βjones] *nm inv* aircraft carrier

portada [por'taða] *nf* (*de revista*) cover

portador, a [porta'ðor, a] *nm/f* carrier, bearer; (*Com*) bearer, payee

portaequipajes [portaeki'paxes] *nm inv* (*Auto: maletero*) boot; (*: baca*) luggage rack

portafolio [porta'foljo] (*LAM*) *nm* briefcase

portal [por'tal] *nm* (*entrada*) vestibule, hall; (*portada*) porch, doorway; (*puerta de entrada*) main door; (*Internet*) portal; **portales** *nmpl* (*LAM*) arcade *sg*

portamaletas [portama'letas] *nm inv* (*Auto: maletero*) boot; (*: baca*) roof rack

portarse [por'tarse] *vr* to behave, conduct o.s.

portátil [por'tatil] *adj* portable

portavoz [porta'βoθ] *nmf* spokesman/woman

portazo [por'taθo] *nm*: **dar un ~** to slam the door

porte ['porte] *nm* (*Com*) transport; (*precio*) transport charges *pl*

portentoso, -a [porten'toso, a] *adj* marvellous, extraordinary

porteño, -a [por'teɲo, a] *adj* of o from Buenos Aires

portería [porte'ria] *nf* (*oficina*) porter's office; (*Deporte*) goal

portero, -a [por'tero, a] *nm/f* porter; (*conserje*) caretaker; (*ujier*) doorman; (*Deporte*) goalkeeper; **portero automático** (*ESP*) entry phone

pórtico ['portiko] *nm* (*patio*) portico, porch; (*fig*) gateway; (*arcada*) arcade

portorriqueño, -a [portorri'keɲo, a] *adj* Puerto Rican

Portugal [portu'xal] *nm* Portugal; **portugués, -esa** *adj*, *nm/f* Portuguese ▷ *nm* (*Ling*) Portuguese

porvenir [porβe'nir] *nm* future

pos [pos] *prep*: **en ~ de** after, in pursuit of

posaderas [posa'ðeras] *nfpl* backside *sg*, buttocks

posar [po'sar] *vt* (*en el suelo*) to lay down, put down; (*la mano*) to place, put gently ▷ *vi* (*modelo*) to sit, pose; **posarse** *vr* to settle; (*pájaro*) to perch; (*avión*) to land, come down

posavasos [posa'basos] *nm inv* coaster; (*para cerveza*) beermat

posdata [pos'ðata] *nf* postscript

pose ['pose] *nf* pose

poseedor, a [posee'ðor, a] *nm/f* owner, possessor; (*de récord, puesto*) holder

poseer [pose'er] *vt* to possess, own; (*ventaja*) to enjoy; (*récord, puesto*) to hold

posesivo, -a [pose'siβo, a] *adj* possessive

posibilidad [posiβili'ðað] *nf*
possibility; (*oportunidad*) chance;
  posibilitar *vt* to make possible; (*hacer
  realizable*) to make feasible
posible [po'siβle] *adj* possible;
  (*realizable*) feasible; **de ser ~** if possible;
  en lo ~ as far as possible
posición [posi'θjon] *nf* position;
  (*rango social*) status
positivo, -a [posi'tiβo, a] *adj*
positive
poso ['poso] *nm* sediment; (*heces*)
dregs *pl*
posponer [pospo'ner] *vt* (*relegar*)
to put behind/below; (*aplazar*) to
postpone
posta ['posta] *nf*: **a ~** deliberately,
on purpose
postal [pos'tal] *adj* postal ▷ *nf*
postcard
poste ['poste] *nm* (*de telégrafos etc*)
post, pole; (*columna*) pillar
póster ['poster] (*pl* **-es, ~s**) *nm* poster
posterior [poste'rjor] *adj* back, rear;
  (*siguiente*) following, subsequent; (*más
  tarde*) later
postgrado [post'graðo] *nm* =
  posgrado
postizo, -a [pos'tiθo, a] *adj* false,
artificial ▷ *nm* hairpiece
postre ['postre] *nm* sweet, dessert
póstumo, -a ['postumo, a] *adj*
posthumous
postura [pos'tura] *nf* (*del cuerpo*)
posture, position; (*fig*) attitude,
position
potable [po'taβle] *adj* drinkable;
  agua ~ drinking water
potaje [po'taxe] *nm* thick vegetable
soup
potencia [po'tenθja] *nf* power;
  potencial [poten'θjal] *adj, nm*
  potential
potente [po'tente] *adj* powerful
potro, -a ['potro, a] *nm/f* (*Zool*) colt/
filly ▷ *nm* (*de gimnasia*) vaulting horse
pozo ['poθo] *nm* well; (*de río*) deep
pool; (*de mina*) shaft

PP (*ESP*) *nm abr* = **Partido Popular**
práctica ['praktika] *nf* practice;
  (*método*) method; (*arte, capacidad*) skill;
  en la ~ in practice
practicable [prakti'kaβle] *adj*
practicable; (*camino*) passable
practicante [prakti'kante] *nmf*
  (*Med: ayudante de doctor*) medical
  assistant; (: *enfermero*) nurse; (*quien
  practica algo*) practitioner ▷ *adj*
  practising
practicar [prakti'kar] *vt* to practise;
  (*Deporte*) to play; (*realizar*) to carry out,
  perform
práctico, -a ['praktiko, a] *adj*
practical; (*instruído: persona*) skilled,
expert
practique *etc vb* V **practicar**
pradera [pra'ðera] *nf* meadow; (*US
etc*) prairie
prado ['praðo] *nm* (*campo*) meadow,
field; (*pastizal*) pasture
Praga ['praɣa] *n* Prague
pragmático, -a [praɣ'matiko, a] *adj*
pragmatic
precario, -a [pre'karjo, a] *adj*
precarious
precaución [prekau'θjon] *nf* (*medida
  preventiva*) preventive measure,
  precaution; (*prudencia*) caution,
  wariness
precedente [preθe'ðente] *adj*
preceding; (*anterior*) former ▷ *nm*
precedent
preceder [preθe'ðer] *vt, vi* to
precede, go before, come before
precepto [pre'θepto] *nm* precept
precinto [pre'θinto] *nm* (*tb*: **~ de
  garantía**) seal
precio ['preθjo] *nm* price; (*costo*)
cost; (*valor*) value, worth; (*de viaje*)
fare; **precio al contado/de coste/de
oportunidad** cash/cost/bargain
price; **precio al por menor** retail price;
precio de ocasión bargain price;
precio de venta al público retail price;
precio tope top price
preciosidad [preθjosi'ðað] *nf* (*valor*)

(high) value, (great) worth; (*encanto*) charm; (*cosa bonita*) beautiful thing; **es una ~** it's lovely, it's really beautiful

precioso, -a [pɾe'θjoso, a] *adj* precious; (*de mucho valor*) valuable; (*fam*) lovely, beautiful

precipicio [pɾeθi'piθjo] *nm* cliff, precipice; (*fig*) abyss

precipitación [pɾeθipita'θjon] *nf* haste; (*lluvia*) rainfall

precipitado, -a [pɾeθipi'taðo, a] *adj* (*conducta*) hasty, rash; (*salida*) hasty, sudden

precipitar [pɾeθipi'tar] *vt* (*arrojar*) to hurl down, throw; (*apresurar*) to hasten; (*acelerar*) to speed up, accelerate; **precipitarse** *vr* to throw o.s.; (*apresurarse*) to rush; (*actuar sin pensar*) to act rashly

precisamente [pɾeθisa'mente] *adv* precisely; (*exactamente*) precisely, exactly

precisar [pɾeθi'sar] *vt* (*necesitar*) to need, require; (*fijar*) to determine exactly, fix; (*especificar*) to specify

precisión [pɾeθi'sjon] *nf* (*exactitud*) precision

preciso, -a [pɾe'θiso, a] *adj* (*exacto*) precise; (*necesario*) necessary, essential

preconcebido, -a [pɾekonθe'βiðo, a] *adj* preconceived

precoz [pɾe'koθ] *adj* (*persona*) precocious; (*calvicie etc*) premature

predecir [pɾeðe'θir] *vt* to predict, forecast

predestinado, -a [pɾeðesti'naðo, a] *adj* predestined

predicar [pɾeði'kar] *vt, vi* to preach

predicción [pɾeðik'θjon] *nf* prediction

predilecto, -a [pɾeði'lekto, a] *adj* favourite

predisposición [pɾeðisposi'θjon] *nf* inclination; prejudice, bias

predominar [pɾeðomi'nar] *vt* to dominate ▷ *vi* to predominate; (*prevalecer*) to prevail; **predominio** *nm* predominance; prevalence

preescolar [pɾe(e)sko'lar] *adj* preschool

prefabricado, -a [pɾefaβri'kaðo, a] *adj* prefabricated

prefacio [pɾe'faθjo] *nm* preface

preferencia [pɾefe'renθja] *nf* preference; **de ~** preferably, for preference

preferible [pɾefe'riβle] *adj* preferable

preferir [pɾefe'rir] *vt* to prefer

prefiero *etc vb* V **preferir**

prefijo [pɾe'fixo] *nm* (*Tel*) (dialling) code

pregunta [pɾe'ɣunta] *nf* question; **hacer una ~** to ask a question; **preguntas frecuentes** FAQs, frequently asked questions

preguntar [pɾeɣun'tar] *vt* to ask; (*cuestionar*) to question ▷ *vi* to ask; **preguntarse** *vr* to wonder; **preguntar por algn** to ask for sb; **preguntón, -ona** [pɾeɣun'ton, ona] *adj* inquisitive

prehistórico, -a [pɾeis'toriko, a] *adj* prehistoric

prejuicio [pɾe'xwiθjo] *nm* (*acto*) prejudgement; (*idea preconcebida*) preconception; (*parcialidad*) prejudice, bias

preludio [pɾe'luðjo] *nm* prelude

prematuro, -a [pɾema'turo, a] *adj* premature

premeditar [pɾemeði'tar] *vt* to premeditate

premiar [pɾe'mjar] *vt* to reward; (*en un concurso*) to give a prize to

premio ['pɾemjo] *nm* reward; prize; (*Com*) premium

prenatal [pɾena'tal] *adj* antenatal, prenatal

prenda ['pɾenda] *nf* (*ropa*) garment, article of clothing; (*garantía*) pledge; **prendas** *nfpl* (*talentos*) talents, gifts

prender [pɾen'der] *vt* (*captar*) to catch, capture; (*detener*) to arrest; (*Costura*) to pin, attach; (*sujetar*) to fasten ▷ *vi* to catch; (*arraigar*) to take root; **prenderse** *vr* (*encenderse*) to catch fire

prendido, -a [pren'diðo, a] (LAM) adj
(luz etc) on

prensa ['prensa] nf press; **la ~** the
press

preñado, -a [pre'ɲaðo, a] adj
pregnant; **~ de** pregnant with, full of

preocupación [preokupa'θjon] nf
worry, concern; (ansiedad) anxiety

preocupado, -a [preoku'paðo,
a] adj worried, concerned; (ansioso)
anxious

preocupar [preoku'par] vt to worry;
preocuparse vr to worry; **~se de algo**
(hacerse cargo) to take care of sth

preparación [prepara'θjon] nf
(acto) preparation; (estado) readiness;
(entrenamiento) training

preparado, -a [prepa'raðo, a] adj
(dispuesto) prepared; (Culin) ready (to
serve) ▷ nm preparation

preparar [prepa'rar] vt (disponer)
to prepare, get ready; (Tec: tratar) to
prepare, process; (entrenar) to teach,
train; **prepararse** vr: **~se a** o **para**
to prepare to o for, get ready to o for;
preparativo, -a adj preparatory,
preliminary; **preparativos** nmpl
preparations; **preparatoria** (MÉX) nf
sixth-form college (BRIT), senior high
school (US)

presa ['presa] nf (cosa apresada) catch;
(víctima) victim; (de animal) prey; (de
agua) dam

presagiar [presa'xjar] vt to presage,
forebode; **presagio** nm omen

prescindir [presθin'dir] vi: **~ de**
(privarse de) to do o go without;
(descartar) to dispense with

prescribir [preskri'βir] vt to
prescribe

presencia [pre'senθja] nf presence;
presenciar vt to be present at; (asistir
a) to attend; (ver) to see, witness

presentación [presenta'θjon]
nf presentation; (introducción)
introduction

presentador, a [presenta'ðor, a]

nm/f presenter, compère

presentar [presen'tar] vt to present;
(ofrecer) to offer; (mostrar) to show,
display; (a una persona) to introduce;
presentarse vr (llegar inesperadamente)
to appear, turn up; (ofrecerse: como
candidato) to run, stand; (aparecer) to
show, appear; (solicitar empleo) to apply

presente [pre'sente] adj present
▷ nm present; **hacer ~** to state, declare;
tener ~ to remember, bear in mind

presentimiento [presenti'mjento]
nm premonition, presentiment

presentir [presen'tir] vt to have a
premonition of

preservación [preserβa'θjon] nf
protection, preservation

preservar [preser'βar] vt to protect,
preserve; **preservativo** nm sheath,
condom

presidencia [presi'ðenθja] nf
presidency; (de comité) chairmanship

presidente [presi'ðente] nmf
president; (de comité) chairman/
woman

presidir [presi'ðir] vt (dirigir) to
preside at, preside over; (: comité)
to take the chair at; (dominar) to
dominate, rule ▷ vi to preside; to take
the chair

presión [pre'sjon] nf pressure;
presión atmosférica atmospheric
o air pressure; **presionar** vt to
press; (fig) to press, put pressure on
▷ vi: **presionar para** to press for

preso, -a ['preso, a] nm/f prisoner;
tomar o **llevar ~ a algn** to arrest sb,
take sb prisoner

prestación [presta'θjon] nf service;
(subsidio) benefit; **prestaciones** nfpl
(Tec, Auto) performance features

prestado, -a [pres'taðo, a] adj on
loan; **pedir ~** to borrow

prestamista [presta'mista] nmf
moneylender

préstamo ['prestamo] nm loan;
préstamo hipotecario mortgage

prestar [pres'tar] vt to lend, loan;

(*atención*) to pay; (*ayuda*) to give

prestigio [pres'tixjo] *nm* prestige; **prestigioso, -a** *adj* (*honorable*) prestigious; (*famoso, renombrado*) renowned, famous

presumido, -a [presu'miðo, a] *adj* (*persona*) vain

presumir [presu'mir] *vt* to presume ▷ *vi* (*tener aires*) to be conceited; **presunto, -a** *adj* (*supuesto*) supposed, presumed; (*así llamado*) so-called; **presuntuoso, -a** *adj* conceited, presumptuous

presupuesto [presu'pwesto] *pp de* **presuponer** ▷ *nm* (*Finanzas*) budget; (*estimación: de costo*) estimate

pretencioso, -a [preten'θjoso, a] *adj* pretentious

pretender [preten'der] *vt* (*intentar*) to try to, seek to; (*reivindicar*) to claim; (*buscar*) to seek, try for; (*cortejar*) to woo, court; **~ que** to expect that

▌ No confundir **pretender** con la palabra inglesa *pretend*.

pretendiente *nmf* (*amante*) suitor; (*al trono*) pretender; **pretensión** *nf* (*aspiración*) aspiration; (*reivindicación*) claim; (*orgullo*) pretension

pretexto [pre'teksto] *nm* pretext; (*excusa*) excuse

prevención [preβen'θjon] *nf* prevention; (*precaución*) precaution

prevenido, -a [preβe'niðo, a] *adj* prepared, ready; (*cauteloso*) cautious

prevenir [preβe'nir] *vt* (*impedir*) to prevent; (*predisponer*) to prejudice, bias; (*avisar*) to warn; (*preparar*) to prepare, get ready; **prevenirse** *vr* to get ready, prepare; **~se contra** to take precautions against; **preventivo, -a** *adj* preventive, precautionary

prever [pre'βer] *vt* to foresee

previo, -a ['preβjo, a] *adj* (*anterior*) previous; (*preliminar*) preliminary ▷ *prep*: **~ acuerdo de los otros** subject to the agreement of the others

previsión [preβi'sjon] *nf* (*perspicacia*) foresight; (*predicción*) forecast;

previsto, -a *adj* anticipated, forecast

prima ['prima] *nf* (*Com*) bonus; (*de seguro*) premium; V *tb* **primo**

primario, -a [pri'marjo, a] *adj* primary

primavera [prima'βera] *nf* spring(-time)

primera [pri'mera] *nf* (*Auto*) first gear; (*Ferro: tb*: **~ clase**) first class; **de ~** (*fam*) first-class, first-rate

primero, -a [pri'mero, a] (*adj* **primer**) first; (*principal*) prime *adv* first; (*más bien*) sooner, rather; **primera plana** front page

primitivo, -a [primi'tiβo, a] *adj* primitive; (*original*) original

primo, -a ['primo, a] *adj* prime ▷ *nm/f* cousin; (*fam*) fool, idiot; **materias primas** raw materials; **primo hermano** first cousin

primogénito, -a [primo'xenito, a] *adj* first-born

primoroso, -a [primo'roso, a] *adj* exquisite, delicate

princesa [prin'θesa] *nf* princess

principal [prinθi'pal] *adj* principal, main ▷ *nm* (*jefe*) chief, principal

príncipe ['prinθipe] *nm* prince

principiante [prinθi'pjante] *nmf* beginner

principio [prin'θipjo] *nm* (*comienzo*) beginning, start; (*origen*) origin; (*primera etapa*) rudiment, basic idea; (*moral*) principle; **desde el ~** from the first; **en un ~** at first; **a ~s de** at the beginning of

pringue ['pringe] *nm* (*grasa*) grease, fat, dripping

prioridad [priori'ðað] *nf* priority

prisa ['prisa] *nf* (*apresuramiento*) hurry, haste; (*rapidez*) speed; (*urgencia*) (sense of) urgency; **a o de ~** quickly; **correr ~** to be urgent; **darse ~** to hurry up; **tener ~** to be in a hurry

prisión [pri'sjon] *nf* (*cárcel*) prison; (*período de cárcel*) imprisonment; **prisionero, -a** *nm/f* prisoner

prismáticos [pris'matikos] *nmpl*

binoculars

privado, -a [pri'βaðo, a] *adj* private

privar [pri'βar] *vt* to deprive; **privativo, -a** *adj* exclusive

privilegiar [priβile'xjar] *vt* to grant a privilege to; (*favorecer*) to favour

privilegio [priβi'lexjo] *nm* privilege; (*concesión*) concession

pro [pro] *nm o f* profit, advantage ▷ *prep*: **asociación ~ ciegos** association for the blind ▷ *prefijo*: **~ americano** pro-American; **en ~ de** on behalf of, for; **los ~s y los contras** the pros and cons

proa ['proa] *nf* bow, prow; **de ~** bow *cpd*, fore

probabilidad [proβaβili'ðað] *nf* probability, likelihood; (*oportunidad, posibilidad*) chance, prospect; **probable** *adj* probable, likely

probador [proβa'ðor] *nm* (*en tienda*) fitting room

probar [pro'βar] *vt* (*demostrar*) to prove; (*someter a prueba*) to test, try out; (*ropa*) to try on; (*comida*) to taste ▷ *vi* to try; **~se un traje** to try on a suit

probeta [pro'βeta] *nf* test tube

problema [pro'βlema] *nm* problem

procedente [proθe'ðente] *adj* (*razonable*) reasonable; (*conforme a derecho*) proper, fitting; **~ de** coming from, originating in

proceder [proθe'ðer] *vi* (*avanzar*) to proceed; (*actuar*) to act; (*ser correcto*) to be right (and proper), be fitting ▷ *nm* (*comportamiento*) behaviour, conduct; **~ de** to come from, originate in; **procedimiento** *nm* procedure; (*proceso*) process; (*método*) means *pl*, method

procesador [proθesa'ðor] *nm* processor; **procesador de textos** word processor

procesar [proθe'sar] *vt* to try, put on trial

procesión [proθe'sjon] *nf* procession

proceso [pro'θeso] *nm* process; (*Jur*) trial

proclamar [prokla'mar] *vt* to proclaim

procrear [prokre'ar] *vt, vi* to procreate

procurador, a [prokura'ðor, a] *nm/f* attorney

procurar [proku'rar] *vt* (*intentar*) to try, endeavour; (*conseguir*) to get, obtain; (*asegurar*) to secure; (*producir*) to produce

prodigio [pro'ðixjo] *nm* prodigy; (*milagro*) wonder, marvel; **prodigioso, -a** *adj* prodigious, marvellous

pródigo, -a ['proðiɣo, a] *adj*: **hijo ~** prodigal son

producción [proðuk'θjon] *nf* (*gen*) production; (*producto*) output; **producción en serie** mass production

producir [proðu'θir] *vt* to produce; (*causar*) to cause, bring about; **producirse** *vr* (*cambio*) to come about; (*accidente*) to take place; (*problema etc*) to arise; (*hacerse*) to be produced, be made; (*estallar*) to break out

productividad [proðuktiβi'ðað] *nf* productivity; **productivo, -a** *adj* productive; (*provechoso*) profitable

producto [pro'ðukto] *nm* product

productor, a [proðuk'tor, a] *adj* productive, producing ▷ *nm/f* producer

proeza [pro'eθa] *nf* exploit, feat

profano, -a [pro'fano, a] *adj* profane ▷ *nm/f* layman/woman

profecía [profe'θia] *nf* prophecy

profesión [profe'sjon] *nf* profession; (*en formulario*) occupation; **profesional** *adj* professional

profesor, a [profe'sor, a] *nm/f* teacher; **profesorado** *nm* teaching profession

profeta [pro'feta] *nmf* prophet

prófugo, -a ['profuɣo, a] *nm/f* fugitive; (*Mil: desertor*) deserter

profundidad [profundi'ðað] *nf* depth; **profundizar** *vi*: **profundizar en** to go deeply into; **profundo, -a** *adj* deep; (*misterio, pensador*) profound

progenitor [proxeni'tor] *nm*
ancestor; **progenitores** *nmpl* (*padres*)
parents

programa [pro'xrama] *nm*
programme (BRIT), program (US);
programa de estudios curriculum,
syllabus; **programación** *nf*
programming; **programador, a**
nm/f programmer; **programar** *vt* to
program

progresar [proxre'sar] *vi* to
progress, make progress; **progresista**
adj, *nmf* progressive; **progresivo,
-a** *adj* progressive; (*gradual*) gradual;
(*continuo*) continuous; **progreso** *nm*
progress

prohibición [proiβi'θjon] *nf*
prohibition, ban

prohibir [proi'βir] *vt* to prohibit, ban,
forbid; **prohibido o se prohibe fumar**
no smoking; **"prohibido el paso"**
"no entry"

prójimo, -a ['proximo, a] *nm/f*
fellow man; (*vecino*) neighbour

prólogo ['proloxo] *nm* prologue

prolongar [prolon'xar] *vt* to extend;
(*reunión etc*) to prolong; (*calle, tubo*)
to extend

promedio [pro'meðjo] *nm* average;
(*de distancia*) middle, mid-point

promesa [pro'mesa] *nf* promise

prometer [prome'ter] *vt* to promise
▷ *vi* to show promise; **prometerse** *vr*
(*novios*) to get engaged; **prometido,
-a** *adj* promised; engaged ▷ *nm/f*
fiancé/fiancée

prominente [promi'nente] *adj*
prominent

promoción [promo'θjon] *nf*
promotion

promotor [promo'tor] *nm* promoter;
(*instigador*) instigator

promover [promo'βer] *vt* to
promote; (*causar*) to cause; (*instigar*) to
instigate, stir up

promulgar [promul'xar] *vt* to
promulgate; (*anunciar*) to proclaim

pronombre [pro'nombre] *nm*
pronoun

pronosticar [pronosti'kar] *vt* to
predict, foretell, forecast; **pronóstico**
nm prediction, forecast; **pronóstico
del tiempo** weather forecast

pronto, -a ['pronto, a] *adj* (*rápido*)
prompt, quick; (*preparado*) ready ▷ *adv*
quickly, promptly; (*en seguida*) at once,
right away; (*dentro de poco*) soon;
(*temprano*) early ▷ *nm*: **tiene unos
~s muy malos** he gets ratty all of a
sudden (*inf*); **de ~** suddenly; **por lo ~**
meanwhile, for the present

pronunciación [pronunθja'θjon] *nf*
pronunciation

pronunciar [pronun'θjar] *vt* to
pronounce; (*discurso*) to make, deliver;
pronunciarse *vr* to revolt, rebel;
(*declararse*) to declare o.s.

propagación [propaxa'θjon] *nf*
propagation

propaganda [propa'xanda] *nf* (*Pol*)
propaganda; (*Com*) advertising

propenso, -a [pro'penso, a] *adj*
inclined to; **ser ~ a** to be inclined to,
have a tendency to

propicio, -a [pro'piθjo, a] *adj*
favourable, propitious

propiedad [propje'ðað] *nf* property;
(*posesión*) possession, ownership;
propiedad particular private property

propietario, -a [propje'tarjo, a]
nm/f owner, proprietor

propina [pro'pina] *nf* tip

propio, -a ['propjo, a] *adj* own,
of one's own; (*característico*)
characteristic, typical; (*debido*) proper;
(*mismo*) selfsame, very; **el ~ ministro**
the minister himself; **¿tienes casa
propia?** have you a house of your own?

proponer [propo'ner] *vt* to propose,
put forward; (*problema*) to pose;
proponerse *vr* to propose, intend

proporción [propor'θjon] *nf*
proportion; (*Mat*) ratio; **proporciones**
nfpl (*dimensiones*) dimensions;
(*fig*) size *sg*; **proporcionado,
-a** *adj* proportionate; (*regular*)

medium, middling; (*justo*) just right;
proporcionar *vt* (*dar*) to give, supply,
provide
proposición [proposi'θjon] *nf*
proposition; (*propuesta*) proposal
propósito [pro'posito] *nm* purpose;
(*intento*) aim, intention ▷ *adv*: **a ~**
by the way, incidentally; (*a posta*) on
purpose, deliberately; **a ~ de** about,
with regard to
propuesta [pro'pwesta] *vb* V
proponer ▷ *nf* proposal
propulsar [propul'sar] *vt* to drive,
propel; (*fig*) to promote, encourage;
propulsión *nf* propulsion; **propulsión
a chorro** o **por reacción** jet propulsion
prórroga ['prorroxa] *nf* extension;
(*Jur*) stay; (*Com*) deferment; (*Deporte*)
extra time; **prorrogar** *vt* (*período*) to
extend; (*decisión*) to defer, postpone
prosa ['prosa] *nf* prose
proseguir [prose'xir] *vt* to continue,
carry on ▷ *vi* to continue, go on
prospecto [pros'pekto] *nm*
prospectus
prosperar [prospe'rar] *vi* to prosper,
thrive, flourish; **prosperidad** *nf*
prosperity; (*éxito*) success; **próspero,
-a** *adj* prosperous, flourishing; (*que
tiene éxito*) successful
prostíbulo [pros'tiβulo] *nm* brothel
(BRIT), house of prostitution (US)
prostitución [prostitu'θjon] *nf*
prostitution
prostituir [prosti'twir] *vt* to
prostitute; **prostituirse** *vr* to
prostitute o.s., become a prostitute
prostituta [prosti'tuta] *nf*
prostitute
protagonista [protaxo'nista] *nmf*
protagonist
protección [protek'θjon] *nf*
protection
protector, a [protek'tor, a] *adj*
protective, protecting ▷ *nm/f*
protector
proteger [prote'xer] *vt* to protect;
protegido, -a *nm/f* protégé/protégée

proteína [prote'ina] *nf* protein
protesta [pro'testa] *nf* protest;
(*declaración*) protestation
protestante [protes'tante] *adj*
Protestant
protestar [protes'tar] *vt* to protest,
declare ▷ *vi* to protest
protocolo [proto'kolo] *nm* protocol
prototipo [proto'tipo] *nm* prototype
provecho [pro'βetʃo] *nm* advantage,
benefit; (*Finanzas*) profit; **¡buen ~!** bon
appétit!; **en ~ de** to the benefit of;
sacar ~ de to benefit from, profit by
provenir [proβe'nir] *vi*: **~ de** to come
o stem from
proverbio [pro'βerβjo] *nm* proverb
providencia [proβi'ðenθja] *nf*
providence
provincia [pro'βinθja] *nf* province
provisión [proβi'sjon] *nf* provision;
(*abastecimiento*) provision, supply;
(*medida*) measure, step
provisional [proβisjo'nal] *adj*
provisional
provocar [proβo'kar] *vt* to provoke;
(*alentar*) to tempt, invite; (*causar*)
to bring about, lead to; (*promover*)
to promote; (*estimular*) to rouse,
stimulate; **¿te provoca un café?** (CAM)
would you like a coffee?; **provocativo,
-a** *adj* provocative
proxeneta [prokse'neta] *nm* pimp
próximamente [proksima'mente]
adv shortly, soon
proximidad [proksimi'ðað] *nf*
closeness, proximity; **próximo, -a**
adj near, close; (*vecino*) neighbouring;
(*siguiente*) next
proyectar [projek'tar] *vt* (*objeto*) to
hurl, throw; (*luz*) to cast, shed; (*Cine*) to
screen, show; (*planear*) to plan
proyectil [projek'til] *nm* projectile,
missile
proyecto [pro'jekto] *nm* plan;
(*estimación de costo*) detailed estimate
proyector [projek'tor] *nm* (*Cine*)
projector
prudencia [pru'ðenθja] *nf* (*sabiduría*)

wisdom; (*cuidado*) care; **prudente** *adj*
sensible, wise; (*conductor*) careful
prueba *etc* ['prweβa] *vb* V **probar** ⊳ *nf*
proof; (*ensayo*) test, trial; (*degustación*)
tasting, sampling; (*de ropa*) fitting; **a
~ on** trial; **a ~ de** proof against; **a ~ de
agua/fuego** waterproof/fireproof;
someter a ~ to put to the test
psico... [siko] *prefijo* psycho...;
psicología *nf* psychology;
psicológico, -a *adj* psychological;
psicólogo, -a *nm/f* psychologist;
psicópata *nmf* psychopath; **psicosis**
nf inv psychosis
psiquiatra [si'kjatra] *nmf*
psychiatrist; **psiquiátrico, -a** *adj*
psychiatric
PSOE [pe'soe] (*ESP*) *nm abr* = **Partido
Socialista Obrero Español**
púa ['pua] *nf* (*Bot, Zool*) prickle, spine;
(*para guitarra*) plectrum (*BRIT*), pick
(*US*); **alambre de ~** barbed wire
pubertad [puβer'taδ] *nf* puberty
publicación [puβlika'θjon] *nf*
publication
publicar [puβli'kar] *vt* (*editar*) to
publish; (*hacer público*) to publicize;
(*divulgar*) to make public, divulge
publicidad [puβliθi'δaδ] *nf*
publicity; (*Com: propaganda*)
advertising; **publicitario, -a** *adj*
publicity *cpd*; advertising *cpd*
público, -a ['puβliko, a] *adj* public
⊳ *nm* public; (*Teatro etc*) audience
puchero [pu'tʃero] *nm* (*Culin: guiso*)
stew; (: *olla*) cooking pot; **hacer ~s**
to pout
pucho ['putʃo] (*CS: fam*) *nm* cigarette,
fag (*BRIT*)
pude *etc vb* V **poder**
pudiente [pu'δjente] *adj* (*rico*)
wealthy, well-to-do
pudiera *etc vb* V **poder**
pudor [pu'δor] *nm* modesty
pudrir [pu'δrir] *vt* to rot; **pudrirse** *vr*
to rot, decay
pueblo ['pweβlo] *nm* people; (*nación*)
nation; (*aldea*) village

puedo *etc vb* V **poder**
puente ['pwente] *nm* bridge; **hacer ~**
(*fam*) to take extra days off work between 2
public holidays; to take a long weekend;
puente aéreo shuttle service; **puente
colgante** suspension bridge; **puente
levadizo** drawbridge

● **HACER PUENTE**
●
● When a public holiday in Spain
● falls on a Tuesday or Thursday it is
● common practice for employers
● to make the Monday or Friday
● a holiday as well and to give
● everyone a four-day weekend. This
● is known as **hacer puente**. When
● a named public holiday such as the
● **Día de la Constitución** falls on a
● Tuesday or Thursday, people refer
● to the whole holiday period as e.g.
● the **puente de la Constitución**.

puerco, -a ['pwerko, a] *nm/f* pig/
sow ⊳ *adj* (*sucio*) dirty, filthy; (*obsceno*)
disgusting; **puerco espín** porcupine
pueril [pwe'ril] *adj* childish
puerro ['pwerro] *nm* leek
puerta ['pwerta] *nf* door; (*de jardín*)
gate; (*portal*) doorway; (*fig*) gateway;
(*portería*) goal; **a la ~** at the door; **a ~
cerrada** behind closed doors; **puerta
giratoria** revolving door
puerto ['pwerto] *nm* port; (*paso*)
pass; (*fig*) haven, refuge
Puerto Rico [pwerto'riko] *nm*
Puerto Rico; **puertorriqueño, -a** *adj*,
nm/f Puerto Rican
pues [pwes] *adv* (*entonces*) then;
(*bueno*) well, well then; (*así que*)
so ⊳ *conj* (*ya que*) since; **¡~ sí!** yes!,
certainly!
puesta ['pwesta] *nf* (*apuesta*) bet,
stake; **puesta al día** updating; **puesta
a punto** fine tuning; **puesta de sol**
sunset; **puesta en marcha** starting
puesto, -a ['pwesto, a] *pp de* **poner**
⊳ *adj*: **tener algo ~** to have sth on, be

wearing sth ▷ *nm* (*lugar, posición*)
place; (*trabajo*) post, job; (*Com*) stall
▷ *conj*: **~ que** since, as
púgil ['puxil] *nm* boxer
pulga ['pulɣa] *nf* flea
pulgada [pul'ɣaða] *nf* inch
pulgar [pul'ɣar] *nm* thumb
pulir [pu'lir] *vt* to polish; (*alisar*) to
smooth; (*fig*) to polish up, touch up
pulmón [pul'mon] *nm* lung;
pulmonía *nf* pneumonia
pulpa ['pulpa] *nf* pulp; (*de fruta*) flesh,
soft part
pulpería [pulpe'ria] (*LAM*) *nf* (*tienda*)
small grocery store
púlpito ['pulpito] *nm* pulpit
pulpo ['pulpo] *nm* octopus
pulque ['pulke] *nm* pulque

- **PULQUE**
-
- **Pulque** is a thick, white, alcoholic
- drink which is very popular in
- Mexico. In ancient times it was
- considered sacred by the Aztecs.
- It is produced by fermenting the
- juice of the **maguey**, a Mexican
- cactus similar to the agave. It can
- be drunk by itself or mixed with
- fruit or vegetable juice.

pulsación [pulsa'θjon] *nf* beat;
pulsaciones pulse rate
pulsar [pul'sar] *vt* (*tecla*) to touch,
tap; (*Mús*) to play; (*botón*) to press, push
▷ *vi* to pulsate; (*latir*) to beat, throb
pulsera [pul'sera] *nf* bracelet
pulso ['pulso] *nm* (*Anat*) pulse;
(*fuerza*) strength; (*firmeza*) steadiness,
steady hand
pulverizador [pulβeriθa'ðor] *nm*
spray, spray gun
pulverizar [pulβeri'θar] *vt* to
pulverize; (*líquido*) to spray
puna ['puna] (*CAM*) *nf* mountain
sickness
punta ['punta] *nf* point, tip; (*extremo*)
end; (*fig*) touch, trace; **horas ~** peak o

rush hours; **sacar ~ a** to sharpen
puntada [pun'taða] *nf* (*Costura*)
stitch
puntal [pun'tal] *nm* prop, support
puntapié [punta'pje] *nm* kick
puntería [punte'ria] *nf* (*de arma*)
aim, aiming; (*destreza*) marksmanship
puntero, -a [pun'tero, a] *adj* leading
▷ *nm* (*palo*) pointer
puntiagudo, -a [puntja'ɣuðo, a] *adj*
sharp, pointed
puntilla [pun'tiʎa] *nf* (*encaje*) lace
edging o trim; **(andar) de ~s** (to walk)
on tiptoe
punto ['punto] *nm* (*gen*) point; (*señal
diminuta*) spot, dot; (*Costura, Med*)
stitch; (*lugar*) spot, place; (*momento*)
point, moment; **a ~** ready; **estar a ~ de**
to be on the point of o about to; **en ~** on
the dot; **hasta cierto ~** to some extent;
hacer ~ (*ESP: tejer*) to knit; **dos ~s**
(*Ling*) colon; **punto de interrogación**
question mark; **punto de vista** point
of view, viewpoint; **punto final**
full stop (*BRIT*), period (*US*); **punto
muerto** dead center; (*Auto*) neutral
(gear); **punto y aparte** (*en dictado*) full
stop, new paragraph; **punto y coma**
semicolon
puntocom [punto'kom] *adj inv, nf
inv* dotcom
puntuación [puntwa'θjon] *nf*
punctuation; (*puntos: en examen*)
mark(s) (*pl*); (*Deporte*) score
puntual [pun'twal] *adj* (*a tiempo*)
punctual; (*exacto*) exact, accurate;
puntualidad *nf* punctuality;
exactness, accuracy
puntuar [pun'twar] *vi* (*Deporte*) to
score, count
punzante [pun'θante] *adj* (*dolor*)
shooting, sharp; (*herramienta*) sharp
puñado [pu'ɲaðo] *nm* handful
puñal [pu'ɲal] *nm* dagger; **puñalada**
nf stab
puñetazo [puɲe'taθo] *nm* punch
puño ['puɲo] *nm* (*Anat*) fist; (*cantidad*)
fistful, handful; (*Costura*) cuff; (*de

herramienta) handle

pupila [pu'pila] *nf* pupil

pupitre [pu'pitre] *nm* desk

puré [pu're] *nm* purée; (*sopa*) (thick) soup; **puré de papas** (*LAM*) mashed potatoes; **puré de patatas** (*ESP*) mashed potatoes

purga ['purɣa] *nf* purge; **purgante** *adj, nm* purgative

purgatorio [purɣa'torjo] *nm* purgatory

purificar [purifi'kar] *vt* to purify; (*refinar*) to refine

puritano, -a [puri'tano, a] *adj* (*actitud*) puritanical; (*iglesia, tradición*) puritan ▷ *nm/f* puritan

puro, -a ['puro, a] *adj* pure; (*verdad*) simple, plain ▷ *nm* cigar

púrpura ['purpura] *nf* purple

pus [pus] *nm* pus

puse *etc vb* V **poder**

pusiera *etc vb* V **poder**

puta ['puta] (*fam!*) *nf* whore, prostitute

putrefacción [putrefak'θjon] *nf* rotting, putrefaction

PVP *nm abr* (= *precio de venta al público*) RRP

pyme, PYME ['pime] *nf abr* (= *Pequeña y Mediana Empresa*) SME

○ **PALABRA CLAVE**

que [ke] *conj* **1** (*con oración subordinada: muchas veces no se traduce*) that; **dijo que vendría** he said (that) he would come; **espero que lo encuentres** I hope (that) you find it; V tb **el**

2 (*en oración independiente*): **¡que entre!** send him in; **¡que aproveche!** enjoy your meal!; **¡que se mejore tu padre!** I hope your father gets better

3 (*enfático*): **¿me quieres? – ¡que sí!** do you love me? – of course!

4 (*consecutivo: muchas veces no se traduce*) that; **es tan grande que no lo puedo levantar** it's so big (that) I can't lift it

5 (*comparaciones*) than; **yo que tú/él** if I were you/him; V tb **más, menos, mismo**

6 (*valor disyuntivo*): **que le guste o no** whether he likes it or not; **que venga o que no venga** whether he comes or not

7 (*porque*): **no puedo, que tengo que quedarme en casa** I can't, I've got to stay in
▷ *pron* **1** (*cosa*) that, which; (+ *prep*) which; **el sombrero que te compraste** the hat (that *o* which) you bought; **la cama en que dormí** the bed (that *o* which) I slept in
2 (*persona*: *suj*) that, who; (: *objeto*) that, whom; **el amigo que me acompañó al museo** the friend that *o* who went to the museum with me; **la chica que invité** the girl (that *o* whom) I invited

qué [ke] *adj* what?, which? ▷ *pron* what?; **¡~ divertido!** how funny!; **¿~ edad tienes?** how old are you?; **¿de ~ me hablas?** what are you saying to me?; **¿~ tal?** how are you?, how are things?; **¿~ hay (de nuevo)?** what's new?

quebrado, -a [ke'βraðo, a] *adj* (*roto*) broken ▷ *nm/f* bankrupt ▷ *nm* (*Mat*) fraction

quebrantar [keβran'tar] *vt* (*infringir*) to violate, transgress

quebrar [ke'βrar] *vt* to break, smash ▷ *vi* to go bankrupt

quedar [ke'ðar] *vi* to stay, remain; (*encontrarse*: *sitio*) to be; (*haber aún*) to remain, be left; **quedarse** *vr* to remain, stay (behind); **~se (con) algo** to keep sth; **~ en** (*acordar*) to agree on/to; **~ en nada** to come to nothing; **~ por hacer** to be still to be done; **~ ciego/mudo** to be left blind/dumb; **no te queda bien ese vestido** that dress doesn't suit you; **eso queda muy lejos** that's a long way (away); **quedamos a las seis** we agreed to meet at six

quedo, -a ['keðo, a] *adj* still ▷ *adv* softly, gently

quehacer [kea'θer] *nm* task, job; **quehaceres (domésticos)** *nmpl* household chores

queja ['kexa] *nf* complaint; **quejarse** *vr* (*enfermo*) to moan, groan; (*protestar*) to complain; **quejarse de que** to complain (about the fact) that; **quejido** *nm* moan

quemado, -a [ke'maðo, a] *adj* burnt

quemadura [kema'ðura] *nf* burn, scald

quemar [ke'mar] *vt* to burn; (*fig*: *malgastar*) to burn up, squander ▷ *vi* to be burning hot; **quemarse** *vr* (*consumirse*) to burn (up); (*del sol*) to get sunburnt

quemarropa [kema'rropa]: **a ~** *adv* point-blank

quepo *etc vb* V **caber**

querella [ke'reʎa] *nf* (*Jur*) charge; (*disputa*) dispute

○ **PALABRA CLAVE**

querer [ke'rer] *vt* **1** (*desear*) to want; **quiero más dinero** I want more money; **quisiera** *o* **querría un té** I'd like a tea; **sin querer** unintentionally; **quiero ayudar/que vayas** I want to help/you to go
2 (*preguntas: para pedir algo*): **¿quiere abrir la ventana?** could you open the window?; **¿quieres echarme una mano?** can you give me a hand?
3 (*amar*) to love; (*tener cariño a*) to be fond of; **te quiero** I love you; **quiere mucho a sus hijos** he's very fond of his children
4 le pedí que me dejara ir pero no quiso I asked him to let me go but he refused

querido, -a [ke'riðo, a] *adj* dear ▷ *nm/f* darling; (*amante*) lover

queso ['keso] *nm* cheese; **queso crema** (*LAM*) cream cheese; **queso de untar** (*ESP*) cream cheese; **queso manchego** sheep's milk cheese made in La Mancha; **queso rallado** grated cheese

quicio ['kiθjo] *nm* hinge; **sacar a algn de ~** to get on sb's nerves

quiebra ['kjeβra] *nf* break, split; (*Com*) bankruptcy; (*Econ*) slump

quiebro ['kjeβro] *nm* (*del cuerpo*)

swerve

quien [kjen] *pron* who; **hay ~ piensa que** there are those who think that; **no hay ~ lo haga** no-one will do it

quién [kjen] *pron* who, whom; **¿~ es?** who's there?

quienquiera [kjen'kjera] (*pl* **quienesquiera**) *pron* whoever

quiero *etc vb* V **querer**

quieto, -a ['kjeto, a] *adj* still; (*carácter*) placid

▌ No confundir **quieto** con la palabra inglesa *quiet*.

quietud *nf* stillness

quilate [ki'late] *nm* carat

químico, -a ['kimiko, a] *adj* chemical ▷ *nm/f* chemist ▷ *nf* chemistry

quincalla [kin'kaʎa] *nf* hardware, ironmongery (*BRIT*)

quince ['kinθe] *num* fifteen; **~ días** a fortnight; **quinceañero, -a** *nm/f* teenager; **quincena** *nf* fortnight; (*pago*) fortnightly pay; **quincenal** *adj* fortnightly

quiniela [ki'njela] *nf* football pools *pl*; **quinielas** *nfpl* (*impreso*) pools coupon *sg*

quinientos, -as [ki'njentos, as] *adj*, *num* five hundred

quinto, -a ['kinto, a] *adj* fifth ▷ *nf* country house; (*Mil*) call-up, draft

quiosco ['kjosko] *nm* (*de música*) bandstand; (*de periódicos*) news stand

quirófano [ki'rofano] *nm* operating theatre

quirúrgico, -a [ki'rurxiko, a] *adj* surgical

quise *etc vb* V **querer**

quisiera *etc vb* V **querer**

quisquilloso, -a [kiski'ʎoso, a] *adj* (*susceptible*) touchy; (*meticuloso*) pernickety

quiste ['kiste] *nm* cyst

quitaesmalte [kitaes'malte] *nm* nail-polish remover

quitamanchas [kita'mantʃas] *nm inv* stain remover

quitanieves [kita'njeβes] *nm inv* snowplough (*BRIT*), snowplow (*US*)

quitar [ki'tar] *vt* to remove, take away; (*ropa*) to take off; (*dolor*) to relieve; **¡quita de ahí!** get away!; **quitarse** *vr* to withdraw; (*ropa*) to take off; **se quitó el sombrero** he took off his hat

Quito ['kito] *n* Quito

quizá(s) [ki'θa(s)] *adv* perhaps, maybe

r

rábano ['raβano] *nm* radish; **me importa un ~** I don't give a damn

rabia ['raβja] *nf* (*Med*) rabies *sg*; (*ira*) fury, rage; **rabiar** *vi* to have rabies; to rage, be furious; **rabiar por algo** to long for sth

rabieta [ra'βjeta] *nf* tantrum, fit of temper

rabino [ra'βino] *nm* rabbi

rabioso, -a [ra'βjoso, a] *adj* rabid; (*fig*) furious

rabo ['raβo] *nm* tail

racha ['ratʃa] *nf* gust of wind; **buena/mala ~** spell of good/bad luck

racial [ra'θjal] *adj* racial, race *cpd*

racimo [ra'θimo] *nm* bunch

ración [ra'θjon] *nf* portion; **raciones** *nfpl* rations

racional [raθjo'nal] *adj* (*razonable*) reasonable; (*lógico*) rational

racionar [raθjo'nar] *vt* to ration (out)

racismo [ra'θismo] *nm* racism; **racista** *adj, nm* racist

radar [ra'ðar] *nm* radar

radiador [raðja'ðor] *nm* radiator

radiante [ra'ðjante] *adj* radiant

radical [raði'kal] *adj, nmf* radical

radicar [raði'kar] *vi*: **~ en** (*dificultad, problema*) to lie in; (*solución*) to consist in

radio ['raðjo] *nf* radio; (*aparato*) radio (set) ▷ *nm* (*Mat*) radius; (*Quím*) radium; **radioactividad** *nf* radioactivity; **radioactivo, -a** *adj* radioactive; **radiografía** *nf* X-ray; **radioterapia** *nf* radiotherapy; **radioyente** *nmf* listener

ráfaga ['rafaɣa] *nf* gust; (*de luz*) flash; (*de tiros*) burst

raíz [ra'iθ] *nf* root; **a ~ de** as a result of; **raíz cuadrada** square root

raja ['raxa] *nf* (*de melón etc*) slice; (*grieta*) crack; **rajar** *vt* to split; (*fam*) to slash; **rajarse** *vr* to split, crack; **rajarse de** to back out of

rajatabla [raxa'taβla]: **a ~** *adv* (*estrictamente*) strictly, to the letter

rallador [raʎa'ðor] *nm* grater

rallar [ra'ʎar] *vt* to grate

rama ['rama] *nf* branch; **ramaje** *nm* branches *pl*, foliage; **ramal** *nm* (*de cuerda*) strand; (*Ferro*) branch line (BRIT); (*Auto*) branch (road) (BRIT)

rambla ['rambla] *nf* (*avenida*) avenue

ramo ['ramo] *nm* branch; (*sección*) department, section

rampa ['rampa] *nf* ramp; **rampa de acceso** entrance ramp

rana ['rana] *nf* frog; **salto de ~** leapfrog

ranchero [ran'tʃero] (*MÉX*) *nm* (*hacendado*) rancher; smallholder

rancho ['rantʃo] *nm* (*grande*) ranch; (*pequeño*) small farm

rancio, -a ['ranθjo, a] *adj* (*comestibles*) rancid; (*vino*) aged, mellow; (*fig*) ancient

rango ['rango] *nm* rank, standing

ranura [ra'nura] *nf* groove; (*de teléfono etc*) slot

rapar [ra'par] *vt* to shave; (*los cabellos*) to crop

rapaz [ra'paθ] (*nf ~a*) *nmf* young

boy/girl ▷ *adj* (*Zool*) predatory

rape ['rape] *nm* (*pez*) monkfish; **al ~** cropped

rapé [ra'pe] *nm* snuff

rapidez [rapi'ðeθ] *nf* speed, rapidity; **rápido, -a** *adj* fast, quick ▷ *adv* quickly ▷ *nm* (*Ferro*) express; **rápidos** *nmpl* rapids

rapiña [ra'piɲa] *nm* robbery; **ave de ~** bird of prey

raptar [rap'tar] *vt* to kidnap; **rapto** *nm* kidnapping; (*impulso*) sudden impulse; (*éxtasis*) ecstasy, rapture

raqueta [ra'keta] *nf* racquet

raquítico, -a [ra'kitiko, a] *adj* stunted; (*fig*) poor, inadequate

rareza [ra'reθa] *nf* rarity; (*fig*) eccentricity

raro, -a ['raro, a] *adj* (*poco común*) rare; (*extraño*) odd, strange; (*excepcional*) remarkable

ras [ras] *nm*: **a ~ de** level with; **a ~ de tierra** at ground level

rasar [ra'sar] *vt* (*igualar*) to level

rascacielos [raska'θjelos] *nm inv* skyscraper

rascar [ras'kar] *vt* (*con las uñas etc*) to scratch; (*raspar*) to scrape; **rascarse** *vr* to scratch (o.s.)

rasgar [ras'ɣar] *vt* to tear, rip (up)

rasgo ['rasɣo] *nm* (*con pluma*) stroke; **rasgos** *nmpl* (*facciones*) features, characteristics; **a grandes ~s** in outline, broadly

rasguño [ras'ɣuɲo] *nm* scratch

raso, -a ['raso, a] *adj* (*liso*) flat, level; (*a baja altura*) very low ▷ *nm* satin; **cielo ~** clear sky

raspadura [raspa'ðura] *nf* (*acto*) scrape, scraping; (*marca*) scratch; **raspaduras** *nfpl* (*de papel etc*) scrapings

raspar [ras'par] *vt* to scrape; (*arañar*) to scratch; (*limar*) to file

rastra ['rastra] *nf* (*Agr*) rake; **a ~s** by dragging; (*fig*) unwillingly

rastrear [rastre'ar] *vt* (*seguir*) to track

rastrero, -a [ras'trero, a] *adj* (*Bot*,

Zool) creeping; (*fig*) despicable, mean

rastrillo [ras'triλo] *nm* rake

rastro ['rastro] *nm* (*Agr*) rake; (*pista*) track, trail; (*vestigio*) trace; **el R~** (*ESP*) the Madrid fleamarket

rasurado [rasu'raðo] (*MÉX*) *nm* shaving; **rasuradora** [rasura'ðora] (*MÉX*) *nf* electric shaver; **rasurar** [rasu'rar] (*MÉX*) *vt* to shave; **rasurarse** *vr* to shave

rata ['rata] *nf* rat

ratear [rate'ar] *vt* (*robar*) to steal

ratero, -a [ra'tero, a] *adj* light-fingered ▷ *nm/f* (*carterista*) pickpocket; (*ladrón*) petty thief

rato ['rato] *nm* while, short time; **a ~s** from time to time; **hay para ~** there's still a long way to go; **al poco ~** soon afterwards; **pasar el ~** to kill time; **pasar un buen/mal ~** to have a good/rough time; **en mis ~s libres** in my spare time

ratón [ra'ton] *nm* mouse; **ratonera** *nf* mousetrap

raudal [rau'ðal] *nm* torrent; **a ~es** in abundance

raya ['raja] *nf* line; (*marca*) scratch; (*en tela*) stripe; (*de pelo*) parting; (*límite*) boundary; (*pez*) ray; (*puntuación*) dash; **a ~s** striped; **pasarse de la ~** to go too far; **tener a ~** to keep in check; **rayar** *vt* to line; to scratch; (*subrayar*) to underline ▷ *vi*: **rayar en** *o* **con** to border on

rayo ['rajo] *nm* (*del sol*) ray, beam; (*de luz*) shaft; (*en una tormenta*) (flash of) lightning; **rayos X** X-rays

raza ['raθa] *nf* race; **raza humana** human race

razón [ra'θon] *nf* reason; (*justicia*) right, justice; (*razonamiento*) reasoning; (*motivo*) reason, motive; (*Mat*) ratio; **a ~ de 10 cada día** at the rate of 10 a day; **en ~ de** with regard to; **dar ~ a algn** to agree that sb is right; **tener ~** to be right; **razón de ser** raison d'être; **razón directa/inversa** direct/inverse proportion; **razonable**

adj reasonable; (*justo, moderado*) fair; **razonamiento** *nm* (*juicio*) judg(e)ment; (*argumento*) reasoning; **razonar** *vt, vi* to reason, argue

re [re] *nm* (*Mús*) D

reacción [reak'θjon] *nf* reaction; **avión a ~** jet plane; **reacción en cadena** chain reaction; **reaccionar** *vi* to react

reacio, -a [re'aθjo, a] *adj* stubborn

reactivar [reakti'βar] *vt* to revitalize

reactor [reak'tor] *nm* reactor

real [re'al] *adj* real; (*del rey, fig*) royal

realidad [reali'ðað] *nf* reality, fact; (*verdad*) truth

realista [rea'lista] *nmf* realist

realización [realiθa'θjon] *nf* fulfilment

realizador, a [realiθa'ðor, a] *nm/f* film-maker

realizar [reali'θar] *vt* (*objetivo*) to achieve; (*plan*) to carry out; (*viaje*) to make, undertake; **realizarse** *vr* to come about, come true

realmente [real'mente] *adv* really, actually

realzar [real'θar] *vt* to enhance; (*acentuar*) to highlight

reanimar [reani'mar] *vt* to revive; (*alentar*) to encourage; **reanimarse** *vr* to revive

reanudar [reanu'ðar] *vt* (*renovar*) to renew; (*historia, viaje*) to resume

reaparición [reapari'θjon] *nf* reappearance

rearme [re'arme] *nm* rearmament

rebaja [re'βaxa] *nf* (*Com*) reduction; (: *descuento*) discount; **rebajas** *nfpl* (*Com*) sale; **rebajar** *vt* (*bajar*) to lower; (*reducir*) to reduce; (*disminuir*) to lessen; (*humillar*) to humble

rebanada [reβa'naða] *nf* slice

rebañar [reβa'ɲar] *vt* (*comida*) to scrape up; (*plato*) to scrape clean

rebaño [re'βaɲo] *nm* herd; (*de ovejas*) flock

rebatir [reβa'tir] *vt* to refute

rebeca [re'βeka] *nf* cardigan

rebelarse [reβe'larse] *vr* to rebel, revolt

rebelde [re'βelde] *adj* rebellious; (*niño*) unruly ▷ *nmf* rebel; **rebeldía** *nf* rebelliousness; (*desobediencia*) disobedience

rebelión [reβe'ljon] *nf* rebellion

reblandecer [reβlande'θer] *vt* to soften

rebobinar [reβoβi'nar] *vt* (*cinta, película de video*) to rewind

rebosante [reβo'sante] *adj* overflowing

rebosar [reβo'sar] *vi* (*líquido, recipiente*) to overflow; (*abundar*) to abound, be plentiful

rebotar [reβo'tar] *vt* to bounce; (*rechazar*) to repel ▷ *vi* (*pelota*) to bounce; (*bala*) to ricochet; **rebote** *nm* rebound; **de rebote** on the rebound

rebozado, -a [reβo'θaðo, a] *adj* fried in batter o breadcrumbs

rebozar [reβo'θar] *vt* to wrap up; (*Culin*) to fry in batter o breadcrumbs

rebuscado, -a [reβus'kaðo, a] *adj* (*amanerado*) affected; (*palabra*) recherché; (*idea*) far-fetched

rebuscar [reβus'kar] *vi*: **~ (en/por)** to search carefully (in/for)

recado [re'kaðo] *nm* (*mensaje*) message; (*encargo*) errand; **tomar un ~** (*Tel*) to take a message

recaer [reka'er] *vi* to relapse; **~ en** to fall to o on; (*criminal etc*) to fall back into, relapse into; **recaída** *nf* relapse

recalcar [rekal'kar] *vt* (*fig*) to stress, emphasize

recalentar [rekalen'tar] *vt* (*volver a calentar*) to reheat; (*calentar demasiado*) to overheat

recámara [re'kamara] (*MÉX*) *nf* bedroom

recambio [re'kambjo] *nm* spare; (*de pluma*) refill

recapacitar [rekapaθi'tar] *vi* to reflect

recargado, -a [rekar'ɣaðo, a] *adj* overloaded

recargar [rekar'xar] vt to overload; (*batería*) to recharge; **~ el saldo de** (*Tel*) to top up; **recargo** nm surcharge; (*aumento*) increase

recatado, -a [reka'taðo, a] adj (*modesto*) modest, demure; (*prudente*) cautious

recaudación [rekauða'θjon] nf (*acción*) collection; (*cantidad*) takings pl; (*en deporte*) gate; **recaudador, a** nm/f tax collector

recelar [reθe'lar] vt: **~ que ...** (*sospechar*) to suspect that ...; (*temer*) to fear that ... ▷ vi: **~ de** to distrust; **recelo** nm distrust, suspicion

recepción [reθep'θjon] nf reception; **recepcionista** nmf receptionist

receptor, a [reθep'tor, a] nm/f recipient ▷ nm (*Tel*) receiver

recesión [reθe'sjon] nf (*Com*) recession

receta [re'θeta] nf (*Culin*) recipe; (*Med*) prescription

▌ No confundir **receta** con la palabra inglesa *receipt*.

rechazar [retʃa'θar] vt to reject; (*oferta*) to turn down; (*ataque*) to repel

rechazo [re'tʃaθo] nm rejection

rechinar [retʃi'nar] vi to creak; (*dientes*) to grind

rechistar [retʃis'tar] vi: **sin ~** without a murmur

rechoncho, -a [re'tʃontʃo, a] (*fam*) adj thickset (BRIT), heavy-set (US)

rechupete [retʃu'pete]: **de ~** adj (*comida*) delicious, scrumptious

recibidor [reθiβi'ðor] nm entrance hall

recibimiento [reθiβi'mjento] nm reception, welcome

recibir [reθi'βir] vt to receive; (*dar la bienvenida*) to welcome ▷ vi to entertain; **recibo** nm receipt

reciclable [reθi'klaβle] adj recyclable

reciclar [reθi'klar] vt to recycle

recién [re'θjen] adv recently, newly; **los ~ casados** the newly-weds; **el ~ llegado** the newcomer; **el ~ nacido** the

newborn child

reciente [re'θjente] adj recent; (*fresco*) fresh

recinto [re'θinto] nm enclosure; (*área*) area, place

recio, -a ['reθjo, a] adj strong, tough; (*voz*) loud ▷ adv hard, loud(ly)

recipiente [reθi'pjente] nm receptacle

recíproco, -a [re'θiproco, a] adj reciprocal

recital [reθi'tal] nm (*Mús*) recital; (*Literatura*) reading

recitar [reθi'tar] vt to recite

reclamación [reklama'θjon] nf claim, demand; (*queja*) complaint

reclamar [rekla'mar] vt to claim, demand ▷ vi: **~ contra** to complain about; **reclamo** nm (*anuncio*) advertisement; (*tentación*) attraction

reclinar [rekli'nar] vt to recline, lean; **reclinarse** vr to lean back

reclusión [reklu'sjon] nf (*prisión*) prison; (*refugio*) seclusion

recluta [re'kluta] nmf recruit ▷ nf recruitment; **reclutar** vt (*datos*) to collect; (*dinero*) to collect up; **reclutamiento** nm recruitment

recobrar [reko'βrar] vt (*salud*) to recover; (*rescatar*) to get back; **recobrarse** vr to recover

recodo [re'koðo] nm (*de río, camino*) bend

recogedor [rekoxe'ðor] nm dustpan

recoger [reko'xer] vt to collect; (*Agr*) to harvest; (*levantar*) to pick up; (*juntar*) to gather; (*pasar a buscar*) to come for, get; (*dar asilo*) to give shelter to; (*faldas*) to gather up; (*pelo*) to put up; **recogerse** vr (*retirarse*) to retire; **recogido, -a** adj (*lugar*) quiet, secluded; (*pequeño*) small ▷ nf (*Correos*) collection; (*Agr*) harvest

recolección [rekolek'θjon] nf (*Agr*) harvesting; (*colecta*) collection

recomendación [rekomenda'θjon] nf (*sugerencia*) suggestion, recommendation; (*referencia*) reference

recomendar [rekomen'dar] vt to suggest, recommend; (confiar) to entrust

recompensa [rekom'pensa] nf reward, recompense; **recompensar** vt to reward, recompense

reconciliación [rekonθilja'θjon] nf reconciliation

reconciliar [rekonθi'ljar] vt to reconcile; **reconciliarse** vr to become reconciled

recóndito, -a [re'kondito, a] adj (lugar) hidden, secret

reconocer [rekono'θer] vt to recognize; (registrar) to search; (Med) to examine; **reconocido, -a** adj recognized; (agradecido) grateful; **reconocimiento** nm recognition; search; examination; gratitude; (confesión) admission

reconquista [rekon'kista] nf reconquest; **la R~** the Reconquest (of Spain)

reconstituyente [rekonstitu'jente] nm tonic

reconstruir [rekonstru'ir] vt to reconstruct

reconversión [rekonβer'sjon] nf (reestructuración) restructuring; **reconversión industrial** industrial rationalization

recopilación [rekopila'θjon] nf (resumen) summary; (compilación) compilation; **recopilar** vt to compile

récord ['rekorð] (pl ~s) adj inv, nm record

recordar [rekor'ðar] vt (acordarse de) to remember; (acordar a otro) to remind ▷ vi to remember

    No confundir **recordar** con la palabra inglesa record.

recorrer [reko'rrer] vt (país) to cross, travel through; (distancia) to cover; (registrar) to search; (repasar) to look over; **recorrido** nm run, journey; **tren de largo recorrido** main-line train

recortar [rekor'tar] vt to cut out; **recorte** nm (acción, de prensa) cutting; (de telas, chapas) trimming; **recorte presupuestario** budget cut

recostar [rekos'tar] vt to lean; **recostarse** vr to lie down

recoveco [reko'βeko] nm (de camino, río etc) bend; (en casa) cubby hole

recreación [rekrea'θjon] nf recreation

recrear [rekre'ar] vt (entretener) to entertain; (volver a crear) to recreate; **recreativo, -a** adj recreational; **recreo** nm recreation; (Escol) break, playtime

recriminar [rekrimi'nar] vt to reproach ▷ vi to recriminate; **recriminarse** vr to reproach each other

recrudecer [rekruðe'θer] vt, vi to worsen; **recrudecerse** vr to worsen

recta ['rekta] nf straight line

rectángulo, -a [rek'tangulo, a] adj rectangular ▷ nm rectangle

rectificar [rektifi'kar] vt to rectify; (volverse recto) to straighten ▷ vi to correct o.s.

rectitud [rekti'tuð] nf straightness

recto, -a ['rekto, a] adj straight; (persona) honest, upright; **siga todo ~** go straight on ▷ nm rectum

rector, a [rek'tor, a] adj governing

recuadro [re'kwaðro] nm box; (Tip) inset

recubrir [reku'βrir] vt: **~ (con)** (pintura, crema) to cover (with)

recuento [re'kwento] nm inventory; **hacer el ~ de** to count o reckon up

recuerdo [re'kwerðo] nm souvenir; **recuerdos** nmpl (memorias) memories; **¡~s a tu madre!** give my regards to your mother!

recular [reku'lar] vi to back down

recuperación [rekupera'θjon] nf recovery

recuperar [rekupe'rar] vt to recover; (tiempo) to make up; **recuperarse** vr to recuperate

recurrir [reku'rrir] vi (Jur) to appeal; **~ a** to resort to; (persona) to turn to;

recurso nm resort; (*medios*) means pl, resources pl; (*Jur*) appeal

red [reð] nf net, mesh; (*Ferro etc*) network; (*trampa*) trap; **la R~** (*Internet*) the Net

redacción [reðak'θjon] nf (*acción*) editing; (*personal*) editorial staff; (*Escol*) essay, composition

redactar [reðak'tar] vt to draw up, draft; (*periódico*) to edit

redactor, a [reðak'tor, a] nm/f editor

redada [re'ðaða] nf (*de policía*) raid, round-up

rededor [reðe'ðor] nm: **al** o **en ~** around, round about

redoblar [reðo'βlar] vt to redouble ▷ vi (*tambor*) to roll

redonda [re'ðonda] nf: **a la ~** around, round about

redondear [reðonde'ar] vt to round, round off

redondel [reðon'del] nm (*círculo*) circle; (*Taur*) bullring, arena

redondo, -a [re'ðondo, a] adj (*circular*) round; (*completo*) complete

reducción [reðuk'θjon] nf reduction

reducido, -a [reðu'θiðo, a] adj reduced; (*limitado*) limited; (*pequeño*) small

reducir [reðu'θir] vt to reduce; to limit; **reducirse** vr to diminish

redundancia [reðun'danθja] nf redundancy

reembolsar [re(e)mbol'sar] vt (*persona*) to reimburse; (*dinero*) to repay, pay back; (*depósito*) to refund; **reembolso** nm reimbursement; refund

reemplazar [re(e)mpla'θar] vt to replace; **reemplazo** nm replacement; **de reemplazo** (*Mil*) reserve

reencuentro [re(e)n'kwentro] nm reunion

reescribible [reeskri'βiβle] adj rewritable

refacción [refak'θjon] (*MÉX*) nf spare (part)

referencia [refe'renθja] nf reference; **con ~ a** with reference to

referéndum [refe'rendum] (*pl* ~s) nm referendum

referente [refe'rente] adj: ~ **a** concerning, relating to

réferi ['referi] (*LAM*) nmf referee

referir [refe'rir] vt (*contar*) to tell, recount; (*relacionar*) to refer, relate; **referirse** vr: ~**se a** to refer to

refilón [refi'lon]: **de ~** adv obliquely

refinado, -a [refi'naðo, a] adj refined

refinar [refi'nar] vt to refine; **refinería** nf refinery

reflejar [refle'xar] vt to reflect; **reflejo, -a** adj reflected; (*movimiento*) reflex ▷ nm reflection; (*Anat*) reflex

reflexión [reflek'sjon] nf reflection; **reflexionar** vt to reflect on ▷ vi to reflect; (*detenerse*) to pause (to think)

reflexivo, -a [reflek'siβo, a] adj thoughtful; (*Ling*) reflexive

reforma [re'forma] nf reform; (*Arq etc*) repair; **reforma agraria** agrarian reform

reformar [refor'mar] vt to reform; (*modificar*) to change, alter; (*Arq*) to repair; **reformarse** vr to mend one's ways

reformatorio [reforma'torjo] nm reformatory

reforzar [refor'θar] vt to strengthen; (*Arq*) to reinforce; (*fig*) to encourage

refractario, -a [refrak'tarjo, a] adj (*Tec*) heat-resistant

refrán [re'fran] nm proverb, saying

refregar [refre'xar] vt to scrub

refrescante [refres'kante] adj refreshing, cooling

refrescar [refres'kar] vt to refresh ▷ vi to cool down; **refrescarse** vr to get cooler; (*tomar aire fresco*) to go out for a breath of fresh air; (*beber*) to have a drink

refresco [re'fresko] nm soft drink, cool drink; "**~s**" "refreshments"

refriega [re'frjexa] nf scuffle, brawl

refrigeración [refrixera'θjon] *nf* refrigeration; (*de sala*) air-conditioning

refrigerador [refrixera'ðor] *nm* refrigerator; (BRIT), icebox (US)

refrigerar [refrixe'rar] *vt* to refrigerate; (*sala*) to air-condition

refuerzo [re'fwerθo] *nm* reinforcement; (*Tec*) support

refugiado, -a [refu'xjaðo, a] *nm/f* refugee

refugiarse [refu'xjarse] *vr* to take refuge, shelter

refugio [re'fuxjo] *nm* refuge; (*protección*) shelter

refunfuñar [refunfu'ɲar] *vi* to grunt, growl; (*quejarse*) to grumble

regadera [reɣa'ðera] *nf* watering can

regadío [reɣa'ðio] *nm* irrigated land

regalado, -a [reɣa'laðo, a] *adj* comfortable, luxurious; (*gratis*) free, for nothing

regalar [reɣa'lar] *vt* (*dar*) to give (as a present); (*entregar*) to give away; (*mimar*) to pamper, make a fuss of

regaliz [reɣa'liθ] *nm* liquorice

regalo [re'ɣalo] *nm* (*obsequio*) gift, present; (*gusto*) pleasure

regañadientes [reɣaɲa'ðjentes]: **a ~** *adv* reluctantly

regañar [reɣa'ɲar] *vt* to scold ▷ *vi* to grumble; **regañón, -ona** *adj* nagging

regar [re'ɣar] *vt* to water, irrigate; (*fig*) to scatter, sprinkle

regatear [reɣate'ar] *vt* (*Com*) to bargain over; (*escatimar*) to be mean with ▷ *vi* to bargain, haggle; (*Deporte*) to dribble; **regateo** *nm* bargaining; dribbling; (*del cuerpo*) swerve, dodge

regazo [re'ɣaθo] *nm* lap

regenerar [rexene'rar] *vt* to regenerate

régimen ['reximen] (*pl* **regímenes**) *nm* regime; (*Med*) diet

regimiento [rexi'mjento] *nm* regiment

regio, -a ['rexjo, a] *adj* royal, regal; (*fig: suntuoso*) splendid; (*cs: fam*) great, terrific

región [re'xjon] *nf* region

regir [re'xir] *vt* to govern, rule; (*dirigir*) to manage, run ▷ *vi* to apply, be in force

registrar [rexis'trar] *vt* (*buscar*) to search; (: *en cajón*) to look through; (*inspeccionar*) to inspect; (*anotar*) to register, record; (*Inform*) to log; **registrarse** *vr* to register; (*ocurrir*) to happen

registro [re'xistro] *nm* (*acto*) registration; (*Mús, libro*) register; (*inspección*) inspection, search; **registro civil** registry office

regla ['reɣla] *nf* (*ley*) rule, regulation; (*de medir*) ruler, rule; (*Med: período*) period; **en ~** in order

reglamentación [reɣlamenta'θjon] *nf* (*acto*) regulation; (*lista*) rules *pl*

reglamentar [reɣlamen'tar] *vt* to regulate; **reglamentario, -a** *adj* statutory; **reglamento** *nm* rules *pl*, regulations *pl*

regocijarse [reɣoθi'xarse] *vr* (*alegrarse*) to rejoice; **regocijo** *nm* joy, happiness

regrabadora [reɣraβa'ðora] *nf* rewriter; **regrabadora de DVD** DVD rewriter

regresar [reɣre'sar] *vi* to come back, go back, return; **regreso** *nm* return

reguero [re'ɣero] *nm* (*de sangre etc*) trickle; (*de humo*) trail

regulador [reɣula'ðor] *nm* regulator; (*de radio etc*) knob, control

regular [reɣu'lar] *adj* regular; (*normal*) normal, usual; (*común*) ordinary; (*organizado*) regular, orderly; (*mediano*) average; (*fam*) not bad, so-so ▷ *adv* so-so, alright ▷ *vt* (*controlar*) to control, regulate; (*Tec*) to adjust; **por lo ~** as a rule; **regularidad** *nf* regularity; **regularizar** *vt* to regularize

rehabilitación [reaβilita'θjon] *nf* rehabilitation; (*Arq*) restoration

rehabilitar [reaβili'tar] *vt* to rehabilitate; (*Arq*) to restore; (*reintegrar*) to reinstate

rehacer [rea'θer] vt (reparar) to mend, repair; (volver a hacer) to redo, repeat; **rehacerse** vr (Med) to recover

rehén [re'en] nm hostage

rehuir [reu'ir] vt to avoid, shun

rehusar [reu'sar] vt, vi to refuse

reina ['reina] nf queen; **reinado** nm reign

reinar [rei'nar] vi to reign

reincidir [reinθi'ðir] vi to relapse

reincorporarse [reinkorpo'rarse] vr: ~ **a** to rejoin

reino ['reino] nm kingdom; **reino animal/vegetal** animal/plant kingdom; **el Reino Unido** the United Kingdom

reintegrar [reinte'ɣrar] vt (reconstituir) to reconstruct; (persona) to reinstate; (dinero) to refund, pay back; **reintegrarse** vr: ~se a to return to

reír [re'ir] vi to laugh; **reírse** vr to laugh; ~se de to laugh at

reiterar [reite'rar] vt to reiterate

reivindicación [reißindika'θjon] nf (demanda) claim, demand; (justificación) vindication

reivindicar [reißindi'kar] vt to claim

reja ['rexa] nf (de ventana) grille, bars pl; (en la calle) grating

rejilla [re'xiʎa] nf grating, grille; (muebles) wickerwork; (de ventilación) vent; (de coche etc) luggage rack

rejoneador [rexonea'ðor] nm mounted bullfighter

rejuvenecer [rexuβene'θer] vt, vi to rejuvenate

relación [rela'θjon] nf relation, relationship; (Mat) ratio; (narración) report; **con ~ a, en ~ con** in relation to; **relaciones públicas** public relations; **relacionar** vt to relate, connect; **relacionarse** vr to be connected, be linked

relajación [relaxa'θjon] nf relaxation

relajar [rela'xar] vt to relax; **relajarse** vr to relax

relamerse [rela'merse] vr to lick one's lips

relámpago [re'lampaɣo] nm flash of lightning; **visita ~** lightning visit

relatar [rela'tar] vt to tell, relate

relativo, -a [rela'tiβo, a] adj relative; **en lo ~ a** concerning

relato [re'lato] nm (narración) story, tale

relegar [rele'ɣar] vt to relegate

relevante [rele'βante] adj eminent, outstanding

relevar [rele'βar] vt (sustituir) to relieve; **relevarse** vr to relay; ~ **a algn de un cargo** to relieve sb of his post

relevo [re'leβo] nm relief; **carrera de ~s** relay race

relieve [re'ljeβe] nm (Arte, Tec) relief; (fig) prominence, importance; **bajo ~** bas-relief

religión [reli'xjon] nf religion; **religioso, -a** adj religious ▷ nm/f monk/nun

relinchar [relin'tʃar] vi to neigh

reliquia [re'likja] nf relic; **reliquia de familia** heirloom

rellano [re'ʎano] nm (Arq) landing

rellenar [reʎe'nar] vt (llenar) to fill up; (Culin) to stuff; (Costura) to pad; **relleno, -a** adj full up; stuffed ▷ nm stuffing; (de tapicería) padding

reloj [re'lo(x)] nm clock; **poner el ~ (en hora)** to set one's watch (o the clock); **reloj (de pulsera)** wristwatch; **reloj despertador** alarm (clock); **reloj digital** digital watch; **relojero, -a** nm/f clockmaker; watchmaker

reluciente [relu'θjente] adj brilliant, shining

relucir [relu'θir] vi to shine; (fig) to excel

remachar [rema'tʃar] vt to rivet; (fig) to hammer home, drive home; **remache** nm rivet

remangar [reman'gar] vt to roll up

remanso [re'manso] nm pool

remar [re'mar] vi to row

rematado, -a [rema'taðo, a] adj complete, utter

rematar [rema'tar] *vt* to finish off; (*Com*) to sell off cheap ▷ *vi* to end, finish off; (*Deporte*) to shoot

remate [re'mate] *nm* end, finish; (*punta*) tip; (*Deporte*) shot; (*Arq*) top; **de** *o* **para ~** to crown it all (BRIT), to top it off

remedar [reme'ðar] *vt* to imitate

remediar [reme'ðjar] *vt* to remedy; (*subsanar*) to make good, repair; (*evitar*) to avoid

remedio [re'meðjo] *nm* remedy; (*alivio*) relief, help; (*Jur*) recourse, remedy; **poner ~ a** to correct, stop; **no tener más ~** to have no alternative; **¡qué ~!** there's no choice!; **sin ~** hopeless

remendar [remen'dar] *vt* to repair; (*con parche*) to patch

remiendo [re'mjendo] *nm* mend; (*con parche*) patch; (*cosido*) darn

remilgado, -a [remil'xaðo, a] *adj* prim; (*afectado*) affected

remiso, -a [re'miso, a] *adj* slack, slow

remite [re'mite] *nm* (*en sobre*) name and address of sender

remitir [remi'tir] *vt* to remit, send ▷ *vi* to slacken; (*en carta*): **remite: X** sender: X; **remitente** *nmf* sender

remo ['remo] *nm* (*de barco*) oar; (*Deporte*) rowing

remojar [remo'xar] *vt* to steep, soak; (*galleta etc*) to dip, dunk

remojo [re'moxo] *nm*: **dejar la ropa en ~** to leave clothes to soak

remolacha [remo'latʃa] *nf* beet, beetroot

remolcador [remolka'ðor] *nm* (*Náut*) tug; (*Auto*) breakdown lorry

remolcar [remol'kar] *vt* to tow

remolino [remo'lino] *nm* eddy; (*de agua*) whirlpool; (*de viento*) whirlwind; (*de gente*) crowd

remolque [re'molke] *nm* tow, towing; (*cuerda*) towrope; **llevar a ~** to tow

remontar [remon'tar] *vt* to mend;

remontarse *vr* to soar; **~se a** (*Com*) to amount to; **~ el vuelo** to soar

remorder [remor'ðer] *vt* to distress, disturb; **~le la conciencia a algn** to have a guilty conscience; **remordimiento** *nm* remorse

remoto, -a [re'moto, a] *adj* remote

remover [remo'βer] *vt* to stir; (*tierra*) to turn over; (*objetos*) to move round

remuneración [remunera'θjon] *nf* remuneration

remunerar [remune'rar] *vt* to remunerate; (*premiar*) to reward

renacer [rena'θer] *vi* to be reborn; (*fig*) to revive; **renacimiento** *nm* rebirth; **el Renacimiento** the Renaissance

renacuajo [rena'kwaxo] *nm* (*Zool*) tadpole

renal [re'nal] *adj* renal, kidney *cpd*

rencilla [ren'θiʎa] *nf* quarrel

rencor [ren'kor] *nm* rancour, bitterness; **rencoroso, -a** *adj* spiteful

rendición [rendi'θjon] *nf* surrender

rendido, -a [ren'diðo, a] *adj* (*sumiso*) submissive; (*cansado*) worn-out, exhausted

rendija [ren'dixa] *nf* (*hendedura*) crack, cleft

rendimiento [rendi'mjento] *nm* (*producción*) output; (*Tec, Com*) efficiency

rendir [ren'dir] *vt* (*vencer*) to defeat; (*producir*) to produce; (*dar beneficio*) to yield; (*agotar*) to exhaust ▷ *vi* to pay; **rendirse** *vr* (*someterse*) to surrender; (*cansarse*) to wear o.s. out; **~ homenaje** *o* **culto a** to pay homage to

renegar [rene'xar] *vi* (*renunciar*) to renounce; (*blasfemar*) to blaspheme; (*quejarse*) to complain

RENFE ['renfe] *nf abr* (= *Red Nacional de los Ferrocarriles Españoles*)

renglón [ren'glon] *nm* (*línea*) line; (*Com*) item, article; **a ~ seguido** immediately after

renombre [re'nombre] *nm* renown

renovación [renoβa'θjon] *nf* (*de*

contrato) renewal; (*Arq*) renovation

renovar [reno'βar] *vt* to renew; (*Arq*) to renovate

renta ['renta] *nf* (*ingresos*) income; (*beneficio*) profit; (*alquiler*) rent; **renta vitalicia** annuity; **rentable** *adj* profitable

renuncia [re'nunθja] *nf* resignation; **renunciar** [renun'θjar] *vt* to renounce; (*tabaco, alcohol etc*); **renunciar a** to give up; (*oferta, oportunidad*) to turn down; (*puesto*) to resign ▷ *vi* to resign

reñido, -a [re'ɲiðo, a] *adj* (*batalla*) bitter, hard-fought; **estar ~ con algn** to be on bad terms with sb

reñir [re'ɲir] *vt* (*regañar*) to scold ▷ *vi* (*estar peleado*) to quarrel, fall out; (*combatir*) to fight

reo ['reo] *nmf* culprit, offender; (*acusado*) accused, defendant

reojo [re'oxo] **de ~** *adv* out of the corner of one's eye

reparación [repara'θjon] *nf* (*acto*) mending, repairing; (*Tec*) repair; (*fig*) amends *pl*, reparation

reparar [repa'rar] *vt* to repair; (*fig*) to make amends for; (*observar*) to observe ▷ *vi*: **~ en** (*darse cuenta de*) to notice; (*prestar atención a*) to pay attention to

reparo [re'paro] *nm* (*advertencia*) observation; (*duda*) doubt; (*dificultad*) difficulty; **poner ~s (a)** to raise objections (to)

repartidor, a [reparti'ðor, a] *nm/f* distributor

repartir [repar'tir] *vt* to distribute, share out; (*Correos*) to deliver; **reparto** *nm* distribution; delivery; (*Teatro, Cine*) cast; (*CAM: urbanización*) housing estate (*BRIT*), real estate development (*US*)

repasar [repa'sar] *vt* (*Escol*) to revise; (*Mecánica*) to check, overhaul; (*Costura*) to mend; **repaso** *nm* revision; overhaul, checkup; mending

repecho [re'petʃo] *nm* steep incline

repelente [repe'lente] *adj* repellent, repulsive

repeler [repe'ler] *vt* to repel

repente [re'pente] *nm*: **de ~** suddenly

repentino, -a [repen'tino, a] *adj* sudden

repercusión [reperku'sjon] *nf* repercussion

repercutir [reperku'tir] *vi* (*objeto*) to rebound; (*sonido*) to echo; **~ en** (*fig*) to have repercussions on

repertorio [reper'torjo] *nm* list; (*Teatro*) repertoire

repetición [repeti'θjon] *nf* repetition

repetir [repe'tir] *vt* to repeat; (*plato*) to have a second helping of ▷ *vi* to repeat; (*sabor*) to come back; **repetirse** *vr* (*volver sobre un tema*) to repeat o.s.

repetitivo, -a [repeti'tiβo, a] *adj* repetitive, repetitious

repique [re'pike] *nm* pealing, ringing; **repiqueteo** *nm* pealing; (*de tambor*) drumming

repisa [re'pisa] *nf* ledge, shelf; (*de ventana*) windowsill; **la ~ de la chimenea** the mantelpiece

repito *etc vb* V **repetir**

replantearse [replante'arse] *vr*: **~ un problema** to reconsider a problem

repleto, -a [re'pleto, a] *adj* replete, full up

réplica ['replika] *nf* answer; (*Arte*) replica

replicar [repli'kar] *vi* to answer; (*objetar*) to argue, answer back

repliegue [re'pljeɣe] *nm* (*Mil*) withdrawal

repoblación [repoβla'θjon] *nf* repopulation; (*de río*) restocking; **repoblación forestal** reafforestation

repoblar [repo'βlar] *vt* to repopulate; (*con árboles*) to reafforest

repollito [repo'ʎito] (*cs*) *nm*: **~s de Bruselas** (Brussels) sprouts

repollo [re'poʎo] *nm* cabbage

reponer [repo'ner] *vt* to replace, put back; (*Teatro*) to revive; **reponerse** *vr* to recover; **~ que ...** to reply that ...

reportaje [repor'taxe] *nm* report,

article

reportero, -a [repor'tero, a] *nm/f*
reporter

reposacabezas [reposaka'βeθas]
nm inv headrest

reposar [repo'sar] *vi* to rest, repose

reposera [repo'sera] (*RPL*) *nf* deck
chair

reposición [reposi'θjon] *nf*
replacement; (*Cine*) remake

reposo [re'poso] *nm* rest

repostar [repos'tar] *vt* to replenish;
(*Auto*) to fill up (with petrol (*BRIT*) o
gasoline (*US*))

repostería [reposte'ria] *nf*
confectioner's (shop)

represa [re'presa] *nf* dam; (*lago
artificial*) lake, pool

represalia [repre'salja] *nf* reprisal

representación [representa'θjon]
nf representation; (*Teatro*)
performance; **representante** *nmf*
representative; performer

representar [represen'tar] *vt* to
represent; (*Teatro*) to perform; (*edad*)
to look; **representarse** *vr* to imagine;
representativo, -a *adj* representative

represión [repre'sjon] *nf* repression

reprimenda [repri'menda] *nf*
reprimand, rebuke

reprimir [repri'mir] *vt* to repress

reprobar [repro'βar] *vt* to censure,
reprove

reprochar [repro'tʃar] *vt* to reproach;
reproche *nm* reproach

reproducción [reproðuk'θjon] *nf*
reproduction

reproducir [reproðu'θir] *vt* to
reproduce; **reproducirse** *vr* to breed;
(*situación*) to recur

reproductor, a [reproðuk'tor,
a] *adj* reproductive ▷ *nm* player;
reproductor de CD CD player

reptil [rep'til] *nm* reptile

república [re'puβlika] *nf* republic;
República Dominicana Dominican
Republic; **republicano, -a** *adj, nm*
republican

repudiar [repu'ðjar] *vt* to repudiate;
(*fe*) to renounce

repuesto [re'pwesto] *nm* (*pieza de
recambio*) spare (part); (*abastecimiento*)
supply; **rueda de ~** spare wheel

repugnancia [repuɣ'nanθja]
nf repugnance; **repugnante** *adj*
repugnant, repulsive

repugnar [repuɣ'nar] *vt* to disgust

repulsa [re'pulsa] *nf* rebuff

repulsión [repul'sjon] *nf* repulsion,
aversion; **repulsivo, -a** *adj* repulsive

reputación [reputa'θjon] *nf*
reputation

requerir [reke'rir] *vt* (*pedir*) to ask,
request; (*exigir*) to require; (*llamar*) to
send for, summon

requesón [reke'son] *nm* cottage
cheese

requete... [re'kete] *prefijo* extremely

réquiem ['rekjem] (*pl* **~s**) *nm*
requiem

requisito [reki'sito] *nm* requirement,
requisite

res [res] *nf* beast, animal

resaca [re'saka] *nf* (*de mar*) undertow,
undercurrent; (*fam*) hangover

resaltar [resal'tar] *vi* to project, stick
out; (*fig*) to stand out

resarcir [resar'θir] *vt* to compensate;
resarcirse *vr* to make up for

resbaladero [resβala'ðero] (*MÉX*)
nm slide

resbaladizo, -a [resβala'ðiθo, a]
adj slippery

resbalar [resβa'lar] *vi* to slip, slide;
(*fig*) to slip (up); **resbalarse** *vr* to
slip, slide; to slip (up); **resbalón** *nm*
(*acción*) slip

rescatar [reska'tar] *vt* (*salvar*) to
save, rescue; (*objeto*) to get back,
recover; (*cautivos*) to ransom

rescate [res'kate] *nm* rescue; (*de
objeto*) recovery; **pagar un ~** to pay
a ransom

rescindir [resθin'dir] *vt* to rescind

rescisión [resθi'sjon] *nf* cancellation

resecar [rese'kar] *vt* to dry

thoroughly; (*Med*) to cut out, remove;
resecarse *vr* to dry up

reseco, -a [re'seko, a] *adj* very dry;
(*fig*) skinny

resentido, -a [resen'tiðo, a] *adj*
resentful

resentimiento [resenti'mjento] *nm*
resentment, bitterness

resentirse [resen'tirse] *vr*
(*debilitarse: persona*) to suffer; **~ de**
(*consecuencias*) to feel the effects of; **~
de (o por) algo** to resent sth, be bitter
about sth

reseña [re'seɲa] *nf* (*cuenta*) account;
(*informe*) report; (*Literatura*) review

reseñar [rese'ɲar] *vt* to describe;
(*Literatura*) to review

reserva [re'serβa] *nf* reserve;
(*reservación*) reservation

reservado, -a [reser'βaðo, a] *adj*
reserved; (*retraído*) cold, distant ▷ *nm*
private room

reservar [reser'βar] *vt* (*guardar*) to
keep; (*habitación, entrada*) to reserve;
reservarse *vr* to save o.s.; (*callar*) to
keep to o.s.

resfriado [resfri'aðo] *nm* cold;
resfriarse *vr* to cool; (*Med*) to catch
a cold

resguardar [resɣwar'ðar] *vt* to
protect, shield; **resguardarse** *vr*: **~se
de** to guard against; **resguardo**
nm defence; (*vale*) voucher; (*recibo*)
receipt, slip

residencia [resi'ðenθja] *nf*
residence; **residencia de ancianos**
residential home, old people's
home; **residencia universitaria**
hall of residence; **residencial** *nf*
(*urbanización*) housing estate

residente [resi'ðente] *adj, nmf*
resident

residir [resi'ðir] *vi* to reside, live; **~ en**
to reside in, lie in

residuo [re'siðwo] *nm* residue

resignación [resiɣna'θjon] *nf*
resignation; **resignarse** *vr*: **resignarse
a** *o* **con** to resign o.s. to, be resigned to

resina [re'sina] *nf* resin

resistencia [resis'tenθja] *nf* (*dureza*)
endurance, strength; (*oposición, Elec*)
resistance; **resistente** *adj* strong,
hardy; resistant

resistir [resis'tir] *vt* (*soportar*) to bear;
(*oponerse a*) to resist, oppose; (*aguantar*)
to put up with ▷ *vi* to resist; (*aguantar*)
to last, endure; **resistirse** *vr*: **~se a** to
refuse to, resist

resoluto, -a [reso'luto, a] *adj*
resolute

resolver [resol'βer] *vt* to resolve;
(*solucionar*) to solve, resolve; (*decidir*) to
decide, settle; **resolverse** *vr* to make
up one's mind

resonar [reso'nar] *vi* to ring, echo

resoplar [reso'plar] *vi* to snort;
resoplido *nm* heavy breathing

resorte [re'sorte] *nm* spring; (*fig*)
lever

resortera [resor'tera] (*MÉX*) *nf*
catapult

respaldar [respal'dar] *vt* to back
(up), support; **respaldarse** *vr* to lean
back; **~se con** *o* **en** (*fig*) to take one's
stand on; **respaldo** *nm* (*de sillón*) back;
(*fig*) support, backing

respectivo, -a [respek'tiβo, a] *adj*
respective; **en lo ~ a** with regard to

respecto [res'pekto] *nm*: **al ~** on this
matter; **con ~ a, ~ de** with regard to,
in relation to

respetable [respe'taβle] *adj*
respectable

respetar [respe'tar] *vt* to respect;
respeto *nm* respect; (*acatamiento*)
deference; **respetos** *nmpl* respects;
respetuoso, -a *adj* respectful

respingo [res'pingo] *nm* start, jump

respiración [respira'θjon] *nf*
breathing; (*Med*) respiration;
(*ventilación*) ventilation; **respiración
asistida** artificial respiration (*by
machine*)

respirar [respi'rar] *vi* to breathe;
respiratorio, -a *adj* respiratory;
respiro *nm* breathing; (*fig: descanso*)

respite

resplandecer [resplande'θer]
vi to shine; **resplandeciente** adj
resplendent, shining; **resplandor**
nm brilliance, brightness; (de luz,
fuego) blaze

responder [respon'der] vt to answer
▷ vi to answer; (fig) to respond; (pey) to
answer back; **~ de** o **por** to answer for;
respondón, -ona adj cheeky

responsabilidad [responsaβili'ðað]
nf responsibility

responsabilizarse
[responsaβili'θarse] vr to make o.s.
responsible, take charge

responsable [respon'saβle] adj
responsible

respuesta [res'pwesta] nf answer,
reply

resquebrajar [reskeβra'xar] vt to
crack, split; **resquebrajarse** vr to
crack, split

resquicio [res'kiθjo] nm chink;
(hendedura) crack

resta ['resta] nf (Mat) remainder

restablecer [restaβle'θer] vt to
re-establish, restore; **restablecerse**
vr to recover

restante [res'tante] adj remaining;
lo ~ the remainder

restar [res'tar] vt (Mat) to subtract;
(fig) to take away ▷ vi to remain, be left

restauración [restaura'θjon] nf
restoration

restaurante [restau'rante] nm
restaurant

restaurar [restau'rar] vt to restore

restituir [restitu'ir] vt (devolver) to
return, give back; (rehabilitar) to restore

resto ['resto] nm (residuo) rest,
remainder; (apuesta) stake; **restos**
nmpl remains

restorán [resto'ran] nm (Lam)
restaurant

restregar [restre'ɣar] vt to scrub, rub

restricción [restrik'θjon] nf
restriction

restringir [restrin'xir] vt to restrict,

limit

resucitar [resuθi'tar] vt, vi to
resuscitate, revive

resuelto, -a [re'swelto, a] pp de
resolver ▷ adj resolute, determined

resultado [resul'taðo] nm result;
(conclusión) outcome; **resultante** adj
resulting, resultant

resultar [resul'tar] vi (ser) to be;
(llegar a ser) to turn out to be; (salir bien)
to turn out well; (Com) to amount to;
~ de to stem from; **me resulta difícil
hacerlo** it's difficult for me to do it

resumen [re'sumen] (pl **resúmenes**)
nm summary, résumé; **en ~** in short

resumir [resu'mir] vt to sum
up; (cortar) to abridge, cut down;
(condensar) to summarize

> No confundir **resumir** con la
> palabra inglesa resume.

resurgir [resur'xir] vi (reaparecer)
to reappear

resurrección [resurre(k)'θjon] nf
resurrection

retablo [re'taβlo] nm altarpiece

retaguardia [reta'ɣwarðja] nf
rearguard

retahíla [reta'ila] nf series, string

retal [re'tal] nm remnant

retar [re'tar] vt to challenge; (desafiar)
to defy, dare

retazo [re'taθo] nm snippet (BRIT),
fragment

retención [reten'θjon] nf (tráfico)
hold-up; **retención fiscal** deduction
for tax purposes

retener [rete'ner] vt (intereses) to
withhold

reticente [reti'θente] adj (tono)
insinuating; (postura) reluctant; **ser ~ a
hacer algo** to be reluctant o unwilling
to do sth

retina [re'tina] nf retina

retintín [retin'tin] nm jangle, jingle

retirada [reti'raða] nf (Mil, refugio)
retreat; (de dinero) withdrawal; (de
embajador) recall; **retirado, -a** adj
(lugar) remote; (vida) quiet; (jubilado)

retired
retirar [reti'rar] vt to withdraw; (quitar) to remove; (jubilar) to retire, pension off; **retirarse** vr to retreat, withdraw; to retire; (acostarse) to retire, go to bed; **retiro** nm retreat; retirement; (pago) pension
reto ['reto] nm dare, challenge
retocar [reto'kar] vt (fotografía) to touch up, retouch
retoño [re'toɲo] nm sprout, shoot; (fig) offspring, child
retoque [re'toke] nm retouching
retorcer [retor'θer] vt to twist; (manos, lavado) to wring; **retorcerse** vr to become twisted; (mover el cuerpo) to writhe
retorcido, -a [retor'θiðo, a] adj (persona) devious
retorcijón [retorθi'jon] (LAM) nm (tb: ~ de tripas) stomach cramp
retórica [re'torika] nf rhetoric; (pey) affectedness
retorno [re'torno] nm return
retortijón [retorti'xon] (ESP) nm (tb: ~ de tripas) stomach cramp
retozar [reto'θar] vi (juguetear) to frolic, romp; (saltar) to gambol
retracción [retrak'θjon] nf retraction
retraerse [retra'erse] vr to retreat, withdraw; **retraído, -a** adj shy, retiring; **retraimiento** nm retirement; (timidez) shyness
retransmisión [retransmi'sjon] nf repeat (broadcast)
retransmitir [retransmi'tir] vt (mensaje) to relay; (TV etc) to repeat, retransmit; (: en vivo) to broadcast live
retrasado, -a [retra'saðo, a] adj late; (Med) mentally retarded; (país etc) backward, underdeveloped
retrasar [retra'sar] vt (demorar) to postpone, put off; (retardar) to slow down ▷vi (atrasarse) to be late; (reloj) to be slow; (producción) to fall (off); (quedarse atrás) to lag behind; **retrasarse** vr to be late; to be slow; to

fall (off); to lag behind
retraso [re'traso] nm (demora) delay; (lentitud) slowness; (tardanza) lateness; (atraso) backwardness; **retrasos** nmpl (Finanzas) arrears; **llegar con ~** to arrive late; **retraso mental** mental deficiency
retratar [retra'tar] vt (Arte) to paint the portrait of; (fotografiar) to photograph; (fig) to depict, describe; **retrato** nm portrait; (fig) likeness; **retrato-robot** (ESP) nm Identikit®
retrete [re'trete] nm toilet
retribuir [retri'βwir] vt (recompensar) to reward; (pagar) to pay
retro... ['retro] prefijo retro...
retroceder [retroθe'ðer] vi (echarse atrás) to move back(wards); (fig) to back down
retroceso [retro'θeso] nm backward movement; (Med) relapse; (fig) backing down
retrospectivo, -a [retrospek'tiβo, a] adj retrospective
retrovisor [retroβi'sor] nm (tb: **espejo ~**) rear-view mirror
retumbar [retum'bar] vi to echo, resound
reúma [re'uma], **reuma** ['reuma] nm rheumatism
reunión [reu'njon] nf (asamblea) meeting; (fiesta) party
reunir [reu'nir] vt (juntar) to reunite, join (together); (recoger) to gather (together); (personas) to get together; (cualidades) to combine; **reunirse** vr (personas: en asamblea) to meet, gather
revalidar [reβali'ðar] vt (ratificar) to confirm, ratify
revalorizar [reβalori'θar] vt to revalue, reassess
revancha [re'βantʃa] nf revenge
revelación [reβela'θjon] nf revelation
revelado [reβe'laðo] nm developing
revelar [reβe'lar] vt to reveal; (Foto) to develop
reventa [re'βenta] nf (de

entradas: para concierto) touting

reventar [reβen'tar] *vt* to burst, explode

reventón [reβen'ton] *nm* (*Auto*) blow-out (*BRIT*), flat (*US*)

reverencia [reβe'renθja] *nf* reverence; **reverenciar** *vt* to revere

reverendo, -a [reβe'rendo, a] *adj* reverend

reverente [reβe'rente] *adj* reverent

reversa [re'βersa] (*MÉX, CAM*) *nf* reverse (gear)

reversible [reβer'siβle] *adj* (*prenda*) reversible

reverso [re'βerso] *nm* back, other side; (*de moneda*) reverse

revertir [reβer'tir] *vi* to revert

revés [re'βes] *nm* back, wrong side; (*fig*) reverse, setback; (*Deporte*) backhand; **al ~** the wrong way round; (*de arriba abajo*) upside down; (*ropa*) inside out; **volver algo del ~** to turn sth round; (*ropa*) to turn sth inside out

revisar [reβi'sar] *vt* (*examinar*) to check; (*texto etc*) to revise; **revisión** *nf* revision; **revisión salarial** wage review

revisor, a [reβi'sor, a] *nm/f* inspector; (*Ferro*) ticket collector

revista [re'βista] *nf* magazine, review; (*Teatro*) revue; (*inspección*) inspection; **pasar ~ a** to review, inspect; **revista del corazón** magazine featuring celebrity gossip and real-life romance stories

revivir [reβi'βir] *vi* to revive

revolcarse [reβol'karse] *vr* to roll about

revoltijo [reβol'tixo] *nm* mess, jumble

revoltoso, -a [reβol'toso, a] *adj* (*travieso*) naughty, unruly

revolución [reβolu'θjon] *nf* revolution; **revolucionario, -a** *adj, nm/f* revolutionary

revolver [reβol'βer] *vt* (*desordenar*) to disturb, mess up; (*mover*) to move about ▷ *vi:* **~ en** to go through,

rummage (about) in; **revolverse** *vr* (*volver contra*) to turn on *o* against

revólver [re'βolβer] *nm* revolver

revuelo [re'βwelo] *nm* fluttering; (*fig*) commotion

revuelta [re'βwelta] *nf* (*motín*) revolt; (*agitación*) commotion

revuelto, -a [re'βwelto, a] *pp de* **revolver** ▷ *adj* (*mezclado*) mixed-up, in disorder

rey [rei] *nm* king; **Día de R~es** Twelfth Night; **los R~es Magos** the Three Wise Men, the Magi

● **REYES MAGOS**
●
● On the night before the 6th
● January (the Epiphany), children
● go to bed expecting **los Reyes**
● **Magos** (the Three Wise Men) to
● bring them presents. Twelfth
● Night processions, known as
● **cabalgatas**, take place that
● evening when 3 people dressed
● as **los Reyes Magos** arrive in the
● town by land or sea to the delight
● of the children.

reyerta [re'jerta] *nf* quarrel, brawl

rezagado, -a [reθa'ɣaðo, a] *nm/f* straggler

rezar [re'θar] *vi* to pray; **~ con** (*fam*) to concern, have to do with; **rezo** *nm* prayer

rezumar [reθu'mar] *vt* to ooze

ría ['ria] *nf* estuary

riada [ri'aða] *nf* flood

ribera [ri'βera] *nf* (*de río*) bank; (: *área*) riverside

ribete [ri'βete] *nm* (*de vestido*) border; (*fig*) addition

ricino [ri'θino] *nm:* **aceite de ~** castor oil

rico, -a ['riko, a] *adj* rich; (*adinerado*) wealthy, rich; (*lujoso*) luxurious; (*comida*) delicious; (*niño*) lovely, cute ▷ *nm/f* rich person

ridiculez [riðiku'leθ] *nf* absurdity

ridiculizar [riðikuli'θar] vt to ridicule

ridículo, -a [ri'ðikulo, a] adj ridiculous; **hacer el ~** to make a fool of o.s.; **poner a algn en ~** to make a fool of sb

riego ['rjeɣo] nm (aspersión) watering; (irrigación) irrigation; **riego sanguíneo** blood flow o circulation

riel [rjel] nm rail

rienda ['rjenda] nf rein; **dar ~ suelta a** to give free rein to

riesgo ['rjesɣo] nm risk; **correr el ~ de** to run the risk of

rifa ['rifa] nf (lotería) raffle; **rifar** vt to raffle

rifle ['rifle] nm rifle

rigidez [rixi'ðeθ] nf rigidity, stiffness; (fig) strictness; **rígido, -a** adj rigid, stiff; strict, inflexible

rigor [ri'ɣor] nm strictness, rigour; (inclemencia) harshness; **de ~** de rigueur, essential; **riguroso, -a** adj rigorous; harsh; (severo) severe

rimar [ri'mar] vi to rhyme

rimbombante [rimbom'bante] adj pompous

rímel ['rimel] nm mascara

rímmel ['rimel] nm = **rímel**

rin [rin] (MÉX) nm (wheel) rim

rincón [rin'kon] nm corner (inside)

rinoceronte [rinoθe'ronte] nm rhinoceros

riña ['riɲa] nf (disputa) argument; (pelea) brawl

riñón [ri'ɲon] nm kidney

río etc ['rio] vb V **reír** ▷ nm river; (fig) torrent, stream; **río abajo/arriba** downstream/upstream; **Río de la Plata** River Plate

rioja [ri'oxa] nm (vino) rioja (wine)

rioplatense [riopla'tense] adj of o from the River Plate region

riqueza [ri'keθa] nf wealth, riches pl; (cualidad) richness

risa ['risa] nf laughter; (una risa) laugh; **¡qué ~!** what a laugh!

risco ['risko] nm crag, cliff

ristra ['ristra] nf string

risueño, -a [ri'sweɲo, a] adj (sonriente) smiling; (contento) cheerful

ritmo ['ritmo] nm rhythm; **a ~ lento** slowly; **trabajar a ~ lento** to go slow; **ritmo cardíaco** heart rate

rito ['rito] nm rite

ritual [ri'twal] adj, nm ritual

rival [ri'βal] adj, nmf rival; **rivalidad** nf rivalry; **rivalizar** vi: **rivalizar con** to rival, vie with

rizado, -a [ri'θaðo, a] adj curly ▷ nm curls pl

rizar [ri'θar] vt to curl; **rizarse** vr (pelo) to curl; (agua) to ripple; **rizo** nm curl; ripple

RNE nf abr = **Radio Nacional de España**

robar [ro'βar] vt to rob; (objeto) to steal; (casa etc) to break into; (Naipes) to draw

roble ['roβle] nm oak; **robledal** nm oakwood

robo ['roβo] nm robbery, theft

robot [ro'βot] nm robot; **robot (de cocina)** (ESP) food processor

robustecer [roβuste'θer] vt to strengthen

robusto, -a [ro'βusto, a] adj robust, strong

roca ['roka] nf rock

roce ['roθe] nm (caricia) brush; (Tec) friction; (en la piel) graze; **tener ~ con** to be in close contact with

rociar [ro'θjar] vt to spray

rocín [ro'θin] nm nag, hack

rocío [ro'θio] nm dew

rocola [ro'kola] (LAM) nf jukebox

rocoso, -a [ro'koso, a] adj rocky

rodaballo [roða'βaʎo] nm turbot

rodaja [ro'ðaxa] nf slice

rodaje [ro'ðaxe] nm (Cine) shooting, filming; (Auto): **en ~** running in

rodar [ro'ðar] vt (vehículo) to wheel (along); (escalera) to roll down; (viajar por) to travel (over) ▷ vi to roll; (coche) to go, run; (Cine) to shoot, film

rodear [roðe'ar] vt to surround ▷ vi

to go round; **rodearse** vr: ~**se de amigos** to surround o.s. with friends

rodeo [ro'ðeo] nm (ruta indirecta) detour; (evasión) evasion; (Deporte) rodeo; **hablar sin ~s** to come to the point, speak plainly

rodilla [ro'ðiʎa] nf knee; **de ~s** kneeling; **ponerse de ~s** to kneel (down)

rodillo [ro'ðiʎo] nm roller; (Culin) rolling-pin

roedor, a [roe'ðor, a] adj gnawing ▷ nm rodent

roer [ro'er] vt (masticar) to gnaw; (corroer, fig) to corrode

rogar [ro'xar] vt, vi (pedir) to ask for; (suplicar) to beg, plead; **se ruega no fumar** please do not smoke

rojizo, -a [ro'xiθo, a] adj reddish

rojo, -a ['roxo, a] adj, nm red; **al ~ vivo** red-hot

rol [rol] nm list, roll; (papel) role

rollito [ro'ʎito] nm (tb: ~ **de primavera**) spring roll

rollizo, -a [ro'ʎiθo, a] adj (objeto) cylindrical; (persona) plump

rollo ['roʎo] nm roll; (de cuerda) coil; (madera) log; (ESP: fam) bore; **¡qué ~!** (ESP: fam) what a carry-on!

Roma ['roma] n Rome

romance [ro'manθe] nm (amoroso) romance; (Literatura) ballad

romano, -a [ro'mano, a] adj, nm/f Roman; **a la romana** in batter

romanticismo [romanti'θismo] nm romanticism

romántico, -a [ro'mantiko, a] adj romantic

rombo ['rombo] nm (Geom) rhombus

romería [rome'ria] nf (Rel) pilgrimage; (excursión) trip, outing

romero, -a [ro'mero, a] nm/f pilgrim ▷ nm rosemary

romo, -a ['romo, a] adj blunt; (fig) dull

rompecabezas [rompeka'βeθas] nm inv riddle, puzzle; (juego) jigsaw (puzzle)

rompehuelgas [rompe'welxas] (LAM) nm inv strikebreaker, scab

rompeolas [rompe'olas] nm inv breakwater

romper [rom'per] vt to break; (hacer pedazos) to smash; (papel, tela etc) to tear, rip ▷ vi (olas) to break; (sol, diente) to break through; **romperse** vr to break; ~ **un contrato** to break a contract; ~ **a** (empezar a) to start (suddenly) to; ~ **a llorar** to burst into tears; ~ **con algn** to fall out with sb

ron [ron] nm rum

roncar [ron'kar] vi to snore

ronco, -a ['ronko, a] adj (afónico) hoarse; (áspero) raucous

ronda ['ronda] nf (gen) round; (patrulla) patrol; **rondar** vt to patrol ▷ vi to patrol; (fig) to prowl round

ronquido [ron'kiðo] nm snore, snoring

ronronear [ronrone'ar] vi to purr

roña ['roɲa] nf (Veterinaria) mange; (mugre) dirt, grime; (óxido) rust

roñoso, -a [ro'ɲoso, a] adj (mugriento) filthy; (tacaño) mean

ropa ['ropa] nf clothes pl, clothing; **ropa blanca** linen; **ropa de cama** bed linen; **ropa de color** coloureds pl; **ropa interior** underwear; **ropa sucia** dirty washing; **ropaje** nm gown, robes pl

ropero [ro'pero] nm linen cupboard; (guardarropa) wardrobe

rosa ['rosa] adj pink ▷ nf rose

rosado, -a [ro'saðo, a] adj pink

▷ nm rosé

rosal [ro'sal] nm rosebush

rosario [ro'sarjo] nm (*Rel*) rosary; **rezar el ~** to say the rosary

rosca ['roska] nf (*de tornillo*) thread; (*de humo*) coil, spiral; (*pan, postre*) ring-shaped roll/pastry

rosetón [rose'ton] nm rosette; (*Arq*) rose window

rosquilla [ros'kiʎa] nf doughnut-shaped fritter

rostro ['rostro] nm (*cara*) face

rotativo, -a [rota'tiβo, a] adj rotary

roto, -a ['roto, a] pp de **romper** ▷ adj broken

rotonda [ro'tonda] nf roundabout

rótula ['rotula] nf kneecap; (*Tec*) ball-and-socket joint

rotulador [rotula'ðor] nm felt-tip pen

rótulo ['rotulo] nm heading, title; label; (*letrero*) sign

rotundamente [rotunda'mente] adv (*negar*) flatly; (*responder, afirmar*) emphatically; **rotundo, -a** adj round; (*enfático*) emphatic

rotura [ro'tura] nf (*acto*) breaking; (*Med*) fracture

rozadura [roθa'ðura] nf abrasion, graze

rozar [ro'θar] vt (*frotar*) to rub; (*arañar*) to scratch; (*tocar ligeramente*) to shave, touch lightly; **rozarse** vr to rub (together); **~se con** (*fam*) to rub shoulders with

rte. abr (= remite, remitente) sender

RTVE nf abr = **Radiotelevisión Española**

rubí [ru'βi] nm ruby; (*de reloj*) jewel

rubio, -a ['ruβjo, a] adj fair-haired, blond(e) ▷ nm/f blond/blonde; **tabaco ~** Virginia tobacco

rubor [ru'βor] nm (*sonrojo*) blush; (*timidez*) bashfulness; **ruborizarse** vr to blush

rúbrica ['ruβrika] nf (*de la firma*) flourish; **rubricar** vt (*firmar*) to sign with a flourish; (*concluir*) to sign

and seal

rudimentario, -a [ruðimen'tarjo, a] adj rudimentary

rudo, -a ['ruðo, a] adj (*sin pulir*) unpolished; (*grosero*) coarse; (*violento*) violent; (*sencillo*) simple

rueda ['rweða] nf wheel; (*círculo*) ring, circle; (*rodaja*) slice, round; **rueda de auxilio** (*RPL*) spare tyre; **rueda delantera/trasera/de repuesto** front/back/spare wheel; **rueda de prensa** press conference; **rueda gigante** (*LAM*) big (*BRIT*) o Ferris (*US*) wheel

ruedo ['rweðo] nm (*círculo*) circle; (*Taur*) arena, bullring

ruego etc ['rweɣo] vb V **rogar** ▷ nm request

rugby ['ruɣβi] nm rugby

rugido [ru'xiðo] nm roar

rugir [ru'xir] vi to roar

rugoso, -a [ru'ɣoso, a] adj (*arrugado*) wrinkled; (*áspero*) rough; (*desigual*) ridged

ruido ['rwiðo] nm noise; (*sonido*) sound; (*alboroto*) racket, row; (*escándalo*) commotion, rumpus; **ruidoso, -a** adj noisy, loud; (*fig*) sensational

ruin [rwin] adj contemptible, mean

ruina ['rwina] nf ruin; (*colapso*) collapse; (*de persona*) ruin, downfall

ruinoso, -a [rwi'noso, a] adj ruinous; (*destartalado*) dilapidated, tumbledown; (*Com*) disastrous

ruiseñor [rwise'ɲor] nm nightingale

rulero [ru'lero] nm (*RPL*) roller

ruleta [ru'leta] nf roulette

rulo ['rulo] nm (*para el pelo*) curler

Rumanía [ruma'nia] nf Rumania

rumba ['rumba] nf rumba

rumbo ['rumbo] nm (*ruta*) route, direction; (*ángulo de dirección*) course, bearing; (*fig*) course of events; **ir con ~ a** to be heading for

rumiante [ru'mjante] nm ruminant

rumiar [ru'mjar] vt to chew; (*fig*) to chew over ▷ vi to chew the cud

rumor [ru'mor] *nm* (*ruido sordo*) low sound; (*murmuración*) murmur, buzz; **rumorearse** *vr*: **se rumorea que ...** it is rumoured that ...

rupestre [ru'pestre] *adj* rock *cpd*

ruptura [rup'tura] *nf* rupture

rural [ru'ral] *adj* rural

Rusia ['rusja] *nf* Russia; **ruso, -a** *adj, nm/f* Russian

rústico, -a ['rustiko, a] *adj* rustic; (*ordinario*) coarse, uncouth ▷ *nm/f* yokel

ruta ['ruta] *nf* route

rutina [ru'tina] *nf* routine

S

S *abr* (= *santo, a*) St; (= *sur*) S

s. *abr* (= *siglo*) C.; (= *siguiente*) foll

S.A. *abr* (= *Sociedad Anónima*) Ltd. (BRIT), Inc. (US)

sábado ['saβaðo] *nm* Saturday

sábana ['saβana] *nf* sheet

sabañón [saβa'ɲon] *nm* chilblain

saber [sa'βer] *vt* to know; (*llegar a conocer*) to find out, learn; (*tener capacidad de*) to know how to ▷ *vi*: **~ a** to taste of, taste like ▷ *nm* knowledge, learning; **a ~** namely; **¿sabes conducir/nadar?** can you drive/swim?; **¿sabes francés?** do you speak French?; **~ de memoria** to know by heart; **hacer ~ algo a algn** to inform sb of sth, let sb know sth

sabiduría [saβiðu'ria] *nf* (*conocimientos*) wisdom; (*instrucción*) learning

sabiendas [sa'βjendas]: **a ~** *adv* knowingly

sabio, -a ['saβjo, a] *adj* (*docto*) learned; (*prudente*) wise, sensible

sabor [sa'βor] *nm* taste, flavour;

saborear vt to taste, savour; (fig) to relish

sabotaje [saβo'taxe] nm sabotage

sabré etc vb V **saber**

sabroso, -a [sa'βroso, a] adj tasty; (fig: fam) racy, salty

sacacorchos [saka'kortʃos] nm inv corkscrew

sacapuntas [saka'puntas] nm inv pencil sharpener

sacar [sa'kar] vt to take out; (fig: extraer) to get (out); (quitar) to remove, get out; (hacer salir) to bring out; (conclusión) to draw; (novela etc) to publish, bring out; (ropa) to take off; (obra) to make; (premio) to receive; (entradas) to get; (Tenis) to serve; ~ **adelante** (niño) to bring up; (negocio) to carry on, go on with; ~ **a algn a bailar** to get sb up to dance; ~ **una foto** to take a photo; ~ **la lengua** to stick out one's tongue; ~ **buenas/malas notas** to get good/bad marks

sacarina [saka'rina] nf saccharin(e)

sacerdote [saθer'ðote] nm priest

saciar [sa'θjar] vt (hambre, sed) to satisfy; **saciarse** vr (de comida) to get full up

saco ['sako] nm bag; (grande) sack; (su contenido) bagful; (LAM: chaqueta) jacket; **saco de dormir** sleeping bag

sacramento [sakra'mento] nm sacrament

sacrificar [sakrifi'kar] vt to sacrifice; **sacrificio** nm sacrifice

sacristía [sakris'tia] nf sacristy

sacudida [saku'ðiða] nf (agitación) shake, shaking; (sacudimiento) jolt, bump; **sacudida eléctrica** electric shock

sacudir [saku'ðir] vt to shake; (golpear) to hit

Sagitario [saxi'tarjo] nm Sagittarius

sagrado, -a [sa'ɣraðo, a] adj sacred, holy

Sáhara ['saara] nm: **el ~** the Sahara (desert)

sal [sal] vb V **salir** ▷ nf salt; **sales de**

baño bath salts

sala ['sala] nf room; (tb: ~ **de estar**) living room; (Teatro) house, auditorium; (de hospital) ward; **sala de espera** waiting room; **sala de estar** living room; **sala de fiestas** dance hall

salado, -a [sa'laðo, a] adj salty; (fig) witty, amusing; **agua salada** salt water

salar [sa'lar] vt to salt, add salt to

salario [sa'larjo] nm wage, pay

salchicha [sal'tʃitʃa] nf (pork) sausage; **salchichón** nm (salami-type) sausage

saldo ['saldo] nm (pago) settlement; (de una cuenta) balance; (lo restante) remnant(s) (pl), remainder; (de móvil) credit; **saldos** nmpl (en tienda) sale

saldré etc vb V **salir**

salero [sa'lero] nm salt cellar

salgo etc vb V **salir**

salida [sa'liða] nf (puerta etc) exit, way out; (acto) leaving, going out; (de tren, Aviac) departure; (Tec) output, production; (fig) way out; (Com) opening; (Geo, válvula) outlet; (de gas) leak; **calle sin ~** cul-de-sac; **salida de baño** (RPL) bathrobe; **salida de emergencia/incendios** emergency exit/fire escape

○ **PALABRA CLAVE**

salir [sa'lir] vi **1** (partir: tb: **salir de**) to leave; **Juan ha salido** Juan is out; **salió de la cocina** he came out of the kitchen

2 (aparecer) to appear; (disco, libro) to come out; **anoche salió en la tele** she appeared o was on TV last night; **salió en todos los periódicos** it was in all the papers

3 (resultar): **la muchacha nos salió muy trabajadora** the girl turned out to be a very hard worker; **la comida te ha salido exquisita** the food was delicious; **sale muy caro** it's very expensive

4: salirle a uno algo: **la entrevista que hice me salió bien/mal** the interview I did went o turned out well/badly

5: salir adelante: **no sé como haré para salir adelante** I don't know how I'll get by

salirse vr (líquido) to spill; (animal) to escape

saliva [sa'liβa] nf saliva

salmo ['salmo] nm psalm

salmón [sal'mon] nm salmon

salmonete [salmo'nete] nm red mullet

salón [sa'lon] nm (de casa) living room, lounge; (muebles) lounge suite; **salón de baile** dance hall; **salón de belleza** beauty parlour

salpicadera [salpika'ðera] (MÉX) nf mudguard (BRIT), fender (US)

salpicadero [salpika'ðero] nm (Auto) dashboard

salpicar [salpi'kar] vt (rociar) to sprinkle, spatter; (esparcir) to scatter

salpicón [salpi'kon] nm (tb: ~ de marisco) seafood salad

salsa ['salsa] nf sauce; (con carne asada) gravy; (fig) spice

saltamontes [salta'montes] nm inv grasshopper

saltar [sal'tar] vt to jump (over), leap (over); (dejar de lado) to skip, miss out ▷ vi to jump, leap; (pelota) to bounce; (al aire) to fly up; (quebrarse) to break; (al agua) to dive; (fig) to explode, blow up

salto ['salto] nm jump, leap; (al agua) dive; **salto de agua** waterfall; **salto de altura/longitud** high/long jump

salud [sa'luð] nf health; ¡(a su) ~! cheers!, good health!; **saludable** adj (de buena salud) healthy; (provechoso) good, beneficial

saludar [salu'ðar] vt to greet; (Mil) to salute; **saludo** nm greeting; **"saludos"** (en carta) "best wishes", "regards"

salvación [salβa'θjon] nf salvation; (rescate) rescue

salvado [sal'βaðo] nm bran

salvaje [sal'βaxe] adj wild; (tribu) savage

salvamanteles [salβaman'teles] nm inv table mat

salvamento [salβa'mento] nm rescue

salvapantallas [salβapan'taʎas] nm inv screen saver

salvar [sal'βar] vt (rescatar) to save, rescue; (resolver) to overcome, resolve; (cubrir distancias) to cover, travel; (hacer excepción) to except, exclude; (barco) to salvage

salvavidas [salβa'βiðas] adj inv: **bote/chaleco ~** lifeboat/life jacket

salvo, -a ['salβo, a] adj safe ▷ adv except (for), save; **a ~** out of danger; **~ que** unless

san [san] adj saint; **S~ Juan** St John

sanar [sa'nar] vt (herida) to heal; (persona) to cure ▷ vi (persona) to get well, recover; (herida) to heal

sanatorio [sana'torjo] nm sanatorium

sanción [san'θjon] nf sanction

sancochado, -a [sanko'tʃado, a] (MÉX) adj (Culin) underdone, rare

sandalia [san'dalja] nf sandal

sandía [san'dia] nf watermelon

sandwich ['sandwitʃ] (pl **~s**, **~es**) nm sandwich

sanfermines [sanfer'mines] nmpl festivities in celebration of San Fermín (Pamplona)

● **SANFERMINES**
●
● The **Sanfermines** is a week-long
● festival in Pamplona made famous
● by Ernest Hemingway. From the
● 7th July, the feast of "San Fermín",
● crowds of mainly young people
● take to the streets drinking,
● singing and dancing. Early in
● the morning bulls are released
● along the narrow streets leading

to the bullring, and young men risk serious injury to show their bravery by running out in front of them, a custom which is also typical of many Spanish villages.

sangrar [san'grar] *vt, vi* to bleed; **sangre** *nf* blood

sangría [san'gria] *nf* sangria, *sweetened drink of red wine with fruit*

sangriento, -a [san'grjento, a] *adj* bloody

sanguíneo, -a [san'gineo, a] *adj* blood *cpd*

sanidad [sani'ðað] *nf* (*tb:* ~ **pública**) public health

San Isidro [sani'sidro] *nm patron saint of Madrid*

SAN ISIDRO

San Isidro is the patron saint of Madrid, and gives his name to the week-long festivities which take place around the 15th May. Originally an 18th-century trade fair, the **San Isidro** celebrations now include music, dance, a famous **romería**, theatre and bullfighting.

sanitario, -a [sani'tarjo, a] *adj* health *cpd*; **sanitarios** *nmpl* toilets (*BRIT*), washroom (*US*)

sano, -a ['sano, a] *adj* healthy; (*sin daños*) sound; (*comida*) wholesome; (*entero*) whole, intact; ~ **y salvo** safe and sound

▌ No confundir **sano** con la palabra inglesa *sane*.

Santiago [san'tjaɣo] *nm:* ~ **(de Chile)** Santiago

santiamén [santja'men] *nm:* **en un** ~ in no time at all

santidad [santi'ðað] *nf* holiness, sanctity

santiguarse [santi'ɣwarse] *vr* to make the sign of the cross

santo, -a ['santo, a] *adj* holy; (*fig*) wonderful, miraculous ▷ *nm/f* saint ▷ *nm* saint's day; ~ **y seña** password

santuario [san'twarjo] *nm* sanctuary, shrine

sapo ['sapo] *nm* toad

saque ['sake] *nm* (*Tenis*) service, serve; (*Fútbol*) throw-in; **saque de esquina** corner (kick)

saquear [sake'ar] *vt* (*Mil*) to sack; (*robar*) to loot, plunder; (*fig*) to ransack

sarampión [saram'pjon] *nm* measles *sg*

sarcástico, -a [sar'kastiko, a] *adj* sarcastic

sardina [sar'ðina] *nf* sardine

sargento [sar'xento] *nm* sergeant

sarmiento [sar'mjento] *nm* (*Bot*) vine shoot

sarna ['sarna] *nf* itch; (*Med*) scabies

sarpullido [sarpu'ʎiðo] *nm* (*Med*) rash

sarro ['sarro] *nm* (*en dientes*) tartar, plaque

sartén [sar'ten] *nf* frying pan

sastre ['sastre] *nm* tailor; **sastrería** *nf* (*arte*) tailoring; (*tienda*) tailor's (shop)

Satanás [sata'nas] *nm* Satan

satélite [sa'telite] *nm* satellite

sátira ['satira] *nf* satire

satisfacción [satisfak'θjon] *nf* satisfaction

satisfacer [satisfa'θer] *vt* to satisfy; (*gastos*) to meet; (*pérdida*) to make good; **satisfacerse** *vr* to satisfy o.s., be satisfied; (*vengarse*) to take revenge; **satisfecho, -a** *adj* satisfied; (*contento*) content(ed), happy; (*tb:* **satisfecho de sí mismo**) self-satisfied, smug

saturar [satu'rar] *vt* to saturate; **saturarse** *vr* (*mercado, aeropuerto*) to reach saturation point

sauce ['sauθe] *nm* willow; **sauce llorón** weeping willow

sauna ['sauna] *nf* sauna

savia ['saβja] *nf* sap

saxofón [sakso'fon] *nm* saxophone

sazonar [saθo'nar] vt to ripen; (Culin) to flavour, season

scooter [e'skuter] (ESP) nf scooter

Scotch® [skotʃ] (LAM) nm Sellotape® (BRIT), Scotch tape® (US)

SE abr (= sudeste) SE

○ **PALABRA CLAVE**

se [se] pron **1** (reflexivo: sg: m) himself; (: f) herself; (: pl) themselves; (: cosa) itself; (: de Vd) yourself; (: de Vds) yourselves; **se está preparando** she's preparing herself

2 (con complemento indirecto) to him; to her; to them; to it; to you; **a usted se lo dije ayer** I told you yesterday; **se compró un sombrero** he bought himself a hat; **se rompió la pierna** he broke his leg

3 (uso recíproco) each other, one another; **se miraron (el uno al otro)** they looked at each other o one another

4 (en oraciones pasivas): **se han vendido muchos libros** a lot of books have been sold

5 (impers): **se dice que ...** people say that ..., it is said that ...; **allí se come muy bien** the food there is very good, you can eat very well there

---

sé etc [se] vb V **saber; ser**

sea etc vb V **ser**

sebo ['seβo] nm fat, grease

secador [seka'ðor] nm: **~ de pelo** hair-dryer

secadora [seka'ðora] nf tumble dryer

secar [se'kar] vt to dry; **secarse** vr to dry (off); (río, planta) to dry up

sección [sek'θjon] nf section

seco, -a ['seko, a] adj dry; (carácter) cold; (respuesta) sharp, curt; **parar en ~** to stop dead; **decir algo a secas** to say sth curtly

secretaría [sekreta'ria] nf secretariat

secretario, -a [sekre'tarjo, a] nm/f secretary

secreto, -a [se'kreto, a] adj secret; (persona) secretive ▷ nm secret; (calidad) secrecy

secta ['sekta] nf sect

sector [sek'tor] nm sector

secuela [se'kwela] nf consequence

secuencia [se'kwenθja] nf sequence

secuestrar [sekwes'trar] vt to kidnap; (bienes) to seize, confiscate; **secuestro** nm kidnapping; seizure, confiscation

secundario, -a [sekun'darjo, a] adj secondary

sed [seð] nf thirst; **tener ~** to be thirsty

seda ['seða] nf silk

sedal [se'ðal] nm fishing line

sedán [se'ðan] (LAM) nm saloon (BRIT), sedan (US)

sedante [se'ðante] nm sedative

sede ['seðe] nf (de gobierno) seat; (de compañía) headquarters pl; **Santa S~** Holy See

sedentario, -a [seðen'tario, a] adj sedentary

sediento, -a [se'ðjento, a] adj thirsty

sedimento [seði'mento] nm sediment

seducción [seðuk'θjon] nf seduction

seducir [seðu'θir] vt to seduce; (cautivar) to charm, fascinate; (atraer) to attract; **seductor, a** adj seductive; charming, fascinating; attractive ▷ nm/f seducer

segar [se'xar] vt (mies) to reap, cut; (hierba) to mow, cut

seglar [se'xlar] adj secular, lay

seguida [se'xiða] nf: **en ~** at once, right away

seguido, -a [se'xiðo, a] adj (continuo) continuous, unbroken; (recto) straight ▷ adv (directo) straight (on); (después) after; (LAM: a menudo) often; **~s** consecutive, successive; **5 días ~s** 5 days running, 5 days in a row

seguir [se'xir] vt to follow; (venir

después) to follow on, come after;
(*proseguir*) to continue; (*perseguir*) to
chase, pursue ▷ *vi* (*gen*) to follow;
(*continuar*) to continue, carry *o* go
on; **seguirse** *vr* to follow; **sigo sin
comprender** I still don't understand;
sigue lloviendo it's still raining

según [se'ɣun] *prep* according to
▷ *adv*: **¿irás? - ~** are you going? – it all
depends ▷ *conj* as; **~ caminamos**
while we walk

segundo, -a [se'ɣundo, a] *adj*
second ▷ *nm* second ▷ *nf* second
meaning; **de segunda mano** secondhand; **segunda (clase)** second class;
segunda (marcha) (*Auto*) second
(gear)

seguramente [seɣura'mente] *adv*
surely; (*con certeza*) for sure, with
certainty

seguridad [seɣuri'ðaθ] *nf* safety;
(*del estado, de casa etc*) security;
(*certidumbre*) certainty; (*confianza*)
confidence; (*estabilidad*) stability;
seguridad social social security

seguro, -a [se'ɣuro, a] *adj* (*cierto*)
sure, certain; (*fiel*) trustworthy; (*libre
de peligro*) safe; (*bien defendido, firme*)
secure ▷ *adv* for sure, certainly ▷ *nm*
(*Com*) insurance; **seguro contra
terceros/a todo riesgo** third party/
comprehensive insurance; **seguros
sociales** social security *sg*

seis [seis] *num* six

seísmo [se'ismo] *nm* tremor,
earthquake

selección [selek'θjon] *nf* selection;
seleccionar *vt* to pick, choose, select

selectividad [selektiβi'ðaθ] (*ESP*) *nf*
university entrance examination

selecto, -a [se'lekto, a] *adj* select,
choice; (*escogido*) selected

sellar [se'ʎar] *vt* (*documento oficial*) to
seal; (*pasaporte, visado*) to stamp

sello ['seʎo] *nm* stamp; (*precinto*) seal

selva ['selβa] *nf* (*bosque*) forest,
woods *pl*; (*jungla*) jungle

semáforo [se'maforo] *nm* (*Auto*)

traffic lights *pl*; (*Ferro*) signal

semana [se'mana] *nf* week; **entre
~** during the week; **Semana Santa**
Holy Week; **semanal** *adj* weekly;
semanario *nm* weekly magazine

- **SEMANA SANTA**
-
- In Spain celebrations for **Semana
- Santa** (Holy Week) are often
- spectacular. "Viernes Santo",
- "Sábado Santo" and "Domingo de
- Resurrección" (Good Friday, Holy
- Saturday, Easter Sunday) are all
- national public holidays, with
- additional days being given as
- local holidays. There are fabulous
- **procesiones** all over the country,
- with members of "cofradías"
- (brotherhoods) dressing in hooded
- robes and parading their "pasos"
- (religious floats and sculptures)
- through the streets. Seville has
- the most famous Holy Week
- processions.

sembrar [sem'brar] *vt* to sow;
(*objetos*) to sprinkle, scatter about;
(*noticias etc*) to spread

semejante [seme'xante] *adj*
(*parecido*) similar ▷ *nm* fellow man,
fellow creature; **~s** alike, similar;
nunca hizo cosa ~ he never did any
such thing; **semejanza** *nf* similarity,
resemblance

semejar [seme'xar] *vi* to seem like,
resemble; **semejarse** *vr* to look alike,
be similar

semen ['semen] *nm* semen

semestral [semes'tral] *adj* half-
yearly, bi-annual

semicírculo [semi'θirkulo] *nm*
semicircle

semidesnatado, -a
[semiðesna'taðo, a] *adj* semi-
skimmed

semifinal [semifi'nal] *nf* semifinal

semilla [se'miʎa] *nf* seed

seminario [semi'narjo] nm (Rel) seminary; (Escol) seminar

sémola ['semola] nf semolina

senado [se'naðo] nm senate; **senador, a** nm/f senator

sencillez [senθi'ʎeθ] nf simplicity; (de persona) naturalness; **sencillo, -a** adj simple; natural, unaffected

senda ['senda] nf path, track

senderismo [sende'rismo] nm hiking

sendero [sen'dero] nm path, track

sendos, -as ['sendos, as] adj pl: **les dio ~ golpes** he hit both of them

senil [se'nil] adj senile

seno ['seno] nm (Anat) bosom, bust; (fig) bosom; **~s** breasts

sensación [sensa'θjon] nf sensation; (sentido) sense; (sentimiento) feeling; **sensacional** adj sensational

sensato, -a [sen'sato, a] adj sensible

sensible [sen'sible] adj sensitive; (apreciable) perceptible, appreciable; (pérdida) considerable

> No confundir **sensible** con la palabra inglesa sensible.

sensiblero, -a adj sentimental

sensitivo, -a [sensi'tiβo, a] adj sense cpd

sensorial [senso'rjal] adj sensory

sensual [sen'swal] adj sensual

sentada [sen'taða] nf sitting; (protesta) sit-in

sentado, -a [sen'taðo, a] adj: **estar ~** to sit, be sitting (down); **dar por ~** to take for granted, assume

sentar [sen'tar] vt to sit, seat; (fig) to establish ▷ vi (vestido) to suit; (alimento): **~ bien/mal a** to agree/ disagree with; **sentarse** vr (persona) to sit, sit down; (los depósitos) to settle

sentencia [sen'tenθja] nf (máxima) maxim, saying; (Jur) sentence; **sentenciar** vt to sentence

sentido, -a [sen'tiðo, a] adj (pérdida) regrettable; (carácter) sensitive ▷ nm sense; (sentimiento) feeling; (significado) sense, meaning; (dirección) direction;

mi más ~ pésame my deepest sympathy; **tener ~** to make sense; **sentido común** common sense; **sentido del humor** sense of humour; **sentido único** one-way (street)

sentimental [sentimen'tal] adj sentimental; **vida ~** love life

sentimiento [senti'mjento] nm feeling

sentir [sen'tir] vt to feel; (percibir) to perceive, sense; (lamentar) to regret, be sorry for ▷ vi (tener la sensación) to feel; (lamentarse) to feel sorry ▷ nm opinion, judgement; **~se bien/mal** to feel well/ill; **lo siento** I'm sorry

seña ['seɲa] nf sign; (Mil) password; **señas** nfpl (dirección) address sg; **señas personales** personal description sg

señal [se'ɲal] nf sign; (síntoma) symptom; (Ferro, Tel) signal; (marca) mark; (Com) deposit; **en ~ de** as a token o sign of; **señalar** vt to mark; (indicar) to point out, indicate

señor [se'ɲor] nm (hombre) man; (caballero) gentleman; (dueño) owner, master; (trato: antes de nombre propio) Mr; (: hablando directamente) sir; **muy ~ mío** Dear Sir; **el ~ alcalde/presidente** the mayor/president

señora [se'ɲora] nf (dama) lady; (trato: antes de nombre propio) Mrs; (: hablando directamente) madam; (esposa) wife; **Nuestra S~** Our Lady

señorita [seɲo'rita] nf (con nombre y/o apellido) Miss; (mujer joven) young lady

señorito [seɲo'rito] nm young gentleman; (pey) rich kid

sepa etc vb V **saber**

separación [separa'θjon] nf separation; (división) division; (hueco) gap

separar [sepa'rar] vt to separate; (dividir) to divide; **separarse** vr (parte) to come away; (partes) to come apart; (persona) to leave, go away; (matrimonio) to separate; **separatismo** nm separatism

sepia ['sepja] nf cuttlefish

septentrional [septentrjo'nal] adj
northern

septiembre [sep'tjembre] nm
September

séptimo, -a ['septimo, a] adj, nm
seventh

sepulcral [sepul'kral] adj (fig: silencio,
atmósfera) deadly; **sepulcro** nm tomb,
grave

sepultar [sepul'tar] vt to bury;
sepultura nf (acto) burial; (tumba)
grave, tomb

sequía [se'kia] nf drought

séquito ['sekito] nm (de rey
etc) retinue; (seguidores) followers
pl

🔾 **PALABRA CLAVE**

ser [ser] vi **1** (descripción) to be; **es
médica/muy alta** she's a doctor/very
tall; **la familia es de Cuzco** his (o her
etc) family is from Cuzco; **soy Ana** (Tel)
Ana speaking o here

2 (propiedad): **es de Joaquín** it's
Joaquín's, it belongs to Joaquín

3 (horas, fechas, números): **es la una** it's
one o'clock; **son las seis y media** it's
half-past six; **es el 1 de junio** it's the
first of June; **somos/son seis** there are
six of us/them

4 (en oraciones pasivas): **ha sido
descubierto ya** it's already been
discovered

5: **es de esperar que ...** it is to be
hoped o I etc hope that ...

6 (locuciones con sub): **o sea** that is to
say; **sea él sea su hermana** either him
or his sister

7: **a no ser por él ...** but for him ...

8: **a no ser que: a no ser que tenga
uno ya** unless he's got one already
▷ nm being; **ser humano** human being

sereno, -a [se'reno, a] adj (persona)
calm, unruffled; (el tiempo) fine, settled;
(ambiente) calm, peaceful ▷ nm night

watchman

serial [ser'jal] nm serial

serie ['serje] nf series; (cadena)
sequence, succession; **fuera de ~**
out of order; (fig) special, out of the
ordinary; **fabricación en ~** mass
production

seriedad [serje'ðað] nf seriousness;
(formalidad) reliability; **serio, -a** adj
serious; reliable, dependable; grave,
serious; **en serio** adv seriously

serigrafía [seriɣra'fia] nf silk-screen
printing

sermón [ser'mon] nm (Rel) sermon

seropositivo, -a [seroposi'tiβo] adj
HIV positive

serpentear [serpente'ar] vi to
wriggle; (camino, río) to wind, snake

serpentina [serpen'tina] nf
streamer

serpiente [ser'pjente] nf snake;
serpiente de cascabel rattlesnake

serranía [serra'nia] nf mountainous
area

serrar [se'rrar] vt =**aserrar**

serrín [se'rrin] nm sawdust

serrucho [se'rrutʃo] nm saw

service ['serβis] (RPL) nm (Auto)
service

servicio [ser'βiθjo] nm service; (LAM
Auto) service; **servicios** nmpl (ESP)
toilet(s); **servicio incluido** service
charge included; **servicio militar**
military service

servidumbre [serβi'ðumbre] nf
(sujeción) servitude; (criados) servants
pl, staff

servil [ser'βil] adj servile

servilleta [serβi'ʎeta] nf serviette,
napkin

servir [ser'βir] vt to serve ▷ vi to
serve; (tener utilidad) to be of use, be
useful; **servirse** vr to serve o help o.s.;
~se de algo to make use of sth, use sth;
sírvase pasar please come in

sesenta [se'senta] num sixty

sesión [se'sjon] nf (Pol) session,
sitting; (Cine) showing

seso ['seso] *nm* brain; **sesudo, -a** *adj* sensible, wise

seta ['seta] *nf* mushroom; **seta venenosa** toadstool

setecientos, -as [sete'θjentos, as] *adj, num* seven hundred

setenta [se'tenta] *num* seventy

seto ['seto] *nm* hedge

severo, -a [se'βero, a] *adj* severe

Sevilla [se'βiʎa] *n* Seville; **sevillano, -a** *adj* of o from Seville ▷ *nm/f* native o inhabitant of Seville

sexo ['sekso] *nm* sex

sexto, -a ['seksto, a] *adj, nm* sixth

sexual [sek'swal] *adj* sexual; **vida ~** sex life

si [si] *conj* if ▷ *nm* (*Mús*) B; **me pregunto ~ ...** I wonder if o whether ...

sí [si] *adv* yes ▷ *nm* consent ▷ *pron* (*uso impersonal*) oneself; (*sg: m*) himself; (: *f*) herself; (: *de cosa*) itself; (*de usted*) yourself; (*pl*) themselves; (*de ustedes*) yourselves; (*recíproco*) each other; **él no quiere pero yo ~** he doesn't want to but I do; **ella ~ vendrá** she will certainly come, she is sure to come; **claro que ~** of course; **creo que ~** I think so

siamés, -esa [sja'mes, esa] *adj, nm/f* Siamese

SIDA ['siða] *nm abr* (= *Síndrome de Inmunodeficiencia Adquirida*) AIDS

siderúrgico, -a [siðe'rurxiko, a] *adj* iron and steel *cpd*

sidra ['siðra] *nf* cider

siembra ['sjembra] *nf* sowing

siempre ['sjempre] *adv* always; (*todo el tiempo*) all the time; **~ que** (*cada vez*) whenever; (*dado que*) provided that; **como ~** as usual; **para ~** for ever

sien [sjen] *nf* temple

siento *etc* ['sjento] *vb* V **sentar; sentir**

sierra ['sjerra] *nf* (*Tec*) saw; (*cadena de montañas*) mountain range

siervo, -a ['sjerβo, a] *nm/f* slave

siesta ['sjesta] *nf* siesta, nap; **echar la ~** to have an afternoon nap o a siesta

siete ['sjete] *num* seven

sifón [si'fon] *nm* syphon

sigla ['siɣla] *nf* abbreviation; acronym

siglo ['siɣlo] *nm* century; (*fig*) age

significado [siɣnifi'kaðo] *nm* (*de palabra etc*) meaning

significar [siɣnifi'kar] *vt* to mean, signify; (*notificar*) to make known, express

signo ['siɣno] *nm* sign; **signo de admiración** o **exclamación** exclamation mark; **signo de interrogación** question mark

sigo *etc vb* V **seguir**

siguiente [si'ɣjente] *adj* next, following

siguió *etc vb* V **seguir**

sílaba ['silaβa] *nf* syllable

silbar [sil'βar] *vt, vi* to whistle; **silbato** *nm* whistle; **silbido** *nm* whistle, whistling

silenciador [silenθja'ðor] *nm* silencer

silenciar [silen'θjar] *vt* (*persona*) to silence; (*escándalo*) to hush up; **silencio** *nm* silence, quiet; **silencioso, -a** *adj* silent, quiet

silla ['siʎa] *nf* (*asiento*) chair; (*tb:* **~ de montar**) saddle; **silla de ruedas** wheelchair

sillón [si'ʎon] *nm* armchair, easy chair

silueta [si'lweta] *nf* silhouette; (*de edificio*) outline; (*figura*) figure

silvestre [sil'βestre] *adj* wild

simbólico, -a [sim'boliko, a] *adj* symbolic(al)

simbolizar [simboli'θar] *vt* to symbolize

símbolo ['simbolo] *nm* symbol

similar [simi'lar] *adj* similar

simio ['simjo] *nm* ape

simpatía [simpa'tia] *nf* liking; (*afecto*) affection; (*amabilidad*) kindness; **simpático, -a** *adj* nice, pleasant; kind

▪ No confundir **simpático** con la palabra inglesa *sympathetic*.

simpatizante [simpati'θante] *nmf* sympathizer

simpatizar [simpati'θar] vi: **~ con** to get on well with

simple ['simple] adj simple; (*elemental*) simple, easy; (*mero*) mere; (*puro*) pure, sheer ▷ nmf simpleton; **simpleza** nf simpleness; (*necedad*) silly thing; **simplificar** vt to simplify

simposio [sim'posjo] nm symposium

simular [simu'lar] vt to simulate

simultáneo, -a [simul'taneo, a] adj simultaneous

sin [sin] prep without; **la ropa está ~ lavar** the clothes are unwashed; **~ que** without; **~ embargo** however, still

sinagoga [sina'xoxa] nf synagogue

sinceridad [sinθeri'ðað] nf sincerity; **sincero, -a** adj sincere

sincronizar [sinkroni'θar] vt to synchronize

sindical [sindi'kal] adj union cpd, trade-union cpd; **sindicalista** adj, nmf trade unionist

sindicato [sindi'kato] nm (*de trabajadores*) trade(s) union; (*de negociantes*) syndicate

síndrome ['sinðrome] nm (*Med*) syndrome; **síndrome de abstinencia** (*Med*) withdrawal symptoms; **síndrome de la clase turista** (*Med*) economy-class syndrome

sinfín [sin'fin] nm: **un ~ de** a great many, no end of

sinfonía [sinfo'nia] nf symphony

singular [singu'lar] adj singular; (*fig*) outstanding, exceptional; (*raro*) peculiar, odd

siniestro, -a [si'njestro, a] adj sinister ▷ nm (*accidente*) accident

sinnúmero [sin'numero] nm = **sinfín**

sino ['sino] nm fate, destiny ▷ conj (*pero*) but; (*salvo*) except, save

sinónimo, -a [si'nonimo, a] adj synonymous ▷ nm synonym

síntesis ['sintesis] nf synthesis; **sintético, -a** adj synthetic

sintió vb V **sentir**

síntoma ['sintoma] nm symptom

sintonía [sinto'nia] nf (*Radio, Mús: de programa*) tuning; **sintonizar** vt (*Radio: emisora*) to tune (in)

sinvergüenza [simber'xwenθa] nmf rogue, scoundrel; **¡es un ~!** he's got a nerve!

siquiera [si'kjera] conj even if, even though ▷ adv at least; **ni ~** not even

Siria ['sirja] nf Syria

sirviente, -a [sir'βjente, a] nm/f servant

sirvo etc vb V **servir**

sistema [sis'tema] nm system; (*método*) method; **sistema educativo** education system; **sistemático, -a** adj systematic

● **SISTEMA EDUCATIVO**
●
● The reform of the Spanish **sistema**
● **educativo** (education system)
● begun in the early 90s has replaced
● the courses **EGB**, **BUP** and **COU**
● with the following: "Primaria" a
● compulsory 6 years; "Secundaria"
● a compulsory 4 years and
● "Bachillerato" an optional 2-year
● secondary school course, essential
● for those wishing to go on to higher
● education.

sitiar [si'tjar] vt to besiege, lay siege to

sitio ['sitjo] nm (*lugar*) place; (*espacio*) room, space; (*Mil*) siege; **sitio de taxis** (*MÉX: parada*) taxi stand o rank (*BRIT*); **sitio web** (*Inform*) website

situación [sitwa'θjon] nf situation, position; (*estatus*) position, standing

situado, -a [situ'aðo] adj situated, placed

situar [si'twar] vt to place, put; (*edificio*) to locate, situate

slip [slip] nm pants pl, briefs pl

smoking ['smokin, es'mokin] (*pl* **~s**) nm dinner jacket (*BRIT*), tuxedo (*US*)
▌ No confundir **smoking** con la palabra inglesa *smoking*.

SMS nm (mensaje) text message, SMS message

snob [es'nob] = **esnob**

SO abr (= suroeste) SW

sobaco [so'βako] nm armpit

sobar [so'βar] vt (ropa) to rumple; (comida) to play around with

soberanía [soβera'nia] nf sovereignty; **soberano, -a** adj sovereign; (fig) supreme ▷ nm/f sovereign

soberbia [so'βerβja] nf pride; haughtiness, arrogance; magnificence

soberbio, -a [so'βerβjo, a] adj (orgulloso) proud; (altivo) arrogant; (estupendo) magnificent, superb

sobornar [soβor'nar] vt to bribe; **soborno** nm bribe

sobra ['soβra] nf excess, surplus; **sobras** nfpl left-overs, scraps; **de ~** surplus, extra; **tengo de ~** I've more than enough; **sobrado, -a** adj (más que suficiente) more than enough; (superfluo) excessive; **sobrante** adj remaining, extra ▷ nm surplus, remainder

sobrar [so'βrar] vt to exceed, surpass ▷ vi (tener de más) to be more than enough; (quedar) to remain, be left (over)

sobrasada [soβra'saða] nf pork sausage spread

sobre ['soβre] prep (gen) on; (encima) on (top of); (por encima de, arriba de) over, above; (más que) more than; (además) in addition to, besides; (alrededor de) about ▷ nm envelope; **~ todo** above all

sobrecama [soβre'kama] nf bedspread

sobrecargar [soβrekar'ɣar] vt (camión) to overload; (Com) to surcharge

sobredosis [soβre'ðosis] nf inv overdose

sobreentender [soβre(e)nten'der] vt to deduce, infer; **sobreentenderse** vr: **se sobreentiende que ...** it is

implied that ...

sobrehumano, -a [soβreu'mano, a] adj superhuman

sobrellevar [soβreʎe'βar] vt to bear, endure

sobremesa [soβre'mesa] nf: **durante la ~** after dinner

sobrenatural [soβrenatu'ral] adj supernatural

sobrenombre [soβre'nombre] nm nickname

sobrepasar [soβrepa'sar] vt to exceed, surpass

sobreponerse [soβrepo'nerse] vr: **~ a** to overcome

sobresaliente [soβresa'ljente] adj outstanding, excellent

sobresalir [soβresa'lir] vi to project, jut out; (fig) to stand out, excel

sobresaltar [soβresal'tar] vt (asustar) to scare, frighten; (sobrecoger) to startle; **sobresalto** nm (movimiento) start; (susto) scare; (turbación) sudden shock

sobretodo [soβre'toðo] nm overcoat

sobrevenir [soβreβe'nir] vi (ocurrir) to happen (unexpectedly); (resultar) to follow, ensue

sobrevivir [soβreβi'βir] vi to survive

sobrevolar [soβreβo'lar] vt to fly over

sobriedad [soβrje'ðað] nf sobriety, soberness; (moderación) moderation, restraint

sobrino, -a [so'βrino, a] nm/f nephew/niece

sobrio, -a ['soβrjo, a] adj sober; (moderado) moderate, restrained

socarrón, -ona [soka'rron, ona] adj (sarcástico) sarcastic, ironic(al)

socavón [soka'βon] nm (hoyo) hole

sociable [so'θjaβle] adj (persona) sociable, friendly; (animal) social

social [so'θjal] adj social; (Com) company cpd

socialdemócrata [soθjalde'mokrata] nmf social democrat

socialista [soθja'lista] *adj, nm* socialist

socializar [soθjali'θar] *vt* to socialize

sociedad [soθje'ðað] *nf* society; (*Com*) company; **sociedad anónima** limited company; **sociedad de consumo** consumer society

socio, -a ['soθjo, a] *nm/f* (*miembro*) member; (*Com*) partner

sociología [soθjolo'xia] *nf* sociology; **sociólogo, -a** *nm/f* sociologist

socorrer [soko'rrer] *vt* to help; **socorrista** *nmf* first aider; (*en piscina, playa*) lifeguard; **socorro** *nm* (*ayuda*) help, aid; (*Mil*) relief; **¡socorro!** help!

soda ['soða] *nf* (*sosa*) soda; (*bebida*) soda (water)

sofá [so'fa] (*pl* ~s) *nm* sofa, settee; **sofá-cama** *nm* studio couch; sofa bed

sofocar [sofo'kar] *vt* to suffocate; (*apagar*) to smother, put out; **sofocarse** *vr* to suffocate; (*fig*) to blush, feel embarrassed; **sofoco** *nm* suffocation; embarrassment

sofreír [sofre'ir] *vt* (*Culin*) to fry lightly

soga ['soxa] *nf* rope

sois *etc vb* V **ser**

soja ['soxa] *nf* soya

sol [sol] *nm* sun; (*luz*) sunshine, sunlight; (*Mús*) G; **hace ~** it's sunny

solamente [sola'mente] *adv* only, just

solapa [so'lapa] *nf* (*de chaqueta*) lapel; (*de libro*) jacket

solapado, -a [sola'paðo, a] *adj* (*intenciónes*) underhand; (*gestos, movimiento*) sly

solar [so'lar] *adj* solar, sun *cpd*

soldado [sol'daðo] *nm* soldier; **soldado raso** private

soldador [solda'ðor] *nm* soldering iron; (*persona*) welder

soldar [sol'dar] *vt* to solder, weld

soleado, -a [sole'aðo, a] *adj* sunny

soledad [sole'ðað] *nf* solitude; (*estado infeliz*) loneliness

solemne [so'lemne] *adj* solemn

soler [so'ler] *vi* to be in the habit of, be accustomed to; **suele salir a las ocho** she usually goes out at eight o'clock

solfeo [sol'feo] *nm* solfa

solicitar [soliθi'tar] *vt* (*permiso*) to ask for, seek; (*puesto*) to apply for; (*votos*) to canvass for; (*atención*) to attract

solícito, -a [so'liθito, a] *adj* (*diligente*) diligent; (*cuidadoso*) careful; **solicitud** *nf* (*calidad*) great care; (*petición*) request; (*a un puesto*) application

solidaridad [soliðari'ðað] *nf* solidarity; **solidario, -a** *adj* (*participación*) joint, common; (*compromiso*) mutually binding

sólido, -a ['soliðo, a] *adj* solid

soliloquio [soli'lokjo] *nm* soliloquy

solista [so'lista] *nmf* soloist

solitario, -a [soli'tarjo, a] *adj* (*persona*) lonely, solitary; (*lugar*) lonely, desolate ▷ *nm/f* (*recluso*) recluse; (*en la sociedad*) loner ▷ *nm* solitaire

sollozar [soλo'θar] *vi* to sob; **sollozo** *nm* sob

solo, -a ['solo, a] *adj* (*único*) single, sole; (*sin compañía*) alone; (*solitario*) lonely; **hay una sola dificultad** there is just one difficulty; **a solas** alone, by oneself

sólo ['solo] *adv* only, just

solomillo [solo'miλo] *nm* sirloin

soltar [sol'tar] *vt* (*dejar ir*) to let go of; (*desprender*) to unfasten, loosen; (*librar*) to release, set free; (*risa etc*) to let out

soltero, -a [sol'tero, a] *adj* single, unmarried ▷ *nm/f* bachelor/single woman; **solterón, -ona** *nm/f* old bachelor/spinster

soltura [sol'tura] *nf* looseness, slackness; (*de los miembros*) agility, ease of movement; (*en el hablar*) fluency, ease

soluble [so'luβle] *adj* (*Quím*) soluble; (*problema*) solvable; **~ en agua** soluble in water

solución [solu'θjon] *nf* solution; **solucionar** *vt* (*problema*) to solve;

(*asunto*) to settle, resolve

solventar [solβen'tar] *vt* (*pagar*) to settle, pay; (*resolver*) to resolve; **solvente** *adj* (*Econ: empresa, persona*) solvent

sombra ['sombra] *nf* shadow; (*como protección*) shade; **sombras** *nfpl* (*oscuridad*) darkness *sg*, shadows; **tener buena/mala ~** to be lucky/unlucky

sombrero [som'brero] *nm* hat

sombrilla [som'briʎa] *nf* parasol, sunshade

sombrío, -a [som'brio, a] *adj* (*oscuro*) dark; (*triste*) sombre, sad; (*persona*) gloomy

someter [some'ter] *vt* (*país*) to conquer; (*persona*) to subject to one's will; (*informe*) to present, submit; **someterse** *vr* to give in, yield, submit; **~ a** to subject to

somier [so'mjer] (*pl* **~s**) *n* spring mattress

somnífero [som'nifero] *nm* sleeping pill

somos *vb* V **ser**

son [son] *vb* V **ser** ▷ *nm* sound

sonaja [so'naxa] (*MÉX*) *nf* = **sonajero**

sonajero [sona'xero] *nm* (baby's) rattle

sonambulismo [sonambu'lismo] *nm* sleepwalking; **sonámbulo, -a** *nm/f* sleepwalker

sonar [so'nar] *vt* to ring ▷ *vi* to sound; (*hacer ruido*) to make a noise; (*pronunciarse*) to be sounded, be pronounced; (*ser conocido*) to sound familiar; (*campana*) to ring; (*reloj*) to strike, chime; **sonarse** *vr*: **~se (las narices)** to blow one's nose; **me suena ese nombre** that name rings a bell

sonda ['sonda] *nf* (*Náut*) sounding; (*Tec*) bore, drill; (*Med*) probe

sondear [sonde'ar] *vt* to sound; to bore (into), drill; to probe, sound; (*fig*) to sound out; **sondeo** *nm* sounding; boring, drilling; (*fig*) poll, enquiry

sonido [so'niðo] *nm* sound

sonoro, -a [so'noro, a] *adj* sonorous;

(*resonante*) loud, resonant

sonreír [sonre'ir] *vi* to smile; **sonreírse** *vr* to smile; **sonriente** *adj* smiling; **sonrisa** *nf* smile

sonrojarse [sonro'xarse] *vr* to blush, go red; **sonrojo** *nm* blush

soñador, a [soɲa'ðor, a] *nm/f* dreamer

soñar [so'ɲar] *vt, vi* to dream; **~ con** to dream about o of

soñoliento, -a [soɲo'ljento, a] *adj* sleepy, drowsy

sopa ['sopa] *nf* soup

soplar [so'plar] *vt* (*polvo*) to blow away, blow off; (*inflar*) to blow up; (*vela*) to blow out ▷ *vi* to blow; **soplo** *nm* blow, puff; (*de viento*) puff, gust

soplón, -ona [so'plon, ona] (*fam*) *nm/f* (*niño*) telltale; (*de policía*) grass (*fam*)

soporífero [sopo'rifero] *nm* sleeping pill

soportable [sopor'taβle] *adj* bearable

soportar [sopor'tar] *vt* to bear, carry; (*fig*) to bear, put up with

▌ No confundir **soportar** con la palabra inglesa *support*.

soporte *nm* support; (*fig*) pillar, support

soprano [so'prano] *nf* soprano

sorber [sor'βer] *vt* (*chupar*) to sip; (*absorber*) to soak up, absorb

sorbete [sor'βete] *nm* iced fruit drink

sorbo ['sorβo] *nm* (*trago: grande*) gulp, swallow; (*: pequeño*) sip

sordera [sor'ðera] *nf* deafness

sórdido, -a ['sorðiðo, a] *adj* dirty, squalid

sordo, -a ['sorðo, a] *adj* (*persona*) deaf ▷ *nm/f* deaf person; **sordomudo, -a** *adj* deaf and dumb

sorna ['sorna] *nf* sarcastic tone

soroche [so'rotʃe] (*CAM*) *nm* mountain sickness

sorprendente [sorpren'dente] *adj* surprising

sorprender [sorpren'der] *vt* to

surprise; **sorpresa** nf surprise

sortear [sorte'ar] vt to draw lots for; (rifar) to raffle; (dificultad) to avoid; **sorteo** nm (en lotería) draw; (rifa) raffle

sortija [sor'tixa] nf ring; (rizo) ringlet, curl

sosegado, -a [sose'ɣaðo, a] adj quiet, calm

sosiego [so'sjeɣo] nm quiet(ness), calm(ness)

soso, -a ['soso, a] adj (Culin) tasteless; (aburrido) dull, uninteresting

sospecha [sos'petʃa] nf suspicion; **sospechar** vt to suspect; **sospechoso, -a** adj suspicious; (testimonio, opinión) suspect ▷ nm/f suspect

sostén [sos'ten] nm (apoyo) support; (sujetador) bra; (alimentación) sustenance, food

sostener [soste'ner] vt to support; (mantener) to keep up, maintain; (alimentar) to sustain, keep going; **sostenerse** vr to support o.s.; (seguir) to continue, remain; **sostenido, -a** adj continuous, sustained; (prolongado) prolonged

sotana [so'tana] nf (Rel) cassock

sótano ['sotano] nm basement

soy [soi] vb V **ser**

soya ['soja] (LAM) nf soya (BRIT), soy (US)

Sr. abr (= Señor) Mr

Sra. abr (= Señora) Mrs

Sres. abr (= Señores) Messrs

Srta. abr (= Señorita) Miss

Sta. abr (= Santa) St

Sto. abr (= Santo) St

su [su] pron (de él) his; (de ella) her; (de una cosa) its; (de ellos, ellas) their; (de usted, ustedes) your

suave ['swaβe] adj gentle; (superficie) smooth; (trabajo) easy; (música, voz) soft, sweet; **suavidad** nf gentleness; smoothness; softness, sweetness; **suavizante** nm (de ropa) softener; (del pelo) conditioner; **suavizar** vt to soften; (quitar la aspereza) to smooth

(out)

subasta [su'βasta] nf auction; **subastar** vt to auction (off)

subcampeón, -ona [suβkampe'on, ona] nm/f runner-up

subconsciente [suβkon'sθjente] adj, nm subconscious

subdesarrollado, -a [suβðesarro'ʎaðo, a] adj underdeveloped

subdesarrollo [suβðesa'rroʎo] nm underdevelopment

subdirector, a [suβðirek'tor, a] nm/f assistant director

súbdito, -a ['suβðito, a] nm/f subject

subestimar [suβesti'mar] vt to underestimate, underrate

subida [su'βiða] nf (de montaña etc) ascent, climb; (de precio) rise, increase; (pendiente) slope, hill

subir [su'βir] vt (objeto) to raise, lift up; (cuesta, calle) to go up; (colina, montaña) to climb; (precio) to raise, put up ▷ vi to go up, come up; (a un coche) to get in; (a un autobús, tren o avión) to get on, board; (precio) to rise, go up; (río, marea) to rise; **subirse** vr to get up, climb

súbito, -a ['suβito, a] adj (repentino) sudden; (imprevisto) unexpected

subjetivo, -a [suβxe'tiβo, a] adj subjective

sublevar [suβle'βar] vt to rouse to revolt; **sublevarse** vr to revolt, rise

sublime [su'βlime] adj sublime

submarinismo [suβmari'nismo] nm scuba diving

submarino, -a [suβma'rino, a] adj underwater ▷ nm submarine

subnormal [suβnor'mal] adj subnormal ▷ nmf subnormal person

subordinado, -a [suβorði'naðo, a] adj, nm/f subordinate

subrayar [suβra'jar] vt to underline

subsanar [suβsa'nar] vt to rectify

subsidio [suβ'siðjo] nm (ayuda) aid, financial help; (subvención) subsidy,

grant; (*de enfermedad, paro etc*) benefit,
allowance

subsistencia [suβsis'tenθja] *nf*
subsistence

subsistir [suβsis'tir] *vi* to subsist;
(*sobrevivir*) to survive, endure

subte ['suβte] (*RPL*) *nm* underground
(*BRIT*), subway (*US*)

subterráneo, -a [suβte'rraneo, a]
adj underground, subterranean ▷ *nm*
underpass, underground passage

subtítulo [suβ'titulo] *nm* (*Cine*)
subtitle

suburbio [su'βurβjo] *nm* (*barrio*)
slum quarter

subvención [suββen'θjon] *nf* (*Econ*)
subsidy, grant; **subvencionar** *vt* to
subsidize

sucedáneo, -a [suθe'ðaneo, a] *adj*
substitute ▷ *nm* substitute (food)

suceder [suθe'ðer] *vt*, *vi* to happen;
(*seguir*) to succeed, follow; **lo que
sucede es que ...** the fact is that
...; **sucesión** *nf* succession; (*serie*)
sequence, series

sucesivamente [suθesiβa'mente]
adv: **y así ~** and so on

sucesivo, -a [suθe'siβo, a] *adj*
successive, following; **en lo ~** in future,
from now on

suceso [su'θeso] *nm* (*hecho*) event,
happening; (*incidente*) incident

▌ No confundir **suceso** con la palabra
inglesa *success*.

suciedad [suθje'ðað] *nf* (*estado*)
dirtiness; (*mugre*) dirt, filth

sucio, -a ['suθjo, a] *adj* dirty

suculento, -a [suku'lento, a] *adj*
succulent

sucumbir [sukum'bir] *vi* to succumb

sucursal [sukur'sal] *nf* branch
(office)

sudadera [suða'ðera] *nf* sweatshirt

Sudáfrica [suð'afrika] *nf* South
Africa

Sudamérica [suða'merika] *nf* South
America; **sudamericano, -a** *adj*, *nm/f*
South American

sudar [su'ðar] *vt*, *vi* to sweat

sudeste [su'ðeste] *nm* south-east

sudoeste [suðo'este] *nm* south-west

sudor [su'ðor] *nm* sweat; **sudoroso,
-a** *adj* sweaty, sweating

Suecia ['sweθja] *nf* Sweden; **sueco,
-a** *adj* Swedish ▷ *nm/f* Swede

suegro, -a ['sweɣro, a] *nm/f* father-/
mother-in-law

suela ['swela] *nf* sole

sueldo ['sweldo] *nm* pay, wage(s) (*pl*)

suele *etc vb* V **soler**

suelo ['swelo] *nm* (*tierra*) ground; (*de
casa*) floor

suelto, -a ['swelto, a] *adj* loose;
(*libre*) free; (*separado*) detached; (*ágil*)
quick, agile ▷ *nm* (*loose*) change,
small change

sueñito [swe'ɲito] (*LAM*) *nm* nap

sueño *etc* ['sweɲo] *vb* V **soñar**
▷ *nm* sleep; (*somnolencia*) sleepiness,
drowsiness; (*lo soñado*, *fig*) dream;
tener ~ to be sleepy

suero ['swero] *nm* (*Med*) serum; (*de
leche*) whey

suerte ['swerte] *nf* (*fortuna*) luck;
(*azar*) chance; (*destino*) fate, destiny;
(*especie*) sort, kind; **tener ~** to be lucky

suéter ['sweter] *nm* sweater

suficiente [sufi'θjente] *adj* enough,
sufficient ▷ *nm* (*Escol*) pass

sufragio [su'fraxjo] *nm* (*voto*) vote;
(*derecho de voto*) suffrage

sufrido, -a [su'friðo, a] *adj* (*persona*)
tough; (*paciente*) long-suffering,
patient

sufrimiento [sufri'mjento] *nm*
(*dolor*) suffering

sufrir [su'frir] *vt* (*padecer*) to suffer;
(*soportar*) to bear, put up with; (*apoyar*)
to hold up, support ▷ *vi* to suffer

sugerencia [suxe'renθja] *nf*
suggestion

sugerir [suxe'rir] *vt* to suggest;
(*sutilmente*) to hint

sugestión [suxes'tjon] *nf*
suggestion; (*sutil*) hint; **sugestionar**
vt to influence

sugestivo, -a [suxes'tiβo, a] *adj*
stimulating; (*fascinante*) fascinating

suicida [sui'θiða] *adj* suicidal ▷ *nmf*
suicidal person; (*muerto*) suicide,
person who has committed suicide;
suicidarse *vr* to commit suicide, kill
o.s.; **suicidio** *nm* suicide

Suiza ['swiθa] *nf* Switzerland; **suizo,
-a** *adj, nm/f* Swiss

sujeción [suxe'θjon] *nf* subjection

sujetador [suxeta'ðor] *nm* (*sostén*)
bra

sujetar [suxe'tar] *vt* (*fijar*) to fasten;
(*detener*) to hold down; **sujetarse** *vr* to
subject o.s.; **sujeto, -a** *adj* fastened,
secure ▷ *nm* subject; (*individuo*)
individual; **sujeto a** subject to

suma ['suma] *nf* (*cantidad*) total,
sum; (*de dinero*) sum; (*acto*) adding (up),
addition; **en ~** in short

sumamente [suma'mente] *adv*
extremely, exceedingly

sumar [su'mar] *vt* to add (up) ▷ *vi*
to add up

sumergir [sumer'xir] *vt* to
submerge; (*hundir*) to sink

suministrar [sumini'strar] *vt* to
supply, provide; **suministro** *nm*
supply; (*acto*) supplying, providing

sumir [su'mir] *vt* to sink, submerge;
(*fig*) to plunge

sumiso, -a [su'miso, a] *adj*
submissive, docile

sumo, -a ['sumo, a] *adj* great,
extreme; (*autoridad*) highest, supreme

suntuoso, -a [sun'twoso, a] *adj*
sumptuous, magnificent

supe *etc vb* V **saber**

super... [super] *prefijo* super..., over...

superbueno, -a [super'bweno, a]
adj great, fantastic

súper ['super] *nf* (*gasolina*) four-star
(petrol)

superar [supe'rar] *vt* (*sobreponerse
a*) to overcome; (*rebasar*) to surpass,
do better than; (*pasar*) to go beyond;
superarse *vr* to excel o.s.

superficial [superfi'θjal] *adj*

superficial; (*medida*) surface *cpd*, of
the surface

superficie [super'fiθje] *nf* surface;
(*área*) area

superfluo, -a [su'perflwo, a] *adj*
superfluous

superior [supe'rjor] *adj* (*piso, clase*)
upper; (*temperatura, número, nivel*)
higher; (*mejor: calidad, producto*)
superior, better ▷ *nmf* superior;
superioridad *nf* superiority

supermercado [supermer'kaðo] *nm*
supermarket

superponer [superpo'ner] *vt* to
superimpose

superstición [supersti'θjon] *nf*
superstition; **supersticioso, -a** *adj*
superstitious

supervisar [superβi'sar] *vt* to
supervise

supervivencia [superβi'βenθja]
nf survival

superviviente [superβi'βjente] *adj*
surviving

supiera *etc vb* V **saber**

suplantar [suplan'tar] *vt* to
supplant

suplemento [suple'mento] *nm*
supplement

suplente [su'plente] *adj, nm*
substitute

supletorio, -a [suple'torjo, a] *adj*
supplementary ▷ *nm* supplement;
teléfono ~ extension

súplica ['suplika] *nf* request; (*Jur*)
petition

suplicar [supli'kar] *vt* (*cosa*) to
beg (for), plead for; (*persona*) to beg,
plead with

suplicio [su'pliθjo] *nm* torture

suplir [su'plir] *vt* (*compensar*) to make
good, make up for; (*reemplazar*) to
replace, substitute ▷ *vi*: **~ a** to take the
place of, substitute for

supo *etc vb* V **saber**

suponer [supo'ner] *vt* to suppose;
suposición *nf* supposition

suprimir [supri'mir] *vt* to suppress;

(*derecho, costumbre*) to abolish; (*palabra etc*) to delete; (*restricción*) to cancel, lift

supuesto, -a [su'pwesto, a] *pp de*
suponer ▷ *adj* (*hipotético*) supposed
▷ *nm* assumption, hypothesis; **~ que**
since; **por ~** of course

sur [sur] *nm* south

surcar [sur'kar] *vt* to plough; **surco**
nm (*en metal, disco*) groove; (*Agr*) furrow

surgir [sur'xir] *vi* to arise, emerge;
(*dificultad*) to come up, crop up

suroeste [suro'este] *nm* south-west

surtido, -a [sur'tiðo, a] *adj* mixed,
assorted ▷ *nm* (*selección*) selection,
assortment; (*abastecimiento*) supply,
stock; **surtidor** *nm* (*tb*: **surtidor de
gasolina**) petrol pump (BRIT), gas
pump (US)

surtir [sur'tir] *vt* to supply, provide
▷ *vi* to spout, spurt

susceptible [susθep'tiβle] *adj*
susceptible; (*sensible*) sensitive; **~ de**
capable of

suscitar [susθi'tar] *vt* to cause,
provoke; (*interés, sospechas*) to arouse

suscribir [suskri'βir] *vt* (*firmar*)
to sign; (*respaldar*) to subscribe to,
endorse; **suscribirse** *vr* to subscribe;
suscripción *nf* subscription

susodicho, -a [suso'ðitʃo, a] *adj*
above-mentioned

suspender [suspen'der] *vt* (*objeto*)
to hang (up), suspend; (*trabajo*) to stop,
suspend; (*Escol*) to fail; (*interrumpir*) to
adjourn; (*atrasar*) to postpone

suspense [sus'pense] (ESP) *nm*
suspense; **película/novela de ~**
thriller

suspensión [suspen'sjon] *nf*
suspension; (*fig*) stoppage, suspension

suspenso, -a [sus'penso, a] *adj*
hanging, suspended; (ESP Escol) failed
▷ *nm* (ESP Escol) fail; **película o novela
de ~** (LAM) thriller; **quedar o estar en ~**
to be pending

suspicaz [suspi'kaθ] *adj* suspicious,
distrustful

suspirar [suspi'rar] *vi* to sigh;

suspiro *nm* sigh

sustancia [sus'tanθja] *nf* substance

sustento [sus'tento] *nm* support;
(*alimento*) sustenance, food

sustituir [sustitu'ir] *vt* to
substitute, replace; **sustituto, -a** *nm/f*
substitute, replacement

susto ['susto] *nm* fright, scare

sustraer [sustra'er] *vt* to remove,
take away; (*Mat*) to subtract

susurrar [susu'rrar] *vi* to whisper;
susurro *nm* whisper

sutil [su'til] *adj* (*aroma, diferencia*)
subtle; (*tenue*) thin; (*inteligencia,
persona*) sharp

suyo, -a ['sujo, a] (*con artículo o
después del verbo* **ser**) *adj* (*de él*) his; (*de
ella*) hers; (*de ellos, ellas*) theirs; (*de Ud,
Uds*) yours; **un amigo ~** a friend of his (*o
hers o theirs o yours*)

t

Tabacalera [taβaka'lera] *nf Spanish state tobacco monopoly*

tabaco [ta'βako] *nm* tobacco; (*ESP: fam*) cigarettes *pl*

tabaquería [tabake'ria] (*LAM*) *nf* tobacconist's (shop) (*BRIT*), smoke shop (*US*); **tabaquero, -a** (*LAM*) *nm/f* tobacconist

taberna [ta'βerna] *nf* bar, pub (*BRIT*)

tabique [ta'βike] *nm* partition (wall)

tabla ['taβla] *nf* (*de madera*) plank; (*estante*) shelf; (*de vestido*) pleat; (*Arte*) panel; **tablas** *nfpl*: **estar** *o* **quedar en ~s** to draw; **tablado** *nm* (*plataforma*) platform; (*Teatro*) stage

tablao [ta'βlao] *nm* (*tb: ~ flamenco*) flamenco show

tablero [ta'βlero] *nm* (*de madera*) plank, board; (*de ajedrez, damas*) board; **tablero de mandos** (*LAM Auto*) dashboard

tableta [ta'βleta] *nf* (*Med*) tablet; (*de chocolate*) bar

tablón [ta'βlon] *nm* (*de suelo*) plank; (*de techo*) beam; **tablón de anuncios** notice (*BRIT*) *o* bulletin (*US*) board

tabú [ta'βu] *nm* taboo

taburete [taβu'rete] *nm* stool

tacaño, -a [ta'kaɲo, a] *adj* mean

tacha ['tatʃa] *nf* flaw; (*Tec*) stud; **tachar** *vt* (*borrar*) to cross out; **tachar de** to accuse of

tacho ['tatʃo] (*cs*) *nm* (*balde*) bucket; **tacho de la basura** rubbish bin (*BRIT*), trash can (*US*)

taco ['tako] *nm* (*Billar*) cue; (*de billetes*) book; (*cs: de zapato*) heel; (*tarugo*) peg; (*palabrota*) swear word

tacón [ta'kon] *nm* heel; **de ~ alto** high-heeled

táctica ['taktika] *nf* tactics *pl*

táctico, -a ['taktiko, a] *adj* tactical

tacto ['takto] *nm* (*fig*) tact

tajada [ta'xaða] *nf* slice

tajante [ta'xante] *adj* sharp

tajo ['taxo] *nm* (*corte*) cut; (*Geo*) cleft

tal [tal] *adj* such ▷ *pron* (*persona*) someone, such a one; (*cosa*) something, such a thing ▷ *adv*: **~ como** (*igual*) just as ▷ *conj*: **con ~ de que** provided that; **~ cual** (*como es*) just as it is; **~ vez** perhaps; **~ como** such as; **~ para cual** (*dos iguales*) two of a kind; **¿qué ~?** how are things?; **¿qué ~ te gusta?** how do you like it?

taladrar [tala'ðrar] *vt* to drill; **taladro** *nm* drill

talante [ta'lante] *nm* (*humor*) mood; (*voluntad*) will, willingness

talar [ta'lar] *vt* to fell, cut down; (*devastar*) to devastate

talco ['talko] *nm* (*polvos*) talcum powder

talento [ta'lento] *nm* talent; (*capacidad*) ability

TALGO ['talxo] (*ESP*) *nm abr* (= *tren articulado ligero Goicoechea-Oriol*) ≈ HST (*BRIT*)

talismán [talis'man] *nm* talisman

talla ['taʎa] *nf* (*estatura, fig, Med*) height, stature; (*palo*) measuring rod; (*Arte*) carving; (*medida*) size

tallar [ta'ʎar] *vt* (*madera*) to carve;

(*metal etc*) to engrave; (*medir*) to measure

tallarines [taʎaˈrines] *nmpl* noodles

talle [ˈtaʎe] *nm* (*Anat*) waist; (*fig*) appearance

taller [taˈʎer] *nm* (*Tec*) workshop; (*de artista*) studio

tallo [ˈtaʎo] *nm* (*de planta*) stem; (*de hierba*) blade; (*brote*) shoot

talón [taˈlon] *nm* (*Anat*) heel; (*Com*) counterfoil; (*cheque*) cheque (BRIT), check (US)

talonario [taloˈnarjo] *nm* (*de cheques*) chequebook (BRIT), checkbook (US); (*de recibos*) receipt book

tamaño, -a [taˈmaɲo, a] *adj* (*tan grande*) such a big; (*tan pequeño*) such a small ▷ *nm* size; **de ~ natural** full-size

tamarindo [tamaˈrindo] *nm* tamarind

tambalearse [tambaleˈarse] *vr* (*persona*) to stagger; (*vehículo*) to sway

también [tamˈbjen] *adv* (*igualmente*) also, too, as well; (*además*) besides

tambor [tamˈbor] *nm* drum; (*Anat*) eardrum; **tambor del freno** brake drum

tamizar [tamiˈθar] *vt* to sieve

tampoco [tamˈpoko] *adv* nor, neither; **yo ~ lo compré** I didn't buy it either

tampón [tamˈpon] *nm* tampon

tan [tan] *adv* so; **~ es así que ...** so much so that ...

tanda [ˈtanda] *nf* (*gen*) series; (*turno*) shift

tangente [tanˈxente] *nf* tangent

tangerina [tanxeˈrina] (LAM) *nf* tangerine

tangible [tanˈxiβle] *adj* tangible

tanque [ˈtanke] *nm* (*cisterna, Mil*) tank; (*Auto*) tanker

tantear [tanteˈar] *vt* (*calcular*) to reckon (up); (*medir*) to take the measure of; (*probar*) to test, try out; (*tomar la medida: persona*) to take the measurements of; (*situación*) to weigh up; (*persona: opinión*) to sound out ▷ *vi*

(*Deporte*) to score; **tanteo** *nm* (*cálculo*) (rough) calculation; (*prueba*) test, trial; (*Deporte*) scoring

tanto, -a [ˈtanto, a] *adj* (*cantidad*) so much, as much ▷ *adv* (*cantidad*) so much, as much; (*tiempo*) so long, as long ▷ *conj*: **en ~ que** while ▷ *nm* (*suma*) certain amount; (*proporción*) so much; (*punto*) point; (*gol*) goal; **un ~ perezoso** somewhat lazy ▷ *pron*: **cado uno paga ~** each one pays so much; **~s** so many, as many; **20 y ~s** 20-odd; **hasta ~ (que)** until such time as; **~ tú como yo** both you and I; **~ como eso** as much as that; **~ más ... cuanto que** all the more ... because; **~ mejor/peor** so much the better/the worse; **~ si viene como si va** whether he comes or whether he goes; **~ es así que** so much so that; **por (lo) ~** therefore; **entre ~** meanwhile; **estar al ~** to be up to date; **me he vuelto ronco de o con ~ hablar** I have become hoarse from so much talking; **a ~s de agosto** on such and such a day in August

tapa [ˈtapa] *nf* (*de caja, olla*) lid; (*de botella*) top; (*de libro*) cover; (*comida*) snack

tapadera [tapaˈðera] *nf* lid, cover

tapar [taˈpar] *vt* (*cubrir*) to cover; (*envolver*) to wrap o cover up; (*la vista*) to obstruct; (*persona, falta*) to conceal; (*MÉX, CAM: diente*) to fill; **taparse** *vr* to wrap o.s. up

taparrabo [tapaˈrraβo] *nm* loincloth

tapete [taˈpete] *nm* table cover

tapia [ˈtapja] *nf* (*garden*) wall

tapicería [tapiθeˈria] *nf* tapestry; (*para muebles*) upholstery; (*tienda*) upholsterer's (shop)

tapiz [taˈpiθ] *nm* (*alfombra*) carpet; (*tela tejida*) tapestry; **tapizar** *vt* (*muebles*) to upholster

tapón [taˈpon] *nm* (*de botella*) top; (*de lavabo*) plug; **tapón de rosca** screw-top

taquigrafía [takiɣraˈfia] *nf* shorthand; **taquígrafo, -a** *nm/f* shorthand writer, stenographer

taquilla [ta'kiʎa] nf (donde se compra) booking office; (suma recogida) takings pl

tarántula [ta'rantula] nf tarantula

tararear [tarare'ar] vi to hum

tardar [tar'ðar] vi (tomar tiempo) to take a long time; (llegar tarde) to be late; (demorar) to delay; **¿tarda mucho el tren?** does the train take (very) long?; **a más ~** at the latest; **no tardes en venir** come soon

tarde ['tarðe] adv late ▷ nf (de día) afternoon; (al anochecer) evening; **de ~ en ~** from time to time; **¡buenas ~s!** good afternoon!; **a o por la ~** in the afternoon; in the evening

tardío, -a [tar'ðio, a] adj (retrasado) late; (lento) slow to arrive

tarea [ta'rea] nf task; (faena) chore; (Escol) homework

tarifa [ta'rifa] nf (lista de precios) price list; (precio) tariff

tarima [ta'rima] nf (plataforma) platform

tarjeta [tar'xeta] nf card; **tarjeta de crédito/de Navidad/postal/ telefónica** credit card/Christmas card/postcard/phonecard; **tarjeta de embarque** boarding pass; **tarjeta de memoria** memory card; **tarjeta prepago** top-up card; **tarjeta SIM** SIM card

tarro ['tarro] nm jar, pot

tarta ['tarta] nf (pastel) cake; (de base dura) tart

tartamudear [tartamuðe'ar] vi to stammer; **tartamudo, -a** adj stammering ▷ nm/f stammerer

tártaro, -a ['tartaro, a] adj: **salsa tártara** tartar(e) sauce

tasa ['tasa] nf (precio) (fixed) price, rate; (valoración) valuation; (medida, norma) measure, standard; **tasa de cambio/interés** exchange/interest rate; **tasas de aeropuerto** airport tax; **tasas universitarias** university fees

tasar [ta'sar] vt (arreglar el precio) to fix a price for; (valorar) to value, assess

tasca ['taska] (fam) nf pub

tatarabuelo, -a [tatara'βwelo, a] nm/f great-great-grandfather/mother

tatuaje [ta'twaxe] nm (dibujo) tattoo; (acto) tattooing

tatuar [ta'twar] vt to tattoo

taurino, -a [tau'rino, a] adj bullfighting cpd

Tauro ['tauro] nm Taurus

tauromaquia [tauro'makja] nf tauromachy, (art of) bullfighting

taxi ['taksi] nm taxi; **taxista** [tak'sista] nmf taxi driver

taza ['taθa] nf cup; (de retrete) bowl; **~ para café** coffee cup; **taza de café** cup of coffee; **tazón** nm (taza grande) mug, large cup; (de fuente) basin

te [te] pron (complemento de objeto) you; (complemento indirecto) (to) you; (reflexivo) (to) yourself; **¿~ duele mucho el brazo?** does your arm hurt a lot?; **~ equivocas** you're wrong; **¡cálma~!** calm down!

té [te] nm tea

teatral [tea'tral] adj theatre cpd; (fig) theatrical

teatro [te'atro] nm theatre; (Literatura) plays pl, drama

tebeo [te'βeo] nm comic

techo ['tetʃo] nm (externo) roof; (interno) ceiling; **techo corredizo** sunroof

tecla ['tekla] nf key; **teclado** nm keyboard; **teclear** vi (Mús) to strum; (con los dedos) to tap ▷ vt (Inform) to key in

técnica ['teknika] nf technique; (tecnología) technology; V tb **técnico**

técnico, -a ['tekniko, a] adj technical ▷ nm/f technician; (experto) expert

tecnología [teknolo'xia] nf technology; **tecnológico, -a** adj technological

tecolote [teko'lote] (MÉX) nm owl

tedioso, -a [te'ðjoso, a] adj boring, tedious

teja ['texa] nf tile; (Bot) lime (tree);

tejado nm (tiled) roof
tejemaneje [texema'nexe] nm (lío) fuss; (intriga) intrigue
tejer [te'xer] vt to weave; (hacer punto) to knit; (fig) to fabricate; **tejido** nm (tela) material, fabric; (telaraña) web; (Anat) tissue
tel [tel] abr (= teléfono) tel
tela ['tela] nf (tejido) material; (telaraña) web; (en líquido) skin; **telar** nm (máquina) loom
telaraña [tela'raŋa] nf cobweb
tele ['tele] (fam) nf telly (BRIT), tube (US)
tele... ['tele] prefijo tele...; **telebasura** nf trash TV; **telecomunicación** nf telecommunication; **telediario** nm television news; **teledirigido, -a** adj remote-controlled
teleférico [tele'feriko] nm (de esquí) ski-lift
telefonear [telefone'ar] vi to telephone
telefónico, -a [tele'foniko, a] adj telephone cpd
telefonillo [telefo'niʎo] nm (de puerta) intercom
telefonista [telefo'nista] nmf telephonist
teléfono [te'lefono] nm (tele)phone; **estar hablando al ~** to be on the phone; **llamar a algn por ~** to ring sb (up) o phone sb (up); **teléfono celular** (LAM) mobile phone; **teléfono con cámara** camera phone; **teléfono inalámbrico** cordless phone; **teléfono móvil** (ESP) mobile phone
telégrafo [te'leɣrafo] nm telegraph
telegrama [tele'ɣrama] nm telegram
tele: telenovela nf soap (opera); **teleobjetivo** nm telephoto lens; **telepatía** nf telepathy; **telepático, -a** adj telepathic; **telerrealidad** nf reality TV; **telescopio** nm telescope; **telesilla** nm chairlift; **telespectador, a** nm/f viewer; **telesquí** nm ski-lift; **teletarjeta** nf phonecard; **teletipo**

nm teletype; **teletrabajador, a** nm/f teleworker; **teletrabajo** nm teleworking; **televentas** nfpl telesales
televidente [teleβi'ðente] nmf viewer
televisar [teleβi'sar] vt to televise
televisión [teleβi'sjon] nf television; **televisión digital** digital television
televisor [teleβi'sor] nm television set
télex ['teleks] nm inv telex
telón [te'lon] nm curtain; **telón de acero** (Pol) iron curtain; **telón de fondo** backcloth, background
tema ['tema] nm (asunto) subject, topic; (Mús) theme; **temático, -a** adj thematic
temblar [tem'blar] vi to shake, tremble; (por frío) to shiver; **temblor** nm trembling; (de tierra) earthquake; **tembloroso, -a** adj trembling
temer [te'mer] vt to fear ▷ vi to be afraid; **temo que llegue tarde** I am afraid he may be late
temible [te'miβle] adj fearsome
temor [te'mor] nm (miedo) fear; (duda) suspicion
témpano ['tempano] nm (tb: ~ de hielo) ice-floe
temperamento [tempera'mento] nm temperament
temperatura [tempera'tura] nf temperature
tempestad [tempes'taδ] nf storm
templado, -a [tem'plaδo, a] adj (moderado) moderate; (frugal) frugal; (agua) lukewarm; (clima) mild; (Mús) well-tuned; **templanza** nf moderation; mildness
templar [tem'plar] vt (moderar) to moderate; (furia) to restrain; (calor) to reduce; (afinar) to tune (up); (acero) to temper; (tuerca) to tighten up; **temple** nm (ajuste) tempering; (afinación) tuning; (pintura) tempera
templo ['templo] nm (iglesia) church; (pagano etc) temple

temporada [tempo'raða] *nf* time, period; (*estación*) season

temporal [tempo'ral] *adj* (*no permanente*) temporary ▷ *nm* storm

temprano, -a [tem'prano, a] *adj* early; (*demasiado pronto*) too soon, too early

ten *vb* V **tener**

tenaces [te'naθes] *adj pl* V **tenaz**

tenaz [te'naθ] *adj* (*material*) tough; (*persona*) tenacious; (*creencia, resistencia*) stubborn

tenaza(s) [te'naθa(s)] *nf(pl)* (*Med*) forceps; (*Tec*) pliers; (*Zool*) pincers

tendedero [tende'ðero] *nm* (*para ropa*) drying place; (*cuerda*) clothes line

tendencia [ten'denθja] *nf* tendency; **tener ~ a** to tend to, have a tendency to

tender [ten'der] *vt* (*extender*) to spread out; (*colgar*) to hang out; (*vía férrea, cable*) to lay; (*estirar*) to stretch ▷ *vi*: **~ a** to have a tendency towards; **tenderse** *vr* to lie down; **~ la cama/mesa** (*LAM*) to make the bed/lay (*BRIT*) *o* set (*US*) the table

tenderete [tende'rete] *nm* (*puesto*) stall; (*exposición*) display of goods

tendero, -a [ten'dero, a] *nm/f* shopkeeper

tendón [ten'don] *nm* tendon

tendré *etc vb* V **tener**

tenebroso, -a [tene'βroso, a] *adj* (*oscuro*) dark; (*fig*) gloomy

tenedor [tene'ðor] *nm* (*Culin*) fork

tenencia [te'nenθja] *nf* (*de casa*) tenancy; (*de oficio*) tenure; (*de propiedad*) possession

○ **PALABRA CLAVE**

tener [te'ner] *vt* **1** (*poseer, gen*) to have; (*en la mano*) to hold; **¿tienes un boli?** have you got a pen?; **va a tener un niño** she's going to have a baby; **¡ten (*o* tenga)!, ¡aquí tienes (*o* tiene)!** here you are!

2 (*edad, medidas*) to be; **tiene 7 años** she's 7 (years old); **tiene 15 cm de largo** it's 15 cm long; V **calor; hambre** etc

3 (*considerar*): **lo tengo por brillante** I consider him to be brilliant; **tener en mucho a algn** to think very highly of sb

4 (*+ pp*: = *pretérito*): **tengo terminada ya la mitad del trabajo** I've done half the work already

5: **tener que hacer algo** to have to do sth; **tengo que acabar este trabajo hoy** I have to finish this job today

6: **¿qué tienes, estás enfermo?** what's the matter with you, are you ill?

tenerse *vr* **1 tenerse en pie** to stand up

2 tenerse por to think o.s.

tengo *etc vb* V **tener**

tenia ['tenja] *nf* tapeworm

teniente [te'njente] *nm* (*rango*) lieutenant; (*ayudante*) deputy

tenis ['tenis] *nm* tennis; **tenis de mesa** table tennis; **tenista** *nmf* tennis player

tenor [te'nor] *nm* (*sentido*) meaning; (*Mús*) tenor; **a ~ de** on the lines of

tensar [ten'sar] *vt* to tighten; (*arco*) to draw

tensión [ten'sjon] *nf* tension; (*Tec*) stress; **tener la ~ alta** to have high blood pressure; **tensión arterial** blood pressure

tenso, -a ['tenso, a] *adj* tense

tentación [tenta'θjon] *nf* temptation

tentáculo [ten'takulo] *nm* tentacle

tentador, a [tenta'ðor, a] *adj* tempting

tentar [ten'tar] *vt* (*seducir*) to tempt; (*atraer*) to attract

tentempié [tentem'pje] *nm* snack

tenue ['tenwe] *adj* (*delgado*) thin, slender; (*neblina*) light; (*lazo, vínculo*) slight

teñir [te'nir] *vt* to dye; (*fig*) to tinge; **teñirse** *vr* to dye; **~se el pelo** to dye one's hair

teología [teolo'xia] *nf* theology

teoría [teo'ria] *nf* theory; **en ~** in

theory; **teórico, -a** adj theoretic(al)
▷ nm/f theoretician, theorist; **teorizar**
vi to theorize
terapéutico, -a [tera'peutiko, a] adj
therapeutic
terapia [te'rapja] nf therapy
tercer adj V **tercero**
tercermundista [terθermun'dista]
adj Third World
tercero, -a [ter'θero, a] (delante de
nmsg: **tercer**) adj third ▷ nm (Jur)
third party
terceto [ter'θeto] nm trio
terciar [ter'θjar] vi (participar) to
take part; (hacer de árbitro) to mediate;
terciario, -a adj tertiary
tercio ['terθjo] nm third
terciopelo [terθjo'pelo] nm velvet
terco, -a ['terko, a] adj obstinate
tergal® [ter'xal] nm type of polyester
tergiversar [terxiβer'sar] vt to
distort
termal [ter'mal] adj thermal
termas ['termas] nfpl hot springs
térmico, -a ['termiko, a] adj
thermal
terminal [termi'nal] adj, nm, nf
terminal
terminante [termi'nante] adj
(final) final, definitive; (tajante)
categorical; **terminantemente**
adv: **terminantemente prohibido**
strictly forbidden
terminar [termi'nar] vt (completar)
to complete, finish; (concluir) to end
▷ vi (llegar a su fin) to end; (parar) to
stop; (acabar) to finish; **terminarse** vr
to come to an end; **~ por hacer algo** to
end up (by) doing sth
término ['termino] nm end,
conclusion; (parada) terminus; (límite)
boundary; **en último ~** (a fin de cuentas)
in the last analysis; (como último
recurso) as a last resort; **término medio**
average; (fig) middle way
termómetro [ter'mometro] nm
thermometer
termo(s)® ['termo(s)] nm Thermos®

termostato [termo'stato] nm
thermostat
ternero, -a [ter'nero, a] nm/f
(animal) calf ▷ nf (carne) veal
ternura [ter'nura] nf (trato)
tenderness; (palabra) endearment;
(cariño) fondness
terrado [te'rraðo] nm terrace
terraplén [terra'plen] nm
embankment
terrateniente [terrate'njente] nmf
landowner
terraza [te'rraθa] nf (balcón) balcony;
(tejado) (flat) roof; (Agr) terrace
terremoto [terre'moto] nm
earthquake
terrenal [terre'nal] adj earthly
terreno [te'rreno] nm (tierra) land;
(parcela) plot; (suelo) soil; (fig) field; **un ~**
a piece of land
terrestre [te'rrestre] adj terrestrial;
(ruta) land cpd
terrible [te'rriβle] adj terrible, awful
territorio [terri'torjo] nm territory
terrón [te'rron] nm (de azúcar) lump;
(de tierra) clod, lump
terror [te'rror] nm terror; **terrorífico,
-a** adj terrifying; **terrorista** adj, nmf
terrorist; **terrorista suicida** suicide
bomber
terso, -a ['terso, a] adj (liso) smooth;
(pulido) polished
tertulia [ter'tulja] nf (reunión
informal) social gathering; (grupo)
group, circle
tesis ['tesis] nf inv thesis
tesón [te'son] nm (firmeza) firmness;
(tenacidad) tenacity
tesorero, -a [teso'rero, a] nm/f
treasurer
tesoro [te'soro] nm treasure; (Com,
Pol) treasury
testamento [testa'mento] nm will
testarudo, -a [testa'ruðo, a] adj
stubborn
testículo [tes'tikulo] nm testicle
testificar [testifi'kar] vt to testify;
(fig) to attest ▷ vi to give evidence

testigo [tes'tiɣo] *nmf* witness;
  testigo de cargo/descargo witness
  for the prosecution/defence; **testigo
  ocular** eye witness
testimonio [testi'monjo] *nm*
  testimony
teta ['teta] *nf* (*de biberón*) teat;
  (*Anat: fam*) breast
tétanos ['tetanos] *nm* tetanus
tetera [te'tera] *nf* teapot
tétrico, -a ['tetriko, a] *adj* gloomy,
  dismal
textil [teks'til] *adj* textile
texto ['teksto] *nm* text; **textual** *adj*
  textual
textura [teks'tura] *nf* (*de tejido*)
  texture
tez [teθ] *nf* (*cutis*) complexion
ti [ti] *pron* you; (*reflexivo*) yourself
tía ['tia] *nf* (*pariente*) aunt; (*fam*)
  chick, bird
tibio, -a ['tiβjo, a] *adj* lukewarm
tiburón [tiβu'ron] *nm* shark
tic [tik] *nm* (*ruido*) click; (*de reloj*) tick;
  (*Med*): **~ nervioso** nervous tic
tictac [tik'tak] *nm* (*de reloj*) tick tock
tiempo ['tjempo] *nm* time; (*época,
  período*) age, period; (*Meteorología*)
  weather; (*Ling*) tense; (*Deporte*) half; **a ~**
  in time; **a un o al mismo ~** at the same
  time; **al poco ~** very soon (after); **se
  quedó poco ~** he didn't stay very long;
  hace poco ~ not long ago; **mucho ~** a
  long time; **de ~ en ~** from time to time;
  hace buen/mal ~ the weather is fine/
  bad; **estar a ~** to be in time; **hace ~**
  some time ago; **hacer ~** to while away
  the time; **motor de 2 ~s** two-stroke
  engine; **primer ~** first half
tienda ['tjenda] *nf* shop, store;
  tienda de abarrotes (*MÉX, CAM*)
  grocer's (*BRIT*), grocery store
  (*US*); **tienda de alimentación** o
  comestibles grocer's (*BRIT*), grocery
  store (*US*); **tienda de campaña** tent
tienes *etc vb* V **tener**
tienta *etc* ['tjenta] *vb* V **tentar**
  ▷ *nf*: **andar a ~s** to grope one's way

along
tiento *etc* ['tjento] *vb* V **tentar** ▷ *nm*
  (*tacto*) touch; (*precaución*) wariness
tierno, -a ['tjerno, a] *adj* (*blando*)
  tender; (*fresco*) fresh; (*amable*) sweet
tierra ['tjerra] *nf* earth; (*suelo*) soil;
  (*mundo*) earth, world; (*país*) country,
  land; **~ adentro** inland
tieso, -a ['tjeso, a] *adj* (*rígido*) rigid;
  (*duro*) stiff; (*fam: orgulloso*) conceited
tiesto ['tjesto] *nm* flowerpot
tifón [ti'fon] *nm* typhoon
tifus ['tifus] *nm* typhus
tigre ['tiɣre] *nm* tiger
tijera [ti'xera] *nf* scissors *pl*; (*Zool*)
  claw; **tijeras** *nfpl* scissors; (*para
  plantas*) shears
tila ['tila] *nf* lime blossom tea
tildar [til'dar] *vt*: **~ de** to brand as
tilde ['tilde] *nf* (*Tip*) tilde
tilín [ti'lin] *nm* tinkle
timar [ti'mar] *vt* (*estafar*) to swindle
timbal [tim'bal] *nm* small drum
timbre ['timbre] *nm* (*sello*) stamp;
  (*campanilla*) bell; (*tono*) timbre; (*Com*)
  stamp duty
timidez [timi'ðeθ] *nf* shyness;
  tímido, -a *adj* shy
timo ['timo] *nm* swindle
timón [ti'mon] *nm* helm, rudder;
  timonel *nm* helmsman
tímpano ['timpano] *nm* (*Anat*)
  eardrum; (*Mús*) small drum
tina ['tina] *nf* tub; (*baño*) bath(tub);
  tinaja *nf* large jar
tinieblas [ti'njeβlas] *nfpl* darkness
  sg; (*sombras*) shadows
tino ['tino] *nm* (*habilidad*) skill; (*juicio*)
  insight
tinta ['tinta] *nf* ink; (*Tec*) dye; (*Arte*)
  colour
tinte ['tinte] *nm* dye
tintero [tin'tero] *nm* inkwell
tinto ['tinto] *nm* red wine
tintorería [tintore'ria] *nf* dry
  cleaner's
tío ['tio] *nm* (*pariente*) uncle;
  (*fam: individuo*) bloke (*BRIT*), guy

tiovivo [tio'βiβo] *nm* merry-go-round

típico, -a ['tipiko, a] *adj* typical

tipo ['tipo] *nm* (*clase*) type, kind; (*hombre*) fellow; (*Anat: de hombre*) build; (: *de mujer*) figure; (*Imprenta*) type; **tipo bancario/de descuento/de interés/de cambio** bank/discount/interest/exchange rate

tipografía [tipoɣra'fia] *nf* printing *cpd*

tíquet ['tiket] (*pl* **~s**) *nm* ticket; (*en tienda*) cash slip

tiquismiquis [tikis'mikis] *nm inv* fussy person ▷ *nmpl* (*querellas*) squabbling *sg*; (*escrúpulos*) silly scruples

tira ['tira] *nf* strip; (*fig*) abundance; **tira y afloja** give and take

tirabuzón [tiraβu'θon] *nm* (*rizo*) curl

tirachinas [tira'tʃinas] *nm inv* catapult

tirada [ti'raða] *nf* (*acto*) cast, throw; (*serie*) series; (*Tip*) printing, edition; **de una ~** at one go

tirado, -a [ti'raðo, a] *adj* (*barato*) dirt-cheap; (*fam: fácil*) very easy

tirador [tira'ðor] *nm* (*mango*) handle

tirano, -a [ti'rano, a] *adj* tyrannical ▷ *nm/f* tyrant

tirante [ti'rante] *adj* (*cuerda etc*) tight, taut; (*relaciónes*) strained ▷ *nm* (*Arq*) brace; (*Tec*) stay; **tirantes** *nmpl* (*de pantalón*) braces (*BRIT*), suspenders (*US*); **tirantez** *nf* tightness; (*fig*) tension

tirar [ti'rar] *vt* to throw; (*dejar caer*) to drop; (*volcar*) to upset; (*derribar*) to knock down *o* over; (*desechar*) to throw out *o* away; (*dinero*) to squander; (*imprimir*) to print ▷ *vi* (*disparar*) to shoot; (*de la puerta etc*) to pull; (*fam: andar*) to go; (*tender a, buscar realizar*) to tend to; (*Deporte*) to shoot; **tirarse** *vr* to throw o.s.; **~ abajo** to bring down, destroy; **tira más a su padre** he takes more after his father; **ir tirando** to manage

tirita [ti'rita] *nf* (sticking) plaster

(*BRIT*), Bandaid® (*US*)

tiritar [tiri'tar] *vi* to shiver

tiro ['tiro] *nm* (*lanzamiento*) throw; (*disparo*) shot; (*Deporte*) shot; (*Golf, Tenis*) drive; (*alcance*) range; **caballo de ~** cart-horse; **tiro al blanco** target practice

tirón [ti'ron] *nm* (*sacudida*) pull, tug; **de un ~** in one go, all at once

tiroteo [tiro'teo] *nm* exchange of shots, shooting

tisis ['tisis] *nf inv* consumption, tuberculosis

títere ['titere] *nm* puppet

titubear [tituβe'ar] *vi* to stagger; to stammer; (*fig*) to hesitate; **titubeo** *nm* staggering; stammering; hesitation

titulado, -a [titu'laðo, a] *adj* (*libro*) entitled; (*persona*) titled

titular [titu'lar] *adj* titular ▷ *nmf* holder ▷ *nm* headline ▷ *vt* to title; **titularse** *vr* to be entitled; **título** *nm* title; (*de diario*) headline; (*certificado*) professional qualification; (*universitario*) (university) degree; **a título de** in the capacity of

tiza ['tiθa] *nf* chalk

toalla [to'aʎa] *nf* towel

tobillo [to'βiʎo] *nm* ankle

tobogán [toβo'ɣan] *nm* (*montaña rusa*) roller-coaster; (*de niños*) chute, slide

tocadiscos [toka'ðiskos] *nm inv* record player

tocado, -a [to'kaðo, a] *adj* (*fam*) touched ▷ *nm* headdress

tocador [toka'ðor] *nm* (*mueble*) dressing table; (*cuarto*) boudoir; (*fam*) ladies' toilet (*BRIT*) *o* room (*US*)

tocar [to'kar] *vt* to touch; (*Mús*) to play; (*referirse a*) to allude to; (*timbre*) to ring; (*a la puerta*) to knock (on *o* at the door); (*ser de turno*) to fall to, be the turn of; (*ser hora*) to be due; **tocarse** *vr* (*cubrirse la cabeza*) to cover one's head; (*tener contacto*) to touch (each other); **por lo que a mí me toca** as far as I am concerned; **te toca a ti** it's your turn

tocayo, -a [to'kajo, a] *nm/f*
namesake

tocino [to'θino] *nm* bacon

todavía [toða'βia] *adv* (*aun*) even;
(*aún*) still, yet; **~ más** yet more; **~ no**
not yet

○ **PALABRA CLAVE**

todo, -a ['toðo, a] *adj* **1** (*con artículo
sg*) all; **toda la carne** all the meat; **toda
la noche** all night, the whole night;
todo el libro the whole book; **toda
una botella** a whole bottle; **todo lo
contrario** quite the opposite; **está
toda sucia** she's all dirty; **por todo
el país** throughout the whole
country

2 (*con artículo pl*) all; every; **todos los
libros** all the books; **todas las noches**
every night; **todos los que quieran
salir** all those who want to leave

▷ *pron* **1** everything, all; **todos**
everyone, everybody; **lo sabemos
todo** we know everything; **todos
querían más tiempo** everybody *o*
everyone wanted more time; **nos
marchamos todos** all of us left

2: **con todo: con todo él me sigue
gustando** even so I still like him

▷ *adv* all; **vaya todo seguido** keep
straight on *o* ahead

▷ *nm*: **como un todo** as a whole; **del
todo: no me agrada del todo** I don't
entirely like it

todopoderoso, -a [toðopoðe'roso,
a] *adj* all powerful; (*Rel*) almighty

todoterreno [toðote'rreno] *sm inv*
four-wheel drive, SUV (*ESP US*)

toga ['toɣa] *nf* toga; (*Escol*) gown

Tokio ['tokjo] *n* Tokyo

toldo ['toldo] *nm* (*para el sol*)
sunshade (*BRIT*), parasol; (*tienda*)
marquee

tolerancia [tole'ranθja] *nf*
tolerance; **tolerante** *adj* (*sociedad*)
liberal; (*persona*) open-minded

tolerar [tole'rar] *vt* to tolerate;
(*resistir*) to endure

toma ['toma] *nf* (*acto*) taking; (*Med*)
dose; **toma de corriente** socket; **toma
de tierra** earth (wire); **tomacorriente**
(*LAM*) *nm* socket

tomar [to'mar] *vt* to take; (*aspecto*)
to take on; (*beber*) to drink ▷ *vi* to take;
(*LAM*: *beber*) to drink; **tomarse** *vr* to
take; **~se por** to consider o.s. to be; **~
a bien/mal** to take well/badly; **~ en
serio** to take seriously; **~ el pelo a algn**
to pull sb's leg; **~la con algn** to pick a
quarrel with sb; **¡tome!** here you are!; **~
el sol** to sunbathe

tomate [to'mate] *nm* tomato

tomillo [to'miʎo] *nm* thyme

tomo ['tomo] *nm* (*libro*) volume

ton [ton] *abr* = **tonelada** ▷ *nm*: **sin ~
ni son** without rhyme or reason

tonalidad [tonali'ðað] *nf* tone

tonel [to'nel] *nm* barrel

tonelada [tone'laða] *nf* ton;
tonelaje *nm* tonnage

tónica ['tonika] *nf* (*Mús*) tonic; (*fig*)
keynote

tónico, -a ['toniko, a] *adj* tonic ▷ *nm*
(*Med*) tonic

tono ['tono] *nm* tone; **fuera de ~**
inappropriate

tontería [tonte'ria] *nf* (*estupidez*)
foolishness; (*cosa*) stupid thing; (*acto*)
foolish act; **tonterías** *nfpl* (*disparates*)
rubbish *sg*, nonsense *sg*

tonto, -a ['tonto, a] *adj* stupid, silly
▷ *nm/f* fool

topar [to'par] *vi*: **~ contra** *o* **en** to run
into; **~ con** to run up against

tope ['tope] *adj* maximum ▷ *nm* (*fin*)
end; (*límite*) limit; (*Ferro*) buffer; (*Auto*)
bumper; **al ~** end to end

tópico, -a ['topiko, a] *adj* topical
▷ *nm* platitude

topo ['topo] *nm* (*Zool*) mole; (*fig*)
blunderer

toque *etc* ['toke] *vb* V **tocar** ▷ *nm*
touch; (*Mús*) beat; (*de campana*) peal;
dar un ~ a to warn; **toque de queda**

curfew

toqué etc vb V **tocar**

toquetear [tokete'ar] vt to finger

toquilla [to'kiʎa] nf (pañuelo)
headscarf; (chal) shawl

tórax ['toraks] nm thorax

torbellino [torbe'ʎino] nm
whirlwind; (fig) whirl

torcedura [torθe'ðura] nf twist;
(Med) sprain

torcer [tor'θer] vt to twist; (la esquina)
to turn; (Med) to sprain ▷ vi (desviar) to
turn off; **torcerse** vr (ladearse) to bend;
(desviarse) to go astray; (fracasar) to go
wrong; **torcido, -a** adj twisted; (fig)
crooked ▷ nm curl

tordo, -a ['torðo, a] adj dappled
▷ nm thrush

torear [tore'ar] vt (fig: evadir) to avoid;
(jugar con) to tease ▷ vi to fight bulls;
toreo nm bullfighting; **torero, -a**
nm/f bullfighter

tormenta [tor'menta] nf storm;
(fig: confusión) turmoil

tormento [tor'mento] nm torture;
(fig) anguish

tornar [tor'nar] vt (devolver) to return,
give back; (transformar) to transform
▷ vi to go back

tornasolado, -a [tornaso'laðo, a]
adj (brillante) iridescent; (reluciente)
shimmering

torneo [tor'neo] nm tournament

tornillo [tor'niʎo] nm screw

torniquete [torni'kete] nm (Med)
tourniquet

torno ['torno] nm (Tec) winch; (café) to
(tambor) drum; **en ~ (a)** round, about

toro ['toro] nm bull; (fam) he-man; **los
~s** bullfighting

toronja [to'ronxa] nf grapefruit

torpe ['torpe] adj (poco hábil) clumsy,
awkward; (necio) dim; (lento) slow

torpedo [tor'peðo] nm torpedo

torpeza [tor'peθa] nf (falta de agilidad)
clumsiness; (lentitud) slowness; (error)
mistake

torre ['torre] nf tower; (de petróleo)

derrick

torrefacto, -a [torre'facto, a] adj
roasted

torrente [to'rrente] nm torrent

torrija [to'rrixa] nf French toast

torsión [tor'sjon] nf twisting

torso ['torso] nm torso

torta ['torta] nf cake; (fam) slap

tortícolis [tor'tikolis] nm inv stiff
neck

tortilla [tor'tiʎa] nf omelette; (LAM: de
maíz) maize pancake; **tortilla de papas**
(LAM) potato omelette; **tortilla de
patatas** (ESP) potato omelette; **tortilla
francesa** (ESP) plain omelette

tórtola ['tortola] nf turtledove

tortuga [tor'tuxa] nf tortoise

tortuoso, -a [tor'twoso, a] adj
winding

tortura [tor'tura] nf torture;
torturar vt to torture

tos [tos] nf cough; **tos ferina**
whooping cough

toser [to'ser] vi to cough

tostada [tos'taða] nf piece of toast;
tostado, -a adj toasted; (por el sol)
dark brown; (piel) tanned

tostador [tosta'ðor] (ESP) nm
toaster; **tostadora** (LAM) nf =
tostador

tostar [tos'tar] vt to toast; (café) to
roast; (persona) to tan; **tostarse** vr to
get brown

total [to'tal] adj total ▷ adv in short;
(al fin y al cabo) when all is said and
done ▷ nm total; **en ~** in all; **~ que ...**
to cut (BRIT) o make (US) a long story
short ...

totalidad [totali'ðað] nf whole

totalitario, -a [totali'tarjo, a] adj
totalitarian

tóxico, -a ['toksiko, a] adj toxic
▷ nm poison; **toxicómano, -a** nm/f
drug addict

toxina [to'ksina] nf toxin

tozudo, -a [to'θuðo, a] adj obstinate

trabajador, a [traβaxa'ðor, a]
adj hard-working ▷ nm/f worker;

trabajador autónomo o **por cuenta propia** self-employed person
trabajar [traβa'xar] vt to work; (Agr) to till; (empeñarse en) to work at; (convencer) to persuade ▷ vi to work; (esforzarse) to strive; **trabajo** nm work; (tarea) task; (Pol) labour; (fig) effort; **tomarse el trabajo de** to take the trouble to; **trabajo a destajo** piecework; **trabajo en equipo** teamwork; **trabajo por turnos** shift work; **trabajos forzados** hard labour sg
trabalenguas [traβa'lengwas] nm inv tongue twister
tracción [trak'θjon] nf traction; **tracción delantera/trasera** front-wheel/rear-wheel drive
tractor [trak'tor] nm tractor
tradición [traði'θjon] nf tradition; **tradicional** adj traditional
traducción [traðuk'θjon] nf translation
traducir [traðu'θir] vt to translate; **traductor, a** nm/f translator
traer [tra'er] vt to bring; (llevar) to carry; (llevar puesto) to wear; (incluir) to carry; (causar) to cause; **traerse** vr: **~se algo** to be up to sth
traficar [trafi'kar] vi to trade
tráfico ['trafiko] nm (Com) trade; (Auto) traffic
tragaluz [traɣa'luθ] nm skylight
tragamonedas [traɣamo'neðas] (LAM) nf inv slot machine
tragaperras [traɣa'perras] (ESP) nf inv slot machine
tragar [tra'ɣar] vt to swallow; (devorar) to devour, bolt down; **tragarse** vr to swallow
tragedia [tra'xeðja] nf tragedy; **trágico, -a** adj tragic
trago ['traɣo] nm (líquido) drink; (bocado) gulp; (fam: de bebida) swig; (desgracia) blow; **echar un ~** to have a drink
traición [trai'θjon] nf treachery; (Jur) treason; (una traición) act of treachery;

traicionar vt to betray
traidor, a [trai'ðor, a] adj treacherous ▷ nm/f traitor
traigo etc vb V **traer**
traje ['traxe] vb V **traer** ▷ nm (de hombre) suit; (de mujer) dress; (vestido típico) costume; **traje de baño/chaqueta** swimsuit/suit; **traje de etiqueta** dress suit; **traje de luces** bullfighter's costume
trajera etc vb V **traer**
trajín [tra'xin] nm (fam: movimiento) bustle; **trajinar** vi (moverse) to bustle about
trama ['trama] nf (intriga) plot; (de tejido) weft (BRIT), woof (US); **tramar** vt to plot; (Tec) to weave
tramitar [trami'tar] vt (asunto) to transact; (negociar) to negotiate
trámite ['tramite] nm (paso) step; (Jur) transaction; **trámites** nmpl (burocracia) procedure sg; (Jur) proceedings
tramo ['tramo] nm (de tierra) plot; (de escalera) flight; (de vía) section
trampa ['trampa] nf trap; (en el suelo) trapdoor; (truco) trick; (engaño) fiddle; **trampear** vt, vi to cheat
trampolín [trampo'lin] nm (de piscina etc) diving board
tramposo, -a [tram'poso, a] adj crooked, cheating ▷ nm/f crook, cheat
tranca ['tranka] nf (palo) stick; (de puerta, ventana) bar; **trancar** vt to bar
trance ['tranθe] nm (momento difícil) difficult moment o juncture; (estado hipnotizado) trance
tranquilidad [trankili'ðað] nf (calma) calmness, stillness; (paz) peacefulness
tranquilizar [trankili'θar] vt (calmar) to calm (down); (asegurar) to reassure; **tranquilizarse** vr to calm down; **tranquilo, -a** adj (calmado) calm; (apacible) peaceful; (mar) calm; (mente) untroubled
transacción [transak'θjon] nf transaction

transbordador [transβorða'ðor]
nm ferry

transbordo [trans'βorðo] nm
transfer; **hacer ~** to change (trains etc)

transcurrir [transku'rrir] vi (tiempo)
to pass; (hecho) to take place

transcurso [trans'kurso] nm: **~ del
tiempo** lapse (of time)

transeúnte [transe'unte] nmf
passer-by

transferencia [transfe'renθja] nf
transference; (Com) transfer

transferir [transfe'rir] vt to transfer

transformador [transforma'ðor]
nm (Elec) transformer

transformar [transfor'mar] vt to
transform; (convertir) to convert

transfusión [transfu'sjon] nf
transfusion

transgénico, -a [trans'xeniko, a]
adj genetically modified, GM

transición [transi'θjon] nf transition

transigir [transi'xir] vi to
compromise, make concessions

transitar [transi'tar] vi to go (from
place to place); **tránsito** nm transit;
(Auto) traffic; **transitorio, -a** adj
transitory

transmisión [transmi'sjon] nf (Tec)
transmission; (transferencia) transfer;
transmisión exterior/en directo
outside/live broadcast

transmitir [transmi'tir] vt to
transmit; (Radio, TV) to broadcast

transparencia [transpa'renθja]
nf transparency; (claridad) clearness,
clarity; (foto) slide

transparentar [transparen'tar]
vt to reveal ▷ vi to be transparent;
transparente adj transparent;
(claro) clear

transpirar [transpi'rar] vi to perspire

transportar [transpor'tar] vt to
transport; (llevar) to carry; **transporte**
nm transport; (Com) haulage

transversal [transβer'sal] adj
transverse, cross

tranvía [tram'bia] nm tram

trapeador [trapea'ðor] (LAM) nm
mop; **trapear** (LAM) vt to mop

trapecio [tra'peθjo] nm trapeze;
trapecista nmf trapeze artist

trapero, -a [tra'pero, a] nm/f
ragman

trapicheo [trapi'tʃeo] (fam) nm
scheme, fiddle

trapo ['trapo] nm (tela) rag; (de
cocina) cloth

tráquea ['trakea] nf windpipe

traqueteo [trake'teo] nm rattling

tras [tras] prep (detrás) behind;
(después) after

trasatlántico [trasat'lantiko] nm
(barco) (cabin) cruiser

trascendencia [trasθen'denθja] nf
(importancia) importance; (Filosofía)
transcendence

trascendental [trasθenden'tal] adj
important; (Filosofía) transcendental

trasero, -a [tra'sero, a] adj back,
rear ▷ nm (Anat) bottom

trasfondo [tras'fondo] nm
background

trasgredir [trasɣre'ðir] vt to
contravene

trashumante [trasu'mante] adj
(animales) migrating

trasladar [trasla'ðar] vt to move;
(persona) to transfer; (postergar) to
postpone; (copiar) to copy; **trasladarse**
vr (mudarse) to move; **traslado** nm
move; (mudanza) move, removal

traslucir [traslu'θir] vt to show

trasluz [tras'luθ] nm reflected light;
al ~ against o up to the light

trasnochador, a [trasnotʃa'ðor, a]
nm/f night owl

trasnochar [trasno'tʃar] vi (acostarse
tarde) to stay up late

traspapelar [traspape'lar] vt
(documento, carta) to mislay, misplace

traspasar [traspa'sar] vt (suj: bala
etc) to pierce, go through; (propiedad)
to sell, transfer; (calle) to cross over;
(límites) to go beyond; (ley) to break;
traspaso nm (venta) transfer, sale

traspatio [tras'patjo] (*LAM*) *nm* backyard

traspié [tras'pje] *nm* (*tropezón*) trip; (*error*) blunder

trasplantar [trasplan'tar] *vt* to transplant

traste ['traste] *nm* (*Mús*) fret; **dar al ~ con algo** to ruin sth

trastero [tras'tero] *nm* storage room

trastienda [tras'tjenda] *nf* back of shop

trasto ['trasto] (*pey*) *nm* (*cosa*) piece of junk; (*persona*) dead loss

trastornado, -a [trastor'naðo, a] *adj* (*loco*) mad, crazy

trastornar [trastor'nar] *vt* (*fig: planes*) to disrupt; (: *nervios*) to shatter; (: *persona*) to drive crazy; **trastornarse** *vr* (*volverse loco*) to go mad *o* crazy; **trastorno** *nm* (*acto*) overturning; (*confusión*) confusion

tratable [tra'taβle] *adj* friendly

tratado [tra'taðo] *nm* (*Pol*) treaty; (*Com*) agreement

tratamiento [trata'mjento] *nm* treatment; **tratamiento de textos** (*Inform*) word processing *cpd*

tratar [tra'tar] *vt* (*ocuparse de*) to treat; (*manejar, Tec*) to handle; (*Med*) to treat; (*dirigirse a: persona*) to address ▷ *vi*: **~ de** (*hablar sobre*) to deal with, be about; (*intentar*) to try to; **tratarse** *vr* to treat each other; **~ con** (*Com*) to trade in; (*negociar*) to negotiate with; (*tener contactos*) to have dealings with; **¿de qué se trata?** what's it about?; **trato** *nm* dealings *pl*; (*relaciónes*) relationship; (*comportamiento*) manner; (*Com*) agreement

trauma ['trauma] *nm* trauma

través [tra'βes] *nm* (*fig*) reverse; **al ~** across, crossways; **a ~ de** across; (*sobre*) over; (*por*) through

travesaño [traβe'saɲo] *nm* (*Arq*) crossbeam; (*Deporte*) crossbar

travesía [traβe'sia] *nf* (*calle*) cross-street; (*Náut*) crossing

travesura [traβe'sura] *nf* (*broma*) prank; (*ingenio*) wit

travieso, -a [tra'βjeso, a] *adj* (*niño*) naughty

trayecto [tra'jekto] *nm* (*ruta*) road, way; (*viaje*) journey; (*tramo*) stretch; **trayectoria** *nf* trajectory; (*fig*) path

traza ['traθa] *nf* (*aspecto*) looks *pl*; (*señal*) sign; **trazado, -a** *adj*: **bien trazado** shapely, well-formed ▷ *nm* (*Arq*) plan, design; (*fig*) outline

trazar [tra'θar] *vt* (*Arq*) to plan; (*Arte*) to sketch; (*fig*) to trace; (*plan*) to draw up; **trazo** *nm* (*línea*) line; (*bosquejo*) sketch

trébol ['treβol] *nm* (*Bot*) clover

trece ['treθe] *num* thirteen

trecho ['tretʃo] *nm* (*distancia*) distance; (*tiempo*) while

tregua ['treɣwa] *nf* (*Mil*) truce; (*fig*) respite

treinta ['treinta] *num* thirty

tremendo, -a [tre'mendo, a] *adj* (*terrible*) terrible; (*imponente: cosa*) imposing; (*fam: fabuloso*) tremendous

tren [tren] *nm* train; **tren de aterrizaje** undercarriage; **tren de cercanías** suburban train

trenca ['trenka] *nf* duffel coat

trenza ['trenθa] *nf* (*de pelo*) plait (*BRIT*), braid (*US*)

trepadora [trepa'ðora] *nf* (*Bot*) climber

trepar [tre'par] *vt*, *vi* to climb

tres [tres] *num* three

tresillo [tre'siʎo] *nm* three-piece suite; (*Mús*) triplet

treta ['treta] *nf* trick

triángulo ['trjangulo] *nm* triangle

tribu ['triβu] *nf* tribe

tribuna [tri'βuna] *nf* (*plataforma*) platform; (*Deporte*) (grand)stand

tribunal [triβu'nal] *nm* (*Jur*) court; (*comisión, fig*) tribunal; **~ popular** jury

tributo [tri'βuto] *nm* (*Com*) tax

trigal [tri'ɣal] *nm* wheat field

trigo ['triɣo] *nm* wheat

trigueño, -a [tri'ɣeɲo, a] *adj* (*pelo*) corn-coloured

trillar [tri'ʎar] vt (Agr) to thresh

trimestral [trimes'tral] adj quarterly; (Escol) termly

trimestre [tri'mestre] nm (Escol) term

trinar [tri'nar] vi (pájaros) to sing; (rabiar) to fume, be angry

trinchar [trin'tʃar] vt to carve

trinchera [trin'tʃera] nf (fosa) trench

trineo [tri'neo] nm sledge

trinidad [trini'ðað] nf trio; (Rel): **la T~** the Trinity

tripa ['tripa] nf (Anat) intestine; (fam: tb: **~s**) insides pl

triple ['triple] adj triple

triplicado, -a [tripli'kaðo, a] adj: **por ~** in triplicate

tripulación [tripula'θjon] nf crew

tripulante [tripu'lante] nmf crewman/woman

tripular [tripu'lar] vt (barco) to man; (Auto) to drive

triquiñuela [triki'ɲwela] nf trick

tris [tris] nm inv crack

triste ['triste] adj sad; (lamentable) sorry, miserable; **tristeza** nf (aflicción) sadness; (melancolía) melancholy

triturar [tritu'rar] vt (moler) to grind; (mascar) to chew

triunfar [trjun'far] vi (tener éxito) to triumph; (ganar) to win; **triunfo** nm triumph

trivial [tri'βjal] adj trivial

triza ['triθa] nf: **hacer ~s** to smash to bits; (papel) to tear to shreds

trocear [troθe'ar] vt (carne, manzana) to cut up, cut into pieces

trocha ['trotʃa] nf short cut

trofeo [tro'feo] nm (premio) trophy; (éxito) success

tromba ['tromba] nf downpour

trombón [trom'bon] nm trombone

trombosis [trom'bosis] nf inv thrombosis

trompa ['trompa] nf horn; (trompo) humming top; (hocico) snout; (fam): **cogerse una ~** to get tight

trompazo [trom'paθo] nm bump, bang

trompeta [trom'peta] nf trumpet; (clarín) bugle

trompicón [trompi'kon]: **a trompicones** adv in fits and starts

trompo ['trompo] nm spinning top

trompón [trom'pon] nm bump

tronar [tro'nar] vt (MÉX, CAM: fusilar) to shoot; (MÉX: examen) to flunk ⊳ vi to thunder; (fig) to rage

tronchar [tron'tʃar] vt (árbol) to chop down; (fig: vida) to cut short; (: esperanza) to shatter; (persona) to tire out; **troncharse** vr to fall down

tronco ['tronko] nm (de árbol, Anat) trunk

trono ['trono] nm throne

tropa ['tropa] nf (Mil) troop; (soldados) soldiers pl

tropezar [trope'θar] vi to trip, stumble; (errar) to slip up; **~ con** to run into; (topar con) to bump into; **tropezón** nm trip; (fig) blunder

tropical [tropi'kal] adj tropical

trópico ['tropiko] nm tropic

tropiezo [tro'pjeθo] vb V **tropezar** ⊳ nm (error) slip, blunder; (desgracia) misfortune; (obstáculo) snag

trotamundos [trota'mundos] nm inv globetrotter

trotar [tro'tar] vi to trot; **trote** nm trot; (fam) travelling; **de mucho trote** hard-wearing

trozar [tro'θar] vt (LAM) to cut up, cut into pieces

trozo ['troθo] nm bit, piece

trucha ['trutʃa] nf trout

truco ['truko] nm (habilidad) knack; (engaño) trick

trueno ['trweno] nm thunder; (estampido) bang

trueque etc ['trweke] vb V **trocar** ⊳ nm exchange; (Com) barter

trufa ['trufa] nf (Bot) truffle

truhán, -ana [tru'an, ana] nm/f rogue

truncar [trun'kar] vt (cortar) to truncate; (fig: la vida etc) to cut short; (: el desarrollo) to stunt

tu [tu] *adj* your

tú [tu] *pron* you

tubérculo [tu'βerkulo] *nm* (*Bot*) tuber

tuberculosis [tuβerku'losis] *nf inv* tuberculosis

tubería [tuβe'ria] *nf* pipes *pl*; (*conducto*) pipeline

tubo ['tuβo] *nm* tube, pipe; **tubo de ensayo** test tube; **tubo de escape** exhaust (pipe)

tuerca ['twerka] *nf* nut

tuerto, -a ['twerto, a] *adj* blind in one eye ▷ *nm/f* one-eyed person

tuerza *etc vb* V **torcer**

tuétano [tu'wetano] *nm* marrow; (*Bot*) pith

tufo ['tufo] *nm* (*hedor*) stench

tul [tul] *nm* tulle

tulipán [tuli'pan] *nm* tulip

tullido, -a [tu'ʎiðo, a] *adj* crippled

tumba ['tumba] *nf* (*sepultura*) tomb

tumbar [tum'bar] *vt* to knock down; **tumbarse** *vr* (*echarse*) to lie down; (*extenderse*) to stretch out

tumbo ['tumbo] *nm*: **dar ~s** to stagger

tumbona [tum'bona] *nf* (*butaca*) easy chair; (*de playa*) deckchair (BRIT), beach chair (US)

tumor [tu'mor] *nm* tumour

tumulto [tu'multo] *nm* turmoil

tuna ['tuna] *nf* (*Mús*) student music group; V *tb* **tuno**

● **TUNA**
●
● A **tuna** is a musical group made
● up of university students or
● former students who dress up
● in costumes from the "Edad de
● Oro", the Spanish Golden Age.
● These groups go through the
● town playing their guitars, lutes
● and tambourines and serenade
● the young ladies in the halls of
● residence or make impromptu
● appearances at weddings or
● parties singing traditional
● Spanish songs for a few coins.

tunante [tu'nante] *nmf* rascal

tunear [tune'ar] *vt* (*Auto*) to style, mod (*inf*)

túnel ['tunel] *nm* tunnel

tuning ['tunin] *nm* (*Auto*) car styling, modding (*inf*)

tuno, -a ['tuno, a] *nm/f* (*fam*) rogue ▷ *nm* member of student music group

tupido, -a [tu'piðo, a] *adj* (*denso*) dense; (*tela*) close-woven

turbante [tur'βante] *nm* turban

turbar [tur'βar] *vt* (*molestar*) to disturb; (*incomodar*) to upset

turbina [tur'βina] *nf* turbine

turbio, -a ['turβjo, a] *adj* cloudy; (*tema etc*) confused

turbulencia [turβu'lenθja] *nf* turbulence; (*fig*) restlessness; **turbulento, -a** *adj* turbulent; (*fig: intranquilo*) restless; (: *ruidoso*) noisy

turco, -a ['turko, a] *adj* Turkish ▷ *nm/f* Turk

turismo [tu'rismo] *nm* tourism; (*coche*) car; **turista** *nmf* tourist; **turístico, -a** *adj* tourist *cpd*

turnar [tur'nar] *vi* to take (it in) turns; **turnarse** *vr* to take (it in) turns; **turno** *nm* (*de trabajo*) shift; (*en juegos etc*) turn

turquesa [tur'kesa] *nf* turquoise

Turquía [tur'kia] *nf* Turkey

turrón [tu'rron] *nm* (*dulce*) nougat

tutear [tute'ar] *vt* to address as familiar "tú"; **tutearse** *vr* to be on familiar terms

tutela [tu'tela] *nf* (*legal*) guardianship; **tutelar** *adj* tutelary ▷ *vt* to protect

tutor, a [tu'tor, a] *nm/f* (*legal*) guardian; (*Escol*) tutor

tuve *etc vb* V **tener**

tuviera *etc vb* V **tener**

tuyo, -a ['tujo, a] *adj* yours, of yours ▷ *pron* yours; **un amigo ~** a friend of yours; **los ~s** (*fam*) your relations o family

TV *nf abr* (= *televisión*) TV

TVE *nf abr* = **Televisión Española**

u [u] *conj* or

ubicar [uβi'kar] *vt* to place, situate; (*LAM: encontrar*) to find; **ubicarse** *vr* (*LAM: encontrarse*) to lie, be located

ubre ['uβre] *nf* udder

UCI *nf abr* (= *Unidad de Cuidados Intensivos*) ICU

Ud(s) *abr* = **usted(es)**

UE *nf abr* (= *Unión Europea*) EU

ufanarse [ufa'narse] *vr* to boast; **ufano, -a** *adj* (*arrogante*) arrogant; (*presumido*) conceited

UGT (*ESP*) *nf abr* = **Unión General de Trabajadores**

úlcera ['ulθera] *nf* ulcer

ulterior [ulte'rjor] *adj* (*más allá*) farther, further; (*subsecuente, siguiente*) subsequent

últimamente ['ultimamente] *adv* (*recientemente*) lately, recently

ultimar [ulti'mar] *vt* to finish; (*finalizar*) to finalize; (*LAM: matar*) to kill

ultimátum [ulti'matum] (*pl* **~s**) *nm* ultimatum

último, -a ['ultimo, a] *adj* last; (*más reciente*) latest, most recent; (*más bajo*) bottom; (*más alto*) top; **en las últimas** on one's last legs; **por ~** finally

ultra ['ultra] *adj* ultra ▷ *nmf* extreme right-winger

ultraje [ul'traxe] *nm* outrage; insult

ultramar [ultra'mar] *nm*: **de** *o* **en ~** abroad, overseas

ultramarinos [ultrama'rinos] *nmpl* groceries; **tienda de ~** grocer's (shop)

ultranza [ul'tranθa]: **a ~** *adv* (*a todo trance*) at all costs; (*completo*) outright

umbral [um'bral] *nm* (*gen*) threshold

O **PALABRA CLAVE**

un, una [un, 'una] *art indef* a; (*antes de vocal*) an; **una mujer/naranja** a woman/an orange
▷ *adj*: **unos** (*o* **unas**): **hay unos regalos para ti** there are some presents for you; **hay unas cervezas en la nevera** there are some beers in the fridge

unánime [u'nanime] *adj* unanimous; **unanimidad** *nf* unanimity

undécimo, -a [un'deθimo, a] *adj* eleventh

ungir [un'xir] *vt* to anoint

ungüento [un'gwento] *nm* ointment

único, -a ['uniko, a] *adj* only, sole; (*sin par*) unique

unidad [uni'ðað] *nf* unity; (*Com, Tec etc*) unit

unido, -a [u'niðo, a] *adj* joined, linked; (*fig*) united

unificar [unifi'kar] *vt* to unite, unify

uniformar [unifor'mar] *vt* to make uniform, level up; (*persona*) to put into uniform

uniforme [uni'forme] *adj* uniform, equal; (*superficie*) even ▷ *nm* uniform

unilateral [unilate'ral] *adj* unilateral

unión [u'njon] *nf* union; (*acto*) uniting, joining; (*unidad*) unity; (*Tec*) joint; **Unión Europea** European Union

unir [u'nir] *vt* (*juntar*) to join, unite;

(*atar*) to tie, fasten; (*combinar*) to combine; **unirse** *vr* to join together, unite; (*empresas*) to merge

unísono [u'nisono] *nm*: **al ~** in unison

universal [uniβer'sal] *adj* universal; (*mundial*) world *cpd*

universidad [uniβersi'ðað] *nf* university

universitario, -a [uniβersi'tarjo, a] *adj* university *cpd* ▷ *nm/f* (*profesor*) lecturer; (*estudiante*) (university) student; (*graduado*) graduate

universo [uni'βerso] *nm* universe

○ **PALABRA CLAVE**

uno, -a ['uno, a] *adj* one; **unos pocos** a few; **unos cien** about a hundred ▷ *pron* **1** one; **quiero sólo uno** I only want one; **uno de ellos** one of them
2 (*alguien*) somebody, someone; **conozco a uno que se te parece** I know somebody o someone who looks like you; **uno mismo** oneself; **unos querían quedarse** some (people) wanted to stay
3 (**los**) **unos ...** (**los**) **otros ...** some ... others ▷ *nf* one; **es la una** it's one o'clock ▷ *nm* (number) one

untar [un'tar] *vt* (*mantequilla*) to spread; (*engrasar*) to grease, oil

uña ['uɲa] *nf* (*Anat*) nail; (*garra*) claw; (*casco*) hoof; (*arrancaclavos*) claw

uranio [u'ranjo] *nm* uranium

urbanización [urβaniθa'θjon] *nf* (*barrio, colonia*) housing estate

urbanizar [urβani'θar] *vt* (*zona*) to develop, urbanize

urbano, -a [ur'βano, a] *adj* (*de ciudad*) urban; (*cortés*) courteous, polite

urbe ['urβe] *nf* large city

urdir [ur'ðir] *vt* to warp; (*complot*) to plot, contrive

urgencia [ur'xenθja] *nf* urgency; (*prisa*) haste, rush; (*emergencia*) emergency; **servicios de ~** emergency

services; **"U~s"** "Casualty"; **urgente** *adj* urgent

urgir [ur'xir] *vi* to be urgent; **me urge** I'm in a hurry for it

urinario, -a [uri'narjo, a] *adj* urinary ▷ *nm* urinal

urna ['urna] *nf* urn; (*Pol*) ballot box

urraca [u'rraka] *nf* magpie

URSS [urs] *nf* (*Hist*): **la URSS** the USSR

Uruguay [uru'ɣwai] *nm* (*tb*: **el ~**) Uruguay; **uruguayo, -a** *adj, nm/f* Uruguayan

usado, -a [u'saðo, a] *adj* used; (*de segunda mano*) secondhand

usar [u'sar] *vt* to use; (*ropa*) to wear; (*tener costumbre*) to be in the habit of; **usarse** *vr* to be used; **uso** *nm* use; wear; (*costumbre*) usage, custom; (*moda*) fashion; **al uso** in keeping with custom; **al uso de** in the style of; **de uso externo** (*Med*) for external use

usted [us'teð] *pron* (*sg*) you *sg*; (*pl*): **~es** you *pl*

usual [u'swal] *adj* usual

usuario, -a [usu'arjo, a] *nm/f* user

usura [u'sura] *nf* usury; **usurero, -a** *nm/f* usurer

usurpar [usur'par] *vt* to usurp

utensilio [uten'siljo] *nm* tool; (*Culin*) utensil

útero ['utero] *nm* uterus, womb

útil ['util] *adj* useful ▷ *nm* tool; **utilidad** *nf* usefulness; (*Com*) profit; **utilizar** *vt* to use, utilize

utopía [uto'pia] *nf* Utopia; **utópico, -a** *adj* Utopian

uva ['uβa] *nf* grape

● **LAS UVAS**

In Spain **Las uvas** play a big part on New Year's Eve (**Nochevieja**), when on the stroke of midnight people gather at home, in restaurants or in the **plaza mayor** and eat a grape for each stroke of the clock of the **Puerta del Sol** in Madrid. It is said to bring luck for the following year.

V

v *abr* (=*voltio*) v

va *vb* V **ir**

vaca ['baka] *nf* (*animal*) cow; **carne de ~** beef

vacaciones [baka'θjones] *nfpl* holidays

vacante [ba'kante] *adj* vacant, empty ▷ *nf* vacancy

vaciar [ba'θjar] *vt* to empty out; (*ahuecar*) to hollow out; (*moldear*) to cast; **vaciarse** *vr* to empty

vacilar [baθi'lar] *vi* to be unsteady; (*al hablar*) to falter; (*dudar*) to hesitate, waver; (*memoria*) to fail

vacío, -a [ba'θio, a] *adj* empty; (*puesto*) vacant; (*desocupado*) idle; (*vano*) vain ▷ *nm* emptiness; (*Física*) vacuum; (*un vacío*) (empty) space

vacuna [ba'kuna] *nf* vaccine; **vacunar** *vt* to vaccinate

vacuno, -a [ba'kuno, a] *adj* cow *cpd*; **ganado ~** cattle

vadear [baðe'ar] *vt* (*río*) to ford; **vado** *nm* ford

vagabundo, -a [baɣa'βundo, a] *adj* wandering ▷ *nm* tramp

vagancia [ba'ɣanθja] *nf* (*pereza*) idleness, laziness

vagar [ba'ɣar] *vi* to wander; (*no hacer nada*) to idle

vagina [ba'xina] *nf* vagina

vago, -a ['baɣo, a] *adj* vague; (*perezoso*) lazy ▷ *nm/f* (*vagabundo*) tramp; (*flojo*) lazybones *sg*, idler

vagón [ba'ɣon] *nm* (*Ferro: de pasajeros*) carriage; (: *de mercancías*) wagon

vaho ['bao] *nm* (*vapor*) vapour, steam; (*respiración*) breath

vaina ['baina] *nf* sheath

vainilla [bai'niʎa] *nf* vanilla

vais *vb* V **ir**

vaivén [bai'βen] *nm* to-and-fro movement; (*de tránsito*) coming and going; **vaivenes** *nmpl* (*fig*) ups and downs

vajilla [ba'xiʎa] *nf* crockery, dishes *pl*; (*juego*) service, set

valdré *etc vb* V **valer**

vale ['bale] *nm* voucher; (*recibo*) receipt; (*pagaré*) IOU

valedero, -a [bale'ðero, a] *adj* valid

valenciano, -a [balen'θjano, a] *adj* Valencian

valentía [balen'tia] *nf* courage, bravery

valer [ba'ler] *vt* to be worth; (*Mat*) to equal; (*costar*) to cost ▷ *vi* (*ser útil*) to be useful; (*ser válido*) to be valid; **valerse** *vr* to take care of oneself; **~se de** to make use of, take advantage of; **~ la pena** to be worthwhile; **¿vale?** (*ESP*) OK?; **más vale que nos vayamos** we'd better go; **¡eso a mí no me vale!** (*MÉX: fam: no importar*) I couldn't care less about that

valeroso, -a [bale'roso, a] *adj* brave, valiant

valgo *etc vb* V **valer**

valía [ba'lia] *nf* worth, value

validar [bali'ðar] *vt* to validate; **validez** *nf* validity; **válido, -a** *adj* valid

valiente [ba'ljente] *adj* brave, valiant

▷ *nm* hero

valija [ba'lixa] (*cs*) *nf* (suit)case

valioso, -a [ba'ljoso, a] *adj* valuable

valla ['baʎa] *nf* fence; (*Deporte*) hurdle;
valla publicitaria hoarding; **vallar** *vt*
to fence in

valle ['baʎe] *nm* valley

valor [ba'lor] *nm* value, worth;
(*precio*) price; (*valentía*) valour, courage;
(*importancia*) importance; **valores**
nmpl (*Com*) securities; **valorar** *vt*
to value

vals [bals] *nm inv* waltz

válvula ['balβula] *nf* valve

vamos *vb* V **ir**

vampiro, -resa [bam'piro, 'resa]
nm/f vampire

van *vb* V **ir**

vanguardia [ban'gwardja] *nf*
vanguard; (*Arte etc*) avant-garde

vanidad [bani'ðað] *nf* vanity;
vanidoso, -a *adj* vain, conceited

vano, -a ['bano, a] *adj* vain

vapor [ba'por] *nm* vapour; (*vaho*)
steam; **al ~** (*Culin*) steamed; **vapor de
agua** water vapour; **vaporizador** *nm*
atomizer; **vaporizar** *vt* to vaporize;
vaporoso, -a *adj* vaporous

vaquero, -a [ba'kero, a] *adj* cattle
cpd ▷ *nm* cowboy; **vaqueros** *nmpl*
(*pantalones*) jeans

vaquilla [ba'kiʎa] *nf* (*Zool*) heifer

vara ['bara] *nf* stick; (*Tec*) rod

variable [ba'rjaβle] *adj, nf* variable

variación [barja'θjon] *nf* variation

variar [bar'jar] *vt* to vary; (*modificar*)
to modify; (*cambiar de posición*) to
switch around ▷ *vi* to vary

varicela [bari'θela] *nf* chickenpox

varices [ba'riθes] *nfpl* varicose veins

variedad [barje'ðað] *nf* variety

varilla [ba'riʎa] *nf* stick; (*Bot*) twig;
(*Tec*) rod; (*de rueda*) spoke

vario, -a ['barjo, a] *adj* varied; **~s**
various, several

varita [ba'rita] *nf* (*tb:* **~ mágica**)
magic wand

varón [ba'ron] *nm* male, man; **varonil**

adj manly, virile

Varsovia [bar'soβja] *n* Warsaw

vas *vb* V **ir**

vasco, -a ['basko, a] *adj,*
nm/f Basque; **vascongado, -a**
[baskon'gaðo, a] *adj* Basque; **las
Vascongadas** the Basque Country

vaselina [base'lina] *nf* Vaseline®

vasija [ba'sixa] *nf* container, vessel

vaso ['baso] *nm* glass, tumbler;
(*Anat*) vessel

▌ No confundir **vaso** con la palabra
inglesa *vase*.

vástago ['bastaxo] *nm* (*Bot*) shoot;
(*Tec*) rod; (*fig*) offspring

vasto, -a ['basto, a] *adj* vast, huge

Vaticano [bati'kano] *nm*: **el ~** the
Vatican

vatio ['batjo] *nm* (*Elec*) watt

vaya *etc vb* V **ir**

Vd(s) *abr* = **usted(es)**

ve [be] *vb* V **ir; ver**

vecindad [beθin'dað] *nf*
neighbourhood; (*habitantes*) residents
pl

vecindario [beθin'darjo] *nm*
neighbourhood; residents *pl*

vecino, -a [be'θino, a] *adj*
neighbouring ▷ *nm/f* neighbour;
(*residente*) resident

veda ['beða] *nf* prohibition; **vedar**
[be'ðar] *vt* (*prohibir*) to ban, prohibit;
(*impedir*) to stop, prevent

vegetación [bexeta'θjon] *nf*
vegetation

vegetal [bexe'tal] *adj, nm* vegetable

vegetariano, -a [bexeta'rjano, a]
adj, nm/f vegetarian

vehículo [be'ikulo] *nm* vehicle;
(*Med*) carrier

veía *etc vb* V **ver**

veinte ['beinte] *num* twenty

vejar [be'xar] *vt* (*irritar*) to annoy, vex;
(*humillar*) to humiliate

vejez [be'xeθ] *nf* old age

vejiga [be'xiɣa] *nf* (*Anat*) bladder

vela ['bela] *nf* (*de cera*) candle; (*Náut*)
sail; (*insomnio*) sleeplessness; (*vigilia*)

vigil; (*Mil*) sentry duty; **estar a dos ~s** (*fam*: *sin dinero*) to be skint

velado, -a [be'laðo, a] *adj* veiled; (*sonido*) muffled; (*Foto*) blurred ▷ *nf* soirée

velar [be'lar] *vt* (*vigilar*) to keep watch over ▷ *vi* to stay awake; **~ por** to watch over, look after

velatorio [bela'torjo] *nm* (funeral) wake

velero [be'lero] *nm* (*Náut*) sailing ship; (*Aviac*) glider

veleta [be'leta] *nf* weather vane

veliz [be'lis] (*MÉX*) *nm* (suit)case

vello ['beʎo] *nm* down, fuzz

velo ['belo] *nm* veil

velocidad [beloθi'ðað] *nf* speed; (*Tec*, *Auto*) gear

velocímetro [belo'θimetro] *nm* speedometer

velorio [be'lorjo] (*LAM*) *nm* (funeral) wake

veloz [be'loθ] *adj* fast

ven *vb* V **venir**

vena ['bena] *nf* vein

venado [be'naðo] *nm* deer

vencedor, a [benθe'ðor, a] *adj* victorious ▷ *nm/f* victor, winner

vencer [ben'θer] *vt* (*dominar*) to defeat, beat; (*derrotar*) to vanquish; (*superar*, *controlar*) to overcome, master ▷ *vi* (*triunfar*) to win (through), triumph; (*plazo*) to expire; **vencido, -a** *adj* (*derrotado*) defeated, beaten; (*Com*) due ▷ *adv*: **pagar vencido** to pay in arrears

venda ['benda] *nf* bandage; **vendaje** *nm* bandage, dressing; **vendar** *vt* to bandage; **vendar los ojos** to blindfold

vendaval [benda'βal] *nm* (*viento*) gale

vendedor, a [bende'ðor, a] *nm/f* seller

vender [ben'der] *vt* to sell; **venderse** *vr* (*estar a la venta*) to be on sale; **~ al contado/al por mayor/al por menor** to sell for cash/wholesale/retail; **"se vende"** "for sale"

vendimia [ben'dimja] *nf* grape harvest

vendré *etc vb* V **venir**

veneno [be'neno] *nm* poison; (*de serpiente*) venom; **venenoso, -a** *adj* poisonous; venomous

venerable [bene'raβle] *adj* venerable; **venerar** *vt* (*respetar*) to revere; (*adorar*) to worship

venéreo, -a [be'nereo, a] *adj*: **enfermedad venérea** venereal disease

venezolano, -a [beneθo'lano, a] *adj* Venezuelan

Venezuela [bene'θwela] *nf* Venezuela

venganza [ben'ganθa] *nf* vengeance, revenge; **vengar** *vt* to avenge; **vengarse** *vr* to take revenge; **vengativo, -a** *adj* (*persona*) vindictive

vengo *etc vb* V **venir**

venia ['benja] *nf* (*perdón*) pardon; (*permiso*) consent

venial [be'njal] *adj* venial

venida [be'niða] *nf* (*llegada*) arrival; (*regreso*) return

venidero, -a [beni'ðero, a] *adj* coming, future

venir [be'nir] *vi* to come; (*llegar*) to arrive; (*ocurrir*) to happen; (*fig*): **~ de** to stem from; **~ bien/mal** to be suitable/unsuitable; **el año que viene** next year; **~se abajo** to collapse

venta ['benta] *nf* (*Com*) sale; **"en ~"** "for sale"; **estar a la o en ~** to be (up) for sale o on the market; **venta a domicilio** door-to-door selling; **venta a plazos** hire purchase; **venta al contado/al por mayor/al por menor** cash sale/wholesale/retail

ventaja [ben'taxa] *nf* advantage; **ventajoso, -a** *adj* advantageous

ventana [ben'tana] *nf* window; **ventanilla** *nf* (*de taquilla*) window (*of booking office etc*)

ventilación [bentila'θjon] *nf* ventilation; (*corriente*) draught

ventilador [bentila'ðor] *nm* fan

ventilar [benti'lar] vt to ventilate; (para secar) to put out to dry; (asunto) to air, discuss

ventisca [ben'tiska] nf blizzard

ventrílocuo, -a [ben'trilokwo, a] nm/f ventriloquist

ventura [ben'tura] nf (felicidad) happiness; (buena suerte) luck; (destino) fortune; **a la (buena) ~** at random; **venturoso, -a** adj happy; (afortunado) lucky, fortunate

veo etc vb V **ver**

ver [ber] vt to see; (mirar) to look at, watch; (entender) to understand; (investigar) to look into ▷ vi to see; to understand; **verse** vr (encontrarse) to meet; (dejarse ver) to be seen; (hallarse: en un apuro) to find o.s., be; **(vamos) a ~** let's see; **no tener nada que ~ con** to have nothing to do with; **a mi modo de ~** as I see it; **ya ~emos** we'll see

vera ['bera] nf edge, verge; (de río) bank

veranear [berane'ar] vi to spend the summer; **veraneo** nm summer holiday; **veraniego, -a** adj summer cpd

verano [be'rano] nm summer

veras ['beras] nfpl truth sg; **de ~** really, truly

verbal [ber'βal] adj verbal

verbena [ber'βena] nf (baile) open-air dance

verbo ['berβo] nm verb

verdad [ber'ðað] nf truth; (fiabilidad) reliability; **de ~** real, proper; **a decir ~** to tell the truth; **verdadero, -a** adj (veraz) true, truthful; (fiable) reliable; (fig) real

verde ['berðe] adj green; (chiste) blue, dirty ▷ nm green; **viejo ~** dirty old man; **verdear** vi to turn green; **verdor** nm greenness

verdugo [ber'ðuxo] nm executioner

verdulero, -a [berðu'lero, a] nm/f greengrocer

verduras [ber'ðuras] nfpl (Culin) greens

vereda [be'reða] nf path; (cs: acera) pavement (BRIT), sidewalk (US)

veredicto [bere'ðikto] nm verdict

vergonzoso, -a [berxon'θoso, a] adj shameful; (tímido) timid, bashful

vergüenza [ber'xwenθa] nf shame, sense of shame; (timidez) bashfulness; (pudor) modesty; **me da ~** I'm ashamed

verídico, -a [be'riðiko, a] adj true, truthful

verificar [berifi'kar] vt to check; (corroborar) to verify; (llevar a cabo) to carry out; **verificarse** vr (predicción) to prove to be true

verja ['berxa] nf (cancela) iron gate; (valla) iron railings pl; (de ventana) grille

vermut [ber'mut] (pl ~s) nm vermouth

verosímil [bero'simil] adj likely, probable; (relato) credible

verruga [be'rruxa] nf wart

versátil [ber'satil] adj versatile

versión [ber'sjon] nf version

verso ['berso] nm verse; **un ~** a line of poetry

vértebra ['berteβra] nf vertebra

verter [ber'ter] vt (líquido: adrede) to empty, pour (out); (: sin querer) to spill; (basura) to dump ▷ vi to flow

vertical [berti'kal] adj vertical

vértice ['bertiθe] nm vertex, apex

vertidos [ber'tiðos] nmpl waste sg

vertiente [ber'tjente] nf slope; (fig) aspect

vértigo ['bertixo] nm vertigo; (mareo) dizziness

vesícula [be'sikula] nf blister

vespino® [bes'pino] nm o nf moped

vestíbulo [bes'tiβulo] nm hall; (de teatro) foyer

vestido [bes'tiðo] nm (ropa) clothes pl, clothing; (de mujer) dress, frock ▷ pp de **vestir**; **~ de azul/marinero** dressed in blue/as a sailor

vestidor [besti'ðor] (MÉX) nm (Deporte) changing (BRIT) o locker (US) room

vestimenta [besti'menta] *nf* clothing

vestir [bes'tir] *vt* (*poner: ropa*) to put on; (*llevar: ropa*) to wear; (*proveer de ropa a*) to clothe; (*sastre*) to make clothes for ▷ *vi* to dress; (*verse bien*) to look good; **vestirse** *vr* to get dressed, dress o.s.

vestuario [bes'twarjo] *nm* clothes *pl*, wardrobe; (*Teatro: cuarto*) dressing room; (*Deporte*) changing (BRIT) o locker (US) room

vetar [be'tar] *vt* to veto

veterano, -a [bete'rano, a] *adj, nm* veteran

veterinaria [beteri'narja] *nf* veterinary science; V *tb* **veterinario**

veterinario, -a [beteri'narjo, a] *nm/f* vet(erinary surgeon)

veto ['beto] *nm* veto

vez [beθ] *nf* time; (*turno*) turn; **a la ~ que** at the same time as; **a su ~** in its turn; **otra ~** again; **una ~** once; **de una ~** in one go; **de una ~ para siempre** once and for all; **en ~ de** instead of; **a o algunas veces** sometimes; **una y otra ~** repeatedly; **de ~ en cuando** from time to time; **7 veces 9** 7 times 9; **hacer las veces de** to stand in for; **tal ~** perhaps

vía ['bia] *nf* track, route; (*Ferro*) line; (*fig*) way; (*Anat*) passage, tube ▷ *prep* via, by way of; **por ~ judicial** by legal means; **en ~s de** in the process of; **vía aérea** airway; **Vía Láctea** Milky Way; **vía pública** public road o thoroughfare

viable ['bjaβle] *adj* (*solución, plan, alternativa*) feasible

viaducto [bja'ðukto] *nm* viaduct

viajante [bja'xante] *nm* commercial traveller

viajar [bja'xar] *vi* to travel; **viaje** *nm* journey; (*gira*) tour; (*Náut*) voyage; **estar de viaje** to be on a trip; **viaje de ida y vuelta** round trip; **viaje de novios** honeymoon; **viajero, -a** *adj* travelling; (*Zool*) migratory ▷ *nm/f* (*quien viaja*) traveller; (*pasajero*) passenger

víbora ['biβora] *nf* (*Zool*) viper; (: (*MÉX: venenosa*) poisonous snake

vibración [biβra'θjon] *nf* vibration

vibrar [bi'βrar] *vt, vi* to vibrate

vicepresidente [biθepresi'ðente] *nmf* vice-president

viceversa [biθe'βersa] *adv* vice versa

vicio ['biθjo] *nm* vice; (*mala costumbre*) bad habit; **vicioso, -a** *adj* (*muy malo*) vicious; (*corrompido*) depraved ▷ *nm/f* depraved person

víctima ['biktima] *nf* victim

victoria [bik'torja] *nf* victory; **victorioso, -a** *adj* victorious

vid [bið] *nf* vine

vida ['biða] *nf* (*gen*) life; (*duración*) lifetime; **de por ~** for life; **en la o mi ~** never; **estar con ~** to be still alive; **ganarse la ~** to earn one's living

vídeo ['biðeo] *nm* video ▷ *adj inv*: **película de ~** video film; **videocámara** *nf* camcorder; **videocasete** *nm* video cassette, videotape; **videoclub** *nm* video club; **videojuego** *nm* video game; **videollamada** *nf* video call; **videoteléfono** *nf* videophone

vidrio ['biðrjo] *nm* glass

vieira ['bjeira] *nf* scallop

viejo, -a ['bjexo, a] *adj* old ▷ *nm/f* old man/woman; **hacerse ~** to get old

Viena ['bjena] *n* Vienna

vienes *etc vb* V **venir**

vienés, -esa [bje'nes, esa] *adj* Viennese

viento ['bjento] *nm* wind; **hacer ~** to be windy

vientre ['bjentre] *nm* belly; (*matriz*) womb

viernes ['bjernes] *nm inv* Friday; **Viernes Santo** Good Friday

Vietnam [bjet'nam] *nm* Vietnam; **vietnamita** *adj* Vietnamese

viga ['bixa] *nf* beam, rafter; (*de metal*) girder

vigencia [bi'xenθja] *nf* validity; **estar en ~** to be in force; **vigente** *adj* valid, in force; (*imperante*) prevailing

vigésimo, -a [bi'xesimo, a] *adj* twentieth

vigía [bi'xia] *nm* look-out

vigilancia [bixi'lanθja] *nf*: **tener a algn bajo ~** to keep watch on sb

vigilar [bixi'lar] *vt* to watch over ▷ *vi* (*gen*) to be vigilant; (*hacer guardia*) to keep watch; **~ por** to take care of

vigilia [vi'xilja] *nf* wakefulness, being awake; (*Rel*) fast

vigor [bi'xor] *nm* vigour, vitality; **en ~** in force; **entrar/poner en ~** to come/put into effect; **vigoroso, -a** *adj* vigorous

VIH *nm abr* (= *virus de la inmunodeficiencia humana*) HIV; **VIH negativo/positivo** HIV-negative/-positive

vil [bil] *adj* vile, low

villa ['biʎa] *nf* (*casa*) villa; (*pueblo*) small town; (*municipalidad*) municipality

villancico [biʎan'θiko] *nm* (Christmas) carol

vilo ['bilo]: **en ~** *adv* in the air, suspended; (*fig*) on tenterhooks, in suspense

vinagre [bi'naxre] *nm* vinegar

vinagreta [bina'xreta] *nf* vinaigrette, French dressing

vinculación [binkula'θjon] *nf* (*lazo*) link, bond; (*acción*) linking

vincular [binku'lar] *vt* to link, bind; **vínculo** *nm* link, bond

vine *etc vb* V **venir**

vinicultura [binikul'tura] *nf* wine growing

viniera *etc vb* V **venir**

vino ['bino] *vb* V **venir** ▷ *nm* wine; **vino blanco/tinto** white/red wine

viña ['biɲa] *nf* vineyard; **viñedo** *nm* vineyard

viola ['bjola] *nf* viola

violación [bjola'θjon] *nf* violation; (*sexual*) rape

violar [bjo'lar] *vt* to violate; (*sexualmente*) to rape

violencia [bjo'lenθja] *nf* violence, force; (*incomodidad*) embarrassment; (*acto injusto*) unjust act; **violentar** *vt* to force; (*casa*) to break into; (*agredir*) to assault; (*violar*) to violate; **violento, -a** *adj* violent; (*furioso*) furious; (*situación*) embarrassing; (*acto*) forced, unnatural

violeta [bjo'leta] *nf* violet

violín [bjo'lin] *nm* violin

violón [bjo'lon] *nm* double bass

virar [bi'rar] *vi* to change direction

virgen ['birxen] *adj, nf* virgin

Virgo ['birxo] *nm* Virgo

viril [bi'ril] *adj* virile; **virilidad** *nf* virility

virtud [bir'tuð] *nf* virtue; **en ~ de** by virtue of; **virtuoso, -a** *adj* virtuous ▷ *nm/f* virtuoso

viruela [bi'rwela] *nf* smallpox

virulento, -a [biru'lento, a] *adj* virulent

virus ['birus] *nm inv* virus

visa ['bisa] (*LAM*) *nf* = **visado**

visado [bi'saðo] (*ESP*) *nm* visa

víscera ['bisθera] *nf* (*Anat, Zool*) gut, bowel; **vísceras** *nfpl* entrails

visceral [bisθe'ral] *adj* (*odio*) intense; **reacción ~** gut reaction

visera [bi'sera] *nf* visor

visibilidad [bisiβili'ðað] *nf* visibility; **visible** *adj* visible; (*fig*) obvious

visillos [bi'siʎos] *nmpl* lace curtains

visión [bi'sjon] *nf* (*Anat*) vision, (eye)sight; (*fantasía*) vision, fantasy

visita [bi'sita] *nf* call, visit; (*persona*) visitor; **hacer una ~** to pay a visit; **visitar** [bisi'tar] *vt* to visit, call on

visón [bi'son] *nm* mink

visor [bi'sor] *nm* (*Foto*) viewfinder

víspera ['bispera] *nf*: **la ~ de ...** the day before ...

vista ['bista] *nf* sight, vision; (*capacidad de ver*) (eye)sight; (*mirada*) look(s) (*pl*); **a primera ~** at first glance; **hacer la ~ gorda** to turn a blind eye; **volver la ~** to look back; **está a la ~ que** it's obvious that; **en ~ de** in view of; **en ~ de que** in view of the fact that; **¡hasta la ~!** so long!, see you!; **con ~s**

a with a view to; **vistazo** *nm* glance; **dar** *o* **echar un vistazo a** to glance at

visto, -a ['bisto, a] *pp de* **ver** ▷ *vb* V *tb* **vestir** ▷ *adj* seen; (*considerado*) considered ▷ *nm*: **~ bueno** approval; **por lo ~** apparently; **está ~ que** it's clear that; **está bien/mal ~** it's acceptable/unacceptable; **~ que** since, considering that

vistoso, -a [bis'toso, a] *adj* colourful

visual [bi'swal] *adj* visual

vital [bi'tal] *adj* life *cpd*, living *cpd*; (*fig*) vital; (*persona*) lively, vivacious; **vitalicio, -a** [bita'liθjo, a] *adj* for life; **vitalidad** *nf* (*de persona, negocio*) energy; (*de ciudad*) liveliness

vitamina [bita'mina] *nf* vitamin

vitorear [bitore'ar] *vt* to cheer, acclaim

vitrina [bi'trina] *nf* show case; (*LAM: escaparate*) shop window

viudo, -a ['bjuðo, a] *nm/f* widower/widow

viva ['biβa] *excl* hurrah!; **¡~ el rey!** long live the king!

vivaracho, -a [biβa'ratʃo, a] *adj* jaunty, lively; (*ojos*) bright, twinkling

vivaz [bi'βaθ] *adj* lively

víveres ['biβeres] *nmpl* provisions

vivero [bi'βero] *nm* (*para plantas*) nursery; (*para peces*) fish farm; (*fig*) hotbed

viveza [bi'βeθa] *nf* liveliness; (*agudeza: mental*) sharpness

vivienda [bi'βjenda] *nf* housing; (*una vivienda*) house; (*piso*) flat (BRIT), apartment (US)

viviente [bi'βjente] *adj* living

vivir [bi'βir] *vt, vi* to live ▷ *nm* life, living

vivo, -a ['biβo, a] *adj* living, alive; (*fig: descripción*) vivid; (*persona: astuto*) smart, clever; **en ~** (*transmisión etc*) live

vocablo [bo'kaβlo] *nm* (*palabra*) word; (*término*) term

vocabulario [bokaβu'larjo] *nm* vocabulary

vocación [boka'θjon] *nf* vocation;

vocacional (LAM) *nf* ≈ technical college

vocal [bo'kal] *adj* vocal ▷ *nf* vowel; **vocalizar** *vt* to vocalize

vocero [bo'θero] (LAM) *nmf* spokesman/woman

voces ['boθes] *pl de* **voz**

vodka ['boðka] *nm o f* vodka

vol *abr* = **volumen**

volado [bo'laðo] (MÉX) *adv* in a rush, hastily

volador, a [bola'ðor, a] *adj* flying

volandas [bo'landas]: **en ~** *adv* in the air

volante [bo'lante] *adj* flying ▷ *nm* (*de coche*) steering wheel; (*de reloj*) balance

volar [bo'lar] *vt* (*edificio*) to blow up ▷ *vi* to fly

volátil [bo'latil] *adj* volatile

volcán [bol'kan] *nm* volcano; **volcánico, -a** *adj* volcanic

volcar [bol'kar] *vt* to upset, overturn; (*tumbar, derribar*) to knock over; (*vaciar*) to empty out ▷ *vi* to overturn; **volcarse** *vr* to tip over

voleibol [bolei'βol] *nm* volleyball

volqué *etc vb* V **volcar**

voltaje [bol'taxe] *nm* voltage

voltear [bolte'ar] *vt* to turn over; (*volcar*) to turn upside down

voltereta [bolte'reta] *nf* somersault

voltio ['boltjo] *nm* volt

voluble [bo'luβle] *adj* fickle

volumen [bo'lumen] (*pl* **volúmenes**) *nm* volume; **voluminoso, -a** *adj* voluminous; (*enorme*) massive

voluntad [bolun'tað] *nf* will; (*resolución*) willpower; (*deseo*) desire, wish

voluntario, -a [bolun'tarjo, a] *adj* voluntary ▷ *nm/f* volunteer

volver [bol'βer] *vt* (*gen*) to turn; (*dar vuelta a*) to turn (over); (*voltear*) to turn round, turn upside down; (*poner al revés*) to turn inside out; (*devolver*) to return ▷ *vi* to return, go back, come back; **volverse** *vr* to turn round; **~ la**

espalda to turn one's back; **~ triste** *etc*
a algn to make sb sad *etc*; **~ a hacer**
to do again; **~ en sí** to come to; **~se**
insoportable/muy caro to get *o*
become unbearable/very expensive;
~se loco to go mad

vomitar [bomi'tar] *vt, vi* to vomit;
vómito *nm* vomit

voraz [bo'raθ] *adj* voracious

vos [bos] (*LAM*) *pron* you

vosotros, -as [bo'sotros, as] (*ESP*)
pron you; (*reflexivo*): **entre/para ~**
among/for yourselves

votación [bota'θjon] *nf* (*acto*) voting;
(*voto*) vote

votar [bo'tar] *vi* to vote; **voto** *nm*
vote; (*promesa*) vow; **votos** *nmpl*
(good) wishes

voy *vb* V **ir**

voz [boθ] *nf* voice; (*grito*) shout;
(*rumor*) rumour; (*Ling*) word; **dar voces**
to shout, yell; **de viva ~** verbally; **en ~**
alta aloud; **en ~ baja** in a low voice, in
a whisper; **voz de mando** command

vuelco ['bwelko] *vb* V **volcar** ▷ *nm*
spill, overturning

vuelo ['bwelo] *vb* V **volar** ▷ *nm*
flight; (*encaje*) lace, frill; **coger al ~** to
catch in flight; **vuelo chárter/regular**
charter/scheduled flight; **vuelo libre**
(*Deporte*) hang-gliding

vuelque *etc vb* V **volcar**

vuelta ['bwelta] *nf* (*gen*) turn; (*curva*)
bend, curve; (*regreso*) return; (*revolución*)
revolution; (*de circuito*) lap; (*de papel,*
tela) reverse; (*cambio*) change; **a la ~**
on one's return; **a la ~ (de la esquina)**
round the corner; **a ~ de correo** by
return of post; **dar ~s** (*cabeza*) to spin;
dar(se) la ~ (*volverse*) to turn round;
dar ~s a una idea to turn over an idea
(in one's head); **estar de ~** to be back;
dar una ~ to go for a walk; (*en coche*) to
go for a drive; **vuelta ciclista** (*Deporte*)
(cycle) tour

vuelto ['bwelto] *pp de* **volver**

vuelvo *etc vb* V **volver**

vuestro, -a ['bwestro, a] *adj pos*
your; **un amigo ~** a friend of yours
▷ *pron*: **el ~/la vuestra, los ~s/las**
vuestras yours

vulgar [bul'ɣar] *adj* (*ordinario*)
vulgar; (*común*) common; **vulgaridad**
nf commonness; (*acto*) vulgarity;
(*expresión*) coarse expression

vulnerable [bulne'raβle] *adj*
vulnerable

vulnerar [bulne'rar] *vt* (*ley, acuerdo*)
to violate, breach; (*derechos, intimidad*)
to violate; (*reputación*) to damage

W X

walkie-talkie [walki-'talki] (pl ~s)
   nm walkie-talkie
Walkman® ['walkman] nm
   Walkman®
wáter ['bater] nm (taza) toilet;
   (LAM: lugar) toilet (BRIT), rest room (US)
web [web] nm o f (página) website;
   (red) (World Wide) Web; **webcam**
   nf webcam; **webmaster** nmf
   webmaster; **website** nm website
western ['western] (pl ~s) nm
   western
whisky ['wiski] nm whisky, whiskey
windsurf ['winsurf] nm
   windsurfing; **hacer ~** to go
   windsurfing

xenofobia [kseno'foβja] nf
   xenophobia
xilófono [ksi'lofono] nm xylophone
xocoyote, -a [ksoko'yote, a] (MÉX)
   nm/f baby of the family, youngest child

yuca ['juka] *nf* (*alimento*) cassava, manioc root
Yugoslavia [juɣos'laβja] *nf* (*Hist*) Yugoslavia
yugular [juɣu'lar] *adj* jugular
yunque ['junke] *nm* anvil
yuyo ['jujo] (*RPL*) *nm* (*mala hierba*) weed

y [i] *conj* and
ya [ja] *adv* (*gen*) already; (*ahora*) now; (*en seguida*) at once; (*pronto*) soon ▷ *excl* all right! ▷ *conj* (*ahora que*) now that; **~ lo sé** I know; **~ que ...** since; **¡~ está bien!** that's (quite) enough!; **¡~ voy!** coming!
yacaré [jaka're] (*cs*) *nm* cayman
yacer [ja'θer] *vi* to lie
yacimiento [jaθi'mjento] *nm* (*de mineral*) deposit; (*arqueológico*) site
yanqui ['janki] *adj*, *nmf* Yankee
yate ['jate] *nm* yacht
yazco *etc vb* V **yacer**
yedra ['jeðra] *nf* ivy
yegua ['jeɣwa] *nf* mare
yema ['jema] *nf* (*del huevo*) yolk; (*Bot*) leaf bud; (*fig*) best part; **yema del dedo** fingertip
yerno ['jerno] *nm* son-in-law
yeso ['jeso] *nm* plaster
yo [jo] *pron* I; **soy ~** it's me
yodo ['joðo] *nm* iodine
yoga ['joɣa] *nm* yoga
yogur(t) [jo'ɣur(t)] *nm* yoghurt

Z

zafar [θa'far] *vt* (*soltar*) to untie; (*superficie*) to clear; **zafarse** *vr* (*escaparse*) to escape; (*Tec*) to slip off

zafiro [θa'firo] *nm* sapphire

zaga ['θaɣa] *nf*: **a la ~** behind

zaguán [θa'ɣwan] *nm* hallway

zalamero, -a [θala'mero, a] *adj* flattering; (*cobista*) suave

zamarra [θa'marra] *nf* (*chaqueta*) sheepskin jacket

zambullirse [θambu'ʎirse] *vr* to dive

zampar [θam'par] *vt* to gobble down

zanahoria [θana'orja] *nf* carrot

zancadilla [θanka'ðiʎa] *nf* trip

zanco ['θanko] *nm* stilt

zanja ['θanxa] *nf* ditch; **zanjar** *vt* (*resolver*) to resolve

zapata [θa'pata] *nf* (*Mecánica*) shoe

zapatería [θapate'ria] *nf* (*oficio*) shoemaking; (*tienda*) shoe shop; (*fábrica*) shoe factory; **zapatero, -a** *nm/f* shoemaker

zapatilla [θapa'tiʎa] *nf* slipper; **zapatilla de deporte** training shoe

zapato [θa'pato] *nm* shoe

zapping ['θapin] *nm* channel-hopping; **hacer ~** to channel-hop

zar [θar] *nm* tsar, czar

zarandear [θaranðe'ar] (*fam*) *vt* to shake vigorously

zarpa ['θarpa] *nf* (*garra*) claw

zarpar [θar'par] *vi* to weigh anchor

zarza ['θarθa] *nf* (*Bot*) bramble; **zarzamora** *nf* blackberry

zarzuela [θar'θwela] *nf* Spanish light opera

zigzag [θiɣ'θaɣ] *nm* zigzag

zinc [θink] *nm* zinc

zíper ['θiper] (*MÉX, CAM*) *nm* zip (fastener) (*BRIT*), zipper (*US*)

zócalo ['θokalo] *nm* (*Arq*) plinth, base; (*de pared*) skirting board (*BRIT*), baseboard (*US*); (*MÉX: plaza*) main o public square

zoclo ['θoklo] (*MÉX*) *nm* skirting board (*BRIT*), baseboard (*US*)

zodíaco [θo'ðiako] *nm* zodiac

zona ['θona] *nf* zone; **zona fronteriza** border area; **zona roja** (*LAM*) red-light district

zonzo, -a (*LAM: fam*) ['θonθo, a] *adj* silly ▷ *nm/f* fool

zoo ['θoo] *nm* zoo

zoología [θoolo'xia] *nf* zoology; **zoológico, -a** *adj* zoological ▷ *nm* (*tb: parque zoológico*) zoo; **zoólogo, -a** *nm/f* zoologist

zoom [θum] *nm* zoom lens

zopilote [θopi'lote] (*MÉX, CAM*) *nm* buzzard

zoquete [θo'kete] *nm* (*fam*) blockhead

zorro, -a ['θorro, a] *adj* crafty ▷ *nm/f* fox/vixen

zozobrar [θoθo'βrar] *vi* (*hundirse*) to capsize; (*fig*) to fail

zueco ['θweko] *nm* clog

zumbar [θum'bar] *vt* (*golpear*) to hit ▷ *vi* to buzz; **zumbido** *nm* buzzing

zumo ['θumo] *nm* juice

zurcir [θur'θir] *vt* (*coser*) to darn

zurdo, -a ['θurðo, a] *adj* left-handed

zurrar [θu'rrar] (*fam*) *vt* to wallop

Introduction

The **Verb Tables** in the following section contain 31 tables of the most common Spanish verbs (some regular, some irregular and some which change their stems) in alphabetical order. Each table shows you the following tenses and forms: **Present**, **Preterite**, **Future**, **Present Subjunctive**, **Imperfect**, **Conditional**, **Imperative**, **Past Participle** and **Gerund**.

In order to help you use the verbs shown in the Verb Tables correctly, there are also a number of example phrases at the bottom of each page to show the verb as it is used in context.

In Spanish there are **regular** verbs (their forms follow the normal rules); **irregular** verbs (their forms do not follow the normal rules); and verbs which change a vowel in their stem (the part that is left when you take off the ending) in fairly predictable ways. The regular verbs in these tables are:

hablar (regular -**ar** verb, Verb Table 12)
comer (regular -**er** verb, Verb Table 3)
vivir (regular -**ir** verb, Verb Table 31)
lavarse (regular -**ar** reflexive verb, Verb Table 15)

For a list of other Spanish irregular and stem-changing verb forms see pages 33–34.

The key at the top of page 33 explains which verb tenses or forms are shown on pages 33-34. For instance, **7** refers to the past participle. So, when you see abrir **7** abierto, you know that abrir has the irregular past participle *abierto*. Only irregular forms are listed. So, **4** busqué, at buscar, means that although *busqué* is irregular (the spelling changes to keep the [k] sound before the letter 'e'), the rest of the preterite tense behaves like any regular -**ar** verb: *busqué, buscaste, buscó, buscamos, buscasteis, buscaron*.

▶ **coger** (to take, to catch)

PRESENT

(yo)	cojo
(tú)	coges
(él/ella/usted)	coge
(nosotros/as)	cogemos
(vosotros/as)	cogéis
(ellos/ellas/ustedes)	cogen

PRESENT SUBJUNCTIVE

(yo)	coja
(tú)	cojas
(él/ella/usted)	coja
(nosotros/as)	cojamos
(vosotros/as)	cojáis
(ellos/ellas/ustedes)	cojan

PRETERITE

(yo)	cogí
(tú)	cogiste
(él/ella/usted)	cogió
(nosotros/as)	cogimos
(vosotros/as)	cogisteis
(ellos/ellas/ustedes)	cogieron

IMPERFECT

(yo)	cogía
(tú)	cogías
(él/ella/usted)	cogía
(nosotros/as)	cogíamos
(vosotros/as)	cogíais
(ellos/ellas/ustedes)	cogían

FUTURE

(yo)	cogeré
(tú)	cogerás
(él/ella/usted)	cogerá
(nosotros/as)	cogeremos
(vosotros/as)	cogeréis
(ellos/ellas/ustedes)	cogerán

CONDITIONAL

(yo)	cogería
(tú)	cogerías
(él/ella/usted)	cogería
(nosotros/as)	cogeríamos
(vosotros/as)	cogeríais
(ellos/ellas/ustedes)	cogerían

IMPERATIVE

coge / coged

PAST PARTICIPLE

cogido

GERUND

cogiendo

EXAMPLE PHRASES

*La **cogí** entre mis brazos.* I took her in my arms.
*Estuvimos **cogiendo** setas.* We were picking mushrooms.
*¿Por qué no **coges** el tren de las seis?* Why don't you get the six o'clock train?

Remember that subject pronouns are not used very often in Spanish.

▶ **comer** (to eat)

PRESENT

(yo)	como
(tú)	comes
(él/ella/usted)	come
(nosotros/as)	comemos
(vosotros/as)	coméis
(ellos/ellas/ustedes)	comen

PRESENT SUBJUNCTIVE

(yo)	coma
(tú)	comas
(él/ella/usted)	coma
(nosotros/as)	comamos
(vosotros/as)	comáis
(ellos/ellas/ustedes)	coman

PRETERITE

(yo)	comí
(tú)	comiste
(él/ella/usted)	comió
(nosotros/as)	comimos
(vosotros/as)	comisteis
(ellos/ellas/ustedes)	comieron

IMPERFECT

(yo)	comía
(tú)	comías
(él/ella/usted)	comía
(nosotros/as)	comíamos
(vosotros/as)	comíais
(ellos/ellas/ustedes)	comían

FUTURE

(yo)	comeré
(tú)	comerás
(él/ella/usted)	comerá
(nosotros/as)	comeremos
(vosotros/as)	comeréis
(ellos/ellas/ustedes)	comerán

CONDITIONAL

(yo)	comería
(tú)	comerías
(él/ella/usted)	comería
(nosotros/as)	comeríamos
(vosotros/as)	comeríais
(ellos/ellas/ustedes)	comerían

IMPERATIVE

come / comed

PAST PARTICIPLE

comido

GERUND

comiendo

EXAMPLE PHRASES

*No **come** carne.* He doesn't eat meat.
*No **comas** tan deprisa.* Don't eat so fast.
***Se ha comido** todo.* He's eaten it all.

Remember that subject pronouns are not used very often in Spanish.

▶ **dar** (to give)

PRESENT

(yo)	doy
(tú)	das
(él/ella/usted)	da
(nosotros/as)	damos
(vosotros/as)	dais
(ellos/ellas/ustedes)	dan

PRESENT SUBJUNCTIVE

(yo)	dé
(tú)	des
(él/ella/usted)	dé
(nosotros/as)	demos
(vosotros/as)	deis
(ellos/ellas/ustedes)	den

PRETERITE

(yo)	di
(tú)	diste
(él/ella/usted)	dio
(nosotros/as)	dimos
(vosotros/as)	disteis
(ellos/ellas/ustedes)	dieron

IMPERFECT

(yo)	daba
(tú)	dabas
(él/ella/usted)	daba
(nosotros/as)	dábamos
(vosotros/as)	dabais
(ellos/ellas/ustedes)	daban

FUTURE

(yo)	daré
(tú)	darás
(él/ella/usted)	dará
(nosotros/as)	daremos
(vosotros/as)	daréis
(ellos/ellas/ustedes)	darán

CONDITIONAL

(yo)	daría
(tú)	darías
(él/ella/usted)	daría
(nosotros/as)	daríamos
(vosotros/as)	daríais
(ellos/ellas/ustedes)	darían

IMPERATIVE

da / dad

PAST PARTICIPLE

dado

GERUND

dando

EXAMPLE PHRASES

*Me **da** miedo la oscuridad.* I'm scared of the dark.
*Nos **dieron** un par de entradas gratis.* They gave us a couple of free tickets.
*Te **daré** el número de mi móvil.* I'll give you my mobile-phone number.

Remember that subject pronouns are not used very often in Spanish.

▶ **decir** (to say, to tell)

PRESENT

(yo)	digo
(tú)	dices
(él/ella/usted)	dice
(nosotros/as)	decimos
(vosotros/as)	decís
(ellos/ellas/ustedes)	dicen

PRESENT SUBJUNCTIVE

(yo)	diga
(tú)	digas
(él/ella/usted)	diga
(nosotros/as)	digamos
(vosotros/as)	digáis
(ellos/ellas/ustedes)	digan

PRETERITE

(yo)	dije
(tú)	dijiste
(él/ella/usted)	dijo
(nosotros/as)	dijimos
(vosotros/as)	dijisteis
(ellos/ellas/ustedes)	dijeron

IMPERFECT

(yo)	decía
(tú)	decías
(él/ella/usted)	decía
(nosotros/as)	decíamos
(vosotros/as)	decíais
(ellos/ellas/ustedes)	decían

FUTURE

(yo)	diré
(tú)	dirás
(él/ella/usted)	dirá
(nosotros/as)	diremos
(vosotros/as)	diréis
(ellos/ellas/ustedes)	dirán

CONDITIONAL

(yo)	diría
(tú)	dirías
(él/ella/usted)	diría
(nosotros/as)	diríamos
(vosotros/as)	diríais
(ellos/ellas/ustedes)	dirían

IMPERATIVE

di / decid

PAST PARTICIPLE

dicho

GERUND

diciendo

EXAMPLE PHRASES

¿Qué **dices**? What are you saying?
Me lo **dijo** ayer. He told me yesterday.
¿Te **ha dicho** lo de la boda? Has he told you about the wedding?

Remember that subject pronouns are not used very often in Spanish.

▶ **dormir** (to sleep)

PRESENT

(yo)	duermo
(tú)	duermes
(él/ella/usted)	duerme
(nosotros/as)	dormimos
(vosotros/as)	dormís
(ellos/ellas/ustedes)	duermen

PRESENT SUBJUNCTIVE

(yo)	duerma
(tú)	duermas
(él/ella/usted)	duerma
(nosotros/as)	durmamos
(vosotros/as)	durmáis
(ellos/ellas/ustedes)	duerman

PRETERITE

(yo)	dormí
(tú)	dormiste
(él/ella/usted)	durmió
(nosotros/as)	dormimos
(vosotros/as)	dormisteis
(ellos/ellas/ustedes)	durmieron

IMPERFECT

(yo)	dormía
(tú)	dormías
(él/ella/usted)	dormía
(nosotros/as)	dormíamos
(vosotros/as)	dormíais
(ellos/ellas/ustedes)	dormían

FUTURE

(yo)	dormiré
(tú)	dormirás
(él/ella/usted)	dormirá
(nosotros/as)	dormiremos
(vosotros/as)	dormiréis
(ellos/ellas/ustedes)	dormirán

CONDITIONAL

(yo)	dormiría
(tú)	dormirías
(él/ella/usted)	dormiría
(nosotros/as)	dormiríamos
(vosotros/as)	dormiríais
(ellos/ellas/ustedes)	dormirían

IMPERATIVE

duerme / dormid

PAST PARTICIPLE

dormido

GERUND

durmiendo

EXAMPLE PHRASES

No **duermo** muy bien. I don't sleep very well.
Nos dormimos en el cine. We fell asleep at the cinema.
Durmió durante doce horas. He slept for twelve hours.

Remember that subject pronouns are not used very often in Spanish.

▶ **empezar** (to begin, to start)

PRESENT

(yo)	empiezo
(tú)	empiezas
(él/ella/usted)	empieza
(nosotros/as)	empezamos
(vosotros/as)	empezáis
(ellos/ellas/ustedes)	empiezan

PRESENT SUBJUNCTIVE

(yo)	empiece
(tú)	empieces
(él/ella/usted)	empiece
(nosotros/as)	empecemos
(vosotros/as)	empecéis
(ellos/ellas/ustedes)	empiecen

PRETERITE

(yo)	empecé
(tú)	empezaste
(él/ella/usted)	empezó
(nosotros/as)	empezamos
(vosotros/as)	empezasteis
(ellos/ellas/ustedes)	empezaron

IMPERFECT

(yo)	empezaba
(tú)	empezabas
(él/ella/usted)	empezaba
(nosotros/as)	empezábamos
(vosotros/as)	empezabais
(ellos/ellas/ustedes)	empezaban

FUTURE

(yo)	empezaré
(tú)	empezarás
(él/ella/usted)	empezará
(nosotros/as)	empezaremos
(vosotros/as)	empezaréis
(ellos/ellas/ustedes)	empezarán

CONDITIONAL

(yo)	empezaría
(tú)	empezarías
(él/ella/usted)	empezaría
(nosotros/as)	empezaríamos
(vosotros/as)	empezaríais
(ellos/ellas/ustedes)	empezarían

IMPERATIVE

empieza / empezad

PAST PARTICIPLE

empezado

GERUND

empezando

EXAMPLE PHRASES

Empieza por aquí. Start here.

¿Cuándo empiezas a trabajar en el sitio nuevo? When do you start work at the new place?

La semana que viene empezaremos un curso nuevo. We'll start a new course next week.

Remember that subject pronouns are not used very often in Spanish.

▶ **entender** (to understand)

PRESENT

(yo)	entiendo
(tú)	entiendes
(él/ella/usted)	entiende
(nosotros/as)	entendemos
(vosotros/as)	entendéis
(ellos/ellas/ustedes)	entienden

PRESENT SUBJUNCTIVE

(yo)	entienda
(tú)	entiendas
(él/ella/usted)	entienda
(nosotros/as)	entendamos
(vosotros/as)	entendáis
(ellos/ellas/ustedes)	entiendan

PRETERITE

(yo)	entendí
(tú)	entendiste
(él/ella/usted)	entendió
(nosotros/as)	entendimos
(vosotros/as)	entendisteis
(ellos/ellas/ustedes)	entendieron

IMPERFECT

(yo)	entendía
(tú)	entendías
(él/ella/usted)	entendía
(nosotros/as)	entendíamos
(vosotros/as)	entendíais
(ellos/ellas/ustedes)	entendían

FUTURE

(yo)	entenderé
(tú)	entenderás
(él/ella/usted)	entenderá
(nosotros/as)	entenderemos
(vosotros/as)	entenderéis
(ellos/ellas/ustedes)	entenderán

CONDITIONAL

(yo)	entendería
(tú)	entenderías
(él/ella/usted)	entendería
(nosotros/as)	entenderíamos
(vosotros/as)	entenderíais
(ellos/ellas/ustedes)	entenderían

IMPERATIVE

entiende / entended

PAST PARTICIPLE

entendido

GERUND

entendiendo

EXAMPLE PHRASES

*No lo **entiendo**.* I don't understand.
*¿**Entendiste** lo que dijo?* Did you understand what she said?
*Con el tiempo lo **entenderás**.* You'll understand one day.

Remember that subject pronouns are not used very often in Spanish.

▶ **enviar** (to send)

PRESENT

(yo)	envío
(tú)	envías
(él/ella/usted)	envía
(nosotros/as)	enviamos
(vosotros/as)	enviáis
(ellos/ellas/ustedes)	envían

PRESENT SUBJUNCTIVE

(yo)	envíe
(tú)	envíes
(él/ella/usted)	envíe
(nosotros/as)	enviemos
(vosotros/as)	enviéis
(ellos/ellas/ustedes)	envíen

PRETERITE

(yo)	envié
(tú)	enviaste
(él/ella/usted)	envió
(nosotros/as)	enviamos
(vosotros/as)	enviasteis
(ellos/ellas/ustedes)	enviaron

IMPERFECT

(yo)	enviaba
(tú)	enviabas
(él/ella/usted)	enviaba
(nosotros/as)	enviábamos
(vosotros/as)	enviabais
(ellos/ellas/ustedes)	enviaban

FUTURE

(yo)	enviaré
(tú)	enviarás
(él/ella/usted)	enviará
(nosotros/as)	enviaremos
(vosotros/as)	enviaréis
(ellos/ellas/ustedes)	enviarán

CONDITIONAL

(yo)	enviaría
(tú)	enviarías
(él/ella/usted)	enviaría
(nosotros/as)	enviaríamos
(vosotros/as)	enviaríais
(ellos/ellas/ustedes)	enviarían

IMPERATIVE

envía / enviad

PAST PARTICIPLE

enviado

GERUND

enviando

EXAMPLE PHRASES

Envíe *todos sus datos personales*. Send all your personal details.
La han **enviado** *a Guatemala*. They've sent her to Guatemala.
Nos **enviarán** *más información*. They'll send us further information.

Remember that subject pronouns are not used very often in Spanish.

▶ **estar** (to be)

PRESENT

(yo)	estoy
(tú)	estás
(él/ella/usted)	está
(nosotros/as)	estamos
(vosotros/as)	estáis
(ellos/ellas/ustedes)	están

PRESENT SUBJUNCTIVE

(yo)	esté
(tú)	estés
(él/ella/usted)	esté
(nosotros/as)	estemos
(vosotros/as)	estéis
(ellos/ellas/ustedes)	estén

PRETERITE

(yo)	estuve
(tú)	estuviste
(él/ella/usted)	estuvo
(nosotros/as)	estuvimos
(vosotros/as)	estuvisteis
(ellos/ellas/ustedes)	estuvieron

IMPERFECT

(yo)	estaba
(tú)	estabas
(él/ella/usted)	estaba
(nosotros/as)	estábamos
(vosotros/as)	estabais
(ellos/ellas/ustedes)	estaban

FUTURE

(yo)	estaré
(tú)	estarás
(él/ella/usted)	estará
(nosotros/as)	estaremos
(vosotros/as)	estaréis
(ellos/ellas/ustedes)	estarán

CONDITIONAL

(yo)	estaría
(tú)	estarías
(él/ella/usted)	estaría
(nosotros/as)	estaríamos
(vosotros/as)	estaríais
(ellos/ellas/ustedes)	estarían

IMPERATIVE

está / estad

GERUND

estando

PAST PARTICIPLE

estado

EXAMPLE PHRASES

Estoy cansado. I'm tired.
Estuvimos en casa de mis padres. We were at my parents' place.
¿A qué hora *estarás* en casa? What time will you be home?

Remember that subject pronouns are not used very often in Spanish.

▶ **haber** (to have (auxiliary))

PRESENT		**PRESENT SUBJUNCTIVE**	
(yo)	he	(yo)	haya
(tú)	has	(tú)	hayas
(él/ella/usted)	ha	(él/ella/usted)	haya
(nosotros/as)	hemos	(nosotros/as)	hayamos
(vosotros/as)	habéis	(vosotros/as)	hayáis
(ellos/ellas/ustedes)	han	(ellos/ellas/ustedes)	hayan

PRETERITE		**IMPERFECT**	
(yo)	hube	(yo)	había
(tú)	hubiste	(tú)	habías
(él/ella/usted)	hubo	(él/ella/usted)	había
(nosotros/as)	hubimos	(nosotros/as)	habíamos
(vosotros/as)	hubisteis	(vosotros/as)	habíais
(ellos/ellas/ustedes)	hubieron	(ellos/ellas/ustedes)	habían

FUTURE		**CONDITIONAL**	
(yo)	habré	(yo)	habría
(tú)	habrás	(tú)	habrías
(él/ella/usted)	habrá	(él/ella/usted)	habría
(nosotros/as)	habremos	(nosotros/as)	habríamos
(vosotros/as)	habréis	(vosotros/as)	habríais
(ellos/ellas/ustedes)	habrán	(ellos/ellas/ustedes)	habrían

IMPERATIVE	**PAST PARTICIPLE**
not used	habido

GERUND

habiendo

EXAMPLE PHRASES

*¿**Has visto** eso?* Did you see that?
*Ya **hemos ido** a ver esa película.* We've already been to see that film.
*Eso nunca **había pasado** antes.* That had never happened before.

Remember that subject pronouns are not used very often in Spanish.

▶ **hablar** (to speak, to talk)

PRESENT

(yo)	hablo
(tú)	hablas
(él/ella/usted)	habla
(nosotros/as)	hablamos
(vosotros/as)	habláis
(ellos/ellas/ustedes)	hablan

PRESENT SUBJUNCTIVE

(yo)	hable
(tú)	hables
(él/ella/usted)	hable
(nosotros/as)	hablemos
(vosotros/as)	habléis
(ellos/ellas/ustedes)	hablen

PRETERITE

(yo)	hablé
(tú)	hablaste
(él/ella/usted)	habló
(nosotros/as)	hablamos
(vosotros/as)	hablasteis
(ellos/ellas/ustedes)	hablaron

IMPERFECT

(yo)	hablaba
(tú)	hablabas
(él/ella/usted)	hablaba
(nosotros/as)	hablábamos
(vosotros/as)	hablabais
(ellos/ellas/ustedes)	hablaban

FUTURE

(yo)	hablaré
(tú)	hablarás
(él/ella/usted)	hablará
(nosotros/as)	hablaremos
(vosotros/as)	hablaréis
(ellos/ellas/ustedes)	hablarán

CONDITIONAL

(yo)	hablaría
(tú)	hablarías
(él/ella/usted)	hablaría
(nosotros/as)	hablaríamos
(vosotros/as)	hablaríais
(ellos/ellas/ustedes)	hablarían

IMPERATIVE

habla / hablad

PAST PARTICIPLE

hablado

GERUND

hablando

EXAMPLE PHRASES

*Hoy **he hablado** con mi hermana.* I've spoken to my sister today.
*No **hables** tan alto.* Don't talk so loud.
*No **se hablan**.* They don't talk to each other.

Remember that subject pronouns are not used very often in Spanish.

▶ **hacer** (to do, to make)

PRESENT

(yo)	hago
(tú)	haces
(él/ella/usted)	hace
(nosotros/as)	hacemos
(vosotros/as)	hacéis
(ellos/ellas/ustedes)	hacen

PRESENT SUBJUNCTIVE

(yo)	haga
(tú)	hagas
(él/ella/usted)	haga
(nosotros/as)	hagamos
(vosotros/as)	hagáis
(ellos/ellas/ustedes)	hagan

PRETERITE

(yo)	hice
(tú)	hiciste
(él/ella/usted)	hizo
(nosotros/as)	hicimos
(vosotros/as)	hicisteis
(ellos/ellas/ustedes)	hicieron

IMPERFECT

(yo)	hacía
(tú)	hacías
(él/ella/usted)	hacía
(nosotros/as)	hacíamos
(vosotros/as)	hacíais
(ellos/ellas/ustedes)	hacían

FUTURE

(yo)	haré
(tú)	harás
(él/ella/usted)	hará
(nosotros/as)	haremos
(vosotros/as)	haréis
(ellos/ellas/ustedes)	harán

CONDITIONAL

(yo)	haría
(tú)	harías
(él/ella/usted)	haría
(nosotros/as)	haríamos
(vosotros/as)	haríais
(ellos/ellas/ustedes)	harían

IMPERATIVE

haz / haced

PAST PARTICIPLE

hecho

GERUND

haciendo

EXAMPLE PHRASES

Lo **haré** yo mismo. *I'll do it myself.*
¿Quién **hizo** eso? *Who did that?*
¿Quieres que **haga** las camas? *Do you want me to make the beds?*

Remember that subject pronouns are not used very often in Spanish.

▶ **ir** (to go)

PRESENT

(yo)	voy
(tú)	vas
(él/ella/usted)	va
(nosotros/as)	vamos
(vosotros/as)	vais
(ellos/ellas/ustedes)	van

PRESENT SUBJUNCTIVE

(yo)	vaya
(tú)	vayas
(él/ella/usted)	vaya
(nosotros/as)	vayamos
(vosotros/as)	vayáis
(ellos/ellas/ustedes)	vayan

PRETERITE

(yo)	fui
(tú)	fuiste
(él/ella/usted)	fue
(nosotros/as)	fuimos
(vosotros/as)	fuisteis
(ellos/ellas/ustedes)	fueron

IMPERFECT

(yo)	iba
(tú)	ibas
(él/ella/usted)	iba
(nosotros/as)	íbamos
(vosotros/as)	ibais
(ellos/ellas/ustedes)	iban

FUTURE

(yo)	iré
(tú)	irás
(él/ella/usted)	irá
(nosotros/as)	iremos
(vosotros/as)	iréis
(ellos/ellas/ustedes)	irán

CONDITIONAL

(yo)	iría
(tú)	irías
(él/ella/usted)	iría
(nosotros/as)	iríamos
(vosotros/as)	iríais
(ellos/ellas/ustedes)	irían

IMPERATIVE

ve / id

PAST PARTICIPLE

ido

GERUND

yendo

EXAMPLE PHRASES

¿*Vamos* a comer al campo? Shall we have a picnic in the country?
El domingo *iré* a Edimburgo. I'll go to Edinburgh on Sunday.
Yo no *voy* con ellos. I'm not going with them.

Remember that subject pronouns are not used very often in Spanish.

▶ **lavarse** (to wash oneself)

PRESENT

(yo)	me lavo
(tú)	te lavas
(él/ella/usted)	se lava
(nosotros/as)	nos lavamos
(vosotros/as)	os laváis
(ellos/ellas/ustedes)	se lavan

PRESENT SUBJUNCTIVE

(yo)	me lave
(tú)	te laves
(él/ella/usted)	se lave
(nosotros/as)	nos lavemos
(vosotros/as)	os lavéis
(ellos/ellas/ustedes)	se laven

PRETERITE

(yo)	me lavé
(tú)	te lavaste
(él/ella/usted)	se lavó
(nosotros/as)	nos lavamos
(vosotros/as)	os lavasteis
(ellos/ellas/ustedes)	se lavaron

IMPERFECT

(yo)	me lavaba
(tú)	te lavabas
(él/ella/usted)	se lavaba
(nosotros/as)	nos lavábamos
(vosotros/as)	os lavabais
(ellos/ellas/ustedes)	se lavaban

FUTURE

(yo)	me lavaré
(tú)	te lavarás
(él/ella/usted)	se lavará
(nosotros/as)	nos lavaremos
(vosotros/as)	os lavaréis
(ellos/ellas/ustedes)	se lavarán

CONDITIONAL

(yo)	me lavaría
(tú)	te lavarías
(él/ella/usted)	se lavaría
(nosotros/as)	nos lavaríamos
(vosotros/as)	os lavaríais
(ellos/ellas/ustedes)	se lavarían

IMPERATIVE

lávate / lavaos

PAST PARTICIPLE

lavado

GERUND

lavándose

EXAMPLE PHRASES

Se lava todos los días. He washes every day.
Ayer me lavé el pelo. I washed my hair yesterday.
Nos lavaremos con agua fría. We'll wash in cold water.

Remember that subject pronouns are not used very often in Spanish.

▶ **leer** (to read)

PRESENT

(yo)	leo
(tú)	lees
(él/ella/usted)	lee
(nosotros/as)	leemos
(vosotros/as)	leéis
(ellos/ellas/ustedes)	leen

PRESENT SUBJUNCTIVE

(yo)	lea
(tú)	leas
(él/ella/usted)	lea
(nosotros/as)	leamos
(vosotros/as)	leáis
(ellos/ellas/ustedes)	lean

PRETERITE

(yo)	leí
(tú)	leíste
(él/ella/usted)	leyó
(nosotros/as)	leímos
(vosotros/as)	leísteis
(ellos/ellas/ustedes)	leyeron

IMPERFECT

(yo)	leía
(tú)	leías
(él/ella/usted)	leía
(nosotros/as)	leíamos
(vosotros/as)	leíais
(ellos/ellas/ustedes)	leían

FUTURE

(yo)	leeré
(tú)	leerás
(él/ella/usted)	leerá
(nosotros/as)	leeremos
(vosotros/as)	leeréis
(ellos/ellas/ustedes)	leerán

CONDITIONAL

(yo)	leería
(tú)	leerías
(él/ella/usted)	leería
(nosotros/as)	leeríamos
(vosotros/as)	leeríais
(ellos/ellas/ustedes)	leerían

IMPERATIVE

lee / leed

PAST PARTICIPLE

leído

GERUND

leyendo

EXAMPLE PHRASES

*Hace mucho tiempo que no **leo**.* I haven't read anything for ages.
*¿**Has leído** esta novela?* Have you read this novel?
*Lo **leí** hace tiempo.* I read it a while ago.

Remember that subject pronouns are not used very often in Spanish.

▶ oír (to hear)

PRESENT

(yo)	oigo
(tú)	oyes
(él/ella/usted)	oye
(nosotros/as)	oímos
(vosotros/as)	oís
(ellos/ellas/ustedes)	oyen

PRESENT SUBJUNCTIVE

(yo)	oiga
(tú)	oigas
(él/ella/usted)	oiga
(nosotros/as)	oigamos
(vosotros/as)	oigáis
(ellos/ellas/ustedes)	oigan

PRETERITE

(yo)	oí
(tú)	oíste
(él/ella/usted)	oyó
(nosotros/as)	oímos
(vosotros/as)	oísteis
(ellos/ellas/ustedes)	oyeron

IMPERFECT

(yo)	oía
(tú)	oías
(él/ella/usted)	oía
(nosotros/as)	oíamos
(vosotros/as)	oíais
(ellos/ellas/ustedes)	oían

FUTURE

(yo)	oiré
(tú)	oirás
(él/ella/usted)	oirá
(nosotros/as)	oiremos
(vosotros/as)	oiréis
(ellos/ellas/ustedes)	oirán

CONDITIONAL

(yo)	oiría
(tú)	oirías
(él/ella/usted)	oiría
(nosotros/as)	oiríamos
(vosotros/as)	oiríais
(ellos/ellas/ustedes)	oirían

IMPERATIVE

oye / oíd

PAST PARTICIPLE

oído

GERUND

oyendo

EXAMPLE PHRASES

*No **oigo** nada.* I can't hear anything.
*Si no **oyes** bien, ve al médico.* If you can't hear properly, go and see the doctor.
*¿**Has oído** eso?* Did you hear that?

Remember that subject pronouns are not used very often in Spanish.

▶ **pedir** (to ask for)

PRESENT

(yo)	pido
(tú)	pides
(él/ella/usted)	pide
(nosotros/as)	pedimos
(vosotros/as)	pedís
(ellos/ellas/ustedes)	piden

PRESENT SUBJUNCTIVE

(yo)	pida
(tú)	pidas
(él/ella/usted)	pida
(nosotros/as)	pidamos
(vosotros/as)	pidáis
(ellos/ellas/ustedes)	pidan

PRETERITE

(yo)	pedí
(tú)	pediste
(él/ella/usted)	pidió
(nosotros/as)	pedimos
(vosotros/as)	pedisteis
(ellos/ellas/ustedes)	pidieron

IMPERFECT

(yo)	pedía
(tú)	pedías
(él/ella/usted)	pedía
(nosotros/as)	pedíamos
(vosotros/as)	pedíais
(ellos/ellas/ustedes)	pedían

FUTURE

(yo)	pediré
(tú)	pedirás
(él/ella/usted)	pedirá
(nosotros/as)	pediremos
(vosotros/as)	pediréis
(ellos/ellas/ustedes)	pedirán

CONDITIONAL

(yo)	pediría
(tú)	pedirías
(él/ella/usted)	pediría
(nosotros/as)	pediríamos
(vosotros/as)	pediríais
(ellos/ellas/ustedes)	pedirían

IMPERATIVE

pide / pedid

PAST PARTICIPLE

pedido

GERUND

pidiendo

EXAMPLE PHRASES

*No nos **pidieron** el pasaporte*. They didn't ask us for our passports.
***Hemos pedido** dos cervezas*. We've ordered two beers.
***Pídele** el teléfono*. Ask her for her telephone number.

Remember that subject pronouns are not used very often in Spanish.

▶ **pensar** (to think)

PRESENT

(yo)	pienso
(tú)	piensas
(él/ella/usted)	piensa
(nosotros/as)	pensamos
(vosotros/as)	pensáis
(ellos/ellas/ustedes)	piensan

PRESENT SUBJUNCTIVE

(yo)	piense
(tú)	pienses
(él/ella/usted)	piense
(nosotros/as)	pensemos
(vosotros/as)	penséis
(ellos/ellas/ustedes)	piensen

PRETERITE

(yo)	pensé
(tú)	pensaste
(él/ella/usted)	pensó
(nosotros/as)	pensamos
(vosotros/as)	pensasteis
(ellos/ellas/ustedes)	pensaron

IMPERFECT

(yo)	pensaba
(tú)	pensabas
(él/ella/usted)	pensaba
(nosotros/as)	pensábamos
(vosotros/as)	pensabais
(ellos/ellas/ustedes)	pensaban

FUTURE

(yo)	pensaré
(tú)	pensarás
(él/ella/usted)	pensará
(nosotros/as)	pensaremos
(vosotros/as)	pensaréis
(ellos/ellas/ustedes)	pensarán

CONDITIONAL

(yo)	pensaría
(tú)	pensarías
(él/ella/usted)	pensaría
(nosotros/as)	pensaríamos
(vosotros/as)	pensaríais
(ellos/ellas/ustedes)	pensarían

IMPERATIVE

piensa / pensad

PAST PARTICIPLE

pensado

GERUND

pensando

EXAMPLE PHRASES

No lo **pienses** más. Don't think any more about it.
Está pensando en comprarse un piso. He's thinking of buying a flat.
Pensaba que vendrías. I thought you'd come.

Remember that subject pronouns are not used very often in Spanish.

▶ **poder** (to be able to)

PRESENT

(yo)	puedo
(tú)	puedes
(él/ella/usted)	puede
(nosotros/as)	podemos
(vosotros/as)	podéis
(ellos/ellas/ustedes)	pueden

PRESENT SUBJUNCTIVE

(yo)	pueda
(tú)	puedas
(él/ella/usted)	pueda
(nosotros/as)	podamos
(vosotros/as)	podáis
(ellos/ellas/ustedes)	puedan

PRETERITE

(yo)	pude
(tú)	pudiste
(él/ella/usted)	pudo
(nosotros/as)	pudimos
(vosotros/as)	pudisteis
(ellos/ellas/ustedes)	pudieron

IMPERFECT

(yo)	podía
(tú)	podías
(él/ella/usted)	podía
(nosotros/as)	podíamos
(vosotros/as)	podíais
(ellos/ellas/ustedes)	podían

FUTURE

(yo)	podré
(tú)	podrás
(él/ella/usted)	podrá
(nosotros/as)	podremos
(vosotros/as)	podréis
(ellos/ellas/ustedes)	podrán

CONDITIONAL

(yo)	podría
(tú)	podrías
(él/ella/usted)	podría
(nosotros/as)	podríamos
(vosotros/as)	podríais
(ellos/ellas/ustedes)	podrían

IMPERATIVE

puede / poded

PAST PARTICIPLE

podido

GERUND

pudiendo

EXAMPLE PHRASES

*¿**Puedo** entrar?* Can I come in?
***Puedes** venir cuando quieras.* You can come when you like.
*¿**Podrías** ayudarme?* Could you help me?

Remember that subject pronouns are not used very often in Spanish.

▶ **poner** (to put)

PRESENT

(yo)	pongo
(tú)	pones
(él/ella/usted)	pone
(nosotros/as)	ponemos
(vosotros/as)	ponéis
(ellos/ellas/ustedes)	ponen

PRESENT SUBJUNCTIVE

(yo)	ponga
(tú)	pongas
(él/ella/usted)	ponga
(nosotros/as)	pongamos
(vosotros/as)	pongáis
(ellos/ellas/ustedes)	pongan

PRETERITE

(yo)	puse
(tú)	pusiste
(él/ella/usted)	puso
(nosotros/as)	pusimos
(vosotros/as)	pusisteis
(ellos/ellas/ustedes)	pusieron

IMPERFECT

(yo)	ponía
(tú)	ponías
(él/ella/usted)	ponía
(nosotros/as)	poníamos
(vosotros/as)	poníais
(ellos/ellas/ustedes)	ponían

FUTURE

(yo)	pondré
(tú)	pondrás
(él/ella/usted)	pondrá
(nosotros/as)	pondremos
(vosotros/as)	pondréis
(ellos/ellas/ustedes)	pondrán

CONDITIONAL

(yo)	pondría
(tú)	pondrías
(él/ella/usted)	pondría
(nosotros/as)	pondríamos
(vosotros/as)	pondríais
(ellos/ellas/ustedes)	pondrían

IMPERATIVE

pon / poned

PAST PARTICIPLE

puesto

GERUND

poniendo

EXAMPLE PHRASES

Ponlo *ahí encima.* Put it on there.
Lo **pondré** *aquí.* I'll put it here.
Todos **nos pusimos** *de acuerdo.* We all agreed.

Remember that subject pronouns are not used very often in Spanish.

▶ **querer** (to want, to love)

PRESENT

(yo)	quiero
(tú)	quieres
(él/ella/usted)	quiere
(nosotros/as)	queremos
(vosotros/as)	queréis
(ellos/ellas/ustedes)	quieren

PRESENT SUBJUNCTIVE

(yo)	quiera
(tú)	quieras
(él/ella/usted)	quiera
(nosotros/as)	queramos
(vosotros/as)	queráis
(ellos/ellas/ustedes)	quieran

PRETERITE

(yo)	quise
(tú)	quisiste
(él/ella/usted)	quiso
(nosotros/as)	quisimos
(vosotros/as)	quisisteis
(ellos/ellas/ustedes)	quisieron

IMPERFECT

(yo)	quería
(tú)	querías
(él/ella/usted)	quería
(nosotros/as)	queríamos
(vosotros/as)	queríais
(ellos/ellas/ustedes)	querían

FUTURE

(yo)	querré
(tú)	querrás
(él/ella/usted)	querrá
(nosotros/as)	querremos
(vosotros/as)	querréis
(ellos/ellas/ustedes)	querrán

CONDITIONAL

(yo)	querría
(tú)	querrías
(él/ella/usted)	querría
(nosotros/as)	querríamos
(vosotros/as)	querríais
(ellos/ellas/ustedes)	querrían

IMPERATIVE

quiere / quered

PAST PARTICIPLE

querido

GERUND

queriendo

EXAMPLE PHRASES

Te **quiero**. I love you.
Quisiera preguntar una cosa. I'd like to ask something.
No **quería** decírmelo. She didn't want to tell me.

Remember that subject pronouns are not used very often in Spanish.

▶ **saber** (to know)

PRESENT

(yo)	sé
(tú)	sabes
(él/ella/usted)	sabe
(nosotros/as)	sabemos
(vosotros/as)	sabéis
(ellos/ellas/ustedes)	saben

PRESENT SUBJUNCTIVE

(yo)	sepa
(tú)	sepas
(él/ella/usted)	sepa
(nosotros/as)	sepamos
(vosotros/as)	sepáis
(ellos/ellas/ustedes)	sepan

PRETERITE

(yo)	supe
(tú)	supiste
(él/ella/usted)	supo
(nosotros/as)	supimos
(vosotros/as)	supisteis
(ellos/ellas/ustedes)	supieron

IMPERFECT

(yo)	sabía
(tú)	sabías
(él/ella/usted)	sabía
(nosotros/as)	sabíamos
(vosotros/as)	sabíais
(ellos/ellas/ustedes)	sabían

FUTURE

(yo)	sabré
(tú)	sabrás
(él/ella/usted)	sabrá
(nosotros/as)	sabremos
(vosotros/as)	sabréis
(ellos/ellas/ustedes)	sabrán

CONDITIONAL

(yo)	sabría
(tú)	sabrías
(él/ella/usted)	sabría
(nosotros/as)	sabríamos
(vosotros/as)	sabríais
(ellos/ellas/ustedes)	sabrían

IMPERATIVE

sabe / sabed

PAST PARTICIPLE

sabido

GERUND

sabiendo

EXAMPLE PHRASES

*No lo **sé**.* I don't know.
*¿**Sabes** una cosa?* Do you know what?
*Pensaba que lo **sabías**.* I thought you knew.

Remember that subject pronouns are not used very often in Spanish.

▶ **seguir** (to follow)

PRESENT

(yo)	sigo
(tú)	sigues
(él/ella/usted)	sigue
(nosotros/as)	seguimos
(vosotros/as)	seguís
(ellos/ellas/ustedes)	siguen

PRESENT SUBJUNCTIVE

(yo)	siga
(tú)	sigas
(él/ella/usted)	siga
(nosotros/as)	sigamos
(vosotros/as)	sigáis
(ellos/ellas/ustedes)	sigan

PRETERITE

(yo)	seguí
(tú)	seguiste
(él/ella/usted)	siguió
(nosotros/as)	seguimos
(vosotros/as)	seguisteis
(ellos/ellas/ustedes)	siguieron

IMPERFECT

(yo)	seguía
(tú)	seguías
(él/ella/usted)	seguía
(nosotros/as)	seguíamos
(vosotros/as)	seguíais
(ellos/ellas/ustedes)	seguían

FUTURE

(yo)	seguiré
(tú)	seguirás
(él/ella/usted)	seguirá
(nosotros/as)	seguiremos
(vosotros/as)	seguiréis
(ellos/ellas/ustedes)	seguirán

CONDITIONAL

(yo)	seguiría
(tú)	seguirías
(él/ella/usted)	seguiría
(nosotros/as)	seguiríamos
(vosotros/as)	seguiríais
(ellos/ellas/ustedes)	seguirían

IMPERATIVE

sigue / seguid

PAST PARTICIPLE

seguido

GERUND

siguiendo

EXAMPLE PHRASES

Siga por esta calle hasta el final. Go on till you get to the end of the street.
*Nos **seguiremos** viendo.* We will go on seeing each other.
*Nos **siguió** todo el camino.* He followed us all the way.

Remember that subject pronouns are not used very often in Spanish.

▶ **sentir** (to feel)

PRESENT

(yo)	siento
(tú)	sientes
(él/ella/usted)	siente
(nosotros/as)	sentimos
(vosotros/as)	sentís
(ellos/ellas/ustedes)	sienten

PRESENT SUBJUNCTIVE

(yo)	sienta
(tú)	sientas
(él/ella/usted)	sienta
(nosotros/as)	sintamos
(vosotros/as)	sintáis
(ellos/ellas/ustedes)	sientan

PRETERITE

(yo)	sentí
(tú)	sentiste
(él/ella/usted)	sintió
(nosotros/as)	sentimos
(vosotros/as)	sentisteis
(ellos/ellas/ustedes)	sintieron

IMPERFECT

(yo)	sentía
(tú)	sentías
(él/ella/usted)	sentía
(nosotros/as)	sentíamos
(vosotros/as)	sentíais
(ellos/ellas/ustedes)	sentían

FUTURE

(yo)	sentiré
(tú)	sentirás
(él/ella/usted)	sentirá
(nosotros/as)	sentiremos
(vosotros/as)	sentiréis
(ellos/ellas/ustedes)	sentirán

CONDITIONAL

(yo)	sentiría
(tú)	sentirías
(él/ella/usted)	sentiría
(nosotros/as)	sentiríamos
(vosotros/as)	sentiríais
(ellos/ellas/ustedes)	sentirían

IMPERATIVE

siente / sentid

PAST PARTICIPLE

sentido

GERUND

sintiendo

EXAMPLE PHRASES

Siento *mucho lo que pasó.* I'm really sorry about what happened.
Sentí *un pinchazo en la pierna.* I felt a sharp pain in my leg.
No creo que lo **sienta**. I don't think she's sorry.

Remember that subject pronouns are not used very often in Spanish.

▶ **ser** (to be)

PRESENT

(yo)	soy
(tú)	eres
(él/ella/usted)	es
(nosotros/as)	somos
(vosotros/as)	sois
(ellos/ellas/ustedes)	son

PRESENT SUBJUNCTIVE

(yo)	sea
(tú)	seas
(él/ella/usted)	sea
(nosotros/as)	seamos
(vosotros/as)	seáis
(ellos/ellas/ustedes)	sean

PRETERITE

(yo)	fui
(tú)	fuiste
(él/ella/usted)	fue
(nosotros/as)	fuimos
(vosotros/as)	fuisteis
(ellos/ellas/ustedes)	fueron

IMPERFECT

(yo)	era
(tú)	eras
(él/ella/usted)	era
(nosotros/as)	éramos
(vosotros/as)	erais
(ellos/ellas/ustedes)	eran

FUTURE

(yo)	seré
(tú)	serás
(él/ella/usted)	será
(nosotros/as)	seremos
(vosotros/as)	seréis
(ellos/ellas/ustedes)	serán

CONDITIONAL

(yo)	sería
(tú)	serías
(él/ella/usted)	sería
(nosotros/as)	seríamos
(vosotros/as)	seríais
(ellos/ellas/ustedes)	serían

IMPERATIVE

sé / sed

PAST PARTICIPLE

sido

GERUND

siendo

EXAMPLE PHRASES

Soy español. I'm Spanish.
¿*Fuiste* tú el que llamó? Was it you who phoned?
Era de noche. It was dark.

Remember that subject pronouns are not used very often in Spanish.

▶ **tener** (to have)

PRESENT

(yo)	tengo
(tú)	tienes
(él/ella/usted)	tiene
(nosotros/as)	tenemos
(vosotros/as)	tenéis
(ellos/ellas/ustedes)	tienen

PRESENT SUBJUNCTIVE

(yo)	tenga
(tú)	tengas
(él/ella/usted)	tenga
(nosotros/as)	tengamos
(vosotros/as)	tengáis
(ellos/ellas/ustedes)	tengan

PRETERITE

(yo)	tuve
(tú)	tuviste
(él/ella/usted)	tuvo
(nosotros/as)	tuvimos
(vosotros/as)	tuvisteis
(ellos/ellas/ustedes)	tuvieron

IMPERFECT

(yo)	tenía
(tú)	tenías
(él/ella/usted)	tenía
(nosotros/as)	teníamos
(vosotros/as)	teníais
(ellos/ellas/ustedes)	tenían

FUTURE

(yo)	tendré
(tú)	tendrás
(él/ella/usted)	tendrá
(nosotros/as)	tendremos
(vosotros/as)	tendréis
(ellos/ellas/ustedes)	tendrán

CONDITIONAL

(yo)	tendría
(tú)	tendrías
(él/ella/usted)	tendría
(nosotros/as)	tendríamos
(vosotros/as)	tendríais
(ellos/ellas/ustedes)	tendrían

IMPERATIVE

ten / tened

PAST PARTICIPLE

tenido

GERUND

teniendo

EXAMPLE PHRASES

Tengo *sed.* I'm thirsty.
No **tenía** *suficiente dinero.* She didn't have enough money.
Tuvimos *que irnos.* We had to leave.

Remember that subject pronouns are not used very often in Spanish.

▶ **traer** (to bring)

PRESENT

(yo)	traigo
(tú)	traes
(él/ella/usted)	trae
(nosotros/as)	traemos
(vosotros/as)	traéis
(ellos/ellas/ustedes)	traen

PRESENT SUBJUNCTIVE

(yo)	traiga
(tú)	traigas
(él/ella/usted)	traiga
(nosotros/as)	traigamos
(vosotros/as)	traigáis
(ellos/ellas/ustedes)	traigan

PRETERITE

(yo)	traje
(tú)	trajiste
(él/ella/usted)	trajo
(nosotros/as)	trajimos
(vosotros/as)	trajisteis
(ellos/ellas/ustedes)	trajeron

IMPERFECT

(yo)	traía
(tú)	traías
(él/ella/usted)	traía
(nosotros/as)	traíamos
(vosotros/as)	traíais
(ellos/ellas/ustedes)	traían

FUTURE

(yo)	traeré
(tú)	traerás
(él/ella/usted)	traerá
(nosotros/as)	traeremos
(vosotros/as)	traeréis
(ellos/ellas/ustedes)	traerán

CONDITIONAL

(yo)	traería
(tú)	traerías
(él/ella/usted)	traería
(nosotros/as)	traeríamos
(vosotros/as)	traeríais
(ellos/ellas/ustedes)	traerían

IMPERATIVE

trae / traed

PAST PARTICIPLE

traído

GERUND

trayendo

EXAMPLE PHRASES

*¿**Has traído** lo que te pedí?* Did you bring what I asked you to?
*No **trajo** el dinero.* He didn't bring the money.
***Trae** eso.* Give that here.

Remember that subject pronouns are not used very often in Spanish.

▶ **venir** (to come)

PRESENT

(yo)	vengo
(tú)	vienes
(él/ella/usted)	viene
(nosotros/as)	venimos
(vosotros/as)	venís
(ellos/ellas/ustedes)	vienen

PRESENT SUBJUNCTIVE

(yo)	venga
(tú)	vengas
(él/ella/usted)	venga
(nosotros/as)	vengamos
(vosotros/as)	vengáis
(ellos/ellas/ustedes)	vengan

PRETERITE

(yo)	vine
(tú)	viniste
(él/ella/usted)	vino
(nosotros/as)	vinimos
(vosotros/as)	vinisteis
(ellos/ellas/ustedes)	vinieron

IMPERFECT

(yo)	venía
(tú)	venías
(él/ella/usted)	venía
(nosotros/as)	veníamos
(vosotros/as)	veníais
(ellos/ellas/ustedes)	venían

FUTURE

(yo)	vendré
(tú)	vendrás
(él/ella/usted)	vendrá
(nosotros/as)	vendremos
(vosotros/as)	vendréis
(ellos/ellas/ustedes)	vendrán

CONDITIONAL

(yo)	vendría
(tú)	vendrías
(él/ella/usted)	vendría
(nosotros/as)	vendríamos
(vosotros/as)	vendríais
(ellos/ellas/ustedes)	vendrían

IMPERATIVE

ven / venid

PAST PARTICIPLE

venido

GERUND

viniendo

EXAMPLE PHRASES

Vengo andando desde la playa. I've walked all the way from the beach.
¿**Vendrás** conmigo al cine? Will you come to the cinema with me?
Prefiero que no **venga**. I'd rather he didn't come.

Remember that subject pronouns are not used very often in Spanish.

▶ **ver** (to see)

PRESENT

(yo)	veo
(tú)	ves
(él/ella/usted)	ve
(nosotros/as)	vemos
(vosotros/as)	veis
(ellos/ellas/ustedes)	ven

PRESENT SUBJUNCTIVE

(yo)	vea
(tú)	veas
(él/ella/usted)	vea
(nosotros/as)	veamos
(vosotros/as)	veáis
(ellos/ellas/ustedes)	vean

PRETERITE

(yo)	vi
(tú)	viste
(él/ella/usted)	vio
(nosotros/as)	vimos
(vosotros/as)	visteis
(ellos/ellas/ustedes)	vieron

IMPERFECT

(yo)	veía
(tú)	veías
(él/ella/usted)	veía
(nosotros/as)	veíamos
(vosotros/as)	veíais
(ellos/ellas/ustedes)	veían

FUTURE

(yo)	veré
(tú)	verás
(él/ella/usted)	verá
(nosotros/as)	veremos
(vosotros/as)	veréis
(ellos/ellas/ustedes)	verán

CONDITIONAL

(yo)	vería
(tú)	verías
(él/ella/usted)	vería
(nosotros/as)	veríamos
(vosotros/as)	veríais
(ellos/ellas/ustedes)	verían

IMPERATIVE

ve / ved

PAST PARTICIPLE

visto

GERUND

viendo

EXAMPLE PHRASES

*No **veo** muy bien*. I can't see very well.
*Los **veía** a todos desde la ventana*. I could see them all from the window.
*¿**Viste** lo que pasó?* Did you see what happened?

Remember that subject pronouns are not used very often in Spanish.

▶ **vivir** (to live)

PRESENT

(yo)	vivo
(tú)	vives
(él/ella/usted)	vive
(nosotros/as)	vivimos
(vosotros/as)	vivís
(ellos/ellas/ustedes)	viven

PRESENT SUBJUNCTIVE

(yo)	viva
(tú)	vivas
(él/ella/usted)	viva
(nosotros/as)	vivamos
(vosotros/as)	viváis
(ellos/ellas/ustedes)	vivan

PRETERITE

(yo)	viví
(tú)	viviste
(él/ella/usted)	vivió
(nosotros/as)	vivimos
(vosotros/as)	vivisteis
(ellos/ellas/ustedes)	vivieron

IMPERFECT

(yo)	vivía
(tú)	vivías
(él/ella/usted)	vivía
(nosotros/as)	vivíamos
(vosotros/as)	vivíais
(ellos/ellas/ustedes)	vivían

FUTURE

(yo)	viviré
(tú)	vivirás
(él/ella/usted)	vivirá
(nosotros/as)	viviremos
(vosotros/as)	viviréis
(ellos/ellas/ustedes)	vivirán

CONDITIONAL

(yo)	viviría
(tú)	vivirías
(él/ella/usted)	viviría
(nosotros/as)	viviríamos
(vosotros/as)	viviríais
(ellos/ellas/ustedes)	vivirían

IMPERATIVE

vive / vivid

PAST PARTICIPLE

vivido

GERUND

viviendo

EXAMPLE PHRASES

Vivo *en Valencia.* I live in Valencia.
Vivieron *juntos dos años.* They lived together for two years.
Hemos vivido *momentos difíciles.* We've had some difficult times.

Remember that subject pronouns are not used very often in Spanish.

▶ **volver** (to return)

PRESENT

(yo)	vuelvo
(tú)	vuelves
(él/ella/usted)	vuelve
(nosotros/as)	volvemos
(vosotros/as)	volvéis
(ellos/ellas/ustedes)	vuelven

PRESENT SUBJUNCTIVE

(yo)	vuelva
(tú)	vuelvas
(él/ella/usted)	vuelva
(nosotros/as)	volvamos
(vosotros/as)	volváis
(ellos/ellas/ustedes)	vuelvan

PRETERITE

(yo)	volví
(tú)	volviste
(él/ella/usted)	volvió
(nosotros/as)	volvimos
(vosotros/as)	volvisteis
(ellos/ellas/ustedes)	volvieron

IMPERFECT

(yo)	volvía
(tú)	volvías
(él/ella/usted)	volvía
(nosotros/as)	volvíamos
(vosotros/as)	volvíais
(ellos/ellas/ustedes)	volvían

FUTURE

(yo)	volveré
(tú)	volverás
(él/ella/usted)	volverá
(nosotros/as)	volveremos
(vosotros/as)	volveréis
(ellos/ellas/ustedes)	volverán

CONDITIONAL

(yo)	volvería
(tú)	volverías
(él/ella/usted)	volvería
(nosotros/as)	volveríamos
(vosotros/as)	volveríais
(ellos/ellas/ustedes)	volverían

IMPERATIVE

vuelve / volved

PAST PARTICIPLE

vuelto

GERUND

volviendo

EXAMPLE PHRASES

Mi padre **vuelve** *mañana.* My father's coming back tomorrow.
No **vuelvas** *por aquí.* Don't come back here.
Ha vuelto *a casa.* He's gone back home.

Remember that subject pronouns are not used very often in Spanish.

1 Gerund **2** Imperative **3** Present **4** Preterite **5** Future **6** Present subjunctive **7** Past participle **8** Imperfect

Etc indicates that the irregular root is used for all persons of the tense, e.g. oír: **6** oiga, oigas, oiga, oigamos, oigáis, oigan

abrir 7 abierto
agradecer 3 agradezco **6** agradezca *etc*
almorzar 2 almuerza **3** almuerzo, almuerzas, almuerza, almuerzan **4** almorcé **6** almuerce, almuerces, almuerce, almorcemos, almorcéis, almuercen
andar 4 anduve, anduviste, anduvo, anduvimos, anduvisteis, anduvieron
aprobar 2 aprueba **3** apruebo, apruebas, aprueba, aprueban **6** apruebe, apruebes, apruebe, aprueben
atravesar 2 atraviesa **3** atravieso, atraviesas, atraviesa, atraviesan **6** atraviese, atravieses, atraviese, atraviesen
buscar 4 busqué **6** busque *etc*
caber 3 quepo **4** cupe, cupiste, cupo, cupimos, cupisteis, cupieron **5** cabré *etc* **6** quepa *etc*
caer 1 cayendo **3** caigo **4** caí, caíste, cayó, caímos, caísteis, cayeron **6** caiga *etc* **7** caído
cerrar 2 cierra **3** cierro, cierras, cierra, cierran **6** cierre, cierres, cierre, cierren
coger *see* Verb Table 2
colgar 2 cuelga **3** cuelgo, cuelgas, cuelga, cuelgan **4** colgué **6** cuelgue, cuelgues, cuelgue, colguemos, colguéis, cuelguen
comer (regular **–er** verb) *see* Verb Table 3
conducir 3 conduzco **4** conduje, condujiste condujo, condujimos, condujisteis, condujeron **6** conduzca *etc*
conocer 3 conozco **6** conozca *etc*
construir 1 construyendo **2** construye **3** construyo, construyes, construye, construyen **4** construyó, construyeron **6** construya *etc*

contar 2 cuenta **3** cuento, cuentas, cuenta, cuentan **6** cuente, cuentes, cuente, cuenten
continuar 2 continúa **3** continúo, continúas, continúa, continúan **6** continúe, continúes, continúe, continúen
corregir 3 corrijo, corriges, corrige, corrigen **4** corrigió, corrigieron, **6** corrija *etc*
creer 1 creyendo **4** creí, creíste, creyó, creímos, creísteis, creyeron **7** creído
cubrir 7 cubierto
dar *see* Verb Table 4
decir *see* Verb Table 5
descubrir 7 descubierto
despertar 2 despierta **3** despierto, despiertas, despierta, despiertan **6** despierte, despiertes, despierte, despierten
dirigir 3 dirijo **6** dirija, dirijas, dirija, dirijamos, dirijáis, dirijan
divertir 1 divirtiendo **2** divierte **3** divierto, diviertes, divierte, divierten **4** divirtió, divirtieron **6** divierta, diviertas, divierta, divirtamos, divirtáis, diviertan
dormir *see* Verb Table 6
empezar *see* Verb Table 7
encontrar 2 encuentra **3** encuentro, encuentras, encuentra, encuentran **6** encuentre, encuentres, encuentre, encuentren
entender *see* Verb Table 8
enviar *see* Verb Table 9
escribir 7 escrito
estar *see* Verb Table 10
freír 1 friendo **2** fríe, freíd **3** frío, fríes, fríe, freímos, freís, fríen **4** freí, freíste, frio, freímos, freísteis, frieron **5** freiré *etc* **6** fría, frías, fría, friamos, frlais, frían **7** frito

haber *see* Verb Table 11

hablar (regular **–ar** verb) *see* Verb Table 12

hacer *see* Verb Table 13

imprimir 7 impreso

instruir 1 instruyendo **2** instruye **3** instruyo, instruyes, instruye, instruyen **4** instruyó, instruyeron **6** instruya *etc*

ir *see* Verb Table 14

jugar 2 juega **3** juego, juegas, juega, juegan **4** jugué **6** juegue *etc*

lavarse (regular **–ar** reflexive verb) *see* Verb Table 15

leer *see* Verb Table 16

marcar 4 marqué **6** marque *etc*

morir 1 muriendo **2** muere **3** muero, mueres, muere, mueren **4** murió, murieron **6** muera, mueras, muera, muramos, muráis, mueran **7** muerto

mover 2 mueve **3** muevo, mueves, mueve, mueven **6** mueva, muevas, mueva, muevan

negar 2 niega **3** niego, niegas, niega, niegan **4** negué **6** niegue, niegues, niegue, neguemos, neguéis, nieguen

oír *see* Verb Table 17

ofrecer 3 ofrezco **6** ofrezca *etc*

oler 2 huele **3** huelo, hueles, huele, huelen **6** huela, huelas, huela, huelan

pagar 4 pagué **6** pague *etc*

parecer 3 parezco **6** parezca *etc*

pedir *see* Verb Table 18

pensar *see* Verb Table 19

perder 2 pierde **3** pierdo, pierdes, pierde, pierden **6** pierda, pierdas, pierda, pierdan

poder *see* Verb Table 20

poner *see* Verb Table 21

preferir 1 prefiriendo **2** prefiere **3** prefiero, prefieres, prefiere, prefieren **4** prefirió, prefirieron **6** prefiera, prefieras, prefiera, prefiramos, prefiráis, prefieran

producir 3 produzco **4** produje, produjiste produjo, produjimos, produjisteis, produjeron **6** produzca *etc*

prohibir 2 prohíbe **3** prohíbo, prohíbes, prohíbe, prohíben **6** prohíba, prohíbas, prohíba, prohíban

querer *see* Verb Table 22

reír 2 ríe **3** río, ríes, ríe, reímos, reís, ríen **4** reí, reíste, rio, reímos, reísteis, rieron **6** ría, rías, ría, riamos, riais, rían

repetir 1 repitiendo **2** repite **3** repito, repites, repite, repiten **4** repitió, repitieron **6** repita *etc*

reunir 2 reúne **3** reúno, reúnes, reúne, reúnen **6** reúna, reúnas, reúna, reúnan

rogar 2 ruega **3** ruego, ruegas, ruega, ruegan **4** rogué **6** ruegue, ruegues, ruegue, roguemos, roguéis, rueguen

romper 7 roto

saber *see* Verb Table 23

sacar 4 saqué **6** saque *etc*

salir 2 sal **3** salgo **5** saldré etc **6** salga *etc*

seguir *see* Verb Table 24

sentar 2 sienta **3** siento, sientas, sienta, sientan **6** siente, sientes, siente, sienten

sentir *see* Verb Table 25

ser *see* Verb Table 26

servir 1 sirviendo **2** sirve **3** sirvo, sirves, sirve, sirven **4** sirvió, sirvieron **6** sirva *etc*

soñar 2 sueña **3** sueño, sueñas, sueña, sueñan **6** sueñe, sueñes, sueñe, sueñen

tener *see* Verb Table 27

torcer 2 tuerce **3** tuerzo, tuerces, tuerce, tuercen **6** tuerza, tuerzas, tuerza, torzamos, torzáis, tuerzan

traer *see* Verb Table 28

valer 2 vale **3** valgo **5** valdré etc **6** valga *etc*

vencer 3 venzo **6** venza *etc*

venir *see* Verb Table 29

ver *see* Verb Table 30

vestir 2 vistiendo **2** viste **3** visto, vistes, viste, visten **4** vistió, vistieron **6** vista *etc*

vivir (regular **–ir** verb) *see* Verb Table 31

volver *see* Verb Table 32

A [eɪ] *n* (*Mus*) la *m*

○ **KEYWORD**

a [ə] (*before vowel or silent h: an*) *indef art*
1 un(a); **a book** un libro; **an apple**
una manzana; **she's a doctor** (ella)
es médica

2 (*instead of the number "one"*) un(a); **a
year ago** hace un año; **a hundred/
thousand** *etc* **pounds** cien/mil *etc*
libras

3 (*in expressing ratios, prices etc*): **3 a
day/week** 3 al día/a la semana; **10 km
an hour** 10 km por hora; **£5 a person** £5
por persona; **30p a kilo** 30p el kilo

A2 (*BRIT: Scol*) *n segunda parte de los
"A levels"*

A.A. *n abbr* (*BRIT:* = *Automobile
Association*) ≈ RACE *m* (*SP*); (= *Alcoholics
Anonymous*) Alcohólicos Anónimos

A.A.A. (*US*) *n abbr* (= *American
Automobile Association*) ≈ RACE *m* (*SP*)

aback [ə'bæk] *adv:* **to be taken ~**
quedar desconcertado

abandon [ə'bændən] *vt* abandonar;
(*give up*) renunciar a

abattoir ['æbətwɑː*] (*BRIT*) *n*
matadero

abbey ['æbɪ] *n* abadía

abbreviation [ə'briːvɪ'eɪʃən] *n* (*short
form*) abreviatura

abdomen ['æbdəmən] *n* abdomen *m*

abduct [æb'dʌkt] *vt* raptar,
secuestrar

abide [ə'baɪd] *vt:* **I can't ~ it/him**
no lo/le puedo ver; **abide by** *vt fus*
atenerse a

ability [ə'bɪlɪtɪ] *n* habilidad *f*,
capacidad *f*; (*talent*) talento

able ['eɪbl] *adj* capaz; (*skilled*) hábil; **to
be ~ to do sth** poder hacer algo

abnormal [æb'nɔːməl] *adj* anormal

aboard [ə'bɔːd] *adv* a bordo ▷ *prep*
a bordo de

abolish [ə'bɔlɪʃ] *vt* suprimir, abolir

abolition [æbəu'lɪʃən] *n* supresión
f, abolición *f*

abort [ə'bɔːt] *vt, vi* abortar; **abortion**
[ə'bɔːʃən] *n* aborto; **to have an
abortion** abortar, hacerse abortar

○ **KEYWORD**

about [ə'baut] *adv* **1** (*approximately*)
más o menos, aproximadamente;
about a hundred/thousand *etc*
unos(unas) cien/mil *etc*; **it takes
about 10 hours** se tarda unas *or* más
o menos 10 horas; **at about 2 o'clock**
sobre las dos; **I've just about finished**
casi he terminado

2 (*referring to place*) por todas partes;
to leave things lying about dejar las
cosas (tiradas) por ahí; **to run about**
correr por todas partes; **to walk about**
pasearse, ir y venir

3: **to be about to do sth** estar a punto
de hacer algo

▷ *prep* **1** (*relating to*) de, sobre, acerca
de; **a book about London** un libro
sobre *or* acerca de Londres; **what is it**

about? ¿de qué se trata?; **we talked
about it** hablamos de eso or ello; **what
or how about doing this?** ¿qué tal si
hacemos esto?
2 (referring to place) por; **to walk about
the town** caminar por la ciudad

above [ə'bʌv] adv encima, por
encima, arriba ▷ prep encima de;
(greater than: in number) más de;
(: in rank) superior a; **mentioned ~**
susodicho; **~ all** sobre todo
abroad [ə'brɔ:d] adv (to be) en el
extranjero; (to go) al extranjero
abrupt [ə'brʌpt] adj (sudden) brusco;
(curt) áspero
abscess ['æbsɪs] n absceso
absence ['æbsəns] n ausencia
absent ['æbsənt] adj ausente;
absent-minded adj distraído
absolute ['æbsəlu:t] adj absoluto;
absolutely [-'lu:tlɪ] adv (totally)
totalmente; (certainly!) ¡por supuesto
(que sí)!
absorb [əb'zɔ:b] vt absorber; **to be
~ed in a book** estar absorto en un libro;
absorbent cotton (US) n algodón m
hidrófilo; **absorbing** adj absorbente
abstain [əb'steɪn] vi: **to ~ (from)**
abstenerse (de)
abstract ['æbstrækt] adj abstracto
absurd [əb'sə:d] adj absurdo
abundance [ə'bʌndəns] n
abundancia
abundant [ə'bʌndənt] adj
abundante
abuse [n ə'bju:s, vb ə'bju:z] n (insults)
insultos mpl, injurias fpl; (ill-treatment)
malos tratos mpl; (misuse) abuso ▷ vt
insultar; maltratar; abusar de; **abusive**
adj ofensivo
abysmal [ə'bɪzməl] adj pésimo;
(failure) garrafal; (ignorance) supino
academic [ækə'dɛmɪk] adj
académico, universitario; (pej: issue)
puramente teórico ▷ n estudioso/a,
profesor(a) m/f universitario/a;
academic year n (Univ) año m

académico; (Scol) año m escolar
academy [ə'kædəmɪ] n (learned body)
academia; (school) instituto, colegio; **~
of music** conservatorio
accelerate [æk'sɛləreɪt] vt, vi
acelerar; **acceleration** [æksɛlə'reɪʃən]
n aceleración f; **accelerator** (BRIT) n
acelerador m
accent ['æksɛnt] n acento; (fig)
énfasis m
accept [ək'sɛpt] vt aceptar;
(responsibility, blame) admitir;
acceptable adj aceptable;
acceptance n aceptación f
access ['æksɛs] n acceso; **to have
~ to** tener libre acceso a; **accessible**
[-'sɛsəbl] adj (place, person) accesible;
(knowledge etc) asequible
accessory [æk'sɛsərɪ] n accesorio;
(Law): **~ to** cómplice de
accident ['æksɪdənt] n accidente
m; (chance event) casualidad f; **by ~**
(unintentionally) sin querer; (by chance)
por casualidad; **accidental** [-'dɛntl]
adj accidental, fortuito; **accidentally**
[-'dɛntəlɪ] adv sin querer; por
casualidad; **Accident and Emergency
Department** n (BRIT) Urgencias fpl;
accident insurance n seguro contra
accidentes
acclaim [ə'kleɪm] vt aclamar,
aplaudir ▷ n aclamación f, aplausos
mpl
accommodate [ə'kɒmədeɪt] vt
(person) alojar, hospedar; (: car, hotel
etc) tener cabida para; (oblige, help)
complacer
accommodation [əkɒmə'deɪʃən] (US
accommodations) n alojamiento
accompaniment [ə'kʌmpənɪmənt]
n acompañamiento
accompany [ə'kʌmpənɪ] vt
acompañar
accomplice [ə'kʌmplɪs] n cómplice
mf
accomplish [ə'kʌmplɪʃ] vt
(finish) concluir; (achieve) lograr;
accomplishment n (skill: gen pl)

talento; (*completion*) realización f
accord [əˈkɔːd] n acuerdo
▷ vt conceder; **of his own ~**
espontáneamente; **accordance**
n: **in accordance with** de acuerdo
con; **according** ▷ **according to** prep
según; (*in accordance with*) conforme
a; **accordingly** adv (*appropriately*)
de acuerdo con esto; (*as a result*) en
consecuencia
account [əˈkaunt] n (*Comm*)
cuenta; (*report*) informe m; **accounts**
npl (*Comm*) cuentas fpl; **of no ~** de
ninguna importancia; **on ~** a cuenta;
on no ~ bajo ningún concepto; **on ~
of** a causa de, por motivo de; **to take
into ~, take ~ of** tener en cuenta;
account for vt fus (*explain*) explicar;
(*represent*) representar; **accountable**
adj: **accountable (to)** responsable
(ante); **accountant** n contable mf,
contador(a) m/f; **account number** n
(*at bank etc*) número de cuenta
accumulate [əˈkjuːmjuleɪt] vt
acumular ▷ vi acumularse
accuracy [ˈækjurəsɪ] n (*of total*)
exactitud f; (*of description etc*)
precisión f
accurate [ˈækjurɪt] adj (*total*) exacto;
(*description*) preciso; (*person*) cuidadoso;
(*device*) de precisión; **accurately** adv
con precisión
accusation [ækjuˈzeɪʃən] n
acusación f
accuse [əˈkjuːz] vt: **to ~ sb (of sth)**
acusar a algn (de algo); **accused** n
(*Law*) acusado/a
accustomed [əˈkʌstəmd] adj: **~ to**
acostumbrado a
ace [eɪs] n as m
ache [eɪk] n dolor m ▷ vi doler; **my
head ~s** me duele la cabeza
achieve [əˈtʃiːv] vt (*aim, result*)
alcanzar; (*success*) lograr, conseguir;
achievement n (*completion*)
realización f; (*success*) éxito
acid [ˈæsɪd] adj ácido; (*taste*) agrio ▷ n
(*Chem, inf: LSD*) ácido

acknowledge [əkˈnɒlɪdʒ] vt
(*letter: also:* **~ receipt of**) acusar recibo
de; (*fact, situation, person*) reconocer;
acknowledgement n acuse m de
recibo
acne [ˈæknɪ] n acné m
acorn [ˈeɪkɔːn] n bellota
acoustic [əˈkuːstɪk] adj acústico
acquaintance [əˈkweɪntəns] n
(*person*) conocido/a; (*with person,
subject*) conocimiento
acquire [əˈkwaɪə*] vt adquirir;
acquisition [ækwɪˈzɪʃən] n
adquisición f
acquit [əˈkwɪt] vt absolver, exculpar;
to ~ o.s. well salir con éxito
acre [ˈeɪkə*] n acre m
acronym [ˈækrənɪm] n siglas fpl
across [əˈkrɒs] prep (*on the other side
of*) al otro lado de, del otro lado de;
(*crosswise*) a través de ▷ adv de un lado
a otro, de una parte a otra; a través, al
través; (*measurement*): **the road is 10m
~** la carretera tiene 10m de ancho; **to
run/swim ~** atravesar corriendo/
nadando; **~ from** enfrente de
acrylic [əˈkrɪlɪk] adj acrílico ▷ n
acrílica
act [ækt] n acto, acción f; (*of play*)
acto; (*in music hall etc*) número;
(*Law*) decreto, ley f ▷ vi (*behave*)
comportarse; (*have effect: drug,
chemical*) hacer efecto; (*Theatre*) actuar;
(*pretend*) fingir; (*take action*) obrar ▷ vt
(*part*) hacer el papel de; **in the ~ of:
catch sb in the ~ of ...** pillar a algn en
el momento en que ...; **to ~ as** actuar
or hacer de; **act up** (*inf*) vi (*person*)
portarse mal; **acting** adj suplente
▷ n (*activity*) actuación f; (*profession*)
profesión f de actor
action [ˈækʃən] n acción f, acto;
(*Mil*) acción f, batalla; (*Law*) proceso,
demanda; **out of ~** (*person*) fuera de
combate; (*thing*) estropeado; **to take ~**
tomar medidas; **action replay** n (*TV*)
repetición f
activate [ˈæktɪveɪt] vt activar

active ['æktɪv] *adj* activo, enérgico; (*volcano*) en actividad; **actively** *adv* (*participate*) activamente; (*discourage, dislike*) enérgicamente

activist ['æktɪvɪst] *n* activista *m/f*

activity [-'tɪvɪtɪ] *n* actividad *f*; **activity holiday** *n* vacaciones con actividades organizadas

actor ['æktə*] *n* actor *m*, actriz *f*

actress ['æktrɪs] *n* actriz *f*

actual ['æktjuəl] *adj* verdadero, real; (*emphatic use*) propiamente dicho

▌ Be careful not to translate **actual** by the Spanish word *actual*.

actually ['æktjuəlɪ] *adv* realmente, en realidad; (*even*) incluso

▌ Be careful not to translate **actually** by the Spanish word *actualmente*.

acupuncture ['ækjupʌŋktʃə*] *n* acupuntura

acute [ə'kju:t] *adj* agudo

ad [æd] *n abbr* = **advertisement**

A.D. *adv abbr* (= *anno Domini*) DC

adamant ['ædəmənt] *adj* firme, inflexible

adapt [ə'dæpt] *vt* adaptar ▷ *vi*: to ~ (to) adaptarse (a), ajustarse (a); **adapter** (*US* **adaptor**) *n* (*Elec*) adaptador *m*; (*for several plugs*) ladrón *m*

add [æd] *vt* añadir, agregar; **add up** *vt* (*figures*) sumar ▷ *vi* (*fig*): **it doesn't add up** no tiene sentido; **add up to** *vt fus* (*Math*) sumar, ascender a; (*fig: mean*) querer decir, venir a ser

addict ['ædɪkt] *n* adicto/a; (*enthusiast*) entusiasta *mf*; **addicted** [ə'dɪktɪd] *adj*: **to be addicted to** ser adicto a, ser fanático de; **addiction** [ə'dɪkʃən] *n* (*to drugs etc*) adicción *f*; **addictive** [ə'dɪktɪv] *adj* que causa adicción

addition [ə'dɪʃən] *n* (*adding up*) adición *f*; (*thing added*) añadidura, añadido; **in ~** además, por añadidura; **in ~ to** además de; **additional** *adj* adicional

additive ['ædɪtɪv] *n* aditivo

address [ə'drɛs] *n* dirección *f*, señas

fpl; (*speech*) discurso ▷ *vt* (*letter*) dirigir; (*speak to*) dirigirse a, dirigir la palabra a; (*problem*) tratar; **address book** *n* agenda (de direcciones)

adequate ['ædɪkwɪt] *adj* (*satisfactory*) adecuado; (*enough*) suficiente

adhere [əd'hɪə*] *vi*: **to ~ to** (*stick to*) pegarse a; (*fig: abide by*) observar; (: *belief etc*) ser partidario de

adhesive [əd'hi:zɪv] *n* adhesivo; **adhesive tape** *n* (*BRIT*) cinta adhesiva; (*US Med*) esparadrapo

adjacent [ə'dʒeɪsənt] *adj*: **~ to** contiguo a, inmediato a

adjective ['ædʒɛktɪv] *n* adjetivo

adjoining [ə'dʒɔɪnɪŋ] *adj* contiguo, vecino

adjourn [ə'dʒə:n] *vt* aplazar ▷ *vi* suspenderse

adjust [ə'dʒʌst] *vt* (*change*) modificar; (*clothing*) arreglar; (*machine*) ajustar ▷ *vi*: **to ~ (to)** adaptarse (a); **adjustable** *adj* ajustable; **adjustment** *n* adaptación *f*; (*to machine, prices*) ajuste *m*

administer [əd'mɪnɪstə*] *vt* administrar; **administration** [-'treɪʃən] *n* (*management*) administración *f*; (*government*) gobierno; **administrative** [-trətɪv] *adj* administrativo

administrator [əd'mɪnɪstreɪtə*] *n* administrador(a) *m/f*

admiral ['ædmərəl] *n* almirante *m*

admiration [ædmə'reɪʃən] *n* admiración *f*

admire [əd'maɪə*] *vt* admirar; **admirer** *n* (*fan*) admirador(a) *m/f*

admission [əd'mɪʃən] *n* (*to university, club*) ingreso; (*entry fee*) entrada; (*confession*) confesión *f*

admit [əd'mɪt] *vt* (*confess*) confesar; (*permit to enter*) dejar entrar, dar entrada a; (*to club, organization*) admitir; (*accept: defeat*) reconocer; **to be ~ted to hospital** ingresar en el hospital; **admit to** *vt fus* confesarse

culpable de; **admittance** n entrada;
admittedly adv es cierto or verdad
que
adolescent [ædəu'lɛsnt] adj, n
adolescente mf
adopt [ə'dɔpt] vt adoptar; **adopted**
adj adoptivo; **adoption** [ə'dɔpʃən] n
adopción f
adore [ə'dɔ:*] vt adorar
adorn [ə'dɔ:n] vt adornar
Adriatic [eɪdrɪ'ætɪk] n: **the ~ (Sea)** el
(Mar) Adriático
adrift [ə'drɪft] adv a la deriva
adult ['ædʌlt] n adulto/a ▷ adj
(grown-up) adulto; (for adults)
para adultos; **adult education** n
educación f para adultos
adultery [ə'dʌltərɪ] n adulterio
advance [əd'va:ns] n (progress)
adelanto, progreso; (money) anticipo,
préstamo; (Mil) avance m ▷ adj: ~
booking venta anticipada; **~ notice,
~ warning** previo aviso ▷ vt (money)
anticipar; (theory, idea) proponer
(para la discusión) ▷ vi avanzar,
adelantarse; **to make ~s (to sb)**
hacer proposiciones (a algn); **in ~** por
adelantado; **advanced** adj avanzado;
(Scol: studies) adelantado
advantage [əd'va:ntɪdʒ] n (also
Tennis) ventaja; **to take ~ of** (person)
aprovecharse de; (opportunity)
aprovechar
advent ['ædvənt] n advenimiento;
A~ Adviento
adventure [əd'vɛntʃə*] n aventura;
adventurous [-tʃərəs] adj atrevido;
aventurero
adverb ['ædvə:b] n adverbio
adversary ['ædvəsərɪ] n adversario,
contrario
adverse ['ædvə:s] adj adverso,
contrario
advert ['ædvə:t] (BRIT) n abbr =
advertisement
advertise ['ædvətaɪz] vi (in newspaper
etc) anunciar, hacer publicidad; **to ~
for** (staff, accommodation etc) buscar

por medio de anuncios ▷ vt anunciar;
advertisement [əd'və:tɪsmənt]
n (Comm) anuncio; **advertiser**
n anunciante mf; **advertising** n
publicidad f, anuncios mpl; (industry)
industria publicitaria
advice [əd'vaɪs] n consejo, consejos
mpl; (notification) aviso; **a piece of ~** un
consejo; **to take legal ~** consultar con
un abogado
advisable [əd'vaɪzəbl] adj
aconsejable, conveniente
advise [əd'vaɪz] vt aconsejar;
(inform): **to ~ sb of sth** informar a algn
de algo; **to ~ sb against sth/doing sth**
desaconsejar algo a algn/aconsejar
a algn que no haga algo; **adviser,
advisor** n consejero/a; (consultant)
asesor(a) m/f; **advisory** adj consultivo
advocate [vb 'ædvəkeɪt, n -kɪt] vt
abogar por ▷ n (lawyer) abogado/a;
(supporter): **~ of** defensor(a) m/f de
Aegean [i:'dʒi:ən] n: **the ~ (Sea)** el
(Mar) Egeo
aerial ['ɛərɪəl] n antena ▷ adj aéreo
aerobics [ɛə'rəubɪks] n aerobic m
aeroplane ['ɛərəpleɪn] (BRIT) n
avión m
aerosol ['ɛərəsɔl] n aerosol m
affair [ə'fɛə*] n asunto; (also: **love ~**)
aventura (amorosa)
affect [ə'fɛkt] vt (influence) afectar,
influir en; (afflict, concern) afectar;
(move) conmover; **affected** adj
afectado; **affection** n afecto, cariño;
affectionate adj afectuoso, cariñoso
afflict [ə'flɪkt] vt afligir
affluent ['æfluənt] adj (wealthy)
acomodado; **the ~ society** la sociedad
opulenta
afford [ə'fɔ:d] vt (provide)
proporcionar; **can we ~ (to buy)
it?** ¿tenemos bastante dinero para
comprarlo?; **affordable** adj asequible
Afghanistan [æf'gænɪstæn] n
Afganistán m
afraid [ə'freɪd] adj: **to be ~ of** (person)
tener miedo a; (thing) tener miedo de;

to be ~ to tener miedo de, temer; **I am ~ that** me temo que; **I am ~ not/so** lo siento, pero no/es así

Africa ['æfrɪkə] n África; **African** adj, n africano/a m/f; **African-American** adj, n afroamericano/a

after ['ɑːftə*] prep (time) después de; (place, order) detrás de, tras ▷ adv después ▷ conj después (de) que; **what/who are you ~?** ¿qué/a quién busca usted?; **~ having done/he left** después de haber hecho/después de que se marchó; **to name sb ~ sb** llamar a algn por algn; **it's twenty ~ eight** (us) son las ocho y veinte; **to ask ~ sb** preguntar por algn; **~ all** después de todo, al fin y al cabo; **~ you!** ¡pase usted!; **after-effects** npl consecuencias fpl, efectos mpl; **aftermath** n consecuencias fpl, resultados mpl; **afternoon** n tarde f; **after-shave (lotion)** n aftershave m; **aftersun (lotion/cream)** n loción f/crema para después del sol, aftersun m; **afterwards** (us **afterward**) adv después, más tarde

again [ə'gɛn] adv otra vez, de nuevo; **to do sth ~** volver a hacer algo; **~ and ~** una y otra vez

against [ə'gɛnst] prep (in opposition to) en contra de; (leaning on, touching) contra, junto a

age [eɪdʒ] n edad f; (period) época ▷ vi envejecer(se) ▷ vt envejecer; **she is 20 years of ~** tiene 20 años; **to come of ~** llegar a la mayoría de edad; **it's been ~s since I saw you** hace siglos que no te veo; **~d 10** de 10 años de edad; **age group** n: **to be in the same age group** tener la misma edad; **age limit** n edad f mínima (or máxima)

agency ['eɪdʒənsɪ] n agencia

agenda [ə'dʒɛndə] n orden m del día

▐ Be careful not to translate **agenda** by the Spanish word *agenda*.

agent ['eɪdʒənt] n agente mf; (Comm: holding concession) representante mf, delegado/a; (Chem,

fig) agente m

aggravate ['ægrəveɪt] vt (situation) agravar; (person) irritar

aggression [ə'grɛʃən] n agresión f

aggressive [ə'grɛsɪv] adj (belligerent) agresivo; (assertive) enérgico

agile ['ædʒaɪl] adj ágil

agitated ['ædʒɪteɪtɪd] adj agitado

AGM n abbr (= annual general meeting) asamblea anual

ago [ə'gəʊ] adv: **2 days ~** hace 2 días; **not long ~** hace poco; **how long ~?** ¿hace cuánto tiempo?

agony ['ægənɪ] n (pain) dolor m agudo; (distress) angustia; **to be in ~** retorcerse de dolor

agree [ə'griː] vt (price, date) acordar, quedar en ▷ vi (have same opinion): **to ~ (with/that)** estar de acuerdo (con/que); (correspond) coincidir, concordar; (consent) acceder; **to ~ with** (person) estar de acuerdo con, ponerse de acuerdo con; (: food) sentar bien a; (Ling) concordar con; **to ~ to sth/to do sth** consentir en algo/aceptar hacer algo; **to ~ that** (admit) estar de acuerdo en que; **agreeable** adj (sensation) agradable; (person) simpático; (willing) de acuerdo, conforme; **agreed** adj (time, place) convenido; **agreement** n acuerdo; (contract) contrato; **in agreement** de acuerdo, conforme

agricultural [ægrɪ'kʌltʃərəl] adj agrícola

agriculture ['ægrɪkʌltʃə*] n agricultura

ahead [ə'hɛd] adv (in front) delante; (into the future): **she had no time to think ~** no tenía tiempo de hacer planes para el futuro; **~ of** delante de; (in advance of) antes de; **~ of time** antes de la hora; **go right** or **straight ~** (direction) siga adelante; (permission) hazlo (or hágalo)

aid [eɪd] n ayuda, auxilio; (device) aparato ▷ vt ayudar, auxiliar; **in ~ of** a beneficio de

aide [eɪd] n (person, also Mil) ayudante

mf

AIDS [eɪdz] *n abbr* (= *acquired immune deficiency syndrome*) SIDA *m*

ailing ['eɪlɪŋ] *adj* (*person, economy*) enfermizo

ailment ['eɪlmənt] *n* enfermedad *f*, achaque *m*

aim [eɪm] *vt* (*gun, camera*) apuntar; (*missile, remark*) dirigir; (*blow*) asestar ▷ *vi* (*also*: **take ~**) apuntar ▷ *n* (*in shooting: skill*) puntería; (*objective*) propósito, meta; **to ~ at** (*with weapon*) apuntar a; (*objective*) aspirar a, pretender; **to ~ to do** tener la intención de hacer

ain't [eɪnt] (*inf*) = **am not; aren't; isn't**

air [ɛə*] *n* aire *m*; (*appearance*) aspecto ▷ *vt* (*room*) ventilar; (*clothes, ideas*) airear ▷ *cpd* aéreo; **to throw sth into the ~** (*ball etc*) lanzar algo al aire; **by ~** (*travel*) en avión; **to be on the ~** (*Radio, TV*) estar en antena; **airbag** *n* airbag *m inv*; **airbed** (*BRIT*) *n* colchón *m* neumático; **airborne** *adj* (*in the air*) en el aire; **as soon as the plane was airborne** tan pronto como el avión estuvo en el aire; **air-conditioned** *adj* climatizado; **air conditioning** *n* aire acondicionado; **aircraft** *n inv* avión *m*; **airfield** *n* campo de aviación; **Air Force** *n* fuerzas *fpl* aéreas, aviación *f*; **air hostess** (*BRIT*) *n* azafata; **airing cupboard** *n* (*BRIT*) armario *m* para oreo; **airlift** *n* puente *m* aéreo; **airline** *n* línea aérea; **airliner** *n* avión *m* de pasajeros; **airmail** *n*: **by airmail** por avión; **airplane** (*US*) *n* avión *m*; **airport** *n* aeropuerto; **air raid** *n* ataque *m* aéreo; **airsick** *adj*: **to be airsick** marearse (en avión); **airspace** *n* espacio aéreo; **airstrip** *n* pista de aterrizaje; **air terminal** *n* terminal *f*; **airtight** *adj* hermético; **air-traffic controller** *n* controlador(a) *m/f* aéreo/a; **airy** *adj* (*room*) bien ventilado; (*fig: manner*) desenfadado

aisle [aɪl] *n* (*of church*) nave *f*; (*of theatre, supermarket*) pasillo; **aisle seat** *n* (*on plane*) asiento de pasillo

ajar [ə'dʒɑ:*] *adj* entreabierto

à la carte [ælæ'kɑ:t] *adv* a la carta

alarm [ə'lɑ:m] *n* (*in shop, bank*) alarma; (*anxiety*) inquietud *f* ▷ *vt* asustar, inquietar; **alarm call** *n* (*in hotel etc*) alarma; **alarm clock** *n* despertador *m*; **alarmed** *adj* (*person*) alarmado, asustado; (*house, car etc*) con alarma; **alarming** *adj* alarmante

Albania [æl'beɪnɪə] *n* Albania

albeit [ɔːl'biːɪt] *conj* aunque

album ['ælbəm] *n* álbum *m*; (*L.P.*) elepé *m*

alcohol ['ælkəhɔl] *n* alcohol *m*; **alcohol-free** *adj* sin alcohol; **alcoholic** [-'hɔlɪk] *adj, n* alcohólico/a *m/f*

alcove ['ælkəuv] *n* nicho, hueco

ale [eɪl] *n* cerveza

alert [ə'lə:t] *adj* (*attentive*) atento; (*to danger, opportunity*) alerta ▷ *n* alerta *m*, alarma ▷ *vt* poner sobre aviso; **to be on the ~** (*also Mil*) estar alerta *or* sobre aviso

algebra ['ældʒɪbrə] *n* álgebra

Algeria [æl'dʒɪərɪə] *n* Argelia

alias ['eɪlɪəs] *adv* alias, conocido por ▷ *n* (*of criminal*) apodo; (*of writer*) seudónimo

alibi ['ælɪbaɪ] *n* coartada

alien ['eɪlɪən] *n* (*foreigner*) extranjero/a; (*extraterrestrial*) extraterrestre *mf* ▷ *adj*: **~ to** ajeno a; **alienate** *vt* enajenar, alejar

alight [ə'laɪt] *adj* ardiendo; (*eyes*) brillante ▷ *vi* (*person*) apearse, bajar; (*bird*) posarse

align [ə'laɪn] *vt* alinear

alike [ə'laɪk] *adj* semejantes, iguales ▷ *adv* igualmente, del mismo modo; **to look ~** parecerse

alive [ə'laɪv] *adj* vivo; (*lively*) alegre

○ **KEYWORD**

all [ɔːl] *adj* (*sg*) todo/a; (*pl*) todos/as; **all day** todo el día; **all night** toda la noche; **all men** todos los hombres;

all five came vinieron los cinco; **all the books** todos los libros; **all his life** toda su vida
▷ *pron* **1** todo; **I ate it all, I ate all of it** me lo comí todo; **all of us went** fuimos todos; **all the boys went** fueron todos los chicos; **is that all?** ¿eso es todo?, ¿algo más?; (*in shop*) ¿algo más?, ¿alguna cosa más?
2 (*in phrases*): **above all** sobre todo; por encima de todo; **after all** después de todo; **at all: not at all** (*in answer to question*) en absoluto; (*in answer to thanks*) ¡de nada!, ¡no hay de qué!; **I'm not at all tired** no estoy nada cansado/a; **anything at all will do** cualquier cosa viene bien; **all in all** a fin de cuentas
▷ *adv*: **all alone** completamente solo/a; **it's not as hard as all that** no es tan difícil como lo pintas; **all the more/the better** tanto más/mejor; **all but** casi; **the score is 2 all** están empatados a 2

Allah ['ælə] *n* Alá *m*
allegation [ælɪ'geɪʃən] *n* alegato
alleged [ə'lɛdʒd] *adj* supuesto, presunto; **allegedly** *adv* supuestamente, según se afirma
allegiance [ə'liːdʒəns] *n* lealtad *f*
allergic [ə'lɜːdʒɪk] *adj*: **~ to** alérgico a
allergy ['ælədʒɪ] *n* alergia
alleviate [ə'liːvɪeɪt] *vt* aliviar
alley ['ælɪ] *n* callejuela
alliance [ə'laɪəns] *n* alianza
allied ['ælaɪd] *adj* aliado
alligator ['ælɪgeɪtə*] *n* (*Zool*) caimán *m*
all-in (*BRIT*) ['ɔːlɪn] *adj, adv* (*charge*) todo incluido
allocate ['æləkeɪt] *vt* (*money etc*) asignar
allot [ə'lɒt] *vt* asignar
all-out ['ɔːlaut] *adj* (*effort etc*) supremo
allow [ə'lau] *vt* permitir, dejar; (*a claim*) admitir; (*sum, time etc*)

dar, conceder; (*concede*): **to ~ that** reconocer que; **to ~ sb to do** permitir a algn hacer; **he is ~ed to ...** se le permite ...; **allow for** *vt fus* tener en cuenta;
allowance *n* subvención *f*; (*welfare payment*) subsidio, pensión *f*; (*pocket money*) dinero de bolsillo; (*tax allowance*) desgravación *f*; **to make allowances for** (*person*) disculpar a; (*thing*) tener en cuenta
all right *adv* bien; (*as answer*) ¡conforme!, ¡está bien!
ally ['ælaɪ] *n* aliado/a ▷ *vt*: **to ~ o.s. with** aliarse con
almighty [ɔːl'maɪtɪ] *adj* todopoderoso; (*row etc*) imponente
almond ['ɑːmənd] *n* almendra
almost ['ɔːlməust] *adv* casi
alone [ə'ləun] *adj, adv* solo; **to leave sb ~** dejar a algn en paz; **to leave sth ~** no tocar algo, dejar algo sin tocar; **let ~ ...** y mucho menos ...
along [ə'lɒŋ] *prep* a lo largo de, por ▷ *adv*: **is he coming ~ with us?** ¿viene con nosotros?; **he was limping ~** iba cojeando; **~ with** junto con; **all ~** (*all the time*) desde el principio; **alongside** *prep* al lado de ▷ *adv* al lado
aloof [ə'luːf] *adj* reservado ▷ *adv*: **to stand ~** mantenerse apartado
aloud [ə'laud] *adv* en voz alta
alphabet ['ælfəbɛt] *n* alfabeto
Alps [ælps] *npl*: **the ~** los Alpes
already [ɔːl'rɛdɪ] *adv* ya
alright ['ɔːl'raɪt] (*BRIT*) *adv* = **all right**
also ['ɔːlsəu] *adv* también, además
altar ['ɔltə*] *n* altar *m*
alter ['ɔltə*] *vt* cambiar, modificar ▷ *vi* cambiar; **alteration** [ɔltə'reɪʃən] *n* cambio; (*to clothes*) arreglo; (*to building*) arreglos *mpl*
alternate [*adj* ɔl'tə:nɪt, *vb* 'ɔltə:neɪt] *adj* (*actions etc*) alternativo; (*events*) alterno; (*US*) = **alternative** ▷ *vi*: **to ~ (with)** alternar (con); **on ~ days** un día sí y otro no
alternative [ɔl'tə:nətɪv] *adj* alternativo ▷ *n* alternativa; **~**

medicine medicina alternativa;
alternatively adv: **alternatively one
could ...** por otra parte se podría ...
although [ɔːlˈðəʊ] conj aunque
altitude [ˈæltɪtjuːd] n altura
altogether [ɔːltəˈgeðə*] adv
completamente, del todo; (on the
whole) en total, en conjunto
aluminium [æljuˈmɪnɪəm] (BRIT),
aluminum [əˈluːmɪnəm] (US) n
aluminio
always [ˈɔːlweɪz] adv siempre
Alzheimer's (disease)
[ˈæltshaɪməz-] n enfermedad f de
Alzheimer
am [æm] vb see **be**
amalgamate [əˈmælgəmeɪt] vi
amalgamarse ▷ vt amalgamar, unir
amass [əˈmæs] vt amontonar,
acumular
amateur [ˈæmətə*] n aficionado/a,
amateur mf
amaze [əˈmeɪz] vt asombrar, pasmar;
to be ~d (at) quedar pasmado (de);
amazed adj asombrado; **amazement**
n asombro, sorpresa; **amazing** adj
extraordinario; (fantastic) increíble
Amazon [ˈæməzən] n (Geo)
Amazonas m
ambassador [æmˈbæsədə*] n
embajador(a) m/f
amber [ˈæmbə*] n ámbar m; **at ~**
(BRIT Aut) en el amarillo
ambiguous [æmˈbɪgjuəs] adj
ambiguo
ambition [æmˈbɪʃən] n ambición f;
ambitious [-ʃəs] adj ambicioso
ambulance [ˈæmbjuləns] n
ambulancia
ambush [ˈæmbuʃ] n emboscada ▷ vt
tender una emboscada a
amen [ɑːˈmɛn] excl amén
amend [əˈmɛnd] vt enmendar; **to
make ~s** dar cumplida satisfacción;
amendment n enmienda
amenities [əˈmiːnɪtɪz] npl
comodidades fpl
America [əˈmɛrɪkə] n (USA)
Estados mpl Unidos; **American** adj, n
norteamericano/a; estadounidense
mf; **American football** n (BRIT) fútbol
m americano
amicable [ˈæmɪkəbl] adj amistoso,
amigable
amid(st) [əˈmɪd(st)] prep entre, en
medio de
ammunition [æmjuˈnɪʃən] n
municiones fpl
amnesty [ˈæmnɪstɪ] n amnistía
among(st) [əˈmʌŋ(st)] prep entre,
en medio de
amount [əˈmaunt] n (gen) cantidad
f; (of bill etc) suma, importe m ▷ vi: **to
~ to** sumar; (be same as) equivaler a,
significar
amp(ère) [ˈæmp(ɛə*)] n amperio
ample [ˈæmpl] adj (large) grande;
(abundant) abundante; (enough)
bastante, suficiente
amplifier [ˈæmplɪfaɪə*] n
amplificador m
amputate [ˈæmpjuteɪt] vt amputar
Amtrak [ˈæmtræk] (US) n empresa
nacional de ferrocarriles de los EEUU
amuse [əˈmjuːz] vt divertir; (distract)
distraer, entretener; **amusement**
n diversión f; (pastime) pasatiempo;
(laughter) risa; **amusement arcade** n
salón m de juegos; **amusement park** n
parque m de atracciones
amusing [əˈmjuːzɪŋ] adj divertido
an [æn] indef art see **a**
anaemia [əˈniːmɪə] (US **anemia**)
n anemia
anaemic [əˈniːmɪk] (US **anemic**) adj
anémico; (fig) soso, insípido
anaesthetic [ænɪsˈθɛtɪk] (US
anesthetic) n anestesia
analog(ue) [ˈænəlɔg] adj (computer,
watch) analógico
analogy [əˈnælədʒɪ] n analogía
analyse [ˈænəlaɪz] (US **analyze**)
vt analizar; **analysis** [əˈnæləsɪs] (pl
analyses) n análisis m inv; **analyst**
[-lɪst] n (political analyst, psychoanalyst)
analista mf

analyze ['ænəlaɪz] (US) vt = **analyse**

anarchy ['ænəkɪ] n anarquía, desorden m

anatomy [ə'nætəmɪ] n anatomía

ancestor ['ænsɪstə*] n antepasado

anchor ['æŋkə*] n ancla, áncora ▷ vi (also: **to drop ~**) anclar ▷ vt anclar; **to weigh ~** levar anclas

anchovy ['æntʃəvɪ] n anchoa

ancient ['eɪnʃənt] adj antiguo

and [ænd] conj y; (before i-, hi- + consonant) e; **men ~ women** hombres y mujeres; **father ~ son** padre e hijo; **trees ~ grass** árboles y hierba; **~ so on** etcétera, y así sucesivamente; **try ~ come** procura venir; **he talked ~ talked** habló sin parar; **better ~ better** cada vez mejor

Andes ['ændi:z] npl: **the ~** los Andes

Andorra [æn'dɔːrə] n Andorra

anemia etc [ə'niːmɪə] (US) = **anaemia** etc

anesthetic [ænɪs'θetɪk] (US) = **anaesthetic**

angel ['eɪndʒəl] n ángel m

anger ['æŋgə*] n cólera

angina [æn'dʒaɪnə] n angina (del pecho)

angle ['æŋgl] n ángulo; **from their ~** desde su punto de vista

angler ['æŋglə*] n pescador(a) m/f (de caña)

Anglican ['æŋglɪkən] adj, n anglicano/a m/f

angling ['æŋglɪŋ] n pesca con caña

angrily ['æŋgrɪlɪ] adv coléricamente, airadamente

angry ['æŋgrɪ] adj enfadado, airado; (wound) inflamado; **to be ~ with sb/at sth** estar enfadado con algn/por algo; **to get ~** enfadarse, enojarse

anguish ['æŋgwɪʃ] n (physical) tormentos mpl; (mental) angustia

animal ['ænɪməl] n animal m; (pej: person) bestia ▷ adj animal

animated [-meɪtɪd] adj animado

animation [ænɪ'meɪʃən] n animación f

aniseed ['ænɪsiːd] n anís m

ankle ['æŋkl] n tobillo

annex [n 'æneks, vb æ'neks] n (BRIT: also: **~e**: building) edificio anexo ▷ vt (territory) anexionar

anniversary [ænɪ'vəːsərɪ] n aniversario

announce [ə'nauns] vt anunciar; **announcement** n anuncio; (official) declaración f; **announcer** n (Radio) locutor(a) m/f; (TV) presentador(a) m/f

annoy [ə'nɔɪ] vt molestar, fastidiar; **don't get ~ed!** ¡no se enfade!; **annoying** adj molesto, fastidioso; (person) pesado

annual ['ænjuəl] adj anual ▷ n (Bot) anual m; (book) anuario; **annually** adv anualmente, cada año

annum ['ænəm] n see **per**

anonymous [ə'nɔnɪməs] adj anónimo

anorak ['ænəræk] n anorak m

anorexia [ænə'reksɪə] n (Med: also: **~ nervosa**) anorexia

anorexic [ænə'reksɪk] adj, n anoréxico/a m/f

another [ə'nʌðə*] adj (one more, a different one) otro ▷ pron otro; see **one**

answer ['ɑːnsə*] n contestación f, respuesta; (to problem) solución f ▷ vi contestar, responder ▷ vt (reply to) contestar a, responder a; (problem) resolver; (prayer) escuchar; **in ~ to your letter** contestando or en contestación a su carta; **to ~ the phone** contestar or coger el teléfono; **to ~ the bell** or **the door** acudir a la puerta; **answer back** vi replicar, ser respondón/ona; **answerphone** n (esp BRIT) contestador m (automático)

ant [ænt] n hormiga

Antarctic [ænt'ɑːktɪk] n: **the ~** el Antártic

antelope ['æntɪləup] n antílope m

antenatal ['æntɪ'neɪtl] adj antenatal, prenatal

antenna [æn'tenə, pl -niː] (pl **antennae**) n antena

anthem ['ænθəm] *n*: **national ~** himno nacional

anthology [æn'θɒlədʒɪ] *n* antología

anthrax ['ænθræks] *n* ántrax *m*

anthropology [ænθrə'pɒlədʒɪ] *n* antropología

anti [æntɪ] *prefix* anti; **antibiotic** [-baɪ'ɒtɪk] *n* antibiótico; **antibody** ['æntɪbɒdɪ] *n* anticuerpo

anticipate [æn'tɪsɪpeɪt] *vt* prever; (*expect*) esperar, contar con; (*look forward to*) esperar con ilusión; (*do first*) anticiparse a, adelantarse a; **anticipation** [-'peɪʃən] *n* (*expectation*) previsión *f*; (*eagerness*) ilusión *f*, expectación *f*

anticlimax [æntɪ'klaɪmæks] *n* decepción *f*

anticlockwise [æntɪ'klɒkwaɪz] (*BRIT*) *adv* en dirección contraria a la de las agujas del reloj

antics ['æntɪks] *npl* gracias *fpl*

anti: antidote ['æntɪdəʊt] *n* antídoto; **antifreeze** ['æntɪfriːz] *n* anticongelante *m*; **antihistamine** [-'hɪstəmiːn] *n* antihistamínico; **antiperspirant** ['æntɪpə:spɪrənt] *n* antitranspirante *m*

antique [æn'tiːk] *n* antigüedad *f* ▷ *adj* antiguo; **antique shop** *n* tienda de antigüedades

antiseptic [æntɪ'septɪk] *adj*, *n* antiséptico

antisocial [æntɪ'səʊʃəl] *adj* antisocial

antivirus [æntɪ'vaɪərəs] *adj* (*program*, *software*) antivirus *inv*

antlers ['æntləz] *npl* cuernas *fpl*, cornamenta *sg*

anxiety [æŋ'zaɪətɪ] *n* inquietud *f*; (*Med*) ansiedad *f*; **~ to do** deseo de hacer

anxious ['æŋkʃəs] *adj* inquieto, preocupado; (*worrying*) preocupante; (*keen*): **to be ~ to do** tener muchas ganas de hacer

○ **KEYWORD**

any ['enɪ] *adj* **1** (*in questions etc*) algún/alguna; **have you any butter/ children?** ¿tienes mantequilla/ hijos?; **if there are any tickets left** si quedan billetes, si queda algún billete

2 (*with negative*): **I haven't any money/ books** no tengo dinero/libros

3 (*no matter which*) cualquier; **any excuse will do** valdrá *o* servirá cualquier excusa; **choose any book you like** escoge el libro que quieras

4 (*in phrases*): **in any case** de todas formas, en cualquier caso; **any day now** cualquier día (de estos); **at any moment** en cualquier momento, de un momento a otro; **at any rate** en todo caso; **any time: come (at) any time** ven cuando quieras; **he might come (at) any time** podría llegar de un momento a otro

▷ *pron* **1** (*in questions etc*): **have you got any?** ¿tienes alguno(s)/a(s)?; **can any of you sing?** ¿sabe cantar alguno de vosotros/ustedes?

2 (*with negative*): **I haven't any (of them)** no tengo ninguno

3 (*no matter which one(s)*): **take any of those books (you like)** toma el libro que quieras de ésos

▷ *adv* **1** (*in questions etc*): **do you want any more soup/sandwiches?** ¿quieres más sopa/bocadillos?; **are you feeling any better?** ¿te sientes algo mejor?

2 (*with negative*): **I can't hear him any more** ya no le oigo; **don't wait any longer** no esperes más

any: anybody *pron* cualquiera; (*in interrogative sentences*) alguien; (*in negative sentences*) alguien; **I don't see anybody** no veo a nadie; **if anybody should phone ...** si llama alguien

...; **anyhow** adv (at any rate) de todos modos, de todas formas; (haphazard): **do it anyhow you like** hazlo como quieras; **she leaves things just anyhow** deja las cosas como quiera or de cualquier modo; **I shall go anyhow** de todos modos iré; **anyone** pron = **anybody**; **anything** pron (in questions etc) algo, alguna cosa; (with negative) nada; **can you see anything?** ¿ves algo?; **if anything happens to me ...** si algo me ocurre ...; (no matter what): **you can say anything you like** puedes decir lo que quieras; **anything will do** vale todo or cualquier cosa; **he'll eat anything** come de todo or lo que sea; **anytime** adv (at any moment) en cualquier momento, de un momento a otro; (whenever) no importa cuándo, cuando quiera; **anyway** adv (at any rate) de todos modos, de todas formas; **I shall go anyway** iré de todos modos; (besides): **anyway, I couldn't come even if I wanted to** además, no podría venir aunque quisiera; **why are you phoning, anyway?** ¿entonces, por qué llamas?, ¿por qué llamas, pues?; **anywhere** adv (in questions etc): **can you see him anywhere?** ¿le ves por algún lado?; **are you going anywhere?** ¿vas a algún sitio?; (with negative): **I can't see him anywhere** no le veo por ninguna parte; **anywhere in the world** (no matter where) en cualquier parte (del mundo); **put the books down anywhere** deja los libros donde quieras

apart [əˈpɑːt] adv (aside) aparte; (situation): **~ (from)** separado (de); (movement): **to pull ~** separar; **10 miles ~** separados por 10 millas; **to take ~** desmontar; **~ from** prep aparte de

apartment [əˈpɑːtmənt] n (US) piso (SP), departamento (LAM), apartamento; (room) cuarto; **apartment building** (US) n edificio de apartamentos

apathy [ˈæpəθɪ] n apatía,

indiferencia

ape [eɪp] n mono ▷ vt imitar, remedar

aperitif [əˈpɛrɪtɪf] n aperitivo

aperture [ˈæpətʃjuə*] n rendija, resquicio; (Phot) abertura

APEX [ˈeɪpɛks] n abbr (= Advanced Purchase Excursion Fare) tarifa f APEX

apologize [əˈpɒlədʒaɪz] vi: **to ~ (for sth to sb)** disculparse (con algn de algo)

apology [əˈpɒlədʒɪ] n disculpa, excusa

▌ Be careful not to translate **apology** by the Spanish word apología.

apostrophe [əˈpɒstrəfɪ] n apóstrofo

appal [əˈpɔːl] (US **appall**) vt horrorizar, espantar; **appalling** adj espantoso; (awful) pésimo

apparatus [æpəˈreɪtəs] n (equipment) equipo; (organization) aparato; (in gymnasium) aparatos mpl

apparent [əˈpærənt] adj aparente; (obvious) evidente; **apparently** adv por lo visto, al parecer

appeal [əˈpiːl] vi (Law) apelar ▷ n (Law) apelación f; (request) llamamiento; (plea) petición f; (charm) atractivo; **to ~ for** reclamar; **to ~ to** (be attractive to) atraer; **it doesn't ~ to me** no me atrae, no me llama la atención; **appealing** adj (attractive) atractivo

appear [əˈpɪə*] vi aparecer, presentarse; (Law) comparecer; (publication) salir (a luz), publicarse; (seem) parecer; **to ~ on TV/in "Hamlet"** salir por la tele/hacer un papel en "Hamlet"; **it would ~ that** parecería que; **appearance** n aparición f; (look) apariencia, aspecto

appendices [əˈpɛndɪsiːz] npl of **appendix**

appendicitis [əpɛndɪˈsaɪtɪs] n apendicitis f

appendix [əˈpɛndɪks] (pl **appendices**) n apéndice m

appetite [ˈæpɪtaɪt] n apetito; (fig) deseo, anhelo

appetizer ['æpɪtaɪzə*] n (drink)
aperitivo; (food) tapas fpl (SP)
applaud [ə'plɔːd] vt, vi aplaudir
applause [ə'plɔːz] n aplausos mpl
apple ['æpl] n manzana; **apple pie**
n pastel m de manzana, pay m de
manzana (LAM)
appliance [ə'plaɪəns] n aparato
applicable [ə'plɪkəbl] adj
(relevant): **to be ~ (to)** referirse (a)
applicant ['æplɪkənt] n candidato/
a; solicitante mf
application [æplɪ'keɪʃən] n
aplicación f; (for a job etc) solicitud
f, petición f; **application form** n
solicitud f
apply [ə'plaɪ] vt (paint etc) poner;
(law etc: put into practice) poner en
vigor ▷ vi: **to ~ to** (ask) dirigirse a;
(be applicable) ser aplicable a; **to ~ for**
(permit, grant, job) solicitar; **to ~ o.s. to**
aplicarse a, dedicarse a
appoint [ə'pɔɪnt] vt (to post)
nombrar a

▌ Be careful not to translate **appoint**
by the Spanish word apuntar.

appointment [ə'pɔɪntmənt] n (with client) cita;
(act) nombramiento; (post) puesto;
(at hairdresser etc): **to have an
appointment** tener hora; **to make
an appointment (with sb)** citarse
(con algn)
appraisal [ə'preɪzl] n valoración f
appreciate [ə'priːʃɪeɪt] vt apreciar,
tener en mucho; (be grateful for)
agradecer; (be aware) comprender
▷ vi (Comm) aumentar(se) en valor;
appreciation [-'eɪʃən] n apreciación
f; (gratitude) reconocimiento,
agradecimiento; (Comm) aumento
en valor
apprehension [æprɪ'hɛnʃən] n
(fear) aprensión f
apprehensive [æprɪ'hɛnsɪv] adj
aprensivo
apprentice [ə'prɛntɪs] n aprendiz(a)
m/f
approach [ə'prəʊtʃ] vi acercarse

▷ vt acercarse a; (ask, apply to) dirigirse
a; (situation, problem) abordar ▷ n
acercamiento; (access) acceso; (to
problem, situation): **~ (to)** actitud f
(ante)
appropriate [adj ə'prəʊprɪɪt, vb
ə'prəʊprɪeɪt] adj apropiado,
conveniente ▷ vt (take) apropiarse de
approval [ə'pruːvəl] n aprobación
f, visto bueno; (permission)
consentimiento; **on ~** (Comm) a prueba
approve [ə'pruːv] vt aprobar;
approve of vt fus (thing) aprobar;
(person): **they don't approve of her**
(ella) no les parece bien
approximate [ə'prɔksɪmɪt] adj
aproximado; **approximately** adv
aproximadamente, más o menos
Apr. abbr (= April) abr
apricot ['eɪprɪkɔt] n albaricoque m,
chabacano (MEX), damasco (RPL)
April ['eɪprəl] n abril m; **April Fools'
Day** n el primero de abril, ≈ día m de
los Inocentes (28 December)
apron ['eɪprən] n delantal m
apt [æpt] adj acertado, apropiado;
(likely): **~ to do** propenso a hacer
aquarium [ə'kwɛərɪəm] n acuario
Aquarius [ə'kwɛərɪəs] n Acuario
Arab ['ærəb] adj, n árabe mf
Arabia [ə'reɪbɪə] n Arabia; **Arabian**
adj árabe; **Arabic** ['ærəbɪk] adj árabe;
(numerals) arábigo ▷ n árabe m
arbitrary ['ɑːbɪtrərɪ] adj arbitrario
arbitration [ɑːbɪ'treɪʃən] n
arbitraje m
arc [ɑːk] n arco
arcade [ɑː'keɪd] n (round a square)
soportales mpl; (shopping mall) galería
comercial
arch [ɑːtʃ] n arco; (of foot) arco del pie
▷ vt arquear
archaeology [ɑːkɪ'ɔlədʒɪ] (US
archeology) n arqueología
archbishop [ɑːtʃ'bɪʃəp] n arzobispo
archeology [ɑːkɪ'ɔlədʒɪ] (US) =
archaeology
architect ['ɑːkɪtɛkt] n arquitecto/a;

architectural [ɑːkɪˈtɛktʃərəl] *adj* arquitectónico; **architecture** *n* arquitectura

archive [ˈɑːkaɪv] *n* (*often pl: also* Comput) archivo

Arctic [ˈɑːktɪk] *adj* ártico ▷ *n*: **the ~** el Ártico

are [ɑː*] *vb see* be

area [ˈɛərɪə] *n* área, región *f*; (*part of place*) zona; (*Math etc*) área, superficie *f*; (*in room: e.g. dining area*) parte *f*; (*of knowledge, experience*) campo; **area code** (*us*) *n* (*Tel*) prefijo

arena [əˈriːnə] *n* estadio; (*of circus*) pista

aren't [ɑːnt] = **are not**

Argentina [ɑːdʒənˈtiːnə] *n* Argentina; **Argentinian** [-ˈtɪnɪən] *adj*, *n* argentino/a *m/f*

arguably [ˈɑːgjuəblɪ] *adv* posiblemente

argue [ˈɑːgjuː] *vi* (*quarrel*) discutir, pelearse; (*reason*) razonar, argumentar; **to ~ that** sostener que

argument [ˈɑːgjumənt] *n* discusión *f*, pelea; (*reasons*) argumento

Aries [ˈɛərɪz] *n* Aries *m*

arise [əˈraɪz] (*pt* **arose**, *pp* **arisen**) *vi* surgir, presentarse

arithmetic [əˈrɪθmətɪk] *n* aritmética

arm [ɑːm] *n* brazo ▷ *vt* armar; **arms** *npl* armas *fpl*; **~ in ~** cogidos del brazo; **armchair** [ˈɑːmtʃɛə*] *n* sillón *m*, butaca

armed [ɑːmd] *adj* armado; **armed robbery** *n* robo a mano armada

armour [ˈɑːmə*] (*us* **armor**) *n* armadura; (*Mil: tanks*) blindaje *m*

armpit [ˈɑːmpɪt] *n* sobaco, axila

armrest [ˈɑːmrɛst] *n* apoyabrazos *m inv*

army [ˈɑːmɪ] *n* ejército; (*fig*) multitud *f*

A road *n* (*BRIT*) ≈ carretera *f* nacional

aroma [əˈrəumə] *n* aroma *m*, fragancia; **aromatherapy** *n* aromaterapia

arose [əˈrəuz] *pt of* **arise**

around [əˈraund] *adv* alrededor; (*in the area*): **there is no one else ~** no hay nadie más por aquí ▷ *prep* alrededor de

arouse [əˈrauz] *vt* despertar; (*anger*) provocar

arrange [əˈreɪndʒ] *vt* arreglar, ordenar; (*organize*) organizar; **to ~ to do sth** quedar en hacer algo; **arrangement** *n* arreglo; (*agreement*) acuerdo; **arrangements** *npl* (*preparations*) preparativos *mpl*

array [əˈreɪ] *n*: **~ of** (*things*) serie *f* de; (*people*) conjunto de

arrears [əˈrɪəz] *npl* atrasos *mpl*; **to be in ~ with one's rent** estar retrasado en el pago del alquiler

arrest [əˈrɛst] *vt* detener; (*sb's attention*) llamar ▷ *n* detención *f*; **under ~** detenido

arrival [əˈraɪvəl] *n* llegada; **new ~** recién llegado/a; (*baby*) recién nacido

arrive [əˈraɪv] *vi* llegar; (*baby*) nacer; **arrive at** *vt fus* (*decision, solution*) llegar a

arrogance [ˈærəgəns] *n* arrogancia, prepotencia (*LAM*)

arrogant [ˈærəgənt] *adj* arrogante

arrow [ˈærəu] *n* flecha

arse [ɑːs] (*BRIT: inf!*) *n* culo, trasero

arson [ˈɑːsn] *n* incendio premeditado

art [ɑːt] *n* arte *m*; (*skill*) destreza; **art college** *n* escuela *f* de Bellas Artes

artery [ˈɑːtərɪ] *n* arteria

art gallery *n* pinacoteca; (*saleroom*) galería de arte

arthritis [ɑːˈθraɪtɪs] *n* artritis *f*

artichoke [ˈɑːtɪtʃəuk] *n* alcachofa; **Jerusalem ~** aguaturma

article [ˈɑːtɪkl] *n* artículo

articulate [*adj* ɑːˈtɪkjulɪt, *vb* ɑːˈtɪkjuleɪt] *adj* claro, bien expresado ▷ *vt* expresar

artificial [ɑːtɪˈfɪʃəl] *adj* artificial; (*affected*) afectado

artist [ˈɑːtɪst] *n* artista *mf*; (*Mus*) intérprete *mf*; **artistic** [ɑːˈtɪstɪk] *adj*

artístico
art school n escuela de bellas artes

○ **KEYWORD**

as [æz] conj **1** (referring to time) cuando, mientras; a medida que; **as the years went by** con el paso de los años; **he came in as I was leaving** entró cuando me marchaba; **as from tomorrow** desde or a partir de mañana
2 (in comparisons): **as big as** tan grande como; **twice as big as** el doble de grande que; **as much money/many books as** tanto dinero/tantos libros como; **as soon as** en cuanto
3 (since, because) como, ya que; **he left early as he had to be home by 10** se fue temprano ya que tenía que estar en casa a las 10
4 (referring to manner, way): **do as you wish** haz lo que quieras; **as she said** como dijo; **he gave it to me as a present** me lo dio de regalo
5 (in the capacity of): **he works as a barman** trabaja de barman; **as chairman of the company, he ...** como presidente de la compañía ...
6 (concerning): **as for** or **to that** por or en lo que respecta a eso
7: **as if** or **though** como si; **he looked as if he was ill** parecía como si estuviera enfermo, tenía aspecto de enfermo; see also **long; such; well**

a.s.a.p. abbr (= as soon as possible) cuanto antes
asbestos [æz'bɛstəs] n asbesto, amianto
ascent [ə'sɛnt] n subida; (slope) cuesta, pendiente f
ash [æʃ] n ceniza; (tree) fresno
ashamed [ə'ʃeɪmd] adj avergonzado, apenado (LAM); **to be ~ of** avergonzarse de
ashore [ə'ʃɔ:*] adv en tierra; (swim etc) a tierra

ashtray ['æʃtreɪ] n cenicero
Ash Wednesday n miércoles m de Ceniza
Asia ['eɪʃə] n Asia; **Asian** adj, n asiático/a m/f
aside [ə'saɪd] adv a un lado ▷ n aparte m
ask [ɑ:sk] vt (question) preguntar; (invite) invitar; **to ~ sb sth/to do sth** preguntar algo a algn/pedir a algn que haga algo; **to ~ sb about sth** preguntar algo a algn; **to ~ (sb) a question** hacer una pregunta (a algn); **to ~ sb out to dinner** invitar a cenar a algn; **ask for** vt fus pedir; (trouble) buscar
asleep [ə'sli:p] adj dormido; **to fall ~** dormirse, quedarse dormido
asparagus [əs'pærəgəs] n (plant) espárrago; (food) espárragos mpl
aspect ['æspɛkt] n aspecto, apariencia; (direction in which a building etc faces) orientación f
aspirations [æspə'reɪʃənz] npl aspiraciones fpl; (ambition) ambición f
aspire [əs'paɪə*] vi: **to ~ to** aspirar a, ambicionar
aspirin ['æsprɪn] n aspirina
ass [æs] n asno, burro; (inf: idiot) imbécil mf; (us: inf!) culo, trasero
assassin [ə'sæsɪn] n asesino/a; **assassinate** vt asesinar
assault [ə'sɔ:lt] n asalto; (Law) agresión f ▷ vt asaltar, atacar; (sexually) violar
assemble [ə'sɛmbl] vt reunir, juntar; (Tech) montar ▷ vi reunirse, juntarse
assembly [ə'sɛmblɪ] n reunión f, asamblea; (parliament) parlamento; (construction) montaje m
assert [ə'sə:t] vt afirmar; (authority) hacer valer; **assertion** [-ʃən] n afirmación f
assess [ə'sɛs] vt valorar, calcular; (tax, damages) fijar; (for tax) gravar; **assessment** n valoración f; (for tax) gravamen m
asset ['æsɛt] n ventaja; **assets** npl (Comm) activo; (property, funds)

fondos *mpl*

assign [ə'saɪn] *vt*: **to ~ (to)** (*date*) fijar (para); (*task*) asignar (a); (*resources*) destinar (a); **assignment** *n* tarea

assist [ə'sɪst] *vt* ayudar; **assistance** *n* ayuda, auxilio; **assistant** *n* ayudante *mf*; (BRIT: *also*: **shop assistant**) dependiente/a *m/f*

associate [*adj, n* ə'səʊʃiɪt, *vb* ə'səʊʃieɪt] *adj* asociado ▷ *n* (*at work*) colega *mf* ▷ *vt* asociar; (*ideas*) relacionar ▷ *vi*: **to ~ with sb** tratar con algn

association [əsəʊsɪ'eɪʃən] *n* asociación *f*

assorted [ə'sɔ:tɪd] *adj* surtido, variado

assortment [ə'sɔ:tmənt] *n* (*of shapes, colours*) surtido; (*of books*) colección *f*; (*of people*) mezcla

assume [ə'sju:m] *vt* suponer; (*responsibilities*) asumir; (*attitude*) adoptar, tomar

assumption [ə'sʌmpʃən] *n* suposición *f*, presunción *f*; (*of power etc*) toma

assurance [ə'ʃʊərəns] *n* garantía, promesa; (*confidence*) confianza, aplomo; (*insurance*) seguro

assure [ə'ʃʊə*] *vt* asegurar

asterisk ['æstərɪsk] *n* asterisco

asthma ['æsmə] *n* asma

astonish [ə'stɒnɪʃ] *vt* asombrar, pasmar; **astonished** *adj* estupefacto, pasmado; **to be astonished (at)** asombrarse (de); **astonishing** *adj* asombroso, pasmoso; **I find it astonishing that ...** me asombra or pasma que ...; **astonishment** *n* asombro, sorpresa

astound [ə'staund] *vt* asombrar, pasmar

astray [ə'streɪ] *adv*: **to go ~** extraviarse; **to lead ~** (*morally*) llevar por mal camino

astrology [æs'trɒlədʒɪ] *n* astrología

astronaut ['æstrənɔ:t] *n* astronauta *mf*

astronomer [əs'trɒnəmə*] *n* astrónomo/a

astronomical [æstrə'nɒmɪkəl] *adj* astronómico

astronomy [æs'trɒnəmɪ] *n* astronomía

astute [əs'tju:t] *adj* astuto

asylum [ə'saɪləm] *n* (*refuge*) asilo; (*mental hospital*) manicomio

○ **KEYWORD**

at [æt] *prep* **1** (*referring to position*) en; (*direction*) a; **at the top** en lo alto; **at home/school** en casa/la escuela; **to look at sth/sb** mirar algo/a algn

2 (*referring to time*): **at 4 o'clock** a las 4; **at night** por la noche; **at Christmas** en Navidad; **at times** a veces

3 (*referring to rates, speed etc*): **at £1 a kilo** a una libra el kilo; **two at a time** de dos en dos; **at 50 km/h** a 50 km/h

4 (*referring to manner*): **at a stroke** de un golpe; **at peace** en paz

5 (*referring to activity*): **to be at work** estar trabajando; (*in the office etc*) estar en el trabajo; **to play at cowboys** jugar a los vaqueros; **to be good at sth** ser bueno en algo

6 (*referring to cause*): **shocked/ surprised/annoyed at sth** asombrado/sorprendido/fastidiado por algo; **I went at his suggestion** fui a instancias suyas

7 (*symbol*) arroba

ate [eɪt] *pt of* **eat**

atheist ['eɪθɪɪst] *n* ateo/a

Athens ['æθɪnz] *n* Atenas

athlete ['æθli:t] *n* atleta *mf*

athletic [æθ'letɪk] *adj* atlético; **athletics** *n* atletismo

Atlantic [ət'læntɪk] *adj* atlántico ▷ *n*: **the ~ (Ocean)** el (Océano) Atlántico

atlas ['ætləs] *n* atlas *m inv*

A.T.M. *n abbr* (= *automated telling*

machine) cajero automático
atmosphere ['ætməsfɪə*] n
atmósfera; (*of place*) ambiente m
atom ['ætəm] n átomo; **atomic**
[ə'tɒmɪk] adj atómico; **atom(ic)
bomb** n bomba atómica
A to Z® n (*map*) callejero
atrocity [ə'trɒsɪtɪ] n atrocidad f
attach [ə'tætʃ] vt (*fasten*) atar;
(*join*) unir, sujetar; (*document,
letter*) adjuntar; (*importance etc*)
dar, conceder; **to be ~ed to sb/sth**
(*to like*) tener cariño a algn/algo;
attachment (*tool*) accesorio;
(*Comput*) archivo, documento adjunto;
(*love*): **attachment (to)** apego (a)
attack [ə'tæk] vt (*Mil*) atacar;
(*criminal*) agredir, asaltar; (*criticize*)
criticar; (*task*) emprender ▷ n ataque
m, asalto; (*on sb's life*) atentado;
(*fig: criticism*) crítica; (*of illness*) ataque
m; **heart ~** infarto (de miocardio);
attacker n agresor(a) m/f, asaltante
mf
attain [ə'teɪn] vt (*also: ~ to*) alcanzar;
(*achieve*) lograr, conseguir
attempt [ə'tɛmpt] n tentativa,
intento; (*attack*) atentado ▷ vt
intentar
attend [ə'tɛnd] vt asistir a; (*patient*)
atender; **attend to** vt fus ocuparse
de; (*customer, patient*) atender a;
attendance n asistencia, presencia;
(*people present*) concurrencia;
attendant n ayudante mf; (*in garage
etc*) encargado/a ▷ adj (*dangers*)
concomitante
attention [ə'tɛnʃən] n atención
f; (*care*) atenciones fpl ▷ excl (*Mil*)
¡firme(s)!; **for the ~ of ...** (*Admin*)
atención ...
attic ['ætɪk] n desván m
attitude ['ætɪtjuːd] n actitud f;
(*disposition*) disposición f
attorney [ə'tə:nɪ] n (*lawyer*)
abogado/a; **Attorney General** n
(*BRIT*) ≈ Presidente m del Consejo del
Poder Judicial (*SP*); (*US*) ≈ ministro

de Justicia
attract [ə'trækt] vt atraer; (*sb's
attention*) llamar; **attraction**
[ə'trækʃən] n encanto; (*gen
pl: amusements*) diversiones fpl;
(*Physics*) atracción f; (*fig: towards sb,
sth*) atractivo; **attractive** adj guapo;
(*interesting*) atrayente
attribute [n 'ætrɪbjuːt, vb ə'trɪbjuːt]
n atributo ▷ vt: **to ~ sth to** atribuir
algo a
aubergine ['əubəʒiːn] (*BRIT*) n
berenjena f; (*colour*) morado
auburn ['ɔːbən] adj color castaño
rojizo
auction ['ɔːkʃən] n (*also: sale by ~*)
subasta ▷ vt subastar
audible ['ɔːdɪbl] adj audible, que se
puede oír
audience ['ɔːdɪəns] n público;
(*Radio*) radioescuchas mpl; (*TV*)
telespectadores mpl; (*interview*)
audiencia
audit ['ɔːdɪt] vt revisar, intervenir
audition [ɔː'dɪʃən] n audición f
auditor ['ɔːdɪtə*] n interventor(a)
m/f, censor(a) m/f de cuentas
auditorium [ɔːdɪ'tɔːrɪəm] n
auditorio
Aug. abbr (= *August*) ag
August ['ɔːgəst] n agosto
aunt [ɑːnt] n tía; **auntie** n diminutive
of **aunt**; **aunty** n diminutive of **aunt**
au pair ['əu'pɛə*] n (*also: ~ girl*)
(chica) au pair f
aura ['ɔːrə] n aura; (*atmosphere*)
ambiente m
austerity [ɔ'stɛrɪtɪ] n austeridad f
Australia [ɔs'treɪlɪə] n Australia;
Australian adj, n australiano/a m/f
Austria ['ɔstrɪə] n Austria; **Austrian**
adj, n austríaco/a m/f
authentic [ɔː'θɛntɪk] adj auténtico
author ['ɔːθə*] n autor(a) m/f
authority [ɔː'θɔrɪtɪ] n autoridad f;
(*official permission*) autorización f; **the
authorities** npl las autoridades
authorize ['ɔːθəraɪz] vt autorizar

auto ['ɔːtəu] (US) n coche m (SP), carro (LAM), automóvil m

auto: autobiography [ɔːtəbaɪ'ɒgrəfɪ] n autobiografía; **autograph** ['ɔːtəgrɑːf] n autógrafo ▷ vt (photo etc) dedicar; (programme) firmar; **automatic** [ɔːtə'mætɪk] adj automático ▷ n (gun) pistola automática; (car) coche m automático; **automatically** adv automáticamente; **automobile** ['ɔːtəməbiːl] (US) n coche m (SP), carro (LAM), automóvil m; **autonomous** [ɔː'tɒnəməs] adj autónomo; **autonomy** [ɔː'tɒnəmɪ] n autonomía

autumn ['ɔːtəm] n otoño

auxiliary [ɔːg'zɪlɪərɪ] adj, n auxiliar mf

avail [ə'veɪl] vt: **to ~ o.s. of** aprovechar(se) de ▷ n: **to no ~** en vano, sin resultado

availability [əveɪlə'bɪlɪtɪ] n disponibilidad f

available [ə'veɪləbl] adj disponible; (unoccupied) libre; (person: unattached) soltero y sin compromiso

avalanche ['ævəlɑːnʃ] n alud m, avalancha

Ave. abbr = **avenue**

avenue ['ævənjuː] n avenida; (fig) camino

average ['ævərɪdʒ] n promedio, término medio ▷ adj medio, de término medio; (ordinary) regular, corriente ▷ vt sacar un promedio de; **on ~** por regla general

avert [ə'vɜːt] vt prevenir; (blow) desviar; (one's eyes) apartar

avid ['ævɪd] adj ávido

avocado [ævə'kɑːdəu] n (also BRIT: **~ pear**) aguacate m, palta (SC)

avoid [ə'vɔɪd] vt evitar, eludir

await [ə'weɪt] vt esperar, aguardar

awake [ə'weɪk] (pt **awoke**, pp **awoken** or **awaked**) adj despierto ▷ vt despertar ▷ vi despertarse; **to be ~** estar despierto

award [ə'wɔːd] n premio;

(Law: damages) indemnización f ▷ vt otorgar, conceder; (Law: damages) adjudicar

aware [ə'wɛə*] adj: **~ (of)** consciente (de); **to become ~ of/that** (realize) darse cuenta de/de que; (learn) enterarse de/de que; **awareness** n conciencia; (knowledge) conocimiento

away [ə'weɪ] adv fuera; (movement): **she went ~** se marchó; **far ~** lejos; **two kilometres ~** a dos kilómetros de distancia; **two hours ~ by car** a dos horas en coche; **the holiday was two weeks ~** faltaban dos semanas para las vacaciones; **he's ~ for a week** estará ausente una semana; **to take ~ (from)** quitar (a); (subtract) substraer (de); **to work/pedal ~** seguir trabajando/pedaleando; **to fade ~** (colour) desvanecerse; (sound) apagarse

awe [ɔː] n admiración f respetuosa; **awesome** ['ɔːsəm] (US) adj (excellent) formidable

awful ['ɔːfəl] adj horroroso; (quantity): **an ~ lot (of)** cantidad (de); **awfully** adv (very) terriblemente

awkward ['ɔːkwəd] adj desmañado, torpe; (shape) incómodo; (embarrassing) delicado, difícil

awoke [ə'wəuk] pt of **awake**

awoken [ə'wəukən] pp of **awake**

axe [æks] (US **ax**) n hacha ▷ vt (project) cortar; (jobs) reducir

axle ['æksl] n eje m, árbol m

ay(e) [aɪ] excl sí

azalea [ə'zeɪlɪə] n azalea

b

B [biː] n (Mus) si m

B.A. abbr = **Bachelor of Arts**

baby ['beɪbɪ] n bebé mf; (us: inf: darling) mi amor; **baby carriage** (us) n cochecito; **baby-sit** vi hacer de canguro; **baby-sitter** n canguro/a; **baby wipe** n toallita húmeda (para bebés)

bachelor ['bætʃələ*] n soltero; **B~ of Arts/Science** licenciado/a en Filosofía y Letras/Ciencias

back [bæk] n (of person) espalda; (of animal) lomo; (of hand) dorso; (as opposed to front) parte f de atrás; (of chair) respaldo; (of page) reverso; (of book) final m; (Football) defensa m; (of crowd): **the ones at the ~** los del fondo ▷ vt (candidate: also: **~ up**) respaldar, apoyar; (horse: at races) apostar a; (car) dar marcha atrás a or con ▷ vi (car etc) ir (or salir or entrar) marcha atrás ▷ adj (payment, rent) atrasado; (seats, wheels) de atrás ▷ adv (not forward) (hacia) atrás; (returned): **he's ~** está de vuelta, ha vuelto; **he ran ~** volvió corriendo; (restitution): **throw the ball ~** devuelve la pelota; **can I have it ~?** ¿me lo devuelve?; (again): **he called ~** llamó de nuevo; **back down** vi echarse atrás; **back out** vi (of promise) volverse atrás; **back up** vt (person) apoyar, respaldar; (theory) defender; (Comput) hacer una copia preventiva or de reserva; **backache** n dolor m de espalda; **backbencher** (BRIT) n miembro del parlamento sin cargo relevante; **backbone** n columna vertebral; **back door** n puerta f trasera; **backfire** vi (Aut) petardear; (plans) fallar, salir mal; **backgammon** n backgammon m; **background** n fondo; (of events) antecedentes mpl; (basic knowledge) bases fpl; (experience) conocimientos mpl, educación f; **family background** origen m, antecedentes mpl; **backing** n (fig) apoyo, respaldo; **backlog** n: **backlog of work** trabajo atrasado; **backpack** n mochila; **backpacker** n mochilero/a; **backslash** n pleca, barra inversa; **backstage** adv entre bastidores; **backstroke** n espalda; **backup** adj suplementario; (Comput) de reserva ▷ n (support) apoyo; (also: **backup file**) copia preventiva or de reserva; **backward** adj (person, country) atrasado; **backwards** adv hacia atrás; (read a list) al revés; (fall) de espaldas; **backyard** n traspatio

bacon ['beɪkən] n tocino, beicon m

bacteria [bæk'tɪərɪə] npl bacterias fpl

bad [bæd] adj malo; (mistake, accident) grave; (food) podrido, pasado; **his ~ leg** su pierna lisiada; (of food) pasarse

badge [bædʒ] n insignia; (policeman's) chapa, placa

badger ['bædʒə*] n tejón m

badly ['bædlɪ] adv mal; **to reflect ~ on sb** influir negativamente en la reputación de algn; **~ wounded** gravemente herido; **he needs it ~** le hace gran falta; **to be ~ off (for money)** andar mal de dinero

bad-mannered ['bæd'mænəd] adj

mal educado

badminton ['bædmɪntən] n
bádminton m

bad-tempered ['bæd'tɛmpəd] adj
de mal genio or carácter; (temporarily)
de mal humor

bag [bæg] n bolsa; (handbag) bolso;
(satchel) mochila; (case) maleta; **~s
of** (inf) un montón de; **baggage** n
equipaje m; **baggage allowance** n
límite m de equipaje; **baggage
reclaim** n recogida de equipajes;
baggy adj amplio; **bagpipes** npl
gaita

bail [beɪl] n fianza ▷ vt
(prisoner: gen: grant bail to) poner en
libertad bajo fianza; (boat: also: **~ out**)
achicar; **on ~** (prisoner) bajo fianza; **to
~ sb out** obtener la libertad de algn
bajo fianza

bait [beɪt] n cebo ▷ vt poner cebo en;
(tease) tomar el pelo a

bake [beɪk] vt cocer (al horno) ▷ vi
cocerse; **baked beans** npl judías fpl
en salsa de tomate; **baked potato** n
patata al horno; **baker** n panadero;
bakery n panadería; (for cakes)
pastelería; **baking** n (act) amasar m;
(batch) hornada; **baking powder** n
levadura (en polvo)

balance ['bæləns] n equilibrio;
(Comm: sum) balance m; (remainder)
resto; (scales) balanza ▷ vt equilibrar;
(budget) nivelar; (account) saldar;
(make equal) equilibrar; **~ of trade/
payments** balanza de comercio/
pagos; **balanced** adj (personality, diet)
equilibrado; (report) objetivo; **balance
sheet** n balance m

balcony ['bælkənɪ] n (open) balcón m;
(closed) galería; (in theatre) anfiteatro

bald [bɔːld] adj calvo; (tyre) liso

Balearics [bælɪ'ærɪks] npl: **the ~** las
Baleares

ball [bɔːl] n pelota; (football) balón m;
(of wool, string) ovillo; (dance) baile m; **to
play ~** (fig) cooperar

ballerina [bælə'riːnə] n bailarina

ballet ['bæleɪ] n ballet m; **ballet
dancer** n bailarín/ina m/f

balloon [bə'luːn] n globo

ballot ['bælət] n votación f

ballpoint (pen) ['bɔːlpɔɪnt-] n
bolígrafo

ballroom ['bɔːlrum] n salón m
de baile

Baltic ['bɔːltɪk] n: **the ~ (Sea)** el (Mar)
Báltico

bamboo [bæm'buː] n bambú m

ban [bæn] n prohibición f,
proscripción f ▷ vt prohibir, proscribir

banana [bə'nɑːnə] n plátano, banana
(LAM), banano (CAM)

band [bænd] n grupo; (strip) faja, tira;
(stripe) lista; (Mus: jazz) orquesta; (: rock)
grupo; (Mil) banda

bandage ['bændɪdʒ] n venda,
vendaje m ▷ vt vendar

Band-Aid® ['bændeɪd] (US) n tirita

bandit ['bændɪt] n bandido

bang [bæŋ] n (of gun, exhaust)
estallido, detonación f; (of door)
portazo; (blow) golpe m ▷ vt (door)
cerrar de golpe; (one's head) golpear ▷ vi
estallar; (door) cerrar de golpe

Bangladesh [bɑːŋglə'dɛʃ] n
Bangladesh m

bangle ['bæŋgl] n brazalete m,
ajorca

bangs [bæŋz] (US) npl flequillo

banish ['bænɪʃ] vt desterrar

banister(s) ['bænɪstə(z)] n(pl)
barandilla, pasamanos m inv

banjo ['bændʒəʊ] (pl **~es** or **~s**) n
banjo

bank [bæŋk] n (Comm) banco; (of river,
lake) ribera, orilla; (of earth) terraplén
m ▷ vi (Aviat) ladearse; **bank on** vt fus
contar con; **bank account** n cuenta
de banco; **bank balance** n saldo;
bank card n tarjeta bancaria; **bank
charges** npl comisión fsg; **banker** n
banquero; **bank holiday** n (BRIT) día m
festivo or de fiesta; **banking** n banca;
bank manager n director(a) m/f
(de sucursal) de banco; **banknote** n

billete *m* de banco

bankrupt ['bæŋkrʌpt] *adj* quebrado,
insolvente; **to go ~** hacer bancarrota;
to be ~ estar en quiebra; **bankruptcy**
n quiebra

bank statement *n* balance *m* or
detalle *m* de cuenta

banner ['bænə*] *n* pancarta

bannister(s) ['bænɪstə(z)] *n(pl)* =
banister(s)

banquet ['bæŋkwɪt] *n* banquete *m*

baptism ['bæptɪzəm] *n* bautismo;
(*act*) bautizo

baptize [bæp'taɪz] *vt* bautizar

bar [bɑ:*] *n* (*pub*) bar *m*; (*counter*)
mostrador *m*; (*rod*) barra; (*of window,
cage*) reja; (*of soap*) pastilla; (*of
chocolate*) tableta; (*fig: hindrance*)
obstáculo; (*prohibition*) proscripción
f; (*Mus*) barra ▷ *vt* (*road*) obstruir;
(*person*) excluir; (*activity*) prohibir; **the
B~** (*Law*) la abogacía; **behind ~s** entre
rejas; **~ none** sin excepción

barbaric [bɑ:'bærɪk] *adj* bárbaro

barbecue ['bɑ:bɪkju:] *n* barbacoa

barbed wire ['bɑ:bd-] *n* alambre
m de púas

barber ['bɑ:bə*] *n* peluquero,
barbero; **barber's (shop)** (*us* **barber
(shop)**) *n* peluquería

bar code *n* código de barras

bare [bɛə*] *adj* desnudo; (*trees*) sin
hojas; (*necessities etc*) básico ▷ *vt*
desnudar; (*teeth*) enseñar; **barefoot**
adj, adv descalzo; **barely** *adv* apenas

bargain ['bɑ:gɪn] *n* pacto, negocio;
(*good buy*) ganga ▷ *vi* negociar; (*haggle*)
regatear; **into the ~** además, por
añadidura; **bargain for** *vt fus*: **he got
more than he bargained for** le resultó
peor de lo que esperaba

barge [bɑ:dʒ] *n* barcaza; **barge in**
vi irrumpir; (*interrupt: conversation*)
interrumpir

bark [bɑ:k] *n* (*of tree*) corteza; (*of dog*)
ladrido ▷ *vi* ladrar

barley ['bɑ:lɪ] *n* cebada

barmaid ['bɑ:meɪd] *n* camarera

barman ['bɑ:mən] (*irreg*) *n* camarero,
barman *m*

barn [bɑ:n] *n* granero

barometer [bə'rɒmɪtə*] *n*
barómetro

baron ['bærən] *n* barón *m*; (*press baron
etc*) magnate *m*; **baroness** *n* baronesa

barracks ['bærəks] *npl* cuartel *m*

barrage ['bærɑ:ʒ] *n* (*Mil*) descarga,
bombardeo; (*dam*) presa; (*of criticism*)
lluvia, aluvión *m*

barrel ['bærəl] *n* barril *m*; (*of gun*)
cañón *m*

barren ['bærən] *adj* estéril

barrette [bə'rɛt] (*us*) *n* pasador *m*
(*LAM, SP*), broche *m* (*MEX*)

barricade [bærɪ'keɪd] *n* barricada

barrier ['bærɪə*] *n* barrera

barring ['bɑ:rɪŋ] *prep* excepto, salvo

barrister ['bærɪstə*] (*BRIT*) *n*
abogado/a

barrow ['bærəu] *n* (*cart*) carretilla
(de mano)

bartender ['bɑ:tɛndə*] (*us*) *n*
camarero, barman *m*

base [beɪs] *n* base f ▷ *vt*: **to ~ sth on**
basar or fundar algo en ▷ *adj* bajo,
infame

baseball ['beɪsbɔ:l] *n* béisbol *m*;
baseball cap *n* gorra f de béisbol

basement ['beɪsmənt] *n* sótano

bases¹ ['beɪsi:z] *npl of* **basis**

bases² ['beɪsɪz] *npl of* **base**

bash [bæʃ] (*inf*) *vt* golpear

basic ['beɪsɪk] *adj* básico; **basically**
adv fundamentalmente, en el fondo;
(*simply*) sencillamente; **basics** *npl:* **the
basics** los fundamentos

basil ['bæzl] *n* albahaca

basin ['beɪsn] *n* cuenco, tazón *m*;
(*Geo*) cuenca; (*also:* **wash~**) lavabo

basis ['beɪsɪs] (*pl* **bases**) *n* base *f;* **on a
part-time/trial ~** a tiempo parcial/a
prueba

basket ['bɑːskɪt] *n* cesta, cesto;
canasta; **basketball** *n* baloncesto

bass [beɪs] *n* (*Mus: instrument*) bajo;
(*double bass*) contrabajo; (*singer*) bajo

bastard ['bɑːstəd] *n* bastardo; (*inf!*)
hijo de puta (*!*)

bat [bæt] *n* (*Zool*) murciélago; (*for ball
games*) palo; (*BRIT: for table tennis*) pala
▷ *vt:* **he didn't ~ an eyelid** ni pestañeó

batch [bætʃ] *n* (*of bread*) hornada; (*of
letters etc*) lote *m*

bath [bɑːθ, *pl* bɑːðz] *n* (*action*) baño;
(*bathtub*) bañera (*SP*), tina (*LAM*),
bañadera (*RPL*) ▷ *vt* bañar; **to have a ~**
bañarse, tomar un baño; *see also* **baths**

bathe [beɪð] *vi* bañarse ▷ *vt* (*wound*)
lavar

bathing ['beɪðɪŋ] *n* el bañarse;
bathing costume (*US* **bathing suit**) *n*
traje *m* de baño

bath: bathrobe *n* (*man's*) batín
m; (*woman's*) bata; **bathroom** *n*
(cuarto *m* de) baño; **baths** [bɑːðz] *npl*
(*also:* **swimming baths**) piscina; **bath
towel** *n* toalla de baño; **bathtub**
n bañera

baton ['bætən] *n* (*Mus*) batuta;
(*Athletics*) testigo; (*weapon*) porra

batter ['bætə*] *vt* maltratar; (*rain
etc*) azotar ▷ *n* masa (para rebozar);
battered *adj* (*hat, pan*) estropeado

battery ['bætərɪ] *n* (*Aut*) batería; (*of
torch*) pila; **battery farming** *n* cría
intensiva

battle ['bætl] *n* batalla; (*fig*) lucha
▷ *vi* luchar; **battlefield** *n* campo *m*
de batalla

bay [beɪ] *n* (*Geo*) bahía; **B~ of Biscay**

≈ mar Cantábrico; **to hold sb at ~**
mantener a algn a raya

bazaar [bə'zɑː*] *n* bazar *m*; (*fete*) venta
con fines benéficos

B. & B. *n abbr* = **bed and breakfast**;
(*place*) pensión *f;* (*terms*) cama y
desayuno

BBC *n abbr* (= British Broadcasting
Corporation) cadena de radio y televisión
estatal británica

B.C. *adv abbr* (= before Christ) a. de C.

○ **KEYWORD**

be [biː] (*pt* **was, were**, *pp* **been**) *aux
vb* **1** (*with present participle: forming
continuous tenses*): **what are you
doing?** ¿qué estás haciendo?, ¿qué
haces?; **they're coming tomorrow**
vienen mañana; **I've been waiting for
you for hours** llevo horas esperándote
2 (*with pp: forming passives*) ser (*but
often replaced by active or reflexive
constructions*); **to be murdered** ser
asesinado; **the box had been opened**
habían abierto la caja; **the thief was
nowhere to be seen** no se veía al
ladrón por ninguna parte
3 (*in tag questions*): **it was fun, wasn't
it?** fue divertido, ¿no? *or* ¿verdad?; **he's
good-looking, isn't he?** es guapo, ¿no
te parece?; **she's back again, is she?**
entonces, ¿ha vuelto?
4 (*+to +infin*): **the house is to be sold**
(*necessity*) hay que vender la casa;
(*future*) van a vender la casa; **he's
not to open it** no tiene que abrirlo
▷ *vb +complement* **1** (*with n or num
complement, but see also 3, 4, 5 and impers
vb below*) ser; **he's a doctor** es médico;
2 and 2 are 4 2 y 2 son 4
2 (*with adj complement: expressing
permanent or inherent quality*) ser;
(: *expressing state seen as temporary
or reversible*) estar; **I'm English** soy
inglés/esa; **she's tall/pretty** es
alta/bonita; **he's young** es joven; **be
careful/good/quiet** ten cuidado/

pórtate bien/cállate; **I'm tired** estoy cansado/a; **it's dirty** está sucio/a
3 (of health) estar; **how are you?** ¿cómo estás?; **he's very ill** está muy enfermo; **I'm better now** ya estoy mejor
4 (of age) tener; **how old are you?** ¿cuántos años tienes?; **I'm sixteen (years old)** tengo dieciséis años
5 (cost) costar; ser; **how much was the meal?** ¿cuánto fue or costó la comida?; **that'll be £5.75, please** son £5.75, por favor; **this shirt is £17** esta camisa cuesta £17
▷ vi **1** (exist, occur etc) existir, haber; **the best singer that ever was** el mejor cantante que existió jamás; **is there a God?** ¿hay un Dios?, ¿existe Dios?; **be that as it may** sea como sea; **so be it** así sea
2 (referring to place) estar; **I won't be here tomorrow** no estaré aquí mañana
3 (referring to movement): **where have you been?** ¿dónde has estado?
▷ impers vb **1** (referring to time): **it's 5 o'clock** son las 5; **it's the 28th of April** estamos a 28 de abril
2 (referring to distance): **it's 10 km to the village** el pueblo está a 10 km
3 (referring to the weather): **it's too hot/cold** hace demasiado calor/frío; **it's windy today** hace viento hoy
4 (emphatic): **it's me** soy yo; **it was Maria who paid the bill** fue María la que pagó la cuenta

beach [biːtʃ] n playa ▷ vt varar
beacon ['biːkən] n (lighthouse) faro; (marker) guía
bead [biːd] n cuenta; (of sweat etc) gota; **beads** npl (necklace) collar m
beak [biːk] n pico
beam [biːm] n (Arch) viga, travesaño; (of light) rayo, haz m de luz ▷ vi brillar; (smile) sonreír
bean [biːn] n judía; **runner/broad ~** habichuela/haba; **coffee ~** grano de café; **beansprouts** npl brotes

mpl de soja
bear [bɛə*] (pt **bore**, pp **borne**) n oso ▷ vt (weight etc) llevar; (cost) pagar; (responsibility) tener; (endure) soportar, aguantar; (children) parir, tener; (fruit) dar ▷ vi: **to ~ right/left** torcer a la derecha/izquierda
beard [bɪəd] n barba
bearer ['bɛərə*] n portador(a) m/f
bearing ['bɛərɪŋ] n porte m, comportamiento; (connection) relación f
beast [biːst] n bestia; (inf) bruto, salvaje m
beat [biːt] (pt **~**, pp **beaten**) n (of heart) latido; (Mus) ritmo, compás m; (of policeman) ronda ▷ vt pegar, golpear; (eggs) batir; (defeat: opponent) vencer, derrotar; (: record) sobrepasar ▷ vi (heart) latir; (drum) redoblar; (rain, wind) azotar; **off the ~en track** aislado; **to ~ it** (inf) largarse; **beat up** vt (attack) dar una paliza a; **beating** n paliza
beautiful ['bjuːtɪful] adj precioso, hermoso, bello; **beautifully** adv maravillosamente
beauty ['bjuːtɪ] n belleza; **beauty parlour** (US **beauty parlor**) n salón m de belleza; **beauty salon** n salón m de belleza; **beauty spot** n (Tourism) lugar m pintoresco
beaver ['biːvə*] n castor m
became [bɪ'keɪm] pt of **become**
because [bɪ'kɔz] conj porque; **~ of** debido a, a causa de
beckon ['bɛkən] vt (also: **~ to**) llamar con señas
become [bɪ'kʌm] (pt **became**, pp **~**) vt (suit) favorecer, sentar bien a ▷ vi (+ n) hacerse, llegar a ser; (+ adj) ponerse, volverse; **to ~ fat** engordar
bed [bɛd] n cama; (of flowers) macizo; (of coal, clay) capa; (of river) lecho; (of sea) fondo; **to go to ~** acostarse; **bed and breakfast** n (place) pensión f; (terms) cama y desayuno; **bedclothes** npl ropa de cama; **bedding** n ropa de cama; **bed linen** n (BRIT) ropa f

de cama

bed: **bedroom** n dormitorio; **bedside**
n: **at the bedside of** a la cabecera de;
bedside lamp n lámpara de noche;
bedside table n mesilla de noche;
bedsit(ter) (BRIT) n cuarto de alquiler;
bedspread n cubrecama m, colcha;
bedtime n hora de acostarse
bee [biː] n abeja
beech [biːtʃ] n haya
beef [biːf] n carne f de vaca; **roast ~**
rosbif m; **beefburger** n hamburguesa;
Beefeater n alabardero de la Torre
de Londres
been [biːn] pp of **be**
beer [bɪə*] n cerveza; **beer garden**
n (BRIT) terraza f de verano, jardín m
(de un bar)
beet [biːt] (US) n (also: **red ~**)
remolacha
beetle ['biːtl] n escarabajo
beetroot ['biːtruːt] (BRIT) n
remolacha
before [bɪ'fɔː*] prep (of time) antes
de; (of space) delante de ▷ conj antes
(de) que ▷ adv antes, anteriormente;
delante, adelante; **~ going** antes de
marcharse; **~ she goes** antes de que se
vaya; **the week ~** la semana anterior;
I've never seen it ~ no lo he visto
nunca; **beforehand** adv de antemano,
con anticipación
beg [beg] vi pedir limosna ▷ vt pedir,
rogar; (entreat) suplicar; **to ~ sb to do
sth** rogar a algn que haga algo; see
also **pardon**

began [bɪ'gæn] pt of **begin**
beggar ['begə*] n mendigo/a
begin [bɪ'gɪn] (pt **began**, pp **begun**) vt,
vi empezar, comenzar; **to ~ doing** or **to
do sth** empezar a hacer algo; **beginner**
n principiante mf; **beginning** n
principio, comienzo
begun [bɪ'gʌn] pp of **begin**
behalf [bɪ'hɑːf] n: **on ~ of** en nombre
de, por; (for benefit of) en beneficio de;
on my/his ~ por mí/él
behave [bɪ'heɪv] vi (person)
portarse, comportarse; (well: also:
~ o.s.) portarse bien; **behaviour**
(US **behavior**) n comportamiento,
conducta
behind [bɪ'haɪnd] prep detrás de;
(supporting): **to be ~ sb** apoyar a
algn ▷ adv detrás, por detrás, atrás
▷ n trasero; **to be ~ (schedule)** ir
retrasado; **~ the scenes** (fig) entre
bastidores
beige [beɪʒ] adj color beige
Beijing ['beɪ'dʒɪŋ] n Pekín m
being ['biːɪŋ] n ser m; (existence): **in ~**
existente; **to come into ~** aparecer
belated [bɪ'leɪtɪd] adj atrasado,
tardío
belch [beltʃ] vi eructar ▷ vt (gen: belch
out: smoke etc) arrojar
Belgian ['beldʒən] adj, n belga mf
Belgium ['beldʒəm] n Bélgica
belief [bɪ'liːf] n opinión f; (faith) fe f
believe [bɪ'liːv] vt, vi creer; **to ~ in**
creer en; **believer** n partidario/a; (Rel)
creyente mf, fiel mf
bell [bel] n campana; (small)
campanilla; (on door) timbre m
bellboy ['belbɔɪ] (BRIT) n botones
m inv
bellhop ['belhɔp] (US) n = **bellboy**
bellow ['beləu] vi bramar; (person)
rugir
bell pepper n (esp US) pimiento,
pimentón m (LAM)
belly ['belɪ] n barriga, panza; **belly
button** (inf) n ombligo
belong [bɪ'lɔŋ] vi: **to ~ to** pertenecer

a; (*club etc*) ser socio de; **this book ~s here** este libro va aquí; **belongings** *npl* pertenencias *fpl*

beloved [bɪ'lʌvɪd] *adj* querido/a

below [bɪ'ləu] *prep* bajo, debajo de; (*less than*) inferior a ▷ *adv* abajo, (por) debajo; **see ~** véase más abajo

belt [bɛlt] *n* cinturón *m*; (*Tech*) correa, cinta *f* ▷ *vt* (*thrash*) pegar con correa; **beltway** (*US*) *n* (*Aut*) carretera de circunvalación

bemused [bɪ'mju:zd] *adj* perplejo

bench [bɛntʃ] *n* banco; (*BRIT Pol*): **the Government/Opposition ~es** (los asientos de) los miembros del Gobierno/de la Oposición; **the B~** (*Law: judges*) magistratura

bend [bɛnd] (*pt, pp* **bent**) *vt* doblar ▷ *vi* inclinarse ▷ *n* (*BRIT: in road, river*) curva; (*in pipe*) codo; **bend down** *vi* inclinarse, doblarse; **bend over** *vi* inclinarse

beneath [bɪ'ni:θ] *prep* bajo, debajo de; (*unworthy*) indigno de ▷ *adv* abajo, (por) debajo

beneficial [bɛnɪ'fɪʃəl] *adj* beneficioso

benefit ['bɛnɪfɪt] *n* beneficio; (*allowance of money*) subsidio ▷ *vt* beneficiar ▷ *vi*: **he'll ~ from it** le sacará provecho

benign [bɪ'naɪn] *adj* benigno; (*smile*) afable

bent [bɛnt] *pt, pp of* **bend** ▷ *n* inclinación *f* ▷ *adj*: **to be ~ on** estar empeñado en

bereaved [bɪ'ri:vd] *npl*: **the ~** los íntimos de una persona afligidos por su muerte

beret ['bɛreɪ] *n* boina

Berlin [bə:'lɪn] *n* Berlín

Bermuda [bə:'mju:də] *n* las Bermudas

berry ['bɛrɪ] *n* baya

berth [bə:θ] *n* (*bed*) litera; (*cabin*) camarote *m*; (*for ship*) amarradero ▷ *vi* atracar, amarrar

beside [bɪ'saɪd] *prep* junto a, al lado de; **to be ~ o.s. with anger** estar fuera

de sí; **that's ~ the point** eso no tiene nada que ver; **besides** *adv* además ▷ *prep* además de

best [bɛst] *adj* (el/la) mejor ▷ *adv* (lo) mejor; **the ~ part of** (*quantity*) la mayor parte de; **at ~** en el mejor de los casos; **to make the ~ of sth** sacar el mejor partido de algo; **to do one's ~** hacer todo lo posible; **to the ~ of my knowledge** que yo sepa; **to the ~ of my ability** como mejor puedo; **best-before date** *n* fecha de consumo preferente; **best man** (*irreg*) *n* padrino de boda; **bestseller** *n* éxito de librería, bestseller *m*

bet [bɛt] (*pt, pp* **~** *or* **~ted**) *n* apuesta ▷ *vt*: **to ~ money on** apostar dinero por ▷ *vi* apostar; **to ~ sb sth** apostar algo a algn

betray [bɪ'treɪ] *vt* traicionar; (*trust*) faltar a

better ['bɛtə*] *adj, adv* mejor ▷ *vt* superar ▷ *n*: **to get the ~ of sb** quedar por encima de algn; **you had ~ do it** más vale que lo hagas; **he thought ~ of it** cambió de parecer; **to get ~** (*Med*) mejorar(se)

betting ['bɛtɪŋ] *n* juego, el apostar; **betting shop** (*BRIT*) *n* agencia de apuestas

between [bɪ'twi:n] *prep* entre ▷ *adv* (*time*) mientras tanto; (*place*) en medio

beverage ['bɛvərɪdʒ] *n* bebida

beware [bɪ'wɛə*] *vi*: **to ~ (of)** tener cuidado (con); **"~ of the dog"** "perro peligroso"

bewildered [bɪ'wɪldəd] *adj* aturdido, perplejo

beyond [bɪ'jɔnd] *prep* más allá de; (*past: understanding*) fuera de; (*after: date*) después de, más allá de; (*above*) superior a ▷ *adv* (*in space*) más allá; (*in time*) posteriormente; **~ doubt** fuera de toda duda; **~ repair** irreparable

bias ['baɪəs] *n* (*prejudice*) prejuicio, pasión *f*; (*preference*) predisposición *f*; **bias(s)ed** *adj* parcial

bib [bɪb] n babero
Bible ['baɪbl] n Biblia
bicarbonate of soda [baɪ'kɑ:bənɪt-] n bicarbonato sódico
biceps ['baɪsɛps] n bíceps m
bicycle ['baɪsɪkl] n bicicleta; **bicycle pump** n bomba de bicicleta
bid [bɪd] (pt **bade** or ~, pp **bidden** or ~) n oferta, postura; (in tender) licitación f; (attempt) tentativa, conato ▷ vi hacer una oferta ▷ vt (offer) ofrecer; **to ~ sb good day** dar a algn los buenos días; **bidder** n: **the highest bidder** el mejor postor
bidet ['bi:deɪ] n bidet m
big [bɪg] adj grande; (brother, sister) mayor; **bigheaded** adj engreído; **big toe** n dedo gordo (del pie)
bike [baɪk] n bici f; **bike lane** n carril-bici m
bikini [bɪ'ki:nɪ] n bikini m
bilateral [baɪ'lætərl] adj (agreement) bilateral
bilingual [baɪ'lɪŋgwəl] adj bilingüe
bill [bɪl] n cuenta; (invoice) factura; (Pol) proyecto de ley; (us: banknote) billete n; (of bird) pico; (of show) programa m; **"post no ~s"** prohibido fijar carteles"; **to fit** or **fill the ~** (fig) cumplir con los requisitos; **billboard** (us) n cartelera; **billfold** ['bɪlfəuld] (us) n cartera
billiards ['bɪljədz] n billar m
billion ['bɪljən] n (BRIT) billón n (millón de millones); (us) mil millones mpl
bin [bɪn] n (for rubbish) cubo or bote m (MEX) or tacho (sc) de la basura; (container) recipiente m
bind [baɪnd] (pt, pp **bound**) vt atar; (book) encuadernar; (oblige) obligar ▷ n (inf: nuisance) lata
binge [bɪndʒ] (inf) n: **to go on a ~** ir de juerga
bingo ['bɪŋgəu] n bingo m
binoculars [bɪ'nɔkjuləz] npl prismáticos mpl
bio... [baɪə] prefix: **biochemistry** n

bioquímica; **biodegradable** [baɪəudɪ'greɪdəbl] adj biodegradable;
biography [baɪ'ɔgrəfɪ] n biografía;
biological adj biológico; **biology** [baɪ'ɔlədʒɪ] n biología; **biometric** [baɪə'mɛtrɪk] adj biométrico
birch [bə:tʃ] n (tree) abedul m
bird [bə:d] n ave f, pájaro; (BRIT: inf: girl) chica; **bird flu** n gripe f aviar; **bird of prey** n ave f de presa; **birdwatching** n: **he likes to go birdwatching on Sundays** los domingos le gusta ir a ver pájaros
Biro® ['baɪrəu] n boli
birth [bə:θ] n nacimiento; **to give ~ to** parir, dar a luz; **birth certificate** n partida de nacimiento; **birth control** n (policy) control m de natalidad; (methods) métodos mpl anticonceptivos; **birthday** n cumpleaños m inv ▷ cpd (cake, card etc) de cumpleaños; **birthmark** n antojo, marca de nacimiento; **birthplace** n lugar m de nacimiento
biscuit ['bɪskɪt] (BRIT) n galleta
bishop ['bɪʃəp] n obispo; (Chess) alfil n
bistro ['bi:strəu] n café-bar m
bit [bɪt] pt of **bite** ▷ n trozo, pedazo, pedacito; (Comput) bit m, bitio; (for horse) freno, bocado; **a ~ of** un poco de; **a ~ mad** un poco loco; **~ by ~** poco a poco
bitch [bɪtʃ] n perra; (inf!: woman) zorra (!)
bite [baɪt] (pt **bit**, pp **bitten**) vt, vi morder; (insect etc) picar ▷ n (insect bite) picadura; (mouthful) bocado; **to ~ one's nails** comerse las uñas; **let's have a ~ (to eat)** (inf) vamos a comer algo
bitten ['bɪtn] pp of **bite**
bitter ['bɪtə*] adj amargo; (wind) cortante, penetrante; (battle) encarnizado ▷ n (BRIT: beer) cerveza típica británica a base de lúpulos
bizarre [bɪ'zɑ:*] adj raro, extraño
black [blæk] adj negro; (tea, coffee) solo ▷ n color m negro; (person): **B~**

negro/a ▷ vt (BRIT Industry) boicotear;
to give sb a ~ eye ponerle a algn
el ojo morado; **~ and blue** (bruised)
amoratado; **to be in the ~** (bank
account) estar en números negros;
black out vi (faint) desmayarse;
blackberry n zarzamora; **blackbird**
n mirlo; **blackboard** n pizarra; **black
coffee** n café m solo; **blackcurrant**
n grosella negra; **black ice** n hielo
invisible en la carretera; **blackmail**
n chantaje m ▷ vt chantajear; **black
market** n mercado negro; **blackout**
n (Mil) oscurecimiento; (power cut)
apagón m; (TV, Radio) interrupción f de
programas; (fainting) desvanecimiento;
black pepper n pimienta f negra;
black pudding n morcilla; **Black Sea**
n: **the Black Sea** el Mar Negro
bladder ['blædə*] n vejiga
blade [bleɪd] n hoja; (of propeller)
paleta; **a ~ of grass** una brizna de
hierba
blame [bleɪm] n culpa ▷ vt: **to ~ sb
for sth** echar a algn la culpa de algo; **to
be to ~ (for)** tener la culpa (de)
bland [blænd] adj (music, taste) soso
blank [blæŋk] adj en blanco; (look) sin
expresión ▷ n (of memory): **my mind is
a ~** no puedo recordar nada; (on form)
blanco, espacio en blanco; (cartridge)
cartucho sin bala or de fogueo
blanket ['blæŋkɪt] n manta (SP),
cobija (LAM); (of snow) capa; (of fog)
manto
blast [blɑːst] n (of wind) ráfaga, soplo;
(of explosive) explosión f ▷ vt (blow
up) volar
blatant ['bleɪtənt] adj descarado
blaze [bleɪz] n (fire) fuego; (fig: of
colour) despliegue m; (: of glory)
esplendor m ▷ vi arder en llamas; (fig)
brillar ▷ vt: **to ~ a trail** (fig) abrir (un)
camino; **in a ~ of publicity** con gran
publicidad
blazer ['bleɪzə*] n chaqueta de uniforme
de colegial o de socio de club
bleach [bliːtʃ] n (also: **household ~**)

lejía ▷ vt blanquear; **bleachers** (US)
npl (Sport) gradas fpl al sol
bleak [bliːk] adj (countryside) desierto;
(prospect) poco prometedor(a);
(weather) crudo; (smile) triste
bled [bled] pt, pp of **bleed**
bleed [bliːd] (pt, pp **bled**) vt, vi
sangrar; **my nose is ~ing** me está
sangrando la nariz
blemish ['blemɪʃ] n marca, mancha;
(on reputation) tacha
blend [blend] n mezcla ▷ vt mezclar;
(colours etc) combinar, mezclar ▷ vi
(colours etc: also: **~ in**) combinarse,
mezclarse; **blender** n (Culin) batidora
bless [bles] (pt, pp **~ed** or **blest**) vt
bendecir; **~ you!** (after sneeze) ¡Jesús!;
blessing n (approval) aprobación f;
(godsend) don m del cielo, bendición f;
(advantage) beneficio, ventaja
blew [bluː] pt of **blow**
blight [blaɪt] vt (hopes etc) frustrar,
arruinar
blind [blaɪnd] adj ciego; (fig): **~ (to)**
ciego (a) ▷ n (for window) persiana ▷ vt
cegar; (dazzle) deslumbrar; (deceive): **to
~ sb to ...** cegar a algn a ...; **the blind**
npl los ciegos; **blind alley** n callejón
m sin salida; **blindfold** n venda ▷ adv
con los ojos vendados ▷ vt vendar
los ojos a
blink [blɪŋk] vi parpadear, pestañear;
(light) oscilar
bliss [blɪs] n felicidad f
blister ['blɪstə*] n ampolla ▷ vi
(paint) ampollarse
blizzard ['blɪzəd] n ventisca
bloated ['bləʊtɪd] adj hinchado;
(person: full) ahíto
blob [blɔb] n (drop) gota; (indistinct
object) bulto
block [blɔk] n bloque m; (in pipes)
obstáculo; (of buildings) manzana
(SP), cuadra (LAM) ▷ vt obstruir,
cerrar; (progress) estorbar; **~ of flats**
(BRIT) bloque m de pisos; **mental ~**
bloqueo mental; **block up** vt tapar,
obstruir; (pipe) atascar; **blockade**

[-'keɪd] n bloqueo ▷ vt bloquear;
blockage n estorbo, obstrucción f;
blockbuster n (book) bestseller m;
(film) éxito de público; **block capitals**
npl mayúsculas fpl; **block letters** npl
mayúsculas fpl

blog [blɔg] n blog m

bloke [bləʊk] (BRIT: inf) n tipo, tío

blond(e) [blɔnd] adj, n rubio/a m/f

blood [blʌd] n sangre f; **blood donor**
n donante mf de sangre; **blood group**
n grupo sanguíneo; **blood poisoning**
n envenenamiento de la sangre; **blood
pressure** n presión f sanguínea;
bloodshed n derramamiento de
sangre; **bloodshot** adj inyectado en
sangre; **bloodstream** n corriente
f sanguínea; **blood test** n análisis
m inv de sangre; **blood transfusion**
n transfusión f de sangre; **blood
type** n grupo sanguíneo; **blood
vessel** n vaso sanguíneo; **bloody**
adj sangriento; (nose etc) lleno de
sangre; (BRIT: inf!): **this bloody ...**
este condenado o puñetero ... (!)
▷ adv: **bloody strong/good** (BRIT: inf!)
terriblemente fuerte/bueno

bloom [bluːm] n flor f ▷ vi florecer

blossom ['blɔsəm] n flor f ▷ vi
florecer

blot [blɔt] n borrón m; (fig) mancha
▷ vt (stain) manchar

blouse [blaʊz] n blusa

blow [bləʊ] (pt **blew**, pp **blown**) n
golpe m; (with sword) espadazo ▷ vi
soplar; (dust, sand etc) volar; (fuse)
fundirse ▷ vt (wind) llevarse; (fuse)
quemar; (instrument) tocar; **to ~ one's
nose** sonarse; **blow away** vt llevarse,
arrancar; **blow out** vi apagarse; **blow
up** vi estallar ▷ vt volar; (tyre) inflar;
(Phot) ampliar; **blow-dry** n moldeado
(con secador)

blown [bləʊn] pp of **blow**

blue [bluː] adj azul; (depressed)
deprimido; **~ film/joke** película/chiste
m verde; **out of the ~** (fig) de repente;
bluebell n campanilla, campánula

azul; **blueberry** n arándano; **blue
cheese** n queso azul; **blues** npl: **the
blues** (Mus) el blues; **to have the blues**
estar triste; **bluetit** n herrerillo m
(común)

bluff [blʌf] vi tirarse un farol, farolear
▷ n farol m; **to call sb's ~** coger a algn
la palabra

blunder ['blʌndə*] n patinazo,
metedura de pata ▷ vi cometer un
error, meter la pata

blunt [blʌnt] adj (pencil) despuntado;
(knife) desafilado, romo; (person) franco,
directo

blur [blə:*] n (shape): **to become
a ~** hacerse borroso ▷ vt (vision)
enturbiar; (distinction) borrar; **blurred**
adj borroso

blush [blʌʃ] vi ruborizarse, ponerse
colorado ▷ n rubor m; **blusher** n
colorete m

board [bɔːd] n (cardboard) cartón m;
(wooden) tabla, tablero; (on wall) tablón
m; (for chess etc) tablero; (committee)
junta, consejo; (in firm) mesa o junta
directiva; (Naut, Aviat): **on ~** a bordo
▷ vt (ship) embarcarse en; (train) subir
a; **full ~** (BRIT) pensión completa; **half
~** (BRIT) media pensión; **to go by the ~**
(fig) ser abandonado o olvidado; **board
game** n juego de tablero; **boarding
card** (BRIT) n tarjeta de embarque;
boarding pass (US) n = **boarding
card**; **boarding school** n internado;
board room n sala de juntas

boast [bəʊst] vi: **to ~ (about or of)**
alardear (de)

boat [bəʊt] n barco, buque m; (small)
barca, bote m

bob [bɔb] vi (also: **~ up and down**)
menearse, balancearse

bobby pin ['bɔbɪ-] (US) n horquilla

body ['bɔdɪ] n cuerpo; (corpse) cadáver
m; (of car) caja, carrocería; (fig: group)
grupo; (: organization) organismo;
body-building n culturismo;
bodyguard n guardaespaldas m inv;
bodywork n carrocería

bog [bɔg] *n* pantano, ciénaga ▷ *vt*: **to get ~ged down** (*fig*) empantanarse, atascarse

bogus ['bəugəs] *adj* falso, fraudulento

boil [bɔɪl] *vt* (*water*) hervir; (*eggs*) pasar por agua, cocer ▷ *vi* hervir; (*fig: with anger*) estar furioso; (: *with heat*) asfixiarse ▷ *n* (*Med*) furúnculo, divieso; **to come to the ~, to come to a ~** (*us*) comenzar a hervir; **to ~ down to** (*fig*) reducirse a; **boil over** *vi* salirse, rebosar; (*anger etc*) llegar al colmo; **boiled egg** *n* (*soft*) huevo tibio (*MEX*) *or* pasado por agua *or* a la copa (*sc*); (*hard*) huevo duro; **boiled potatoes** *npl* patatas *fpl* (*sp*) *or* papas *fpl* (*LAM*) cocidas; **boiler** *n* caldera; **boiling** ['bɔɪlɪŋ] *adj*: **I'm boiling (hot)** (*inf*) estoy asado; **boiling point** *n* punto de ebullición

bold [bəuld] *adj* valiente, audaz; (*pej*) descarado; (*colour*) llamativo

Bolivia [bə'lɪvɪə] *n* Bolivia; **Bolivian** *adj, n* boliviano/a *m/f*

bollard ['bɔləd] (*BRIT*) *n* (*Aut*) poste *m*

bolt [bəult] *n* (*lock*) cerrojo; (*with nut*) perno, tornillo ▷ *adv*: **~ upright** rígido, erguido ▷ *vt* (*door*) echar el cerrojo a; (*also*: **~ together**) sujetar con tornillos; (*food*) engullir ▷ *vi* fugarse; (*horse*) desbocarse

bomb [bɔm] *n* bomba ▷ *vt* bombardear; **bombard** [bɔm'bɑːd] *vt* bombardear; (*fig*) asediar; **bomber** *n* (*Aviat*) bombardero; **bomb scare** *n* amenaza de bomba

bond [bɔnd] *n* (*promise*) fianza; (*Finance*) bono; (*link*) vínculo, lazo; (*Comm*): **in ~** en depósito bajo fianza; **bonds** *npl* (*chains*) cadenas *fpl*

bone [bəun] *n* hueso; (*of fish*) espina ▷ *vt* deshuesar; quitar las espinas a

bonfire ['bɔnfaɪə*] *n* hoguera, fogata

bonnet ['bɔnɪt] *n* gorra; (*BRIT*: *of car*) capó *m*

bonus ['bəunəs] *n* (*payment*) paga extraordinaria, plus *m*; (*fig*) bendición *f*

boo [buː] *excl* ¡uh! ▷ *vt* abuchear, rechiflar

book [buk] *n* libro; (*of tickets*) taco; (*of stamps etc*) librito ▷ *vt* (*ticket*) sacar; (*seat, room*) reservar; **books** *npl* (*Comm*) cuentas *fpl*, contabilidad *f*; **book in** *vi* (*at hotel*) registrarse; **book up** *vt*: **to be booked up** (*hotel*) estar completo; **bookcase** *n* librería, estante *m* para libros; **booking** *n* reserva; **booking office** *n* (*BRIT Rail*) despacho de billetes (*SP*) *or* boletos (*LAM*); (*Theatre*) taquilla (*SP*), boletería (*LAM*); **book-keeping** *n* contabilidad *f*; **booklet** *n* folleto; **bookmaker** *n* corredor *m* de apuestas; **bookmark** *n* (*also* Comput) marcador; **bookseller** *n* librero; **bookshelf** *n* estante *m* (para libros); **bookshop, book store** *n* librería

boom [buːm] *n* (*noise*) trueno, estampido; (*in prices etc*) alza rápida; (*Econ, in population*) boom *m* ▷ *vi* (*cannon*) hacer gran estruendo, retumbar; (*Econ*) estar en alza

boost [buːst] *n* estímulo, empuje *m* ▷ *vt* estimular, empujar

boot [buːt] *n* bota; (*BRIT*: *of car*) maleta, maletero ▷ *vt* (*Comput*) arrancar; **to ~** (*in addition*) además, por añadidura

booth [buːð] *n* (*telephone booth, voting booth*) cabina

booze [buːz] (*inf*) *n* bebida

border ['bɔːdə*] *n* borde *m*, margen *m*; (*of a country*) frontera; (*for flowers*) arriate *m* ▷ *vt* (*road*) bordear; (*another country*: *also*: **~ on**) lindar con; **borderline** *n*: **on the borderline** en el límite

bore [bɔː*] *pt of* **bear** ▷ *vt* (*hole*) hacer un agujero en; (*well*) perforar; (*person*) aburrir ▷ *n* (*person*) pelmazo, pesado; (*of gun*) calibre *m*; **bored** *adj* aburrido; **he's bored to tears** *or* **to death** *or* **stiff** está aburrido como una ostra, está muerto de aburrimiento; **boredom** *n* aburrimiento

boring ['bɔːrɪŋ] *adj* aburrido

born [bɔːn] *adj*: **to be ~** nacer; **I was ~**

in 1960 nací en 1960

borne [bɔːn] *pp of* **bear**

borough ['bʌrə] *n* municipio

borrow ['bɔrəu] *vt:* **to ~ sth (from sb)** tomar algo prestado (a algn)

Bosnia(-Herzegovina) ['bɔːsnɪə(hɛrzə'gəuviːnə)] *n* Bosnia(-Herzegovina); **Bosnian** ['bɔznɪən] *adj, n* bosnio/a

bosom ['buzəm] *n* pecho

boss [bɔs] *n* jefe *m* ▷ *vt (also:* **~ about or around)** mangonear; **bossy** *adj* mandón/ona

both [bəuθ] *adj, pron* ambos/as, los dos(las dos); **~ of us went, we ~ went** fuimos los dos, ambos fuimos ▷ *adv:* **~ A and B** tanto A como B

bother ['bɔðə*] *vt (worry)* preocupar; *(disturb)* molestar, fastidiar ▷ *vi (also:* **~ o.s.)** molestarse ▷ *n (trouble)* dificultad *f; (nuisance)* molestia, lata; **to ~ doing** tomarse la molestia de hacer

bottle ['bɔtl] *n* botella; *(small)* frasco; *(baby's)* biberón *m* ▷ *vt* embotellar; **bottle bank** *n* contenedor *m* de vidrio; **bottle-opener** *n* abrebotellas *m inv*

bottom ['bɔtəm] *n (of box, sea)* fondo; *(buttocks)* trasero, culo; *(of page)* pie *m; (of list)* final *m; (of class)* último/a ▷ *adj (lowest)* más bajo; *(last)* último

bought [bɔːt] *pt, pp of* **buy**

boulder ['bəuldə*] *n* canto rodado

bounce [bauns] *vi (ball)* (re)botar; *(cheque)* ser rechazado ▷ *vt* hacer (re)botar ▷ *n (rebound)* (re)bote *m;* **bouncer** *(inf) n* gorila *m (que echa a los alborotadores de un bar, club etc)*

bound [baund] *pt, pp of* **bind** ▷ *n (leap)* salto; *(gen pl: limit)* límite *m* ▷ *vi (leap)* saltar ▷ *vt (border)* rodear ▷ *adj:* **~ by** rodeado de; **to be ~ to do sth** *(obliged)* tener el deber de hacer algo; **he's ~ to come** es seguro que vendrá; **out of ~s** prohibido el paso; **~ for** con destino a

boundary ['baundrɪ] *n* límite *m*

bouquet ['bukeɪ] *n (of flowers)* ramo

bourbon ['buəbən] *(US) n (also:* **~**

whiskey) whisky *m* americano, bourbon *m*

bout [baut] *n (of malaria etc)* ataque *m; (of activity)* período; *(Boxing etc)* combate *m*, encuentro

boutique [buːˈtiːk] *n* boutique *f,* tienda de ropa

bow¹ [bəu] *n (knot)* lazo; *(weapon, Mus)* arco

bow² [bau] *n (of the head)* reverencia; *(Naut: also:* **~s)** proa ▷ *vi* inclinarse, hacer una reverencia

bowels [bauəlz] *npl* intestinos *mpl*, vientre *m; (fig)* entrañas *fpl*

bowl [bəul] *n* tazón *m*, cuenco; *(ball)* bola ▷ *vi (Cricket)* arrojar la pelota; *see also* **bowls; bowler** *n (Cricket)* lanzador *m* (de la pelota); *(BRIT: also:* **bowler hat)** hongo, bombín *m;* **bowling** *n (game)* bochas *fpl*, bolos *mpl;* **bowling alley** *n* bolera; **bowling green** *n* pista para bochas; **bowls** *n* juego de las bochas, bolos *mpl*

bow tie ['bəu-] *n* corbata de lazo, pajarita

box [bɔks] *n (also:* **cardboard ~)** caja, cajón *m; (Theatre)* palco ▷ *vt* encajonar ▷ *vi (Sport)* boxear; **boxer** ['bɔksə*] *n (person)* boxeador *m;* **boxer shorts** ['bɔksəfɔːts] *pl n* bóxers; **a pair of boxer shorts** unos bóxers; **boxing** ['bɔksɪŋ] *n (Sport)* boxeo; **Boxing Day** *(BRIT) n día en que se dan los aguinaldos, 26 de diciembre;* **boxing gloves** *npl* guantes *mpl* de boxeo; **boxing ring** *n* ring *m*, cuadrilátero; **box office** *n* taquilla *(SP)*, boletería *(LAM)*

boy [bɔɪ] *n (young)* niño; *(older)* muchacho, chico; *(son)* hijo; **boy band** *n* boy band *m (grupo musical de chicos)*

boycott ['bɔɪkɔt] *n* boicot *m* ▷ *vt* boicotear

boyfriend ['bɔɪfrɛnd] *n* novio

bra [brɑː] *n* sostén *m*, sujetador *m*

brace [breɪs] *n (BRIT: also:* **~s:** *on teeth)* corrector *m*, aparato; *(tool)* berbiquí *m* ▷ *vt (knees, shoulders)* tensionar; **braces** *npl (BRIT)* tirantes *mpl;* **to ~ o.s.** *(fig)* prepararse

bracelet ['breɪslɪt] n pulsera, brazalete m

bracket ['brækɪt] n (*Tech*) soporte m, puntal m; (*group*) clase f, categoría; (*also*: **brace ~**) soporte m, abrazadera; (*also*: **round ~**) paréntesis m inv; (*also*: **square ~**) corchete m ▷ vt (*word etc*) poner entre paréntesis

brag [bræg] vi jactarse

braid [breɪd] n (*trimming*) galón m; (*of hair*) trenza

brain [breɪn] n cerebro; **brains** npl sesos mpl; **she's got ~s** es muy lista

braise [breɪz] vt cocer a fuego lento

brake [breɪk] n (*on vehicle*) freno ▷ vi frenar; **brake light** n luz f de frenado

bran [bræn] n salvado

branch [brɑːntʃ] n rama; (*Comm*) sucursal f; **branch off** vi: **a small road branches off to the right** hay una carretera pequeña que sale hacia la derecha; **branch out** vi (*fig*) extenderse

brand [brænd] n marca; (*fig: type*) tipo ▷ vt (*cattle*) marcar con hierro candente; **brand name** n marca; **brand-new** adj flamante, completamente nuevo

brandy ['brændɪ] n coñac m

brash [bræʃ] adj (*forward*) descarado

brass [brɑːs] n latón m; **the ~** (*Mus*) los cobres; **brass band** n banda de metal

brat [bræt] (*pej*) n mocoso/a

brave [breɪv] adj valiente, valeroso ▷ vt (*face up to*) desafiar; **bravery** n valor m, valentía

brawl [brɔːl] n pelea, reyerta

Brazil [brə'zɪl] n (el) Brasil; **Brazilian** adj, n brasileño/a m/f

breach [briːtʃ] vt abrir brecha en ▷ n (*gap*) brecha; (*breaking*): **~ of contract** infracción f de contrato; **~ of the peace** perturbación f del órden público

bread [brɛd] n pan m; **breadbin** n panera; **breadbox** (us) n panera; **breadcrumbs** npl migajas fpl; (*Culin*) pan rallado

breadth [brɛtθ] n anchura; (*fig*) amplitud f

break [breɪk] (*pt* **broke**, *pp* **broken**) vt romper; (*promise*) faltar a; (*law*) violar, infringir; (*record*) batir ▷ vi romperse, quebrarse; (*storm*) estallar; (*weather*) cambiar; (*dawn*) despuntar; (*news etc*) darse a conocer ▷ n (*gap*) abertura; (*fracture*) fractura; (*time*) intervalo; (: *at school*) (período de) recreo; (*chance*) oportunidad f; **to ~ the news to sb** comunicar la noticia a algn; **break down** vt (*figures, data*) analizar, descomponer ▷ vi (*machine*) estropearse; (*Aut*) averiarse; (*person*) romper a llorar; (*talks*) fracasar; **break in** vt (*horse etc*) domar ▷ vi (*burglar*) forzar una entrada; (*interrupt*) interrumpir; **break into** vt fus (*house*) forzar; **break off** vi (*speaker*) pararse, detenerse; (*branch*) partir; **break out** vi estallar; (*prisoner*) escaparse; **to break out in spots** salirle a algn granos; **break up** vi (*ship*) hacerse pedazos; (*crowd, meeting*) disolverse; (*marriage*) deshacerse; (*Scol*) terminar (el curso); (*line*) cortarse ▷ vt (*rocks etc*) partir; (*journey*) partir; (*fight etc*) acabar con; **the line's** *or* **you're breaking up** se corta; **breakdown** n (*Aut*) avería; (*in communications*) interrupción f; (*Med: also*: **nervous breakdown**) colapso, crisis f nerviosa; (*of marriage, talks*) fracaso; (*of statistics*) análisis m inv; **breakdown truck, breakdown van** n (camión m) grúa

breakfast ['brɛkfəst] n desayuno

break: break-in n robo con allanamiento de morada;

breakthrough n (*also fig*) avance m

breast [brɛst] n (*of woman*) pecho, seno; (*chest*) pecho; (*of bird*) pechuga; **breast-feed** (*pt, pp* **breast-fed**) vt, vi amamantar, criar a los pechos; **breast-stroke** n braza (de pecho)

breath [brɛθ] n aliento, respiración f; **to take a deep ~** respirar hondo; **out of ~** sin aliento, sofocado

Breathalyser® ['brɛθəlaɪzə*] (BRIT)
n alcoholímetro
breathe [bri:ð] vt, vi respirar;
breathe in vt, vi aspirar; **breathe
out** vt, vi espirar; **breathing** n
respiración f
breath: breathless adj sin aliento,
jadeante; **breathtaking** adj
imponente, pasmoso; **breath test** n
prueba de la alcoholemia
bred [bred] pt, pp of **breed**
breed [bri:d] (pt, pp **bred**) vt criar ▷ vi
reproducirse, procrear ▷ n (Zool) raza,
casta; (type) tipo
breeze [bri:z] n brisa
breezy ['bri:zɪ] adj de mucho viento,
ventoso; (person) despreocupado
brew [bru:] vt (tea) hacer; (beer)
elaborar ▷ vi (fig: trouble) prepararse;
(storm) amenazar; **brewery** n fábrica
de cerveza, cervecería
bribe [braɪb] n soborno ▷ vt
sobornar, cohechar; **bribery** n
soborno, cohecho
bric-a-brac ['brɪkabræk] n inv
baratijas fpl
brick [brɪk] n ladrillo; **bricklayer** n
albañil m
bride [braɪd] n novia; **bridegroom** n
novio; **bridesmaid** n dama de honor
bridge [brɪdʒ] n puente m; (Naut)
puente m de mando; (of nose) caballete
m; (Cards) bridge m ▷ vt (fig): **to ~ a gap**
llenar un vacío
bridle ['braɪdl] n brida, freno
brief [bri:f] adj breve, corto ▷ n (Law)
escrito; (task) cometido, encargo
▷ vt informar; **briefs** npl (for men)
calzoncillos mpl; (for women) bragas fpl;
briefcase n cartera (SP), portafolio
(LAM); **briefing** n (Press) informe m;
briefly adv (glance) fugazmente; (say)
en pocas palabras
brigadier [brɪgə'dɪə*] n general m
de brigada
bright [braɪt] adj brillante; (room)
luminoso; (day) de sol; (person: clever)
listo, inteligente; (: lively) alegre;

(colour) vivo; (future) prometedor(a)
brilliant ['brɪljənt] adj brillante; (inf)
fenomenal
brim [brɪm] n borde m; (of hat) ala
brine [braɪn] n (Culin) salmuera
bring [brɪŋ] (pt, pp **brought**) vt (thing,
person: with you) traer; (: to sb) llevar,
conducir; (trouble, satisfaction) causar;
bring about vt ocasionar, producir;
bring back vt volver a traer; (return)
devolver; **bring down** vt (government,
plane) derribar; (price) rebajar; **bring
in** vt (harvest) recoger; (person) hacer
entrar o pasar; (object) traer; (Pol: bill,
law) presentar; (produce: income)
producir, rendir; **bring on** vt (illness,
attack) producir, causar; (player,
substitute) sacar (de la reserva), hacer
salir; **bring out** vt sacar; (book etc)
publicar; (meaning) subrayar; **bring
up** vt subir; (person) educar, criar;
(question) sacar a colación; (food: vomit)
devolver, vomitar
brink [brɪŋk] n borde m
brisk [brɪsk] adj (abrupt: tone) brusco;
(person) enérgico, vigoroso; (pace)
rápido; (trade) activo
bristle ['brɪsl] n cerda ▷ vi: **to ~ in
anger** temblar de rabia
Brit [brɪt] n abbr (inf: = British person)
británico/a
Britain ['brɪtən] n (also: **Great ~**)
Gran Bretaña
British ['brɪtɪʃ] adj británico
▷ npl: **the ~** los británicos; **British Isles**
npl: **the British Isles** las Islas Británicas
Briton ['brɪtən] n británico/a
brittle ['brɪtl] adj quebradizo, frágil
broad [brɔ:d] adj ancho; (range)
amplio; (smile) abierto; (general: outlines
etc) general; (accent) cerrado; **in ~
daylight** en pleno día; **broadband** n
banda ancha; **broad bean** n haba;
broadcast (pt, pp **~**) n emisión f
▷ vt (Radio) emitir; (TV) transmitir
▷ vi emitir, transmitir; **broaden** vt
ampliar ▷ vi ensancharse; **to broaden
one's mind** hacer más tolerante a

algn; **broadly** adv en general; **broad-minded** adj tolerante, liberal
broccoli ['brɒkəlɪ] n brécol m
brochure ['brəʊʃjʊə*] n folleto
broil [brɔɪl] vt (Culin) asar a la parrilla
broiler ['brɔɪlə*] n (grill) parrilla
broke [brəʊk] pt of **break** ▷ adj (inf) pelado, sin blanca
broken ['brəʊkən] pp of **break** ▷ adj roto; (machine: also: **~ down**) averiado; **~ leg** pierna rota; **in ~ English** en un inglés imperfecto
broker ['brəʊkə*] n agente mf, bolsista mf; (insurance broker) agente de seguros
bronchitis [brɒŋ'kaɪtɪs] n bronquitis f
bronze [brɒnz] n bronce m
brooch [brəʊtʃ] n prendedor m, broche m
brood [bru:d] n camada, cría ▷ vi (person) dejarse obsesionar
broom [brum] n escoba; (Bot) retama
Bros. abbr (= Brothers) Hnos
broth [brɒθ] n caldo
brothel ['brɒθl] n burdel m
brother ['brʌðə*] n hermano; **brother-in-law** n cuñado
brought [brɔ:t] pt, pp of **bring**
brow [brau] n (forehead) frente m; (eyebrow) ceja; (of hill) cumbre f
brown [braun] adj (colour) marrón; (hair) castaño; (tanned) bronceado, moreno ▷ n (colour) color m marrón or pardo ▷ vt (Culin) dorar; **brown bread** n pan integral
Brownie ['braunɪ] n niña exploradora
brown rice n arroz m integral
brown sugar n azúcar m terciado
browse [brauz] vi (through book) hojear; (in shop) mirar; **browser** n (Comput) navegador m
bruise [bru:z] n cardenal m (SP), moretón m ▷ vt magullar
brunette [bru:'nɛt] n morena
brush [brʌʃ] n cepillo; (for painting, shaving etc) brocha; (artist's) pincel m;

(with police etc) roce m ▷ vt (sweep) barrer; (groom) cepillar; (also: **~ against**) rozar al pasar
Brussels ['brʌslz] n Bruselas
Brussels sprout n col f de Bruselas
brutal ['bru:tl] adj brutal
B.Sc. abbr (= Bachelor of Science) licenciado en Ciencias
BSE n abbr (= bovine spongiform encephalopathy) encefalopatía espongiforme bovina
bubble ['bʌbl] n burbuja ▷ vi burbujear, borbotar; **bubble bath** n espuma para el baño; **bubble gum** n chicle m de globo; **bubblejet printer** ['bʌbldʒɛt-] n impresora de injección por burbujas
buck [bʌk] n (rabbit) conejo macho; (deer) gamo; (us: inf) dólar m ▷ vi corcovear; **to pass the ~ (to sb)** echar (a algn) el muerto
bucket ['bʌkɪt] n cubo, balde m
buckle ['bʌkl] n hebilla ▷ vt abrochar con hebilla ▷ vi combarse
bud [bʌd] n (of plant) brote m, yema; (of flower) capullo ▷ vi brotar, echar brotes
Buddhism ['budɪzm] n Budismo
Buddhist ['budɪst] adj, n budista m/f
buddy ['bʌdɪ] (us) n compañero, compinche m
budge [bʌdʒ] vt mover; (fig) hacer ceder ▷ vi moverse, ceder
budgerigar ['bʌdʒərɪgɑ:*] n periquito
budget ['bʌdʒɪt] n presupuesto ▷ vi: **to ~ for sth** presupuestar algo
budgie ['bʌdʒɪ] n = **budgerigar**
buff [bʌf] adj (colour) color de ante ▷ n (inf: enthusiast) entusiasta mf
buffalo ['bʌfələu] (pl **~** or **~es**) n (BRIT) búfalo; (us: bison) bisonte m
buffer ['bʌfə*] n (Comput) memoria intermedia; (Rail) tope m
buffet¹ ['bʌfɪt] vt golpear
buffet² ['bufeɪ] n (BRIT: in station) bar m, cafetería; (food) buffet m; **buffet car** (BRIT) n (Rail) coche-comedor m

bug [bʌg] n (esp us: insect) bicho, sabandija; (Comput) error m; (germ) microbio, bacilo; (spy device) micrófono oculto ▷ vt (inf: annoy) fastidiar; (room) poner micrófono oculto en

buggy ['bʌgɪ] n cochecito de niño

build [bɪld] (pt, pp built) n (of person) tipo ▷ vt construir, edificar; **build up** vt (morale, forces, production) acrecentar; (stocks) acumular; **builder** n (contractor) contratista mf; **building** n construcción f; (structure) edificio; **building site** n obra; **building society** (BRIT) n sociedad f inmobiliaria

built [bɪlt] pt, pp de **build**; **built-in** adj (cupboard) empotrado; (device) interior, incorporado; **built-up** adj (area) urbanizado

bulb [bʌlb] n (Bot) bulbo; (Elec) bombilla, foco (MEX), bujía (CAM), bombita (RPL)

Bulgaria [bʌl'gɛərɪə] n Bulgaria; **Bulgarian** adj, n búlgaro/a m/f

bulge [bʌldʒ] n bulto, protuberancia ▷ vi bombearse, pandearse; (pocket etc): **to ~ (with)** rebosar (de)

bulimia [bə'lɪmɪə] n bulimia

bulimic [bjuː'lɪmɪk] adj, n bulímico/a m/f

bulk [bʌlk] n masa, mole f; **in ~** (Comm) a granel; **the ~ of** la mayor parte de; **bulky** adj voluminoso, abultado

bull [bul] n toro; (male elephant, whale) macho

bulldozer ['buldəuzə*] n bulldozer m

bullet ['bulɪt] n bala

bulletin ['bulɪtɪn] n anuncio, parte m; (journal) boletín m; **bulletin board** n (us) tablón m de anuncios; (Comput) tablero de noticias

bullfight ['bulfaɪt] n corrida de toros; **bullfighter** n torero; **bullfighting** n los toros, el toreo

bully ['bulɪ] n valentón m, matón m ▷ vt intimidar, tiranizar

bum [bʌm] n (inf: backside) culo; (esp us: tramp) vagabundo

bumblebee ['bʌmblbiː] n abejorro

bump [bʌmp] n (blow) tope m, choque m; (jolt) sacudida; (on road etc) bache m; (on head etc) chichón m ▷ vt (strike) chocar contra; **bump into** vt fus chocar contra, tropezar con; (person) topar con; **bumper** n (Aut) parachoques m inv ▷ adj: **bumper crop** or **harvest** cosecha abundante; **bumpy** adj (road) lleno de baches

bun [bʌn] n (BRIT: cake) pastel m; (us: bread) bollo; (of hair) moño

bunch [bʌntʃ] n (of flowers) ramo; (of keys) manojo; (of bananas) piña; (of people) grupo; (pej) pandilla; **bunches** npl (in hair) coletas fpl

bundle ['bʌndl] n bulto, fardo; (of sticks) haz m; (of papers) legajo ▷ vt (also: ~ **up**) atar, envolver; **to ~ sth/sb into** meter algo/a algn precipitadamente en

bungalow ['bʌngələu] n bungalow m, chalé m

bungee jumping ['bʌndʒiː'dʒʌmpɪŋ] n puenting m, banyi m

bunion ['bʌnjən] n juanete m

bunk [bʌŋk] n litera; **bunk beds** npl literas fpl

bunker ['bʌŋkə*] n (coal store) carbonera; (Mil) refugio; (Golf) bunker m

bunny ['bʌnɪ] n (inf: also: ~ **rabbit**) conejito

buoy [bɔɪ] n boya; **buoyant** adj (ship) capaz de flotar; (economy) boyante; (person) optimista

burden ['bəːdn] n carga ▷ vt cargar

bureau [bjuə'rəu] (pl **-x**) n (BRIT: writing desk) escritorio, buró m; (us: chest of drawers) cómoda; (office) oficina, agencia

bureaucracy [bjuə'rɔkrəsɪ] n burocracia

bureaucrat ['bjuərəkræt] n burócrata m/f

bureau de change [-də'ʃɑ̃ʒ] (pl **bureaux de change**) n caja f de cambio

bureaux ['bjuərəuz] npl of **bureau**

burger ['bəːgə*] n hamburguesa
burglar ['bəːglə*] n ladrón/ona m/f;
  burglar alarm n alarma f antirrobo;
  burglary n robo con allanamiento,
  robo de una casa
burial ['bɛrɪəl] n entierro
burn [bəːn] (pt, pp **-ed** or **~t**) vt
  quemar; (house) incendiar ▷ vi
  quemarse, arder; incendiarse; (sting)
  escocer ▷ n quemadura; **burn down**
  vt incendiar; **burn out** vt (writer
  etc): **to burn o.s. out** agotarse;
  burning adj (building etc) en llamas;
  (hot: sand etc) abrasador(a); (ambition)
  ardiente
Burns' Night [bəːnz-] n ver recuadro

burnt [bəːnt] pt, pp of **burn**
burp [bəːp] (inf) n eructo ▷ vi eructar
burrow ['bʌrəu] n madriguera ▷ vi
  hacer una madriguera; (rummage)
  hurgar
burst [bəːst] (pt, pp **~**) vt reventar;
  (river: banks etc) romper ▷ vi
  reventarse; (tyre) pincharse ▷ n (of
  gunfire) ráfaga; (also: **~ pipe**) reventón
  m; **a ~ of energy/speed/enthusiasm**
  una explosión de energía/un
  ímpetu de velocidad/un arranque
  deentusiasmo; **to ~ into flames**

estallar en llamas; **to ~ into tears**
  deshacerse en lágrimas; **to ~ out**
  laughing soltar la carcajada; **to ~**
  open abrirse de golpe; **to be ~ing with**
  (container) estar lleno a rebosar de;
  (: person) reventar por o de; **burst into**
  vt fus (room etc) irrumpir en
bury ['bɛrɪ] vt enterrar; (body)
  enterrar, sepultar
bus [bʌs] (pl **~es**) n autobús m; **bus**
  conductor n cobrador(a) m/f
bush [buʃ] n arbusto; (scrub land)
  monte m; **to beat about the ~**
  andar(se) con rodeos
business ['bɪznɪs] n (matter) asunto;
  (trading) comercio, negocios mpl; (firm)
  empresa, casa; (occupation) oficio;
  to be away on ~ estar en viaje de
  negocios; **it's my ~ to ...** me toca or
  corresponde ...; **it's none of my ~** yo no
  tengo nada que ver; **he means ~** habla
  en serio; **business class** n (Aer) clase f
  preferente; **businesslike** adj eficiente;
  businessman (irreg) n hombre m de
  negocios; **business trip** n viaje m de
  negocios; **businesswoman** (irreg) n
  mujer f de negocios
busker ['bʌskə*] (BRIT) n músico/a
  ambulante
bus: bus pass n bonobús m; **bus shelter**
  n parada cubierta; **bus station** n
  estación f de autobuses; **bus-stop** n
  parada de autobús
bust [bʌst] n (Anat) pecho; (sculpture)
  busto ▷ adj (inf: broken) roto,
  estropeado; **to go ~** quebrar
bustling ['bʌslɪŋ] adj (town)
  animado, bullicioso
busy ['bɪzɪ] adj ocupado, atareado;
  (shop, street) concurrido, animado;
  (Tel: line) comunicando ▷ vt: **to ~ o.s.**
  with ocuparse en; **busy signal** (US) n
  (Tel) señal f de comunicando

○ **KEYWORD**

but [bʌt] conj **1** pero; **he's not very**
  bright, but he's hard-working no es

muy inteligente, pero es trabajador
2 (*in direct contradiction*) sino; **he's not English but French** no es inglés sino francés; **he didn't sing but he shouted** no cantó sino que gritó
3 (*showing disagreement, surprise etc*): **but that's far too expensive!** ¡pero eso es carísimo!; **but it does work!** ¡(pero) sí que funciona!
▷ *prep* (*apart from, except*) menos, salvo; **we've had nothing but trouble** no hemos tenido más que problemas; **no-one but him can do it** nadie más que él puede hacerlo; **who but a lunatic would do such a thing?** ¡sólo un loco haría una cosa así!; **but for you/your help** si no fuera por ti/tu ayuda; **anything but that** cualquier cosa menos eso
▷ *adv* (*just, only*) **she's but a child** no es más que una niña; **had I but known** si lo hubiera sabido; **I can but try** al menos lo puedo intentar; **it's all but finished** está casi acabado

butcher ['bʊtʃə*] *n* carnicero ▷ *vt* hacer una carnicería con; (*cattle etc*) matar; **butcher's(shop)** *n* carnicería
butler ['bʌtlə*] *n* mayordomo
butt [bʌt] *n* (*barrel*) tonel *m*; (*of gun*) culata; (*of cigarette*) colilla; (BRIT: *fig: target*) blanco ▷ *vt* dar cabezadas contra, top(et)ar
butter ['bʌtə*] *n* mantequilla ▷ *vt* untar con mantequilla; **buttercup** *n* botón *m* de oro
butterfly ['bʌtəflaɪ] *n* mariposa; (*Swimming: also*: **~ stroke**) braza de mariposa
buttocks ['bʌtəks] *npl* nalgas *fpl*
button ['bʌtn] *n* botón *m*; (US) placa, chapa ▷ *vt* (*also*: **~ up**) abotonar, abrochar ▷ *vi* abrocharse
buy [baɪ] (*pt, pp* **bought**) *vt* comprar ▷ *n* compra; **to ~ sb sth/sth from sb** comprarle algo a algn; **to ~ sb a drink** invitar a algn a tomar algo; **buy out** *vt*

(*partner*) comprar la parte de; **buy up** *vt* (*property*) acaparar; (*stock*) comprar todas las existencias de; **buyer** *n* comprador(a) *m/f*
buzz [bʌz] *n* zumbido; (*inf: phone call*) llamada (por teléfono) ▷ *vi* zumbar; **buzzer** *n* timbre *m*

○ **KEYWORD**

by [baɪ] *prep* **1** (*referring to cause, agent*) por; de; **killed by lightning** muerto por un relámpago; **a painting by Picasso** un cuadro de Picasso
2 (*referring to method, manner, means*): **by bus/car/train** en autobús/coche/tren; **to pay by cheque** pagar con un cheque; **by moonlight/candlelight** a la luz de la luna/una vela; **by saving hard he ...** ahorrando ...
3 (*via, through*) por; **we came by Dover** vinimos por Dover
4 (*close to, past*): **the house by the river** la casa junto al río; **she rushed by me** pasó a mi lado como una exhalación; **I go by the post office every day** paso por delante de Correos todos los días
5 (*time: not later than*) para; (: *during*): **by daylight** de día; **by 4 o'clock** para las cuatro; **by this time tomorrow** mañana a estas horas; **by the time I got here it was too late** cuando llegué ya era demasiado tarde
6 (*amount*): **by the metre/kilo** por metro/kilo; **paid by the hour** pagado por hora
7 (*Math, measure*): **to divide/multiply by 3** dividir/multiplicar por 3; **a room 3 metres by 4** una habitación de 3 metros por 4; **it's broader by a metre** es un metro más ancho
8 (*according to*) según, de acuerdo con; **it's 3 o'clock by my watch** según mi reloj, son las tres; **it's all right by me** por mí, está bien
9: **(all) by oneself** *etc* todo solo; **he did it (all) by himself** lo hizo él solo;

he was standing (all) by himself in a corner estaba de pie solo en un rincón **10**: **by the way** a propósito, por cierto; **this wasn't my idea, by the way** pues, no fue idea mía
▷ adv **1** see **go**; **pass** etc
2: **by and by** finalmente; **they'll come back by and by** acabarán volviendo; **by and large** en líneas generales, en general

bye(-bye) ['baı('baı)] *excl* adiós, hasta luego
by-election (*BRIT*) *n* elección *f* parcial
bypass ['baıpɑ:s] *n* carretera de circunvalación; (*Med*) (operación *f* de) by-pass *f* ▷ *vt* evitar
byte [baıt] *n* (*Comput*) byte *m*, octeto

C [si:] *n* (*Mus*) do *m*
cab [kæb] *n* taxi *m*; (*of truck*) cabina
cabaret ['kæbəreɪ] *n* cabaret *m*
cabbage ['kæbɪdʒ] *n* col *f*, berza
cabin ['kæbɪn] *n* cabaña; (*on ship*) camarote *m*; (*on plane*) cabina; **cabin crew** *n* tripulación *f* de cabina
cabinet ['kæbɪnɪt] *n* (*Pol*) consejo de ministros; (*furniture*) armario; (*also*: **display ~**) vitrina; **cabinet minister** *n* ministro/a (del gabinete)
cable ['keɪbl] *n* cable *m* ▷ *vt* cablegrafiar; **cable car** *n* teleférico; **cable television** *n* televisión *f* por cable
cactus ['kæktəs] (*pl* **cacti**) *n* cacto
café ['kæfeɪ] *n* café *m*
cafeteria [kæfɪ'tɪərɪə] *n* cafetería
caffein(e) ['kæfi:n] *n* cafeína
cage [keɪdʒ] *n* jaula
cagoule [kə'gu:l] *n* chubasquero
cake [keɪk] *n* (*Culin*: *large*) tarta; (: *small*) pastel *m*; (*of soap*) pastilla
calcium ['kælsɪəm] *n* calcio
calculate ['kælkjuleɪt] *vt* calcular;

calculation [-'leɪʃən] n cálculo, cómputo; **calculator** n calculadora

calendar ['kæləndə*] n calendario

calf [kɑːf] (pl **calves**) n (of cow) ternero, becerro; (of other animals) cría; (also: **~skin**) piel f de becerro; (Anat) pantorrilla

calibre ['kælɪbə*] (us **caliber**) n calibre m

call [kɔːl] vt llamar; (meeting) convocar ▷ vi (shout) llamar; (Tel) llamar (por teléfono); (visit: also: **~ in, ~ round**) hacer una visita ▷ n llamada; (of bird) canto; **to be ~ed** llamarse; **on ~** (on duty) de guardia; **call back** vi (return) volver; (Tel) volver a llamar; **call for** vt fus (demand) pedir, exigir; (fetch) pasar a recoger; **call in** vt (doctor, expert, police) llamar; **call off** vt (cancel: meeting, race) cancelar; (: deal) anular; (: strike) desconvocar; **call on** vt fus (visit) visitar; (turn to) acudir a; **call out** vi gritar; **call up** vt (Mil) llamar al servicio militar; (Tel) llamar; **callbox** (BRIT) n cabina telefónica; **call centre** (us **call center**) n centro de atención al cliente; **caller** n visita; (Tel) usuario/a

callous ['kæləs] adj insensible, cruel

calm [kɑːm] adj tranquilo; (sea) liso, en calma ▷ n calma, tranquilidad f ▷ vt calmar, tranquilizar; **calm down** vi calmarse, tranquilizarse ▷ vt calmar, tranquilizar; **calmly** ['kɑːmlɪ] adv tranquilamente, con calma

Calor gas® ['kælə*-] n butano

calorie ['kælərɪ] n caloría

calves [kɑːvz] npl of **calf**

camcorder ['kæmkɔːdə*] n videocámara

came [keɪm] pt of **come**

camel ['kæməl] n camello

camera ['kæmərə] n máquina fotográfica; (Cinema, TV) cámara; **in ~** (Law) a puerta cerrada; **cameraman** (irreg) n cámara m; **camera phone** n teléfono con cámara

camouflage ['kæməflɑːʒ] n camuflaje m ▷ vt camuflar

camp [kæmp] n campamento, camping m; (Mil) campamento; (for prisoners) campo; (fig: faction) bando ▷ vi acampar ▷ adj afectado, afeminado

campaign [kæm'peɪn] n (Mil, Pol etc) campaña ▷ vi hacer campaña; **campaigner** n: **campaigner for** defensor(a) m/f de

camp: campbed (BRIT) n cama de campaña; **camper** n campista mf; (vehicle) caravana; **campground** (us) n camping m, campamento; **camping** n camping m; **to go camping** hacer camping; **campsite** n camping m

campus ['kæmpəs] n ciudad f universitaria

can¹ [kæn] n (of oil, water) bidón m; (tin) lata, bote m ▷ vt enlatar

○ **KEYWORD**

can² [kæn] (negative **cannot, can't**, conditional and pt **could**) aux vb **1** (be able to) poder; **you can do it if you try** puedes hacerlo si lo intentas; **I can't see you** no te veo

2 (know how to) saber; **I can swim/play tennis/drive** sé nadar/jugar al tenis/ conducir; **can you speak French?** ¿hablas or sabes hablar francés?

3 (may) poder; **can I use your phone?** ¿me dejas or puedo usar tu teléfono?

4 (expressing disbelief, puzzlement etc): **it can't be true!** ¡no puede ser (verdad)!; **what CAN he want?** ¿qué querrá?

5 (expressing possibility, suggestion etc): **he could be in the library** podría estar en la biblioteca; **she could have been delayed** pudo haberse retrasado

Canada ['kænədə] n (el) Canadá; **Canadian** [kə'neɪdɪən] adj, n canadiense mf

canal [kə'næl] n canal m

canary [kə'nɛərɪ] n canario

Canary Islands [kə'nɛərɪ'aɪləndz]

npl: **the ~** las (Islas) Canarias
cancel ['kænsəl] *vt* cancelar; (*train*)
suprimir; (*cross out*) tachar, borrar;
cancellation [-'leɪʃən] *n* cancelación
f; supresión *f*
Cancer ['kænsə*] *n* (*Astrology*)
Cáncer *m*
cancer ['kænsə*] *n* cáncer *m*
candidate ['kændɪdeɪt] *n*
candidato/a
candle ['kændl] *n* vela; (*in church*)
cirio; **candlestick** *n* (*single*) candelero;
(*low*) palmatoria; (*bigger, ornate*)
candelabro
candy ['kændɪ] *n* azúcar *m* cande;
(*US*) caramelo; **candy bar** (*US*) *n*
barrita (*dulce*); **candyfloss** (*BRIT*) *n*
algodón *m* (azucarado)
cane [keɪn] *n* (*Bot*) caña; (*stick*) vara,
palmeta; (*for furniture*) mimbre *f* ▷ *vt*
(*BRIT: Scol*) castigar (con vara)
canister ['kænɪstə*] *n* bote *m*, lata;
(*of gas*) bombona
cannabis ['kænəbɪs] *n* marijuana
canned [kænd] *adj* en lata, de lata
cannon ['kænən] (*pl ~ or ~s*) *n*
cañón *m*
cannot ['kænɔt] = **can not**
canoe [kə'nuː] *n* canoa; (*Sport*)
piragua; **canoeing** *n* piragüismo
canon ['kænən] *n* (*clergyman*)
canónigo; (*standard*) canon *m*
can-opener ['kænəupnə*] *n*
abrelatas *m inv*
can't [kænt] = **can not**
canteen [kæn'tiːn] *n* (*eating place*)
cantina; (*BRIT: of cutlery*) juego
canter ['kæntə*] *vi* ir a medio galope
canvas ['kænvəs] *n* (*material*) lona;
(*painting*) lienzo; (*Naut*) velas *fpl*
canvass ['kænvəs] *vi* (*Pol*): **to ~
for** solicitar votos por ▷ *vt* (*Comm*)
sondear
canyon ['kænjən] *n* cañón *m*
cap [kæp] *n* (*hat*) gorra; (*of pen*)
capuchón *m*; (*of bottle*) tapa, tapón *m*;
(*contraceptive*) diafragma *m*; (*for toy gun*)
cápsula ▷ *vt* (*outdo*) superar; (*limit*)

recortar
capability [keɪpə'bɪlɪtɪ] *n* capacidad
f
capable ['keɪpəbl] *adj* capaz
capacity [kə'pæsɪtɪ] *n* capacidad *f*;
(*position*) calidad *f*
cape [keɪp] *n* capa; (*Geo*) cabo
caper ['keɪpə*] *n* (*Culin: gen pl*)
alcaparra; (*prank*) broma
capital ['kæpɪtl] *n* (*also:* **~ city**)
capital *f*; (*money*) capital *m*; (*also:*
~ letter) mayúscula; **capitalism**
n capitalismo; **capitalist** *adj*, *n*
capitalista *mf*; **capital punishment** *n*
pena de muerte
Capitol ['kæpɪtl] *n* ver recuadro

● **CAPITOL**
●
● El Capitolio **(Capitol)** es el edificio
● del Congreso **(Congress)** de
● los Estados Unidos, situado en
● la ciudad de Washington. Por
● extensión, también se suele llamar
● así al edificio en el que tienen lugar
● las sesiones parlamentarias de
● la cámara de representantes de
● muchos de los estados.

Capricorn ['kæprɪkɔːn] *n*
Capricornio
capsize [kæp'saɪz] *vt* volcar, hacer
zozobrar ▷ *vi* volcarse, zozobrar
capsule ['kæpsjuːl] *n* cápsula
captain ['kæptɪn] *n* capitán *m*
caption ['kæpʃən] *n* (*heading*) título;
(*to picture*) leyenda
captivity [kæp'tɪvɪtɪ] *n* cautiverio
capture ['kæptʃə*] *vt* prender,
apresar; (*animal, Comput*) capturar;
(*place*) tomar; (*attention*) captar, llamar
▷ *n* apresamiento; captura; toma;
(*data capture*) formulación *f* de datos
car [kɑː*] *n* coche *m*, carro (*LAM*),
automóvil *m*; (*US Rail*) vagón *m*
carafe [kə'ræf] *n* jarra
caramel ['kærəməl] *n* caramelo
carat ['kærət] *n* quilate *m*

caravan ['kærəvæn] n (BRIT)
caravana, rulóf; (in desert) caravana;
caravan site (BRIT) n camping m para
caravanas
carbohydrate [kɑːbəʊ'haɪdreɪt] n
hidrato de carbono; (food) fécula
carbon ['kɑːbən] n carbono; **carbon
dioxide** n dióxido de carbono,
anhídrido carbónico; **carbon
monoxide** n monóxido de carbono
car boot sale n mercadillo organizado
en un aparcamiento, en el que se
exponen las mercancías en el maletero
del coche
carburettor [kɑːbju'rɛtə*] (US
carburetor) n carburador m
card [kɑːd] n (material) cartulina;
(index card etc) ficha; (playing card) carta,
naipe m; (visiting card, greetings card etc)
tarjeta; **cardboard** n cartón m; **card
game** n juego de naipes or cartas
cardigan ['kɑːdɪgən] n rebeca
cardinal ['kɑːdɪnl] adj cardinal;
(importance, principal) esencial ▷ n
cardenal m
cardphone ['kɑːdfəʊn] n cabina que
funciona con tarjetas telefónicas
care [kɛə*] n cuidado; (worry)
inquietud f; (charge) cargo, custodia
▷ vi: **to ~ about** (person, animal) tener
cariño a; (thing, idea) preocuparse por; **~
of** en casa de, al cuidado de; **in sb's ~** a
cargo de algn; **to take ~ to** cuidarse de,
tener cuidado de; **to take ~ of** cuidar;
(problem etc) ocuparse de; **I don't ~** no
me importa; **I couldn't ~ less** eso me
trae sin cuidado; **care for** vt fus cuidar
a; (like) querer
career [kə'rɪə*] n profesión f; (in work,
school) carrera ▷ vi (also: **~ along**)
correr a toda velocidad
care: carefree adj despreocupado;
careful adj cuidadoso; (cautious)
cauteloso; **(be) careful!** ¡tenga
cuidado!; **carefully** adv con cuidado,
cuidadosamente; con cautela;
caregiver (US) n (professional)
enfermero/a m/f; (unpaid) persona que

cuida a un pariente o vecino; **careless**
adj descuidado; (heedless) poco
atento; **carelessness** n descuido,
falta de atención; **carer** ['kɛərə*] n
(professional) enfermero/a m/f; (unpaid)
persona que cuida a un pariente o vecino;
caretaker n portero/a, conserje mf
car-ferry ['kɑːfɛrɪ] n transbordador
m para coches
cargo ['kɑːgəʊ] (pl **~es**) n
cargamento, carga
car hire n alquiler m de automóviles
Caribbean [kærɪ'biːən] n: **the ~ (Sea)**
el (Mar) Caribe
caring ['kɛərɪŋ] adj humanitario;
(behaviour) afectuoso
carnation [kɑː'neɪʃən] n clavel m
carnival ['kɑːnɪvəl] n carnaval m;
(US: funfair) parque m de atracciones
carol ['kærəl] n: **(Christmas) ~**
villancico
carousel [kærə'sɛl] (US) n tiovivo,
caballitos mpl
car park (BRIT) n aparcamiento,
parking m
carpenter ['kɑːpɪntə*] n
carpintero/a
carpet ['kɑːpɪt] n alfombra; (fitted)
moqueta ▷ vt alfombrar
car rental (US) n alquiler m de coches
carriage ['kærɪdʒ] n (BRIT Rail) vagón
m; (horse-drawn) coche m; (of goods)
transporte m; (: cost) porte m, flete m;
carriageway (BRIT) n (part of road)
calzada
carrier ['kærɪə*] n (transport company)
transportista, empresa de transportes;
(Med) portador/a m/f; **carrier bag**
(BRIT) n bolsa de papel or plástico
carrot ['kærət] n zanahoria
carry ['kærɪ] vt (person)
llevar; (transport) transportar;
(involve: responsibilities etc) entrañar,
implicar; (Med) ser portador de ▷ vi
(sound) oírse; **to get carried away** (fig)
entusiasmarse; **carry on** vi (continue)
seguir (adelante), continuar ▷ vt
proseguir, continuar; **carry out** vt

(*orders*) cumplir; (*investigation*) llevar a cabo, realizar

cart [kɑːt] n carro, carreta ▷ vt (*inf: transport*) acarrear

carton ['kɑːtən] n (*box*) caja (de cartón); (*of milk etc*) bote m; (*of yogurt*) tarrina

cartoon [kɑː'tuːn] n (*Press*) caricatura; (*comic strip*) tira cómica; (*film*) dibujos mpl animados

cartridge ['kɑːtrɪdʒ] n cartucho; (*of pen*) recambio

carve [kɑːv] vt (*meat*) trinchar; (*wood, stone*) cincelar, esculpir; (*initials etc*) grabar; **carving** n (*object*) escultura; (*design*) talla; (*art*) tallado

car wash n lavado de coches

case [keɪs] n (*container*) caja; (*Med*) caso; (*for jewels etc*) estuche m; (*Law*) causa, proceso; (*BRIT: also:* **suit~**) maleta; **in ~ of** en caso de; **in any ~** en todo caso; **just in ~** por si acaso

cash [kæʃ] n dinero en efectivo, dinero contante ▷ vt cobrar, hacer efectivo; **to pay (in) ~** pagar al contado; **~ on delivery** cóbrese al entregar; **cashback** n (*discount*) devolución f; (*at supermarket etc*) retirada de dinero en efectivo de un establecimiento donde se ha pagado con tarjeta; *también* dinero retirado; **cash card** n tarjeta f dinero; **cash desk** (*BRIT*) n caja; **cash dispenser** n cajero automático

cashew [kæ'ʃuː] n (*also:* **~ nut**) anacardo

cashier [kæ'ʃɪə*] n cajero/a

cashmere ['kæʃmɪə*] n cachemira

cash point n cajero automático

cash register n caja

casino [kə'siːnəu] n casino

casket ['kɑːskɪt] n cofre m, estuche m; (*US: coffin*) ataúd m

casserole ['kæsərəul] n (*food, pot*) cazuela

cassette [kæ'sɛt] n casete f; **cassette player, cassette recorder** n casete m

cast [kɑːst] (*pt, pp* **~**) vt (*throw*) echar, arrojar, lanzar; (*glance, eyes*) dirigir;

(*Theatre*): **to ~ sb as Othello** dar a algn el papel de Otelo ▷ vi (*Fishing*) lanzar ▷ n (*Theatre*) reparto; (*also:* **plaster ~**) vaciado; **to ~ one's vote** votar; **to ~ doubt on** suscitar dudas acerca de; **cast off** vi (*Naut*) desamarrar; (*Knitting*) cerrar (los puntos)

castanets [kæstə'nɛts] npl castañuelas fpl

caster sugar ['kɑːstə*-] (*BRIT*) n azúcar m extrafino

Castile [kæs'tiːl] n Castilla; **Castilian** adj, n castellano/a m/f

cast-iron ['kɑːstaɪən] adj (*lit*) (hecho) de hierro fundido; (*fig: case*) irrebatible

castle ['kɑːsl] n castillo; (*Chess*) torre f

casual ['kæʒjul] adj fortuito; (*irregular: work etc*) eventual, temporero; (*unconcerned*) despreocupado; (*clothes*) informal

▌ Be careful not to translate **casual** by the Spanish word casual.

casualty ['kæʒjultɪ] n víctima, herido/a; (*dead*) muerto/a; (*Med: department*) urgencias fpl

cat [kæt] n gato; (*big cat*) felino

Catalan ['kætəlæn] adj, n catalán/ana m/f

catalogue ['kætəlɔg] (*US* **catalog**) n catálogo ▷ vt catalogar

Catalonia [kætə'ləunɪə] n Cataluña

catalytic converter [kætə'lɪtɪkkən'vɜːtə*] n catalizador m

cataract ['kætərækt] n (*Med*) cataratas fpl

catarrh [kə'tɑː*] n catarro

catastrophe [kə'tæstrəfɪ] n catástrofe f

catch [kætʃ] (*pt, pp* **caught**) vt coger (*SP*), agarrar (*LAM*); (*arrest*) detener; (*grasp*) asir; (*breath*) contener; (*surprise: person*) sorprender; (*attract: attention*) captar; (*hear*) oír; (*Med*) contagiarse de, coger; (*also:* **~ up**) alcanzar ▷ vi (*fire*) encenderse; (*in branches etc*) enredarse ▷ n (*fish etc*) pesca; (*act of catching*) cogida; (*hidden problem*) dificultad f; (*game*) pilla-pilla; (of lock) pestillo, cerradura; **to ~ fire** encenderse; **to ~ sight of** divisar; **catch up** vi (fig) ponerse al día; **catching** ['kætʃɪŋ] adj (Med) contagioso

category ['kætɪgərɪ] n categoría, clase f

cater ['keɪtə*] vi: **to ~ for** (BRIT) abastecer a; (needs) atender a; (Comm: parties etc) proveer comida a

caterpillar ['kætəpɪlə*] n oruga, gusano

cathedral [kə'θi:drəl] n catedral f

Catholic ['kæθəlɪk] adj, n (Rel) católico/a m/f

Catseye® ['kæts'aɪ] (BRIT) n (Aut) catafoto

cattle ['kætl] npl ganado

catwalk ['kætwɔ:k] n pasarela

caught [kɔ:t] pt, pp of **catch**

cauliflower ['kɒlɪflauə*] n coliflor f

cause [kɔ:z] n causa, motivo, razón f; (principle: also Pol) causa ▷ vt causar

caution ['kɔ:ʃən] n cautela, prudencia; (warning) advertencia, amonestación f ▷ vt amonestar; **cautious** adj cauteloso, prudente, precavido

cave [keɪv] n cueva, caverna; **cave in** vi (roof etc) derrumbarse, hundirse

caviar(e) ['kævɪɑ:*] n caviar m

cavity ['kævɪtɪ] n hueco, cavidad f

cc abbr (= cubic centimetres) c.c.; (= carbon copy) copia hecha con papel del carbón

CCTV n abbr (= closed-circuit television) circuito cerrado de televisión

CD n abbr (= compact disc) CD m; (player) (reproductor m de) CD; **CD player** n reproductor m de CD; **CD-ROM** [si:di:'rɔm] n abbr CD-ROM m; **CD writer** n grabadora de CD

cease [si:s] vt, vi cesar; **ceasefire** n alto m el fuego

cedar ['si:də*] n cedro

ceilidh ['keɪlɪ] n baile con música y danzas tradicionales escocesas o irlandesas

ceiling ['si:lɪŋ] n techo; (fig) límite m

celebrate ['sɛlɪbreɪt] vt celebrar ▷ vi

divertirse; **celebration** [-'breɪʃən] n fiesta, celebración f

celebrity [sɪ'lɛbrɪtɪ] n celebridad f

celery ['sɛlərɪ] n apio

cell [sɛl] n celda; (Biol) célula; (Elec) elemento

cellar ['sɛlə*] n sótano; (for wine) bodega

cello ['tʃɛləu] n violoncelo

Cellophane® ['sɛləfeɪn] n celofán m

cellphone ['sɛlfəun] n teléfono celular

Celsius ['sɛlsɪəs] adj centígrado

Celtic ['kɛltɪk] adj celta

cement [sə'mɛnt] n cemento

cemetery ['sɛmɪtrɪ] n cementerio

censor ['sɛnsə*] n censor m ▷vt (cut) censurar; **censorship** n censura

census ['sɛnsəs] n censo

cent [sɛnt] n (unit of dollar) centavo, céntimo; (unit of euro) céntimo; see also **per**

centenary [sɛn'ti:nərɪ] n centenario

centennial [sɛn'tɛnɪəl] (US) n centenario

center ['sɛntə*] (US) = **centre**

centi... [sɛntɪ] prefix: **centigrade** adj centígrado; **centimetre** (US **centimeter**) n centímetro; **centipede** ['sɛntɪpi:d] n ciempiés m inv

central ['sɛntrəl] adj central; (of house etc) céntrico; **Central America** n Centroamérica; **central heating** n calefacción f central; **central reservation** n (BRIT Aut) mediana

centre ['sɛntə*] (US **center**) n centro; (fig) núcleo ▷ vt centrar; **centre-forward** n (Sport) delantero centro; **centre-half** n (Sport) medio centro

century ['sɛntjurɪ] n siglo; **20th ~** siglo veinte

CEO n abbr = **chief executive officer**

ceramic [sɪ'ræmɪk] adj cerámico

cereal ['si:rɪəl] n cereal m

ceremony ['sɛrɪmənɪ] n ceremonia; **to stand on ~** hacer ceremonias, estar de cumplido

certain ['sə:tən] adj seguro;

(*person*): **a ~ Mr Smith** un tal Sr. Smith;
(*particular, some*) cierto; **for ~** a ciencia
cierta; **certainly** *adv* (*undoubtedly*)
ciertamente; (*of course*) desde luego,
por supuesto; **certainty** *n* certeza,
certidumbre *f*, seguridad *f*; (*inevitability*)
certeza

certificate [sə'tɪfɪkɪt] *n* certificado
certify ['sə:tɪfaɪ] *vt* certificar; (*award
diploma to*) conceder un diploma a;
(*declare insane*) declarar loco

cf. *abbr* (= *compare*) cfr

CFC *n abbr* (= *chlorofluorocarbon*) CFC *m*

chain [tʃeɪn] *n* cadena; (*of mountains*)
cordillera; (*of events*) sucesión *f* ▷ *vt*
(*also:* **~ up**) encadenar; **chain-smoke** *vi*
fumar un cigarrillo tras otro

chair [tʃɛə*] *n* silla; (*armchair*) sillón
m, butaca; (*of university*) cátedra;
(*of meeting etc*) presidencia ▷ *vt*
(*meeting*) presidir; **chairlift** *n* telesilla;
chairman (*irreg*) *n* presidente *m*;
chairperson *n* presidente/a *m/f*;
chairwoman (*irreg*) *n* presidenta

chalet ['ʃæleɪ] *n* chalet *m* (de madera)

chalk [tʃɔ:k] *n* (*Geo*) creta; (*for writing*)
tiza, gis *m* (*MEX*); **chalkboard** (*US*) *n*
pizarrón (*LAM*), pizarra (*SP*)

challenge ['tʃælɪndʒ] *n* desafío, reto
▷ *vt* desafiar, retar; (*statement, right*)
poner en duda; **to ~ sb to do sth** retar a
algn a que haga algo; **challenging** *adj*
exigente; (*tone*) de desafío

chamber ['tʃeɪmbə*] *n* cámara,
sala; (*Pol*) cámara; (*BRIT Law: gen pl*)
despacho; **~ of commerce** cámara de
comercio; **chambermaid** *n* camarera

champagne [ʃæm'peɪn] *n*
champaña *m*, champán *m*

champion ['tʃæmpiən] *n* campeón/
ona *m/f*; (*of cause*) defensor(a) *m/f*;
championship *n* campeonato

chance [tʃɑːns] *n* (*opportunity*)
ocasión *f*, oportunidad *f*; (*likelihood*)
posibilidad *f*; (*risk*) riesgo ▷ *vt*
arriesgar, probar ▷ *adj* fortuito,
casual; **to ~ it** arriesgarse, intentarlo;
to take a ~ arriesgarse; **by ~** por

casualidad

chancellor ['tʃɑːnsələ*] *n* canciller
m; **Chancellor of the Exchequer** (*BRIT*)
n Ministro de Hacienda

chandelier [ʃændə'lɪə*] *n* araña
(de luces)

change [tʃeɪndʒ] *vt* cambiar;
(*replace*) cambiar, reemplazar; (*gear,
clothes, job*) cambiar de; (*transform*)
transformar ▷ *vi* cambiar(se); (*change
trains*) hacer transbordo; (*traffic lights*)
cambiar de color; (*be transformed*): **to
~ into** transformarse en ▷ *n*
cambio; (*alteration*) modificación *f*;
(*transformation*) transformación *f*; (*of
clothes*) muda; (*coins*) suelto, sencillo;
(*money returned*) vuelta; **to ~ gear** (*Aut*)
cambiar de marcha; **to ~ one's mind**
cambiar de opinión *or* idea; **for a ~** para
variar; **change over** *vi* (*from sth to sth*)
cambiar; (*players etc*) cambiar(se) ▷ *vt*
cambiar; **changeable** *adj* (*weather*)
cambiable; **change machine**
máquina de cambio; **changing room**
(*BRIT*) *n* vestuario

channel ['tʃænl] *n* (*TV*) canal *m*;
(*of river*) cauce *m*; (*groove*) conducto;
(*fig: medium*) medio ▷ *vt* (*river etc*)
encauzar; **the (English) C~** el Canal
(de la Mancha); **the C~ Islands** las Islas
Normandas; **Channel Tunnel** *n*: **the
Channel Tunnel** el túnel del Canal de la
Mancha, el Eurotúnel

chant [tʃɑːnt] *n* (*of crowd*) gritos *mpl*;
(*Rel*) canto ▷ *vt* (*slogan, word*) repetir
a gritos

chaos ['keɪɔs] *n* caos *m*

chaotic [keɪ'ɔtɪk] *adj* caótico

chap [tʃæp] (*BRIT: inf*) *n* (*man*) tío, tipo

chapel ['tʃæpəl] *n* capilla

chapped [tʃæpt] *adj* agrietado

chapter ['tʃæptə*] *n* capítulo

character ['kærɪktə*] *n* carácter *m*,
naturaleza, índole *f*; (*moral strength,
personality*) carácter; (*in novel, film*)
personaje *m*; **characteristic** [-'rɪstɪk]
adj característico ▷ *n* característica;
characterize ['kærɪktəraɪz] *vt*

caracterizar
charcoal ['tʃɑːkəul] *n* carbón *m*
vegetal; (*Art*) carboncillo
charge [tʃɑːdʒ] *n* (*Law*) cargo,
acusación *f*; (*cost*) precio, coste *m*;
(*responsibility*) cargo ▷ *vt* (*Law*): **to ~
(with)** acusar (de); (*battery*) cargar;
(*price*) pedir; (*customer*) cobrar ▷ *vi*
precipitarse; (*Mil*) cargar, atacar;
charge card *n* tarjeta de cuenta;
charger *n* (*also*: **battery charger**)
cargador *m* (de baterías)
charismatic [kærɪz'mætɪk] *adj*
carismático
charity ['tʃærɪtɪ] *n* caridad *f*;
(*organization*) sociedad *f* benéfica;
(*money, gifts*) limosnas *fpl*; **charity
shop** *n* (*BRIT*) tienda de artículos de
segunda mano que dedica su recaudación a
causas benéficas
charm [tʃɑːm] *n* encanto, atractivo;
(*talisman*) hechizo; (*on bracelet*) dije
m ▷ *vt* encantar; **charming** *adj*
encantador(a)
chart [tʃɑːt] *n* (*diagram*) cuadro;
(*graph*) gráfica; (*map*) carta de
navegación ▷ *vt* (*course*) trazar;
(*progress*) seguir; **charts** *npl* (*Top
40*): **the ~s** ≈ los 40 principales (*SP*)
charter ['tʃɑːtə*] *vt* (*plane*) alquilar;
(*ship*) fletar ▷ *n* (*document*) carta; (*of
university, company*) estatutos *mpl*;
chartered accountant (*BRIT*) *n*
contable *m/f* diplomado/a; **charter
flight** *n* vuelo chárter
chase [tʃeɪs] *vt* (*pursue*) perseguir;
(*also*: **~ away**) ahuyentar ▷ *n*
persecución *f*
chat [tʃæt] *vi* (*also*: **have a ~**) charlar;
(*on Internet*) chatear ▷ *n* charla; **chat
up** *vt* (*inf: girl*) ligar con, enrollarse
con; **chat room** *n* (*Internet*) chat *m*,
canal *m* de charla; **chat show** (*BRIT*) *n*
programa *m* de entrevistas
chatter ['tʃætə*] *vi* (*person*) charlar;
(*teeth*) castañetear ▷ *n* (*of birds*)
parloteo; (*of people*) charla, cháchara
chauffeur ['ʃəufə*] *n* chófer *m*

chauvinist ['ʃəuvɪnɪst] *n* (*male
chauvinist*) machista *m*; (*nationalist*)
chovinista *mf*
cheap [tʃiːp] *adj* barato; (*joke*) de mal
gusto; (*poor quality*) de mala calidad
▷ *adv* barato; **cheap day return**
n billete de ida y vuelta el mismo día;
cheaply *adv* barato, a bajo precio
cheat [tʃiːt] *vi* hacer trampa ▷ *vt*: **to
~ sb (out of sth)** estafar (algo) a algn
▷ *n* (*person*) tramposo/a; **cheat on** *vt
fus* engañar
Chechnya [tʃitʃˈnjɑː] *n* Chechenia
check [tʃɛk] *vt* (*examine*) controlar;
(*facts*) comprobar; (*halt*) parar, detener;
(*restrain*) refrenar, restringir ▷ *n*
(*inspection*) control *m*, inspección *f*;
(*curb*) freno; (*US*: bill) nota, cuenta;
(*US*) = **cheque**; (*pattern: gen pl*) cuadro;
check in *vi* (*at hotel*) firmar el registro;
(*at airport*) facturar el equipaje ▷ *vt*
(*luggage*) facturar; **check off** *vt* (*esp
US: check*) comprobar; (*cross off*) tachar;
check out *vi* (*of hotel*) marcharse;
check up *vi*: **to check up on sth**
comprobar algo; **to check up on sb**
investigar a algn; **checkbook** (*US*) =
chequebook; checked *adj* a cuadros;
checkers (*US*) *n* juego de damas;
check-in *n* (*also*: **check-in desk**: *at
airport*) mostrador *m* de facturación;
checking account (*US*) *n* cuenta
corriente; **checklist** *n* lista (de
control); **checkmate** *n* jaque *m*
mate; **checkout** *n* caja; **checkpoint**
n (punto de) control *m*; **checkroom**
(*US*) *n* consigna; **checkup** *n* (*Med*)
reconocimiento general
cheddar ['tʃedə*] *n* (*also*: **~ cheese**)
queso *m* cheddar
cheek [tʃiːk] *n* mejilla; (*impudence*)
descaro; **what a ~!** ¡qué cara!;
cheekbone *n* pómulo; **cheeky** *adj*
fresco, descarado
cheer [tʃɪə*] *vt* vitorear, aplaudir;
(*gladden*) alegrar, animar ▷ *vi* dar vivas
▷ *n* viva *m*; **cheer up** *vi* animarse ▷ *vt*
alegrar, animar; **cheerful** *adj* alegre

cheerio [tʃɪərɪˈəu] (BRIT) excl ¡hasta luego!

cheerleader ['tʃɪəliːdə*] n animador(a) m/f

cheese [tʃiːz] n queso; **cheeseburger** n hamburguesa con queso; **cheesecake** n pastel m de queso

chef [ʃɛf] n jefe/a m/f de cocina

chemical ['kɛmɪkəl] adj químico ▷ n producto químico

chemist ['kɛmɪst] n (BRIT: pharmacist) farmacéutico/a; (scientist) químico/a; **chemistry** n química; **chemist's (shop)** (BRIT) n farmacia

cheque [tʃɛk] (US **check**) n cheque m; **chequebook** n talonario de cheques (SP), chequera (LAM); **cheque card** n tarjeta de cheque

cherry ['tʃɛrɪ] n cereza; (also: **~ tree**) cerezo

chess [tʃɛs] n ajedrez m

chest [tʃɛst] n (Anat) pecho; (box) cofre m, cajón m

chestnut ['tʃɛsnʌt] n castaña; (also: **~ tree**) castaño

chest of drawers n cómoda

chew [tʃuː] vt mascar, masticar; **chewing gum** n chicle m

chic [ʃiːk] adj elegante

chick [tʃɪk] n pollito, polluelo; (inf: girl) chica

chicken ['tʃɪkɪn] n gallina, pollo; (food) pollo; (inf: coward) gallina mf; **chicken out** (inf) vi rajarse; **chickenpox** n varicela

chickpea ['tʃɪkpiː] n garbanzo

chief [tʃiːf] n jefe/a m/f ▷ adj principal; **chief executive (officer)** n director(a) m/f general; **chiefly** adv principalmente

child [tʃaɪld] (pl **~ren**) n niño/a; (offspring) hijo/a; (with violence) malos tratos mpl a niños; (sexual) abuso m sexual de niños; **child benefit** n (BRIT) subsidio por cada hijo pequeño; **childbirth** n parto; **child-care** n cuidado de los niños; **childhood** n niñez f, infancia; **childish**

adj pueril, aniñado; **child minder** (BRIT) n madre f de día; **children** ['tʃɪldrən] npl of **child**

Chile ['tʃɪlɪ] n Chile m; **Chilean** adj, n chileno/a m/f

chill [tʃɪl] n frío; (Med) resfriado ▷ vt enfriar; (Culin) congelar; **chill out** vi (esp US: inf) tranquilizarse

chil(l)i ['tʃɪlɪ] (BRIT) n chile m, ají m (SC)

chilly ['tʃɪlɪ] adj frío

chimney ['tʃɪmnɪ] n chimenea

chimpanzee [tʃɪmpæn'ziː] n chimpancé m

chin [tʃɪn] n mentón m, barbilla

China ['tʃaɪnə] n China

china ['tʃaɪnə] n porcelana; (crockery) loza

Chinese [tʃaɪ'niːz] adj chino ▷ n inv chino/a m/f; (Ling) chino

chip [tʃɪp] n (gen pl: Culin: BRIT) patata (SP) or papa (LAM) frita; (: US: also: **potato ~**) patata or papa frita; (of wood) astilla; (of glass, stone) lasca; (at poker) ficha; (Comput) chip m ▷ vt (cup, plate) desconchar; **chip shop** pescadería (donde se vende principalmente pescado rebozado y patatas fritas)

chiropodist [kɪ'rɔpədɪst] (BRIT) n pedicuro/a, callista m/f

chisel ['tʃɪzl] n (for wood) escoplo; (for stone) cincel m

chives [tʃaɪvz] npl cebollinos mpl

chlorine ['klɔːriːn] n cloro

choc-ice ['tʃɔkaɪs] n (BRIT) helado m cubierto de chocolate

chocolate ['tʃɔklɪt] n chocolate m; (sweet) bombón m

choice [tʃɔɪs] n elección f, selección f; (option) opción f; (preference) preferencia ▷ adj escogido

choir ['kwaɪə*] n coro

choke [tʃəuk] vi ahogarse; (on food) atragantarse ▷ vt estrangular, ahogar; (block): **to be ~d with** estar atascado de ▷ n (Aut) estárter m

cholesterol [kə'lɛstərul] n colesterol m

choose [tʃuːz] (pt **chose**, pp **chosen**)

vt escoger, elegir; (*team*) seleccionar;
to ~ to do sth optar por hacer algo
chop [tʃɒp] *vt* (*wood*) cortar, tajar;
(*Culin: also:* **~ up**) picar ▷ *n* (*Culin*)
chuleta; **chop down** *vt* (*tree*) talar;
chop off *vt* cortar (de un tajo);
chopsticks ['tʃɒpstɪks] *npl* palillos
mpl
chord [kɔːd] *n* (*Mus*) acorde *m*
chore [tʃɔː*] *n* faena, tarea; (*routine
task*) trabajo rutinario
chorus ['kɔːrəs] *n* coro; (*repeated part
of song*) estribillo
chose [tʃəuz] *pt of* **choose**
chosen ['tʃəuzn] *pp of* **choose**
Christ [kraɪst] *n* Cristo
christen ['krɪsn] *vt* bautizar;
christening *n* bautizo
Christian ['krɪstɪən] *adj, n*
cristiano/a *m/f*; **Christianity** [-'ænɪtɪ]
n cristianismo; **Christian name** *n*
nombre *m* de pila
Christmas ['krɪsməs] *n* Navidad *f*;
Merry ~! ¡Felices Pascuas!; **Christmas
card** *n* crismas *m inv*, tarjeta de
Navidad; **Christmas carol** *n* villancico
m; **Christmas Day** *n* día *m* de Navidad;
Christmas Eve *n* Nochebuena;
Christmas pudding *n* (*esp BRIT*) pudin
m de Navidad; **Christmas tree** *n* árbol
m de Navidad
chrome [krəum] *n* cromo
chronic ['krɒnɪk] *adj* crónico
chrysanthemum [krɪ'sænθəməm]
n crisantemo
chubby ['tʃʌbɪ] *adj* regordete
chuck [tʃʌk] (*inf*) *vt* lanzar, arrojar;
(*BRIT: also:* **~ up**) abandonar; **chuck
out** *vt* (*person*) echar (fuera); (*rubbish
etc*) tirar
chuckle ['tʃʌkl] *vi* reírse entre dientes
chum [tʃʌm] *n* compañero/a
chunk [tʃʌŋk] *n* pedazo, trozo
church [tʃəːtʃ] *n* iglesia; **churchyard**
n cementerio
churn [tʃəːn] *n* (*for butter*)
mantequera; (*for milk*) lechera
chute [ʃuːt] *n* (*also:* **rubbish ~**)

vertedero; (*for coal etc*) rampa de caída
chutney ['tʃʌtnɪ] *n* condimento a base
de frutas de la India
CIA (*us*) *n abbr* (= *Central Intelligence
Agency*) CIA *f*
CID (*BRIT*) *n abbr* (= *Criminal
Investigation Department*) ≈ B.I.C. *f* (*SP*)
cider ['saɪdə*] *n* sidra
cigar [sɪ'gɑː*] *n* puro
cigarette [sɪgə'rɛt] *n* cigarrillo;
cigarette lighter *n* mechero
cinema ['sɪnəmə] *n* cine *m*
cinnamon ['sɪnəmən] *n* canela
circle ['səːkl] *n* círculo; (*in theatre*)
anfiteatro ▷ *vi* dar vueltas ▷ *vt*
(*surround*) rodear, cercar; (*move round*)
dar la vuelta a
circuit ['səːkɪt] *n* circuito; (*tour*) gira;
(*track*) pista; (*lap*) vuelta
circular ['səːkjulə*] *adj* circular ▷ *n*
circular *f*
circulate ['səːkjuleɪt] *vi* circular;
(*person: at party etc*) hablar con los
invitados ▷ *vt* poner en circulación;
circulation [-'leɪʃən] *n* circulación *f*;
(*of newspaper*) tirada
circumstances ['səːkəmstənsɪz] *npl*
circunstancias *fpl*; (*financial condition*)
situación *f* económica
circus ['səːkəs] *n* circo
cite [saɪt] *vt* citar
citizen ['sɪtɪzn] *n* (*Pol*) ciudadano/a;
(*of city*) vecino/a, habitante *mf*;
citizenship *n* ciudadanía; (*BRIT: Scol*)
civismo
citrus fruits ['sɪtrəs-] *npl* agrios *mpl*
city ['sɪtɪ] *n* ciudad *f*; **the C~** centro
financiero de Londres; **city centre** (*BRIT*)
n centro de la ciudad; **city technology
college** *n* centro de formación
profesional (*centro de enseñanza
secundaria que da especial importancia a la
ciencia y tecnología.*)
civic ['sɪvɪk] *adj* cívico; (*authorities*)
municipal
civil ['sɪvɪl] *adj* civil; (*polite*) atento,
cortés; **civilian** [sɪ'vɪlɪən] *adj* civil (*no
militar*) ▷ *n* civil *mf*, paisano/a

civilization [sɪvɪlaɪˈzeɪʃən] *n*
civilización *f*
civilized [ˈsɪvɪlaɪzd] *adj* civilizado
civil: civil law *n* derecho civil; **civil
rights** *npl* derechos *mpl* civiles; **civil
servant** *n* funcionario/a del Estado;
Civil Service *n* administración *f*
pública; **civil war** *n* guerra civil
CJD *n abbr* (= *Creutzfeldt-Jakob disease*)
enfermedad de Creutzfeldt-Jakob
claim [kleɪm] *vt* exigir, reclamar;
(*rights etc*) reivindicar; (*assert*)
pretender ▷ *vi* (*for insurance*) reclamar
▷ *n* reclamación *f*; pretensión *f*; **claim
form** *n* solicitud *f*
clam [klæm] *n* almeja
clamp [klæmp] *n* abrazadera,
grapa ▷ *vt* (*two things together*) cerrar
fuertemente; (*one thing on another*)
afianzar (con abrazadera); (*Aut: wheel*)
poner el cepo a
clan [klæn] *n* clan *m*
clap [klæp] *vi* aplaudir
claret [ˈklærət] *n* burdeos *m inv*
clarify [ˈklærɪfaɪ] *vt* aclarar
clarinet [klærɪˈnɛt] *n* clarinete *m*
clarity [ˈklærɪtɪ] *n* claridad *f*
clash [klæʃ] *n* enfrentamiento;
choque *m*; desacuerdo; estruendo ▷ *vi*
(*fight*) enfrentarse; (*beliefs*) chocar;
(*disagree*) estar en desacuerdo; (*colours*)
desentonar; (*two events*) coincidir
clasp [klɑːsp] *n* (*hold*) apretón *m*; (*of
necklace, bag*) cierre *m* ▷ *vt* apretar;
abrazar
class [klɑːs] *n* clase *f* ▷ *vt* clasificar
classic [ˈklæsɪk] *adj*, *n* clásico;
classical *adj* clásico
classification [klæsɪfɪˈkeɪʃən] *n*
clasificación *f*
classify [ˈklæsɪfaɪ] *vt* clasificar
classmate [ˈklɑːsmeɪt] *n*
compañero/a de clase
classroom [ˈklɑːsruːm] *n* aula;
classroom assistant *n* profesor(a)
m/f de apoyo
classy [ˈklɑːsɪ] *adj* (*inf*) elegante,
con estilo

clatter [ˈklætə*] *n* estrépito ▷ *vi*
hacer ruido *or* estrépito
clause [klɔːz] *n* cláusula; (*Ling*)
oración *f*
claustrophobic [klɔːstrəˈfəʊbɪk]
adj claustrofóbico; **I feel ~** me entra
claustrofobia
claw [klɔː] *n* (*of cat*) uña; (*of bird of
prey*) garra; (*of lobster*) pinza
clay [kleɪ] *n* arcilla
clean [kliːn] *adj* limpio; (*record,
reputation*) bueno, intachable; (*joke*)
decente ▷ *vt* limpiar; (*hands etc*) lavar;
clean up *vt* limpiar, asear; **cleaner**
n (*person*) asistenta; (*substance*)
producto para la limpieza; **cleaner's** *n*
tintorería; **cleaning** *n* limpieza
cleanser [ˈklɛnzə*] *n* (*for face*) crema
limpiadora
clear [klɪə*] *adj* claro; (*road, way*)
libre; (*conscience*) limpio, tranquilo;
(*skin*) terso; (*sky*) despejado ▷ *vt*
(*space*) despejar, limpiar; (*Law: suspect*)
absolver; (*obstacle*) salvar, saltar por
encima de; (*cheque*) aceptar ▷ *vi* (*fog
etc*) despejarse ▷ *adv*: **~ of** a distancia
de; **to ~ the table** recoger *or* levantar
la mesa; **clear away** *vt* (*things, clothes
etc*) quitar (de en medio); (*dishes*)
retirar; **clear up** *vt* limpiar; (*mystery*)
aclarar, resolver; **clearance** *n* (*removal*)
despeje *m*; (*permission*) acreditación *f*;
clear-cut *adj* bien definido, nítido;
clearing *n* (*in wood*) claro; **clearly**
adv claramente; (*evidently*) sin duda;
clearway (*BRIT*) *n* carretera donde no
se puede parar
clench [klɛntʃ] *vt* apretar, cerrar
clergy [ˈklɜːdʒɪ] *n* clero
clerk [klɑːk, (*US*) klɜːrk] *n* (*BRIT*)
oficinista *mf*; (*US*) dependiente/a *m/f*
clever [ˈklɛvə*] *adj* (*intelligent*)
inteligente, listo; (*skilful*) hábil; (*device,
arrangement*) ingenioso
cliché [ˈkliːʃeɪ] *n* cliché *m*, frase *f*
hecha
click [klɪk] *vt* (*tongue*) chasquear;
(*heels*) taconear ▷ *vi* (*Comput*) hacer

clic; **to ~ on an icon** hacer clic en un icono

client ['klaɪənt] n cliente m/f

cliff [klɪf] n acantilado

climate ['klaɪmɪt] n clima m; **climate change** n cambio climático

climax ['klaɪmæks] n (of battle, career) apogeo; (of film, book) punto culminante; (sexual) orgasmo

climb [klaɪm] vi subir; (plant) trepar; (move with effort): **to ~ over a wall/into a car** trepar a una tapia/subir a un coche ▷ vt (stairs) subir; (tree) trepar a; (mountain) escalar ▷ n subida; **climb down** vi (fig) volverse atrás; **climber** n alpinista mf (SP, MEX), andinista mf (LAM); **climbing** n alpinismo (SP, MEX), andinismo (LAM)

clinch [klɪntʃ] vt (deal) cerrar; (argument) remachar

cling [klɪŋ] (pt, pp **clung**) vi: **to ~ to** agarrarse a; (clothes) pegarse a

Clingfilm® ['klɪŋfɪlm] n plástico adherente

clinic ['klɪnɪk] n clínica

clip [klɪp] n (for hair) horquilla; (also: **paper ~**) sujetapapeles m inv, clip m; (TV, Cinema) fragmento ▷ vt (cut) cortar; (also: **~ together**) unir; **clipping** n (newspaper) recorte m

cloak [kləuk] n capa, manto ▷ vt (fig) encubrir, disimular; **cloakroom** n guardarropa; (BRIT: WC) lavabo (SP), aseos mpl (SP), baño (LAM)

clock [klɔk] n reloj m; **clock in or on** vi (with card) fichar, picar; (start work) entrar a trabajar; **clock off or out** vi (with card) fichar or picar la salida; (leave work) salir del trabajar; **clockwise** adv en el sentido de las agujas del reloj; **clockwork** n aparato de relojería ▷ adj (toy) de cuerda

clog [klɔg] n zueco, chanclo ▷ vt atascar ▷ vi (also: **~ up**) atascarse

clone [kləun] n clon m ▷ vt clonar

close¹ [kləus] adj (near): **~ (to)** cerca (de); (friend) íntimo; (connection) estrecho; (examination) detallado,

minucioso; (weather) bochornoso ▷ adv cerca; **~ by, ~ at hand** muy cerca; **to have a ~ shave** (fig) escaparse por un pelo

close² [kləuz] vt (shut) cerrar; (end) concluir, terminar ▷ vi (shop etc) cerrarse; (end) concluirse, terminarse ▷ n (end) fin m, final m, conclusión f; **close down** vi cerrar definitivamente; **closed** adj (shop etc) cerrado

closely ['kləuslɪ] adv (study) con detalle; (watch) de cerca; (resemble) estrechamente

closet ['klɔzɪt] n armario

close-up ['kləusʌp] n primer plano

closing time n hora de cierre

closure ['kləuʒə*] n cierre m

clot [klɔt] n (gen) coágulo; (inf: idiot) imbécil m/f ▷ vi (blood) coagularse

cloth [klɔθ] n (material) tela, paño; (rag) trapo

clothes [kləuðz] npl ropa; **clothes line** n cuerda (para tender la ropa); **clothes peg** (us **clothes pin**) n pinza

clothing ['kləuðɪŋ] n = **clothes**

cloud [klaud] n nube f; **cloud over** vi (also fig) nublarse; **cloudy** adj nublado, nuboso; (liquid) turbio

clove [kləuv] n clavo; **~ of garlic** diente m de ajo

clown [klaun] n payaso ▷ vi (also: **~ about, ~ around**) hacer el payaso

club [klʌb] n (society) club m; (weapon) porra, cachiporra; (also: **golf ~**) palo ▷ vt aporrear ▷ vi: **to ~ together** (for gift) comprar entre todos; **clubs** npl (Cards) tréboles mpl; **club class** n (Aviat) clase f preferente

clue [kluː] n pista; (in crosswords) indicación f; **I haven't a ~** no tengo ni idea

clump [klʌmp] n (of trees) grupo

clumsy ['klʌmzɪ] adj (person) torpe, desmañado; (tool) difícil de manejar; (movement) desgarbado

clung [klʌŋ] pt, pp of **cling**

cluster ['klʌstə*] n grupo ▷ vi

agruparse, apiñarse
clutch [klʌtʃ] n (Aut) embrague m;
(grasp): **~es** garras fpl ▷ vt asir; agarrar
cm abbr (= centimetre) cm
Co. abbr (= county; company)
c/o abbr (= care of) c/a, a/c
coach [kəʊtʃ] n autocar m (SP),
coche m de línea; (horse-drawn) coche
m; (of train) vagón m, coche m; (Sport)
entrenador(a) m/f, instructor(a) m/f;
(tutor) profesor(a) m/f particular ▷ vt
(Sport) entrenar; (student) preparar,
enseñar; **coach station** n (BRIT)
estación f de autobuses etc; **coach trip**
n excursión f en autocar
coal [kəʊl] n carbón m
coalition [kəʊəˈlɪʃən] n coalición f
coarse [kɔːs] adj basto, burdo; (vulgar)
grosero, ordinario
coast [kəʊst] n costa, litoral m ▷ vi
(Aut) ir en punto muerto; **coastal**
adj costero, costanero; **coastguard**
n guardacostas m inv; **coastline** n
litoral m
coat [kəʊt] n abrigo; (of animal)
pelaje m, lana; (of paint) mano f, capa
▷ vt cubrir, revestir; **coat hanger** n
percha (SP), gancho (LAM); **coating** n
capa, baño
coax [kəʊks] vt engatusar
cob [kɔb] n see **corn**
cobbled [ˈkɔbld] adj: **~ street** calle f
empedrada, calle f adoquinada
cobweb [ˈkɔbwɛb] n telaraña
cocaine [kəˈkeɪn] n cocaína
cock [kɔk] n (rooster) gallo; (male bird)
macho ▷ vt (gun) amartillar; **cockerel**
n gallito
cockney [ˈkɔknɪ] n habitante de ciertos
barrios de Londres
cockpit [ˈkɔkpɪt] n cabina
cockroach [ˈkɔkrəʊtʃ] n cucaracha
cocktail [ˈkɔkteɪl] n coctel m,
cóctel m
cocoa [ˈkəʊkəʊ] n cacao; (drink)
chocolate m
coconut [ˈkəʊkənʌt] n coco
cod [kɔd] n bacalao

C.O.D. abbr (= cash on delivery) C.A.E.
code [kəʊd] n código; (cipher) clave
f; (dialling code) prefijo; (post code)
código postal
coeducational [kəʊɛdjuˈkeɪʃənl]
adj mixto
coffee [ˈkɔfɪ] n café m; **coffee bar**
(BRIT) n cafetería; **coffee bean**
n grano de café; **coffee break** n
descanso (para tomar café); **coffee
maker** n máquina de hacer café,
cafetera; **coffeepot** n cafetera; **coffee
shop** n café m; **coffee table** n mesita
(para servir el café)
coffin [ˈkɔfɪn] n ataúd m
cog [kɔg] n (wheel) rueda dentada;
(tooth) diente m
cognac [ˈkɔnjæk] n coñac m
coherent [kəʊˈhɪərənt] adj
coherente
coil [kɔɪl] n rollo; (Elec) bobina, carrete
m; (contraceptive) espiral f ▷ vt enrollar
coin [kɔɪn] n moneda ▷ vt (word)
inventar, idear
coincide [kəʊɪnˈsaɪd] vi coincidir;
(agree) estar de acuerdo; **coincidence**
[kəʊˈɪnsɪdəns] n casualidad f
Coke® [kəʊk] n Coca-Cola®
coke [kəʊk] n (coal) coque m
colander [ˈkɔləndə*] n colador m,
escurridor m
cold [kəʊld] adj frío ▷ n frío; (Med)
resfriado; **it's ~** hace frío; **to be ~**
(person) tener frío; **to catch (a) ~**
resfriarse; **in ~ blood** a sangre fría; **cold
sore** n herpes mpl or fpl
coleslaw [ˈkəʊlslɔː] n especie de
ensalada de col
colic [ˈkɔlɪk] n cólico
collaborate [kəˈlæbəreɪt] vi
colaborar
collapse [kəˈlæps] vi hundirse,
derrumbarse; (Med) sufrir un colapso
▷ n hundimiento, derrumbamiento;
(Med) colapso
collar [ˈkɔlə*] n (of coat, shirt) cuello;
(of dog etc) collar; **collarbone** n
clavícula

colleague [ˈkɔliːg] n colega mf; (at work) compañero/a

collect [kəˈlɛkt] vt (litter, mail etc) recoger; (as a hobby) coleccionar; (BRIT: call and pick up) recoger; (debts, subscriptions etc) recaudar ▷ vi reunirse; (dust) acumularse; **to call ~** (US Tel) llamar a cobro revertido; **collection** [kəˈlɛkʃən] n colección f; (of mail, for charity) recogida; **collective** [kəˈlɛktɪv] adj colectivo; **collector** n coleccionista mf

college [ˈkɔlɪdʒ] n colegio mayor; (of agriculture, technology) escuela universitaria

collide [kəˈlaɪd] vi chocar

collision [kəˈlɪʒən] n choque m

cologne [kəˈləun] n (also: **eau de ~**) (agua de) colonia

Colombia [kəˈlɔmbɪə] n Colombia; **Colombian** adj, n colombiano/a

colon [ˈkəulən] n (sign) dos puntos; (Med) colon m

colonel [ˈkəːnl] n coronel m

colonial [kəˈləunɪəl] adj colonial

colony [ˈkɔlənɪ] n colonia

colour etc [ˈkʌlə*] (US **color** etc) n color m ▷ vt color(e)ar; (dye) teñir; (fig: account) adornar; (: judgement) distorsionar ▷ vi (blush) sonrojarse; **colour in** vt colorear; **colour-blind** adj daltónico; **coloured** adj de color; (photo) en color; **colour film** n película en color; **colourful** adj lleno de color; (story) fantástico; (person) excéntrico; **colouring** n (complexion) tez f; (in food) colorante m; **colour television** n televisión f en color

column [ˈkɔləm] n columna

coma [ˈkəumə] n coma m

comb [kəum] n peine m; (ornamental) peineta ▷ vt (hair) peinar; (area) registrar a fondo

combat [ˈkɔmbæt] n combate m ▷ vt combatir

combination [kɔmbɪˈneɪʃən] n combinación f

combine [vb kəmˈbaɪn, n ˈkɔmbaɪn]

vt combinar; (qualities) reunir ▷ vi combinarse ▷ n (Econ) cartel m

○ **KEYWORD**

come [kʌm] (pt **came**, pp **come**) vi
1 (movement towards) venir; **to come running** venir corriendo
2 (arrive) llegar; **he's come here to work** ha venido aquí para trabajar; **to come home** volver a casa
3 (reach): **to come to** llegar a; **the bill came to £40** la cuenta ascendía a cuarenta libras
4 (occur): **an idea came to me** se me ocurrió una idea
5 (be, become): **to come loose/undone** etc aflojarse/desabrocharse/desatarse etc; **I've come to like him** por fin ha llegado a gustarme

come across vt fus (person) topar con; (thing) dar con

come along vi (BRIT: progress) ir

come back vi (return) volver

come down vi (price) bajar; (tree, building) ser derribado

come from vt fus (place, source) ser de

come in vi (visitor) entrar; (train, report) llegar; (fashion) ponerse de moda; (on deal etc) entrar

come off vi (button) soltarse, desprenderse; (attempt) salir bien

come on vi (pupil) progresar; (work, project) desarrollarse; (lights) encenderse; (electricity) volver; **come on!** ¡vamos!

come out vi (fact) salir a la luz; (book, sun) salir; (stain) quitarse

come round vi (after faint, operation) volver en sí

come to vi (wake) volver en sí

come up vi (sun) salir; (problem) surgir; (event) aproximarse; (in conversation) mencionarse

come up with vt fus (idea) sugerir; (money) conseguir

comeback [ˈkʌmbæk] n: **to make a ~**

(*Theatre*) volver a las tablas
comedian [kə'mi:diən] *n* humorista *mf*
comedy ['kɔmɪdɪ] *n* comedia; (*humour*) comicidad *f*
comet ['kɔmɪt] *n* cometa *m*
comfort ['kʌmfət] *n* bienestar *m*; (*relief*) alivio ▷ *vt* consolar;
comfortable *adj* cómodo; (*financially*) acomodado; (*easy*) fácil; **comfort station** (*us*) *n* servicios *mpl*
comic ['kɔmɪk] *adj* (*also*: **~al**) cómico ▷ *n* (*comedian*) cómico; (*brit*: *for children*) tebeo; (*brit*: *for adults*) comic *m*; **comic book** (*us*) *n* libro *m* de cómics; **comic strip** *n* tira cómica
comma ['kɔmə] *n* coma
command [kə'mɑːnd] *n* orden *f*, mandato; (*Mil*: *authority*) mando; (*mastery*) dominio ▷ *vt* (*troops*) mandar; (*give orders to*): **to ~ sb to do** mandar *or* ordenar a algn hacer; **commander** *n* (*Mil*) comandante *mf*, jefe/a *m/f*
commemorate [kə'mɛmərəit] *vt* conmemorar
commence [kə'mɛns] *vt*, *vi* comenzar, empezar; **commencement** (*us*) *n* (*Univ*) (ceremonia de) graduación *f*
commend [kə'mɛnd] *vt* elogiar, alabar; (*recommend*) recomendar
comment ['kɔmɛnt] *n* comentario ▷ *vi*: **to ~ on** hacer comentarios sobre; **"no ~"** (*written*) "sin comentarios"; (*spoken*) "no tengo nada que decir"; **commentary** ['kɔməntərɪ] *n* comentario; **commentator** ['kɔmənteɪtə*] *n* comentarista *mf*
commerce ['kɔmə:s] *n* comercio
commercial [kə'mə:ʃəl] *adj* comercial ▷ *n* (*TV, Radio*) anuncio; **commercial break** *n* intermedio para publicidad
commission [kə'mɪʃən] *n* (*committee, fee*) comisión *f* ▷ *vt* (*work of art*) encargar; **out of ~** fuera de servicio; **commissioner** *n* (*Police*) comisario de policía

commit [kə'mɪt] *vt* (*act*) cometer; (*resources*) dedicar; (*to sb's care*) entregar; **to ~ o.s. (to do)** comprometerse (a hacer); **to ~ suicide** suicidarse; **commitment** *n* compromiso; (*to ideology etc*) entrega
committee [kə'mɪtɪ] *n* comité *m*
commodity [kə'mɔdɪtɪ] *n* mercancía
common ['kɔmən] *adj* común; (*pej*) ordinario ▷ *n* campo común; **commonly** *adv* comúnmente; **commonplace** *adj* de lo más común; **Commons** (*brit*) *npl* (*Pol*): **the Commons** (la Cámara de) los Comunes; **common sense** *n* sentido común; **Commonwealth** *n*: **the Commonwealth** la Commonwealth
communal ['kɔmju:nl] *adj* (*property*) comunal; (*kitchen*) común
commune [*n* kə'mju:n, *vb* kə'mju:n] *n* (*group*) comuna ▷ *vi*: **to ~ with** comulgar *or* conversar con
communicate [kə'mju:nɪkeɪt] *vt* comunicar ▷ *vi*: **to ~ (with)** comunicarse (con); (*in writing*) estar en contacto (con)
communication [kəmju:nɪ'keɪʃən] *n* comunicación *f*
communion [kə'mju:nɪən] *n* (*also*: **Holy ~**) comunión *f*
communism ['kɔmjunɪzəm] *n* comunismo; **communist** *adj*, *n* comunista *mf*
community [kə'mju:nɪtɪ] *n* comunidad *f*; (*large group*) colectividad *f*; **community centre** (*us* **community center**) *n* centro social; **community service** *n* trabajo *m* comunitario (*prestado en lugar de cumplir una pena de prisión*)
commute [kə'mju:t] *vi* viajar a diario de la casa al trabajo ▷ *vt* conmutar; **commuter** *n* persona que viaja a diario de la casa al trabajo
compact [*adj* kəm'pækt, *n* 'kɔmpækt] *adj* compacto ▷ *n* (*also*: **powder ~**)

polvera; **compact disc** n compact
disc m; **compact disc player** n
reproductor m de disco compacto,
compact disc m
companion [kəm'pænɪən] n
compañero/a
company ['kʌmpənɪ] n compañía;
(*Comm*) sociedad f, compañía; **to keep
sb ~** acompañar a algn; **company car**
n coche m de la empresa; **company
director** n director(a) m/f de empresa
comparable ['kɔmpərəbl] adj
comparable
comparative [kəm'pærətɪv]
adj relativo; (*study*) comparativo;
comparatively adv (*relatively*)
relativamente
compare [kəm'pɛə*] vt: **to ~ sth/sb
with** or **to** comparar algo/a algn
con ▷ vi: **to ~ (with)** compararse
(con); **comparison** [-'pærɪsn] n
comparación f
compartment [kəm'pɑːtmənt] n
(*also: Rail*) compartim(i)ento
compass ['kʌmpəs] n brújula;
compasses npl (*Math*) compás m
compassion [kəm'pæʃən] n
compasión f
compatible [kəm'pætɪbl] adj
compatible
compel [kəm'pɛl] vt obligar;
compelling adj (*fig: argument*)
convincente
compensate ['kɔmpənseɪt] vt
compensar ▷ vi: **to ~ for** compensar;
compensation [-'seɪʃən] n (*for loss*)
indemnización f
compete [kəm'piːt] vi (*take part*)
tomar parte, concurrir; (*vie with*): **to ~
with** competir con, hacer competencia
a
competent ['kɔmpɪtənt] adj
competente, capaz
competition [kɔmpɪ'tɪʃə
n] n (*contest*) concurso; (*rivalry*)
competencia
competitive [kəm'pɛtɪtɪv] adj (*Econ,
Sport*) competitivo

competitor [kəm'pɛtɪtə*] n (*rival*)
competidor(a) m/f; (*participant*)
concursante mf
complacent [kəm'pleɪsənt] adj
autocomplaciente
complain [kəm'pleɪn] vi quejarse;
(*Comm*) reclamar; **complaint** n queja;
reclamación f; (*Med*) enfermedad f
complement [n 'kɔmplɪmənt,
vb 'kɔmplɪment] n complemento;
(*esp of ship's crew*) dotación
f ▷ vt (*enhance*) complementar;
complementary [kɔmplɪ'mentərɪ]
adj complementario
complete [kəm'pliːt] adj (*full*)
completo; (*finished*) acabado ▷ vt
(*fulfil*) completar; (*finish*) acabar;
(*a form*) llenar; **completely** adv
completamente; **completion**
[-'pliːʃən] n terminación f; (*of contract*)
realización f
complex ['kɔmplɛks] adj, n complejo
complexion [kəm'plɛkʃən] n (*of
face*) tez f, cutis m
compliance [kəm'plaɪəns] n
(*submission*) sumisión f; (*agreement*)
conformidad f; **in ~ with** de acuerdo
con
complicate ['kɔmplɪkeɪt] vt
complicar; **complicated** adj
complicado; **complication** [-'keɪʃən]
n complicación f
compliment ['kɔmplɪmənt] n
(*formal*) cumplido ▷ vt felicitar;
complimentary [-'mentərɪ] adj
lisonjero; (*free*) de favor
comply [kəm'plaɪ] vi: **to ~ with**
cumplir con
component [kəm'pəunənt] adj
componente ▷ n (*Tech*) pieza
compose [kəm'pəuz] vt: **to be ~d of**
componerse de; (*music etc*) componer;
to ~ o.s. tranquilizarse; **composer** n
(*Mus*) compositor(a) m/f; **composition**
[kɔmpə'zɪʃən] n composición f
composure [kəm'pəuʒə*] n
serenidad f, calma
compound ['kɔmpaund] n (*Chem*)

compuesto; (*Ling*) palabra compuesta; (*enclosure*) recinto ▷ *adj* compuesto; (*fracture*) complicado

comprehension [-'hɛnʃən] *n* comprensión *f*

comprehensive [kɔmprɪ'hɛnsɪv] *adj* exhaustivo; (*Insurance*) contra todo riesgo; **comprehensive (school)** *n* *centro estatal de enseñanza secundaria* ≈ Instituto Nacional de Bachillerato (*SP*)

compress [*vb* kəm'prɛs, *n* 'kɔmprɛs] *vt* comprimir; (*information*) condensar ▷ *n* (*Med*) compresa

comprise [kəm'praɪz] *vt* (*also*: **be ~d of**) comprender, constar de; (*constitute*) constituir

compromise ['kɔmprəmaɪz] *n* (*agreement*) arreglo ▷ *vt* comprometer ▷ *vi* transigir

compulsive [kəm'pʌlsɪv] *adj* compulsivo; (*viewing, reading*) obligado

compulsory [kəm'pʌlsərɪ] *adj* obligatorio

computer [kəm'pju:tə*] *n* ordenador *m*, computador *m*, computadora *f*; **computer game** *n* juego para ordenador; **computer-generated** *adj* realizado por ordenador, creado por ordenador; **computerize** *vt* (*data*) computerizar; (*system*) informatizar; **we're computerized now** ya nos hemos informatizado; **computer programmer** *n* programador(a) *m/f*; **computer programming** *n* programación *f*; **computer science** *n* informática; **computer studies** *npl* informática *fsg*, computación *fsg* (*LAM*); **computing** [kəm'pju:tɪŋ] *n* (*activity, science*) informática

con [kɔn] *vt* (*deceive*) engañar; (*cheat*) estafar ▷ *n* estafa

conceal [kən'si:l] *vt* ocultar

concede [kən'si:d] *vt* (*point, argument*) reconocer; (*territory*) ceder; **to ~ (defeat)** darse por vencido; **to ~ that** admitir que

conceited [kən'si:tɪd] *adj* presumido

conceive [kən'si:v] *vt, vi* concebir

concentrate ['kɔnsəntreɪt] *vi* concentrarse ▷ *vt* concentrar

concentration [kɔnsən'treɪʃən] *n* concentración *f*

concept ['kɔnsɛpt] *n* concepto

concern [kən'sə:n] *n* (*matter*) asunto; (*Comm*) empresa; (*anxiety*) preocupación *f* ▷ *vt* (*worry*) preocupar; (*involve*) afectar; (*relate to*) tener que ver con; **to be ~ed (about)** interesarse (por), preocuparse (por); **concerning** *prep* sobre, acerca de

concert ['kɔnsət] *n* concierto; **concert hall** *n* sala de conciertos

concerto [kən'tʃɔ:təu] *n* concierto

concession [kən'sɛʃən] *n* concesión *f*; **tax ~** privilegio fiscal

concise [kən'saɪs] *adj* conciso

conclude [kən'klu:d] *vt* concluir; (*treaty etc*) firmar; (*agreement*) llegar a; (*decide*) llegar a la conclusión de; **conclusion** [-'klu:ʒən] *n* conclusión *f*; firma

concrete ['kɔnkri:t] *n* hormigón *m* ▷ *adj* de hormigón; (*fig*) concreto

concussion [kən'kʌʃən] *n* conmoción *f* cerebral

condemn [kən'dɛm] *vt* condenar; (*building*) declarar en ruina

condensation [kɔndɛn'seɪʃən] *n* condensación *f*

condense [kən'dɛns] *vi* condensarse ▷ *vt* condensar, abreviar

condition [kən'dɪʃən] *n* condición *f*, estado; (*requirement*) condición *f* ▷ *vt* condicionar; **on ~ that** a condición (de) que; **conditional** [kən'dɪʃənl] *adj* condicional; **conditioner** *n* suavizante

condo ['kɔndəu] (*US*) *n* (*inf*) = **condominium**

condom ['kɔndəm] *n* condón *m*

condominium [kɔndə'mɪnɪəm] (*US*) *n* (*building*) bloque *m* de pisos or apartamentos (*propiedad de quienes lo habitan*), condominio (*LAM*); (*apartment*) piso or apartamento (en propiedad), condominio (LAM)

condone [kən'dəun] vt condonar

conduct [n 'kɔndʌkt, vb kən'dʌkt] n conducta, comportamiento ▷ vt (lead) conducir; (manage) llevar a cabo, dirigir; (Mus) dirigir; **to ~ o.s.** comportarse; **conducted tour** (BRIT) n visita acompañada; **conductor** n (of orchestra) director m; (US: on train) revisor(a) m/f; (on bus) cobrador m; (Elec) conductor m

cone [kəun] n cono; (pine cone) piña; (on road) pivote m; (for ice-cream) cucurucho

confectionery [kən'fɛkʃənRɪ] n dulces mpl

confer [kən'fə:*] vt: **to ~ sth on** otorgar algo a ▷ vi conferenciar

conference ['kɔnfərns] n (meeting) reunión f; (convention) congreso

confess [kən'fɛs] vt confesar ▷ vi admitir; **confession** [-'fɛʃən] n confesión f

confide [kən'faɪd] vi: **to ~ in** confiar en

confidence ['kɔnfɪdns] n (also: **self-~**) confianza; (secret) confidencia; **in ~** (speak, write) en confianza; **confident** adj seguro de sí mismo; (certain) seguro; **confidential** [kɔnfɪ'dɛnʃəl] adj confidencial

confine [kən'faɪn] vt (limit) limitar; (shut up) encerrar; **confined** adj (space) reducido

confirm [kən'fə:m] vt confirmar; **confirmation** [kɔnfə'meɪʃən] n confirmación f

confiscate ['kɔnfɪskeɪt] vt confiscar

conflict [n 'kɔnflɪkt, vb kən'flɪkt] n conflicto ▷ vi (opinions) chocar

conform [kən'fɔ:m] vi conformarse; **to ~ to** ajustarse a

confront [kən'frʌnt] vt (problems) hacer frente a; (enemy, danger) enfrentarse con; **confrontation** [kɔnfrən'teɪʃən] n enfrentamiento

confuse [kən'fju:z] vt (perplex) aturdir, desconcertar; (mix up)

confundir; (complicate) complicar; **confused** adj confuso; (person) perplejo; **confusing** adj confuso; **confusion** [-'fju:ʒən] n confusión f

congestion [kən'dʒɛstʃən] n congestión f

congratulate [kən'grætjuleɪt] vt: **to ~ sb (on)** felicitar a algn (por); **congratulations** [-'leɪʃənz] npl felicitaciones fpl; **congratulations!** ¡enhorabuena!

congregation [-'geɪʃən] n (of a church) feligreses mpl

congress ['kɔngrɛs] n congreso; (US): **C~** Congreso; **congressman** (irreg: US) n miembro del Congreso; **congresswoman** (irreg: US) n diputada, miembro f del Congreso

conifer ['kɔnɪfə*] n conífera

conjugate ['kɔndʒugeɪt] vt conjugar

conjugation [kɔndʒə'geɪʃən] n conjugación f

conjunction [kən'dʒʌŋkʃən] n conjunción f; **in ~ with** junto con

conjure ['kʌndʒə*] vi hacer juegos de manos

connect [kə'nɛkt] vt juntar, unir; (Elec) conectar; (Tel: subscriber) poner; (: caller) poner al habla; (fig) relacionar, asociar ▷ vi: **to ~ with** (train) enlazar con; **to be ~ed with** (associated) estar relacionado con; **connecting flight** n vuelo m de enlace; **connection** [-ʃən] n juntura, unión f; (Elec) conexión f; (Rail) enlace m; (Tel) comunicación f; (fig) relación f

conquer ['kɔŋkə*] vt (territory) conquistar; (enemy, feelings) vencer

conquest ['kɔŋkwɛst] n conquista

cons [kɔnz] npl see **convenience; pro; mod**

conscience ['kɔnʃəns] n conciencia

conscientious [kɔnʃɪ'ɛnʃəs] adj concienzudo; (objection) de conciencia

conscious ['kɔnʃəs] adj (deliberate) deliberado; (awake, aware) consciente; **consciousness** n conciencia; (Med) conocimiento

consecutive [kən'sɛkjutɪv] adj
consecutivo; **on 3 ~ occasions** en 3
ocasiones consecutivas

consensus [kən'sɛnsəs] n consenso

consent [kən'sɛnt] n
consentimiento ▷ vi: **to ~ (to)**
consentir (en)

consequence ['kɔnsɪkwəns]
n consecuencia; (significance)
importancia

consequently ['kɔnsɪkwəntlɪ] adv
por consiguiente

conservation [kɔnsə'veɪʃən] n
conservación f

conservative [kən'sə:vətɪv]
adj conservador(a); (estimate etc)
cauteloso; **Conservative** (BRIT) adj, n
(Pol) conservador(a) m/f

conservatory [kən'sə:vətrɪ] n
invernadero; (Mus) conservatorio

consider [kən'sɪdə*] vt considerar;
(take into account) tener en cuenta;
(study) estudiar, examinar; **to ~
doing sth** pensar en (la posibilidad
de) hacer algo; **considerable** adj
considerable; **considerably** adv
notablemente; **considerate** adj
considerado; **consideration** [-'reɪʃə
n] n consideración f; (factor) factor
m; **to give sth further consideration**
estudiar algo más a fondo;
considering prep teniendo en cuenta

consignment [kən'saɪnmənt]
n envío

consist [kən'sɪst] vi: **to ~ of** consistir
en

consistency [kən'sɪstənsɪ]
n (of argument etc) coherencia;
consecuencia; (thickness) consistencia

consistent [kən'sɪstənt] adj (person)
consecuente; (argument etc) coherente

consolation [kɔnsə'leɪʃən] n
consuelo

console[1] [kən'səul] vt consolar

console[2] ['kɔnsəul] n consola

consonant ['kɔnsənənt] n
consonante f

conspicuous [kən'spɪkjuəs] adj

(visible) visible

conspiracy [kən'spɪrəsɪ] n conjura,
complot m

constable ['kʌnstəbl] (BRIT) n policía
mf; **chief ~** ≈ jefe m de policía

constant ['kɔnstənt] adj constante;
constantly adv constantemente

constipated ['kɔnstɪpeɪtəd] adj
estreñido

> Be careful not to translate
> **constipated** by the Spanish word
> constipado.

constipation [kɔnstɪ'peɪʃən] n
estreñimiento

constituency [kən'stɪtjuənsɪ] n
(Pol: area) distrito electoral; (: electors)
electorado

constitute ['kɔnstɪtjuːt] vt
constituir

constitution [kɔnstɪ'tjuːʃən] n
constitución f

constraint [kən'streɪnt] n
obligación f; (limit) restricción f

construct [kən'strʌkt] vt construir;
construction [-ʃən] n construcción f;
constructive adj constructivo

consul ['kɔnsl] n cónsul mf;
consulate ['kɔnsjulɪt] n consulado

consult [kən'sʌlt] vt consultar;
consultant n (BRIT Med) especialista
mf; (other specialist) asesor(a)
m/f; **consultation** [kɔnsəl'teɪʃən] n
consulta; **consulting room** (BRIT) n
consultorio

consume [kən'sjuːm] vt (eat)
comerse; (drink) beberse; (fire etc,
Comm) consumir; **consumer** n
consumidor(a) m/f

consumption [kən'sʌmpʃən] n
consumo

cont. abbr (= continued) sigue

contact ['kɔntækt] n contacto;
(person) contacto; (: pej) enchufe m ▷ vt
ponerse en contacto con; **contact
lenses** npl lentes fpl de contacto

contagious [kən'teɪdʒəs] adj
contagioso

contain [kən'teɪn] vt contener;

to ~ o.s. contenerse; **container**
n recipiente m; (for shipping etc)
contenedor m

contaminate [kən'tæmɪneɪt] vt
contaminar

cont'd abbr (=continued) sigue

contemplate ['kɔntəmpleɪt] vt
contemplar; (reflect upon) considerar

contemporary [kən'tempərərɪ] adj,
n contemporáneo/a m/f

contempt [kən'tempt] n desprecio;
~ of court (Law) desacato (a los
tribunales)

contend [kən'tend] vt (argue) afirmar
▷ vi: **to ~ with/for** luchar contra/por

content [adj, vb kən'tent, n
'kɔntent] adj (happy) contento;
(satisfied) satisfecho ▷ vt contentar;
satisfacer ▷ n contenido; **contents**
npl contenido; **(table of) ~s** índice m
de materias; **contented** adj contento;
satisfecho

contest [n 'kɔntest, vb kən'test] n
lucha; (competition) concurso ▷ vt
(dispute) impugnar; (Pol) presentarse
como candidato/a en

▌ Be careful not to translate **contest**
by the Spanish word contestar.

contestant [kən'testənt] n
concursante mf; (in fight) contendiente
mf

context ['kɔntekst] n contexto

continent ['kɔntɪnənt] n continente
m; **the C~** (BRIT) el continente
europeo; **continental** [-'nentl] adj
continental; **continental breakfast** n
desayuno estilo europeo; **continental
quilt** (BRIT) n edredón m

continual [kən'tɪnjuəl] adj
continuo; **continually** adv
constantemente

continue [kən'tɪnjuː] vi, vt seguir,
continuar

continuity [kɔntɪ'njuɪtɪ] n (also
Cine) continuidad f

continuous [kən'tɪnjuəs] adj
continuo; **continuous assessment**
n (BRIT) evaluación f continua;

continuously adv continuamente

contour ['kɔntuə*] n contorno; (also:
~ line) curva de nivel

contraception [kɔntrə'sepʃən] n
contracepción f

contraceptive [kɔntrə'septɪv] adj, n
anticonceptivo

contract [n 'kɔntrækt, vb kən'trækt]
n contrato ▷ vi (Comm): **to ~ to do
sth** comprometerse por contrato a
hacer algo; (become smaller) contraerse,
encogerse ▷ vt contraer; **contractor**
n contratista mf

contradict [kɔntrə'dɪkt] vt
contradecir; **contradiction** [-ʃən]
contradicción f

contrary[1] ['kɔntrərɪ] adj contrario
▷ n lo contrario; **on the ~** al contrario;
unless you hear to the ~ a no ser que
le digan lo contrario

contrary[2] [kən'treərɪ] adj (perverse)
terco

contrast [n 'kɔntrɑːst, vt kən'trɑːst]
n contraste m ▷ vt comparar; **in ~ to**
en contraste con

contribute [kən'trɪbjuːt] vi
contribuir ▷ vt: **to ~ £10/an article to**
contribuir con 10 libras/un artículo
a; **to ~ to** (charity) donar a; (newspaper)
escribir para; (discussion) intervenir en;
contribution [kɔntrɪ'bjuːʃən]
n (donation) donativo; (BRIT: for social
security) cotización f; (to debate)
intervención f; (to journal) colaboración
f; **contributor** n contribuyente mf; (to
newspaper) colaborador(a) m/f

control [kən'trəul] vt controlar;
(process etc) dirigir; (machinery)
manejar; (temper) dominar; (disease)
contener ▷ n control m; **controls** npl
(of vehicle) instrumentos mpl de mando;
(of radio) controles mpl; (governmental)
medidas fpl de control; **under ~** bajo
control; **to be in ~ of** tener el mando
de; **the car went out of ~** se perdió
el control del coche; **control tower** n
(Aviat) torre f de control

controversial [kɔntrə'vəːʃl] adj

polémico

controversy ['kɔntrəvə:sɪ] n
polémica

convenience [kən'vi:nɪəns] n
(easiness) comodidad f; (suitability)
idoneidad f; (advantage) ventaja; **at
your ~** cuando le sea conveniente;
all modern ~s, all mod cons (BRIT)
todo confort

convenient [kən'vi:nɪənt] adj
(useful) útil; (place, time) conveniente

convent ['kɔnvənt] n convento

convention [kən'vɛnʃən] n
convención f; (meeting) asamblea;
(agreement) convenio; **conventional**
adj convencional

conversation [kɔnvə'seɪʃən] n
conversación f

conversely [-'və:slɪ] adv a la inversa

conversion [kən'və:ʃən] n
conversión f

convert [vb kən'və:t, n 'kɔnvə:t] vt
(Rel, Comm) convertir; (alter): **to ~ sth
into/to** transformar algo en/convertir
algo a ▷ n converso/a; **convertible**
adj convertible ▷ n descapotable m

convey [kən'veɪ] vt llevar; (thanks)
comunicar; (idea) expresar; **conveyor
belt** n cinta transportadora

convict [vb kən'vɪkt, n 'kɔnvɪkt] vt
(find guilty) declarar culpable a ▷ n
presidiario/a; **conviction** [-ʃən] n
condena; (belief, certainty) convicción f

convince [kən'vɪns] vt convencer;
convinced adj: **convinced of/that**
convencido de/de que; **convincing** adj
convincente

convoy ['kɔnvɔɪ] n convoy m

cook [kuk] vt (stew etc) guisar; (meal)
preparar ▷ vi cocer; (person) cocinar
▷ n cocinero/a; **cook book** n libro de
cocina; **cooker** n cocina; **cookery** n
cocina; **cookery book** (BRIT) n = **cook
book**; **cookie** (US) n galleta; **cooking**
n cocina

cool [ku:l] adj fresco; (not afraid)
tranquilo; (unfriendly) frío ▷ vt enfriar
▷ vi enfriarse; **cool down** vi enfriarse;

(fig: person, situation) calmarse; **cool
off** vi (become calmer) calmarse,
apaciguarse; (lose enthusiasm) perder
(el) interés, enfriarse

cop [kɔp] (inf) n poli mf(SP), tira
mf(MEX)

cope [kəup] vi: **to ~ with** (problem)
hacer frente a

copper ['kɔpə*] n (metal) cobre m;
(BRIT: inf) poli mf, tira mf(MEX)

copy ['kɔpɪ] n copia; (of book etc)
ejemplar m ▷ vt copiar; **copyright** n
derechos mpl de autor

coral ['kɔrəl] n coral m

cord [kɔ:d] n cuerda; (Elec) cable
m; (fabric) pana; **cords** npl (trousers)
pantalones mpl de pana; **cordless** adj
sin hilos

corduroy ['kɔ:dərɔɪ] n pana

core [kɔ:*] n centro, núcleo; (of fruit)
corazón m; (of problem) meollo ▷ vt
quitar el corazón de

coriander [kɔrɪ'ændə*] n culantro

cork [kɔ:k] n corcho; (tree) alcornoque
m; **corkscrew** n sacacorchos m inv

corn [kɔ:n] n (BRIT: cereal crop) trigo;
(US: maize) maíz m; (on foot) callo; **~ on
the cob** (Culin) mazorca, elote m (MEX),
choclo (SC)

corned beef ['kɔ:nd-] n carne f
acecinada (en lata)

corner ['kɔ:nə*] n (outside) esquina;
(inside) rincón m; (in road) curva;
(Football) córner m; (Boxing) esquina
▷ vt (trap) arrinconar; (Comm) acaparar
▷ vi (in car) tomar las curvas; **corner
shop** (BRIT) tienda de la esquina

cornflakes ['kɔ:nfleɪks] npl copos
mpl de maíz, cornflakes mpl

cornflour ['kɔ:nflauə*] (BRIT) n
harina de maíz

cornstarch ['kɔ:nstɑ:tʃ] (US) n =
cornflour

Cornwall ['kɔ:nwəl] n Cornualles m

coronary ['kɔrənərɪ] n (also: **~
thrombosis**) infarto

coronation [kɔrə'neɪʃən] n
coronación f

coroner ['kɔrənə*] n juez mf de instrucción

corporal ['kɔ:pərl] n cabo ▷ adj: **~ punishment** castigo corporal

corporate ['kɔ:pərɪt] adj (action, ownership) colectivo; (finance, image) corporativo

corporation [kɔ:pə'reɪʃən] n (of town) ayuntamiento; (Comm) corporación f

corps [kɔ:*, pl kɔ:z] n inv cuerpo; **diplomatic ~** cuerpo diplomático; **press ~** gabinete m de prensa

corpse [kɔ:ps] n cadáver m

correct [kə'rekt] adj justo, exacto; (proper) correcto ▷ vt corregir; (exam) corregir, calificar; **correction** [-ʃən] n (act) corrección f; (instance) rectificación f

correspond [kɔrɪs'pɔnd] vi (write): **to ~ (with)** escribirse (con); (be equivalent to): **to ~ (to)** corresponder (a); (be in accordance): **to ~ (with)** corresponder (con); **correspondence** n correspondencia; **correspondent** n corresponsal mf; **corresponding** adj correspondiente

corridor ['kɔrɪdɔ:*] n pasillo

corrode [kə'rəud] vt corroer ▷ vi corroerse

corrupt [kə'rʌpt] adj (person) corrupto; (Comput) corrompido ▷ vt corromper; (Comput) degradar; **corruption** n corrupción f; (of data) alteración f

Corsica ['kɔ:sɪkə] n Córcega

cosmetic [kɔz'metɪk] adj, n cosmético; **cosmetic surgery** n cirugía f estética

cosmopolitan [kɔzmə'pɔlɪtn] adj cosmopolita

cost [kɔst] (pt, pp **~**) n (price) precio ▷ vi costar, valer ▷ vt preparar el presupuesto de; **how much does it ~?** ¿cuánto cuesta?; **to ~ sb time/effort** costarle a algn tiempo/esfuerzo; **it ~ him his life** le costó la vida; **at all ~s** cueste lo que cueste; **costs** npl (Comm)

costes mpl; (Law) costas fpl

co-star ['kəustɑ:*] n coprotagonista mf

Costa Rica ['kɔstə'ri:kə] n Costa Rica; **Costa Rican** adj, n costarriqueño/a

costly ['kɔstlɪ] adj costoso

cost of living n costo or coste m (Sp) de la vida

costume ['kɔstju:m] n traje m; (BRIT: also: **swimming ~**) traje de baño

cosy ['kəuzɪ] (US **cozy**) adj (person) cómodo; (room) acogedor(a)

cot [kɔt] n (BRIT: child's) cuna; (US: campbed) cama de campaña

cottage ['kɔtɪdʒ] n casita de campo; (rustic) barraca; **cottage cheese** n requesón m

cotton ['kɔtn] n algodón m; (thread) hilo; **cotton on** vi (inf): **to cotton on (to sth)** caer en la cuenta (de algo); **cotton bud** (BRIT) n bastoncillo m de algodón; **cotton candy** (US) n algodón m (azucarado); **cotton wool** (BRIT) n algodón m (hidrófilo)

couch [kautʃ] n sofá m; (doctor's etc) diván m

cough [kɔf] vi toser ▷ n tos f; **cough mixture** n jarabe m para la tos

could [kud] pt of **can²**; **couldn't** = **could not**

council ['kaunsl] n consejo; **city or town ~** consejo municipal; **council estate** (BRIT) n urbanización de viviendas municipales de alquiler; **council house** (BRIT) n vivienda municipal de alquiler; **councillor** (US **councilor**) n concejal(a) m/f; **council tax** (BRIT) n contribución f municipal (dependiente del valor de la vivienda)

counsel ['kaunsl] n (advice) consejo; (lawyer) abogado/a ▷ vt aconsejar; **counselling** (US **counseling**) n (Psych) asistencia f psicológica; **counsellor** (US **counselor**) n consejero/a, abogado/a

count [kaunt] vt contar; (include) incluir ▷ vi contar ▷ n cuenta; (of votes) escrutinio; (level) nivel m;

(*nobleman*) conde *m*; **count in** (*inf*) *vt*: **to count sb in on sth** contar con algn para algo; **count on** *vt fus* contar con; **countdown** *n* cuenta atrás

counter ['kauntə*] *n* (*in shop*) mostrador *m*; (*in games*) ficha ▷ *vt* contrarrestar ▷ *adv*: **to run ~ to** ser contrario a, ir en contra de; **counter clockwise** (*us*) *adv* en sentido contrario al de las agujas del reloj

counterfeit ['kauntəfɪt] *n* falsificación *f*, simulación *f* ▷ *vt* falsificar ▷ *adj* falso, falsificado

counterpart ['kauntəpɑ:t] *n* homólogo/a

countess ['kauntɪs] *n* condesa

countless ['kauntlɪs] *adj* innumerable

country ['kʌntrɪ] *n* país *m*; (*native land*) patria; (*as opposed to town*) campo; (*region*) región *f*, tierra; **country and western (music)** *n* música country; **country house** *n* casa de campo; **countryside** *n* campo

county ['kauntɪ] *n* condado

coup [ku:] (*pl* **~s**) *n* (*also*: **~ d'état**) golpe *m* (de estado); (*achievement*) éxito

couple ['kʌpl] *n* (*of things*) par *m*; (*of people*) pareja; (*married couple*) matrimonio; **a ~ of** un par de

coupon ['ku:pɔn] *n* cupón *m*; (*voucher*) valé *m*

courage ['kʌrɪdʒ] *n* valor *m*, valentía; **courageous** [kə'reɪdʒəs] *adj* valiente

courgette [kuə'ʒɛt] (*brit*) *n* calabacín *m*, calabacita (*mex*)

courier ['kurɪə*] *n* mensajero/a; (*for tourists*) guía *mf* (de turismo)

course [kɔ:s] *n* (*direction*) dirección *f*; (*of river, Scol*) curso; (*process*) transcurso; (*Med*): **~ of treatment** tratamiento; (*of ship*) rumbo; (*part of meal*) plato; (*Golf*) campo; **of ~** desde luego, naturalmente; **of ~!** ¡claro!

court [kɔ:t] *n* (*royal*) corte *f*; (*Law*) tribunal *m*, juzgado; (*Tennis etc*) pista, cancha ▷ *vt* (*woman*) cortejar a; **to take to ~** demandar

courtesy ['kə:təsɪ] *n* cortesía; **(by) ~ of** por cortesía de; **courtesy bus, courtesy coach** *n* autobús *m* gratuito

court: court-house ['kɔ:thaus] (*us*) *n* palacio de justicia; **courtroom** ['kɔ:trum] *n* sala de justicia; **courtyard** ['kɔ:tjɑ:d] *n* patio

cousin ['kʌzn] *n* primo/a; **first ~** primo/a carnal, primo/a hermano/a

cover ['kʌvə*] *vt* cubrir; (*feelings, mistake*) ocultar; (*with lid*) tapar; (*book etc*) forrar; (*distance*) recorrer; (*include*) abarcar; (*protect: also: Insurance*) cubrir; (*Press*) investigar; (*discuss*) tratar ▷ *n* cubierta; (*lid*) tapa; (*for chair etc*) funda; (*envelope*) sobre *m*; (*for book*) forro; (*of magazine*) portada; (*shelter*) abrigo; (*Insurance*) cobertura; (*of spy*) cobertura; **covers** *npl* (*on bed*) sábanas; mantas; **to take ~** (*shelter*) protegerse, resguardarse; **under ~** (*indoors*) bajo techo; **under ~ of darkness** al amparo de la oscuridad; **under separate ~** (*Comm*) por separado; **cover up** *vi*: **to cover up for sb** encubrir a algn; **coverage** *n* (*TV, Press*) cobertura; **cover charge** *n* precio del cubierto; **cover-up** *n* encubrimiento

cow [kau] *n* vaca; (*infl: woman*) bruja ▷ *vt* intimidar

coward ['kauəd] *n* cobarde *mf*; **cowardly** *adj* cobarde

cowboy ['kaubɔɪ] *n* vaquero

cozy ['kəuzɪ] (*us*) *adj* = **cosy**

crab [kræb] *n* cangrejo

crack [kræk] *n* grieta; (*noise*) crujido; (*drug*) crack *m* ▷ *vt* agrietar, romper; (*nut*) cascar; (*solve: problem*) resolver; (*: code*) descifrar; (*whip etc*) chasquear; (*knuckles*) crujir; (*joke*) contar ▷ *adj* (*expert*) de primera; **crack down on** *vt fus* adoptar fuertes medidas contra; **cracked** *adj* (*cup, window*) rajado; (*wall*) resquebrajado; **cracker** *n* (*biscuit*) cráquer *m*; (*Christmas cracker*) petardo sorpresa

crackle ['krækl] *vi* crepitar

cradle ['kreɪdl] *n* cuna

craft [krɑ:ft] n (skill) arte m; (trade) oficio; (cunning) astucia; (boat: pl inv) barco; (plane: pl inv) avión m; **craftsman** (irreg) n artesano; **craftsmanship** n (quality) destreza

cram [kræm] vt (fill): **to ~ sth with** llenar algo (a reventar) de; (put): **to ~ sth into** meter algo a la fuerza en ▷ vi (for exams) empollar

cramp [kræmp] n (Med) calambre m; **cramped** adj apretado, estrecho

cranberry ['krænbərɪ] n arándano agrio

crane [kreɪn] n (Tech) grúa; (bird) grulla

crap [kræp] n (inf!) mierda (!)

crash [kræʃ] n (noise) estrépito; (of cars etc) choque m; (of plane) accidente m de aviación; (Comm) quiebra ▷ vt (car, plane) estrellar ▷ vi (car, plane) estrellarse; (two cars) chocar; (Comm) quebrar; **crash course** n curso acelerado; **crash helmet** n casco (protector)

crate [kreɪt] n cajón m de embalaje; (for bottles) caja

crave [kreɪv] vt, vi: **to ~ (for)** ansiar, anhelar

crawl [krɔ:l] vi (drag o.s.) arrastrarse; (child) andar a gatas, gatear; (vehicle) avanzar (lentamente) ▷ n (Swimming) crol m

crayfish ['kreɪfɪʃ] n inv (freshwater) cangrejo de río; (saltwater) cigala

crayon ['kreɪən] n lápiz m de color

craze [kreɪz] n (fashion) moda

crazy ['kreɪzɪ] adj (person) loco; (idea) disparatado; (inf: keen): **~ about sb/sth** loco por algn/algo

creak [kri:k] vi (floorboard) crujir; (hinge etc) chirriar, rechinar

cream [kri:m] n (of milk) nata, crema; (lotion) crema; (fig) flor f y nata ▷ adj (colour) color crema; **cream cheese** n queso blanco; **creamy** adj cremoso; (colour) color crema

crease [kri:s] n (fold) pliegue m; (in trousers) raya; (wrinkle) arruga ▷ vt (wrinkle) arrugar ▷ vi (wrinkle up) arrugarse

create [kri:'eɪt] vt crear; **creation** [-ʃən] n creación f; **creative** adj creativo; **creator** n creador(a) m/f

creature ['kri:tʃə*] n (animal) animal m, bicho; (person) criatura

crèche [krɛʃ] n guardería (infantil)

credentials [krɪ'dɛnʃlz] npl (references) referencias fpl; (identity papers) documentos mpl de identidad

credibility [krɛdɪ'bɪlɪtɪ] n credibilidad f

credible ['krɛdɪbl] adj creíble; (trustworthy) digno de confianza

credit ['krɛdɪt] n crédito; (merit) honor m, mérito ▷ vt (Comm) abonar; (believe: also: **give ~ to**) creer, prestar fe a ▷ adj crediticio; **credits** npl (Cinema) fichas fpl técnicas; **to be in ~** (person) tener saldo a favor; **to ~ sb with** (fig) reconocer a algn el mérito de; **credit card** n tarjeta de crédito

creek [kri:k] n cala, ensenada; (us) riachuelo

creep [kri:p] (pt, pp crept) vi arrastrarse

cremate [krɪ'meɪt] vt incinerar

crematorium [krɛmə'tɔ:rɪəm] (pl **crematoria**) n crematorio

crept [krɛpt] pt, pp of **creep**

crescent ['krɛsnt] n media luna; (street) calle f (en forma de semicírculo)

cress [krɛs] n berro

crest [krɛst] n (of bird) cresta; (of hill) cima, cumbre f; (of coat of arms) blasón m

crew [kru:] n (of ship etc) tripulación f; (TV, Cinema) equipo; **crew-neck** n cuello a la caja

crib [krɪb] n cuna ▷ vt (inf) plagiar

cricket ['krɪkɪt] n (insect) grillo; (game) críquet m; **cricketer** n jugador(a) m/f de críquet

crime [kraɪm] n (no pl: illegal activities) crimen m; (illegal action) delito; **criminal** ['krɪmɪnl] n criminal mf, delincuente mf ▷ adj criminal; (illegal)

delictivo; (*law*) penal
crimson ['krɪmzn] *adj* carmesí
cringe [krɪndʒ] *vi* agacharse,
encogerse
cripple ['krɪpl] *n* lisiado/a, cojo/a
▷ *vt* lisiar, mutilar
crisis ['kraɪsɪs] (*pl* **crises**) *n* crisis *f inv*
crisp [krɪsp] *adj* fresco; (*vegetables
etc*) crujiente; (*manner*) seco; **crispy**
adj crujiente
criterion [kraɪ'tɪərɪən] (*pl* **criteria**)
n criterio
critic ['krɪtɪk] *n* crítico/a; **critical**
adj crítico; (*illness*) grave; **criticism**
['krɪtɪsɪzm] *n* crítica; **criticize**
['krɪtɪsaɪz] *vt* criticar
Croat ['krəuæt] *adj, n* = **Croatian**
Croatia [krəu'eɪʃə] *n* Croacia;
Croatian *adj, n* croata *m/f* ▷ *n* (*Ling*)
croata *m*
crockery ['krɒkərɪ] *n* loza, vajilla
crocodile ['krɒkədaɪl] *n* cocodrilo
crocus ['krəukəs] *n* croco, crocus *m*
croissant ['krwasŋ] *n* croissant *m*,
medialuna (*esp* LAM)
crook [kruk] *n* ladrón/ona *m/f*; (*of
shepherd*) cayado; **crooked** ['krukɪd]
adj torcido; (*dishonest*) nada honrado
crop [krɒp] *n* (*produce*) cultivo;
(*amount produced*) cosecha; (*riding crop*)
látigo de montar ▷ *vt* cortar, recortar;
crop up *vi* surgir, presentarse
cross [krɒs] *n* cruz *f*; (*hybrid*) cruce
m ▷ *vt* (*street etc*) cruzar, atravesar
▷ *adj* de mal humor, enojado; **cross
off** *vt* tachar; **cross out** *vt* tachar;
cross over *vi* cruzar; **cross-Channel
ferry** ['krɒs'tʃænl-] *n* transbordador
m que cruza el Canal de la Mancha;
crosscountry (race) *n* carrera a
campo traviesa, cross *m*; (*crossing
n (sea passage*) travesía; (*also:
**pedestrian crossing*) paso para
peatones; **crossing guard** (*us*) *n*
*persona encargada de ayudar a los niños a
cruzar la calle*; **crossroads** *n* cruce *m*,
encrucijada; **crosswalk** (*us*) *n* paso de
peatones; **crossword** *n* crucigrama *m*

crotch [krɒtʃ] *n* (*Anat, of garment*)
entrepierna
crouch [krautʃ] *vi* agacharse,
acurrucarse
crouton ['kru:tɒn] *n* cubito de
pan frito
crow [krəu] *n* (*bird*) cuervo; (*of cock*)
canto, cacareo ▷ *vi* (*cock*) cantar
crowd [kraud] *n* muchedumbre
f, multitud *f* ▷ *vt* (*fill*) llenar ▷ *vi*
(*gather*): **to ~ round** reunirse en torno
a; (*cram*): **to ~ in** entrar en tropel;
crowded *adj* (*full*) atestado; (*densely
populated*) superpoblado
crown [kraun] *n* corona; (*of head*)
coronilla; (*for tooth*) funda; (*of hill*)
cumbre *f* ▷ *vt* coronar; (*fig*) completar,
rematar; **crown jewels** *npl* joyas
fpl reales
crucial ['kru:ʃl] *adj* decisivo
crucifix ['kru:sɪfɪks] *n* crucifijo
crude [kru:d] *adj* (*materials*) bruto;
(*fig: basic*) tosco; (*: vulgar*) ordinario;
crude (oil) *n* (petróleo) crudo
cruel ['kru:əl] *adj* cruel; **cruelty** *n*
crueldad *f*
cruise [kru:z] *n* crucero ▷ *vi* (*ship*)
hacer un crucero; (*car*) ir a velocidad
de crucero
crumb [krʌm] *n* miga, migaja
crumble ['krʌmbl] *vt* desmenuzar
▷ *vi* (*building, also fig*) desmoronarse
crumpet ['krʌmpɪt] *n* ≈bollo para
tostar
crumple ['krʌmpl] *vt* (*paper*) estrujar;
(*material*) arrugar
crunch [krʌntʃ] *vt* (*with teeth*)
mascar; (*underfoot*) hacer crujir ▷ *n*
(*fig*) hora *or* momento de la verdad;
crunchy *adj* crujiente
crush [krʌʃ] *n* (*crowd*) aglomeración
f; (*infatuation*): **to have a ~ on sb**
estar loco por algn; (*drink*): **lemon
~** limonada ▷ *vt* aplastar; (*paper*)
estrujar; (*cloth*) arrugar; (*fruit*) exprimir;
(*opposition*) aplastar; (*hopes*) destruir
crust [krʌst] *n* corteza; (*of snow, ice*)
costra; **crusty** *adj* (*bread*) crujiente;

(*person*) de mal carácter
crutch [krʌtʃ] *n* muleta
cry [kraɪ] *vi* llorar ⊳ *n* (*shriek*) chillido; (*shout*) grito; **cry out** *vi* (*call out, shout*) lanzar un grito, echar un grito ⊳ *vt* gritar
crystal ['krɪstl] *n* cristal *m*
cub [kʌb] *n* cachorro; (*also*: **~ scout**) niño explorador
Cuba ['kju:bə] *n* Cuba; **Cuban** *adj*, *n* cubano/a *m/f*
cube [kju:b] *n* cubo ⊳ *vt* (*Math*) cubicar
cubicle ['kju:bɪkl] *n* (*at pool*) caseta; (*for bed*) cubículo
cuckoo ['kuku:] *n* cuco
cucumber ['kju:kʌmbə*] *n* pepino
cuddle ['kʌdl] *vt* abrazar ⊳ *vi* abrazarse
cue [kju:] *n* (*snooker cue*) taco; (*Theatre etc*) señal *f*
cuff [kʌf] *n* (*of sleeve*) puño; (*US: of trousers*) vuelta; (*blow*) bofetada ⊳ **off the ~** *adv* de improviso; **cufflinks** *npl* gemelos *mpl*
cuisine [kwɪ'zi:n] *n* cocina
cul-de-sac ['kʌldəsæk] *n* callejón *m* sin salida
cull [kʌl] *vt* (*idea*) sacar ⊳ *n* (*of animals*) matanza selectiva
culminate ['kʌlmɪneɪt] *vi*: **to ~ in** terminar en
culprit ['kʌlprɪt] *n* culpable *mf*
cult [kʌlt] *n* culto
cultivate ['kʌltɪveɪt] *vt* cultivar
cultural ['kʌltʃərəl] *adj* cultural
culture ['kʌltʃə*] *n* (*also fig*) cultura; (*Biol*) cultivo
cumin ['kʌmɪn] *n* (*spice*) comino
cunning ['kʌnɪŋ] *n* astucia ⊳ *adj* astuto
cup [kʌp] *n* taza; (*as prize*) copa
cupboard ['kʌbəd] *n* armario; (*in kitchen*) alacena
cup final *n* (*Football*) final *f* de copa
curator [kjuə'reɪtə*] *n* director(a) *m/f*
curb [kə:b] *vt* refrenar; (*person*)

reprimir ⊳ *n* freno; (*US*) bordillo
curdle ['kə:dl] *vi* cuajarse
cure [kjuə*] *vt* curar ⊳ *n* cura, curación *f*; (*fig: solution*) remedio
curfew ['kə:fju:] *n* toque *m* de queda
curiosity [kjuərɪ'ɒsɪtɪ] *n* curiosidad *f*
curious ['kjuərɪəs] *adj* curioso; (*person: interested*): **to be ~** sentir curiosidad
curl [kə:l] *n* rizo ⊳ *vt* (*hair*) rizar ⊳ *vi* rizarse; **curl up** *vi* (*person*) hacerse un ovillo; **curler** *n* rulo; **curly** *adj* rizado
currant ['kʌrnt] *n* pasa (de Corinto); (*blackcurrant, redcurrant*) grosella
currency ['kʌrnsɪ] *n* moneda; **to gain ~** (*fig*) difundirse
current ['kʌrnt] *n* corriente *f* ⊳ *adj* (*accepted*) corriente; (*present*) actual; **current account** (*BRIT*) *n* cuenta corriente; **current affairs** *npl* noticias *fpl* de actualidad; **currently** *adv* actualmente
curriculum [kə'rɪkjuləm] (*pl* **~s** *or* **curricula**) *n* plan *m* de estudios; **curriculum vitae** *n* currículum *m*
curry ['kʌrɪ] *n* curry *m* ⊳ *vt*: **to ~ favour with** buscar favores con; **curry powder** *n* curry *m* en polvo
curse [kə:s] *vi* soltar tacos ⊳ *vt* maldecir ⊳ *n* maldición *f*; (*swearword*) palabrota, taco
cursor ['kə:sə*] *n* (*Comput*) cursor *m*
curt [kə:t] *adj* corto, seco
curtain ['kə:tn] *n* cortina; (*Theatre*) telón *m*
curve [kə:v] *n* curva ⊳ *vi* (*road*) hacer una curva; (*line etc*) curvarse; **curved** *adj* curvo
cushion ['kuʃən] *n* cojín *m*; (*of air*) colchón *m* ⊳ *vt* (*shock*) amortiguar
custard ['kʌstəd] *n* natillas *fpl*
custody ['kʌstədɪ] *n* custodia; **to take into ~** detener
custom ['kʌstəm] *n* costumbre *f*; (*Comm*) clientela
customer ['kʌstəmə*] *n* cliente *m/f*
customized ['kʌstəmaɪzd] *adj* (*car etc*) hecho a encargo

customs ['kʌstəmz] npl aduana;
customs officer n aduanero/a
cut [kʌt] (pt, pp ~) vt cortar; (price)
rebajar; (text, programme) acortar;
(reduce) reducir ▷ vi cortar ▷ n (of
garment) corte m; (in skin) cortadura;
(in salary etc) rebaja; (in spending)
reducción f, recorte m; (slice of meat)
tajada; **to ~ a tooth** echar un diente;
to ~ and paste (Comput) cortar y pegar;
cut back vt (plants) podar; (production,
expenditure) reducir; **cut down** vt
(tree) derribar; (reduce) reducir; **cut
off** vt cortar; (person, place) aislar;
(Tel) desconectar; **cut out** vt (shape)
recortar; (stop: activity etc) dejar;
(remove) quitar; **cut up** vt cortar (en
pedazos); **cutback** n reducción f
cute [kjuːt] adj mono
cutlery ['kʌtlərɪ] n cubiertos mpl
cutlet ['kʌtlɪt] n chuleta; (nut etc
cutlet) plato vegetariano hecho con nueces
y verdura en forma de chuleta
cut-price ['kʌt'praɪs] (BRIT) adj a
precio reducido
cut-rate ['kʌt'reɪt] (US) adj =
cut-price
cutting ['kʌtɪŋ] adj (remark) mordaz
▷ n (BRIT: from newspaper) recorte m;
(from plant) esqueje m
CV n abbr = **curriculum vitae**
cwt abbr = **hundredweight(s)**
cybercafé ['saɪbəkæfeɪ] n cibercafé
m
cyberspace ['saɪbəspeɪs] n
ciberespacio
cycle ['saɪkl] n ciclo; (bicycle) bicicleta
▷ vi ir en bicicleta; **cycle hire** n
alquiler m de bicicletas; **cycle lane** n
carril-bici m; **cycle path** n carril-bici
m; **cycling** n ciclismo; **cyclist** n
ciclista mf
cyclone ['saɪkləun] n ciclón m
cylinder ['sɪlɪndə*] n cilindro; (of gas)
bombona
cymbal ['sɪmbl] n címbalo, platillo
cynical ['sɪnɪkl] adj cínico
Cypriot ['sɪprɪət] adj, n chipriota m/f

Cyprus ['saɪprəs] n Chipre f
cyst [sɪst] n quiste m; **cystitis**
[-'taɪtɪs] n cistitis f
czar [zɑː*] n zar m
Czech [tʃɛk] adj, n checo/a m/f; **Czech
Republic** n: **the Czech Republic** la
República Checa

D [diː] n (Mus) re m

dab [dæb] vt (eyes, wound) tocar (ligeramente); (paint, cream) poner un poco de

dad [dæd] n = **daddy**

daddy ['dædɪ] n papá m

daffodil ['dæfədɪl] n narciso

daft [dɑːft] adj tonto

dagger ['dægə*] n puñal m, daga

daily ['deɪlɪ] adj diario, cotidiano ▷ adv todos los días, cada día

dairy ['dɛərɪ] n (shop) lechería; (on farm) vaquería; **dairy produce** n productos mpl lácteos

daisy ['deɪzɪ] n margarita

dam [dæm] n presa ▷ vt construir una presa sobre, represar

damage ['dæmɪdʒ] n lesión f; daño; (dents etc) desperfectos mpl; (fig) perjuicio ▷ vt dañar, perjudicar; (spoil, break) estropear; **damages** npl (Law) daños mpl y perjuicios

damn [dæm] vt condenar; (curse) maldecir ▷ n (inf): **I don't give a ~** me importa un pito ▷ adj (inf: also: **~ed**) maldito; **~ (it)!** ¡maldito sea!

damp [dæmp] adj húmedo, mojado ▷ n humedad f ▷ vt (also: **~en**: cloth, rag) mojar; (: enthusiasm) enfriar

dance [dɑːns] n baile m ▷ vi bailar; **dance floor** n pista f de baile; **dancer** n bailador(a) m/f; (professional) bailarín/ina m/f; **dancing** n baile m

dandelion ['dændɪlaɪən] n diente m de león

dandruff ['dændrəf] n caspa

Dane [deɪn] n danés/esa m/f

danger ['deɪndʒə*] n peligro; (risk) riesgo; **~!** (on sign) ¡peligro de muerte!; **to be in ~** correr riesgo de; **dangerous** adj peligroso

dangle ['dæŋgl] vt colgar ▷ vi pender, colgar

Danish ['deɪnɪʃ] adj danés/esa ▷ n (Ling) danés m

dare [dɛə*] vt: **to ~ sb to do** desafiar a algn a hacer ▷ vi: **to ~ (to) do sth** atreverse a hacer algo; **I ~ say** (I suppose) puede ser (que); **daring** adj atrevido, osado ▷ n atrevimiento, osadía

dark [dɑːk] adj oscuro; (hair, complexion) moreno ▷ n: **in the ~** a oscuras; **to be in the ~ about** (fig) no saber nada de; **after ~** después del anochecer; **darken** vt (colour) hacer más oscuro ▷ vi oscurecerse; **darkness** n oscuridad f; **darkroom** n cuarto oscuro

darling ['dɑːlɪŋ] adj, n querido/a m/f

dart [dɑːt] n dardo; (in sewing) sisa ▷ vi precipitarse; **dartboard** n diana; **darts** n (game) dardos mpl

dash [dæʃ] n (small quantity: of liquid) gota, chorrito; (sign) raya ▷ vt (throw) tirar; (hopes) defraudar ▷ vi precipitarse, ir de prisa

dashboard ['dæʃbɔːd] n (Aut) salpicadero

data ['deɪtə] npl datos mpl; **database** n base f de datos; **data processing** n proceso de datos

date [deɪt] n (day) fecha; (with

friend) cita; (*fruit*) dátil *m* ▷ *vt* fechar; (*person*) salir con; **~ of birth** fecha de nacimiento; **to ~** *adv* hasta la fecha; **dated** *adj* anticuado

daughter ['dɔːtə*] *n* hija; **daughter-in-law** *n* nuera, hija política

daunting ['dɔːntɪŋ] *adj* desalentador(a)

dawn [dɔːn] *n* alba, amanecer *m*; (*fig*) nacimiento ▷ *vi* (*day*) amanecer; (*fig*): **it ~ed on him that ...** cayó en la cuenta de que ...

day [deɪ] *n* día *m*; (*working day*) jornada; (*heyday*) tiempos *mpl*, días *mpl*; **the ~ before/after** el día anterior/siguiente; **the ~ after tomorrow** pasado mañana; **the ~ before yesterday** anteayer; **the following ~** el día siguiente; **by ~** de día; **day-care centre** ['deɪkɛə-] *n* centro de día; (*for children*) guardería infantil; **daydream** *vi* soñar despierto; **daylight** *n* luz *f* (del día); **day return** (*BRIT*) *n* billete *m* de ida y vuelta (en un día); **daytime** *n* día *m*; **day-to-day** *adj* cotidiano; **day trip** *n* excursión *f* (de un día)

dazed [deɪzd] *adj* aturdido

dazzle ['dæzl] *vt* deslumbrar; **dazzling** *adj* (*light*, *smile*) deslumbrante; (*colour*) fuerte

DC *abbr* (= *direct current*) corriente *f* continua

dead [dɛd] *adj* muerto; (*limb*) dormido; (*telephone*) cortado; (*battery*) agotado ▷ *adv* (*completely*) totalmente; (*exactly*) exactamente; **to shoot sb ~** matar a algn a tiros; **~ tired** muerto (de cansancio); **to stop ~** parar en seco; **dead end** *n* callejón *m* sin salida; **deadline** *n* fecha (*or* hora) tope; **deadly** *adj* mortal, fatal; **Dead Sea** *n*: **the Dead Sea** el Mar Muerto

deaf [dɛf] *adj* sordo; **deafen** *vt* ensordecer; **deafening** *adj* ensordecedor/a

deal [diːl] (*pt*, *pp* **~t**) *n* (*agreement*) pacto, convenio; (*business deal*) trato ▷ *vt* dar; (*card*) repartir; **a great ~**

(*of*) bastante, mucho; **deal with** *vt fus* (*people*) tratar con; (*problem*) ocuparse de; (*subject*) tratar de; **dealer** *n* comerciante *m/f*; (*Cards*) mano *f*; **dealings** *npl* (*Comm*) transacciones *fpl*; (*relations*) relaciones *fpl*

dealt [dɛlt] *pt*, *pp* of **deal**

dean [diːn] *n* (*Rel*) deán *m*; (*Scol*: *BRIT*) decano; (: *US*) decano; rector *m*

dear [dɪə*] *adj* querido; (*expensive*) caro ▷ *n*: **my ~** mi querido/a ▷ *excl*: **~ me!** ¡Dios mío!; **D~ Sir/Madam** (*in letter*) Muy Señor Mío, Estimado Señor/Estimada Señora; **D~ Mr/Mrs X** Estimado/a Señor(a) X; **dearly** *adv* (*love*) mucho; (*pay*) caro

death [dɛθ] *n* muerte *f*; **death penalty** *n* pena de muerte; **death sentence** *n* condena a muerte

debate [dɪ'beɪt] *n* debate *m* ▷ *vt* discutir

debit ['dɛbɪt] *n* debe *m* ▷ *vt*: **to ~ a sum to sb** *or* **to sb's account** cargar una suma en cuenta a algn; **debit card** *n* tarjeta *f* de débito

debris ['dɛbriː] *n* escombros *mpl*

debt [dɛt] *n* deuda; **to be in ~** tener deudas

debut [deɪ'bjuː] *n* presentación *f*

Dec. *abbr* (= *December*) dic

decade ['dɛkeɪd] *n* decenio, década

decaffeinated [dɪ'kæfɪneɪtɪd] *adj* descafeinado

decay [dɪ'keɪ] *n* (*of building*) desmoronamiento; (*of tooth*) caries *f inv* ▷ *vi* (*rot*) pudrirse

deceased [dɪ'siːst] *n*: **the ~** el(la) difunto/a

deceit [dɪ'siːt] *n* engaño; **deceive** [dɪ'siːv] *vt* engañar

December [dɪ'sɛmbə*] *n* diciembre *m*

decency ['diːsənsɪ] *n* decencia

decent ['diːsənt] *adj* (*proper*) decente; (*person*: *kind*) amable, bueno

deception [dɪ'sɛpʃən] *n* engaño

deceptive [dɪ'sɛptɪv] *adj* engañoso

Be careful not to translate **deception** by the Spanish word *decepción*.

decide [dɪˈsaɪd] vt (person) decidir; (question, argument) resolver ▷ vi decidir; **to ~ to do/that** decidir hacer/que; **to ~ on sth** decidirse por algo

decimal [ˈdɛsɪməl] adj decimal ▷ n decimal m

decision [dɪˈsɪʒən] n decisión f

decisive [dɪˈsaɪsɪv] adj decisivo; (person) decidido

deck [dɛk] n (Naut) cubierta; (of bus) piso; (record deck) platina; (of cards) baraja; **deckchair** n tumbona

declaration [dɛkləˈreɪʃən] n declaración f

declare [dɪˈklɛə*] vt declarar

decline [dɪˈklaɪn] n disminución f, descenso ▷ vt rehusar ▷ vi (person, business) decaer; (strength) disminuir

decorate [ˈdɛkəreɪt] vt (adorn): **to ~ (with)** adornar (de), decorar (de); (paint) pintar; (paper) empapelar; **decoration** [-ˈreɪʃən] n adorno; (act) decoración f; (medal) condecoración f; **decorator** n (workman) pintor m (decorador)

decrease [n ˈdiːkriːs, vb diˈkriːs] n: **~ (in)** disminución f (de) ▷ vt disminuir, reducir ▷ vi reducirse

decree [dɪˈkriː] n decreto

dedicate [ˈdɛdɪkeɪt] vt dedicar; **dedicated** adj dedicado; (Comput) especializado; **dedicated word processor** procesador m de textos especializado or dedicado; **dedication** [-ˈkeɪʃən] n (devotion) dedicación f; (in book) dedicatoria

deduce [dɪˈdjuːs] vt deducir

deduct [dɪˈdʌkt] vt restar; descontar; **deduction** [dɪˈdʌkʃən] n (amount deducted) descuento; (conclusion) deducción f, conclusión f

deed [diːd] n hecho, acto; (feat) hazaña; (Law) escritura

deem [diːm] vt (formal) juzgar, considerar

deep [diːp] adj profundo; (expressing measurements) de profundidad; (voice) bajo; (breath) profundo; (colour) intenso ▷ adv: **the spectators stood 20 ~** los espectadores se formaron de 20 en fondo; **to be 4 metres ~** tener 4 metros de profundidad; **deep-fry** vt freír en aceite abundante; **deeply** adv (breathe) a pleno pulmón; (interested, moved, grateful) profundamente, hondamente

deer [dɪə*] n inv ciervo

default [dɪˈfɔːlt] n: **by ~** (win) por incomparecencia ▷ adj (Comput) por defecto

defeat [dɪˈfiːt] n derrota ▷ vt derrotar, vencer

defect [n ˈdiːfɛkt, vb dɪˈfɛkt] n defecto ▷ vi: **to ~ to the enemy** pasarse al enemigo; **defective** [dɪˈfɛktɪv] adj defectuoso

defence [dɪˈfɛns] (us **defense**) n defensa

defend [dɪˈfɛnd] vt defender; **defendant** n acusado/a; (in civil case) demandado/a; **defender** n defensor(a) m/f; (Sport) defensa mf

defense [dɪˈfɛns] (us) = **defence**

defensive [dɪˈfɛnsɪv] adj defensivo ▷ n: **on the ~** a la defensiva

defer [dɪˈfəː*] vt aplazar

defiance [dɪˈfaɪəns] n desafío; **in ~ of** en contra de; **defiant** [dɪˈfaɪənt] adj (challenging) desafiante, retador(a)

deficiency [dɪˈfɪʃənsɪ] n (lack) falta; (defect) defecto; **deficient** [dɪˈfɪʃənt] adj deficiente

deficit [ˈdɛfɪsɪt] n déficit m

define [dɪˈfaɪn] vt (word etc) definir; (limits etc) determinar

definite [ˈdɛfɪnɪt] adj (fixed) determinado; (obvious) claro; (certain) indudable; **he was ~ about it** no dejó lugar a dudas (sobre ello); **definitely** adv desde luego, por supuesto

definition [dɛfɪˈnɪʃən] n definición f; (clearness) nitidez f

deflate [diːˈfleɪt] vt desinflar

deflect [dɪˈflɛkt] vt desviar

defraud [dɪˈfrɔːd] vt: **to ~ sb of sth** estafar algo a algn

defrost [diːˈfrɒst] vt descongelar

defuse [diːˈfjuːz] vt desactivar; (situation) calmar

defy [dɪˈfaɪ] vt (resist) oponerse a; (challenge) desafiar; (fig): **it defies description** resulta imposible describirlo

degree [dɪˈɡriː] n grado; (Scol) título; **to have a ~ in maths** tener una licenciatura en matemáticas; **by ~s** (gradually) poco a poco, por etapas; **to some ~** hasta cierto punto

dehydrated [diːhaɪˈdreɪtɪd] adj deshidratado; (milk) en polvo

de-icer [diːˈaɪsə*] n descongelador m

delay [dɪˈleɪ] vt demorar, aplazar; (person) entretener; (train) retrasar ▷ vi tardar ▷ n demora, retraso; **to be ~ed** retrasarse; **without ~** en seguida, sin tardar

delegate [n ˈdɛlɪɡɪt, vb ˈdɛlɪɡeɪt] n delegado/a ▷ vt (person) delegar en; (task) delegar

delete [dɪˈliːt] vt suprimir, tachar

deli [ˈdɛlɪ] n = **delicatessen**

deliberate [adj dɪˈlɪbərɪt, vb dɪˈlɪbəreɪt] adj (intentional) intencionado; (slow) pausado, lento ▷ vi deliberar; **deliberately** adv (on purpose) a propósito

delicacy [ˈdɛlɪkəsɪ] n delicadeza; (choice food) manjar m

delicate [ˈdɛlɪkɪt] adj delicado; (fragile) frágil

delicatessen [dɛlɪkəˈtɛsn] n ultramarinos mpl finos

delicious [dɪˈlɪʃəs] adj delicioso

delight [dɪˈlaɪt] n (feeling) placer m, deleite m; (person, experience etc) encanto, delicia ▷ vt encantar, deleitar; **to take ~ in** deleitarse en; **delighted** adj: **delighted (at or with/to do)** encantado (con/de hacer); **delightful** adj encantador(a), delicioso

delinquent [dɪˈlɪŋkwənt] adj, n delincuente mf

deliver [dɪˈlɪvə*] vt (distribute)

repartir; (hand over) entregar; (message) comunicar; (speech) pronunciar; (Med) asistir al parto de; **delivery** n reparto; entrega; (of speaker) modo de expresarse; (Med) parto, alumbramiento; **to take delivery of** recibir

delusion [dɪˈluːʒən] n ilusión f, engaño

de luxe [dəˈlʌks] adj de lujo

delve [dɛlv] vi: **to ~ into** hurgar en

demand [dɪˈmɑːnd] vt (gen) exigir; (rights) reclamar ▷ n exigencia; (claim) reclamación f; (Econ) demanda; **to be in ~** ser muy solicitado; **on ~** a solicitud; **demanding** adj (boss) exigente; (work) absorbente

demise [dɪˈmaɪz] n (death) fallecimiento

demo [ˈdɛməu] (inf) n abbr (= demonstration) manifestación f

democracy [dɪˈmɔkrəsɪ] n democracia; **democrat** [ˈdɛməkræt] n demócrata mf; **democratic** [dɛməˈkrætɪk] adj democrático; (us) demócrata

demolish [dɪˈmɔlɪʃ] vt derribar, demoler; (fig: argument) destruir

demolition [dɛməˈlɪʃən] n derribo, demolición f

demon [ˈdiːmən] n (evil spirit) demonio

demonstrate [ˈdɛmənstreɪt] vt demostrar; (skill, appliance) mostrar ▷ vi manifestarse; **demonstration** [-ˈstreɪʃən] n (Pol) manifestación f; (proof, exhibition) demostración f; **demonstrator** n (Pol) manifestante mf; (Comm) demostrador(a) m/f; vendedor(a) m/f

demote [dɪˈməut] vt degradar

den [dɛn] n (of animal) guarida; (room) habitación f

denial [dɪˈnaɪəl] n (refusal) negativa; (of report etc) negación f

denim [ˈdɛnɪm] n tela vaquera; **denims** npl vaqueros mpl

Denmark [ˈdɛnmɑːk] n Dinamarca

denomination [dɪnɔmɪ'neɪʃən] n
valor m; (Rel) confesión f

denounce [dɪ'nauns] vt denunciar

dense [dɛns] adj (crowd) denso; (thick)
espeso; (: foliage etc) tupido; (inf: stupid)
torpe

density ['dɛnsɪtɪ] n densidad f
▷ **single/double-~ disk** n (Comput)
disco de densidad sencilla/de doble
densidad

dent [dɛnt] n abolladura ▷ vt
(also: **make a ~ in**) abollar

dental ['dɛntl] adj dental; **dental
floss** [-flɔs] n seda dental; **dental
surgery** n clínica f dental, consultorio
m dental

dentist ['dɛntɪst] n dentista mf

dentures ['dɛntʃəz] npl dentadura
(postiza)

deny [dɪ'naɪ] vt negar; (charge)
rechazar

deodorant [di:'əudərənt] n
desodorante m

depart [dɪ'pɑ:t] vi irse, marcharse;
(train) salir; **to ~ from** (fig: differ from)
apartarse de

department [dɪ'pɑ:tmənt] n
(Comm) sección f; (Scol) departamento;
(Pol) ministerio; **department store** n
gran almacén m

departure [dɪ'pɑ:tʃə*] n partida, ida;
(of train) salida; (of employee) marcha;
a new ~ un nuevo rumbo; **departure
lounge** n (at airport) sala de embarque

depend [dɪ'pɛnd] vi: **to ~ on** depender
de; (rely on) contar con; **it ~s** depende,
según; **~ing on the result** según el
resultado; **dependant** n dependiente
mf; **dependent** adj: **to be dependent
on** depender de ▷ n = **dependant**

depict [dɪ'pɪkt] vt (in picture) pintar;
(describe) representar

deport [dɪ'pɔ:t] vt deportar

deposit [dɪ'pɔzɪt] n depósito; (Chem)
sedimento; (of ore, oil) yacimiento ▷ vt
(gen) depositar; **deposit account** (BRIT)
n cuenta de ahorros

depot ['dɛpəu] n (storehouse)

depósito; (for vehicles) parque m; (US)
estación f

depreciate [dɪ'pri:ʃɪeɪt] vi
depreciarse, perder valor

depress [dɪ'prɛs] vt deprimir; (wages
etc) hacer bajar; (press down) apretar;
depressed adj deprimido; **depressing**
adj deprimente; **depression**
[dɪ'prɛʃən] n depresión f

deprive [dɪ'praɪv] vt: **to ~ sb of** privar
a algn de; **deprived** adj necesitado

dept. abbr (= department) dto

depth [dɛpθ] n profundidad f; (of
cupboard) fondo; **to be in the ~s of
despair** sentir la mayor desesperación;
to be out of one's ~ (in water) no hacer
pie; (fig) sentirse totalmente perdido

deputy ['dɛpjutɪ] adj: **~ head**
subdirector(a) m/f ▷ n sustituto/a,
suplente mf; (US Pol) diputado/a;
(US: also: **~ sheriff**) agente m del sheriff

derail [dɪ'reɪl] vt: **to be ~ed**
descarrilarse

derelict ['dɛrɪlɪkt] adj abandonado

derive [dɪ'raɪv] vt (benefit etc) obtener
▷ vi: **to ~ from** derivarse de

descend [dɪ'sɛnd] vt, vi descender,
bajar; **to ~ from** descender de; **to
~ to** rebajarse a; **descendant** n
descendiente mf

descent [dɪ'sɛnt] n descenso; (origin)
descendencia

describe [dɪs'kraɪb] vt describir;
description [-'krɪpʃən] n descripción
f; (sort) clase f, género

desert [n 'dɛzət, vb dɪ'zə:t] n desierto
▷ vt abandonar ▷ vi (Mil) desertar;
deserted [dɪ'zə:tɪd] adj desierto

deserve [dɪ'zə:v] vt merecer, ser
digno de

design [dɪ'zaɪn] n (sketch) bosquejo;
(layout, shape) diseño; (pattern) dibujo;
(intention) intención f ▷ vt diseñar;
design and technology (BRIT: Scol) n
≈ dibujo y tecnología

designate [vb 'dɛzɪgneɪt, adj
'dɛzɪgnɪt] vt (appoint) nombrar;
(destine) designar ▷ adj designado

designer [dɪˈzaɪnə*] n diseñador(a)
m/f; (fashion designer) modisto/a,
diseñador(a) m/f de moda
desirable [dɪˈzaɪərəbl] adj (proper)
deseable; (attractive) atractivo
desire [dɪˈzaɪə*] n deseo ▷ vt desear
desk [dɛsk] n (in office) escritorio;
(for pupil) pupitre m; (in hotel, at airport)
recepción f; (BRIT: in shop, restaurant)
caja; **desk-top publishing** [ˈdɛsktɔp-]
n autoedición f
despair [dɪsˈpɛə*] n desesperación f
▷ vi: **to ~ of** perder la esperanza de
despatch [dɪsˈpætʃ] n, vt = **dispatch**
desperate [ˈdɛspərɪt] adj
desesperado; (fugitive) peligroso;
to be ~ for sth/to do necesitar
urgentemente algo/hacer;
desperately adv desesperadamente;
(very) terriblemente, gravemente
desperation [dɛspəˈreɪʃən]
n desesperación f; **in (sheer) ~**
(absolutamente) desesperado
despise [dɪsˈpaɪz] vt despreciar
despite [dɪsˈpaɪt] prep a pesar de,
pese a
dessert [dɪˈzɜːt] n postre m;
dessertspoon n cuchara (de postre)
destination [dɛstɪˈneɪʃən] n destino
destined [ˈdɛstɪnd] adj: **~ for London**
con destino a Londres
destiny [ˈdɛstɪnɪ] n destino
destroy [dɪsˈtrɔɪ] vt destruir; (animal)
sacrificar
destruction [dɪsˈtrʌkʃən] n
destrucción f
destructive [dɪsˈtrʌktɪv] adj
destructivo, destructor(a)
detach [dɪˈtætʃ] vt separar; (unstick)
despegar; **detached** adj (attitude)
objetivo, imparcial; **detached house**
n ≈ chalé m, ≈ chalet m
detail [ˈdiːteɪl] n detalle m; (no pl;
(: in picture etc) detalles mpl; (trifle)
pequeñez f ▷ vt detallar; (Mil)
destacar; **in ~** detalladamente;
detailed adj detallado
detain [dɪˈteɪn] vt retener; (in

captivity) detener
detect [dɪˈtɛkt] vt descubrir; (Med,
Police) identificar; (Mil, Radar, Tech)
detectar; **detection** [dɪˈtɛkʃən] n
descubrimiento; identificación f;
detective n detective mf; **detective
story** n novela policíaca
detention [dɪˈtɛnʃən] n detención f,
arresto; (Scol) castigo
deter [dɪˈtɜː*] vt (dissuade) disuadir
detergent [dɪˈtɜːdʒənt] n
detergente m
deteriorate [dɪˈtɪərɪəreɪt] vi
deteriorarse
determination [dɪtɜːmɪˈneɪʃən] n
resolución f
determine [dɪˈtɜːmɪn] vt
determinar; **determined** adj (person)
resuelto, decidido; **determined to do**
resuelto a hacer
deterrent [dɪˈtɛrənt] n (Mil) fuerza
de disuasión
detest [dɪˈtɛst] vt aborrecer
detour [ˈdiːtuə*] n (gen, US Aut)
desviación f
detract [dɪˈtrækt] vt: **to ~ from** quitar
mérito a, desvirtuar
detrimental [dɛtrɪˈmɛntl] adj: **~ (to)**
perjudicial (a)
devastating [ˈdɛvəsteɪtɪŋ] adj
devastador(a); (fig) arrollador(a)
develop [dɪˈvɛləp] vt desarrollar;
(Phot) revelar; (disease) coger;
(habit) adquirir; (fault) empezar a
tener ▷ vi desarrollarse; (advance)
progresar; (facts, symptoms) aparecer;
developing country n país m en
(vías de) desarrollo; **development**
n desarrollo; (advance) progreso; (of
affair, case) desenvolvimiento; (of land)
urbanización f
device [dɪˈvaɪs] n (apparatus) aparato,
mecanismo
devil [ˈdɛvl] n diablo, demonio
devious [ˈdiːvɪəs] adj taimado
devise [dɪˈvaɪz] vt idear, inventar
devote [dɪˈvəut] vt: **to ~ sth to**
dedicar algo a; **devoted** adj (loyal)

leal, fiel; **to be devoted to sb** querer con devoción a algn; **the book is devoted to politics** el libro trata de la política; **devotion** n dedicación f; (Rel) devoción f

devour [dɪ'vauə*] vt devorar

devout [dɪ'vaut] adj devoto

dew [dju:] n rocío

diabetes [daɪə'bi:ti:z] n diabetes f

diabetic [daɪə'bɛtɪk] adj, n diabético/a m/f

diagnose ['daɪəgnəuz] vt diagnosticar

diagnosis [daɪəg'nəusɪs] (pl -ses) n diagnóstico

diagonal [daɪ'ægənl] adj, n diagonal f

diagram ['daɪəgræm] n diagrama m, esquema m

dial ['daɪəl] n esfera (SP), cara (LAM); (on radio etc) dial m; (of phone) disco ▷ vt (number) marcar

dialect ['daɪəlɛkt] n dialecto

dialling code ['daɪəlɪŋ-] n prefijo

dialling tone (US **dial tone**) n (BRIT) señal f or tono de marcar

dialogue ['daɪəlɒg] (US **dialog**) n diálogo

diameter [daɪ'æmɪtə*] n diámetro

diamond ['daɪəmənd] n diamante m; (shape) rombo; **diamonds** npl (Cards) diamantes mpl

diaper ['daɪəpə*] (US) n pañal m

diarrhoea [daɪə'ri:ə] (US **diarrhea**) n diarrea

diary ['daɪərɪ] n (daily account) diario; (book) agenda

dice [daɪs] n inv dados mpl ▷ vt (Culin) cortar en cuadritos

dictate [dɪk'teɪt] vt dictar; (conditions) imponer; **dictation** [-'teɪʃən] n dictado; (giving of orders) órdenes fpl

dictator [dɪk'teɪtə*] n dictador m

dictionary ['dɪkʃənrɪ] n diccionario

did [dɪd] pt of **do**

didn't ['dɪdənt] = **did not**

die [daɪ] vi morir; (fig: fade) desvanecerse, desaparecer; **to be dying for sth/to do sth** morirse por algo/de ganas de hacer algo; **die down** vi apagarse; (wind) amainar; **die out** vi desaparecer

diesel ['di:zəl] n vehículo con motor Diesel

diet ['daɪət] n dieta; (restricted food) régimen m ▷ vi (also: **be on a ~**) estar a dieta, hacer régimen

differ ['dɪfə*] vi: **to ~ (from)** (be different) ser distinto (a), diferenciarse (de); (disagree) discrepar (de); **difference** n diferencia; (disagreement) desacuerdo; **different** adj diferente, distinto; **differentiate** [-'rɛnʃɪeɪt] vi: **to differentiate (between)** distinguir (entre); **differently** adv de otro modo, en forma distinta

difficult ['dɪfɪkəlt] adj difícil; **difficulty** n dificultad f

dig [dɪg] (pt, pp **dug**) vt (hole, ground) cavar ▷ n (prod) empujón m; (archaeological) excavación f; (remark) indirecta; **to ~ one's nails into** clavar las uñas en; **dig up** vt (information) desenterrar; (plant) desarraigar

digest [vb daɪ'dʒɛst, n 'daɪdʒɛst] vt (food) digerir; (facts) asimilar ▷ n resumen m; **digestion** [dɪ'dʒɛstʃən] n digestión f

digit ['dɪdʒɪt] n (number) dígito; (finger) dedo; **digital** adj digital; **digital camera** n cámara digital; **digital TV** n televisión f digital

dignified ['dɪgnɪfaɪd] adj grave, solemne

dignity ['dɪgnɪtɪ] n dignidad f

digs [dɪgz] (BRIT: inf) npl pensión f, alojamiento

dilemma [daɪ'lɛmə] n dilema m

dill [dɪl] n eneldo

dilute [daɪ'lu:t] vt diluir

dim [dɪm] adj (light) débil; (outline) indistinto; (room) oscuro; (inf: stupid) lerdo ▷ vt (light) bajar

dime [daɪm] (US) n moneda de diez centavos

dimension [dɪˈmɛnʃən] n dimensión f

diminish [dɪˈmɪnɪʃ] vt, vi disminuir

din [dɪn] n estruendo, estrépito

dine [daɪn] vi cenar; **diner** n (person) comensal mf

dinghy [ˈdɪŋɡɪ] n bote m; (also: **rubber ~**) lancha (neumática)

dingy [ˈdɪndʒɪ] adj (room) sombrío; (colour) sucio

dining car [ˈdaɪnɪŋ-] (BRIT) n (Rail) coche-comedor m

dining room [ˈdaɪnɪŋ-] n comedor m

dining table n mesa f de comedor

dinner [ˈdɪnə*] n (evening meal) cena; (lunch) comida; (public) cena, banquete m; **dinner jacket** n smoking m; **dinner party** n cena; **dinner time** n (evening) hora de cenar; (midday) hora de comer

dinosaur [ˈdaɪnəsɔ:*] n dinosaurio

dip [dɪp] n (slope) pendiente m; (in sea) baño; (Culin) salsa ▷ vt (in water) mojar; (ladle etc) meter; (BRIT Aut): **to ~ one's lights** poner luces de cruce ▷ vi (road etc) descender, bajar

diploma [dɪˈpləumə] n diploma m

diplomacy [dɪˈpləuməsɪ] n diplomacia

diplomat [ˈdɪpləmæt] n diplomático/a; **diplomatic** [dɪpləˈmætɪk] adj diplomático

dipstick [ˈdɪpstɪk] (BRIT) n (Aut) varilla de nivel (del aceite)

dire [daɪə*] adj calamitoso

direct [daɪˈrɛkt] adj directo; (challenge) claro; (person) franco ▷ vt dirigir; (order): **to ~ sb to do sth** mandar a algn hacer algo ▷ adv derecho; **can you ~ me to ...?** ¿puede indicarme dónde está ...?; **direct debit** (BRIT) n domiciliación f bancaria de recibos

direction [dɪˈrɛkʃən] n dirección f; **sense of ~** sentido de la dirección; **directions** npl (instructions) instrucciones fpl; **~s for use** modo de empleo

directly [dɪˈrɛktlɪ] adv (in straight line)

directamente; (at once) en seguida

director [dɪˈrɛktə*] n director(a) m/f

directory [dɪˈrɛktərɪ] n (Tel) guía (telefónica); (Comput) directorio; **directory enquiries** (US **directory assistance**) n (servicio de) información f

dirt [də:t] n suciedad f; (earth) tierra; **dirty** adj sucio; (joke) verde, colorado (MEX) ▷ vt ensuciar; (stain) manchar

disability [dɪsəˈbɪlɪtɪ] n incapacidad f

disabled [dɪsˈeɪbld] adj: **to be physically ~** ser minusválido/a; **to be mentally ~** ser deficiente mental

disadvantage [dɪsədˈvɑ:ntɪdʒ] n desventaja, inconveniente m

disagree [dɪsəˈgri:] vi (differ) discrepar; **to ~ (with)** no estar de acuerdo (con); **disagreeable** adj desagradable; (person) antipático; **disagreement** n desacuerdo

disappear [dɪsəˈpɪə*] vi desaparecer; **disappearance** n desaparición f

disappoint [dɪsəˈpɔɪnt] vt decepcionar, defraudar; **disappointed** adj decepcionado; **disappointing** adj decepcionante; **disappointment** n decepción f

disapproval [dɪsəˈpru:vəl] n desaprobación f

disapprove [dɪsəˈpru:v] vi: **to ~ of** ver mal

disarm [dɪsˈɑ:m] vt desarmar; **disarmament** [dɪsˈɑ:məmənt] n desarme m

disaster [dɪˈzɑ:stə*] n desastre m

disastrous [dɪˈzɑ:strəs] adj desastroso

disbelief [dɪsbəˈli:f] n incredulidad f

disc [dɪsk] n disco; (Comput) = **disk**

discard [dɪsˈkɑ:d] vt (old things) tirar; (fig) descartar

discharge [vb dɪsˈtʃɑ:dʒ, n ˈdɪstʃɑ:dʒ] vt (task, duty) cumplir; (waste) verter; (patient) dar de alta; (employee) despedir; (soldier) licenciar; (defendant) poner en libertad ▷ n (Elec) descarga; (*Med*) supuración f; (*dismissal*) despedida; (*of duty*) desempeño; (*of debt*) pago, descargo

discipline ['dısıplın] n disciplina ▷ vt disciplinar; (*punish*) castigar

disc jockey n pinchadiscos *mf inv*

disclose [dıs'kləuz] vt revelar

disco ['dıskəu] n *abbr* discoteca

discoloured [dıs'kʌləd] (*US* **discolored**) adj descolorido

discomfort [dıs'kʌmfət] n incomodidad f; (*unease*) inquietud f; (*physical*) malestar m

disconnect [dıskə'nɛkt] vt separar; (*Elec etc*) desconectar

discontent [dıskən'tɛnt] n descontento

discontinue [dıskən'tınju:] vt interrumpir; (*payments*) suspender; **"~d"** (*Comm*) "ya no se fabrica"

discount [n 'dıskaunt, vb dıs'kaunt] n descuento ▷ vt descontar

discourage [dıs'kʌrıdʒ] vt desalentar; (*advise against*): **to ~ sb from doing** disuadir a algn de hacer

discover [dıs'kʌvə*] vt descubrir; (*error*) darse cuenta de; **discovery** n descubrimiento

discredit [dıs'krɛdıt] vt desacreditar

discreet [dı'skri:t] adj (*tactful*) discreto; (*careful*) prudente

discrepancy [dı'skrɛpənsı] n . diferencia

discretion [dı'skrɛʃən] n (*tact*) discreción f; **at the ~ of** a criterio de

discriminate [dı'skrımıneıt] vi: **to ~ between** distinguir entre; **to ~ against** discriminar contra; **discrimination** [-'neıʃən] n (*discernment*) perspicacia; (*bias*) discriminación f

discuss [dı'skʌs] vt discutir; (*a theme*) tratar; **discussion** [dı'skʌʃən] n discusión f

disease [dı'zi:z] n enfermedad f

disembark [dısım'ba:k] vt, vi desembarcar

disgrace [dıs'greıs] n ignominia;

(*shame*) vergüenza, escándalo ▷ vt deshonrar; **disgraceful** adj vergonzoso

disgruntled [dıs'grʌntld] adj disgustado, descontento

disguise [dıs'gaız] n disfraz m ▷ vt disfrazar; **in ~** disfrazado

disgust [dıs'gʌst] n repugnancia ▷ vt repugnar, dar asco a

▌ Be careful not to translate **disgust** by the Spanish word *disgustar*.

disgusted [dıs'gʌstıd] adj indignado

▌ Be careful not to translate **disgusted** by the Spanish word *disgustado*.

disgusting [dıs'gʌstıŋ] adj repugnante, asqueroso; (*behaviour etc*) vergonzoso

dish [dıʃ] n (*gen*) plato; **to do** or **wash the ~es** fregar los platos; **dishcloth** n estropajo

dishonest [dıs'ɔnıst] adj (*person*) poco honrado, tramposo; (*means*) fraudulento

dishtowel ['dıʃtauəl] (*US*) n estropajo

dishwasher ['dıʃwɔʃə*] n lavaplatos *m inv*

disillusion [dısı'lu:ʒən] vt desilusionar

disinfectant [dısın'fɛktənt] n desinfectante m

disintegrate [dıs'ıntıgreıt] vi disgregarse, desintegrarse

disk [dısk] n (*esp US*) = **disc**; (*Comput*) disco, disquete m; **single-/double-sided ~** disco de una cara/dos caras; **disk drive** n disc drive m; **diskette** n = **disk**

dislike [dıs'laık] n antipatía, aversión f ▷ vt tener antipatía a

dislocate ['dısləkeıt] vt dislocar

disloyal [dıs'lɔıəl] adj desleal

dismal ['dızml] adj (*gloomy*) deprimente, triste; (*very bad*) malísimo, fatal

dismantle [dıs'mæntl] vt desmontar, desarmar

dismay [dɪs'meɪ] n consternación f
▷ vt consternar

dismiss [dɪs'mɪs] vt (worker)
despedir; (pupils) dejar marchar;
(soldiers) dar permiso para irse; (idea,
Law) rechazar; (possibility) descartar;
dismissal n despido

disobedient [dɪsə'biːdɪənt] adj
desobediente

disobey [dɪsə'beɪ] vt desobedecer

disorder [dɪs'ɔːdə*] n desorden m;
(rioting) disturbios mpl; (Med) trastorno

disorganized [dɪs'ɔːgənaɪzd] adj
desorganizado

disown [dɪs'əun] vt (action) renegar
de; (person) negar cualquier tipo de
relación con

dispatch [dɪs'pætʃ] vt enviar ▷ n
(sending) envío; (Press) informe m; (Mil)
parte m

dispel [dɪs'pɛl] vt disipar

dispense [dɪs'pɛns] vt (medicines)
preparar; **dispense with** vt fus
prescindir de; **dispenser** n (container)
distribuidor m automático

disperse [dɪs'pəːs] vt dispersar ▷ vi
dispersarse

display [dɪs'pleɪ] n (in shop window)
escaparate m; (exhibition) exposición
f; (Comput) visualización f; (of feeling)
manifestación f ▷ vt exponer;
manifestar; (ostentatiously) lucir

displease [dɪs'pliːz] vt (offend)
ofender; (annoy) fastidiar

disposable [dɪs'pəuzəbl] adj
desechable; (income) disponible

disposal [dɪs'pəuzl] n (of rubbish)
destrucción f; **at one's ~** a su
disposición

dispose [dɪs'pəuz] vi: **to ~ of**
(unwanted goods) deshacerse de;
(problem etc) resolver; **disposition**
[dɪspə'zɪʃən] n (nature)
temperamento; (inclination)
propensión f

disproportionate [dɪsprə'pɔːʃənət]
adj desproporcionado

dispute [dɪs'pjuːt] n disputa; (also:

industrial ~) conflicto (laboral) ▷ vt
(argue) disputar, discutir; (question)
cuestionar

disqualify [dɪs'kwɒlɪfaɪ] vt (Sport)
desclasificar; **to ~ sb for sth/from
doing sth** incapacitar a algn para
algo/hacer algo

disregard [dɪsrɪ'gɑːd] vt (ignore) no
hacer caso de

disrupt [dɪs'rʌpt] vt (plans)
desbaratar, trastornar; (conversation)
interrumpir; **disruption**
[dɪs'rʌpʃən] n trastorno,
desbaratamiento; interrupción f

dissatisfaction [dɪssætɪs'fækʃən] n
disgusto, descontento

dissatisfied [dɪs'sætɪsfaɪd] adj
insatisfecho

dissect [dɪ'sɛkt] vt disecar

dissent [dɪ'sɛnt] n disensión f

dissertation [dɪsə'teɪʃən] n tesina

dissolve [dɪ'zɔlv] vt disolver
▷ vi disolverse; **to ~ in(to) tears**
deshacerse en lágrimas

distance ['dɪstəns] n distancia; **in
the ~** a lo lejos

distant ['dɪstənt] adj lejano; (manner)
reservado, frío

distil [dɪs'tɪl] (us **distill**) vt destilar;
distillery n destilería

distinct [dɪs'tɪŋkt] adj (different)
distinto; (clear) claro; (unmistakeable)
inequívoco; **as ~ from** a diferencia
de; **distinction** [dɪs'tɪŋkʃən] n
distinción f; (honour) honor m; (in
exam) sobresaliente m; **distinctive** adj
distintivo

distinguish [dɪs'tɪŋgwɪʃ] vt
distinguir; **to ~ o.s.** destacarse;
distinguished adj (eminent)
distinguido

distort [dɪs'tɔːt] vt distorsionar;
(shape, image) deformar

distract [dɪs'trækt] vt distraer;
distracted adj distraído; **distraction**
[dɪs'trækʃən] n distracción f;
(confusion) aturdimiento

distraught [dɪs'trɔːt] adj loco de

inquietud

distress [dɪs'trɛs] n (anguish)
angustia, aflicción f ▷ vt afligir;
distressing adj angustioso; doloroso

distribute [dɪs'trɪbjuːt] vt distribuir;
(share out) repartir; **distribution**
[-'bjuːʃən] n distribución f, reparto;
distributor n (Aut) distribuidor m;
(Comm) distribuidora

district ['dɪstrɪkt] n (of country)
zona, región f; (of town) barrio; (Admin)
distrito; **district attorney** (US) n
fiscal mf

distrust [dɪs'trʌst] n desconfianza
▷ vt desconfiar de

disturb [dɪs'təːb] vt (person: bother,
interrupt) molestar; (: upset)
perturbar, inquietar; (disorganize)
alterar; **disturbance** n (upheaval)
perturbación f; (political etc: gen
pl) disturbio; (of mind) trastorno;
disturbed adj (worried, upset)
preocupado, angustiado; **emotionally
disturbed** trastornado; (childhood)
inseguro; **disturbing** adj inquietante,
perturbador(a)

ditch [dɪtʃ] n zanja; (irrigation ditch)
acequia ▷ vt (inf: partner) deshacerse
de; (: plan, car etc) abandonar

ditto ['dɪtəu] adv ídem, lo mismo

dive [daɪv] n (from board) salto;
(underwater) buceo; (of submarine)
sumersión f ▷ vi (swimmer: into water)
saltar; (: under water) zambullirse,
bucear; (fish, submarine) sumergirse;
(bird) lanzarse en picado; **to ~ into** (bag
etc) meter la mano en; (place) meterse
de prisa en; **diver** n (underwater) buzo

diverse [daɪ'vəːs] adj diversos/as,
varios/as

diversion [daɪ'vəːʃən] n (BRIT Aut)
desviación f; (distraction, Mil) diversión
f; (of funds) distracción f

diversity [daɪ'vəːsɪtɪ] n diversidad f

divert [daɪ'vəːt] vt (turn aside) desviar

divide [dɪ'vaɪd] vt dividir; (separate)
separar ▷ vi dividirse; (road)
bifurcarse; **divided highway** (US) n

carretera de doble calzada

divine [dɪ'vaɪn] adj (also fig) divino

diving ['daɪvɪŋ] n (Sport) salto;
(underwater) buceo; **diving board** n
trampolín m

division [dɪ'vɪʒən] n división f;
(sharing out) reparto; (disagreement)
diferencias fpl; (Comm) sección f

divorce [dɪ'vɔːs] n divorcio
▷ vt divorciarse de; **divorced** adj
divorciado; **divorcee** [-'siː] n
divorciado/a

D.I.Y. (BRIT) adj, n abbr = **do-it-
yourself**

dizzy ['dɪzɪ] adj (spell) de mareo; **to
feel ~** marearse

DJ n abbr = **disc jockey**

DNA n abbr (= deoxyribonucleic acid)
ADN m

○ **KEYWORD**

do [duː] (pt **did**, pp **done**) n (inf: party
etc): **we're having a little do on
Saturday** damos una fiestecita el
sábado; **it was rather a grand do** fue
un acontecimiento a lo grande
▷ aux vb **1** (in negative constructions: not
translated): **I don't understand** no
entiendo

2 (to form questions: not translated):
didn't you know? ¿no lo sabías?; **what
do you think?** ¿qué opinas?

3 (for emphasis, in polite expressions):
**people do make mistakes
sometimes** sí que se cometen errores
a veces; **she does seem rather late**
a mí también me parece que se ha
retrasado; **do sit down/help yourself**
siéntate/sírvete por favor; **do take
care!** ¡ten cuidado(, te pido)!

4 (used to avoid repeating vb): **she sings
better than I do** canta mejor que yo;
do you agree? – yes, I do/no, I don't
¿estás de acuerdo? – sí (lo estoy)/no
(lo estoy); **she lives in Glasgow – so
do I** vive en Glasgow – yo también; **he
didn't like it and neither did we** no

le gustó y a nosotros tampoco; **who made this mess? – I did** ¿quién hizo esta chapuza? – yo; **he asked me to help him and I did** me pidió que le ayudara y lo hice

5 (*in question tags*): **you like him, don't you?** te gusta, ¿verdad? or ¿no?; **I don't know him, do I?** creo que no le conozco

▷ *vt* **1** (*gen, carry out, perform etc*): **what are you doing tonight?** ¿qué haces esta noche?; **what can I do for you?** ¿en qué puedo servirle?; **to do the washing-up/cooking** fregar los platos/cocinar; **to do one's teeth/hair/nails** lavarse los dientes/arreglarse el pelo/arreglarse las uñas

2 (*Aut etc*): **the car was doing 100** el coche iba a 100; **we've done 200 km already** ya hemos hecho 200 km; **he can do 100 in that car** puede ir a 100 en ese coche

▷ *vi* **1** (*act, behave*) hacer; **do as I do** haz como yo

2 (*get on, fare*): **he's doing well/badly at school** va bien/mal en la escuela; **the firm is doing well** la empresa anda *or* va bien; **how do you do?** mucho gusto; (*less formal*) ¿qué tal?

3 (*suit*): **will it do?** ¿sirve?, ¿está *or* va bien?

4 (*be sufficient*) bastar; **will £10 do?** ¿será bastante con £10?; **that'll do** así está bien; **that'll do!** (*in annoyance*) ¡ya está bien!, ¡basta ya!; **to make do (with)** arreglárselas (con)

do up *vt* (*laces*) atar; (*zip, dress, shirt*) abrochar; (*renovate: room, house*) renovar

do with *vt fus* (*need*): **I could do with a drink/some help** no me vendría mal un trago/un poco de ayuda; (*be connected*) tener que ver con; **what has it got to do with you?** ¿qué tiene que ver contigo?

do without *vi* pasar sin; **if you're late for tea then you'll do without** si llegas tarde tendrás que quedarte sin cenar

▷ *vt fus* pasar sin; **I can do without a car** puedo pasar sin coche

dock [dɔk] *n* (*Naut*) muelle *m*; (*Law*) banquillo (de los acusados) ▷ *vi* (*enter dock*) atracar (la) muelle; (*Space*) acoplarse; **docks** *npl* (*Naut*) muelles *mpl*, puerto *sg*

doctor ['dɔktə*] *n* médico/a; (*Ph. D. etc*) doctor(a) *m/f* ▷ *vt* (*drink etc*) adulterar; **Doctor of Philosophy** *n* Doctor en Filosofía y Letras

document ['dɔkjumənt] *n* documento; **documentary** [-'mɛntərɪ] *adj* documental ▷ *n* documental *m*; **documentation** [-mɛn'teɪʃən] *n* documentación *f*

dodge [dɔdʒ] *n* (*fig*) truco ▷ *vt* evadir; (*blow*) esquivar

dodgy ['dɔdʒɪ] *adj* (*inf: uncertain*) dudoso; (*suspicious*) sospechoso; (*risky*) arriesgado

does [dʌz] *vb see* **do**

doesn't ['dʌznt] = **does not**

dog [dɔg] *n* perro ▷ *vt* seguir los pasos de; (*bad luck*) perseguir; **doggy bag** ['dɔgɪ-] *n* bolsa para llevarse las sobras de la comida

do-it-yourself ['du:ɪtjɔ:'sɛlf] *n* bricolaje *m*

dole [dəul] (*BRIT*) *n* (*payment*) subsidio de paro; **on the ~** parado

doll [dɔl] *n* muñeca; (*US: inf: woman*) muñeca, gachí *f*

dollar ['dɔlə*] *n* dólar *m*

dolphin ['dɔlfɪn] *n* delfín *m*

dome [dəum] *n* (*Arch*) cúpula

domestic [də'mɛstɪk] *adj* (*animal, duty*) doméstico; (*flight, policy*) nacional; **domestic appliance** *n* aparato *m* doméstico, aparato *m* de uso doméstico

dominant ['dɔmɪnənt] *adj* dominante

dominate ['dɔmɪneɪt] *vt* dominar

domino ['dɔmɪnəu] (*pl* **~es**) *n* ficha de dominó; **dominoes** *n* (*game*) dominó

donate [də'neɪt] vt donar; **donation** [də'neɪʃən] n donativo

done [dʌn] pp of **do**

donkey ['dɔŋkɪ] n burro

donor ['dəʊnə*] n donante mf; **donor card** n carnet m de donante

don't [dəʊnt] = **do not**

donut ['dəʊnʌt] (US) n = **doughnut**

doodle ['du:dl] vi hacer dibujitos or garabatos

doom [du:m] n (fate) suerte f ▷ vt: **to be ~ed to failure** estar condenado al fracaso

door [dɔ:*] n puerta; **doorbell** n timbre m; **door handle** n tirador m; (of car) manija; **doorknob** n pomo m de la puerta, manilla f (LAM); **doorstep** n peldaño; **doorway** n entrada, puerta

dope [dəʊp] n (inf: illegal drug) droga; (: person) imbécil mf ▷ vt (horse etc) drogar

dormitory ['dɔ:mɪtrɪ] n (BRIT) dormitorio; (US) colegio mayor

DOS n abbr (= disk operating system) DOS m

dosage ['dəʊsɪdʒ] n dosis f inv

dose [dəʊs] n dosis f inv

dot [dɔt] n punto ▷ vi: **~ted with** salpicado de; **on the ~** en punto; **dotcom** n [dɔt'kɔm] n puntocom f inv; **dotted line** ['dɔtɪd-] n: **to sign on the dotted line** firmar

double ['dʌbl] adj doble ▷ adv (twice): **to cost ~** costar el doble ▷ n doble m ▷ vt doblar ▷ vi doblarse; **on the ~, at the ~** (BRIT) corriendo; **double back** vi (person) volver sobre sus pasos; **double bass** n contrabajo; **double bed** n cama de matrimonio; **double-check** vt volver a revisar ▷ vi: **I'll double-check** voy a revisarlo otra vez; **double-click** vi (Comput) hacer doble clic; **double-cross** vt (trick) engañar; (betray) traicionar; **doubledecker** n autobús m de dos pisos; **double glazing** (BRIT) n doble acristalamiento; **double room** n

habitación f doble; **doubles** n (Tennis) juego de dobles; **double yellow lines** npl (BRIT: Aut) línea doble amarilla de prohibido aparcar, ≈ línea fsg amarilla continua

doubt [daʊt] n duda ▷ vt dudar; (suspect) dudar de; **to ~ that** dudar que; **doubtful** adj dudoso; (person): **to be doubtful about sth** tener dudas sobre algo; **doubtless** adv sin duda

dough [dəʊ] n masa, pasta; **doughnut** (US **donut**) n ≈ rosquilla

dove [dʌv] n paloma

down [daʊn] n (feathers) plumón m, flojel m ▷ adv (downwards) abajo, hacia abajo; (on the ground) por or en tierra ▷ prep abajo ▷ vt (inf: drink) beberse; **~ with X!** ¡abajo X!; **down-and-out** n vagabundo/a; **downfall** n caída, ruina; **downhill** adv: **to go downhill** (also fig) ir cuesta abajo

Downing Street ['daʊnɪŋ-] n (BRIT) Downing Street f

down: download vt (Comput) bajar; **downright** adj (nonsense, lie) manifiesto; (refusal) terminante

Down's syndrome ['daʊnz-] n síndrome m de Down

down: downstairs adv (below) (en el piso de) abajo; (downwards) escaleras abajo; **down-to-earth** adj práctico; **downtown** adv en el centro de la ciudad; **down under** adv en Australia (or Nueva Zelanda); **downward** [-wəd] adj, adv hacia abajo; **downwards** [-wədz] adv hacia abajo

doz. abbr = **dozen**

doze [dəʊz] vi dormitar

dozen ['dʌzn] n docena; **a ~ books** una docena de libros; **~s of** cantidad de

Dr. abbr = **doctor**; **drive**

drab [dræb] adj gris, monótono

draft [drɑ:ft] n (first copy) borrador m; (Pol: of bill) anteproyecto; (US: call-up) quinta ▷ vt (plan) preparar; (write roughly) hacer un borrador de; see also **draught**

drag [dræg] vt arrastrar; (river) dragar;

rastrear ▷vi (time) pasar despacio;
(play, film etc) hacerse pesado ▷n (inf)
lata; (women's clothing): **in ~** vestido
de travesti; **to ~ and drop** (Comput)
arrastrar y soltar

dragon ['drægən] n dragón m

dragonfly ['drægənflaɪ] n libélula

drain [dreɪn] n desaguadero; (in
street) sumidero; (source of loss): **to be
a ~ on** consumir, agotar ▷vt (land,
marshes) desaguar; (reservoir) desecar;
(vegetables) escurrir ▷vi escurrirse;
drainage n (act) desagüe m; (Med,
Agr) drenaje m; (sewage) alcantarillado;
drainpipe n tubo de desagüe

drama ['drɑːmə] n (art) teatro;
(play) drama m; (excitement) emoción f;
dramatic [drə'mætɪk] adj dramático;
(sudden, marked) espectacular

drank [dræŋk] pt of **drink**

drape [dreɪp] vt (cloth) colocar; (flag)
colgar; **drapes** npl (us) cortinas fpl

drastic ['dræstɪk] adj (measure)
severo; (change) radical, drástico

draught [drɑːft] (us **draft**) n (of
air) corriente f de aire; (Naut) calado;
on ~ (beer) de barril; **draught beer** n
cerveza de barril; **draughts** (BRIT) n
(game) juego de damas

draw [drɔː] (pt **drew**, pp **drawn**) vt
(picture) dibujar; (cart) tirar de; (curtain)
correr; (take out) sacar; (attract) atraer;
(money) retirar; (wages) cobrar ▷vi
(Sport) empatar ▷n (Sport) empate m;
(lottery) sorteo; **draw out** vi (lengthen)
alargarse ▷vt sacar; **draw up** vi (stop)
pararse ▷vt (chair) acercar; (document)
redactar; **drawback** n inconveniente
m, desventaja

drawer [drɔː*] n cajón m

drawing ['drɔːɪŋ] n dibujo; **drawing
pin** (BRIT) n chincheta; **drawing room**
n salón m

drawn [drɔːn] pp of **draw**

dread [dred] n pavor m, terror m ▷vt
temer, tener miedo or pavor a; **dreadful**
adj horroroso

dream [driːm] (pt, pp **~ed** or **~t**) n

sueño ▷vt, vi soñar; **dreamer** n
soñador(a) m/f

dreamt [dremt] pt, pp of **dream**

dreary ['drɪərɪ] adj monótono

drench [drentʃ] vt empapar

dress [dres] n vestido; (clothing)
ropa ▷vt vestir; (wound) vendar ▷vi
vestirse; **to get ~ed** vestirse; **dress
up** vi vestirse de etiqueta; (in fancy
dress) disfrazarse; **dress circle** (BRIT)
n principal m; **dresser** n (furniture)
aparador m; (: us) cómoda (con espejo);
dressing n (Med) vendaje m; (Culin)
aliño; **dressing gown** (BRIT) n bata;
dressing room n (Theatre) camarín
m; (Sport) vestuario; **dressing table** n
tocador m; **dressmaker** n modista,
costurera

drew [druː] pt of **draw**

dribble ['drɪbl] vi (baby) babear ▷vt
(ball) regatear

dried [draɪd] adj (fruit) seco; (milk)
en polvo

drier ['draɪə*] n = **dryer**

drift [drɪft] n (of current etc) flujo;
(of snow) ventisquero; (meaning)
significado ▷vi (boat) ir a la deriva;
(sand, snow) amontonarse

drill [drɪl] n (drill bit) broca; (tool for
DIY etc) taladro; (of dentist) fresa; (for
mining etc) perforadora, barrena; (Mil)
instrucción f ▷vt perforar, taladrar;
(troops) enseñar la instrucción a ▷vi
(for oil) perforar

drink [drɪŋk] (pt **drank**, pp **drunk**) n
bebida; (sip) trago ▷vt, vi beber; **to
have a ~** tomar algo; tomar una copa
or un trago; **a ~ of water** un trago de
agua; **drink-driving** n: **to be charged
with drink-driving** ser acusado de
conducir borracho or en estado de
embriaguez; **drinker** n bebedor(a)
m/f; **drinking water** n agua potable

drip [drɪp] n (act) goteo; (one drip)
gota; (Med) gota a gota m ▷vi gotear

drive [draɪv] (pt **drove**, pp **driven**)
n (journey) viaje m (en coche); (also:
~way) entrada; (energy) energía,

vigor m; (*Comput: also:* **disk ~**) drive
m ▷ vt (*car*) conducir (*SP*), manejar
(*LAM*); (*nail*) clavar; (*push*) empujar;
(*Tech: motor*) impulsar ▷ vi (*Aut: at
controls*) conducir; (: *travel*) pasearse en
coche; **left-/right-hand ~** conducción
f a la izquierda/derecha; **to ~ sb mad**
volverle loco a algn; **drive out** vt (*force
out*) expulsar, echar; **drive-in** adj (*esp
US*): **drive-in cinema** autocine m

driven ['drɪvn] pp of **drive**

driver ['draɪvə*] n conductor(a) m/f
(*SP*), chofer m (*LAM*); (*of taxi, bus*) chófer
mf (*SP*), chofer mf (*LAM*); **driver's license**
(*US*) n carnet m de conducir

driveway ['draɪvweɪ] n entrada

driving ['draɪvɪŋ] n el conducir (*SP*),
el manejar (*LAM*); **driving instructor**
n profesor(a) m/f de autoescuela (*SP*),
instructor(a) m/f de manejo (*LAM*);
driving lesson n clase f de conducir
(*SP*) or manejar (*LAM*); **driving licence**
(*BRIT*) n licencia de manejo (*LAM*),
carnet m de conducir (*SP*); **driving
test** n examen m de conducir (*SP*) or
manejar (*LAM*)

drizzle ['drɪzl] n llovizna

droop [druːp] vi (*flower*) marchitarse;
(*shoulders*) encorvarse; (*head*) inclinarse

drop [drɒp] n (*of water*) gota;
(*lessening*) baja; (*fall*) caída ▷ vt dejar
caer; (*voice, eyes, price*) bajar; (*passenger*)
dejar; (*omit*) omitir ▷ vi (*object*) caer;
(*wind*) amainar; **drop in** vi (*inf: visit*): **to
drop in (on)** pasar por casa (de); **drop
off** vi (*sleep*) dormirse ▷ vt (*passenger*)
dejar; **drop out** vi (*withdraw*) retirarse

drought [draʊt] n sequía

drove [drəʊv] pt of **drive**

drown [draʊn] vt ahogar ▷ vi
ahogarse

drowsy ['draʊzɪ] adj soñoliento; **to
be ~** tener sueño

drug [drʌg] n medicamento; (*narcotic*)
droga ▷ vt drogar; **to be on ~s**
drogarse; **drug addict** n drogadicto/
a; **drug dealer** n traficante mf de
drogas; **druggist** (*US*) n farmacéutico;

drugstore (*US*) n farmacia

drum [drʌm] n tambor m; (*for oil,
petrol*) bidón m; **drums** npl batería;
drummer n tambor m

drunk [drʌŋk] pp of **drink** ▷ adj
borracho ▷ n (*also:* **~ard**) borracho/a;
drunken adj borracho; (*laughter, party*)
de borrachos

dry [draɪ] adj seco; (*day*) sin lluvia;
(*climate*) árido, seco ▷ vt secar; (*tears*)
enjugarse ▷ vi secarse; **dry off** vi
secarse ▷ vt secar; **dry up** vi (*river*)
secarse; **dry-cleaner's** n tintorería;
dry-cleaning n lavado en seco; **dryer**
n (*for hair*) secador m; (*US: for clothes*)
secadora

DSS n abbr **= Department of Social
Security**

D & T (*BRIT: Scol*) n abbr (= *design and
technology*) ≈ dibujo y tecnología

DTP n abbr (= *desk-top publishing*)
autoedición f

dual ['djuəl] adj doble; **dual
carriageway** (*BRIT*) n carretera de
doble calzada

dubious ['djuːbɪəs] adj indeciso;
(*reputation, company*) sospechoso

duck [dʌk] n pato ▷ vi agacharse

due [djuː] adj (*owed*): **he is ~ £10** se le
deben 10 libras; (*expected: event*): **the
meeting is ~ on Wednesday** la
reunión tendrá lugar el miércoles;
(: *arrival*): **the train is ~ at 8am** el tren
tiene su llegada para las 8; (*proper*)
debido ▷ n: **to give sb his** (*or* **her**) **~** ser
justo con algn ▷ adv: **~ north** derecho
al norte

duel ['djuəl] n duelo

duet [djuːˈɛt] n dúo

dug [dʌg] pt, pp of **dig**

duke [djuːk] n duque m

dull [dʌl] adj (*light*) débil; (*stupid*)
torpe; (*boring*) pesado; (*sound, pain*)
sordo; (*weather, day*) gris ▷ vt (*pain,
grief*) aliviar; (*mind, senses*) entorpecer

dumb [dʌm] adj mudo; (*pej: stupid*)
estúpido

dummy ['dʌmɪ] n (*tailor's dummy*)

maniquí *m*; (*mock-up*) maqueta; (BRIT: *for baby*) chupete *m* ▷ *adj* falso, postizo

dump [dʌmp] *n* (*also*: **rubbish ~**) basurero, vertedero; (*inf: place*) cuchitril *m* ▷ *vt* (*put down*) dejar; (*get rid of*) deshacerse de; (*Comput: data*) transferir

dumpling ['dʌmplɪŋ] *n bola de masa hervida*

dune [djuːn] *n* duna

dungarees [dʌŋgə'riːz] *npl* mono

dungeon ['dʌndʒən] *n* calabozo

duplex ['djuːplɛks] *n* dúplex *m*

duplicate [*n* 'djuːplɪkət, *vb* 'djuːplɪkeɪt] *n* duplicado ▷ *vt* duplicar; (*photocopy*) fotocopiar; (*repeat*) repetir; **in ~** por duplicado

durable ['djuərəbl] *adj* duradero

duration [djuə'reɪʃən] *n* duración *f*

during ['djuərɪŋ] *prep* durante

dusk [dʌsk] *n* crepúsculo, anochecer *m*

dust [dʌst] *n* polvo ▷ *vt* quitar el polvo a, desempolvar; (*cake etc*) **to ~ with** espolvorear de; **dustbin** (BRIT) *n* cubo *or* bote *m* (MEX) *or* tacho (SC) de la basura; **duster** *n* paño, trapo; **dustman** (BRIT: *irreg*) *n* basurero; **dustpan** *n* cogedor *m*; **dusty** *adj* polvoriento

Dutch [dʌtʃ] *adj* holandés/esa ▷ *n* (*Ling*) holandés *m*; **the Dutch** *npl* los holandeses; **to go ~** (*inf*) pagar cada uno lo suyo; **Dutchman** (*irreg*) *n* holandés *m*; **Dutchwoman** (*irreg*) *n* holandésa

duty ['djuːtɪ] *n* deber *m*; (*tax*) derechos *mpl* de aduana; **on ~** de servicio; (*at night etc*) de guardia; **off ~** libre (de servicio); **duty-free** *adj* libre de impuestos

duvet ['duːveɪ] (BRIT) *n* edredón *m*

DVD *n abbr* (= *digital versatile or video disc*) DVD *m*; **DVD player** *n* lector *m* de DVD; **DVD writer** *n* grabadora de DVD

dwarf [dwɔːf] (*pl* **dwarves**) *n* enano/a ▷ *vt* empequeñecer

dwell [dwɛl] (*pt, pp* **dwelt**) *vi* morar; **dwell on** *vt fus* explayarse en

dwelt [dwɛlt] *pt, pp of* **dwell**

dwindle ['dwɪndl] *vi* disminuir

dye [daɪ] *n* tinte *m* ▷ *vt* teñir

dying ['daɪɪŋ] *adj* moribundo

dynamic [daɪ'næmɪk] *adj* dinámico

dynamite ['daɪnəmaɪt] *n* dinamita

dyslexia [dɪs'lɛksɪə] *n* dislexia

dyslexic [dɪs'lɛksɪk] *adj, n* disléxico/a *m/f*

e

E [i:] *n* (*Mus*) mi *m*

E111 *n abbr* (= *form E111*) impreso E111

each [i:tʃ] *adj* cada *inv* ▷ *pron* cada uno; **~ other** el uno al otro; **they hate ~ other** se odian (entre ellos *or* mutuamente); **they have 2 books ~** tienen 2 libros por persona

eager ['i:gə*] *adj* (*keen*) entusiasmado; **to be ~ to do sth** tener muchas ganas de hacer algo, impacientarse por hacer algo; **to be ~ for** tener muchas ganas de

eagle ['i:gl] *n* águila

ear [iə*] *n* oreja; oído; (*of corn*) espiga; **earache** *n* dolor *m* de oídos; **eardrum** *n* tímpano

earl [ə:l] *n* conde *m*

earlier ['ə:liə*] *adj* anterior ▷ *adv* antes

early ['ə:li] *adv* temprano; (*before time*) con tiempo, con anticipación ▷ *adj* temprano; (*settlers etc*) primitivo; (*death, departure*) prematuro; (*reply*) pronto; **to have an ~ night** acostarse temprano; **in the ~** *or* **~ in the spring/19th century** a principios de primavera/del siglo diecinueve; **early retirement** *n* jubilación *f* anticipada

earmark ['iəmɑ:k] *vt*: **to ~ (for)** reservar (para), destinar (a)

earn [ə:n] *vt* (*salary*) percibir; (*interest*) devengar; (*praise*) merecerse

earnest ['ə:nist] *adj* (*wish*) fervoroso; (*person*) serio, formal; **in ~** en serio

earnings ['ə:niŋz] *npl* (*personal*) sueldo, ingresos *mpl*; (*company*) ganancias *fpl*

ear: earphones *npl* auriculares *mpl*; **earplugs** *npl* tapones *mpl* para los oídos; **earring** *n* pendiente *m*, arete *m*

earth [ə:θ] *n* tierra; (*BRIT Elec*) cable *m* de toma de tierra ▷ *vt* (*BRIT Elec*) conectar a tierra; **earthquake** *n* terremoto

ease [i:z] *n* facilidad *f*; (*comfort*) comodidad *f* ▷ *vt* (*lessen: problem*) mitigar; (: *pain*) aliviar; (: *tension*) reducir; **to ~ sth in/out** meter/sacar algo con cuidado; **at ~!** (*Mil*) ¡descansen!

easily ['i:zili] *adv* fácilmente

east [i:st] *n* este *m* ▷ *adj* del este, oriental; (*wind*) este ▷ *adv* al este, hacia el este; **the E~** el Oriente; (*Pol*) los países del Este; **eastbound** *adj* en dirección este

Easter ['i:stə*] *n* Pascua (de Resurrección); **Easter egg** *n* huevo de Pascua

eastern ['i:stən] *adj* del este, oriental; (*oriental*) oriental

Easter Sunday *n* Domingo de Resurrección

easy ['i:zi] *adj* fácil; (*simple*) sencillo; (*comfortable*) holgado, cómodo; (*relaxed*) tranquilo ▷ *adv*: **to take it** *or* **things ~** (*not worry*) tomarlo con calma; (*rest*) descansar; **easy-going** *adj* acomodadizo

eat [i:t] (*pt* **ate**, *pp* **eaten**) *vt* comer; **eat out** *vi* comer fuera

eavesdrop ['i:vzdrɔp] *vi*: **to ~ (on)** escuchar a escondidas

e-book ['i:buk] n libro electrónico
e-business ['i:bɪznɪs] n (company) negocio electrónico; (commerce) comercio electrónico
EC n abbr (= European Community) CE f
eccentric [ɪk'sentrɪk] adj, n excéntrico/a m/f
echo ['ekəu] (pl **-es**) n eco ▷ vt (sound) repetir ▷ vi resonar, hacer eco
eclipse [ɪ'klɪps] n eclipse m
eco-friendly ['i:kəufrendlɪ] adj ecológico
ecological [i:kə'lɔdʒɪkl] adj ecológico
ecology [ɪ'kɔlədʒɪ] n ecología
e-commerce n abbr comercio electrónico
economic [i:kə'nɔmɪk] adj económico; (business etc) rentable; **economical** adj económico; **economics** n (Scol) economía ▷ npl (of project etc) rentabilidad f
economist [ɪ'kɔnəmɪst] n economista m/f
economize [ɪ'kɔnəmaɪz] vi economizar, ahorrar
economy [ɪ'kɔnəmɪ] n economía; **economy class** n (Aviat) clase f económica; **economy class syndrome** n síndrome m de la clase turista
ecstasy ['ekstəsɪ] n éxtasis m inv; (drug) éxtasis m inv; **ecstatic** [eks'tætɪk] adj extático
eczema ['eksɪmə] n eczema m
edge [edʒ] n (of knife) filo; (of object) borde m; (of lake) orilla ▷ vt (Sewing) ribetear; **on ~** (fig) = edgy; **to ~ away from** alejarse poco a poco de
edgy ['edʒɪ] adj nervioso, inquieto
edible ['edɪbl] adj comestible
Edinburgh ['edɪnbərə] n Edimburgo
edit ['edɪt] vt (be the editor of) dirigir; (text, report) corregir, preparar; **edition** [ɪ'dɪʃən] n edición f; **editor** n (of newspaper) director(a) m/f; (of column): **foreign/political editor** encargado de la sección de extranjero/política; (of book) redactor(a) m/f;

editorial [-'tɔ:rɪəl] adj editorial ▷ n editorial m
educate ['edjukeɪt] vt (gen) educar; (instruct) instruir; **educated** ['edjukeɪtɪd] adj culto
education [edju'keɪʃən] n educación f; (schooling) enseñanza; (Scol) pedagogía; **educational** adj (policy etc) educacional; (experience) docente; (toy) educativo
eel [i:l] n anguila
eerie ['ɪərɪ] adj misterioso
effect [ɪ'fekt] n efecto ▷ vt efectuar, llevar a cabo; **to take ~** (law) entrar en vigor or vigencia; (drug) surtir efecto; **in ~** en realidad; **effects** npl (property) efectos mpl; **effective** adj eficaz; (actual) verdadero; **effectively** adv eficazmente; (in reality) efectivamente
efficiency [ɪ'fɪʃənsɪ] n eficiencia; rendimiento
efficient [ɪ'fɪʃənt] adj eficiente; (machine) de buen rendimiento; **efficiently** adv eficientemente, de manera eficiente
effort ['efət] n esfuerzo; **effortless** adj sin ningún esfuerzo; (style) natural
e.g. adv abbr (= exempli gratia) p. ej.
egg [eg] n huevo; **hard-boiled/soft-boiled ~** huevo duro/pasado por agua; **eggcup** n huevera; **eggplant** (esp US) n berenjena; **eggshell** n cáscara de huevo; **egg white** n clara de huevo; **egg yolk** n yema de huevo
ego ['i:gəu] n ego
Egypt ['i:dʒɪpt] n Egipto; **Egyptian** [ɪ'dʒɪpʃən] adj, n egipcio/a m/f
eight [eɪt] num ocho; **eighteen** num diez y ocho, dieciocho; **eighteenth** adj decimoctavo; **the eighteenth floor** la planta dieciocho; **the eighteenth of August** el dieciocho de agosto; **eighth** num octavo; **eightieth** ['eɪtɪɪθ] adj octogésimo
eighty ['eɪtɪ] num ochenta
Eire ['eərə] n Eire m
either ['aɪðə*] adj cualquiera de los dos; (both, each) cada ▷ pron: **~ (of**

them) cualquiera (de los dos) ▷ *adv* tampoco ▷ *conj*: **~ yes or no** o sí o no; **on ~ side** en ambos lados; **I don't like ~** no me gusta ninguno/a de los(las) dos; **no, I don't ~** no, yo tampoco

eject [ɪ'dʒɛkt] *vt* echar, expulsar; (*tenant*) desahuciar

elaborate [*adj* ɪ'læbərɪt, *vb* ɪ'læbəreɪt] *adj* (*complex*) complejo ▷ *vt* (*expand*) ampliar; (*refine*) refinar ▷ *vi* explicar con más detalles

elastic [ɪ'læstɪk] *n* elástico ▷ *adj* elástico; (*fig*) flexible; **elastic band** (*BRIT*) *n* gomita

elbow ['ɛlbəʊ] *n* codo

elder ['ɛldə*] *adj* mayor ▷ *n* (*tree*) saúco; (*person*) mayor; **elderly** *adj* de edad, mayor ▷ *npl*: **the elderly** los mayores

eldest ['ɛldɪst] *adj, n* el/la mayor

elect [ɪ'lɛkt] *vt* elegir ▷ *adj*: **the president ~** el presidente electo; **to ~ to do** optar por hacer; **election** *n* elección *f*; **electoral** *adj* electoral; **electorate** *n* electorado

electric [ɪ'lɛktrɪk] *adj* eléctrico; **electrical** *adj* eléctrico; **electric blanket** *n* manta eléctrica; **electric fire** *n* estufa eléctrica; **electrician** [ɪlɛk'trɪʃən] *n* electricista *mf*; **electricity** [ɪlɛk'trɪsɪtɪ] *n* electricidad *f*; **electric shock** *n* electrochoque *m*; **electrify** [ɪ'lɛktrɪfaɪ] *vt* (*Rail*) electrificar; (*fig: audience*) electrizar

electronic [ɪlɛk'trɔnɪk] *adj* electrónico; **electronic mail** *n* correo electrónico; **electronics** *n* electrónica

elegance ['ɛlɪɡəns] *n* elegancia

elegant ['ɛlɪɡənt] *adj* elegante

element ['ɛlɪmənt] *n* elemento; (*of kettle etc*) resistencia

elementary [ɛlɪ'mɛntərɪ] *adj* elemental; (*primitive*) rudimentario; **elementary school** (*US*) *n* escuela de enseñanza primaria

elephant ['ɛlɪfənt] *n* elefante *m*

elevate ['ɛlɪveɪt] *vt* (*gen*) elevar; (*in rank*) ascender

elevator ['ɛlɪveɪtə*] (*US*) *n* ascensor *m*; (*in warehouse etc*) montacargas *m inv*

eleven [ɪ'lɛvn] *num* once; **eleventh** *num* undécimo

eligible ['ɛlɪdʒəbl] *adj*: **an ~ young man/woman** un buen partido; **to be ~ for sth** llenar los requisitos para algo

eliminate [ɪ'lɪmɪneɪt] *vt* (*suspect, possibility*) descartar

elm [ɛlm] *n* olmo

eloquent ['ɛləkwənt] *adj* elocuente

else [ɛls] *adv*: **something ~** otra cosa; **somewhere ~** en otra parte; **everywhere ~** en todas partes menos aquí; **where ~?** ¿dónde más?, ¿en qué otra parte?; **there was little ~ to do** apenas quedaba otra cosa que hacer; **nobody ~ spoke** no habló nadie más; **elsewhere** *adv* (*be*) en otra parte; (*go*) a otra parte

elusive [ɪ'luːsɪv] *adj* esquivo; (*quality*) difícil de encontrar

e-mail ['iːmeɪl] *n abbr* (= *electronic mail*) correo electrónico, e-mail *m*; **e-mail address** *n* dirección *f* electrónica, email *m*

embankment [ɪm'bæŋkmənt] *n* terraplén *m*

embargo [ɪm'bɑːɡəʊ] (*pl* **~es**) *n* (*Comm, Naut*) embargo; (*prohibition*) prohibición *f*; **to put an ~ on sth** poner un embargo en algo

embark [ɪm'bɑːk] *vi* embarcarse ▷ *vt* embarcar; **to ~ on** (*journey*) emprender; (*course of action*) lanzarse a

embarrass [ɪm'bærəs] *vt* avergonzar; (*government etc*) dejar en mal lugar; **embarrassed** *adj* (*laugh, silence*) embarazoso

> ▌Be careful not to translate **embarrassed** by the Spanish word *embarazada*.

embarrassing *adj* (*situation*) violento; (*question*) embarazoso; **embarrassment** *n* (*shame*) vergüenza; (*problem*) **to be an embarrassment for sb** poner en un aprieto a algn

embassy ['embəsɪ] n embajada
embrace [ɪm'breɪs] vt abrazar, dar un abrazo a; (include) abarcar ▷ vi abrazarse ▷ n abrazo
embroider [ɪm'brɔɪdə*] vt bordar; **embroidery** n bordado
embryo ['embrɪəu] n embrión m
emerald ['emərəld] n esmeralda
emerge [ɪ'məːdʒ] vi salir; (arise) surgir
emergency [ɪ'məːdʒənsɪ] n crisis f inv; **in an ~** en caso de urgencia; **state of ~** estado de emergencia; **emergency brake** (us) n freno de mano; **emergency exit** n salida de emergencia; **emergency landing** n aterrizaje m forzoso; **emergency room** (us: Med) n sala f de urgencias; **emergency services** npl (fire, police, ambulance) servicios mpl de urgencia or emergencia
emigrate ['emɪɡreɪt] vi emigrar; **emigration** [emɪ'ɡreɪʃən] n emigración f
eminent ['emɪnənt] adj eminente
emissions [ɪ'mɪʃənz] npl emisión f
emit [ɪ'mɪt] vt emitir; (smoke) arrojar; (smell) despedir; (sound) producir
emotion [ɪ'məuʃən] n emoción f; **emotional** adj (needs) emocional; (person) sentimental; (scene) conmovedor(a), emocionante; (speech) emocionado
emperor ['empərə*] n emperador m
emphasis ['emfəsɪs] (pl **-ses**) n énfasis m inv
emphasize ['emfəsaɪz] vt (word, point) subrayar, recalcar; (feature) hacer resaltar
empire ['empaɪə*] n imperio
employ [ɪm'plɔɪ] vt emplear; **employee** [-'iː] n empleado/a; **employer** n patrón/ona m/f; empresario; **employment** n (work) trabajo; **employment agency** n agencia de colocaciones
empower [ɪm'pauə*] vt: **to ~ sb to do sth** autorizar a algn para hacer algo
empress ['emprɪs] n emperatriz f

emptiness ['emptɪnɪs] n vacío; (of life etc) vaciedad f
empty ['emptɪ] adj vacío; (place) desierto; (house) desocupado; (threat) vano ▷ vt vaciar; (place) dejar vacío ▷ vi vaciarse; (house etc) quedar desocupado; **empty-handed** adj con las manos vacías
EMU n abbr (= European Monetary Union) UME f
emulsion [ɪ'mʌlʃən] n emulsión f; (also: **~ paint**) pintura emulsión
enable [ɪ'neɪbl] vt: **to ~ sb to do sth** permitir a algn hacer algo
enamel [ɪ'næməl] n esmalte m; (also: **~ paint**) pintura esmaltada
enchanting [ɪn'tʃɑːntɪŋ] adj encantador(a)
encl. abbr (= enclosed) adj
enclose [ɪn'kləuz] vt (land) cercar; (letter etc) adjuntar; **please find ~d** le mandamos adjunto
enclosure [ɪn'kləuʒə*] n cercado, recinto
encore [ɔŋ'kɔː*] excl ¡otra!, ¡bis! ▷ n bis m
encounter [ɪn'kauntə*] n encuentro ▷ vt encontrar, encontrarse con; (difficulty) tropezar con
encourage [ɪn'kʌrɪdʒ] vt alentar, animar; (activity) fomentar; (growth) estimular; **encouragement** n estímulo; (of industry) fomento
encouraging [ɪn'kʌrɪdʒɪŋ] adj alentador(a)
encyclop(a)edia [ensaɪkləu'piːdɪə] n enciclopedia
end [end] n fin m; (of table) extremo; (of street) final m; (Sport) lado ▷ vt terminar, acabar; (also: **bring to an ~, put an ~ to**) acabar con ▷ vi terminar, acabar; **in the ~** al fin; **on ~** (object) de punta, de cabeza; **to stand on ~** (hair) erizarse; **for hours on ~** hora tras hora; **end up** vi: **to end up in** terminar en; (place) ir a parar en
endanger [ɪn'deɪndʒə*] vt poner en peligro; **an ~ed species** una especie en

peligro de extinción

endearing [ɪnˈdɪərɪŋ] adj simpático, atractivo

endeavour [ɪnˈdɛvə*] (US **endeavor**) n esfuerzo; (attempt) tentativa ▷ vi: **to ~ to do** esforzarse por hacer; (try) procurar hacer

ending [ˈɛndɪŋ] n (of book) desenlace m; (Ling) terminación f

endless [ˈɛndlɪs] adj interminable, inacabable

endorse [ɪnˈdɔːs] vt (cheque) endosar; (approve) aprobar; **endorsement** n (on driving licence) nota de inhabilitación

endurance [ɪnˈdjuərəns] n resistencia

endure [ɪnˈdjuə*] vt (bear) aguantar, soportar ▷ vi (last) durar

enemy [ˈɛnəmɪ] adj, n enemigo/a m/f

energetic [ɛnəˈdʒɛtɪk] adj enérgico

energy [ˈɛnədʒɪ] n energía

enforce [ɪnˈfɔːs] vt (Law) hacer cumplir

engaged [ɪnˈgeɪdʒd] adj (BRIT: busy, in use) ocupado; (betrothed) prometido; **to get ~** prometerse; **engaged tone** (BRIT) n (Tel) señal f de comunicando

engagement [ɪnˈgeɪdʒmənt] n (appointment) compromiso, cita; (booking) contratación f; (to marry) compromiso; (period) noviazgo; **engagement ring** n anillo de prometida

engaging [ɪnˈgeɪdʒɪŋ] adj atractivo

engine [ˈɛndʒɪn] n (Aut) motor m; (Rail) locomotora

engineer [ɛndʒɪˈnɪə*] n ingeniero; (BRIT: for repairs) mecánico; (on ship, US Rail) maquinista m; **engineering** n ingeniería

England [ˈɪŋglənd] n Inglaterra

English [ˈɪŋglɪʃ] adj inglés/esa ▷ n (Ling) inglés m; **the English** npl los ingleses mpl; **English Channel** n: **the English Channel** (el Canal de) la Mancha; **Englishman** (irreg) n inglés m; **Englishwoman** (irreg) n inglesa

engrave [ɪnˈgreɪv] vt grabar

engraving [ɪnˈgreɪvɪŋ] n grabado

enhance [ɪnˈhɑːns] vt (gen) aumentar; (beauty) realzar

enjoy [ɪnˈdʒɔɪ] vt (health, fortune) disfrutar de, gozar de; (like) gustarle a algn; **to ~ o.s.** divertirse; **enjoyable** adj agradable; (amusing) divertido; **enjoyment** n (joy) placer m; (activity) diversión f

enlarge [ɪnˈlɑːdʒ] vt aumentar; (broaden) extender; (Phot) ampliar ▷ vi: **to ~ on** (subject) tratar con más detalles; **enlargement** n (Phot) ampliación f

enlist [ɪnˈlɪst] vt alistar; (support) conseguir ▷ vi alistarse

enormous [ɪˈnɔːməs] adj enorme

enough [ɪˈnʌf] adj: **~ time/books** bastante tiempo/bastantes libros ▷ pron bastante(s) ▷ adv: **big ~** bastante grande; **he has not worked ~** no ha trabajado bastante; **have you got ~?** ¿tiene usted bastante(s)?; **~ to eat** (lo) suficiente or (lo) bastante para comer; **~!** ¡basta ya!; **that's ~, thanks** con eso basta, gracias; **I've had ~ of him** estoy harto de él; **... which, funnily** or **oddly ~ ...** ... lo que, por extraño que parezca ...

enquire [ɪnˈkwaɪə*] vt, vi = **inquire**

enquiry [ɪnˈkwaɪərɪ] n (official investigation) investigación f

enrage [ɪnˈreɪdʒ] vt enfurecer

enrich [ɪnˈrɪtʃ] vt enriquecer

enrol [ɪnˈrəul] (US **enroll**) vt (members) inscribir; (Scol) matricular ▷ vi inscribirse; matricularse; **enrolment** (US **enrollment**) n inscripción f; matriculación f

en route [ɔnˈruːt] adv durante el viaje

en suite [ɔnˈswiːt] adj: **with ~ bathroom** con baño

ensure [ɪnˈʃuə*] vt asegurar

entail [ɪnˈteɪl] vt suponer

enter [ˈɛntə*] vt (room) entrar en; (club) hacerse socio de; (army) alistarse en; (sb for a competition) inscribir; (write

down) anotar, apuntar; (*Comput*) meter
▷ *vi* entrar
enterprise [ˈɛntəpraɪz] *n*
empresa; (*spirit*) iniciativa; **free
~ la** libre empresa; **private ~ la**
iniciativa privada; **enterprising** *adj*
emprendedor(a)
entertain [ɛntəˈteɪn] *vt* (*amuse*)
divertir; (*invite: guest*) invitar (a casa);
(*idea*) abrigar; **entertainer** *n* artista
mf; **entertaining** *adj* divertido,
entretenido; **entertainment** *n*
(*amusement*) diversión *f*; (*show*)
espectáculo
enthusiasm [ɪnˈθuːzɪæzəm] *n*
entusiasmo
enthusiast [ɪnˈθuːzɪæst] *n*
entusiasta *mf*; **enthusiastic** [-ˈæstɪk]
adj entusiasta; **to be enthusiastic
about** entusiasmarse por
entire [ɪnˈtaɪə*] *adj* entero; **entirely**
adv totalmente
entitle [ɪnˈtaɪtl] *vt*: **to ~ sb to sth** dar
a algn derecho a algo; **entitled** *adj*
(*book*) titulado; **to be entitled to do**
tener derecho a hacer
entrance [*n* ˈɛntrəns, *vb* ɪnˈtrɑːns] *n*
entrada ▷ *vt* encantar, hechizar; **to
gain ~ to** (*university etc*) ingresar en;
entrance examination *n* examen
m de ingreso; **entrance fee** *n* cuota;
entrance ramp (*us*) *n* (*Aut*) rampa
de acceso
entrant [ˈɛntrənt] *n* (*in race,
competition*) participante *mf*; (*in
examination*) candidato/a
entrepreneur [ɔntrəprəˈnəː] *n*
empresario
entrust [ɪnˈtrʌst] *vt*: **to ~ sth to sb**
confiar algo a algn
entry [ˈɛntrɪ] *n* entrada; (*in
competition*) participación *f*; (*in
register*) apunte *m*; (*in account*) partida;
(*in reference book*) artículo; **"no ~"**
"prohibido el paso"; (*Aut*) "dirección
prohibida"; **entry phone** *n* portero
automático
envelope [ˈɛnvələup] *n* sobre *m*

envious [ˈɛnvɪəs] *adj* envidioso; (*look*)
de envidia
environment [ɪnˈvaɪərnmənt] *n*
(*surroundings*) entorno; (*natural world*):
the ~ el medio ambiente;
environmental [-ˈmɛntl] *adj*
ambiental; medioambiental;
environmentally [-ˈmɛntəlɪ]
adv: **environmentally sound/friendly**
ecológico
envisage [ɪnˈvɪzɪdʒ] *vt* prever
envoy [ˈɛnvɔɪ] *n* enviado
envy [ˈɛnvɪ] *n* envidia ▷ *vt* tener
envidia a; **to ~ sb sth** envidiar algo
a algn
epic [ˈɛpɪk] *n* épica ▷ *adj* épico
epidemic [ɛpɪˈdɛmɪk] *n* epidemia
epilepsy [ˈɛpɪlɛpsɪ] *n* epilepsia
epileptic [ɛpɪˈlɛptɪk] *adj, n*
epiléptico/a *m/f*; **epileptic fit**
[ɛpɪˈlɛptɪk-] *n* ataque *m* de epilepsia,
acceso *m* epiléptico
episode [ˈɛpɪsəud] *n* episodio
equal [ˈiːkwl] *adj* igual; (*treatment*)
equitativo ▷ *n* igual *mf* ▷ *vt* ser igual
a; (*fig*) igualar; **to be ~ to** (*task*) estar
a la altura de; **equality** [iːˈkwɔlɪtɪ]
n igualdad *f*; **equalize** *vi* (*Sport*)
empatar; **equally** *adv* igualmente;
(*share etc*) a partes iguales
equation [ɪˈkweɪʒən] *n* (*Math*)
ecuación *f*
equator [ɪˈkweɪtə*] *n* ecuador *m*
equip [ɪˈkwɪp] *vt* equipar; (*person*)
proveer; **to be well ~ped** estar bien
equipado; **equipment** *n* equipo;
(*tools*) avíos *mpl*
equivalent [ɪˈkwɪvələnt] *adj*: **~ (to)**
equivalente (a) ▷ *n* equivalente *m*
ER *abbr* (*BRIT*: = *Elizabeth Regina*) *la reina
Isabel*; (*us*: *Med*) = **emergency room**
era [ˈɪərə] *n* era, época
erase [ɪˈreɪz] *vt* borrar; **eraser** *n*
goma de borrar
erect [ɪˈrɛkt] *adj* erguido ▷ *vt* erigir,
levantar; (*assemble*) montar; **erection**
[-ʃən] *n* construcción *f*; (*assembly*)
montaje *m*; (*Physiol*) erección *f*

ERM *n abbr* (= *Exchange Rate Mechanism*) tipo de cambio europeo

erode [ɪ'rəud] *vt* (*Geo*) erosionar; (*metal*) corroer, desgastar; (*fig*) desgastar

erosion [ɪ'rəuʒən] *n* erosión *f*; desgaste *m*

erotic [ɪ'rɔtɪk] *adj* erótico

errand ['ɛrnd] *n* recado (*SP*), mandado (*LAM*)

erratic [ɪ'rætɪk] *adj* desigual, poco uniforme

error ['ɛrə*] *n* error *m*, equivocación *f*

erupt [ɪ'rʌpt] *vi* entrar en erupción; (*fig*) estallar; **eruption** [ɪ'rʌpʃən] *n* erupción *f*; (*of war*) estallido

escalate ['ɛskəleɪt] *vi* extenderse, intensificarse

escalator ['ɛskəleɪtə*] *n* escalera móvil

escape [ɪ'skeɪp] *n* fuga ▷ *vi* escaparse; (*flee*) huir, evadirse; (*leak*) fugarse ▷ *vt* (*responsibility etc*) evitar, eludir; (*consequences*) escapar a; (*elude*): **his name ~s me** no me sale su nombre; **to ~ from** (*place*) escaparse de; (*person*) escaparse a

escort [*n* 'ɛskɔːt, *vb* ɪ'skɔːt] *n* acompañante *mf*; (*Mil*) escolta *mf* ▷ *vt* acompañar

especially [ɪ'spɛʃlɪ] *adv* (*above all*) sobre todo; (*particularly*) en particular, especialmente

espionage ['ɛspɪənɑːʒ] *n* espionaje *m*

essay ['ɛseɪ] *n* (*Literature*) ensayo; (*Scol: short*) redacción *f*; (: *long*) trabajo

essence ['ɛsns] *n* esencia

essential [ɪ'sɛnʃl] *adj* (*necessary*) imprescindible; (*basic*) esencial; **essentially** *adv* esencialmente; **essentials** *npl* lo imprescindible, lo esencial

establish [ɪ'stæblɪʃ] *vt* establecer; (*prove*) demostrar; (*relations*) entablar; (*reputation*) ganarse; **establishment** *n* establecimiento; **the Establishment** la clase dirigente

estate [ɪ'steɪt] *n* (*land*) finca, hacienda; (*inheritance*) herencia; (*BRIT: also:* **housing ~**) urbanización *f*; **estate agent** (*BRIT*) *n* agente *mf* inmobiliario/a; **estate car** (*BRIT*) *n* furgoneta

estimate [*n* 'ɛstɪmət, *vb* 'ɛstɪmeɪt] *n* estimación *f*, apreciación *f*; (*assessment*) tasa, cálculo; (*Comm*) presupuesto ▷ *vt* estimar, tasar; calcular

etc *abbr* (= *et cetera*) etc

eternal [ɪ'təːnl] *adj* eterno

eternity [ɪ'təːnɪtɪ] *n* eternidad *f*

ethical ['ɛθɪkl] *adj* ético; **ethics** ['ɛθɪks] *n* ética ▷ *npl* moralidad *f*

Ethiopia [iːθɪ'əupɪə] *n* Etiopía

ethnic ['ɛθnɪk] *adj* étnico; **ethnic minority** *n* minoría étnica

e-ticket ['iːtɪkɪt] *n* billete *m* electrónico (*SP*), boleto electrónico (*LAM*)

etiquette ['ɛtɪkɛt] *n* etiqueta

EU *n abbr* (= *European Union*) UE *f*

euro *n* euro

Europe ['juərəp] *n* Europa; **European** [-'piːən] *adj, n* europeo/a *m/f*; **European Community** *n* Comunidad *f* Europea; **European Union** *n* Unión *f* Europea

Eurostar® ['juərəustɑː*] *n* Eurostar® *m*

evacuate [ɪ'vækjueɪt] *vt* (*people*) evacuar; (*place*) desocupar

evade [ɪ'veɪd] *vt* evadir, eludir

evaluate [ɪ'væljueɪt] *vt* evaluar; (*value*) tasar; (*evidence*) interpretar

evaporate [ɪ'væpəreɪt] *vi* evaporarse; (*fig*) desvanecerse

eve [iːv] *n*: **on the ~ of** en vísperas de

even ['iːvn] *adj* (*level*) llano; (*smooth*) liso; (*speed, temperature*) uniforme; (*number*) par ▷ *adv* hasta, incluso; (*introducing a comparison*) aún, todavía; **~ if, ~ though** aunque +*subjun*; **~ more** aun más; **~ so** aun así; **not ~** ni siquiera; **~ he was there** hasta él estuvo allí; **~ on Sundays** incluso los domingos; **to get ~ with sb** ajustar cuentas con algn

evening ['i:vnɪŋ] n tarde f; (late) noche f; **in the ~** por la tarde; **evening class** n clase f nocturna; **evening dress** n (no pl: formal clothes) traje m de etiqueta; (woman's) traje m de noche

event [ɪ'vɛnt] n suceso, acontecimiento; (Sport) prueba; **in the ~ of** en caso de; **eventful** adj (life) activo; (day) ajetreado

eventual [ɪ'vɛntʃuəl] adj final

Be careful not to translate **eventual** by the Spanish word *eventual*.

eventually adv (finally) finalmente; (in time) con el tiempo

ever ['ɛvə*] adv (at any time) nunca, jamás; (at all times) siempre; (in question) **why ~ not?** ¿y por qué no?; **the best ~** lo nunca visto; **have you ~ seen it?** ¿lo ha visto usted alguna vez?; **better than ~** mejor que nunca; **~ since** adv desde entonces ▷ conj después de que; **evergreen** n árbol m de hoja perenne

○ **KEYWORD**

every ['ɛvrɪ] adj 1 (each) cada; **every one of them** (persons) todos ellos/as; (objects) cada uno de ellos/as; **every shop in the town was closed** todas las tiendas de la ciudad estaban cerradas

2 (all possible) todo/a; **I gave you every assistance** te di toda la ayuda posible; **I have every confidence in him** tiene toda mi confianza; **we wish you every success** te deseamos toda suerte de éxitos

3 (showing recurrence) todo/a; **every day/week** todos los días/todas las semanas; **every other car had been broken into** habían forzado uno de cada dos coches; **she visits me every other/third day** me visita cada dos/tres días; **every now and then** de vez en cuando

every: everybody pron = **everyone**; **everyday** adj (daily) cotidiano, de todos los días; (usual) acostumbrado; **everyone** pron todos/as, todo el mundo; **everything** pron todo; **this shop sells everything** esta tienda vende de todo; **everywhere** adv: **I've been looking for you everywhere** te he estado buscando por todas partes; **everywhere you go you meet ...** en todas partes encuentras ...

evict [ɪ'vɪkt] vt desahuciar

evidence ['ɛvɪdəns] n (proof) prueba; (of witness) testimonio; (sign) indicios mpl; **to give ~** prestar declaración, dar testimonio

evident ['ɛvɪdənt] adj evidente, manifiesto; **evidently** adv por lo visto

evil ['i:vl] adj malo; (influence) funesto ▷ n mal m

evoke [ɪ'vəuk] vt evocar

evolution [i:və'lu:ʃən] n evolución f

evolve [ɪ'vɒlv] vt desarrollar ▷ vi evolucionar, desarrollarse

ewe [ju:] n oveja

ex [ɛks] (inf) n: **my ~** mi ex

ex- [ɛks] prefix ex

exact [ɪg'zækt] adj exacto; (person) meticuloso ▷ vt: **to ~ sth (from)** exigir algo (de); **exactly** adv exactamente; (indicating agreement) exacto

exaggerate [ɪg'zædʒəreɪt] vt, vi exagerar; **exaggeration** [-'reɪʃən] n exageración f

exam [ɪg'zæm] n abbr (Scol) = **examination**

examination [ɪgzæmɪ'neɪʃən] n examen m; (Med) reconocimiento

examine [ɪg'zæmɪn] vt examinar; (inspect) inspeccionar, escudriñar; (Med) reconocer; **examiner** n examinador(a) m/f

example [ɪg'zɑ:mpl] n ejemplo; **for ~** por ejemplo

exasperated [ɪg'zɑ:spəreɪtɪd] adj exasperado

excavate ['ɛkskəveɪt] vt excavar

exceed [ɪk'si:d] vt (amount) exceder;

(*number*) pasar de; (*speed limit*) sobrepasar; (*powers*) excederse en; (*hopes*) superar; **exceedingly** *adv* sumamente, sobremanera

excel [ɪk'sɛl] *vi* sobresalir; **to ~ o.s** lucirse

excellence ['ɛksələns] *n* excelencia

excellent ['ɛksələnt] *adj* excelente

except [ɪk'sɛpt] *prep* (*also*: **~ for, ~ing**) excepto, salvo ▷ *vt* exceptuar, excluir; **~ if/when** excepto si/cuando; **~ that** salvo que; **exception** [ɪk'sɛpʃən] *n* excepción *f*; **to take exception to** ofenderse por; **exceptional** [ɪk'sɛpʃənl] *adj* excepcional; **exceptionally** [ɪk'sɛpʃənəlɪ] *adv* excepcionalmente, extraordinariamente

excerpt ['ɛksəːpt] *n* extracto

excess [ɪk'sɛs] *n* exceso; **excess baggage** *n* exceso de equipaje; **excessive** *adj* excesivo

exchange [ɪks'tʃeɪndʒ] *n* intercambio; (*conversation*) diálogo; (*also*: **telephone ~**) central *f* (telefónica) ▷ *vt*: **to ~ (for)** cambiar (por); **exchange rate** *n* tipo de cambio

excite [ɪk'saɪt] *vt* (*stimulate*) estimular; (*arouse*) excitar; **excited** *adj*: **to get excited** emocionarse; **excitement** *n* (*agitation*) excitación *f*; (*exhilaration*) emoción *f*; **exciting** *adj* emocionante

exclaim [ɪk'skleɪm] *vi* exclamar; **exclamation** [ɛksklə'meɪʃən] *n* exclamación *f*; **exclamation mark** *n* punto de admiración; **exclamation point** (*us*) = **exclamation mark**

exclude [ɪk'sklu:d] *vt* excluir; exceptuar

excluding [ɪks'klu:dɪŋ] *prep*: **~ VAT** IVA no incluido

exclusion [ɪk'sklu:ʒən] *n* exclusión *f*; **to the ~ of** con exclusión de

exclusive [ɪk'sklu:sɪv] *adj* exclusivo; (*club, district*) selecto; **~ of tax** excluyendo impuestos; **exclusively** *adv* únicamente

excruciating [ɪk'skru:ʃɪeɪtɪŋ] *adj* (*pain*) agudísimo, atroz; (*noise, embarrassment*) horrible

excursion [ɪk'skəːʃən] *n* (*tourist excursion*) excursión *f*

excuse [*n* ɪk'skju:s, *vb* ɪk'skju:z] *n* disculpa, excusa; (*pretext*) pretexto ▷ *vt* (*justify*) justificar; (*forgive*) disculpar, perdonar; **to ~ sb from doing sth** dispensar a algn de hacer algo; **~ me!** (*attracting attention*) ¡por favor!; (*apologizing*) ¡perdón!; **if you will ~ me** con su permiso

ex-directory ['ɛksdɪ'rɛktərɪ] (*BRIT*) *adj* que no consta en la guía

execute ['ɛksɪkju:t] *vt* (*plan*) realizar; (*order*) cumplir; (*person*) ajusticiar, ejecutar; **execution** [-'kju:ʃən] *n* realización *f*; cumplimiento; ejecución *f*

executive [ɪg'zɛkjutɪv] *n* (*person, committee*) ejecutivo; (*Pol: committee*) poder *m* ejecutivo ▷ *adj* ejecutivo

exempt [ɪg'zɛmpt] *adj*: **~ from** exento de ▷ *vt*: **to ~ sb from** eximir a algn de

exercise ['ɛksəsaɪz] *n* ejercicio ▷ *vt* (*patience*) usar de; (*right*) valerse de; (*dog*) llevar de paseo; (*mind*) preocupar ▷ *vi* (*also*: **to take ~**) hacer ejercicio(s); **exercise book** *n* cuaderno

exert [ɪg'zəːt] *vt* ejercer; **to ~ o.s** esforzarse; **exertion** [-ʃən] *n* esfuerzo

exhale [ɛks'heɪl] *vt* despedir ▷ *vi* exhalar

exhaust [ɪg'zɔːst] *n* (*Aut: also*: **~ pipe**) escape *m*; (: *fumes*) gases *mpl* de escape ▷ *vt* agotar; **exhausted** *adj* agotado; **exhaustion** [ɪg'zɔːstʃən] *n* agotamiento; **nervous exhaustion** postración *f* nerviosa

exhibit [ɪg'zɪbɪt] *n* (*Art*) obra expuesta; (*Law*) objeto expuesto ▷ *vt* (*show: emotions*) manifestar; (: *courage, skill*) demostrar; (*paintings*) exponer; **exhibition** [ɛksɪ'bɪʃən] *n* exposición *f*; (*of talent etc*) demostración *f*

exhilarating [ɪg'zɪləreɪtɪŋ] *adj* estimulante, tónico

exile ['ɛksaɪl] n exilio; (*person*) exiliado/a ▷ vt desterrar, exiliar

exist [ɪg'zɪst] vi existir; (*live*) vivir; **existence** n existencia; **existing** adj existente, actual

exit ['ɛksɪt] n salida ▷ vi (*Theatre*) hacer mutis; (*Comput*) salir (del sistema)

> ▌ Be careful not to translate **exit** by the Spanish word *éxito*.

exit ramp (us) n (*Aut*) vía de acceso

exotic [ɪg'zɔtɪk] adj exótico

expand [ɪk'spænd] vt ampliar; (*number*) aumentar ▷ vi (*population*) aumentar; (*trade etc*) expandirse; (*gas, metal*) dilatarse

expansion [ɪk'spænʃən] n (*of population*) aumento; (*of trade*) expansión f

expect [ɪk'spɛkt] vt esperar; (*require*) contar con; (*suppose*) suponer ▷ vi: **to be ~ing** (*pregnant woman*) estar embarazada; **expectation** [ɛkspɛk'teɪʃən] n (*hope*) esperanza; (*belief*) expectativa

expedition [ɛkspə'dɪʃən] n expedición f

expel [ɪk'spɛl] vt arrojar; (*from place*) expulsar

expenditure [ɪks'pɛndɪtʃə*] n gastos mpl, desembolso; consumo

expense [ɪk'spɛns] n gasto, gastos mpl; (*high cost*) costa; **expenses** npl (*Comm*) gastos mpl; **at the ~ of** a costa de; **expense account** n cuenta de gastos

expensive [ɪk'spɛnsɪv] adj caro, costoso

experience [ɪk'spɪərɪəns] n experiencia ▷ vt experimentar; (*suffer*) sufrir; **experienced** adj experimentado

experiment [ɪk'spɛrɪmənt] n experimento ▷ vi hacer experimentos; **experimental** [-'mɛntl] adj experimental; **the process is still at the experimental stage** el proceso está todavía en prueba

expert ['ɛkspə:t] adj experto, perito ▷ n experto/a, perito/a; (*specialist*) especialista mf; **expertise** [-'ti:z] n pericia

expire [ɪk'spaɪə*] vi caducar, vencer; **expiry** n vencimiento; **expiry date** n (*of medicine, food item*) fecha de caducidad

explain [ɪk'spleɪn] vt explicar; **explanation** [ɛksplə'neɪʃən] n explicación f

explicit [ɪk'splɪsɪt] adj explícito

explode [ɪk'spləud] vi estallar, explotar; (*population*) crecer rápidamente; (*with anger*) reventar

exploit [n 'ɛksplɔɪt, vb ɪk'splɔɪt] n hazaña ▷ vt explotar; **exploitation** [-'teɪʃən] n explotación f

explore [ɪk'splɔ:*] vt explorar; (*fig*) examinar; investigar; **explorer** n explorador(a) m/f

explosion [ɪk'spləuʒən] n explosión f; **explosive** [ɪks'pləusɪv] adj, n explosivo

export [vb ɛk'spɔ:t, n, cpd 'ɛkspɔ:t] vt exportar ▷ n (*process*) exportación f; (*product*) producto de exportación ▷ cpd de exportación; **exporter** n exportador m

expose [ɪk'spəuz] vt exponer; (*unmask*) desenmascarar; **exposed** adj expuesto

exposure [ɪk'spəuʒə*] n exposición f; (*publicity*) publicidad f; (*Phot: speed*) velocidad f de obturación; (: *shot*) fotografía; **to die from ~** (*Med*) morir de frío

express [ɪk'sprɛs] adj (*definite*) expreso, explícito; (BRIT: *letter etc*) urgente ▷ n (*train*) rápido ▷ vt expresar; **expression** [ɪk'sprɛʃən] n expresión f; (*of actor etc*) sentimiento; **expressway** (us) n (*urban motorway*) autopista

exquisite [ɛk'skwɪzɪt] adj exquisito

extend [ɪk'stɛnd] vt (*visit, street*) prolongar; (*building*) ampliar; (*invitation*) ofrecer ▷ vi (*land*) extenderse; (*period of time*) prolongarse

extension [ɪk'stɛnʃən] *n* extensión *f*; (*building*) ampliación *f*; (*of time*) prolongación *f*; (*Tel: in private house*) línea derivada; (: *in office*) extensión *f*; **extension lead** *n* alargador *m*, alargadera

extensive [ɪk'stɛnsɪv] *adj* extenso; (*damage*) importante; (*knowledge*) amplio

extent [ɪk'stɛnt] *n* (*breadth*) extensión *f*; (*scope*) alcance *m*; **to some ~** hasta cierto punto; **to the ~ of ...** hasta el punto de ...; **to such an ~ that ...** hasta tal punto que ...; **to what ~?** ¿hasta qué punto?

exterior [ɛk'stɪərɪə*] *adj* exterior, externo ▷ *n* exterior *m*

external [ɛk'stəːnl] *adj* externo

extinct [ɪk'stɪŋkt] *adj* (*volcano*) extinguido; (*race*) extinto; **extinction** *n* extinción *f*

extinguish [ɪk'stɪŋgwɪʃ] *vt* extinguir, apagar

extra ['ɛkstrə] *adj* adicional ▷ *adv* (*in addition*) de más ▷ *n* (*luxury, addition*) extra *m*; (*Cinema, Theatre*) extra *mf*, comparsa *mf*

extract [*vb* ɪk'strækt, *n* 'ɛkstrækt] *vt* sacar; (*tooth*) extraer; (*money, promise*) obtener ▷ *n* extracto

extradite ['ɛkstrədaɪt] *vt* extraditar

extraordinary [ɪk'strɔːdnrɪ] *adj* extraordinario; (*odd*) raro

extravagance [ɪk'strævəgəns] *n* derroche *m*, despilfarro; (*thing bought*) extravagancia

extravagant [ɪk'strævəgənt] *adj* (*lavish: person*) pródigo; (: *gift*) (demasiado) caro; (*wasteful*) despilfarrador(a)

extreme [ɪk'striːm] *adj* extremo, extremado ▷ *n* extremo; **extremely** *adv* sumamente, extremadamente

extremist [ɪk'striːmɪst] *adj, n* extremista *m/f*

extrovert ['ɛkstrəvəːt] *n* extrovertido/a

eye [aɪ] *n* ojo ▷ *vt* mirar de soslayo, ojear; **to keep an ~ on** vigilar; **eyeball** *n* globo ocular; **eyebrow** *n* ceja; **eyedrops** *npl* gotas *fpl* para los ojos, colino; **eyelash** *n* pestaña; **eyelid** *n* párpado; **eyeliner** *n* delineador *m* (de ojos); **eyeshadow** *n* sombreador *m* de ojos; **eyesight** *n* vista; **eye witness** *n* testigo *mf* presencial

f

F [ɛf] n (Mus) fa m

fabric ['fæbrɪk] n tejido, tela
  Be careful not to translate **fabric** by
  the Spanish word *fábrica*.

fabulous ['fæbjuləs] adj fabuloso

face [feɪs] n (Anat) cara, rostro;
  (of clock) esfera (SP), cara (LAM); (of
  mountain) cara, ladera; (of building)
  fachada ▷ vt (direction) estar de cara
  a; (situation) hacer frente a; (facts)
  aceptar; **~ down** (person, card) boca
  abajo; **to lose ~** desprestigiarse; **to
  make** or **pull a ~** hacer muecas; **in the
  ~ of** (difficulties etc) ante; **on the ~ of it**
  a primera vista; **~ to ~** cara a cara; **face
  up to** vt fus hacer frente a, arrostrar;
  face cloth (BRIT) n manopla; **face
  pack** n (BRIT) mascarilla

facial ['feɪʃəl] adj de la cara ▷ n
  (also: **beauty ~**) tratamiento facial,
  limpieza

facilitate [fə'sɪlɪteɪt] vt facilitar

facilities [fə'sɪlɪtɪz] npl (buildings)
  instalaciones fpl; (equipment) servicios
  mpl; **credit ~** facilidades fpl de crédito

fact [fækt] n hecho; **in ~** en realidad

faction ['fækʃən] n facción f

factor ['fæktə*] n factor m

factory ['fæktərɪ] n fábrica

factual ['fæktjuəl] adj basado en
  los hechos

faculty ['fækəltɪ] n facultad f;
  (US: teaching staff) personal m docente

fad [fæd] n novedad f, moda

fade [feɪd] vi desteñirse; (sound, smile)
  desvanecerse; (light) apagarse; (flower)
  marchitarse; (hope, memory) perderse;
  fade away vi (sound) apagarse

fag [fæg] (BRIT: inf) n (cigarette) pitillo
  (SP), cigarro

Fahrenheit ['fɑːrənhaɪt] n
  Fahrenheit m

fail [feɪl] vt (candidate, test) suspender
  (SP), reprobar (LAM); (memory etc) fallar a
  ▷ vi suspender (SP), reprobar (LAM); (be
  unsuccessful) fracasar; (strength, brakes)
  fallar; (light) acabarse; **to ~ to do sth**
  (neglect) dejar de hacer algo; (be unable)
  no poder hacer algo; **without ~** sin
  falta; **failing** n falta, defecto ▷ prep a
  falta de; **failure** ['feɪljə*] n fracaso;
  (person) fracasado/a; (mechanical
  etc) fallo

faint [feɪnt] adj débil; (recollection)
  vago; (mark) apenas visible ▷ n
  desmayo ▷ vi desmayarse; **to feel ~**
  estar mareado, marearse; **faintest**
  adj: **I haven't the faintest idea** no
  tengo la más remota idea; **faintly** adv
  débilmente; (vaguely) vagamente

fair [fɛə*] adj justo; (hair, person) rubio;
  (weather) bueno; (good enough) regular;
  (considerable) considerable ▷ adv
  (play) limpio ▷ n feria; (BRIT: funfair)
  parque m de atracciones; **fairground** n
  recinto ferial; **fair-haired** adj (person)
  rubio; **fairly** adv (justly) con justicia;
  (quite) bastante; **fair trade** n comercio
  justo; **fairway** n (Golf) calle f

fairy ['fɛərɪ] n hada; **fairy tale** n
  cuento de hadas

faith [feɪθ] n fe f; (trust) confianza;
  (sect) religión f; **faithful** adj

(*loyal: troops etc*) leal; (*spouse*) fiel; (*account*) exacto; **faithfully** *adv* fielmente; **yours faithfully** (*BRIT: in letters*) le saluda atentamente

fake [feɪk] *n* (*painting etc*) falsificación f; (*person*) impostor/a *m/f* ▷ *adj* falso ▷ *vt* fingir; (*painting etc*) falsificar

falcon ['fɔːlkən] *n* halcón *m*

fall [fɔːl] (*pt* **fell**, *pp* **fallen**) *n* caída; (*in price etc*) descenso; (*US*) otoño ▷ *vi* caer(se); (*price*) bajar, descender; **falls** *npl* (*waterfall*) cascada, salto de agua; **to ~ flat** (*on one's face*) caerse (boca abajo); (*plan*) fracasar; (*joke, story*) no hacer gracia; **fall apart** *vi* deshacerse; **fall down** *vi* (*person*) caerse; (*building, hopes*) derrumbarse; **fall for** *vt fus* (*trick*) dejarse engañar por; (*person*) enamorarse de; **fall off** *vi* caerse; (*diminish*) disminuir; **fall out** *vi* (*friends etc*) reñir; (*hair, teeth*) caerse; **fall over** *vi* caer(se); **fall through** *vi* (*plan, project*) fracasar

fallen ['fɔːlən] *pp of* **fall**

fallout ['fɔːlaut] *n* lluvia radioactiva

false [fɔːls] *adj* falso; **under ~ pretences** con engaños; **false alarm** *n* falsa alarma; **false teeth** (*BRIT*) *npl* dentadura postiza

fame [feɪm] *n* fama

familiar [fə'mɪlɪə*] *adj* conocido, familiar; (*tone*) de confianza; **to be ~ with** (*subject*) conocer (bien); **familiarize** [fə'mɪlɪəraɪz] *vt*: **to familiarize o.s. with** familiarizarse con

family ['fæmɪlɪ] *n* familia; **family doctor** *n* médico/a de cabecera; **family planning** *n* planificación f familiar

famine ['fæmɪn] *n* hambre f, hambruna

famous ['feɪməs] *adj* famoso, célebre

fan [fæn] *n* abanico; (*Elec*) ventilador *m*; (*of pop star*) fan *mf*; (*Sport*) hincha *mf* ▷ *vt* abanicar; (*fire, quarrel*) atizar

fanatic [fə'nætɪk] *n* fanático/a

fan belt *n* correa del ventilador

fan club *n* club *m* de fans

fancy ['fænsɪ] *n* (*whim*) capricho, antojo; (*imagination*) imaginación f ▷ *adj* (*luxury*) lujoso, de lujo ▷ *vt* (*feel like, want*) tener ganas de; (*imagine*) imaginarse; (*think*) creer; **to take a ~ to sb** tomar cariño a algn; **he fancies her** (*inf*) le gusta (ella) mucho; **fancy dress** *n* disfraz *m*

fan heater *n* calefactor *m* de aire

fantasize ['fæntəsaɪz] *vi* fantasear, hacerse ilusiones

fantastic [fæn'tæstɪk] *adj* (*enormous*) enorme; (*strange, wonderful*) fantástico

fantasy ['fæntəzɪ] *n* (*dream*) sueño; (*unreality*) fantasía

fanzine ['fænziːn] *n* fanzine *m*

FAQs *abbr* (= *frequently asked questions*) preguntas frecuentes

far [fɑː*] *adj* (*distant*) lejano ▷ *adv* lejos; (*much, greatly*) mucho; **~ away, ~ off** (a lo) lejos; **~ better** mucho mejor; **~ from** lejos de; **by ~** con mucho; **go as ~ as the farm** vaya hasta la granja; **as ~ as I know** que yo sepa; **how ~?** ¿hasta dónde?; (*fig*) ¿hasta qué punto?

farce [fɑːs] *n* farsa

fare [fɛə*] *n* (*on trains, buses*) precio (del billete); (*in taxi: cost*) tarifa; (*food*) comida; **half ~** medio pasaje *m*; **full ~** pasaje completo

Far East *n*: **the ~** el Extremo Oriente

farewell [fɛə'wɛl] *excl, n* adiós *m*

farm [fɑːm] *n* cortijo (*SP*), hacienda (*LAM*), rancho (*MEX*), estancia (*RPL*) ▷ *vt* cultivar; **farmer** *n* granjero, hacendado (*LAM*), ranchero (*MEX*), estanciero (*RPL*); **farmhouse** *n* granja, casa del hacendado (*LAM*), rancho (*MEX*), casco de la estancia (*RPL*); **farming** *n* agricultura; (*of crops*) cultivo; (*of animals*) cría; **farmyard** *n* corral *m*

far-reaching [fɑː'riːtʃɪŋ] *adj* (*reform, effect*) de gran alcance

fart [fɑːt] (*inf!*) *vi* tirarse un pedo (!)

farther ['fɑːðə*] *adv* más lejos, más allá ▷ *adj* más lejano

farthest ['fɑːðɪst] *superlative of* **far**

fascinate ['fæsɪneɪt] *vt* fascinar; **fascinated** *adj* fascinado

fascinating ['fæsɪneɪtɪŋ] *adj* fascinante

fascination [-'neɪʃən] *n* fascinación f

fascist ['fæʃɪst] *adj, n* fascista *m/f*

fashion ['fæʃən] *n* moda; (*fashion industry*) industria de la moda; (*manner*) manera ▷ *vt* formar; **in ~** a la moda; **out of ~** pasado de moda; **fashionable** *adj* de moda; **fashion show** *n* desfile *m* de modelos

fast [fɑːst] *adj* rápido; (*dye, colour*) resistente; (*clock*): **to be ~** estar adelantado ▷ *adv* rápidamente, de prisa; (*stuck, held*) firmemente ▷ *n* ayuno ▷ *vi* ayunar; **~ asleep** profundamente dormido

fasten ['fɑːsn] *vt* atar, sujetar; (*coat, belt*) abrochar ▷ *vi* atarse; abrocharse

fast food *n* comida rápida, platos *mpl* preparados

fat [fæt] *adj* gordo; (*book*) grueso; (*profit*) grande, pingüe ▷ *n* grasa; (*on person*) carnes *fpl*; (*lard*) manteca

fatal ['feɪtl] *adj* (*mistake*) fatal; (*injury*) mortal; **fatality** [fə'tælɪtɪ] *n* (*road death etc*) víctima; **fatally** *adv* fatalmente; mortalmente

fate [feɪt] *n* destino; (*of person*) suerte f

father ['fɑːðə*] *n* padre *m*; **Father Christmas** *n* Papá *m* Noel; **father-in-law** *n* suegro

fatigue [fə'tiːg] *n* fatiga, cansancio

fattening ['fætnɪŋ] *adj* (*food*) que hace engordar

fatty ['fætɪ] *adj* (*food*) graso ▷ *n* (*inf*) gordito/a, gordinflón/ona *m/f*

faucet ['fɔːsɪt] (*us*) *n* grifo (*sp*), llave f, canilla (*RPL*)

fault [fɔːlt] *n* (*blame*) culpa; (*defect: in person, machine*) defecto; (*Geo*) falla ▷ *vt* criticar; **it's my ~** es culpa mía; **to find ~ with** criticar, poner peros a; **at ~** culpable; **faulty** *adj* defectuoso

fauna ['fɔːnə] *n* fauna

favour *etc* ['feɪvə*] (*us* **favor** *etc*) *n* favor *m*; (*approval*) aprobación f ▷ *vt* (*proposition*) estar a favor de, aprobar; (*assist*) ser propicio a; **to do sb a ~** hacer un favor a algn; **to find ~ with sb** caer en gracia a algn; **in ~ of** a favor de; **favourable** *adj* favorable; **favourite** ['feɪvrɪt] *adj, n* favorito, preferido

fawn [fɔːn] *n* cervato ▷ *adj* (*also*: **~-coloured**) color de cervato, leonado ▷ *vi*: **to ~ (up)on** adular

fax [fæks] *n* (*document*) fax *m*; (*machine*) telefax *m* ▷ *vt* mandar por telefax

FBI (*us*) *n abbr* (= *Federal Bureau of Investigation*) ≈ BIC f (*SP*)

fear [fɪə*] *n* miedo, temor *m* ▷ *vt* tener miedo de, temer; **for ~ of** por si; **fearful** *adj* temeroso, miedoso; (*awful*) terrible; **fearless** *adj* audaz

feasible ['fiːzəbl] *adj* factible

feast [fiːst] *n* banquete *m*; (*Rel: also*: **~ day**) fiesta ▷ *vi* festejar

feat [fiːt] *n* hazaña

feather ['feðə*] *n* pluma

feature ['fiːtʃə*] *n* característica; (*article*) artículo de fondo ▷ *vt* (*film*) presentar ▷ *vi*: **to ~ in** tener un papel destacado en; **features** *npl* (*of face*) facciones *fpl*; **feature film** *n* largometraje *m*

Feb. *abbr* (= *February*) feb

February ['fɛbruərɪ] *n* febrero

fed [fɛd] *pt, pp of* **feed**

federal ['fɛdərəl] *adj* federal

federation [fɛdə'reɪʃən] *n* federación f

fed up [fɛd'ʌp] *adj*: **to be ~ (with)** estar harto (de)

fee [fiː] *n* pago; (*professional*) derechos *mpl*, honorarios *mpl*; (*of club*) cuota; **school ~s** matrícula

feeble ['fiːbl] *adj* débil; (*joke*) flojo

feed [fiːd] *n* (*pt, pp* **fed**) *n* comida; (*of animal*) pienso; (*on printer*) dispositivo de alimentación ▷ *vt* alimentar; (*BRIT: baby: breastfeed*) dar el pecho a; (*animal*) dar de comer a; (*data,*

information): **to ~ into** meter en;
feedback *n* reacción *f*, feedback *m*
feel [fi:l] (*pt, pp* **felt**) *n* (*sensation*)
sensación *f*; (*sense of touch*) tacto;
(*impression*): **to have the ~ of** parecerse
a ▷ *vt* tocar; (*pain etc*) sentir; (*think,
believe*) creer; **to ~ hungry/cold** tener
hambre/frío; **to ~ lonely/better**
sentirse solo/mejor; **I don't ~ well**
no me siento bien; **it ~s soft** es suave
al tacto; **to ~ like** (*want*) tener ganas
de; **feeling** *n* (*physical*) sensación *f*;
(*foreboding*) presentimiento; (*emotion*)
sentimiento
feet [fi:t] *npl of* **foot**
fell [fɛl] *pt of* **fall** ▷ *vt* (*tree*) talar
fellow ['fɛləu] *n* tipo, tío (*SP*);
(*comrade*) compañero; (*of learned
society*) socio/a; **fellow citizen** *n*
conciudadano/a; **fellow countryman**
(*irreg*) *n* compatriota *m*; **fellow men**
npl semejantes *mpl*; **fellowship** *n*
compañerismo; (*grant*) beca
felony ['fɛlənɪ] *n* crimen *m*
felt [fɛlt] *pt, pp of* **feel** ▷ *n* fieltro;
felt-tip *n* (*also*: **felt-tip pen**)
rotulador *m*
female ['fi:meɪl] *n* (*pej*: *woman*) mujer
f, tía; (*Zool*) hembra ▷ *adj* femenino;
hembra
feminine ['fɛmɪnɪn] *adj* femenino
feminist ['fɛmɪnɪst] *n* feminista
fence [fɛns] *n* valla, cerca ▷ *vt* (*also*: **~
in**) cercar ▷ *vi* (*Sport*) hacer esgrima;
fencing *n* esgrima
fend [fɛnd] *vi*: **to ~ for o.s.** valerse por
sí mismo; **fend off** *vt* (*attack*) rechazar;
(*questions*) evadir
fender ['fɛndə*] (*US*) *n* guardafuego;
(*Aut*) parachoques *m inv*
fennel ['fɛnl] *n* hinojo
ferment [*vb* fə'mɛnt, *n* 'fə:mɛnt] *vi*
fermentar ▷ *n* (*fig*) agitación *f*
fern [fə:n] *n* helecho
ferocious [fə'rəuʃəs] *adj* feroz
ferret ['fɛrɪt] *n* hurón *m*
ferry ['fɛrɪ] *n* (*small*) barca (de pasaje),
balsa; (*large*: *also*: **~boat**) transbordador

m, ferry *m* ▷ *vt* transportar
fertile ['fə:taɪl] *adj* fértil; (*Biol*)
fecundo; **fertilize** ['fə:tɪlaɪz] *vt* (*Biol*)
fecundar; (*Agr*) abonar; **fertilizer** *n*
abono
festival ['fɛstɪvəl] *n* (*Rel*) fiesta; (*Art,
Mus*) festival *m*
festive ['fɛstɪv] *adj* festivo; **the ~
season** (*BRIT*: *Christmas*) las Navidades
fetch [fɛtʃ] *vt* ir a buscar; (*sell for*)
venderse por
fête [feɪt] *n* fiesta
fetus ['fi:təs] (*US*) *n* = **foetus**
feud [fju:d] *n* (*hostility*) enemistad *f*;
(*quarrel*) disputa
fever ['fi:və*] *n* fiebre *f*; **feverish**
adj febril
few [fju:] *adj* (*not many*) pocos ▷ *pron*
pocos; algunos; **a ~** *adj* unos pocos,
algunos; **fewer** *adj* menos; **fewest** *adj*
los(las) menos
fiancé [fɪ'ã:ŋseɪ] *n* novio, prometido;
fiancée *n* novia, prometida
fiasco [fɪ'æskəu] *n* fiasco
fib [fɪb] *n* mentirilla
fibre ['faɪbə*] (*US* **fiber**) *n* fibra;
fibreglass (*US* **Fiberglass**®) *n* fibra
de vidrio
fickle ['fɪkl] *adj* inconstante
fiction ['fɪkʃən] *n* ficción *f*; **fictional**
adj novelesco
fiddle ['fɪdl] *n* (*Mus*) violín *m*;
(*cheating*) trampa ▷ *vt* (*BRIT*: *accounts*)
falsificar; **fiddle with** *vt fus* juguetear
con
fidelity [fɪ'dɛlɪtɪ] *n* fidelidad *f*
field [fi:ld] *n* campo; (*fig*) campo,
esfera; (*Sport*) campo (*SP*), cancha (*LAM*);
field marshal *n* mariscal *m*
fierce [fɪəs] *adj* feroz; (*wind, heat*)
fuerte; (*fighting, enemy*) encarnizado
fifteen [fɪf'ti:n] *num* quince;
fifteenth *adj* decimoquinto; **the
fifteenth floor** la planta quince;
the fifteenth of August el quince
de agosto
fifth [fɪfθ] *num* quinto
fiftieth ['fɪftɪɪθ] *adj* quincuagésimo

fifty ['fɪftɪ] *num* cincuenta; **fifty-fifty** *adj* (*deal, split*) a medias ▷ *adv* a medias, mitad por mitad

fig [fɪg] *n* higo

fight [faɪt] (*pt, pp* **fought**) *n* (*gen*) pelea; (*Mil*) combate *m*; (*struggle*) lucha ▷ *vt* luchar contra; (*cancer, alcoholism*) combatir; (*election*) intentar ganar; (*emotion*) resistir ▷ *vi* pelear, luchar; **fight back** *vi* defenderse; (*after illness*) recuperarse ▷ *vt* (*tears*) contener; **fight off** *vt* (*attack, attacker*) rechazar; (*disease, sleep, urge*) luchar contra; **fighting** *n* combate *m*, pelea

figure ['fɪgə*] *n* (*Drawing, Geom*) figura, dibujo; (*number, cipher*) cifra; (*body, outline*) tipo; (*personality*) figura ▷ *vt* (*esp US*) imaginar ▷ *vi* (*appear*) figurar; **figure out** *vt* (*work out*) resolver

file [faɪl] *n* (*tool*) lima; (*dossier*) expediente *m*; (*folder*) carpeta; (*Comput*) fichero; (*row*) fila ▷ *vt* limar; (*Law: claim*) presentar; (*store*) archivar; **filing cabinet** *n* fichero, archivador *m*

Filipino [fɪlɪ'pi:nəu] *adj* filipino ▷ *n* (*person*) filipino/a *m/f*; (*Ling*) tagalo

fill [fɪl] *vt* (*space*): **to ~ (with)** llenar (de); (*vacancy, need*) cubrir ▷ *n*: **to eat one's ~** llenarse; **fill in** *vt* rellenar; **fill out** *vt* (*form, receipt*) rellenar; **fill up** *vt* llenar (hasta el borde) ▷ *vi* (*Aut*) poner gasolina

fillet ['fɪlɪt] *n* filete *m*; **fillet steak** *n* filete *m* de ternera

filling ['fɪlɪŋ] *n* (*Culin*) relleno; (*for tooth*) empaste *m*; **filling station** *n* estación *f* de servicio

film [fɪlm] *n* película ▷ *vt* (*scene*) filmar ▷ *vi* rodar (una película); **film star** *n* astro, estrella de cine

filter ['fɪltə*] *n* filtro ▷ *vt* filtrar; **filter lane** (*BRIT*) *n* carril *m* de selección

filth [fɪlθ] *n* suciedad *f*; **filthy** *adj* sucio; (*language*) obsceno

fin [fɪn] *n* (*gen*) aleta

final ['faɪnl] *adj* (*last*) final, último; (*definitive*) definitivo, terminante ▷ *n* (*BRIT Sport*) final *f*; **finals** *npl* (*Scol*) examen *m* final; (*US Sport*) final *f*

finale [fɪ'nɑ:lɪ] *n* final *m*

final: finalist *n* (*Sport*) finalista *mf*; **finalize** *vt* concluir, completar; **finally** *adv* (*lastly*) por último, finalmente; (*eventually*) por fin

finance [faɪ'næns] *n* (*money*) fondos *mpl* ▷ *vt* financiar; **finances** *npl* finanzas *fpl*; (*personal finances*) situación *f* económica; **financial** [-'nænʃəl] *adj* financiero; **financial year** *n* ejercicio (financiero)

find [faɪnd] (*pt, pp* **found**) *vt* encontrar, hallar; (*come upon*) descubrir ▷ *n* hallazgo; descubrimiento; **to ~ sb guilty** (*Law*) declarar culpable a algn; **find out** *vt* averiguar; (*truth, secret*) descubrir; **to find out about** (*subject*) informarse sobre; (*by chance*) enterarse de; **findings** *npl* (*Law*) veredicto, fallo; (*of report*) recomendaciones *fpl*

fine [faɪn] *adj* excelente; (*thin*) fino ▷ *adv* (*well*) bien ▷ *n* (*Law*) multa ▷ *vt* (*Law*) multar; **to be ~** (*person*) estar bien; (*weather*) hacer buen tiempo; **fine arts** *npl* bellas artes *fpl*

finger ['fɪŋgə*] *n* dedo ▷ *vt* (*touch*) manosear; **little/index ~** (dedo) meñique *m*/índice *m*; **fingernail** *n* uña; **fingerprint** *n* huella dactilar; **fingertip** *n* yema del dedo

finish ['fɪnɪʃ] *n* (*end*) fin *m*; (*Sport*) meta; (*polish etc*) acabado ▷ *vt, vi* terminar; **to ~ doing sth** acabar de hacer algo; **to ~ third** llegar el tercero; **finish off** *vt* acabar, terminar; (*kill*) acabar con; **finish up** *vt* acabar, terminar ▷ *vi* ir a parar, terminar

Finland ['fɪnlənd] *n* Finlandia

Finn [fɪn] *n* finlandés/esa *m/f*; **Finnish** *adj* finlandés/esa ▷ *n* (*Ling*) finlandés *m*

fir [fə:*] *n* abeto

fire ['faɪə*] *n* fuego; (*in hearth*) lumbre *f*; (*accidental*) incendio; (*heater*) estufa ▷ *vt* (*gun*) disparar; (*interest*) despertar; (*inf: dismiss*) despedir ▷ *vi* (*shoot*)

disparar; **on ~** ardiendo, en llamas;
fire alarm n alarma de incendios;
firearm n arma de fuego; **fire brigade**
(US **fire department**) n (cuerpo de)
bomberos mpl; **fire engine** (BRIT) n
coche m de bomberos; **fire escape**
n escalera de incendios; **fire exit** n
salida de incendios; **fire extinguisher**
n extintor m (de incendios); **fireman**
(irreg) n bombero; **fireplace** n
chimenea; **fire station** n parque m
de bomberos; **firetruck** (US) n = **fire
engine**; **firewall** n (Internet) firewall
m; **firewood** n leña; **fireworks** npl
fuegos mpl artificiales
firm [fə:m] adj firme; (look, voice)
resuelto ▷ n firma, empresa; **firmly**
adv firmemente; resueltamente
first [fə:st] adj primero ▷ adv (before
others) primero; (when listing reasons
etc) en primer lugar, primeramente
▷ n (person: in race) primero/a; (Aut)
primera; (BRIT Scol) título de licenciado
con calificación de sobresaliente; **at ~** al
principio; **~ of all** ante todo; **first aid** n
primera ayuda, primeros auxilios mpl;
first-aid kit n botiquín m; **first-class**
adj (excellent) de primera (categoría);
(ticket etc) de primera clase; **first-hand**
adj de primera mano; **first lady** n
(esp US) primera dama; **firstly** adv en
primer lugar; **first name** n nombre m
(de pila); **first-rate** adj estupendo
fiscal ['fɪskəl] adj fiscal; **fiscal year** n
año fiscal, ejercicio
fish [fɪʃ] n inv pez m; (food) pescado
▷ vt, vi pescar; **to go ~ing** ir de pesca;
~ and chips pescado frito con patatas
fritas; **fisherman** (irreg) n pescador
m; **fish fingers** (BRIT) npl croquetas
fpl de pescado; **fishing** n pesca;
fishing boat n barca de pesca; **fishing
line** n sedal m; **fishmonger** n (BRIT)
pescadero/a; **fishmonger's (shop)**
(BRIT) n pescadería; **fish sticks** (US)
npl = **fish fingers**; **fishy** (inf) adj
sospechoso
fist [fɪst] n puño

fit [fɪt] adj (healthy) en (buena)
forma; (proper) adecuado, apropiado
▷ vt (clothes) estar or sentar bien a;
(instal) poner; (equip) proveer, dotar;
(facts) cuadrar or corresponder con
▷ vi (clothes) sentar bien; (in space,
gap) caber; (facts) coincidir ▷ n (Med)
ataque m; **~ to** (ready) a punto de; **~ for**
apropiado para; **a ~ of anger/pride**
un arranque de cólera/orgullo; **this
dress is a good ~** este vestido me
sienta bien; **by ~s and starts** a rachas;
fit in vi (fig: person) llevarse bien
(con todos); **fitness** n (Med) salud
f; **fitted** adj (jacket, shirt) entallado;
(sheet) de cuatro picos; **fitted carpet**
n moqueta; **fitted kitchen** n cocina
amueblada; **fitting** adj apropiado ▷ n
(of dress) prueba; (of piece of equipment)
instalación f; **fitting room** n probador
m; **fittings** npl instalaciones fpl
five [faɪv] num cinco; **fiver** (inf) n
(BRIT) billete m de cinco libras; (US)
billete m de cinco dólares
fix [fɪks] vt (secure) fijar, asegurar;
(mend) arreglar; (prepare) preparar
▷ n: **to be in a ~** estar en un aprieto; **fix
up** vt (meeting) arreglar; **to fix sb up
with sth** proveer a algn de algo; **fixed**
adj (prices etc) fijo; **fixture** n (Sport)
encuentro
fizzy ['fɪzɪ] adj (drink) gaseoso
flag [flæg] n bandera; (stone) losa ▷ vi
decaer ▷ vt: **to ~ sb down** hacer señas
a algn para que se pare; **flagpole** n
asta de bandera
flair [flɛə*] n aptitud f especial
flak [flæk] n (Mil) fuego antiaéreo;
(inf: criticism) lluvia de críticas
flake [fleɪk] n (of rust, paint) escama;
(of snow, soap powder) copo ▷ vi (also: ~
off) desconcharse
flamboyant [flæm'bɔɪənt] adj
(dress) vistoso; (person)
extravagante
flame [fleɪm] n llama
flamingo [flə'mɪŋgəʊ] n flamenco
flammable ['flæməbl] adj

inflamable

flan [flæn] (BRIT) n tarta

▮ Be careful not to translate **flan** by the Spanish word *flan*.

flank [flæŋk] n (*of animal*) ijar m; (*of army*) flanco ▷ vt flanquear

flannel ['flænl] n (BRIT: *also*: **face ~**) manopla; (*fabric*) franela

flap [flæp] n (*of pocket, envelope*) solapa ▷ vt (*wings, arms*) agitar ▷ vi (*sail, flag*) ondear

flare [flɛə*] n llamarada; (*Mil*) bengala; (*in skirt etc*) vuelo; **flares** npl (*trousers*) pantalones mpl de campana; **flare up** vi encenderse; (*fig: person*) encolerizarse; (: *revolt*) estallar

flash [flæʃ] n relámpago; (*also*: **news ~**) noticias fpl de última hora; (*Phot*) flash m ▷ vt (*light, headlights*) lanzar un destello con; (*news, message*) transmitir; (*smile*) lanzar ▷ vi brillar; (*hazard light etc*) lanzar destellos; **in a ~** en un instante; **he ~ed by** or **past** pasó como un rayo; **flashback** n (*Cinema*) flashback m; **flashbulb** n bombilla fusible; **flashlight** n linterna

flask [flɑːsk] n frasco; (*also*: **vacuum ~**) termo

flat [flæt] adj llano; (*smooth*) liso; (*tyre*) desinflado; (*battery*) descargado; (*beer*) muerto; (*refusal etc*) rotundo; (*Mus*) desafinado; (*rate*) fijo ▷ n (BRIT: *apartment*) piso (SP), departamento (LAM), apartamento; (*Aut*) pinchazo; (*Mus*) bemol m; **to work ~ out** trabajar a toda mecha; **flatten** vt (*also*: **flatten out**) allanar; (*smooth out*) alisar; (*building, plants*) arrasar

flatter ['flætə*] vt adular, halagar; **flattering** adj halagüeño; (*dress*) que favorece

flaunt [flɔːnt] vt ostentar, lucir

flavour etc ['fleɪvə*] (US **flavor** etc) n sabor m, gusto ▷ vt sazonar, condimentar; **strawberry-flavoured** con sabor a fresa; **flavouring** n (*in product*) aromatizante m

flaw [flɔː] n defecto; **flawless** adj

impecable

flea [fliː] n pulga; **flea market** n rastro, mercadillo

flee [fliː] (*pt, pp* **fled**) vt huir de ▷ vi huir, fugarse

fleece [fliːs] n vellón m; (*wool*) lana; (*top*) forro polar ▷ vt (*inf*) desplumar

fleet [fliːt] n flota; (*of lorries etc*) escuadra

fleeting ['fliːtɪŋ] adj fugaz

Flemish ['flɛmɪʃ] adj flamenco

flesh [flɛʃ] n carne f; (*skin*) piel f; (*of fruit*) pulpa

flew [fluː] pt of **fly**

flex [flɛks] n cordón m ▷ vt (*muscles*) tensar; **flexibility** n flexibilidad f; **flexible** adj flexible; **flexitime** (US **flextime**) n horario flexible

flick [flɪk] n capirotazo; chasquido ▷ vt (*with hand*) dar un capirotazo a; (*whip etc*) chasquear; (*switch*) accionar; **flick through** vt fus hojear

flicker ['flɪkə*] vi (*light*) parpadear; (*flame*) vacilar

flies [flaɪz] npl of **fly**

flight [flaɪt] n vuelo; (*escape*) huida, fuga; (*also*: **~ of steps**) tramo (de escaleras); **flight attendant** n auxiliar mf de vuelo

flimsy ['flɪmzɪ] adj (*thin*) muy ligero; (*building*) endeble; (*excuse*) flojo

flinch [flɪntʃ] vi encogerse; **to ~ from** retroceder ante

fling [flɪŋ] (*pt, pp* **flung**) vt arrojar

flint [flɪnt] n pedernal m; (*in lighter*) piedra

flip [flɪp] vt dar la vuelta a; (*switch: turn on*) encender; (*turn*) apagar; (*coin*) echar a cara o cruz

flip-flops ['flɪpflɔps] npl (*esp* BRIT) chancletas fpl

flipper ['flɪpə*] n aleta

flirt [flɜːt] vi coquetear, flirtear ▷ n coqueta

float [fləut] n flotador m; (*in procession*) carroza; (*money*) reserva ▷ vi flotar; (*swimmer*) hacer la plancha

flock [flɔk] n (*of sheep*) rebaño; (*of*

birds) bandada ▷ *vi*: **to ~ to** acudir
en tropel a
flood [flʌd] *n* inundación *f*; (*of
letters, imports etc*) avalancha ▷ *vt*
inundar ▷ *vi* (*place*) inundarse;
(*people*): **to ~ into** inundar; **flooding** *n*
inundaciones *fpl*; **floodlight** *n* foco
floor [flɔ:*] *n* suelo; (*storey*) piso; (*of
sea*) fondo ▷ *vt* (*question*) dejar sin
respuesta; (: *blow*) derribar; **ground ~,
first ~** (*us*) planta baja; **first ~, second
~** (*us*) primer piso; **floorboard** *n* tabla;
flooring *n* suelo; (*material*) solería;
floor show *n* cabaret *m*
flop [flɔp] *n* fracaso ▷ *vi* (*fail*)
fracasar; (*fall*) derrumbarse; **floppy** *adj*
flojo ▷ *n* (*Comput: also*: **floppy disk**)
floppy *m*
flora ['flɔ:rə] *n* flora
floral ['flɔ:rl] *adj* (*pattern*) floreado
florist ['flɔrɪst] *n* florista *mf*; **florist's
(shop)** *n* floristería
flotation [fləu'teɪʃən] *n* (*of shares*)
emisión *f*; (*of company*) lanzamiento
flour ['flauə*] *n* harina
flourish ['flʌrɪʃ] *vi* florecer ▷ *n*
ademán *m*, movimiento (ostentoso)
flow [fləu] *n* (*movement*) flujo; (*of
traffic*) circulación *f*; (*tide*) corriente *f*
▷ *vi* (*river, blood*) fluir; (*traffic*) circular
flower ['flauə*] *n* flor *f* ▷ *vi* florecer;
flower bed *n* macizo; **flowerpot**
n tiesto
flown [fləun] *pp of* **fly**
fl. oz. *abbr* (= *fluid ounce*)
flu [flu:] *n*: **to have ~** tener la gripe
fluctuate ['flʌktjueɪt] *vi* fluctuar
fluent ['flu:ənt] *adj* (*linguist*) que
habla perfectamente; (*speech*)
elocuente; **he speaks ~ French, he's ~
in French** domina el francés
fluff [flʌf] *n* pelusa; **fluffy** *adj* de
pelo suave
fluid ['flu:ɪd] *adj* (*movement*) fluido,
líquido; (*situation*) inestable ▷ *n* fluido,
líquido; **fluid ounce** *n* onza *f* líquida
fluke [flu:k] (*inf*) *n* chiripa
flung [flʌŋ] *pt, pp of* **fling**

fluorescent [fluə'rɛsnt] *adj*
fluorescente
fluoride ['fluəraɪd] *n* fluoruro
flurry ['flʌrɪ] *n* (*of snow*) temporal *m*; **~
of activity** frenesí *m* de actividad
flush [flʌʃ] *n* rubor *m*; (*fig: of youth
etc*) resplandor *m* ▷ *vt* limpiar con
agua ▷ *vi* ruborizarse ▷ *adj*: **~ with** a
ras de; **to ~ the toilet** hacer funcionar
la cisterna
flute [flu:t] *n* flauta
flutter ['flʌtə*] *n* (*of wings*) revoloteo,
aleteo; (*fig*): **a ~ of panic/excitement**
una oleada de pánico/excitación ▷ *vi*
revolotear
fly [flaɪ] (*pt* **flew**, *pp* **flown**) *n* mosca;
(*on trousers: also*: **flies**) bragueta ▷ *vt*
(*plane*) pilot(e)ar; (*cargo*) transportar
(en avión); (*distances*) recorrer (en
avión) ▷ *vi* volar; (*passengers*) ir en
avión; (*escape*) evadirse; (*flag*) ondear;
fly away, fly off *vi* emprender el
vuelo; **fly-drive** *n*: **fly-drive holiday**
*vacaciones que incluyen vuelo y alquiler
de coche*; **flying** *n* (*activity*) (el) volar;
(*action*) vuelo ▷ *adj*: **flying visit** visita
relámpago; **with flying colours** con
lucimiento; **flying saucer** *n* platillo
volante; **flyover** (*BRIT*) *n* paso a
desnivel *or* superior
FM *abbr* (*Radio*) (= *frequency modulation*)
FM
foal [fəul] *n* potro
foam [fəum] *n* espuma ▷ *vi* hacer
espuma
focus ['fəukəs] (*pl* **-es**) *n* foco; (*centre*)
centro ▷ *vt* (*field glasses etc*) enfocar
▷ *vi*: **to ~ (on)** enfocar (a); (*issue etc*)
centrarse en; **in/out of ~** enfocado/
desenfocado
foetus ['fi:təs] (*us* **fetus**) *n* feto
fog [fɔg] *n* niebla; **foggy** *adj*: **it's
foggy** hay niebla, está brumoso;
fog lamp (*us* **fog light**) *n* (*Aut*) faro
de niebla
foil [fɔɪl] *vt* frustrar ▷ *n* hoja; (*kitchen
foil*) papel *m* (de) aluminio; (*complement*)
complemento; (*Fencing*) florete *m*

fold [fəuld] n (bend, crease) pliegue
m; (Agr) redil m ▷vt doblar; (arms)
cruzar; **fold up** vi plegarse, doblarse;
(business) quebrar ▷vt (map etc) plegar;
folder n (for papers) carpeta; (Comput)
directorio; **folding** adj (chair, bed)
plegable

foliage ['fəulɪɪdʒ] n follaje m

folk [fəuk] npl gente f ▷adj popular,
folklórico; **folks** npl (family) familia sg,
parientes mpl; **folklore** ['fəuklɔː*] n
folklore m; **folk music** n música folk;
folk song n canción f popular

follow ['fɔləu] vt seguir ▷vi seguir;
(result) resultar; **to ~ suit** hacer lo
mismo; **follow up** vt (letter, offer)
responder a; (case) investigar; **follower**
n (of person, belief) partidario/a;
following adj siguiente ▷n afición
f, partidarios mpl; **follow-up** n
continuación f

fond [fɔnd] adj (memory, smile etc)
cariñoso; (hopes) ilusorio; **to be ~
of** tener cariño a; (pastime, food) ser
aficionado a

food [fuːd] n comida; **food mixer**
n batidora; **food poisoning** n
intoxicación f alimenticia; **food
processor** n robot m de cocina; **food
stamp** (US) n vale m para comida

fool [fuːl] n tonto/a; (Culin) puré m de
frutas con nata ▷vt engañar ▷vi (gen)
bromear; **fool about, fool around**
vi hacer el tonto; **foolish** adj tonto;
(careless) imprudente; **foolproof** adj
(plan etc) infalible

foot [fut] (pl **feet**) n pie m; (measure)
pie m (= 304 m); (of animal) pata ▷vt
(bill) pagar; **on ~** a pie; **footage** n
(Cinema) imágenes fpl; **foot-and-
mouth (disease)** [futənd'mauθ-]
n fiebre f aftosa; **football** n balón
m; (game: BRIT) fútbol m; (: US) fútbol
m americano; **footballer** n (BRIT) =
football player; **football match** n
partido de fútbol; **football player** n
(BRIT) futbolista mf; (US) jugador m
de fútbol americano; **footbridge** n

puente m para peatones; **foothills**
npl estribaciones fpl; **foothold** n pie
m firme; **footing** n (fig) posición f;
to lose one's footing perder el pie;
footnote n nota (al pie de la página);
footpath n sendero; **footprint** n
huella, pisada; **footstep** n paso;
footwear n calzado

○ **KEYWORD**

for [fɔː] prep **1** (indicating destination,
intention) para; **the train for London** el
tren con destino a or de Londres; **he left
for Rome** marchó para Roma; **he went
for the paper** fue por el periódico; **is
this for me?** ¿es esto para mí?; **it's time
for lunch** es la hora de comer
2 (indicating purpose) para; **what('s it)
for?** ¿para qué (es)?; **to pray for peace**
rezar por la paz
3 (on behalf of, representing): **the MP
for Hove** el diputado por Hove; **he
works for the government/a local
firm** trabaja para el gobierno/en una
empresa local; **I'll ask him for you** se
lo pediré por ti; **G for George** G de
Gerona
4 (because of) por esta razón; **for fear
of being criticized** por temor a ser
criticado
5 (with regard to) para; **it's cold for
July** hace frío para julio; **he has a gift
for languages** tiene don de lenguas
6 (in exchange for) por; **I sold it for £5**
lo vendí por £5; **to pay 50 pence for a
ticket** pagar 50 peniques por un billete
7 (in favour of): **are you for or
against us?** ¿estás con nosotros o
contra nosotros?; **I'm all for it** estoy
totalmente a favor; **vote for X** vote
(a) X
8 (referring to distance): **there are
roadworks for 5 km** hay obras en 5
km; **we walked for miles** caminamos
kilómetros y kilómetros
9 (referring to time): **he was away for
two years** estuvo fuera (durante) dos

años; **it hasn't rained for 3 weeks** no ha llovido durante *or* en 3 semanas; **I have known her for years** la conozco desde hace años; **can you do it for tomorrow?** ¿lo podrás hacer para mañana?
10 (*with infinitive clauses*): **it is not for me to decide** la decisión no es cosa mía; **it would be best for you to leave** sería mejor que te fueras; **there is still time for you to do it** todavía te queda tiempo para hacerlo; **for this to be possible ...** para que esto sea posible ...
11 (*in spite of*) a pesar de; **for all his complaints** a pesar de sus quejas ▷ *conj* (*since, as*: *rather formal*) puesto que

forbid [fəˈbɪd] (*pt* **forbad(e)**, *pp* **forbidden**) *vt* prohibir; **to ~ sb to do sth** prohibir a algn hacer algo; **forbidden** *pt of* **forbid** ▷ *adj* (*food, area*) prohibido; (*word, subject*) tabú
force [fɔːs] *n* fuerza ▷ *vt* forzar; (*push*) meter a la fuerza; **to ~ o.s. to do** hacer un esfuerzo por hacer; **forced** *adj* forzado; **forceful** *adj* enérgico
ford [fɔːd] *n* vado
fore [fɔː*] *n*: **to come to the ~** empezar a destacar; **forearm** *n* antebrazo; **forecast** (*pt, pp* **forecast**) *n* pronóstico ▷ *vt* pronosticar; **forecourt** *n* patio; **forefinger** *n* (dedo) índice *m*; **forefront** *n*: **in the forefront of** en la vanguardia de; **foreground** *n* primer plano; **forehead** [ˈfɒrɪd] *n* frente *f*
foreign [ˈfɒrɪn] *adj* extranjero; (*trade*) exterior; (*object*) extraño; **foreign currency** *n* divisas *fpl*; **foreigner** *n* extranjero/a; **foreign exchange** *n* divisas *fpl*; **Foreign Office** (*BRIT*) *n* Ministerio de Asuntos Exteriores; **Foreign Secretary** (*BRIT*) *n* Ministro de Asuntos Exteriores
fore: foreman (*irreg*) *n* capataz *m*; (*in construction*) maestro de obras; **foremost** *adj* principal ▷ *adv*: **first**

and foremost ante todo; **forename** *n* nombre *m* (de pila)
forensic [fəˈrɛnsɪk] *adj* forense
foresee [fɔːˈsiː] (*pt* **foresaw**, *pp* **foreseen**) *vt* prever; **foreseeable** *adj* previsible
forest [ˈfɒrɪst] *n* bosque *m*; **forestry** *n* silvicultura
forever [fəˈrɛvə*] *adv* para siempre; (*endlessly*) constantemente
foreword [ˈfɔːwəːd] *n* prefacio
forfeit [ˈfɔːfɪt] *vt* perder
forgave [fəˈgeɪv] *pt of* **forgive**
forge [fɔːdʒ] *n* herrería ▷ *vt* (*signature, money*) falsificar; (*metal*) forjar; **forger** *n* falsificador(a) *m/f*; **forgery** *n* falsificación *f*
forget [fəˈgɛt] (*pt* **forgot**, *pp* **forgotten**) *vt* olvidar ▷ *vi* olvidarse; **forgetful** *adj* despistado
forgive [fəˈgɪv] (*pt* **forgave**, *pp* **forgiven**) *vt* perdonar; **to ~ sb for sth** perdonar algo a algn
forgot [fəˈgɒt] *pt of* **forget**
forgotten [fəˈgɒtn] *pp of* **forget**
fork [fɔːk] *n* (*for eating*) tenedor *m*; (*for gardening*) horca; (*of roads*) bifurcación *f* ▷ *vi* (*road*) bifurcarse
forlorn [fəˈlɔːn] *adj* (*person*) triste, melancólico; (*place*) abandonado; (*attempt, hope*) desesperado
form [fɔːm] *n* forma; (*BRIT Scol*) clase *f*; (*document*) formulario ▷ *vt* formar; (*idea*) concebir; (*habit*) adquirir; **in top ~** en plena forma; **to ~ a queue** hacer cola
formal [ˈfɔːməl] *adj* (*offer, receipt*) por escrito; (*person etc*) correcto; (*occasion, dinner*) de etiqueta; (*dress*) correcto; (*garden*) (de estilo) clásico; **formality** [-ˈmælɪtɪ] *n* (*procedure*) trámite *m*; corrección *f*; etiqueta
format [ˈfɔːmæt] *n* formato ▷ *vt* (*Comput*) formatear
formation [fɔːˈmeɪʃən] *n* formación *f*
former [ˈfɔːmə*] *adj* anterior; (*earlier*) antiguo; (*ex*) ex; **the ~ ... the latter ...** aquél ... éste ...; **formerly** *adv* antes

formidable ['fɔ:mɪdəbl] *adj*
formidable

formula ['fɔ:mjulə] *n* fórmula

fort [fɔ:t] *n* fuerte *m*

forthcoming [fɔ:θ'kʌmɪŋ] *adj*
próximo, venidero; (*help, information*)
disponible; (*character*) comunicativo

fortieth ['fɔ:tɪɪθ] *adj* cuadragésimo

fortify ['fɔ:tɪfaɪ] *vt* (*city*) fortificar;
(*person*) fortalecer

fortnight ['fɔ:tnaɪt] (*BRIT*) *n* quince
días *mpl*; quincena; **fortnightly** *adj*
de cada quince días, quincenal ▷ *adv*
cada quince días, quincenalmente

fortress ['fɔ:trɪs] *n* fortaleza

fortunate ['fɔ:tʃənɪt] *adj*
afortunado; **it is ~ that ...** (es una)
suerte que ...; **fortunately** *adv*
afortunadamente

fortune ['fɔ:tʃən] *n* suerte *f*; (*wealth*)
fortuna; **fortune-teller** *n* adivino/a

forty ['fɔ:tɪ] *num* cuarenta

forum ['fɔ:rəm] *n* foro

forward ['fɔ:wəd] *adj* (*movement,
position*) avanzado; (*front*) delantero;
(*in time*) adelantado; (*not shy*) atrevido
▷ *n* (*Sport*) delantero ▷ *vt* (*letter*)
remitir; (*career*) promocionar; **to move
~** avanzar; **forwarding address** *n*
destinatario; **forward(s)** *adv* (hacia)
adelante; **forward slash** *n* barra
diagonal

fossil ['fɔsl] *n* fósil *m*

foster ['fɔstə*] *vt* (*child*) acoger en
una familia; fomentar; **foster child** *n*
hijo/a adoptivo/a; **foster mother** *n*
madre *f* adoptiva

fought [fɔ:t] *pt, pp of* fight

foul [faul] *adj* sucio, puerco; (*weather,
smell etc*) asqueroso; (*language*) grosero;
(*temper*) malísimo ▷ *n* (*Sport*) falta
▷ *vt* (*dirty*) ensuciar; **foul play** *n* (*Law*)
muerte *f* violenta

found [faund] *pt, pp of* find ▷ *vt*
fundar; **foundation** [-'deɪʃən]
n (*act*) fundación *f*; (*basis*) base *f*;
(*also*: **foundation cream**) crema
base; **foundations** *npl* (*of building*)

cimientos *mpl*

founder ['faundə*] *n* fundador(a) *m/f*
▷ *vi* hundirse

fountain ['fauntɪn] *n* fuente *f*;
fountain pen *n* (pluma) estilográfica
(*SP*), pluma-fuente *f* (*LAM*)

four [fɔ:*] *num* cuatro; **on all ~s** a
gatas; **four-letter word** *n* taco; **four-
poster** *n* (*also*: **four-poster bed**) cama
de columnas; **fourteen** *num* catorce;
fourteenth *adj* decimocuarto; **fourth**
num cuarto; **four-wheel drive** *n*
tracción *f* a las cuatro ruedas

fowl [faul] *n* ave *f* (de corral)

fox [fɔks] *n* zorro ▷ *vt* confundir

foyer ['fɔɪeɪ] *n* vestíbulo

fraction ['frækʃən] *n* fracción *f*

fracture ['fræktʃə*] *n* fractura

fragile ['frædʒaɪl] *adj* frágil

fragment ['frægmənt] *n* fragmento

fragrance ['freɪɡrəns] *n* fragancia

frail [freɪl] *adj* frágil; (*person*) débil

frame [freɪm] *n* (*Tech*) armazón *m*;
(*of person*) cuerpo; (*of picture, door etc*)
marco; (*of spectacles: also*: **~s**) montura
▷ *vt* enmarcar; **framework** *n* marco

France [frɑ:ns] *n* Francia

franchise ['fræntʃaɪz] *n* (*Pol*) derecho
de votar, sufragio; (*Comm*) licencia,
concesión *f*

frank [fræŋk] *adj* franco ▷ *vt* (*letter*)
franquear; **frankly** *adv* francamente

frantic ['fræntɪk] *adj* (*distraught*)
desesperado; (*hectic*) frenético

fraud [frɔ:d] *n* fraude *m*; (*person*)
impostor(a) *m/f*

fraught [frɔ:t] *adj*: **~ with** lleno de

fray [freɪ] *vi* deshilacharse

freak [fri:k] *n* (*person*) fenómeno;
(*event*) suceso anormal

freckle ['frɛkl] *n* peca

free [fri:] *adj* libre; (*gratis*) gratuito
▷ *vt* (*prisoner etc*) poner en libertad;
(*jammed object*) soltar; **~ (of charge),
for ~** gratis; **freedom** *n* libertad
f; **Freefone®** *n* número gratuito;
free gift *n* prima; **free kick** *n* tiro
libre; **freelance** *adj* independiente

▷ *adv* por cuenta propia; **freely** *adv*
libremente; (*liberally*) generosamente;
Freepost® *n* porte *m* pagado;
free-range *adj* (*hen, eggs*) de granja;
freeway (*US*) *n* autopista; **free will** *n*
libre albedrío; **of one's own free will**
por su propia voluntad

freeze [fri:z] (*pt* **froze**, *pp* **frozen**) *vi*
(*weather*) helar; (*liquid, pipe, person*)
helarse, congelarse ▷ *vt* helar; (*food,
prices, salaries*) congelar ▷ *n* helada; (*on
arms, wages*) congelación *f*; **freezer** *n*
congelador *m*, freezer *m* (*SC*)

freezing ['fri:zɪŋ] *adj* helado; **three
degrees below ~** tres grados bajo
cero; **freezing point** *n* punto de
congelación

freight [freɪt] *n* (*goods*) carga; (*money
charged*) flete *m*; **freight train** (*US*) *n*
tren *m* de mercancías

French [frɛntʃ] *adj* francés/esa ▷ *n*
(*Ling*) francés *m*; **the French** *npl* los
franceses; **French bean** *n* judía
verde; **French bread** *n* pan *m* francés;
French dressing *n* (*Culin*) vinagreta;
French fried potatoes, French fries
(*US*) *npl* patatas *fpl* (*SP*) or papas *fpl*
(*LAM*) fritas; **Frenchman** (*irreg*) *n*
francés *m*; **Frenchwoman** (*irreg*) *n*
francésa; **French stick** *n* barra de pan;
French window *n* puerta de cristal

frenzy ['frɛnzɪ] *n* frenesí *m*

frequency ['fri:kwənsɪ] *n* frecuencia

frequent [*adj* 'fri:kwənt, *vb*
frɪ'kwɛnt] *adj* frecuente ▷ *vt*
frecuentar; **frequently** [-əntlɪ] *adv*
frecuentemente, a menudo

fresh [frɛʃ] *adj* fresco; (*bread*) tierno;
(*new*) nuevo; **freshen** *vi* (*wind, air*)
soplar más recio; **freshen up** *vi*
(*person*) arreglarse, lavarse; **fresher**
(*BRIT: inf*) *n* (*Univ*) estudiante *mf* de
primer año; **freshly** *adv* (*made, painted
etc*) recién; **freshman** (*US: irreg*) *n* =
fresher; **freshwater** *adj* (*fish*) de
agua dulce

fret [frɛt] *vi* inquietarse

Fri *abbr* (= *Friday*) vier

friction ['frɪkʃən] *n* fricción *f*

Friday ['fraɪdɪ] *n* viernes *m inv*

fridge [frɪdʒ] (*BRIT*) *n* frigorífico
(*SP*), nevera (*SP*), refrigerador *m* (*LAM*),
heladera (*RPL*)

fried [fraɪd] *adj* frito

friend [frɛnd] *n* amigo/a; **friendly**
adj simpático; (*government*) amigo;
(*place*) acogedor(a); (*match*) amistoso;
friendship *n* amistad *f*

fries [fraɪz] (*esp US*) *npl* = **French fried
potatoes**

frigate ['frɪgɪt] *n* fragata

fright [fraɪt] *n* (*terror*) terror *m*; (*scare*)
susto; **to take ~** asustarse; **frighten**
vt asustar; **frightened** *adj* asustado;
frightening *adj* espantoso; **frightful**
adj espantoso, horrible

frill [frɪl] *n* volante *m*

fringe [frɪndʒ] *n* (*BRIT: of hair*)
flequillo; (*on lampshade etc*) flecos *mpl*;
(*of forest etc*) borde *m*, margen *m*

Frisbee® ['frɪzbɪ] *n* frisbee® *m*

fritter ['frɪtə*] *n* buñuelo

frivolous ['frɪvələs] *adj* frívolo

fro [frəu] *see* **to**

frock [frɔk] *n* vestido

frog [frɔg] *n* rana; **frogman** (*irreg*) *n*
hombre-rana *m*

○ **KEYWORD**

from [frɔm] *prep* **1** (*indicating starting
place*) de, desde; **where do you come
from?** ¿de dónde eres?; **from London
to Glasgow** de Londres a Glasgow;
to escape from sth/sb escaparse de
algo/algn
2 (*indicating origin etc*) de; **a letter/
telephone call from my sister** una
carta/llamada de mi hermana; **tell
him from me that ...** dígale de mi
parte que ...
3 (*indicating time*): **from one o'clock
to** *or* **until** *or* **till two** de(sde) la una a
or hasta las dos; **from January (on)** a
partir de enero
4 (*indicating distance*) de; **the hotel is**

1 km from the beach el hotel está a 1 km de la playa
5 (*indicating price, number etc*) de; **prices range from £10 to £50** los precios van desde £10 a *or* hasta £50; **the interest rate was increased from 9% to 10%** el tipo de interés fue incrementado de un 9% a un 10%
6 (*indicating difference*) de; **he can't tell red from green** no sabe distinguir el rojo del verde; **to be different from sb/sth** ser diferente a algn/algo
7 (*because of, on the basis of*): **from what he says** por lo que dice; **weak from hunger** debilitado por el hambre

front [frʌnt] *n* (*foremost part*) parte *f* delantera; (*of house*) fachada; (*of dress*) delantero; (*promenade: also:* **sea ~**) paseo marítimo; (*Mil, Pol, Meteorology*) frente *m*; (*fig: appearances*) apariencias *fpl* ▷ *adj* (*wheel, leg*) delantero; (*row, line*) primero; **in ~ (of)** delante (de); **front door** *n* puerta principal; **frontier** ['frʌntiə*] *n* frontera; **front page** *n* primera plana; **front-wheel drive** *n* tracción *f* delantera
frost [frɔst] *n* helada; (*also:* **hoar~**) escarcha; **frostbite** *n* congelación *f*; **frosting** *n* (*esp US: icing*) glaseado *m*; **frosty** *adj* (*weather*) de helada; (*welcome etc*) glacial
froth [frɔθ] *n* espuma
frown [fraun] *vi* fruncir el ceño
froze [frəuz] *pt of* **freeze**
frozen ['frəuzn] *pp of* **freeze**
fruit [fru:t] *n inv* fruta; fruto; (*fig*) fruto; resultados *mpl*; **fruit juice** *n* zumo (SP) *or* jugo (LAM) de fruta; **fruit machine** (BRIT) *n* máquina *f* tragaperras; **fruit salad** *n* macedonia (SP) *or* ensalada (LAM) de frutas
frustrate [frʌs'treɪt] *vt* frustrar; **frustrated** *adj* frustrado
fry [fraɪ] (*pt, pp* **fried**) *vt* freír; **small ~** gente *f* menuda; **frying pan** *n* sartén *f*
ft. *abbr* =**foot; feet**
fudge [fʌdʒ] *n* (*Culin*) caramelo blando

fuel [fjuəl] *n* (*for heating*) combustible *m*; (*coal*) carbón *m*; (*wood*) leña; (*for engine*) carburante *m*; **fuel tank** *n* depósito (de combustible)
fulfil [ful'fɪl] *vt* (*function*) cumplir con; (*condition*) satisfacer; (*wish, desire*) realizar
full [ful] *adj* lleno; (*fig*) pleno; (*complete*) completo; (*maximum*) máximo; (*information*) detallado; (*price*) íntegro; (*skirt*) amplio ▷ *adv*: **to know ~ well that** saber perfectamente que; **I'm ~ (up)** no puedo más; **~ employment** pleno empleo; **a ~ two hours** dos horas completas; **at ~ speed** a máxima velocidad; **in ~** (*reproduce, quote*) íntegramente; **full-length** *adj* (*novel etc*) entero; (*coat*) largo; (*portrait*) de cuerpo entero; **full moon** *n* luna llena; **full-scale** *adj* (*attack, war*) en gran escala; (*model*) de tamaño natural; **full stop** *n* punto; **full-time** *adj* (*work*) de tiempo completo ▷ *adv*: **to work full-time** trabajar a tiempo completo; **fully** *adv* completamente; (*at least*) por lo menos
fumble ['fʌmbl] *vi*: **to ~ with** manejar torpemente
fume [fju:m] *vi* (*rage*) estar furioso; **fumes** *npl* humo, gases *mpl*
fun [fʌn] *n* (*amusement*) diversión *f*; **to have ~** divertirse; **for ~** en broma; **to make ~ of** burlarse de
function ['fʌŋkʃən] *n* función *f* ▷ *vi* funcionar
fund [fʌnd] *n* fondo; (*reserve*) reserva; **funds** *npl* (*money*) fondos *mpl*
fundamental [fʌndə'mɛntl] *adj* fundamental
funeral ['fju:nərəl] *n* (*burial*) entierro; (*ceremony*) funerales *mpl*; **funeral director** *n* director(a) *m/f* de pompas fúnebres; **funeral parlour** (BRIT) *n* funeraria
funfair ['fʌnfɛə*] (BRIT) *n* parque *m* de atracciones
fungus ['fʌŋgəs] (*pl* **fungi**) *n* hongo; (*mould*) moho

funnel ['fʌnl] *n* embudo; *(of ship)* chimenea

funny ['fʌnɪ] *adj* gracioso, divertido; *(strange)* curioso, raro

fur [fə:*] *n* piel *f*; *(BRIT: in kettle etc)* sarro; **fur coat** *n* abrigo de pieles

furious ['fjʊərɪəs] *adj* furioso; *(effort)* violento

furnish ['fə:nɪʃ] *vt* amueblar; *(supply)* suministrar; *(information)* facilitar; **furnishings** *npl* muebles *mpl*

furniture ['fə:nɪtʃə*] *n* muebles *mpl*; **piece of ~** mueble *m*

furry ['fə:rɪ] *adj* peludo

further ['fə:ðə*] *adj* *(new)* nuevo, adicional ▷ *adv* más lejos; *(more)* más; *(moreover)* además ▷ *vt* promover, adelantar; **further education** *n* educación *f* superior; **furthermore** *adv* además

furthest ['fə:ðɪst] *superlative of* **far**

fury ['fjʊərɪ] *n* furia

fuse [fju:z] *(us* **fuze***)* *n* fusible *m*; *(for bomb etc)* mecha ▷ *vt* *(metal)* fundir; *(fig)* fusionar ▷ *vi* fundirse; fusionarse; *(BRIT Elec)*: **to ~ the lights** fundir los plomos; **fuse box** *n* caja de fusibles

fusion ['fju:ʒən] *n* fusión *f*

fuss [fʌs] *n* *(excitement)* conmoción *f*; *(trouble)* alboroto; **to make a ~** armar un lío *or* jaleo; **to make a ~ of sb** mimar a algn; **fussy** *adj* *(person)* exigente; *(too ornate)* recargado

future ['fju:tʃə*] *adj* futuro; *(coming)* venidero ▷ *n* futuro; *(prospects)* porvenir *m*; **in ~** de ahora en adelante; **futures** *npl* *(Comm)* operaciones *fpl* a término, futuros *mpl*

fuze [fju:z] *(us)* = **fuse**

fuzzy ['fʌzɪ] *adj* *(Phot)* borroso; *(hair)* muy rizado

G [dʒi:] *n* *(Mus)* sol *m*

g. *abbr* (= *gram(s)*) gr

gadget ['gædʒɪt] *n* aparato

Gaelic ['geɪlɪk] *adj, n* *(Ling)* gaélico

gag [gæg] *n* *(on mouth)* mordaza; *(joke)* chiste *m* ▷ *vt* amordazar

gain [geɪn] *n*: **~ (in)** aumento (de); *(profit)* ganancia ▷ *vt* ganar ▷ *vi* *(watch)* adelantarse; **to ~ from/by sth** sacar provecho de algo; **to ~ on sb** ganar terreno a algn; **to ~ 3 lbs (in weight)** engordar 3 libras

gal. *abbr* = **gallon**

gala ['gɑ:lə] *n* fiesta

galaxy ['gæləksɪ] *n* galaxia

gale [geɪl] *n* *(wind)* vendaval *m*

gall bladder ['gɔ:l-] *n* vesícula biliar

gallery ['gælərɪ] *n* *(also:* **art ~**: *public)* pinacoteca; *(: private)* galería de arte; *(for spectators)* tribuna

gallon ['gæln] *n* galón *m* *(BRIT = 4,546 litros, US = 3,785 litros)*

gallop ['gæləp] *n* galope *m* ▷ *vi* galopar

gallstone ['gɔ:lstəun] *n* cálculo

biliario

gamble ['gæmbl] n (risk) riesgo
▷ vt jugar, apostar ▷ vi (take a risk)
jugárselas; (bet) apostar; **to ~ on**
apostar a; (success etc) contar con;
gambler n jugador(a) m/f; **gambling**
n juego

game [geɪm] n juego; (match)
partido; (of cards) partida; (Hunting)
caza ▷ adj (willing): **to be ~ for
anything** atreverse a todo; **big ~** caza
mayor (contest) juegos; (BRIT: Scol)
deportes mpl; **games console**
[geɪmz-] n consola de juegos; **game
show** n programa m concurso m,
concurso

gammon ['gæmən] n (bacon) tocino
ahumado; (ham) jamón m ahumado

gang [gæŋ] n (of criminals) pandilla;
(of friends etc) grupo; (of workmen)
brigada

gangster ['gæŋstə*] n gángster m

gap [gæp] n vacío (SP), hueco (LAM);
(in trees, traffic) claro; (in time) intervalo;
(difference): **~ (between)** diferencia
(entre)

gape [geɪp] vi mirar boquiabierto;
(shirt etc) abrirse (completamente)

gap year n año sabático (antes de
empezar a estudiar en la universidad)

garage ['gærɑːʒ] n garaje m; (for
repairs) taller m; **garage sale** n venta
de objetos usados (en el jardín de una
casa particular)

garbage ['gɑːbɪdʒ] (US) n basura;
(inf: nonsense) tonterías fpl; **garbage
can** n cubo or bote m (MEX) or tacho
(SC) de la basura; **garbage collector**
(US) n basurero/a

garden ['gɑːdn] n jardín m; **gardens**
npl (park) parque m; **garden centre**
(BRIT) n centro de jardinería;
gardener n jardinero/a; **gardening**
n jardinería

garlic ['gɑːlɪk] n ajo

garment ['gɑːmənt] n prenda (de
vestir)

garnish ['gɑːnɪʃ] vt (Culin) aderezar

garrison ['gærɪsn] n guarnición f

gas [gæs] n gas m; (fuel) combustible
m; (US: gasoline) gasolina ▷ vt asfixiar
con gas; **gas cooker** (BRIT) n cocina de
gas; **gas cylinder** n bombona de gas;
gas fire n estufa de gas

gasket ['gæskɪt] n (Aut) junta de
culata

gasoline ['gæsəliːn] (US) n gasolina

gasp [gɑːsp] n boqueada; (of shock etc)
grito sofocado ▷ vi (pant) jadear

gas: gas pedal n (esp US) acelerador
m; **gas station** (US) n gasolinera;
gas tank (US) n (Aut) depósito (de
gasolina)

gate [geɪt] n puerta; (iron gate) verja

gateau ['gætəʊ] (pl ~x) n tarta

gatecrash ['geɪtkræʃ] (BRIT) vt
colarse en

gateway ['geɪtweɪ] n puerta

gather ['gæðə*] vt (flowers, fruit)
coger (SP), recoger; (assemble) reunir;
(pick up) recoger; (Sewing) fruncir;
(understand) entender ▷ vi (assemble)
reunirse; **to ~ speed** ganar velocidad;
gathering n reunión f, asamblea

gauge [geɪdʒ] n (instrument)
indicador m ▷ vt medir; (fig) juzgar

gave [geɪv] pt of **give**

gay [geɪ] adj (homosexual) gay; (joyful)
alegre; (colour) vivo

gaze [geɪz] n mirada fija ▷ vi: **to ~ at
sth** mirar algo fijamente

GB abbr = **Great Britain**

GCSE (BRIT) n abbr (= General Certificate
of Secondary Education) examen de
reválida que se hace a los 16 años

gear [gɪə*] n equipo, herramientas
fpl; (Tech) engranaje m; (Aut) velocidad
f, marcha ▷ vt (fig: adapt): **to ~ sth to**
adaptar or ajustar algo a; **top** or **high
(US)/low ~** cuarta/primera velocidad;
in ~ en marcha; **gear up** vi prepararse;
gear box n caja de cambios; **gear
lever** n palanca de cambio; **gear
shift** (US) n = **gear lever**; **gear stick**
(BRIT) palanca de cambios

geese [giːs] npl of **goose**

gel [dʒɛl] n gel m

gem [dʒɛm] n piedra preciosa

Gemini ['dʒɛmɪnaɪ] n Géminis m,
Gemelos mpl

gender ['dʒɛndə*] n género

gene [dʒiːn] n gen(e) m

general ['dʒɛnrl] n general m ▷ adj
general; **in ~** en general; **general
anaesthetic** (us **general anesthetic**)
n anestesia general; **general
election** n elecciones fpl generales;
generalize vi generalizar; **generally**
adv generalmente, en general; **general
practitioner** n médico general;
general store n tienda (que vende de
todo) (LAM, SP), almacén m (SC, SP)

generate ['dʒɛnəreɪt] vt (Elec)
generar; (jobs, profits) producir

generation [dʒɛnə'reɪʃən] n
generación f

generator ['dʒɛnəreɪtə*] n
generador m

generosity [dʒɛnə'rɒsɪtɪ] n
generosidad f

generous ['dʒɛnərəs] adj generoso

genetic [dʒɪ'nɛtɪk] adj: **~ engineering**
ingeniería genética; **~ fingerprinting**
identificación f genética; **genetically
modified** adj transgénico; **genetics**
n genética

genitals ['dʒɛnɪtlz] npl (órganos mpl)
genitales mpl

genius ['dʒiːnɪəs] n genio

genome ['giːnəum] n genoma m

gent [dʒɛnt] n abbr (BRIT inf)
= gentleman

gentle ['dʒɛntl] adj apacible, dulce;
(animal) manso; (breeze, curve etc) suave

▌Be careful not to translate **gentle** by
the Spanish word gentil.

gentleman ['dʒɛntlmən] (irreg) n
señor m; (well-bred man) caballero

gently ['dʒɛntlɪ] adv dulcemente;
suavemente

gents [dʒɛnts] n aseos mpl (de
caballeros)

genuine ['dʒɛnjuɪn] adj auténtico;
(person) sincero; **genuinely** adv

sinceramente

geographic(al) [dʒɪə'græfɪk(l)] adj
geográfico

geography [dʒɪ'ɔgrəfɪ] n geografía

geology [dʒɪ'ɔlədʒɪ] n geología

geometry [dʒɪ'ɔmətrɪ] n geometría

geranium [dʒɪ'reɪnjəm] n geranio

geriatric [dʒɛrɪ'ætrɪk] adj, n
geriátrico/a

germ [dʒəːm] n (microbe) microbio,
bacteria; (seed, fig) germen m

German ['dʒəːmən] adj alemán/ana
▷ n alemán/ana m/f; (Ling) alemán m;
German measles n rubéola

Germany ['dʒəːmənɪ] n Alemania

gesture ['dʒɛstjə*] n gesto; (symbol)
muestra

○ **KEYWORD**

get [gɛt] (pt, pp **got**, pp **gotten** (US)) vi
1 (become, be) ponerse, volverse; **to get
old/tired** envejecer/cansarse; **to get
drunk** emborracharse; **to get dirty**
ensuciarse; **to get married** casarse;
when do I get paid? ¿cuándo me
pagan or se me paga?; **it's getting late**
se está haciendo tarde

2 (go): **to get to/from** llegar a/de; **to
get home** llegar a casa

3 (begin) empezar a; **to get to know sb**
(llegar a) conocer a algn; **I'm getting
to like him** me está empezando a
gustar; **let's get going** or **started**
¡vamos (a empezar)!

4 (modal aux vb): **you've got to do it**
tienes que hacerlo

▷ vt **1**: **to get sth done** (finish) terminar
algo; (have done) mandar hacer algo; **to
get one's hair cut** cortarse el pelo; **to
get the car going** or **to go** arrancar el
coche; **to get sb to do sth** conseguir
or hacer que algn haga algo; **to get
sth/sb ready** preparar algo/a algn

2 (obtain: money, permission, results)
conseguir; (find: job, flat) encontrar;
(fetch: person, doctor) buscar; (object)
ir a buscar, traer; **to get sth for sb**

conseguir algo para algn; **get me Mr Jones, please** (*Tel*) póngame (*SP*) or comuníqueme (*LAM*) con el Sr. Jones, por favor; **can I get you a drink?** ¿quieres algo de beber?

3 (*receive: present, letter*) recibir; (*acquire: reputation*) alcanzar; (: *prize*) ganar; **what did you get for your birthday?** ¿qué te regalaron por tu cumpleaños?; **how much did you get for the painting?** ¿cuánto sacaste por el cuadro?

4 (*catch*) coger (*SP*), agarrar (*LAM*); (*hit: target etc*) dar en; **to get sb by the arm/throat** coger or agarrar a algn por el brazo/cuello; **get him!** ¡cógelo! (*SP*), ¡atrápalo! (*LAM*); **the bullet got him in the leg** la bala le dio en la pierna

5 (*take, move*) llevar; **to get sth to sb** hacer llegar algo a algn; **do you think we'll get it through the door?** ¿crees que lo podremos meter por la puerta?

6 (*catch, take: plane, bus etc*) coger (*SP*), tomar (*LAM*); **where do I get the train for Birmingham?** ¿dónde se coge or se toma el tren para Birmingham?

7 (*understand*) entender; (*hear*) oír; **I've got it!** ¡ya lo tengo!, ¡eureka!; **I don't get your meaning** no te entiendo; **I'm sorry, I didn't get your name** lo siento, no cogí tu nombre

8 (*have, possess*): **to have got** tener

get away *vi* marcharse; (*escape*) escaparse

get away with *vt fus* hacer impunemente

get back *vi* (*return*) volver ▷ *vt* recobrar

get in *vi* entrar; (*train*) llegar; (*arrive home*) volver a casa, regresar

get into *vt fus* entrar en; (*vehicle*) subir a; **to get into a rage** enfadarse

get off *vi* (*from train etc*) bajar; (*depart: person, car*) marcharse ▷ *vt* (*remove*) quitar ▷ *vt fus* (*train, bus*) bajar de

get on *vi* (*at exam etc*): **how are you getting on?** ¿cómo te va?; (*agree*): **to**

get on (with) llevarse bien (con) ▷ *vt fus* subir a

get out *vi* salir; (*of vehicle*) bajar ▷ *vt* sacar

get out of *vt fus* salir de; (*duty etc*) escaparse de

get over *vt fus* (*illness*) recobrarse de

get through *vi* (*Tel*) (lograr) comunicarse

get up *vi* (*rise*) levantarse ▷ *vt fus* subir

getaway ['gɛtəweɪ] *n* fuga
Ghana ['gɑːnə] *n* Ghana
ghastly ['gɑːstlɪ] *adj* horrible
ghetto ['gɛtəu] *n* gueto
ghost [gəust] *n* fantasma *m*
giant ['dʒaɪənt] *n* gigante *mf* ▷ *adj* gigantesco, gigante
gift [gɪft] *n* regalo; (*ability*) talento; **gifted** *adj* dotado; **gift shop** (*US* **gift store**) *n* tienda de regalos; **gift token, gift voucher** *n* vale *m* canjeable por un regalo
gig [gɪg] *n* (*inf: concert*) actuación *f*
gigabyte ['dʒɪgəbaɪt] *n* gigabyte *m*
gigantic [dʒaɪ'gæntɪk] *adj* gigantesco
giggle ['gɪgl] *vi* reírse tontamente
gills [gɪlz] *npl* (*of fish*) branquias *fpl*, agallas *fpl*
gilt [gɪlt] *adj, n* dorado
gimmick ['gɪmɪk] *n* truco
gin [dʒɪn] *n* ginebra
ginger ['dʒɪndʒə*] *n* jengibre *m*
gipsy ['dʒɪpsɪ] *n* = **gypsy**
giraffe [dʒɪ'rɑːf] *n* jirafa
girl [gəːl] *n* (*small*) niña; (*young woman*) chica, joven *f*, muchacha; (*daughter*) hija; **an English ~** una (chica) inglesa; **girl band** *n* girl band *m* (*grupo musical de chicas*); **girlfriend** *n* (*of girl*) amiga; (*of boy*) novia; **Girl Scout** (*US*) *n* = **Girl Guide**
gist [dʒɪst] *n* lo esencial
give [gɪv] (*pt* **gave**, *pp* **given**) *vt* dar; (*deliver*) entregar; (*as gift*) regalar ▷ *vi* (*break*) romperse; (*stretch: fabric*) dar

de sí; **to ~ sb sth, ~ sth to sb** dar
algo a algn; **give away** vt (give free)
regalar; (betray) traicionar; (disclose)
revelar; **give back** vt devolver; **give
in** vi ceder ▷ vt entregar; **give out** vt
distribuir; **give up** vi rendirse, darse
por vencido ▷ vt renunciar a; **to give
up smoking** dejar de fumar; **to give
o.s. up** entregarse

given ['gɪvn] pp of **give** ▷ adj
(fixed: time, amount) determinado
▷ conj: **~ (that) ...** dado (que) ...; **~
the circumstances ...** dadas las
circunstancias ...

glacier ['glæsɪə*] n glaciar m

glad [glæd] adj contento; **gladly** ['-lɪ]
adv con mucho gusto

glamour ['glæmər] (US **glamor**) n
encanto, atractivo; **glamorous** adj
encantador(a), atractivo

glance [glɑːns] n ojeada, mirada
▷ vi: **to ~ at** echar una ojeada a

gland [glænd] n glándula

glare [glɛə*] n (of anger) mirada feroz;
(of light) deslumbramiento, brillo; **to
be in the ~ of publicity** ser el foco de
la atención pública ▷ vi deslumbrar;
to ~ at mirar con odio a; **glaring** adj
(mistake) manifiesto

glass [glɑːs] n vidrio, cristal m;
(for drinking) vaso; (: with stem) copa;
glasses npl (spectacles) gafas fpl

glaze [gleɪz] vt (window) poner
cristales a; (pottery) vidriar ▷ n
vidriado

gleam [gliːm] vi brillar

glen [glɛn] n cañada

glide [glaɪd] vi deslizarse; (Aviat: birds)
planear; **glider** n (Aviat) planeador m

glimmer ['glɪmə*] n luz f tenue; (of
interest) muestra; (of hope) rayo

glimpse [glɪmps] n vislumbre m ▷ vt
vislumbrar, entrever

glint [glɪnt] vi centellear

glisten ['glɪsn] vi relucir, brillar

glitter ['glɪtə*] vi relucir, brillar

global ['gləʊbl] adj mundial;
globalization n globalización f;

global warming n (re)calentamiento
global or de la tierra

globe [gləʊb] n globo; (model) globo
terráqueo

gloom [gluːm] n oscuridad f; (sadness)
tristeza; **gloomy** adj (dark) oscuro;
(sad) triste; (pessimistic) pesimista

glorious ['glɔːrɪəs] adj glorioso;
(weather etc) magnífico

glory ['glɔːrɪ] n gloria

gloss [glɒs] n (shine) brillo; (paint)
pintura de aceite

glossary ['glɒsərɪ] n glosario

glossy ['glɒsɪ] adj lustroso; (magazine)
de lujo

glove [glʌv] n guante m; **glove
compartment** n (Aut) guantera

glow [gləʊ] vi brillar

glucose ['gluːkəʊs] n glucosa

glue [gluː] n goma (de pegar),
cemento ▷ vt pegar

GM adj abbr (= genetically modified)
transgénico

gm abbr (= gram) g

GMO n abbr (= genetically modified
organism) organismo transgénico

GMT abbr (= Greenwich Mean Time) GMT

gnaw [nɔː] vt roer

go [gəʊ] (pt **went**, pp **gone**, pl
~es) vi ir; (travel) viajar; (depart)
irse, marcharse; (work) funcionar,
marchar; (be sold) venderse; (time)
pasar; (fit, suit): **to ~ with** hacer juego
con; (become) ponerse; (break etc)
estropearse, romperse ▷ n: **to have
a ~ (at)** probar suerte (con); **to be
on the ~** no parar; **whose ~ is it?** ¿a
quién le toca?; **he's ~ing to do it** va a
hacerlo; **to ~ for a walk** ir de paseo;
to ~ dancing ir a bailar; **how did it ~?**
¿qué tal salió or resultó?, ¿cómo ha ido?;
to ~ round the back pasar por detrás;
go ahead vi seguir adelante; **go away**
vi irse, marcharse; **go back** vi volver;
go by vi (time) pasar ▷ vt fus guiarse
por; **go down** vi bajar; (ship) hundirse;
(sun) ponerse ▷ vt fus bajar; **go for** vt
fus (fetch) ir por; (like) gustar; (attack)

atacar; **go in** vi entrar; **go into** vt fus entrar en; (investigate) investigar; (embark on) dedicarse a; **go off** vi irse, marcharse; (food) pasarse; (explode) estallar; (event) realizarse ▷ vt fus dejar de gustar; **I'm going off him/the idea** ya no me gusta tanto él/la idea; **go on** vi (continue) seguir, continuar; (happen) pasar, ocurrir; **to go on doing sth** seguir haciendo algo; **go out** vi salir; (fire, light) apagarse; **go over** vi (ship) zozobrar ▷ vt fus (check) revisar; **go past** vi, vt fus pasar; **go round** vi (circulate: news, rumour) correr; (suffice) alcanzar, bastar; (revolve) girar, dar vueltas; (visit): **to go round (to sb's)** pasar a ver (a algn); **to go round (by)** (make a detour) dar la vuelta (por); **go through** vt fus (town etc) atravesar; **go up** vi, vt fus subir; **go with** vt fus (accompany) ir con, acompañar a; **go without** vt fus pasarse sin

go-ahead ['gəʊəhɛd] adj (person) dinámico; (firm) innovador(a) ▷ n luz f verde

goal [gəʊl] n meta; (score) gol m; **goalkeeper** n portero; **goal-post** n poste m (de la portería)

goat [gəʊt] n cabra

gobble ['gɔbl] vt (also: ~ **down**, ~ **up**) tragarse, engullir

God [gɔd] n Dios m; **godchild** n ahijado/a; **goddaughter** n ahijada; **goddess** n diosa; **godfather** n padrino; **godmother** n madrina; **godson** n ahijado

goggles ['gɔglz] npl gafas fpl

going ['gəʊɪŋ] n (conditions) estado del terreno ▷ adj: **the ~ rate** la tarifa corriente or en vigor

gold [gəʊld] n oro ▷ adj de oro; **golden** adj (made of gold) de oro; (gold in colour) dorado; **goldfish** n pez m de colores; **goldmine** n (also fig) mina de oro; **gold-plated** adj chapado en oro

golf [gɔlf] n golf m; **golf ball** n (for game) pelota de golf; (on typewriter) esfera; **golf club** n club m de golf;

(stick) palo (de golf); **golf course** n campo de golf; **golfer** n golfista mf

gone [gɔn] pp of **go**

gong [gɔŋ] n gong m

good [gʊd] adj bueno; (pleasant) agradable; (kind) bueno, amable; (well-behaved) educado ▷ n bien m, provecho; **goods** npl (Comm) mercancías fpl; ~! ¡qué bien!; **to be ~ at** tener aptitud para; **to be ~ for** servir para; **it's ~ for you** te hace bien; **would you be ~ enough to ...?** ¿podría hacerme el favor de ...?, ¿sería tan amable de ...?; **a ~ deal (of)** mucho; **a ~ many** muchos; **to make ~** reparar; **it's no ~ complaining** no vale la pena (de) quejarse; **for ~** para siempre, definitivamente; **~ morning/afternoon!** ¡buenos días/buenas tardes!; **~ evening!** ¡buenas noches!; **~ night!** ¡buenas noches!

goodbye [gʊd'baɪ] excl ¡adiós!; **to say ~ (to)** (person) despedirse (de)

good: Good Friday n Viernes m Santo; **good-looking** adj guapo; **good-natured** adj amable, simpático; **goodness** n (of person) bondad f; **for goodness sake!** ¡por Dios!; **goodness gracious!** ¡Dios mío!; **goods train** (BRIT) n tren m de mercancías; **goodwill** n buena voluntad f

Google® ['guːgəl] n Google® m ▷ vi hacer búsquedas en Internet ▷ vt buscar información en Internet sobre

goose [guːs] (pl **geese**) n ganso, oca

gooseberry ['gʊzbəri] n grosella espinosa; **to play ~** hacer de carabina

goose bumps, goose pimples npl carne f de gallina

gorge [gɔːdʒ] n barranco ▷ vr: **to ~ o.s. (on)** atracarse (de)

gorgeous ['gɔːdʒəs] adj (thing) precioso; (weather) espléndido; (person) guapísimo

gorilla [gə'rɪlə] n gorila m

gosh [gɔʃ] (inf) excl ¡cielos!

gospel ['gɔspl] n evangelio

gossip ['gɔsɪp] n (scandal)

cotilleo, chismes *mpl*; (*chat*) charla;
(*scandalmonger*) cotilla *m/f*, chismoso/a
▷ *vi* cotillear; **gossip column** *n* ecos
mpl de sociedad

got [gɔt] *pt, pp of* **get**

gotten (US) ['gɔtn] *pp of* **get**

gourmet ['guəmeɪ] *n* gastrónomo/a
m/f

govern ['gʌvən] *vt* gobernar;
(*influence*) dominar; **government** *n*
gobierno; **governor** *n* gobernador(a)
m/f; (*of school etc*) miembro del consejo;
(*of jail*) director(a) *m/f*

gown [gaun] *n* traje *m*; (*of teacher*,
BRIT: of judge) toga

G.P. *n abbr* = **general practitioner**

grab [græb] *vt* coger (SP), agarrar
(LAM), arrebatar ▷ *vi*: **to ~ at** intentar
agarrar

grace [greɪs] *n* gracia ▷ *vt* honrar;
(*adorn*) adornar; **5 days' ~** un plazo de
5 días; **graceful** *adj* grácil, ágil; (*style*,
shape) elegante, gracioso; **gracious**
['greɪʃəs] *adj* amable

grade [greɪd] *n* (*quality*) clase
f, calidad *f*; (*in hierarchy*) grado;
(*Scol: mark*) nota; (US: *school class*) curso
▷ *vt* clasificar; **grade crossing** (US)
n paso a nivel; **grade school** (US) *n*
escuela primaria

gradient ['greɪdɪənt] *n* pendiente *f*

gradual ['grædjuəl] *adj* paulatino;
gradually *adv* paulatinamente

graduate [*n* 'grædjuɪt, *vb* 'grædjueɪt]
n (US: *of high school*) graduado/a; (*of
university*) licenciado/a ▷ *vi* graduarse;
licenciarse; **graduation** [-'eɪʃən] *n*
(*ceremony*) entrega del título

graffiti [grə'fiːtɪ] *n* pintadas *fpl*

graft [grɑːft] *n* (*Agr, Med*) injerto;
(*BRIT: inf*) trabajo duro; (*bribery*)
corrupción *f* ▷ *vt* injertar

grain [greɪn] *n* (*single particle*) grano;
(*corn*) granos *mpl*, cereales *mpl*; (*of
wood*) fibra

gram [græm] *n* gramo

grammar ['græmə*] *n* gramática;
grammar school (BRIT) *n* ≈ instituto

de segunda enseñanza, liceo (SP)

gramme [græm] *n* = **gram**

gran [græn] (*inf*) *n* (BRIT) abuelita

grand [grænd] *adj* magnífico,
imponente; (*wonderful*) estupendo;
(*gesture etc*) grandioso; **grandad**
(*inf*) *n* = **granddad**; **grandchild**
(*pl* **grandchildren**) *n* nieto/a
m/f; **granddad** (*inf*) *n* yayo, abuelito;
granddaughter *n* nieta; **grandfather**
n abuelo; **grandma** (*inf*) *n* yaya,
abuelita; **grandmother** *n* abuela;
grandpa (*inf*) *n* = **granddad**;
grandparents *npl* abuelos *mpl*; **grand
piano** *n* piano de cola; **Grand Prix**
['grɑ̃:'priː] *n* (*Aut*) gran premio, Grand
Prix *m*; **grandson** *n* nieto

granite ['grænɪt] *n* granito

granny ['grænɪ] (*inf*) *n* abuelita, yaya

grant [grɑːnt] *vt* (*concede*) conceder;
(*admit*) reconocer ▷ *n* (*Scol*) beca;
(*Admin*) subvención *f*; **to take sth/sb
for ~ed** dar algo por sentado/no hacer
ningún caso a algn

grape [greɪp] *n* uva

grapefruit ['greɪpfruːt] *n* pomelo
(SP, SC), toronja (LAM)

graph [grɑːf] *n* gráfica; **graphic**
['græfɪk] *adj* gráfico; **graphics** *n*
artes *fpl* gráficas ▷ *npl* (*drawings*)
dibujos *mpl*

grasp [grɑːsp] *vt* agarrar, asir;
(*understand*) comprender ▷ *n*
(*grip*) asimiento; (*understanding*)
comprensión *f*

grass [grɑːs] *n* hierba; (*lawn*) césped
m; **grasshopper** *n* saltamontes *m inv*

grate [greɪt] *n* parrilla de chimenea
▷ *vi*: **to ~ (on)** chirriar (sobre) ▷ *vt*
(*Culin*) rallar

grateful ['greɪtful] *adj* agradecido

grater ['greɪtə*] *n* rallador *m*

gratitude ['grætɪtjuːd] *n*
agradecimiento

grave [greɪv] *n* tumba ▷ *adj* serio,
grave

gravel ['grævl] *n* grava

gravestone ['greɪvstəun] *n* lápida

graveyard ['greɪvjɑːd] *n* cementerio

gravity ['grævɪtɪ] *n* gravedad *f*

gravy ['greɪvɪ] *n* salsa de carne

gray [greɪ] *adj* = **grey**

graze [greɪz] *vi* pacer ▷ *vt* (*touch lightly*) rozar; (*scrape*) raspar ▷ *n* (*Med*) abrasión *f*

grease [griːs] *n* (*fat*) grasa; (*lubricant*) lubricante *m* ▷ *vt* engrasar; lubrificar; **greasy** *adj* grasiento

great [greɪt] *adj* grande; (*inf*) magnífico, estupendo; **Great Britain** *n* Gran Bretaña; **great-grandfather** *n* bisabuelo; **great-grandmother** *n* bisabuela; **greatly** *adv* muy; (*with verb*) mucho

Greece [griːs] *n* Grecia

greed [griːd] *n* (*also:* **~iness**) codicia, avaricia; (*for food*) gula; (*for power etc*) avidez *f*; **greedy** *adj* avaro; (*for food*) glotón/ona

Greek [griːk] *adj* griego ▷ *n* griego/a; (*Ling*) griego

green [griːn] *adj* (*also Pol*) verde; (*inexperienced*) novato ▷ *n* verde *m*; (*stretch of grass*) césped *m*; (*Golf*) green; *m* **greens** *npl* (*vegetables*) verduras *fpl*; **green card** *n* (*Aut*) carta verde; (*us: work permit*) permiso de trabajo para los extranjeros en EE. UU.; **greengage** *n* (*ciruela*) claudia; **greengrocer** (*BRIT*) *n* verdulero/a; **greenhouse** *n* invernadero; **greenhouse effect** *n* efecto invernadero

Greenland ['griːnlənd] *n* Groenlandia

green salad *n* ensalada *f* (*de lechuga, pepino, pimiento verde, etc*)

greet [griːt] *vt* (*welcome*) dar la bienvenida a; (*receive: news*) recibir; **greeting** *n* (*welcome*) bienvenida; **greeting(s) card** *n* tarjeta de felicitación

grew [gruː] *pt of* **grow**

grey [greɪ] (*US* **gray**) *adj* gris; (*weather*) sombrío; **grey-haired** *adj* canoso; **greyhound** *n* galgo

grid [grɪd] *n* reja; (*Elec*) red *f*; **gridlock** *n* (*traffic jam*) retención *f*

grief [griːf] *n* dolor *m*, pena

grievance ['griːvəns] *n* motivo de queja, agravio

grieve [griːv] *vi* afligirse, acongojarse ▷ *vt* dar pena a; **to ~ for** llorar por

grill [grɪl] *n* (*on cooker*) parrilla; (*also:* **mixed ~**) parrillada ▷ *vt* (*BRIT*) asar a la parrilla; (*inf: question*) interrogar

grille [grɪl] *n* reja; (*Aut*) rejilla

grim [grɪm] *adj* (*place*) sombrío; (*situation*) triste; (*person*) ceñudo

grime [graɪm] *n* mugre *f*, suciedad *f*

grin [grɪn] *n* sonrisa abierta ▷ *vi* sonreír abiertamente

grind [graɪnd] (*pt, pp* **ground**) *vt* (*coffee, pepper etc*) moler; (*us: meat*) picar; (*make sharp*) afilar ▷ *n* (*work*) rutina

grip [grɪp] *n* (*hold*) asimiento; (*control*) control *m*, dominio; (*of tyre etc*): **to have a good/bad ~** agarrarse bien/mal; (*handle*) asidero; (*holdall*) maletín *m* ▷ *vt* agarrar; (*viewer, reader*) fascinar; **to get to ~s with** enfrentarse con; **gripping** *adj* absorbente

grit [grɪt] *n* gravilla; (*courage*) valor *m* ▷ *vt* (*road*) poner gravilla en; **to ~ one's teeth** apretar los dientes

grits [grɪts] (*US*) *npl* maíz *msg* a medio moler

groan [grəun] *n* gemido; quejido ▷ *vi* gemir; quejarse

grocer ['grəusə*] *n* tendero (de ultramarinos (*SP*)); **groceries** *npl* comestibles *mpl*; **grocer's (shop)** *n* tienda de comestibles *or* (*MEX, CAM*), abarrotes, almacén (*SC*); **grocery** *n* (*shop*) tienda de ultramarinos

groin [grɔɪn] *n* ingle *f*

groom [gruːm] *n* mozo/a de cuadra; (*also:* **bride~**) novio ▷ *vt* (*horse*) almohazar; (*fig*): **to ~ sb for** preparar a algn para; **well-~ed** de buena presencia

groove [gruːv] *n* ranura, surco

grope [grəup] *vi*: **to ~ for** buscar a tientas

gross [grəus] *adj* (*neglect, injustice*) grave; (*vulgar: behaviour*) grosero;

(: *appearance*) de mal gusto; (*Comm*) bruto; **grossly** *adv* (*greatly*) enormemente

grotesque [grə'tɛsk] *adj* grotesco

ground [graund] *pt, pp of* **grind** ▷*n* suelo, tierra; (*Sport*) campo, terreno; (*reason: gen pl*) causa, razón *f*; (*us: also:* **~ wire**) tierra ▷*vt* (*plane*) mantener en tierra; (*us Elec*) conectar con tierra; **grounds** *npl* (*of coffee etc*) poso; (*gardens etc*) jardines *mpl*, parque *m*; **on the ~** en el suelo; **to the ~** al suelo; **to gain/lose ~** ganar/perder terreno; **ground floor** *n* (*BRIT*) planta baja; **groundsheet** (*BRIT*) *n* tela impermeable; suelo; **groundwork** *n* preparación *f*

group [gru:p] *n* grupo; (*musical*) conjunto ▷*vt* (*also:* **~ together**) agrupar ▷*vi* (*also:* **~ together**) agruparse

grouse [graus] *n inv* (*bird*) urogallo ▷*vi* (*complain*) quejarse

grovel ['grɔvl] *vi* (*fig*): **to ~ before** humillarse ante

grow [grəu] (*pt* **grew**, *pp* **grown**) *vi* crecer; (*increase*) aumentar; (*expand*) desarrollarse; (*become*) volverse; **to ~ rich/weak** enriquecerse/debilitarse ▷*vt* cultivar; (*hair, beard*) dejar crecer; **grow on** *vt fus*: **that painting is growing on me** ese cuadro me gusta cada vez más; **grow up** *vi* crecer, hacerse hombre/mujer

growl [graul] *vi* gruñir

grown [grəun] *pp of* **grow**; **grown-up** *n* adulto/a, mayor *mf*

growth [grəuθ] *n* crecimiento, desarrollo; (*what has grown*) brote *m*; (*Med*) tumor *m*

grub [grʌb] *n* larva, gusano; (*inf: food*) comida

grubby ['grʌbɪ] *adj* sucio, mugriento

grudge [grʌdʒ] *n* (motivo de) rencor *m* ▷*vt*: **to ~ sb sth** dar algo a algn de mala gana; **to bear sb a ~** guardar rencor a algn

gruelling ['gruəlɪŋ] (*us* **grueling**) *adj*

penoso, duro

gruesome ['gru:səm] *adj* horrible

grumble ['grʌmbl] *vi* refunfuñar, quejarse

grumpy ['grʌmpɪ] *adj* gruñón/ona

grunt [grʌnt] *vi* gruñir

guarantee [gærən'ti:] *n* garantía ▷*vt* garantizar

guard [gɑ:d] *n* (*squad*) guardia; (*one man*) guardia *mf*; (*BRIT Rail*) jefe *m* de tren; (*on machine*) dispositivo de seguridad; (*also:* **fire~**) rejilla de protección ▷*vt* guardar; (*prisoner*) vigilar; **to be on one's ~** estar alerta; **guardian** *n* guardián/ana *m/f*; (*of minor*) tutor(a) *m/f*

guerrilla [gə'rɪlə] *n* guerrillero/a

guess [gɛs] *vi* adivinar; (*us*) suponer ▷*vt* adivinar; suponer ▷*n* suposición *f*, conjetura; **to take** *or* **have a ~** tratar de adivinar

guest [gɛst] *n* invitado/a; (*in hotel*) huésped *mf*; **guest house** *n* casa de huéspedes, pensión *f*; **guest room** *n* cuarto de huéspedes

guidance ['gaɪdəns] *n* (*advice*) consejos *mpl*

guide [gaɪd] *n* (*person*) guía *mf*; (*book, fig*) guía; (*also:* **Girl ~**) guía ▷*vt* (*round museum etc*) guiar; (*lead*) conducir; (*direct*) orientar; **guidebook** *n* guía; **guide dog** *n* perro *m* guía; **guided tour** *n* visita *f* con guía; **guidelines** *npl* (*advice*) directrices *fpl*

guild [gɪld] *n* gremio

guilt [gɪlt] *n* culpabilidad *f*; **guilty** *adj* culpable

guinea pig ['gɪnɪ-] *n* cobaya; (*fig*) conejillo de Indias

guitar [gɪ'tɑ:*] *n* guitarra; **guitarist** *n* guitarrista *m/f*

gulf [gʌlf] *n* golfo; (*abyss*) abismo

gull [gʌl] *n* gaviota

gulp [gʌlp] *vi* tragar saliva ▷*vt* (*also:* **~ down**) tragarse

gum [gʌm] *n* (*Anat*) encía; (*glue*) goma, cemento; (*sweet*) caramelo de goma; (*also:* **chewing-~**) chicle *m* ▷*vt* pegar con goma

gun [gʌn] n (small) pistola, revólver m; (shotgun) escopeta; (rifle) fusil m; (cannon) cañón m; **gunfire** n disparos mpl; **gunman** (irreg) n pistolero; **gunpoint** n: **at gunpoint** a mano armada; **gunpowder** n pólvora; **gunshot** n escopetazo

gush [gʌʃ] vi salir a raudales; (person) deshacerse en efusiones

gust [gʌst] n (of wind) ráfaga

gut [gʌt] n intestino; **guts** npl (Anat) tripas fpl; (courage) valor m

gutter ['gʌtə*] n (of roof) canalón m; (in street) cuneta

guy [gaɪ] n (also: **~rope**) cuerda; (inf: man) tío (SP), tipo; (figure) monigote m

Guy Fawkes' Night [gaɪ'fɔːks-] n ver recuadro

gym [dʒɪm] n gimnasio; **gymnasium** n gimnasio mf; **gymnast** n gimnasta mf; **gymnastics** n gimnasia; **gym shoes** npl zapatillas fpl (de deporte)

gynaecologist [gaɪnɪ'kɔlədʒɪst] (us **gynecologist**) n ginecólogo/a

gypsy ['dʒɪpsɪ] n gitano/a

h

haberdashery [hæbə'dæʃərɪ] (BRIT) n mercería

habit ['hæbɪt] n hábito, costumbre f; (drug habit) adicción f; (costume) hábito

habitat ['hæbɪtæt] n hábitat m

hack [hæk] vt (cut) cortar; (slice) tajar ▷ n (pej: writer) escritor(a) m/f a sueldo; **hacker** n (Comput) pirata mf informático/a

had [hæd] pt, pp of **have**

haddock ['hædək] (pl ~ or ~s) n especie de merluza

hadn't ['hædnt] = **had not**

haemorrhage ['hɛmərɪdʒ] (us **hemorrhage**) n hemorragia

haemorrhoids ['hɛmərɔɪdz] (us **hemorrhoids**) npl hemorroides fpl

haggle ['hægl] vi regatear

Hague [heɪg] n: **The ~** La Haya

hail [heɪl] n granizo; (fig) lluvia ▷ vt saludar; (taxi) llamar a; (acclaim) aclamar ▷ vi granizar; **hailstone** n (piedra de) granizo

hair [hɛə*] n pelo, cabellos mpl; (one hair) pelo, cabello; (on legs etc) vello;

to do one's ~ arreglarse el pelo; **to have grey ~** tener canas *fpl*; **hairband** *n* cinta; **hairbrush** *n* cepillo (para el pelo); **haircut** *n* corte *m* (de pelo); **hairdo** *n* peinado; **hairdresser** *n* peluquero/a; **hairdresser's** *n* peluquería; **hair dryer** *n* secador *m* de pelo; **hair gel** *n* fijador; **hair spray** *n* laca; **hairstyle** *n* peinado; **hairy** *adj* peludo; velludo; (*inf: frightening*) espeluznante

hake [heɪk] (*pl ~ or ~s*) *n* merluza

half [hɑːf] (*pl* **halves**) *n* mitad *f*; (*of beer*) ≈ caña (*SP*), media pinta; (*Rail, Bus*) billete *m* de niño ▷ *adj* medio ▷ *adv* medio, a medias; **two and a ~** dos y media; **~ a dozen** media docena; **~ a pound** media libra; **to cut sth in ~** cortar algo por la mitad; **half board** *n* (*BRIT: in hotel*) media pensión; **half-brother** *n* hermanastro; **half day** *n* medio día *m*, media jornada; **half fare** *n* medio pasaje *m*; **half-hearted** *adj* indiferente, poco entusiasta; **half-hour** *n* media hora; **half-price** *adj, adv* a mitad de precio; **half term** (*BRIT*) *n* (*Scol*) *vacaciones de mediados del trimestre*; **half-time** *n* descanso; **halfway** *adv* a medio camino; **halfway through** a mitad de

hall [hɔːl] *n* (*for concerts*) sala; (*entrance way*) hall *m*; vestíbulo

hallmark ['hɔːlmɑːk] *n* sello

hallo [hə'ləʊ] *excl* = **hello**

hall of residence (*BRIT*) *n* residencia

Hallowe'en [hæləʊ'iːn] *n* víspera de Todos los Santos

● **HALLOWE'EN**
●
● La tradición anglosajona dice
● que en la noche del 31 de octubre,
● **Hallowe'en**, víspera de Todos los
● Santos, es posible ver a brujas y
● fantasmas. En este día los niños
● se disfrazan y van de puerta en
● puerta llevando un farol hecho con
● una calabaza en forma de cabeza

● humana. Cuando se les abre la
● puerta gritan "trick or treat",
● amenazando con gastar una
● broma a quien no les dé golosinas
● o algo de calderilla.

hallucination [həluːsɪ'neɪʃən] *n* alucinación *f*

hallway ['hɔːlweɪ] *n* vestíbulo

halo ['heɪləʊ] *n* (*of saint*) halo, aureola

halt [hɔːlt] *n* (*stop*) alto, parada ▷ *vt* parar; interrumpir ▷ *vi* pararse

halve [hɑːv] *vt* partir por la mitad

halves [hɑːvz] *npl of* **half**

ham [hæm] *n* jamón *m* (cocido)

hamburger ['hæmbəːgə*] *n* hamburguesa

hamlet ['hæmlɪt] *n* aldea

hammer ['hæmə*] *n* martillo ▷ *vt* (*nail*) clavar; (*force*): **to ~ an idea into sb/a message home** meter una idea en la cabeza a algn/machacar una idea ▷ *vi* dar golpes

hammock ['hæmək] *n* hamaca

hamper ['hæmpə*] *vt* estorbar ▷ *n* cesto

hamster ['hæmstə*] *n* hámster *m*

hamstring ['hæmstrɪŋ] *n* (*Anat*) tendón *m* de la corva

hand [hænd] *n* mano *f*; (*of clock*) aguja; (*writing*) letra; (*worker*) obrero ▷ *vt* dar, pasar; **to give** *or* **lend sb a ~** echar una mano a algn, ayudar a algn; **at ~** a mano; **in ~** (*time*) libre; (*job etc*) entre manos; **on ~** (*person, services*) a mano, al alcance; **to ~** (*information etc*) a mano; **on the one ~ ..., on the other ~ ...** por una parte ... por otra (parte) ...; **hand down** *vt* pasar, bajar; (*tradition*) transmitir; (*heirloom*) dejar en herencia; (*US: sentence, verdict*) imponer; **hand in** *vt* entregar; **hand out** *vt* distribuir; **hand over** *vt* (*deliver*) entregar; **handbag** *n* bolso (*SP*), cartera (*LAM*), bolsa (*MEX*); **hand baggage** *n* = **hand luggage**; **handbook** *n* manual *m*; **handbrake** *n* freno de mano; **handcuffs** *npl* esposas *fpl*; **handful**

n puñado

handicap ['hændɪkæp] *n* minusvalía; (*disadvantage*) desventaja; (*Sport*) handicap *m* ▷ *vt* estorbar; **to be mentally ~ped** ser mentalmente *m/f* discapacitado; **to be physically ~ped** ser minusválido/a

handkerchief ['hæŋkətʃɪf] *n* pañuelo

handle ['hændl] *n* (*of door etc*) tirador *m*; (*of cup etc*) asa; (*of knife etc*) mango; (*for winding*) manivela ▷ *vt* (*touch*) tocar; (*deal with*) encargarse de; (*treat: people*) manejar; **"~ with care"** "(manéjese) con cuidado"; **to fly off the ~** perder los estribos; **handlebar(s)** *n(pl)* manillar *m*

hand: **hand luggage** *n* equipaje *m* de mano; **handmade** *adj* hecho a mano; **handout** *n* (*money etc*) limosna; (*leaflet*) folleto; **hands-free** *adj* (*phone*) manos libres *inv*; **hands-free kit** *n* manos libres *m inv*

handsome ['hænsəm] *adj* guapo; (*building*) bello; (*fig: profit*) considerable

handwriting ['hændraɪtɪŋ] *n* letra

handy ['hændɪ] *adj* (*close at hand*) a la mano; (*tool etc*) práctico; (*skilful*) hábil, diestro

hang [hæŋ] (*pt, pp* **hung**) *vt* colgar; (*criminal: pt, pp* **hanged**) ahorcar ▷ *vi* (*painting, coat etc*) colgar; (*hair, drapery*) caer; **to get the ~ of sth** (*inf*) lograr dominar algo; **hang about** or **around** *vi* haraganear; **hang down** *vi* colgar, pender; **hang on** *vi* (*wait*) esperar; **hang out** *vt* (*washing*) tender, colgar ▷ *vi* (*inf: live*) vivir; (*spend time*) pasar el rato; **to hang out of sth** colgar fuera de algo; **hang round** *vi* = **hang around**; **hang up** *vi* (*Tel*) colgar ▷ *vt* colgar

hanger ['hæŋə*] *n* percha

hang-gliding ['-glaɪdɪŋ] *n* vuelo libre

hangover ['hæŋəuvə*] *n* (*after drinking*) resaca

hankie, hanky ['hæŋkɪ] *n abbr* = **handkerchief**

happen ['hæpən] *vi* suceder, ocurrir; (*chance*): **he ~ed to hear/see** dió la casualidad de que oyó/vió; **as it ~s** da la casualidad de que

happily ['hæpɪlɪ] *adv* (*luckily*) afortunadamente; (*cheerfully*) alegremente

happiness ['hæpɪnɪs] *n* felicidad *f*; (*cheerfulness*) alegría

happy ['hæpɪ] *adj* feliz; (*cheerful*) alegre; **to be ~ (with)** estar contento (con); **to be ~ to do** estar encantado de hacer; **~ birthday!** ¡feliz cumpleaños!

harass ['hærəs] *vt* acosar, hostigar; **harassment** *n* persecución *f*

harbour ['hɑːbə*] (*US* **harbor**) *n* puerto ▷ *vt* (*fugitive*) dar abrigo a; (*hope etc*) abrigar

hard [hɑːd] *adj* duro; (*difficult*) difícil; (*work*) arduo; (*person*) severo; (*fact*) innegable ▷ *adv* (*work*) mucho, duro; (*think*) profundamente; **to look ~ at** clavar los ojos en; **to try ~** esforzarse; **no ~ feelings!** ¡sin rencor(es)!; **to be ~ of hearing** ser duro de oído; **to be ~ done by** ser tratado injustamente; **hardback** *n* libro en cartoné; **hardboard** *n* aglomerado *m* (*de madera*); **hard disk** *n* (*Comput*) disco duro or rígido; **harden** *vt* endurecer; (*fig*) curtir ▷ *vi* endurecerse; curtirse

hardly ['hɑːdlɪ] *adv* apenas; **~ ever** casi nunca

hard: **hardship** *n* privación *f*; **hard shoulder** (*BRIT*) *n* (*Aut*) arcén *m*; **hard-up** (*inf*) *adj* sin un duro (*SP*), pelado, sin un centavo (*MEX*), pato (*SC*); **hardware** *n* ferretería; (*Comput*) hardware *m*; (*Mil*) armamento; **hardware shop** (*US* **hardware store**) ferretería; **hard-working** *adj* trabajador(a)

hardy ['hɑːdɪ] *adj* fuerte; (*plant*) resistente

hare [hɛə*] *n* liebre *f*

harm [hɑːm] *n* daño, mal *m* ▷ *vt* (*person*) hacer daño a; (*health, interests*) perjudicar; (*thing*) dañar; **out of ~'s**

way a salvo; **harmful** adj dañino;
harmless adj (person) inofensivo; (joke
etc) inocente

harmony ['hɑːmənɪ] n armonía

harness ['hɑːnɪs] n arreos mpl; (for
child) arnés m; (safety harness) arneses
mpl ▷ vt (horse) enjaezar; (resources)
aprovechar

harp [hɑːp] n arpa ▷ vi: **to ~ on**
(**about**) machacar (con)

harsh [hɑːʃ] adj (cruel) duro, cruel;
(severe) severo; (sound) áspero; (light)
deslumbrador(a)

harvest ['hɑːvɪst] n (harvest time)
siega; (of cereals etc) cosecha; (of grapes)
vendimia ▷ vt cosechar

has [hæz] vb see **have**

hasn't ['hæznt] = **has not**

hassle ['hæsl] (inf) n lata

haste [heɪst] n prisa; **hasten** ['heɪsn]
vt acelerar ▷ vi darse prisa; **hastily**
adv de prisa; precipitadamente; **hasty**
adj apresurado; (rash) precipitado

hat [hæt] n sombrero

hatch [hætʃ] n (Naut: also: **~way**)
escotilla; (also: **service ~**) ventanilla
▷ vi (bird) salir del cascarón ▷ vt
incubar; (plot) tramar; **5 eggs have ~ed**
han salido 5 pollos

hatchback ['hætʃbæk] n (Aut) tres or
cinco puertas m

hate [heɪt] vt odiar, aborrecer ▷ n
odio; **hatred** ['heɪtrɪd] n odio

haul [hɔːl] vt tirar ▷ n (of fish) redada;
(of stolen goods etc) botín m

haunt [hɔːnt] vt (ghost) aparecerse
en; (obsess) obsesionar ▷ n guarida;
haunted adj (castle etc) embrujado;
(look) de angustia

○ **KEYWORD**

have [hæv] (pt, pp **had**) aux vb **1** (gen)
haber; **to have arrived/eaten** haber
llegado/comido; **having finished** or
when he had finished, he left cuando
hubo acabado, se fue
2 (in tag questions): **you've done it,**

haven't you? lo has hecho, ¿verdad?
or ¿no?
3 (in short answers and questions): **I
haven't** no; **so I have** pues, es verdad;
we haven't paid - yes we have!
no hemos pagado – ¡sí que hemos
pagado!; **I've been there before, have
you?** he estado allí antes, ¿y tú?
▷ modal aux vb (be obliged): **to have
(got) to do sth** tener que hacer algo;
you haven't to tell her no hay que or
no debes decírselo
▷ vt **1** (possess): **he has (got) blue
eyes/dark hair** tiene los ojos azules/el
pelo negro
2 (referring to meals etc): **to have
breakfast/lunch/dinner** desayunar/
comer/cenar; **to have a drink/a
cigarette** tomar algo/fumar un
cigarrillo
3 (receive) recibir; (obtain) obtener; **may
I have your address?** ¿puedes darme
tu dirección?; **you can have it for
£5** te lo puedes quedar por £5; **I must
have it by tomorrow** lo necesito para
mañana; **to have a baby** tener un
niño or bebé
4 (maintain, allow): **I won't have it/this
nonsense!** ¡no lo permitiré!/¡no
permitiré estas tonterías!; **we can't
have that** no podemos permitir eso
5 to have sth done hacer or mandar
hacer algo; **to have one's hair cut**
cortarse el pelo; **to have sb do sth**
hacer que algn haga algo
6 (experience, suffer): **to have a cold/flu**
tener un resfriado/la gripe; **she had
her bag stolen/her arm broken** le
robaron el bolso/se rompió un brazo;
to have an operation operarse
7 (+ noun): **to have a swim/walk/
bath/rest** nadar/dar un paseo/darse
un baño/descansar; **let's have a look**
vamos a ver; **to have a meeting/
party** celebrar una reunión/una fiesta;
let me have a try déjame intentarlo

haven ['heɪvn] n puerto; (fig) refugio

haven't ['hævnt] = **have not**

havoc ['hævək] n estragos mpl

Hawaii [hə'waɪi:] n (Islas fpl) Hawai fpl

hawk [hɔ:k] n halcón m

hawthorn ['hɔ:θɔ:n] n espino

hay [heɪ] n heno; **hay fever** n fiebre f del heno; **haystack** n almiar m

hazard ['hæzəd] n peligro ▷ vt aventurar; **hazardous** adj peligroso; **hazard warning lights** npl (Aut) señales fpl de emergencia

haze [heɪz] n neblina

hazel ['heɪzl] n (tree) avellano ▷ adj (eyes) color m de avellano; **hazelnut** n avellana

hazy ['heɪzɪ] adj brumoso; (idea) vago

he [hi:] pron él; ~ **who** ... él que ..., quien ...

head [hɛd] n cabeza; (leader) jefe/a m/f; (of school) director(a) m/f ▷ vt (list) encabezar; (group) capitanear; (company) dirigir; ~**s (or tails)** cara (o cruz); ~ **first** de cabeza; ~ **over heels** (in love) perdidamente; **to** ~ **the ball** cabecear (la pelota); **head for** vt fus dirigirse a; (disaster) ir camino de; **head off** vt (threat, danger) evitar; **headache** n dolor m de cabeza; **heading** n título; **headlamp** (BRIT) n = **headlight**; **headlight** n faro; **headline** n titular m; **head office** n oficina central, central f; **headphones** npl auriculares mpl; **headquarters** npl sede f central; (Mil) cuartel m general; **headroom** n (in car) altura interior; (under bridge) (límite m de) altura; **headscarf** n pañuelo; **headset** n cascos mpl; **headteacher** n director(directora); **head waiter** n maître m

heal [hi:l] vt curar ▷ vi cicatrizarse

health [hɛlθ] n salud f; **health care** n asistencia sanitaria; **health centre** (BRIT) n ambulatorio, centro médico; **health food** n alimentos mpl orgánicos; **Health Service** (BRIT) n el servicio de salud pública, ≈ el Insalud (SP); **healthy** adj sano, saludable

heap [hi:p] n montón m ▷ vt: **to** ~ **(up)** amontonar; **to** ~ **sth with** llenar algo hasta arriba de; ~**s of** un montón de

hear [hɪə*] (pt, pp ~**d**) vt (also Law) oír; (news) saber ▷ vi oír; **to** ~ **about** oír hablar de; **to** ~ **from sb** tener noticias de algn

heard [hə:d] pt, pp of **hear**

hearing ['hɪərɪŋ] n (sense) oído; (Law) vista; **hearing aid** n audífono

hearse [hə:s] n coche m fúnebre

heart [hɑ:t] n corazón m; (fig) valor m; (of lettuce) cogollo; **hearts** npl (Cards) corazones mpl; **to lose/take** ~ descorazonarse/cobrar ánimo; **at** ~ en el fondo; **by** ~ (learn, know) de memoria; **heart attack** n infarto (de miocardio); **heartbeat** n latido (del corazón); **heartbroken** adj: **she was heartbroken about it** esto le partió el corazón; **heartburn** n acedía; **heart disease** n enfermedad f cardíaca

hearth [hɑ:θ] n (fireplace) chimenea

heartless ['hɑ:tlɪs] adj despiadado

hearty ['hɑ:tɪ] adj (person) campechano; (laugh) sano; (dislike, support) absoluto

heat [hi:t] n calor m; (Sport: also: **qualifying** ~) prueba eliminatoria ▷ vt calentar; **heat up** vi calentarse ▷ vt calentar; **heated** adj caliente; (fig) acalorado; **heater** n estufa; (in car) calefacción f

heather ['hɛðə*] n brezo

heating ['hi:tɪŋ] n calefacción f

heatwave ['hi:tweɪv] n ola de calor

heaven ['hɛvn] n cielo; (fig) una maravilla; **heavenly** adj celestial; (fig) maravilloso

heavily ['hɛvɪlɪ] adv pesadamente; (drink, smoke) con exceso; (sleep, sigh) profundamente; (depend) mucho

heavy ['hɛvɪ] adj pesado; (work, blow) duro; (sea, rain, meal) fuerte; (drinker, smoker) grande; (responsibility) grave; (schedule) ocupado; (weather) bochornoso

Hebrew ['hi:bru:] *adj, n* (*Ling*) hebreo

hectare ['hɛktɑ:*] *n* (*BRIT*) hectárea

hectic ['hɛktɪk] *adj* agitado

he'd [hi:d] = **he would; he had**

hedge [hɛdʒ] *n* seto ▷ *vi* contestar con evasivas; **to ~ one's bets** (*fig*) cubrirse

hedgehog ['hɛdʒhɔg] *n* erizo

heed [hi:d] *vt* (*also:* **take ~**: *pay attention to*) hacer caso de

heel [hi:l] *n* talón *m*; (*of shoe*) tacón *m* ▷ *vt* (*shoe*) poner tacón a

hefty ['hɛftɪ] *adj* (*person*) fornido; (*parcel, profit*) gordo

height [haɪt] *n* (*of person*) estatura; (*of building*) altura; (*high ground*) cerro; (*altitude*) altitud *f*; (*fig: of season*): **at the ~ of summer** en los días más calurosos del verano; (: *of power etc*) cúspide *f*; (: *of stupidity etc*) colmo; **heighten** *vt* elevar; (*fig*) aumentar

heir [ɛə*] *n* heredero; **heiress** *n* heredera

held [hɛld] *pt, pp of* **hold**

helicopter ['hɛlɪkɔptə*] *n* helicóptero

hell [hɛl] *n* infierno; **~!** (*inf*) ¡demonios!

he'll [hi:l] = **he will; he shall**

hello [hə'ləʊ] *excl* ¡hola!; (*to attract attention*) ¡oiga!; (*surprise*) ¡caramba!

helmet ['hɛlmɪt] *n* casco

help [hɛlp] *n* ayuda; (*cleaner etc*) criada, asistenta ▷ *vt* ayudar; **~!** ¡socorro!; **~ yourself** sírvete; **he can't ~ it** no es culpa suya; **help out** *vi* ayudar, echar una mano ▷ *vt*: **to help sb out** ayudar a algn, echar una mano a algn; **helper** *n* ayudante *mf*; **helpful** *adj* útil; (*person*) servicial; (*advice*) útil; **helping** *n* ración *f*; **helpless** *adj* (*incapable*) incapaz; (*defenceless*) indefenso; **helpline** *n* teléfono de asistencia al público

hem [hɛm] *n* dobladillo ▷ *vt* poner or coser el dobladillo en

hemisphere ['hɛmɪsfɪə*] *n* hemisferio

hemorrhage ['hɛmərɪdʒ] (*US*) *n* = **haemorrhage**

hemorrhoids ['hɛmərɔɪdz] (*US*) *npl* = **haemorrhoids**

hen [hɛn] *n* gallina; (*female bird*) hembra

hence [hɛns] *adv* (*therefore*) por lo tanto; **2 years ~** de aquí a 2 años

hen night, hen party *n* (*inf*) despedida de soltera

hepatitis [hɛpə'taɪtɪs] *n* hepatitis *f*

her [hə:*] *pron* (*direct*) la; (*indirect*) le; (*stressed, after prep*) ella ▷ *adj* su; *see also* **me; my**

herb [hə:b] *n* hierba; **herbal** *adj* de hierbas; **herbal tea** *n* infusión *f* de hierbas

herd [hə:d] *n* rebaño

here [hɪə*] *adv* aquí; (*at this point*) en este punto; **~!** (*present*) ¡presente!; **~ is/are** aquí está/están; **~ she is** aquí está

hereditary [hɪ'rɛdɪtrɪ] *adj* hereditario

heritage ['hɛrɪtɪdʒ] *n* patrimonio

hernia ['hə:nɪə] *n* hernia

hero ['hɪərəʊ] (*pl* **~es**) *n* héroe *m*; (*in book, film*) protagonista *m*; **heroic** [hɪ'rəʊɪk] *adj* heroico

heroin ['hɛrəʊɪn] *n* heroína

heroine ['hɛrəʊɪn] *n* heroína; (*in book, film*) protagonista

heron ['hɛrən] *n* garza

herring ['hɛrɪŋ] *n* arenque *m*

hers [hə:z] *pron* (el) suyo((la) suya) *etc*; *see also* **mine**[1]

herself [hə:'sɛlf] *pron* (*reflexive*) se; (*emphatic*) ella misma; (*after prep*) sí (misma); *see also* **oneself**

he's [hi:z] = **he is; he has**

hesitant ['hɛzɪtənt] *adj* vacilante

hesitate ['hɛzɪteɪt] *vi* vacilar; (*in speech*) titubear; (*be unwilling*) resistirse a; **hesitation** ['-teɪʃən] *n* indecisión *f*; titubeo; dudas *fpl*

heterosexual [hɛtərəʊ'sɛksjʊəl] *adj* heterosexual

hexagon ['hɛksəgən] *n* hexágono

hey [heɪ] *excl* ¡oye!, ¡oiga!
heyday ['heɪdeɪ] *n*: **the ~ of** el
apogeo de
HGV *n abbr* (= *heavy goods vehicle*)
vehículo pesado
hi [haɪ] *excl* ¡hola!; (*to attract attention*)
¡oiga!
hibernate ['haɪbəneɪt] *vi* invernar
hiccough ['hɪkʌp] = **hiccup**
hiccup ['hɪkʌp] *vi* hipar
hid [hɪd] *pt of* **hide**
hidden ['hɪdn] *pp of* **hide** ▷ *adj*: **~
agenda** plan *m* encubierto
hide [haɪd] (*pt* **hid**, *pp* **hidden**) *n* (*skin*)
piel *f* ▷ *vt* esconder, ocultar ▷ *vi*: **to
~ (from sb)** esconderse *or* ocultarse
(de algn)
hideous ['hɪdɪəs] *adj* horrible
hiding ['haɪdɪŋ] *n* (*beating*) paliza; **to
be in ~** (*concealed*) estar escondido
hi-fi ['haɪfaɪ] *n* estéreo, hifi *m* ▷ *adj*
de alta fidelidad
high [haɪ] *adj* alto; (*speed, number*)
grande; (*price*) elevado; (*wind*) fuerte;
(*voice*) agudo ▷ *adv* alto, a gran altura;
it is 20 m ~ tiene 20 m de altura; **~
in the air** en las alturas; **highchair**
n silla alta; **high-class** *adj* (*hotel*)
de lujo; (*person*) distinguido, de
categoría; (*food*) de alta categoría;
higher education *n* educación *f*
or enseñanza superior; **high heels**
npl (*heels*) tacones *mpl* altos; (*shoes*)
zapatos *mpl* de tacón; **high jump** *n*
(*Sport*) salto de altura; **highlands**
['haɪləndz] *npl* tierras *fpl* altas; **the
Highlands** (*in Scotland*) las Tierras Altas
de Escocia; **highlight** *n* (*fig: of event*)
punto culminante ▷ *vt* subrayar;
highlights *npl* (*in hair*) reflejos *mpl*;
highlighter *n* rotulador; **highly** *adv*
(*paid*) muy bien; (*critical, confidential*)
sumamente; (*a lot*): **to speak/think
highly of** hablar muy bien de/tener
en mucho a; **highness** *n* altura;
Her/His Highness Su Alteza; **high-rise**
n (*also*: **High-rise block, high-rise
building**) torre *f* de pisos; **high school**

n ≈ Instituto Nacional de Bachillerato
(*SP*); **high season** (*BRIT*) *n* temporada
alta; **high street** (*BRIT*) *n* calle *f* mayor;
high-tech (*inf*) *adj* al-tec (*inf*), de alta
tecnología; **highway** *n* carretera;
(*US*) carretera nacional; autopista;
Highway Code (*BRIT*) *n* código de la
circulación
hijack ['haɪdʒæk] *vt* secuestrar;
hijacker *n* secuestrador(a) *m/f*
hike [haɪk] *vi* (*go walking*) ir de
excursión (a pie) ▷ *n* caminata;
hiker *n* excursionista *mf*; **hiking** *n*
senderismo
hilarious [hɪ'lɛərɪəs] *adj*
divertidísimo
hill [hɪl] *n* colina; (*high*) montaña;
(*slope*) cuesta; **hillside** *n* ladera; **hill
walking** *n* senderismo (de montaña);
hilly *adj* montañoso
him [hɪm] *pron* (*direct*) le, lo; (*indirect*)
le; (*stressed, after prep*) él; *see also* **me**;
himself *pron* (*reflexive*) se; (*emphatic*)
él mismo; (*after prep*) sí (mismo); *see
also* **oneself**
hind [haɪnd] *adj* posterior
hinder ['hɪndə*] *vt* estorbar, impedir
hindsight ['haɪndsaɪt] *n*: **with ~** en
retrospectiva
Hindu ['hɪnduː] *n* hindú *mf*;
Hinduism *n* (*Rel*) hinduismo
hinge [hɪndʒ] *n* bisagra, gozne *m* ▷ *vi*
(*fig*): **to ~ on** depender de
hint [hɪnt] *n* indirecta; (*advice*)
consejo; (*sign*) dejo ▷ *vt*: **to ~ that**
insinuar que ▷ *vi*: **to ~ at** hacer
alusión a
hip [hɪp] *n* cadera
hippie ['hɪpɪ] *n* hippie *m/f*, jipi *m/f*
hippo ['hɪpəu] (*pl* **~s**) *n* hipopótamo
hippopotamus [hɪpə'pɔtəməs] (*pl*
~es *or* **hippopotami**) *n* hipopótamo
hippy ['hɪpɪ] *n* = **hippie**
hire ['haɪə*] *vt* (*BRIT: car, equipment*)
alquilar; (*worker*) contratar ▷ *n* alquiler
m; **for ~** se alquila; (*taxi*) libre; **hire(d)
car** (*BRIT*) *n* coche *m* de alquiler; **hire
purchase** (*BRIT*) *n* compra a plazos

his [hɪz] *pron* (el) suyo((la) suya) *etc*
▷ *adj* su; *see also* **mine¹; my**
Hispanic [hɪs'pænɪk] *adj* hispánico
hiss [hɪs] *vi* silbar
historian [hɪ'stɔːrɪən] *n*
historiador(a) *m/f*
historic(al) [hɪ'stɔrɪk(l)] *adj*
histórico
history ['hɪstərɪ] *n* historia
hit [hɪt] (*pt, pp* ~) *vt* (*strike*) golpear,
pegar; (*reach: target*) alcanzar; (*collide
with: car*) chocar contra; (*fig: affect*)
afectar ▷ *n* golpe *m*; (*success*) éxito;
(*on website*) visita; (*in web search*)
correspondencia; **to ~ it off with
sb** llevarse bien con algn; **hit back**
vi defenderse; (*fig*) devolver golpe
por golpe
hitch [hɪtʃ] *vt* (*fasten*) atar, amarrar;
(*also:* ~ **up**) remangar ▷ *n* (*difficulty*)
dificultad *f*; **to ~ a lift** hacer
autostop
hitch-hike ['hɪtʃhaɪk] *vi* hacer
autostop; **hitch-hiker** *n* autostopista
m/f; **hitch-hiking** *n* autostop *m*
hi-tech [haɪ'tɛk] *adj* de alta
tecnología
hitman ['hɪtmæn] (*irreg*) *n* asesino
a sueldo
HIV *n abbr* (= *human immunodeficiency
virus*) VIH *m*; **~-negative/positive**
VIH negativo/positivo
hive [haɪv] *n* colmena
hoard [hɔːd] *n* (*treasure*) tesoro;
(*stockpile*) provisión *f* ▷ *vt* acumular;
(*goods in short supply*) acaparar
hoarse [hɔːs] *adj* ronco
hoax [həʊks] *n* trampa
hob [hɔb] *n* quemador *m*
hobble ['hɔbl] *vi* cojear
hobby ['hɔbɪ] *n* pasatiempo, afición
f
hobo ['həʊbəʊ] (*US*) *n* vagabundo
hockey ['hɔkɪ] *n* hockey *m*; **hockey
stick** *n* palo *m* de hockey
hog [hɔg] *n* cerdo, puerco ▷ *vt* (*fig*)
acaparar; **to go the whole ~** poner
toda la carne en el asador

Hogmanay [hɔgmə'neɪ] *n ver
recuadro*

● **HOGMANAY**
●
● La Nochevieja o "New Year's Eve"
● se conoce como "Hogmanay"
● en Escocia, donde se festeje de
● forma especial. La familia y los
● amigos se suelen juntar para oír
● las campanadas del reloj y luego se
● hace el "first-footing", costumbre
● que consiste en visitar a los amigos
● y vecinos llevando algo de beber
● (generalmente whisky) y un trozo
● de carbón que se supone que traerá
● buena suerte para el año entrante.

hoist [hɔɪst] *n* (*crane*) grúa ▷ *vt*
levantar, alzar; (*flag, sail*) izar
hold [həʊld] (*pt, pp* **held**) *vt* sostener;
(*contain*) contener; (*have: power,
qualification*) tener; (*keep back*) retener;
(*believe*) sostener; (*consider*) considerar;
(*keep in position*): **to ~ one's head up**
mantener la cabeza alta; (*meeting*)
celebrar ▷ *vi* (*withstand pressure*)
resistir; (*be valid*) valer ▷ *n* (*grasp*)
asimiento; (*fig*) dominio; **~ the line!**
(*Tel*) ¡no cuelgue!; **to ~ one's own** (*fig*)
defenderse; **to catch** *or* **get (a) ~ of**
agarrarse *or* asirse de; **hold back** *vt*
retener; (*secret*) ocultar; **hold on** *vi*
agarrarse bien; (*wait*) esperar; **hold
on!** (*Tel*) ¡(espere) un momento!; **hold
out** *vt* ofrecer ▷ *vi* (*resist*) resistir;
hold up *vt* (*raise*) levantar; (*support*)
apoyar; (*delay*) retrasar; (*rob*) asaltar;
holdall (*BRIT*) *n* bolsa; **holder** *n*
(*container*) receptáculo; (*of ticket, record*)
poseedor(a) *m/f*; (*of office, title etc*)
titular *mf*
hole [həʊl] *n* agujero
holiday ['hɔlədɪ] *n* vacaciones
fpl; (*public holiday*) (día *m* de) fiesta,
día *m* feriado; **on ~** de vacaciones;
holiday camp *n* (*BRIT: also:* **holiday
centre**) centro de vacaciones; **holiday**

job n (BRIT) trabajillo extra para las
vacaciones; **holiday-maker** (BRIT) n
turista mf; **holiday resort** n centro
turístico
Holland ['hɔlənd] n Holanda
hollow ['hɔləu] adj hueco; (claim)
vacío; (eyes) hundido; (sound) sordo
▷ n hueco; (in ground) hoyo ▷ vt: **to ~
out** excavar
holly ['hɔlɪ] n acebo
Hollywood ['hɔlɪwud] n Hollywood
m
holocaust ['hɔləkɔ:st] n holocausto
holy ['həulɪ] adj santo, sagrado;
(water) bendito
home [həum] n casa; (country) patria;
(institution) asilo ▷ cpd (domestic)
casero, de casa; (Econ, Pol) nacional
▷ adv (direction) a casa; (right in: nail
etc) a fondo; **at ~** en casa; (in country)
en el país; (fig) como pez en el agua;
to go/come ~ ir/volver a casa; **make
yourself at ~** ¡estás en tu casa!; **home
address** n domicilio; **homeland** n
tierra natal; **homeless** adj sin hogar,
sin casa; **homely** adj (simple) sencillo;
home-made adj casero; **home
match** n partido en casa; **Home
Office** (BRIT) n Ministerio del Interior;
home owner n propietario/a m/f
de una casa; **home page** n página
de inicio; **Home Secretary** (BRIT) n
Ministro del Interior; **homesick** adj: **to
be homesick** sentir morriña, sentir
nostalgia; **home town** n ciudad f
natal; **homework** n deberes mpl
homicide ['hɔmɪsaɪd] (US) n
homicidio
homoeopathic [həumɪɔ'pəθɪk] (US
homeopathic) adj homeopático
homoeopathy [həumɪ'ɔpəθɪ] (US
homeopathy) n homeopatía
homosexual [hɔməu'sɛksjuəl] adj, n
homosexual mf
honest ['ɔnɪst] adj honrado;
(sincere) franco, sincero; **honestly** adv
honradamente; francamente; **honesty**
n honradez f

honey ['hʌnɪ] n miel f; **honeymoon**
n luna de miel; **honeysuckle** n
madreselva
Hong Kong ['hɔŋ'kɔŋ] n Hong-
Kong m
honorary ['ɔnərərɪ] adj (member,
president) de honor; (title) honorífico; **~
degree** doctorado honoris causa
honour ['ɔnə*] (US **honor**) vt honrar;
(commitment, promise) cumplir con ▷ n
honor m, honra; **to graduate with ~s**
≈ licenciarse con matrícula (de honor);
honourable (US **honorable**) adj
honorable; **honours degree** n (Scol)
título de licenciado con calificación alta
hood [hud] n capucha; (BRIT Aut)
capota; (US Aut) capó m; (of cooker)
campana de humos; **hoodie** n (top)
jersey m con capucha
hoof [hu:f] (pl **hooves**) n pezuña
hook [huk] n gancho; (on dress)
corchete m, broche m; (for fishing)
anzuelo ▷ vt enganchar; (fish) pescar
hooligan ['hu:lɪgən] n gamberro
hoop [hu:p] n aro
hooray [hu:'reɪ] excl = **hurray**
hoot [hu:t] (BRIT) vi (Aut) tocar el pito,
pitar; (siren) (hacer) sonar; (owl) ulular
Hoover® ['hu:və*] (BRIT) n
aspiradora ▷ vt: **to hoover** pasar la
aspiradora por
hooves [hu:vz] npl of **hoof**
hop [hɔp] vi saltar, brincar; (on one
foot) saltar con un pie
hope [həup] vt, vi esperar ▷ n
esperanza; **I ~ so/not** espero
que sí/no; **hopeful** adj (person)
optimista; (situation) prometedor(a);
hopefully adv con esperanza; (one
hopes): **hopefully he will recover**
esperamos que se recupere; **hopeless**
adj desesperado; (person): **to be
hopeless** ser un desastre
hops [hɔps] npl lúpulo
horizon [hə'raɪzn] n horizonte m;
horizontal [hɔrɪ'zɔntl] adj horizontal
hormone ['hɔ:məun] n hormona
horn [hɔ:n] n cuerno; (Mus: also:

French ~) trompa; (*Aut*) pito, claxon *m*

horoscope ['hɔrəskəup] *n* horóscopo

horrendous [hɔ'rɛndəs] *adj* horrendo

horrible ['hɔrɪbl] *adj* horrible

horrid ['hɔrɪd] *adj* horrible, horroroso

horrific [hɔ'rɪfɪk] *adj* (*accident*) horroroso; (*film*) horripilante

horrifying ['hɔrɪfaɪɪŋ] *adj* horroroso

horror ['hɔrə*] *n* horror *m*; **horror film** *n* película de horror

hors d'œuvre [ɔ:'də:vrə] *n* entremeses *mpl*

horse [hɔ:s] *n* caballo; **horseback** *n*: **on horseback** a caballo; **horse chestnut** *n* (*tree*) castaño de Indias; (*nut*) castaña de Indias; **horsepower** *n* caballo (de fuerza); **horse-racing** *n* carreras *fpl* de caballos; **horseradish** *n* rábano picante; **horse riding** *n* (BRIT) equitación *f*

hose [həuz] *n* manguera; **hosepipe** *n* manguera

hospital ['hɔspɪtl] *n* hospital *m*

hospitality [hɔspɪ'tælɪtɪ] *n* hospitalidad *f*

host [həust] *n* anfitrión *m*; (*TV, Radio*) presentador *m*; (*Rel*) hostia; (*large number*): **a ~ of** multitud de

hostage ['hɔstɪdʒ] *n* rehén *m*

hostel ['hɔstl] *n* hostal *m*; **(youth) ~** albergue *m* juvenil

hostess ['həustɪs] *n* anfitriona; (BRIT: *air hostess*) azafata; (*TV, Radio*) presentadora

hostile ['hɔstaɪl] *adj* hostil

hostility [hɔ'stɪlɪtɪ] *n* hostilidad *f*

hot [hɔt] *adj* caliente; (*weather*) caluroso, de calor; (*as opposed to warm*) muy caliente; (*spicy*) picante; **to be ~** (*person*) tener calor; (*object*) estar caliente; (*weather*) hacer calor; **hot dog** *n* perro caliente

hotel [həu'tɛl] *n* hotel *m*

hot-water bottle [hɔt'wɔ:tə*-] *n* bolsa de agua caliente

hound [haund] *vt* acosar ▷ *n* perro

(de caza)

hour ['auə*] *n* hora, **hourly** *adj* (de) cada hora

house [*n* haus, *pl* 'hauzɪz, *vb* hauz] *n* (*gen, firm*) casa; (*Pol*) cámara; (*Theatre*) sala ▷ *vt* (*person*) alojar; (*collection*) albergar; **on the ~** (*fig*) la casa invita; **household** *n* familia; (*home*) casa; **householder** *n* propietario/a; (*head of house*) cabeza de familia; **housekeeper** *n* ama de llaves; **housekeeping** *n* (*work*) trabajos *mpl* domésticos; **housewife** (*irreg*) *n* ama de casa; **house wine** *n* vino *m* de la casa; **housework** *n* faenas *fpl* (de la casa)

housing ['hauzɪŋ] *n* (*act*) alojamiento; (*houses*) viviendas *fpl*; **housing development, housing estate** (BRIT) *n* urbanización *f*

hover ['hɔvə*] *vi* flotar (en el aire); **hovercraft** *n* aerodeslizador *m*

how [hau] *adv* (*in what way*) cómo; **~ are you?** ¿cómo estás?; **~ much milk/ many people?** ¿cuánta leche/gente?; **~ much does it cost?** ¿cuánto cuesta?; **~ long have you been here?** ¿cuánto hace que estás aquí?; **~ old are you?** ¿cuántos años tienes?; **~ tall is he?** ¿cómo es de alto?; **~ is school?** ¿cómo (te) va (en) la escuela?; **~ was the film?** ¿qué tal la película?; **~ lovely/awful!** ¡qué bonito/horror!

however [hau'ɛvə*] *adv*: **~ I do it** lo haga como lo haga; **~ cold it is** por mucho frío que haga; **~ fast he runs** por muy rápido que corra; **~ did you do it?** ¿cómo lo hiciste? ▷ *conj* sin embargo, no obstante

howl [haul] *n* aullido ▷ *vi* aullar; (*person*) dar alaridos; (*wind*) ulular

H.P. *n abbr* = **hire purchase**

h.p. *abbr* = **horsepower**

HQ *n abbr* = **headquarters**

hr(s) *abbr* (= *hour(s)*) h

HTML *n abbr* (= *hypertext markup language*) lenguaje *m* de hipertexto

hubcap ['hʌbkæp] *n* tapacubos *m inv*

huddle ['hʌdl] *vi*: **to ~ together**

acurrucarse

huff [hʌf] n: **in a ~** enojado

hug [hʌg] vt abrazar; (thing) apretar con los brazos

huge [hju:dʒ] adj enorme

hull [hʌl] n (of ship) casco

hum [hʌm] vt tararear, canturrear ▷ vi tararear, canturrear; (insect) zumbar

human ['hju:mən] adj, n humano

humane [hju:'meɪn] adj humano, humanitario

humanitarian [hju:mænɪ'tɛərɪən] adj humanitario

humanity [hju:'mænɪtɪ] n humanidad f

human rights npl derechos mpl humanos

humble ['hʌmbl] adj humilde

humid ['hju:mɪd] adj húmedo; **humidity** [-'mɪdɪtɪ] n humedad f

humiliate [hju:'mɪlɪeɪt] vt humillar

humiliating [hju:'mɪlɪeɪtɪŋ] adj humillante, vergonzoso

humiliation [hju:mɪlɪ'eɪʃən] n humillación f

hummus ['huməs] n paté de garbanzos

humorous ['hju:mərəs] adj gracioso, divertido

humour ['hju:mə*] (US **humor**) n humorismo, sentido del humor; (mood) humor m ▷ vt (person) complacer

hump [hʌmp] n (in ground) montículo; (camel's) giba

hunch [hʌntʃ] n (premonition) presentimiento

hundred ['hʌndrəd] num ciento; (before n) cien; **~s of** centenares de; **hundredth** [-ɪdθ] adj centésimo

hung [hʌŋ] pt, pp of **hang**

Hungarian [hʌŋ'gɛərɪən] adj, n húngaro/a m/f

Hungary ['hʌŋgərɪ] n Hungría

hunger ['hʌŋgə*] n hambre f ▷ vi: **to ~ for** (fig) tener hambre de, anhelar

hungry ['hʌŋgrɪ] adj: **~ (for)** hambriento (de); **to be ~** tener hambre

hunt [hʌnt] vt (seek) buscar; (Sport) cazar ▷ vi (search): **to ~ (for)** buscar; (Sport) cazar ▷ n búsqueda; caza, cacería; **hunter** n cazador(a) m/f; **hunting** n caza

hurdle ['hə:dl] n (Sport) valla; (fig) obstáculo

hurl [hə:l] vt lanzar, arrojar

hurrah [hu:'rɑ:] excl = **hurray**

hurray [hu'reɪ] excl ¡viva!

hurricane ['hʌrɪkən] n huracán m

hurry ['hʌrɪ] n prisa ▷ vt (also: ~ **up**: person) dar prisa a; (: work) apresurar; hacer de prisa; **to be in a ~** tener prisa; **hurry up** vi darse prisa, apurarse (LAM)

hurt [hə:t] (pt, pp ~) vt hacer daño a ▷ vi doler ▷ adj lastimado

husband ['hʌzbənd] n marido

hush [hʌʃ] n silencio ▷ vt hacer callar; **~!** ¡chitón!, ¡cállate!

husky ['hʌskɪ] adj ronco ▷ n perro esquimal

hut [hʌt] n cabaña; (shed) cobertizo

hyacinth ['haɪəsɪnθ] n jacinto

hydrangea [haɪ'dreɪnʒə] n hortensia

hydrofoil ['haɪdrəfɔɪl] n aerodeslizador m

hydrogen ['haɪdrədʒən] n hidrógeno

hygiene ['haɪdʒi:n] n higiene f; **hygienic** [-'dʒi:nɪk] adj higiénico

hymn [hɪm] n himno

hype [haɪp] (inf) n bombardeo publicitario

hyphen ['haɪfn] n guión m

hypnotize ['hɪpnətaɪz] vt hipnotizar

hypocrite ['hɪpəkrɪt] n hipócrita mf

hypocritical [hɪpə'krɪtɪkl] adj hipócrita

hypothesis [haɪ'pɔθɪsɪs] (pl **hypotheses**) n hipótesis f inv

hysterical [hɪ'stɛrɪkl] adj histérico; (funny) para morirse de risa

hysterics [hɪ'stɛrɪks] npl histeria; **to be in ~** (fig) morirse de risa

they're ideally suited hacen una pareja ideal

identical [aɪ'dɛntɪkl] *adj* idéntico

identification [aɪdɛntɪfɪ'keɪʃən] *n* identificación *f*; **(means of) ~** documentos *mpl* personales

identify [aɪ'dɛntɪfaɪ] *vt* identificar

identity [aɪ'dɛntɪtɪ] *n* identidad *f*; **identity card** *n* carnet *m* de identidad; **identity theft** *n* robo de identidad

ideology [aɪdɪ'ɔlədʒɪ] *n* ideología

idiom ['ɪdɪəm] *n* modismo; *(style of speaking)* lenguaje *m*

> ▌Be careful not to translate **idiom** by the Spanish word *idioma*.

idiot ['ɪdɪət] *n* idiota *mf*

idle ['aɪdl] *adj (inactive)* ocioso; *(lazy)* holgazán/ana; *(unemployed)* parado, desocupado; *(machinery etc)* parado; *(talk etc)* frívolo ▷ *vi (machine)* marchar en vacío

idol ['aɪdl] *n* ídolo

idyllic [ɪ'dɪlɪk] *adj* idílico

i.e. *abbr* (= *that is*) esto es

if [ɪf] *conj* si; **~ necessary** si fuera necesario, si hiciese falta; **~ I were you** yo en tu lugar; **~ so/not** de ser así/si no; **~ only I could!** ¡ojalá pudiera!; *see also* **as; even**

ignite [ɪg'naɪt] *vt (set fire to)* encender ▷ *vi* encenderse

ignition [ɪg'nɪʃən] *n (Aut: process)* ignición *f*; (: *mechanism*) encendido; **to switch on/off the ~** arrancar/apagar el motor

ignorance ['ɪgnərəns] *n* ignorancia

ignorant ['ɪgnərənt] *adj* ignorante; **to be ~ of** ignorar

ignore [ɪg'nɔː*] *vt (person, advice)* no hacer caso de; *(fact)* pasar por alto

I'll [aɪl] = **I will; I shall**

ill [ɪl] *adj* enfermo, malo ▷ *n* mal *m* ▷ *adv* mal; **to be taken ~** ponerse enfermo

illegal [ɪ'liːgl] *adj* ilegal

illegible [ɪ'lɛdʒɪbl] *adj* ilegible

illegitimate [ɪlɪ'dʒɪtɪmət] *adj*

I [aɪ] *pron* yo

ice [aɪs] *n* hielo; *(ice cream)* helado ▷ *vt (cake)* alcorzar ▷ *vi (also: ~ over, ~ up)* helarse; **iceberg** *n* iceberg *m*; **ice cream** *n* helado; **ice cube** *n* cubito de hielo; **ice hockey** *n* hockey *m* sobre hielo

Iceland ['aɪslənd] *n* Islandia; **Icelander** *n* islandés/esa *m/f*; **Icelandic** [aɪs'lændɪk] *adj* islandés/esa ▷ *n (Ling)* islandés *m*

ice: ice lolly (BRIT) *n* polo; **ice rink** *n* pista de hielo; **ice skating** *n* patinaje *m* sobre hielo

icing ['aɪsɪŋ] *n (Culin)* alcorza; **icing sugar** (BRIT) *n* azúcar *m* glas(eado)

icon ['aɪkɔn] *n* icono

ICT (BRIT: *Scol*) *n abbr* (= *information and communications technology*) informática

icy ['aɪsɪ] *adj* helado

I'd [aɪd] = **I would; I had**

ID card *n (identity card)* DNI *m*

idea [aɪ'dɪə] *n* idea

ideal [aɪ'dɪəl] *n* ideal *m* ▷ *adj* ideal; **ideally** [-dɪəlɪ] *adv* idealmente;

ilegítimo

ill health n mala salud f; **to be in ~** estar mal de salud

illiterate [ɪ'lɪtərət] adj analfabeto

illness ['ɪlnɪs] n enfermedad f

illuminate [ɪ'lu:mɪneɪt] vt (room, street) iluminar, alumbrar

illusion [ɪ'lu:ʒən] n ilusión f; (trick) truco

illustrate ['ɪləstreɪt] vt ilustrar

illustration [ɪlə'streɪʃən] n (act of illustrating) ilustración f; (example) ejemplo, ilustración f; (in book) lámina

I'm [aɪm] = **I am**

image ['ɪmɪdʒ] n imagen f

imaginary [ɪ'mædʒɪnərɪ] adj imaginario

imagination [ɪmædʒɪ'neɪʃən] n imaginación f; (inventiveness) inventiva

imaginative [ɪ'mædʒɪnətɪv] adj imaginativo

imagine [ɪ'mædʒɪn] vt imaginarse

imbalance [ɪm'bæləns] n desequilibrio

imitate ['ɪmɪteɪt] vt imitar; **imitation** [ɪmɪ'teɪʃən] n imitación f; (copy) copia

immaculate [ɪ'mækjulət] adj inmaculado

immature [ɪmə'tjuə*] adj (person) inmaduro

immediate [ɪ'mi:dɪət] adj inmediato; (pressing) urgente, apremiante; (nearest: family) próximo; (: neighbourhood) inmediato; **immediately** adv (at once) en seguida; (directly) inmediatamente; **immediately next to** muy junto a

immense [ɪ'mɛns] adj inmenso, enorme; (importance) enorme; **immensely** adv enormemente

immerse [ɪ'mə:s] vt (submerge) sumergir; **to be ~d in** (fig) estar absorto en

immigrant ['ɪmɪgrənt] n inmigrante mf; **immigration** [ɪmɪ'greɪʃən] n inmigración f

imminent ['ɪmɪnənt] adj inminente

immoral [ɪ'mɒrl] adj inmoral

immortal [ɪ'mɔ:tl] adj inmortal

immune [ɪ'mju:n] adj: **~ (to)** inmune (a); **immune system** n sistema m inmunitario

immunize ['ɪmjunaɪz] vt inmunizar

impact ['ɪmpækt] n impacto

impair [ɪm'pɛə*] vt perjudicar

impartial [ɪm'pɑ:ʃl] adj imparcial

impatience [ɪm'peɪʃəns] n impaciencia

impatient [ɪm'peɪʃənt] adj impaciente; **to get** or **grow ~** impacientarse

impeccable [ɪm'pɛkəbl] adj impecable

impending [ɪm'pɛndɪŋ] adj inminente

imperative [ɪm'pɛrətɪv] adj (tone) imperioso; (need) imprescindible ▷ n (Ling: also: **~ tense**)

imperfect [ɪm'pə:fɪkt] adj (goods etc) defectuoso ▷ n (Ling: also: **~ tense**) imperfecto

imperial [ɪm'pɪərɪəl] adj imperial

impersonal [ɪm'pə:sənl] adj impersonal

impersonate [ɪm'pə:səneɪt] vt hacerse pasar por; (Theatre) imitar

impetus ['ɪmpətəs] n ímpetu m; (fig) impulso

implant [ɪm'plɑ:nt] vt (Med) injertar, implantar; (fig: idea, principle) inculcar

implement [n 'ɪmplɪmənt, vb 'ɪmplɪmɛnt] n herramienta; (for cooking) utensilio ▷ vt (regulation) hacer efectivo; (plan) realizar

implicate ['ɪmplɪkeɪt] vt (compromise) comprometer; **to ~ sb in sth** comprometer a algn en algo

implication [ɪmplɪ'keɪʃən] n consecuencia; **by ~** indirectamente

implicit [ɪm'plɪsɪt] adj implícito; (belief, trust) absoluto

imply [ɪm'plaɪ] vt (involve) suponer; (hint) dar a entender que

impolite [ɪmpə'laɪt] adj mal educado

import [vb ɪmˈpɔːt, n ˈɪmpɔːt] vt
importar ▷ n (Comm) importación
f; (: article) producto importado;
(meaning) significado, sentido
importance [ɪmˈpɔːtəns] n
importancia
important [ɪmˈpɔːtənt] adj
importante; **it's not ~** no importa, no
tiene importancia
importer [ɪmˈpɔːtə*] n
importador(a) m/f
impose [ɪmˈpəʊz] vt imponer
▷ vi: **to ~ on sb** abusar de algn;
imposing adj imponente,
impresionante
impossible [ɪmˈpɔsɪbl] adj
imposible; (person) insoportable
impotent [ˈɪmpətənt] adj impotente
impoverished [ɪmˈpɔvərɪʃt] adj
necesitado
impractical [ɪmˈpræktɪkl] adj
(person, plan) poco práctico
impress [ɪmˈprɛs] vt impresionar;
(mark) estampar; **to ~ sth on sb** hacer
entender algo a algn
impression [ɪmˈprɛʃən] n
impresión f; (imitation) imitación f; **to
be under the ~ that** tener la impresión
de que
impressive [ɪmˈprɛsɪv] adj
impresionante
imprison [ɪmˈprɪzn] vt encarcelar;
imprisonment n encarcelamiento;
(term of imprisonment) cárcel f
improbable [ɪmˈprɔbəbl] adj
improbable, inverosímil
improper [ɪmˈprɔpə*] adj
(unsuitable: conduct etc) incorrecto;
(: activities) deshonesto
improve [ɪmˈpruːv] vt mejorar;
(foreign language) perfeccionar
▷ vi mejorarse; **improvement** n
mejoramiento; perfección f;
progreso
improvise [ˈɪmprəvaɪz] vt, vi
improvisar
impulse [ˈɪmpʌls] n impulso; **to act
on ~** obrar sin reflexión; **impulsive**

[ɪmˈpʌlsɪv] adj irreflexivo

○ **KEYWORD**

in [ɪn] prep **1** (indicating place,
position, with place names) en; **in the
house/garden** en (la) casa/el jardín;
in here/there aquí/ahí or allí dentro;
in London/England en Londres/
Inglaterra
2 (indicating time) en; **in spring** en (la)
primavera; **in the afternoon** por la
tarde; **at 4 o'clock in the afternoon**
a las 4 de la tarde; **I did it in 3 hours/
days** lo hice en 3 horas/días; **I'll see
you in 2 weeks** or **in 2 weeks' time** te
veré dentro de 2 semanas
3 (indicating manner etc) en; **in a loud/
soft voice** en voz alta/baja; **in pencil/
ink** a lápiz/bolígrafo; **the boy in the
blue shirt** el chico de la camisa azul
4 (indicating circumstances): **in the sun/
shade/rain** al sol/a la sombra/bajo la
lluvia; **a change in policy** un cambio
de política
5 (indicating mood, state): **in tears** en
lágrimas, llorando; **in anger/despair**
enfadado/desesperado; **to live in
luxury** vivir lujosamente
6 (with ratios, numbers): **1 in 10
households, 1 household in 10** una
de cada 10 familias; **20 pence in the
pound** 20 peniques por libra; **they
lined up in twos** se alinearon de dos
en dos
7 (referring to people, works) en; entre;
the disease is common in children la
enfermedad es común entre los niños;
in (the works of) Dickens en (las
obras de) Dickens
8 (indicating profession etc): **to be in
teaching** estar en la enseñanza
9 (after superlative) de; **the best pupil
in the class** el(la) mejor alumno/a
de la clase
10 (with present participle): **in saying
this** al decir esto
▷ adv: **to be in** (person: at home) estar en

casa; (*at work*) estar; (*train, ship, plane*) haber llegado; (*in fashion*) estar de moda; **she'll be in later today** llegará más tarde hoy; **to ask sb in** hacer pasar a algn; **to run/limp** *etc* **in** entrar corriendo/cojeando *etc*
▷ *n*: **the ins and outs** (*of proposal, situation etc*) los detalles

inability [ɪnə'bɪlɪtɪ] *n*: **~ (to do)** incapacidad *f* (de hacer)

inaccurate [ɪn'ækjurət] *adj* inexacto, incorrecto

inadequate [ɪn'ædɪkwət] *adj* (*income, reply etc*) insuficiente; (*person*) incapaz

inadvertently [ɪnəd'vɜːtntlɪ] *adv* por descuido

inappropriate [ɪnə'prəʊprɪət] *adj* inadecuado; (*improper*) poco oportuno

inaugurate [ɪ'nɔ:gjureɪt] *vt* inaugurar; (*president, official*) investir

Inc. (*US*) *abbr* (= *incorporated*) S.A.

incapable [ɪn'keɪpəbl] *adj* incapaz

incense [*n* 'ɪnsɛns, *vb* ɪn'sɛns] *n* incienso ▷ *vt* (*anger*) indignar, encolerizar

incentive [ɪn'sɛntɪv] *n* incentivo, estímulo

inch [ɪntʃ] *n* pulgada; **to be within an ~ of** estar a dos dedos de; **he didn't give an ~** no dio concesión alguna

incidence ['ɪnsɪdns] *n* (*of crime, disease*) incidencia

incident ['ɪnsɪdnt] *n* incidente *m*

incidentally [ɪnsɪ'dɛntəlɪ] *adv* (*by the way*) a propósito

inclination [ɪnklɪ'neɪʃən] *n* (*tendency*) tendencia, inclinación *f*; (*desire*) deseo; (*disposition*) propensión *f*

incline [*n* 'ɪnklaɪn, *vb* ɪn'klaɪn] *n* pendiente *m*, cuesta ▷ *vt* (*head*) poner de lado ▷ *vi* inclinarse; **to be ~d to** (*tend*) tener tendencia a hacer algo

include [ɪn'klu:d] *vt* (*incorporate*) incluir; (*in letter*) adjuntar; **including** *prep* incluso, inclusive

inclusion [ɪn'klu:ʒən] *n* inclusión *f*

inclusive [ɪn'klusɪv] *adj* inclusivo; **~ of tax** incluidos los impuestos

income ['ɪŋkʌm] *n* (*earned*) ingresos *mpl*; (*from property etc*) renta; (*from investment etc*) rédito; **income support** *n* (*BRIT*) ≈ ayuda familiar; **income tax** *n* impuesto sobre la renta

incoming ['ɪnkʌmɪŋ] *adj* (*flight, government etc*) entrante

incompatible [ɪnkəm'pætɪbl] *adj* incompatible

incompetence [ɪn'kɔmpɪtəns] *n* incompetencia

incompetent [ɪn'kɔmpɪtənt] *adj* incompetente

incomplete [ɪnkəm'pli:t] *adj* (*partial: achievement etc*) incompleto; (*unfinished: painting etc*) inacabado

inconsistent [ɪnkən'sɪstənt] *adj* inconsecuente; (*contradictory*) incongruente; **~ with** (que) no concuerda con

inconvenience [ɪnkən'vi:njəns] *n* inconvenientes *mpl*; (*trouble*) molestia, incomodidad *f* ▷ *vt* incomodar

inconvenient [ɪnkən'vi:njənt] *adj* incómodo, poco práctico; (*time, place, visitor*) inoportuno

incorporate [ɪn'kɔ:pəreɪt] *vt* incorporar; (*contain*) comprender; (*add*) agregar

incorrect [ɪnkə'rɛkt] *adj* incorrecto

increase [*n* 'ɪnkri:s, *vb* ɪn'kri:s] *n* aumento ▷ *vi* aumentar; (*grow*) crecer; (*price*) subir ▷ *vt* aumentar; (*price*) subir; **increasingly** *adv* cada vez más, más y más

incredible [ɪn'krɛdɪbl] *adj* increíble; **incredibly** *adv* increíblemente

incur [ɪn'kə:*] *vt* (*expenditure*) incurrir; (*loss*) sufrir; (*anger, disapproval*) provocar

indecent [ɪn'di:snt] *adj* indecente

indeed [ɪn'di:d] *adv* efectivamente, en realidad; (*in fact*) en efecto; (*furthermore*) es más; **yes ~!** ¡claro que sí!

indefinitely [ɪnˈdɛfɪnɪtlɪ] *adv* (*wait*) indefinidamente

independence [ɪndɪˈpɛndns] *n* independencia; **Independence Day** (*US*) *n* Día *m* de la Independencia

● **INDEPENDENCE DAY**
●
● El cuatro de julio es **Independence**
● **Day**, la fiesta nacional de Estados
● Unidos, que se celebra en
● conmemoración de la Declaración
● de Independencia, escrita por
● Thomas Jefferson y aprobada
● en 1776. En ella se proclamaba
● la independencia total de Gran
● Bretaña de las trece colonias
● americanas que serían el origen de
● los Estados Unidos de América.

independent [ɪndɪˈpɛndənt] *adj* independiente; **independent school** *n* (*BRIT*) escuela *f* privada, colegio *m* privado

index [ˈɪndɛks] (*pl* **-es**) *n* (*in book*) índice *m*; (: *in library etc*) catálogo; (*pl* **indices**: *ratio, sign*) exponente *m*

India [ˈɪndɪə] *n* la India; **Indian** *adj, n* indio/a; **Red Indian** piel roja *mf*

indicate [ˈɪndɪkeɪt] *vt* indicar; **indication** [-ˈkeɪʃən] *n* indicio, señal *f*; **indicative** [ɪnˈdɪkətɪv] · *adj*: **to be indicative of** indicar; **indicator** *n* indicador *m*; (*Aut*) intermitente *m*

indices [ˈɪndɪsiːz] *npl of* **index**

indict [ɪnˈdaɪt] *vt* acusar; **indictment** *n* acusación *f*

indifference [ɪnˈdɪfrəns] *n* indiferencia

indifferent [ɪnˈdɪfrənt] *adj* indiferente; (*mediocre*) regular

indigenous [ɪnˈdɪdʒɪnəs] *adj* indígena

indigestion [ɪndɪˈdʒɛstʃən] *n* indigestión *f*

indignant [ɪnˈdɪgnənt] *adj*: **to be ~ at sth/with sb** indignarse por

algo/con algn

indirect [ɪndɪˈrɛkt] *adj* indirecto

indispensable [ɪndɪˈspɛnsəbl] *adj* indispensable, imprescindible

individual [ɪndɪˈvɪdjuəl] *n* individuo ▷ *adj* individual; (*personal*) personal; (*particular*) particular; **individually** *adv* (*singly*) individualmente

Indonesia [ɪndəˈniːzɪə] *n* Indonesia

indoor [ˈɪndɔː*] *adj* (*swimming pool*) cubierto; (*plant*) de interior; (*sport*) bajo cubierta; **indoors** [ɪnˈdɔːz] *adv* dentro

induce [ɪnˈdjuːs] *vt* inducir, persuadir; (*bring about*) producir; (*labour*) provocar

indulge [ɪnˈdʌldʒ] *vt* (*whim*) satisfacer; (*person*) complacer; (*child*) mimar ▷ *vi*: **to ~ in** darse el gusto de; **indulgent** *adj* indulgente

industrial [ɪnˈdʌstrɪəl] *adj* industrial; **industrial estate** (*BRIT*) *n* polígono (*SP*) *or* zona (*LAM*) industrial; **industrialist** *n* industrial *mf*; **industrial park** (*US*) *n* = **industrial estate**

industry [ˈɪndəstrɪ] *n* industria; (*diligence*) aplicación *f*

inefficient [ɪnɪˈfɪʃənt] *adj* ineficaz, ineficiente

inequality [ɪnɪˈkwɔlɪtɪ] *n* desigualdad *f*

inevitable [ɪnˈɛvɪtəbl] *adj* inevitable; **inevitably** *adv* inevitablemente

inexpensive [ɪnɪkˈspɛnsɪv] *adj* económico

inexperienced [ɪnɪkˈspɪərɪənst] *adj* inexperto

inexplicable [ɪnɪkˈsplɪkəbl] *adj* inexplicable

infamous [ˈɪnfəməs] *adj* infame

infant [ˈɪnfənt] *n* niño/a; (*baby*) niño/a pequeño/a, bebé *mf*; (*pej*) aniñado

infantry [ˈɪnfəntrɪ] *n* infantería

infant school (*BRIT*) *n* parvulario

infect [ɪnˈfɛkt] *vt* (*wound*) infectar; (*food*) contaminar; (*person, animal*) contagiar; **infection** [ɪnˈfɛkʃən] *n* infección *f*; (*fig*) contagio; **infectious**

[ɪn'fɛkʃəs] adj (also fig) contagioso

infer [ɪn'fə:*] vt deducir, inferir

inferior [ɪn'fɪərɪə*] adj, n inferior mf

infertile [ɪn'fə:taɪl] adj estéril; (person) infecundo

infertility [ɪnfə:'tɪlɪtɪ] n esterilidad f; infecundidad f

infested [ɪn'fɛstɪd] adj: **~ with** plagado de

infinite ['ɪnfɪnɪt] adj infinito; **infinitely** adv infinitamente

infirmary [ɪn'fə:mərɪ] n hospital m

inflamed [ɪn'fleɪmd] adj: **to become ~** inflamarse

inflammation [ɪnflə'meɪʃən] n inflamación f

inflatable [ɪn'fleɪtəbl] adj (ball, boat) inflable

inflate [ɪn'fleɪt] vt (tyre, price etc) inflar; (fig) hinchar; **inflation** [ɪn'fleɪʃən] n (Econ) inflación f

inflexible [ɪn'flɛksəbl] adj (rule) rígido; (person) inflexible

inflict [ɪn'flɪkt] vt: **to ~ sth on sb** infligir algo en algn

influence ['ɪnfluəns] n influencia ▷ vt influir en, influenciar; **under the ~ of alcohol** en estado de embriaguez; **influential** [-'ɛnʃl] adj influyente

influx ['ɪnflʌks] n afluencia

info (inf) ['ɪnfəu] n = **information**

inform [ɪn'fɔ:m] vt: **to ~ sb of sth** informar a algn sobre or de algo ▷ vi: **to ~ on sb** delatar a algn

informal [ɪn'fɔ:məl] adj (manner, tone) familiar; (dress, interview, occasion) informal; (visit, meeting) extraoficial

information [ɪnfə'meɪʃən] n información f; (knowledge) conocimientos mpl; **a piece of ~** un dato; **information office** n información f; **information technology** n informática

informative [ɪn'fɔ:mətɪv] adj informativo

infra-red [ɪnfrə'rɛd] adj infrarrojo

infrastructure ['ɪnfrəstrʌktʃə*] n (of system etc) infraestructura

infrequent [ɪn'fri:kwənt] adj infrecuente

infuriate [ɪn'fjuərɪeɪt] vt: **to become ~d** ponerse furioso

infuriating [ɪn'fjuərɪeɪtɪŋ] adj (habit, noise) enloquecedor(a)

ingenious [ɪn'dʒi:nɪəs] adj ingenioso

ingredient [ɪn'gri:dɪənt] n ingrediente m

inhabit [ɪn'hæbɪt] vt vivir en; **inhabitant** n habitante mf

inhale [ɪn'heɪl] vt inhalar ▷ vi (breathe in) aspirar; (in smoking) tragar; **inhaler** n inhalador m

inherent [ɪn'hɪərənt] adj: **~ in or to** inherente a

inherit [ɪn'hɛrɪt] vt heredar; **inheritance** n herencia; (fig) patrimonio

inhibit [ɪn'hɪbɪt] vt inhibir, impedir; **inhibition** [-'bɪʃən] n cohibición f

initial [ɪ'nɪʃl] adj primero ▷ n inicial f ▷ vt firmar con las iniciales; **initials** npl (as signature) iniciales fpl; (abbreviation) siglas fpl; **initially** adv al principio

initiate [ɪ'nɪʃɪeɪt] vt iniciar; **to ~ proceedings against sb** (Law) entablar proceso contra algn

initiative [ɪ'nɪʃətɪv] n iniciativa

inject [ɪn'dʒɛkt] vt inyectar; **to ~ sb with sth** inyectar algo a algn; **injection** [ɪn'dʒɛkʃən] n inyección f

injure ['ɪndʒə*] vt (hurt) herir, lastimar; (fig: reputation etc) perjudicar; **injured** adj (person, arm) herido, lastimado; **injury** n herida, lesión f; (wrong) perjuicio, daño

> Be careful not to translate **injury** by the Spanish word *injuria*.

injustice [ɪn'dʒʌstɪs] n injusticia

ink [ɪŋk] n tinta; **ink-jet printer** ['ɪŋkdʒɛt-] n impresora de chorro de tinta

inland [adj 'ɪnlənd, adv ɪn'lænd] adj (waterway, port etc) interior ▷ adv tierra adentro; **Inland Revenue** (BRIT) n departamento de impuestos ≈

Hacienda (SP)

in-laws ['ɪnlɔːz] npl suegros mpl

inmate ['ɪnmeɪt] n (in prison) preso/a, presidiario/a; (in asylum) internado/a

inn [ɪn] n posada, mesón m

inner ['ɪnə*] adj (courtyard, calm) interior; (feelings) íntimo; **inner-city** adj (schools, problems) de las zonas céntricas pobres, de los barrios céntricos pobres

inning ['ɪnɪŋ] n (us: Baseball) inning m, entrada; **~s** (Cricket) entrada, turno

innocence ['ɪnəsns] n inocencia

innocent ['ɪnəsnt] adj inocente

innovation [ɪnəu'veɪʃən] n novedad f

innovative ['ɪnəu'veɪtɪv] adj innovador

in-patient ['ɪnpeɪʃənt] n paciente m/f interno/a

input ['ɪnput] n entrada; (of resources) inversión f; (Comput) entrada de datos

inquest ['ɪnkwɛst] n (coroner's) encuesta judicial

inquire [ɪn'kwaɪə*] vi preguntar ▷ vt: **to ~ whether** preguntar si; **to ~ about** (person) preguntar por; (fact) informarse de; **inquiry** n pregunta; (investigation) investigación f, pesquisa; **"Inquiries"** "Información"

ins. abbr = **inches**

insane [ɪn'seɪn] adj loco; (Med) demente

insanity [ɪn'sænɪtɪ] n demencia, locura

insect ['ɪnsɛkt] n insecto; **insect repellent** n loción f contra insectos

insecure [ɪnsɪ'kjuə*] adj inseguro

insecurity [ɪnsɪ'kjuərɪtɪ] n inseguridad f

insensitive [ɪn'sɛnsɪtɪv] adj insensible

insert [vb ɪn'sɜːt, n 'ɪnsɛːt] vt (into sth) introducir ▷ n encarte m

inside ['ɪn'saɪd] n interior m ▷ adj interior, interno ▷ adv (be) (por) dentro; (go) hacia dentro ▷ prep dentro de; (of time): **~ 10 minutes** en menos

de 10 minutos; **inside lane** n (Aut: in Britain) carril m izquierdo, (: in US, Europe etc) carril m derecho; **inside out** adv (turn) al revés; (know) a fondo

insight ['ɪnsaɪt] n perspicacia

insignificant [ɪnsɪg'nɪfɪknt] adj insignificante

insincere [ɪnsɪn'sɪə*] adj poco sincero

insist [ɪn'sɪst] vi insistir; **to ~ on** insistir en; **to ~ that** insistir en que; (claim) exigir que; **insistent** adj insistente; (noise, action) persistente

insomnia [ɪn'sɔmnɪə] n insomnio

inspect [ɪn'spɛkt] vt inspeccionar, examinar; (troops) pasar revista a; **inspection** [ɪn'spɛkʃən] n inspección f, examen m; (of troops) revista; **inspector** n inspector(a) m/f; (BRIT: on buses, trains) revisor(a) m/f

inspiration [ɪnspə'reɪʃən] n inspiración f; **inspire** [ɪn'spaɪə*] vt inspirar; **inspiring** adj inspirador(a)

instability [ɪnstə'bɪlɪtɪ] n inestabilidad f

install [ɪn'stɔːl] (us **instal**) vt instalar; (official) nombrar; **installation** [ɪnstə'leɪʃən] n instalación f

instalment [ɪn'stɔːlmənt] (us **installment**) n plazo; (of story) entrega; (of TV serial etc) capítulo; **in ~s** (pay, receive) a plazos

instance ['ɪnstəns] n ejemplo, caso; **for ~** por ejemplo; **in the first ~** en primer lugar

instant ['ɪnstənt] n instante m, momento ▷ adj inmediato; (coffee etc) instantáneo; **instantly** adv en seguida; **instant messaging** n mensajería instantánea

instead [ɪn'stɛd] adv en cambio; **~ of** en lugar de, en vez de

instinct ['ɪnstɪŋkt] n instinto; **instinctive** adj instintivo

institute ['ɪnstɪtjuːt] n instituto; (professional body) colegio ▷ vt (begin) iniciar, empezar; (proceedings) entablar; (system, rule) establecer

institution [ɪnstɪ'tjuːʃən] n
institución f; (Med: home) asilo;
(: asylum) manicomio; (of system etc)
establecimiento; (of custom)
iniciación f

instruct [ɪn'strʌkt] vt: **to ~ sb in sth**
instruir a algn en or sobre algo; **to ~ sb**
to do sth dar instrucciones a algn de
hacer algo; **instruction**
[ɪn'strʌkʃən] n (teaching) instrucción f; **instructions**
npl (orders) órdenes fpl; **instructions**
(for use) modo de empleo; **instructor**
n instructor(a) m/f

instrument ['ɪnstrəmənt] n
instrumento; **instrumental** [-'mɛntl]
adj (Mus) instrumental; **to be**
instrumental in ser (el) artífice de

insufficient [ɪnsə'fɪʃənt] adj
insuficiente

insulate ['ɪnsjuleɪt] vt aislar;
insulation [-'leɪʃən] n aislamiento

insulin ['ɪnsjulɪn] n insulina

insult [n 'ɪnsʌlt, vb ɪn'sʌlt] n insulto
▷ vt insultar; **insulting** adj insultante

insurance [ɪn'ʃuərəns] n seguro;
fire/life ~ seguro contra incendios/
sobre la vida; **insurance company**
n compañía f de seguros; **insurance**
policy n póliza (de seguros)

insure [ɪn'ʃuə*] vt asegurar

intact [ɪn'tækt] adj íntegro;
(unharmed) intacto

intake ['ɪnteɪk] n (of food) ingestión f;
(of air) consumo; (BRIT Scol): **an ~ of 200**
a year 200 matriculados al año

integral ['ɪntɪɡrəl] adj (whole)
íntegro; (part) integrante

integrate ['ɪntɪɡreɪt] vt integrar ▷ vi
integrarse

integrity [ɪn'tɛɡrɪtɪ] n honradez f,
rectitud f

intellect ['ɪntəlɛkt] n intelecto;
intellectual [-'lɛktjuəl] adj, n
intelectual mf

intelligence [ɪn'tɛlɪdʒəns] n
inteligencia

intelligent [ɪn'tɛlɪdʒənt] adj
inteligente

intend [ɪn'tɛnd] vt (gift etc): **to ~ sth**
for destinar algo a; **to ~ to do sth** tener
intención de or pensar hacer algo

intense [ɪn'tɛns] adj intenso

intensify [ɪn'tɛnsɪfaɪ] vt intensificar;
(increase) aumentar

intensity [ɪn'tɛnsɪtɪ] n (gen)
intensidad f

intensive [ɪn'tɛnsɪv] adj intensivo;
intensive care n: **to be in intensive**
care estar bajo cuidados intensivos;
intensive care unit n unidad f de
vigilancia intensiva

intent [ɪn'tɛnt] n propósito; (Law)
premeditación f ▷ adj (absorbed)
absorto; (attentive) atento; **to all ~s**
and purposes prácticamente; **to**
be ~ on doing sth estar resuelto a
hacer algo

intention [ɪn'tɛnʃən] n intención f,
propósito; **intentional** adj deliberado

interact [ɪntər'ækt] vi influirse
mutuamente; **interaction**
[ɪntər'ækʃən] n interacción f, acción
f recíproca; **interactive** adj (Comput)
interactivo

intercept [ɪntə'sɛpt] vt interceptar;
(stop) detener

interchange ['ɪntətʃeɪndʒ] n
intercambio; (on motorway)
intersección f

intercourse ['ɪntəkɔːs] n (sexual)
relaciones fpl sexuales

interest ['ɪntrɪst] n (also Comm)
interés m ▷ vt interesar; **interested**
adj interesado; **to be interested**
in interesarse por; **interesting** adj
interesante; **interest rate** n tipo or
tasa de interés

interface ['ɪntəfeɪs] n (Comput)
junción f

interfere [ɪntə'fɪə*] vi: **to ~ in**
entrometerse en; **to ~ with** (hinder)
estorbar; (damage) estropear

interference [ɪntə'fɪərəns] n
intromisión f; (Radio, TV) interferencia

interim ['ɪntərɪm] n: **in the ~** en el
ínterin ▷ adj provisional

interior [ɪn'tɪərɪə*] n interior
m ▷ adj interior; **interior design**
n interiorismo, decoración f de
interiores

intermediate [ɪntə'miːdɪət] adj
intermedio

intermission [ɪntə'mɪʃən] n
intermisión f; (Theatre) descanso

intern [vb ɪn'tɜːn, n 'ɪntɜːn] (US) vt
internar ▷ n interno/a

internal [ɪn'tɜːnl] adj (layout, pipes,
security) interior; (injury, structure,
memo) internal; **Internal Revenue
Service** (US) n departamento de
impuestos, ≈ Hacienda (SP)

international [ɪntə'næʃənl] adj
internacional ▷ n (BRIT: match) partido
internacional

Internet ['ɪntənɛt] n: **the ~** Internet
m or f; **Internet café** n cibercafé
m; **Internet Service Provider** n
proveedor m de (acceso a) Internet;
Internet user n internauta mf

interpret [ɪn'tɜːprɪt] vt interpretar;
(translate) traducir; (understand)
entender ▷ vi hacer de intérprete;
interpretation [ɪntɜːprɪ'teɪʃən]
n interpretación f; traducción f;
interpreter n intérprete mf

interrogate [ɪn'tɛrəuɡeɪt] vt
interrogar; **interrogation** [-'ɡeɪʃən] n
interrogatorio

interrogative [ɪntə'rɔɡətɪv] adj
interrogativo

interrupt [ɪntə'rʌpt] vt, vi
interrumpir; **interruption** [-'rʌpʃən] n
interrupción f

intersection [ɪntə'sɛkʃən] n (of
roads) cruce m

interstate ['ɪntəsteɪt] (US) n
carretera interestatal

interval ['ɪntəvl] n intervalo; (BRIT
Theatre, Sport) descanso; (Scol) recreo;
at ~s a ratos, de vez en cuando

intervene [ɪntə'viːn] vi intervenir;
(event) interponerse; (time) transcurrir

interview ['ɪntəvjuː] n entrevista
▷ vt entrevistarse con; **interviewer** n

entrevistador(a) m/f

intimate [adj 'ɪntɪmət, vb 'ɪntɪmeɪt]
adj íntimo; (friendship) estrecho;
(knowledge) profundo ▷ vt dar a
entender

intimidate [ɪn'tɪmɪdeɪt] vt
intimidar, amedrentar

intimidating [ɪn'tɪmɪdeɪtɪŋ] adj
amedrentador, intimidante

into ['ɪntuː] prep en; (towards) a;
(inside) hacia el interior de; **~ 3 pieces/
French** en 3 pedazos/al francés

intolerant [ɪn'tɔlərənt] adj: **~ (of)**
intolerante (con or para)

intranet ['ɪntrənɛt] n intranet f

intransitive [ɪn'trænsɪtɪv] adj
intransitivo

intricate ['ɪntrɪkət] adj (design,
pattern) intrincado

intrigue [ɪn'triːɡ] n intriga ▷ vt
fascinar; **intriguing** adj fascinante

introduce [ɪntrə'djuːs] vt introducir,
meter; (speaker, TV show etc) presentar;
to ~ sb (to sb) presentar a algn (a
algn); **to ~ sb to** (pastime, technique)
introducir a algn a; **introduction**
[-'dʌkʃən] n introducción f; (of person)
presentación f; **introductory**
[-'dʌktərɪ] adj introductorio; (lesson,
offer) de introducción

intrude [ɪn'truːd] vi (person)
entrometerse; **to ~ on** estorbar;
intruder n intruso/a

intuition [ɪntjuː'ɪʃən] n intuición f

inundate ['ɪnʌndeɪt] vt: **to ~ with**
inundar de

invade [ɪn'veɪd] vt invadir

invalid [n 'ɪnvəlɪd, adj ɪn'vælɪd] n
(Med) minusválido/a ▷ adj (not valid)
inválido, nulo

invaluable [ɪn'væljuəbl] adj
inestimable

invariably [ɪn'veərɪəblɪ] adv sin
excepción, siempre; **she is ~ late**
siempre llega tarde

invasion [ɪn'veɪʒən] n invasión f

invent [ɪn'vɛnt] vt inventar;
invention [ɪn'vɛnʃən] n invento;

(lie) ficción f, mentira; **inventor** n inventor(a) m/f

inventory ['ɪnvəntrɪ] n inventario

inverted commas [ɪn'vəːtɪd-] (BRIT) npl comillas fpl

invest [ɪn'vɛst] vt invertir ▷ vi: **to ~ in** *(company etc)* invertir dinero en; *(fig: sth useful)* comprar

investigate [ɪn'vɛstɪgeɪt] vt investigar; **investigation** [-'geɪʃən] n investigación f, pesquisa

investigator [ɪn'vɛstɪgeɪtə*] n investigador(a) m/f; **private ~** investigador(a) m/f privado/a

investment [ɪn'vɛstmənt] n inversión f

investor [ɪn'vɛstə*] n inversionista mf

invisible [ɪn'vɪzɪbl] adj invisible

invitation [ɪnvɪ'teɪʃən] n invitación f

invite [ɪn'vaɪt] vt invitar; *(opinions etc)* solicitar, pedir; **inviting** adj atractivo; *(food)* apetitoso

invoice ['ɪnvɔɪs] n factura ▷ vt facturar

involve [ɪn'vɔlv] vt suponer, implicar; tener que ver con; *(concern, affect)* corresponder; **to ~ sb (in sth)** comprometer a algn (con algo); **involved** adj complicado; **to be involved in** *(take part)* tomar parte en; *(be engrossed)* estar muy metido en; **involvement** n participación f; dedicación f

inward ['ɪnwəd] adj *(movement)* interior, interno; *(thought, feeling)* íntimo; **inward(s)** adv hacia dentro

iPod ® ['aɪpɔd] n iPod ® m

IQ n abbr *(= intelligence quotient)* cociente m intelectual

IRA n abbr *(= Irish Republican Army)* IRA m

Iran [ɪ'rɑːn] n Irán m; **Iranian** [ɪ'reɪnɪən] adj, n iraní mf

Iraq [ɪ'rɑːk] n Iraq; **Iraqi** adj, n iraquí mf

Ireland ['aɪələnd] n Irlanda

iris ['aɪrɪs] *(pl* **~es)** n *(Anat)* iris m;

(Bot) lirio

Irish ['aɪrɪʃ] adj irlandés/esa ▷ npl: **the ~** los irlandeses; **Irishman** *(irreg)* n irlandés m; **Irishwoman** *(irreg)* n irlandésa

iron ['aɪən] n hierro; *(for clothes)* plancha ▷ cpd de hierro ▷ vt *(clothes)* planchar

ironic(al) [aɪ'rɔnɪk(l)] adj irónico; **ironically** adv irónicamente

ironing ['aɪənɪŋ] n *(activity)* planchado; *(clothes: ironed)* ropa planchada; *(: to be ironed)* ropa por planchar; **ironing board** n tabla de planchar

irony ['aɪrənɪ] n ironía

irrational [ɪ'ræʃənl] adj irracional

irregular [ɪ'rɛgjulə*] adj irregular; *(surface)* desigual; *(action, event)* anómalo; *(behaviour)* poco ortodoxo

irrelevant [ɪ'rɛləvənt] adj fuera de lugar, inoportuno

irresistible [ɪrɪ'zɪstɪbl] adj irresistible

irresponsible [ɪrɪ'spɔnsɪbl] adj *(act)* irresponsable; *(person)* poco serio

irrigation [ɪrɪ'geɪʃən] n riego

irritable ['ɪrɪtəbl] adj *(person)* de mal humor

irritate ['ɪrɪteɪt] vt fastidiar; *(Med)* picar; **irritating** adj fastidioso; **irritation** [-'teɪʃən] n fastidio; enfado; picazón f

IRS (US) n abbr = **Internal Revenue Service**

is [ɪz] vb see **be**

ISDN n abbr *(= Integrated Services Digital Network)* RDSI f

Islam ['ɪzlɑːm] n Islam m; **Islamic** [ɪz'læmɪk] adj islámico

island ['aɪlənd] n isla; **islander** n isleño/a

isle [aɪl] n isla

isn't ['ɪznt] = **is not**

isolated ['aɪsəleɪtɪd] adj aislado

isolation [aɪsə'leɪʃən] n aislamiento

ISP n abbr = **Internet Service Provider**

Israel ['ɪzreɪl] n Israel m; **Israeli**

[ız'reılı] *adj, n* israelí *mf*

issue ['ısjuː] *n* (*problem, subject*)
cuestión f; (*outcome*) resultado; (*of banknotes etc*) emisión f; (*of newspaper etc*) edición f ▷ *vt* (*rations, equipment*)
distribuir, repartir; (*orders*) dar;
(*certificate, passport*) expedir; (*decree*)
promulgar; (*magazine*) publicar;
(*cheques*) extender; (*banknotes, stamps*)
emitir; **at ~** en cuestión; **to take ~
with sb (over)** estar en desacuerdo
con algn (sobre); **to make an ~ of sth**
hacer una cuestión de algo

IT *n abbr* = **information technology**

○ **KEYWORD**

it [ıt] *pron* **1** (*specific subject: not generally
translated*) él (ella); (: *direct object*) lo, la;
(: *indirect object*) le; (*after prep*) él (ella);
(*abstract concept*) ello; **it's on the table**
está en la mesa; **I can't find it** no lo (*or*
la) encuentro; **give it to me** dámelo
(*or* dámela); **I spoke to him about
it** le hablé del asunto; **what did you
learn from it?** ¿qué aprendiste de él (*or*
ella)?; **did you go to it?** (*party, concert
etc*) ¿fuiste?
2 (*impersonal*): **it's raining** llueve, está
lloviendo; **it's 6 o'clock/the 10th of
August** son las 6/es el 10 de agosto;
**how far is it? – it's 10 miles/2 hours
on the train** ¿a qué distancia está? – a
10 millas/2 horas en tren; **who is it?
– it's me** ¿quién es? – soy yo

Italian [ı'tæljən] *adj* italiano ▷ *n*
italiano/a; (*Ling*) italiano
italics [ı'tælıks] *npl* cursiva
Italy ['ıtəlı] *n* Italia
itch [ıtʃ] *n* picazón f ▷ *vi* (*part of body*)
picar; **to ~ to do sth** rabiar por hacer
algo; **itchy** *adj*: **my hand is itchy** me
pica la mano
it'd ['ıtd] = **it would; it had**
item ['aıtəm] *n* artículo; (*on agenda*)
asunto (a tratar); (*also*: **news ~**) noticia
itinerary [aı'tınərərı] *n* itinerario

it'll ['ıtl] = **it will; it shall**
its [ıts] *adj* su; sus *pl*
it's [ıts] = **it is; it has**
itself [ıt'sɛlf] *pron* (*reflexive*) sí mismo/
a; (*emphatic*) él mismo (ella misma)
ITV *n abbr* (BRIT: = *Independent
Television*) cadena de televisión comercial
independiente del Estado
I've [aıv] = **I have**
ivory ['aıvərı] *n* marfil *m*
ivy ['aıvı] *n* (*Bot*) hiedra

J

jab [dʒæb] vt: **to ~ sth into sth** clavar algo en algo ▷ n (inf: Med) pinchazo
jack [dʒæk] n (Aut) gato; (Cards) sota
jacket ['dʒækɪt] n chaqueta, americana (SP), saco (LAM); (of book) sobrecubierta; **jacket potato** n patata asada (con piel)
jackpot ['dʒækpɔt] n premio gordo
Jacuzzi® [dʒə'ku:zɪ] n jacuzzi® m
jagged ['dʒægɪd] adj dentado
jail [dʒeɪl] n cárcel f ▷ vt encarcelar; **jail sentence** n pena f de cárcel
jam [dʒæm] n mermelada; (also: **traffic ~**) embotellamiento; (inf: difficulty) apuro ▷ vt (passage etc) obstruir; (mechanism, drawer etc) atascar; (Radio) interferir ▷ vi atascarse, trabarse; **to ~ sth into sth** meter algo a la fuerza en algo
Jamaica [dʒə'meɪkə] n Jamaica
jammed [dʒæmd] adj atascado
Jan abbr (= January) ene
janitor ['dʒænɪtə*] n (caretaker) portero, conserje m
January ['dʒænjuərɪ] n enero

Japan [dʒə'pæn] n (el) Japón; **Japanese** [dʒæpə'ni:z] adj japonés/esa ▷ n inv japonés/esa m/f; (Ling) japonés m
jar [dʒɑ:*] n tarro, bote m ▷ vi (sound) chirriar; (colours) desentonar
jargon ['dʒɑ:gən] n jerga
javelin ['dʒævlɪn] n jabalina
jaw [dʒɔ:] n mandíbula
jazz [dʒæz] n jazz m
jealous ['dʒɛləs] adj celoso; (envious) envidioso; **jealousy** n celos mpl; envidia
jeans [dʒi:nz] npl vaqueros mpl, tejanos mpl
Jello® ['dʒɛləu] (US) n gelatina
jelly ['dʒɛlɪ] n (jam) jalea; (dessert etc) gelatina; **jellyfish** n inv medusa, aguaviva (RPL)
jeopardize ['dʒɛpədaɪz] vt arriesgar, poner en peligro
jerk [dʒə:k] n (jolt) sacudida; (wrench) tirón m; (inf) imbécil mf ▷ vt tirar bruscamente de ▷ vi (vehicle) traquetear
jersey ['dʒə:zɪ] n Jersey m
jersey ['dʒə:zɪ] n jersey m; (fabric) (tejido de) punto
Jesus ['dʒi:zəs] n Jesús m
jet [dʒɛt] n (of gas, liquid) chorro; (Aviat) avión m a reacción; **jet lag** n desorientación f después de un largo vuelo; **jet-ski** vi practicar el motociclismo acuático
jetty ['dʒɛtɪ] n muelle m, embarcadero
Jew [dʒu:] n judío/a
jewel ['dʒu:əl] n joya; (in watch) rubí m; **jeweller** (US **jeweler**) n joyero/a; **jeweller's (shop)** (US **jewelry store**) n joyería; **jewellery** (US **jewelry**) n joyas fpl, alhajas fpl
Jewish ['dʒu:ɪʃ] adj judío
jigsaw ['dʒɪgsɔ:] n (also: **~ puzzle**) rompecabezas m inv, puzle m
job [dʒɔb] n (task) tarea; (post) empleo; **it's not my ~** no me incumbe a mí; **it's a good ~ that ...** menos mal que

...; **just the ~!** ¡estupendo!; **job centre** (BRIT) n oficina estatal de colocaciones; **jobless** adj sin trabajo

jockey ['dʒɔkɪ] n jockey mf ▷ vi: **to ~ for position** maniobrar para conseguir una posición

jog [dʒɔg] vt empujar (ligeramente) ▷ vi (run) hacer footing; **to ~ sb's memory** refrescar la memoria a algn; **jogging** n footing m

join [dʒɔɪn] vt (things) juntar, unir; (club) hacerse socio de; (Pol: party) afiliarse a; (queue) ponerse en; (meet: people) reunirse con ▷ vi (roads) juntarse; (rivers) confluir ▷ n juntura; **join in** vi tomar parte, participar ▷ vt fus tomar parte or participar en; **join up** vi reunirse; (Mil) alistarse

joiner ['dʒɔɪnə*] (BRIT) n carpintero/a

joint [dʒɔɪnt] n (Tech) junta, unión f; (Anat) articulación f; (BRIT Culin) pieza de carne (para asar); (inf: place) tugurio; (: of cannabis) porro ▷ adj (common) común; (combined) combinado; **joint account** n (with bank etc) cuenta común; **jointly** adv (gen) en común; (together) conjuntamente

joke [dʒəʊk] n chiste m; (also: **practical ~**) broma ▷ vi bromear; **to play a ~ on** gastar una broma a; **joker** n (Cards) comodín m

jolly ['dʒɔlɪ] adj (merry) alegre; (enjoyable) divertido ▷ adv (BRIT: inf) muy, terriblemente

jolt [dʒəʊlt] n (jerk) sacudida; (shock) susto ▷ vt (physically) sacudir; (emotionally) asustar

Jordan ['dʒɔːdən] n (country) Jordania; (river) Jordán m

journal ['dʒəːnl] n (magazine) revista; (diary) periódico, diario; **journalism** n periodismo; **journalist** n periodista mf, reportero/a

journey ['dʒəːnɪ] n viaje m; (distance covered) trayecto

joy [dʒɔɪ] n alegría; **joyrider** n gamberro que roba un coche para dar una vuelta y luego abandonarlo; **joy stick** n

(Aviat) palanca de mando; (Comput) palanca de control

Jr abbr = **junior**

judge [dʒʌdʒ] n juez mf; (fig: expert) perito ▷ vt juzgar; (consider) considerar

judo ['dʒuːdəʊ] n judo

jug [dʒʌg] n jarra

juggle ['dʒʌgl] vi hacer juegos malabares; **juggler** n malabarista mf

juice [dʒuːs] n zumo (SP), jugo (LAM); **juicy** adj jugoso

Jul abbr (= July) jul

July [dʒuː'laɪ] n julio

jumble ['dʒʌmbl] n revoltijo ▷ vt (also: **~ up**) revolver; **jumble sale** (BRIT) n venta de objetos usados con fines benéficos

○
● **JUMBLE SALE**
●
● Los **jumble sales** son unos
● mercadillos que se organizan con
● fines benéficos en los locales de
● un colegio, iglesia u otro centro
● público. En ellos puede comprarse
● todo tipo de artículos baratos de
● segunda mano, sobre todo ropa,
● juguetes, libros, vajillas o muebles.

jumbo ['dʒʌmbəʊ] n (also: **~ jet**) jumbo

jump [dʒʌmp] vi saltar, dar saltos; (with fear etc) pegar un bote; (increase) aumentar ▷ vt saltar ▷ n salto; aumento; **to ~ the queue** (BRIT) colarse

jumper ['dʒʌmpə*] n (BRIT: pullover) suéter m, jersey m; (US: dress) mandil m

jumper cables (US) npl = **jump leads**

jump leads (BRIT) npl cables mpl puente de batería

Jun. abbr = **junior**

junction ['dʒʌŋkʃən] n (BRIT: of roads) cruce m; (Rail) empalme m

June [dʒuːn] n junio

jungle ['dʒʌŋgl] n selva, jungla

junior ['dʒuːnɪə*] adj (in age) menor, más joven; (brother/sister etc): **seven**

years her ~ siete años menor que ella; (*position*) subalterno ▷ *n* menor *mf*; joven *mf*; **junior high school** (US) *n* centro de educación secundaria; see also **high school**; **junior school** (BRIT) *n* escuela primaria

junk [dʒʌŋk] *n* (*cheap goods*) baratijas *fpl*; (*rubbish*) basura; **junk food** *n* alimentos preparados y envasados de escaso valor nutritivo

junkie ['dʒʌŋkɪ] (*inf*) *n* drogadicto/a, yonqui *mf*

junk mail *n* propaganda de buzón

Jupiter ['dʒuːpɪtə*] *n* (*Mythology, Astrology*) Júpiter *m*

jurisdiction [dʒuərɪs'dɪkʃən] *n* jurisdicción *f*; **it falls** *or* **comes within/ outside our ~** es/no es de nuestra competencia

jury ['dʒuərɪ] *n* jurado

just [dʒʌst] *adj* justo ▷ *adv* (*exactly*) exactamente; (*only*) sólo, solamente; **he's ~ done it/left** acaba de hacerlo/ irse; **~ right** perfecto; **~ two o'clock** las dos en punto; **she's ~ as clever as you** (ella) es tan lista como tú; **~ as well that ...** menos mal que ...; **~ as he was leaving** en el momento en que se marchaba; **~ before/enough** justo antes/lo suficiente; **~ here** aquí mismo; **he ~ missed** ha fallado por poco; **~ listen to this** escucha esto un momento

justice ['dʒʌstɪs] *n* justicia; (US: *judge*) juez *mf*; **to do ~ to** (*fig*) hacer justicia a

justification [dʒʌstɪfɪ'keɪʃən] *n* justificación *f*

justify ['dʒʌstɪfaɪ] *vt* justificar; (*text*) alinear

jut [dʒʌt] *vi* (*also:* **~ out**) sobresalir

juvenile ['dʒuːvənaɪl] *adj* (*court*) de menores; (*humour, mentality*) infantil ▷ *n* menor *m* de edad

K *abbr* (= *one thousand*) mil; (= *kilobyte*) kilobyte *m*, kilooocteto

kangaroo [kæŋgə'ruː] *n* canguro

karaoke [kɑ:rə'əʊkɪ] *n* karaoke

karate [kə'rɑ:tɪ] *n* karate *m*

kebab [kə'bæb] *n* pincho moruno

keel [ki:l] *n* quilla; **on an even ~** (*fig*) en equilibrio

keen [ki:n] *adj* (*interest, desire*) grande, vivo; (*eye, intelligence*) agudo; (*competition*) reñido; (*edge*) afilado; (*eager*) entusiasta; **to be ~ to do** *or* **on doing sth** tener muchas ganas de hacer algo; **to be ~ on sth/sb** interesarse por algo/algn

keep [ki:p] (*pt, pp* **kept**) *vt* (*preserve, store*) guardar; (*hold back*) quedarse con; (*maintain*) mantener; (*detain*) detener; (*shop*) ser propietario de; (*feed: family etc*) mantener; (*promise*) cumplir; (*chickens, bees etc*) criar; (*accounts*) llevar; (*diary*) escribir; (*prevent*): **to ~ sb from doing sth** impedir a algn hacer algo ▷ *vi* (*food*) conservarse; (*remain*) seguir, continuar ▷ *n* (*of* *castle*) torreón *m*; (*food etc*) comida, subsistencia; (*inf*): **for ~s** para siempre; **to ~ doing sth** seguir haciendo algo; **to ~ sb happy** tener a algn contento; **to ~ a place tidy** mantener un lugar limpio; **to ~ sth to o.s.** guardar algo para sí mismo; **to ~ sth (back) from sb** ocultar algo a algn; **to ~ time** (*clock*) mantener la hora exacta; **keep away** *vt*: **to keep sth/sb away from sb** mantener algo/a algn apartado de algn ▷ *vi*: **to keep away (from)** mantenerse apartado (de); **keep back** *vt* (*crowd, tears*) contener; (*money*) quedarse con; (*conceal: information*): **to keep sth back from sb** ocultar algo a algn ▷ *vi* hacerse a un lado; **keep off** *vt* (*dog, person*) mantener a distancia ▷ *vi*: **if the rain keeps off** so no lleuve; **keep your hands off!** ¡no toques!; **"keep off the grass"** "prohibido pisar el césped"; **keep on** *vi*: **to keep on doing** seguir *or* continuar haciendo; **to keep on (about sth)** no parar de hablar (de algo); **keep out** *vi* (*stay out*) permanecer fuera; **"keep out"** "prohibida la entrada"; **keep up** *vt* mantener, conservar ▷ *vi* no retrasarse; **to keep up with** (*pace*) ir al paso de; (*level*) mantenerse a la altura de; **keeper** *n* guardián/ana *m/f*; **keeping** *n* (*care*) cuidado; **in keeping with** de acuerdo con

kennel ['kɛnl] *n* perrera; **kennels** *npl* residencia canina

Kenya ['kɛnjə] *n* Kenia

kept [kɛpt] *pt, pp of* **keep**

kerb [kə:b] (*BRIT*) *n* bordillo

kerosene ['kɛrəsi:n] *n* keroseno

ketchup ['kɛtʃəp] *n* salsa de tomate, catsup *m*

kettle ['kɛtl] *n* hervidor *m* de agua

key [ki:] *n* llave *f*; (*Mus*) tono; (*of piano, typewriter*) tecla ▷ *adj* (*issue etc*) clave *inv* ▷ *vt* (*also*: **~ in**) teclear; **keyboard** *n* teclado; **keyhole** *n* ojo (de la cerradura); **keyring** *n* llavero

kg *abbr* (= *kilogram*) kg

khaki ['kɑːkɪ] *n* caqui

kick [kɪk] *vt* dar una patada *or* un puntapié a; (*inf: habit*) quitarse de ▷ *vi* (*horse*) dar coces ▷ *n* patada; puntapié *m*; (*of animal*) coz *f*; (*thrill*): **he does it for ~s** lo hace por pura diversión; **kick off** *vi* (*Sport*) hacer el saque inicial; **kick-off** *n* saque inicial; **the kick-off is at 10 o'clock** el partido empieza a las diez

kid [kɪd] *n* (*inf: child*) chiquillo/a; (*animal*) cabrito; (*leather*) cabritilla ▷ *vi* (*inf*) bromear

kidnap ['kɪdnæp] *vt* secuestrar; **kidnapping** *n* secuestro

kidney ['kɪdnɪ] *n* riñón *m*; **kidney bean** *n* judía, alubia

kill [kɪl] *vt* matar; (*murder*) asesinar ▷ *n* matanza; **to ~ time** matar el tiempo; **killer** *n* asesino/a; **killing** *n* (*one*) asesinato; (*several*) matanza; **to make a killing** (*fig*) hacer su agosto

kiln [kɪln] *n* horno

kilo ['ki:ləu] *n* kilo; **kilobyte** *n* (*Comput*) kilobyte *m*, kiloocteto; **kilogram(me)** *n* kilo, kilogramo; **kilometre** ['kɪləmi:tə*] (*US* **kilometer**) *n* kilómetro; **kilowatt** *n* kilovatio

kilt [kɪlt] *n* falda escocesa

kin [kɪn] *n* see **next-of-kin**

kind [kaɪnd] *adj* amable, atento ▷ *n* clase *f*, especie *f*; (*species*) género; **in ~** (*Comm*) en especie; **a ~ of** una especie de; **to be two of a ~** ser tal para cual

kindergarten ['kɪndəgɑːtn] *n* jardín *m* de la infancia

kindly ['kaɪndlɪ] *adj* bondadoso; cariñoso ▷ *adv* bondadosamente, amablemente; **will you ~ ...** sea usted tan amable de ...

kindness ['kaɪndnɪs] *n* (*quality*) bondad *f*, amabilidad *f*; (*act*) favor *m*

king [kɪŋ] *n* rey *m*; **kingdom** *n* reino; **kingfisher** *n* martín *m* pescador; **king-size(d) bed** *n* cama de matrimonio extragrande

kiosk ['ki:ɔsk] *n* quiosco; (*BRIT Tel*) cabina

kipper ['kɪpə*] *n* arenque *m* ahumado

kiss [kɪs] n beso ▷ vt besar; **to ~ (each other)** besarse; **kiss of life** n respiración f boca a boca

kit [kɪt] n (equipment) equipo; (tools etc) (caja de) herramientas fpl; (assembly kit) juego de armar

kitchen ['kɪtʃɪn] n cocina

kite [kaɪt] n (toy) cometa

kitten ['kɪtn] n gatito/a

kiwi ['kiːwiː-] n (also: ~ **fruit**) kiwi m

km abbr (= kilometre) km

km/h abbr (= kilometres per hour) km/h

knack [næk] n: **to have the ~ of doing sth** tener el don de hacer algo

knee [niː] n rodilla; **kneecap** n rótula

kneel [niːl] (pt, pp **knelt**) vi (also: ~ **down**) arrodillarse

knelt [nɛlt] pt, pp of **kneel**

knew [njuː] pt of **know**

knickers ['nɪkəz] (BRIT) npl bragas fpl

knife [naɪf] (pl **knives**) n cuchillo ▷ vt acuchillar

knight [naɪt] n caballero; (Chess) caballo

knit [nɪt] vt tejer, tricotar ▷ vi hacer punto, tricotar; (bones) soldarse; **to ~ one's brows** fruncir el ceño; **knitting** n labor f de punto; **knitting needle** n aguja de hacer punto; **knitwear** n prendas fpl de punto

knives [naɪvz] npl of **knife**

knob [nɔb] n (of door) tirador m; (of stick) puño; (on radio, TV) botón m

knock [nɔk] vt (strike) golpear; (bump into) chocar contra; (inf) criticar ▷ vi (at door etc): **to ~ at/on** llamar a ▷ n golpe m; (on door) llamada; **knock down** vt atropellar; **knock off** (inf) vi (finish) salir del trabajo ▷ vt (from price) descontar; (inf: steal) birlar; **knock out** vt dejar sin sentido; (Boxing) poner fuera de combate, dejar K.O.; (in competition) eliminar; **knock over** vt (object) tirar; (person) atropellar; **knockout** n (Boxing) K.O. m, knockout m ▷ cpd (competition etc) eliminatorio

knot [nɔt] n nudo ▷ vt anudar

know [nəu] (pt **knew**, pp **known**)
vt (facts) saber; (be acquainted with) conocer; (recognize) reconocer, conocer; **to ~ how to swim** saber nadar; **to ~ about** or **of sb/sth** saber de algn/algo; **know-all** n sabelotodo mf; **know-how** n conocimientos mpl; **knowing** adj (look) de complicidad; **knowingly** adv (purposely) adrede; (smile, look) con complicidad; **know-it-all** (US) n = **know-all**

knowledge ['nɔlɪdʒ] n conocimiento; (learning) saber m, conocimientos mpl; **knowledgeable** adj entendido

known [nəun] pp of **know** ▷ adj (thief, facts) conocido; (expert) reconocido

knuckle ['nʌkl] n nudillo

koala [kəu'ɑːlə] n (also: ~ **bear**) koala m

Koran [kɔ'rɑːn] n Corán m

Korea [kə'rɪə] n Corea; **Korean** adj, n coreano/a m/f

kosher ['kəuʃə*] adj autorizado por la ley judía

Kosovar ['kɔsəvɑ*], **Kosovan** ['kɔːsəvən] adj kosovar

Kosovo ['kɔsəvəu] n Kosovo

Kremlin ['krɛmlɪn] n: **the ~** el Kremlin

Kuwait [ku'weɪt] n Kuwait m

L (BRIT) *abbr* = **learner driver**

l. *abbr* (= litre) l

lab [læb] *n abbr* = **laboratory**

label ['leɪbl] *n* etiqueta ▷*vt* poner etiqueta a

labor *etc* ['leɪbə*] (US) = **labour** *etc*

laboratory [lə'bɔrətərɪ] *n* laboratorio

Labor Day (US) *n* día *m* de los trabajadores (*primer lunes de septiembre*)

labor union (US) *n* sindicato

labour ['leɪbə*] (US **labor**) *n* (*hard work*) trabajo; (*labour force*) mano *f* de obra; (*Med*): **to be in ~** estar de parto ▷*vi*: **to ~ (at sth)** trabajar (en algo) ▷*vt*: **to ~ a point** insistir en un punto; **L~, the L~ party** (BRIT) el partido laborista, los laboristas *mpl*; **labourer** *n* peón *m*; **farm labourer** peón *m*; (*day labourer*) jornalero

lace [leɪs] *n* encaje *m*; (*of shoe etc*) cordón *m* ▷*vt* (*shoes: also: ~ up*) atarse (los zapatos)

lack [læk] *n* (*absence*) falta ▷*vt* faltarle a algn, carecer de; **through** or **for ~ of** por falta de; **to be ~ing** faltar, no haber; **to be ~ing in sth** faltarle a algn algo

lacquer ['lækə*] *n* laca

lacy ['leɪsɪ] *adj* (*of lace*) de encaje; (*like lace*) como de encaje

lad [læd] *n* muchacho, chico

ladder ['lædə*] *n* escalera (de mano); (BRIT: *in tights*) carrera

ladle ['leɪdl] *n* cucharón *m*

lady ['leɪdɪ] *n* señora; (*dignified, graceful*) dama; **"ladies and gentlemen ..."** "señoras y caballeros ..."; **young ~** señorita; **the ladies' (room)** los servicios de señoras; **ladybird** (US **ladybug**) *n* mariquita

lag [læg] *n* retraso ▷*vi* (*also: ~ behind*) retrasarse, quedarse atrás ▷*vt* (*pipes*) revestir

lager ['lɑːgə*] *n* cerveza (rubia)

lagoon [lə'guːn] *n* laguna

laid [leɪd] *pt, pp of* **lay**; **laid back** (*inf*) *adj* relajado

lain [leɪn] *pp of* **lie**

lake [leɪk] *n* lago

lamb [læm] *n* cordero; (*meat*) (carne *f* de) cordero

lame [leɪm] *adj* cojo; (*excuse*) poco convincente

lament [lə'mɛnt] *n* quejo ▷*vt* lamentarse de

lamp [læmp] *n* lámpara; **lamppost** (BRIT) *n* (poste *m* de) farol *m*; **lampshade** *n* pantalla

land [lænd] *n* tierra; (*country*) país *m*; (*piece of land*) terreno; (*estate*) tierras *fpl*, finca ▷*vi* (*from ship*) desembarcar; (*Aviat*) aterrizar; (*fig: fall*) caer, terminar ▷*vt* (*passengers, goods*) desembarcar; **to ~ sb with sth** (*inf*) hacer cargar a algn con algo; **landing** *n* aterrizaje *m*; (*of staircase*) rellano; **landing card** *n* tarjeta de desembarque; **landlady** *n* (*of rented house, pub etc*) dueña; **landlord** *n* propietario; (*of pub etc*) patrón *m*; **landmark** *n* lugar *m* conocido; **to be a landmark** (*fig*) marcar un hito histórico; **landowner** *n* terrateniente *mf*; **landscape** *n* paisaje *m*; **landslide** *n* (*Geo*) corrimiento de tierras; (*fig: Pol*) victoria arrolladora

lane [leɪn] *n* (*in country*) camino; (*Aut*) carril *m*; (*in race*) calle *f*

language ['læŋgwɪdʒ] *n* lenguaje *m*; (*national tongue*) idioma *m*, lengua; **bad ~** palabrotas *fpl*; **language laboratory** *n* laboratorio de idiomas; **language school** *n* academia de idiomas

lantern ['læntn] *n* linterna, farol *m*

lap [læp] *n* (*of track*) vuelta; (*of body*) regazo ▷ *vt* (*also: ~ up*) beber a lengüetadas ▷ *vi* (*waves*) chapotear; **to sit on sb's ~** sentarse en las rodillas de algn

lapel [lə'pɛl] *n* solapa

lapse [læps] *n* fallo; (*moral*) desliz *m*; (*of time*) intervalo ▷ *vi* (*expire*) caducar; (*time*) pasar, transcurrir; **to ~ into bad habits** caer en malos hábitos

laptop (computer) ['læptɒp-] *n* (ordenador *m*) portátil *m*

lard [lɑːd] *n* manteca (de cerdo)

larder ['lɑːdə*] *n* despensa

large [lɑːdʒ] *adj* grande; **at ~** (*free*) en libertad; (*generally*) en general

▌ Be careful not to translate **large** by the Spanish word *largo*.

largely *adv* (*mostly*) en su mayor parte; (*introducing reason*) en gran parte; **large-scale** *adj* (*map*) en gran escala; (*fig*) importante

lark [lɑːk] *n* (*bird*) alondra; (*joke*) broma

laryngitis [lærɪn'dʒaɪtɪs] *n* laringitis *f*

lasagne [lə'zænjə] *n* lasaña

laser ['leɪzə*] *n* láser *m*; **laser printer** *n* impresora (por) láser

lash [læʃ] *n* latigazo; (*also: eye~*) pestaña ▷ *vt* azotar; (*tie*): **to ~ to/ together** atar a/atar; **lash out** *vi*: **to lash out (at sb)** (*hit*) arremeter (contra algn); **to lash out against sb** lanzar invectivas contra algn

lass [læs] (*BRIT*) *n* chica

last [lɑːst] *adj* último; (*end: of series etc*) final ▷ *adv* (*most recently*) la última vez; (*finally*) por último ▷ *vi* durar; (*continue*) continuar, seguir; **~ night** anoche; **~ week** la semana pasada; **at ~** por fin; **~ but one** penúltimo; **lastly** *adv* por último, finalmente; **last-minute** *adj* de última hora

latch [lætʃ] *n* pestillo; **latch onto** *vt fus* (*person, group*) pegarse a; (*idea*) agarrarse a

late [leɪt] *adj* (*far on: in time, process etc*) al final de; (*not on time*) tarde, atrasado; (*dead*) fallecido ▷ *adv* tarde; (*behind time, schedule*) con retraso; **of ~** últimamente; **~ at night** a última hora de la noche; **in ~ May** hacia fines de mayo; **the ~ Mr X** el difunto Sr X; **latecomer** *n* recién llegado/a; **lately** *adv* últimamente; **later** *adj* (*date etc*) posterior; (*version etc*) más reciente ▷ *adv* más tarde, después; **latest** ['leɪtɪst] *adj* último; **at the latest** a más tardar

lather ['lɑːðə*] *n* espuma (de jabón) ▷ *vt* enjabonar

Latin ['lætɪn] *n* latín *m* ▷ *adj* latino; **Latin America** *n* América latina; **Latin American** *adj, n* latinoamericano/a *m/f*

latitude ['lætɪtjuːd] *n* latitud *f*; (*fig*) libertad *f*

latter ['lætə*] *adj* último; (*of two*) segundo ▷ *n*: **the ~** el último, éste

laugh [lɑːf] *n* risa ▷ *vi* reír(se); **(to do sth) for a ~** (hacer algo) en broma; **laugh at** *vt fus* reírse de; **laughter** *n* risa

launch [lɔːntʃ] *n* lanzamiento; (*boat*) lancha ▷ *vt* (*ship*) botar; (*rocket etc*) lanzar; (*fig*) comenzar; **launch into** *vt fus* lanzarse a

launder [lɔːndə*] *vt* lavar

Launderette® [lɔːn'drɛt] (*BRIT*) *n* lavandería (automática)

Laundromat® ['lɔːndrəmæt] (*US*) *n* = **Launderette**

laundry ['lɔːndrɪ] *n* (*dirty*) ropa sucia; (*clean*) colada; (*room*) lavadero

lava ['lɑːvə] n lava

lavatory ['lævətərɪ] n wáter m

lavender ['lævəndə*] n lavanda

lavish ['lævɪʃ] adj (amount) abundante; (person): ~ with pródigo en ▷ vt: **to ~ sth on sb** colmar a algn de algo

law [lɔː] n ley f; (Scol) derecho; (a rule) regla; (professions connected with law) jurisprudencia; **lawful** adj legítimo, lícito; **lawless** adj (action) criminal

lawn [lɔːn] n césped m; **lawnmower** n cortacésped m

lawsuit ['lɔːsuːt] n pleito

lawyer ['lɔːjə*] n abogado/a; (for sales, wills etc) notario/a

lax [læks] adj laxo

laxative ['læksətɪv] n laxante m

lay [leɪ] (pt, pp **laid**) pt of **lie** ▷ adj laico; (not expert) lego ▷ vt (place) colocar; (eggs, table) poner; (cable) tender; (carpet) extender; **lay down** vt (pen etc) dejar; (rules etc) establecer; **to lay down the law** (pej) imponer las normas; **lay off** vt (workers) despedir; **lay on** vt (meal, facilities) proveer; **lay out** vt (spread out) disponer, exponer; **lay-by** n (BRIT Aut) área de aparcamiento

layer ['leɪə*] n capa

layman ['leɪmən] (irreg) n lego

layout ['leɪaut] n (design) plan m, trazado; (Press) composición f

lazy ['leɪzɪ] adj perezoso, vago; (movement) lento

lb. abbr = **pound** (weight)

lead¹ [liːd] (pt, pp **led**) n (front position) delantera; (clue) pista; (Elec) cable m; (for dog) correa; (Theatre) papel m principal ▷ vt (walk etc in front) ir a la cabeza de; (guide): **to ~ sb somewhere** conducir a algn a algún sitio; (be leader) dirigir; (start, guide: activity) protagonizar ▷ vi (road, pipe etc) conducir a; (Sport) ir primero; **to be in the ~** (Sport) llevar la delantera; (fig) ir a la cabeza; **to ~ the way** llevar la delantera; **lead up to** vt fus (events)

conducir a; (in conversation) preparar el terreno para

lead² [lɛd] n (metal) plomo; (in pencil) mina

leader ['liːdə*] n jefe/a m/f, líder mf; (Sport) líder mf; **leadership** n dirección f; (position) mando; (quality) iniciativa

lead-free ['lɛdfriː] adj sin plomo

leading ['liːdɪŋ] adj (main) principal; (first) primero; (front) delantero

lead singer [liːd-] n cantante mf

leaf [liːf] (pl **leaves**) n hoja ▷ vi: **to ~ through** hojear; **to turn over a new ~** reformarse

leaflet ['liːflɪt] n folleto

league [liːg] n sociedad f; (Football) liga; **to be in ~ with** haberse confabulado con

leak [liːk] n (of liquid, gas) escape m, fuga; (in pipe) agujero; (in roof) gotera; (in security) filtración f ▷ vi (shoes, ship) hacer agua; (pipe) tener (un) escape; (roof) gotear; (liquid, gas) escaparse, fugarse; (fig) divulgarse ▷ vt (fig) filtrar

lean [liːn] (pt, pp **~ed** or **~t**) adj (thin) flaco; (meat) magro ▷ vt: **to ~ sth on sth** apoyar algo en algo ▷ vi (slope) inclinarse; **to ~ against** apoyarse contra; **to ~ on** apoyarse en; **lean forward** vi inclinarse hacia adelante; **lean over** vi inclinarse; **leaning** n: **leaning (towards)** inclinación f (hacia)

leant [lɛnt] pt, pp of **lean**

leap [liːp] (pt, pp **~ed** or **~t**) n salto ▷ vi saltar

leapt [lɛpt] pt, pp of **leap**

leap year n año bisiesto

learn [ləːn] (pt, pp **~ed** or **~t**) vt aprender ▷ vi aprender; **to ~ about sth** enterarse de algo; **to ~ to do sth** aprender a hacer algo; **learner** n (BRIT: also: **learner driver**) principiante mf; **learning** n el saber m, conocimientos mpl

learnt [ləːnt] pp of **learn**

lease [liːs] n arriendo ▷ vt arrendar

leash [liːʃ] n correa

least [liːst] adj: **the ~** (slightest) el menor, el más pequeño; (smallest amount of) mínimo ▷ adv (+ vb) menos; (+ adj): **the ~ expensive** el (la) menos costoso/a; **the ~ possible effort** el menor esfuerzo posible; **at ~** por lo menos, al menos; **you could at ~ have written** por lo menos podías haber escrito; **not in the ~** en absoluto

leather ['lɛðə*] n cuero

leave [liːv] (pt, pp **left**) vt dejar; (go away from) abandonar; (place etc: permanently) salir de ▷ vi irse; (train etc) salir ▷ n permiso; **to ~ sth to sb** (money etc) legar algo a algn; (responsibility etc) encargar a algn de algo; **to be left** quedar, sobrar; **there's some milk left over** sobra or queda algo de leche; **on ~** de permiso; **leave behind** vt (on purpose) dejar; (accidentally) dejarse; **leave out** vt omitir

leaves [liːvz] npl of **leaf**

Lebanon ['lɛbənən] n: **the ~** el Líbano

lecture ['lɛktʃə*] n conferencia; (Scol) clase f ▷ vi dar una clase ▷ vt (scold): **to ~ sb on** or **about sth** echar una reprimenda a algn por algo; **to give a ~ on** dar una conferencia sobre; **lecture hall** n sala de conferencias; (Univ) aula; **lecturer** n conferenciante mf; (BRIT: at university) profesor(a) m/f; **lecture theatre** n = **lecture hall**

led [lɛd] pt, pp of **lead**[1]

ledge [lɛdʒ] n repisa; (of window) alféizar m; (of mountain) saliente m

leek [liːk] n puerro

left [lɛft] pt, pp of **leave** ▷ adj izquierdo; (remaining): **there are two ~** quedan dos ▷ n izquierda ▷ adv a la izquierda; **on** or **to the ~** a la izquierda; **the L~** (Pol) la izquierda; **left-hand** adj: **the left-hand side** la izquierda; **left-hand drive** adj: **a left-hand drive car** un coche con el volante a la izquierda; **left-handed** adj zurdo; **left-luggage locker** n (BRIT) consigna f automática; **left-luggage**

(office) (BRIT) n consigna; **left-overs** npl sobras fpl; **left-wing** adj (Pol) de izquierdas, izquierdista

leg [lɛg] n pierna; (of animal, chair) pata; (trouser leg) pernera; (Culin: of lamb) pierna; (: of chicken) pata; (of journey) etapa

legacy ['lɛgəsɪ] n herencia

legal ['liːgl] adj (permitted by law) lícito; (of law) legal; **legal holiday** (US) n fiesta oficial; **legalize** vt legalizar; **legally** adv legalmente

legend ['lɛdʒənd] n (also fig: person) leyenda; **legendary** [-ərɪ] adj legendario

leggings ['lɛgɪŋz] npl mallas fpl, leggins mpl

legible ['lɛdʒəbl] adj legible

legislation [lɛdʒɪs'leɪʃən] n legislación f

legislative ['lɛdʒɪslətɪv] adj legislativo

legitimate [lɪ'dʒɪtɪmət] adj legítimo

leisure ['lɛʒə*] n ocio, tiempo libre; **at ~** con tranquilidad; **leisure centre** (BRIT) n centro de recreo; **leisurely** adj sin prisa; lento

lemon ['lɛmən] n limón m; **lemonade** n (fizzy) gaseosa; **lemon tea** n té m con limón

lend [lɛnd] (pt, pp **lent**) vt: **to ~ sth to sb** prestar algo a algn

length [lɛŋθ] n (size) largo, longitud f; (distance): **the ~ of** todo lo largo de; (of swimming pool, cloth) largo; (of wood, string) trozo; (amount of time) duración f; **at ~** (at last) por fin, finalmente; (lengthily) largamente; **lengthen** vt alargar ▷ vi alargarse; **lengthways** adv a lo largo; **lengthy** adj largo, extenso

lens [lɛnz] n (of spectacles) lente f; (of camera) objetivo

Lent [lɛnt] n Cuaresma

lent [lɛnt] pt, pp of **lend**

lentil ['lɛntl] n lenteja

Leo ['liːəu] n Leo

leopard ['lɛpəd] n leopardo

leotard ['li:əta:d] n mallas fpl
leprosy ['leprəsɪ] n lepra
lesbian ['lɛzbɪən] n lesbiana
less [lɛs] adj (in size, degree etc)
menor; (in quality) menos ▷ pron, adv
menos ▷ prep: **~ tax/10% discount**
menos impuestos/el 10 por ciento
de descuento; **~ than half** menos
de la mitad; **~ than ever** menos que
nunca; **~ and ~** cada vez menos; **the
~ he works ...** cuanto menos trabaja
...; **lessen** vi disminuir, reducirse ▷ vt
disminuir, reducir; **lesser** ['lɛsə*] adj
menor; **to a lesser extent** en menor
grado
lesson ['lɛsn] n clase f; (warning)
lección f
let [lɛt] (pt, pp **~**) vt (allow) dejar,
permitir; (BRIT: lease) alquilar; **to ~ sb
do sth** dejar que algn haga algo; **to ~
sb know sth** comunicar algo a algn;
~'s go ¡vamos!; **~ him come** que venga;
"to ~" "se alquila"; **let down** vt (tyre)
desinflar; (disappoint) defraudar; **let in**
vt dejar entrar; (visitor etc) hacer pasar;
let off vt (culprit) dejar escapar; (gun)
disparar; (bomb) accionar; (firework)
hacer estallar; **let out** vt dejar salir;
(sound) soltar
lethal ['li:θl] adj (weapon) mortífero;
(poison, wound) mortal
letter ['lɛtə*] n (of alphabet) letra;
(correspondence) carta; **letterbox** (BRIT)
n buzón m
lettuce ['lɛtɪs] n lechuga
leukaemia [lu:'ki:mɪə] (US **leukemia**)
n leucemia
level ['lɛvl] adj (flat) llano ▷ adv: **to
draw ~ with** llegar a la altura de ▷ n
nivel m; (height) altura ▷ vt nivelar;
allanar; (destroy: building) derribar;
(: forest) arrasar; **to be ~ with** estar
a nivel de; **A ~s** (BRIT) ≈ exámenes
mpl de bachillerato superior, B.U.P.;
AS ~ (BRIT) asignatura aprobada entre
los "GCSEs" y los "A levels"; **on the ~**
(fig: honest) serio; **level crossing** (BRIT)
n paso a nivel

lever ['li:və*] n (also fig) palanca
▷ vt: **to ~ up** levantar con palanca;
leverage n (using bar etc)
apalancamiento; (fig: influence)
influencia
levy ['lɛvɪ] n impuesto ▷ vt exigir,
recaudar
liability [laɪə'bɪlətɪ] n (pej: person,
thing) estorbo, lastre m; (Jur:
responsibility) responsabilidad f
liable ['laɪəbl] adj (subject): **~ to** sujeto
a; (responsible): **~ for** responsable de;
(likely): **~ to do** propenso a hacer
liaise [lɪ'eɪz] vi: **to ~ with** enlazar con
liar ['laɪə*] n mentiroso/a
liberal ['lɪbərəl] adj liberal; (offer,
amount etc) generoso; **Liberal
Democrat** n (BRIT) demócrata m/f
liberal
liberate ['lɪbəreɪt] vt (people: from
poverty etc) librar; (prisoner) libertar;
(country) liberar
liberation [lɪbə'reɪʃən] n liberación f
liberty ['lɪbətɪ] n libertad f; **to be at
~** (criminal) estar en libertad; **to be at
~ to do** estar libre para hacer; **to take
the ~ of doing sth** tomarse la libertad
de hacer algo
Libra ['li:brə] n Libra
librarian [laɪ'brɛərɪən] n
bibliotecario/a
library ['laɪbrərɪ] n biblioteca
　Be careful not to translate **library**
　by the Spanish word librería.
Libya ['lɪbɪə] n Libia
lice [laɪs] npl of **louse**
licence ['laɪsəns] (US **license**) n
licencia; (permit) permiso; (also: **driving
~**) carnet m de conducir (SP), licencia de
manejo (LAM)
license ['laɪsəns] n (US) = **licence** ▷ vt
autorizar, dar permiso a; **licensed** adj
(for alcohol) autorizado para vender
bebidas alcohólicas; (car) matriculado;
license plate (US) n placa (de
matrícula); **licensing hours** (BRIT) npl
horas durante las cuales se permite la venta
y consumo de alcohol (en un bar etc)

lick [lɪk] *vt* lamer; *(inf: defeat)* dar una paliza a; **to ~ one's lips** relamerse

lid [lɪd] *n (of box, case)* tapa; *(of pan)* tapadera

lie [laɪ] *(pt* **lay**, *pp* **lain***) vi (rest)* estar echado, estar acostado; *(of object: be situated)* estar, encontrarse; *(tell lies: pt, pp* **lied***)* mentir ▷ *n* mentira; **to ~ low** *(fig)* mantenerse a escondidas; **lie about** *or* **around** *vi (things)* estar tirado; *(BRIT: people)* estar tumbado; **lie down** *vi* echarse, tumbarse

Liechtenstein ['lɪktənstaɪn] *n* Liechtenstein *m*

lie-in ['laɪɪn] *(BRIT) n*: **to have a ~** quedarse en la cama

lieutenant [lɛf'tɛnənt, *US* luː'tɛnənt] *n (Mil)* teniente *mf*

life [laɪf] *(pl* **lives***) n* vida; **to come to ~** animarse; **life assurance** *(BRIT) n* seguro de vida; **lifeboat** *n* lancha de socorro; **lifeguard** *n* vigilante *mf*, socorrista *mf*; **life insurance** *n* **= life assurance**; **life jacket** *n* chaleco salvavidas; **lifelike** *adj (model etc)* que parece vivo; *(realistic)* realista; **life preserver** *(US) n* cinturón *m*/chaleco salvavidas; **life sentence** *n* cadena perpetua; **lifestyle** *n* estilo de vida; **lifetime** *n (of person)* vida; *(of thing)* período de vida

lift [lɪft] *vt* levantar; *(end: ban, rule)* levantar, suprimir ▷ *vi (fog)* disiparse ▷ *n (BRIT: machine)* ascensor *m*; **to give sb a ~** *(BRIT)* llevar a algn en el coche; **lift up** *vt* levantar; **lift-off** *n* despegue *m*

light [laɪt] *(pt, pp* **~ed** *or* **lit***) n* luz *f*; *(lamp)* luz *f*, lámpara; *(Aut)* faro; *(for cigarette etc)*: **have you got a ~?** ¿tienes fuego? ▷ *vt (candle, cigarette, fire)* encender *(SP)*, prender *(LAM)*; *(room)* alumbrar ▷ *adj (colour)* claro; *(not heavy, also fig)* ligero; *(room)* con mucha luz; *(gentle, graceful)* ágil; **lights** *npl (traffic lights)* semáforos *mpl*; **to come to ~** salir a luz; **in the ~ of** *(new evidence etc)* a la luz de; **light up** *vi*

(smoke) encender un cigarrillo; *(face)* iluminarse ▷ *vt (illuminate)* iluminar, alumbrar; *(set fire to)* encender; **light bulb** *n* bombilla *(SP)*, foco *(MEX)*, bujía *(CAM)*, bombita *(RPL)*; **lighten** *vt (make less heavy)* aligerar; **lighter** *n (also:* **cigarette lighter***)* encendedor *m*, mechero; **light-hearted** *adj (person)* alegre; *(remark etc)* divertido; **lighthouse** *n* faro; **lighting** *n (system)* alumbrado; **lightly** *adv* ligeramente; *(not seriously)* con poca seriedad; **to get off lightly** ser castigado con poca severidad

lightning ['laɪtnɪŋ] *n* relámpago, rayo

lightweight ['laɪtweɪt] *adj (suit)* ligero ▷ *n (Boxing)* peso ligero

like [laɪk] *vt* gustarle a algn ▷ *prep* como ▷ *adj* parecido, semejante ▷ *n*: **and the ~** y otros por el estilo; **his ~s and dislikes** sus gustos y aversiones; **I would ~, I'd ~** me gustaría; *(for purchase)* quisiera; **would you ~ a coffee?** ¿te apetece un café?; **I ~ swimming** me gusta nadar; **she ~s apples** le gustan las manzanas; **to be** *or* **look ~ sb/sth** parecerse a algn/algo; **what does it look/taste/sound ~?** ¿cómo es/a qué sabe/cómo suena?; **that's just ~ him** es muy de él, es característico de él; **do it ~ this** hazlo así; **it is nothing ~ ...** no tiene parecido alguno con ...; **likeable** *adj* simpático, agradable

likelihood ['laɪklɪhud] *n* probabilidad *f*

likely ['laɪklɪ] *adj* probable; **he's ~ to leave** es probable que se vaya; **not ~!** ¡ni hablar!

likewise ['laɪkwaɪz] *adv* igualmente; **to do ~** hacer lo mismo

liking ['laɪkɪŋ] *n*: **~ (for)** *(person)* cariño (a); *(thing)* afición (a); **to be to sb's ~** ser del gusto de algn

lilac ['laɪlək] *n (tree)* lilo; *(flower)* lila

Lilo® ['laɪləu] *n* colchoneta inflable

lily ['lɪlɪ] *n* lirio, azucena; **~ of the**

valley lirio de los valles
limb [lɪm] n miembro
limbo ['lɪmbəu] n: **to be in ~** (fig) quedar a la expectativa
lime [laɪm] n (tree) limero; (fruit) lima; (Geo) cal f
limelight ['laɪmlaɪt] n: **to be in the ~** (fig) ser el centro de atención
limestone ['laɪmstəun] n piedra caliza
limit ['lɪmɪt] n límite m ▷ vt limitar; **limited** adj limitado; **to be limited to** limitarse a
limousine ['lɪməziːn] n limusina
limp [lɪmp] n: **to have a ~** tener cojera ▷ vi cojear ▷ adj flojo; (material) fláccido
line [laɪn] n línea; (rope) cuerda; (for fishing) sedal m; (wire) hilo; (row, series) fila, hilera; (of writing) renglón m, línea; (of song) verso; (on face) arruga; (Rail) vía ▷ vt (road etc) llenar; (Sewing) forrar; **to ~ the streets** llenar las aceras; **in ~ with** alineado con; (according to) de acuerdo con; **line up** vi hacer cola ▷ vt alinear; (prepare) preparar; organizar
linear ['lɪnɪə*] adj lineal
linen ['lɪnɪn] n ropa blanca; (cloth) lino
liner ['laɪnə*] n vapor m de línea, transatlántico; (for bin) bolsa (de basura)
line-up ['laɪnʌp] n (us: queue) cola; (Sport) alineación f
linger ['lɪŋgə*] vi retrasarse, tardar en marcharse; (smell, tradition) persistir
lingerie ['lænʒəriː] n lencería
linguist ['lɪŋgwɪst] n lingüista mf; **linguistic** adj lingüístico
lining ['laɪnɪŋ] n forro; (Anat) (membrana) mucosa
link [lɪŋk] n (of a chain) eslabón m; (relationship) relación f, vínculo; (Internet) link m, enlace m ▷ vt vincular, unir; (associate): **to ~ with** or **to** relacionar con; **links** npl (Golf) campo de golf; **link up** vt acoplar ▷ vi unirse
lion ['laɪən] n león m; **lioness** n leona

lip [lɪp] n labio; **lipread** vi leer los labios; **lip salve** n crema protectora para labios; **lipstick** n lápiz m de labios, carmín m
liqueur [lɪ'kjuə*] n licor m
liquid ['lɪkwɪd] adj, n líquido; **liquidizer** [-aɪzə*] n licuadora
liquor ['lɪkə*] n licor m, bebidas fpl alcohólicas; **liquor store** (us) n bodega, tienda de vinos y bebidas alcohólicas
Lisbon ['lɪzbən] n Lisboa
lisp [lɪsp] n ceceo ▷ vi cecear
list [lɪst] n lista ▷ vt (mention) enumerar; (put on a list) poner en una lista
listen ['lɪsn] vi escuchar, oír; **to ~ to sb/sth** escuchar a algn/algo; **listener** n oyente mf; (Radio) radioyente mf
lit [lɪt] pt, pp of **light**
liter ['liːtə*] (us) n = **litre**
literacy ['lɪtərəsɪ] n capacidad f de leer y escribir
literal ['lɪtərl] adj literal; **literally** adv literalmente
literary ['lɪtərərɪ] adj literario
literate ['lɪtərət] adj que sabe leer y escribir; (educated) culto
literature ['lɪtərɪtʃə*] n literatura; (brochures etc) folletos mpl
litre ['liːtə*] (us **liter**) n litro
litter ['lɪtə*] n (rubbish) basura; (young animals) camada, cría; **litter bin** (BRIT) n papelera; **littered** adj: **littered with** (scattered) lleno de
little ['lɪtl] adj (small) pequeño; (not much) poco ▷ adv poco; **a ~** un poco (de); **~ house/bird** casita/pajarito; **a ~ bit** un poquito; **~ by ~** poco a poco; **little finger** n dedo meñique
live¹ [laɪv] adj (animal) vivo; (wire) conectado; (broadcast) en directo; (shell) cargado
live² [lɪv] vi vivir; **live together** vi vivir juntos; **live up to** vt fus (fulfil) cumplir con
livelihood ['laɪvlɪhud] n sustento
lively ['laɪvlɪ] adj vivo;

(*interesting: place, book etc*) animado
liven up ['laɪvn-] vt animar ▷vi
animarse
liver ['lɪvə*] n hígado
lives [laɪvz] npl of **life**
livestock ['laɪvstɔk] n ganado
living ['lɪvɪŋ] adj (*alive*) vivo ▷n: **to
earn** or **make a ~** ganarse la vida;
living room n sala (de estar)
lizard ['lɪzəd] n lagarto; (*small*)
lagartija
load [ləud] n carga; (*weight*) peso ▷vt
(*Comput*) cargar; (*also:* **~ up**) **to ~ (with)**
cargar (con or de); **a ~ of rubbish** (*inf*)
tonterías fpl; **a ~ of, ~s of** (*fig*) (gran)
cantidad de, montones de; **loaded**
adj (*vehicle*): **to be loaded with** estar
cargado de
loaf [ləuf] (pl **loaves**) n (barra de)
pan m
loan [ləun] n préstamo ▷vt prestar;
on ~ prestado
loathe [ləuð] vt aborrecer; (*person*)
odiar
loaves [ləuvz] npl of **loaf**
lobby ['lɔbɪ] n vestíbulo, sala de
espera; (*Pol: pressure group*) grupo de
presión ▷vt presionar
lobster ['lɔbstə*] n langosta
local ['ləukl] adj local ▷n (*pub*) bar m;
the locals npl los vecinos, los del lugar;
local anaesthetic n (*Med*) anestesia
local; **local authority** n municipio,
ayuntamiento (sp); **local government**
n gobierno municipal; **locally** [-kəlɪ]
adv en la vecindad; por aquí
locate [ləu'keɪt] vt (*find*) localizar;
(*situate*): **to be ~d in** estar situado en
location [ləu'keɪʃən] n situación f;
on ~ (*Cinema*) en exteriores
loch [lɔx] n lago
lock [lɔk] n (*of door, box*) cerradura;
(*of canal*) esclusa; (*of hair*) mechón m
▷vt (*with key*) cerrar (con llave) ▷vi
(*door etc*) cerrarse (con llave); (*wheels*)
trabarse; **lock in** vt encerrar; **lock out**
vt (*person*) cerrar la puerta a; **lock up**
vt (*criminal*) meter en la cárcel; (*mental*

patient) encerrar; (*house*) cerrar (con
llave) ▷vi echar la llave
locker ['lɔkə*] n casillero; **locker-
room** (us) n (*Sport*) vestuario
locksmith ['lɔksmɪθ] n cerrajero/a
locomotive [ləukə'məutɪv] n
locomotora
lodge [lɔdʒ] n casita (del guarda)
▷vi (*person*): **to ~ (with)** alojarse (en
casa de); (*bullet, bone*) incrustarse ▷vt
presentar; **lodger** n huésped mf
lodging ['lɔdʒɪŋ] n alojamiento,
hospedaje m
loft [lɔft] n desván m
log [lɔg] n (*of wood*) leño, tronco;
(*written account*) diario ▷vt anotar;
log in, log on vi (*Comput*) entrar en el
sistema; **log off, log out** vi (*Comput*)
salir del sistema
logic ['lɔdʒɪk] n lógica; **logical** adj
lógico
logo ['ləugəu] n logotipo
lollipop ['lɔlɪpɔp] n pirulí m; **lollipop
man/lady** (BRIT: *irreg*) n persona
encargada de ayudar a los niños a cruzar
la calle
lolly ['lɔlɪ] n (*inf: ice cream*) polo;
(: *lollipop*) piruleta; (: *money*) guita
London ['lʌndən] n Londres;
Londoner n londinense mf
lone [ləun] adj solitario
loneliness ['ləunlɪnɪs] n soledad f;
aislamiento
lonely ['ləunlɪ] adj (*situation*)
solitario; (*person*) solo; (*place*) aislado
long [lɔŋ] adj largo ▷adv mucho
tiempo, largamente ▷vi: **to ~ for sth**
anhelar algo; **so** or **as ~ as** mientras,
con tal que; **don't be ~!** ¡no tardes!,
¡vuelve pronto!; **how ~ is the street?**
¿cuánto tiene la calle de largo?; **how ~
is the lesson?** ¿cuánto dura la clase?;
6 metres ~ que mide 6 metros, de
6 metros de largo; **6 months ~** que
dura 6 meses, de 6 meses de duración;
all night ~ toda la noche; **he no ~er
comes** ya no viene; **I can't stand it
any ~er** ya no lo aguanto más; **~ before**

mucho antes; **before ~** (+ *future*) dentro
de poco; (+ *past*) poco tiempo después;
at ~ last al fin, por fin; **long-distance**
adj (*race*) de larga distancia; (*call*)
interurbano; **long-haul** *adj* (*flight*)
de larga distancia; **longing** *n* anhelo,
ansia; (*nostalgia*) nostalgia ▷ *adj*
anhelante

longitude ['lɒŋgɪtjuːd] *n* longitud *f*

long: long jump *n* salto de
longitud; **long-life** *adj* (*batteries*)
de larga duración; (*milk*) uperizado;
long-sighted (BRIT) *adj* présbita;
long-standing *adj* de mucho tiempo;
long-term *adj* a largo plazo

loo [luː] (BRIT: *inf*) *n* wáter *m*

look [lʊk] *vi* mirar; (*seem*) parecer;
(*building etc*): **to ~ south/on to the sea**
dar al sur/al mar ▷ *n* (*gen*): **to have a
~** mirar; (*glance*) mirada; (*appearance*)
aire *m*, aspecto; **looks** *npl* (*good looks*)
belleza; **~ (here)!** (*expressing annoyance
etc*) ¡oye!; **~!** (*expressing surprise*) ¡mira!;
look after *vt fus* (*care for*) cuidar a;
(*deal with*) encargarse de; **look around**
vi echar una mirada alrededor; **look
at** *vt fus* mirar; (*read quickly*) echar
un vistazo a; **look back** *vi* mirar
hacia atrás; **look down on** *vt fus* (*fig*)
despreciar, mirar con desprecio; **look
for** *vt fus* buscar; **look forward to** *vt
fus* esperar con ilusión; (*in letters*): **we
look forward to hearing from you**
quedamos a la espera de sus gratas
noticias; **look into** *vt* investigar; **look
out** *vi* (*beware*): **to look out (for)** tener
cuidado (de); **look out for** *vt fus* (*seek*)
buscar; (*await*) esperar; **look round**
vi volver la cabeza; **look through** *vt
fus* (*examine*) examinar; **look up** *vi*
mirar hacia arriba; (*improve*) mejorar
▷ *vt* (*word*) buscar; **look up to** *vt fus*
admirar; **lookout** *n* (*tower etc*) puesto
de observación; (*person*) vigía *mf*; **to
be on the lookout for sth** estar al
acecho de algo

loom [luːm] *vi*: **~ (up)** (*threaten*)
surgir, amenazar; (*event: approach*)

aproximarse

loony ['luːnɪ] (*inf*) *n*, *adj* loco/a *m/f*

loop [luːp] *n* lazo ▷ *vt*: **to ~ sth round
sth** pasar algo alrededor de algo;
loophole *n* escapatoria

loose [luːs] *adj* suelto; (*clothes*)
ancho; (*morals, discipline*) relajado; **to
be on the ~** estar en libertad; **to be
at a ~ end** *or* **at ~ ends** (US) no saber
qué hacer; **loosely** *adv* libremente,
aproximadamente; **loosen** *vt* aflojar

loot [luːt] *n* botín *m* ▷ *vt* saquear

lop-sided ['lɒp'saɪdɪd] *adj* torcido

lord [lɔːd] *n* señor *m*; **L~ Smith**
Lord Smith; **the L~** el Señor; **my ~**
(*to bishop*) Ilustrísima; (*to noble etc*)
Señor; **good L~!** ¡Dios mío!; **Lords** *npl*
(BRIT: *Pol*): **the (House of) Lords** la
Cámara de los Lores

lorry ['lɒrɪ] (BRIT) *n* camión *m*; **lorry
driver** (BRIT) *n* camionero/a

lose [luːz] (*pt, pp* **lost**) *vt* perder ▷ *vi*
perder, ser vencido; **to ~ (time)** (*clock*)
atrasarse; **lose out** *vi* salir perdiendo;
loser *n* perdedor(a) *m/f*

loss [lɒs] *n* pérdida; **heavy ~es** (*Mil*)
grandes pérdidas; **to be at a ~** no saber
qué hacer; **to make a ~** sufrir pérdidas

lost [lɒst] *pt, pp of* **lose** ▷ *adj* perdido;
lost property (US **lost and found**) *n*
objetos *mpl* perdidos

lot [lɒt] *n* (*group: of things*) grupo; (*at
auctions*) lote *m*; **the ~** el todo, todos;
a ~ (*large number: of books etc*) muchos;
(*a great deal*) mucho, bastante; **a ~
of, ~s of** mucho(s) (*pl*); **I read a ~** leo
bastante; **to draw ~s (for sth)** echar
suertes (para decidir algo)

lotion ['ləʊʃən] *n* loción *f*

lottery ['lɒtərɪ] *n* lotería

loud [laʊd] *adj* (*voice, sound*)
fuerte; (*laugh, shout*) estrepitoso;
(*condemnation etc*) enérgico; (*gaudy*)
chillón/ona ▷ *adv* (*speak etc*) fuerte;
out ~ en voz alta; **loudly** *adv* (*noisily*)
fuerte; (*aloud*) en voz alta; **loudspeaker**
n altavoz *m*

lounge [laʊndʒ] *n* salón *m*, sala (de

estar); (*at airport etc*) sala; (BRIT: *also*:
~-bar) salón-bar *m* ▷ *vi* (*also*: **~ about**
or **around**) reposar, holgazanear
louse [laus] (*pl* **lice**) *n* piojo
lousy ['lauzɪ] (*inf*) *adj* (*bad quality*)
malísimo, asqueroso; (*ill*) fatal
love [lʌv] *n* (*romantic, sexual*) amor *m*;
(*kind, caring*) cariño ▷ *vt* amar, querer;
(*thing, activity*) encantarle a algn; **"~
from Anne"** (*on letter*) "un abrazo (de)
Anne"; **to ~ to do** encantarle a algn
hacer; **to be/fall in ~ with** estar
enamorado/enamorarse de; **to make
~** hacer el amor; **for the ~ of** por amor
de; **"15 ~"** (*Tennis*) "15 a cero"; **I ~ you** te
quiero; **I ~ paella** me encanta la paella;
love affair *n* aventura sentimental;
love life (*on letter*) vida sentimental
lovely ['lʌvlɪ] *adj* (*delightful*)
encantador(a); (*beautiful*) precioso
lover ['lʌvə*] *n* amante *mf*; (*person in
love*) enamorado; (*amateur*): **a ~ of** un(a)
aficionado/a *or* un(a) amante de
loving ['lʌvɪŋ] *adj* amoroso, cariñoso;
(*action*) tierno
low [ləu] *adj, adv* bajo ▷ *n*
(*Meteorology*) área de baja presión;
to be ~ on (*supplies etc*) andar mal de;
to feel ~ sentirse deprimido; **to turn
(down)** ▷ bajar; **low-alcohol** *adj* de
bajo contenido en alcohol; **low-calorie**
adj bajo en calorías
lower ['ləuə*] *adj* más bajo; (*less
important*) menos importante ▷ *vt*
bajar; (*reduce*) reducir ▷ *vr*: **to ~ o.s. to**
(*fig*) rebajarse a
low-fat *adj* (*milk, yoghurt*) desnatado;
(*diet*) bajo en calorías
loyal ['lɔɪəl] *adj* leal; **loyalty** *n* lealtad
f; **loyalty card** *n* tarjeta cliente
L.P. *n abbr* (= *long-playing record*) elepé *m*
L-plates ['ɛl-] (BRIT) *npl* placas *fpl* de
aprendiz de conductor

- **L-PLATES**
-
- En el Reino Unido las personas
- que están aprendiendo a conducir

- deben llevar en la parte delantera
- y trasera de su vehículo unas
- placas blancas con una L en rojo
- conocidas como **L-Plates** (de
- **learner**). No es necesario que
- asistan a clases teóricas sino que,
- desde el principio, se le sentrega
- un carnet de conducir provisional
- ("provisional driving licence")
- para que realicen sus prácticas,
- aunque no pueden circular por
- las autopistas y deben ir siempre
- acompañadas por un conductor
- con carnet definitivo ("full driving
- licence").

Lt *abbr* (= *lieutenant*) Tte.
Ltd *abbr* (= *limited company*) S.A.
luck [lʌk] *n* suerte *f*; **bad ~** mala
suerte; **good ~!** ¡que tengas suerte!,
¡suerte!; **bad** *or* **hard** *or* **tough ~!** ¡qué
pena!; **luckily** *adv* afortunadamente;
lucky *adj* afortunado; (*at cards etc*) con
suerte; (*object*) que trae suerte
lucrative ['lu:krətɪv] *adj* lucrativo
ludicrous ['lu:dɪkrəs] *adj* absurdo
luggage ['lʌgɪdʒ] *n* equipaje
m; **luggage rack** *n* (*on car*) baca,
portaequipajes *m inv*
lukewarm ['lu:kwɔ:m] *adj* tibio
lull [lʌl] *n* tregua ▷ *vt*: **to ~ sb to sleep**
arrullar a algn; **to ~ sb into a false
sense of security** dar a algn una falsa
sensación de seguridad
lullaby ['lʌləbaɪ] *n* nana
lumber ['lʌmbə*] *n* (*junk*) trastos *mpl*
viejos; (*wood*) maderos *mpl*
luminous ['lu:mɪnəs] *adj* luminoso
lump [lʌmp] *n* terrón *m*; (*fragment*)
trozo; (*swelling*) bulto ▷ *vt* (*also*: **~
together**) juntar; **lump sum** *n* suma
global; **lumpy** *adj* (*sauce*) lleno de
grumos; (*mattress*) lleno de bultos
lunatic ['lu:nətɪk] *adj* loco
lunch [lʌntʃ] *n* almuerzo, comida ▷ *vi*
almorzar; **lunch break, lunch hour** *n*
hora del almuerzo; **lunch time** *n* hora
de comer

lung [lʌŋ] *n* pulmón *m*
lure [luə*] *n* (*attraction*) atracción *f*
▷ *vt* tentar
lurk [lə:k] *vi* (*person, animal*) estar al
acecho; (*fig*) acechar
lush [lʌʃ] *adj* exuberante
lust [lʌst] *n* lujuria; (*greed*) codicia
Luxembourg ['lʌksəmbə:g] *n*
Luxemburgo
luxurious [lʌg'zjuəriəs] *adj* lujoso
luxury ['lʌkʃəri] *n* lujo ▷ *cpd* de lujo
Lycra® ['laikrə] *n* licra®
lying ['laiiŋ] *n* mentiras *fpl* ▷ *adj*
mentiroso
lyrics ['liriks] *npl* (*of song*) letra

m. *abbr* = **metre; mile; million**
M.A. *abbr* = **Master of Arts**
ma (*inf*) [mɑ:] *n* mamá
mac [mæk] (*BRIT*) *n* impermeable *m*
macaroni [mækə'rəuni] *n*
macarrones *mpl*
Macedonia [mæsi'dəuniə] *n*
Macedonia; **Macedonian** [-'dəuniən]
adj macedonio ▷ *n* macedonio/a;
(*Ling*) macedonio
machine [mə'ʃi:n] *n* máquina
▷ *vt* (*dress etc*) coser a máquina;
(*Tech*) hacer a máquina; **machine
gun** *n* ametralladora; **machinery**
n maquinaria; (*fig*) mecanismo;
machine washable *adj* lavable a
máquina
macho ['mætʃəu] *adj* machista
mackerel ['mækrl] *n inv* caballa
mackintosh ['mækintɔʃ] (*BRIT*) *n*
impermeable *m*
mad [mæd] *adj* loco; (*idea*)
disparatado; (*angry*) furioso; (*keen*): **to
be ~ about sth** volverle loco a algn algo
Madagascar [mædə'gæskə*] *n*

Madagascar m

madam ['mædəm] n señora

mad cow disease n encefalopatía espongiforme bovina

made [meɪd] pt, pp of **make**; **made-to-measure** (BRIT) adj hecho a la medida; **made-up** ['meɪdʌp] adj (story) ficticio

madly ['mædlɪ] adv locamente

madman ['mædmən] (irreg) n loco

madness ['mædnɪs] n locura

Madrid [mə'drɪd] n Madrid

Mafia ['mæfɪə] n Mafia

mag [mæg] n abbr (BRIT inf) = **magazine**

magazine [mægə'ziːn] n revista; (Radio, TV) programa m magazina

maggot ['mægət] n gusano

magic ['mædʒɪk] n magia ▷ adj mágico; **magical** adj mágico; **magician** [mə'dʒɪʃən] n mago/a; (conjurer) prestidigitador(a) m/f

magistrate ['mædʒɪstreɪt] n juez mf (municipal)

magnet ['mægnɪt] n imán m; **magnetic** [-'nɛtɪk] adj magnético; (personality) atrayente

magnificent [mæg'nɪfɪsənt] adj magnífico

magnify ['mægnɪfaɪ] vt (object) ampliar; (sound) aumentar; **magnifying glass** n lupa

magpie ['mægpaɪ] n urraca

mahogany [mə'hɔgənɪ] n caoba

maid [meɪd] n criada; **old ~** (pej) solterona

maiden name n nombre m de soltera

mail [meɪl] n correo; (letters) cartas fpl ▷ vt echar al correo; **mailbox** (US) n buzón m; **mailing list** n lista de direcciones; **mailman** (US: irreg) n cartero; **mail-order** n pedido postal

main [meɪn] adj principal, mayor ▷ n (pipe) cañería maestra; (US) red f eléctrica ▷ **the ~s** npl (BRIT Elec) la red eléctrica; **in the ~** en general; **main course** n (Culin) plato principal; **mainland** n tierra firme; **mainly**

adv principalmente; **main road** n carretera; **mainstream** n corriente f principal; **main street** n calle f mayor

maintain [meɪn'teɪn] vt mantener; **maintenance** ['meɪntənəns] n mantenimiento; (Law) manutención f

maisonette [meɪzə'nɛt] n dúplex m

maize [meɪz] (BRIT) n maíz m, choclo (SC)

majesty ['mædʒɪstɪ] n majestad f; (title): **Your M~** Su Majestad

major ['meɪdʒə*] n (Mil) comandante mf ▷ adj principal; (Mus) mayor

Majorca [mə'jɔːkə] n Mallorca

majority [mə'dʒɔrɪtɪ] n mayoría

make [meɪk] (pt, pp **made**) vt hacer; (manufacture) fabricar; (mistake) cometer; (speech) pronunciar; (cause to be): **to ~ sb sad** poner triste a algn; (force): **to ~ sb do sth** obligar a algn a hacer algo; (earn) ganar; (equal): **2 and 2 ~ 4** 2 y 2 son 4 ▷ n marca; **to ~ the bed** hacer la cama; **to ~ a fool of sb** poner a algn en ridículo; **to ~ a profit/loss** obtener ganancias/sufrir pérdidas; **to ~ it** (arrive) llegar; (achieve sth) tener éxito; **what time do you ~ it?** ¿qué hora tienes?; **to ~ do with** contentarse con; **make off** vi largarse; **make out** vt (decipher) descifrar; (understand) entender; (see) distinguir; (cheque) extender; **make up** vt (invent) inventar; (prepare) hacer; (constitute) constituir ▷ vi reconciliarse; (with cosmetics) maquillarse; **make up for** vt fus compensar; **makeover** ['meɪkəuvə*] n (by beautician) sesión f de maquillaje y peluquería; (change of image) lavado de cara; **maker** n fabricante mf; (of film, programme) autor(a) m/f; **makeshift** adj improvisado; **make-up** n maquillaje m

making ['meɪkɪŋ] n (fig): **in the ~** en vías de formación; **to have the ~s of** (person) tener madera de

malaria [mə'lɛərɪə] n malaria

Malaysia [mə'leɪzɪə] n Malasia,

Malaysia

male [meɪl] *n* (*Biol*) macho ▷ *adj* (*sex, attitude*) masculino; (*child etc*) varón

malicious [mə'lɪʃəs] *adj* malicioso; rencoroso

malignant [mə'lɪgnənt] *adj* (*Med*) maligno

mall [mɔːl] (*US*) *n* (*also:* **shopping ~**) centro comercial

mallet ['mælɪt] *n* mazo

malnutrition [mælnju:'trɪʃən] *n* desnutrición *f*

malpractice [mæl'præktɪs] *n* negligencia profesional

malt [mɔːlt] *n* malta; (*whisky*) whisky *m* de malta

Malta ['mɔːltə] *n* Malta; **Maltese** [-'tiːz] *adj, n inv* maltés/esa *m/f*

mammal ['mæml] *n* mamífero

mammoth ['mæməθ] *n* mamut *m* ▷ *adj* gigantesco

man [mæn] (*pl* **men**) *n* hombre *m*; (*mankind*) el hombre ▷ *vt* (*Naut*) tripular; (*Mil*) guarnecer; (*operate: machine*) manejar; **an old ~** un viejo; **~ and wife** marido y mujer

manage ['mænɪdʒ] *vi* arreglárselas, ir tirando ▷ *vt* (*be in charge of*) dirigir; (*control: person*) manejar; (*: ship*) gobernar; **manageable** *adj* manejable; **management** *n* dirección *f*; **manager** *n* director(a) *m/f*; (*of pop star*) mánager *m/f*; (*Sport*) entrenador(a) *m/f*; **manageress** *n* directora, entrenadora; **managerial** [-ə'dʒɪərɪəl] *adj* directivo; **managing director** *n* director(a) *m/f* general

mandarin ['mændərɪn] *n* (*also:* **~ orange**) mandarina; (*person*) mandarín *m*

mandate ['mændeɪt] *n* mandato

mandatory ['mændətərɪ] *adj* obligatorio

mane [meɪn] *n* (*of horse*) crin *f*; (*of lion*) melena

maneuver [mə'nu:və*] (*US*) = **manoeuvre**

mangetout [mɔnʒ'tu:] *n* tirabeque

m

mango ['mæŋgəʊ] (*pl* **~es**) *n* mango

man: manhole *n* agujero de acceso; **manhood** *n* edad *f* viril; (*state*) virilidad *f*

mania ['meɪnɪə] *n* manía; **maniac** ['meɪnɪæk] *n* maníaco/a; (*fig*) maniático

manic ['mænɪk] *adj* frenético

manicure ['mænɪkjuə*] *n* manicura

manifest ['mænɪfest] *vt* manifestar, mostrar ▷ *adj* manifiesto

manifesto [mænɪ'festəu] *n* manifiesto

manipulate [mə'nɪpjuleɪt] *vt* manipular

man: mankind [mæn'kaɪnd] *n* humanidad *f*, género humano; **manly** *adj* varonil; **man-made** *adj* artificial

manner ['mænə*] *n* manera, modo; (*behaviour*) conducta, manera de ser; (*type*) **all ~ of things** toda clase de cosas; **manners** *npl* (*behaviour*) modales *mpl*; **bad ~s** mala educación

manoeuvre [mə'nu:və*] (*us* **maneuver**) *vt, vi* maniobrar ▷ *n* maniobra

manpower ['mænpauə*] *n* mano *f* de obra

mansion ['mænʃən] *n* palacio, casa grande

manslaughter ['mænslɔ:tə*] *n* homicidio no premeditado

mantelpiece ['mæntlpi:s] *n* repisa, chimenea

manual ['mænjuəl] *adj* manual ▷ *n* manual *m*

manufacture [mænju'fæktʃə*] *vt* fabricar ▷ *n* fabricación *f*; **manufacturer** *n* fabricante *mf*

manure [mə'njuə*] *n* estiércol *m*

manuscript ['mænjuskrɪpt] *n* manuscrito

many ['menɪ] *adj, pron* muchos/as; **a great ~** muchísimos, un buen número de; **~ a time** muchas veces

map [mæp] *n* mapa *m* ▷ **to ~ out** *vt* proyectar

maple ['meɪpl] n arce m, maple m (LAM)

Mar abbr (= March) mar

mar [mɑ:*] vt estropear

marathon ['mærəθən] n maratón m

marble ['mɑ:bl] n mármol m; (toy) canica

March [mɑ:tʃ] n marzo

march [mɑ:tʃ] vi (Mil) marchar; (demonstrators) manifestarse ▷ n marcha; (demonstration) manifestación f

mare [mɛə*] n yegua

margarine [mɑ:dʒə'ri:n] n margarina

margin ['mɑ:dʒɪn] n margen m; (Comm: profit margin) margen m de beneficios; **marginal** adj marginal; **marginally** adv ligeramente

marigold ['mærɪgəʊld] n caléndula

marijuana [mærɪ'wɑ:nə] n marijuana

marina [mə'ri:nə] n puerto deportivo

marinade [mærɪ'neɪd] n adobo

marinate ['mærɪneɪt] vt marinar

marine [mə'ri:n] adj marino ▷ n soldado de marina

marital ['mærɪtl] adj matrimonial; **marital status** n estado m civil

maritime ['mærɪtaɪm] adj marítimo

marjoram ['mɑ:dʒərəm] n mejorana

mark [mɑ:k] n marca, señal f; (in snow, mud etc) huella; (stain) mancha; (BRIT Scol) nota ▷ vt marcar; manchar; (damage: furniture) rayar; (indicate: place etc) señalar; (BRIT Scol) calificar, corregir; **to ~ time** marcar el paso; (fig) marcar(se) un ritmo; **marked** adj (obvious) marcado, acusado; **marker** n (sign) marcador m; (bookmark) señal f (de libro)

market ['mɑ:kɪt] n mercado ▷ vt (Comm) comercializar; **marketing** n márketing m; **marketplace** n mercado; **market research** n análisis m inv de mercados

marmalade ['mɑ:məleɪd] n mermelada de naranja

maroon [mə'ru:n] vt: **to be ~ed** quedar aislado; (fig) quedar abandonado ▷ n (colour) granate m

marquee [mɑ:'ki:] n entoldado

marriage ['mærɪdʒ] n (relationship, institution) matrimonio; (wedding) boda; (act) casamiento; **marriage certificate** n partida de casamiento

married ['mærɪd] adj casado; (life, love) conyugal

marrow ['mærəʊ] n médula; (vegetable) calabacín m

marry ['mærɪ] vt casarse con; (father, priest etc) casar ▷ vi (also: **get married**) casarse

Mars [mɑ:z] n Marte m

marsh [mɑ:ʃ] n pantano; (salt marsh) marisma

marshal ['mɑ:ʃl] n (Mil) mariscal m; (at sports meeting etc) oficial m; (US: of police, fire department) jefe/a m/f ▷ vt (thoughts etc) ordenar; (soldiers) formar

martyr ['mɑ:tə*] n mártir mf

marvel ['mɑ:vl] n maravilla, prodigio ▷ vi: **to ~ (at)** maravillarse (de); **marvellous** (US **marvelous**) adj maravilloso

Marxism ['mɑ:ksɪzəm] n marxismo

Marxist ['mɑ:ksɪst] adj, n marxista mf

marzipan ['mɑ:zɪpæn] n mazapán m

mascara [mæs'kɑ:rə] n rímel m

mascot ['mæskət] n mascota

masculine ['mæskjulɪn] adj masculino

mash [mæʃ] vt machacar; **mashed potato(es)** n(pl) puré m de patatas (SP) or papas (LAM)

mask [mɑ:sk] n máscara ▷ vt (cover): **to ~ one's face** ocultarse la cara; (hide: feelings) esconder

mason ['meɪsn] n (also: **stone~**) albañil m; (also: **free~**) masón m; **masonry** n (in building) mampostería

mass [mæs] n (people) muchedumbre f; (of air, liquid etc) masa; (of detail, hair etc) gran cantidad f; (Rel) misa ▷ cpd

masivo ▷ *vi* reunirse; concentrarse;
the masses *npl* las masas; **~es of** (*inf*)
montones de
massacre ['mæsəkə*] *n* masacre *f*
massage ['mæsɑːʒ] *n* masaje *m* ▷ *vt*
dar masaje en
massive ['mæsɪv] *adj* enorme;
(*support, changes*) masivo
mass media *npl* medios *mpl* de
comunicación
mass-produce ['mæsprə'djuːs] *vt*
fabricar en serie
mast [mɑːst] *n* (*Naut*) mástil *m*; (*Radio
etc*) torre *f*
master ['mɑːstə*] *n* (*of servant*)
amo; (*of situation*) dueño, maestro;
(*in primary school*) maestro; (*in
secondary school*) profesor *m*; (*title for
boys*): **M~ X** Señorito X ▷ *vt* dominar;
mastermind *n* inteligencia superior
▷ *vt* dirigir, planear; **Master of
Arts/Science** *n* licenciatura superior
en Letras/Ciencias; **masterpiece** *n*
obra maestra
masturbate ['mæstəbeɪt] *vi*
masturbarse
mat [mæt] *n* estera; (*also*: **door~**)
felpudo; (*also*: **table ~**) salvamanteles *m
inv*, posavasos *m inv* ▷ *adj* = **matt**
match [mætʃ] *n* cerilla, fósforo;
(*game*) partido; (*equal*) igual *m/f* ▷ *vt*
(*go well with*) hacer juego con; (*equal*)
igualar; (*correspond to*) corresponderse
con; (*pair*: *also*: **~ up**) casar con ▷ *vi*
hacer juego; **to be a good ~** hacer
juego; **matchbox** *n* caja de cerillas;
matching *adj* que hace juego
mate [meɪt] *n* (*workmate*) colega *mf*;
(*inf*: *friend*) amigo/a; (*animal*) macho/
hembra; (*in merchant navy*) segundo
de a bordo ▷ *vi* acoplarse, aparearse
▷ *vt* aparear
material [mə'tɪərɪəl] *n* (*substance*)
materia; (*information*) material *m*;
(*cloth*) tela, tejido ▷ *adj* material;
(*important*) esencial; **materials** *npl*
materiales *mpl*
materialize [mə'tɪərɪəlaɪz] *vi*

materializarse
maternal [mə'təːnl] *adj* maternal
maternity [mə'təːnɪtɪ] *n*
maternidad *f*; **maternity hospital** *n*
hospital *m* de maternidad; **maternity
leave** *n* baja por maternidad
math [mæθ] (*US*) *n* = **mathematics**
mathematical [mæθə'mætɪkl] *adj*
matemático
mathematician [mæθəmə'tɪʃən] *n*
matemático/a
mathematics [mæθə'mætɪks] *n*
matemáticas *fpl*
maths [mæθs] (*BRIT*) *n* =
mathematics
matinée ['mætɪneɪ] *n* sesión *f* de
tarde
matron ['meɪtrən] *n* enfermera *f* jefe;
(*in school*) ama de llaves
matt [mæt] *adj* mate
matter ['mætə*] *n* cuestión *f*, asunto;
(*Physics*) sustancia, materia; (*reading
matter*) material *m*; (*Med: pus*) pus *m*
▷ *vi* importar; **matters** *npl* (*affairs*)
asuntos *mpl*, temas *mpl*; **it doesn't ~**
no importa; **what's the ~?** ¿qué pasa?;
no ~ what pase lo que pase; **as a ~
of course** por rutina; **as a ~ of fact**
de hecho
mattress ['mætrɪs] *n* colchón *m*
mature [mə'tjuə*] *adj* maduro
▷ *vi* madurar; **mature student** *n*
estudiante de más de 21 años; **maturity**
n madurez *f*
maul [mɔːl] *vt* magullar
mauve [məuv] *adj* de color malva (*SP*)
or guinda (*LAM*)
max *abbr* = **maximum**
maximize ['mæksɪmaɪz] *vt* (*profits
etc*) llevar al máximo; (*chances*)
maximizar
maximum ['mæksɪməm] (*pl.*
maxima) *adj* máximo ▷ *n* máximo
May [meɪ] *n* mayo
may [meɪ] (*conditional* **might**) *vi*
(*indicating possibility*): **he ~ come** puede
que venga; (*be allowed to*): **~ I smoke?**
¿puedo fumar?; (*wishes*): **~ God bless**

you! ¡que Dios le bendiga!; **you ~ as well go** bien puedes irte

maybe ['meɪbi:] *adv* quizá(s)

May Day *n* el primero de Mayo

mayhem ['meɪhɛm] *n* caos *m* total

mayonnaise [meɪə'neɪz] *n* mayonesa

mayor [mɛə*] *n* alcalde *m*; **mayoress** *n* alcaldesa

maze [meɪz] *n* laberinto

MD *n abbr* = **managing director**

me [mi:] *pron* (*direct*) me; (*stressed, after pron*) mí; **can you hear ~?** ¿me oyes?; **he heard ME** ¡me oyó a mí!; **it's ~** soy yo; **give them to ~** dámelos/las; **with/without ~** conmigo/sin mí

meadow ['mɛdəu] *n* prado, pradera

meagre ['mi:gə*] (*US* **meager**) *adj* escaso, pobre

meal [mi:l] *n* comida; (*flour*) harina; **mealtime** *n* hora de comer

mean [mi:n] (*pt, pp* **~t**) *adj* (*with money*) tacaño; (*unkind*) mezquino, malo; (*shabby*) humilde; (*average*) medio ▷ *vt* (*signify*) querer decir, significar; (*refer to*) referirse a; (*intend*): **to ~ to do sth** pensar *or* pretender hacer algo ▷ *n* medio, término medio; **means** *npl* (*way*) medio, manera; (*money*) recursos *mpl*, medios *mpl*; **by ~s of** mediante, por medio de; **by all ~s!** ¡naturalmente!, ¡claro que sí!; **do you ~ it?** ¿lo dices en serio?; **what do you ~?** ¿qué quiere decir?; **to be ~t for sb/sth** ser para algn/algo

meaning ['mi:nɪŋ] *n* significado, sentido; (*purpose*) sentido, propósito; **meaningful** *adj* significativo; **meaningless** *adj* sin sentido

meant [mɛnt] *pt, pp of* **mean**

meantime ['mi:ntaɪm] *adv* (*also*: **in the ~**) mientras tanto

meanwhile ['mi:nwaɪl] *adv* = **meantime**

measles ['mi:zlz] *n* sarampión *m*

measure ['mɛʒə*] *vt, vi* medir ▷ *n* medida; (*ruler*) regla; **measurement** ['mɛʒəmənt] *n* (*measure*) medida; (*act*) medición *f*; **to take sb's measurements** tomar las medidas a algn

meat [mi:t] *n* carne *f*; **cold ~** fiambre *m*; **meatball** *n* albóndiga

Mecca ['mɛkə] *n* La Meca

mechanic [mɪ'kænɪk] *n* mecánico/a; **mechanical** *adj* mecánico

mechanism ['mɛkənɪzəm] *n* mecanismo

medal ['mɛdl] *n* medalla; **medallist** (*US* **medalist**) *n* (*Sport*) medallista *mf*

meddle ['mɛdl] *vi*: **to ~ in** entrometerse en; **to ~ with sth** manosear algo

media ['mi:dɪə] *npl* medios *mpl* de comunicación ▷ *npl of* **medium**

mediaeval [mɛdɪ'i:vl] *adj* = **medieval**

mediate ['mi:dɪeɪt] *vi* mediar

medical ['mɛdɪkl] *adj* médico ▷ *n* reconocimiento médico; **medical certificate** *n* certificado *m* médico

medicated ['mɛdɪkeɪtɪd] *adj* medicinal

medication [mɛdɪ'keɪʃən] *n* medicación *f*

medicine ['mɛdsɪn] *n* medicina; (*drug*) medicamento

medieval [mɛdɪ'i:vl] *adj* medieval

mediocre [mi:dɪ'əukə*] *adj* mediocre

meditate ['mɛdɪteɪt] *vi* meditar

meditation [mɛdɪ'teɪʃən] *n* meditación *f*

Mediterranean [mɛdɪtə'reɪnɪən] *adj* mediterráneo; **the ~ (Sea)** el (Mar) Mediterráneo

medium ['mi:dɪəm] (*pl* **media**) *adj* mediano, regular ▷ *n* (*means*) medio; (*pl* **mediums**: *person*) médium *mf*; **medium-sized** *adj* de tamaño mediano; (*clothes*) de (la) talla mediana; **medium wave** *n* onda media

meek [mi:k] *adj* manso, sumiso

meet [mi:t] (*pt, pp* **met**) *vt* encontrar; (*accidentally*) encontrarse con, tropezar con; (*by arrangement*) reunirse con; (*for the first time*) conocer; (*go and fetch*) ir a buscar; (*opponent*) enfrentarse con; (*obligations*) cumplir; (*encounter: problem*) hacer frente a; (*need*) satisfacer ▷ *vi* encontrarse; (*in session*) reunirse; (*join: objects*) unirse; (*for the first time*) conocerse; **meet up** *vi*: **to meet up with sb** reunirse con algn; **meet with** *vt fus* (*difficulty*) tropezar con; **to meet with success** tener éxito; **meeting** *n* encuentro; (*arranged*) cita, compromiso; (*business meeting*) reunión *f*; (*Pol*) mitin *m*; **meeting place** *n* lugar *m* de reunión *or* encuentro

megabyte ['mɛgəbaɪt] *n* (*Comput*) megabyte *m*, megaocteto

megaphone ['mɛgəfəʊn] *n* megáfono

megapixel ['mɛgəpɪksl] *n* megapíxel *m*

melancholy ['mɛlənkəlɪ] *n* melancolía ▷ *adj* melancólico

melody ['mɛlədɪ] *n* melodía

melon ['mɛlən] *n* melón *m*

melt [mɛlt] *vi* (*metal*) fundirse; (*snow*) derretirse ▷ *vt* fundir

member ['mɛmbə*] *n* (*gen, Anat*) miembro; (*of club*) socio/a; **Member of Congress** (*US*) *n* miembro *mf* del Congreso; **Member of Parliament** *n* (*BRIT*) diputado/a *m/f*, parlamentario/a *m/f*; **Member of the European Parliament** *n* diputado/a *m/f* del Parlamento Europeo, eurodiputado/a *m/f*; **Member of the Scottish Parliament** (*BRIT*) diputado/a del Parlamento escocés; **membership** *n* (*members*) número de miembros; (*state*) filiación *f*; **membership card** *n* carnet *m* de socio

memento [mə'mɛntəʊ] *n* recuerdo

memo ['mɛməʊ] *n* apunte *m*, nota

memorable ['mɛmərəbl] *adj* memorable

memorandum [mɛmə'rændəm] (*pl* **memoranda**) *n* apunte *m*, nota; (*official note*) acta

memorial [mɪ'mɔːrɪəl] *n* monumento conmemorativo ▷ *adj* conmemorativo

memorize ['mɛməraɪz] *vt* aprender de memoria

memory ['mɛmərɪ] *n* (*also: Comput*) memoria; (*instance*) recuerdo; (*of dead person*): **in ~ of** a la memoria de; **memory card** *n* (*for digital camera*) tarjeta de memoria

men [mɛn] *npl of* **man**

menace ['mɛnəs] *n* amenaza ▷ *vt* amenazar

mend [mɛnd] *vt* reparar, arreglar; (*darn*) zurcir ▷ *vi* reponerse ▷ *n* arreglo, reparación *f* zurcido ▷ *n*: **to be on the ~** ir mejorando; **to ~ one's ways** enmendarse

meningitis [mɛnɪn'dʒaɪtɪs] *n* meningitis *f*

menopause ['mɛnəʊpɔːz] *n* menopausia

men's room (*US*) *n*: **the ~** el servicio de caballeros

menstruation [mɛnstru'eɪʃən] *n* menstruación *f*

menswear ['mɛnzwɛə*] *n* confección *f* de caballero

mental ['mɛntl] *adj* mental; **mental hospital** *n* (*hospital m*) psiquiátrico; **mentality** [mɛn'tælɪtɪ] *n* mentalidad *f*; **mentally** *adv*: **to be mentally ill** tener una enfermedad mental

menthol ['mɛnθɔl] *n* mentol *m*

mention ['mɛnʃən] *n* mención *f* ▷ *vt* mencionar; (*speak*) hablar de; **don't ~ it!** ¡de nada!

menu ['mɛnjuː] *n* (*set menu*) menú *m*; (*printed*) carta; (*Comput*) menú *m*

MEP *n abbr* = **Member of the European Parliament**

mercenary ['məːsɪnərɪ] *adj, n* mercenario/a

merchandise ['məːtʃəndaɪz] *n* mercancías *fpl*

merchant ['məːtʃənt] *n* comerciante *mf*; **merchant navy** (*US*), **merchant marine** *n* marina mercante

merciless ['mə:sɪlɪs] *adj* despiadado

mercury ['mə:kjʊrɪ] *n* mercurio

mercy ['mə:sɪ] *n* compasión *f*; (*Rel*) misericordia; **at the ~ of** a la merced de

mere [mɪə*] *adj* simple, mero; **merely** *adv* simplemente, sólo

merge [mə:dʒ] *vt* (*join*) unir ▷ *vi* unirse; (*Comm*) fusionarse; (*colours etc*) fundirse; **merger** *n* (*Comm*) fusión *f*

meringue [mə'ræŋ] *n* merengue *m*

merit ['mɛrɪt] *n* mérito ▷ *vt* merecer

mermaid ['mə:meɪd] *n* sirena

merry ['mɛrɪ] *adj* alegre; **M~ Christmas!** ¡Felices Pascuas!; **merry-go-round** *n* tiovivo

mesh [mɛʃ] *n* malla

mess [mɛs] *n* (*muddle: of situation*) confusión *f*; (: *of room*) revoltijo; (*dirt*) porquería; (*Mil*) comedor *m*; **mess about** *or* **around** (*inf*) *vi* perder el tiempo; (*pass the time*) entretenerse; **mess up** *vt* (*spoil*) estropear; (*dirty*) ensuciar; **mess with** (*inf*) *vt fus* (*challenge, confront*) meterse con (*inf*); (*interfere with*) interferir con

message ['mɛsɪdʒ] *n* recado, mensaje *m*

messenger ['mɛsɪndʒə*] *n* mensajero/a

Messrs *abbr* (*on letters*) (= *Messieurs*) Sres

messy ['mɛsɪ] *adj* (*dirty*) sucio; (*untidy*) desordenado

met [mɛt] *pt, pp of* **meet**

metabolism [mɛ'tæbəlɪzəm] *n* metabolismo

metal ['mɛtl] *n* metal *m*; **metallic** [-'tælɪk] *adj* metálico

metaphor ['mɛtəfə*] *n* metáfora

meteor ['mi:tɪə*] *n* meteoro; **meteorite** [-aɪt] *n* meteorito

meteorology [mi:tɪə'rɔlədʒɪ] *n* meteorología

meter ['mi:tə*] *n* (*instrument*) contador *m*; (*US: unit*) = **metre** ▷ *vt* (*US Post*) franquear

method ['mɛθəd] *n* método; **methodical** [mɪ'θɔdɪkl] *adj* metódico

meths [mɛθs] *n* (*BRIT*) alcohol *m* metilado *or* desnaturalizado

meticulous [mɛ'tɪkjʊləs] *adj* meticuloso

metre ['mi:tə*] (*US* **meter**) *n* metro

metric ['mɛtrɪk] *adj* métrico

metro ['mɛtrəʊ] *n* metro

metropolitan [mɛtrə'pɔlɪtən] *adj* metropolitano; **the M~ Police** (*BRIT*) la policía londinense

Mexican ['mɛksɪkən] *adj, n* mexicano/a , mejicano/a

Mexico ['mɛksɪkəʊ] *n* México, Méjico (*SP*)

mg *abbr* (= *milligram*) mg

mice [maɪs] *npl of* **mouse**

micro... [maɪkrəʊ] *prefix* micro...; **microchip** *n* microplaqueta; **microphone** *n* micrófono; **microscope** *n* microscopio; **microwave** *n* (*also:* **microwave oven**) horno microondas

mid [mɪd] *adj*: **in ~ May** a mediados de mayo; **in ~ afternoon** a media tarde; **in ~ air** en el aire; **midday** *n* mediodía *m*

middle ['mɪdl] *n* centro; (*half-way point*) medio; (*waist*) cintura ▷ *adj* de en medio; (*course, way*) intermedio; **in the ~ of the night** en plena noche; **middle-aged** *adj* de mediana edad; **Middle Ages** *npl*: **the Middle Ages** la Edad Media; **middle-class** *adj* de clase media; **the middle class(es)** la clase media; **Middle East** *n* Oriente *m* Medio; **middle name** *n* segundo nombre; **middle school** *n* (*US*) colegio para niños de doce a catorce años; (*BRIT*) colegio para niños de ocho o nueve a doce o trece años

midge [mɪdʒ] *n* mosquito

midget ['mɪdʒɪt] *n* enano/a

midnight ['mɪdnaɪt] *n* medianoche *f*

midst [mɪdst] *n*: **in the ~ of** (*crowd*) en medio de; (*situation, action*) en mitad de

midsummer [mɪd'sʌmə*] *n*: **in ~** en pleno verano

midway [mɪd'weɪ] *adj, adv*: **~ (between)** a medio camino (entre); **~**

through a la mitad (de)

midweek [mɪd'wiːk] *adv* entre semana

midwife ['mɪdwaɪf] (*irreg*) *n* comadrona, partera

midwinter [mɪd'wɪntə*] *n*: **in ~** en pleno invierno

might [maɪt] *vb see* **may** ▷ *n* fuerza, poder *m*; **mighty** *adj* fuerte, poderoso

migraine ['miːgreɪn] *n* jaqueca

migrant ['maɪgrənt] *n, adj* (*bird*) migratorio; (*worker*) emigrante

migrate [maɪ'greɪt] *vi* emigrar

migration [maɪ'greɪʃən] *n* emigración *f*

mike [maɪk] *n abbr* (= microphone) micro

mild [maɪld] *adj* (*person*) apacible; (*climate*) templado; (*slight*) ligero; (*taste*) suave; (*illness*) leve; **mildly** ['-lɪ] *adv* ligeramente; suavemente; **to put it mildly** para no decir más

mile [maɪl] *n* milla; **mileage** *n* número de millas ≈ kilometraje *m*; **mileometer** [maɪ'lɔmɪtə*] *n* ≈ cuentakilómetros *m inv*; **milestone** *n* mojón *m*

military ['mɪlɪtərɪ] *adj* militar

militia [mɪ'lɪʃə] *n* milicia

milk [mɪlk] *n* leche *f* ▷ *vt* (*cow*) ordeñar; (*fig*) chupar; **milk chocolate** *n* chocolate *m* con leche; **milkman** (*irreg*) *n* lechero; **milky** *adj* lechoso

mill [mɪl] *n* (*windmill etc*) molino; (*coffee mill*) molinillo; (*factory*) fábrica ▷ *vt* moler ▷ *vi* (*also:* **~ about**) arremolinarse

millennium [mɪ'lɛnɪəm] (*pl* **~s** or **millennia**) *n* milenio, milenario

milli... ['mɪlɪ] *prefix*: **milligram(me)** *n* miligramo; **millilitre** (*us* **milliliter**) ['mɪlɪliːtə*] *n* mililitro; **millimetre** (*us* **millimeter**) *n* milímetro

million ['mɪljən] *n* millón *m*; **a ~ times** un millón de veces; **millionaire** [-jə'nɛə*] *n* millonario/a; **millionth** [-θ] *adj* millonésimo

milometer [maɪ'lɔmɪtə*] (*BRIT*) *n* =

mileometer

mime [maɪm] *n* mímica; (*actor*) mimo/a ▷ *vt* remedar ▷ *vi* actuar de mimo

mimic ['mɪmɪk] *n* imitador(a) *m/f* ▷ *adj* mímico ▷ *vt* remedar, imitar

min. *abbr* = **minimum**; **minute(s)**

mince [mɪns] *vt* picar ▷ *n* (*BRIT Culin*) carne *f* picada; **mincemeat** *n* conserva de fruta picada; (*us: meat*) carne *f* picada; **mince pie** *n* empanadilla rellena de fruta picada

mind [maɪnd] *n* mente *f*; (*intellect*) intelecto; (*contrasted with matter*) espíritu *m* ▷ *vt* (*attend to, look after*) ocuparse de, cuidar; (*be careful*) tener cuidado con; (*object to*): **I don't ~ the noise** no me molesta el ruido; **it is on my ~** me preocupa; **to bear sth in ~** tomar *or* tener algo en cuenta; **to make up one's ~** decidirse; **I don't ~** me es igual; **~ you ...** te advierto que ...; **never ~!** ¡es igual!, ¡no importa!; (*don't worry*) ¡no te preocupes!; **"~ the step"** "cuidado con el escalón"; **mindless** *adj* (*crime*) sin motivo; (*work*) de autómata

mine¹ [maɪn] *pron* el mío/la mía etc; **a friend of ~** un(a) amigo/a mío/mía ▷ *adj*: **this book is ~** este libro es mío

mine² [maɪn] *n* mina ▷ *vt* (*coal*) extraer; (*bomb: beach etc*) minar; **minefield** *n* campo de minas; **miner** *n* minero/a

mineral ['mɪnərəl] *adj* mineral ▷ *n* mineral *m*; **mineral water** *n* agua mineral

mingle ['mɪŋgl] *vi*: **to ~ with** mezclarse con

miniature ['mɪnətʃə*] *adj* (en) miniatura ▷ *n* miniatura

minibar ['mɪnɪbɑː*] *n* minibar *m*

minibus ['mɪnɪbʌs] *n* microbús *m*

minicab ['mɪnɪkæb] *n* taxi *m* (*que sólo puede pedirse por teléfono*)

minimal ['mɪnɪml] *adj* mínimo

minimize ['mɪnɪmaɪz] *vt* minimizar; (*play down*) empequeñecer

minimum ['mɪnɪməm] (*pl* **minima**)

n, adj mínimo

mining ['maɪnɪŋ] *n* explotación *f* minera

miniskirt ['mɪnɪskə:t] *n* minifalda

minister ['mɪnɪstə*] *n* (*BRIT Pol*) ministro/a (*SP*), secretario/a (*LAM*); (*Rel*) pastor *m* ▷ *vi*: **to ~ to** atender a

ministry ['mɪnɪstrɪ] *n* (*BRIT Pol*) ministerio, secretaría (*MEX*); (*Rel*) sacerdocio

minor ['maɪnə*] *adj* (*repairs, injuries*) leve; (*poet, planet*) menor; (*Mus*) menor ▷ *n* (*Law*) menor *m* de edad

Minorca [mɪ'nɔ:kə] *n* Menorca

minority [maɪ'nɔrɪtɪ] *n* minoría

mint [mɪnt] *n* (*plant*) menta, hierbabuena; (*sweet*) caramelo de menta ▷ *vt* (*coins*) acuñar; **the (Royal) M~, the (US) M~** la Casa de la Moneda; **in ~ condition** en perfecto estado

minus ['maɪnəs] *n* (*also*: **~ sign**) signo de menos ▷ *prep* menos; **12 ~ 6 equals 6** 12 menos 6 son 6; **~ 24°C** menos 24 grados

minute¹ ['mɪnɪt] *n* minuto; (*fig*) momento; **minutes** *npl* (*of meeting*) actas *fpl*; **at the last ~** a última hora

minute² [maɪ'nju:t] *adj* diminuto; (*search*) minucioso

miracle ['mɪrəkl] *n* milagro

miraculous [mɪ'rækjuləs] *adj* milagroso

mirage ['mɪrɑ:ʒ] *n* espejismo

mirror ['mɪrə*] *n* espejo; (*in car*) retrovisor *m*

misbehave [mɪsbɪ'heɪv] *vi* portarse mal

misc. *abbr* = **miscellaneous**

miscarriage ['mɪskærɪdʒ] *n* (*Med*) aborto; **~ of justice** error *m* judicial

miscellaneous [mɪsɪ'leɪnɪəs] *adj* varios/as, diversos/as

mischief ['mɪstʃɪf] *n* travesuras *fpl*, diabluras *fpl*; (*maliciousness*) malicia; **mischievous** [-ʃɪvəs] *adj* travieso

misconception [mɪskən'sɛpʃən] *n* idea equivocada; equivocación *f*

misconduct [mɪs'kɔndʌkt] *n* mala conducta; **professional ~** falta profesional

miser ['maɪzə*] *n* avaro/a

miserable ['mɪzərəbl] *adj* (*unhappy*) triste, desgraciado; (*unpleasant, contemptible*) miserable

misery ['mɪzərɪ] *n* tristeza; (*wretchedness*) miseria, desdicha

misfortune [mɪs'fɔ:tʃən] *n* desgracia

misgiving [mɪs'gɪvɪŋ] *n* (*apprehension*) presentimiento; **to have ~s about sth** tener dudas acerca de algo

misguided [mɪs'gaɪdɪd] *adj* equivocado

mishap ['mɪshæp] *n* desgracia, contratiempo

misinterpret [mɪsɪn'tə:prɪt] *vt* interpretar mal

misjudge [mɪs'dʒʌdʒ] *vt* juzgar mal

mislay [mɪs'leɪ] *vt* extraviar, perder

mislead [mɪs'li:d] *vt* llevar a conclusiones erróneas; **misleading** *adj* engañoso

misplace [mɪs'pleɪs] *vt* extraviar

misprint ['mɪsprɪnt] *n* errata, error *m* de imprenta

misrepresent [mɪsrɛprɪ'zɛnt] *vt* falsificar

Miss [mɪs] *n* Señorita

miss [mɪs] *vt* (*train etc*) perder; (*fail to hit: target*) errar; (*regret the absence of*): **I ~ him** (yo) le echo de menos *or* a faltar; (*fail to see*): **you can't ~ it** no tiene pérdida ▷ *vi* fallar ▷ *n* (*shot*) tiro fallido *or* perdido; **miss out** (*BRIT*) *vt* omitir; **miss out on** *vt fus* (*fun, party, opportunity*) perderse

missile ['mɪsaɪl] *n* (*Aviat*) mísil *m*; (*object thrown*) proyectil *m*

missing ['mɪsɪŋ] *adj* (*pupil*) ausente; (*thing*) perdido; (*Mil*): **~ in action** desaparecido en combate

mission ['mɪʃən] *n* misión *f*; (*official representation*) delegación *f*; **missionary** *n* misionero/a

misspell [mɪs'spɛl] (*pt, pp* **misspelt** (*BRIT*) *or* **~ed**) *vt* escribir mal

mist [mɪst] *n* (*light*) neblina; (*heavy*) niebla; (*at sea*) bruma ▷ *vi* (*eyes: also:* **~ over, ~ up**) llenarse de lágrimas; (*BRIT: windows: also:* **~ over, ~ up**) empañarse

mistake [mɪs'teɪk] (*vt: irreg*) *n* error *m* ▷ *vt* entender mal; **by ~** por equivocación; **to make a ~** equivocarse; **to ~ A for B** confundir A con B; **mistaken** *pp of* **mistake** ▷ *adj* equivocado; **to be mistaken** equivocarse, engañarse

mister ['mɪstə*] (*inf*) *n* señor *m*; *see* **Mr**

mistletoe ['mɪsltəu] *n* muérdago

mistook [mɪs'tuk] *pt of* **mistake**

mistress ['mɪstrɪs] *n* (*lover*) amante *f*; (*of house*) señora (de la casa); (*BRIT: in primary school*) maestra; (*in secondary school*) profesora; (*of situation*) dueña

mistrust [mɪs'trʌst] *vt* desconfiar de

misty ['mɪstɪ] *adj* (*day*) de niebla; (*glasses etc*) empañado

misunderstand [mɪsʌndə'stænd] (*irreg*) *vt, vi* entender mal; **misunderstanding** *n* malentendido

misunderstood [mɪsʌndə'stud] *pt, pp of* **misunderstand** ▷ *adj* (*person*) incomprendido

misuse [*n* mɪs'juːs, *vb* mɪs'juːz] *n* mal uso; (*of power*) abuso; (*of funds*) malversación *f* ▷ *vt* abusar de; malversar

mitt(en) ['mɪt(n)] *n* manopla

mix [mɪks] *vt* mezclar; (*combine*) unir ▷ *vi* mezclarse; (*people*) llevarse bien ▷ *n* mezcla; **mix up** *vt* mezclar; (*confuse*) confundir; **mixed** *adj* mixto; (*feelings etc*) encontrado; **mixed grill** *n* (*BRIT*) parrillada mixta; **mixed salad** *n* ensalada mixta; **mixed-up** *adj* (*confused*) confuso, revuelto; **mixer** *n* (*for food*) licuadora; (*for drinks*) coctelera; (*person*): **he's a good mixer** tiene don de gentes; **mixture** *n* mezcla; (*also:* **cough mixture**) jarabe

m; **mix-up** *n* confusión *f*

ml *abbr* (= *millilitre(s)*) ml

mm *abbr* (= *millimetre*) mm

moan [məun] *n* gemido ▷ *vi* gemir; (*inf: complain*): **to ~ (about)** quejarse (de)

moat [məut] *n* foso

mob [mɔb] *n* multitud *f* ▷ *vt* acosar

mobile ['məubaɪl] *adj* móvil ▷ *n* móvil *m*; **mobile home** *n* caravana; **mobile phone** *n* teléfono móvil

mobility [məu'bɪlɪtɪ] *n* movilidad *f*

mobilize ['məubɪlaɪz] *vt* movilizar

mock [mɔk] *vt* (*ridicule*) ridiculizar; (*laugh at*) burlarse de ▷ *adj* fingido; **~ exam** examen preparatorio antes de los exámenes oficiales® (*BRIT: Scol: inf*) exámenes *mpl* de prueba; **mockery** *n* burla

mod cons ['mɔd'kɔnz] *npl abbr* (= *modern conveniences*) *see* **convenience**

mode [məud] *n* modo

model ['mɔdl] *n* modelo; (*fashion model, artist's model*) modelo *mf* ▷ *adj* modelo ▷ *vt* (*with clay etc*) modelar; (*copy*): **to ~ o.s. on** tomar como modelo a ▷ *vi* ser modelo; **to ~ clothes** pasar modelos, ser modelo

modem ['məudəm] *n* modem *m*

moderate [*adj* 'mɔdərət, *vb* 'mɔdəreɪt] *adj* moderado/a ▷ *vi* moderarse, calmarse ▷ *vt* moderar

moderation [mɔdə'reɪʃən] *n* moderación *f*; **in ~** con moderación

modern ['mɔdən] *adj* moderno; **modernize** *vt* modernizar; **modern languages** *npl* lenguas *fpl* modernas

modest ['mɔdɪst] *adj* modesto; (*small*) módico; **modesty** *n* modestia

modification [mɔdɪfɪ'keɪʃən] *n* modificación *f*

modify ['mɔdɪfaɪ] *vt* modificar

module ['mɔdjuːl] *n* (*unit, component, Space*) módulo

mohair ['məuhɛə*] *n* mohair *m*

Mohammed [mə'hæmɛd] *n* Mahoma *m*

moist [mɔɪst] *adj* húmedo; **moisture**
['mɔɪstʃə*] *n* humedad *f*; **moisturizer**
['mɔɪstʃəraɪzə*] *n* crema hidratante
mold *etc* [məuld] (*US*) = **mould** *etc*
mole [məul] *n* (*animal, spy*) topo;
(*spot*) lunar *m*
molecule ['mɔlɪkjuːl] *n* molécula
molest [məu'lɛst] *vt* importunar;
(*assault sexually*) abusar sexualmente
de

> Be careful not to translate **molest**
> by the Spanish word *molestar*.

molten ['məultən] *adj* fundido;
(*lava*) líquido
mom [mɔm] (*US*) *n* = **mum**
moment ['məumənt] *n* momento;
at the ~ de momento, por ahora;
momentarily ['məuməntrɪlɪ] *adv*
momentáneamente; (*US: very soon*) de
un momento a otro; **momentary** *adj*
momentáneo; **momentous** [-'mɛntə
s] *adj* trascendental, importante
momentum [məu'mɛntəm] *n*
momento; (*fig*) ímpetu *m*; **to gather ~**
cobrar velocidad; (*fig*) ganar fuerza
mommy ['mɔmɪ] (*US*) *n* = **mummy**
Mon *abbr* (= *Monday*) lun
Monaco ['mɔnəkəu] *n* Mónaco
monarch ['mɔnək] *n* monarca *mf*;
monarchy *n* monarquía
monastery ['mɔnəstərɪ] *n*
monasterio
Monday ['mʌndɪ] *n* lunes *m inv*
monetary ['mʌnɪtərɪ] *adj* monetario
money ['mʌnɪ] *n* dinero; (*currency*)
moneda; **to make ~** ganar dinero;
money belt *n* riñonera; **money
order** *n* giro
mongrel ['mʌŋgrəl] *n* (*dog*) perro
mestizo
monitor ['mɔnɪtə*] *n* (*Scol*) monitor
m; (*also:* **television ~**) receptor *m* de
control; (*of computer*) monitor *m* ▷ *vt*
controlar
monk [mʌŋk] *n* monje *m*
monkey ['mʌŋkɪ] *n* mono
monologue ['mɔnələg] *n* monólogo
monopoly [mə'nɔpəlɪ] *n* monopolio

monosodium glutamate
[mɔnə'səudɪəm'gluːtəmeɪt] *n*
glutamato monosódico
monotonous [mə'nɔtənəs] *adj*
monótono
monsoon [mɔn'suːn] *n* monzón *m*
monster ['mɔnstə*] *n* monstruo
month [mʌnθ] *n* mes *m*; **monthly**
adj mensual ▷ *adv* mensualmente
monument ['mɔnjumənt] *n*
monumento
mood [muːd] *n* humor *m*; (*of crowd,
group*) clima *m*; **to be in a good/bad ~**
estar de buen/mal humor; **moody** *adj*
(*changeable*) de humor variable; (*sullen*)
malhumorado
moon [muːn] *n* luna; **moonlight** *n*
luz *f* de la luna
moor [muə*] *n* páramo ▷ *vt* (*ship*)
amarrar ▷ *vi* echar las amarras
moose [muːs] *n inv* alce *m*
mop [mɔp] *n* fregona; (*of hair*)
greña, melena ▷ *vt* fregar; **mop up**
vt limpiar
mope [məup] *vi* estar *or* andar
deprimido
moped ['məupɛd] *n* ciclomotor *m*
moral ['mɔrl] *adj* moral ▷ *n*
moraleja; **morals** *npl* moralidad *f*,
moral *f*
morale [mɔ'rɑːl] *n* moral *f*
morality [mə'rælɪtɪ] *n* moralidad *f*
morbid ['mɔːbɪd] *adj* (*interest*)
morboso; (*Med*) mórbido

○ **KEYWORD**

more [mɔː*] *adj* **1** (*greater in number
etc*) más; **more people/work
than before** más gente/trabajo
que antes
2 (*additional*) más; **do you want
(some) more tea?** ¿quieres más té?; **is
there any more wine?** ¿queda vino?;
it'll take a few more weeks tardará
unas semanas más; **it's 2 kms more
to the house** faltan 2 kms para la casa;
more time/letters than we expected

más tiempo del que/más cartas de las que esperábamos
▷ *pron* (*greater amount, additional amount*) más; **more than 10** más de 10; **it cost more than the other one/than we expected** costó más que el otro/más de lo que esperábamos; **is there any more?** ¿hay más?; **many/much more** muchos(as)/mucho(a) más
▷ *adv* más; **more dangerous/easily (than)** más peligroso/fácilmente (que); **more and more expensive** cada vez más caro; **more or less** más o menos; **more than ever** más que nunca

moreover [mɔː'rəuvə*] *adv* además, por otra parte
morgue [mɔːg] *n* depósito de cadáveres
morning ['mɔːnɪŋ] *n* mañana; (*early morning*) madrugada ▷ *cpd* matutino, de la mañana; **in the ~** por la mañana; **7 o'clock in the ~** las 7 de la mañana; **morning sickness** *n* náuseas *fpl* matutinas
Moroccan [mə'rɔkən] *adj, n* marroquí *m/f*
Morocco [mə'rɔkəu] *n* Marruecos *m*
moron ['mɔːrɔn] (*inf*) *n* imbécil *mf*
morphine ['mɔːfiːn] *n* morfina
Morse [mɔːs] *n* (*also: ~ code*) (código) Morse
mortal ['mɔːtl] *adj, n* mortal *m*
mortar ['mɔːtə*] *n* argamasa
mortgage ['mɔːgɪdʒ] *n* hipoteca ▷ *vt* hipotecar
mortician [mɔː'tɪʃən] (*US*) *n* director/a *m/f* de pompas fúnebres
mortified ['mɔːtɪfaɪd] *adj*: **I was ~** me dio muchísima vergüenza
mortuary ['mɔːtjuərɪ] *n* depósito de cadáveres
mosaic [məu'zeɪɪk] *n* mosaico
Moslem ['mɔzləm] *adj, n* = **Muslim**
mosque [mɔsk] *n* mezquita
mosquito [mɔs'kiːtəu] (*pl* **~es**) *n*

mosquito (*SP*), zancudo (*LAM*)
moss [mɔs] *n* musgo
most [məust] *adj* la mayor parte de, la mayoría de ▷ *pron* la mayor parte, la mayoría ▷ *adv* el más; (*very*) muy; **the ~** (*also:* + *adj*) el más; **~ of them** la mayor parte de ellos; **I saw the ~** yo vi el que más; **at the (very) ~** a lo sumo, todo lo más; **to make the ~ of** aprovechar (al máximo); **a ~ interesting book** un libro interesantísimo; **mostly** *adv* en su mayor parte, principalmente
MOT (*BRIT*) *n abbr* = **Ministry of Transport**; **the ~ (test)** inspección (*anual*) obligatoria de coches y camiones
motel [məu'tɛl] *n* motel *m*
moth [mɔθ] *n* mariposa nocturna; (*clothes moth*) polilla
mother ['mʌðə*] *n* madre *f* ▷ *adj* materno ▷ *vt* (*care for*) cuidar (como una madre); **motherhood** *n* maternidad *f*; **mother-in-law** *n* suegra; **mother-of-pearl** *n* nácar *m*; **Mother's Day** *n* Día *m* de la Madre; **mother-to-be** *n* futura madre *f*; **mother tongue** *n* lengua materna
motif [məu'tiːf] *n* motivo
motion ['məuʃən] *n* movimiento; (*gesture*) ademán *m*, señal *f*; (*at meeting*) moción *f* ▷ *vt, vi*: **to ~ (to) sb to do sth** hacer señas a algn para que haga algo; **motionless** *adj* inmóvil; **motion picture** *n* película
motivate ['məutɪveɪt] *vt* motivar
motivation [məutɪ'veɪʃən] *n* motivación *f*
motive ['məutɪv] *n* motivo
motor ['məutə*] *n* motor *m*; (*BRIT: inf: vehicle*) coche *m* (*SP*), carro (*LAM*), automóvil *m* ▷ *adj* motor (*f: motora or motriz*); **motorbike** *n* moto *f*; **motorboat** *n* lancha motora; **motorcar** (*BRIT*) *n* coche *m*, carro, automóvil *m*; **motorcycle** *n* motocicleta; **motorcyclist** *n* motociclista *mf*; **motoring** (*BRIT*) *n* automovilismo; **motorist** *n* conductor(a) *m/f*, automovilista *mf*;

motor racing (BRIT) n carreras fpl de coches, automovilismo; **motorway** (BRIT) n autopista

motto ['mɔtəu] (pl ~es) n lema m; (watchword) consigna

mould [məuld] (US **mold**) n molde m; (mildew) moho ▷ vt moldear; (fig) formar; **mouldy** adj enmohecido

mound [maund] n montón m, montículo

mount [maunt] n monte m ▷ vt montar, subir a; (jewel) engarzar; (picture) enmarcar; (exhibition etc) organizar ▷ vi (increase) aumentar; **mount up** vi aumentar

mountain ['mauntin] n montaña ▷ cpd de montaña; **mountain bike** n bicicleta de montaña; **mountaineer** n alpinista mf (SP, MEX), andinista mf (LAM); **mountaineering** n alpinismo (SP, MEX), andinismo (LAM); **mountainous** adj montañoso; **mountain range** n sierra

mourn [mɔːn] vt llorar, lamentar ▷ vi: **to ~ for** llorar la muerte de; **mourner** n doliente mf; dolorido/a; **mourning** n luto; **in mourning** de luto

mouse [maus] (pl **mice**) n (Zool, Comput) ratón m; **mouse mat** n (Comput) alfombrilla

moussaka [mu'sɑːkə] n musaca

mousse [muːs] n (Culin) crema batida; (for hair) espuma (moldeadora)

moustache [məs'tɑːʃ] (US **mustache**) n bigote m

mouth [mauð, pl mauðz] n boca; (of river) desembocadura; **mouthful** n bocado; **mouth organ** n armónica; **mouthpiece** n (of musical instrument) boquilla; (spokesman) portavoz mf; **mouthwash** n enjuague m

move [muːv] n (movement) movimiento; (in game) jugada; (: turn to play) turno; (change: of house) mudanza; (: of job) cambio de trabajo ▷ vt mover; (emotionally) conmover; (Pol: resolution etc) proponer ▷ vi moverse; (traffic)

circular; (also: ~ **house**) trasladarse, mudarse; **to ~ sb to do sth** mover a algn a hacer algo; **to get a ~ on** darse prisa; **move back** vi retroceder; **move in** vi (to a house) instalarse; (police, soldiers) intervenir; **move off** vi ponerse en camino; **move on** vi ponerse en camino; **move out** vi (of house) mudarse; **move over** vi apartarse, hacer sitio; **move up** vi (employee) ser ascendido; **movement** n movimiento

movie ['muːvɪ] n película; **to go to the ~s** ir al cine; **movie theater** (US) n cine m

moving ['muːvɪŋ] adj (emotional) conmovedor(a); (that moves) móvil

mow [məu] (pt ~**ed**, pp **mowed** or **mown**) vt (grass, corn) cortar, segar; **mower** n (also: **lawnmower**) cortacéspedes m inv

Mozambique [məuzæm'biːk] n Mozambique m

MP n abbr = **Member of Parliament**

MP3 n MP3; **MP3 player** n reproductor m (de) MP3

mpg n abbr = **miles per gallon**

m.p.h. abbr = **miles per hour** (60 m.p.h. = 96 k.p.h.)

Mr ['mɪstə*] (US **Mr.**) n: ~ **Smith** (el) Sr. Smith

Mrs ['mɪsɪz] (US **Mrs.**) n: ~ **Smith** (la) Sra. Smith

Ms [mɪz] (US **Ms.**) n = **Miss** or **Mrs**; ~ **Smith** (la) Sr(t)a. Smith

MSP n abbr = **Member of the Scottish Parliament**

Mt abbr (Geo) (= mount) m

much [mʌtʃ] adj mucho ▷ adv mucho; (before pp) muy ▷ n or pron mucho; **how ~ is it?** ¿cuánto es?, ¿cuánto cuesta?; **too ~** demasiado; **it's not ~** no es mucho; **as ~ as** tanto como; **however ~ he tries** por mucho que se esfuerce

muck [mʌk] n suciedad f; **muck up** (inf) vt arruinar, estropear; **mucky** adj (dirty) sucio

mucus ['mju:kəs] n mucosidad
f, moco

mud [mʌd] n barro, lodo

muddle ['mʌdl] n desorden m,
confusión f; (mix-up) embrollo, lío ▷ vt
(also: ~ up) embrollar, confundir

muddy ['mʌdɪ] adj fangoso, cubierto
de lodo

mudguard ['mʌdgɑ:d] n
guardabarros m inv

muesli ['mju:zlɪ] n muesli m

muffin ['mʌfɪn] n panecillo dulce

muffled ['mʌfld] adj (noise etc)
amortiguado, apagado

muffler (US) ['mʌflə*] n (Aut)
silenciador m

mug [mʌg] n taza grande (sin platillo);
(for beer) jarra; (inf: face) jeta ▷ vt
(assault) asaltar; **mugger** ['mʌgə*] n
atracador(a) m/f; **mugging** n asalto

muggy ['mʌgɪ] adj bochornoso

mule [mju:l] n mula

multicoloured ['mʌltɪkʌləd] (US),
multicolored adj multicolor

multimedia ['mʌltɪ'mi:dɪə] adj
multimedia

multinational [mʌltɪ'næʃənl] n
multinacional f ▷ adj multinacional

multiple ['mʌltɪpl] adj múltiple
▷ n múltiplo; **multiple choice (test)**
n examen m de tipo test; **multiple
sclerosis** n esclerosis f múltiple

multiplex cinema ['mʌltɪplɛks-] n
multicines mpl

multiplication [mʌltɪplɪ'keɪʃən] n
multiplicación f

multiply ['mʌltɪplaɪ] vt multiplicar
▷ vi multiplicarse

multistorey [mʌltɪ'stɔ:rɪ] (BRIT) adj
de muchos pisos

mum [mʌm] (BRIT: inf) n mamá
▷ adj: **to keep ~** mantener la boca
cerrada

mumble ['mʌmbl] vt, vi hablar entre
dientes, refunfuñar

mummy ['mʌmɪ] n (BRIT: mother)
mamá; (embalmed) momia

mumps [mʌmps] n paperas fpl

munch [mʌntʃ] vt, vi mascar

municipal [mju:'nɪsɪpl] adj
municipal

mural ['mjuərl] n (pintura) mural m

murder ['mə:də*] n asesinato; (in
law) homicidio ▷ vt asesinar, matar;
murderer n asesino

murky ['mə:kɪ] adj (water) turbio;
(street, night) lóbrego

murmur ['mə:mə*] n murmullo ▷ vt,
vi murmurar

muscle ['mʌsl] n músculo;
(fig: strength) garra, fuerza; **muscular**
['mʌskjulə*] adj muscular; (person)
musculoso

museum [mju:'zɪəm] n museo

mushroom ['mʌʃrum] n seta,
hongo; (Culin) champiñón m ▷ vi
crecer de la noche a la mañana

music ['mju:zɪk] n música; **musical**
adj musical; (sound) melodioso;
(person) con talento musical ▷ n
(show) comedia musical; **musical
instrument** n instrumento musical;
musician [-'zɪʃən] n músico/a

Muslim ['mʌzlɪm] adj, n musulmán/
ana m/f

muslin ['mʌzlɪn] n muselina

mussel ['mʌsl] n mejillón m

must [mʌst] aux vb (obligation): **I ~
do it** debo hacerlo, tengo que hacerlo;
(probability): **he ~ be there by now**
ya debe (de) estar allí ▷ n: **it's a ~** es
imprescindible

mustache ['mʌstæʃ] (US) n =
moustache

mustard ['mʌstəd] n mostaza

mustn't ['mʌsnt] = **must not**

mute [mju:t] adj, n mudo/a m/f

mutilate ['mju:tɪleɪt] vt mutilar

mutiny ['mju:tɪnɪ] n motín m ▷ vi
amotinarse

mutter ['mʌtə*] vt, vi murmurar

mutton ['mʌtn] n carne f de cordero

mutual ['mju:tʃuəl] adj mutuo;
(interest) común

muzzle ['mʌzl] n hocico; (for dog)
bozal m; (of gun) boca ▷ vt (dog) poner

un bozal a

my [maɪ] *adj* mi(s); **~ house/brother/ sisters** mi casa/mi hermano/mis hermanas; **I've washed ~ hair/cut ~ finger** me he lavado el pelo/cortado un dedo; **is this ~ pen or yours?** ¿es este bolígrafo mío o tuyo?

myself [maɪ'sɛlf] *pron* (*reflexive*) me; (*emphatic*) yo mismo; (*after prep*) mí (mismo); *see also* **oneself**

mysterious [mɪs'tɪərɪəs] *adj* misterioso

mystery ['mɪstərɪ] *n* misterio

mystical ['mɪstɪkl] *adj* místico

mystify ['mɪstɪfaɪ] *vt* (*perplex*) dejar perplejo

myth [mɪθ] *n* mito; **mythology** [mɪ'θɔlədʒɪ] *n* mitología

n/a *abbr* (= *not applicable*) no interesa

nag [næg] *vt* (*scold*) regañar

nail [neɪl] *n* (*human*) uña; (*metal*) clavo ▷ *vt* clavar; **to ~ sth to sth** clavar algo en algo; **to ~ sb down to doing sth** comprometer a algn a que haga algo; **nailbrush** *n* cepillo para las uñas; **nailfile** *n* lima para las uñas; **nail polish** *n* esmalte *m* or laca para las uñas; **nail polish remover** *n* quitaesmalte *m*; **nail scissors** *npl* tijeras *fpl* para las uñas; **nail varnish** (*BRIT*) *n* = **nail polish**

naïve [naɪ'iːv] *adj* ingenuo

naked ['neɪkɪd] *adj* (*nude*) desnudo; (*flame*) expuesto al aire

name [neɪm] *n* nombre *m*; (*surname*) apellido; (*reputation*) fama, renombre *m* ▷ *vt* (*child*) poner nombre a; (*criminal*) identificar; (*price, date etc*) fijar; **what's your ~?** ¿cómo se llama?; **by ~** de nombre; **in the ~ of** en nombre de; **to give one's ~ and address** dar sus señas; **namely** *adv* a saber

nanny ['nænɪ] *n* niñera

nap [næp] *n* (*sleep*) sueñecito, siesta

napkin ['næpkɪn] *n* (*also*: **table ~**) servilleta

nappy ['næpɪ] (*BRIT*) *n* pañal *m*

narcotics *npl* (*illegal drugs*) estupefacientes *mpl*, narcóticos *mpl*

narrative ['nærətɪv] *n* narrativa ▷ *adj* narrativo

narrator [nə'reɪtə*] *n* narrador(a) *m/f*

narrow ['nærəu] *adj* estrecho, angosto; (*fig: majority etc*) corto; (: *ideas etc*) estrecho ▷ *vi* (*road*) estrecharse; (*diminish*) reducirse; **to have a ~ escape** escaparse por los pelos; **narrow down** *vt* (*search, investigation, possibilities*) restringir, limitar; (*list*) reducir; **narrowly** *adv* (*miss*) por poco; **narrow-minded** *adj* de miras estrechas

nasal ['neɪzl] *adj* nasal

nasty ['nɑːstɪ] *adj* (*remark*) feo; (*person*) antipático; (*revolting: taste, smell*) asqueroso; (*wound, disease etc*) peligroso, grave

nation ['neɪʃən] *n* nación *f*

national ['næʃənl] *adj, n* nacional *m/f*; **national anthem** *n* himno nacional; **national dress** *n* vestido nacional; **National Health Service** (*BRIT*) *n* servicio nacional de salud pública ≈ Insalud *m* (*SP*); **National Insurance** (*BRIT*) *n* seguro social nacional; **nationalist** *adj, n* nacionalista *mf*; **nationality** [-'nælɪtɪ] *n* nacionalidad *f*; **nationalize** *vt* nacionalizar; **national park** (*BRIT*) *n* parque *m* nacional; **National Trust** *n* (*BRIT*) *organización encargada de preservar el patrimonio histórico británico*

nationwide ['neɪʃənwaɪd] *adj* en escala *or* a nivel nacional

native ['neɪtɪv] *n* (*local inhabitant*) natural *mf*, nacional *mf* ▷ *adj* (*indigenous*) indígena; (*country*) natal; (*innate*) natural, innato; **a ~ of Russia** un(a) natural *mf* de Rusia; **Native American** *adj, n* americano/a

indígena, amerindio/a; **native speaker** *n* hablante *mf* nativo/a

NATO ['neɪtəu] *n abbr* (= *North Atlantic Treaty Organization*) OTAN *f*

natural ['nætʃrəl] *adj* natural; **natural gas** *n* gas *m* natural; **natural history** *n* historia natural; **naturally** *adv* (*speak etc*) naturalmente; (*of course*) desde luego, por supuesto; **natural resources** *npl* recursos *mpl* naturales

nature ['neɪtʃə*] *n* (*also*: **N~**) naturaleza; (*group, sort*) género, clase *f*; (*character*) carácter *m*, genio; **by ~** por *or* de naturaleza; **nature reserve** *n* reserva natural

naughty ['nɔːtɪ] *adj* (*child*) travieso

nausea ['nɔːsɪə] *n* náuseas *fpl*

naval ['neɪvl] *adj* naval, de marina

navel ['neɪvl] *n* ombligo

navigate ['nævɪgeɪt] *vt* gobernar ▷ *vi* navegar; (*Aut*) ir de copiloto; **navigation** [-'geɪʃən] *n* (*action*) navegación *f*; (*science*) náutica

navy ['neɪvɪ] *n* marina de guerra; (*ships*) armada, flota

Nazi ['nɑːtsɪ] *n* nazi *mf*

NB *abbr* (= *nota bene*) nótese

near [nɪə*] *adj* (*place, relation*) cercano; (*time*) próximo ▷ *adv* cerca ▷ *prep* (*also*: **~ to**: *space*) cerca de, junto a; (: *time*) cerca de ▷ *vt* acercarse a, aproximarse a; **nearby** [nɪə'baɪ] *adj* cercano, próximo ▷ *adv* cerca; **nearly** *adv* casi, por poco; **I nearly fell** por poco me caigo; **near-sighted** *adj* miope, corto de vista

neat [niːt] *adj* (*place*) ordenado, bien cuidado; (*person*) pulcro; (*plan*) ingenioso; (*spirits*) solo; **neatly** *adv* (*tidily*) con esmero; (*skilfully*) ingeniosamente

necessarily ['nɛsɪsrɪlɪ] *adv* necesariamente

necessary ['nɛsɪsrɪ] *adj* necesario, preciso

necessity [nɪ'sɛsɪtɪ] *n* necesidad *f*

neck [nɛk] *n* (*of person, garment, bottle*) cuello; (*of animal*) pescuezo ▷ *vi*

(inf) besQuearse; **~ and ~** parejos;
necklace ['nɛklɪs] n collar m; **necktie**
['nɛktaɪ] n corbata

nectarine ['nɛktərɪn] n nectarina

need [niːd] n (lack) escasez f, falta;
(necessity) necesidad f ▷ vt (require)
necesitar; **I ~ to do it** tengo que or debo
hacerlo; **you don't ~ to go** no hace
falta que (te) vayas

needle ['niːdl] n aguja ▷ vt (fig: inf)
picar, fastidiar

needless ['niːdlɪs] adj innecesario; **~
to say** huelga decir que

needlework ['niːdlwəːk] n (activity)
costura, labor f de aguja

needn't ['niːdnt] = **need not**

needy ['niːdɪ] adj necesitado

negative ['nɛgətɪv] n (Phot)
negativo; (Ling) negación f ▷ adj
negativo

neglect [nɪ'glɛkt] vt (one's duty) faltar
a, no cumplir con; (child) descuidar,
desatender ▷ n (of house, garden etc)
abandono; (of child) desatención f; (of
duty) incumplimiento

negotiate [nɪ'gəuʃɪeɪt] vt (treaty,
loan) negociar; (obstacle) franquear;
(bend in road) tomar ▷ vi: **to ~ (with)**
negociar (con)

negotiations [nɪgəuʃɪ'eɪʃənz] pl n
negociaciones

negotiator [nɪ'gəuʃɪeɪtə*] n
negociador(a) m/f

neighbour ['neɪbə*] (US **neighbor** etc)
n vecino/a; **neighbourhood** n (place)
vecindad f, barrio; (people) vecindario;
neighbouring adj vecino

neither ['naɪðə*] adj ni ▷ conj: **I
didn't move and ~ did John** no me
he movido, ni Juan tampoco ▷ pron
ninguno ▷ adv: **~ good nor bad** ni
bueno ni malo; **~ is true** ninguno/a de
los(las) dos es cierto/a

neon ['niːɔn] n neón m

Nepal [nɪ'pɔːl] n Nepal m

nephew ['nɛvjuː] n sobrino

nerve [nəːv] n (Anat) nervio; (courage)
valor m; (impudence) descaro, frescura

(nervousness) nerviosismo msg, nervios
mpl; **a fit of ~s** un ataque de nervios

nervous ['nəːvəs] adj (anxious, Anat)
nervioso; (timid) tímido, miedoso;
nervous breakdown n crisis f
nerviosa

nest [nɛst] n (of bird) nido; (wasps'
nest) avispero ▷ vi anidar

net [nɛt] n (gen) red f; (fabric) tul m
▷ adj (Comm) neto, líquido ▷ vt coger
(SP) or agarrar (LAM) con red; (Sport)
marcar; **netball** n básquet m

Netherlands ['nɛðələndz] npl: **the ~**
los Países Bajos

nett [nɛt] adj = **net**

nettle ['nɛtl] n ortiga

network ['nɛtwəːk] n red f

neurotic [njuə'rɔtɪk] adj neurótico/a

neuter ['njuːtə*] adj (Ling) neutro
▷ vt castrar, capar

neutral ['njuːtrəl] adj (person)
neutral; (colour etc, Elec) neutro ▷ n
(Aut) punto muerto

never ['nɛvə*] adv nunca, jamás;
I ~ went no fui nunca; **~ in my life**
jamás en la vida; see also **mind**; **never-
ending** adj interminable, sin fin;
nevertheless [nɛvəðə'lɛs] adv sin
embargo, no obstante

new [njuː] adj nuevo; (brand new) a
estrenar; (recent) reciente; **New Age**
n Nueva Era; **newborn** adj recién
nacido; **newcomer** ['njuːkʌmə*] n
recién venido/a or llegado/a; **newly**
adv nuevamente, recién

news [njuːz] n noticias fpl; **a piece
of ~** una noticia; **the ~** (Radio, TV) las
noticias fpl; **news agency** n agencia
de noticias; **newsagent** (BRIT) n
vendedor(a) m/f de periódicos;
newscaster n presentador(a) m/f,
locutor(a) m/f; **news dealer** (US)
= **newsagent**; **newsletter** n hoja
informativa, boletín m; **newspaper**
n periódico, diario; **newsreader** n =
newscaster

newt [njuːt] n tritón m

New Year n Año Nuevo; **New Year's**

Day n Día m de Año Nuevo; **New Year's Eve** n Nochevieja

New Zealand [njuːˈziːlənd] n Nueva Zelanda; **New Zealander** n neozelandés/esa m/f

next [nɛkst] adj (house, room) vecino; (bus stop, meeting) próximo; (following: page etc) siguiente ▷ adv después; **the ~ day** el día siguiente; **~ time** la próxima vez; **~ year** el año próximo or que viene; **~ to** junto a, al lado de; **~ to nothing** casi nada; **~ please!** ¡el siguiente!; **next door** adv en la casa del lado ▷ adj vecino, de al lado; **next-of-kin** n pariente m más cercano

NHS n abbr = **National Health Service**

nibble [ˈnɪbl] vt mordisquear, mordiscar

nice [naɪs] adj (likeable) simpático; (kind) amable; (pleasant) agradable; (attractive) bonito, lindo (LAM); **nicely** adv amablemente; bien

niche [niːʃ] n (Arch) nicho, hornacina

nick [nɪk] n (wound) rasguño; (cut, indentation) mella, muesca ▷ vt (inf) birlar, robar; **in the ~ of time** justo a tiempo

nickel [ˈnɪkl] n níquel m; (US) moneda de 5 centavos

nickname [ˈnɪkneɪm] n apodo, mote m ▷ vt apodar

nicotine [ˈnɪkətiːn] n nicotina

niece [niːs] n sobrina

Nigeria [naɪˈdʒɪərɪə] n Nigeria

night [naɪt] n noche f; (evening) tarde f; **the ~ before last** anteanoche; **at ~, by ~** de noche, por la noche; **night club** n cabaret m; **nightdress** (BRIT) n camisón m; **nightie** [ˈnaɪtɪ] n = **nightdress**; **nightlife** n vida nocturna; **nightly** adj de todas las noches ▷ adv todas las noches, cada noche; **nightmare** n pesadilla; **night school** n clase(s) f(pl) nocturna(s); **night shift** n turno nocturno or de noche; **night-time** n noche f

nil [nɪl] (BRIT) n (Sport) cero, nada

nine [naɪn] num nueve; **nineteen** num diecinueve, diez y nueve; **nineteenth** [naɪnˈtiːnθ] adj decimonoveno, decimonono; **ninetieth** [ˈnaɪntɪɪθ] adj nonagésimo; **ninety** num noventa

ninth [naɪnθ] adj noveno

nip [nɪp] vt (pinch) pellizcar; (bite) morder

nipple [ˈnɪpl] n (Anat) pezón m

nitrogen [ˈnaɪtrədʒən] n nitrógeno

○ **KEYWORD**

no [nəʊ] (pl noes) adv (opposite of "yes") no; **are you coming? – no (I'm not)** ¿vienes? – no; **would you like some more? – no thank you** ¿quieres más? – no gracias ▷ adj (not any): **I have no money/time/books** no tengo dinero/tiempo/libros; **no other man would have done it** ningún otro lo hubiera hecho; **"no entry"** "prohibido el paso"; **"no smoking"** "prohibido fumar" ▷ n no m

nobility [nəʊˈbɪlɪtɪ] n nobleza

noble [ˈnəʊbl] adj noble

nobody [ˈnəʊbədɪ] pron nadie

nod [nɔd] vi saludar con la cabeza; (in agreement) decir que sí con la cabeza; (doze) dar cabezadas ▷ vt: **to ~ one's head** inclinar la cabeza ▷ n inclinación f de cabeza; **nod off** vi dar cabezadas

noise [nɔɪz] n ruido; (din) escándalo, estrépito; **noisy** adj ruidoso; (child) escandaloso

nominal [ˈnɔmɪnl] adj nominal

nominate [ˈnɔmɪneɪt] vt (propose) proponer; (appoint) nombrar; **nomination** [nɔmɪˈneɪʃən] n propuesta; nombramiento; **nominee** [-ˈniː] n candidato/a

none [nʌn] pron ninguno/a ▷ adv de ninguna manera; **~ of you** ninguno de vosotros; **I've ~ left** no me queda ninguno/a; **he's ~ the worse for it** no le ha hecho ningún mal

nonetheless [nʌnðə'lɛs] *adv* sin embargo, no obstante

non-fiction [nɔn'fɪkʃən] *n* literatura no novelesca

nonsense ['nɔnsəns] *n* tonterías *fpl*, disparates *fpl*; **~!** ¡qué tonterías!

non: non-smoker *n* no fumador(a) *m/f*; **non-smoking** *adj* (de) no fumador; **non-stick** *adj* (*pan, surface*) antiadherente

noodles ['nu:dlz] *npl* tallarines *mpl*

noon [nu:n] *n* mediodía *m*

no-one ['nəuwʌn] *pron* = **nobody**

nor [nɔ:*] *conj* = **neither** ▷ *adv see* **neither**

norm [nɔ:m] *n* norma

normal ['nɔ:ml] *adj* normal; **normally** *adv* normalmente

north [nɔ:θ] *n* norte *m* ▷ *adj* del norte, norteño ▷ *adv* al or hacia el norte; **North America** *n* América del Norte; **North American** *adj*, *n* norteamericano/a *m/f*; **northbound** ['nɔ:θbaund] *adj* (*traffic*) que se dirige al norte; (*carriageway*) de dirección norte; **north-east** *n* nor(d)este *m*; **northeastern** *adj* nor(d)este, del nor(d)este; **northern** ['nɔ:ðən] *adj* norteño, del norte; **Northern Ireland** *n* Irlanda del Norte; **North Korea** *n* Corea del Norte; **North Pole** *n* Polo Norte; **North Sea** *n* Mar *m* del Norte; **north-west** *n* nor(d)oeste *m*; **northwestern** ['nɔ:θ'westən] *adj* noroeste, del noroeste

Norway ['nɔ:weɪ] *n* Noruega; **Norwegian** [-'wi:dʒən] *adj* noruego/ a ▷ *n* noruego/a; (*Ling*) noruego

nose [nəuz] *n* (*Anat*) nariz *f*; (*Zool*) hocico; (*sense of smell*) olfato ▷ *vi*: **to ~ about** curiosear; **nosebleed** *n* hemorragia nasal; **nosey** (*inf*) *adj* curioso, fisgón/ona

nostalgia [nɔs'tældʒɪə] *n* nostalgia

nostalgic [nɔs'tældʒɪk] *adj* nostálgico

nostril ['nɔstrɪl] *n* ventana de la nariz

nosy ['nəuzɪ] (*inf*) *adj* = **nosey**

not [nɔt] *adv* no; **~ that ...** no es que ...; **it's too late, isn't it?** es demasiado tarde, ¿verdad *or* no?; **~ yet/now** todavía/ahora no; **why ~?** ¿por qué no?; *see also* **all; only**

notable ['nəutəbl] *adj* notable; **notably** *adv* especialmente

notch [nɔtʃ] *n* muesca, corte *m*

note [nəut] *n* (*Mus, record, letter*) nota; (*banknote*) billete *m*; (*tone*) tono ▷ *vt* (*observe*) notar, observar; (*write down*) apuntar, anotar; **notebook** *n* libreta, cuaderno; **noted** ['nəutɪd] *adj* célebre, conocido; **notepad** *n* bloc *m*; **notepaper** *n* papel *m* para cartas

nothing ['nʌθɪŋ] *n* nada; (*zero*) cero; **he does ~** no hace nada; **~ new** nada nuevo; **~ much** no mucho; **for ~** (*free*) gratis, sin pago; (*in vain*) en balde

notice ['nəutɪs] *n* (*announcement*) anuncio; (*warning*) aviso; (*dismissal*) despido; (*resignation*) dimisión *f*; (*period of time*) plazo ▷ *vt* (*observe*) notar, observar; **to bring sth to sb's ~** (*attention*) llamar la atención de algn sobre algo; **to take ~ of** tomar nota de, prestar atención a; **at short ~** con poca anticipación; **until further ~** hasta nuevo aviso; **to hand in one's ~** dimitir

▐ Be careful not to translate **notice** by the Spanish word *noticia*.

noticeable *adj* evidente, obvio

notify ['nəutɪfaɪ] *vt*: **to ~ sb (of sth)** comunicar (algo) a algn

notion ['nəuʃən] *n* idea; (*opinion*) opinión *f*; **notions** *npl* (*US*) mercería

notorious [nəu'tɔ:rɪəs] *adj* notorio

notwithstanding [nɔtwɪθ'stændɪŋ] *adv* no obstante, sin embargo; **~ this** a pesar de esto

nought [nɔ:t] *n* cero

noun [naun] *n* nombre *m*, sustantivo

nourish ['nʌrɪʃ] *vt* nutrir; (*fig*) alimentar; **nourishment** *n* alimento, sustento

Nov. *abbr* (= *November*) nov

novel ['nɔvl] *n* novela ▷ *adj* (*new*)

nuevo, original; (*unexpected*) insólito;
novelist *n* novelista *mf*: **novelty** *n*
novedad *f*
November [nəu'vɛmbə*] *n*
noviembre *m*
novice ['nɔvɪs] *n* (*Rel*) novicio/a
now [nau] *adv* (*at the present time*)
ahora; (*these days*) actualmente, hoy
día ▷ *conj*: **~ (that)** ya que, ahora que;
right ~ ahora mismo; **by ~** ya; **just
~** ahora mismo; **~ and then, ~ and
again** de vez en cuando; **from ~ on** de
ahora en adelante; **nowadays** ['nauə
deɪz] *adv* hoy (en) día, actualmente
nowhere ['nəuwɛə*] *adv* (*direction*)
a ninguna parte; (*location*) en ninguna
parte
nozzle ['nɔzl] *n* boquilla
nr *abbr* (*BRIT*) = **near**
nuclear ['nju:klɪə*] *adj* nuclear
nucleus ['nju:klɪəs] (*pl* **nuclei**) *n*
núcleo
nude [nju:d] *adj*, *n* desnudo/a *m/f*; **in
the ~** desnudo
nudge [nʌdʒ] *vt* dar un codazo a
nudist ['nju:dɪst] *n* nudista *mf*
nudity ['nju:dɪtɪ] *n* desnudez *f*
nuisance ['nju:sns] *n* molestia,
fastidio; (*person*) pesado, latoso; **what
a ~!** ¡qué lata!
numb [nʌm] *adj*: **~ with cold/fear**
entumecido por el frío/paralizado
de miedo
number ['nʌmbə*] *n* número;
(*quantity*) cantidad *f* ▷ *vt* (*pages etc*)
numerar, poner número a; (*amount to*)
sumar, ascender a; **to be ~ed among**
figurar entre; **a ~ of** varios, algunos;
they were ten in ~ eran diez; **number
plate** (*BRIT*) *n* matrícula, placa;
Number Ten *n* (*BRIT*: 10 *Downing
Street*) residencia del primer ministro
numerical [nju:'mɛrɪkl] *adj*
numérico
numerous ['nju:mərəs] *adj*
numeroso
nun [nʌn] *n* monja, religiosa
nurse [nə:s] *n* enfermero/a; (*also*:

~maid) niñera ▷ *vt* (*patient*) cuidar,
atender
nursery ['nə:sərɪ] *n* (*institution*)
guardería infantil; (*room*) cuarto de los
niños; (*for plants*) criadero, semillero;
nursery rhyme *n* canción *f* infantil;
nursery school *n* parvulario, escuela
de párvulos; **nursery slope** (*BRIT*) *n*
(*Ski*) cuesta para principiantes
nursing ['nə:sɪŋ] *n* (*profession*)
profesión *f* de enfermera; (*care*)
asistencia, cuidado; **nursing home** *n*
clínica de reposo
nurture ['nə:tʃə*] *vt* (*child, plant*)
alimentar, nutrir
nut [nʌt] *n* (*Tech*) tuerca; (*Bot*) nuez *f*
nutmeg ['nʌtmɛg] *n* nuez *f* moscada
nutrient ['nju:trɪənt] *adj* nutritivo
▷ *n* elemento nutritivo
nutrition [nju:'trɪʃən] *n* nutrición *f*,
alimentación *f*
nutritious [nju:'trɪʃəs] *adj* nutritivo,
alimenticio
nuts [nʌts] (*inf*) *adj* loco
NVQ *n abbr* (*BRIT*) = **National
Vocational Qualification**
nylon ['naɪlɔn] *n* nilón *m* ▷ *adj* de
nilón

O

oath [əuθ] n juramento; (*swear word*) palabrota; **on** (*BRIT*) or **under ~** bajo juramento

oak [əuk] n roble m ▷ adj de roble

O.A.P. (*BRIT*) n, abbr = **old-age pensioner**

oar [ɔ:*] n remo

oasis [əu'eɪsɪs] (pl **oases**) n oasis m inv

oath [əuθ] n juramento; (*swear word*) palabrota; **on** (*BRIT*) or **under ~** bajo juramento

oatmeal ['əutmi:l] n harina de avena

oats [əuts] npl avena

obedience [ə'bi:dɪəns] n obediencia

obedient [ə'bi:dɪənt] adj obediente

obese [əu'bi:s] adj obeso

obesity [əu'bi:sɪtɪ] n obesidad f

obey [ə'beɪ] vt obedecer; (*instructions, regulations*) cumplir

obituary [ə'bɪtjuərɪ] n necrología

object [n 'ɔbdʒɪkt, vb əb'dʒekt] n objeto; (*purpose*) objeto, propósito; (*Ling*) complemento ▷ vi: **to ~ to** estar en contra de; (*proposal*) oponerse a; **to ~ that** objetar que; **expense is no ~** no importa cuánto cuesta; **I ~!** ¡yo protesto!; **objection** [əb'dʒekʃən] n protesta; **I have no objection to ...** no tengo inconveniente en que ...; **objective** adj, n objetivo

obligation [ɔblɪ'geɪʃən] n obligación f; (*debt*) deber m; **without ~** sin compromiso

obligatory [ə'blɪgətərɪ] adj obligatorio

oblige [ə'blaɪdʒ] vt (*do a favour for*) complacer, hacer un favor a; **to ~ sb to do sth** forzar or obligar a algn a hacer algo; **to be ~d to sb for sth** estarle agradecido a algn por algo

oblique [ə'bli:k] adj oblicuo; (*allusion*) indirecto

obliterate [ə'blɪtəreɪt] vt borrar

oblivious [ə'blɪvɪəs] adj: **~ of** inconsciente de

oblong ['ɔblɔŋ] adj rectangular ▷ n rectángulo

obnoxious [əb'nɔkʃəs] adj odioso, detestable; (*smell*) nauseabundo

oboe ['əubəu] n oboe m

obscene [əb'si:n] adj obsceno

obscure [əb'skjuə*] adj oscuro ▷ vt oscurecer; (*hide: sun*) esconder

observant [əb'zə:vnt] adj observador(a)

observation [ɔbzə'veɪʃən] n observación f; (*Med*) examen m

observatory [əb'zə:vətrɪ] n observatorio

observe [əb'zə:v] vt observar; (*rule*) cumplir; **observer** n observador(a) m/f

obsess [əb'ses] vt obsesionar; **obsession** [əb'seʃən] n obsesión f; **obsessive** adj obsesivo; obsesionante

obsolete ['ɔbsəli:t] adj: **to be ~** estar en desuso

obstacle ['ɔbstəkl] n obstáculo; (*nuisance*) estorbo

obstinate ['ɔbstɪnɪt] adj terco, porfiado; (*determined*) obstinado

obstruct [əb'strʌkt] vt obstruir; (*hinder*) estorbar, obstaculizar; **obstruction** [əb'strʌkʃən] n (*action*) obstrucción f; (*object*) estorbo, obstáculo

obtain [əb'teɪn] vt obtener; (*achieve*)
conseguir

obvious ['ɒbvɪəs] adj obvio, evidente;
obviously adv evidentemente,
naturalmente; **obviously not** por
supuesto que no

occasion [ə'keɪʒən] n oportunidad
f, ocasión f; (*event*) acontecimiento;
occasional adj poco frecuente,
ocasional; **occasionally** adv de vez
en cuando

occult [ɔ'kʌlt] adj (*gen*) oculto

occupant ['ɔkjupənt] n (*of house*)
inquilino/a; (*of car*) ocupante mf

occupation [ɔkju'peɪʃən] n
ocupación f; (*job*) trabajo; (*pastime*)
ocupaciones fpl

occupy ['ɔkjupaɪ] vt (*seat, post, time*)
ocupar; (*house*) habitar; **to ~ o.s. in
doing** pasar el tiempo haciendo

occur [ə'kɔː*] vi pasar, suceder; **to ~
to sb** ocurrírsele a algn; **occurrence**
[ə'kʌrəns] n acontecimiento;
(*existence*) existencia

ocean ['əuʃən] n océano

o'clock [ə'klɔk] adv: **it is 5 ~** son las 5

Oct. abbr (= October) oct

October [ɔk'təubə*] n octubre m

octopus ['ɔktəpəs] n pulpo

odd [ɔd] adj extraño, raro; (*number*)
impar; (*sock, shoe etc*) suelto; **60-~** 60 y
pico; **at ~ times** de vez en cuando; **to
be the ~ one out** estar de más; **oddly**
adv curiosamente, extrañamente;
see also **enough**; **odds** npl (*in betting*)
puntos mpl de ventaja; **it makes no
odds** da lo mismo; **at odds** reñidos/as;
odds and ends minucias fpl

odometer [ɔ'dɔmɪtə*] (*US*) n
cuentakilómetros m inv

odour ['əudə*] (*US* odor) n olor m;
(*unpleasant*) hedor m

⭕ **KEYWORD**

of [ɒv, əv] prep **1** (*gen*) de; **a friend of
ours** un amigo nuestro; **a boy of 10** un

chico de 10 años; **that was kind of you**
eso fue muy amable por or de tu parte
2 (*expressing quantity, amount, dates
etc*) de; **a kilo of flour** un kilo de
harina; **there were three of them**
había tres; **three of us went** tres de
nosotros fuimos; **the 5th of July** el
5 de julio
3 (*from, out of*) de; **made of wood**
(hecho) de madera

off [ɒf] adj, adv (*engine*) desconectado;
(*light*) apagado; (*tap*) cerrado;
(*BRIT: food: bad*) pasado, malo; (: *milk*)
cortado; (*cancelled*) cancelado ▷ prep
de; **to be ~** (*to leave*) irse, marcharse;
to be ~ sick estar enfermo or de baja;
a day ~ un día libre or sin trabajar; **to
have an ~ day** tener un día malo; **he
had his coat ~** se había quitado el
abrigo; **10% ~** (*Comm*) (con el) 10% de
descuento; **5 km ~ (the road)** a 5 km
(de la carretera); **~ the coast** frente a la
costa; **I'm ~ meat** (*no longer eat/like it*)
paso de la carne; **on the ~ chance** por
si acaso; **~ and on** and **on and off** de vez en cuando

offence [ə'fɛns] (*US* offense) n (*crime*)
delito; **to take ~ at** ofenderse por

offend [ə'fɛnd] vt (*person*) ofender;
offender n delincuente mf

offense [ə'fɛns] (*US*) n = **offence**

offensive [ə'fɛnsɪv] adj ofensivo;
(*smell etc*) repugnante ▷ n (*Mil*)
ofensiva

offer ['ɔfə*] n oferta, ofrecimiento;
(*proposal*) propuesta ▷ vt ofrecer;
(*opportunity*) facilitar; **"on ~"** (*Comm*)
"en oferta"

offhand [ɔf'hænd] adj informal ▷ adv
de improviso

office ['ɔfɪs] n (*place*) oficina; (*room*)
despacho; (*position*) carga, oficio;
doctor's ~ (*US*) consultorio; **to take
~** entrar en funciones; **office block**
(*US*), **office building** n bloque m de
oficinas; **office hours** npl horas fpl de
oficina; (*US Med*) horas fpl de consulta

officer ['ɔfɪsə*] n (*Mil etc*) oficial mf;

(*also*: **police ~**) agente *mf* de policía; (*of organization*) director(a) *m/f*
office worker *n* oficinista *mf*
official [ə'fɪʃl] *adj* oficial, autorizado ▷ *n* funcionario/a, oficial *mf*
off: off-licence (*BRIT*) *n* (*shop*) bodega *tienda de vinos y bebidas alcohólicas*; **off-line** *adj*, *adv* (*Comput*) fuera de línea; **off-peak** *adj* (*electricity*) de banda económica; (*ticket*) billete de precio reducido por viajar fuera de las horas punta; **off-putting** (*BRIT*) *adj* (*person*) asqueroso; (*remark*) desalentador(a); **off-season** *adj*, *adv* fuera de temporada

- **OFF-LICENCE**
- En el Reino Unido la venta
- de bebidas alcohólicas está
- estrictamente regulada
- y se necesita una licencia
- especial, con la que cuentan
- los bares, restaurantes y los
- establecimientos de **off-licence**,
- los únicos lugares en donde
- se pueden adquirir bebidas
- alcohólicas para su consumo
- fuera del local, de donde viene
- su nombre. También venden
- bebidas no alcohólicas, tabaco,
- chocolatinas, patatas fritas, etc.
- y a menudo forman parte de una
- cadena nacional.

offset ['ɔfsɛt] *vt* contrarrestar, compensar
offshore [ɔf'ʃɔ:*] *adj* (*breeze*, *island*) costera; (*fishing*) de bajura
offside ['ɔf'saɪd] *adj* (*Sport*) fuera de juego; (*Aut*: *in UK*) del lado derecho; (: *in US*, *Europe etc*) del lado izquierdo
offspring ['ɔfsprɪŋ] *n inv* descendencia
often ['ɔfn] *adv* a menudo, con frecuencia; **how ~ do you go?** ¿cada cuánto vas?

oh [əu] *excl* ¡ah!
oil [ɔɪl] *n* aceite *m*; (*petroleum*) petróleo; (*for heating*) aceite *m* combustible ▷ *vt* engrasar; **oil filter** *n* (*Aut*) filtro de aceite; **oil painting** *n* pintura al óleo; **oil refinery** *n* refinería de petróleo; **oil rig** *n* torre *f* de perforación; **oil slick** *n* marea negra; **oil tanker** *n* petrolero; (*truck*) camión *m* cisterna; **oil well** *n* pozo (de petróleo); **oily** *adj* aceitoso; (*food*) grasiento
ointment ['ɔɪntmənt] *n* ungüento
O.K., okay ['əu'keɪ] *excl* ¡O.K.!, ¡está bien!, ¡vale! (*SP*) ▷ *adj* bien ▷ *vt* dar el visto bueno a
old [əuld] *adj* viejo; (*former*) antiguo; **how ~ are you?** ¿cuántos años tienes?, ¿qué edad tienes?; **he's 10 years ~** tiene 10 años; **~er brother** hermano mayor; **old age** *n* vejez *f*; **old-age pension** *n* (*BRIT*) jubilación *f*, pensión *f*; **old-age pensioner** (*BRIT*) *n* jubilado/a; **old-fashioned** *adj* anticuado, pasado de moda; **old people's home** *n* (*esp BRIT*) residencia *f* de ancianos
olive ['ɔlɪv] *n* (*fruit*) aceituna; (*tree*) olivo ▷ *adj* (*also*: **~-green**) verde oliva; **olive oil** *n* aceite *m* de oliva
Olympic [əu'lɪmpɪk] *adj* olímpico; **the ~ Games, the ~s** las Olimpiadas
omelet(te) ['ɔmlɪt] *n* tortilla francesa (*SP*), omelette *f* (*LAM*)
omen ['əumɛn] *n* presagio
ominous ['ɔmɪnəs] *adj* de mal agüero, amenazador(a)
omit [əu'mɪt] *vt* omitir

○ **KEYWORD**

on [ɔn] *prep* **1** (*indicating position*) en; sobre; **on the wall** en la pared; **it's on the table** está sobre *or* en la mesa; **on the left** a la izquierda
2 (*indicating means*, *method*, *condition etc*): **on foot** a pie; **on the train/**

plane (go) en tren/avión; (be) en el tren/el avión; **on the radio/television/telephone** por or en la radio/televisión/al teléfono; **to be on drugs** drogarse; (Med) estar a tratamiento; **to be on holiday/business** estar de vacaciones/en viaje de negocios
3 (referring to time): **on Friday** el viernes; **on Fridays** los viernes; **on June 20th** el 20 de junio; **a week on Friday** del viernes en una semana; **on arrival** al llegar; **on seeing this** al ver esto
4 (about, concerning) sobre, acerca de; **a book on physics** un libro de or sobre física
▷ adv **1** (referring to dress): **to have one's coat on** tener or llevar el abrigo puesto; **she put her gloves on** se puso los guantes
2 (referring to covering): **"screw the lid on tightly"** "cerrar bien la tapa"
3 (further, continuously): **to walk** etc **on** seguir caminando etc
▷ adj **1** (functioning, in operation: machine, radio, TV, light) encendido/a (SP), prendido/a (LAM); (: tap) abierto/a; (: brakes) echado/a, puesto/a; **is the meeting still on?** (in progress) ¿todavía continúa la reunión?; (not cancelled) ¿va a haber reunión al fin?; **there's a good film on at the cinema** ponen una buena película en el cine
2 that's not on! (inf: not possible) ¡eso ni hablar!; (: not acceptable) ¡eso no se hace!

once [wʌns] adv una vez; (formerly) antiguamente ▷ conj una vez que; **~ he had left/it was done** una vez que se había marchado/se hizo; **at ~** en seguida, inmediatamente; (simultaneously) a la vez; **~ a week** una vez por semana; **~ more** otra vez; **~ and for all** de una vez por todas; **~ upon a time** érase una vez
oncoming ['ɒnkʌmɪŋ] adj (traffic)

que viene de frente

🔵 **KEYWORD**

one [wʌn] num un(o)/una; **one hundred and fifty** ciento cincuenta; **one by one** uno a uno
▷ adj **1** (sole) único; **the one book which** el único libro que; **the one man who** el único que
2 (same) mismo/a; **they came in the one car** vinieron en un solo coche
▷ pron **1** this one éste(ésta); that one ése(ésa); (more remote) aquél(aquella); **I've already got (a red) one** ya tengo uno/a rojo/a; **one by one** uno/a por uno/a
2 one another os (SP), se (+ el uno al otro, unos a otros etc); **do you two ever see one another?** ¿vosotros dos os veis alguna vez? (SP), ¿se ven ustedes dos alguna vez?; **the boys didn't dare look at one another** los chicos no se atrevieron a mirarse (el uno al otro); **they all kissed one another** se besaron unos a otros
3 (impers): **one never knows** nunca se sabe; **to cut one's finger** cortarse el dedo; **one needs to eat** hay que comer
one-off (BRIT: inf) n (event) acontecimiento único

oneself [wʌn'sɛlf] pron (reflexive) se; (after prep) sí; (emphatic) uno/a mismo/a; **to hurt ~** hacerse daño; **to keep sth for ~** guardarse algo; **to talk to ~** hablar solo
one: **one-shot** [wʌn'ʃɒt] (US) n = **one-off**; **one-sided** adj (argument) parcial; **one-to-one** adj (relationship) de dos; **one-way** adj (street) de sentido único
ongoing ['ɒŋgəʊɪŋ] adj continuo
onion ['ʌnjən] n cebolla
on-line ['ɒnlaɪn] adj, adv (Comput) en línea
onlooker ['ɒnlʊkə*] n espectador(a) m/f

only ['əunlı] adv solamente, sólo ▷ adj único, solo ▷ conj solamente que, pero; **an ~ child** un hijo único; **not ~ ... but also ...** no sólo ... sino también ...

on-screen [ɔn'skri:n] adj (Comput etc) en pantalla; (romance, kiss) cinematográfico

onset ['ɔnset] n comienzo

onto ['ɔntu] prep = **on to**

onward(s) ['ɔnwəd(z)] adv (move) (hacia) adelante; **from that time ~** desde entonces en adelante

oops [ups] excl (also: **~-a-daisy!**) ¡huy!

ooze [u:z] vi rezumar

opaque [əu'peɪk] adj opaco

open ['əupn] adj abierto; (car) descubierto; (road, view) despejado; (meeting) público; (admiration) manifiesto ▷ vt abrir ▷ vi abrirse; (book etc: commence) empezar; **in the ~ (air)** al aire libre; **open up** vt abrir; (blocked road) despejar ▷ vi abrirse, empezar; **open-air** adj al aire libre; **opening** n abertura; (start) comienzo; (opportunity) oportunidad f; **opening hours** npl horario de apertura; **open learning** n enseñanza flexible a tiempo parcial; **openly** adv abiertamente; **open-minded** adj imparcial; **open-necked** adj (shirt) desabrochado; sin corbata; **open-plan** adj: **open-plan office** gran oficina sin particiones; **Open University** n (BRIT) ≈ Universidad f Nacional de Enseñanza a Distancia, UNED f

opera ['ɔpərə] n ópera; **opera house** n teatro de la ópera; **opera singer** n cantante m/f de ópera

operate ['ɔpəreɪt] vt (machine) hacer funcionar; (company) dirigir ▷ vi funcionar; **to ~ on sb** (Med) operar a algn

operating room ['ɔpəreɪtɪŋ-] (US) n quirófano, sala de operaciones

operating theatre (BRIT) n sala de operaciones

operation [ɔpə'reɪʃən] n operación f; (of machine) funcionamiento; **to be in ~** estar funcionando or en funcionamiento; **to have an ~** (Med) ser operado; **operational** adj operacional, en buen estado

operative ['ɔpərətɪv] adj en vigor

operator ['ɔpəreɪtə*] n (of machine) maquinista mf, operario/a; (Tel) operador(a) m/f, telefonista mf

opinion [ə'pɪnɪən] n opinión f; **in my ~** en mi opinión, a mi juicio; **opinion poll** n encuesta, sondeo

opponent [ə'pəunənt] n adversario/a, contrincante mf

opportunity [ɔpə'tju:nɪtɪ] n oportunidad f; **to take the ~ of doing** aprovechar la ocasión para hacer

oppose [ə'pəuz] vt oponerse a; **to be ~d to sth** oponerse a algo; **as ~d to** a diferencia de

opposite ['ɔpəzɪt] adj opuesto, contrario a; (house etc) de enfrente ▷ adv en frente ▷ prep en frente de, frente a ▷ n lo contrario

opposition [ɔpə'zɪʃən] n oposición f

oppress [ə'prɛs] vt oprimir

opt [ɔpt] vi: **to ~ for** optar por; **to ~ to do** optar por hacer; **opt out** vi: **to opt out of** optar por no hacer

optician [ɔp'tɪʃən] n óptico m/f

optimism ['ɔptɪmɪzəm] n optimismo

optimist ['ɔptɪmɪst] n optimista mf;

optimistic [-'mɪstɪk] *adj* optimista
optimum ['ɔptɪməm] *adj* óptimo
option ['ɔpʃən] *n* opción *f*; **optional**
adj facultativo, discrecional
or [ɔ:*] *conj* o; (*before o, ho*) u; (*with
negative*): **he hasn't seen ~ heard
anything** no ha visto ni oído nada; **~
else** si no
oral ['ɔ:rəl] *adj* oral ▷ *n* examen *m* oral
orange ['ɔrɪndʒ] *n* (*fruit*) naranja
▷ *adj* color naranja; **orange juice** *n*
jugo *m* de naranja, zumo *m* de naranja
(*SP*); **orange squash** *n* naranjada
orbit ['ɔ:bɪt] *n* órbita ▷ *vt, vi* orbitar
orchard ['ɔ:tʃəd] *n* huerto
orchestra ['ɔ:kɪstrə] *n* orquesta;
(*us: seating*) platea
orchid ['ɔ:kɪd] *n* orquídea
ordeal [ɔ:'di:l] *n* experiencia
horrorosa
order ['ɔ:də*] *n* orden *m*; (*command*)
orden *f*; (*good order*) buen estado;
(*Comm*) pedido ▷ *vt* (*also*: **put in ~**)
arreglar, poner en orden; (*Comm*)
pedir; (*command*) mandar, ordenar;
in ~ en orden; (*of document*) en regla;
in (working) ~ en funcionamiento;
in ~ to do/that para hacer/que;
on ~ (*Comm*) pedido; **to be out of ~**
estar desordenado; (*not working*) no
funcionar; **to ~ sb to do sth** mandar
a algn hacer algo; **order form** *n* hoja
de pedido; **orderly** *n* (*Mil*) ordenanza
m; (*Med*) enfermero/a (auxiliar) ▷ *adj*
ordenado
ordinary ['ɔ:dnrɪ] *adj* corriente,
normal; (*pej*) común y corriente; **out of
the ~** fuera de lo común
ore [ɔ:*] *n* mineral *m*
oregano [ɔrɪ'gɑ:nəu] *n* orégano
organ ['ɔ:gən] *n* órgano; **organic**
[ɔ:'gænɪk] *adj* orgánico; **organism** *n*
organismo
organization [ɔ:gənaɪ'zeɪʃən] *n*
organización *f*
organize ['ɔ:gənaɪz] *vt* organizar;
organized ['ɔ:gənaɪzd] *adj*
organizado; **organizer** *n*

organizador(a) *m/f*
orgasm ['ɔ:gæzəm] *n* orgasmo
orgy ['ɔ:dʒɪ] *n* orgía
oriental [ɔ:rɪ'entl] *adj* oriental
orientation [ɔ:rɪen'teɪʃən] *n*
orientación *f*
origin ['ɔrɪdʒɪn] *n* origen *m*
original [ə'rɪdʒɪnl] *adj* original; (*first*)
primero; (*earlier*) primitivo ▷ *n* original
m; **originally** *adv* al principio
originate [ə'rɪdʒɪneɪt] *vi*: **to ~ from,
to ~ in** surgir de, tener su origen en
Orkneys ['ɔ:knɪz] *npl*: **the ~** (*also*: **the
Orkney Islands**) las Orcadas
ornament ['ɔ:nəmənt] *n* adorno;
(*trinket*) chuchería; **ornamental**
[-'mentl] *adj* decorativo, de adorno
ornate [ɔ:'neɪt] *adj* muy ornado,
vistoso
orphan ['ɔ:fn] *n* huérfano/a
orthodox ['ɔ:θədɔks] *adj* ortodoxo
orthopaedic [ɔ:θə'pi:dɪk] (*us*
orthopedic) *adj* ortopédico
osteopath ['ɔstɪəpæθ] *n* osteópata
mf
ostrich ['ɔstrɪtʃ] *n* avestruz *m*
other ['ʌðə*] *adj* otro ▷ *pron*: **the ~
(one)** el(la) otro/a ▷ *adv*: **~ than** aparte
de; **otherwise** *adv* de otra manera
▷ *conj* (*if not*) si no
otter ['ɔtə*] *n* nutria
ouch [autʃ] *excl* ¡ay!
ought [ɔ:t] (*pt ~*) *aux vb*: **I ~ to do
it** debería hacerlo; **this ~ to have
been corrected** esto debiera haberse
corregido; **he ~ to win** (*probability*)
debe *or* debiera ganar
ounce [auns] *n* onza (28.35*g*)
our ['auə*] *adj* nuestro; *see also* **my**;
ours *pron* (el) nuestro/(la) nuestra
etc; *see also* **mine¹**; **ourselves** *pron pl*
(*reflexive, after prep*) nosotros; (*emphatic*)
nosotros mismos; *see also* **oneself**
oust [aust] *vt* desalojar
out [aut] *adv* fuera, afuera; (*not
at home*) fuera (de casa); (*light, fire*)
apagado; **~ there** allí (fuera); **he's ~**
(*absent*) no está, ha salido; **to be ~ in**

one's calculations equivocarse (en sus cálculos); **to run** ~ salir corriendo; ~ **loud** en alta voz; ~ **of** (*outside*) fuera de; (*because of: anger etc*) por; ~ **of petrol** sin gasolina; "**~ of order**" "no funciona"; **outback** n interior m; **outbound** *adj* (*flight*) de salida; (*flight: not return*) de ida; **outbreak** n (*of war*) comienzo; (*of disease*) epidemia; (*of violence etc*) ola; **outburst** n explosión f, arranque m; **outcast** n paria mf; **outcome** n resultado; **outcry** n protestas fpl; **outdated** *adj* anticuado, fuera de moda; **outdoor** *adj* exterior, de aire libre; (*clothes*) de calle; **outdoors** *adv* al aire libre

outer ['autə*] *adj* exterior, externo; **outer space** n espacio exterior

outfit ['autfɪt] n (*clothes*) conjunto

out: outgoing *adj* (*character*) extrovertido; (*retiring: president etc*) saliente; **outgoings** (BRIT) npl gastos mpl; **outhouse** n dependencia

outing ['autɪŋ] n excursión f, paseo

out: outlaw n proscrito ▷ vt proscribir; **outlay** n inversión f; **outlet** n salida; (*of pipe*) desagüe m; (US Elec) toma de corriente; (*also:* **retail outlet**) punto de venta; **outline** n (*shape*) contorno, perfil m; (*sketch, plan*) esbozo ▷ vt (*plan etc*) esbozar; **in outline** (*fig*) a grandes rasgos; **outlook** n (*fig: prospects*) perspectivas fpl; (: *for weather*) pronóstico; **outnumber** vt superar en número; **out-of-date** *adj* (*passport*) caducado; (*clothes*) pasado de moda; **out-of-doors** *adv* al aire libre; **out-of-the-way** *adj* apartado; **out-of-town** *adj* (*shopping centre etc*) en las afueras; **outpatient** n paciente mf externo/a; **outpost** n puesto avanzado; **output** n (volumen m de) producción m, rendimiento f; (Comput) salida

outrage ['autreɪdʒ] n escándalo; (*atrocity*) atrocidad f ▷ vt ultrajar; **outrageous** [-'reɪdʒəs] *adj* monstruoso

outright [*adv* aut'raɪt, *adj* 'autraɪt] *adv* (*ask, deny*) francamente; (*refuse*) rotundamente; (*win*) de manera absoluta; (*be killed*) en el acto ▷ *adj* franco; rotundo

outset ['autsɛt] n principio

outside [aut'saɪd] n exterior m ▷ *adj* exterior, externo ▷ *adv* fuera ▷ *prep* fuera de; (*beyond*) más allá de; **at the ~** (*fig*) a lo sumo; **outside lane** n (Aut: *in Britain*) carril m de la derecha; (: *in US, Europe etc*) carril m de la izquierda; **outside line** n (Tel) línea (exterior); **outsider** n (*stranger*) extraño, forastero

out: outsize *adj* (*clothes*) de talla grande; **outskirts** npl alrededores mpl, afueras fpl; **outspoken** *adj* muy franco; **outstanding** *adj* excepcional, destacado; (*remaining*) pendiente

outward ['autwəd] *adj* externo; (*journey*) de ida; **outwards** *adv* (esp BRIT) = **outward**

outweigh [aut'weɪ] vt pesar más que

oval ['əuvl] *adj* ovalado ▷ n óvalo

ovary ['əuvərɪ] n ovario

oven ['ʌvn] n horno; **oven glove** n guante m para el horno, manopla para el horno; **ovenproof** *adj* resistente al horno; **oven-ready** *adj* listo para el horno

over ['əuvə*] *adv* encima, por encima ▷ *adj or adv* (*finished*) terminado; (*surplus*) de sobra ▷ *prep* (por) encima de; (*above*) sobre; (*on the other side of*) al otro lado de; (*more than*) más de; (*during*) durante; ~ **here** (por) aquí; ~ **there** (por) allí or allá; **all** ~ (*everywhere*) por todas partes; ~ **and** ~ (**again**) una y otra vez; ~ **and above** además de; **to ask sb** ~ invitar a algn a casa; **to bend** ~ inclinarse

overall [*adj, n* 'əuvərɔːl, *adv* əuvər'ɔːl] *adj* (*length etc*) total; (*study*) de conjunto ▷ *adv* en conjunto ▷ n (BRIT) guardapolvo; **overalls** npl (*boiler suit*) mono (SP) or overol m (LAM) (de trabajo)

overboard *adv* (Naut) por la borda

overcame [əʊvə'keɪm] *pt of*
overcome

overcast ['əʊvəkɑːst] *adj*
encapotado

overcharge [əʊvə'tʃɑːdʒ] *vt*: **to ~ sb**
cobrar un precio excesivo a algn

overcoat ['əʊvəkəʊt] *n* abrigo,
sobretodo

overcome [əʊvə'kʌm] *vt* vencer;
(*difficulty*) superar

over: overcrowded *adj* atestado de
gente; (*city, country*) superpoblado;
overdo (*irreg*) *vt* exagerar; (*overcook*)
cocer demasiado; **to overdo it** (*work
etc*) pasarse; **overdone** [əʊvə'dʌn] *adj*
(*vegetables*) recocido; (*steak*) demasiado
hecho; **overdose** *n* sobredosis *f inv*;
overdraft *n* saldo deudor; **overdrawn**
adj (*account*) en descubierto; **overdue**
adj retrasado; **overestimate** *vt*
sobreestimar

overflow [*vb* əʊvə'fləʊ, *n* 'əʊvəfləʊ]
vi desbordarse ▷ *n* (*also*: **~ pipe**)
(cañería de) desagüe *m*

overgrown [əʊvə'grəʊn] *adj* (*garden*)
invadido por la vegetación

overhaul [*vb* əʊvə'hɔːl, *n* 'əʊvəhɔːl]
vt revisar, repasar ▷ *n* revisión *f*

overhead [*adv* əʊvə'hɛd, *adj*, *n* 'əʊvə
hɛd] *adv* por arriba or encima ▷ *adj*
(*cable*) aéreo ▷ *n* (*us*) = **overheads**;
overhead projector *n* retroproyector;
overheads *npl* (*expenses*) gastos *mpl*
generales

over: overhear (*irreg*) *vt* oír por
casualidad; **overheat** *vi* (*engine*)
recalentarse; **overland** *adj*, *adv*
por tierra; **overlap** [əʊvə'læp] *vi*
traslaparse; **overleaf** *adv* al dorso;
overload *vt* sobrecargar; **overlook**
vt (*have view of*) dar a, tener vistas a;
(*miss: by mistake*) pasar por alto; (*excuse*)
perdonar

overnight [əʊvə'naɪt] *adv* durante
la noche; (*fig*) de la noche a la mañana
▷ *adj* de noche; **to stay ~** pasar la
noche; **overnight bag** *n* fin *m* de
semana, neceser *m* de viaje

overpass (*us*) ['əʊvəpɑːs] *n* paso
superior

overpower [əʊvə'paʊə*]
vt dominar; (*fig*) embargar;
overpowering *adj* (*heat*) agobiante;
(*smell*) penetrante

over: overreact [əʊvərɪ'ækt] *vi*
reaccionar de manera exagerada;
overrule *vt* (*decision*) anular; (*claim*)
denegar; **overrun** (*irreg*) *vt* (*country*)
invadir; (*time limit*) rebasar, exceder

overseas [əʊvə'siːz] *adv* (*abroad*: *live*)
en el extranjero; (*travel*) al extranjero
▷ *adj* (*trade*) exterior; (*visitor*) extranjero

oversee [əʊvə'siː] (*irreg*) *vt* supervisar

overshadow [əʊvə'ʃædəʊ] *vt*: **to be
~ed by** estar a la sombra de

oversight ['əʊvəsaɪt] *n* descuido

oversleep [əʊvə'sliːp] (*irreg*) *vi*
quedarse dormido

overspend [əʊvə'spɛnd] (*irreg*) *vi*
gastar más de la cuenta; **we have
overspent by 5 pounds** hemos
excedido el presupuesto en 5 libras

overt [əʊ'vəːt] *adj* abierto

overtake [əʊvə'teɪk] (*irreg*) *vt*
sobrepasar; (*BRIT Aut*) adelantar

over: overthrow (*irreg*) *vt* (*government*)
derrocar; **overtime** *n* horas *fpl*
extraordinarias

overtook [əʊvə'tʊk] *pt of* **overtake**

over: overturn *vt* volcar; (*fig*: *plan*)
desbaratar; (: *government*) derrocar ▷ *vi*
volcar; **overweight** *adj* demasiado
gordo or pesado; **overwhelm** *vt*
aplastar; (*emotion*) sobrecoger;
overwhelming *adj* (*victory, defeat*)
arrollador(a); (*feeling*) irresistible

ow [aʊ] *excl* ¡ay!

owe [əʊ] *vt*: **to ~ sb sth, to ~ sth to
sb** deber algo a algn; **owing to** *prep*
debido a, por causa de

owl [aʊl] *n* búho, lechuza

own [əʊn] *vt* tener, poseer ▷ *adj*
propio; **a room of my ~** una habitación
propia; **to get one's ~ back** tomar
revancha; **on one's ~** solo, a solas; **own
up** *vi* confesar; **owner** *n* dueño/a;

ownership *n* posesión *f*

ox [ɔks] (*pl* **~en**) *n* buey *m*

Oxbridge ['ɔksbrɪdʒ] *n* universidades de Oxford y Cambridge

oxen ['ɔksən] *npl of* **ox**

oxygen ['ɔksɪdʒən] *n* oxígeno

oyster ['ɔɪstə*] *n* ostra

oz. *abbr* = **ounce(s)**

ozone ['əuzəun] *n* ozono; **ozone friendly** *adj* que no daña la capa de ozono; **ozone layer** *n* capa *f* de ozono

p [piː] *abbr* = **penny; pence**

P.A. *n abbr* = **personal assistant; public address system**

p.a. *abbr* = **per annum**

pace [peɪs] *n* paso ▷ *vi*: **to ~ up and down** pasearse de un lado a otro; **to keep ~ with** llevar el mismo paso que; **pacemaker** *n* (*Med*) regulador *m* cardíaco, marcapasos *m inv*; (*Sport: also:* **pacesetter**) liebre *f*

Pacific [pə'sɪfɪk] *n*: **the ~ (Ocean)** el (Océano) Pacífico

pacifier ['pæsɪfaɪə*] (*US*) *n* (*dummy*) chupete *m*

pack [pæk] *n* (*packet*) paquete *m*; (*of hounds*) jauría; (*of people*) manada, bando; (*of cards*) baraja; (*bundle*) fardo; (*US: of cigarettes*) paquete *m*; (*back pack*) mochila ▷ *vt* (*fill*) llenar; (*in suitcase etc*) meter, poner; (*cram*) llenar, atestar; **to ~ (one's bags)** hacerse la maleta; **to ~ sb off** despachar a algn; **pack in** *vi* (*watch, car*) estropearse ▷ *vt* (*inf*) dejar; **pack it in!** ¡para!, ¡basta ya!; **pack up** *vi* (*inf: machine*) estropearse; (*person*) irse

▷ vt (belongings, clothes) recoger; (goods, presents) empaquetar, envolver

package ['pækɪdʒ] n paquete m; (bulky) bulto; (also: ~ **deal**) acuerdo global; **package holiday** n vacaciones fpl organizadas; **package tour** n viaje m organizado

packaging ['pækɪdʒɪŋ] n envase m

packed [pækt] adj abarrotado; **packed lunch** n almuerzo frío

packet ['pækɪt] n paquete m

packing ['pækɪŋ] n embalaje m

pact [pækt] n pacto

pad [pæd] n (of paper) bloc m; (cushion) cojinete m; (inf: home) casa ▷ vt rellenar; **padded** adj (jacket) acolchado; (bra) reforzado

paddle ['pædl] n (oar) canalete m; (us: for table tennis) paleta ▷ vt impulsar con canalete ▷ vi (with feet) chapotear; **paddling pool** (BRIT) n estanque m de juegos

paddock ['pædək] n corral m

padlock ['pædlɔk] n candado

paedophile ['piːdəufaɪl] (us **pedophile**) adj de pedófilos ▷ n pedófilo/a

page [peɪdʒ] n (of book) página; (of newspaper) plana; (also: ~ **boy**) paje m ▷ vt (in hotel etc) llamar por altavoz a

pager ['peɪdʒə*] n (Tel) busca m

paid [peɪd] pt, pp of **pay** ▷ adj (work) remunerado; (holiday) pagado; (official etc) a sueldo; **to put ~ to** (BRIT) acabar con

pain [peɪn] n dolor m; **to be in ~** sufrir; **to take ~s to do sth** tomarse grandes molestias en hacer algo; **painful** adj doloroso; (difficult) penoso; (disagreeable) desagradable; **painkiller** n analgésico; **painstaking** ['peɪnzteɪkɪŋ] adj (person) concienzudo, esmerado

paint [peɪnt] n pintura ▷ vt pintar; **to ~ the door blue** pintar la puerta de azul; **paintbrush** n (of artist) pincel m; (of decorator) brocha; **painter** n pintor(a) m/f; **painting** n pintura

pair [pɛə*] n (of shoes, gloves etc) par m; (of people) pareja; **a ~ of scissors** unas tijeras; **a ~ of trousers** unos pantalones, un pantalón

pajamas [pə'dʒɑːməz] (us) npl pijama m

Pakistan [pɑːkɪ'stɑːn] n Paquistán m; **Pakistani** adj, n paquistaní mf

pal [pæl] (inf) n compinche mf, compañero/a

palace ['pæləs] n palacio

pale [peɪl] adj (gen) pálido; (colour) claro ▷ n: **to be beyond the ~** pasarse de la raya

Palestine ['pælɪstaɪn] n Palestina; **Palestinian** [-'tɪnɪən] adj, n palestino/a m/f

palm [pɑːm] n (Anat) palma; (also: ~ **tree**) palmera, palma ▷ vt: **to ~ sth off on sb** (inf) encajar algo a algn

pamper ['pæmpə*] vt mimar

pamphlet ['pæmflət] n folleto

pan [pæn] n (also: **sauce~**) cacerola, cazuela, olla; (also: **frying ~**) sartén f

pancake ['pænkeɪk] n crepe f

panda ['pændə] n panda m

pane [peɪn] n cristal m

panel ['pænl] n (of wood etc) panel m; (Radio, TV) panel m de invitados

panhandler ['pænhændlə*] (us) n (inf) mendigo/a

panic ['pænɪk] n terror m pánico ▷ vi dejarse llevar por el pánico

panorama [pænə'rɑːmə] n panorama m

pansy ['pænzɪ] n (Bot) pensamiento; (inf, pej) maricón m

pant [pænt] vi jadear

panther ['pænθə*] n pantera

panties ['pæntɪz] npl bragas fpl, pantis mpl

pantomime ['pæntəmaɪm] (BRIT) n revista musical representada en Navidad, basada en cuentos de hadas

● **PANTOMIME**
●
● En época navideña se ponen en

- escena en los teatros británicos
- las llamadas **pantomimes**, que
- son versiones libres de cuentos
- tradicionales como Aladino
- o El gato con botas. En ella
- nunca faltan personajes como
- la dama ("dame"), papel que
- siempre interpreta un actor, el
- protagonista joven ("principal
- boy"), normalmente interpretado
- por una actriz, y el malvado
- ("villain"). Es un espectáculo
- familiar en el que se anima al
- público a participar y aunque
- va dirigido principalmente a los
- niños, cuenta con grandes dosis de
- humor para adultos.

pants [pænts] n (BRIT: underwear: woman's) bragas fpl; (: man's) calzoncillos mpl; (US: trousers) pantalones mpl

paper ['peɪpə*] n papel m; (also: **news~**) periódico, diario; (academic essay) ensayo; (exam) examen m ▷ adj de papel ▷ vt empapelar, tapizar (MEX); **papers** npl (also: **identity ~s**) papeles mpl, documentos mpl; **paperback** n libro en rústica; **paper bag** n bolsa de papel; **paper clip** n clip m; **paper shop** (BRIT) n tienda de periódicos; **paperwork** n trabajo administrativo

paprika ['pæprɪkə] n pimentón m

par [pɑː*] n par f; (Golf) par m; **to be on a ~ with** estar a la par con

paracetamol [pærə'siːtəmɒl] (BRIT) n paracetamol m

parachute ['pærəʃuːt] n paracaídas m inv

parade [pə'reɪd] n desfile m ▷ vt (show) hacer alarde de ▷ vi desfilar; (Mil) pasar revista

paradise ['pærədaɪs] n paraíso

paradox ['pærədɒks] n paradoja

paraffin ['pærəfɪn] (BRIT) n (also: ~ **oil**) parafina

paragraph ['pærəɡrɑːf] n párrafo

parallel ['pærəlɛl] adj en paralelo;

(fig) semejante ▷ n (line) paralela; (fig, Geo) paralelo

paralysed ['pærəlaɪzd] adj paralizado

paralysis [pə'rælɪsɪs] n parálisis f inv

paramedic [pærə'mɛdɪk] n auxiliar m/f sanitario/a

paranoid ['pærənɔɪd] adj (person, feeling) paranoico

parasite ['pærəsaɪt] n parásito/a

parcel ['pɑːsl] n paquete m ▷ vt (also: ~ **up**) empaquetar, embalar

pardon ['pɑːdn] n (Law) indulto ▷ vt perdonar; **~ me!**, **I beg your ~!** (I'm sorry!) ¡perdone usted!; **(I beg your) ~?**, **~ me?** (US: what did you say?) ¿cómo?

parent ['pɛərənt] n (mother) madre f; (father) padre m; **parents** npl padres mpl

▌ Be careful not to translate **parent** by the Spanish word pariente.

parental [pə'rɛntl] adj paternal/ maternal

Paris ['pærɪs] n París

parish ['pærɪʃ] n parroquia

Parisian [pə'rɪziən] adj, n parisiense mf

park [pɑːk] n parque m ▷ vt aparcar, estacionar ▷ vi aparcar, estacionarse

parking ['pɑːkɪŋ] n aparcamiento, estacionamiento; **"no ~"** "prohibido estacionarse"; **parking lot** (US) n parking m; **parking meter** n parquímetro; **parking ticket** n multa de aparcamiento

parkway ['pɑːkweɪ] (US) n alameda

parliament ['pɑːləmənt] n parlamento; (Spanish) Cortes fpl; **parliamentary** [-'mɛntərɪ] adj parlamentario

- **PARLIAMENT**

- El Parlamento británico
- (**Parliament**) tiene como sede
- el palacio de Westminster,
- también llamado "Houses of
- Parliament" y consta de dos

cámaras. La Cámara de los
Comunes ("House of Commons"),
compuesta por 650 diputados
(**Members of Parliament**)
elegidos por sufragio universal
en su respectiva circunscripción
electoral (constituency), se reúne
175 días al año y sus sesiones son
moderadas por el Presidente de
la Cámara (**Speaker**). La cámara
alta es la Cámara de los Lores
("House of Lords") y está formada
por miembros que han sido
nombrados por el monarca o que
han heredado su escaño. Su poder
es limitado, aunque actúa como
tribunal supremo de apelación,
excepto en Escocia.

Parmesan [pɑːmɪˈzæn] n (also: ~
cheese) queso parmesano
parole [pəˈrəul] n: **on ~** libre bajo
palabra
parrot [ˈpærət] n loro, papagayo
parsley [ˈpɑːslɪ] n perejil m
parsnip [ˈpɑːsnɪp] n chirivía
parson [ˈpɑːsn] n cura m
part [pɑːt] n (gen, Mus) parte f; (bit)
trozo; (of machine) pieza; (Theatre etc)
papel m; (of serial) entrega; (US: in hair)
raya ▷ adv = **partly** ▷ vt separar ▷ vi
(people) separarse; (crowd) apartarse; **to
take ~ in** tomar parte or participar en;
to take sth in good ~ tomar algo en
buena parte; **to take sb's ~** defender
a algn; **for my ~** por mi parte; **for the
most ~** en su mayor parte; **to ~ one's
hair** hacerse la raya; **part with** vt fus
ceder, entregar; (money) pagar; **part
of speech** n parte f de la oración,
categoría f gramatical
partial [ˈpɑːʃl] adj parcial; **to be ~ to**
ser aficionado a
participant [pɑːˈtɪsɪpənt] n (in
competition) concursante mf; (in
campaign etc) participante mf
participate [pɑːˈtɪsɪpeɪt] vi: **to ~ in**
participar en

particle [ˈpɑːtɪkl] n partícula; (of
dust) grano
particular [pəˈtɪkjulə*] adj (special)
particular; (concrete) concreto; (given)
determinado; (fussy) quisquilloso;
(demanding) exigente; **in ~** en
particular; **particularly** adv (in
particular) sobre todo; (difficult, good
etc) especialmente; **particulars**
npl (information) datos mpl; (details)
pormenores mpl
parting [ˈpɑːtɪŋ] n (act) separación f;
(farewell) despedida; (BRIT: in hair) raya
▷ adj de despedida
partition [pɑːˈtɪʃən] n (Pol) división f;
(wall) tabique m
partly [ˈpɑːtlɪ] adv en parte
partner [ˈpɑːtnə*] n (Comm)
socio/a; (Sport, at dance) pareja; (spouse)
cónyuge mf; (lover) compañero/a;
partnership n asociación f; (Comm)
sociedad f
partridge [ˈpɑːtrɪdʒ] n perdiz f
part-time [ˈpɑːtˈtaɪm] adj, adv a
tiempo parcial
party [ˈpɑːtɪ] n (Pol) partido;
(celebration) fiesta; (group) grupo;
(Law) parte f interesada ▷ cpd (Pol)
de partido
pass [pɑːs] vt (time, object) pasar;
(place) pasar por; (overtake) rebasar;
(exam) aprobar; (approve) aprobar ▷ vi
pasar; (Scol) aprobar, ser aprobado
▷ n (permit) permiso; (membership
card) carnet m; (in mountains) puerto,
desfiladero; (Sport) pase m; (Scol: also:
~ **mark**): **to get a ~ in** aprobar en;
to ~ sth through sth pasar algo por
algo; **to make a ~ at sb** (inf) hacer
proposiciones a algn; **pass away** vi
fallecer; **pass by** vi pasar ▷ vt (ignore)
pasar por alto; **pass on** vt transmitir;
pass out vi desmayarse; **pass over**
vi, vt omitir, pasar por alto; **pass up** vt
(opportunity) renunciar a; **passable** adj
(road) transitable; (tolerable) pasable
passage [ˈpæsɪdʒ] n (also: ~**way**)
pasillo; (act of passing) tránsito; (fare,

in book) pasaje *m*; (*by boat*) travesía; (*Anat*) tubo

passenger ['pæsɪndʒə*] *n* pasajero/a, viajero/a

passer-by [pɑːsə'baɪ] *n* transeúnte *mf*

passing place *n* (*Aut*) apartadero

passion ['pæʃən] *n* pasión *f*; **passionate** *adj* apasionado; **passion fruit** *n* fruta de la pasión, granadilla

passive ['pæsɪv] *adj* (*gen, also Ling*) pasivo

passport ['pɑːspɔːt] *n* pasaporte *m*; **passport control** *n* control *m* de pasaporte; **passport office** *n* oficina de pasaportes

password ['pɑːswəːd] *n* contraseña

past [pɑːst] *prep* (*in front of*) por delante de; (*further than*) más allá de; (*later than*) después de ▷ *adj* pasado; (*president etc*) antiguo ▷ *n* (*time*) pasado; (*of person*) antecedentes *mpl*; **he's ~ forty** tiene más de cuarenta años; **ten/quarter ~ eight** las ocho y diez/cuarto; **for the ~ few/3 days** durante los últimos días/últimos 3 días; **to run ~ sb** pasar a algn corriendo

pasta ['pæstə] *n* pasta

paste [peɪst] *n* pasta; (*glue*) engrudo ▷ *vt* pegar

pastel ['pæstl] *adj* pastel; (*painting*) al pastel

pasteurized ['pæstəraɪzd] *adj* pasteurizado

pastime ['pɑːstaɪm] *n* pasatiempo

pastor ['pɑːstə*] *n* pastor *m*

past participle [-'pɑːtɪsɪpl] *n* (*Ling*) participio *m* (de) pasado *or* (de) pretérito *or* pasivo

pastry ['peɪstrɪ] *n* (*dough*) pasta; (*cake*) pastel *m*

pasture ['pɑːstʃə*] *n* pasto

pasty¹ ['pæstɪ] *n* empanada

pasty² ['peɪstɪ] *adj* (*complexion*) pálido

pat [pæt] *vt* dar una palmadita a; (*dog etc*) acariciar

patch [pætʃ] *n* (*of material,*: *eye patch*) parche *m*; (*mended part*) remiendo; (*of

land) terreno ▷ *vt* remendar; **(to go through) a bad ~** (pasar por) una mala racha; **patchy** *adj* desigual

pâté ['pæteɪ] *n* paté *m*

patent ['peɪtnt] *n* patente *f* ▷ *vt* patentar ▷ *adj* patente, evidente

paternal [pə'təːnl] *adj* paternal; (*relation*) paterno

paternity leave [pə'təːnɪtɪ-] *n* permiso *m* por paternidad, licencia por paternidad

path [pɑːθ] *n* camino, sendero; (*trail, track*) pista; (*of missile*) trayectoria

pathetic [pə'θetɪk] *adj* patético, lastimoso; (*very bad*) malísimo

pathway ['pɑːθweɪ] *n* sendero, vereda

patience ['peɪʃns] *n* paciencia; (*BRIT Cards*) solitario

patient ['peɪʃnt] *n* paciente *mf* ▷ *adj* paciente, sufrido

patio ['pætɪəu] *n* patio

patriotic [pætrɪ'ɔtɪk] *adj* patriótico

patrol [pə'trəul] *n* patrulla ▷ *vt* patrullar por; **patrol car** *n* coche *m* patrulla

patron ['peɪtrən] *n* (*in shop*) cliente *mf*; (*of charity*) patrocinador(a) *m/f*; **~ of the arts** mecenas *m*

patronizing ['pætrənaɪzɪŋ] *adj* condescendiente

pattern ['pætən] *n* (*Sewing*) patrón *m*; (*design*) dibujo; **patterned** *adj* (*material*) estampado

pause [pɔːz] *n* pausa ▷ *vi* hacer una pausa

pave [peɪv] *vt* pavimentar; **to ~ the way for** preparar el terreno para

pavement ['peɪvmənt] (*BRIT*) *n* acera, banqueta (*MEX*), andén *m* (*CAM*), vereda (*SC*)

pavilion [pə'vɪlɪən] *n* (*Sport*) caseta

paving ['peɪvɪŋ] *n* pavimento, enlosado

paw [pɔː] *n* pata

pawn [pɔːn] *n* (*Chess*) peón *m*; (*fig*) instrumento ▷ *vt* empeñar; **pawn broker** *n* prestamista *mf*

pay [peɪ] (*pt, pp* **paid**) *n* (*wage etc*) sueldo, salario ▷ *vt* pagar ▷ *vi* (*be profitable*) rendir; **to ~ attention (to)** prestar atención (a); **to ~ sb a visit** hacer una visita a algn; **to ~ one's respects to sb** presentar sus respetos a algn; **pay back** *vt* (*money*) reembolsar; (*person*) pagar; **pay for** *vt fus* pagar; **pay in** *vt* ingresar; **pay off** *vt* saldar ▷ *vi* (*scheme, decision*) dar resultado; **pay out** *vt* (*money*) gastar, desembolsar; **pay up** *vt* pagar (de mala gana); **payable** *adj*: **payable to** pagadero a; **pay day** *n* día *m* de paga; **pay envelope** (*US*) *n* = **pay packet**; **payment** *n* pago; **monthly payment** mensualidad *f*; **payout** *n* pago; (*in competition*) premio en metálico; **pay packet** (*BRIT*) *n* sobre *m* (de paga); **pay phone** *n* teléfono público; **payroll** *n* nómina; **pay slip** *n* recibo de sueldo; **pay television** *n* televisión *f* de pago

PC *n abbr* = **personal computer**; (*BRIT*) (= *police constable*) policía *mf* ▷ *adv abbr* = **politically correct**

p.c. *abbr* = **per cent**

PDA *n abbr* (= *personal digital assistant*) agenda electrónica

PE *n abbr* (= *physical education*) ed. física

pea [pi:] *n* guisante *m* (*SP*), arveja (*LAM*), chícharo (*MEX, CAM*)

peace [pi:s] *n* paz *f*; (*calm*) paz *f*, tranquilidad *f*; **peaceful** *adj* (*gentle*) pacífico; (*calm*) tranquilo, sosegado

peach [pi:tʃ] *n* melocotón *m* (*SP*), durazno (*LAM*)

peacock [ˈpi:kɔk] *n* pavo real

peak [pi:k] *n* (*of mountain*) cumbre *f*, cima; (*of cap*) visera; (*fig*) cumbre *f*; **peak hours** *npl* horas *fpl* punta

peanut [ˈpi:nʌt] *n* cacahuete *m* (*SP*), maní *m* (*LAM*), cacahuate *m* (*MEX*); **peanut butter** *n* manteca de cacahuete *or* maní

pear [pɛə*] *n* pera

pearl [pə:l] *n* perla

peasant [ˈpɛznt] *n* campesino/a

peat [pi:t] *n* turba

pebble [ˈpɛbl] *n* guijarro

peck [pɛk] *vt* (*also*: **~ at**) picotear ▷ *n* picotazo; (*kiss*) besito; **peckish** (*BRIT: inf*) *adj*: **I feel peckish** tengo ganas de picar algo

peculiar [pɪˈkju:lɪə*] *adj* (*odd*) extraño, raro; (*typical*) propio, característico; **~ to** propio de

pedal [ˈpɛdl] *n* pedal *m* ▷ *vi* pedalear

pedalo [ˈpɛdələu] *n* patín *m* a pedal

pedestal [ˈpɛdəstl] *n* pedestal *m*

pedestrian [pɪˈdɛstrɪən] *n* peatón/ ona *m/f* ▷ *adj* pedestre; **pedestrian crossing** (*BRIT*) *n* paso de peatones; **pedestrianized** *adj*: **a pedestrianized street** una calle peatonal; **pedestrian precinct** (*US* **pedestrian zone**) *n* zona peatonal

pedigree [ˈpɛdɪgri:] *n* genealogía; (*of animal*) raza, pedigrí *m* ▷ *cpd* (*animal*) de raza, de casta

pedophile [ˈpi:dəufaɪl] (*US*) *n* = **paedophile**

pee [pi:] (*inf*) *vi* mear

peek [pi:k] *vi* mirar a hurtadillas

peel [pi:l] *n* piel *f*; (*of orange, lemon*) cáscara; (: *removed*) peladuras *fpl* ▷ *vt* pelar ▷ *vi* (*paint etc*) desconcharse; (*wallpaper*) despegarse, desprenderse; (*skin*) pelar

peep [pi:p] *n* (*BRIT: look*) mirada furtiva; (*sound*) pío ▷ *vi* (*BRIT: look*) mirar furtivamente

peer [pɪə*] *vi*: **to ~ at** esudriñar ▷ *n* (*noble*) par *m*; (*equal*) igual *m*; (*contemporary*) contemporáneo/a

peg [pɛg] *n* (*for coat etc*) gancho, colgadero; (*BRIT: also*: **clothes ~**) pinza

pelican [ˈpɛlɪkən] *n* pelícano; **pelican crossing** (*BRIT*) *n* (*Aut*) paso de peatones señalizado

pelt [pɛlt] *vt*: **to ~ sb with sth** arrojarle algo a algn ▷ *vi* (*rain*) llover a cántaros; (*inf: run*) correr ▷ *n* pellejo

pelvis [ˈpɛlvɪs] *n* pelvis *f*

pen [pɛn] *n* (*fountain pen*) pluma; (*ballpoint pen*) bolígrafo; (*for sheep*) redil *m*

penalty ['pɛnltɪ] n (gen) pena; (fine) multa

pence [pɛns] npl of **penny**

pencil ['pɛnsl] n lápiz m; **pencil in** vt (appointment) apuntar con carácter provisional; **pencil case** n estuche m; **pencil sharpener** n sacapuntas m inv

pendant ['pɛndnt] n pendiente m

pending ['pɛndɪŋ] prep antes de ▷ adj pendiente

penetrate ['pɛnɪtreɪt] vt penetrar

penfriend ['pɛnfrɛnd] (BRIT) n amigo/a por carta

penguin ['pɛŋgwɪn] n pingüino

penicillin [pɛnɪ'sɪlɪn] n penicilina

peninsula [pə'nɪnsjulə] n península

penis ['piːnɪs] n pene m

penitentiary [pɛnɪ'tɛnʃərɪ] (US) n cárcel f, presidio

penknife ['pɛnnaɪf] n navaja

penniless ['pɛnɪlɪs] adj sin dinero

penny ['pɛnɪ] (pl **pennies** or **pence**) (BRIT) n penique m; (US) centavo

penpal ['pɛnpæl] n amigo/a por carta

pension ['pɛnʃən] n (state benefit) jubilación f; **pensioner** (BRIT) n jubilado/a

pentagon ['pɛntəgən] (US) n: **the P~** (Pol) el Pentágono

- **PENTAGON**
-
- Se conoce como **Pentagon** al
- edificio de planta pentagonal
- que acoge las dependencias
- del Ministerio de Defensa
- estadounidense ("Department of
- Defense") en Arlington, Virginia.
- En lenguaje periodístico se aplica
- también a la dirección militar
- del país.

penthouse ['pɛnthaus] n ático de lujo

penultimate [pɛ'nʌltɪmət] adj penúltimo

people ['piːpl] npl gente f; (citizens) pueblo, ciudadanos mpl; (Pol): **the ~** el pueblo ▷ n (nation, race) pueblo, nación f; **several ~ came** vinieron varias personas; **~ say that ...** dice la gente que ...

pepper ['pɛpə*] n (spice) pimienta; (vegetable) pimiento ▷ vt: **to ~ with** (fig) salpicar de; **peppermint** n (sweet) pastilla de menta

per [pə:*] prep por; **~ day/~son** por día/persona; **~ annum** al año

perceive [pə'siːv] vt percibir; (realize) darse cuenta de

per cent n por ciento

percentage [pə'sɛntɪdʒ] n porcentaje m

perception [pə'sɛpʃən] n percepción f; (insight) perspicacia; (opinion etc) opinión f

perch [pə:tʃ] n (fish) perca; (for bird) percha ▷ vi: **to ~ (on)** (bird) posarse (en); (person) encaramarse en

percussion [pə'kʌʃən] n percusión f

perfect [adj, n 'pə:fɪkt, vb pə'fɛkt] adj perfecto ▷ n (also: **~ tense**) perfecto ▷ vt perfeccionar; **perfection** [pə'fɛkʃən] n perfección f; **perfectly** ['pə:fɪktlɪ] adv perfectamente

perform [pə'fɔ:m] vt (carry out) realizar, llevar a cabo; (Theatre) representar; (piece of music) interpretar ▷ vi (well, badly) funcionar; **performance** n (of a play) representación f; (of actor, athlete etc) actuación f; (of car, engine, company) rendimiento; (of economy) resultados mpl; **performer** n (actor) actor m, actriz f

perfume ['pə:fjuːm] n perfume m

perhaps [pə'hæps] adv quizá(s), tal vez

perimeter [pə'rɪmɪtə*] n perímetro

period ['pɪərɪəd] n período; (Scol) clase f; (full stop) punto; (Med) regla ▷ adj (costume, furniture) de época; **periodical** [pɪərɪ'ɔdɪkl] n periódico; **periodically** adv de vez en cuando, cada cierto tiempo

perish ['pɛrɪʃ] vi perecer; (decay) echarse a perder

perjury ['pə:dʒərɪ] n (Law) perjurio

perk [pə:k] n extra m

perm [pə:m] n permanente f

permanent ['pə:mənənt] adj permanente; **permanently** adv (lastingly) para siempre, de modo definitivo; (all the time) permanentemente

permission [pə'mɪʃən] n permiso

permit [n 'pə:mɪt, vt pə'mɪt] n permiso, licencia ▷ vt permitir

perplex [pə'plɛks] vt dejar perplejo

persecute ['pə:sɪkju:t] vt perseguir

persecution [pə:sɪ'kju:ʃən] n persecución f

persevere [pə:sɪ'vɪə*] vi persistir

Persian ['pə:ʃən] adj, n persa mf; **the ~ Gulf** el Golfo Pérsico

persist [pə'sɪst] vi: **to ~ (in doing sth)** persistir (en hacer algo); **persistent** adj persistente; (determined) porfiado

person ['pə:sn] n persona; **in ~** en persona; **personal** adj personal; individual; (visit) en persona; **personal assistant** n ayudante mf personal; **personal computer** n ordenador m personal; **personality** [-'nælɪtɪ] n personalidad f; **personally** adv personalmente; (in person) en persona; **to take sth personally** tomarse algo a mal; **personal organizer** n agenda; **personal stereo** n Walkman® m

personnel [pə:sə'nɛl] n personal m

perspective [pə'spɛktɪv] n perspectiva

perspiration [pə:spɪ'reɪʃən] n transpiración f

persuade [pə'sweɪd] vt: **to ~ sb to do sth** persuadir a algn para que haga algo

persuasion [pə'sweɪʒən] n persuasión f; (persuasiveness) persuasiva

persuasive [pə'sweɪsɪv] adj persuasivo

perverse [pə'və:s] adj perverso; (wayward) travieso

pervert [n 'pə:və:t, vb pə'və:t] n pervertido/a ▷ vt pervertir; (truth, sb's words) tergiversar

pessimism ['pɛsɪmɪzəm] n pesimismo

pessimist ['pɛsɪmɪst] n pesimista mf; **pessimistic** [-'mɪstɪk] adj pesimista

pest [pɛst] n (insect) insecto nocivo; (fig) lata, molestia

pester ['pɛstə*] vt molestar, acosar

pesticide ['pɛstɪsaɪd] n pesticida m

pet [pɛt] n animal m doméstico ▷ cpd favorito ▷ vt acariciar; **teacher's ~** favorito/a (del profesor); **~ hate** manía

petal ['pɛtl] n pétalo

petite [pə'ti:t] adj chiquita

petition [pə'tɪʃən] n petición f

petrified ['pɛtrɪfaɪd] adj horrorizado

petrol ['pɛtrəl] (BRIT) n gasolina

petroleum [pə'trəulɪəm] n petróleo

petrol: petrol pump (BRIT) n (in garage) surtidor m de gasolina; **petrol station** (BRIT) n gasolinera; **petrol tank** (BRIT) n depósito (de gasolina)

petticoat ['pɛtɪkəut] n enaguas fpl

petty ['pɛtɪ] adj (mean) mezquino; (unimportant) insignificante

pew [pju:] n banco

pewter ['pju:tə*] n peltre m

phantom ['fæntəm] n fantasma m

pharmacist ['fɑ:məsɪst] n farmacéutico/a

pharmacy ['fɑ:məsɪ] n farmacia

phase [feɪz] n fase f; **phase in** vt introducir progresivamente; **phase out** vt (machinery, product) retirar progresivamente; (job, subsidy) eliminar por etapas

Ph.D. abbr = **Doctor of Philosophy**

pheasant ['fɛznt] n faisán m

phenomena [fə'nɔmɪnə] npl of **phenomenon**

phenomenal [fɪ'nɔmɪnl] adj fenomenal, extraordinario

phenomenon [fə'nɔmɪnən] (pl **phenomena**) n fenómeno

Philippines ['fɪlɪpi:nz] npl: **the ~** las

Filipinas

philosopher [fɪ'lɔsəfə*] n filósofo/a

philosophical [fɪlə'sɔfɪkl] adj
filosófico

philosophy [fɪ'lɔsəfɪ] n filosofía

phlegm [flɛm] n flema

phobia ['fəubjə] n fobia

phone [fəun] n teléfono ▷ vt
telefonear, llamar por teléfono; **to be
on the ~** tener teléfono; (be calling)
estar hablando por teléfono; **phone
back** vt, vi volver a llamar; **phone up**
vt, vi llamar por teléfono; **phone book**
n guía telefónica; **phone booth**
n cabina telefónica; **phone box** (BRIT) n
= **phone booth; phone call** n llamada
(telefónica); **phonecard** n teletarjeta;
phone number n número de teléfono

phonetics [fə'nɛtɪks] n fonética

phoney ['fəunɪ] adj falso

photo ['fəutəu] n foto f; **photo album**
n álbum m de fotos; **photocopier**
n fotocopiadora; **photocopy** n
fotocopia ▷ vt fotocopiar

photograph ['fəutəgrɑːf]
n fotografía ▷ vt fotografiar;
photographer [fə'tɔgrəfə*] n
fotógrafo; **photography** [fə'tɔgrəfɪ]
n fotografía

phrase [freɪz] n frase f ▷ vt expresar;
phrase book n libro de frases

physical ['fɪzɪkl] adj físico; **physical
education** n educación f física;
physically adv físicamente

physician [fɪ'zɪʃən] n médico m

physicist ['fɪzɪsɪst] n físico/a

physics ['fɪzɪks] n física

physiotherapist [fɪzɪəu'θerəpɪst] n
fisioterapeuta

physiotherapy [fɪzɪəu'θerəpɪ] n
fisioterapia

physique [fɪ'ziːk] n físico

pianist ['piːənɪst] n pianista mf

piano [pɪ'ænəu] n piano

pick [pɪk] n (tool: also: **~-axe**) pico,
piqueta ▷ vt (select) elegir, escoger;
(gather) coger (SP), recoger; (remove,
take out) sacar, quitar; (lock) abrir con

ganzúa; **take your ~** escoja lo que
quiera; **the ~ of** lo mejor de; **to ~ one's
nose/teeth** hurgarse las narices/
limpiarse los dientes; **to ~ a quarrel
with sb** meterse con algn; **pick on** vt
fus (person) meterse con; **pick out** vt
escoger; (distinguish) identificar; **pick
up** vi (improve: sales) ir mejor; (: patient)
reponerse; (Finance) recobrarse ▷ vt
recoger; (learn) aprender; (Police: arrest)
detener; (person: for sex) ligar; (Radio)
captar; **to pick up speed** acelerarse; **to
pick o.s. up** levantarse

pickle ['pɪkl] n (also: **~s**: as condiment)
escabeche m; (fig: mess) apuro ▷ vt
encurtir

pickpocket ['pɪkpɔkɪt] n carterista
mf

pick-up ['pɪkʌp] n (also: **~ truck**)
furgoneta, camioneta

picnic ['pɪknɪk] n merienda ▷ vi ir
de merienda; **picnic area** n zona de
picnic; (Aut) área de descanso

picture ['pɪktʃə*] n cuadro; (painting)
pintura; (photograph) fotografía; (TV)
imagen f; (film) película; (fig: description)
descripción f; (: situation) situación
f ▷ vt (imagine) imaginar; **pictures**
npl: **the ~s** (BRIT) el cine; **picture frame**
n marco; **picture messaging** n (envío
de) mensajes con imágenes

picturesque [pɪktʃə'rɛsk] adj
pintoresco

pie [paɪ] n pastel m; (open) tarta;
(small: of meat) empanada

piece [piːs] n pedazo, trozo; (of
cake) trozo; (item): **a ~ of clothing/
furniture/advice** una prenda (de
vestir)/un mueble/un consejo ▷ vt: **to
~ together** juntar; (Tech) armar; **to
take to ~s** desmontar

pie chart n gráfico de sectores or
tarta

pier [pɪə*] n muelle m, embarcadero

pierce [pɪəs] vt perforar; **pierced**
adj: **I've got pierced ears** tengo los
agujeros hechos en las orejas

pig [pɪg] n cerdo, chancho (LAM);

(*pej: unkind person*) asqueroso; (: *greedy person*) glotón/ona *m/f*
pigeon ['pɪdʒən] *n* paloma; (*as food*) pichón *m*
piggy bank ['pɪgɪ-] *n* hucha (*en forma de cerdito*)
pigsty ['pɪgstaɪ] *n* pocilga
pigtail *n* (*girl's*) trenza
pike [paɪk] *n* (*fish*) lucio
pilchard ['pɪltʃəd] *n* sardina
pile [paɪl] *n* montón *m*; (*of carpet, cloth*) pelo; **pile up** *vi +adv* (*accumulate: work*) amontonarse, acumularse ▷*vt +adv* (*put in a heap: books, clothes*) apilar, amontonar; (*accumulate*) acumular; **piles** *npl* (*Med*) almorranas *fpl*, hemorroides *mpl*; **pile-up** *n* (*Aut*) accidente *m* múltiple
pilgrimage ['pɪlgrɪmɪdʒ] *n* peregrinación *f*, romería
pill [pɪl] *n* píldora; **the ~** la píldora
pillar ['pɪlə*] *n* pilar *m*
pillow ['pɪləu] *n* almohada; **pillowcase** *n* funda
pilot ['paɪlət] *n* piloto ▷*cpd* (*scheme etc*) piloto ▷*vt* pilotar; **pilot light** *n* piloto
pimple ['pɪmpl] *n* grano
PIN *n abbr* (= *personal identification number*) número personal
pin [pɪn] *n* alfiler *m* ▷*vt* prender (con alfiler); **~s and needles** hormigueo; **to ~ sb down** (*fig*) hacer que algn concrete; **to ~ sth on sb** (*fig*) colgarle a algn el sambenito de algo
pinafore ['pɪnəfɔ:*] *n* delantal *m*
pinch [pɪntʃ] *n* (*of salt etc*) pizca ▷*vt* pellizcar; (*inf: steal*) birlar; **at a ~** en caso de apuro
pine [paɪn] *n* (*also: ~ tree*) pino ▷*vi*: **to ~ for** suspirar por
pineapple ['paɪnæpl] *n* piña, ananás *m*
ping [pɪŋ] *n* (*noise*) sonido agudo; **ping-pong**® *n* pingpong® *m*
pink [pɪŋk] *adj* rosado, (color de) rosa ▷*n* (*colour*) rosa; (*Bot*) clavel *m*, clavellina

pinpoint ['pɪnpɔɪnt] *vt* precisar
pint [paɪnt] *n* pinta (BRIT = 568cc, US = 473cc); (BRIT: *inf: of beer*) pinta de cerveza ≈ jarra (SP)
pioneer [paɪə'nɪə*] *n* pionero/a
pious ['paɪəs] *adj* piadoso, devoto
pip [pɪp] *n* (*seed*) pepita; **the ~s** (BRIT) la señal
pipe [paɪp] *n* tubo, caño; (*for smoking*) pipa ▷*vt* conducir en cañerías; **pipeline** *n* (*for oil*) oleoducto; (*for gas*) gasoducto; **piper** *n* gaitero/a
pirate ['paɪərət] *n* pirata *mf* ▷*vt* (*cassette, book*) piratear
Pisces ['paɪsi:z] *n* Piscis *m*
piss [pɪs] (*inf!*) *vi* mear; **pissed** (*inf!*) *adj* (*drunk*) borracho
pistol ['pɪstl] *n* pistola
piston ['pɪstən] *n* pistón *m*, émbolo
pit [pɪt] *n* hoyo; (*also:* **coal ~**) mina; (*in garage*) foso de inspección; (*also:* **orchestra ~**) platea ▷*vt*: **to ~ one's wits against sb** medir fuerzas con algn
pitch [pɪtʃ] *n* (*Mus*) tono; (BRIT *Sport*) campo, terreno; (*fig*) punto; (*tar*) brea ▷*vt* (*throw*) arrojar, lanzar ▷*vi* (*fall*) caer(se); **to ~ a tent** montar una tienda (de campaña); **pitch-black** *adj* negro como boca de lobo
pitfall ['pɪtfɔ:l] *n* riesgo
pith [pɪθ] *n* (*of orange*) médula
pitiful ['pɪtɪful] *adj* (*touching*) lastimoso, conmovedor(a)
pity ['pɪtɪ] *n* compasión *f*, piedad *f* ▷*vt* compadecer(se de); **what a ~!** ¡qué pena!
pizza ['pi:tsə] *n* pizza
placard ['plækɑ:d] *n* letrero; (*in march etc*) pancarta
place [pleɪs] *n* lugar *m*, sitio; (*seat*) plaza, asiento; (*post*) puesto; (*home*): **at/to his ~** en/a su casa; (*role: in society etc*) papel *m* ▷*vt* (*object*) poner, colocar; (*identify*) reconocer; **to take ~** tener lugar; **to be ~d** (*in race, exam*) colocarse; **out of ~** (*not suitable*) fuera de lugar; **in the first ~** en primer lugar; **to change ~s with sb** cambiarse de

sitio con algn; **~ of birth** lugar *m* de nacimiento; **place mat** *n* (*wooden etc*) salvamanteles *m inv*; (*linen etc*) mantel *m* individual; **placement** *n* (*positioning*) colocación *f*; (*at work*) emplazamiento

placid ['plæsɪd] *adj* apacible

plague [pleɪg] *n* plaga; (*Med*) peste *f* ▷ *vt* (*fig*) acosar, atormentar

plaice [pleɪs] *n inv* platija

plain [pleɪn] *adj* (*unpatterned*) liso; (*clear*) claro, evidente; (*simple*) sencillo; (*not handsome*) poco atractivo ▷ *adv* claramente ▷ *n* llano, llanura; **plain chocolate** *n* chocolate *m* amargo; **plainly** *adv* claramente

plaintiff ['pleɪntɪf] *n* demandante *mf*

plait [plæt] *n* trenza

plan [plæn] *n* (*drawing*) plano; (*scheme*) plan *m*, proyecto ▷ *vt* proyectar, planificar ▷ *vi* hacer proyectos; **to ~ to do** pensar hacer

plane [pleɪn] *n* (*Aviat*) avión *m*; (*Math, fig*) plano; (*also: ~ tree*) plátano; (*tool*) cepillo

planet ['plænɪt] *n* planeta *m*

plank [plæŋk] *n* tabla

planning ['plænɪŋ] *n* planificación *f*; **family ~** planificación familiar

plant [plɑːnt] *n* planta; (*machinery*) maquinaria; (*factory*) fábrica ▷ *vt* plantar; (*field*) sembrar; (*bomb*) colocar

plantation [plæn'teɪʃən] *n* plantación *f*; (*estate*) hacienda

plaque [plæk] *n* placa

plaster ['plɑːstə*] *n* (*for walls*) yeso; (*also: ~ of Paris*) yeso mate, escayola (SP); (BRIT: *also: sticking ~*) tirita (SP), curita (LAM) ▷ *vt* enyesar; (*cover*): **to ~ with** llenar *or* cubrir de; **plaster cast** *n* (*Med*) escayola; (*model, statue*) vaciado de yeso

plastic ['plæstɪk] *n* plástico ▷ *adj* de plástico; **plastic bag** *n* bolsa de plástico; **plastic surgery** *n* cirugía plástica

plate [pleɪt] *n* (*dish*) plato; (*metal, in book*) lámina; (*dental plate*) placa de

dentadura postiza

plateau ['plætəu] (*pl* **~s** *or* **~x**) *n* meseta, altiplanicie *f*

platform ['plætfɔːm] *n* (Rail) andén *m*; (*stage*, BRIT: *on bus*) plataforma; (*at meeting*) tribuna; (Pol) programa *m* (electoral)

platinum ['plætɪnəm] *adj*, *n* platino

platoon [plə'tuːn] *n* pelotón *m*

platter ['plætə*] *n* fuente *f*

plausible ['plɔːzɪbl] *adj* verosímil; (*person*) convincente

play [pleɪ] *n* (Theatre) obra, comedia ▷ *vt* (*game*) jugar; (*compete against*) jugar contra; (*instrument*) tocar; (*part: in play etc*) hacer el papel de; (*tape, record*) poner ▷ *vi* jugar; (*band*) tocar; (*tape, record*) sonar; **to ~ safe** ir a lo seguro; **play back** *vt* (*tape*) poner; **play up** *vi* (*cause trouble to*) dar guerra; **player** *n* jugador(a) *m/f*; (Theatre) actor(actriz) *m/f*; (Mus) músico/a; **playful** *adj* juguetón/ona; **playground** *n* (*in school*) patio de recreo; (*in park*) parque *m* infantil; **playgroup** *n* jardín *m* de niños; **playing card** *n* naipe *m*, carta; **playing field** *n* campo de deportes; **playschool** *n* =**playgroup**; **playtime** *n* (Scol) recreo; **playwright** *n* dramaturgo/a

plc *abbr* (= *public limited company*) ≈ S.A.

plea [pliː] *n* súplica, petición *f*; (Law) alegato, defensa

plead [pliːd] *vt* (Law): **to ~ sb's case** defender a algn; (*give as excuse*) poner como pretexto ▷ *vi* (Law) declararse; (*beg*): **to ~ with sb** suplicar *or* rogar a algn

pleasant ['plɛznt] *adj* agradable

please [pliːz] *excl* ¡por favor! ▷ *vt* (*give pleasure to*) dar gusto a, agradar ▷ *vi* (*think fit*): **do as you ~** haz lo que quieras; **~ yourself!** (*inf*) ¡haz lo que quieras!, ¡como quieras!; **pleased** *adj* (*happy*) alegre, contento; **pleased (with)** satisfecho (de); **pleased to meet you** ¡encantado!, ¡tanto gusto!

pleasure ['plɛʒə*] *n* placer *m*, gusto;

"it's a ~" "el gusto es mío"

pleat [pli:t] n pliegue m

pledge [plɛdʒ] n (*promise*) promesa, voto ▷ vt prometer

plentiful ['plɛntɪful] adj copioso, abundante

plenty ['plɛntɪ] n: **~ of** mucho(s)/a(s)

pliers ['plaɪəz] npl alicates mpl, tenazas fpl

plight [plaɪt] n situación f difícil

plod [plɒd] vi caminar con paso pesado; (*fig*) trabajar laboriosamente

plonk [plɒŋk] (*inf*) n (BRIT: *wine*) vino peleón ▷ vt: **to ~ sth down** dejar caer algo

plot [plɒt] n (*scheme*) complot m, conjura; (*of story, play*) argumento; (*of land*) terreno ▷ vt (*mark out*) trazar; (*conspire*) tramar, urdir ▷ vi conspirar

plough [plaʊ] (US **plow**) n arado ▷ vt (*earth*) arar; **to ~ money into** invertir dinero en; **ploughman's lunch** (BRIT) n almuerzo de pub a base de pan, queso y encurtidos

plow [plaʊ] (US) = **plough**

ploy [plɔɪ] n truco, estratagema

pluck [plʌk] vt (*fruit*) coger (SP), recoger (LAM); (*musical instrument*) puntear; (*bird*) desplumar; (*eyebrows*) depilar; **to ~ up courage** hacer de tripas corazón

plug [plʌg] n tapón m; (*Elec*) enchufe m, clavija; (*Aut: also*: **spark(ing) ~**) bujía ▷ vt (*hole*) tapar; (*inf: advertise*) dar publicidad a; **plug in** vt (*Elec*) enchufar; **plughole** n desagüe m

plum [plʌm] n (*fruit*) ciruela

plumber ['plʌmə*] n fontanero/a (SP, CAM), plomero/a (LAM)

plumbing ['plʌmɪŋ] n (*trade*) fontanería, plomería; (*piping*) cañería

plummet ['plʌmɪt] vi: **to ~ (down)** caer a plomo

plump [plʌmp] adj rechoncho, rollizo ▷ vi: **to ~ for** (*inf: choose*) optar por

plunge [plʌndʒ] n zambullida ▷ vt sumergir, hundir ▷ vi (*fall*) caer; (*dive*) saltar; (*person*) arrojarse; **to take the**

~ lanzarse

plural ['plʊərl] adj plural ▷ n plural m

plus [plʌs] n (*also*: **~ sign**) signo más ▷ prep más, y, además de; **ten/twenty ~** más de diez/veinte

ply [plaɪ] vt (*a trade*) ejercer ▷ vi (*ship*) ir y venir ▷ n (*of wool, rope*) cabo; **to ~ sb with drink** insistir en ofrecer a algn muchas copas; **plywood** n madera contrachapada

P.M. n abbr = **Prime Minister**

p.m. adv abbr (= *post meridiem*) de la tarde or noche

PMS n abbr (= *premenstrual syndrome*) SPM m

PMT n abbr (= *premenstrual tension*) SPM m

pneumatic drill [njuːˈmætɪk-] n martillo neumático

pneumonia [njuːˈməʊnɪə] n pulmonía

poach [pəʊtʃ] vt (*cook*) escalfar; (*steal*) cazar (or pescar) en vedado ▷ vi cazar (or pescar) en vedado; **poached** adj escalfado

P.O. Box n abbr (= *Post Office Box*) apdo., aptdo.

pocket ['pɒkɪt] n bolsillo; (*fig: small area*) bolsa ▷ vt meter en el bolsillo; (*steal*) embolsar; **to be out of ~** (BRIT) salir perdiendo; **pocketbook** (US) n cartera; **pocket money** n asignación f

pod [pɒd] n vaina

podiatrist [pɒˈdiːətrɪst] (US) n pedicuro/a

podium ['pəʊdɪəm] n podio

poem ['pəʊɪm] n poema m

poet ['pəʊɪt] n poeta m/f; **poetic** [-ˈɛtɪk] adj poético; **poetry** n poesía

poignant ['pɔɪnjənt] adj conmovedor(a)

point [pɔɪnt] n punto; (*tip*) punta; (*purpose*) fin m, propósito; (*use*) utilidad f; (*significant part*) lo significativo; (*moment*) momento; (*Elec*) toma (de corriente); (*also*: **decimal ~**): **2 ~ 3 (2.3)** dos coma tres (2,3) ▷ vt señalar; (*gun etc*): **to ~ sth at sb** apuntar algo

a algn ▷ vi: **to ~ at** señalar; **points**
npl (Aut) contactos mpl; (Rail) agujas
fpl; **to be on the ~ of doing sth** estar
a punto de hacer algo; **to make a ~ of**
poner empeño en; **to get/miss the
~** comprender/no comprender; **to
come to the ~** ir al meollo; **there's no
~ (in doing)** no tiene sentido (hacer);
point out vt señalar; **point-blank**
adv (say, refuse) sin más hablar; (also:
at point-blank range) a quemarropa;
pointed adj (shape) puntiagudo,
afilado; (remark) intencionado; **pointer**
n (needle) aguja, indicador m; **pointless**
adj sin sentido; **point of view** n punto
de vista

poison ['pɔɪzn] n veneno ▷ vt
envenenar; **poisonous** adj venenoso;
(fumes etc) tóxico

poke [pəuk] vt (jab with finger, stick
etc) empujar; (put): **to ~ sth in(to)**
introducir algo en; **poke about** or
around vi fisgonear; **poke out** vi
(stick out) salir

poker ['pəukə*] n atizador m; (Cards)
póker m

Poland ['pəulənd] n Polonia

polar ['pəulə*] adj polar; **polar bear**
n oso polar

Pole [pəul] n polaco/a

pole [pəul] n palo; (fixed) poste m;
(Geo) polo; **pole bean** (US) n ≈ judía
verde; **pole vault** n salto con pértiga

police [pə'li:s] n policía ▷ vt vigilar;
police car n coche-patrulla m; **police
constable** (BRIT) n guardia m, policía
m; **police force** n cuerpo de policía;
policeman (irreg) n policía m, guardia
m; **police officer** n guardia m, policía
m; **police station** n comisaría;
policewoman (irreg) n mujer f policía

policy ['pɔlɪsɪ] n política; (also:
insurance ~) póliza

polio ['pəulɪəu] n polio f

Polish ['pəulɪʃ] adj polaco ▷ n (Ling)
polaco

polish ['pɔlɪʃ] n (for shoes) betún m;
(for floor) cera (de lustrar); (shine) brillo,

lustre m; (fig: refinement) educación f
▷ vt (shoes) limpiar; (make shiny) pulir,
sacar brillo a; **polish off** vt (food)
despachar; **polished** adj (fig: person)
elegante

polite [pə'laɪt] adj cortés, atento;
politeness n cortesía

political [pə'lɪtɪkl] adj político;
politically adv políticamente;
politically correct políticamente
correcto

politician [pɔlɪ'tɪʃən] n político/a

politics ['pɔlɪtɪks] n política

poll [pəul] n (election) votación f; (also:
opinion ~) sondeo, encuesta ▷ vt
encuestar; (votes) obtener

pollen ['pɔlən] n polen m

polling station ['pəulɪŋ-] n centro
electoral

pollute [pə'lu:t] vt contaminar

pollution [pə'lu:ʃən] n polución f,
contaminación f del medio ambiente

polo ['pəuləu] n (sport) polo; **polo-
neck** adj de cuello vuelto ▷ n (sweater)
suéter m de cuello vuelto; **polo shirt**
n polo, niqui m

polyester [pɔlɪ'estə*] n poliéster m

polystyrene [pɔlɪ'staɪri:n] n
poliestireno

polythene ['pɔlɪθi:n] (BRIT) n
politeno; **polythene bag** n bolsa de
plástico

pomegranate ['pɔmɪgrænɪt] n
granada

pompous ['pɔmpəs] adj pomposo

pond [pɔnd] n (natural) charca;
(artificial) estanque m

ponder ['pɔndə*] vt meditar

pony ['pəunɪ] n poni m; **ponytail**
n coleta; **pony trekking** (BRIT) n
excursión f a caballo

poodle ['pu:dl] n caniche m

pool [pu:l] n (natural) charca; (also:
swimming ~) piscina, alberca (MEX),
pileta (RPL); (fig: of light etc) charco;
(Sport) chapolín m ▷ vt juntar; **pools**
npl quinielas fpl

poor [puə*] adj pobre; (bad) de mala

calidad ▷ *npl*: **the ~** los pobres; **poorly** *adj* mal, enfermo ▷ *adv* mal

pop [pɒp] *n* (*sound*) ruido seco; (*Mus*) (música) pop *m*; (*inf*: *father*) papá *m*; (*drink*) gaseosa ▷ *vt* (*put quickly*) meter (de prisa) ▷ *vi* reventar; (*cork*) saltar; **pop in** *vi* entrar un momento; **pop out** *vi* salir un momento; **popcorn** *n* palomitas *fpl*

poplar ['pɒplə*] *n* álamo

popper ['pɒpə*] (*BRIT*) *n* automático

poppy ['pɒpɪ] *n* amapola

Popsicle® ['pɒpsɪkl] (*US*) *n* polo

pop star *n* estrella del pop

popular ['pɒpjulə*] *adj* popular; **popularity** [pɒpju'lærɪtɪ] *n* popularidad *f*

population [pɒpju'leɪʃən] *n* población *f*

pop-up ['pɒpʌp] (*Comput*) *adj* (*menu, window*) emergente ▷ *n* ventana emergente, (ventana *f*) pop-up *f*

porcelain ['pɔːslɪn] *n* porcelana

porch [pɔːtʃ] *n* pórtico, entrada; (*US*) veranda

pore [pɔː*] *n* poro ▷ *vi*: **to ~ over** engolfarse en

pork [pɔːk] *n* carne *f* de cerdo *or* (*LAM*) chancho; **pork chop** *n* chuleta de cerdo; **pork pie** *n* (*BRIT*: *Culin*) empanada de carne de cerdo

porn [pɔːn] *adj* (*inf*) porno *inv* ▷ *n* porno; **pornographic** [pɔːnə'græfɪk] *adj* pornográfico; **pornography** [pɔː'nɔgrəfɪ] *n* pornografía

porridge ['pɒrɪdʒ] *n* gachas *fpl* de avena

port [pɔːt] *n* puerto; (*Naut*: *left side*) babor *m*; (*wine*) vino de Oporto; **~ of call** puerto de escala

portable ['pɔːtəbl] *adj* portátil

porter ['pɔːtə*] *n* (*for luggage*) maletero; (*doorkeeper*) portero/a, conserje *m/f*

portfolio [pɔːt'fəuliəu] *n* cartera

portion ['pɔːʃən] *n* porción *f*; (*of food*) ración *f*

portrait ['pɔːtreɪt] *n* retrato

portray [pɔː'treɪ] *vt* retratar; (*actor*) representar

Portugal ['pɔːtjugl] *n* Portugal *m*

Portuguese [pɔːtju'giːz] *adj* portugués/esa ▷ *n inv* portugués/esa *m/f*; (*Ling*) portugués *m*

pose [pəuz] *n* postura, actitud *f* ▷ *vi* (*pretend*): **to ~ as** hacerse pasar por ▷ *vt* (*question*) plantear; **to ~ for** posar para

posh [pɒʃ] (*inf*) *adj* elegante, de lujo

position [pə'zɪʃən] *n* posición *f*; (*job*) puesto; (*situation*) situación *f* ▷ *vt* colocar

positive ['pɒzɪtɪv] *adj* positivo; (*certain*) seguro; (*definite*) definitivo; **positively** *adv* (*affirmatively, enthusiastically*) de forma positiva; (*inf*: *really*) absolutamente

possess [pə'zɛs] *vt* poseer; **possession** [pə'zɛʃən] *n* posesión *f*; **possessions** *npl* (*belongings*) pertenencias *fpl*; **possessive** *adj* posesivo

possibility [pɒsɪ'bɪlɪtɪ] *n* posibilidad *f*

possible ['pɒsɪbl] *adj* posible; **as big as ~** lo más grande posible; **possibly** *adv* posiblemente; **I cannot possibly come** me es imposible venir

post [pəust] *n* (*BRIT*: *system*) correos *mpl*; (*BRIT*: *letters, delivery*) correo; (*job, situation*) puesto; (*pole*) poste *m* ▷ *vt* (*BRIT*: *send by post*) echar al correo; (*BRIT*: *appoint*): **to ~ to** enviar a; **postage** *n* porte *m*, franqueo; **postal** *adj* postal, de correos; **postal order** *n* giro postal; **postbox** (*BRIT*) *n* buzón *m*; **postcard** *n* tarjeta postal; **postcode** (*BRIT*) *n* código postal

poster ['pəustə*] *n* cartel *m*

postgraduate ['pəust'grædjuət] *n* posgraduado/a

postman ['pəustmən] (*BRIT*: *irreg*) *n* cartero

postmark ['pəustmɑːk] *n* matasellos *m inv*

post-mortem [-'mɔːtəm] *n* autopsia

post office n (building) (oficina de) correos m; (organization): **the Post Office** Correos m inv (SP), Dirección f General de Correos (LAM)

postpone [pəs'pəun] vt aplazar

posture ['pɒstʃə*] n postura, actitud f

postwoman ['pəustwumən] (BRIT: irreg) n cartera

pot [pɒt] n (for cooking) olla; (teapot) tetera; (coffeepot) cafetera; (for flowers) maceta; (for jam) tarro, pote m; (inf: marijuana) chocolate m ⊳ vt (plant) poner en tiesto; **to go to ~** (inf) irse al traste

potato [pə'teɪtəu] (pl ~es) n patata (SP), papa (LAM); **potato peeler** n pelapatatas m inv

potent ['pəutnt] adj potente, poderoso; (drink) fuerte

potential [pə'tɛnʃl] adj potencial, posible ⊳ n potencial m

pothole ['pɒthəul] n (in road) bache m; (BRIT: underground) gruta

pot plant ['pɒtplɑːnt] n planta de interior

potter ['pɒtə*] n alfarero/a ⊳ vi: **to ~ around** or **about** (BRIT) hacer trabajitos; **pottery** n cerámica; (factory) alfarería

potty ['pɒtɪ] n orinal m de niño

pouch [pautʃ] n (Zool) bolsa; (for tobacco) petaca

poultry ['pəultrɪ] n aves fpl de corral; (meat) pollo

pounce [pauns] vi: **to ~ on** precipitarse sobre

pound [paund] n libra (weight = 453g or 16oz; money = 100 pence) ⊳ vt (beat) golpear; (crush) machacar ⊳ vi (heart) latir; **pound sterling** n libra esterlina

pour [pɔː*] vt echar; (tea etc) servir ⊳ vi correr, fluir; **to ~ sb a drink** servirle a algn una copa; **pour in** vi (people) entrar en tropel; **pour out** vi salir en tropel ⊳ vt (drink) echar, servir; (fig): **to pour out one's feelings** desahogarse; **pouring** adj: **pouring rain** lluvia torrencial

pout [paut] vi hacer pucheros

poverty ['pɒvətɪ] n pobreza, miseria

powder ['paudə*] n polvo; (also: **face ~**) polvos mpl ⊳ vt polvorear; **to ~ one's face** empolvarse la cara; **powdered milk** n leche f en polvo

power ['pauə*] n poder m; (strength) fuerza; (nation, Tech) potencia; (drive) empuje m; (Elec) fuerza, energía ⊳ vt impulsar; **to be in ~** (Pol) estar en el poder; **power cut** (BRIT) n apagón m; **power failure** n = **power cut**; **powerful** adj poderoso; (engine) potente; (speech etc) convincente; **powerless** adj: **powerless (to do)** incapaz (de hacer); **power point** (BRIT) n enchufe m; **power station** n central f eléctrica

p.p. abbr (= per procurationem); **p.p. J. Smith** p.p. (por poder de) J. Smith; (= pages) págs

PR n abbr = **public relations**

practical ['præktɪkl] adj práctico; **practical joke** n broma pesada; **practically** adv (almost) casi

practice ['præktɪs] n (habit) costumbre f; (exercise) práctica, ejercicio; (training) adiestramiento; (Med: of profession) práctica, ejercicio; (Med, Law: business) consulta ⊳ vt, vi (US) = **practise**; **in ~** (in reality) en la práctica; **out of ~** desentrenado

practise ['præktɪs] (US **practice**) vt (carry out) practicar; (profession) ejercer; (train at) practicar ⊳ vi ejercer; (train) practicar; **practising** adj (Christian etc) practicante; (lawyer) en ejercicio

practitioner [præk'tɪʃənə*] n (Med) médico/a

pragmatic [præg'mætɪk] adj pragmático

prairie ['preərɪ] n pampa

praise [preɪz] n alabanza(s) f(pl), elogio(s) m(pl) ⊳ vt alabar, elogiar

pram [præm] (BRIT) n cochecito de niño

prank [præŋk] n travesura

prawn [prɔːn] n gamba; **prawn**

cocktail n cóctel m de gambas
pray [preɪ] vi rezar; **prayer** [prɛə*] n
oración f, rezo; (entreaty) ruego, súplica
preach [pri:tʃ] vi predicar; **preacher**
n predicador(a) m/f
precarious [prɪ'kɛərɪəs] adj precario
precaution [prɪ'kɔ:ʃən] n
precaución f
precede [prɪ'si:d] vt, vi preceder;
precedent ['prɛsɪdənt] n precedente
m; **preceding** [prɪ'si:dɪŋ] adj anterior
precinct ['pri:sɪŋkt] n recinto
precious ['prɛʃəs] adj precioso
precise [prɪ'saɪs] adj preciso,
exacto; **precisely** adv precisamente,
exactamente
precision [prɪ'sɪʒən] n precisión f
predator ['prɛdətə*] n depredador m
predecessor ['pri:dɪsɛsə*] n
antecesor(a) m/f
predicament [prɪ'dɪkəmənt] n
apuro
predict [prɪ'dɪkt] vt pronosticar;
predictable adj previsible; **prediction**
[-'dɪkʃən] n predicción f
predominantly [prɪ'dɔmɪnəntlɪ]
adv en su mayoría
preface ['prɛfəs] n prefacio
prefect ['pri:fɛkt] (BRIT) n (in school)
monitor(a) m/f
prefer [prɪ'fə:*] vt preferir; **to ~ doing**
or **to do** preferir hacer; **preferable**
['prɛfrəbl] adj preferible; **preferably**
['prɛfrəblɪ] adv de preferencia;
preference ['prɛfrəns] n preferencia;
(priority) prioridad f
prefix ['pri:fɪks] n prefijo
pregnancy ['prɛgnənsɪ] n (of woman)
embarazo; (of animal) preñez f
pregnant ['prɛgnənt] adj (woman)
embarazada; (animal) preñada
prehistoric ['pri:hɪs'tɔrɪk] adj
prehistórico
prejudice ['prɛdʒudɪs] n prejuicio;
prejudiced adj (person) predispuesto
preliminary [prɪ'lɪmɪnərɪ] adj
preliminar
prelude ['prɛlju:d] n preludio

premature ['prɛmətʃuə*] adj
prematuro
premier ['prɛmɪə*] adj primero,
principal ▷ n (Pol) primer(a)
ministro/a
première ['prɛmɪɛə*] n estreno
Premier League [prɛmɪə'li:g] n
primera división
premises ['prɛmɪsɪz] npl (of business
etc) local m; **on the ~** en el lugar mismo
premium ['pri:mɪəm] n premio;
(insurance) prima; **to be at a ~** ser muy
solicitado
premonition [prɛmə'nɪʃən] n
presentimiento
preoccupied [pri:'ɔkjupaɪd] adj
ensimismado
prepaid [pri:'peɪd] adj porte pagado
preparation [prɛpə'reɪʃən] n
preparación f; **preparations** npl
preparativos mpl
preparatory school [prɪ'pærətərɪ-]
n escuela preparatoria
prepare [prɪ'pɛə*] vt preparar,
disponer; (Culin) preparar ▷ vi: **to ~ for**
(action) prepararse or disponerse para;
(event) hacer preparativos para; **~d to**
dispuesto a; **~d for** listo para
preposition [prɛpə'zɪʃən] n
preposición f
prep school [prɛp-] n = **preparatory
school**
prerequisite [pri:'rɛkwɪzɪt] n
requisito
preschool ['pri:'sku:l] adj preescolar
prescribe [prɪ'skraɪb] vt (Med)
recetar
prescription [prɪ'skrɪpʃən] n (Med)
receta
presence ['prɛzns] n presencia; **in
sb's ~** en presencia de algn; **~ of mind**
aplomo
present [adj, n 'prɛznt, vb prɪ'zɛnt] adj
(in attendance) presente; (current) actual
▷ n (gift) regalo; (actuality): **the ~** la
actualidad, el presente ▷ vt (introduce,
describe) presentar; (expound) exponer;
(give) presentar, dar, ofrecer; (Theatre)

representar; **to give sb a ~** regalar algo a algn; **at ~** actualmente; **presentable** [prɪˈzɛntəbl] *adj*: **to make o.s. presentable** arreglarse; **presentation** [-ˈteɪʃən] *n* presentación *f*; (*of report etc*) exposición *f*; (*formal ceremony*) entrega de un regalo; **present-day** *adj* actual; **presenter** [prɪˈzɛntə*] *n* (*Radio, TV*) locutor(a) *m/f*; **presently** *adv* (*soon*) dentro de poco; (*now*) ahora; **present participle** *n* participio (de) presente

preservation [prɛzəˈveɪʃən] *n* conservación *f*

preservative [prɪˈzəːvətɪv] *n* conservante *m*

preserve [prɪˈzəːv] *vt* (*keep safe*) preservar, proteger; (*maintain*) mantener; (*food*) conservar ▷ *n* (*for game*) coto, vedado; (*often pl: jam*) conserva, confitura

preside [prɪˈzaɪd] *vi* presidir

president [ˈprɛzɪdənt] *n* presidente *m/f*; **presidential** [-ˈdɛnʃl] *adj* presidencial

press [prɛs] *n* (*newspapers*): **the P~** la prensa; (*printer's*) imprenta; (*of button*) pulsación *f* ▷ *vt* empujar; (*button etc*) apretar; (*clothes: iron*) planchar; (*put pressure on: person*) presionar; (*insist*): **to ~ sth on sb** insistir en que algn acepte algo ▷ *vi* (*squeeze*) apretar; (*pressurize*): **to ~ for** presionar por; **we are ~ed for time/money** estamos apurados de tiempo/dinero; **press conference** *n* rueda de prensa; **pressing** *adj* apremiante; **press stud** (*BRIT*) *n* botón *m* de presión; **press-up** (*BRIT*) *n* plancha

pressure [ˈprɛʃə*] *n* presión *f*; **to put ~ on sb** presionar a algn; **pressure cooker** *n* olla a presión; **pressure group** *n* grupo de presión

prestige [prɛsˈtiːʒ] *n* prestigio

prestigious [prɛsˈtɪdʒəs] *adj* prestigioso

presumably [prɪˈzjuːməblɪ] *adv* es de suponer que, cabe presumir que

presume [prɪˈzjuːm] *vt*: **to ~ (that)** presumir (que), suponer (que)

pretence [prɪˈtɛns] (*US* **pretense**) *n* fingimiento; **under false ~s** con engaños

pretend [prɪˈtɛnd] *vt, vi* (*feign*) fingir

▌Be careful not to translate **pretend** by the Spanish word *pretender*.

pretense [prɪˈtɛns] (*US*) *n* = **pretence**

pretentious [prɪˈtɛnʃəs] *adj* presumido; (*ostentatious*) ostentoso, aparatoso

pretext [ˈpriːtɛkst] *n* pretexto

pretty [ˈprɪtɪ] *adj* bonito, lindo (*LAM*) ▷ *adv* bastante

prevail [prɪˈveɪl] *vi* (*gain mastery*) prevalecer; (*be current*) predominar; **prevailing** *adj* (*dominant*) predominante

prevalent [ˈprɛvələnt] *adj* (*widespread*) extendido

prevent [prɪˈvɛnt] *vt*: **to ~ sb from doing sth** impedir a algn hacer algo; **to ~ sth from happening** evitar que ocurra algo; **prevention** [prɪˈvɛnʃən] *n* prevención *f*; **preventive** *adj* preventivo

preview [ˈpriːvjuː] *n* (*of film*) preestreno

previous [ˈpriːvɪəs] *adj* previo, anterior; **previously** *adv* antes

prey [preɪ] *n* presa ▷ *vi*: **to ~ on** (*feed on*) alimentarse de; **it was ~ing on his mind** le preocupaba, le obsesionaba

price [praɪs] *n* precio ▷ *vt* (*goods*) fijar el precio de; **priceless** *adj* que no tiene precio; **price list** *n* tarifa

prick [prɪk] *n* (*sting*) picadura ▷ *vt* pinchar; (*hurt*) picar; **to ~ up one's ears** aguzar el oído

prickly [ˈprɪklɪ] *adj* espinoso; (*fig: person*) enojadizo

pride [praɪd] *n* orgullo; (*pej*) soberbia ▷ *vt*: **to ~ o.s. on** enorgullecerse de

priest [priːst] *n* sacerdote *m*

primarily [ˈpraɪmərɪlɪ] *adv* ante todo

primary [ˈpraɪmərɪ] *adj* (*first in importance*) principal ▷ *n* (*US Pol*)

elección f primaria; **primary school**
(BRIT) n escuela primaria
prime [praɪm] adj primero, principal;
(excellent) selecto, de primera clase
▷ n: **in the ~ of life** en la flor de la vida
▷ vt (wood: fig) preparar; **~ example**
ejemplo típico; **Prime Minister** n
primer(a) ministro/a
primitive ['prɪmɪtɪv] adj primitivo;
(crude) rudimentario
primrose ['prɪmrəʊz] n primavera,
prímula
prince [prɪns] n príncipe m
princess [prɪn'sɛs] n princesa
principal ['prɪnsɪpl] adj principal,
mayor ▷ n director(a) m/f; **principally**
adv principalmente
principle ['prɪnsɪpl] n principio; **in ~**
en principio; **on ~** por principio
print [prɪnt] n (footprint) huella;
(fingerprint) huella dactilar; (letters)
letra de molde; (fabric) estampado;
(Art) grabado; (Phot) impresión
f ▷ vt imprimir; (cloth) estampar;
(write in capitals) escribir en letras de
molde; **out of ~** agotado; **print out** vt
(Comput) imprimir; **printer** n (person)
impresor(a) m/f; (machine) impresora;
printout n (Comput) impresión f
prior ['praɪə*] adj anterior, previo;
(more important) más importante; **~**
to antes de
priority [praɪ'ɔrɪtɪ] n prioridad f; **to**
have ~ (over) tener prioridad (sobre)
prison ['prɪzn] n cárcel f, prisión f
▷ cpd carcelario; **prisoner** n (in prison)
preso/a; (captured person) prisionero;
prisoner-of-war n prisionero de
guerra
pristine ['prɪstiːn] adj pristino
privacy ['prɪvəsɪ] n intimidad f
private ['praɪvɪt] adj (personal)
particular; (property, industry, discussion
etc) privado; (person) reservado; (place)
tranquilo ▷ n soldado raso; **"~"** (on
envelope) "confidencial"; (on door)
"prohibido el paso"; **in ~** en privado;
privately adv en privado; (in o.s.)

en secreto; **private property** n
propiedad f privada; **private school** n
colegio particular
privatize ['praɪvɪtaɪz] vt privatizar
privilege ['prɪvɪlɪdʒ] n privilegio;
(prerogative) prerrogativa
prize [praɪz] n premio ▷ adj de
primera clase ▷ vt apreciar, estimar;
prize-giving n distribución f de
premios; **prizewinner** n premiado/a
pro [prəʊ] n (Sport) profesional mf
▷ prep a favor de; **the ~s and cons** los
pros y los contras
probability [prɔbə'bɪlɪtɪ] n
probabilidad f; **in all ~** con toda
probabilidad
probable ['prɔbəbl] adj probable
probably ['prɔbəblɪ] adv
probablemente
probation [prə'beɪʃən] n: **on ~**
(employee) a prueba; (Law) en libertad
condicional
probe [prəʊb] n (Med, Space) sonda;
(enquiry) encuesta, investigación f ▷ vt
sondar; (investigate) investigar
problem ['prɔbləm] n problema m
procedure [prə'siːdʒə*] n
procedimiento; (bureaucratic) trámites
mpl
proceed [prə'siːd] vi (do
afterwards): **to ~ to do sth** proceder
a hacer algo; (continue): **to ~ (with)**
continuar or seguir (con); **proceedings**
npl acto(s) (pl); (Law) proceso;
proceeds ['prəʊsiːdz] npl (money)
ganancias fpl, ingresos mpl
process ['prəʊsɛs] n proceso ▷ vt
tratar, elaborar
procession [prə'sɛʃən] n desfile m;
funeral ~ cortejo fúnebre
proclaim [prə'kleɪm] vt (announce)
anunciar
prod [prɔd] vt empujar ▷ n empujón
m
produce [n 'prɔdjuːs, vt prə'djuːs]
n (Agr) productos mpl agrícolas ▷ vt
producir; (play, film, programme)
presentar; **producer** n productor(a)

m/f; (*of film, programme*) director(a) *m/f*; (*of record*) productor(a) *m/f*

product ['prɒdʌkt] *n* producto; **production** [prə'dʌkʃən] *n* producción *f*; (*Theatre*) presentación *f*; **productive** [prə'dʌktɪv] *adj* productivo; **productivity** [prɒdʌk'tɪvɪtɪ] *n* productividad *f*

Prof. [prɒf] *abbr* (= *professor*) Prof

profession [prə'fɛʃən] *n* profesión *f*; **professional** *adj* profesional ▷ *n* profesional *mf*; (*skilled person*) perito

professor [prə'fɛsə*] *n* (*BRIT*) catedrático/a; (*US, CANADA*) profesor(a) *m/f*

profile ['prəufaɪl] *n* perfil *m*

profit ['prɒfɪt] *n* (*Comm*) ganancia ▷ *vi*: **to ~ by** *or* **from** aprovechar *or* sacar provecho de; **profitable** *adj* (*Econ*) rentable

profound [prə'faund] *adj* profundo

programme ['prəugræm] (*us* **program**) *n* programa *m* ▷ *vt* programar; **programmer** (*us* **programer**) *n* programador(a) *m/f*; **programming** (*us* **programing**) *n* programación *f*

progress [*n* 'prəugrɛs, *vi* prə'grɛs] *n* progreso; (*development*) desarrollo ▷ *vi* progresar, avanzar; **in ~** en curso; **progressive** [-'grɛsɪv] *adj* progresivo; (*person*) progresista

prohibit [prə'hɪbɪt] *vt* prohibir; **to ~ sb from doing sth** prohibir a algn hacer algo

project [*n* 'prɒdʒɛkt, *vb* prə'dʒɛkt] *n* proyecto ▷ *vt* proyectar ▷ *vi* (*stick out*) salir, sobresalir; **projection** [prə'dʒɛkʃən] *n* proyección *f*; (*overhang*) saliente *m*; **projector** [prə'dʒɛktə*] *n* proyector *m*

prolific [prə'lɪfɪk] *adj* prolífico

prolong [prə'lɒŋ] *vt* prolongar, extender

prom [prɒm] *n abbr* = **promenade** (*us: ball*) baile *m* de gala; **the P~s** ver recuadro

promenade [prɒmə'nɑːd] *n* (*by sea*) paseo marítimo

prominent ['prɒmɪnənt] *adj* (*standing out*) saliente; (*important*) eminente, importante

promiscuous [prə'mɪskjuəs] *adj* (*sexually*) promiscuo

promise ['prɒmɪs] *n* promesa ▷ *vt*, *vi* prometer; **promising** *adj* prometedor(a)

promote [prə'məut] *vt* (*employee*) ascender; (*product, pop star*) hacer propaganda por; (*ideas*) fomentar; **promotion** [-'məuʃən] *n* (*advertising campaign*) campaña *f* de promoción; (*in rank*) ascenso

prompt [prɒmpt] *adj* rápido ▷ *adv*: **at 6 o'clock ~** a las seis en punto ▷ *n* (*Comput*) aviso ▷ *vt* (*urge*) mover, incitar; (*when talking*) instar; (*Theatre*) apuntar; **to ~ sb to do sth** instar a algn a hacer algo; **promptly** *adv* rápidamente; (*exactly*) puntualmente

prone [prəun] *adj* (*lying*) postrado; **~ to** propenso a

prong [prɒŋ] *n* diente *m*, punta

pronoun ['prəunaun] *n* pronombre

m

pronounce [prə'nauns] vt
pronunciar

pronunciation [prənʌnsɪ'eɪʃən] n
pronunciación f

proof [pru:f] n prueba ▷ adj: **~
against** a prueba de

prop [prɔp] n apoyo; (fig) sostén m
accesorios mpl, at(t)rezzo msg; **prop up**
vt (roof, structure) apuntalar; (economy)
respaldar

propaganda [prɔpə'gændə] n
propaganda

propeller [prə'pɛlə*] n hélice f

proper ['prɔpə*] adj (suited, right)
propio; (exact) justo; (seemly) correcto,
decente; (authentic) verdadero;
(referring to place): **the village ~**
el pueblo mismo; **properly** adv
(adequately) correctamente; (decently)
decentemente; **proper noun** n
nombre m propio

property ['prɔpətɪ] n propiedad f;
(personal) bienes mpl muebles

prophecy ['prɔfɪsɪ] n profecía

prophet ['prɔfɪt] n profeta m

proportion [prə'pɔ:ʃən] n
proporción f; (share) parte f;
proportions npl (size) dimensiones fpl;
proportional adj: **proportional (to)**
en proporción (con)

proposal [prə'pəuzl] n (offer of
marriage) oferta de matrimonio; (plan)
proyecto

propose [prə'pəuz] vt proponer ▷ vi
declararse; **to ~ to do** tener intención
de hacer

proposition [prɔpə'zɪʃən] n
propuesta

proprietor [prə'praɪətə*] n
propietario/a, dueño/a

prose [prəuz] n prosa

prosecute ['prɔsɪkju:t] vt (Law)
procesar; **prosecution** [-'kju:ʃən]
n proceso, causa; (accusing
side) acusación f; **prosecutor** n
acusador(a) m/f; (also: **public
prosecutor**) fiscal mf

prospect [n 'prɔspɛkt, vb
prə'spɛkt] n (possibility) posibilidad
f; (outlook) perspectiva ▷ vi: **to ~
for** buscar; **prospects** npl (for work
etc) perspectivas fpl; **prospective**
[prə'spɛktɪv] adj futuro

prospectus [prə'spɛktəs] n
prospecto

prosper ['prɔspə*] vi prosperar;
prosperity [-'spɛrɪtɪ] n prosperidad f;
prosperous adj próspero

prostitute ['prɔstɪtju:t] n
prostituta; (male) hombre que se dedica a
la prostitución

protect [prə'tɛkt] vt proteger;
protection [-'tɛkʃən] n protección f;
protective adj protector(a)

protein ['prəuti:n] n proteína

protest [n 'prəutɛst, vb prə'tɛst] n
protesta ▷ vi: **to ~ about** or **at/against**
protestar de/contra ▷ vt (insist): **to ~
(that)** insistir en (que)

Protestant ['prɔtɪstənt] adj, n
protestante mf

protester [prə'tɛstə*] n
manifestante mf

protractor [prə'træktə*] n (Geom)
transportador m

proud [praud] adj orgulloso; (pej)
soberbio, altanero

prove [pru:v] vt probar; (show)
demostrar ▷ vi: **to ~ (to be) correct**
resultar correcto; **to ~ o.s.** probar
su valía

proverb ['prɔvə:b] n refrán m

provide [prə'vaɪd] vt proporcionar,
dar; **to ~ sb with sth** proveer a algn
de algo; **provide for** vt fus (person)
mantener a; (problem etc) tener en
cuenta; **provided** conj: **provided
(that)** con tal de que, a condición
de que; **providing** [prə'vaɪdɪŋ]
conj: **providing (that)** a condición de
que, con tal de que

province ['prɔvɪns] n provincia; (fig)
esfera; **provincial** [prə'vɪnʃəl] adj
provincial; (pej) provinciano

provision [prə'vɪʒən] n (supplying)

suministro, abastecimiento; (of
contract etc) disposición f; **provisions**
npl (food) comestibles mpl; **provisional**
adj provisional

provocative [prə'vɒkətɪv] adj
provocativo

provoke [prə'vəuk] vt (cause)
provocar, incitar; (anger) enojar

prowl [praul] vi (also: **~ about, ~
around**) merodear ▷ n: **on the ~** de
merodeo

proximity [prɒk'sɪmɪtɪ] n
proximidad f

proxy ['prɒksɪ] n: **by ~** por poderes

prudent ['pru:dənt] adj prudente

prune [pru:n] n ciruela pasa ▷ vt
podar

pry [praɪ] vi: **to ~ (into)** entrometerse
(en)

PS n abbr (= postscript) P.D.

pseudonym ['sju:dəunɪm] n
seudónimo

PSHE (BRIT: Scol) n abbr (= personal,
social and health education) formación
social y sanitaria

psychiatric [saɪkɪ'ætrɪk] adj
psiquiátrico

psychiatrist [saɪ'kaɪətrɪst] n
psiquiatra mf

psychic ['saɪkɪk] adj (also: **~al**)
psíquico

psychoanalysis [saɪkəuə'nælɪsɪs] n
psicoanálisis m inv

psychological [saɪkə'lɒdʒɪkl] adj
psicológico

psychologist [saɪ'kɒlədʒɪst] n
psicólogo/a

psychology [saɪ'kɒlədʒɪ] n
psicología

psychotherapy [saɪkəu'θerəpɪ] n
psicoterapia

pt abbr = **pint(s); point(s)**

PTO abbr (= please turn over) sigue

pub [pʌb] n abbr (= public house) pub
m, bar m

puberty ['pju:bətɪ] n pubertad f

public ['pʌblɪk] adj público ▷ n: **the ~**
el público; **in ~** en público; **to make ~**

hacer público

publication [pʌblɪ'keɪʃən] n
publicación f

public: public company n sociedad
f anónima; **public convenience** (BRIT)
n aseos mpl públicos (SP), sanitarios
mpl (LAM); **public holiday** n (día m de)
fiesta (SP), (día m) feriado (LAM); **public
house** (BRIT) n bar m, pub m

publicity [pʌb'lɪsɪtɪ] n publicidad f

publicize ['pʌblɪsaɪz] vt publicitar

public: public limited company n
sociedad f anónima (S.A.); **publicly**
adv públicamente, en público;
public opinion n opinión f pública;
public relations n relaciones fpl
públicas; **public school** n (BRIT)
escuela privada; (US) instituto; **public
transport** n transporte m público

publish ['pʌblɪʃ] vt publicar;
publisher n (person) editor(a)
m/f; (firm) editorial f; **publishing** n
(industry) industria del libro

pub lunch n almuerzo que se sirve en
un pub; **to go for a ~** almorzar o comer
en un pub

pudding ['pudɪŋ] n pudín m;
(BRIT: dessert) postre m; **black ~** morcilla

puddle ['pʌdl] n charco

Puerto Rico [pwɛ:təu'ri:kəu] n
Puerto Rico

puff [pʌf] n soplo; (of smoke, air)
bocanada; (of breathing) resoplido
▷ vt: **to ~ one's pipe** chupar la pipa ▷ vi
(pant) jadear; **puff pastry** n hojaldre m

pull [pul] n (tug): **to give sth a ~**
dar un tirón a algo ▷ vt tirar de;
(press: trigger) apretar; (haul) tirar,
arrastrar; (close: curtain) echar ▷ vi
tirar; **to ~ to pieces** hacer pedazos;
not to ~ one's punches no andarse
con bromas; **to ~ one's weight**
hacer su parte; **to ~ o.s. together**
sobreponerse; **to ~ sb's leg** tomar
el pelo a algn; **pull apart** vt (break)
romper; **pull away** vi (vehicle: move off)
salir, arrancar; (draw back) apartarse
bruscamente; **pull back** vt (lever etc)

tirar hacia sí; (*curtains*) descorrer ▷ *vi* (*refrain*) contenerse; (*Mil: withdraw*) retirarse; **pull down** *vt* (*building*) derribar; **pull in** *vi* (*car etc*) parar (junto a la acera); (*train*) llegar a la estación; **pull off** *vt* (*deal etc*) cerrar; **pull out** *vi* (*car, train etc*) salir ▷ *vt* sacar, arrancar; **pull over** *vi* (*Aut*) hacerse a un lado; **pull up** *vi* (*stop*) parar ▷ *vt* (*raise*) levantar; (*uproot*) arrancar, desarraigar

pulley ['pulɪ] *n* polea

pullover ['puləuvə*] *n* jersey *m*, suéter *m*

pulp [pʌlp] *n* (*of fruit*) pulpa

pulpit ['pulpɪt] *n* púlpito

pulse [pʌls] *n* (*Anat*) pulso; (*rhythm*) pulsación *f*; (*Bot*) legumbre *f*; **pulses** *pl n* legumbres

puma ['pju:mə] *n* puma *m*

pump [pʌmp] *n* bomba; (*shoe*) zapatilla ▷ *vt* sacar con una bomba; **pump up** *vt* inflar

pumpkin ['pʌmpkɪn] *n* calabaza

pun [pʌn] *n* juego de palabras

punch [pʌntʃ] *n* (*blow*) golpe *m*, puñetazo; (*tool*) punzón *m*; (*drink*) ponche *m* ▷ *vt* (*hit*): **to ~ sb/sth** dar un puñetazo *or* golpear a algn/algo; **punch-up** (*BRIT: inf*) *n* riña

punctual ['pʌŋktjuəl] *adj* puntual

punctuation [pʌŋktjuˈeɪʃən] *n* puntuación *f*

puncture ['pʌŋktʃə*] (*BRIT*) *n* pinchazo ▷ *vt* pinchar

punish ['pʌnɪʃ] *vt* castigar; **punishment** *n* castigo

punk [pʌŋk] *n* (*also:* **~ rocker**) punki *mf*; (*also:* **~ rock**) música punk; (*US: inf: hoodlum*) rufián *m*

pup [pʌp] *n* cachorro

pupil ['pju:pl] *n* alumno/a; (*of eye*) pupila

puppet ['pʌpɪt] *n* títere *m*

puppy ['pʌpɪ] *n* cachorro, perrito

purchase ['pə:tʃɪs] *n* compra ▷ *vt* comprar

pure [pjuə*] *adj* puro; **purely** *adv* puramente

purify ['pjuərɪfaɪ] *vt* purificar, depurar

purity ['pjuərɪtɪ] *n* pureza

purple ['pə:pl] *adj* purpúreo; morado

purpose ['pə:pəs] *n* propósito; **on ~** a propósito, adrede

purr [pə:*] *vi* ronronear

purse [pə:s] *n* monedero; (*US: handbag*) bolso (*SP*), cartera (*LAM*), bolsa (*MEX*) ▷ *vt* fruncir

pursue [pəˈsju:] *vt* seguir

pursuit [pəˈsju:t] *n* (*chase*) caza; (*occupation*) actividad *f*

pus [pʌs] *n* pus *m*

push [puʃ] *n* empuje *m*, empujón *m*; (*of button*) presión *f*; (*drive*) empuje *m* ▷ *vt* empujar; (*button*) apretar; (*promote*) promover ▷ *vi* empujar; (*demand*): **to ~ for** luchar por; **push in** *vi* colarse; **push off** (*inf*) *vi* largarse; **push on** *vi* seguir adelante; **push over** *vt* (*cause to fall*) hacer caer, derribar; (*knock over*) volcar; **push through** *vi* (*crowd*) abrirse paso a empujones ▷ *vt* (*measure*) despachar; **pushchair** (*BRIT*) *n* sillita de ruedas; **pusher** *n* (*drug pusher*) traficante *mf* de drogas; **push-up** (*US*) *n* plancha

pussy(-cat) ['pusɪ-] (*inf*) *n* minino (*inf*)

put [put] (*pt, pp* **~**) *vt* (*place*) poner, colocar; (*put into*) meter; (*say*) expresar; (*a question*) hacer; (*estimate*) estimar; **put aside** *vt* (*lay down: book etc*) dejar *or* poner a un lado; (*save*) ahorrar; (*in shop*) guardar; **put away** *vt* (*store*) guardar; **put back** *vt* (*replace*) devolver a su lugar; (*postpone*) aplazar; **put by** *vt* (*money*) guardar; **put down** *vt* (*on ground*) poner en el suelo; (*animal*) sacrificar; (*in writing*) apuntar; (*revolt etc*) sofocar; (*attribute*): **to put sth down to** atribuir algo a; **put forward** *vt* (*ideas*) presentar, proponer; **put in** *vt* (*complaint*) presentar; (*time*) dedicar; **put off** *vt* (*postpone*) aplazar; (*discourage*) desanimar; **put on** *vt*

ponerse; (*light etc*) encender; (*play etc*)
presentar; (*gain*): **to put on weight**
engordar; (*brake*) echar; (*record, kettle
etc*) poner; (*assume*) adoptar; **put out**
vt (*fire, light*) apagar; (*rubbish etc*) sacar;
(*cat etc*) echar; (*one's hand*) alargar;
(*inf: person*): **to be put out** alterarse;
put through *vt* (*Tel*) poner; (*plan etc*)
hacer aprobar; **put together** *vt* unir,
reunir; (*assemble: furniture*) armar,
montar; (*meal*) preparar; **put up** *vt*
(*raise*) levantar, alzar; (*hang*) colgar;
(*build*) construir; (*increase*) aumentar;
(*accommodate*) alojar; **put up with** *vt
fus* aguantar

putt [pʌt] *n* putt *m*, golpe *m* corto;
putting green *n* green *m*; minigolf *m*
puzzle [ˈpʌzl] *n* rompecabezas *m
inv*; (*also:* **crossword ~**) crucigrama
m; (*mystery*) misterio ▷ *vt* dejar
perplejo, confundir ▷ *vi*: **to ~ over sth**
devanarse los sesos con algo; **puzzled**
adj perplejo; **puzzling** *adj* misterioso,
extraño
pyjamas [pɪˈdʒɑːməz] (*BRIT*) *npl*
pijama *m*
pylon [ˈpaɪlən] *n* torre *f* de
conducción eléctrica
pyramid [ˈpɪrəmɪd] *n* pirámide *f*

q

quack [kwæk] *n* graznido; (*pej: doctor*)
curandero/a
quadruple [kwɔˈdruːpl] *vt, vi*
cuadruplicar
quail [kweɪl] *n* codorniz *f* ▷ *vi*: **to ~ at**
or **before** amedrentarse ante
quaint [kweɪnt] *adj* extraño;
(*picturesque*) pintoresco
quake [kweɪk] *vi* temblar ▷ *n abbr* =
earthquake
qualification [kwɔlɪfɪˈkeɪʃən] *n*
(*ability*) capacidad *f*; (*often pl: diploma
etc*) título; (*reservation*) salvedad *f*
qualified [ˈkwɔlɪfaɪd] *adj*
capacitado; (*professionally*) titulado;
(*limited*) limitado
qualify [ˈkwɔlɪfaɪ] *vt* (*make competent*)
capacitar; (*modify*) modificar ▷ *vi* (*in
competition*): **to ~ (for)** calificarse
(para); (*pass examination(s)*: **to ~ (as)**
calificarse (de), graduarse (en); (*be
eligible*): **to ~ (for)** reunir los requisitos
(para)
quality [ˈkwɔlɪtɪ] *n* calidad *f*; (*of
person*) cualidad *f*

qualm [kwɑːm] n escrúpulo
quantify ['kwɒntɪfaɪ] vt cuantificar
quantity ['kwɒntɪtɪ] n cantidad f; **in ~** en grandes cantidades
quarantine ['kwɒrntiːn] n cuarentena
quarrel ['kwɒrl] n riña, pelea ▷ vi reñir, pelearse
quarry ['kwɒrɪ] n cantera
quart [kwɔːt] n ≈ litro
quarter ['kwɔːtə*] n cuarto, cuarta parte f; (us: coin) moneda de 25 centavos; (of year) trimestre m; (district) barrio ▷ vt dividir en cuartos; (Mil: lodge) alojar; **quarters** npl (barracks) cuartel m; (living quarters) alojamiento; **a ~ of an hour** un cuarto de hora; **quarter final** n cuarto de final; **quarterly** adj trimestral ▷ adv cada 3 meses, trimestralmente
quartet(te) [kwɔː'tɛt] n cuarteto
quartz [kwɔːts] n cuarzo
quay [kiː] n (also: **~side**) muelle m
queasy ['kwiːzɪ] adj: **to feel ~** tener náuseas
queen [kwiːn] n reina; (Cards etc) dama
queer [kwɪə*] adj raro, extraño ▷ n (inf: highly offensive) maricón m
quench [kwɛntʃ] vt: **to ~ one's thirst** apagar la sed
query ['kwɪərɪ] n (question) pregunta ▷ vt dudar de
quest [kwɛst] n busca, búsqueda
question ['kwɛstʃən] n pregunta; (doubt) duda; (matter) asunto, cuestión f ▷ vt (doubt) dudar de; (interrogate) interrogar, hacer preguntas a; **beyond ~** fuera de toda duda; **out of the ~** imposible; ni hablar; **questionable** adj dudoso; **question mark** n punto de interrogación; **questionnaire** [-'nɛə*] n cuestionario
queue [kjuː] (BRIT) n cola ▷ vi (also: **~ up**) hacer cola
quiche [kiːʃ] n quiche m
quick [kwɪk] adj rápido; (agile) ágil; (mind) listo ▷ n: **cut to the ~** (fig) herido

en lo vivo; **be ~!** ¡date prisa!; **quickly** adv rápidamente, de prisa
quid [kwɪd] (BRIT: inf) n inv libra
quiet ['kwaɪət] adj (voice, music etc) bajo; (person, place) tranquilo; (ceremony) íntimo ▷ n silencio; (calm) tranquilidad f ▷ vt, vi (us) = **quieten**

> ▌ Be careful not to translate **quiet** by the Spanish word quieto.

quietly adv tranquilamente; (silently) silenciosamente
quilt [kwɪlt] n edredón m
quirky ['kwɜːkɪ] adj raro, estrafalario
quit [kwɪt] (pt, pp ~ or **~ted**) vt dejar, abandonar; (premises) desocupar ▷ vi (give up) renunciar; (resign) dimitir
quite [kwaɪt] adv (rather) bastante; (entirely) completamente; **that's not ~ big enough** no acaba de ser lo bastante grande; **~ a few of them** un buen número de ellos; **~ (so)!** ¡así es!, ¡exactamente!
quits [kwɪts] adj: **~ (with)** en paz (con); **let's call it ~** dejémoslo en tablas
quiver ['kwɪvə*] vi estremecerse
quiz [kwɪz] n concurso ▷ vt interrogar
quota ['kwəutə] n cuota
quotation [kwəu'teɪʃən] n cita; (estimate) presupuesto; **quotation marks** npl comillas fpl
quote [kwəut] n cita; (estimate) presupuesto ▷ vt citar; (price) cotizar ▷ vi: **to ~ from** citar de; **quotes** npl (inverted commas) comillas fpl

r

rabbi ['ræbaɪ] n rabino
rabbit ['ræbɪt] n conejo
rabies ['reɪbiːz] n rabia
RAC (BRIT) n abbr (= Royal Automobile Club) ≈ RACE m
rac(c)oon [rə'kuːn] n mapache m
race [reɪs] n carrera; (species) raza ▷ vt (horse) hacer correr; (engine) acelerar ▷ vi (compete) competir; (run) correr; (pulse) latir a ritmo acelerado; **race car** (US) n = **racing car**; **racecourse** n hipódromo; **racehorse** n caballo de carreras; **racetrack** n pista; (for cars) autódromo
racial ['reɪʃl] adj racial
racing ['reɪsɪŋ] n carreras fpl; **racing car** (BRIT) n coche m de carreras; **racing driver** (BRIT) n piloto mf de carreras
racism ['reɪsɪzəm] n racismo; **racist** [-sɪst] adj, n racista mf
rack [ræk] n (also: **luggage ~**) rejilla; (shelf) estante m; (also: **roof ~**) baca, portaequipajes m inv; (dish rack) escurreplatos m inv; (clothes rack) percha ▷ vt atormentar; **to ~ one's brains** devanarse los sesos
racket ['rækɪt] n (for tennis) raqueta; (noise) ruido, estrépito; (swindle) estafa, timo
racquet ['rækɪt] n raqueta
radar ['reɪdɑː*] n radar m
radiation [reɪdɪ'eɪʃən] n radiación f
radiator ['reɪdɪeɪtə*] n radiador m
radical ['rædɪkl] adj radical
radio ['reɪdɪəu] n radio f; **on the ~** por radio; **radioactive** adj radioactivo; **radio station** n emisora
radish ['rædɪʃ] n rábano
RAF n abbr (= Royal Air Force) las Fuerzas Aéreas Británicas
raffle ['ræfl] n rifa, sorteo
raft [rɑːft] n balsa; (also: **life ~**) balsa salvavidas
rag [ræg] n (piece of cloth) trapo; (torn cloth) harapo; (pej: newspaper) periodicucho; (for charity) actividades estudiantiles benéficas; **rags** npl (torn clothes) harapos mpl
rage [reɪdʒ] n rabia, furor m ▷ vi (person) rabiar, estar furioso; (storm) bramar; **it's all the ~** (very fashionable) está muy de moda
ragged ['rægɪd] adj (edge) desigual, mellado; (appearance) andrajoso, harapiento
raid [reɪd] n (Mil) incursión f; (criminal) asalto; (by police) redada ▷ vt invadir, atacar; asaltar
rail [reɪl] n (on stair) barandilla, pasamanos m inv; (on bridge, balcony) pretil m; (of ship) barandilla; (also: **towel ~**) toallero; **railcard** n (BRIT) tarjeta para obtener descuentos en el tren; **railing(s)** n(pl) vallado; **railroad** (US) n = **railway**; **railway** (BRIT) n ferrocarril m, vía férrea; **railway line** (BRIT) n línea (de ferrocarril); **railway station** (BRIT) n estación f de ferrocarril
rain [reɪn] n lluvia ▷ vi llover; **in the ~** bajo la lluvia; **it's ~ing** llueve, está lloviendo; **rainbow** n arco iris;

raincoat n impermeable m; **raindrop**
n gota de lluvia; **rainfall** n lluvia;
rainforest n selvas fpl tropicales;
rainy adj lluvioso

raise [reɪz] n aumento ▷ vt levantar;
(increase) aumentar; (improve: morale)
subir; (: standards) mejorar; (doubts)
suscitar; (a question) plantear; (cattle,
family) criar; (crop) cultivar; (army)
reclutar; (loan) obtener; **to ~ one's
voice** alzar la voz

raisin ['reɪzn] n pasa de Corinto

rake [reɪk] n (tool) rastrillo; (person)
libertino ▷ vt (garden) rastrillar

rally ['rælɪ] n (Pol etc) reunión f, mitin
m; (Aut) rallye m; (Tennis) peloteo ▷ vt
reunir ▷ vi recuperarse

RAM [ræm] n abbr (= random access
memory) RAM f

ram [ræm] n carnero; (also: **battering
~**) ariete m ▷ vt (crash into) dar contra,
chocar con; (push: fist etc) empujar
con fuerza

Ramadan [ræmə'dæn] n ramadán m

ramble ['ræmbl] n caminata,
excursión f en el campo ▷ vi (pej: also: ~
on) divagar; **rambler** n excursionista
mf; (Bot) trepadora; **rambling** adj
(speech) inconexo; (house) laberíntico;
(Bot) trepador(a)

ramp [ræmp] n rampa; **on/off ~** (US
Aut) vía de acceso/salida

rampage [ræm'peɪdʒ] n: **to be
on the ~** desmandarse ▷ vi: **they
went rampaging through the
town** recorrieron la ciudad armando
alboroto

ran [ræn] pt of **run**

ranch [rɑːntʃ] n hacienda, estancia

random ['rændəm] adj fortuito, sin
orden; (Comput, Math) aleatorio ▷ n: **at
~** al azar

rang [ræŋ] pt of **ring**

range [reɪndʒ] n (of mountains)
cadena de montañas, cordillera; (of
missile) alcance m; (of voice) registro;
(series) serie f; (of products) surtido;
(Mil: also: **shooting ~**) campo de tiro;

(also: **kitchen ~**) fogón m ▷ vt (place)
colocar; (arrange) arreglar ▷ vi: **to ~
over** (extend) extenderse por; **to ~ from
... to ...** oscilar entre ... y ...

ranger [reɪndʒə*] n guardabosques
mf inv

rank [ræŋk] n (row) fila; (Mil) rango;
(status) categoría; (BRIT: also: **taxi
~**) parada de taxis ▷ vi: **to ~ among**
figurar entre ▷ adj fétido, rancio; **the ~
and file** (fig) la base

ransom ['rænsəm] n rescate m; **to
hold to ~** (fig) hacer chantaje a

rant [rænt] vi divagar, desvariar

rap [ræp] vt golpear, dar un golpecito
en ▷ n (music) ráp m

rape [reɪp] n violación f; (Bot) colza
▷ vt violar

rapid ['ræpɪd] adj rápido; **rapidly**
adv rápidamente; **rapids** npl (Geo)
rápidos mpl

rapist ['reɪpɪst] n violador m

rapport [ræ'pɔː*] n simpatía

rare [reə*] adj raro, poco común;
(Culin: steak) poco hecho; **rarely** adv
pocas veces

rash [ræʃ] adj imprudente,
precipitado ▷ n (Med) sarpullido,
erupción f (cutánea); (of events) serie f

rasher ['ræʃə*] n lonja

raspberry ['rɑːzbərɪ] n frambuesa

rat [ræt] n rata

rate [reɪt] n (ratio) razón f; (price)
precio; (: of hotel etc) tarifa; (of interest)
tipo; (speed) velocidad f ▷ vt (value)
tasar; (estimate) estimar; **rates** npl
(BRIT: property tax) impuesto municipal;
(fees) tarifa; **to ~ sth/sb as** considerar
algo/a algn como

rather ['rɑːðə*] adv: **it's ~ expensive**
es algo caro; (too much) es demasiado
caro; (to some extent) más bien; **there's
~ a lot** hay bastante; **I would** or **I'd ~ go**
preferiría ir; **or ~** mejor dicho

rating ['reɪtɪŋ] n tasación f; (score)
índice m; (of ship) clase f; **ratings** npl
(Radio, TV) niveles mpl de audiencia

ratio ['reɪʃɪəu] n razón f; **in the ~ of**

100 to 1 a razón de 100 a 1

ration ['ræʃən] n ración f ⊳ vt racionar; **rations** npl víveres mpl

rational ['ræʃənl] adj (solution, reasoning) lógico, razonable; (person) cuerdo, sensato

rattle ['rætl] n golpeteo; (of train etc) traqueteo; (for baby) sonaja, sonajero ⊳ vi castañetear; (car, bus): **to ~ along** traquetear ⊳ vt hacer sonar agitando

rave [reɪv] vi (in anger) encolerizarse; (with enthusiasm) entusiasmarse; (Med) delirar, desvariar ⊳ n (inf: party) rave m

raven ['reɪvən] n cuervo

ravine [rə'viːn] n barranco

raw [rɔː] adj crudo; (not processed) bruto; (sore) vivo; (inexperienced) novato, inexperto; **~ materials** materias primas

ray [reɪ] n rayo; **~ of hope** (rayo de) esperanza

razor ['reɪzə*] n (open) navaja; (safety razor) máquina de afeitar; (electric razor) máquina (eléctrica) de afeitar; **razor blade** n hoja de afeitar

Rd abbr = **road**

RE n abbr (BRIT) = **religious education**

re [riː] prep con referencia a

reach [riːtʃ] n alcance m; (of river etc) extensión f entre dos recodos ⊳ vt alcanzar, llegar a; (achieve) lograr ⊳ vi extenderse; **within ~** al alcance (de la mano); **out of ~** fuera del alcance; **reach out** vt (hand) tender ⊳ vi: **to reach out for sth** alargar or tender la mano para tomar algo

react [riː'ækt] vi reaccionar; **reaction** [-'ækʃən] n reacción f; **reactor** [riː'æktə*] n (also: **nuclear reactor**) reactor m (nuclear)

read [riːd, pt, pp red] (pt, pp **~**) vi leer ⊳ vt leer; (understand) entender; (study) estudiar; **read out** vt leer en alta voz; **reader** n lector(a) m/f; (BRIT: at university) profesor(a) m/f adjunto/a

readily ['redɪlɪ] adv (willingly) de buena gana; (easily) fácilmente; (quickly) en seguida

reading ['riːdɪŋ] n lectura; (on instrument) indicación f

ready ['redɪ] adj listo, preparado; (willing) dispuesto; (available) disponible ⊳ adv: **~-cooked** listo para comer ⊳ n: **at the ~** (Mil) listo para tirar ⊳ **to get ~** vi prepararse ⊳ **to get ~** vt preparar; **ready-made** adj confeccionado

real [rɪəl] adj verdadero, auténtico; **in ~ terms** en términos reales; **real ale** n cerveza elaborada tradicionalmente; **real estate** n bienes mpl raíces; **realistic** [-'lɪstɪk] adj realista; **reality** [riː'ælɪtɪ] n realidad f; **reality TV** n telerrealidad f

realization [rɪəlaɪ'zeɪʃən] n comprensión f; (fulfilment, Comm) realización f

realize ['rɪəlaɪz] vt (understand) darse cuenta de

really ['rɪəlɪ] adv realmente; (for emphasis) verdaderamente; (actually): **what ~ happened** lo que pasó en realidad; **~?** ¿de veras?; **~!** (annoyance) ¡vamos!, ¡por favor!

realm [relm] n reino; (fig) esfera

realtor ['rɪəltɔː*] (US) n agente mf inmobiliario/a

reappear [riːə'pɪə*] vi reaparecer

rear [rɪə*] adj trasero ⊳ n parte f trasera ⊳ vt (cattle, family) criar ⊳ vi (also: **~ up**: animal) encabritarse

rearrange [riːə'reɪndʒ*] vt ordenar or arreglar de nuevo

rear: **rear-view mirror** n (Aut) (espejo) retrovisor m; **rear-wheel drive** n tracción f trasera

reason ['riːzn] n razón f ⊳ vi: **to ~ with sb** tratar de que algn entre en razón; **it stands to ~ that ...** es lógico que ...; **reasonable** adj razonable; (sensible) sensato; **reasonably** adv razonablemente; **reasoning** n razonamiento, argumentos mpl

reassurance [riːə'ʃuərəns] n consuelo

reassure [riːə'ʃuə*] vt tranquilizar,

alentar; **to ~ sb that ...** tranquilizar a algn asegurando que ...

rebate ['ri:beɪt] n (on tax etc) desgravación f

rebel [n 'rɛbl, vi rɪ'bɛl] n rebelde mf ▷ vi rebelarse, sublevarse; **rebellion** [rɪ'bɛljən] n rebelión f, sublevación f; **rebellious** [rɪ'bɛljəs] adj rebelde; (child) revoltoso

rebuild [ri:'bɪld] vt reconstruir

recall [vb rɪ'kɔ:l, n 'ri:kɔl] vt (remember) recordar; (ambassador etc) retirar ▷ n recuerdo; retirada

rec'd abbr (= received) rbdo

receipt [rɪ'si:t] n (document) recibo; (for parcel etc) acuse m de recibo; (act of receiving) recepción f; **receipts** npl (Comm) ingresos mpl

Be careful not to translate **receipt** by the Spanish word receta.

receive [rɪ'si:v] vt recibir; (guest) acoger; (wound) sufrir; **receiver** n (Tel) auricular m; (Radio) receptor m; (of stolen goods) perista mf; (Comm) administrador m jurídico

recent ['ri:snt] adj reciente; **recently** adv recientemente; **recently arrived** recién llegado

reception [rɪ'sɛpʃən] n recepción f; (welcome) acogida; **reception desk** n recepción f; **receptionist** n recepcionista mf

recession [rɪ'sɛʃən] n recesión f

recharge [ri:'tʃɑ:dʒ] vt (battery) recargar

recipe ['rɛsɪpɪ] n receta; (for disaster, success) fórmula

recipient [rɪ'sɪpɪənt] n recibidor(a) m/f; (of letter) destinatario/a

recital [rɪ'saɪtl] n recital m

recite [rɪ'saɪt] vt (poem) recitar

reckless ['rɛkləs] adj temerario, imprudente; (driving, driver) peligroso

reckon ['rɛkən] vt calcular; (consider) considerar; (think): **I ~ that ...** me parece que ...

reclaim [rɪ'kleɪm] vt (land, waste) recuperar; (land: from sea) rescatar;

(demand back) reclamar

recline [rɪ'klaɪn] vi reclinarse

recognition [rɛkəg'nɪʃən] n reconocimiento; **transformed beyond ~** irreconocible

recognize ['rɛkəgnaɪz] vt: **to ~ (by/as)** reconocer (por/como)

recollection [rɛkə'lɛkʃən] n recuerdo

recommend [rɛkə'mɛnd] vt recomendar; **recommendation** [rɛkə mɛn'deɪʃən] n recomendación f

reconcile ['rɛkənsaɪl] vt (two people) reconciliar; (two facts) compaginar; **to ~ o.s. to sth** conformarse a algo

reconsider [ri:kən'sɪdə*] vt repensar

reconstruct [ri:kən'strʌkt] vt reconstruir

record [n, adj 'rɛkɔ:d, vt rɪ'kɔ:d] n (Mus) disco; (of meeting etc) acta; (register) registro, partida; (file) archivo; (also: **criminal ~**) antecedentes mpl; (written) expediente m; (Sport, Comput) récord m ▷ adj récord, sin precedentes ▷ vt registrar; (Mus: song etc) grabar; **in ~ time** en un tiempo récord; **off the ~** adj no oficial ▷ adv confidencialmente; **recorded delivery** (BRIT) n (Post) entrega con acuse de recibo; **recorder** n (Mus) flauta de pico; **recording** n (Mus) grabación f; **record player** n tocadiscos m inv

recount [rɪ'kaunt] vt contar

recover [rɪ'kʌvə*] vt recuperar ▷ vi (from illness, shock) recuperarse; **recovery** n recuperación f

recreate [ri:krɪ'eɪt] vt recrear

recreation [rɛkrɪ'eɪʃən] n recreo; **recreational vehicle** (US) n caravan or rulota pequeña; **recreational drug** droga recreativa

recruit [rɪ'kru:t] n recluta mf ▷ vt reclutar; (staff) contratar; **recruitment** n reclutamiento

rectangle ['rɛktæŋgl] n rectángulo; **rectangular** [-'tæŋgjulə*] adj rectangular

rectify ['rɛktɪfaɪ] vt rectificar

rector ['rɛktə*] n (Rel) párroco
recur [rɪ'kə:*] vi repetirse; (pain, illness) producirse de nuevo; **recurring** adj (problem) repetido, constante
recyclable [ri:'saɪkləbl] adj reciclable
recycle [ri:'saɪkl] vt reciclar
recycling [ri:'saɪklɪŋ] n reciclaje
red [rɛd] n rojo ▷adj rojo; (hair) pelirrojo; (wine) tinto; **to be in the ~** (account) estar en números rojos; (business) tener un saldo negativo; **to give sb the ~ carpet treatment** recibir a algn con todos los honores; **Red Cross** n Cruz f Roja; **redcurrant** n grosella roja
redeem [rɪ'di:m] vt redimir; (promises) cumplir; (sth in pawn) desempeñar; (fig, also Rel) rescatar
red: red-haired adj pelirrojo; **redhead** n pelirrojo/a; **red-hot** adj candente; **red light** n: **to go through a red light** (Aut) pasar la luz roja; **red-light district** n barrio chino
red meat n carne f roja
reduce [rɪ'dju:s] vt reducir; **to ~ sb to tears** hacer llorar a algn; **"~ speed now"** (Aut) "reduzca la velocidad"; **reduced** adj (decreased) reducido, rebajado; **at a reduced price** con rebaja or descuento; **"greatly reduced prices"** "grandes rebajas"; **reduction** [rɪ'dʌkʃən] n reducción f; (of price) rebaja; (discount) descuento; (smaller-scale copy) copia reducida
redundancy [rɪ'dʌndənsɪ] n (dismissal) despido; (unemployment) desempleo
redundant [rɪ'dʌndnt] adj (BRIT: worker) parado, sin trabajo; (detail, object) superfluo; **to be made ~** quedar(se) sin trabajo
reed [ri:d] n (Bot) junco, caña; (Mus) lengüeta
reef [ri:f] n (at sea) arrecife m
reel [ri:l] n carrete m, bobina; (of film) rollo; (dance) baile escocés ▷vt (also: ~ up) devanar; (also: ~ in) sacar ▷vi

(sway) tambalear(se)
ref [rɛf] (inf) n abbr = **referee**
refectory [rɪ'fɛktərɪ] n comedor m
refer [rɪ'fə:*] vt (send: patient) referir; (: matter) remitir ▷vi: **to ~ to** (allude to) referirse a, aludir a; (apply to) relacionarse con; (consult) consultar
referee [rɛfə'ri:] n árbitro; (BRIT: for job application): **to be a ~ for sb** proporcionar referencias a algn ▷vt (match) arbitrar en
reference ['rɛfrəns] n referencia; (for job application: letter) carta de recomendación; **with ~ to** (Comm: in letter) me remito a; **reference number** n número de referencia
refill [vt ri:'fɪl, n 'ri:fɪl] vt rellenar ▷n repuesto, recambio
refine [rɪ'faɪn] vt refinar; **refined** adj (person) fino; **refinery** n refinería
reflect [rɪ'flɛkt] vt reflejar ▷vi (think) reflexionar, pensar; **it ~s badly/well on him** le perjudica/le hace honor; **reflection** [-'flɛkʃən] n (act) reflexión f; (image) reflejo; (criticism) crítica; **on reflection** pensándolo bien
reflex ['ri:flɛks] adj, n reflejo
reform [rɪ'fɔ:m] n reforma ▷vt reformar
refrain [rɪ'freɪn] vi: **to ~ from doing** abstenerse de hacer ▷n estribillo
refresh [rɪ'frɛʃ] vt refrescar; **refreshing** adj refrescante; **refreshments** npl refrescos mpl
refrigerator [rɪ'frɪdʒəreɪtə*] n frigorífico (SP), nevera (SP), refrigerador m (LAM), heladera (RPL)
refuel [ri:'fjuəl] vi repostar (combustible)
refuge ['rɛfju:dʒ] n refugio, asilo; **to take ~ in** refugiarse en; **refugee** [rɛfju'dʒi:] n refugiado/a
refund [n 'ri:fʌnd, vb rɪ'fʌnd] n reembolso ▷vt devolver, reembolsar
refurbish [ri:'fə:bɪʃ] vt restaurar, renovar
refusal [rɪ'fju:zəl] n negativa; **to have first ~ on** tener la primera

opción a

refuse¹ ['rɛfjuːs] n basura

refuse² [rɪ'fjuːz] vt rechazar;
(*invitation*) declinar; (*permission*)
denegar ▷ vi: **to ~ to do sth** negarse a
hacer algo; (*horse*) rehusar

regain [rɪ'geɪn] vt recobrar, recuperar

regard [rɪ'gɑːd] n mirada; (*esteem*)
respeto; (*attention*) consideración f ▷ vt
(*consider*) considerar; **to give one's ~s
to** saludar de su parte a; **"with kindest
~s"** "con muchos recuerdos"; **as ~s,
with ~ to** con respecto a, en cuanto
a; **regarding** prep con respecto a, en
cuanto a; **regardless** adv a pesar de
todo; **regardless of** sin reparar en

regenerate [rɪ'dʒɛnəreɪt] vt
regenerar

reggae ['rɛgeɪ] n reggae m

regiment ['rɛdʒɪmənt] n regimiento

region ['riːdʒən] n región f; **in the
~ of** (*fig*) alrededor de; **regional** adj
regional

register ['rɛdʒɪstə*] n registro
▷ vt registrar; (*birth*) declarar;
(*car*) matricular; (*letter*) certificar;
(*instrument*) marcar, indicar ▷ vi
(*at hotel*) registrarse; (*as student*)
matricularse; (*make impression*)
producir impresión; **registered** adj
(*letter, parcel*) certificado

registrar ['rɛdʒɪstrɑː*] n secretario/a
(del registro civil)

registration [rɛdʒɪs'treɪʃən] n (*act*)
declaración f; (*Aut: also: ~ number*)
matrícula

registry office ['rɛdʒɪstrɪ-] (BRIT) n
registro civil; **to get married in a ~**
casarse por lo civil

regret [rɪ'grɛt] n sentimiento, pesar
m ▷ vt sentir, lamentar; **regrettable**
adj lamentable

regular ['rɛgjulə*] adj regular;
(*soldier*) profesional; (*usual*) habitual;
(: *doctor*) de cabecera ▷ n (*client etc*)
cliente/a m/f habitual; **regularly** adv
con regularidad; (*often*) repetidas veces

regulate ['rɛgjuleɪt] vt controlar;

regulation [-'leɪʃən] n (*rule*) regla,
reglamento

rehabilitation ['riːəbɪlɪ'teɪʃən] n
rehabilitación f

rehearsal [rɪ'həːsəl] n ensayo

rehearse [rɪ'həːs] vt ensayar

reign [reɪn] n reinado; (*fig*)
predominio ▷ vi reinar; (*fig*) imperar

reimburse [riːɪm'bəːs] vt reembolsar

rein [reɪn] n (*for horse*) rienda

reincarnation [riːɪnkɑː'neɪʃən] n
reencarnación f

reindeer ['reɪndɪə*] n inv reno

reinforce [riːɪn'fɔːs] vt reforzar;
reinforcements npl (*Mil*) refuerzos
mpl

reinstate [riːɪn'steɪt] vt reintegrar;
(*tax, law*) reinstaurar

reject [n 'riːdʒɛkt, vb rɪ'dʒɛkt] n
(*thing*) desecho ▷ vt rechazar;
(*suggestion*) descartar; (*coin*) expulsar;
rejection [rɪ'dʒɛkʃən] n rechazo

rejoice [rɪ'dʒɔɪs] vi: **to ~ at** or **over**
regocijarse or alegrarse de

relate [rɪ'leɪt] vt (*tell*) contar,
relatar; (*connect*) relacionar ▷ vi
relacionarse; **related** adj afín; (*person*)
emparentado; **related to** (*subject*)
relacionado con; **relating to** prep
referente a

relation [rɪ'leɪʃən] n (*person*) familiar
mf, pariente mf; (*link*) relación f;
relations npl (*relatives*) familiares
mpl; **relationship** n relación f;
(*personal*) relaciones fpl; (*also:* **family
relationship**) parentesco

relative ['rɛlətɪv] n pariente mf,
familiar mf ▷ adj relativo; **relatively**
adv (*comparatively*) relativamente

relax [rɪ'læks] vi descansar; (*unwind*)
relajarse ▷ vt (*one's grip*) soltar,
aflojar; (*control*) relajar; (*mind, person*)
descansar; **relaxation** [riːlæk'seɪʃə
n] n descanso; (*of rule, control*)
relajamiento; (*entertainment*) diversión
f; **relaxed** adj relajado; (*tranquil*)
tranquilo; **relaxing** adj relajante

relay ['riːleɪ] n (*race*) carrera de relevos

▷ *vt* (*Radio, TV*) retransmitir

release [rɪ'liːs] *n* (*liberation*) liberación f; (*from prison*) puesta en libertad; (*of gas etc*) escape m; (*of film etc*) estreno; (*of record*) lanzamiento ▷ *vt* (*prisoner*) poner en libertad; (*gas*) despedir, arrojar; (*from wreckage*) soltar; (*catch, spring etc*) desenganchar; (*film*) estrenar; (*book*) publicar; (*news*) difundir

relegate ['relɪgeɪt] *vt* relegar; (*BRIT Sport*): **to be ~d to** bajar a

relent [rɪ'lent] *vi* ablandarse; **relentless** *adj* implacable

relevant ['relɪvənt] *adj* (*fact*) pertinente; **~ to** relacionado con

reliable [rɪ'laɪəbl] *adj* (*person, firm*) de confianza, de fiar; (*method, machine*) seguro; (*source*) fidedigno

relic ['relɪk] *n* (*Rel*) reliquia; (*of the past*) vestigio

relief [rɪ'liːf] *n* (*from pain, anxiety*) alivio; (*help, supplies*) socorro, ayuda; (*Art, Geo*) relieve m

relieve [rɪ'liːv] *vt* (*pain*) aliviar; (*bring help to*) ayudar, socorrer; (*take over from*) sustituir; (: *guard*) relevar; **to ~ sb of sth** quitar algo a algn; **to ~ o.s.** hacer sus necesidades; **relieved** *adj*: **to be relieved** sentir un gran alivio

religion [rɪ'lɪdʒən] *n* religión f

religious [rɪ'lɪdʒəs] *adj* religioso; **religious education** *n* educación f religiosa

relish ['relɪʃ] *n* (*Culin*) salsa; (*enjoyment*) entusiasmo ▷ *vt* (*food etc*) saborear; (*enjoy*): **to ~ sth** hacerle mucha ilusión a algn algo

relocate [riːləʊ'keɪt] *vt* cambiar de lugar, mudar ▷ *vi* mudarse

reluctance [rɪ'lʌktəns] *n* renuencia

reluctant [rɪ'lʌktənt] *adj* renuente; **reluctantly** *adv* de mala gana

rely on [rɪ'laɪ-] *vt fus* depender de; (*trust*) contar con

remain [rɪ'meɪn] *vi* (*survive*) quedar; (*be left*) sobrar; (*continue*) quedar(se), permanecer; **remainder** *n* resto;

remaining *adj* que queda(n); (*surviving*) restante(s); **remains** *npl* restos *mpl*

remand [rɪ'mɑːnd] *n*: **on ~** detenido (bajo custodia) ▷ *vt*: **to be ~ed in custody** quedar detenido bajo custodia

remark [rɪ'mɑːk] *n* comentario ▷ *vt* comentar; **remarkable** *adj* (*outstanding*) extraordinario

remarry [riː'mærɪ] *vi* volver a casarse

remedy ['remədɪ] *n* remedio ▷ *vt* remediar, curar

remember [rɪ'membə*] *vt* recordar, acordarse de; (*bear in mind*) tener presente; (*send greetings to*): **~ me to him** dale recuerdos de mi parte; **Remembrance Day** *n* ≈ día en el que se recuerda a los caídos en las dos guerras mundiales

● **REMEMBRANCE DAY**
●
● En el Reino Unido el domingo
● más próximo al 11 de noviembre
● se conoce como **Remembrance**
● **Sunday** o **Remembrance**
● **Day**, aniversario de la firma del
● armisticio de 1918 que puso fin a
● la Primera Guerra Mundial. Ese
● día, a las once de la mañana (hora
● en que se firmó el armisticio), se
● recuerda a los que murieron en
● las dos guerras mundiales con
● dos minutos de silencio ante los
● monumentos a los caídos. Allí se
● colocan coronas de amapolas,
● flor que también se suele llevar
● prendida en el pecho tras pagar un
● donativo destinado a los inválidos
● de guerra.

remind [rɪ'maɪnd] *vt*: **to ~ sb to do sth** recordar a algn que haga algo; **to ~ sb of sth** (*of fact*) recordar algo a algn; **she ~s me of her mother** me recuerda a su madre; **reminder** *n* notificación f; (*memento*) recuerdo

reminiscent [remɪ'nɪsnt] *adj*: **to be ~ of sth** recordar algo

remnant ['remnənt] *n* resto; (*of cloth*) retal *m*

remorse [rɪ'mɔːs] *n* remordimientos *mpl*

remote [rɪ'məut] *adj* (*distant*) lejano; (*person*) distante; **remote control** *n* telecontrol *m*; **remotely** *adv* remotamente; (*slightly*) levemente

removal [rɪ'muːvəl] *n* (*taking away*) el quitar; (*BRIT: from house*) mudanza; (*from office: dismissal*) destitución *f*; (*Med*) extirpación *f*; **removal man** (*irreg*) *n* (*BRIT*) mozo de mudanzas; **removal van** (*BRIT*) *n* camión *m* de mudanzas

remove [rɪ'muːv] *vt* quitar; (*employee*) destituir; (*name: from list*) tachar, borrar; (*doubt*) disipar; (*abuse*) suprimir, acabar con; (*Med*) extirpar

Renaissance [rɪ'neɪsāns] *n*: **the ~** el Renacimiento

rename [riː'neɪm] *vt* poner nuevo nombre a

render ['rendə*] *vt* (*thanks*) dar; (*aid*) proporcionar, prestar; (*make*): **to ~ sth useless** hacer algo inútil

rendezvous ['rɒndɪvuː] *n* cita

renew [rɪ'njuː] *vt* renovar; (*resume*) reanudar; (*loan etc*) prorrogar

renovate ['renəveɪt] *vt* renovar

renowned [rɪ'naund] *adj* renombrado

rent [rent] *n* (*for house*) arriendo, renta ▷ *vt* alquilar; **rental** *n* (*for television, car*) alquiler *m*

reorganize [riː'ɔːɡənaɪz] *vt* reorganizar

rep [rep] *n abbr* = **representative**

repair [rɪ'peə*] *n* reparación *f*, compostura ▷ *vt* reparar, componer; (*shoes*) remendar; **in good/bad ~** en buen/mal estado; **repair kit** *n* caja de herramientas

repay [riː'peɪ] *vt* (*money*) devolver, reembolsar; (*person*) pagar; (*debt*) liquidar; (*sb's efforts*) devolver,

corresponder a; **repayment** *n* reembolso, devolución *f*; (*sum of money*) recompensa

repeat [rɪ'piːt] *n* (*Radio, TV*) reposición *f* ▷ *vt* repetir ▷ *vi* repetirse; **repeatedly** *adv* repetidas veces; **repeat prescription** *n* (*BRIT*) receta renovada

repellent [rɪ'pɛlənt] *adj* repugnante ▷ *n*: **insect ~** crema *or* loción *f* anti-insectos

repercussions [riːpə'kʌʃənz] *npl* consecuencias *fpl*

repetition [repɪ'tɪʃən] *n* repetición *f*

repetitive [rɪ'pɛtɪtɪv] *adj* repetitivo

replace [rɪ'pleɪs] *vt* (*put back*) devolver a su sitio; (*take the place*) reemplazar, sustituir; **replacement** *n* (*act*) reposición *f*; (*thing*) recambio; (*person*) suplente *mf*

replay ['riːpleɪ] *n* (*Sport*) desempate *m*; (*of tape, film*) repetición *f*

replica ['replɪkə] *n* copia, reproducción *f* (exacta)

reply [rɪ'plaɪ] *n* respuesta, contestación *f* ▷ *vi* contestar, responder

report [rɪ'pɔːt] *n* informe *m*; (*Press etc*) reportaje *m*; (*BRIT: also*: **school ~**) boletín *m* escolar; (*of gun*) estallido ▷ *vt* informar de; (*Press etc*) hacer un reportaje sobre; (*notify: accident, culprit*) denunciar ▷ *vi* (*make a report*) presentar un informe; (*present o.s.*): **to ~ (to sb)** presentarse (ante algn); **report card** *n* (*US, SCOTTISH*) cartilla escolar; **reportedly** *adv* según se dice; **reporter** *n* periodista *mf*

represent [reprɪ'zent] *vt* representar; (*Comm*) ser agente de; (*describe*): **to ~ sth as** describir algo como; **representation** [-'teɪʃən] *n* representación *f*; **representative** *n* representante *mf*; (*US Pol*) diputado/a *m/f* ▷ *adj* representativo

repress [rɪ'pres] *vt* reprimir; **repression** [-'preʃən] *n* represión *f*

reprimand ['reprɪmɑːnd] *n*

reprimenda ▷ vt reprender

reproduce [riːprəˈdjuːs] vt reproducir ▷ vi reproducirse; **reproduction** [-ˈdʌkʃən] n reproducción f

reptile [ˈrɛptaɪl] n reptil m

republic [rɪˈpʌblɪk] n república; **republican** adj, n republicano/a m/f

reputable [ˈrɛpjutəbl] adj (make etc) de renombre

reputation [rɛpjuˈteɪʃən] n reputación f

request [rɪˈkwɛst] n petición f; (formal) solicitud f ▷ vt: **to ~ sth of** or **from sb** solicitar algo a algn; **request stop** (BRIT) n parada discrecional

require [rɪˈkwaɪə*] vt (need: person) necesitar, tener necesidad de; (: thing, situation) exigir; (want) pedir; **to ~ sb to do sth** pedir a algn que haga algo; **requirement** n requisito; (need) necesidad f

resat [riːˈsæt] pt, pp of **resit**

rescue [ˈrɛskjuː] n rescate m ▷ vt rescatar

research [rɪˈsəːtʃ] n investigaciones fpl ▷ vt investigar

resemblance [rɪˈzɛmbləns] n parecido m

resemble [rɪˈzɛmbl] vt parecerse a

resent [rɪˈzɛnt] vt tomar a mal; **resentful** adj resentido; **resentment** n resentimiento

reservation [rɛzəˈveɪʃən] n reserva; **reservation desk** (US) n (in hotel) recepción f

reserve [rɪˈzəːv] n reserva; (Sport) suplente mf ▷ vt (seats etc) reservar; **reserved** adj reservado

reservoir [ˈrɛzəvwɑː*] n (artificial lake) embalse m, tank; (small) depósito

residence [ˈrɛzɪdəns] n (formal: home) domicilio; (length of stay) permanencia; **residence permit** (BRIT) n permiso de permanencia

resident [ˈrɛzɪdənt] n (of area) vecino/a; (in hotel) huésped mf ▷ adj (population) permanente; (doctor)

residente; **residential** [-ˈdɛnʃəl] adj residencial

residue [ˈrɛzɪdjuː] n resto

resign [rɪˈzaɪn] vt renunciar a ▷ vi dimitir; **to ~ o.s. to** (situation) resignarse a; **resignation** [rɛzɪgˈneɪʃən] n dimisión f; (state of mind) resignación f

resin [ˈrɛzɪn] n resina

resist [rɪˈzɪst] vt resistir, oponerse a; **resistance** n resistencia

resit [ˈriːsɪt] (BRIT) (pt, pp **resat**) vt (exam) volver a presentarse a; (subject) recuperar, volver a examinarse de (SP)

resolution [rɛzəˈluːʃən] n resolución f

resolve [rɪˈzɔlv] n resolución f ▷ vt resolver ▷ vi: **to ~ to do** resolver hacer

resort [rɪˈzɔːt] n (town) centro turístico; (recourse) recurso ▷ vi: **to ~ to** recurrir a; **in the last ~** como último recurso

resource [rɪˈsɔːs] n recurso; **resourceful** adj despabilado, ingenioso

respect [rɪsˈpɛkt] n respeto ▷ vt respetar; **respectable** adj respetable; (large: amount) apreciable; (passable) tolerable; **respectful** adj respetuoso; **respective** adj respectivo; **respectively** adv respectivamente

respite [ˈrɛspaɪt] n respiro

respond [rɪsˈpɔnd] vi responder; (react) reaccionar; **response** [-ˈpɔns] n respuesta; reacción f

responsibility [rɪspɔnsɪˈbɪlɪtɪ] n responsabilidad f

responsible [rɪsˈpɔnsɪbl] adj (character) serio, formal; (job) de confianza; (liable): **~ (for)** responsable (de); **responsibly** adv con seriedad

responsive [rɪsˈpɔnsɪv] adj sensible

rest [rɛst] n descanso, reposo; (Mus, pause) pausa, silencio; (support) apoyo; (remainder) resto ▷ vi descansar; (be supported): **to ~ on** descansar sobre ▷ vt: **to ~ sth on/against** apoyar algo en or sobre/contra; **the ~ of them** (*people, objects*) los demás; **it ~s with him to ...** depende de él el que ...

restaurant ['rɛstərɔŋ] *n* restaurante *m*; **restaurant car** (*BRIT*) *n* (*Rail*) coche-comedor *m*

restless ['rɛstlɪs] *adj* inquieto

restoration [rɛstə'reɪʃən] *n* restauración *f*; devolución *f*

restore [rɪ'stɔ:*] *vt* (*building*) restaurar; (*sth stolen*) devolver; (*health*) restablecer; (*to power*) volver a poner a

restrain [rɪs'treɪn] *vt* (*feeling*) contener, refrenar; (*person*): **to ~ (from doing)** disuadir (de hacer); **restraint** *n* (*restriction*) restricción *f*; (*moderation*) moderación *f*; (*of manner*) reserva

restrict [rɪs'trɪkt] *vt* restringir, limitar; **restriction** [-kʃən] *n* restricción *f*, limitación *f*

rest room (*US*) *n* aseos *mpl*

restructure [ri:'strʌktʃə*] *vt* reestructurar

result [rɪ'zʌlt] *n* resultado ▷ *vi*: **to ~ in** terminar en, tener por resultado; **as a ~ of** a consecuencia de

resume [rɪ'zju:m] *vt* reanudar ▷ *vi* comenzar de nuevo

◼ Be careful not to translate **resume** by the Spanish word *resumir*.

résumé ['reɪzju:meɪ] *n* resumen *m*; (*US*) currículum *m*

resuscitate [rɪ'sʌsɪteɪt] *vt* (*Med*) resucitar

retail ['ri:teɪl] *adj, adv* al por menor; **retailer** *n* detallista *mf*

retain [rɪ'teɪn] *vt* (*keep*) retener, conservar

retaliation [rɪtælɪ'eɪʃən] *n* represalias *fpl*

retarded [rɪ'tɑ:dɪd] *adj* retrasado

retire [rɪ'taɪə*] *vi* (*give up work*) jubilarse; (*withdraw*) retirarse; (*go to bed*) acostarse; **retired** *adj* (*person*) jubilado; **retirement** *n* (*giving up work: state*) retiro; (*: act*) jubilación *f*

retort [rɪ'tɔ:t] *vi* contestar

retreat [rɪ'tri:t] *n* (*place*) retiro; (*Mil*)

retirada ▷ *vi* retirarse

retrieve [rɪ'tri:v] *vt* recobrar; (*situation, honour*) salvar; (*Comput*) recuperar; (*error*) reparar

retrospect ['rɛtrəspɛkt] *n*: **in ~** retrospectivamente; **retrospective** [-'spɛktɪv] *adj* retrospectivo; (*law*) retroactivo

return [rɪ'tə:n] *n* (*going or coming back*) vuelta, regreso; (*of sth stolen etc*) devolución *f*; (*Finance: from land, shares*) ganancia, ingresos *mpl* ▷ *cpd* (*journey*) de regreso; (*BRIT: ticket*) de ida y vuelta; (*match*) de vuelta ▷ *vi* (*person etc: come or go back*) volver, regresar; (*symptoms etc*) reaparecer; (*regain*): **to ~ to** recuperar ▷ *vt* devolver; (*favour, love etc*) corresponder a; (*verdict*) pronunciar; (*Pol: candidate*) elegir; **returns** *npl* (*Comm*) ingresos *mpl*; **in ~ (for)** a cambio (de); **by ~ of post** a vuelta de correo; **many happy ~s (of the day)!** ¡feliz cumpleaños!; **return ticket** *n* (*esp BRIT*) billete *m* (*SP*) or boleto *m* (*LAM*) de ida y vuelta, billete *m* redondo (*MEX*)

reunion [ri:'ju:nɪən] *n* (*of family*) reunión *f*; (*of two people, school*) reencuentro

reunite [ri:ju:'naɪt] *vt* reunir; (*reconcile*) reconciliar

revamp [ri:'væmp] *vt* renovar

reveal [rɪ'vi:l] *vt* revelar; **revealing** *adj* revelador(a)

revel ['rɛvl] *vi*: **to ~ in sth/in doing sth** gozar de algo/con hacer algo

revelation [rɛvə'leɪʃən] *n* revelación *f*

revenge [rɪ'vɛndʒ] *n* venganza; **to take ~ on** vengarse de

revenue ['rɛvənju:] *n* ingresos *mpl*, rentas *fpl*

Reverend ['rɛvərənd] *adj* (*in titles*): **the ~ John Smith** (*Anglican*) el Reverendo John Smith; (*Catholic*) el Padre John Smith; (*Protestant*) el Pastor John Smith

reversal [rɪ'və:sl] *n* (*of order*)

inversión f; (of direction, policy) cambio; (of decision) revocación f

reverse [rɪ'vəːs] n (opposite) contrario; (back: of cloth) revés m; (: of coin) reverso; (: of paper) dorso; (Aut: also: ~ **gear**) marcha atrás, revés m ▷ adj (order) inverso; (direction) contrario; (process) opuesto ▷ vt (decision, Aut) dar marcha atrás a; (position, function) invertir ▷ vi (BRIT Aut) dar marcha atrás; **reverse-charge call** (BRIT) n llamada a cobro revertido; **reversing lights** (BRIT) npl (Aut) luces fpl de retroceso

revert [rɪ'vəːt] vi: **to ~ to** volver a

review [rɪ'vjuː] n (magazine, Mil) revista; (of book, film) reseña; (US: examination) repaso, examen m ▷ vt repasar, examinar; (Mil) pasar revista a; (book, film) reseñar

revise [rɪ'vaɪz] vt (manuscript) corregir; (opinion) modificar; (price, procedure) revisar ▷ vi (study) repasar; **revision** [rɪ'vɪʒən] n corrección f; modificación f; (for exam) repaso

revival [rɪ'vaɪvəl] n (recovery) reanimación f; (of interest) renacimiento; (Theatre) reestreno; (of faith) despertar m

revive [rɪ'vaɪv] vt resucitar; (custom) restablecer; (hope) despertar; (play) reestrenar ▷ vi (person) volver en sí; (business) reactivarse

revolt [rɪ'vəult] n rebelión f ▷ vi rebelarse, sublevarse ▷ vt dar asco a, repugnar; **revolting** adj asqueroso, repugnante

revolution [rɛvə'luːʃən] n revolución f; **revolutionary** adj, n revolucionario/a m/f

revolve [rɪ'vɔlv] vi dar vueltas, girar; (life, discussion): **to ~ (a)round** girar en torno a

revolver [rɪ'vɔlvə*] n revólver m

reward [rɪ'wɔːd] n premio, recompensa ▷ vt: **to ~ (for)** recompensar o premiar (por); **rewarding** adj (fig) valioso

rewind [riː'waɪnd] vt rebobinar

rewritable [riː'raɪtəbl] adj (CD, DVD) reescribible

rewrite [riː'raɪt] (pt **rewrote**, pp **rewritten**) vt reescribir

rheumatism ['ruːmətɪzəm] n reumatismo, reúma m

rhinoceros [raɪ'nɔsərəs] n rinoceronte m

rhubarb ['ruːbɑːb] n ruibarbo

rhyme [raɪm] n rima; (verse) poesía

rhythm ['rɪðm] n ritmo

rib [rɪb] n (Anat) costilla ▷ vt (mock) tomar el pelo a

ribbon ['rɪbən] n cinta; **in ~s** (torn) hecho trizas

rice [raɪs] n arroz m; **rice pudding** n arroz m con leche

rich [rɪtʃ] adj rico; (soil) fértil; (food) pesado; (: sweet) empalagoso; (abundant): **~ in** (minerals etc) rico en

rid [rɪd] (pt, pp ~) vt: **to ~ sb of sth** librar a algn de algo; **to get ~ of** deshacerse o desembarazarse de

riddle ['rɪdl] n (puzzle) acertijo; (mystery) enigma m, misterio ▷ vt: **to be ~d with** ser lleno o plagado de

ride [raɪd] (pt **rode**, pp **ridden**) n paseo; (distance covered) viaje m, recorrido ▷ vi (as sport) montar; (go somewhere: on horse, bicycle) dar un paseo, pasearse; (travel: on bicycle, motorcycle, bus) viajar ▷ vt (a horse) montar a; (a bicycle, motorcycle) andar en; (distance) recorrer; **to take sb for a ~** (fig) engañar a algn; **rider** n (on horse) jinete mf; (on bicycle) ciclista mf; (on motorcycle) motociclista mf

ridge [rɪdʒ] n (of hill) cresta; (of roof) caballete m; (wrinkle) arruga

ridicule ['rɪdɪkjuːl] n irrisión f, burla ▷ vt poner en ridículo, burlarse de; **ridiculous** [-'dɪkjuləs] adj ridículo

riding ['raɪdɪŋ] n equitación f; **I like ~** me gusta montar a caballo; **riding school** n escuela de equitación

rife [raɪf] adj: **to be ~** ser muy común; **to be ~ with** abundar en

rifle ['raifl] n rifle m, fusil m ▷ vt saquear

rift [rift] n (in clouds) claro; (fig: disagreement) desavenencia

rig [rig] n (also: **oil ~**: at sea) plataforma petrolera ▷ vt (election etc) amañar

right [rait] adj (correct) correcto, exacto; (suitable) indicado, debido; (proper) apropiado; (just) justo; (morally good) bueno; (not left) derecho ▷ n bueno; (title, claim) derecho; (not left) derecha ▷ adv bien, correctamente; (not left) a la derecha; (exactly): **~ now** ahora mismo ▷ vt enderezar; (correct) corregir ▷ excl ¡bueno!, ¡está bien!; **to be ~** (person) tener razón; (answer) ser correcto; **is that the ~ time?** (of clock) ¿es esa la hora buena?; **by ~s** en justicia; **on the ~** a la derecha; **to be in the ~** tener razón; **~ away** en seguida; **~ in the middle** exactamente en el centro; **right angle** n ángulo recto; **rightful** adj legítimo; **right-hand** adj: **right-hand drive** conducción f por la derecha; **the right-hand side** derecha; **right-handed** adj diestro; **rightly** adv correctamente, debidamente; (with reason) con razón; **right of way** n (on path etc) derecho de paso; (Aut) prioridad f; **right-wing** adj (Pol) derechista

rigid ['ridʒid] adj rígido; (person, ideas) inflexible

rigorous ['rigərəs] adj riguroso

rim [rim] n borde m; (of spectacles) aro; (of wheel) llanta

rind [raind] n (of bacon) corteza; (of lemon etc) cáscara; (of cheese) costra

ring [riŋ] (pt **rang**, pp **rung**) n (of metal) aro; (on finger) anillo; (of people) corro; (of objects) círculo; (gang) banda; (for boxing) cuadrilátero; (of circus) pista; (bull ring) ruedo, plaza; (sound of bell) toque m ▷ vi (on telephone) llamar por teléfono; (bell) repicar; (doorbell, phone) sonar; (also: **~ out**) sonar; (ears) zumbar ▷ vt (Brit Tel) llamar, telefonear; (bell etc) hacer sonar; (doorbell) tocar; **to give sb a ~** (Brit Tel) llamar or telefonear a algn; **ring back** (Brit) vt, vi (Tel) devolver la llamada; **ring off** (Brit) vi (Tel) colgar, cortar la comunicación; **ring up** (Brit) vt (Tel) llamar, telefonear; **ringing tone** n (Tel) tono de llamada; **ringleader** n (of gang) cabecilla m; **ring road** (Brit) n carretera periférica or de circunvalación; **ringtone** n (on mobile) tono de llamada

rink [riŋk] n (also: **ice ~**) pista de hielo

rinse [rins] n aclarado; (dye) tinte m ▷ vt aclarar; (mouth) enjuagar

riot ['raiət] n motín m, disturbio ▷ vi amotinarse; **to run ~** desmandarse

rip [rip] n rasgón m, rasgadura ▷ vt rasgar, desgarrar ▷ vi rasgarse, desgarrarse; **rip off** vt (inf: cheat) estafar; **rip up** vt hacer pedazos

ripe [raip] adj maduro

rip-off ['ripɔf] n (inf): **it's a ~!** ¡es una estafa!, ¡es un timo!

ripple ['ripl] n onda, rizo; (sound) murmullo ▷ vi rizarse

rise [raiz] (pt **rose**, pp **risen**) n (slope) cuesta, pendiente f; (hill) altura; (Brit: in wages) aumento; (in prices, temperature) subida; (fig: to power etc) ascenso ▷ vi subir; (waters) crecer; (sun, moon) salir; (person: from bed etc) levantarse; (also: **~ up**: rebel) sublevarse; (in rank) ascender; **to give ~ to** dar lugar or origen a; **to ~ to the occasion** ponerse a la altura de las circunstancias; **risen** ['rizn] pp of **rise**; **rising** adj (increasing: number) creciente; (: prices) en aumento or alza; (tide) creciente; (sun, moon) naciente

risk [risk] n riesgo, peligro ▷ vt arriesgar; (run the risk of) exponerse a; **to take** or **run the ~ of doing** correr el riesgo de hacer; **at ~** en peligro; **at one's own ~** bajo su propia responsabilidad; **risky** adj arriesgado, peligroso

rite [rait] n rito; **last ~s** exequias fpl

ritual ['ritjuəl] adj ritual ▷ n ritual

m, rito

rival ['raɪvl] *n* rival *mf*; (*in business*) competidor(a) *m/f* ▷ *adj* rival, opuesto ▷ *vt* competir con; **rivalry** *n* competencia

river ['rɪvə*] *n* río ▷ *cpd* (*port*) de río; (*traffic*) fluvial; **up/down ~** río arriba/abajo; **riverbank** *n* orilla (del río)

rivet ['rɪvɪt] *n* roblón *m*, remache *m* ▷ *vt* (*fig*) captar

road [rəud] *n* camino; (*motorway etc*) carretera; (*in town*) calle *f* ▷ *cpd* (*accident*) de tráfico; **major/minor ~** carretera principal/secundaria; **roadblock** *n* barricada; **road map** *n* mapa *m* de carreteras; **road rage** *n* agresividad en la carretera; **road safety** *n* seguridad *f* vial; **roadside** *n* borde *m* (del camino); **roadsign** *n* señal *f* de tráfico; **road tax** *n* (BRIT) impuesto de rodaje; **roadworks** *npl* obras *fpl*

roam [rəum] *vi* vagar

roar [rɔ:*] *n* rugido; (*of vehicle, storm*) estruendo; (*of laughter*) carcajada ▷ *vi* rugir; hacer estruendo; **to ~ with laughter** reírse a carcajadas; **to do a ~ing trade** hacer buen negocio

roast [rəust] *n* carne *f* asada, asado ▷ *vt* asar; (*coffee*) tostar; **roast beef** *n* rosbif *m*

rob [rɔb] *vt* robar; **to ~ sb of sth** robar algo a algn; (*fig: deprive*) quitar algo a algn; **robber** *n* ladrón/ona *m/f*; **robbery** *n* robo

robe [rəub] *n* (*for ceremony etc*) toga; (*also:* **bath~**) albornoz *m*

robin ['rɔbɪn] *n* petirrojo

robot ['rəubɔt] *n* robot *m*

robust [rəu'bʌst] *adj* robusto, fuerte

rock [rɔk] *n* roca; (*boulder*) peña, peñasco; (*us: small stone*) piedrecita; (*BRIT: sweet*) ≈ pirulí ▷ *vt* (*swing gently: cradle*) balancear, mecer; (: *child*) arrullar; (*shake*) sacudir ▷ *vi* mecerse, balancearse; sacudirse; **on the ~s** (*drink*) con hielo; (*marriage etc*) en ruinas; **rock and roll** *n* rocanrol *m*; **rock climbing** *n* (*Sport*) escalada

rocket ['rɔkɪt] *n* cohete *m*; **rocking chair** ['rɔkɪŋ-] *n* mecedora

rocky ['rɔkɪ] *adj* rocoso

rod [rɔd] *n* vara, varilla; (*also:* **fishing ~**) caña

rode [rəud] *pt of* **ride**

rodent ['rəudnt] *n* roedor *m*

rogue [rəug] *n* pícaro, pillo

role [rəul] *n* papel *m*; **role-model** *n* modelo a imitar

roll [rəul] *n* rollo; (*of bank notes*) fajo; (*also:* **bread ~**) panecillo; (*register, list*) lista, nómina; (*sound of drums etc*) redoble *m* ▷ *vt* hacer rodar; (*also:* **~ up**: *string*) enrollar; (*cigarette*) liar; (*also:* **~ out**: *pastry*) aplanar; (*flatten: road, lawn*) apisonar ▷ *vi* rodar; (*drum*) redoblar; (*ship*) balancearse; **roll over** *vi* dar una vuelta; **roll up** *vi* (*inf: arrive*) aparecer ▷ *vt* (*carpet*) arrollar; (: *sleeves*) arremangar; **roller** *n* rodillo; (*wheel*) rueda; (*for road*) apisonadora; (*for hair*) rulo; **Rollerblades®** *npl* patines *mpl* en línea; **roller coaster** *n* montaña rusa; **roller skates** *npl* patines *mpl* de rueda; **roller-skating** *n* patinaje sobre ruedas; **to go roller-skating** ir a patinar (*sobre ruedas*); **rolling pin** *n* rodillo (de cocina)

ROM [rɔm] *n abbr* (*Comput*: = *read only memory*) ROM *f*

Roman ['rəumən] (*irreg*) *adj* romano/a; **Roman Catholic** (*irreg*) *adj*, *n* católico/a *m/f* (romano/a)

romance [rə'mæns] *n* (*love affair*) amor *m*; (*charm*) lo romántico; (*novel*) novela de amor

Romania *etc* [ru:'meɪnɪə] *n* = **Rumania** *etc*

Roman numeral *n* número romano

romantic [rə'mæntɪk] *adj* romántico

Rome [rəum] *n* Roma

roof [ru:f] (*pl* **~s**) *n* techo; (*of house*) techo, tejado ▷ *vt* techar, poner techo a; **the ~ of the mouth** el paladar; **roof rack** *n* (*Aut*) baca, portaequipajes *m inv*

rook [ruk] *n* (*bird*) graja; (*Chess*) torre *f*

room [ruːm] n cuarto, habitación f; (also: **bed~**) dormitorio, recámara (MEX), pieza (SC); (in school etc) sala; (space, scope) sitio, cabida; **roommate** n compañero/a de cuarto; **room service** n servicio de habitaciones; **roomy** adj espacioso; (garment) amplio

rooster ['ruːstə*] n gallo

root [ruːt] n raíz f ▷ vi arraigarse

rope [rəup] n cuerda; (Naut) cable m ▷ vt (tie) atar or amarrar con (una) cuerda; (climbers: also: **~ together**) encordarse; (an area: also: **~ off**) acordonar; **to know the ~s** (fig) conocer los trucos (del oficio)

rose [rəuz] pt of **rise** ▷ n rosa; (shrub) rosal m; (on watering can) roseta

rosé ['rəuzeɪ] n vino rosado

rosemary ['rəuzmərɪ] n romero

rosy ['rəuzɪ] adj rosado, sonrosado; **a ~ future** un futuro prometedor

rot [rɒt] n podredumbre f; (fig: pej) tonterías fpl ▷ vt pudrir ▷ vi pudrirse

rota ['rəutə] n (sistema m de) turnos m

rotate [rəu'teɪt] vt (revolve) hacer girar, dar vueltas a; (jobs) alternar ▷ vi girar, dar vueltas

rotten ['rɒtn] adj podrido; (dishonest) corrompido; (inf: bad) pocho; **to feel ~** (ill) sentirse fatal

rough [rʌf] adj (skin, surface) áspero; (terrain) quebrado; (road) desigual; (voice) bronco; (person, manner) tosco, grosero; (weather) borrascoso; (treatment) brutal; (sea) picado; (town, area) peligroso; (cloth) basto; (plan) preliminar; (guess) aproximado ▷ n (Golf): **in the ~** en las hierbas altas; **to ~ it** vivir sin comodidades; **to sleep ~** (BRIT) pasar la noche al raso; **roughly** adv (handle) torpemente; (make) toscamente; (speak) groseramente; (approximately) aproximadamente

roulette [ruː'lɛt] n ruleta

round [raund] adj redondo ▷ n círculo; (BRIT: of toast) rebanada; (of policeman) ronda; (of milkman) recorrido; (of doctor) visitas fpl; (game: of cards, in competition) partida; (of ammunition) cartucho; (Boxing) asalto; (of talks) ronda ▷ vt (corner) doblar ▷ prep alrededor de; (surrounding): **~ his neck/the table** en su cuello/alrededor de la mesa; (in a circular movement): **to move ~ the room/sail ~ the world** dar una vuelta a la habitación/circunnavegar el mundo; (in various directions): **to move ~ a room/house** moverse por toda la habitación/casa; (approximately) alrededor de ▷ adv: **all ~** por todos lados; **the long way ~** por el camino menos directo; **all (the) year ~** durante todo el año; **it's just ~ the corner** (fig) está a la vuelta de la esquina; **~ the clock** adv las 24 horas; **to go ~ to sb's (house)** ir a casa de algn; **to go ~ the back** pasar por atrás; **enough to go ~** bastante (para todos); **a ~ of applause** una salva de aplausos; **a ~ of drinks/sandwiches** una ronda de bebidas/bocadillos; **round off** vt (speech etc) acabar, poner término a; **round up** vt (cattle) acorralar; (people) reunir; (price) redondear; **roundabout** (BRIT) n (Aut) isleta; (at fair) tiovivo ▷ adj (route, means) indirecto; **round trip** n viaje m de ida y vuelta; **roundup** n rodeo; (of criminals) redada; (of news) resumen m

rouse [rauz] vt (wake up) despertar; (stir up) suscitar

route [ruːt] n ruta, camino; (of bus) recorrido; (of shipping) derrota

routine [ruː'tiːn] adj rutinario ▷ n rutina; (Theatre) número

row¹ [rəu] n (line) fila, hilera; (Knitting) pasada ▷ vi (in boat) remar ▷ vt conducir remando; **4 days in a ~** 4 días seguidos

row² [rau] n (racket) escándalo; (dispute) bronca, pelea; (scolding) regaño ▷ vi pelear(se)

rowboat ['rəubəut] (US) = **rowing boat**

rowing ['rəʊɪŋ] n remo; **rowing boat** (BRIT) n bote m de remos

royal ['rɔɪəl] adj real; **royalty** n (royal persons) familia real; (payment to author) derechos mpl de autor

rpm abbr (= revs per minute) r.p.m.

R.S.V.P. abbr (= répondez s'il vous plaôt) SRC

Rt. Hon. abbr (BRIT) (= Right Honourable) título honorífico de diputado

rub [rʌb] vt frotar; (scrub) restregar ▷ n: **to give sth a ~** frotar algo; **to ~ sb up** o **sb** (US) **the wrong way** entrarle algn por mal ojo; **rub in** vt (ointment) aplicar frotando; **rub off** vi borrarse; **rub out** vt borrar

rubber ['rʌbə*] n caucho, goma; (BRIT: eraser) goma de borrar; **rubber band** n goma, gomita; **rubber gloves** npl guantes mpl de goma

rubbish ['rʌbɪʃ] (BRIT) n basura; (waste) desperdicios mpl; (fig: pej) tonterías fpl; (junk) pacotilla; **rubbish bin** (BRIT) n cubo o bote m (MEX) o tacho (SC) de la basura; **rubbish dump** (BRIT) n vertedero, basurero

rubble ['rʌbl] n escombros mpl

ruby ['ru:bɪ] n rubí m

rucksack ['rʌksæk] n mochila

rudder ['rʌdə*] n timón m

rude [ru:d] adj (impolite: person) mal educado; (: word, manners) grosero; (crude) crudo; (indecent) indecente

ruffle ['rʌfl] vt (hair) despeinar; (clothes) arrugar; **to get ~d** (fig: person) alterarse

rug [rʌg] n alfombra; (BRIT: blanket) manta

rugby ['rʌgbɪ] n rugby m

rugged ['rʌgɪd] adj (landscape) accidentado; (features) robusto

ruin ['ru:ɪn] n ruina ▷ vt arruinar; (spoil) estropear; **ruins** npl ruinas fpl, restos mpl

rule [ru:l] n (norm) norma, costumbre f; (regulation, ruler) regla; (government) dominio ▷ vt (country, person) gobernar ▷ vi gobernar; (Law) fallar;

as a ~ por regla general; **rule out** vt excluir; **ruler** n (sovereign) soberano; (for measuring) regla; **ruling** adj (party) gobernante; (class) dirigente ▷ n (Law) fallo, decisión f

rum [rʌm] n ron m

Rumania [ru:'meɪnɪə] n Rumanía; **Rumanian** adj rumano/a ▷ n rumano/a m/f; (Ling) rumano

rumble ['rʌmbl] n (noise) ruido sordo ▷ vi retumbar, hacer un ruido sordo; (stomach, pipe) sonar

rumour ['ru:mə*] (US **rumor**) n rumor m ▷ vt: **it is ~ed that ...** se rumorea que ...

rump steak n filete m de lomo

run [rʌn] (pt **ran**, pp **run**) n (fast pace): **at a ~** corriendo; (Sport, in tights) carrera; (outing) paseo, excursión f; (distance travelled) trayecto; (series) serie f; (Theatre) temporada; (Ski) pista ▷ vt correr; (operate: business) dirigir; (: competition, course) organizar; (: hotel, house) administrar, llevar; (Comput) ejecutar; (pass: hand) pasar; (Press: feature) publicar ▷ vi correr; (work: machine) funcionar, marchar; (bus, train: operate) circular, ir; (: travel) ir; (continue: play) seguir; (contract) ser válido; (flow: river) fluir; (colours, washing) desteñirse; (in election) ser candidato; **there was a ~ on** (meat, tickets) hubo mucha demanda de; **in the long ~** a la larga; **on the ~** en fuga; **I'll ~ you to the station** te llevaré a la estación (en coche); **to ~ a risk** correr un riesgo; **to ~ a bath** llenar la bañera; **run after** vt fus (to catch up) correr tras; (chase) perseguir; **run away** vi huir; **run down** vt (production) ir reduciendo; (factory) ir restringiendo la producción en; (car) atropellar; (criticize) criticar; **to be run down** (person: tired) estar debilitado; **run into** vt fus (meet: person, trouble) tropezar con; (collide with) chocar con; **run off** vt (water) dejar correr; (copies) sacar ▷ vi huir corriendo; **run out** vi (person) salir corriendo; (*liquid*) irse; (*lease*) caducar, vencer; (*money etc*) acabarse; **run out of** *vt fus* quedar sin; **run over** *vt* (*Aut*) atropellar ▷ *vt fus* (*revise*) repasar; **run through** *vt fus* (*instructions*) repasar; **run up** *vt* (*debt*) contraer; **to run up against** (*difficulties*) tropezar con; **runaway** *adj* (*horse*) desbocado; (*truck*) sin frenos; (*child*) escapado de casa

rung [rʌŋ] *pp of* **ring** ▷ *n* (*of ladder*) escalón *m*, peldaño

runner ['rʌnə*] *n* (*in race: person*) corredor(a) *m/f*; (: *horse*) caballo; (*on sledge*) patín *m*; **runner bean** (BRIT) *n* ≈ judía verde; **runner-up** *n* subcampeón/ona *m/f*

running ['rʌnɪŋ] *n* (*sport*) atletismo; (*of business*) administración *f* ▷ *adj* (*water, costs*) corriente; (*commentary*) continuo; **to be in/out of the ~ for sth** tener/no tener posibilidades de ganar algo; **6 days ~** 6 días seguidos

runny ['rʌnɪ] *adj* fluido; (*nose, eyes*) gastante

run-up ['rʌnʌp] *n*: **~ to** (*election etc*) período previo a

runway ['rʌnweɪ] *n* (*Aviat*) pista de aterrizaje

rupture ['rʌptʃə*] *n* (*Med*) hernia ▷ *vt*: **to ~ o.s** causarse una hernia

rural ['ruərl] *adj* rural

rush [rʌʃ] *n* ímpetu *m*; (*hurry*) prisa; (*Comm*) demanda repentina; (*current*) corriente *f* fuerte; (*of feeling*) torrente *m*; (*Bot*) junco ▷ *vt* apresurar; (*work*) hacer de prisa ▷ *vi* correr, precipitarse; **rush hour** *n* horas *fpl* punta

Russia ['rʌʃə] *n* Rusia; **Russian** *adj* ruso/a ▷ *n* ruso/a *m/f*; (*Ling*) ruso

rust [rʌst] *n* herrumbre *f*, moho ▷ *vi* oxidarse

rusty ['rʌstɪ] *adj* oxidado

ruthless ['ruːθlɪs] *adj* despiadado

RV (US) *n abbr* = **recreational vehicle**

rye [raɪ] *n* centeno

S

Sabbath ['sæbəθ] *n* domingo; (*Jewish*) sábado

sabotage ['sæbətɑːʒ] *n* sabotaje *m* ▷ *vt* sabotear

saccharin(e) ['sækərɪn] *n* sacarina

sachet ['sæʃeɪ] *n* sobrecito

sack [sæk] *n* (*bag*) saco, costal *m* ▷ *vt* (*dismiss*) despedir; (*plunder*) saquear; **to get the ~** ser despedido

sacred ['seɪkrɪd] *adj* sagrado, santo

sacrifice ['sækrɪfaɪs] *n* sacrificio ▷ *vt* sacrificar

sad [sæd] *adj* (*unhappy*) triste; (*deplorable*) lamentable

saddle ['sædl] *n* silla (de montar); (*of cycle*) sillín *m* ▷ *vt* (*horse*) ensillar; **to be ~d with sth** (*inf*) quedar cargado con algo

sadistic [səˈdɪstɪk] *adj* sádico

sadly ['sædlɪ] *adv* lamentablemente; **to be ~ lacking in** estar por desgracia carente de

sadness ['sædnɪs] *n* tristeza

s.a.e. *abbr* (= *stamped addressed envelope*) *sobre con las propias señas de* *uno y con sello*

safari [sə'fɑːrɪ] *n* safari *m*

safe [seɪf] *adj* (*out of danger*) fuera de peligro; (*not dangerous, sure*) seguro; (*unharmed*) ileso ▷ *n* caja de caudales, caja fuerte; **~ and sound** sano y salvo; **(just) to be on the ~ side** para mayor seguridad; **safely** *adv* seguramente, con seguridad; **to arrive safely** llegar bien; **safe sex** *n* sexo seguro *or* sin riesgo

safety ['seɪftɪ] *n* seguridad *f*; **safety belt** *n* cinturón *m* (de seguridad); **safety pin** *n* imperdible *m*, seguro (*MEX*), alfiler *m* de gancho (*sc*)

saffron ['sæfrən] *n* azafrán *m*

sag [sæg] *vi* aflojarse

sage [seɪdʒ] *n* (*herb*) salvia; (*man*) sabio

Sagittarius [sædʒɪ'tɛərɪəs] *n* Sagitario

Sahara [sə'hɑːrə] *n*: **the ~ (Desert)** el (desierto del) Sáhara

said [sɛd] *pt, pp* of **say**

sail [seɪl] *n* (*on boat*) vela; (*trip*): **to go for a ~** dar un paseo en barco ▷ *vt* (*boat*) gobernar ▷ *vi* (*travel: ship*) navegar; (*Sport*) hacer vela; (*begin voyage*) salir; **they ~ed into Copenhagen** arribaron a Copenhague; **sailboat** (*US*) *n* = **sailing boat**; **sailing** *n* (*Sport*) vela; **to go sailing** hacer vela; **sailing boat** *n* barco de vela; **sailor** *n* marinero, marino

saint [seɪnt] *n* santo

sake [seɪk] *n*: **for the ~ of** por

salad ['sæləd] *n* ensalada; **salad cream** (*BRIT*) *n* (especie *f* de) mayonesa; **salad dressing** *n* aliño

salami [sə'lɑːmɪ] *n* salami *m*, salchichón *m*

salary ['sælərɪ] *n* sueldo

sale [seɪl] *n* venta; (*at reduced prices*) liquidación *f*, saldo; (*auction*) subasta; **sales** *npl* (*total amount sold*) ventas *fpl*, facturación *f*; **"for ~"** "se vende"; **on ~** en venta; **on ~ or return** (*goods*) venta por reposición; **sales assistant** (*US*),

sales clerk *n* dependiente/a *m/f*; **salesman/woman** (*irreg*) *n* (*in shop*) dependiente/a *m/f*; **salesperson** (*irreg*) *n* vendedor(a) *m/f*, dependiente/a *m/f*; **sales rep** *n* representante *mf*, agente *mf* comercial

saline ['seɪlaɪn] *adj* salino

saliva [sə'laɪvə] *n* saliva

salmon ['sæmən] *n inv* salmón *m*

salon ['sælɔn] *n* (*hairdressing salon*) peluquería; (*beauty salon*) salón *m* de belleza

saloon [sə'luːn] *n* (*US*) bar *m*, taberna; (*BRIT Aut*) coche *m* (de) turismo; (*ship's lounge*) cámara, salón *m*

salt [sɔlt] *n* sal *f* ▷ *vt* salar; (*put salt on*) poner sal en; **saltwater** *adj* de agua salada; **salty** *adj* salado

salute [sə'luːt] *n* saludo; (*of guns*) salva ▷ *vt* saludar

salvage ['sælvɪdʒ] *n* (*saving*) salvamento, recuperación *f*; (*things saved*) objetos *mpl* salvados ▷ *vt* salvar

Salvation Army [sæl'veɪʃən-] *n* Ejército de Salvación

same [seɪm] *adj* mismo ▷ *pron*: **the ~** el(la) mismo/a, los(las) mismos/as; **the ~ book as** el mismo libro que; **at the ~ time** (*at the same moment*) al mismo tiempo; (*yet*) sin embargo; **all** *or* **just the ~** sin embargo, aun así; **to do the ~ (as sb)** hacer lo mismo (que algn); **the ~ to you!** ¡igualmente!

sample ['sɑːmpl] *n* muestra ▷ *vt* (*food*) probar; (*wine*) catar

sanction ['sæŋkʃən] *n* aprobación *f* ▷ *vt* sancionar; aprobar; **sanctions** *npl* (*Pol*) sanciones *fpl*

sanctuary ['sæŋktjuərɪ] *n* santuario; (*refuge*) asilo, refugio; (*for wildlife*) reserva

sand [sænd] *n* arena; (*beach*) playa ▷ *vt* (*also*: **~ down**) lijar

sandal ['sændl] *n* sandalia

sand: sandbox (*US*) *n* = **sandpit**; **sandcastle** *n* castillo de arena; **sand dune** *n* duna; **sandpaper** *n* papel *m* de lija; **sandpit** *n* (*for children*) cajón *m*

de arena; **sands** npl playa sg de arena;
sandstone ['sændstəʊn] n piedra
arenlsca
sandwich ['sændwɪtʃ] n sandwich
m ▷ vt intercalar; **~ed between**
apretujado entre; **cheese/ham ~**
sandwich de queso/jamón
sandy ['sændɪ] adj arenoso; (colour)
rojizo
sane [seɪn] adj cuerdo; (sensible)
sensato

▌ Be careful not to translate **sane** by
the Spanish word sano.

sang [sæŋ] pt of **sing**
sanitary towel (us **sanitary napkin**)
n paño higiénico, compresa
sanity ['sænɪtɪ] n cordura; (of
judgment) sensatez f
sank [sæŋk] pt of **sink**
Santa Claus [sæntə'klɔːz] n San
Nicolás, Papá Noel
sap [sæp] n (of plants) savia ▷ vt
(strength) minar, agotar
sapphire ['sæfaɪə*] n zafiro
sarcasm ['sɑːkæzm] n sarcasmo
sarcastic [sɑː'kæstɪk] adj sarcástico
sardine [sɑː'diːn] n sardina
SASE (us) n abbr (= self-addressed
stamped envelope) sobre con las propias
señas de uno y con sello
Sat. abbr (= Saturday) sáb
sat [sæt] pt, pp of **sit**
satchel ['sætʃl] n (child's) mochila,
cartera (sp)
satellite ['sætəlaɪt] n satélite m;
satellite dish n antena de televisión
por satélite; **satellite television** n
televisión f vía satélite
satin ['sætɪn] n raso ▷ adj de raso
satire ['sætaɪə*] n sátira
satisfaction [sætɪs'fækʃən] n
satisfacción f
satisfactory [sætɪs'fæktərɪ] adj
satisfactorio
satisfied ['sætɪsfaɪd] adj satisfecho;
to be ~ (with sth) estar satisfecho
(de algo)
satisfy ['sætɪsfaɪ] vt satisfacer;

(convince) convencer
Saturday ['sætədɪ] n sábado
sauce [sɔːs] n salsa; (sweet) crema;
jarabe m; **saucepan** n cacerola, olla
saucer ['sɔːsə*] n platillo; **Saudi
Arabia** n Arabia Saudí or Saudita
sauna ['sɔːnə] n sauna
sausage ['sɒsɪdʒ] n salchicha;
sausage roll n empanadita de
salchicha
sautéed ['səʊteɪd] adj salteado
savage ['sævɪdʒ] adj (cruel, fierce)
feroz, furioso; (primitive) salvaje ▷ n
salvaje mf ▷ vt (attack) embestir
save [seɪv] vt (rescue) salvar, rescatar;
(money, time) ahorrar; (put by, keep: seat)
guardar; (Comput) salvar (y guardar),
(avoid: trouble) evitar; (Sport) parar ▷ vi
(also: ~ up) ahorrar ▷ n (Sport) parada
▷ prep salvo, excepto
savings ['seɪvɪŋz] npl ahorros mpl;
savings account n cuenta de ahorros;
savings and loan association (us)
sociedad f de ahorro y préstamo
savoury ['seɪvərɪ] (us **savory**) adj
sabroso; (dish: not sweet) salado
saw [sɔː] (pt **~ed**, pp **~ed** or **~n**) pt
of **see** ▷ n (tool) sierra ▷ vt serrar;
sawdust n (a)serrín m
sawn [sɔːn] pp of **saw**
saxophone ['sæksəfəʊn] n saxófono
say [seɪ] (pt, pp said) n: **to have one's
~** expresar su opinión ▷ vt decir; **to
have a or some ~ in sth** tener voz or
tener que ver en algo; **to ~ yes/no** decir
que sí/no; **could you ~ that again?**
¿podría repetir eso?; **that is to ~** es
decir; **that goes without ~ing** ni que
decir tiene; **saying** n dicho, refrán m
scab [skæb] n costra; (pej) esquirol m
scaffolding ['skæfəldɪŋ] n andamio,
andamiaje m
scald [skɔːld] n escaldadura ▷ vt
escaldar
scale [skeɪl] n (gen, Mus) escala;
(of fish) escama; (of salaries, fees
etc) escalafón m ▷ vt (mountain)
escalar; (tree) trepar; **scales** npl (for

weighing: small) balanza; (: *large*) báscula; **on a large ~** en gran escala; **~ of charges** tarifa, lista de precios

scallion ['skæljən] (*US*) *n* cebolleta

scallop ['skɔləp] *n* (*Zool*) venera; (*Sewing*) festón *m*

scalp [skælp] *n* cabellera ▷ *vt* escalpar

scalpel ['skælpl] *n* bisturí *m*

scam [skæm] *n* (*inf*) estafa, timo

scampi ['skæmpɪ] *npl* gambas *fpl*

scan [skæn] *vt* (*examine*) escudriñar; (*glance at quickly*) dar un vistazo a; (*TV, Radar*) explorar, registrar ▷ *n* (*Med*): **to have a ~** pasar por el escáner

scandal ['skændl] *n* escándalo; (*gossip*) chismes *mpl*

Scandinavia [skændɪ'neɪvɪə] *n* Escandinavia; **Scandinavian** *adj, n* escandinavo/a *m/f*

scanner ['skænə*] *n* (*Radar, Med*) escáner *m*

scapegoat ['skeɪpgəut] *n* cabeza de turco, chivo expiatorio

scar [skɑ:] *n* cicatriz *f*; (*fig*) señal *f* ▷ *vt* dejar señales en

scarce [skɛəs] *adj* escaso; **to make o.s. ~** (*inf*) esfumarse; **scarcely** *adv* apenas

scare [skɛə*] *n* susto, sobresalto; (*panic*) pánico ▷ *vt* asustar, espantar; **to ~ sb stiff** dar a algn un susto de muerte; **bomb ~** amenaza de bomba; **scarecrow** *n* espantapájaros *inv*; **scared** *adj*: **to be scared** estar asustado

scarf [skɑ:f] (*pl* **~s** *or* **scarves**) *n* (*long*) bufanda; (*square*) pañuelo

scarlet ['skɑ:lɪt] *adj* escarlata

scarves [skɑ:vz] *npl of* **scarf**

scary ['skɛərɪ] (*inf*) *adj* espeluznante

scatter ['skætə*] *vt* (*spread*) esparcir, desparramar; (*put to flight*) dispersar ▷ *vi* desparramarse; dispersarse

scenario [sɪ'nɑ:rɪəu] *n* (*Theatre*) argumento; (*Cinema*) guión *m*; (*fig*) escenario

scene [si:n] *n* (*Theatre, fig etc*) escena; (*of crime etc*) escenario; (*view*) panorama *m*; (*fuss*) escándalo; **scenery** *n* (*Theatre*) decorado; (*landscape*) paisaje *m*

> Be careful not to translate **scenery** by the Spanish word *escenario*.

scenic *adj* pintoresco

scent [sɛnt] *n* perfume *m*, olor *m*; (*fig: track*) rastro, pista

sceptical ['skɛptɪkl] *adj* escéptico

schedule ['ʃɛdju:l] (*US*) ['skɛdju:l] *n* (*timetable*) horario; (*of events*) programa *m*; (*list*) lista ▷ *vt* (*visit*) fijar la hora de; **to arrive on ~** llegar a la hora debida; **to be ahead of/behind ~** estar adelantado/en retraso; **scheduled flight** *n* vuelo regular

scheme [ski:m] *n* (*plan*) plan *m*, proyecto; (*plot*) intriga; (*arrangement*) disposición *f*; (*pension scheme etc*) sistema *m* ▷ *vi* (*intrigue*) intrigar

schizophrenic [skɪtzə'frɛnɪk] *adj* esquizofrénico

scholar ['skɔlə*] *n* (*pupil*) alumno/a; (*learned person*) sabio/a, erudito/a; **scholarship** *n* erudición *f*; (*grant*) beca

school [sku:l] *n* escuela, colegio; (*in university*) facultad *f* ▷ *cpd* escolar; **schoolbook** *n* libro de texto; **schoolboy** *n* alumno; **school children** *npl* alumnos *mpl*; **schoolgirl** *n* alumna; **schooling** *n* enseñanza; **schoolteacher** *n* (*primary*) maestro/a; (*secondary*) profesor(a) *m/f*

science ['saɪəns] *n* ciencia; **science fiction** *n* ciencia-ficción *f*; **scientific** [-'tɪfɪk] *adj* científico; **scientist** *n* científico/a

sci-fi ['saɪfaɪ] *n abbr* (*inf*) = **science fiction**

scissors ['sɪzəz] *npl* tijeras *fpl*; **a pair of ~** unas tijeras

scold [skəuld] *vt* regañar

scone [skɔn] *n* pastel de pan

scoop [sku:p] *n* (*for flour etc*) pala; (*Press*) exclusiva

scooter ['sku:tə*] *n* moto *f*; (*toy*) patinete *m*

scope [skəʊp] n (of plan) ámbito;
(of person) competencia; (opportunity)
libertad f (de acción)

scorching ['skɔ:tʃɪŋ] adj (heat, sun)
abrasador(a)

score [skɔ:*] n (points etc) puntuación
f; (Mus) partitura; (twenty) veintena
▷ vt (goal, point) ganar; (mark) rayar;
(achieve: success) conseguir ▷ vi marcar
un tanto; (Football) marcar (un) gol;
(keep score) llevar el tanteo; **~s of**
(lots of) decenas de; **on that ~** en lo
que se refiere a eso; **to ~ 6 out of 10**
obtener una puntuación de 6 sobre
10; **score out** vt tachar; **scoreboard**
n marcador m; **scorer** n marcador
m; (keeping score) encargado/a del
marcador

scorn [skɔ:n] n desprecio

Scorpio ['skɔ:pɪəʊ] n Escorpión m

scorpion ['skɔ:pɪən] n alacrán m

Scot [skɒt] n escocés/esa m/f

Scotch tape® (us) n cinta adhesiva,
celo, scotch® m

Scotland ['skɒtlənd] n Escocia

Scots [skɒts] adj escocés/esa;
Scotsman (irreg) n escocés;
Scotswoman (irreg) n escocésa;
Scottish ['skɒtɪʃ] adj escocés/esa;
Scottish Parliament n Parlamento
escocés

scout [skaut] n (Mil: also: **boy
~**) explorador m; **girl ~** (us) niña
exploradora

scowl [skaul] vi fruncir el ceño; **to ~
at sb** mirar con ceño a algn

scramble ['skræmbl] n (climb)
subida (difícil); (struggle) pelea ▷ vi: **to
~ through/out** abrirse paso/salir
con dificultad; **to ~ for** pelear por;
scrambled eggs npl huevos mpl
revueltos

scrap [skræp] n (bit) pedacito; (fig)
pizca; (fight) riña, bronca; (also: **~ iron**)
chatarra, hierro viejo ▷ vt (discard)
desechar, descartar ▷ vi reñir, armar
una bronca; **scraps** npl (waste) sobras
fpl, desperdicios mpl; **scrapbook** n

álbum m de recortes

scrape [skreip] n: **to get into a ~**
meterse en un lío ▷ vt raspar; (skin etc)
rasguñar; (scrape against) rozar ▷ vi: **to
~ through** (exam) aprobar por los pelos;
scrap paper n pedazos mpl de papel

scratch [skrætʃ] n rasguño; (from
claw) arañazo ▷ vt (paint, car) rayar;
(with claw, nail) rasguñar, arañar;
(rub: nose etc) rascarse ▷ vi rascarse;
to start from ~ partir de cero; **to be
up to ~** cumplir con los requisitos;
scratch card n (BRIT) tarjeta f de
"rasque y gane"

scream [skri:m] n chillido ▷ vi
chillar

screen [skri:n] n (Cinema, TV)
pantalla; (movable barrier) biombo
▷ vt (conceal) tapar; (from the wind etc)
proteger; (film) proyectar; (candidates
etc) investigar a; **screening** n (Med)
investigación f médica; **screenplay**
n guión m; **screen saver** n (Comput)
protector m de pantalla

screw [skru:] n tornillo ▷ vt (also: **~
in**) atornillar; **screw up** vt (paper
etc) arrugar; **to screw up one's eyes**
arrugar el entrecejo; **screwdriver** n
destornillador m

scribble ['skrɪbl] n garabatos mpl
▷ vt, vi garabatear

script [skrɪpt] n (Cinema etc) guión m;
(writing) escritura, letra

scroll [skrəʊl] n rollo

scrub [skrʌb] n (land) maleza ▷ vt
fregar, restregar; (inf: reject) cancelar,
anular

scruffy ['skrʌfɪ] adj desaliñado,
piojoso

scrum(mage) ['skrʌm(mɪdʒ)] n
(Rugby) melée f

scrutiny ['skru:tɪnɪ] n escrutinio,
examen m

scuba diving ['sku:bə'daɪvɪŋ] n
submarinismo

sculptor ['skʌlptə*] n escultor(a) m/f

sculpture ['skʌlptʃə*] n escultura

scum [skʌm] n (on liquid) espuma;

(pej: people) escoria

scurry ['skʌrɪ] vi correr; **to ~ off** escabullirse

sea [si:] n mar m ▷cpd de mar, marítimo; **by ~** (travel) en barco; **on the ~** (boat) en el mar; (town) junto al mar; **to be all at ~** (fig) estar despistado; **out to ~, at ~** en alta mar; **seafood** n mariscos mpl; **sea front** n paseo marítimo; **seagull** n gaviota

seal [si:l] n (animal) foca; (stamp) sello ▷vt (close) cerrar; **seal off** vt (area) acordonar

sea level n nivel m del mar

seam [si:m] n costura; (of metal) juntura; (of coal) veta, filón m

search [sə:tʃ] n (for person, thing) busca, búsqueda; (Comput) búsqueda; (inspection: of sb's home) registro ▷vt (look in) buscar en; (examine) examinar; (person, place) registrar ▷vi: **to ~ for** buscar; **in ~ of** en busca de; **search engine** n (Comput) buscador m; **search party** n pelotón m de salvamento

sea: seashore n playa, orilla del mar; **seasick** adj mareado; **seaside** n playa, orilla del mar; **seaside resort** n centro turístico costero

season ['si:zn] n (of year) estación f; (sporting etc) temporada; (of films etc) ciclo ▷vt (food) sazonar; **in/out of ~** en sazón/fuera de temporada; **seasonal** adj estacional; **seasoning** n condimento, aderezo; **season ticket** n abono

seat [si:t] n (in bus, train) asiento; (chair) silla; (Parliament) escaño; (buttocks) culo, trasero; (of trousers) culera ▷vt sentar; (have room for) tener cabida para; **to be ~ed** sentarse; **seat belt** n cinturón m de seguridad; **seating** n asientos mpl

sea: sea water n agua del mar; **seaweed** n alga marina

sec. abbr = **second(s)**

secluded [sɪ'klu:dɪd] adj retirado

second ['sɛkənd] adj segundo ▷adv en segundo lugar ▷n segundo;

(Aut: also: **~ gear**) segunda; (Comm) artículo con algún desperfecto; (BRIT Scol: degree) título de licenciado con calificación de notable ▷vt (motion) apoyar; **secondary** adj secundario; **secondary school** n escuela secundaria; **second-class** adj de segunda clase ▷adv (Rail) en segunda; **secondhand** adj de segunda mano, usado; **secondly** adv en segundo lugar; **second-rate** adj de segunda categoría; **second thoughts**: **to have second thoughts** cambiar de opinión; **on second thoughts** or **thought** (US) pensándolo bien

secrecy ['si:krəsɪ] n secreto

secret ['si:krɪt] adj, n secreto; **in ~** en secreto

secretary ['sɛkrətərɪ] n secretario/a; **S~ of State (for)** (BRIT Pol) Ministro (de)

secretive ['si:krətɪv] adj reservado, sigiloso

secret service n servicio secreto

sect [sɛkt] n secta

section ['sɛkʃən] n sección f; (part) parte f; (of document) artículo; (of opinion) sector m; (cross-section) corte m transversal

sector ['sɛktə*] n sector m

secular ['sɛkjulə*] adj secular, seglar

secure [sɪ'kjuə*] adj seguro; (firmly fixed) firme, fijo ▷vt (fix) asegurar, afianzar; (get) conseguir

security [sɪ'kjuərɪtɪ] n seguridad f; (for loan) fianza; (: object) prenda; **securities** npl (Comm) valores mpl, títulos mpl; **security guard** n guardia m/f de seguridad

sedan [sɪ'dæn] (US) n (Aut) sedán m

sedate [sɪ'deɪt] adj tranquilo ▷vt tratar con sedantes

sedative ['sɛdɪtɪv] n sedante m, sedativo

seduce [sɪ'dju:s] vt seducir; **seductive** [-'dʌktɪv] adj seductor(a)

see [si:] (pt **saw**, pp **seen**) vt ver; (accompany): **to ~ sb to the door**

acompañar a algn a la puerta;
(*understand*) ver, comprender ▷ *vi* ver
▷ *n* (*arz*)obispado; **to ~ that** (*ensure*)
asegurar que; **~ you soon!** ¡hasta
pronto!; **see off** *vt* despedir; **see out**
vt (*take to the door*) acompañar hasta la
puerta; **see through** *vt fus* (*fig*) calar
▷ *vt* (*plan*) llevar a cabo; **see to** *vt fus*
atender a, encargarse de

seed [siːd] *n* semilla; (*in fruit*) pepita;
(*fig: gen pl*) germen *m*; (*Tennis etc*)
preseleccionado/a; **to go to ~** (*plant*)
granar; (*fig*) descuidarse

seeing [ˈsiːɪŋ] *conj*: **~ (that)** visto que,
en vista de que

seek [siːk] (*pt, pp* **sought**) *vt* buscar;
(*post*) solicitar

seem [siːm] *vi* parecer; **there ~s to
be ...** parece que hay ...; **seemingly** *adv*
aparentemente, según parece

seen [siːn] *pp of* **see**

seesaw [ˈsiːsɔː] *n* subibaja

segment [ˈsɛgmənt] *n* (*part*) sección
f; (*of orange*) gajo

segregate [ˈsɛgrɪgeɪt] *vt* segregar

seize [siːz] *vt* (*grasp*) agarrar,
asir; (*take possession of*) secuestrar;
(: *territory*) apoderarse de; (*opportunity*)
aprovecharse de

seizure [ˈsiːʒə*] *n* (*Med*) ataque *m*;
(*Law, of power*) incautación *f*

seldom [ˈsɛldəm] *adv* rara vez

select [sɪˈlɛkt] *adj* selecto, escogido
▷ *vt* escoger, elegir; (*Sport*) seleccionar;
selection *n* selección *f*, elección
f; (*Comm*) surtido; **selective** *adj*
selectivo

self [sɛlf] (*pl* **selves**) *n* uno mismo;
the ~ el yo ▷ *prefix* auto...; **self-
assured** *adj* seguro de sí mismo;
self-catering (*BRIT*) *adj* (*flat etc*)
con cocina; **self-centred** (*US*
self-centered) *adj* egocéntrico;
self-confidence *n* confianza en sí
mismo; **self-confident** *adj* seguro
de sí (mismo), lleno de confianza en sí
mismo; **self-conscious** *adj* cohibido;
self-contained (*BRIT*) *adj* (*flat*) con

entrada particular; **self-control** *n*
autodominio; **self-defence** (*US* **self-
defense**) *n* defensa propia; **self-drive**
adj (*BRIT*) sin chofer *or* (*SP*) chófer; **self-
employed** *adj* que trabaja por cuenta
propia; **self-esteem** *n* amor *m* propio;
self-indulgent *adj* autocomplaciente;
self-interest *n* egoísmo; **selfish**
adj egoísta; **self-pity** *n* lástima de
sí mismo; **self-raising** [sɛlfˈreɪzɪŋ]
(*US* **self-rising**) *adj*: **self-raising flour**
harina con levadura; **self-respect** *n*
amor *m* propio; **self-service** *adj* de
autoservicio

sell [sɛl] (*pt, pp* **sold**) *vt* vender ▷ *vi*
venderse; **to ~ at** *or* **for £10** venderse a
10 libras; **sell off** *vt* liquidar; **sell out**
vi: **to sell out of tickets/milk** vender
todas las entradas/toda la leche; **sell-
by date** *n* fecha de caducidad; **seller**
n vendedor(a) *m/f*

Sellotape® [ˈsɛləuteɪp] (*BRIT*) *n* celo
(*SP*), cinta Scotch® (*LAM*) *or* Dúrex®
(*MEX, ARG*)

selves [sɛlvz] *npl of* **self**

semester [sɪˈmɛstə*] (*US*) *n*
semestre *m*

semi... [sɛmɪ] *prefix* semi...,
medio...; **semicircle** *n* semicírculo;
semidetached (house) *n* (*casa*)
semiseparada; **semi-final** *n* semi-
final *m*

seminar [ˈsɛmɪnɑː*] *n* seminario

semi-skimmed [sɛmɪˈskɪmd] *adj*
semidesnatado; **semi-skimmed
(milk)** *n* leche semidesnatada

senate [ˈsɛnɪt] *n* senado; **the S~** (*US*)
el Senado; **senator** *n* senador(a) *m/f*

send [sɛnd] (*pt, pp* **sent**) *vt* mandar,
enviar; (*signal*) transmitir; **send back**
vt devolver; **send for** *vt fus* mandar
traer; **send in** *vt* (*report, application,
resignation*) mandar; **send off** *vt*
(*goods*) despachar; (*BRIT Sport: player*)
expulsar; **send on** *vt* (*letter, luggage*)
remitir; (*person*) mandar; **send out**
vt (*invitation*) mandar; (*signal*) emitir;
send up *vt* (*person, price*) hacer subir;

(BRIT: *parody*) parodiar; **sender** n
remitente *mf*; **send-off** n: **a good
send-off** una buena despedida

senile ['si:naɪl] *adj* senil

senior ['si:nɪə*] *adj* (*older*) mayor, más
viejo; (: *on staff*) de más antigüedad; (*of
higher rank*) superior; **senior citizen** n
persona de la tercera edad; **senior high
school** (US) n ≈ instituto de enseñanza
media; *see also* **high school**

sensation [sɛn'seɪʃən] n sensación *f*;
sensational *adj* sensacional

sense [sɛns] n (*faculty, meaning*)
sentido; (*feeling*) sensación *f*; (*good
sense*) sentido común, juicio ▷ *vt*
sentir, percibir; **it makes ~** tiene
sentido; **senseless** *adj* estúpido,
insensato; (*unconscious*) sin
conocimiento; **sense of humour** (BRIT)
n sentido del humor

sensible ['sɛnsɪbl] *adj* sensato;
(*reasonable*) razonable, lógico

  Be careful not to translate **sensible**
  by the Spanish word *sensible*.

sensitive ['sɛnsɪtɪv] *adj* sensible;
(*touchy*) susceptible

sensual ['sɛnsjuəl] *adj* sensual

sensuous ['sɛnsjuəs] *adj* sensual

sent [sɛnt] *pt, pp of* **send**

sentence ['sɛntns] n (*Ling*) oración
f; (*Law*) sentencia, fallo ▷ *vt*: **to ~ sb to
death/to 5 years (in prison)** condenar
a algn a muerte/a 5 años de cárcel

sentiment ['sɛntɪmənt] n
sentimiento; (*opinion*) opinión
f; **sentimental** [-'mɛntl] *adj*
sentimental

Sep. *abbr* (= *September*) sep., set.

separate [*adj* 'sɛprɪt, *vb* 'sɛpəreɪt]
adj separado; (*distinct*) distinto ▷ *vt*
separar; (*part*) dividir ▷ *vi* separarse;
separately *adv* por separado;
separates *npl* (*clothes*) coordinados
mpl; **separation** [-'reɪʃən] n
separación *f*

September [sɛp'tɛmbə*] n
se(p)tiembre *m*

septic ['sɛptɪk] *adj* séptico; **septic

tank** n fosa séptica

sequel ['si:kwl] n consecuencia,
resultado; (*of story*) continuación *f*

sequence ['si:kwəns] n sucesión *f*,
serie *f*; (*Cinema*) secuencia

sequin ['si:kwɪn] n lentejuela

Serb [sə:b] *adj, n* = **Serbian**

Serbian ['sə:bɪən] *adj* serbio ▷ *n*
serbio/a; (*Ling*) serbio

sergeant ['sɑːdʒənt] n sargento

serial ['sɪərɪəl] n (*TV*) telenovela, serie
f televisiva; (*Book*) serie *f*; **serial killer** n
asesino/a múltiple; **serial number** n
número de serie

series ['sɪəri:s] n *inv* serie *f*

serious ['sɪərɪəs] *adj* serio; (*grave*)
grave; **seriously** *adv* en serio; (*ill,
wounded etc*) gravemente

sermon ['sə:mən] n sermón *m*

servant ['sə:vənt] n servidor(a) *m/f*;
(*house servant*) criado/a

serve [sə:v] *vt* servir; (*customer*)
atender; (*train*) pasar por;
(*apprenticeship*) hacer; (*prison term*)
cumplir ▷ *vi* (*at table*) servir; (*Tennis*)
sacar; **to ~ as/for/to do** servir
de/para/para hacer ▷ *n* (*Tennis*) saque
m; **it ~s him right** se lo tiene merecido;
server n (*Comput*) servidor *m*

service ['sə:vɪs] n servicio; (*Rel*)
misa; (*Aut*) mantenimiento; (*dishes
etc*) juego ▷ *vt* (*car etc*) revisar;
(: *repair*) reparar; **to be of ~ to sb** ser
útil a algn; **~ included/not included**
servicio incluido/no incluido
(*Econ: tertiary sector*) sector *m* terciario
or (de) servicios; (BRIT: *on motorway*)
área de servicio; (*Mil*): **the S~s** las
fuerzas armadas; **service area** n (*on
motorway*) área de servicio; **service
charge** (BRIT) n servicio; **serviceman**
(*irreg*) n militar *m*; **service station** n
estación *f* de servicio

serviette [sə:vɪ'ɛt] (BRIT) n servilleta

session ['sɛʃən] n sesión *f*; **to be in ~**
estar en sesión

set [sɛt] (*pt, pp* ~) n juego; (*Radio*)
aparato; (*TV*) televisor *m*; (*of utensils*)

batería; (of cutlery) cubierto; (of books) colección f; (Tennis) set m; (group of people) grupo; (Cinema) plató m; (Theatre) decorado; (Hairdressing) marcado ▷ adj (fixed) fijo; (ready) listo ▷ vt (place) poner, colocar; (fix) fijar; (adjust) ajustar, arreglar; (decide: rules etc) establecer, decidir ▷ vi (sun) ponerse; (jam, jelly) cuajarse; (concrete) fraguar; (bone) componerse; **to be ~ on doing sth** estar empeñado en hacer algo; **to ~ to music** poner música a; **to ~ on fire** incendiar, poner fuego a; **to ~ free** poner en libertad; **to ~ sth going** poner algo en marcha; **to ~ sail** zarpar, hacerse a la vela; **set aside** vt poner aparte, dejar de lado; (money, time) reservar; **set down** vt (bus, train) dejar; **set in** vi (infection) declararse; (complications) comenzar; **the rain has set in for the day** parece que va a llover todo el día; **set off** vi partir ▷ vt (bomb) hacer estallar; (events) poner en marcha; (show up well) hacer resaltar; **set out** vi partir ▷ vt (arrange) disponer; (state) exponer; **to set out to do sth** proponerse hacer algo; **set up** vt establecer; **setback** n revés m, contratiempo; **set menu** n menú m

settee [sɛ'tiː] n sofá m

setting ['sɛtɪŋ] n (scenery) marco; (position) disposición f; (of sun) puesta; (of jewel) engaste m, montadura

settle ['sɛtl] vt (argument) resolver; (accounts) ajustar, liquidar; (Med: calm) calmar, sosegar ▷ vi (dust etc) depositarse; (weather) serenarse; **to ~ for sth** convenir en aceptar algo; **to ~ on sth** decidirse por algo; **settle down** vi (get comfortable) ponerse cómodo, acomodarse; (calm down) calmarse, tranquilizarse; (live quietly) echar raíces; **settle in** vi instalarse; **settle up** vi: **to settle up with sb** ajustar cuentas con algn; **settlement** n (payment) liquidación f; (agreement) acuerdo, convenio; (village etc) pueblo

setup ['sɛtʌp] n sistema m; (situation) situación f

seven ['sɛvn] num siete; **seventeen** num diez y siete, diecisiete; **seventeenth** [sɛvn'tiːnθ] adj decimoséptimo; **seventh** num séptimo; **seventieth** ['sɛvntɪɪθ] adj septuagésimo; **seventy** num setenta

sever ['sɛvə*] vt cortar; (relations) romper

several ['sɛvərl] adj, pron varios/as m/fpl, algunos/as m/fpl; **~ of us** varios de nosotros

severe [sɪ'vɪə*] adj severo; (serious) grave; (hard) duro; (pain) intenso

sew [səu] (pt **~ed**, pp **~n**) vt, vi coser

sewage ['suːɪdʒ] n aguas fpl residuales

sewer ['suːə*] n alcantarilla, cloaca

sewing ['səuɪŋ] n costura; **sewing machine** n máquina de coser

sewn [səun] pp of **sew**

sex [sɛks] n sexo; (lovemaking): **to have ~** hacer el amor; **sexism** ['sɛksɪzəm] n sexismo; **sexist** adj, n sexista mf; **sexual** ['sɛksjuəl] adj sexual; **sexual intercourse** n relaciones fpl sexuales; **sexuality** [sɛksju'ælɪtɪ] n sexualidad f; **sexy** adj sexy

shabby ['ʃæbɪ] adj (person) desharrapado; (clothes) raído, gastado; (behaviour) ruin inv

shack [ʃæk] n choza, chabola

shade [ʃeɪd] n sombra; (for lamp) pantalla; (for eyes) visera; (of colour) matiz m, tonalidad f; (small quantity): **a ~ (too big/more)** un poquitín (grande/más) ▷ vt dar sombra a; (eyes) proteger del sol; **in the ~** en la sombra; **shades** npl (sunglasses) gafas fpl de sol

shadow ['ʃædəu] n sombra ▷ vt (follow) seguir y vigilar; **shadow cabinet** (BRIT) n (Pol) gabinete paralelo formado por el partido de oposición

shady ['ʃeɪdɪ] adj sombreado; (fig: dishonest) sospechoso; (: deal) turbio

shaft [ʃɑːft] n (of arrow, spear) astil m; (Aut, Tech) eje m, árbol m; (of mine) pozo;

(of lift) hueco, caja; (of light) rayo

shake [ʃeɪk] (pt **shook**, pp **shaken**) vt sacudir; (building) hacer temblar; (bottle, cocktail) agitar ▷ vi (tremble) temblar; **to ~ one's head** (in refusal) negar con la cabeza; (in dismay) mover or menear la cabeza, incrédulo; **to ~ hands with sb** estrechar la mano a algn; **shake off** vt sacudirse; (fig) deshacerse de; **shake up** vt agitar; (fig) reorganizar; **shaky** adj (hand, voice) trémulo; (building) inestable

shall [ʃæl] aux vb: **~ I help you?** ¿quieres que te ayude?; **I'll buy three, ~ I?** compro tres, ¿no te parece?

shallow ['ʃæləʊ] adj poco profundo; (fig) superficial

sham [ʃæm] n fraude m, engaño

shambles ['ʃæmblz] n confusión f

shame [ʃeɪm] n vergüenza ▷ vt avergonzar; **it is a ~ that/to do** es una lástima que/hacer; **what a ~!** ¡qué lástima!; **shameful** adj vergonzoso; **shameless** adj desvergonzado

shampoo [ʃæm'puː] n champú m ▷ vt lavar con champú

shandy ['ʃændɪ] n mezcla de cerveza con gaseosa

shan't [ʃɑːnt] = **shall not**

shape [ʃeɪp] n forma ▷ vt formar, dar forma a; (sb's ideas) formar; (sb's life) determinar; **to take ~** tomar forma

share [ʃeə*] n (part) parte f, porción f; (contribution) cuota; (Comm) acción f ▷ vt dividir; (have in common) compartir; **to ~ out (among or between)** repartir (entre); **shareholder** (BRIT) n accionista mf

shark [ʃɑːk] n tiburón m

sharp [ʃɑːp] adj (blade, nose) afilado; (point) puntiagudo; (outline) definido; (pain) intenso; (Mus) desafinado; (contrast) marcado; (voice) agudo; (person: quick-witted) astuto; (: dishonest) poco escrupuloso ▷ n (Mus) sostenido ▷ adv: **at 2 o'clock ~** a las 2 en punto; **sharpen** vt afilar; (pencil) sacar punta a; (fig) agudizar;

sharpener n (also: **pencil sharpener**) sacapuntas m inv; **sharply** adv (turn, stop) bruscamente; (stand out, contrast) claramente; (criticize, retort) severamente

shatter ['ʃætə*] vt hacer añicos or pedazos; (fig: ruin) destruir, acabar con ▷ vi hacerse añicos; **shattered** adj (grief-stricken) destrozado, deshecho; (exhausted) agotado, hecho polvo

shave [ʃeɪv] vt afeitar, rasurar ▷ vi afeitarse, rasurarse ▷ n: **to have a ~** afeitarse; **shaver** n (also: **electric shaver**) máquina de afeitar (eléctrica)

shavings ['ʃeɪvɪŋz] npl (of wood etc) virutas fpl

shaving cream ['ʃeɪvɪŋ-] n crema de afeitar

shaving foam n espuma de afeitar

shawl [ʃɔːl] n chal m

she [ʃiː] pron ella

sheath [ʃiːθ] n vaina; (contraceptive) preservativo

shed [ʃed] (pt, pp **~**) n cobertizo ▷ vt (skin) mudar; (tears, blood) derramar; (load) derramar; (workers) despedir

she'd [ʃiːd] = **she had**; **she would**

sheep [ʃiːp] n inv oveja; **sheepdog** n perro pastor; **sheepskin** n piel f de carnero

sheer [ʃɪə*] adj (utter) puro, completo; (steep) escarpado; (material) diáfano ▷ adv verticalmente

sheet [ʃiːt] n (on bed) sábana; (of paper) hoja; (of glass, metal) lámina; (of ice) capa

sheik(h) [ʃeɪk] n jeque m

shelf [ʃelf] (pl **shelves**) n estante m

shell [ʃel] n (on beach) concha; (of egg, nut etc) cáscara; (explosive) proyectil m, obús m; (of building) armazón f ▷ vt (peas) desenvainar; (Mil) bombardear

she'll [ʃiːl] = **she will**; **she shall**

shellfish ['ʃelfɪʃ] n inv crustáceo; (as food) mariscos mpl

shelter ['ʃeltə*] n abrigo, refugio ▷ vt (aid) amparar, proteger; (give lodging to) abrigar ▷ vi abrigarse, refugiarse;

sheltered adj (life) protegido; (spot) abrigado

shelves [ʃɛlvz] npl of **shelf**

shelving [ʃɛlvɪŋ] n estantería

shepherd [ʃɛpəd] n pastor m ⊳vt (guide) guiar, conducir; **shepherd's pie** (BRIT) n pastel de carne y patatas

sheriff [ʃɛrɪf] (US) n sheriff m

sherry [ʃɛrɪ] n jerez m

she's [ʃiːz] = **she is**; **she has**

Shetland [ʃɛtlənd] n (also: **the ~s, the ~ Isles**) las Islas de Zetlandia

shield [ʃiːld] n escudo; (protection) blindaje m ⊳vt: **to ~ (from)** proteger (de)

shift [ʃɪft] n (change) cambio; (at work) turno ⊳vt trasladar; (remove) quitar ⊳vi moverse

shin [ʃɪn] n espinilla

shine [ʃaɪn] (pt, pp **shone**) n brillo, lustre m ⊳vi brillar, relucir ⊳vt (shoes) lustrar, sacar brillo a; **to ~ a torch on sth** dirigir una linterna hacia algo

shingles [ʃɪŋglz] n (Med) herpes mpl o fpl

shiny [ʃaɪnɪ] adj brillante, lustroso

ship [ʃɪp] n buque m, barco ⊳vt (goods) embarcar; (send) transportar or enviar por vía marítima; **shipment** n (goods) envío; **shipping** n (act) embarque m; (traffic) buques mpl; **shipwreck** n naufragio ⊳vt: **to be shipwrecked** naufragar; **shipyard** n astillero

shirt [ʃəːt] n camisa; **in (one's) ~ sleeves** en mangas de camisa

shit [ʃɪt] (inf!) excl ¡mierda! (!)

shiver [ʃɪvə*] n escalofrío ⊳vi temblar, estremecerse; (with cold) tiritar

shock [ʃɔk] n (impact) choque m; (Elec) descarga (eléctrica); (emotional) conmoción f; (start) sobresalto, susto; (Med) postración f nerviosa ⊳vt dar un susto a; (offend) escandalizar; **shocking** adj (awful) espantoso; (outrageous) escandaloso

shoe [ʃuː] (pt, pp **shod**) n zapato; (for horse) herradura ⊳vt (horse) herrar; **shoelace** n cordón m; **shoe polish** n betún m; **shoeshop** n zapatería

shone [ʃɔn] pt, pp of **shine**

shook [ʃuk] pt of **shake**

shoot [ʃuːt] (pt, pp **shot**) n (on branch, seedling) retoño, vástago ⊳vt disparar; (kill) matar a tiros; (wound) pegar un tiro; (execute) fusilar; (film) rodar, filmar ⊳vi (Football) chutar; **shoot down** vt (plane) derribar; **shoot up** vi (prices) dispararse; **shooting** n (shots) tiros mpl; (Hunting) caza con escopeta

shop [ʃɔp] n tienda; (workshop) taller m ⊳vi (also: **go ~ping**) ir de compras; **shop assistant** (BRIT) n dependiente/a m/f; **shopkeeper** n tendero/a; **shoplifting** n mechería; **shopping** n (goods) compras fpl; **shopping bag** n bolsa (de compras); **shopping centre** (US **shopping center**) n centro comercial; **shopping mall** n centro comercial; **shopping trolley** n (BRIT) carrito de la compra; **shop window** n escaparate m (SP), vidriera (LAM)

shore [ʃɔː*] n orilla ⊳vt: **to ~ (up)** reforzar; **on ~** en tierra

short [ʃɔːt] adj corto; (in time) breve, de corta duración; (person) bajo; (curt) brusco, seco; (insufficient) insuficiente; **(a pair of) ~s** (unos) pantalones mpl cortos; **to be ~ of sth** estar falto de algo; **in ~** en pocas palabras; **~ of doing ...** fuera de hacer ...; **it is ~ for** es la forma abreviada de; **to cut ~** (speech, visit) interrumpir, terminar inesperadamente; **everything ~ of ...** todo menos ...; **to fall ~ of** no alcanzar; **to run ~** quedarle a algn poco; **to stop ~** parar en seco; **to stop ~ of** detenerse antes de; **shortage** n: **a shortage of** una falta de; **shortbread** n especie de mantecada; **shortcoming** n defecto, deficiencia; **short(crust) pastry** (BRIT) n pasta quebradiza; **shortcut** n atajo; **shorten** vt acortar; (visit) interrumpir; **shortfall** n déficit m; **shorthand** (BRIT) n

taquigrafía; **short-lived** adj efímero;
shortly adv en breve, dentro de poco;
shorts npl pantalones mpl cortos; (us)
calzoncillos mpl; **short-sighted** (BRIT)
adj miope; (fig) imprudente; **short-
sleeved** adj de manga corta; **short
story** n cuento; **short-tempered** adj
enojadizo; **short-term** adj (effect) a
corto plazo

shot [ʃɔt] pt, pp of **shoot** ▷ n (sound)
tiro, disparo; (try) tentativa; (injection)
inyección f; (Phot) toma, fotografía;
to be a good/poor ~ (person) tener
buena/mala puntería; **like a ~** (without
any delay) como un rayo; **shotgun** n
escopeta

should [ʃud] aux vb: **I ~ go now** debo
irme ahora; **he ~ be there now** debe
de haber llegado (ya); **I ~ go if I were
you** yo en tu lugar me iría; **I ~ like to**
me gustaría

shoulder [ˈʃəuldə*] n hombro ▷ vt
(fig) cargar con; **shoulder blade** n
omóplato

shouldn't [ˈʃudnt] = **should not**

shout [ʃaut] n grito ▷ vt gritar ▷ vi
gritar, dar voces

shove [ʃʌv] n empujón m ▷ vt
empujar; (inf: put): **to ~ sth in** meter
algo a empellones

shovel [ˈʃʌvl] n pala; (mechanical)
excavadora ▷ vt mover con pala

show [ʃəu] (pt ~ed, pp ~n) n (of
emotion) demostración f; (semblance)
apariencia; (exhibition) exposición
f; (Theatre) función f, espectáculo;
(TV) show m ▷ vt mostrar, enseñar;
(courage etc) manifestar;
(exhibit) exponer; (film) proyectar ▷ vi
mostrarse; (appear) aparecer; **for ~**
para impresionar; **on ~** (exhibits etc)
expuesto; **show in** vt (person) hacer
pasar; **show off** (pej) vi presumir ▷ vt
(display) lucir; **show out** vt: **to show
sb out** acompañar a algn a la puerta;
show up vi (stand out) destacar;
(inf: turn up) aparecer ▷ vt (unmask)
desenmascarar; **show business** n

mundo del espectáculo

shower [ˈʃauə*] n (rain) chaparrón
m, chubasco; (of stones etc) lluvia;
(for bathing) ducha, regadera (MEX)
▷ vi llover ▷ vt (fig): **to ~ sb with sth**
colmar a algn de algo; **ducharse**; **shower cap** n gorro de
baño; **shower gel** n gel m de ducha

showing [ˈʃəuɪŋ] n (of film)
proyección f

show jumping n hípica

shown [ʃəun] pp of **show**

show: **show-off** (inf) n (person)
presumido/a; **showroom** n sala de
muestras

shrank [ʃræŋk] pt of **shrink**

shred [ʃred] n (gen pl) triza, jirón m
▷ vt hacer trizas; (Culin) desmenuzar

shrewd [ʃru:d] adj astuto

shriek [ʃri:k] n chillido ▷ vi chillar

shrimp [ʃrimp] n camarón m

shrine [ʃrain] n santuario, sepulcro

shrink [ʃriŋk] (pt **shrank**, pp **shrunk**)
vi encogerse; (be reduced) reducirse;
(also: **~ away**) retroceder ▷ vt encoger
▷ n (inf, pej) loquero/a; **to ~ from
(doing) sth** no atreverse a hacer algo

shrivel [ˈʃrivl] (also: **~ up**) vt (dry) secar
▷ vi secarse

shroud [ʃraud] n sudario ▷ vt: **~ed in
mystery** envuelto en el misterio

Shrove Tuesday [ˈʃrəuv-] n martes
m de carnaval

shrub [ʃrʌb] n arbusto

shrug [ʃrʌg] n encogimiento
de hombros ▷ vt, vi: **to ~ (one's
shoulders)** encogerse de hombros;
shrug off vt negar importancia a

shrunk [ʃrʌŋk] pp of **shrink**

shudder [ˈʃʌdə*] n estremecimiento,
escalofrío ▷ vi estremecerse

shuffle [ˈʃʌfl] vt (cards) barajar ▷ vi: **to
~ (one's feet)** arrastrar los pies

shun [ʃʌn] vt rehuir, esquivar

shut [ʃʌt] (pt, pp **~**) vt cerrar ▷ vi
cerrarse; **shut down** vt, vi cerrar;
shut up vi (inf: keep quiet) callarse
▷ vt (close) cerrar; (silence) hacer callar;

shutter n contraventana; (Phot) obturador m

shuttle ['ʃʌtl] n lanzadera; (also: ~ **service**) servicio rápido y continuo entre dos puntos; (Aviat) puente m aéreo; **shuttlecock** n volante m

shy [ʃaɪ] adj tímido

sibling ['sɪblɪŋ] n (formal) hermano/a

Sicily ['sɪsɪlɪ] n Sicilia

sick [sɪk] adj (ill) enfermo; (nauseated) mareado; (humour) negro; (vomiting): **to be ~** (BRIT) vomitar; **to feel ~** tener náuseas; **to be ~ of** (fig) estar harto de; **sickening** adj (fig) asqueroso; **sick leave** n baja por enfermedad; **sickly** adj enfermizo; (smell) nauseabundo; **sickness** n enfermedad f, mal m; (vomiting) náuseas fpl

side [saɪd] n (gen) lado m; (of body) costado; (of lake) orilla; (of hill) ladera; (team) equipo ▷ adj (door, entrance) lateral ▷ vi: **to ~ with sb** tomar el partido de algn; **by the ~ of** al lado de; **~ by ~** juntos/as; **from ~ to ~** de un lado para otro; **from all ~s** de todos lados; **to take ~s (with)** tomar partido (con); **sideboard** n aparador m; **sideboards** (BRIT) npl = **sideburns; sideburns** npl patillas fpl; **sidelight** n (Aut) luz f lateral; **sideline** n (Sport) línea de banda; (fig) empleo suplementario; **side order** n plato de acompañamiento; **side road** n (BRIT) calle f lateral; **side street** n calle f lateral; **sidetrack** vt (fig) desviar (de su propósito); **sidewalk** (US) n acera; **sideways** adv de lado

siege [siːdʒ] n cerco, sitio

sieve [sɪv] n colador m ▷ vt cribar

sift [sɪft] vt cribar; (fig: information) escudriñar

sigh [saɪ] n suspiro ▷ vi suspirar

sight [saɪt] n (faculty) vista; (spectacle) espectáculo; (on gun) mira, alza ▷ vt divisar; **in ~** a la vista; **out of ~** fuera de (la) vista; **on ~** (shoot) sin previo aviso; **sightseeing** n excursionismo, turismo; **to go sightseeing** hacer turismo

sign [saɪn] n (with hand) señal f, seña; (trace) huella, rastro; (notice) letrero; (written) signo ▷ vt firmar; (Sport) fichar; **to ~ sth over to sb** firmar el traspaso de algo a algn; **sign for** vt fus (item) firmar el recibo de; **sign in** vi firmar el registro (al entrar); **sign on** vi (BRIT: as unemployed) registrarse como desempleado; (for course) inscribirse ▷ vt (Mil) alistar; (employee) contratar; **sign up** vi (Mil) alistarse; (for course) inscribirse ▷ vt (player) fichar

signal ['sɪgnl] n señal f ▷ vi señalizar ▷ vt (person) hacer señas a; (message) comunicar por señales

signature ['sɪgnətʃə*] n firma

significance [sɪg'nɪfɪkəns] n (importance) trascendencia

significant [sɪg'nɪfɪkənt] adj significativo; (important) trascendente

signify ['sɪgnɪfaɪ] vt significar

sign language n lenguaje m para sordomudos

signpost ['saɪnpəust] n indicador m

Sikh [siːk] adj, n sij mf

silence ['saɪlns] n silencio ▷ vt acallar; (guns) reducir al silencio

silent ['saɪlnt] adj silencioso; (not speaking) callado; (film) mudo; **to remain ~** guardar silencio

silhouette [sɪluːˈɛt] n silueta

silicon chip ['sɪlɪkən-] n plaqueta de silicio

silk [sɪlk] n seda ▷ adj de seda

silly ['sɪlɪ] adj (person) tonto; (idea) absurdo

silver ['sɪlvə*] n plata; (money) moneda suelta ▷ adj de plata; (colour) plateado; **silver-plated** adj plateado

similar ['sɪmɪlə*] adj: **~ (to)** parecido or semejante (a); **similarity** [-ˈlærɪtɪ] n semejanza; **similarly** adv del mismo modo

simmer ['sɪmə*] vi hervir a fuego lento

simple ['sɪmpl] adj (easy) sencillo; (foolish, Comm: interest) simple;

simplicity [-'plɪsɪtɪ] n sencillez f;
simplify ['sɪmplɪfaɪ] vt simplificar;
simply adv (live, talk) sencillamente;
(just, merely) sólo
simulate ['sɪmjuːleɪt] vt fingir,
simular
simultaneous [sɪməl'teɪnɪəs] adj
simultáneo; **simultaneously** adv
simultáneamente
sin [sɪn] n pecado ▷ vi pecar
since [sɪns] adv desde entonces,
después ▷ prep desde ▷ conj (time)
desde que; (because) ya que, puesto
que; **~ then**, **ever ~** desde entonces
sincere [sɪn'sɪə*] adj sincero;
sincerely adv: **yours sincerely** (in
letters) le saluda atentamente
sing [sɪŋ] (pt **sang**, pp **sung**) vt, vi
cantar
Singapore [sɪŋə'pɔː*] n Singapur m
singer ['sɪŋə*] n cantante mf
singing ['sɪŋɪŋ] n canto
single ['sɪŋgl] adj único, solo;
(unmarried) soltero; (not double) simple,
sencillo ▷ n (BRIT: also: **~ ticket**) billete
m sencillo; (record) sencillo, single
m; **singles** npl (Tennis) individual
m; **single out** vt (choose) escoger;
single bed n cama individual; **single
file** n: **in single file** en fila de uno;
single-handed adv sin ayuda; **single-
minded** adj resuelto, firme; **single
parent** n padre m soltero, madre f
soltera (o divorciado etc); **single parent
family** familia monoparental; **single
room** n cuarto individual
singular ['sɪŋgjulə*] adj (odd) raro,
extraño; (outstanding) excepcional ▷ n
(Ling) singular m
sinister ['sɪnɪstə*] adj siniestro
sink [sɪŋk] (pt **sank**, pp **sunk**) n
fregadero ▷ vt (ship) hundir, echar
a pique; (foundations) excavar ▷ vi
hundirse; **to ~ sth into** hundir algo en;
sink in vi (fig) penetrar, calar
sinus ['saɪnəs] n (Anat) seno
sip [sɪp] n sorbo ▷ vt sorber, beber
a sorbitos

sir [sə*] n señor m; **S~ John Smith** Sir
John Smith; **yes ~** sí, señor
siren ['saɪərn] n sirena
sirloin ['səːlɔɪn] n (also: **~ steak**)
solomillo
sister ['sɪstə*] n hermana;
(BRIT: nurse) enfermera jefe; **sister-in-
law** n cuñada
sit [sɪt] (pt, pp **sat**) vi sentarse; (be
sitting) estar sentado; (assembly)
reunirse; (for painter) posar ▷ vt (exam)
presentarse a; **sit back** vi (in seat)
recostarse; **sit down** vi sentarse;
sit on vt fus (jury, committee) ser
miembro de, formar parte de; **sit up** vi
incorporarse; (not go to bed) velar
sitcom ['sɪtkɔm] n abbr (= situation
comedy) comedia de situación
site [saɪt] n sitio; (also: **building ~**)
solar m ▷ vt situar
sitting ['sɪtɪŋ] n (of assembly etc)
sesión f; (in canteen) turno; **sitting
room** n sala de estar
situated ['sɪtjueɪtɪd] adj situado
situation [sɪtju'eɪʃən] n situación f;
"~s vacant" "ofrecen trabajo"
six [sɪks] num seis; **sixteen** num diez
y seis, dieciséis; **sixteenth** [sɪks'tiːnθ]
adj decimosexto; **sixth** [sɪksθ] num
sexto; **sixth form** n (BRIT) clase f de
alumnos del sexto año (de 16 a 18 años de
edad); **sixth-form college** n instituto
m para alumnos de 16 a 18 años;
sixtieth ['sɪkstɪθ] adj sexagésimo;
sixty num sesenta
size [saɪz] n tamaño; (extent)
extensión f; (of clothing) talla; (of shoes)
número; **sizeable** adj importante,
considerable
sizzle ['sɪzl] vi crepitar
skate [skeɪt] n patín m; (fish: pl
inv) raya ▷ vi patinar; **skateboard**
n monopatín m; **skateboarding** n
monopatín m; **skater** n patinador(a)
m/f; **skating** n patinaje m; **skating
rink** n pista de patinaje
skeleton ['skelɪtn] n esqueleto;
(Tech) armazón f; (outline) esquema m

skeptical ['skɛptɪkl] (US) = **sceptical**

sketch [skɛtʃ] n (drawing) dibujo; (outline) esbozo, bosquejo; (Theatre) sketch m ▷ vt dibujar; (plan etc: also: ~ out) esbozar

skewer ['skjuːə*] n broqueta

ski: [skiː] n esquí m ▷ vi esquiar; **ski boot** n bota de esquí

skid [skɪd] n patinazo ▷ vi patinar

ski: skier n esquiador(a) m/f; **skiing** n esquí m

skilful ['skɪlful] (US **skillful**) adj diestro, experto

ski lift n telesilla m, telesquí m

skill [skɪl] n destreza, pericia; técnica; **skilled** adj hábil, diestro; (worker) cualificado

skim [skɪm] vt (milk) desnatar; (glide over) rozar, rasar ▷ vi: **to ~ through** (book) hojear; **skimmed milk** (US **skim milk**) n leche f desnatada

skin [skɪn] n piel f; (complexion) cutis m ▷ vt (fruit etc) pelar; (animal) despellejar; **skinhead** n cabeza m/f rapada, skin(head) m/f; **skinny** adj flaco

skip [skɪp] n brinco, salto; (BRIT: container) contenedor m ▷ vi brincar; (with rope) saltar a la comba ▷ vt saltarse

ski: ski pass n forfait m (de esquí); **ski pole** n bastón m de esquiar

skipper ['skɪpə*] n (Naut, Sport) capitán m

skipping rope ['skɪpɪŋ-] (US **skip rope**) n comba

skirt [skəːt] n falda, pollera (SC) ▷ vt (go round) ladear

skirting board ['skəːtɪŋ-] (BRIT) n rodapié m

ski slope n pista de esquí

ski suit n traje m de esquiar

skull [skʌl] n calavera; (Anat) cráneo

skunk [skʌŋk] n mofeta

sky [skaɪ] n cielo; **skyscraper** n rascacielos m inv

slab [slæb] n (stone) bloque m; (flat) losa; (of cake) trozo

slack [slæk] adj (loose) flojo; (slow) de poca actividad; (careless) descuidado; **slacks** npl pantalones mpl

slain [sleɪn] pp of **slay**

slam [slæm] vt (throw) arrojar (violentamente); (criticize) criticar duramente ▷ vi (door) cerrarse de golpe; **to ~ the door** dar un portazo

slander ['slɑːndə*] n calumnia, difamación f

slang [slæŋ] n argot m; (jargon) jerga

slant [slɑːnt] n sesgo, inclinación f; (fig) interpretación f

slap [slæp] n palmada; (in face) bofetada ▷ vt dar una palmada or bofetada a; (paint etc): **to ~ sth on sth** embadurnar algo con algo ▷ adv (directly) exactamente, directamente

slash [slæʃ] vt acuchillar; (fig: prices) fulminar

slate [sleɪt] n pizarra ▷ vt (fig: criticize) criticar duramente

slaughter ['slɔːtə*] n (of animals) matanza; (of people) carnicería ▷ vt matar; **slaughterhouse** n matadero

Slav [slɑːv] adj eslavo

slave [sleɪv] n esclavo/a ▷ vi (also: ~ away) sudar tinta; **slavery** n esclavitud f

slay [sleɪ] (pt **slew**, pp **slain**) vt matar

sleazy ['sliːzɪ] adj de mala fama

sled [slɛd] (US) = **sledge**

sledge [slɛdʒ] n trineo

sleek [sliːk] adj (shiny) lustroso; (car etc) elegante

sleep [sliːp] (pt, pp **slept**) n sueño ▷ vi dormir; **to go to ~** quedarse dormido; **sleep in** vi (oversleep) quedarse dormido; **sleep together** vi (have sex) acostarse juntos; **sleeper** n (person) durmiente m/f; (BRIT Rail: on track) traviesa; (: train) coche-cama m; **sleeping bag** n saco de dormir; **sleeping car** n coche-cama m; **sleeping pill** n somnífero; **sleepover** n: **we're having a sleepover at Jo's** nos vamos a quedar a dormir en casa de Jo; **sleepwalk** vi caminar dormido;

(*habitually*) ser sonámbulo; **sleepy** *adj*
soñoliento; (*place*) soporífero
sleet [sli:t] *n* aguanieve *f*
sleeve [sli:v] *n* manga; (*Tech*)
manguito; (*of record*) portada;
sleeveless *adj* sin mangas
sleigh [sleɪ] *n* trineo
slender ['slɛndə*] *adj* delgado;
(*means*) escaso
slept [slɛpt] *pt, pp of* **sleep**
slew [slu:] *pt of* **slay** ▷ *vi* (*BRIT: veer*)
torcerse
slice [slaɪs] *n* (*of meat*) tajada; (*of
bread*) rebanada; (*of lemon*) rodaja;
(*utensil*) pala ▷ *vt* cortar (en tajos),
rebanar
slick [slɪk] *adj* (*skilful*) hábil, diestro;
(*clever*) astuto ▷ *n* (*also: **oil ~***) marea
negra
slide [slaɪd] (*pt, pp* **slid**) *n* (*movement*)
descenso, desprendimiento; (*in
playground*) tobogán *m*; (*Phot*)
diapositiva, (*BRIT: also: **hair ~***) pasador
m ▷ *vt* correr, deslizar ▷ *vi* (*slip*)
resbalarse; (*glide*) deslizarse; **sliding**
adj (*door*) corredizo
slight [slaɪt] *adj* (*slim*) delgado;
(*frail*) delicado; (*pain etc*) leve; (*trivial*)
insignificante; (*small*) pequeño
▷ *n* desaire *m* ▷ *vt* (*insult*) ofender,
desairar; **not in the ~est** en absoluto;
slightly *adv* ligeramente, un poco
slim [slɪm] *adj* delgado, esbelto;
(*fig: chance*) remoto ▷ *vi* adelgazar;
slimming *n* adelgazamiento
slimy ['slaɪmɪ] *adj* cenagoso
sling [slɪŋ] (*pt, pp* **slung**) *n* (*Med*)
cabestrillo; (*weapon*) honda ▷ *vt* tirar,
arrojar
slip [slɪp] *n* (*slide*) resbalón *m*; (*mistake*)
descuido; (*underskirt*) combinación *f*;
(*of paper*) papelito ▷ *vt* (*slide*) deslizar
▷ *vi* deslizarse; (*stumble*) resbalar(se);
(*decline*) decaer; (*move smoothly*): **to ~
into/out of** (*room etc*) introducirse
en/salirse de; **to give sb the ~** eludir a
algn; **a ~ of the tongue** un lapsus; **to
~ sth on/off** ponerse/quitarse algo;

slip up *vi* (*make mistake*) equivocarse;
meter la pata
slipper ['slɪpə*] *n* zapatilla, pantufla
slippery ['slɪpərɪ] *adj* resbaladizo;
slip road (*BRIT*) *n* carretera de acceso
slit [slɪt] (*pt, pp ~*) *n* raja; (*cut*) corte *m*
▷ *vt* rajar; cortar
slog [slɔg] (*BRIT*) *vi* sudar tinta; **it was
a ~** costó trabajo (hacerlo)
slogan ['sləugən] *n* eslogan *m*,
lema *m*
slope [sləup] *n* (*up*) cuesta, pendiente
f; (*down*) declive *m*; (*side of mountain*)
falda, vertiente *m* ▷ *vi*: **to ~ down** estar
en declive; **to ~ up** inclinarse; **sloping**
adj en pendiente; en declive; (*writing*)
inclinado
sloppy ['slɔpɪ] *adj* (*work*) descuidado;
(*appearance*) desaliñado
slot [slɔt] *n* ranura ▷ *vt*: **to ~
into** encajar en; **slot machine** *n*
(*BRIT: vending machine*) distribuidor *m*
automático; (*for gambling*) tragaperras
m inv
Slovakia [sləuˈvækɪə] *n* Eslovaquia
Slovene [sləuˈviːn] *adj* esloveno ▷ *n*
esloveno/a; (*Ling*) esloveno; **Slovenia**
[sləuˈviːnɪə] *n* Eslovenia; **Slovenian**
adj, n = **Slovene**
slow [sləu] *adj* lento; (*not clever*)
lerdo; (*watch*): **to be ~** atrasar ▷ *adv*
lentamente, despacio ▷ *vt, vi*
retardar; **"~"** (*road sign*) "disminuir
velocidad"; **slow down** *vi* reducir
la marcha; **slowly** *adv* lentamente,
despacio; **slow motion** *n*: **in slow
motion** a cámara lenta
slug [slʌg] *n* babosa; (*bullet*) posta;
sluggish *adj* lento; (*person*) perezoso
slum [slʌm] *n* casucha
slump [slʌmp] *n* (*economic*) depresión
f ▷ *vi* hundirse; (*prices*) caer en picado
slung [slʌŋ] *pt, pp of* **sling**
slur [slə:*] *n*: **to cast a ~ on** insultar
▷ *vt* (*speech*) pronunciar mal
sly [slaɪ] *adj* astuto; (*smile*) taimado
smack [smæk] *n* bofetada ▷ *vt* dar
con la mano a; (*child, on face*) abofetear

▷ *vi*: **to ~ of** saber a, oler a

small [smɔːl] *adj* pequeño; **small ads** (*BRIT*) *npl* anuncios *mpl* por palabras; **small change** *n* suelto, cambio

smart [smɑːt] *adj* elegante; (*clever*) listo, inteligente; (*quick*) rápido, vivo ▷ *vi* escocer, picar; **smartcard** *n* tarjeta inteligente

smash [smæʃ] *n* (*also*: **~-up**) choque *m*; (*Mus*) exitazo ▷ *vt* (*break*) hacer pedazos; (*car etc*) estrellar; (*Sport: record*) batir ▷ *vi* hacerse pedazos; (*against wall etc*) estrellarse; **smashing** (*inf*) *adj* estupendo

smear [smɪə*] *n* mancha; (*Med*) frotis *m inv* ▷ *vt* untar; **smear test** *n* (*Med*) citología, frotis *m inv* (cervical)

smell [smɛl] (*pt, pp* **smelt** *or* **~ed**) *n* olor *m*; (*sense*) olfato ▷ *vt, vi* oler; **smelly** *adj* maloliente

smelt [smɛlt] *pt, pp of* **smell**

smile [smaɪl] *n* sonrisa ▷ *vi* sonreír

smirk [smɜːk] *n* sonrisa falsa *or* afectada

smog [smɔg] *n* esmog *m*

smoke [sməuk] *n* humo ▷ *vi* fumar; (*chimney*) echar humo ▷ *vt* (*cigarettes*) fumar; **smoke alarm** *n* detector *m* de humo, alarma contra incendios; **smoked** *adj* (*bacon, glass*) ahumado; **smoker** *n* fumador(a) *m/f*; (*Rail*) coche *m* fumador; **smoking** *n*: **"no smoking"** "prohibido fumar"

▍ Be careful not to translate **smoking** by the Spanish word *smoking*.

smoky *adj* (*room*) lleno de humo; (*taste*) ahumado

smooth [smuːð] *adj* liso; (*sea*) tranquilo; (*flavour, movement*) suave; (*sauce*) fino; (*person: pej*) meloso ▷ *vt* (*also*: **~ out**) alisar; (*creases, difficulties*) allanar

smother ['smʌðə*] *vt* sofocar; (*repress*) contener

SMS *n abbr* (= *short message service*) (servicio) SMS; **SMS message** *n* (mensaje *m*) SMS

smudge [smʌdʒ] *n* mancha ▷ *vt*

manchar

smug [smʌg] *adj* presumido; orondo

smuggle ['smʌgl] *vt* pasar de contrabando; **smuggling** *n* contrabando

snack [snæk] *n* bocado; **snack bar** *n* cafetería

snag [snæg] *n* problema *m*

snail [sneɪl] *n* caracol *m*

snake [sneɪk] *n* serpiente *f*

snap [snæp] *n* (*sound*) chasquido; (*photograph*) foto *f* ▷ *adj* (*decision*) instantáneo ▷ *vt* (*break*) quebrar; (*fingers*) castañetear ▷ *vi* quebrarse; (*fig: speak sharply*) contestar bruscamente; **to ~ shut** cerrarse de golpe; **snap at** *vt fus* (*dog*) intentar morder; **snap up** *vt* agarrar; **snapshot** *n* foto *f* (instantánea)

snarl [snɑːl] *vi* gruñir

snatch [snætʃ] *n* (*small piece*) fragmento ▷ *vt* (*snatch away*) arrebatar; (*fig*) agarrar; **to ~ some sleep** encontrar tiempo para dormir

sneak [sniːk] (*pt (us)* **snuck**) *vi*: **to ~ in/out** entrar/salir a hurtadillas ▷ *n* (*inf*) soplón/ona *m/f*; **to ~ up on sb** aparecérsele de improviso a algn; **sneakers** *npl* zapatos *mpl* de lona

sneer [snɪə*] *vi* reír con sarcasmo; (*mock*): **to ~ at** burlarse de

sneeze [sniːz] *vi* estornudar

sniff [snɪf] *vi* sollozar ▷ *vt* husmear, oler; (*drugs*) esnifar

snigger ['snɪgə*] *vi* reírse con disimulo

snip [snɪp] *n* tijeretazo; (*BRIT: inf: bargain*) ganga ▷ *vt* tijeretear

sniper ['snaɪpə*] *n* francotirador(a) *m/f*

snob [snɔb] *n* (e)snob *mf*

snooker ['snuːkə*] *n* especie de billar

snoop [snuːp] *vi*: **to ~ about** fisgonear

snooze [snuːz] *n* siesta ▷ *vi* echar una siesta

snore [snɔː*] *n* ronquido ▷ *vi* roncar

snorkel ['snɔːkl] *n* (tubo) respirador *m*

snort [snɔːt] n bufido ▷ vi bufar

snow [snəu] n nieve f ▷ vi nevar;
snowball n bola de nieve ▷ vi (fig)
agrandirse, ampliarse; **snowstorm** n
nevada, nevasca

snub [snʌb] vt (person) desairar ▷ n
desaire m, repulsa

snug [snʌg] adj (cosy) cómodo; (fitted)
ajustado

○ **KEYWORD**

so [səu] adv 1 (thus, likewise) así, de este
modo; **if so** de ser así; **I like swimming
– so do I** a mí me gusta nadar – a mí
también; **I've got work to do – so has
Paul** tengo trabajo que hacer – Paul
también; **it's 5 o'clock – so it is!** son las
cinco – ¡pues es verdad!; **I hope/think
so** espero/creo que sí; **so far** hasta
ahora; (in past) hasta este momento
2 (in comparisons etc: to such a degree)
tan; **so quickly (that)** tan rápido (que);
so big (that) tan grande (que); **she's
not so clever as her brother** no es
tan lista como su hermano; **we
were so worried** estábamos
preocupadísimos
3 : **so much** adj, adv tanto; **so many**
tantos/as
4 (phrases): **10 or so** unos 10, 10 o así; **so
long!** (inf: goodbye) ¡hasta luego!
▷ conj 1 (expressing purpose): **so as to do**
para hacer; **so (that)** para que +subjun
2 (expressing result) así que, **so you see,
I could have gone** así que ya ves, (yo)
podría haber ido

soak [səuk] vt (drench) empapar;
(steep in water) remojar ▷ vi remojarse,
estar a remojo; **soak up** vt absorber;
soaking adj (also: **soaking wet**)
calado or empapado (hasta los huesos
or el tuétano)

so-and-so ['səuənsəu] n (somebody)
fulano/a de tal

soap [səup] n jabón m; **soap opera**
n telenovela; **soap powder** n jabón
m en polvo

soar [sɔː*] vi (on wings) remontarse;
(rocket: prices) dispararse; (building etc)
elevarse

sob [sɔb] n sollozo ▷ vi sollozar

sober ['səubə*] adj (serious) serio; (not
drunk) sobrio; (colour, style) discreto;
sober up vt quitar la borrachera

so-called ['səu'kɔːld] adj así llamado

soccer ['sɔkə*] n fútbol m

sociable ['səuʃəbl] adj sociable

social ['səuʃl] adj social ▷ n velada,
fiesta; **socialism** n socialismo;
socialist adj, n socialista mf; **socialize**
vi: **to socialize (with)** alternar (con);
social life n vida social; **socially**
adv socialmente; **social security** n
seguridad f social; **social services** npl
servicios mpl sociales; **social work**
n asistencia social; **social worker** n
asistente/a m/f social

society [sə'saɪətɪ] n sociedad f;
(club) asociación f; (also: **high ~**) alta
sociedad

sociology [səusɪ'ɔlədʒɪ] n sociología

sock [sɔk] n calcetín m

socket ['sɔkɪt] n cavidad f; (BRIT Elec)
enchufe m

soda ['səudə] n (Chem) sosa; (also: **~
water**) soda; (US: also: **~ pop**) gaseosa

sodium ['səudɪəm] n sodio

sofa ['səufə] n sofá m; **sofa bed** n
sofá-cama m

soft [sɔft] adj (lenient, not hard) blando;
(gentle, not bright) suave; **soft drink** n
bebida no alcohólica; **soft drugs** npl
drogas fpl blandas; **soften** ['sɔfn] vt
ablandar; suavizar; (effect) amortiguar
▷ vi ablandarse; suavizarse; **softly** adv
suavemente; (gently) delicadamente,
con delicadeza; **software** n (Comput)
software m

soggy ['sɔgɪ] adj empapado

soil [sɔɪl] n (earth) tierra, suelo ▷ vt
ensuciar

solar ['səulə*] adj solar; **solar power**
n energía solar; **solar system** n
sistema m solar

sold [səʊld] *pt, pp of* **sell**

soldier ['səʊldʒə*] *n* soldado; (*army man*) militar *m*

sold out *adj* (Comm) agotado

sole [səʊl] *n* (*of foot*) planta; (*of shoe*) suela; (*fish: pl inv*) lenguado ▷ *adj* único; **solely** *adv* únicamente, sólo, solamente; **I will hold you solely responsible** le consideraré el único responsable

solemn ['sɔləm] *adj* solemne

solicitor [sə'lɪsɪtə*] (BRIT) *n* (*for wills etc*) ≈ notario/a; (*in court*) ≈ abogado/a

solid ['sɔlɪd] *adj* sólido; (*gold etc*) macizo ▷ *n* sólido

solitary ['sɔlɪtərɪ] *adj* solitario, solo

solitude ['sɔlɪtjuːd] *n* soledad *f*

solo ['səʊləʊ] *n* solo ▷ *adv* (*fly*) en solitario; **soloist** *n* solista *m/f*

soluble ['sɔljuːbl] *adj* soluble

solution [sə'luːʃən] *n* solución *f*

solve [sɔlv] *vt* resolver, solucionar

solvent ['sɔlvənt] *adj* (Comm) solvente ▷ *n* (Chem) solvente *m*

sombre ['sɔmbə*] (US **somber**) *adj* sombrío

○ **KEYWORD**

some [sʌm] *adj* **1** (*a certain amount or number*): **some tea/water/biscuits** té/agua/(unas) galletas; **there's some milk in the fridge** hay leche en el frigo; **there were some people outside** había algunas personas fuera; **I've got some money, but not much** tengo algo de dinero, pero no mucho

2 (*certain: in contrasts*) algunos/as; **some people say that ...** hay quien dice que ...; **some films were excellent, but most were mediocre** hubo películas excelentes, pero la mayoría fueron mediocres

3 (*unspecified*): **some woman was asking for you** una mujer estuvo preguntando por ti; **he was asking for some book (or other)** pedía un libro;

some day algún día; **some day next week** un día de la semana que viene ▷ *pron* **1** (*a certain number*): **I've got some** (*books etc*) tengo algunos/as **2** (*a certain amount*) algo; **I've got some** (*money, milk*) tengo algo; **could I have some of that cheese?** ¿me puede dar un poco de ese queso?; **I've read some of the book** he leído parte del libro ▷ *adv*: **some 10 people** unas 10 personas, una decena de personas

some: somebody ['sʌmbədɪ] *pron* = **someone**; **somehow** *adv* de alguna manera; (*for some reason*) por una u otra razón; **someone** *pron* alguien; **someplace** (*US*) *adv* = **somewhere**; **something** *pron* algo; **would you like something to eat/drink?** ¿te gustaría cenar/tomar algo?; **sometime** *adv* (*in future*) algún día, en algún momento; (*in past*): **sometime last month** durante el mes pasado; **sometimes** *adv* a veces; **somewhat** *adv* algo; **somewhere** *adv* (*be*) en alguna parte; (*go*) a alguna parte; **somewhere else** (*be*) en otra parte; (*go*) a otra parte

son [sʌn] *n* hijo

song [sɔŋ] *n* canción *f*

son-in-law ['sʌnɪnlɔː] *n* yerno

soon [suːn] *adv* pronto, dentro de poco; **~ afterwards** poco después; *see also* **as**; **sooner** *adv* (*time*) antes, más temprano; (*preference: rather*): **I would sooner do that** preferiría hacer eso; **sooner or later** tarde o temprano

soothe [suːð] *vt* tranquilizar; (*pain*) aliviar

sophisticated [sə'fɪstɪkeɪtɪd] *adj* sofisticado

sophomore ['sɔfəmɔː*] (*US*) *n* estudiante *mf* de segundo año

soprano [sə'prɑːnəʊ] *n* soprano *f*

sorbet ['sɔːbeɪ] *n* sorbete *m*

sordid ['sɔːdɪd] *adj* (*place etc*) sórdido; (*motive etc*) mezquino

sore [sɔː*] *adj* (*painful*) doloroso, que duele ▷ *n* llaga

sorrow ['sɔrəu] n pena, dolor m

sorry ['sɔrɪ] adj (regretful) arrepentido; (condition, excuse) lastimoso; **~!** ¡perdón!, ¡perdone!; **~?** ¿cómo?; **to feel ~ for sb** tener lástima a algn; **I feel ~ for him** me da lástima

sort [sɔːt] n clase f, género, tipo; **sort out** vt (papers) clasificar; (organize) ordenar, organizar; (resolve: problem, situation etc) arreglar, solucionar

SOS n SOS m

so-so ['səusəu] adv regular, así así

sought [sɔːt] pt, pp of **seek**

soul [səul] n alma

sound [saund] n (noise) sonido, ruido; (volume: on TV etc) volumen m; (Geo) estrecho ▷ adj (healthy) sano; (safe, not damaged) en buen estado; (reliable: person) digno de confianza; (sensible) sensato, razonable; (secure: investment) seguro ▷ adv: **~ asleep** profundamente dormido ▷ vt (alarm) sonar ▷ vi sonar, resonar; (fig: seem) parecer; **to ~ like** sonar a; **soundtrack** n (of film) banda sonora

soup [suːp] n (thick) sopa; (thin) caldo

sour ['sauə*] adj agrio; (milk) cortado; **it's ~ grapes** (fig) están verdes

source [sɔːs] n fuente f

south [sauθ] n sur m ▷ adj del sur, sureño ▷ adv al sur, hacia el sur; **South Africa** n África del Sur; **South African** adj, n sudafricano/a m/f; **South America** n América del Sur, Sudamérica; **South American** adj, n sudamericano/a m/f; **southbound** adj (con) rumbo al sur; **southeastern** [sauθ'iːstən] adj sureste, del sureste; **southern** ['sʌðən] adj del sur, meridional; **South Korea** n Corea del Sur; **South Pole** n Polo Sur; **southward(s)** adv hacia el sur; **southwest** [sauθ'west] n suroeste m; **southwestern** [sauθ'westən] adj suroeste

souvenir [suːvə'nɪə*] n recuerdo

sovereign(s) ['sɔvrɪn] adj, n soberano/a m/f

sow¹ [səu] (pt **~ed**, pp **sown**) vt sembrar

sow² [sau] n cerda, puerca

soya ['sɔɪə] (BRIT) n soja

spa [spɑː] n balneario

space [speɪs] n espacio; (room) sitio ▷ cpd espacial ▷ vt (also: **~ out**) espaciar; **spacecraft** n nave f espacial; **spaceship** n = **spacecraft**

spacious ['speɪʃəs] adj amplio

spade [speɪd] n (tool) pala, laya; **spades** npl (Cards: British) picas fpl; (: Spanish) espadas fpl

spaghetti [spə'getɪ] n espaguetis mpl, fideos mpl

Spain [speɪn] n España

spam [spæm] n (junk e-mail) spam m

span [spæn] n (of bird, plane) envergadura; (of arch) luz f; (in time) lapso ▷ vt extenderse sobre, cruzar; (fig) abarcar

Spaniard ['spænjəd] n español(a) m/f

Spanish ['spænɪʃ] adj español(a) ▷ n (Ling) español m, castellano; **the Spanish** npl los españoles

spank [spæŋk] vt zurrar

spanner ['spænə*] (BRIT) n llave f (inglesa)

spare [speə*] adj de reserva; (surplus) sobrante, de más ▷ n = **spare part** ▷ vt (do without) pasarse sin; (refrain from hurting) perdonar; **to ~** (surplus) sobrante, de sobra; **spare part** n pieza de repuesto; **spare room** n cuarto de los invitados; **spare time** n tiempo libre; **spare tyre** (US **spare tire**) n (Aut) neumático or llanta (LAM) de recambio; **spare wheel** n (Aut) rueda de recambio

spark [spɑːk] n chispa; (fig) chispazo; **spark(ing) plug** n bujía

sparkle ['spɑːkl] n centelleo, destello ▷ vi (shine) relucir, brillar

sparrow ['spærəu] n gorrión m

sparse [spɑːs] adj esparcido, escaso

spasm ['spæzəm] n (Med) espasmo

spat [spæt] pt, pp of **spit**

spate [speɪt] n (fig): **a ~ of** un

torrente de
spatula ['spætjulə] n espátula
speak [spi:k] (pt **spoke**, pp **spoken**)
vt (language) hablar; (truth) decir ▷ vi
hablar; (make a speech) intervenir; **to
~ to sb/of** or **about sth** hablar con
algn/de or sobre algo; **~ up!** ¡habla
fuerte!; **speaker** n (in public) orador(a)
m/f; (also: **loudspeaker**) altavoz m; (for
stereo etc) bafle m; (Pol): **the Speaker**
(BRIT) el Presidente de la Cámara de los
Comunes; (US) el Presidente del Congreso
spear [spɪə*] n lanza ▷ vt alancear
special ['spɛʃl] adj especial; (edition
etc) extraordinario; (delivery) urgente;
special delivery n (Post): **by special
delivery** por entrega urgente;
special effects npl (Cine) efectos mpl
especiales; **specialist** n especialista
mf; **speciality** [spɛʃɪ'ælɪtɪ] (BRIT)
n especialidad f; **specialize** vi: **to
specialize (in)** especializarse
(en); **specially** adv sobre todo,
en particular; **special needs** npl
(BRIT): **children with special needs**
niños que requieren una atención
diferenciada; **special offer** n (Comm)
oferta especial; **special school** n
(BRIT) colegio m de educación especial;
specialty (US) n = **speciality**
species ['spi:ʃi:z] n inv especie f
specific [spə'sɪfɪk] adj específico;
specifically adv específicamente
specify ['spɛsɪfaɪ] vt, vi especificar,
precisar
specimen ['spɛsɪmən] n ejemplar m;
(Med: of urine) espécimen m; (: of blood)
muestra
speck [spɛk] n grano, mota
spectacle ['spɛktəkl] n espectáculo;
spectacles npl (BRIT: glasses) gafas
fpl (SP), anteojos mpl; **spectacular**
[-'tækjulə*] adj espectacular; (success)
impresionante
spectator [spɛk'teɪtə*] n
espectador(a) m/f
spectrum ['spɛktrəm] (pl **spectra**)
n espectro

speculate ['spɛkjuleɪt] vi: **to ~ (on)**
especular (en)
sped [spɛd] pt, pp of **speed**
speech [spi:tʃ] n (faculty) habla;
(formal talk) discurso; (spoken language)
lenguaje m; **speechless** adj mudo,
estupefacto
speed [spi:d] n velocidad f; (haste)
prisa; (promptness) rapidez f; **at full** or
top ~ a máxima velocidad; **speed up** vi
acelerarse ▷ vt acelerar; **speedboat**
n lancha motora; **speeding** n (Aut)
exceso de velocidad; **speed limit** n
límite m de velocidad, velocidad f
máxima; **speedometer** [spɪ'dɒmɪtə*]
n velocímetro; **speedy** adj (fast) veloz,
rápido; (prompt) pronto
spell [spɛl] (pt, pp **spelt** (BRIT) or **~ed**)
n (also: **magic ~**) encanto, hechizo;
(period of time) rato, período ▷ vt
deletrear; (fig) anunciar, presagiar;
to cast a ~ on sb hechizar a algn;
he can't ~ pone faltas de ortografía;
spell out vt (explain): **to spell sth out
for sb** explicar algo a algn en detalle;
spellchecker ['spɛltʃekə*] n corrector
m ortográfico; **spelling** n ortografía
spelt [spɛlt] pt, pp of **spell**
spend [spɛnd] (pt, pp **spent**) vt
(money) gastar; (time) pasar; (life)
dedicar; **spending** n: **government
spending** gastos mpl del gobierno
spent [spɛnt] pt, pp of **spend** ▷ adj
(cartridge, bullets, match) usado
sperm [spə:m] n esperma
sphere [sfɪə*] n esfera
spice [spaɪs] n especia ▷ vt
condimentar
spicy ['spaɪsɪ] adj picante
spider ['spaɪdə*] n araña
spike [spaɪk] n (point) punta; (Bot)
espiga
spill [spɪl] (pt, pp **spilt** or **~ed**) vt
derramar, verter ▷ vi derramarse; **to ~
over** desbordarse
spin [spɪn] (pt, pp **spun**) n (Aviat)
barrena; (trip in car) paseo (en coche);
(on ball) efecto ▷ vt (wool etc) hilar; (ball

etc) hacer girar ▷ *vi* girar, dar vueltas

spinach ['spinitʃ] *n* espinaca; (*as food*) espinacas *fpl*

spinal ['spaɪnl] *adj* espinal

spin doctor *n* informador(a) parcial al servicio de un partido político *etc*

spin-dryer (BRIT) *n* secador *m* centrífugo

spine [spaɪn] *n* espinazo, columna vertebral; (*thorn*) espina

spiral ['spaɪərl] *n* espiral *f* ▷ *vi* (*fig: prices*) subir desorbitadamente

spire ['spaɪə*] *n* aguja, chapitel *m*

spirit ['spirit] *n* (*soul*) alma; (*ghost*) fantasma *m*; (*attitude, sense*) espíritu *m*; (*courage*) valor *m*, ánimo; **spirits** *npl* (*drink*) licor(es) *m(pl)*; **in good ~s** alegre, de buen ánimo

spiritual ['spiritjuəl] *adj* espiritual ▷ *n* espiritual *m*

spit [spit] (*pt, pp* **spat**) *n* (*for roasting*) asador *m*, espetón *m*; (*saliva*) saliva ▷ *vi* escupir; (*sound*) chisporrotear; (*rain*) lloviznar

spite [spaɪt] *n* rencor *m*, ojeriza ▷ *vt* causar pena a, mortificar; **in ~ of** a pesar de, pese a; **spiteful** *adj* rencoroso, malévolo

splash [splæʃ] *n* (*sound*) chapoteo; (*of colour*) mancha ▷ *vt* salpicar ▷ *vi* (*also: ~ about*) chapotear; **splash out** (*inf*) *vi* (BRIT) derrochar dinero

splendid ['splendɪd] *adj* espléndido

splinter ['splɪntə*] *n* (*of wood etc*) astilla; (*in finger*) espigón *m* ▷ *vi* astillarse, hacer astillas

split [split] (*pt, pp* **~**) *n* hendedura, raja; (*fig*) división *f*; (*Pol*) escisión *f* ▷ *vt* partir, rajar; (*party*) dividir; (*share*) repartir ▷ *vi* dividirse, escindirse; **split up** *vi* (*couple*) separarse; (*meeting*) acabarse

spoil [spɔɪl] (*pt, pp* **~t** *or* **~ed**) *vt* (*damage*) dañar; (*mar*) estropear; (*child*) mimar, consentir

spoilt [spɔɪlt] *pt, pp of* **spoil** ▷ *adj* (*child*) mimado, consentido; (*ballot paper*) invalidado

spoke [spəuk] *pt of* **speak** ▷ *n* rayo, radio

spoken ['spəukn] *pp of* **speak**

spokesman ['spəuksmən] (*irreg*) *n* portavoz *m*

spokesperson ['spəukspə:sn] (*irreg*) *n* portavoz *m/f*, vocero/a (LAM)

spokeswoman ['spəukswumən] (*irreg*) *n* portavoz *f*

sponge [spʌndʒ] *n* esponja; (*also: ~ cake*) bizcocho ▷ *vt* (*wash*) lavar con esponja ▷ *vi*: **to ~ off** *or* **on sb** vivir a costa de algn; **sponge bag** (BRIT) *n* esponjera

sponsor ['spɔnsə*] *n* patrocinador(a) *m/f* ▷ *vt* (*applicant, proposal etc*) proponer; **sponsorship** *n* patrocinio

spontaneous [spɔn'teɪnɪəs] *adj* espontáneo

spooky ['spu:kɪ] (*inf*) *adj* espeluznante, horripilante

spoon [spu:n] *n* cuchara; **spoonful** *n* cucharada

sport [spɔ:t] *n* deporte *m*; (*person*): **to be a good ~** ser muy majo ▷ *vt* (*wear*) lucir, ostentar; **sport jacket** (US) *n* = **sports jacket**; **sports car** *n* coche *m* deportivo; **sports centre** (BRIT) *n* polideportivo; **sports jacket** (BRIT) *n* chaqueta deportiva; **sportsman** (*irreg*) *n* deportista *m*; **sports utility vehicle** *n* todoterreno *m inv*; **sportswear** *n* trajes *mpl* de deporte *or* sport; **sportswoman** (*irreg*) *n* deportista; **sporty** *adj* deportista

spot [spɔt] *n* sitio, lugar *m*; (*dot: on pattern*) punto, mancha; (*pimple*) grano; (*Radio*) cuña publicitaria; (*TV*) espacio publicitario; (*small amount*): **a ~ of** un poquito de ▷ *vt* (*notice*) notar, observar; **on the ~** allí mismo; **spotless** *adj* perfectamente limpio; **spotlight** *n* foco, reflector *m*; (*Aut*) faro auxiliar

spouse [spauz] *n* cónyuge *mf*

sprain [spreɪn] *n* torcedura ▷ *vt*: **to ~ one's ankle/wrist** torcerse el tobillo/la muñeca

sprang [spræŋ] *pt of* **spring**

sprawl [sprɔːl] vi tumbarse

spray [spreɪ] n rociada; (of sea) espuma; (container) atomizador m; (for paint etc) pistola rociadora; (of flowers) ramita ▷vt rociar; (crops) regar

spread [sprɛd] (pt, pp ~) n extensión f; (for bread etc) pasta para untar; (inf: food) comilona ▷vt extender; (butter) untar; (wings, sails) desplegar; (work, wealth) repartir; (scatter) esparcir ▷vi (also: ~ out: stain) extenderse; (news) diseminarse; **spread out** vi (move apart) separarse; **spreadsheet** n hoja electrónica or de cálculo

spree [spriː] n: **to go on a ~** ir de juerga

spring [sprɪŋ] (pt **sprang**, pp **sprung**) n (season) primavera; (leap) salto, brinco; (coiled metal) resorte m; (of water) fuente f, manantial m ▷vi saltar, brincar; **spring up** vi (thing: appear) aparecer; (problem) surgir; **spring onion** n cebolleta

sprinkle ['sprɪŋkl] vt (pour: liquid) rociar; (: salt, sugar) espolvorear; **to ~ water etc on, ~ with water etc** rociar or salpicar de agua etc

sprint [sprɪnt] n esprint m ▷vi esprintar

sprung [sprʌŋ] pp of **spring**

spun [spʌn] pt, pp of **spin**

spur [spəː*] n espuela; (fig) estímulo, aguijón m ▷vt (also: ~ on) estimular, incitar; **on the ~ of the moment** de improviso

spurt [spəːt] n chorro; (of energy) arrebato ▷vi chorrear

spy [spaɪ] n espía mf ▷vi: **to ~ on** espiar a ▷vt (see) divisar, lograr ver

sq. abbr = **square**

squabble ['skwɔbl] vi reñir, pelear

squad [skwɔd] n (Mil) pelotón m; (Police) brigada; (Sport) equipo

squadron ['skwɔdrn] n (Mil) escuadrón m; (Aviat, Naut) escuadra

squander ['skwɔndə*] vt (money) derrochar, despilfarrar; (chances) desperdiciar

square [skwɛə*] n cuadro; (in town) plaza; (inf: person) carca m/f ▷adj cuadrado; (inf: Ideas, tastes) trasnochado ▷vt (arrange) arreglar; (Math) cuadrar; (reconcile) compaginar; **all ~** igual(es); **to have a ~ meal** comer caliente; **2 metres ~** 2 metros en cuadro; **2 ~ metres** 2 metros cuadrados; **square root** n raíz f cuadrada

squash [skwɔʃ] n (BRIT: drink): **lemon/orange ~** zumo (SP) or jugo (LAM) de limón/naranja; (US Bot) calabacín m; (Sport) squash m ▷vt aplastar

squat [skwɔt] adj achaparrado ▷vi (also: ~ down) agacharse, sentarse en cuclillas; **squatter** n okupa mf (SP)

squeak [skwiːk] vi (hinge) chirriar, rechinar; (mouse) chillar

squeal [skwiːl] vi chillar, dar gritos agudos

squeeze [skwiːz] n presión f; (of hand) apretón m; (Comm) restricción f ▷vt (hand, arm) apretar

squid [skwɪd] n inv calamar m; (Culin) calamares mpl

squint [skwɪnt] vi bizquear, ser bizco ▷n (Med) estrabismo

squirm [skwəːm] vi retorcerse, revolverse

squirrel ['skwɪrəl] n ardilla

squirt [skwəːt] vi salir a chorros ▷vt chiscar

Sr abbr = **senior**

Sri Lanka [srɪ'læŋkə] n Sri Lanka m

St abbr = **saint**; **street**

stab [stæb] n (with knife) puñalada; (of pain) pinchazo; (inf: try): **to have a ~ at (doing) sth** intentar (hacer) algo ▷vt apuñalar

stability [stə'bɪlɪtɪ] n estabilidad f

stable ['steɪbl] adj estable ▷n cuadra, caballeriza

stack [stæk] n montón m, pila ▷vt amontonar, apilar

stadium ['steɪdɪəm] n estadio

staff [stɑːf] n (work force) personal m,

plantilla; (*BRIT Scol*) cuerpo docente
▷ *vt* proveer de personal
stag [stæg] *n* ciervo, venado
stage [steɪdʒ] *n* escena; (*point*) etapa;
(*platform*) plataforma; (*profession*): **the
~** el teatro ▷ *vt* (*play*) poner en escena,
representar; (*organize*) montar,
organizar; **in ~s** por etapas
stagger [ˈstægəʳ] *vi* tambalearse
▷ *vt* (*amaze*) asombrar; (*hours, holidays*)
escalonar; **staggering** *adj* asombroso
stagnant [ˈstægnənt] *adj* estancado
stag night, stag party *n*
despedida de soltero
stain [steɪn] *n* mancha; (*colouring*)
tintura ▷ *vt* manchar; (*wood*) teñir;
stained glass *n* vidrio *m* de color;
stainless steel *n* acero inoxidable
staircase [ˈstɛəkeɪs] *n* = **stairway**
stairs [stɛəz] *npl* escaleras *fpl*
stairway [ˈstɛəweɪ] *n* escalera
stake [steɪk] *n* estaca, poste *m*;
(*Comm*) interés *m*; (*Betting*) apuesta
▷ *vt* (*money*) apostar; (*life*) arriesgar;
(*reputation*) poner en juego; (*claim*)
presentar una reclamación; **to be at ~**
estar en juego
stale [steɪl] *adj* (*bread*) duro; (*food*)
pasado; (*smell*) rancio; (*beer*) agrio
stalk [stɔːk] *n* tallo, caña ▷ *vt*
acechar, cazar al acecho
stall [stɔːl] *n* (*in market*) puesto; (*in
stable*) casilla (de establo) ▷ *vt* (*Aut*)
calar; (*fig*) dar largas a ▷ *vi* (*Aut*)
calarse; (*fig*) andarse con rodeos
stamina [ˈstæmɪnə] *n* resistencia
stammer [ˈstæməʳ] *n* tartamudeo
▷ *vi* tartamudear
stamp [stæmp] *n* sello (*SP*),
estampilla (*LAM*), timbre *m* (*MEX*); (*mark*)
marca, huella; (*on document*) timbre
m ▷ *vi* (*also*: **~ one's foot**) patear ▷ *vt*
(*mark*) marcar; (*letter*) franquear; (*with
rubber stamp*) sellar; **stamp out** *vt* (*fire*)
apagar con el pie; (*crime, opposition*)
acabar con; **stamped addressed
envelope** *n* (*BRIT*) sobre *m* sellado con
las señas propias

stampede [stæmˈpiːd] *n* estampida
stance [stæns] *n* postura
stand [stænd] (*pt, pp* **stood**) *n*
(*position*) posición *f*, postura; (*for
taxis*) parada; (*hall stand*) perchero;
(*music stand*) atril *m*; (*Sport*) tribuna;
(*at exhibition*) stand *m* ▷ *vi* (*be*) estar,
encontrarse; (*be on foot*) estar de pie;
(*rise*) levantarse; (*remain*) quedar en
pie; (*in election*) presentar candidatura
▷ *vt* (*place*) poner, colocar; (*withstand*)
aguantar, soportar; (*invite to*) invitar;
to make a ~ (*fig*) mantener una
postura firme; **to ~ for parliament**
(*BRIT*) presentarse (como candidato) a
las elecciones; **stand back** *vi* retirarse;
stand by *vi* (*be ready*) estar listo
▷ *vt fus* (*opinion*) aferrarse a; (*person*)
apoyar; **stand down** *vi* (*withdraw*)
ceder el puesto; **stand for** *vt fus*
(*signify*) significar; (*tolerate*) aguantar,
permitir; **stand in for** *vt fus* suplir a;
stand out *vi* destacarse; **stand up** *vi*
levantarse, ponerse de pie; **stand up
for** *vt fus* defender; **stand up to** *vt fus*
hacer frente a
standard [ˈstændəd] *n* patrón *m*,
norma; (*level*) nivel *m*; (*flag*) estandarte
m ▷ *adj* (*size etc*) normal, corriente;
(*text*) básico; **standards** *npl* (*morals*)
valores *mpl* morales; **standard of
living** *n* nivel *m* de vida
standing [ˈstændɪŋ] *adj* (*on foot*) de
pie, en pie; (*permanent*) permanente
▷ *n* reputación *f*; **of many years' ~**
que lleva muchos años; **standing
order** (*BRIT*) *n* (*at bank*) orden *f* de pago
permanente
stand: standpoint *n* punto de vista;
standstill *n*: **at a standstill** (*industry,
traffic*) paralizado; (*car*) parado;
to come to a standstill quedar
paralizado; pararse
stank [stæŋk] *pt of* **stink**
staple [ˈsteɪpl] *n* (*for papers*) grapa
▷ *adj* (*food etc*) básico ▷ *vt* grapar
star [stɑːʳ] *n* estrella; (*celebrity*)
estrella, astro ▷ *vt* (*Theatre, Cinema*)

ser el/la protagonista de; **the stars** npl
(Astrology) el horóscopo

starboard ['stɑːbəd] n estribor m

starch [stɑːtʃ] n almidón m

stardom ['stɑːdəm] n estrellato

stare [stɛə*] n mirada fija ▷ vi: **to ~
at** mirar fijo

stark [stɑːk] adj (bleak) severo,
escueto ▷ adv: **~ naked** en cueros

start [stɑːt] n principio, comienzo;
(departure) salida; (sudden movement)
salto, sobresalto; (advantage) ventaja
▷ vt empezar, comenzar; (cause)
causar; (found) fundar; (engine) poner
en marcha ▷ vi comenzar, empezar;
(with fright) asustarse, sobresaltarse;
(train etc) salir; **to ~ doing** or **to do
sth** empezar a hacer algo; **start off**
vi empezar, comenzar; (leave) salir,
ponerse en camino; **start out** vi
(begin) empezar; (set out) partir, salir;
start up vi comenzar; (car) ponerse
en marcha ▷ vt comenzar; poner en
marcha; **starter** n (Aut) botón m de
arranque; (Sport: official) juez mf de
salida; (BRIT Culin) entrante m; **starting
point** n punto de partida

startle ['stɑːtl] vt asustar,
sobrecoger; **startling** adj alarmante

starvation [stɑːˈveɪʃən] n hambre f

starve [stɑːv] vi tener mucha
hambre; (to death) morir de hambre
▷ vt hacer pasar hambre

state [steɪt] n estado ▷ vt (say,
declare) afirmar; **the S~s** los Estados
Unidos; **to be in a ~** estar agitado;
statement n afirmación f; **state
school** n escuela or colegio estatal;
statesman (irreg) n estadista m

static ['stætɪk] n (Radio) parásitos mpl
▷ adj estático

station ['steɪʃən] n estación f; (Radio)
emisora; (rank) posición f social ▷ vt
colocar, situar; (Mil) apostar

stationary ['steɪʃnərɪ] adj
estacionario, fijo

stationer's (shop) (BRIT) n
papelería

stationery [-nərɪ] n papel m de
escribir, artículos mpl de escritorio

station wagon (US) n ranchera

statistic [stəˈtɪstɪk] n estadística;
statistics n (science) estadística

statue ['stætjuː] n estatua

stature ['stætʃə*] n estatura; (fig)
talla

status ['steɪtəs] n estado; (reputation)
estatus m; **status quo** n (e)statu
quo m

statutory ['stætjutrɪ] adj
estatutario

staunch [stɔːntʃ] adj leal,
incondicional

stay [steɪ] n estancia ▷ vi quedar(se);
(as guest) hospedarse; **to ~** seguir
en el mismo sitio; **to ~ the night/5
days** pasar la noche/estar 5 días;
stay away vi (from person, building)
no acercarse; (from event) no acudir;
stay behind vi quedar atrás; **stay
in** vi quedarse en casa; **stay on** vi
quedarse; **stay out** vi (of house) no
volver a casa; (on strike) permanecer
en huelga; **stay up** vi (at night) velar,
no acostarse

steadily ['stedɪlɪ] adv
constantemente; (firmly) firmemente;
(work, walk) sin parar; (gaze) fijamente

steady ['stedɪ] adj (firm) firme;
(regular) regular; (person, character)
sensato, juicioso; (boyfriend) formal;
(look, voice) tranquilo ▷ vt (stabilize)
estabilizar; (nerves) calmar

steak [steɪk] n filete m; (beef) bistec m

steal [stiːl] (pt **stole**, pp **stolen**) vt
robar ▷ vi robar; (move secretly) andar
a hurtadillas

steam [stiːm] n vapor m; (mist) vaho,
humo ▷ vt (Culin) cocer al vapor ▷ vi
echar vapor; **steam up** vi (window)
empañarse; **to get steamed up
about sth** (fig) ponerse negro por algo;
steamy adj (room) lleno de vapor;
(window) empañado; (heat, atmosphere)
bochornoso

steel [stiːl] n acero ▷ adj de acero

steep [sti:p] *adj* escarpado, abrupto; (*stair*) empinado; (*price*) exorbitante, excesivo ▷ *vt* empapar, remojar

steeple ['sti:pl] *n* aguja

steer [stɪə*] *vt* (*car*) conducir (*SP*), manejar (*LAM*); (*person*) dirigir ▷ *vi* conducir, manejar; **steering** *n* (*Aut*) dirección *f*; **steering wheel** *n* volante *m*

stem [stɛm] *n* (*of plant*) tallo; (*of glass*) pie *m* ▷ *vt* detener; (*blood*) restañar

step [stɛp] *n* paso; (*on stair*) peldaño, escalón *m* ▷ *vi*: **to ~ forward/back** dar un paso adelante/hacia atrás; **steps** *npl* (*BRIT*) = **stepladder; in/out of ~ (with)** acorde/en disonancia (con); **step down** *vi* (*fig*) retirarse; **step in** *vi* entrar; (*fig*) intervenir; **step up** *vt* (*increase*) aumentar; **stepbrother** *n* hermanastro; **stepchild** (*pl* **stepchildren**) *n* hijastro/a *m/f*; **stepdaughter** *n* hijastra; **stepfather** *n* padrastro; **stepladder** *n* escalera doble *or* de tijera; **stepmother** *n* madrastra; **stepsister** *n* hermanastra; **stepson** *n* hijastro

stereo ['stɛrɪəu] *n* estéreo ▷ *adj* (*also:* **~phonic**) estéreo, estereofónico

stereotype ['stɪərɪətaɪp] *n* estereotipo ▷ *vt* estereotipar

sterile ['stɛraɪl] *adj* estéril; **sterilize** ['stɛrɪlaɪz] *vt* esterilizar

sterling ['stə:lɪŋ] *adj* (*silver*) de ley ▷ *n* (*Econ*) libras *fpl* esterlinas *fpl*; **one pound ~** una libra esterlina

stern [stə:n] *adj* severo, austero ▷ *n* (*Naut*) popa

steroid ['stɪərɔɪd] *n* esteroide *m*

stew [stju:] *n* estofado, guiso ▷ *vt* estofar, guisar; (*fruit*) cocer

steward ['stju:əd] *n* camarero; **stewardess** *n* (*esp on plane*) azafata

stick [stɪk] (*pt, pp* **stuck**) *n* palo; (*of dynamite*) barreno; (*as weapon*) porra; (*also:* **walking ~**) bastón *m* ▷ *vt* (*glue*) pegar; (*inf: put*) meter; (: *tolerate*) aguantar, soportar; (*thrust*): **to ~ sth into** clavar *or* hincar algo en ▷ *vi*

pegarse; (*be unmoveable*) quedarse parado; (*in mind*) quedarse grabado; **stick out** *vi* sobresalir; **stick up** *vi* sobresalir; **stick up for** *vt fus* defender; **sticker** *n* (*label*) etiqueta engomada; (*with slogan*) pegatina; **sticking plaster** *n* esparadrapo; **stick shift** (*US*) *n* (*Aut*) palanca de cambios

sticky ['stɪkɪ] *adj* pegajoso; (*label*) engomado; (*fig*) difícil

stiff [stɪf] *adj* rígido, tieso; (*hard*) duro; (*manner*) estirado; (*difficult*) difícil; (*person*) inflexible; (*price*) exorbitante ▷ *adv*: **scared/bored ~** muerto de miedo/aburrimiento

stifling ['staɪflɪŋ] *adj* (*heat*) sofocante, bochornoso

stigma ['stɪgmə] *n* (*fig*) estigma *m*

stiletto [stɪ'lɛtəu] (*BRIT*) *n* (*also:* **~ heel**) tacón *m* de aguja

still [stɪl] *adj* inmóvil, quieto ▷ *adv* todavía; (*even*) aun; (*nonetheless*) sin embargo, aun así

stimulate ['stɪmjuleɪt] *vt* estimular

stimulus ['stɪmjuləs] (*pl* **stimuli**) *n* estímulo, incentivo

sting [stɪŋ] (*pt, pp* **stung**) *n* picadura; (*pain*) escozor *m*, picazón *f*; (*organ*) aguijón *m* ▷ *vt*, *vi* picar

stink [stɪŋk] (*pt* **stank**, *pp* **stunk**) *n* hedor *m*, tufo ▷ *vi* heder, apestar

stir [stə:*] *n* (*fig: agitation*) conmoción *f* ▷ *vt* (*tea etc*) remover; (*fig: emotions*) provocar ▷ *vi* moverse; **stir up** *vt* (*trouble*) fomentar; **stir-fry** *vt* sofreír removiendo ▷ *n* plato preparado sofriendo y removiendo los ingredientes

stitch [stɪtʃ] *n* (*Sewing*) puntada; (*Knitting*) punto; (*Med*) punto (de sutura); (*pain*) punzada ▷ *vt* coser; (*Med*) suturar

stock [stɔk] *n* (*Comm: reserves*) existencias *fpl*, stock *m*; (: *selection*) surtido; (*Agr*) ganado, ganadería; (*Culin*) caldo; (*descent*) raza, estirpe *f*; (*Finance*) capital *m* ▷ *adj* (*fig: reply etc*) clásico ▷ *vt* (*have in stock*) tener existencias de; **~s and shares** acciones

y valores; **in ~** en existencia or almacén;
out of ~ agotado; **to take ~ of** (fig)
asesorar, examinar; **stockbroker**
['stɔkbrəukə*] n agente mf or corredor
mf de bolsa(a); **stock cube** (BRIT) n
pastilla de caldo; **stock exchange** n
bolsa; **stockholder** ['stɔkhəuldə*] (US)
n accionista m/f

stocking ['stɔkɪŋ] n media

stock market n bolsa (de valores)

stole [stəul] pt of **steal** ▷ n estola

stolen ['stəuln] pp of **steal**

stomach ['stʌmək] n (Anat)
estómago; (belly) vientre m ▷ vt tragar,
aguantar; **stomachache** n dolor m
de estómago

stone [stəun] n piedra; (in fruit) hueso
(= 6.348 kg; 14 libras) ▷ adj de piedra
▷ vt apedrear; (fruit) deshuesar

stood [stud] pt, pp of **stand**

stool [stu:l] n taburete m

stoop [stu:p] vi (also: ~ down)
doblarse, agacharse; (also: have a ~)
ser cargado de espaldas

stop [stɔp] n parada; (in punctuation)
punto ▷ vt parar, detener; (break)
suspender; (block: pay) suspender;
(: cheque) invalidar; (also: **put a ~
to**) poner término a ▷ vi pararse,
detenerse; (end) acabarse; **to ~ doing
sth** dejar de hacer algo; **stop by** vi
pasar por; **stop off** vi interrumpir
el viaje; **stopover** n parada; (Aviat)
escala; **stoppage** n (strike) paro;
(blockage) obstrucción f

storage ['stɔːrɪdʒ] n almacenaje m

store [stɔː*] n (stock) provisión f;
(depot (BRIT: large shop) almacén m; (US)
tienda; (reserve) reserva, repuesto ▷ vt
almacenar; **stores** npl víveres mpl;
to be in ~ for sb (fig) esperarle a algn;
storekeeper n tendero/a

storey ['stɔːrɪ] (US **story**) n piso

storm [stɔːm] n tormenta; (fig: of
applause) salva; (: of criticism) nube f
▷ vi (fig) rabiar ▷ vt tomar por asalto;
stormy adj tempestuoso

story ['stɔːrɪ] n historia; (lie) mentira;

(US) = **storey**

stout [staut] adj (strong) sólido; (fat)
gordo, corpulento; (resolute) resuelto
▷ n cerveza negra

stove [stəuv] n (for cooking) cocina;
(for heating) estufa

straight [streɪt] adj recto,
derecho; (frank) franco, directo;
(simple) sencillo ▷ adv derecho,
directamente; (drink) sin mezcla; **to
put** or **get sth ~** dejar algo en claro; **~
away, ~ off** en seguida; **straighten**
vt (also: **straighten out**) enderezar,
poner derecho ▷ vi (also: **straighten
up**) enderezarse, ponerse derecho;
straightforward adj (simple) sencillo;
(honest) honrado, franco

strain [streɪn] n tensión f; (Tech)
presión f; (Med) torcedura; (breed) tipo,
variedad f ▷ vt (back etc) torcerse;
(resources) agotar; (stretch) estirar;
(food, tea) colar; **strained** adj (muscle)
torcido; (laugh) forzado; (relations)
tenso; **strainer** n colador m

strait [streɪt] n (Geo) estrecho; (fig): **to
be in dire ~s** estar en un gran apuro

strand [strænd] n (of thread) hebra;
(of hair) trenza; (of rope) ramal m;
stranded adj (person: without money)
desamparado; (: without transport)
colgado

strange [streɪndʒ] adj (not known)
desconocido; (odd) extraño, raro;
strangely adv de un modo raro;
stranger n desconocido/a; (from
another area) forastero/a

■ Be careful not to translate **stranger**
by the Spanish word extranjero.

strangle ['stræŋgl] vt estrangular

strap [stræp] n correa; (of slip, dress)
tirante m

strategic [strə'tiːdʒɪk] adj
estratégico

strategy ['strætɪdʒɪ] n estrategia

straw [strɔː] n paja; (drinking straw)
caña, pajita; **that's the last ~!** ¡eso
es el colmo!

strawberry ['strɔːbərɪ] n fresa,

frutilla (sc)

stray [streɪ] adj (animal) extraviado; (bullet) perdido; (scattered) disperso ▷ vi extraviarse, perderse

streak [striːk] n raya; (in hair) raya ▷ vt rayar ▷ vi: **to ~ past** pasar como un rayo

stream [striːm] n riachuelo, arroyo; (of people, vehicles) riada, caravana; (of smoke, insults etc) chorro ▷ vt (Scol) dividir en grupos por habilidad ▷ vi correr, fluir; **to ~ in/out** (people) entrar/salir en tropel

street [striːt] n calle f; **streetcar** (us) n tranvía m; **street light** n farol m (LAM), farola (sP); **street map** n plano (de la ciudad); **street plan** n plano

strength [strɛŋθ] n fuerza; (of girder, knot etc) resistencia; (fig: power) poder m; **strengthen** vt fortalecer, reforzar

strenuous ['strɛnjuəs] adj (energetic, determined) enérgico

stress [strɛs] n presión f; (mental strain) estrés m; (accent) acento ▷ vt subrayar, recalcar; (syllable) acentuar; **stressed** adj (tense) estresado, agobiado; (syllable) acentuado; **stressful** adj (job) estresante

stretch [strɛtʃ] n (of sand etc) trecho ▷ vi estirarse; (extend): **to ~ to or as far as** extenderse hasta ▷ vt extender, estirar; (make demands) exigir el máximo esfuerzo a; **stretch out** vi tenderse ▷ vt (arm etc) extender; (spread) estirar

stretcher ['strɛtʃə*] n camilla

strict [strɪkt] adj severo; (exact) estricto; **strictly** adv severamente; estrictamente

stride [straɪd] (pt **strode**, pp **stridden**) n zancada, tranco ▷ vi dar zancadas, andar a trancos

strike [straɪk] (pt, pp **struck**) n huelga; (of oil etc) descubrimiento; (attack) ataque m ▷ vt golpear, pegar; (oil etc) descubrir; (bargain, deal) cerrar ▷ vi declarar la huelga; (attack) atacar; (clock) dar la hora; **on ~** (workers)

en huelga; **to ~ a match** encender un fósforo; **striker** n huelguista mf; (Sport) delantero; **striking** adj llamativo

string [strɪŋ] (pt, pp **strung**) n cuerda; (row) hilera ▷ vt: **to ~ together** ensartar; **to ~ out** extenderse; **the strings** npl (Mus) los instrumentos de cuerda; **to pull ~s** (fig) mover palancas

strip [strɪp] n tira; (of land) franja; (of metal) cinta, lámina ▷ vt desnudar; (paint) quitar; (also: **~ down**: machine) desmontar ▷ vi desnudarse; **strip off** vt (paint etc) quitar ▷ vi (person) desnudarse

stripe [straɪp] n raya; (Mil) galón m; **striped** adj a rayas, rayado

stripper ['strɪpə*] n artista mf de striptease

strip-search ['strɪpsəːtʃ] vt: **to ~ sb** desnudar y registrar a algn

strive [straɪv] (pt **strove**, pp **striven**) vi: **to ~ for sth/to do sth** luchar por conseguir/hacer algo

strode [strəud] pt of **stride**

stroke [strəuk] n (blow) golpe m; (Swimming) brazada; (Med) apoplejía; (of paintbrush) toque m ▷ vt acariciar; **at a ~** de un solo golpe

stroll [strəul] n paseo, vuelta ▷ vi dar un paseo or una vuelta; **stroller** (us) n (for child) sillita de ruedas

strong [strɒŋ] adj fuerte; **they are 50 ~** son 50; **stronghold** n fortaleza; (fig) baluarte m; **strongly** adv fuertemente, con fuerza; (believe) firmemente

strove [strəuv] pt of **strive**

struck [strʌk] pt, pp of **strike**

structure ['strʌktʃə*] n estructura; (building) construcción f

struggle ['strʌgl] n lucha ▷ vi luchar

strung [strʌŋ] pt, pp of **string**

stub [stʌb] n (of ticket etc) talón m; (of cigarette) colilla; **to ~ one's toe on sth** dar con el dedo (del pie) contra algo; **stub out** vt apagar

stubble ['stʌbl] n rastrojo; (on chin)

barba (incipiente)

stubborn ['stʌbən] *adj* terco, testarudo

stuck [stʌk] *pt, pp of* **stick** ▷ *adj* (*jammed*) atascado

stud [stʌd] *n* (*shirt stud*) corchete *m*; (*of boot*) taco; (*earring*) pendiente *m* (de bolita); (*also:* **~ farm**) caballeriza; (*also:* **~ horse**) caballo semental ▷ *vt* (*fig*): **~ded with** salpicado de

student ['stju:dənt] *n* estudiante *mf* ▷ *adj* estudiantil; **student driver** (*US*) *n* conductor(a) *mf* en prácticas; **students' union** (*building*) centro de estudiantes; (*BRIT: association*) federación *f* de estudiantes

studio ['stju:dɪəu] *n* estudio; (*artist's*) taller *m*; **studio flat** *n* estudio

study ['stʌdɪ] *n* estudio ▷ *vt* estudiar; (*examine*) examinar, investigar ▷ *vi* estudiar

stuff [stʌf] *n* materia; (*substance*) material *m*, sustancia; (*things*) cosas *fpl* ▷ *vt* llenar; (*Culin*) rellenar; (*animals*) disecar; (*inf: push*) meter; **stuffing** *n* relleno; **stuffy** *adj* (*room*) mal ventilado; (*person*) de miras estrechas

stumble ['stʌmbl] *vi* tropezar, dar un traspié; **to ~ across**, **~ on** (*fig*) tropezar con

stump [stʌmp] *n* (*of tree*) tocón *m*; (*of limb*) muñón *m* ▷ *vt*: **to be ~ed for an answer** no saber qué contestar

stun [stʌn] *vt* dejar sin sentido

stung [stʌŋ] *pt, pp of* **sting**

stunk [stʌŋk] *pp of* **stink**

stunned [stʌnd] *adj* (*dazed*) aturdido, atontado; (*amazed*) pasmado; (*shocked*) anonadado

stunning ['stʌnɪŋ] *adj* (*fig: news*) pasmoso; (: *outfit etc*) sensacional

stunt [stʌnt] *n* (*in film*) escena peligrosa; (*publicity stunt*) truco publicitario

stupid ['stju:pɪd] *adj* estúpido, tonto; **stupidity** [-'pɪdɪtɪ] *n* estupidez *f*

sturdy ['stə:dɪ] *adj* robusto, fuerte

stutter ['stʌtə*] *n* tartamudeo ▷ *vi* tartamudear

style [staɪl] *n* estilo; **stylish** *adj* elegante, a la moda; **stylist** *n* (*hair stylist*) peluquero/a

sub... [sʌb] *prefix* sub...; **subconscious** *adj* subconsciente

subdued [səb'dju:d] *adj* (*light*) tenue; (*person*) sumiso, manso

subject [*n* 'sʌbdʒɪkt, *vb* səb'dʒekt] *n* súbdito; (*Scol*) asignatura; (*matter*) tema *m*; (*Grammar*) sujeto ▷ *vt*: **to ~ sb to sth** someter a algn a algo; **to be ~ to** (*law*) estar sujeto a; (*person*) ser propenso a; **subjective** [-'dʒektɪv] *adj* subjetivo; **subject matter** *n* (*content*) contenido

subjunctive [səb'dʒʌŋktɪv] *adj, n* subjuntivo

submarine [sʌbmə'ri:n] *n* submarino

submission [səb'mɪʃən] *n* sumisión *f*

submit [səb'mɪt] *vt* someter ▷ *vi*: **to ~ to sth** someterse a algo

subordinate [sə'bɔ:dɪnət] *adj, n* subordinado/a *m/f*

subscribe [səb'skraɪb] *vi* suscribir; **to ~ to** (*opinion, fund*) suscribir, aprobar; (*newspaper*) suscribirse a

subscription [səb'skrɪpʃən] *n* abono; (*to magazine*) suscripción *f*

subsequent ['sʌbsɪkwənt] *adj* subsiguiente, posterior; **subsequently** *adv* posteriormente, más tarde

subside [səb'saɪd] *vi* hundirse; (*flood*) bajar; (*wind*) amainar

subsidiary [səb'sɪdɪərɪ] *adj* secundario ▷ *n* sucursal *f*, filial *f*

subsidize ['sʌbsɪdaɪz] *vt* subvencionar

subsidy ['sʌbsɪdɪ] *n* subvención *f*

substance ['sʌbstəns] *n* sustancia

substantial [səb'stænʃl] *adj* sustancial, sustancioso; (*fig*) importante

substitute ['sʌbstɪtju:t] *n* (*person*) suplente *mf*; (*thing*) sustituto ▷ *vt*: **to ~ A for B** sustituir A por B, reemplazar B por A; **substitution** *n* sustitución *f*

subtle ['sʌtl] adj sutil

subtract [səb'trækt] vt restar, sustraer

suburb ['sʌbə:b] n barrio residencial; **the ~s** las afueras (de la ciudad); **suburban** [sə'bə:bən] adj suburbano; (*train etc*) de cercanías

subway ['sʌbweɪ] n (BRIT) paso subterráneo or inferior; (US) metro

succeed [sək'si:d] vi (*person*) tener éxito; (*plan*) salir bien ⊳vt suceder a; **to ~ in doing** lograr hacer

success [sək'sɛs] n éxito

> Be careful not to translate **success** by the Spanish word *suceso*.

successful adj exitoso; (*business*) próspero; **to be successful (in doing)** lograr (hacer); **successfully** adv con éxito

succession [sək'sɛʃən] n sucesión f, serie f

successive [sək'sɛsɪv] adj sucesivo, consecutivo

successor [sək'sɛsə*] n sucesor(a) m/f

succumb [sə'kʌm] vi sucumbir

such [sʌtʃ] adj tal, semejante; (*of that kind*): **~ a book** tal libro; (*so much*): **~ courage** tanto valor ⊳adv tan; **~ a long trip** un viaje tan largo; **~ a lot of** tanto(s)/a(s); **~ as** (*like*) tal como; **as ~** como tal; **such-and-such** adj tal o cual

suck [sʌk] vt chupar; (*bottle*) sorber; (*breast*) mamar

Sudan [su'dæn] n Sudán m

sudden ['sʌdn] adj (*rapid*) repentino, súbito; (*unexpected*) imprevisto; **all of a ~** de repente; **suddenly** adv de repente

sue [su:] vt demandar

suede [sweɪd] n ante m, gamuza

suffer ['sʌfə*] vt sufrir, padecer; (*tolerate*) aguantar, soportar ⊳vi sufrir; **to ~ from** (*illness etc*) padecer; **suffering** n sufrimiento

suffice [sə'faɪs] vi bastar, ser suficiente

sufficient [sə'fɪʃənt] adj suficiente, bastante

suffocate ['sʌfəkeɪt] vi ahogarse, asfixiarse

sugar ['ʃugə*] n azúcar m ⊳vt echar azúcar a, azucarar

suggest [sə'dʒɛst] vt sugerir; **suggestion** [-'dʒɛstʃən] n sugerencia

suicide ['suɪsaɪd] n suicidio; (*person*) suicida mf; *see also* **commit**; **suicide attack** n atentado suicida; **suicide bomber** n terrorista mf suicida; **suicide bombing** n atentado suicida

suit [su:t] n (*man's*) traje m; (*woman's*) conjunto; (*Law*) pleito; (*Cards*) palo ⊳vt convenir; (*clothes*) sentar a, ir bien a; (*adapt*): **to ~ sth to** adaptar or ajustar algo a; **well ~ed** (*well matched: couple*) hecho el uno para el otro; **suitable** adj conveniente; (*apt*) indicado; **suitcase** n maleta, valija (RPL)

suite [swi:t] n (*of rooms, Mus*) suite f; (*furniture*): **bedroom/dining room ~** (juego de) dormitorio/comedor; *see also* **three-piece suite**

sulfur ['sʌlfə*] (US) n =**sulphur**

sulk [sʌlk] vi estar de mal humor

sulphur ['sʌlfə*] (US **sulfur**) n azufre m

sultana [sʌl'tɑ:nə] n (*fruit*) pasa de Esmirna

sum [sʌm] n suma; (*total*) total m; **sum up** vt resumir ⊳vi hacer un resumen

summarize ['sʌməraɪz] vt resumir

summary ['sʌməɪ] n resumen m ⊳adj (*justice*) sumario

summer ['sʌmə*] n verano ⊳cpd de verano; **in ~** en verano; **summer holidays** npl vacaciones fpl de verano; **summertime** n (*season*) verano

summit ['sʌmɪt] n cima, cumbre f; (*also*: **~ conference**, **~ meeting**) (conferencia) cumbre f

summon ['sʌmən] vt (*person*) llamar; (*meeting*) convocar; (*Law*) citar

Sun. abbr (= *Sunday*) dom

sun [sʌn] n sol m; **sunbathe** vi tomar el sol; **sunbed** n cama solar;

sunblock n filtro solar; **sunburn** n (painful) quemadura; (tan) bronceado; **sunburned, sunburnt** adj (painfully) quemado por el sol; (tanned) bronceado

Sunday ['sʌndɪ] n domingo

sunflower ['sʌnflauə*] n girasol m

sung [sʌŋ] pp of **sing**

sunglasses ['sʌnglɑːsɪz] npl gafas fpl (SP) or anteojos fpl (LAM) de sol

sunk [sʌŋk] pp of **sink**

sun: sunlight n luz f del sol; **sun lounger** n tumbona, perezosa (LAM); **sunny** adj soleado; (day) de sol; (fig) alegre; **sunrise** n salida del sol; **sun roof** n (Aut) techo corredizo; **sunscreen** n protector m solar; **sunset** n puesta del sol; **sunshade** n (over table) sombrilla; **sunshine** n sol m; **sunstroke** n insolación f; **suntan** n bronceado; **suntan lotion** n bronceador m; **suntan oil** n aceite m bronceador

super ['suːpə*] (inf) adj genial

superb [suːˈpəːb] adj magnífico, espléndido

superficial [suːpəˈfɪʃəl] adj superficial

superintendent [suːpərɪnˈtɛndənt] n director(a) m/f; (Police) subjefe a m/f

superior [suˈpɪərɪə*] adj superior; (smug) desdeñoso ▷ n superior m

superlative [suˈpəːlətɪv] n superlativo

supermarket ['suːpəmɑːkɪt] n supermercado

supernatural [suːpəˈnætʃərəl] adj sobrenatural ▷ n: **the ~** lo sobrenatural

superpower ['suːpəpauə*] n (Pol) superpotencia

superstition [suːpəˈstɪʃən] n superstición f

superstitious [suːpəˈstɪʃəs] adj supersticioso

superstore ['suːpəstɔː*] n (BRIT) hipermercado

supervise ['suːpəvaɪz] vt supervisar; **supervision** [-ˈvɪʒən] n supervisión f; **supervisor** n supervisor(a) m/f

supper ['sʌpə*] n cena

supple ['sʌpl] adj flexible

supplement [n 'sʌplɪmənt, vb sʌplɪˈmɛnt] n suplemento ▷ vt suplir

supplier [səˈplaɪə*] n (Comm) distribuidor(a) m/f

supply [səˈplaɪ] vt (provide) suministrar; (equip): **to ~ (with)** proveer (de) ▷ n provisión f; (of gas, water etc) suministro; **supplies** npl (food) víveres mpl; (Mil) pertrechos mpl

support [səˈpɔːt] n apoyo; (Tech) soporte m ▷ vt apoyar; (financially) mantener; (uphold, Tech) sostener

■ Be careful not to translate **support** by the Spanish word soportar.

supporter n (Pol etc) partidario/a; (Sport) aficionado/a

suppose [səˈpəuz] vt suponer; (imagine) imaginarse; (duty): **to be ~d to do sth** deber hacer algo; **supposedly** [səˈpəuzɪdlɪ] adv según cabe suponer; **supposing** conj en caso de que

suppress [səˈprɛs] vt suprimir; (yawn) ahogar

supreme [suˈpriːm] adj supremo

surcharge ['səːtʃɑːdʒ] n sobretasa, recargo

sure [ʃuə*] adj seguro; (definite, convinced) cierto; **to make ~ of sth/that** asegurarse de algo/asegurar que; **~!** (of course) ¡claro!, ¡por supuesto!; **~ enough** efectivamente; **surely** adv (certainly) seguramente

surf [səːf] n olas fpl ▷ vt: **to ~ the Net** navegar por Internet

surface ['səːfɪs] n superficie f ▷ vt (road) revestir ▷ vi salir a la superficie; **by ~ mail** por vía terrestre

surfboard ['səːfbɔːd] n tabla (de surf)

surfer ['səːfə*] n (in sea) surfista mf; **web** or **net ~** internauta mf

surfing ['səːfɪŋ] n surf m

surge [səːdʒ] n oleada, oleaje m ▷ vi (wave) romper; (people) avanzar en tropel

surgeon ['səːdʒən] n cirujano/a

surgery ['sə:dʒərɪ] n cirugía;
(BRIT: room) consultorio
surname ['sə:neɪm] n apellido
surpass [sə:'pɑ:s] vt superar, exceder
surplus ['sə:pləs] n excedente m;
(Comm) superávit m ▷ adj excedente,
sobrante
surprise [sə'praɪz] n sorpresa ▷ vt
sorprender; **surprised** adj (look,
smile) de sorpresa; **to be surprised**
sorprenderse; **surprising** adj
sorprendente; **surprisingly** adv: **it was
surprisingly easy** me etc sorprendió lo
fácil que fue
surrender [sə'rɛndə*] n rendición f,
entrega ▷ vi rendirse, entregarse
surround [sə'raund] vt rodear,
circundar; (Mil etc) cercar; **surrounding**
adj circundante; **surroundings** npl
alrededores mpl, cercanías fpl
surveillance [sə:'veɪləns] n
vigilancia
survey [n 'sə:veɪ, vb sə:'veɪ] n
inspección f, reconocimiento; (inquiry)
encuesta ▷ vt examinar, inspeccionar;
(look at) mirar, contemplar; **surveyor** n
agrimensor(a) m/f
survival [sə'vaɪvl] n supervivencia
survive [sə'vaɪv] vi sobrevivir;
(custom etc) perdurar ▷ vt sobrevivir a;
survivor n superviviente mf
suspect [adj, n 'sʌspɛkt, vb səs'pɛkt]
adj, n sospechoso/a m/f ▷ vt (person)
sospechar de; (think) sospechar
suspend [səs'pɛnd] vt suspender;
suspended sentence n (Law) libertad
f condicional; **suspenders** npl (BRIT)
ligas fpl; (US) tirantes mpl
suspense [səs'pɛns] n
incertidumbre f, duda; (in film etc)
suspense m; **to keep sb in ~** mantener
a algn en suspense
suspension [səs'pɛnʃən] n (gen,
Aut) suspensión f; (of driving licence)
privación f; **suspension bridge** n
puente m colgante
suspicion [səs'pɪʃən] n sospecha;
(distrust) recelo; **suspicious** adj

receloso; (causing suspicion) sospechoso
sustain [səs'teɪn] vt sostener,
apoyar; (suffer) sufrir, padecer
SUV (esp US) n abbr (= sports utility
vehicle) todoterreno m inv, 4x4 m
swallow ['swɔləu] n (bird) golondrina
▷ vt tragar; (fig.: pride) tragarse
swam [swæm] pt of **swim**
swamp [swɔmp] n pantano, ciénaga
▷ vt (with water etc) inundar; (fig)
abrumar, agobiar
swan [swɔn] n cisne m
swap [swɔp] n canje m, intercambio
▷ vt: **to ~ (for)** cambiar (por)
swarm [swɔ:m] n (of bees) enjambre
m; (fig) multitud f ▷ vi (bees) formar un
enjambre; (people) pulular; **to be ~ing
with** ser un hervidero de
sway [sweɪ] vi mecerse, balancearse
▷ vt (influence) mover, influir en
swear [swɛə*] (pt **swore**, pp **sworn**)
vi (curse) maldecir; (promise) jurar
▷ vt jurar; **swear in** vt: **to be sworn
in** prestar juramento; **swearword** n
taco, palabrota
sweat [swɛt] n sudor m ▷ vi sudar
sweater ['swɛtə*] n suéter m
sweatshirt ['swɛtʃə:t] n suéter m
sweaty ['swɛtɪ] adj sudoroso
Swede [swi:d] n sueco/a
swede [swi:d] (BRIT) n nabo
Sweden ['swi:dn] n Suecia; **Swedish**
['swi:dɪʃ] adj sueco ▷ n (Ling) sueco
sweep [swi:p] (pt, pp **swept**) n
(act) barrido; (also: **chimney ~**)
deshollinador(a) m/f ▷ vt barrer; (with
arm) empujar; (current) arrastrar ▷ vi
barrer; (arm etc) moverse rápidamente;
(wind) soplar con violencia
sweet [swi:t] n (candy) dulce m,
caramelo; (BRIT: pudding) postre m
▷ adj dulce; (fig: kind) dulce, amable;
(: attractive) mono; **sweetcorn** n maíz
m; **sweetener** ['swi:tnə*] n (Culin)
edulcorante m; **sweetheart** n novio/
a; **sweetshop** n (BRIT) confitería,
bombonería
swell [swɛl] (pt **~ed**, pp **swollen** or **~ed**)

n (*of sea*) marejada, oleaje *m* ▷ *adj*
(*US*: *inf*: *excellent*) estupendo, fenomenal
▷ *vt* hinchar, inflar ▷ *vi* (*also*: **~ up**)
hincharse; (*numbers*) aumentar; (*sound,
feeling*) ir aumentando; **swelling** *n*
(*Med*) hinchazón *f*

swept [swɛpt] *pt, pp of* **sweep**

swerve [swə:v] *vi* desviarse
bruscamente

swift [swɪft] *n* (*bird*) vencejo ▷ *adj*
rápido, veloz

swim [swɪm] (*pt* **swam**, *pp* **swum**)
n: **to go for a ~** ir a nadar *or* a bañarse
▷ *vi* nadar; (*head, room*) dar vueltas
▷ *vt* nadar; (*the Channel etc*) cruzar a
nado; **swimmer** *n* nadador(a) *m/f*;
swimming *n* natación *f*; **swimming
costume** (*BRIT*) *n* bañador *m*, traje *m*
de baño; **swimming pool** *n* piscina,
alberca (*MEX*), pileta (*RPL*); **swimming
trunks** *npl* bañador *m* (de hombre);
swimsuit *n* = **swimming costume**

swing [swɪŋ] (*pt, pp* **swung**) *n* (*in
playground*) columpio; (*movement*)
balanceo, vaivén *m*; (*change of
direction*) viraje *m*; (*rhythm*) ritmo ▷ *vt*
balancear; (*also*: **~ round**) voltear, girar
▷ *vi* balancearse, columpiarse; (*also*: **~
round**) dar media vuelta; **to be in full ~**
estar en plena marcha

swipe card [swaɪp-] *n* tarjeta
magnética deslizante, tarjeta swipe

swirl [swə:l] *vi* arremolinarse

Swiss [swɪs] *adj, n inv* suizo/a *m/f*

switch [swɪtʃ] *n* (*for light etc*)
interruptor *m*; (*change*) cambio ▷ *vt*
(*change*) cambiar de; **switch off** *vt*
apagar; (*engine*) parar; **switch on** *vt*
encender (*SP*), prender (*LAM*); (*engine,
machine*) arrancar; **switchboard** *n* (*Tel*)
centralita (*SP*), conmutador *m* (*LAM*)

Switzerland ['swɪtsələnd] *n* Suiza

swivel ['swɪvl] *vi* (*also*: **~ round**) girar

swollen ['swəʊlən] *pp of* **swell**

swoop [swu:p] *n* (*by police etc*) redada
▷ *vi* (*also*: **~ down**) calarse

swop [swɔp] = **swap**

sword [sɔ:d] *n* espada; **swordfish** *n*
pez *m* espada

swore [swɔ:*] *pt of* **swear**

sworn [swɔ:n] *pp of* **swear** ▷ *adj*
(*statement*) bajo juramento; (*enemy*)
implacable

swum [swʌm] *pp of* **swim**

swung [swʌŋ] *pt, pp of* **swing**

syllable ['sɪləbl] *n* sílaba

syllabus ['sɪləbəs] *n* programa *m*
de estudios

symbol ['sɪmbl] *n* símbolo;
symbolic(al) [sɪm'bɔlɪk(l)] *adj*
simbólico; **to be symbolic(al) of sth**
simbolizar algo

symmetrical [sɪ'mɛtrɪkl] *adj*
simétrico

symmetry ['sɪmɪtrɪ] *n* simetría

sympathetic [sɪmpə'θɛtɪk] *adj*
(*understanding*) comprensivo; (*showing
support*): **~ to(wards)** bien dispuesto
hacia

> Be careful not to translate
> **sympathetic** by the Spanish word
> *simpático*.

sympathize ['sɪmpəθaɪz] *vi*: **to
~ with** (*person*) compadecerse de;
(*feelings*) comprender; (*cause*) apoyar

sympathy ['sɪmpəθɪ] *n* (*pity*)
compasión *f*

symphony ['sɪmfənɪ] *n* sinfonía

symptom ['sɪmptəm] *n* síntoma
m, indicio

synagogue ['sɪnəgɔg] *n* sinagoga

syndicate ['sɪndɪkɪt] *n* sindicato; (*of
newspapers*) agencia (de noticias)

syndrome ['sɪndrəʊm] *n* síndrome
m

synonym ['sɪnənɪm] *n* sinónimo

synthetic [sɪn'θɛtɪk] *adj* sintético

Syria ['sɪrɪə] *n* Siria

syringe [sɪ'rɪndʒ] *n* jeringa

syrup ['sɪrəp] *n* jarabe *m*; (*also*:
golden ~) almíbar *m*

system ['sɪstəm] *n* sistema *m*; (*Anat*)
organismo; **systematic** [-'mætɪk]
adj sistemático, metódico; **systems
analyst** *n* analista *mf* de sistemas

t

ta [tɑː] (BRIT: inf) excl ¡gracias!
tab [tæb] n lengüeta; (label) etiqueta;
to keep ~s on (fig) vigilar
table ['teɪbl] n mesa; (of statistics etc)
cuadro, tabla ▷ vt (BRIT: motion etc)
presentar; **to lay** or **set the ~** poner la
mesa; **tablecloth** n mantel m; **table
d'hôte** [tɑːbl'dəut] adj del menú;
table lamp n lámpara de mesa;
tablemat n (for plate) posaplatos
m inv; (for hot dish) salvamantel m;
tablespoon n cuchara de servir;
(also: **tablespoonful**: as measurement)
cucharada
tablet ['tæblɪt] n (Med) pastilla,
comprimido; (of stone) lápida
table tennis n ping-pong m, tenis
m de mesa
tabloid ['tæblɔɪd] n periódico
popular sensacionalista

taboo [tə'buː] adj, n tabú m
tack [tæk] n (nail) tachuela; (fig)
rumbo ▷ vt (nail) clavar con tachuelas;
(stitch) hilvanar ▷ vi virar
tackle ['tækl] n (fishing tackle)
aparejo (de pescar); (for lifting)
aparejo ▷ vt (difficulty) enfrentarse
con; (challenge: person) hacer frente a;
(grapple with) agarrar; (Football) cargar;
(Rugby) placar
tacky ['tækɪ] adj pegajoso; (pej) cutre
tact [tækt] n tacto, discreción f;
tactful adj discreto, diplomático
tactics ['tæktɪks] npl táctica
tactless ['tæktlɪs] adj indiscreto
tadpole ['tædpəul] n renacuajo
taffy ['tæfɪ] (US) n melcocha
tag [tæg] n (label) etiqueta
tail [teɪl] n cola; (of shirt, coat) faldón m
▷ vt (follow) vigilar a; **tails** npl (formal
suit) levita
tailor ['teɪlə*] n sastre m
Taiwan [taɪ'wɑːn] n Taiwán m;
Taiwanese [taɪwə'niːz] adj, n
taiwanés/esa m/f
take [teɪk] (pt **took**, pp **taken**) vt
tomar; (grab) coger (SP), agarrar (LAM);
(gain: prize) ganar; (require: effort,
courage) exigir; (tolerate: pain etc)
aguantar; (hold: passengers etc) tener
cabida para; (accompany, bring, carry)
llevar; (exam) presentarse a; **to ~ sth
from** (drawer etc) sacar algo de; (person)
quitar algo a; **I ~ it that ...** supongo

que ...; **take after** vt fus parecerse a;
take apart vt desmontar; **take away**
vt (remove) quitar; (carry) llevar; (Math)
restar; **take back** vt (return) devolver;
(one's words) retractarse de; **take
down** vt (building) derribar; (letter etc)
apuntar; **take in** vt (deceive) engañar;
(understand) entender; (include) abarcar;
(lodger) acoger, recibir; **take off** vi
(Aviat) despegar ▷ vt (remove) quitar;
take on vt (work) aceptar; (employee)
contratar; (opponent) desafiar; **take out**
vt sacar; **take over** vt (business) tomar
posesión de; (country) tomar el poder
▷ vi: **to take over from sb** reemplazar
a algn; **take up** vt (a dress) acortar;
(occupy: time, space) ocupar; (engage
in: hobby etc) dedicarse a; (accept): **to
take sb up on** aceptar algo de algn;
takeaway (BRIT) adj (food) para llevar
▷ n tienda or restaurante m de comida
para llevar; **taken** pp of **take**; **takeoff**
n (Aviat) despegue m; **takeout** (US)
n = **takeaway**; **takeover** n (Comm)
absorción f; **takings** npl (Comm)
ingresos mpl
talc [tælk] n (also: **~um powder**)
(polvos de) talco
tale [teɪl] n (story) cuento; (account)
relación f; **to tell ~s** (fig) chivarse
talent ['tælnt] n talento; **talented**
adj de talento
talk [tɔːk] n charla; (conversation)
conversación f; (gossip) habladurías
fpl ▷ vi hablar; **talks** npl
(Pol etc) conversaciones fpl; **to ~ about**
hablar de; **to ~ sb into doing sth**
convencer a algn para que haga algo;
to ~ sb out of doing sth disuadir a
algn de que haga algo; **to ~ shop** hablar
del trabajo; **talk over** vt discutir; **talk
show** n programa m de entrevistas
tall [tɔːl] adj alto; (object) grande; **to
be 6 feet ~** (person) ≈ medir 1 metro 80
tambourine [tæmbə'riːn] n
pandereta
tame [teɪm] adj domesticado; (fig)
mediocre

tamper ['tæmpə*] vi: **to ~ with** tocar,
andar con
tampon ['tæmpən] n tampón m
tan [tæn] n (also: **sun~**) bronceado
▷ vi ponerse moreno ▷ adj (colour)
marrón
tandem ['tændəm] n tándem m
tangerine [tændʒə'riːn] n
mandarina
tangle ['tæŋgl] n enredo; **to get
in(to) a ~** enredarse
tank [tæŋk] n (water tank) depósito,
tanque m; (for fish) acuario; (Mil)
tanque m
tanker ['tæŋkə*] n (ship) buque m,
cisterna; (truck) camión m cisterna
tanned [tænd] adj (skin) moreno
tantrum ['tæntrəm] n rabieta
Tanzania [tænzə'nɪə] n Tanzania
tap [tæp] n (BRIT: on sink etc) grifo (SP),
llave f, canilla (RPL); (gas tap) llave f;
(gentle blow) golpecito ▷ vt (hit gently)
dar golpecitos en; (resources) utilizar,
explotar; (telephone) intervenir; **on ~**
(fig: resources) a mano; **tap dancing**
n claqué m
tape [teɪp] n (also: **magnetic ~**)
cinta magnética; (cassette) cassette
f, cinta; (sticky tape) cinta adhesiva;
(for tying) cinta ▷ vt (record) grabar
(en cinta); (stick with tape) pegar con
cinta adhesiva; **tape measure** n cinta
métrica, metro; **tape recorder** n
grabadora
tapestry ['tæpɪstrɪ] n (object) tapiz
m; (art) tapicería
tar [tɑː] n alquitrán m, brea
target ['tɑːgɪt] n blanco
tariff ['tærɪf] n (on goods) arancel m;
(BRIT: in hotels etc) tarifa
tarmac ['tɑːmæk] n (BRIT: on road)
asfaltado; (Aviat) pista (de aterrizaje)
tarpaulin [tɑː'pɔːlɪn] n lona
impermeabilizada
tarragon ['tærəgən] n estragón m
tart [tɑːt] n (Culin) tarta;
(BRIT: inf: prostitute) puta ▷ adj agrio,
ácido

tartan ['tɑːtn] n tejido escocés m

tartar(e) sauce ['tɑːtə-] n salsa tártara

task [tɑːsk] n tarea; **to take to ~** reprender

taste [teɪst] n (sense) gusto; (flavour) sabor m; (sample): **have a ~!** ¡prueba un poquito!; (fig) muestra, idea ▷ vt probar ▷ vi: **to ~ of** or **like** (fish, garlic etc) saber a; **you can ~ the garlic (in it)** se nota el sabor a ajo; **in good/bad ~** de buen/mal gusto; **tasteful** adj de buen gusto; **tasteless** adj (food) soso; (remark etc) de mal gusto; **tasty** adj sabroso, rico

tatters ['tætəz] npl: **in ~** hecho jirones

tattoo [tə'tuː] n tatuaje m; (spectacle) espectáculo militar ▷ vt tatuar

taught [tɔːt] pt, pp de **teach**

taunt [tɔːnt] n burla ▷ vt burlarse de

Taurus ['tɔːrəs] n Tauro

taut [tɔːt] adj tirante, tenso

tax [tæks] n impuesto ▷ vt gravar (con un impuesto); (fig: memory) poner a prueba; (: patience) agotar; **tax-free** adj libre de impuestos

taxi ['tæksɪ] n taxi m ▷ vi (Aviat) rodar por la pista; **taxi driver** n taxista mf; **taxi rank** (BRIT) n = **taxi stand**; **taxi stand** n parada de taxis

tax payer n contribuyente mf

TB n abbr = **tuberculosis**

tea [tiː] n té m; (BRIT: meal) ≈ merienda (SP); cena; **high ~** (BRIT) merienda-cena (SP); **tea bag** n bolsita de té; **tea break** (BRIT) n descanso para el té

teach [tiːtʃ] (pt, pp **taught**) vt: **to ~ sb sth, ~ sth to sb** enseñar algo a algn ▷ vi (be a teacher) ser profesor(a), enseñar; **teacher** n (in secondary school) profesor(a) m/f; (in primary school) maestro/a, profesor(a) de EGB; **teaching** n enseñanza

tea: tea cloth n (BRIT) paño de cocina, trapo de cocina (LAM); **teacup** n taza para el té

tea leaves npl hojas de té

team [tiːm] n equipo; (of horses) tiro;

team up vi asociarse

teapot ['tiːpɔt] n tetera

tear¹ [tɪə*] n lágrima; **in ~s** llorando

tear² [tɛə*] (pt **tore**, pp **torn**) n rasgón m, desgarrón m ▷ vt romper, rasgar ▷ vi rasgarse; **tear apart** vt (also fig) hacer pedazos; **tear down** vt +adv (building, statue) derribar; (poster, flag) arrancar; **tear off** vt (sheet of paper etc) arrancar; (one's clothes) quitarse a tirones; **tear up** vt (sheet of paper etc) romper

tearful ['tɪəfəl] adj lloroso

tear gas ['tɪə-] n gas m lacrimógeno

tearoom ['tiːruːm] n salón m de té

tease [tiːz] vt tomar el pelo a

tea: teaspoon n cucharita; (also: **teaspoonful**: as measurement) cucharadita; **teatime** n hora del té; **tea towel** (BRIT) n paño de cocina

technical ['tɛknɪkl] adj técnico

technician [tɛk'nɪʃn] n técnico/a

technique [tɛk'niːk] n técnica

technology [tɛk'nɔlədʒɪ] n tecnología

teddy (bear) ['tɛdɪ-] n osito de felpa

tedious ['tiːdɪəs] adj pesado, aburrido

tee [tiː] n (Golf) tee m

teen [tiːn] adj = **teenage** ▷ n (US) = **teenager**

teenage ['tiːneɪdʒ] adj (fashions etc) juvenil; (children) quinceañero; **teenager** n adolescente mf

teens [tiːnz] npl: **to be in one's ~** ser adolescente

teeth [tiːθ] npl of **tooth**

teetotal ['tiː'təutl] adj abstemio

telecommunications [tɛlɪkəmjuːnɪ'keɪʃənz] n telecomunicaciones fpl

telegram ['tɛlɪgræm] n telegrama m

telegraph pole ['tɛlɪgrɑː-f] n poste m telegráfico

telephone ['tɛlɪfəun] n teléfono ▷ vt llamar por teléfono, telefonear; (message) dar por teléfono; **to be on the ~** (talking) hablar por teléfono; (possessing telephone) tener teléfono;

telephone book n guía f telefónica;
telephone booth, telephone box
(BRIT) n cabina telefónica; **telephone
call** n llamada (telefónica); **telephone
directory** n guía (telefónica);
telephone number n número de
teléfono

telesales ['tɛlɪseɪlz] npl televenta(s)
(f(pl))

telescope ['tɛlɪskəʊp] n telescopio

televise ['tɛlɪvaɪz] vt televisar

television ['tɛlɪvɪʒən] n televisión
f; **on ~** en la televisión; **television
programme** n programa m de
televisión

tell [tɛl] (pt, pp **told**) vt decir;
(relate: story) contar; (distinguish): **to
~ sth from** distinguir algo de ▷ vi
(talk): **to ~ (of)** contar; (have effect)
tener efecto; **to ~ sb to do sth** mandar
a algn hacer algo; **tell off** vt: **to tell sb
off** regañar a algn; **teller** n (in bank)
cajero/a

telly ['tɛlɪ] (BRIT: inf) n abbr
(= television) tele f

temp [tɛmp] n abbr (BRIT)
(= temporary) temporero/a

temper ['tɛmpə*] n (nature) carácter
m; (mood) humor m; (bad temper) (mal)
genio; (fit of anger) acceso de ira ▷ vt
(moderate) moderar; **to be in a ~** estar
furioso; **to lose one's ~** enfadarse,
enojarse

temperament ['tɛmprəmə
nt] n (nature) temperamento;
temperamental [tɛmprə'mɛntl] adj
temperamental

temperature ['tɛmprətʃə*] n
temperatura; **to have** or **run a ~**
tener fiebre

temple ['tɛmpl] n (building) templo;
(Anat) sien f

temporary ['tɛmpərərɪ] adj
provisional; (passing) transitorio;
(worker) temporero; (job) temporal

tempt [tɛmpt] vt tentar; **to ~ sb into
doing sth** tentar o inducir a algn a
hacer algo; **temptation** n tentación

f; **tempting** adj tentador(a); (food)
apetitoso/a

ten [tɛn] num diez

tenant ['tɛnənt] n inquilino/a

tend [tɛnd] vt cuidar ▷ vi: **to ~ to
do sth** tener tendencia a hacer algo;
tendency ['tɛndənsɪ] n tendencia

tender ['tɛndə*] adj (person, care)
tierno, cariñoso; (meat) tierno; (sore)
sensible ▷ n (Comm: offer) oferta;
(money): **legal ~** moneda de curso legal
▷ vt ofrecer

tendon ['tɛndən] n tendón m

tenner ['tɛnə*] n (inf) (billete m de)
diez libras m

tennis ['tɛnɪs] n tenis m; **tennis
ball** n pelota de tenis; **tennis court**
n cancha de tenis; **tennis match** n
partido de tenis; **tennis player** n
tenista mf; **tennis racket** n raqueta
de tenis

tenor ['tɛnə*] n (Mus) tenor m

tenpin bowling ['tɛnpɪn-] n (juego
de los) bolos

tense [tɛns] adj (person) nervioso;
(moment, atmosphere) tenso; (muscle)
tenso, en tensión ▷ n (Ling) tiempo

tension ['tɛnʃən] n tensión f

tent [tɛnt] n tienda (de campaña)
(SP), carpa (LAM)

tentative ['tɛntətɪv] adj (person,
smile) indeciso; (conclusion, plans)
provisional

tenth [tɛnθ] num décimo

tent: tent peg n clavija, estaca; **tent
pole** n mástil m

tepid ['tɛpɪd] adj tibio

term [tə:m] n (word) término;
(period) período; (Scol) trimestre m ▷ vt
llamar; **terms** npl (conditions, Comm)
condiciones fpl; **in the short/long ~**
a corto/largo plazo; **to be on good
~s with sb** llevarse bien con algn; **to
come to ~s with** (problem) aceptar

terminal ['tə:mɪnl] adj (disease)
mortal; (patient) terminal ▷ n (Elec)
borne m; (Comput) terminal m; (also:
air ~) terminal f; (BRIT: also: **coach ~**)

estación f terminal f
terminate ['tə:mɪneɪt] vt terminar
termini ['tə:mɪnaɪ] npl of **terminus**
terminology [tə:mɪ'nɔlədʒɪ] n
terminología
terminus ['tə:mɪnəs] (pl **termini**) n
término, (estación f) terminal f
terrace ['terəs] n terraza; (BRIT: row of
houses) hilera de casas adosadas; **the
~s** (BRIT Sport) las gradas fpl; **terraced**
adj (garden) en terrazas; (house)
adosado
terrain [tɛ'reɪn] n terreno
terrestrial [tɪ'restrɪəl] adj (life)
terrestre; (BRIT: channel) de transmisión
(por) vía terrestre
terrible ['terɪbl] adj terrible, horrible;
(inf) atroz; **terribly** adv terriblemente;
(very badly) malísimamente
terrier ['terɪə*] n terrier m
terrific [tə'rɪfɪk] adj (very great)
tremendo; (wonderful) fantástico,
fenomenal
terrified ['terɪfaɪd] adj aterrorizado
terrify ['terɪfaɪ] vt aterrorizar;
terrifying adj aterrador(a)
territorial [terɪ'tɔ:rɪəl] adj territorial
territory ['terɪtərɪ] n territorio
terror ['terə*] n terror m; **terrorism**
n terrorismo; **terrorist** n terrorista
mf; **terrorist attack** n atentado
(terrorista)
test [test] n (gen, Chem) prueba; (Med)
examen m; (Scol) examen m, test m;
(also: **driving ~**) examen m de conducir
▷ vt probar, poner a prueba; (Med, Scol)
examinar
testicle ['testɪkl] n testículo
testify ['testɪfaɪ] vi (Law) prestar
declaración; **to ~ to sth** atestiguar
algo
testimony ['testɪmənɪ] n (Law)
testimonio
test: test match n (Cricket, Rugby)
partido internacional; **test tube** n
probeta
tetanus ['tetənəs] n tétano
text [tekst] n texto; (on mobile phone)

mensaje m de texto ▷ vt: **to ~ sb** (inf)
enviar un mensaje (de texto) or un SMS
a algn; **textbook** n libro de texto
textile ['tekstaɪl] n textil m, tejido
text message n mensaje m de texto
text messaging [-'mesɪdʒɪŋ] n
(envío de) mensajes mpl de texto
texture ['tekstʃə*] n textura
Thai [taɪ] adj, n tailandés/esa m/f
Thailand ['taɪlænd] n Tailandia
than [ðæn] conj (in comparisons):
more ~ 10/once más de 10/una vez;
I have more/less ~ you/Paul tengo
más/menos que tú/Paul; **she is older
~ you think** es mayor de lo que piensas
thank [θæŋk] vt dar las gracias a,
agradecer; **~ you (very much)** muchas
gracias; **~ God!** ¡gracias a Dios! ▷ excl
(also: **many ~s, ~s a lot**) ¡gracias! ▷ **~s
to** prep gracias a; **thanks** npl gracias
fpl; **thankfully** adv (fortunately)
afortunadamente; **Thanksgiving
(Day)** n día m de Acción de Gracias

THANKSGIVING (DAY)

En Estados Unidos el cuarto jueves
de noviembre es **Thanksgiving
Day**, fiesta oficial en la que se
recuerda la celebración que
hicieron los primeros colonos
norteamericanos ("Pilgrims"
o "Pilgrim Fathers") tras la
estupenda cosecha de 1621, por
la que se dan gracias a Dios. En
Canadá se celebra una fiesta
semejante el segundo lunes
de octubre, aunque no está
relacionada con dicha fecha
histórica.

KEYWORD

that [ðæt] (pl **those**) adj
(demonstrative) ese/a; (pl) esos/as; (more
remote) aquel(aquella); (pl) aquellos/as;
leave those books on the table deja

esos libros sobre la mesa; **that one** ése(ésa); (*more remote*) aquél(aquélla); **that one over there** ése(ésa) de ahí; aquél(aquélla) de allí ▷ *pron* **1** (*demonstrative*) ése/a; (*pl*) ésos/as; (*neuter*) eso; (*more remote*) aquél(aquélla); (*pl*) aquéllos/as; (*neuter*) aquello; **what's that?** ¿qué es eso (*or* aquello)?; **who's that?** ¿quién es ése/a (*or* aquél (aquella))?; **is that you?** ¿eres tú?; **will you eat all that?** ¿vas a comer todo eso?; **that's my house** ésa es mi casa; **that's what he said** eso es lo que dijo; **that is (to say)** es decir **2** (*relative: subject, object*) que; (*with preposition*) (el (la)) que *etc*, el(la) cual *etc*; **the book (that) I read** el libro que leí; **the books that are in the library** los libros que están en la biblioteca; **all (that) I have** todo lo que tengo; **the box (that) I put it in** la caja en la que or donde lo puse; **the people (that) I spoke to** la gente con la que hablé **3** (*relative: of time*) que; **the day (that) he came** el día (en) que vino ▷ *conj* que; **he thought that I was ill** creyó que yo estaba enfermo ▷ *adv* (*demonstrative*): **I can't work that much** no puedo trabajar tanto; **I didn't realise it was that bad** no creí que fuera tan malo; **that high** así de alto

thatched [θætʃt] *adj* (*roof*) de paja; (*cottage*) con tejado de paja
thaw [θɔ:] *n* deshielo ▷ *vi* (*ice*) derretirse; (*food*) descongelarse ▷ *vt* (*food*) descongelar

○ **KEYWORD**

the [ði:, ðə] *def art* **1** (*gen*) el *f*, la *pl*, los *fpl*, las (NB 'el' immediately before f n beginning with stressed (h)*a*; *a+ el =al*; *de + el = del*); **the boy/girl** el chico/la chica; **the books/flowers** los libros/las flores; **to the postman/from the drawer** al cartero/del cajón; **I haven't the time/money** no tengo

tiempo/dinero **2** (*+adj to form n*) los; lo; **the rich and the poor** los ricos y los pobres; **to attempt the impossible** intentar lo imposible **3** (*in titles*): **Elizabeth the First** Isabel primera; **Peter the Great** Pedro el Grande **4** (*in comparisons*): **the more he works the more he earns** cuanto más trabaja más gana

theatre [ˈθɪətə*] (*us* **theater**) *n* teatro; (*also:* **lecture ~**) aula; (*Med: also:* **operating ~**) quirófano
theft [θɛft] *n* robo
their [ðɛə*] *adj* su; **theirs** *pron* (el) suyo((la) suya etc); *see also* **my; mine**[1]
them [ðɛm, ðəm] *pron* (*direct*) los/las; (*indirect*) les; (*stressed, after prep*) ellos(ellas); *see also* **me**
theme [θi:m] *n* tema *m*; **theme park** *n* parque de atracciones (*en torno a un tema central*)
themselves [ðəm'sɛlvz] *pl pron* (*subject*) ellos mismos(ellas mismas); (*complement*) se; (*after prep*) sí (mismos(as)); *see also* **oneself**
then [ðɛn] *adv* (*at that time*) entonces; (*next*) después; (*later*) luego, después; (*and also*) además ▷ *conj* (*therefore*) en ese caso, entonces ▷ *adj*: **the ~ president** el entonces presidente; **by ~** para entonces; **from ~ on** desde entonces
theology [θɪˈɔlədʒɪ] *n* teología
theory [ˈθɪərɪ] *n* teoría
therapist [ˈθɛrəpɪst] *n* terapeuta *mf*
therapy [ˈθɛrəpɪ] *n* terapia

○ **KEYWORD**

there [ðɛə*] *adv* **1 there is, there are** hay; **there is no-one here/no bread left** no hay nadie aquí/no queda pan; **there has been an accident** ha habido un accidente **2** (*referring to place*) ahí; (*distant*) allí; **it's**

there está ahí; **put it in/on/up/down
there** ponlo ahí dentro/encima/
arriba/abajo; **I want that book there**
quiero ese libro de ahí; **there he is!**
¡ahí está!

3 there, there (*esp to child*) ea, ea

there: thereabouts *adv* por ahí;
thereafter *adv* después; **thereby**
adv así, de ese modo; **therefore** *adv* por lo
tanto; **there's** = **there is**; **there has**

thermal ['θə:ml] *adj* termal; (*paper*)
térmico

thermometer [θə'mɔmɪtə*] *n*
termómetro

thermostat ['θə:məustæt] *n*
termostato

these [ði:z] *pl adj* estos/as ▷ *pl pron*
éstos/as

thesis ['θi:sɪs] (*pl* **theses**) *n* tesis *f inv*

they [ðeɪ] *pl pron* ellos(ellas); (*stressed*)
ellos (mismos)(ellas (mismas)); **~
say that …** (*it is said that*) se dice que
…; **they'd** = **they had; they would;
they'll** = **they shall; they will; they're**
= **they are; they've** = **they have**

thick [θɪk] *adj* (*in consistency*) espeso;
(*in size*) grueso; (*stupid*) torpe ▷ *n*: **in
the ~ of the battle** en lo más reñido
de la batalla; **it's 20 cm ~** tiene 20
cm de espesor; **thicken** *vi* espesarse
▷ *vt* (*sauce etc*) espesar; **thickness** *n*
espesor *m*; grueso

thief [θi:f] (*pl* **thieves**) *n* ladrón/ona
m/f

thigh [θaɪ] *n* muslo

thin [θɪn] *adj* (*person, animal*) flaco;
(*in size*) delgado; (*in consistency*) poco
espeso; (*hair, crowd*) escaso ▷ *vt*: **to ~
(down)** diluir

thing [θɪŋ] *n* cosa; (*object*) objeto,
artículo; (*matter*) asunto; (*mania*): **to
have a ~ about sb/sth** estar
obsesionado con algn/algo; **things** *npl*
(*belongings*) efectos *mpl* (personales);
the best ~ would be to … lo mejor
sería …; **how are ~s?** ¿qué tal?

think [θɪŋk] (*pt, pp* **thought**) *vi*

pensar ▷ *vt* pensar, creer; **what did
you ~ of them?** ¿qué te parecieron?; **to
~ about sth/sb** pensar en algo/algn;
I'll ~ about it lo pensaré; **to ~ of doing
sth** pensar en hacer algo; **I ~ so/not**
creo que sí/no; **to ~ well of sb** tener
buen concepto de algn; **think over** *vt*
reflexionar sobre, meditar; **think up** *vt*
(*plan etc*) idear

third [θə:d] *adj* (*before n*) tercer(a);
(*following n*) tercero/a ▷ *n* tercero/a;
(*fraction*) tercio; (BRIT Scol: *degree*) título
de licenciado con calificación de aprobado;
thirdly *adv* en tercer lugar; **third
party insurance** (BRIT) *n* seguro
contra terceros; **Third World** *n* Tercer
Mundo

thirst [θə:st] *n* sed *f*; **thirsty** *adj*
(*person, animal*) sediento; (*work*) que da
sed; **to be thirsty** tener sed

thirteen ['θə:'ti:n] *num* trece;
thirteenth [-'ti:nθ] *adj*
decimotercero

thirtieth ['θə:tɪəθ] *adj* trigésimo

thirty ['θə:tɪ] *num* treinta

○ **KEYWORD**

this [ðɪs] (*pl* **these**) *adj*
(*demonstrative*) este/a *pl*; estos/as;
(*neuter*) esto; **this man/woman** este
hombre(esta mujer); **these children/
flowers** estos chicos/estas flores; **this
one (here)** éste/a, esto (de aquí)
▷ *pron* (*demonstrative*) éste/a *pl*, éstos/
as; (*neuter*) esto; **who is this?** ¿quién
es éste/ésta?; **what is this?** ¿qué es
esto?; **this is where I live** aquí vivo;
this is what he said esto es lo que
dijo; **this is Mr Brown** (*in introductions*)
le presento al Sr. Brown; (*photo*) éste
es el Sr. Brown; (*on telephone*) habla el
Sr. Brown
▷ *adv* (*demonstrative*): **this high/long**
etc así de alto/largo *etc*; **this far**
hasta aquí

thistle ['θɪsl] *n* cardo

thorn [θɔ:n] n espina

thorough ['θʌrə] adj (search) minucioso; (wash) a fondo; (knowledge, research) profundo; (person) meticuloso; **thoroughly** adv (search) minuciosamente; (study) profundamente; (wash) a fondo; (utterly: bad, wet etc) completamente, totalmente

those [ðəuz] pl adj esos(esas); (more remote) aquellos/as

though [ðəu] conj aunque ▷ adv sin embargo

thought [θɔ:t] pt, pp of **think** ▷ n pensamiento; (opinion) opinión f; **thoughtful** adj pensativo; (serious) serio; (considerate) atento; **thoughtless** adj desconsiderado

thousand ['θauzənd] num mil; **two ~** dos mil; **~s of** miles de; **thousandth** num milésimo

thrash [θræʃ] vt azotar; (defeat) derrotar

thread [θrɛd] n hilo; (of screw) rosca ▷ vt (needle) enhebrar

threat [θrɛt] n amenaza; **threaten** vi amenazar ▷ vt: **to threaten sb with/ to do** amenazar a algn con/con hacer; **threatening** adj amenazador(a), amenazante

three [θri:] num tres; **three-dimensional** adj tridimensional; **three-piece suite** n tresillo; **three-quarters** npl tres cuartas partes; **three-quarters full** tres cuartas partes lleno

threshold ['θrɛʃhəuld] n umbral m

threw [θru:] pt of **throw**

thrill [θrɪl] n (excitement) emoción f; (shudder) estremecimiento ▷ vt emocionar; **to be ~ed** (with gift etc) estar encantado; **thrilled** adj: **I was thrilled** Estaba emocionada; **thriller** n novela (or obra or película) de suspense; **thrilling** adj emocionante

thriving ['θraɪvɪŋ] adj próspero

throat [θrəut] n garganta; **to have a sore ~** tener dolor de garganta

throb [θrɔb] vi latir; dar punzadas; vibrar

throne [θrəun] n trono

through [θru:] prep por, a través de; (time) durante; (by means of) por medio de, mediante; (owing to) gracias a ▷ adj (ticket, train) directo ▷ adv completamente, de parte a parte; de principio a fin; **to put sb ~ to sb** (Tel) poner or pasar a algn con algn; **to be ~** (Tel) tener comunicación; (have finished) haber terminado; **"no ~ road"** (BRIT) "calle sin salida"; **throughout** prep (place) por todas partes de, por todo; (time) durante todo ▷ adv por or en todas partes

throw [θrəu] (pt **threw**, pp **thrown**) n tiro; (Sport) lanzamiento ▷ vt tirar, echar; (Sport) lanzar; (rider) derribar; (fig) desconcertar; **to ~ a party** dar una fiesta; **throw away** vt tirar; (money) derrochar; **throw in** vt (Sport: ball) sacar; (include) incluir; **throw off** vt deshacerse de; **throw out** vt tirar; (person) echar; expulsar; **throw up** vi vomitar

thru [θru:] (US) = **through**

thrush [θrʌʃ] n zorzal m, tordo

thrust [θrʌst] (pt, pp **~**) vt empujar con fuerza

thud [θʌd] n golpe m sordo

thug [θʌg] n gamberro/a

thumb [θʌm] n (Anat) pulgar m; **to ~ a lift** hacer autostop; **thumbtack** (US) n chincheta (SP)

thump [θʌmp] n golpe m; (sound) ruido seco or sordo ▷ vt golpear ▷ vi (heart etc) palpitar

thunder ['θʌndə*] n trueno ▷ vi tronar; (train etc): **to ~ past** pasar como un trueno; **thunderstorm** n tormenta

Thur(s). abbr (= Thursday) juev

Thursday ['θə:zdɪ] n jueves m inv

thus [ðʌs] adv así, de este modo

thwart [θwɔ:t] vt frustrar

thyme [taɪm] n tomillo

Tibet [tɪ'bɛt] n el Tibet

tick [tɪk] n (sound: of clock) tictac m;

(*mark*) palomita; (*Zool*) garrapata; (*BRIT: inf*): **in a ~** en un instante ▷ vi hacer tictac ▷ vt marcar; **tick off** vt marcar; (*person*) reñir

ticket ['tɪkɪt] n billete m (SP), boleto (LAM); (*for cinema etc*) entrada; (*in shop: on goods*) etiqueta; (*for raffle*) papeleta; (*for library*) tarjeta; (*parking ticket*) multa de aparcamiento (SP) or por estacionamiento (indebido) (LAM); **ticket barrier** n (BRIT: Rail) barrera más allá de la cual se necesita billete/boleto; **ticket collector** n revisor(a) m/f; **ticket inspector** n revisor(a) m/f, inspector(a) m/f de boletos (LAM); **ticket machine** n máquina de billetes (SP) or boletos (LAM); **ticket office** n (*Theatre*) taquilla (SP), boletería (LAM); (*Rail*) mostrador m de billetes (SP) or boletos (LAM)

tickle ['tɪkl] vt hacer cosquillas a ▷ vi hacer cosquillas; **ticklish** adj (*person*) cosquilloso; (*problem*) delicado

tide [taɪd] n marea; (*fig: of events etc*) curso, marcha

tidy ['taɪdɪ] adj (*room etc*) ordenado; (*dress, work*) limpio; (*person*) (bien) arreglado ▷ vt (*also: ~ up*) poner en orden

tie [taɪ] n (*string etc*) atadura; (*BRIT: also:* **neck~**) corbata; (*fig: link*) vínculo, lazo; (*Sport etc: draw*) empate m ▷ vt atar ▷ vi (*Sport etc*) empatar; **to ~ in a bow** atar con un lazo; **to ~ a knot in sth** hacer un nudo en algo; **tie down** vt (*fig: person: restrict*) atar; (: *to price, date etc*) obligar a; **tie up** vt (*dog, person*) atar; (*arrangements*) concluir; **to be tied up** (*busy*) estar ocupado

tier [tɪə*] n grada; (*of cake*) piso

tiger ['taɪgə*] n tigre m

tight [taɪt] adj (*rope*) tirante; (*money*) escaso; (*clothes*) ajustado; (*bend*) cerrado; (*shoes, schedule*) apretado; (*budget*) ajustado; (*security*) estricto; (*inf: drunk*) borracho ▷ adv (*squeeze*) muy fuerte; (*shut*) bien; **tighten** vt (*rope*) estirar; (*screw, grip*) apretar;

(*security*) reforzar ▷ vi estirarse; apretarse; **tightly** adv (*grasp*) muy fuerte; **tights** (BRIT) npl panti mpl

tile [taɪl] n (*on roof*) teja; (*on floor*) baldosa; (*on wall*) azulejo

till [tɪl] n caja (registradora) ▷ vt (*land*) cultivar ▷ prep, conj = **until**

tilt [tɪlt] vt inclinar ▷ vi inclinarse

timber ['tɪmbə*] n (*material*) madera

time [taɪm] n tiempo; (*epoch: often pl*) época; (*by clock*) hora; (*moment*) momento; (*occasion*) vez f; (*Mus*) compás m ▷ vt calcular or medir el tiempo de; (*race*) cronometrar; (*remark, visit etc*) elegir el momento para; **a long ~** mucho tiempo; **4 at a ~** de 4 en 4; 4 a la vez; **for the ~ being** de momento, por ahora; **from ~ to ~** de vez en cuando; **at ~s** a veces; **in ~** (*soon enough*) a tiempo; (*after some time*) con el tiempo; (*Mus*) al compás; **in a week's ~** dentro de una semana; **in no ~** en un abrir y cerrar de ojos; **any ~** cuando sea; **on ~** a la hora; **5 ~s 5** 5 por 5; **what ~ is it?** ¿qué hora es?; **to have a good ~** pasarlo bien, divertirse; **time limit** n plazo; **timely** adj oportuno; **timer** n (*in kitchen etc*) programador m horario; **time-share** n apartamento (or casa) a tiempo compartido; **timetable** n horario; **time zone** n huso horario

timid ['tɪmɪd] adj tímido

timing ['taɪmɪŋ] n (*Sport*) cronometraje m; **the ~ of his resignation** el momento que eligió para dimitir

tin [tɪn] n estaño; (*also: ~ plate*) hojalata; (*BRIT: can*) lata; **tinfoil** n papel m de estaño

tingle ['tɪŋgl] vi (*person*): **to ~ (with)** estremecerse (de); (*hands etc*) hormiguear

tinker ['tɪŋkə*]: **~ with** vt fus jugar con, tocar

tinned [tɪnd] (BRIT) adj (*food*) en lata, en conserva

tin opener [-əupnə*] (BRIT) n abrelatas m inv

tint [tɪnt] n matiz m; (for hair) tinte m; **tinted** adj (hair) teñido; (glass, spectacles) ahumado

tiny ['taɪnɪ] adj minúsculo, pequeñito

tip [tɪp] n (end) punta; (gratuity) propina; (BRIT: for rubbish) vertedero; (advice) consejo ▷ vt (waiter) dar una propina a; (tilt) inclinar; (empty: also: ~ **out**) vaciar, echar; (overturn: also: ~ **over**) volcar; **tip off** vt avisar, poner sobreaviso a

tiptoe ['tɪptəʊ] n: **on** ~ de puntillas

tire ['taɪə*] n (US) =**tyre** ▷ vt cansar ▷ vi cansarse; (become bored) aburrirse; **tired** adj cansado; **to be tired of sth** estar harto de algo; **tire pressure** (US) = **tyre pressure**; **tiring** adj cansado

tissue ['tɪʃuː] n tejido; (paper handkerchief) pañuelo de papel, kleenex® m; **tissue paper** n papel m de seda

tit [tɪt] n (bird) herrerillo común; **to give ~ for tat** dar ojo por ojo

title ['taɪtl] n título

T-junction ['tiː'dʒʌŋkʃən] n cruce m en T

TM abbr =**trademark**

○ **KEYWORD**

to [tuː, tə] prep **1** (direction) a; **to go to France/London/school/the station** ir a Francia/Londres/al colegio/a la estación; **to go to Claude's/the doctor's** ir a casa de Claude/al médico; **the road to Edinburgh** la carretera de Edimburgo

2 (as far as) hasta, a; **from here to London** de aquí a or hasta Londres; **to count to 10** contar hasta 10; **from 40 to 50 people** entre 40 y 50 personas

3 (with expressions of time): **a quarter/twenty to 5** las 5 menos cuarto/veinte

4 (for, of): **the key to the front door** la llave de la puerta principal; **she is secretary to the director** es la secretaría del director; **a letter to his wife** una carta a or para su mujer

5 (expressing indirect object) a; **to give sth to sb** darle algo a algn; **to talk to sb** hablar con algn; **to be a danger to sb** ser un peligro para algn; **to carry out repairs to sth** hacer reparaciones en algo

6 (in relation to): **3 goals to 2** 3 goles a 2; **30 miles to the gallon** ≈ 94 litros a los cien (kms)

7 (purpose, result): **to come to sb's aid** venir en auxilio or ayuda de algn; **to sentence sb to death** condenar a algn a muerte; **to my great surprise** con gran sorpresa mía

▷ with vb **1** (simple infin): **to go/eat** ir/comer

2 (following another vb): **to want/try/start to do** querer/intentar/empezar a hacer

3 (with vb omitted): **I don't want to** no quiero

4 (purpose, result) para; **I did it to help you** lo hice para ayudarte; **he came to see you** vino a verte

5 (equivalent to relative clause): **I have things to do** tengo cosas que hacer; **the main thing is to try** lo principal es intentarlo

6 (after adj etc): **ready to go** listo para irse; **too old to ...** demasiado viejo (como) para ...

▷ adv: **pull/push the door to** tirar de/empujar la puerta

toad [təʊd] n sapo; **toadstool** n hongo venenoso

toast [təʊst] n (Culin) tostada; (drink, speech) brindis m ▷ vt (Culin) tostar; (drink to) brindar por; **toaster** n tostador m

tobacco [tə'bækəʊ] n tabaco

toboggan [tə'bɔgən] n tobogán m

today [tə'deɪ] adv, n (also fig) hoy m

toddler ['tɔdlə*] n niño/a (que empieza a andar)

toe [təʊ] n dedo (del pie); (of shoe) punta; **to ~ the line** (fig) conformarse;

toenail n uña del pie

toffee ['tɒfɪ] n toffee m

together [tə'gɛðə*] adv juntos; (at same time) al mismo tiempo, a la vez; **~ with** junto con

toilet ['tɔɪlət] n inodoro; (BRIT: room) (cuarto de) baño, servicio ▷ cpd (soap etc) de aseo; **toilet bag** n neceser m, bolsa de aseo; **toilet paper** n papel m higiénico; **toiletries** npl artículos mpl de tocador; **toilet roll** n rollo de papel higiénico

token ['təukən] n (sign) señal f, muestra; (souvenir) recuerdo; (disc) ficha ▷ adj (strike, payment etc) simbólico; **book/record ~** (BRIT) vale m para comprar libros/discos; **gift ~** (BRIT) vale-regalo

Tokyo ['təukjəu] n Tokio, Tokío

told [təuld] pt, pp of **tell**

tolerant ['tɒlərnt] adj: **~ of** tolerante con

tolerate ['tɒləreɪt] vt tolerar

toll [təul] n (of casualties) número de víctimas; (tax, charge) peaje m ▷ vi (bell) doblar; **toll call** n (US Tel) conferencia, llamada interurbana; **toll-free** (US) adj, adv gratis

tomato [tə'mɑːtəu] (pl **~es**) n tomate m; **tomato sauce** n salsa de tomate

tomb [tuːm] n tumba; **tombstone** n lápida

tomorrow [tə'mɔrəu] adv, n (also: fig) mañana; **the day after ~** pasado mañana; **~ morning** mañana por la mañana

ton [tʌn] n tonelada (BRIT = 1016 kg; US = 907 kg); (metric ton) tonelada métrica; **~s of** (inf) montones de

tone [təun] n tono ▷ vi (also: **~ in**) armonizar; **tone down** vt (criticism) suavizar; (colour) atenuar

tongs [tɒŋz] npl (for coal) tenazas fpl; (curling tongs) tenacillas fpl

tongue [tʌŋ] n lengua; **~ in cheek** irónicamente

tonic ['tɒnɪk] n (Med) tónico; (also: **~ water**) (agua) tónica

tonight [tə'naɪt] adv, n esta noche; esta tarde

tonne [tʌn] n tonelada (métrica) (1.000kg)

tonsil ['tɒnsl] n amígdala; **tonsillitis** [-'laɪtɪs] n amigdalitis f

too [tuː] adv (excessively) demasiado; (also) también; **~ much** demasiado; **~ many** demasiados/as

took [tuk] pt of **take**

tool [tuːl] n herramienta; **tool box** n caja de herramientas; **tool kit** n juego de herramientas

tooth [tuːθ] (pl **teeth**) n (Anat, Tech) diente m; (molar) muela; **toothache** n dolor m de muelas; **toothbrush** n cepillo de dientes; **toothpaste** n pasta de dientes; **toothpick** n palillo

top [tɒp] n (of mountain) cumbre f, cima; (of tree) copa; (of head) coronilla; (of ladder, page) lo alto; (of table) superficie f; (of cupboard) parte f de arriba; (lid: of box) tapa; (: of bottle, jar) tapón m; (of list etc) cabeza; (toy) peonza; (garment) blusa; camiseta ▷ adj de arriba; (in rank) principal, primero; (best) mejor ▷ vt (exceed) exceder; (be first in) encabezar; **on ~ of** (above) sobre, encima de; (in addition to) además de; **from ~ to bottom** de pies a cabeza; **top up** vt llenar; (mobile phone) recargar (el saldo de); **top floor** n último piso; **top hat** n sombrero de copa

topic ['tɒpɪk] n tema m; **topical** adj actual

topless ['tɒplɪs] adj (bather, bikini) topless inv

topping ['tɒpɪŋ] n (Culin): **with a ~ of cream** con nata por encima

topple ['tɒpl] vt derribar ▷ vi caerse

top-up card n (for mobile phone) tarjeta prepago

torch [tɔːtʃ] n antorcha; (BRIT: electric) linterna

tore [tɔː*] pt of **tear²**

torment [n 'tɔːmɛnt, vt tɔː'mɛnt] n tormento ▷ vt atormentar; (fig: annoy) fastidiar

torn [tɔːn] *pp of* **tear²**

tornado [tɔːˈneɪdəu] (*pl* ~**es**) *n*
tornado

torpedo [tɔːˈpiːdəu] (*pl* ~**es**) *n*
torpedo

torrent [ˈtɔrnt] *n* torrente *m*;
torrential [tɔˈrenʃl] *adj* torrencial

tortoise [ˈtɔːtəs] *n* tortuga ▷ *vt*

torture [ˈtɔːtʃə*] *n* tortura ▷ *vt*
torturar; (*fig*) atormentar

Tory [ˈtɔːrɪ] (BRIT) *adj, n* (*Pol*)
conservador(a) *m/f*

toss [tɔs] *vt* tirar, echar; (*one's head*)
sacudir; **to ~ a coin** echar a cara o cruz;
to ~ up for sth jugar a cara o cruz algo;
to ~ and turn (*in bed*) dar vueltas

total [ˈtəutl] *adj* total, entero;
(*emphatic: failure etc*) completo, total
▷ *n* total *m*, suma ▷ *vt* (*add up*) sumar;
(*amount to*) ascender a

totalitarian [təutælɪˈtɛərɪən] *adj*
totalitario

totally [ˈtəutəlɪ] *adv* totalmente

touch [tʌtʃ] *n* tacto; (*contact*)
contacto ▷ *vt* tocar; (*emotionally*)
conmover; **a ~ of** (*fig*) un poquito
de; **to get in ~ with sb** ponerse en
contacto con algn; **to lose ~** (*friends*)
perder contacto; **touch down** *vi*
(*on land*) aterrizar; **touchdown** *n*
aterrizaje *m*; (*on sea*) amerizaje *m*; (*US
Football*) ensayo; **touched** *adj* (*moved*)
conmovido; **touching** *adj* (*moving*)
conmovedor(a); **touchline** *n* (*Sport*)
línea de banda; **touch-sensitive** *adj*
sensible al tacto

tough [tʌf] *adj* (*material*) resistente;
(*meat*) duro; (*problem etc*) difícil; (*policy,
stance*) inflexible; (*person*) fuerte

tour [ˈtuə*] *n* viaje *m*, vuelta; (*also:*
package ~) viaje *m* todo comprendido;
(*of town, museum*) visita; (*by band etc*)
gira ▷ *vt* recorrer, visitar; **tour guide**
n guía *mf* turístico/a

tourism [ˈtuərɪzm] *n* turismo

tourist [ˈtuərɪst] *n* turista *mf* ▷ *cpd*
turístico; **tourist office** *n* oficina
de turismo

tournament [ˈtuənəmənt] *n* torneo

tour operator *n* touroperador(a)
m/f, operador(a) *m/f* turístico/a

tow [təu] *vt* remolcar; **"on** *or* **in** (US)
~" (*Aut*) "a remolque"; **tow away** *vt*
llevarse a remolque

toward(s) [təˈwɔːd(z)] *prep* hacia;
(*attitude*) respecto a, con; (*purpose*) para

towel [ˈtauəl] *n* toalla; **towelling** *n*
(*fabric*) felpa

tower [ˈtauə*] *n* torre *f*; **tower block**
(BRIT) *n* torre *f* (de pisos)

town [taun] *n* ciudad *f*; **to go to
~** ir a la ciudad; (*fig*) echar la casa
por la ventana; **town centre** (BRIT)
n centro de la ciudad; **town hall** *n*
ayuntamiento

tow truck (US) *n* camión *m* grúa

toxic [ˈtɔksɪk] *adj* tóxico

toy [tɔɪ] *n* juguete *m*; **toy with** *vt fus*
jugar con; (*idea*) acariciar; **toyshop** *n*
juguetería

trace [treɪs] *n* rastro ▷ *vt* (*draw*)
trazar, delinear; (*locate*) encontrar;
(*follow*) seguir la pista de

track [træk] *n* (*mark*) huella, pista;
(*path: gen*) camino, senda; (: *of bullet
etc*) trayectoria; (: *of suspect, animal*)
pista, rastro; (*Rail*) vía; (*Sport*) pista;
(*on tape, record*) canción *f* ▷ *vt* seguir
la pista de; **to keep ~ of** mantenerse al
tanto de, seguir; **track down** *vt* (*prey*)
seguir el rastro de; (*sth lost*) encontrar;
tracksuit *n* chandal *m*

tractor [ˈtræktə*] *n* tractor *m*

trade [treɪd] *n* comercio; (*skill, job*)
oficio ▷ *vi* negociar, comerciar ▷ *vt*
(*exchange*): **to ~ sth (for sth)** cambiar
algo (por algo); **trade in** *vt* (*old car
etc*) ofrecer como parte del pago;
trademark *n* marca de fábrica; **trader**
n comerciante *mf*; **tradesman** (*irreg*)
n (*shopkeeper*) tendero; **trade union**
n sindicato

trading [ˈtreɪdɪŋ] *n* comercio

tradition [trəˈdɪʃən] *n* tradición *f*;
traditional *adj* tradicional

traffic [ˈtræfɪk] *n* (*gen, Aut*) tráfico,

circulación f ▷ vi: **to ~ in** (pej: liquor, drugs) traficar en; **traffic circle** (US) n isleta; **traffic island** n refugio, isleta; **traffic jam** n embotellamiento; **traffic lights** npl semáforo; **traffic warden** n guardia mf de tráfico

tragedy ['trædʒədɪ] n tragedia

tragic ['trædʒɪk] adj trágico

trail [treɪl] n (tracks) rastro, pista; (path) camino, sendero; (dust, smoke) estela ▷ vt (drag) arrastrar; (follow) seguir la pista de ▷ vi arrastrar; (in contest etc) ir perdiendo; **trailer** n (Aut) remolque m; (caravan) caravana; (Cinema) trailer m, avance m

train [treɪn] n tren m; (of dress) cola; (series) serie f ▷ vt (educate, teach skills to) formar; (sportsman) entrenar; (dog) adiestrar; (point: gun etc): **to ~ on** apuntar a ▷ vi (Sport) entrenarse; (learn a skill): **to ~ as a teacher** etc estudiar para profesor etc; **one's ~ of thought** el razonamiento de algn; **trainee** [treɪ'niː] n aprendiz(a) m/f; **trainer** n (Sport: coach) entrenador(a) m/f; (of animals) domador(a) m/f; **trainers** npl (shoes) zapatillas fpl (de deporte); **training** n formación f; entrenamiento; **to be in training** (Sport) estar entrenando; **training course** n curso de formación; **training shoes** npl zapatillas fpl (de deporte)

trait [treɪt] n rasgo

traitor ['treɪtə*] n traidor(a) m/f

tram [træm] (BRIT) n (also: **~car**) tranvía m

tramp [træmp] n (person) vagabundo/a; (inf: pej: woman) puta

trample ['træmpl] vt: **to ~ (underfoot)** pisotear

trampoline ['træmpəliːn] n trampolín m

tranquil ['træŋkwɪl] adj tranquilo; **tranquillizer** (US **tranquilizer**) n (Med) tranquilizante m

transaction [træn'zækʃən] n transacción f, operación f

transatlantic ['trænzət'læntɪk] adj transatlántico

transcript ['trænskrɪpt] n copia

transfer [n 'trænsfə:*, vb træns'fə:*] n (of employees) traslado; (of money, power) transferencia; (Sport) traspaso; (picture, design) calcomanía ▷ vt trasladar; transferir; **to ~ the charges** (BRIT Tel) llamar a cobro revertido

transform [træns'fɔ:m] vt transformar; **transformation** n transformación f

transfusion [træns'fjuːʒən] n transfusión f

transit ['trænzɪt] n: **in ~** en tránsito

transition [træn'zɪʃən] n transición f

transitive ['trænzɪtɪv] adj (Ling) transitivo

translate [trænz'leɪt] vt traducir; **translation** [-'leɪʃən] n traducción f; **translator** n traductor(a) m/f

transmission [trænz'mɪʃən] n transmisión f

transmit [trænz'mɪt] vt transmitir; **transmitter** n transmisor m

transparent [træns'pærnt] adj transparente

transplant ['trænsplɑ:nt] n (Med) transplante m

transport [n 'trænspɔ:t, vb træns'pɔ:t] n transporte m; (car) coche m (SP), carro (LAM), automóvil m ▷ vt transportar; **transportation** [-'teɪʃən] n transporte m

transvestite [trænz'vestaɪt] n travestí mf

trap [træp] n (snare, trick) trampa; (carriage) cabriolé m ▷ vt coger (SP) or agarrar (LAM) (en una trampa); (trick) engañar; (confine) atrapar

trash [træʃ] n (rubbish) basura; (nonsense) tonterías fpl; (pej): **the book/ film is ~** el libro/la película no vale nada; **trash can** (US) n cubo or bote m (MEX) or tacho (SC) de la basura

trauma ['trɔ:mə] n trauma m; **traumatic** [trɔ:'mætɪk] adj traumático

travel ['trævl] n el viajar ▷ vi viajar
▷ vt (distance) recorrer; **travel agency**
n agencia de viajes; **travel agent** n
agente mf de viajes; **travel insurance**
n seguro de viaje; **traveller** (US
traveler) n viajero/a; **traveller's
cheque** (US **traveler's check**) n
cheque m de viajero; **travelling** (US
traveling) n los viajes, el viajar;
travel-sick adj: **to get travel-sick**
marearse al viajar; **travel sickness**
n mareo

tray [treɪ] n bandeja; (on desk) cajón m

treacherous ['trɛtʃərəs] adj traidor,
traicionero; (dangerous) peligroso

treacle ['triːkl] (BRIT) n melaza

tread [trɛd] (pt **trod**, pp **trodden**)
n (step) paso, pisada; (sound) ruido
de pasos; (of stair) escalón m; (of tyre)
banda de rodadura ▷ vi pisar; **tread
on** vt fus pisar

treasure ['trɛʒə*] n tesoro ▷ vt
(value: object, friendship) apreciar;
(: memory) guardar; **treasurer** n
tesorero/a

treasury ['trɛʒərɪ] n: **the T~** el
Ministerio de Hacienda

treat [triːt] n (present) regalo ▷ vt
tratar; **to ~ sb to sth** invitar a algn a
algo; **treatment** n tratamiento

treaty ['triːtɪ] n tratado

treble ['trɛbl] adj triple ▷ vt triplicar
▷ vi triplicarse

tree [triː] n árbol m; **~ trunk** tronco
(de árbol)

trek [trɛk] n (long journey) viaje m
largo y difícil; (tiring walk) caminata

tremble ['trɛmbl] vi temblar

tremendous [trɪ'mɛndəs] adj
tremendo, enorme; (excellent)
estupendo

trench [trɛntʃ] n zanja

trend [trɛnd] n (tendency) tendencia;
(of events) curso; (fashion) moda; **trendy**
adj de moda

trespass ['trɛspəs] vi: **to ~ on** entrar
sin permiso en; **"no ~ing"** "prohibido
el paso"

trial ['traɪəl] n (Law) juicio, proceso;
(test: of machine etc) prueba; **trial
period** n periodo de prueba

triangle ['traɪæŋgl] n (Math, Mus)
triángulo

triangular [traɪ'æŋgjulə*] adj
triangular

tribe [traɪb] n tribu f

tribunal [traɪ'bjuːnl] n tribunal m

tribute ['trɪbjuːt] n homenaje m,
tributo; **to pay ~ to** rendir homenaje a

trick [trɪk] n (skill, knack) tino, truco;
(conjuring trick) truco; (joke) broma;
(Cards) baza ▷ vt engañar; **to play a
~ on sb** gastar una broma a algn; **that
should do the ~** a ver si funciona así

trickle ['trɪkl] n (of water etc) goteo
▷ vi gotear

tricky ['trɪkɪ] adj difícil; delicado

tricycle ['traɪsɪkl] n triciclo

trifle ['traɪfl] n bagatela; (Culin) dulce
de bizcocho borracho, gelatina, fruta y
natillas ▷ adv: **a ~ long** un poquito largo

trigger ['trɪgə*] n (of gun) gatillo

trim [trɪm] adj (house, garden) en
buen estado; (person, figure) esbelto
▷ n (haircut etc) recorte m; (on car)
guarnición f ▷ vt (neaten) arreglar; (cut)
recortar; (decorate) adornar; (Naut: a
sail) orientar

trio ['triːəu] n trío

trip [trɪp] n viaje m; (excursion)
excursión f; (stumble) traspié m ▷ vi
(stumble) tropezar; (go lightly) andar a
paso ligero; **on a ~** de viaje; **trip up** vi
tropezar, caerse ▷ vt hacer tropezar
or caer

triple ['trɪpl] adj triple

triplets ['trɪplɪts] npl trillizos/as
mpl/fpl

tripod ['traɪpɔd] n trípode m

triumph ['traɪʌmf] n triunfo
▷ vi: **to ~ (over)** vencer; **triumphant**
[traɪ'ʌmfənt] adj (team etc)
vencedor(a); (wave, return) triunfal

trivial ['trɪvɪəl] adj insignificante;
(commonplace) banal

trod [trɔd] pt of **tread**

trodden ['trɒdn] *pp of* **tread**

trolley ['trɒlɪ] *n* carrito; (*also*: **~ bus**) trolebús *m*

trombone [trɒm'bəʊn] *n* trombón *m*

troop [truːp] *n* grupo, banda; **troops** *npl* (*Mil*) tropas *fpl*

trophy ['trəʊfɪ] *n* trofeo

tropical ['trɒpɪkl] *adj* tropical

trot [trɒt] *n* trote *m* ▷ *vi* trotar; **on the ~** (*BRIT*: *fig*) seguidos/as

trouble ['trʌbl] *n* problema *m*, dificultad *f*; (*worry*) preocupación *f*; (*bother*, *effort*) molestia, esfuerzo; (*unrest*) inquietud *f*; (*Med*): **stomach** *etc* **~** problemas *mpl* gástricos *etc* ▷ *vt* (*disturb*) molestar; (*worry*) preocupar, inquietar ▷ *vi*: **to ~ to do sth** molestarse en hacer algo; **troubles** *npl* (*Pol etc*) conflictos *mpl*; (*personal*) problemas *mpl*; **to be in ~** estar en un apuro; **it's no ~!** ¡no es molestia (ninguna)!; **what's the ~?** (*with broken TV etc*) ¿cuál es el problema?; (*doctor to patient*) ¿qué pasa?; **troubled** *adj* (*person*) preocupado; (*country*, *epoch*, *life*) agitado; **troublemaker** *n* agitador(a) *m/f*; (*child*) alborotador *m*; **troublesome** *adj* molesto

trough [trɒf] *n* (*also*: **drinking ~**) abrevadero; (*also*: **feeding ~**) comedero; (*depression*) depresión *f*

trousers ['traʊzəz] *npl* pantalones *mpl*; **short ~** pantalones *mpl* cortos

trout [traʊt] *n inv* trucha

trowel ['traʊəl] *n* (*of gardener*) palita; (*of builder*) paleta

truant ['truənt] *n*: **to play ~** (*BRIT*) hacer novillos

truce [truːs] *n* tregua

truck [trʌk] *n* (*lorry*) camión *m*; (*Rail*) vagón *m*; **truck driver** *n* camionero

true [truː] *adj* verdadero; (*accurate*) exacto; (*genuine*) auténtico; (*faithful*) fiel; **to come ~** realizarse

truly ['truːlɪ] *adv* (*really*) realmente; (*truthfully*) verdaderamente; (*faithfully*): **yours ~** (*in letter*) le saluda atentamente

trumpet ['trʌmpɪt] *n* trompeta

trunk [trʌŋk] *n* (*of tree*, *person*) tronco; (*of elephant*) trompa; (*case*) baúl *m*; (*US Aut*) maletero; **trunks** *npl* (*also*: **swimming ~s**) bañador *m* (de hombre)

trust [trʌst] *n* confianza; (*responsibility*) responsabilidad *f*; (*Law*) fideicomiso ▷ *vt* (*rely on*) tener confianza en; (*hope*) esperar; (*entrust*): **to ~ sth to sb** confiar algo a algn; **to take sth on ~** fiarse de algo; **trusted** *adj* de confianza; **trustworthy** *adj* digno de confianza

truth [truːθ, *pl* truːðz] *n* verdad *f*; **truthful** *adj* veraz

try [traɪ] *n* tentativa, intento; (*Rugby*) ensayo ▷ *vt* (*attempt*) intentar; (*test*: *also*: **~ out**) probar, someter a prueba; (*Law*) juzgar, procesar; (*strain*: *patience*) hacer perder ▷ *vi* probar; **to have a ~** probar suerte; **to ~ to do sth** intentar hacer algo; **~ again!** ¡vuelve a probar!; **~ harder!** ¡esfuérzate más!; **well, I tried** al menos lo intenté; **try on** *vt* (*clothes*) probarse; **trying** *adj* (*experience*) cansado; (*person*) pesado

T-shirt ['tiːʃəːt] *n* camiseta

tub [tʌb] *n* cubo (*SP*), cubeta (*SP*, *MEX*), balde *m* (*LAM*); (*bath*) bañera (*SP*), tina (*LAM*), bañadera (*RPL*)

tube [tjuːb] *n* tubo; (*BRIT*: *underground*) metro; (*for tyre*) cámara de aire

tuberculosis [tjʊbəːkjuˈləʊsɪs] *n* tuberculosis *f inv*

tube station (*BRIT*) *n* estación *f* de metro

tuck [tʌk] *vt* (*put*) poner; **tuck away** *vt* (*money*) guardar; (*building*): **to be tucked away** esconderse, ocultarse; **tuck in** *vt* meter dentro; (*child*) arropar ▷ *vi* (*eat*) comer con apetito; **tuck shop** *n* (*Scol*) tienda ≈ bar *m* (del colegio) (*SP*)

Tue(s). *abbr* (= *Tuesday*) mart

Tuesday ['tjuːzdɪ] *n* martes *m inv*

tug [tʌg] *n* (*ship*) remolcador *m* ▷ *vt* tirar de

tuition [tjuːˈɪʃən] *n* (*BRIT*) enseñanza;

(: *private tuition*) clases *fpl* particulares; (*us: school fees*) matrícula

tulip ['tjuːlɪp] *n* tulipán *m*

tumble ['tʌmbl] *n* (*fall*) caída ▷ *vi* caer; **to ~ to sth** (*inf*) caer en la cuenta de algo; **tumble dryer** (BRIT) *n* secadora

tumbler ['tʌmblə*] *n* (*glass*) vaso

tummy ['tʌmɪ] (*inf*) *n* barriga, tripa

tumour ['tjuːmə*] (*us* **tumor**) *n* tumor *m*

tuna ['tjuːnə] *n inv* (*also:* **~ fish**) atún *m*

tune [tjuːn] *n* melodía ▷ *vt* (*Mus*) afinar; (*Radio, TV, Aut*) sintonizar; **to be in/out of ~** (*instrument*) estar afinado/desafinado; (*singer*) cantar afinadamente/desafinar; **to be in/out of ~ with** (*fig*) estar de acuerdo/en desacuerdo con; **tune in** *vi*: **to tune in (to)** (*Radio, TV*) sintonizar (con); **tune up** *vi* (*musician*) afinar (su instrumento)

tunic ['tjuːnɪk] *n* túnica

Tunisia [tjuːˈnɪzɪə] *n* Túnez *m*

tunnel ['tʌnl] *n* túnel *m*; (*in mine*) galería ▷ *vi* construir un túnel/una galería

turbulence ['təːbjʊləns] *n* (*Aviat*) turbulencia

turf [təːf] *n* césped *m*; (*clod*) tepe *m* ▷ *vt* cubrir con césped

Turk [təːk] *n* turco/a

Turkey ['təːkɪ] *n* Turquía

turkey ['təːkɪ] *n* pavo

Turkish ['təːkɪʃ] *adj, n* turco; (*Ling*) turco

turmoil ['təːmɔɪl] *n*: **in ~** revuelto

turn [təːn] *n* turno; (*in road*) curva; (*of mind, events*) rumbo; (*Theatre*) número; (*Med*) ataque *m* ▷ *vt* girar, volver; (*collar, steak*) dar la vuelta a; (*page*) pasar; (*change*): **to ~ sth into** convertir algo en ▷ *vi* volver; (*person: look back*) volverse; (*reverse direction*) dar la vuelta; (*milk*) cortarse; (*become*): **to ~ nasty/forty** ponerse feo/cumplir los cuarenta; **a good ~** un favor; **it gave me quite a ~** me dio un susto; **"no left ~"** (*Aut*) "prohibido girar a la izquierda"; **it's your ~** te toca a ti; **in ~** por turnos; **to take ~s (at)** turnarse (en); **turn around** *vi* (*person*) volverse, darse la vuelta ▷ *vt* (*object*) dar la vuelta a, voltear (LAM); **turn away** *vi* apartar la vista ▷ *vi* rechazar; **turn back** *vi* volverse atrás ▷ *vt* hacer retroceder; (*clock*) retrasar; **turn down** *vt* (*refuse*) rechazar; (*reduce*) bajar; (*fold*) doblar; **turn in** *vi* (*inf: go to bed*) acostarse ▷ *vt* (*fold*) doblar hacia dentro; **turn off** *vi* (*from road*) desviarse ▷ *vt* (*light, radio etc*) apagar; (*tap*) cerrar; (*engine*) parar; **turn on** *vt* (*light, radio etc*) encender (SP), prender (LAM); (*tap*) abrir; (*engine*) poner en marcha; **turn out** *vt* (*light, gas*) apagar; (*produce*) producir ▷ *vi* (*voters*) concurrir; **to turn out to be ...** resultar ser ...; **turn over** *vi* (*person*) volverse ▷ *vt* (*object*) dar la vuelta a; (*page*) volver; **turn round** *vi* volverse; (*rotate*) girar; **turn to** *vt fus*: **to turn to sb** acudir a algn; **turn up** *vi* (*person*) llegar, presentarse; (*lost object*) aparecer ▷ *vt* (*gen*) subir; **turning** *n* (*in road*) vuelta; **turning point** *n* (*fig*) momento decisivo

turnip ['təːnɪp] *n* nabo

turn: turnout *n* concurrencia; **turnover** *n* (*Comm: amount of money*) volumen *m* de ventas; (: *of goods*) movimiento; **turnstile** *n* torniquete *m*; **turn-up** (BRIT) *n* (*on trousers*) vuelta

turquoise ['təːkwɔɪz] *n* (*stone*) turquesa ▷ *adj* color turquesa

turtle ['təːtl] *n* galápago; **turtleneck (sweater)** *n* jersey *m* de cuello vuelto

tusk [tʌsk] *n* colmillo

tutor ['tjuːtə*] *n* profesor(a) *m/f*; **tutorial** [-ˈtɔːrɪəl] *n* (*Scol*) seminario

tuxedo [tʌkˈsiːdəʊ] (*us*) *n* smóking *m*, esmoquin *m*

TV [tiːˈviː] *n abbr* (= *television*) tele *f*

tweed [twiːd] *n* tweed *m*

tweezers ['twiːzəz] *npl* pinzas *fpl* (de depilar)

twelfth [twɛlfθ] num duodécimo
twelve [twɛlv] num doce; **at ~ o'clock** (midday) a mediodía; (midnight) a medianoche
twentieth ['twɛntɪɪθ] adj vigésimo
twenty ['twɛntɪ] num veinte
twice [twaɪs] adv dos veces; **~ as much** dos veces más
twig [twɪg] n ramita
twilight ['twaɪlaɪt] n crepúsculo
twin [twɪn] adj, n gemelo/a m/f ▷ vt hermanar; **twin(-bedded) room** n habitación f doble; **twin beds** npl camas fpl gemelas
twinkle ['twɪŋkl] vi centellear; (eyes) brillar
twist [twɪst] n (action) torsión f; (in road, coil) vuelta; (in wire, flex) doblez f; (in story) giro ▷ vt torcer; (weave) trenzar; (roll around) enrollar; (fig) deformar ▷ vi serpentear
twit [twɪt] (inf) n tonto
twitch [twɪtʃ] n (pull) tirón m; (nervous) tic m ▷ vi crisparse
two [tu:] num dos; **to put ~ and ~ together** (fig) atar cabos
type [taɪp] n (category) tipo, género; (model) tipo; (Typ) tipo, letra ▷ vt (letter etc) escribir a máquina; **typewriter** n máquina de escribir
typhoid ['taɪfɔɪd] n tifoidea
typhoon [taɪ'fu:n] n tifón m
typical ['tɪpɪkl] adj típico; **typically** adv típicamente
typing ['taɪpɪŋ] n mecanografía
typist ['taɪpɪst] n mecanógrafo/a
tyre ['taɪə*] (US tire) n neumático, llanta (LAM); **tyre pressure** (BRIT) n presión f de los neumáticos

UFO ['ju:fəu] n abbr (= unidentified flying object) OVNI m
Uganda [ju:'gændə] n Uganda
ugly ['ʌglɪ] adj feo; (dangerous) peligroso
UHT abbr (= UHT milk) leche f UHT, leche f uperizada
UK n abbr = **United Kingdom**
ulcer ['ʌlsə*] n úlcera; (mouth ulcer) llaga
ultimate ['ʌltɪmət] adj último, final; (greatest) máximo; **ultimately** adv (in the end) por último, al final; (fundamentally) a or en fin de cuentas
ultimatum [ʌltɪ'meɪtəm] (pl ~s or ultimata) n ultimátum m
ultrasound ['ʌltrəsaund] n (Med) ultrasonido
ultraviolet ['ʌltrə'vaɪəlɪt] adj ultravioleta
umbrella [ʌm'brɛlə] n paraguas m inv; (for sun) sombrilla
umpire ['ʌmpaɪə*] n árbitro
UN n abbr (= United Nations) NN. UU.
unable [ʌn'eɪbl] adj: **to be ~ to do sth**

no poder hacer algo
unacceptable [ʌnək'sɛptəbl] *adj*
(*proposal, behaviour, price*) inaceptable;
it's ~ that no se puede aceptar que
unanimous [ju:'nænɪməs] *adj*
unánime
unarmed [ʌn'ɑ:md] *adj* (*defenceless*)
inerme; (*without weapon*) desarmado
unattended [ʌnə'tɛndɪd] *adj*
desatendido
unattractive [ʌnə'træktɪv] *adj* poco
atractivo
unavailable [ʌnə'veɪləbl] *adj* (*article,*
room, book) no disponible; (*person*)
ocupado
unavoidable [ʌnə'vɔɪdəbl] *adj*
inevitable
unaware [ʌnə'wɛə*] *adj*: **to be ~ of**
ignorar; **unawares** *adv*: **to catch sb**
unawares pillar a algn desprevenido
unbearable [ʌn'bɛərəbl] *adj* .
insoportable
unbeatable [ʌn'bi:təbl] *adj* (*team*)
invencible; (*price*) inmejorable; (*quality*)
insuperable
unbelievable [ʌnbɪ'li:vəbl] *adj*
increíble
unborn [ʌn'bɔ:n] *adj* que va a nacer
unbutton [ʌn'bʌtn] *vt* desabrochar
uncalled-for [ʌn'kɔ:ldfɔ:*] *adj*
gratuito, inmerecido
uncanny [ʌn'kænɪ] *adj* extraño
uncertain [ʌn'sə:tn] *adj* incierto;
(*indecisive*) indeciso; **uncertainty** *n*
incertidumbre *f*
unchanged [ʌn'tʃeɪndʒd] *adj* igual,
sin cambios
uncle ['ʌŋkl] *n* tío
unclear [ʌn'klɪə*] *adj* poco claro; **I'm**
still ~ about what I'm supposed to
do todavía no tengo muy claro lo que
tengo que hacer
uncomfortable [ʌn'kʌmfətəbl] *adj*
incómodo; (*uneasy*) inquieto
uncommon [ʌn'kɔmən] *adj* poco
común, raro
unconditional [ʌnkən'dɪʃənl] *adj*
incondicional

unconscious [ʌn'kɔnʃəs] *adj* sin
sentido; (*unaware*): **to be ~ of** no darse
cuenta de ▷ *n*: **the ~** el inconsciente
uncontrollable [ʌnkən'trəuləbl]
adj (*child etc*) incontrolable; (*temper*)
indomable; (*laughter*) incontenible
unconventional [ʌnkən'vɛnʃnl]
adj poco convencional
uncover [ʌn'kʌvə*] *vt* descubrir;
(*take lid off*) destapar
undecided [ʌndɪ'saɪdɪd] *adj*
(*character*) indeciso; (*question*) no
resuelto
undeniable [ʌndɪ'naɪəbl] *adj*
innegable
under ['ʌndə*] *prep* debajo de; (*less*
than) menos de; (*according to*) según,
de acuerdo con; (*sb's leadership*) bajo
▷ *adv* debajo, abajo; **~ there** allí abajo;
~ repair en reparación; **undercover**
adj clandestino; **underdone** *adj*
(*Culin*) poco hecho; **underestimate**
vt subestimar; **undergo** (*irreg*)
vt sufrir; (*treatment*) recibir;
undergraduate *n* estudiante *mf*;
underground *n* (BRIT: *railway*) metro;
(*Pol*) movimiento clandestino ▷ *adj*
(*car park*) subterráneo ▷ *adv* (*work*)
en la clandestinidad; **undergrowth**
n maleza; **underline** *vt* subrayar;
undermine *vt* socavar, minar;
underneath [ʌndə'ni:θ] *adv* debajo
▷ *prep* debajo de, bajo; **underpants**
npl calzoncillos *mpl*; **underpass** (BRIT)
n paso subterráneo; **underprivileged**
adj desposeído; **underscore** *vt*
subrayar; **undershirt** (US) *n* camiseta;
underskirt (BRIT) *n* enaguas *fpl*
understand [ʌndə'stænd] *vt*,
vi entender, comprender; (*assume*)
tener entendido; **understandable**
adj comprensible; **understanding**
adj comprensivo ▷ *n* comprensión *f*,
entendimiento; (*agreement*) acuerdo
understatement ['ʌndəsteɪtmənt]
n modestia (excesiva); **that's an ~!**
¡eso es decir poco!
understood [ʌndə'stud] *pt*, *pp of*

understand ▷ *adj* (*agreed*) acordado; (*implied*): **it is ~ that** se sobreentiende que

undertake [ʌndə'teɪk] (*irreg*) *vt* emprender; **to ~ to do sth** comprometerse a hacer algo

undertaker ['ʌndəteɪkə*] *n* director(a) *m/f* de pompas fúnebres

undertaking ['ʌndəteɪkɪŋ] *n* empresa; (*promise*) promesa

under: underwater *adv* bajo el agua ▷ *adj* submarino; **underway** *adj*: **to be underway** (*meeting*) estar en marcha; (*investigation*) estar llevándose a cabo; **underwear** *n* ropa interior; **underwent** *vb see* **undergo**; **underworld** *n* (*of crime*) hampa, inframundo

undesirable [ʌndɪ'zaɪrəbl] *adj* (*person*) indeseable; (*thing*) poco aconsejable

undisputed [ʌndɪ'spjuːtɪd] *adj* incontestable

undo [ʌn'duː] (*irreg*) *vt* (*laces*) desatar; (*button etc*) desabrochar; (*spoil*) deshacer

undone [ʌn'dʌn] *pp of* **undo** ▷ *adj*: **to come ~** (*clothes*) desabrocharse; (*parcel*) desatarse

undoubtedly [ʌn'daʊtɪdlɪ] *adv* indudablemente, sin duda

undress [ʌn'drɛs] *vi* desnudarse

unearth [ʌn'əːθ] *vt* desenterrar

uneasy [ʌn'iːzɪ] *adj* intranquilo, preocupado; (*feeling*) desagradable; (*peace*) inseguro

unemployed [ʌnɪm'plɔɪd] *adj* parado, sin trabajo ▷ *npl*: **the ~** los parados

unemployment [ʌnɪm'plɔɪmənt] *n* paro, desempleo; **unemployment benefit** *n* (BRIT) subsidio de desempleo *or* paro

unequal [ʌn'iːkwəl] *adj* (*unfair*) desigual; (*size, length*) distinto

uneven [ʌn'iːvn] *adj* desigual; (*road etc*) lleno de baches

unexpected [ʌnɪk'spɛktɪd] *adj* inesperado; **unexpectedly** *adv* inesperadamente

unfair [ʌn'fɛə*] *adj*: **~ (to sb)** injusto (con algn)

unfaithful [ʌn'feɪθful] *adj* infiel

unfamiliar [ʌnfə'mɪlɪə*] *adj* extraño, desconocido; **to be ~ with** desconocer

unfashionable [ʌn'fæʃnəbl] *adj* pasado *or* fuera de moda

unfasten [ʌn'fɑːsn] *vt* (*knot*) desatar; (*dress*) desabrochar; (*open*) abrir

unfavourable [ʌn'feɪvərəbl] (US **unfavorable**) *adj* desfavorable

unfinished [ʌn'fɪnɪʃt] *adj* inacabado, sin terminar

unfit [ʌn'fɪt] *adj* bajo de forma; (*incompetent*): **~ (for)** incapaz (de); **~ for work** no apto para trabajar

unfold [ʌn'fəʊld] *vt* desdoblar ▷ *vi* abrirse

unforgettable [ʌnfə'gɛtəbl] *adj* inolvidable

unfortunate [ʌn'fɔːtʃnət] *adj* desgraciado; (*event, remark*) inoportuno; **unfortunately** *adv* desgraciadamente

unfriendly [ʌn'frɛndlɪ] *adj* antipático; (*behaviour, remark*) hostil, poco amigable

unfurnished [ʌn'fəːnɪʃt] *adj* sin amueblar

unhappiness [ʌn'hæpɪnɪs] *n* tristeza, desdicha

unhappy [ʌn'hæpɪ] *adj* (*sad*) triste; (*unfortunate*) desgraciado; (*childhood*) infeliz; **~ about/with** (*arrangements etc*) poco contento con, descontento de

unhealthy [ʌn'hɛlθɪ] *adj* (*place*) malsano; (*person*) enfermizo; (*fig: interest*) morboso

unheard-of [ʌn'həːdɔv] *adj* inaudito, sin precedente

unhelpful [ʌn'hɛlpful] *adj* (*person*) poco servicial; (*advice*) inútil

unhurt [ʌn'həːt] *adj* ileso

unidentified [ʌnaɪ'dɛntɪfaɪd] *adj* no identificado, sin identificar; *see* *also* **UFO**

uniform ['ju:nɪfɔ:m] *n* uniforme *m*
▷ *adj* uniforme

unify ['ju:nɪfaɪ] *vt* unificar, unir

unimportant [ˌʌnɪm'pɔ:tənt] *adj* sin
importancia

uninhabited [ˌʌnɪn'hæbɪtɪd] *adj*
desierto

unintentional [ˌʌnɪn'tenʃənəl] *adj*
involuntario

union ['ju:njən] *n* unión *f*; (*also*: **trade
~**) sindicato ▷ *cpd* sindical; **Union Jack**
n bandera del Reino Unido

unique [ju:'ni:k] *adj* único

unisex ['ju:nɪseks] *adj* unisex

unit ['ju:nɪt] *n* unidad *f*; (*section*: *of
furniture etc*) elemento; (*team*) grupo;
kitchen ~ módulo de cocina

unite [ju:'naɪt] *vt* unir ▷ *vi* unirse;
united *adj* unido; (*effort*) conjunto;
United Kingdom *n* Reino Unido;
United Nations (Organization) *n*
Naciones *fpl* Unidas; **United States (of
America)** *n* Estados *mpl* Unidos

unity ['ju:nɪtɪ] *n* unidad *f*

universal [ju:nɪ'və:sl] *adj* universal

universe ['ju:nɪvə:s] *n* universo

university [ju:nɪ'və:sɪtɪ] *n*
universidad *f*

unjust [ʌn'dʒʌst] *adj* injusto

unkind [ʌn'kaɪnd] *adj* poco amable;
(*behaviour, comment*) cruel

unknown [ʌn'nəun] *adj*
desconocido

unlawful [ʌn'lɔ:ful] *adj* ilegal, ilícito

unleaded [ʌn'ledɪd] *adj* (*petrol, fuel*)
sin plombo

unleash [ʌn'li:ʃ] *vt* desatar

unless [ʌn'les] *conj* a menos que;
~ he comes a menos que venga; **~
otherwise stated** salvo indicación
contraria

unlike [ʌn'laɪk] *adj* (*not alike*) distinto
de or a; (*not like*) poco propio de ▷ *prep*
a diferencia de

unlikely [ʌn'laɪklɪ] *adj* improbable;
(*unexpected*) inverosímil

unlimited [ʌn'lɪmɪtɪd] *adj* ilimitado

unlisted [ʌn'lɪstɪd] (*US*) *adj* (*Tel*) que
no consta en la guía

unload [ʌn'ləud] *vt* descargar

unlock [ʌn'lɔk] *vt* abrir (con llave)

unlucky [ʌn'lʌkɪ] *adj* desgraciado;
(*object, number*) que da mala suerte; **to
be ~** tener mala suerte

unmarried [ʌn'mærɪd] *adj* soltero

unmistak(e)able [ˌʌnmɪs'teɪkəbl]
adj inconfundible

unnatural [ʌn'nætʃrəl] *adj* (*gen*)
antinatural; (*manner*) afectado; (*habit*)
perverso

unnecessary [ʌn'nesəsərɪ] *adj*
innecesario, inútil

UNO ['ju:nəu] *n abbr* (= *United Nations
Organization*) ONU *f*

unofficial [ʌnə'fɪʃl] *adj* no oficial;
(*news*) sin confirmar

unpack [ʌn'pæk] *vi* deshacer las
maletas ▷ *vt* deshacer

unpaid [ʌn'peɪd] *adj* (*bill, debt*) sin
pagar, impagado; (*Comm*) pendiente;
(*holiday*) sin sueldo; (*work*) sin pago,
voluntario

unpleasant [ʌn'pleznt] *adj*
(*disagreeable*) desagradable; (*person,
manner*) antipático

unplug [ʌn'plʌg] *vt* desenchufar,
desconectar

unpopular [ʌn'pɔpjulə*] *adj*
impopular, poco popular

unprecedented [ʌn'presɪdəntɪd]
adj sin precedentes

unpredictable [ʌnprɪ'dɪktəbl] *adj*
imprevisible

unprotected ['ʌnprə'tektɪd] *adj* (*sex*)
sin protección

unqualified [ʌn'kwɔlɪfaɪd] *adj* sin
título, no cualificado; (*success*) total

unravel [ʌn'rævl] *vt* desenmarañar

unreal [ʌn'rɪəl] *adj* irreal;
(*extraordinary*) increíble

unrealistic [ʌnrɪə'lɪstɪk] *adj* poco
realista

unreasonable [ʌn'ri:znəbl] *adj*
irrazonable; (*demand*) excesivo

unrelated [ʌnrɪ'leɪtɪd] *adj* sin

relación; (*family*) no emparentado

unreliable [ʌnrɪˈlaɪəbl] *adj* (*person*) informal; (*machine*) poco fiable

unrest [ʌnˈrɛst] *n* inquietud *f*, malestar *m*; (*Pol*) disturbios *mpl*

unroll [ʌnˈrəul] *vt* desenrollar

unruly [ʌnˈruːlɪ] *adj* indisciplinado

unsafe [ʌnˈseɪf] *adj* peligroso

unsatisfactory [ˈʌnsætɪsˈfæktərɪ] *adj* poco satisfactorio

unscrew [ʌnˈskruː] *vt* destornillar

unsettled [ʌnˈsɛtld] *adj* inquieto, intranquilo; (*weather*) variable

unsettling [ʌnˈsɛtlɪŋ] *adj* perturbador(a), inquietante

unsightly [ʌnˈsaɪtlɪ] *adj* feo

unskilled [ʌnˈskɪld] *adj* (*work*) no especializado; (*worker*) no cualificado

unspoiled [ˈʌnˈspɔɪld], **unspoilt** [ˈʌnˈspɔɪlt] *adj* (*place*) que no ha perdido su belleza natural

unstable [ʌnˈsteɪbl] *adj* inestable

unsteady [ʌnˈstɛdɪ] *adj* inestable

unsuccessful [ʌnsəkˈsɛsful] *adj* (*attempt*) infructuoso; (*writer, proposal*) sin éxito; **to be ~** (*in attempting sth*) no tener éxito, fracasar

unsuitable [ʌnˈsuːtəbl] *adj* inapropiado; (*time*) inoportuno

unsure [ʌnˈʃuə*] *adj* inseguro, poco seguro

untidy [ʌnˈtaɪdɪ] *adj* (*room*) desordenado; (*appearance*) desaliñado

untie [ʌnˈtaɪ] *vt* desatar

until [ənˈtɪl] *prep* hasta ▷ *conj* hasta que; **~ he comes** hasta que venga; **~ now** hasta ahora; **~ then** hasta entonces

untrue [ʌnˈtruː] *adj* (*statement*) falso

unused [ʌnˈjuːzd] *adj* sin usar

unusual [ʌnˈjuːʒuəl] *adj* insólito, poco común; (*exceptional*) inusitado; **unusually** *adv* (*exceptionally*) excepcionalmente; **he arrived unusually early** llegó más temprano que de costumbre

unveil [ʌnˈveɪl] *vt* (*statue*) descubrir

unwanted [ʌnˈwɒntɪd] *adj* (*clothing*)

viejo; (*pregnancy*) no deseado

unwell [ʌnˈwɛl] *adj*: **to be/feel ~** estar indispuesto/sentirse mal

unwilling [ʌnˈwɪlɪŋ] *adj*: **to be ~ to do sth** estar poco dispuesto a hacer algo

unwind [ʌnˈwaɪnd] (*irreg*) *vt* desenvolver ▷ *vi* (*relax*) relajarse

unwise [ʌnˈwaɪz] *adj* imprudente

unwittingly [ʌnˈwɪtɪŋlɪ] *adv* inconscientemente, sin darse cuenta

unwrap [ʌnˈræp] *vt* desenvolver

unzip [ʌnˈzɪp] *vt* abrir la cremallera de; (*Comput*) descomprimir

○ **KEYWORD**

up [ʌp] *prep*: **to go/be up sth** subir/estar subido en algo; **he went up the stairs/the hill** subió las escaleras/la colina; **we walked/climbed up the hill** subimos la colina; **they live further up the street** viven más arriba en la calle; **go up that road and turn left** sigue por esa calle y gira a la izquierda
▷ *adv* **1** (*upwards, higher*) más arriba; **up in the mountains** en lo alto (de la montaña); **put it a bit higher up** ponlo un poco más arriba or alto; **up there** ahí or allí arriba; **up above** en lo alto, por encima, arriba
2: **to be up** (*out of bed*) estar levantado; (*prices, level*) haber subido
3: **up to** (*as far as*) hasta; **up to now** hasta ahora or la fecha
4: **to be up to: it's up to you** (*depending on*) depende de ti; **he's not up to it** (*job, task etc*) no es capaz de hacerlo, **his work is not up to the required standard** su trabajo no da la talla; (*inf: be doing*): **what is he up to?** ¿que estará tramando?
▷ *n*: **ups and downs** altibajos *mpl*

up-and-coming [ʌpəndˈkʌmɪŋ] *adj* prometedor(a)

upbringing [ˈʌpbrɪŋɪŋ] *n* educación

f

update [ʌp'deɪt] *vt* poner al día

upfront [ʌp'frʌnt] *adj* claro, directo ▷ *adv* a las claras; (*pay*) por adelantado; **to be ~ about sth** admitir algo claramente

upgrade [ʌp'greɪd] *vt* (*house*) modernizar; (*employee*) ascender

upheaval [ʌp'hi:vl] *n* trastornos *mpl*; (*Pol*) agitación *f*

uphill [ʌp'hɪl] *adj* cuesta arriba; (*fig: task*) penoso, difícil ▷ *adv*: **to go ~** ir cuesta arriba

upholstery [ʌp'həulstəri] *n* tapicería

upmarket [ʌp'mɑ:kɪt] *adj* (*product*) de categoría

upon [ə'pɔn] *prep* sobre

upper ['ʌpə*] *adj* superior, de arriba ▷ *n* (*of shoe: also*: **~s**) empeine *m*; **upper-class** *adj* de clase alta

upright ['ʌpraɪt] *adj* derecho; (*vertical*) vertical; (*fig*) honrado

uprising ['ʌpraɪzɪŋ] *n* sublevación *f*

uproar ['ʌprɔ:*] *n* escándalo

upset [*n* 'ʌpsɛt, *vb, adj* ʌp'sɛt] *n* (*to plan etc*) revés *m*, contratiempo; (*Med*) trastorno ▷ *vt irreg* (*glass etc*) volcar; (*plan*) alterar; (*person*) molestar, disgustar ▷ *adj* molesto, disgustado; (*stomach*) revuelto

upside-down [ʌpsaɪd'daun] *adv* al revés; **to turn a place ~** (*fig*) revolverlo todo

upstairs [ʌp'stɛəz] *adv* arriba ▷ *adj* (*room*) de arriba ▷ *n* el piso superior

up-to-date ['ʌptə'deɪt] *adj* al día

uptown ['ʌptaun] (*us*) *adv* hacia las afueras ▷ *adj* exterior, de las afueras

upward ['ʌpwəd] *adj* ascendente; **upward(s)** *adv* hacia arriba; (*more than*): **upward(s) of** más de

uranium [juə'reɪnɪəm] *n* uranio

Uranus [juə'reɪnəs] *n* Urano

urban ['ə:bən] *adj* urbano

urge [ə:dʒ] *n* (*desire*) deseo ▷ *vt*: **to ~ sb to do sth** animar a algn a hacer algo

urgency ['ə:dʒənsɪ] *n* urgencia

urgent ['ə:dʒənt] *adj* urgente; (*voice*) perentorio

urinal ['juərɪnl] *n* (*building*) urinario; (*vessel*) orinal *m*

urinate ['juərɪneɪt] *vi* orinar

urine ['juərɪn] *n* orina, orines *mpl*

US *n abbr* (= *United States*) EE. UU.

us [ʌs] *pron* nos; (*after prep*) nosotros/as; *see also* **me**

USA *n abbr* (= *United States (of America)*) EE.UU.

use [*n* ju:s, *vb* ju:z] *n* uso, empleo; (*usefulness*) utilidad *f* ▷ *vt* usar, emplear; **she ~d to do it** (ella) solía *or* acostumbraba hacerlo; **in ~** en uso; **out of ~** en desuso; **to be of ~** servir; **it's no ~** (*pointless*) es inútil; (*not useful*) no sirve; **to be ~d to** estar acostumbrado a, acostumbrar; **use up** *vt* (*food*) consumir; (*money*) gastar; **used** [ju:zd] *adj* (*car*) usado; **useful** *adj* útil; **useless** *adj* (*unusable*) inservible; (*pointless*) inútil; (*person*) inepto; **user** *n* usuario/a; **user-friendly** *adj* (*computer*) amistoso

usual ['ju:ʒuəl] *adj* normal, corriente; **as ~** como de costumbre; **usually** *adv* normalmente

utensil [ju:'tɛnsl] *n* utensilio; **kitchen ~s** batería de cocina

utility [ju:'tɪlɪtɪ] *n* utilidad *f*; (*public utility*) (empresa de) servicio público

utilize ['ju:tɪlaɪz] *vt* utilizar

utmost ['ʌtməust] *adj* mayor ▷ *n*: **to do one's ~** hacer todo lo posible

utter ['ʌtə*] *adj* total, completo ▷ *vt* pronunciar, proferir; **utterly** *adv* completamente, totalmente

U-turn ['ju:'tə:n] *n* viraje *m* en redondo

V

v. abbr =**verse**; **versus**; (=*volt*) v;
(=*vide*) véase

vacancy ['veɪkənsɪ] n (BRIT: *job*)
vacante f; (*room*) habitación f libre; **"no
vacancies"** "completo"

vacant ['veɪkənt] adj desocupado,
libre; (*expression*) distraído

vacate [və'keɪt] vt (*house, room*)
desocupar; (*job*) dejar (vacante)

vacation [və'keɪʃən] n vacaciones
fpl; **vacationer** (US **vacationist**) n
turista m/f

vaccination [væksɪ'neɪʃən] n
vacunación f

vaccine ['væksi:n] n vacuna

vacuum ['vækjum] n vacío; **vacuum
cleaner** n aspiradora

vagina [və'dʒaɪnə] n vagina

vague [veɪg] adj vago; (*memory*)
borroso; (*ambiguous*) impreciso;
(*person: absent-minded*) distraído;
(: *evasive*): **to be ~** no decir las cosas
claramente

vain [veɪn] adj (*conceited*) presumido;
(*useless*) vano, inútil; **in ~** en vano

Valentine's Day ['væləntaɪnzdeɪ] n
día de los enamorados

valid ['vælɪd] adj válido; (*ticket*)
valedero; (*law*) vigente

valley ['vælɪ] n valle m

valuable ['væljuəbl] adj (*jewel*) de
valor; (*time*) valioso; **valuables** npl
objetos mpl de valor

value ['vælju:] n valor m; (*importance*)
importancia ▷ vt (*fix price of*) tasar,
valorar; (*esteem*) apreciar; **values** npl
(*principles*) principios mpl

valve [vælv] n válvula

vampire ['væmpaɪə*] n vampiro

van [væn] n (Aut) furgoneta,
camioneta

vandal ['vændl] n vándalo/a;
vandalism n vandalismo; **vandalize**
vt dañar, destruir

vanilla [və'nɪlə] n vainilla

vanish ['vænɪʃ] vi desaparecer

vanity ['vænɪtɪ] n vanidad f

vapour ['veɪpə*] (US **vapor**) n vapor
m; (*on breath, window*) vaho

variable ['vɛərɪəbl] adj variable

variant ['vɛərɪənt] n variante f

variation [vɛərɪ'eɪʃən] n variación f

varied ['vɛərɪd] adj variado

variety [və'raɪətɪ] n (*diversity*)
diversidad f; (*type*) variedad f

various ['vɛərɪəs] adj (*several: people*)
varios/as; (*reasons*) diversos/as

varnish ['vɑ:nɪʃ] n barniz m; (*nail
varnish*) esmalte m ▷ vt barnizar; (*nails*)
pintar (con esmalte)

vary ['vɛərɪ] vt variar; (*change*)
cambiar ▷ vi variar

vase [vɑ:z] n jarrón m

> Be careful not to translate **vase** by
> the Spanish word *vaso*.

Vaseline® ['væsɪli:n] n vaselina®

vast [vɑ:st] adj enorme

VAT [væt] (BRIT) n abbr (=*value added
tax*) IVA m

vault [vɔ:lt] n (*of roof*) bóveda;
(*tomb*) panteón m; (*in bank*) cámara
acorazada ▷ vt (*also*: **~ over**) saltar
(por encima de)

VCR n abbr = **video cassette recorder**

VDU n abbr (= visual display unit) UPV f

veal [viːl] n ternera

veer [vɪə*] vi (vehicle) virar; (wind) girar

vegan ['viːgən] n vegetariano/a estricto/a, vegetaliano/a

vegetable ['vɛdʒtəbl] n (Bot) vegetal m; (edible plant) legumbre f, hortaliza ▷ adj vegetal

vegetarian [vɛdʒɪ'tɛərɪən] adj, n vegetariano/a m/f

vegetation [vɛdʒɪ'teɪʃən] n vegetación f

vehicle ['viːɪkl] n vehículo; (fig) medio

veil [veɪl] n velo ▷ vt velar

vein [veɪn] n vena; (of ore etc) veta

Velcro® ['vɛlkrəʊ] n velcro® m

velvet ['vɛlvɪt] n terciopelo

vending machine ['vɛndɪŋ-] n distribuidor m automático

vendor ['vɛndə*] n vendedor(a) m/f; **street ~** vendedor(a) m/f callejero/a

vengeance ['vɛndʒəns] n venganza; **with a ~** (fig) con creces

venison ['vɛnɪsn] n carne f de venado

venom ['vɛnəm] n veneno; (bitterness) odio

vent [vɛnt] n (in jacket) respiradero; (in wall) rejilla (de ventilación) ▷ vt (fig: feelings) desahogar

ventilation [vɛntɪ'leɪʃən] n ventilación f

venture ['vɛntʃə*] n empresa ▷ vt (opinion) ofrecer ▷ vi arriesgarse, lanzarse; **business ~** empresa comercial

venue ['vɛnjuː] n lugar m

Venus ['viːnəs] n Venus m

verb [vəːb] n verbo; **verbal** adj verbal

verdict ['vəːdɪkt] n veredicto, fallo; (fig) opinión f, juicio

verge [vəːdʒ] (BRIT) n borde m; **"soft ~s"** (Aut) "arcén m no asfaltado"; **to be on the ~ of doing sth** estar a punto de hacer algo

verify ['vɛrɪfaɪ] vt comprobar, verificar

versatile ['vəːsətaɪl] adj (person) polifacético; (machine, tool etc) versátil

verse [vəːs] n poesía; (stanza) estrofa; (in bible) versículo

version ['vəːʃən] n versión f

versus ['vəːsəs] prep contra

vertical ['vəːtɪkl] adj vertical

very ['vɛrɪ] adv muy ▷ adj: **the ~ book which** el mismo libro que; **the ~ last** el último de todos; **at the ~ least** al menos; **~ much** muchísimo

vessel ['vɛsl] n (ship) barco; (container) vasija; see **blood**

vest [vɛst] n (BRIT) camiseta; (us: waistcoat) chaleco

vet [vɛt] vt (candidate) investigar ▷ n abbr (BRIT) = **veterinary surgeon**

veteran ['vɛtərn] n excombatiente mf, veterano/a

veterinary surgeon ['vɛtrɪnərɪ-] (us **veterinarian**) n veterinario/a m/f

veto ['viːtəʊ] (pl ~es) n veto ▷ vt prohibir, poner el veto a

via ['vaɪə] prep por, por medio de

viable ['vaɪəbl] adj viable

vibrate [vaɪ'breɪt] vi vibrar

vibration [vaɪ'breɪʃən] n vibración f

vicar ['vɪkə*] n párroco (de la Iglesia Anglicana)

vice [vaɪs] n (evil) vicio; (Tech) torno de banco; **vice-chairman** (irreg) n vicepresidente m

vice versa ['vaɪsɪ'vəːsə] adv viceversa

vicinity [vɪ'sɪnɪtɪ] n: **in the ~ (of)** cercano (a)

vicious ['vɪʃəs] adj (attack) violento; (words) cruel; (horse, dog) resabido

victim ['vɪktɪm] n víctima

victor ['vɪktə*] n vencedor(a) m/f

Victorian [vɪk'tɔːrɪən] adj victoriano

victorious [vɪk'tɔːrɪəs] adj vencedor(a)

victory ['vɪktərɪ] n victoria

video ['vɪdɪəʊ] n vídeo (SP), video (LAM); **video call** n videollamada; **video camera** n videocámara, cámara de vídeo; **video (cassette) recorder** n vídeo (SP), video

(*LAM*); **video game** n videojuego;
videophone n videoteléfono; **video
shop** n videoclub m; **video tape** n
cinta de vídeo
vie [vaɪ] vi: **to ~ (with sb for sth)**
competir (con algn por algo)
Vienna [vɪˈɛnə] n Viena
Vietnam [vjɛtˈnæm] n Vietnam
m; **Vietnamese** [-nəˈmiːz] n inv, adj
vietnamita mf
view [vjuː] n vista; (*outlook*)
perspectiva; (*opinion*) opinión f, criterio
▷ vt (*look at*) mirar; (*fig*) considerar;
on ~ (*in museum etc*) expuesto; **in full
~ (of)** en plena vista (de); **in ~ of the
weather/the fact that** en vista del
tiempo/del hecho de que; **in my ~** en
mi opinión; **viewer** n espectador(a)
m/f; (*TV*) telespectador(a) m/f;
viewpoint n (*attitude*) punto de vista;
(*place*) mirador m
vigilant [ˈvɪdʒɪlənt] adj vigilante
vigorous [ˈvɪgərəs] adj enérgico,
vigoroso
vile [vaɪl] adj vil, infame; (*smell*)
asqueroso; (*temper*) endemoniado
villa [ˈvɪlə] n (*country house*) casa de
campo; (*suburban house*) chalet m
village [ˈvɪlɪdʒ] n aldea; **villager** n
aldeano/a
villain [ˈvɪlən] n (*scoundrel*) malvado/
a; (*in novel*) malo; (*BRIT: criminal*)
maleante mf
vinaigrette [vɪneɪˈgrɛt] n vinagreta
vine [vaɪn] n vid f
vinegar [ˈvɪnɪgə*] n vinagre m
vineyard [ˈvɪnjɑːd] n viña, viñedo
vintage [ˈvɪntɪdʒ] n (*year*) vendimia,
cosecha ▷ cpd de época
vinyl [ˈvaɪnl] n vinilo
viola [vɪˈəʊlə] n (*Mus*) viola
violate [ˈvaɪəleɪt] vt violar
violation [vaɪəˈleɪʃən] n violación f;
in ~ of sth en violación de algo
violence [ˈvaɪələns] n violencia
violent [ˈvaɪələnt] adj violento;
(*intense*) intenso
violet [ˈvaɪələt] adj violado, violeta

▷ n (*plant*) violeta
violin [vaɪəˈlɪn] n violín m
VIP n abbr (= *very important person*) VIP m
virgin [ˈvəːdʒɪn] n virgen f
Virgo [ˈvəːgəʊ] n Virgo
virtual [ˈvəːtjuəl] adj virtual;
virtually adv prácticamente; **virtual
reality** n (*Comput*) mundo or realidad
f virtual
virtue [ˈvəːtjuː] n virtud f; (*advantage*)
ventaja; **by ~ of** en virtud de
virus [ˈvaɪərəs] n (*also Comput*)
virus m inv
visa [ˈviːzə] n visado (*SP*), visa (*LAM*)
vise [vaɪs] (*US*) n (*Tech*) = **vice**
visibility [vɪzɪˈbɪlɪtɪ] n visibilidad f
visible [ˈvɪzəbl] adj visible
vision [ˈvɪʒən] n (*sight*) vista;
(*foresight, in dream*) visión f
visit [ˈvɪzɪt] n visita ▷ vt (*person*
(*US: also*: **~ with**) visitar, hacer una
visita a; (*place*) ir a, conocer;
visiting hours npl (*in hospital etc*)
horas f pl de visita; **visitor** n (*in
museum*) visitante mf; (*invited to house*)
visita; (*tourist*) turista mf; **visitor
centre** (*US* **visitor center**) n centro m
de información
visual [ˈvɪzjuəl] adj visual; **visualize**
vt imaginarse
vital [ˈvaɪtl] adj (*essential*) esencial,
imprescindible; (*dynamic*) dinámico;
(*organ*) vital
vitality [vaɪˈtælɪtɪ] n energía,
vitalidad f
vitamin [ˈvɪtəmɪn] n vitamina
vivid [ˈvɪvɪd] adj (*account*) gráfico;
(*light*) intenso; (*imagination, memory*)
vivo
V-neck [ˈviːnɛk] n cuello de pico
vocabulary [vəʊˈkæbjulərɪ] n
vocabulario
vocal [ˈvəʊkl] adj vocal; (*articulate*)
elocuente
vocational [vəʊˈkeɪʃənl] adj
profesional
vodka [ˈvɔdkə] n vodka m
vogue [vəʊg] n: **in ~** en boga

voice [vɔɪs] n voz f ▷ vt expresar;
voice mail n fonobuzón m
void [vɔɪd] n vacío; (hole) hueco ▷ adj
(invalid) nulo, inválido; (empty): **~ of**
carente or desprovisto de
volatile ['vɔlətaɪl] adj (situation)
inestable; (person) voluble; (liquid)
volátil
volcano [vɔl'keɪnəu] (pl **~es**) n
volcán m
volleyball ['vɔlibɔːl] n vol(e)ibol m
volt [vəult] n voltio; **voltage** n
voltaje m
volume ['vɔljuːm] n (gen) volumen
m; (book) tomo
voluntarily ['vɔləntrɪlɪ] adv
libremente, voluntariamente
voluntary ['vɔləntərɪ] adj voluntario
volunteer [vɔlən'tɪə*] n voluntario/
a ▷ vt (information) ofrecer ▷ vi
ofrecerse (de voluntario); **to ~ to do**
ofrecerse a hacer
vomit ['vɔmɪt] n vómito ▷ vt, vi
vomitar

vote [vəut] n voto; (votes cast)
votación f; (right to vote) derecho
de votar; (franchise) sufragio ▷ vt
(chairman) elegir; (propose): **to ~ that**
proponer que ▷ vi votar, ir a votar; **~
of thanks** voto de gracias; **voter** n
votante mf; **voting** n votación f
voucher ['vautʃə*] n (for meal, petrol)
vale m
vow [vau] n voto ▷ vt: **to ~ to do/
that** jurar hacer/que
vowel ['vauəl] n vocal f
voyage ['vɔɪɪdʒ] n viaje m
vulgar ['vʌlgə*] adj (rude) ordinario,
grosero; (in bad taste) de mal gusto
vulnerable ['vʌlnərəbl] adj
vulnerable
vulture ['vʌltʃə*] n buitre m

waddle ['wɔdl] vi anadear
wade [weɪd] vi: **to ~ through** (water)
vadear; (fig: book) leer con dificultad
wafer ['weɪfə*] n galleta, barquillo
waffle ['wɔfl] n (Culin) gofre m ▷ vi
dar el rollo
wag [wæg] vt menear, agitar ▷ vi
moverse, menearse
wage [weɪdʒ] n (also: **~s**) sueldo,
salario ▷ vt: **to ~ war** hacer la guerra
wag(g)on ['wægən] n (horse-drawn)
carro; (BRIT Rail) vagón m
wail [weɪl] n gemido ▷ vi gemir
waist [weɪst] n cintura, talle m;
waistcoat (BRIT) n chaleco
wait [weɪt] n (interval) pausa ▷ vi
esperar; **to lie in ~ for** acechar a; **I
can't ~ to** (fig) estoy deseando; **to ~
for** esperar (a); **wait on** vt fus servir
a; **waiter** n camarero; **waiting list**
n lista de espera; **waiting room** n
sala de espera; **waitress** ['weɪtrɪs] n
camarera
waive [weɪv] vt suspender
wake [weɪk] (pt **woke** or **~d**, pp **woken**

or **~d**) vt (also: **~ up**) despertar ▷ vi
(also: **~ up**) despertarse ▷ n (for dead
person) vela, velatorio; (Naut) estela
Wales [weɪlz] n País m de Gales; **the
Prince of ~** el príncipe de Gales
walk [wɔːk] n (stroll) paseo; (hike)
excursión f a pie, caminata; (gait) paso,
andar m; (in park etc) paseo, alameda
▷ vi andar, caminar; (for pleasure,
exercise) pasear ▷ vt (distance) recorrer
a pie, andar; (dog) pasear; **10 minutes'
~ from here** a 10 minutos de aquí
andando; **people from all ~s of life**
gente de todas las esferas; **walk out** vi
(audience) salir; (workers) declararse en
huelga; **walker** n (person) paseante mf,
caminante mf; **walkie-talkie**
['wɔːkɪ'tɔːkɪ] n walkie-talkie m;
walking n el andar; **walking shoes**
npl zapatos mpl para andar; **walking
stick** n bastón m; **Walkman®** n
Walkman® m; **walkway** n paseo
wall [wɔːl] n pared f; (exterior) muro;
(city wall etc) muralla
wallet ['wɒlɪt] n cartera, billetera
wallpaper ['wɔːlpeɪpə*] n papel m
pintado ▷ vt empapelar
walnut ['wɔːlnʌt] n nuez f; (tree)
nogal m
walrus ['wɔːlrəs] (pl **~** or **~es**) n morsa
waltz [wɔːlts] n vals m ▷ vi bailar
el vals
wand [wɒnd] n (also: **magic ~**) varita
(mágica)
wander ['wɒndə*] vi (person) vagar;
deambular; (thoughts) divagar ▷ vt
recorrer, vagar por
want [wɒnt] vt querer, desear;
(need) necesitar ▷ n: **for ~ of** por falta
de; **wanted** adj (criminal) buscado;
"wanted" (in advertisements) "se busca"
war [wɔː*] n guerra; **to make ~ (on)**
declarar la guerra (a)
ward [wɔːd] n (in hospital) sala; (Pol)
distrito electoral; (Law: child: also: **~ of
court**) pupilo/a
warden ['wɔːdn] n (BRIT: of institution)
director(a) m/f; (of park, game reserve)

guardián/ana m/f; (BRIT: also: **traffic
~**) guardia mf
wardrobe ['wɔːdrəub] n armario,
ropero; (clothes) vestuario
warehouse ['wɛəhaus] n almacén
m, depósito
warfare ['wɔːfɛə*] n guerra
warhead ['wɔːhɛd] n cabeza armada
warm [wɔːm] adj caliente; (thanks)
efusivo; (clothes etc) abrigado;
(welcome, day) caluroso; **it's ~** hace
calor; **I'm ~** tengo calor; **warm up**
vi (room) calentarse; (person) entrar
en calor; (athlete) hacer ejercicios de
calentamiento ▷ vt calentar; **warmly**
adv afectuosamente; **warmth** n
calor m
warn [wɔːn] vt avisar, advertir;
warning n aviso, advertencia;
warning light n luz f de advertencia
warrant ['wɒrnt] n autorización f;
(Law: to arrest) orden f de detención; (: to
search) mandamiento de registro
warranty ['wɒrəntɪ] n garantía
warrior ['wɒrɪə*] n guerrero/a
Warsaw ['wɔːsɔː] n Varsovia
warship ['wɔːʃɪp] n buque m or barco
de guerra
wart [wɔːt] n verruga
wartime ['wɔːtaɪm] n: **in ~** en
tiempos de guerra, en la guerra
wary ['wɛərɪ] adj cauteloso
was [wɒz] pt of **be**
wash [wɒʃ] vt lavar ▷ vi lavarse;
(sea etc): **to ~ against/over sth** llegar
hasta/cubrir algo ▷ n (clothes etc)
lavado; (of ship) estela; **to have a ~**
lavarse; **wash up** vi (BRIT) fregar los
platos; (US) lavarse; **washbasin** (US) n
lavabo; **wash cloth** (US) n manopla;
washer n (Tech) arandela; **washing**
n (dirty) ropa sucia; (clean) colada;
washing line n cuerda de (colgar) la
ropa; **washing machine** n lavadora;
washing powder (BRIT) n detergente
m (en polvo)
Washington ['wɒʃɪŋtən] n
Washington m

wash: washing-up (BRIT) n fregado, platos mpl (para fregar); **washing-up liquid** (BRIT) n líquido lavavajillas; **washroom** (US) n servicios mpl

wasn't ['wɔznt] = **was not**

wasp [wɔsp] n avispa

waste [weist] n derroche m, despilfarro; (of time) pérdida; (food) sobras fpl; (rubbish) basura, desperdicios mpl ▷ adj (material) de desecho; (left over) sobrante; (land) baldío, descampado ▷ vt malgastar, derrochar; (time) perder; (opportunity) desperdiciar; **waste ground** (BRIT) n terreno baldío; **wastepaper basket** n papelera

watch [wɔtʃ] n (also: **wrist ~**) reloj m; (Mil: group of guards) centinela m; (act) vigilancia; (Naut: spell of duty) guardia ▷ vt (look at) mirar, observar; (: match, programme) ver; (spy on, guard) vigilar; (be careful of) cuidarse de, tener cuidado de ▷ vi ver, mirar; (keep guard) montar guardia; **watch out** vi cuidarse, tener cuidado; **watchdog** n perro guardián; (fig) persona u organismo encargado de asegurarse de que las empresas actúan dentro de la legalidad; **watch strap** n pulsera (de reloj)

water ['wɔ:tə*] n agua ▷ vt (plant) regar ▷ vi (eyes) llorar; (mouth) hacerse la boca agua; **water down** vt (milk etc) aguar; (fig: story) dulcificar, diluir; **watercolour** (US **watercolor**) n acuarela; **watercress** n berro; **waterfall** n cascada, salto de agua; **watering can** n regadera; **watermelon** n sandía; **waterproof** adj impermeable; **water-skiing** n esquí m acuático

watt [wɔt] n vatio

wave [weiv] n (of hand) señal f con la mano; (on water) ola; (Radio, in hair) onda; (fig) oleada ▷ vi agitar la mano; (flag etc) ondear ▷ vt (handkerchief, gun) agitar; **wavelength** n longitud f de onda

waver ['weivə*] vi (voice, love etc)

flaquear; (person) vacilar

wavy ['weivi] adj ondulado

wax [wæks] n cera ▷ vt encerar ▷ vi (moon) crecer

way [wei] n camino; (distance) trayecto, recorrido; (direction) dirección f, sentido; (manner) modo, manera; (habit) costumbre f; **which ~? – this ~** ¿por dónde? or ¿en qué dirección? – por aquí; **on the ~** (en route) en (el) camino; **to be on one's ~** estar en camino; **to be in the ~** bloquear el camino; (fig) estorbar; **to go out of one's ~ to do sth** desvivirse por hacer algo; **under ~** en marcha; **to lose one's ~** extraviarse; **in a ~** en cierto modo or sentido; **no ~!** (inf) ¡de eso nada!; **by the ~ ...** a propósito ...; **"~ in"** (BRIT) "entrada"; **"~ out"** (BRIT) "salida"; **the ~ back** el camino de vuelta; **"give ~"** (BRIT Aut) "ceda el paso"

W.C. n (BRIT) wáter m

we [wi:] pl pron nosotros/as

weak [wi:k] adj débil, flojo; (tea etc) claro; **weaken** vi debilitarse; (give way) ceder ▷ vt debilitar; **weakness** n debilidad f; (fault) punto débil; **to have a weakness for** tener debilidad por

wealth [welθ] n riqueza; (of details) abundancia; **wealthy** adj rico

weapon ['wepən] n arma; **~s of mass destruction** armas de destrucción masiva

wear [wɛə*] (pt **wore**, pp **worn**) n (use) uso; (deterioration through use) desgaste m ▷ vt (clothes) llevar; (shoes) calzar; (damage: through use) gastar, usar ▷ vi (last) durar; (rub through etc) desgastarse; **evening ~** ropa de etiqueta; **sports~/baby~** ropa de deportes/de niños; **wear off** vi (pain etc) pasar, desaparecer; **wear out** vt desgastar; (person, strength) agotar

weary ['wiəri] adj cansado; (dispirited) abatido ▷ vi: **to ~ of** cansarse de

weasel ['wi:zl] n (Zool) comadreja

weather ['wɛðə*] n tiempo ▷ vt (storm, crisis) hacer frente a; **under**

the ~ (fig: ill) indispuesto, pachucho; **weather forecast** n boletín m meteorológico

weave [wiːv] (pt **wove**, pp **woven**) vt (cloth) tejer; (fig) entretejer

web [wɛb] n (of spider) telaraña; (on duck's foot) membrana; (network) red f; **the (World Wide) W~** la Red; **web address** n dirección f de Internet; **webcam** n webcam f; **web page** n (página) web m or f; **website** n sitio web

Wed. abbr (=Wednesday) miérc

wed [wɛd] (pt, pp **~ded**) vt casar ▷ vi casarse

we'd [wiːd] = **we had; we would**

wedding ['wɛdɪŋ] n boda, casamiento; **silver/golden ~ (anniversary)** bodas fpl de plata/de oro; **wedding anniversary** n aniversario de boda; **wedding day** n día m de la boda; **wedding dress** n traje m de novia; **wedding ring** n alianza

wedge [wɛdʒ] n (of wood etc) cuña; (of cake) trozo ▷ vt acuñar; (push) apretar

Wednesday ['wɛdnzdɪ] n miércoles m inv

wee [wiː] (SCOTTISH) adj pequeñito

weed [wiːd] n mala hierba, maleza ▷ vt escardar, desherbar; **weedkiller** n herbicida m

week [wiːk] n semana; **a ~ today/on Friday** de hoy/del viernes en ocho días; **weekday** n día m laborable; **weekend** n fin m de semana; **weekly** adv semanalmente, cada semana ▷ adj semanal ▷ n semanario

weep [wiːp] (pt, pp **wept**) vi, vt llorar

weigh [weɪ] vt, vi pesar; **to ~ anchor** levar anclas; **weigh up** vt sopesar

weight [weɪt] n peso; (metal weight) pesa; **to lose/put on ~** adelgazar/engordar; **weightlifting** n levantamiento de pesas

weir [wɪə*] n presa

weird [wɪəd] adj raro, extraño

welcome ['wɛlkəm] adj bienvenido

▷ n bienvenida ▷ vt dar la bienvenida a; (be glad of) alegrarse de; **thank you – you're ~** gracias – de nada

weld [wɛld] n soldadura ▷ vt soldar

welfare ['wɛlfɛə*] n bienestar m; (social aid) asistencia social; **welfare state** n estado del bienestar

well [wɛl] n fuente f, pozo ▷ adv bien ▷ adj: **to be ~** estar bien (de salud) ▷ excl ¡vaya!, ¡bueno!; **as ~** también; **as ~ as** además de; **~ done!** ¡bien hecho!; **get ~ soon!** ¡que te mejores pronto!; **to do ~** (business) ir bien; (person) tener éxito

we'll [wiːl] = **we will; we shall**

well: well-behaved adj bueno; **well-built** adj (person) fornido; **well-dressed** adj bien vestido

wellies ['wɛlɪz] (inf) npl (BRIT) botas de goma

well: well-known adj (person) conocido; **well-off** adj acomodado; **well-paid** [wɛl'peɪd] adj bien pagado, bien retribuido

Welsh [wɛlʃ] adj galés/esa ▷ n (Ling) galés m; **Welshman** (irreg) n galés m; **Welshwoman** (irreg) n galesa

went [wɛnt] pt of **go**

wept [wɛpt] pt, pp of **weep**

were [wəː*] pt of **be**

we're [wɪə*] = **we are**

weren't [wəːnt] = **were not**

west [wɛst] n oeste m ▷ adj occidental, del oeste ▷ adv al or hacia el oeste; **the W~** el Oeste, el Occidente; **westbound** ['wɛstbaund] adj (traffic, carriageway) con rumbo al oeste; **western** adj occidental ▷ n (Cinema) película del oeste; **West Indian** adj, n antillano/a m/f

wet [wɛt] adj (damp) húmedo; (soaked): **~ through** mojado; (rainy) lluvioso ▷ n (BRIT: Pol) conservador(a) m/f moderado/a; **to get ~** mojarse; **"~ paint"** "recién pintado"; **wetsuit** n traje m térmico

we've [wiːv] = **we have**

whack [wæk] vt dar un buen golpe a

whale [weɪl] n (Zool) ballena

wharf [wɔːf] (*pl* **wharves**) *n* muelle
m

○ KEYWORD

what [wɔt] *adj* **1** (*in direct/indirect
questions*) qué; **what size is he?** ¿qué
talla usa?; **what colour/shape is it?**
¿de qué color/forma es?
2 (*in exclamations*): **what a mess!** ¡qué
desastre!; **what a fool I am!** ¡qué
tonto soy!
▷ *pron* **1** (*interrogative*) qué; **what
are you doing?** ¿qué haces *or* estás
haciendo?; **what is happening?** ¿qué
pasa *or* está pasando?; **what is it
called?** ¿cómo se llama?; **what about
me?** ¿y yo qué?; **what about doing ...?**
¿qué tal si hacemos ...?
2 (*relative*) lo que; **I saw what you
did/was on the table** vi lo que hiciste/
había en la mesa
▷ *excl* (*disbelieving*) ¡cómo!; **what, no
coffee!** ¡que no hay café!

whatever [wɔt'ɛvə*] *adj*: **~ book
you choose** cualquier libro que elijas
▷ *pron*: **do ~ is necessary** haga lo que
sea necesario; **~ happens** pase lo que
pase; **no reason ~ or whatsoever**
ninguna razón sea la que sea; **nothing
~** nada en absoluto
whatsoever [wɔtsəu'ɛvə*] *adj see*
whatever
wheat [wiːt] *n* trigo
wheel [wiːl] *n* rueda; (*Aut: also:*
steering ~) volante *m*; (*Naut*)
timón *m* ▷ *vt* (*pram etc*) empujar
▷ *vi* (*also:* **~ round**) dar la vuelta,
girar; **wheelbarrow** *n* carretilla;
wheelchair *n* silla de ruedas; **wheel
clamp** *n* (*Aut*) cepo
wheeze [wiːz] *vi* resollar

○ KEYWORD

when [wɛn] *adv* cuando; **when did
it happen?** ¿cuándo ocurrió?; **I know**

when it happened sé cuándo
ocurrió
▷ *conj* **1** (*at, during, after the time that*)
cuando; **be careful when you cross
the road** ten cuidado al cruzar la calle;
that was when I needed you fue
entonces que te necesité
2 (*on, at which*): **on the day when I met
him** el día en qué le conocí
3 (*whereas*) cuando

whenever [wɛn'ɛvə*] *conj* cuando;
(*every time that*) cada vez que ▷ *adv*
cuando sea
where [wɛə*] *adv* dónde ▷ *conj*
donde; **this is ~** aquí es donde;
whereabouts ▷ *n*: **nobody
knows his whereabouts** nadie conoce
su paradero; **whereas** *conj* visto que,
mientras; **whereby** *pron* por lo cual;
wherever *conj* dondequiera que;
(*interrogative*) dónde
whether ['wɛðə*] *conj* si; **I don't
know ~ to accept or not** no sé si
aceptar o no; **~ you go or not** vayas
o no vayas

○ KEYWORD

which [wɪtʃ] *adj* **1** (*interrogative: direct,
indirect*) qué; **which picture(s) do you
want?** ¿qué cuadro(s) quieres?; **which
one?** ¿cuál?
2 in which case en cuyo caso; **we got
there at 8 pm, by which time the
cinema was full** llegamos allí a las 8,
cuando el cine estaba lleno
▷ *pron* **1** (*interrogative*) cual; **I don't
mind which** el/la que sea
2 (*relative: replacing noun*) que; (*: replacing
clause*) lo que; (*: after preposition*) (el(la))
que el/la cual etc; **the apple which
you ate/which is on the table** la
manzana que comiste/que está en
la mesa; **the chair on which you are
sitting** la silla en que *or* la cual estás sentado;
**he said he knew, which is true/I
feared** dijo que lo sabía, lo cual *or* lo

que es cierto/me temía

whichever [wɪtʃˈɛvə*] adj: **take ~ book you prefer** coja (SP) el libro que prefiera; **~ book you take** cualquier libro que coja

while [waɪl] n rato, momento ▷ conj mientras; (although) aunque; **for a ~** durante algún tiempo

whilst [waɪlst] conj = **while**

whim [wɪm] n capricho

whine [waɪn] n (of pain) gemido; (of engine) zumbido; (of siren) aullido ▷ vi gemir; zumbar; (fig: complain) gimotear

whip [wɪp] n látigo; (Pol: person) encargado de la disciplina partidaria en el parlamento ▷ vt (Culin): batir; (move quickly): **to ~ sth out/off** sacar/quitar algo de un tirón; **whipped cream** n nata or crema montada

whirl [wə:l] vt hacer girar, dar vueltas a ▷ vi girar, dar vueltas; (leaves etc) arremolinarse

whisk [wɪsk] n (Culin) batidor m ▷ vt (Culin) batir; **to ~ sb away** or **off** llevar volando a algn

whiskers ['wɪskəz] npl (of animal) bigotes mpl; (of man) patillas fpl

whiskey ['wɪskɪ] (US, IRELAND) n = **whisky**

whisky ['wɪskɪ] n whisky m

whisper ['wɪspə*] n susurro ▷ vi, vt susurrar

whistle ['wɪsl] n (sound) silbido; (object) silbato ▷ vi silbar

white [waɪt] adj blanco; (pale) pálido ▷ n blanco; (of egg) clara; **whiteboard** n pizarra blanca; **interactive whiteboard** pizarra interactiva; **White House** (US) n Casa Blanca; **whitewash** n (paint) jalbegue m, cal f ▷ vt blanquear

whiting ['waɪtɪŋ] n inv (fish) pescadilla

Whitsun ['wɪtsn] n pentecostés m

whittle ['wɪtl] vt: **to ~ away**, **~ down** ir reduciendo

whizz [wɪz] vi: **to ~ past** or **by** pasar a toda velocidad

○ **KEYWORD**

who [hu:] pron **1** (interrogative) quién; **who is it?, who's there?** ¿quién es?; **who are you looking for?** ¿a quién buscas?; **I told her who I was** le dije quién era yo
2 (relative) que; **the man/woman who spoke to me** el hombre/la mujer que habló conmigo; **those who can swim** los que saben or sepan nadar

whoever [hu:ˈɛvə*] pron: **~ finds it** cualquiera or quienquiera que lo encuentre; **ask ~ you like** pregunta a quien quieras; **~ he marries** no importa con quién se case

whole [həul] adj (entire) todo, entero; (not broken) intacto ▷ n todo; (all): **the ~ of the town** toda la ciudad, la ciudad entera ▷ n (total) total m; (sum) conjunto; **on the ~, as a ~** en general; **wholefood(s)** n(pl) alimento(s) m(pl) integral(es); **wholeheartedly** [həulˈhɑːtɪdlɪ] adv con entusiasmo; **wholemeal** adj integral; **wholesale** n venta al por mayor ▷ adj al por mayor; (fig: destruction) sistemático; **wholewheat** adj = **wholemeal**; **wholly** adv totalmente, enteramente

○ **KEYWORD**

whom [hu:m] pron **1** (interrogative): **whom did you see?** ¿a quién viste?; **to whom did you give it?** ¿a quién se lo diste?; **tell me from whom you received it** dígame de quién lo recibí
2 (relative) que; **to whom** a quien(es); **of whom** de quien(es), del/de la que etc; **the man whom I saw/to whom I wrote** el hombre que vi/a quien escribí; **the lady about/with whom I was talking** la señora de (la) que/con

quien or (la) que hablaba

whore [hɔː*] (inf, pej) n puta

○ KEYWORD

whose [huːz] adj **1** (possessive: interrogative): **whose book is this?**, **whose is this book?** ¿de quién es este libro?; **whose pencil have you taken?** ¿de quién es el lápiz que has cogido?; **whose daughter are you?** ¿de quién eres hija?
2 (possessive: relative) cuyo/a, pl cuyos/as; **the man whose son you rescued** el hombre cuyo hijo rescataste; **those whose passports I have** aquellas personas cuyos pasaportes tengo; **the woman whose car was stolen** la mujer a quien le robaron el coche ▷ pron de quién; **whose is this?** ¿de quién es esto?; **I know whose it is** sé de quién es

○ KEYWORD

why [waɪ] adv por qué; **why not?** ¿por qué no?; **why not do it now?** ¿por qué no lo haces (or hacemos etc) ahora? ▷ conj: **I wonder why he said that** me pregunto por qué dijo eso; **that's not why I'm here** no es por eso (por lo) que estoy aquí; **the reason why** la razón por la que ▷ excl (expressing surprise, shock, annoyance) ¡hombre!, ¡vaya!; (explaining): **why, it's you!** ¡hombre, eres tú!; **why, that's impossible!** ¡pero sí eso es imposible!

○ KEYWORD

wicked [ˈwɪkɪd] adj malvado, cruel
wicket [ˈwɪkɪt] n (Cricket: stumps) palos mpl; (: grass area) terreno de juego
wide [waɪd] adj ancho; (area, knowledge) vasto, grande; (choice) amplio ▷ adv: **to open ~** abrir de par en par; **to shoot ~** errar el tiro; **widely** adv (travelled) mucho; (spaced) muy; **it is widely believed/known that ...** mucha gente piensa/sabe que ...; **widen** vt ensanchar; (experience) ampliar ▷ vi ensancharse; **wide open** adj abierto de par en par; **widespread** adj extendido, general
widow [ˈwɪdəu] n viuda; **widower** n viudo
width [wɪdθ] n anchura; (of cloth) ancho
wield [wiːld] vt (sword) blandir; (power) ejercer
wife [waɪf] (pl **wives**) n mujer f, esposa
wig [wɪg] n peluca
wild [waɪld] adj (animal) salvaje; (plant) silvestre; (person) furioso, violento; (idea) descabellado; (rough: sea) bravo; (: land) agreste; (: weather) muy revuelto; **wilderness** [ˈwɪldənɪs] n desierto; **wildlife** n fauna; **wildly** adv (behave) locamente; (lash out) a diestro y siniestro; (guess) a lo loco; (happy) a más no poder

○ KEYWORD

will [wɪl] aux vb **1** (forming future tense): **I will finish it tomorrow** lo terminaré or voy a terminar mañana; **I will have finished it by tomorrow** lo habré terminado para mañana; **will you do it?** – **yes I will/no I won't** ¿lo harás? – sí/no
2 (in conjectures, predictions): **he will** or **he'll be there by now** ya habrá or debe (de) haber llegado; **that will be the postman** será or debe ser el cartero
3 (in commands, requests, offers): **will you be quiet!** ¿quieres callarte?; **will you help me?** ¿quieres ayudarme?; **will you have a cup of tea?** ¿te apetece un té?; **I won't put up with it!** ¡no lo soporto! ▷ vt (pt, pp **willed**): **to will sb to do sth** desear que algn haga algo; **he willed himself to go on** con gran fuerza de voluntad, continuó

▷ *n* voluntad *f*; (*testament*) testamento

willing ['wɪlɪŋ] *adj* (*with goodwill*) de buena voluntad; (*enthusiastic*) entusiasta; **he's ~ to do it** está dispuesto a hacerlo; **willingly** *adv* con mucho gusto

willow ['wɪləʊ] *n* sauce *m*

willpower ['wɪlpaʊə*] *n* fuerza de voluntad

wilt [wɪlt] *vi* marchitarse

win [wɪn] (*pt, pp* **won**) *n* victoria, triunfo ▷*vt* ganar; (*obtain*) conseguir, lograr ▷*vi* ganar; **win over** *vt* convencer a

wince [wɪns] *vi* encogerse

wind¹ [wɪnd] *n* viento; (*Med*) gases *mpl* ▷*vt* (*take breath away from*) dejar sin aliento a

wind² [waɪnd] (*pt, pp* **wound**) *vt* enrollar; (*wrap*) envolver; (*clock, toy*) dar cuerda a ▷*vi* (*road, river*) serpentear; **wind down** *vt* (*car window*) bajar; (*fig: production, business*) disminuir; **wind up** *vt* (*clock*) dar cuerda a; (*debate, meeting*) concluir, terminar

windfall ['wɪndfɔ:l] *n* golpe *m* de suerte

winding ['waɪndɪŋ] *adj* (*road*) tortuoso; (*staircase*) de caracol

windmill ['wɪndmɪl] *n* molino de viento

window ['wɪndəʊ] *n* ventana; (*in car, train*) ventanilla; (*in shop etc*) escaparate *m* (*SP*), vidriera (*LAM*); **window box** *n* jardinera de ventana; **window cleaner** *n* (*person*) limpiacristales *mf inv*; **window pane** *n* cristal *m*; **window seat** *n* asiento junto a la ventana; **windowsill** *n* alféizar *m*, repisa

windscreen ['wɪndskri:n] (*Us* **windshield**) *n* parabrisas *m inv*; **windscreen wiper** (*Us* **windshield wiper**) *n* limpiaparabrisas *m inv*

windsurfing ['wɪndsə:fɪŋ] *n* windsurf *m*

windy ['wɪndɪ] *adj* de mucho viento; **it's ~** hace viento

wine [waɪn] *n* vino; **wine bar** *n* enoteca; **wine glass** *n* copa (para vino); **wine list** *n* lista de vinos; **wine tasting** *n* degustación *f* de vinos

wing [wɪŋ] *n* ala; (*Aut*) aleta; **wing mirror** *n* (espejo) retrovisor *m*

wink [wɪŋk] *n* guiño, pestañeo ▷*vi* guiñar, pestañear

winner ['wɪnə*] *n* ganador(a) *m/f*

winning ['wɪnɪŋ] *adj* (*team*) ganador(a); (*goal*) decisivo; (*smile*) encantador(a)

winter ['wɪntə*] *n* invierno ▷*vi* invernar; **winter sports** *npl* deportes *mpl* de invierno; **wintertime** *n* invierno

wipe [waɪp] *n*: **to give sth a ~** pasar un trapo sobre algo ▷*vt* limpiar; (*tape*) borrar; **wipe out** *vt* (*debt*) liquidar; (*memory*) borrar; (*destroy*) destruir; **wipe up** *vt* limpiar

wire ['waɪə*] *n* alambre *m*; (*Elec*) cable *m* (eléctrico); (*Tel*) telegrama *m* ▷*vt* (*house*) poner la instalación eléctrica en; (*also:* **~ up**) conectar; (*person: telegram*) telegrafiar

wiring ['waɪərɪŋ] *n* instalación *f* eléctrica

wisdom ['wɪzdəm] *n* sabiduría, saber *m*; (*good sense*) cordura; **wisdom tooth** *n* muela del juicio

wise [waɪz] *adj* sabio; (*sensible*) juicioso

wish [wɪʃ] *n* deseo ▷*vt* querer; **best ~es** (*on birthday etc*) felicidades *fpl*; **with best ~es** (*in letter*) saludos *mpl*, recuerdos *mpl*; **to ~ sb goodbye** despedirse de algn; **he ~ed me well** me deseó mucha suerte; **to ~ to do/sb to do sth** querer hacer/que algn haga algo; **to ~ for** desear

wistful ['wɪstful] *adj* pensativo

wit [wɪt] *n* ingenio, gracia; (*also:* **~s**) inteligencia; (*person*) chistoso/a

witch [wɪtʃ] *n* bruja

○ **KEYWORD**

with [wɪð, wɪθ] *prep* **1** (*accompanying, in the company of*) con (*con +mí, ti, sí =*

conmigo, contigo, consigo); **I was with him** estaba con él; **we stayed with friends** nos quedamos en casa de unos amigos; **I'm (not) with you** (don't understand) (no) te entiendo; **to be with it** (inf: person: up-to-date) estar al tanto; (: alert) ser despabilado **2** (descriptive, indicating manner etc) con; de; **a room with a view** una habitación con vistas; **the man with the grey hat/blue eyes** el hombre del sombrero gris/de los ojos azules; **red with anger** rojo de ira; **to shake with fear** temblar de miedo; **to fill sth with water** llenar algo de agua

withdraw [wɪθ'drɔ:] vt retirar, sacar ▷ vi retirarse; **to ~ money (from the bank)** retirar fondos (del banco); **withdrawal** n retirada; (of money) reintegro; **withdrawn** pp of **withdraw** ▷ adj (person) reservado, introvertido

withdrew [wɪθ'dru:] pt of **withdraw**

wither ['wɪðə*] vi marchitarse

withhold [wɪθ'həuld] vt (money) retener; (decision) aplazar; (permission) negar; (information) ocultar

within [wɪð'ɪn] prep dentro de ▷ adv dentro; **~ reach (of)** al alcance (de); **~ sight (of)** a la vista (de); **~ the week** antes de acabar la semana; **~ a mile (of)** a menos de una milla (de)

without [wɪð'aut] prep sin; **to go ~ sth** pasar sin algo

withstand [wɪθ'stænd] vt resistir a

witness ['wɪtnɪs] n testigo mf ▷ vt (event) presenciar; (document) atestiguar la veracidad de; **to bear ~ to** (fig) ser testimonio de

witty ['wɪtɪ] adj ingenioso

wives [waɪvz] npl of **wife**

wizard ['wɪzəd] n hechicero

wk abbr = **week**

wobble ['wɔbl] vi temblar; (chair) cojear

woe [wəu] n desgracia

woke [wəuk] pt of **wake**

woken ['wəukən] pp of **wake**

wolf [wulf] n lobo

woman ['wumən] (pl **women**) n mujer f

womb [wu:m] n matriz f, útero

women ['wɪmɪn] npl of **woman**

won [wʌn] pt, pp of **win**

wonder ['wʌndə*] n maravilla, prodigio; (feeling) asombro ▷ vi: **to ~ whether/why** preguntarse si/por qué; **to ~ at** asombrarse de; **to ~ about** pensar sobre or en; **it's no ~ (that)** no es de extrañarse (que +subjun); **wonderful** adj maravilloso

won't [wəunt] = **will not**

wood [wud] n (timber) madera; (forest) bosque m; **wooden** adj de madera; (fig) inexpresivo; **woodwind** n (Mus) instrumentos mpl de viento de madera; **woodwork** n carpintería

wool [wul] n lana; **to pull the ~ over sb's eyes** (fig) engatusar a algn; **woollen** (us **woolen**) adj de lana; **woolly** (us **wooly**) adj lanudo, de lana; (fig: ideas) confuso

word [wə:d] n palabra; (news) noticia; (promise) palabra (de honor) ▷ vt redactar; **in other ~s** en otras palabras; **to break/keep one's ~** faltar a la palabra/cumplir la promesa; **to have ~s with sb** reñir con algn; **wording** n redacción f; **word processing** n proceso de textos; **word processor** n procesador m de textos

wore [wɔ:*] pt of **wear**

work [wə:k] n trabajo; (job) empleo, trabajo; (Art, Literature) obra ▷ vi trabajar; (mechanism) funcionar, marchar; (medicine) ser eficaz, surtir efecto ▷ vt (shape) trabajar; (stone etc) tallar; (mine etc) explotar; (machine) manejar, hacer funcionar ▷ npl (of clock, machine) mecanismo; **to be out of ~** estar parado, no tener trabajo; **to ~ loose** (part) desprenderse; (knot) aflojarse; **works** n (BRIT: factory) fábrica; **work out** vi (plans etc) salir bien, funcionar; **works** vt (problem) resolver; (plan) elaborar; **it works out at £100** suma 100 libras; **worker** n trabajador(a) m/f, obrero/a; **work experience** n: **I'm going to do my work experience in a factory** voy a hacer las prácticas en una fábrica; **workforce** n mano de obra; **working class** n clase f obrera ▷ adj: **working-class** obrero; **working week** n semana laboral; **workman** (irreg) n obrero; **work of art** n obra de arte; **workout** n (Sport) sesión f de ejercicios; **work permit** n permiso de trabajo; **workplace** n lugar m de trabajo; **worksheet** n (Scol) hoja de ejercicios; **workshop** n taller m; **work station** n puesto or estación f de trabajo; **work surface** n encimera; **worktop** n encimera

world [wə:ld] n mundo ▷ cpd (champion) del mundo; (power, war) mundial; **to think the ~ of sb** (fig) tener un concepto muy alto de algn; **World Cup** n (Football): **the World Cup** el Mundial, los Mundiales; **world-wide** adj mundial, universal; **World-Wide Web** n: **the World-Wide Web** el World Wide Web

worm [wə:m] n (also: **earth ~**) lombriz f

worn [wɔ:n] pp of **wear** ▷ adj usado; **worn-out** adj (object) gastado; (person) rendido, agotado

worried ['wʌrɪd] adj preocupado

worry ['wʌrɪ] n preocupación f ▷ vt preocupar, inquietar ▷ vi preocuparse; **worrying** adj inquietante

worse [wə:s] adj, adv peor ▷ n lo peor; **a change for the ~** un empeoramiento; **worsen** vt, vi empeorar; **worse off** adj (financially): **to be worse off** tener menos dinero; (fig): **you'll be worse off this way** de esta forma estarás peor que nunca

worship ['wə:ʃɪp] n adoración f ▷ vt adorar; **Your W~** (BRIT: to mayor) señor

alcalde; (: to judge) señor juez

worst [wə:st] adj, adv peor ▷ n lo peor; **at ~** en lo peor de los casos

worth [wə:θ] n valor m ▷ adj: **to be ~** valer; **it's ~ it** vale or merece la pena; **to be ~ one's while** (to do) merecer la pena (hacer); **worthless** adj sin valor; (useless) inútil; **worthwhile** adj (activity) que merece la pena; (cause) loable

worthy ['wə:ðɪ] adj respetable; (motive) honesto; **~ of** digno de

○ KEYWORD

would [wʊd] aux vb **1** (conditional tense): **if you asked him he would do it** si se lo pidieras, lo haría; **if you had asked him he would have done it** si se lo hubieras pedido, lo habría or hubiera hecho

2 (in offers, invitations, requests): **would you like a biscuit?** ¿quieres una galleta?; (formal) ¿querría una galleta?; **would you ask him to come in?** ¿quiere hacerle pasar?; **would you open the window please?** ¿quiere or podría abrir la ventana, por favor?

3 (in indirect speech): **I said I would do it** dije que lo haría

4 (emphatic): **it would have to snow today!** ¡tenía que nevar precisamente hoy!

5 (insistence): **she wouldn't behave** no quiso comportarse bien

6 (conjecture): **it would have been midnight** sería medianoche; **it would seem so** parece ser que sí

7 (indicating habit): **he would go there on Mondays** iba allí los lunes

wouldn't ['wʊdnt] = **would not**

wound¹ [wu:nd] n herida ▷ vt herir

wound² [waʊnd] pt, pp of **wind²**

wove [wəʊv] pt of **weave**

woven ['wəʊvən] pp of **weave**

wrap [ræp] vt (also: **~ up**) envolver; (gift) envolver, abrigar ▷ vi (dress *warmly*) abrigarse; **wrapper** n (*on chocolate*) papel m; (BRIT: *of book*) sobrecubierta; **wrapping** n envoltura, envase m; **wrapping paper** n papel m de envolver; (*fancy*) papel m de regalo

wreath [riːθ, pl riːðz] n (*funeral wreath*) corona

wreck [rɛk] n (*ship: destruction*) naufragio; (: *remains*) restos mpl del barco; (*pej: person*) ruina ▷ vt (*car etc*) destrozar; (*chances*) arruinar; **wreckage** n restos mpl; (*of building*) escombros mpl

wren [rɛn] n (*Zool*) reyezuelo

wrench [rɛntʃ] n (*Tech*) llave f inglesa; (*tug*) tirón m; (*fig*) dolor m ▷ vt arrancar; **to ~ sth from sb** arrebatar algo violentamente a algn

wrestle ['rɛsl] vi: **to ~ (with sb)** luchar (con or contra algn); **wrestler** n luchador(a) m/f (de lucha libre); **wrestling** n lucha libre

wretched ['rɛtʃɪd] adj miserable

wriggle ['rɪgl] vi (*also: ~ about*) menearse, retorcerse

wring [rɪŋ] (*pt, pp* **wrung**) vt retorcer; (*wet clothes*) escurrir; (*fig*): **to ~ sth out of sb** sacar algo por la fuerza a algn

wrinkle ['rɪŋkl] n arruga ▷ vt arrugar ▷ vi arrugarse

wrist [rɪst] n muñeca

writable ['raɪtəbl] adj (CD, DVD) escribible

write [raɪt] (*pt* **wrote**, *pp* **written**) vt escribir; (*cheque*) extender ▷ vi escribir; **write down** vt escribir; (*note*) apuntar; **write off** vt (*debt*) borrar (como incobrable); (*fig*) desechar por inútil; **write out** vt escribir; **write-off** n siniestro total; **writer** n escritor(a) m/f

writing ['raɪtɪŋ] n escritura; (*handwriting*) letra; (*of author*) obras fpl; **in ~** por escrito; **writing paper** n papel m de escribir

written ['rɪtn] *pp of* **write**

wrong [rɔŋ] adj (*wicked*) malo; (*unfair*) injusto; (*incorrect*) equivocado, incorrecto; (*not suitable*) inoportuno, inconveniente; (*reverse*) del revés ▷ adv equivocadamente ▷ n injusticia ▷ vt ser injusto con; **you are ~ to do it** haces mal en hacerlo; **you are ~ about that, you've got it ~** en eso estás equivocado; **to be in the ~** no tener razón, tener la culpa; **what's ~?** ¿qué pasa?; **to go ~** (*person*) equivocarse; (*plan*) salir mal; (*machine*) estropearse; **wrongly** adv mal, incorrectamente; (*by mistake*) por error; **wrong number** n (*Tel*): **you've got the wrong number** se ha equivocado de número

wrote [rəʊt] *pt of* **write**

wrung [rʌŋ] *pt, pp of* **wring**

WWW n abbr (= World Wide Web) WWW m

X y

XL *abbr* = **extra large**
Xmas ['ɛksməs] *n abbr* = **Christmas**
X-ray ['ɛksreɪ] *n* radiografía ▷*vt*
radiografiar, sacar radiografías de
xylophone ['zaɪləfəun] *n* xilófono

yacht [jɔt] *n* yate *m*; **yachting** *n*
(*sport*) balandrismo
yard [jɑːd] *n* patio; (*measure*) yarda;
yard sale (*us*) *n* venta de objetos
usados (*en el jardín de una casa particular*)
yarn [jɑːn] *n* hilo; (*tale*) cuento,
historia
yawn [jɔːn] *n* bostezo ▷*vi* bostezar
yd. *abbr* (= *yard*) yda
yeah [jɛə] (*inf*) *adv* sí
year [jɪə*] *n* año; **to be 8 ~s old** tener
8 años; **an eight-~-old child** un niño de
ocho años (de edad); **yearly** *adj* anual
▷*adv* anualmente, cada año
yearn [jəːn] *vi*: **to ~ for sth** añorar
algo, suspirar por algo
yeast [jiːst] *n* levadura
yell [jɛl] *n* grito, alarido ▷*vi* gritar
yellow ['jɛləu] *adj* amarillo; **Yellow
Pages**® *npl* páginas *fpl* amarillas
yes [jɛs] *adv* sí ▷*n* sí *m*; **to say/
answer ~** decir/contestar que sí
yesterday ['jɛstədɪ] *adv* ayer ▷*n*
ayer *m*; **~ morning/evening** ayer por
la mañana/tarde; **all day ~** todo el

día de ayer

yet [jɛt] *adv* ya; (*negative*) todavía
▷ *conj* sin embargo, a pesar de todo;
it is not finished ~ todavía no está
acabado; **the best ~** el/la mejor hasta
ahora; **as ~** hasta ahora, todavía

yew [ju:] *n* tejo

Yiddish ['jɪdɪʃ] *n* yiddish *m*

yield [ji:ld] *n* (*Agr*) cosecha; (*Comm*)
rendimiento; (*results*) producir, dar; (*profit*) rendir ▷ *vi*
rendirse, ceder; (*US Aut*) ceder el paso

yob(bo) ['jɔb(bəu)] *n* (*BRIT inf*)
gamberro

yoga ['jəugə] *n* yoga *m*

yog(h)ourt ['jəugət] *n* yogur *m*

yog(h)urt ['jəugət] *n* = **yog(h)ourt**

yolk [jəuk] *n* yema (de huevo)

◯ **KEYWORD**

you [ju:] *pron* **1** (*subject: familiar*) tú;
(*pl*) vosotros/as (*SP*), ustedes (*LAM*);
(*polite*) usted; (*pl*) ustedes; **you are
very kind** eres/es *etc* muy amable; **you
Spanish enjoy your food** a vosotros
(*or* ustedes) los españoles os (*or* les)
gusta la comida; **you and I will go**
iremos tú y yo

2 (*object: direct: familiar*) te; (*pl*) os (*SP*),
les (*LAM*); (*polite*) le; (*pl*) les; (*f*) la; (*pl*) las;
I know you te/le *etc* conozco

3 (*object: indirect: familiar*) te; (*pl*) os (*SP*),
les (*LAM*); (*polite*) le; (*pl*) les; **I gave the
letter to you yesterday** te/os *etc* di
la carta ayer

4 (*stressed*): **I told you to do it** te dije a
ti que lo hicieras, es a ti a quien dije que
lo hicieras; *see also* **3; 5**

5 (*after prep: NB: con +ti =
contigo: familiar*) ti; (*pl*) vosotros/as
(*SP*), ustedes (*LAM*); (*: polite*) usted;
(*pl*) ustedes; **it's for you** es para
ti/vosotros *etc*

6 (*comparisons: familiar*) tú; (*pl*)
vosotros/as (*SP*), ustedes (*LAM*);
(*: polite*) usted; (*pl*) ustedes; **she's
younger than you** es más joven que

tú/vosotros etc

7 (*impersonal: one*): **fresh air does you
good** el aire puro (te) hace bien; **you
never know** nunca se sabe; **you can't
do that!** ¡eso no se hace!

you'd [ju:d] = **you had; you would**

you'll [ju:l] = **you will; you shall**

young [jʌŋ] *adj* joven ▷ *npl* (*of
animal*) cría; (*people*): **the ~** los jóvenes,
la juventud; **youngster** *n* joven *mf*

your [jɔ:*] *adj* tu; (*pl*) vuestro; (*formal*)
su; *see also* **my**

you're [juə*] = **you are**

yours [jɔ:z] *pron* tuyo (*pl*), vuestro;
(*formal*) suyo; *see also* **faithfully; mine¹**
see also **sincerely**

yourself [jɔ:'sɛlf] *pron* tú mismo;
(*complement*) te; (*after prep*) tí (mismo);
(*formal*) usted mismo; (*: complement*)
se; (*: after prep*) sí (mismo); **yourselves**
pl pron vosotros mismos; (*after prep*)
vosotros (mismos); (*formal*) ustedes
(mismos); (*: complement*) se; (*: after prep*)
sí mismos; *see also* **oneself**

youth [*pl* ju:ðz] *n* juventud *f*; (*young
man*) joven *m*; **youth club** *n* club *m*
juvenil; **youthful** *adj* juvenil; **youth
hostel** *n* albergue *m* de juventud

you've [ju:v] = **you have**

Z

zeal [ziːl] *n* celo, entusiasmo
zebra ['ziːbrə] *n* cebra; **zebra crossing** (BRIT) *n* paso de peatones
zero ['zɪərəu] *n* cero
zest [zest] *n* ánimo, vivacidad *f*; (*of orange*) piel *f*
zigzag ['zɪgzæg] *n* zigzag *m* ▷ *vi* zigzaguear, hacer eses
Zimbabwe [zɪm'bɑːbwɪ] *n* Zimbabwe *m*
zinc [zɪŋk] *n* cinc *m*, zinc *m*
zip [zɪp] *n* (*also*: **~ fastener**, (US) **~per**) cremallera (SP), cierre (AM) *m*, zíper *m* (MEX, CAM) ▷ *vt* (*also*: **~ up**) cerrar la cremallera de; (*file*) comprimir; **zip code** (US) *n* código postal; **zip file** *n* (*Comput*) archivo comprimido; **zipper** (US) *n* cremallera
zit [zɪt] *n* grano
zodiac ['zəudɪæk] *n* zodíaco
zone [zəun] *n* zona
zoo [zuː] *n* (jardín *m*) zoo *m*
zoology [zuːˈɔlədʒɪ] *n* zoología
zoom [zuːm] *vi*: **to ~ past** pasar zumbando; **zoom lens** *n* zoom *m*
zucchini [zuːˈkiːnɪ] (US) *n(pl)* calabacín(ines) *m(pl)*